Special Edition

Using

Using

HTML 4

Fourth Edition

Special Edition

Using

Using

HTML 4

Fourth Edition

Mark R. Brown and
Jerry Honeycutt, et al.

Special Edition Using HTML 4, Fourth Edition

Library of Congress Catalog No.: 97-80808

ISBN: 0-7897-1449-3

00 99 98   6 5 4 3 2 1

Interpretation of the printing code: the rightmost double-digit number is the year of the book's printing; the rightmost single-digit number, the number of the book's printing. For example, a printing code of 98-1 shows that the first printing of the book occurred in 1998.

Screen reproductions in this book were created using Collage Plus from Inner Media, Inc., Hollis, NH.

Contents at a Glance

Table of Contents

V Pushing Content

Credits

SENIOR VICE PRESIDENT OF PUBLISHING
Richard K. Swadley

PUBLISHER
Jordan Gold

GENERAL MANAGER
Joe Muldoon

BRAND DIRECTOR
Greg Wiegand

DIRECTOR OF EDITORIAL SERVICES
Lisa Wilson

DIRECTOR OF SOFTWARE AND USER SERVICES
Cheryl D. Willoughby

MANAGER OF PUBLISHING OPERATIONS
Linda H. Buehler

MANAGING EDITOR
Patrick Kanouse

EXECUTIVE EDITOR
Beverly Eppink

ACQUISITIONS EDITORS
David Mayhew
Jeff Taylor

DEVELOPMENT EDITORS
Kelly Murdock

PROJECT EDITOR
Rebecca Mounts

COPY EDITORS
Tonya Maddox
Jean Jameson
Erik Dafforn
Kristine Simmons
June Waldman

Kelli Brooks
Geneil Breeze
Chuck Hutchinson

COORDINATOR OF EDITORIAL SERVICES
Charlotte Clapp

TECHNICAL EDITORS
Brett Bonenberger
Kyle Bryant
Lee Anne Phillips
Bill Vernon

SOFTWARE SPECIALIST
Adam Swetnam

WEBMASTER
Thomas H. Bennett

TEAM COORDINATOR
Michelle Newcomb

EDITORIAL ASSISTANT
Rhonda Tinch-Mize

BRAND COORDINATOR
Trey Frank

BOOK DESIGNERS
Ruth Harvey
Kim Scott

COVER DESIGNER
Sandra Schroeder

PRODUCTION TEAM
Marcia Deboy
Michael Dietsch
Cynthia Fields
Maureen West

INDEXER
Greg Pearson

Composed in *Century Old Style* and *ITC Franklin Gothic* by Que Corporation.

For Alex, David, and Frank—my golfing buddies.

—Jerry Honeycutt

To my wife, Carol, and my daughter, Jenny, who are and have always been my inspiration, my foundation, and my best friends.

—Mark R. Brown

About the Authors

Mark Brown has been writing computer magazine articles, books, and manuals for over 13 years. He was managing editor of *.info* magazine when it was named one of the six best computer magazines of 1991 by the Computer Press Association, and was nominated by the Software Publisher's Association for the 1988 Software Reviewer of the Year award. He is currently the manger of technical publications for Neural Applications Corporation, a major player in applying cutting-edge artificial intelligence techniques to industrial control applications, such as steel making and food processing. A bona fide personal computing pioneer, he hand-built his first PC in 1977, taught himself to program it in hexadecimal, and has since dabbled in dozens of different programming languages. He has been telecomputing since 1983, and is currently Webmaster of two World Wide Web sites: **http://www.neural.com**, and a personal Web site on the topic of airships. Mark is a life-long resident of Iowa. He enjoys reading and writing, gaming, Iowa Hawkeye Big 10 football, walks in the park with his dog, Bosco, and day trips through the Iowa countryside with his wife, Carol.

Jerry Honeycutt provides business-oriented technical leadership to the Internet community and software development industry. He has served companies such as The Travelers, IBM, Nielsen North America, IRM, Howard Systems International, and NCR. Jerry has participated in the industry since before the days of Microsoft Windows 1.0; and is completely hooked on Windows and the Internet.

Jerry is a leading author in the Internet field. He is the author of over a dozen books, each published by QUE, including *Platinum Edition Using Windows NT Server 4.0, Special Edition Using the Internet; Using Netscape Composer; Using the Internet;* and *Windows 95 and NT 4.0 Registry & Customization Handbook.* Many of Jerry's books are sold internationally and have been translated into a variety of foreign languages.

Jerry has also contributed to several other books, including *Platinum Edition Using Office 97, Platinum Edition Using Windows 95; Special Edition Using JavaScript; Special Edition Using Netscape Communicator;* and *Windows NT Server 4.0 Advanced Technical Reference.* He's been printed in Computer Language magazine and is a regular speaker at Windows World, Comdex, and other industry trade shows on topics related to software development, Windows, and the Internet.

Jerry graduated from the University of Texas at Dallas in 1992 with a B.S. degree in Computer Science. He currently lives in the Dallas suburb of Frisco, Texas with two Westies, Corky and Turbo, and a Yorkie named Pompy. Jerry is an avid golfer; and has a passion for fine photography and international travel. Feel free to contact Jerry on the Internet at **jerry@honeycutt.com** or visit his Web site at **http://rampages.onramp.net/~jerry**.

Luke Cassady-Dorion is a software engineer at Metis LLC (**http://www.metisllc.com**), a leading health-care software development firm. With the aid of various distributed-object technologies, including CORBA, Luke has deployed a series of enterprise-wide solutions written entirely in Java. Luke is the author of numerous articles on distributed computing and Java, including the recently published book Industrial Strength Java. Luke can be reached for comment at **luke@luke.org**.

Sue Charlesworth has 14 years experience in PC software development, holding various roles from tester to programmer to team leader responsible for developing quality assurance standards and high-performance test teams. She has a master's degree in international management. Over the years, she has found that her most enjoyable work involves writing and helping others as a knowledge resource. This has led to recent work in HTML Web page development and multimedia courseware authoring. Sue currently works for United Airlines, programming multimedia lessons for pilot ground school.

Pamela Rice Hahn has been writing about computers for over twelve years, during which time she's published more than 100 articles. However, she's worked with computers since her college days back in the punch card era, circa 1969. Now a full-time freelance writer and owner of PRH Pages—a business writing services, typesetting, Web page design, and book doctoring business, Pam also can be found (as Fawnn) during her Virtual Water Cooler breaks on the Undernet chat channel, #Authors, where she is channel manager. (Stop in and she'll gladly tell you about the MBABGDITW—Most Beautiful and Brilliant GrandDaughter In The World. Pam points out she was a young bride and therefore is a very young grandmother; her only child, a married daughter—Lara, works as a nurse and is a published author as well.) Look for her Web pages at **http://www.bright.net/~fawnn01/prh/main.htm** and **http://www.bright.net/~fawnn01/authors/authors.htm**. She can be reached by email at **fawnn01@bright.net**.

Pam is the 1997 winner of The Manny Award for Nonfiction from the MidWest Writers Workshop. She served as an Associate Editor for the literary 'zine, *Dream Forge*, as well as editor for a number of computer-related and business newsletters. She is Publisher and Editor-in-Chief for a literary 'zine that will debut with the Winter 1998 issue, *The Blue Rose Bouquet*. Articles she's book-doctored have appeared in *Glamour*, *Country Living*, and other national publications. In addition, she works as a tech editor for Que Publishing and wrote another chapter on Web page design for them as well.

Mike Morgan is founder and president of DSE, Inc., a full-service Web presence provider and software development shop. The DSE team has developed software for such companies as Intelect, Magnavox, DuPont, the American Biorobotics Corporation, and Satellite Systems Corporation, as well as for the Government of Iceland and the Royal Saudi Air Force. DSE's Web sites include the prestigious Nikka Galleria, an online art gallery. DSE's sites are noted for their effectiveness—one of the company's sites generated sales of over $100,000 within 30 days of being announced.

Mike is a frequent speaker at conferences on Internet technology, and has taught computer science and software engineering at Chaminade University (the University of Honolulu) and in the graduate program of Hawaii Pacific University. He has given seminars for the IEEE, National Seminars Group, the University of Hawaii, Purdue University, and Notre Dame.

Mike holds a Master of Science in Systems Management from the Florida Institute of Technology and a Bachelor of Science in Mathematics from Wheaton College, where he concentrated his studies on computer science. He is currently a student in the Organizational Leadership Ph.D. program at Regent University.

Mike can usually be found in his office at DSE, drinking Diet Pepsi and writing HTML and C++. He lives in Virginia Beach with his wife, Jean, and their six children. You can reach him at **Mike.Morgan@mail.dse.com**.

Melissa Niles is a systems administrator and web programmer for InCommand Inc., a company located in Yakima Washington that specializes in Internet and Intranet applications.

Clayton Walnum, who has a degree in computer science, has been writing about computers for almost 15 years and has published hundreds of articles in major computer publications. He is the former editor of two nationally distributed computer magazines and is also the author of almost 30 books, which cover such diverse topics as programming, computer gaming, and applications programs. His most recent book is *Special Edition Using MFC and ATL*, published by Que. His other titles include the award-winning *Building Windows 95 Applications with Visual Basic 4* (Que), *Windows 95 Game SDK Strategy Guide* (Que), *Datamania: A Child's Computer Organizer* (Alpha Kids), *Master Populous* (Sams), and *Adventures in Artificial Life* (Que). When Clay can't stare at his monitor anymore, he writes and records music in his home studio. You can reach him at his home page, which is located at **http://www.connix.com/ ~cwalnum**.

Acknowledgments

This book took a lot of work by many people. The authors, of course, contributed many hours of bone-racking work to this book. The editors made sure that this book's content was on the up and up. There are a couple of very special folks that we want you to be aware of, though:

- Stephanie McComb, David Mayhew, and Jeff Taylor put together a fine group of contributing authors in order to get this book done.

- Ben Milstead, Jon Steever, and Kelly Murdock are the development editors for this book. They kept their heads cool and allowed the authors to put together the best book possible. Thanks.

- Rebecca Mounts, the project editor for this book, is a joy. I've had many occasions to work with her, and she amazes me every time.

- The technical editors—Kyle Bryant, Brett Bonenberger, Bill Vernon, and Lee Anne Phillips—did a fabulous job of making sure the technical details were correct. They scoured over every line of HTML in this book, as well as the text content. They didn't just verify the facts, either, they often came up with great ideas for new content.

- The copy editors—Tonya Maddox, Jean Jameson, Erik Dafforn, Kristine Simmons, June Waldman, Kelli Brooks, Geneil Breeze, and Chuck Hutchinson—made sure the gibberish the authors banged out on the keyboard was readable and conformed to some sense of English structure.

- The contributing authors—Mike Morgan, Luke Cassady-Dorion, Melissa Niles, Pamela Hahn, Clayton Walnum, and Sue Charlesworth—were shooting at fast-moving targets. They did good.

- The Internet community contributed ideas for content and often provided solutions to problems for which we were stumped.

We'd Like to Hear from You!

As part of our continuing effort to produce books of the highest possible quality, Que would like to hear your comments. To stay competitive, we *really* want you to let us know what you like or dislike most about this book or other Que products.

Please send your comments, ideas, and suggestions for improvement to:

Beverly Eppink

Macmillan Computer Publishing

201 West 103rd Street

Indianapolis, IN 46290-1097

beppink@mcp.com

Introduction

by Jerry Honeycutt

In this chapter

What Is HTML?

You can't build a monument without bricks, and you can't make bricks without straw—everyone who has seen the film *The Ten Commandments* knows that. Likewise, if you plan to establish your own monumental presence on the World Wide Web, you have to start with the straw—HTML.

The World Wide Web is built of Web pages, and those pages are themselves created with HyperText Markup Language, or HTML. Though many folks talk about HTML Programming with a capital P (particularly recruiters), HTML is really not a programming language at all. HTML is exactly what it claims to be: a markup language. You use HTML to mark up a text document, just as you would if you were an editor using a red pencil. The marks you use indicate which format (or style) should be used when displaying the marked text.

If you have ever used an old word processing program (remember WordStar?), you already know how a markup language works. In these old programs, if you wanted text to appear italicized, you surrounded it with control characters. For example, you might surround a phrase with control characters that make it appear as bold text:

```
/Bthis text appears bold/b
```

When you printed the document, the first /B caused the word processor to start using bold characters. It printed all the characters in bold, until it reached /b. The word processor didn't actually print the /B and /b. These just "marked up" the text sandwiched between them.

HTML works the same way. If you want text to appear on the Web page in bold characters, mark it up like this:

```
<b>this text appears bold</b>
```

The <b> turns on bold characters. The </b> turns off bold characters. These tags don't actually appear on the screen, they just cause the text sandwiched between them to display in bold characters.

Why You Need This Book

Everything you create in HTML relies on tags like these. To be a whiz-bang HTML programmer, you need to learn which tags do what. Fortunately, that's what this entire book is about.

A few other topics are covered in this book: page design techniques, the Dynamic HTML object model, graphics creation, scripting, Web casting, and much more. You take a look at HTML and graphics editing tools, HTML code verification, and how to promote your site on the Web. You even take short side trips into Java programming, CGI programming, ActiveX controls, and Virtual Reality Modeling Language (VRML).

You explore these topics only as they relate to the main theme: creating your own Web pages using HTML. This book's major goal is to help you learn as much as possible about HTML itself.

Ultimately, what you get out of this book depends on how advanced you are:

- If you're a beginner, you find information on what other people are doing on the Web, what is appropriate to put on the Web, and how to use basic HTML tags to begin creating your own pages.
- If you're an intermediate user, you find tips, tricks, and techniques for creating Web pages that exploit HTML's full potential.
- If you're an advanced user, you learn how to use powerful extensions to HTML and additional technologies, such as Dynamic HTML, style sheets, and Web casting, to make your Web pages world-class.

What's Changed in the Fourth Edition

The recent evolution of HTML allows you to build documents with which a user can interact, not just view. In the fourth edition, our goal is to help you stay on top of all these changes:

- We've updated our coverage of HTML to include the latest and greatest HTML standards (HTML 4.0).
- We've reorganized the content so that information is easier for you to access.
- We've added an entire part covering Dynamic HTML, which includes topics such as the object model, scripting, style sheets, Web fonts, and more.
- We've added a part covering Web casting for both Internet Explorer 4.0 and Netscape Netcaster.

Aside from the more dramatic changes we've made to this edition, each and every chapter has gone through more subtle changes. We've updated each chapter with new tips. Outdated information has been replaced with new information. Each chapter has been updated with the latest versions of each program.

How This Book Is Organized

Special Edition Using HTML 4.0, Fourth Edition, provides comprehensive information about HTML and related technologies that you can use to build great Web pages. The new edition has eight parts, 46 chapters, four appendixes, and an index. Each part is dedicated to a particular concept, such as Web programming or objects. What follows is an overview of topics you find in each part of this book:

- Part I, "Publishing a Web Site," gives you a brief history of the Internet, World Wide Web, and HTML. In this part, you also learn about an approach to designing and implementing Web pages and how to publish your site to the Internet.
- Part II, "Creating Basic Web Pages with HTML 4.0," introduces you to HTML. You learn how HTML documents are organized and formatted. You also learn how to add frames, forms, and imagemaps to your Web page, as well as a number of other advanced techniques.

■ Part III, "Creating Advanced Web Pages with Dynamic HTML," contains some of this book's biggest enhancements. You learn about Dynamic HTML, including the object model, scripting, and style sheets.

■ Part IV, "Serving Multimedia Content," shows you how to use a variety of multimedia objects on your Web pages. This part covers topics such as streaming audio and video; graphics files, and animation.

■ Part V, "Pushing Content," shows you how to push content and applications to the user's desktop. This part covers technologies for both Internet Explorer 4.0 and Netscape Netcaster.

■ Part VI, "Scripting on the Web Server," introduces you to some of the most exciting technology available for creating dynamic Web pages. You learn how to write CGI scripts, for example, or how to dynamically serve content using Active Server Pages and LiveWire Pro.

■ Part VII, "Managing Your Web Site," shows you how to manage your entire Web site. You learn how to get your pages onto the Internet. You learn how to manage the files on your Web site, get your Web site noticed, and secure your Web site, too.

■ Part VIII, "Learning by Example," contains a variety of real-world examples that reinforce everything you've learned in this book. You find examples such as an intranet, an online magazine, and a personal Web site.

Other Books of Interest

This book focuses on using HTML. Que also publishes books in other specific but related areas, as well as more introductory books about the Internet. Here are some you might find useful:

■ *Special Edition Using Netscape* shows you how to get the absolute most out of Netscape. This is a must-have book for avid Netscape users.

■ *Special Edition Using Java* is a tell-all book that shows you how to create your own Java applications.

■ *Special Edition Using JavaScript* provides all the information you need in order to script great Web pages with JavaScript.

■ *Special Edition Using VBScript* describes how to use Microsoft's VBScript to glue together the objects on a Web page.

■ *Special Edition Using Windows 95* is a tell-all book about Windows 95. If you can buy just one book about Windows 95, this should be it.

■ *Special Edition Using Windows NT* is a similar tell-all book about Windows NT. Again, if you can buy just one book about Windows NT, this should be it.

■ *Special Edition Using Windows* is a similar book about Windows 3.x and Windows for Workgroups.

Special Features in This Book

This book contains a variety of special features to help you find the information you need—fast. Formatting conventions are used to make important keywords or special text obvious. Specific language is used so as to make keyboard and mouse actions clear. A variety of visual elements are used to make important and useful information stand out. The following sections describe the special features used in this book.

Visual Aids

Notes, Tips, Cautions, Troubleshootings, and other visual aids give you useful information. The following are descriptions of each element.

N O T E Notes provide useful information that isn't essential to the discussion. They usually contain more technical information, but can also contain interesting but non-vital technical or non-technical information. ▓

 T I P Tips enhance your experience with Windows 95 by providing hints and tricks you won't find elsewhere.

CAUTION

Cautions warn you that a particular action can cause severe harm to your configuration. Given the consequences of editing your Registry, you shouldn't skip the Cautions in this book.

 TROUBLESHOOTING

I need help with a particular problem. Troubleshooting elements anticipate the problems you might have and provide a solution.

Cross references point you to specific sections within other chapters so that you can get more information that's related to the topic you're reading about. Here is what a cross reference looks like:

▶ **See** "The Web Explosion," **p. 11**

Sidebars Are Interesting Nuggets of Information

Sidebars are detours from the main text. They usually provide background or other interesting information that is relevant but nonessential reading. You might find information that's a bit more technical than the surrounding text, or you might find a brief diversion into the historical aspects of the text.

Keyboard Conventions

In addition to the special features that help you find what you need, this book uses some special conventions to make it easier to read:

Feature	Convention
Hotkeys	Hotkeys are underlined in this book, just as they appear in Windows 95 menus. To use a hotkey, press Alt and the underlined key. For example, the F in File is a hotkey that represents the File menu.
Key combinations	Key combinations are joined with the plus sign (+). Alt+F, for example, means hold down the Alt key, press the F key, and then release both keys.
Menu commands	A comma is used to separate the parts of a pull-down menu command. For example, choosing File, New means to open the File menu and select the New option.

In most cases, special-purpose keys are referred to by the text that actually appears on them (on a standard 101-key keyboard). For example, "press Esc," "press F1," or "press Enter." Some of the keys on your keyboard don't actually have words on them, so here are the conventions used in this book for those keys:

- The Backspace key, which is labeled with a left arrow, is usually located directly above the Enter key. The Tab key is usually labeled with two arrows pointing to lines, with one arrow pointing right and the other arrow pointing left.

- The cursor keys—labeled on most keyboards with arrows pointing up, down, right, and left—are called the up-arrow key, down-arrow key, right-arrow key, and left-arrow key.

- Case is not important unless explicitly stated: "Press A" and "press a" mean the same thing.

Formatting Conventions

This book also uses some special typeface conventions to help you understand what you're reading:

Typeface	Description
Italics	Italics indicate new terms. They also indicate placeholders in commands and addresses.
Bold	Bold indicates text you type. It also indicates addresses on the Internet.
Computer type	This typeface is used for on-screen messages and commands that you type.
MYFILE.DOC	Windows file names and folders are capitalized to help you distinguish them from regular text.

Publishing a Web Site

## CHAPTER 1

HTML on the Internet

by Mark R. Brown

In this chapter

The Birth of the World Wide Web

Contrary to what the media would have you believe, the World Wide Web did not spring into being overnight. Though relatively new in human terms, the Web has a venerable genealogy for a computing technology. It can trace its roots back over 35 years, which is more than half the distance back to the primordial dawn of the electronic computing age.

The World Wide Web is actually just one of many applications that run on the Internet, a world-wide network of computer networks (or *internetwork*) that has been around in one form or another since 1961.

ON THE WEB

If you're curious about the origins of the Internet, read Bruce Sterling's excellent article on the subject at **gopher://oak.zilker.net:70/00/bruces/F_SF_Science_Column/F_SF_Five_**.

By the mid-1970s, many government agencies, research facilities, and universities were on this internetwork (which was then called ARPAnet), but each was running on its own internal network developed by the lowest bidder for their specific project. For example, the Army's system was built by DEC, the Air Force's by IBM, and the Navy's by Unisys. All were capable networks, but all spoke different languages. What was clearly needed to make things work smoothly was a set of networking *protocols* that would tie together disparate networks and enable them to communicate with each other.

In 1974, Vint Cerf and Bob Kahn published a paper titled "A Protocol for Packet Network Internetworking" that detailed a design that would solve the problem. In 1982, this solution was implemented as *TCP/IP.* TCP stands for *Transmission Control Protocol*; IP is the abbreviation for *Internet Protocol.* With the advent of TCP/IP, the word *Internet*—which is a portmanteau word for *interconnected networks*—entered the language.

The Department of Defense quickly declared the TCP/IP suite the standard protocol for internetworking military computers. TCP/IP has been ported to most computer systems, including personal computers, and has become the new standard in internetworking. It is the TCP/IP protocol set that provides the infrastructure for the Internet today.

TCP/IP comprises over 100 different protocols. It includes services for remote logon, file transfers, and data indexing and retrieval, among others.

ON THE WEB

An excellent source of additional information on TCP/IP is the introduction to the TCP/IP Gopher site at the University of California at Davis. Check it out at **gopher://gopher-chem.ucdavis.edu/11/Index/Internet_aw/Intro_the_Internet/intro.to.ip/**.

ON THE WEB

http://www.eff.org/papers/bdgtti/eegtti.html   One of the best online guides to the Internet as a whole is the Electronic Freedom Foundation's Extended Guide to the Internet.

The Web Explosion

There were a plethora of different data-indexing and retrieval experiments in the early days of the Net, but none was all-pervasive until, in 1991, Paul Lindner and Mark P. McCahill at the University of Minnesota created Gopher. Though it suffered from an overly cute (but highly descriptive) name, its technique for organizing files under an intuitive menuing system won it instant acceptance on the Net. The direct precursor in both concept and function to the World Wide Web, Gopher lacked hypertext links or graphic elements (see Figure 1.1). Although Gopher servers sprung up quickly all over the Internet, it was almost immediately apparent that something more was needed.

FIG. 1.1

Most Web browsers, like Netscape Navigator, can also display information on Gopher sites like this.

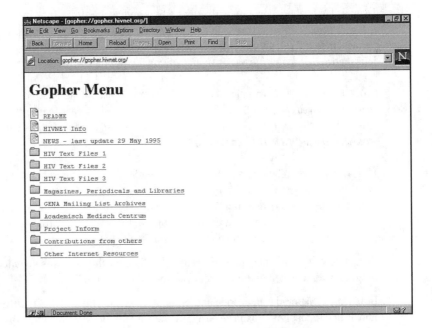

By the time "Gopherspace" began to establish itself on the Net, the European High-Energy Particle Physics Lab (CERN) had become the largest Internet site in Europe and was the driving force in getting the rest of Europe connected to the Net. To help promote and facilitate the concept of distributed computing via the Internet, Tim Berners-Lee created the World Wide Web in 1992.

The Web was an extension of the Gopher idea, but with many, many improvements. Inspired by Ted Nelson's work on Xanadu and the hypertext concept, the World Wide Web incorporated graphics, typographic text styles, and—most importantly—hypertext links.

N O T E   The hypertext concept predates personal computers. It was first proposed by computer visionary Ted Nelson in his ground-breaking, self-published book *Computer Lib/Dream Machines* in 1974.

In a nutshell, electronic hypertext involves adding links to words or phrases. When selected, these links jump you to associated text in the same document or in another document altogether. For example, you could click an unfamiliar term and jump to a definition, or add your own notes that would be optionally displayed when you or someone else selected the note's hyperlink.

The hypertext concept has since been expanded to incorporate the idea of *hypermedia*, in which links can also be added to and from graphics, video, and audio clips. ■

The World Wide Web used three new technologies:

- HTML (HyperText Markup Language) used to write Web pages.
- HTTP (HyperText Transfer Protocol) to transmit those pages.
- A Web browser client program to receive the data, interpret it, and display the results.

Using HTML, almost anyone with a text editor and access to an Internet site can build visually interesting pages that organize and present information in a way seldom seen in other online venues. In fact, Web sites are said to be composed of *pages* because the information on them looks more like magazine pages than traditional computer screens.

N O T E   HTML is, itself, an outgrowth of the much more complex SGML, or Standard Generalized Markup Language. SGML is (rarely) also used for creating pages on the Web, though it takes a different browser to be able to view SGML pages. You can find out all about SGML at **http://www.w3.org/pub/WWW/MarkUp/SGML/**. ■

HTML is a markup language, which means that Web pages can only be viewed by using a specialized Internet terminal program called a *Web browser*. In the beginning, the potential was there for the typical computing "chicken and the egg problem": no one would create Web pages because no one owned a browser program to view them with, and no one would get a browser program because there were no Web pages to view.

Fortunately, this did not happen, because shortly after the Web was invented, a killer browser program was released to the Internet community—free of charge!

In 1993, the National Center for Supercomputing Applications (NCSA) at the University of Illinois at Champaign-Urbana released Mosaic, a Web browser designed by Marc Andreessen and developed by a team of students and staff at the University of Illinois (see Figure 1.2). It spread like wildfire though the Internet community; within a year, an estimated two million users were on the Web with Mosaic. Suddenly, everyone was browsing the Web, and everyone else was creating Web pages. Nothing in the history of computing had grown so fast.

ON THE WEB

http://www.ncsa.uiuc.edu/SDG/Software/Mosaic/   For more information on NCSA Mosaic, check out the NCSA Web site.

FIG. 1.2
NCSA Mosaic, the
browser that drove the
phenomenal growth of
the World Wide Web.

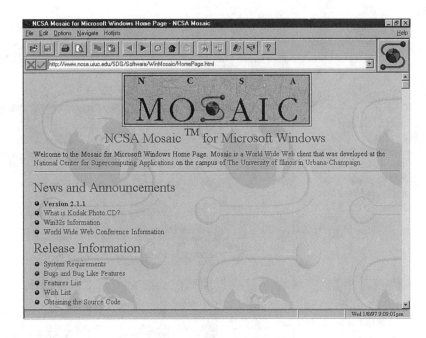

By mid-1993, there were 130 sites on the World Wide Web. Six months later, there were over 600. Today, there may be as many as a million Web sites in the world (depending on whose figures you believe).

Mosaic's success—and the fact that its source code was distributed for free—spawned a wave of new browser introductions. Each topped the previous by adding new HTML commands and features. Marc Andreessen moved on from NCSA and joined with Jim Clark of Silicon Graphics to found Netscape Communications Corporation. They took along most of the NCSA Mosaic development team, which quickly turned out the first version of Netscape Navigator for Windows, Macintosh, and UNIX platforms. Because of its many new features and free trial preview offer, Netscape Navigator quickly became the most popular browser on the Web. The Web's incredible growth even attracted Microsoft's attention, and in 1995, they introduced their Internet Explorer Web browser to coincide with the launch of their new WWW service, the Microsoft Network (MSN).

Established online services like CompuServe, America Online, and Prodigy scrambled to meet their users' demands to add Web access to their systems. Most of them quickly developed their own versions of Mosaic, customized to work in conjunction with their proprietary online services. This enabled millions of established commercial service subscribers to spill over onto the Web virtually overnight; "old-timers" who had been on the Web since its beginning (only a year and a half or so before) suddenly found themselves overtaken by a tidal wave of Web-surfing *newbies*. Even television discovered the Web, and it seemed that every other news report featured a story about surfing the Net.

The World Wide Web didn't get its name by accident. It truly is a web that encompasses just about every topic in the world. A quick look at the premier index to the Web, Yahoo!

(**http://www.yahoo.com**), lists topics as diverse as art, world news, sports, business, libraries, classified advertising, education, TV, science, fitness, and politics (see Figure 1.3). You can't get much more diverse than that! There are literally thousands of sites listed on Yahoo! and other online indexes.

FIG. 1.3

If you really want to know what's on the Web, you need look no further than Yahoo!, which serves as a good example of an excellent Web site itself.

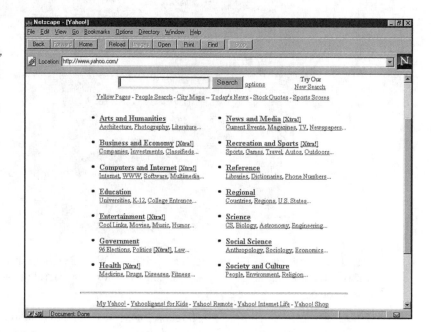

ON THE WEB

http://www.boutell.com/faq   For more information about the World Wide Web, consult the WWW FAQ.

The Rise of the Corporate Intranet

The World Wide Web explosion shows no signs of slowing down. It proved so intuitive and so much fun to use that people almost immediately began to see other uses for the Web browsing "metaphor."

One of the first and most obvious was to build Webs that didn't communicate over the Internet at all, but were confined within the computer systems of individual companies and institutions. A term was quickly coined to distinguish these internal Webs: *intranets*.

The major difference between an intranet and a Web site—besides the obvious fact that the former is constrained to an individual site, while the latter is worldwide—is the audience. On a Web site, the content is aimed at the public, while an intranet addresses the needs of an organization's own employees (see Figure 1.4).

FIG. 1.4
HTML-based corporate intranets like this one give employees quick-and-easy access to company databases

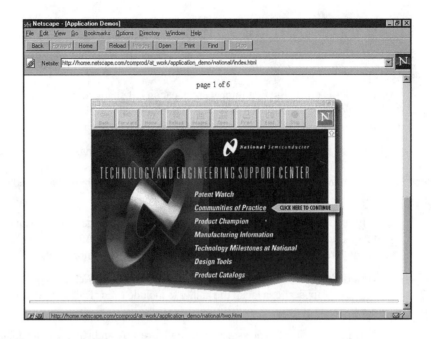

This means that intranets are more likely to contain company-specific—even confidential—data, such as sales reports, customer databases, training materials, and employee manuals.

Though these kinds of data have been available on internal corporate networks for years, the difference with intranets is in the presentation. HTML and associated technologies are used to create user interfaces which are as fun and easy to use as those on most World Wide Web sites. Data which might have previously been locked up in difficult-to-use corporate databases can be made easily accessible to even computer novices.

Even with only a year or two of real-world usage, the utility of corporate intranets has already been proved beyond the shadow of a doubt. Netscape Communications Corporation, a publisher of Web-server and client software and one of the premier advocates of intranet development, says that a resounding majority of their intranet customers report substantial cost savings after installing corporate intranets. Some have claimed 1000% returns on their investments, according to Netscape. In the world of business, this is a phenomenal rate of return, and a claim which has grabbed the attention of the majority of Fortune 500 companies—as well as many that are much, much smaller.

ON THE WEB

http://home.netscape.com/comprod/announce/roi.html   Use this site to read Netscape Communication Corporation's study on intranet return-on-investment.

In fact, interest in intranets is so great that HTML server and client publishers like Netscape and Microsoft predict that the majority of their HTML-related income over the next few years will be generated by intranet development, not the World Wide Web.

HTML in E-Mail and News

HTML is also showing up in many other places you might not expect—electronic mail, for example.

E-mail was one of the first Internet applications. It changed the way scientists collaborated in the mid-60s, and continues to be one of the major applications of Internet technology. Millions more people use the Internet for e-mail than use it for Web surfing.

Perhaps, then, it should come as no surprise that HTML has made its way into e-mail messages. HTML affords the same benefits to e-mail as it does to Web pages or intranets: an easy and fun-to-use interface; integration of text and graphics; hyperlinks; and the ability to integrate video, sound, and applications inline, to name just a few.

Where e-mail is just a way to exchange text, HTML-enhanced e-mail can enhance and reinforce text messages with graphics or other "rich" information. After all, sometimes a picture—or sound bite, or video clip—is worth a thousand words, or more.

Hyperlinks mean the ability to link an e-mail message to Web sites or intranet information. Integrated applications mean the ability to include even "live" spreadsheets or other data into e-mail messages.

Extend this concept to newsgroups (see Figure 1.5), and you have the ability to turn static, all-text news postings into truly collaborative works. One worker can post an HTML message which contains an AutoCAD drawing, for example, and all the other members of the group can comment on it, adding notes or even making changes to the drawing itself.

FIG. 1.5

E-mail messages and newsgroup postings created with HTML can have all the look, feel, and functionality of Web pages.

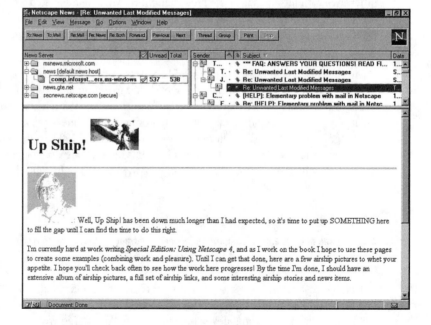

Clearly, HTML in messages—both e-mail and newsgroups—may have as much of an impact on the way people communicate and collaborate online as the Web or intranets have already had.

> **CAUTION**
>
> Not all e-mail programs and newsgroup readers can correctly interpret HTML-enhanced messages. Only use HTML in such messages when you're sure your intended audience can read them properly.

HTML for GUIs

But that's not the end of HTML's potential. Both Microsoft and Netscape are advocating that HTML be used as the basis for creating stand-alone applications, too.

That HTML's user interface is friendly and easy-to-use has certainly been well-established on the Web and corporate intranets. But, because HTML documents can also incorporate *active* objects like ActiveX controls, Java applets, and JavaScript scripts, HTML pages can act as containers for applications. HTML tags can be used to format text, graphics, interactive buttons, forms, and other objects on-screen which interact with the user just as any other GUI (Graphical User Interface). Incorporated into the HTML page are objects such as an ActiveX control or a Java applet (see Figure 1.6).

FIG. 1.6

This JavaScript-based online calculator is just a simple example of using HTML to create the user interface for an application program.

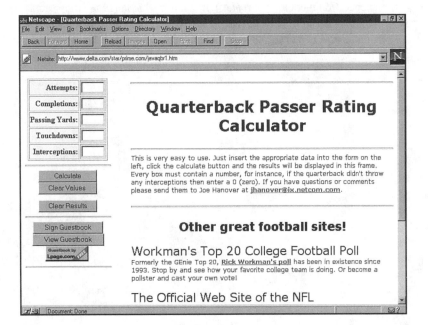

By using HTML as the GUI-development language, the developer gains a whole list of advantages:

■ GUI development is sped up considerably. Rather than using a high-level language like C or C++, the GUI is created quickly with simple HTML.

■ GUIs can be created by end users, or at least by relatively inexperienced personnel, which is cheaper and faster than tying up programmers.

■ GUIs can be easily debugged and modified, further freeing up development resources.

■ GUI development is not tied to application development. Applications can be of any type, from ActiveX controls to Java applets to JavaScript or VBScript applications.

■ It's easy to develop applications that can access data locally, over a corporate intranet, and over the Internet without having to change the code.

■ User interfaces are naturally easy to use and easy to learn, because they use the familiar Web metaphor.

Netscape is actively pushing Sun's Java as its development language of choice, while Microsoft would like to see developers using their ActiveX controls. But each supports the other and—most importantly—both advocate HTML as the GUI-development language.

As this concept catches on, you'll see more applications developed with HTML interfaces, and HTML will become important in its own right as a language for "gluing together" mini-application modules (or *applets*), no matter what language those applets have been written in. In time, it may be the majority of special-purpose software and shareware is written in this way, and even a percentage of commercial applications may be developed in this manner. ●

## CHAPTER 2

HTML Page Design and Implementation

by Mark R. Brown

In this chapter

What HTML Is

It isn't a programming language. HTML is exactly what it claims to be—a markup language. You use HTML to mark up a text document, just as you would if you were an editor with a red pencil. The marks you use indicate which format (or presentation style) should be used when displaying the marked text.

If you have ever used an old word-processor program, you already know how a markup language works. In older word-processing programs, if you wanted text to appear in italics, you might surround it with control characters like this:

```
/Ithis is in italics/i
```

When the document was printed, the /I would kick your line printer into italics mode, and the following text would be printed in italics. The /i would then turn italics off. The printer didn't actually print the /I or /i. They were just codes to tell it what to do. But the "marked up" text in between appeared in italics.

This is exactly how HTML works. If you want text to appear on a Web page in italics, you mark it like this:

```
<I>this is in italics</I>
```

The `<I>` turns italics on; the `</I>` turns them off. The `<I>` and `</I>` tags don't appear on-screen, but the text in between is displayed in italics.

Everything you create in HTML relies on marks, or *tags*. To be a great HTML "programmer," all you need to learn is which tags do what.

Of course, nothing in the real world is ever quite that simple. In truth, simple HTML gets a big boost in real-world page design from add-ons like Java and JavaScript, VBScript, CGI programming, cascading style sheets, ActiveX controls, and other page-design extenders and expanders. But, you can still get started in HTML page design by using nothing but a handful of basic HTML tags and a good text editor.

The Only Tool You Really Need

Because HTML is a tag-oriented text markup language that works with standard ASCII text, all you really need to begin creating HTML pages is a good text editor. If you're using a version of Windows, for example, good old Notepad will do just fine.

Listing 2.1 is a simple HTML document that you can recreate by using Notepad.

Listing 2.1   A Sample HTML Document

```
<HTML>
<HEAD>
<TITLE>A Simple Sample HTML Document</TITLE>
</HEAD>
<BODY>
```

```
<H1>Welcome to the World of HTML</H1>
<HR>
HTML documents can be as simple as this Web page, which consists of just a
single page of <B>text</B> and <I>links</I>, or as complex as a 10,000
page corporate intranet site replete with Java applets and CGI database
access. <P>
In this book, we'll explore the possibilities of HTML, but we'll also
check out what can be done by adding other elements to your documents.<P>
Click <A HREF="sample.htm">HERE</A> to reload this page!<P>
</BODY>
</HTML>
```

Don't worry that you don't know what these markup tags mean for right now—they are explained in the next few chapters. Just type this sample document into your text editor of choice and save it by using the file name **sample.htm**. (Make sure your editor is set to save in simple ASCII text mode.) Then fire up your Web browser and load this file from disk. You should see a display similar to that in Figure 2.1.

 TIP In Netscape Navigator 4, you can load a file from disk by selecting File, Open Page from the menu. In Microsoft Internet Explorer, choose File, Open. Then use the Browse (or Choose File) button to locate the file you want. Other browser programs work similarly.

FIG. 2.1
Netscape Navigator displays the sample HTML file from Listing 2.1.

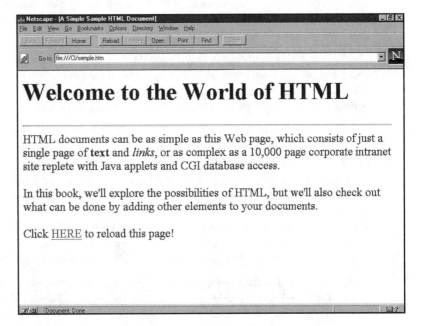

Of course, just as most carpentry projects are easier when you have a selection of power tools rather than a couple of hand tools, the job of creating HTML documents is made easier if you have a selection of software tools to help you along. Chapter 42, "Using HTML and Site Tools,"

discusses a variety of HTML editors that speed and simplify the task of editing HTML, and many of the other chapters in this book describe graphics editors and other software tools to ease the creation of the other elements you'll want to incorporate into your HTML documents.

Image Is Not Everything

Billy Crystal's Fernando character on Saturday Night Live used to say, "As we all know, it is better to look good than to feel good…and you look mahvelous!" Unfortunately, it seems that many HTML developers have a similar attitude: They believe it is more important for their pages to look good than to actually be good. For example, you can find plenty of Web sites that are loaded with colorful graphics and have a multitude of links to click; but, they often lack good, solid content.

It might be better to follow the advice of the 20th Century's most famous architect, Frank Lloyd Wright, who coined the mantra of modern architecture: "Form Follows Function."

Because HTML documents can contain so many flashy elements—graphics, animations, video clips, and even interactive games—it's easy for the message to be overwhelmed. When designing HTML pages, you need to continually ask yourself: "Is this really necessary?"

Before adding a page-design element, you should determine that the element will actually enhance and emphasize the message your document is trying to communicate. What are you trying to say? Does that graphic, sound bite, or table help you communicate your message? If the answer is "no," then you should rethink your page design.

The flip side of this is, of course, that if your HTML pages have excellent content but aren't visually appealing, people aren't likely to stay around long enough to find out just how good they are. People have a tendency to judge a book by its cover, and with so many well-done, attractive HTML documents out there, you're up against some stiff competition.

 A case in point, chosen at random, is the Defense Technical Information Center's Business Process Reengineering Help Desk Web site, found at **http://www.dtic.dla.mil/ bpr-helpdesk/** (see Figure 2.2). Though this government site links to a lot of important information, it's not clear from this page to what kinds of information it leads. Though there's a big, colorful department logo, an animated e-mail icon, and even a nice, subtle American flag background graphic, the menu is a wad of text-link acronyms that convey limited information. There's plenty of room on this page to have organized things better, and to even have included a bit of explanatory text. Unfortunately, most visitors won't have a clue what's available from this site. It just isn't clear. People will need help first in order to use this Help Desk!

If you're going to draw people in, you have to present your pages the way a politician campaigns: You've only got the public's attention for a quick sound bite, so you must make your impression up front.

FIG. 2.2
What's this site all about? How do you get to the information you need? Unfortunately, it's hard to tell.

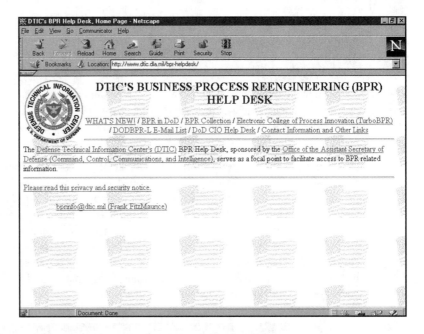

Part
I

Ch
2

N O T E Though you want to strive for good design, don't just shove a bunch of extra elements down your viewers' throats—give them a choice! If you want to add Java applications, animations, sound files, video clips, and even background graphics to your pages, make them optional. Don't make your visitors automatically load a home page that is overloaded with lots of noncritical elements. Viewers with slow modem connections will especially appreciate the opportunity to not view everything on your pages. ■

The Right Stuff

It's been established that looks aren't everything, but that without looks you'll never get your message across. Now, it's time to think about what that message will be.

Keep Focused

Here's your new motto: Keep in-focus!

Your HTML documents should focus on a single topic or, at most, a cluster of closely associated topics. If you're developing a Web site, for example, there are millions of Web surfers out there, and most of them won't even slow down for a generic, generalized site. They want to find information and entertainment that suits their personal needs, wants, and tastes. The odds are that you'll never find even a handful of individuals who share your dual interests in, say, windsurfing and Baroque music. It would be suicide to mix the two on a Web page—those who are interested in one topic will be turned off by the other, and move on. But if you put up a site devoted to one or the other, you'll pull in thousands of like-minded individuals. (And remember, there's nothing to keep you from putting two separate sites on the Web!)

Above all, your pages should be interesting. Whether you're developing a Web site or a corporate intranet, or even if you're just enhancing an e-mail or news message, your HTML documents should appeal to the audience you have identified for them, and should communicate your message clearly. The topic should be focused—the tighter, the better.

There are a million Web sites devoted to music, for example. The odds of drawing much of a crowd with such a generic topic are slim—you're sure to be overwhelmed by other bigger and better established Web sites with more resources to devote to the project.

 However, if your Web site is focused on something specific, such as Lithuanian folk music, you're sure to pull in a devoted following of true, die-hard advocates of the topic. Figure 2.3 is a perfect example of a Web site with a tightly defined subject matter. The St. Augustine page at the University of Pennsylvania (**http://ccat.sas.upenn.edu/jod/augustine.html**) is a scholarly site devoted completely to the study of St. Augustine. There are complete texts (including some in Latin), images, commentaries, and essays, all presented in a well-organized and appealing way. And it's not stuffy—you'll even find the lyrics to Sting's rock-and-roll ballad, "St. Augustine in Hell"! This site won't attract many punk rockers or rocket scientists. However, its intended audience—philosophers and theologians, both amateur and professional—are sure to not only find it, but to keep coming back.

FIG. 2.3

This page, devoted to the study of St. Augustine, is a perfect example of an HTML document that is focused, well-presented, and rich in content.

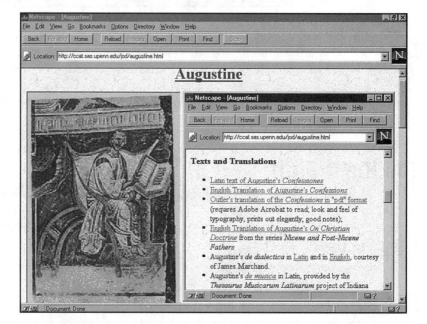

On the Links

Here's another motto for you: Think hyper!

Almost every HTML document features hypertext links; they're what make HTML unique. But, I'm sure you've seen many Web sites which have a huge, unorganized list of links, some of which are more relevant to the topic at hand than others. A well-organized list of links—whether to associated Web pages or to a network database—can be a valuable asset to an HTML document.

For example, Scott Yanoff began his list of must-see sites on the Internet back before the World Wide Web existed. People would download his list of informative Gopher, FTP, and Telnet sites every month or grab it off their UseNet news feed when it was updated. With the advent of the Web, Yanoff added Web sites to his list and set up a site of his own to host the list (**http://www.spectracom.com/islist/**). It is, and always has been, one of the best topically organized lists of resources on the Net (see Figure 2.4). Take a look at his site, and try to do as good a job of organizing your own hypertext link lists.

Part

I

Ch

2

FIG. 2.4
Scott Yanoff's topical list of Internet services is one of the most comprehensive and well-organized lists of resources on the Web.

Timeliness

One of the reasons people love the World Wide Web is because of its capability to deliver new information with an immediacy that can only be matched by other broadcast media such as TV and radio. Whenever news breaks—whether it is a major world event or the release of the latest new software product—you can bet that the Web will have the information first. If you can keep the information on your site up-to-the-minute fresh, you're sure to attract loyal viewers.

Don't let your Web site lag behind. Keep it up-to-date. Always be on the lookout for new information and new links. Make sure to delete or update older information so that your site never, ever presents outdated or stale information. And, even if you're creating an internal intranet, you want to make sure the information contained therein is timely and accurate.

There are hundreds of daily news sites on the Web that do an amazing job of posting the latest news items every day. Even if your site isn't news-oriented, you can learn a few things by checking out how these sites keep up the pace. Figure 2.5 shows the Web site of the *Beloit Daily News,* one of the smaller newspapers keeping a daily presence on the Web—and doing an excellent job of it. Check out their site at **http://www.beloitdailynews.com/**.

FIG. 2.5
The *Beloit Daily News* is just one of hundreds of sites that presents the latest news stories on the Web daily—or even hourly!

ON THE WEB

http://www.cnn.com/   For general news updated on a daily basis, you can't beat CNN's Web pages.

http://www.news.com/   For the best in computer-related daily news, check out c|net's site.

Create a Vortex

So your HTML documents should be appealing, focused, organized, and up-to-date. That's not too much to ask, is it? The whole idea is to create an information vortex that draws in your audience like a spider draws in flies.

You've got to strike a careful balance between form and content, between innovation and familiarity. People long for the new, innovative, and unique—but, conversely, they are more comfortable with the recognizable and familiar. Everything must work together to make your pages appealing.

Everything in your documents should be directed toward delivering your message. All should point to the center: your focus topic. Graphics should illustrate, links should be relevant, and design should set a mood.

 There are people accomplishing this every day on the World Wide Web. For example, take a look at Figure 2.6, the Web site for the Rock and Roll Hall of Fame at **http:// www.rockhall.com**. The home page features a big, colorful, playful, clickable graphic menu that leads to fun and relevant areas of interest—from a tour of the museum itself to a list of the 500 top rock songs of all time. There's even a thoughtful link to the Cleveland home page. (This is a good tie-in because the Rock Hall is a tourist attraction, and potential visitors want to know about travel, hotels, restaurants, and other tourist sites in the area).

Right up front are two very timely items: a link to Rock News and an item right below the menu showing what happened in rock-and-roll history on this date. The first thing you think when you check into this site is, "awesome!" All of the information is relevant and up front, so the site accomplishes its real goal: to entice people to visit the Rock and Roll Hall of Fame.

FIG. 2.6

The Rock and Roll Hall of Fame Web site is the perfect example of what an HTML document should be: entertaining, appealing, and focused, with a clear goal in mind.

The Wrong Stuff

So what shouldn't you put into your HTML documents? That's easy—just turn around everything said so far.

Remember to focus. Don't try to be everything to everybody. This is the number-two problem of many personal sites on the World Wide Web—they haven't defined who or what they are there for. They spew out whatever pops up in whatever areas interest them at the moment. You might see graphics of motorcycles, rock bands, comic book characters, and computer screens all mixed up like a nightmare collage.

"Wait a minute," you protest, "you said that's the number-two problem of personal Web sites. What's number one?"

Even worse than a site that's burdened with everything is one that contains nothing of interest at all. Many personal sites contain next to nothing: lists of CDs or comic books the person owns; pictures of his or her dog, gerbil, or fish; fuzzy photos of the site's owner goofing around with friends; and so on. Let's face it; except for a small circle of your very closest friends, nobody but nobody (not even your significant other) wants to know that much about you. So why put it up in public? It's a waste of bandwidth. It's boring!

What astounds me is many people are aware that it's mind-numbingly boring, and yet they put it up anyway! Some even seem to take pride in how boring they can make their sites, as shown by examples like the following page, appropriately titled "My Boring Life" (see Figure 2.7). Please don't ever put another site like this up on the Web. There are far too many of them already.

FIG. 2.7

There are already too many boring sites on the Web. Make sure yours isn't one of them.

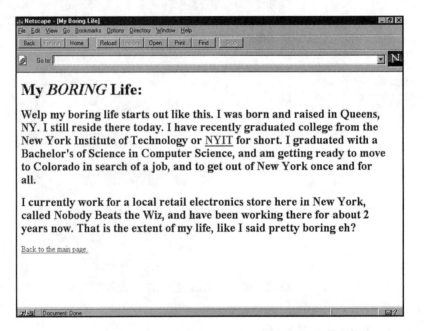

 The number one rule of writing is this: Have something to say. If a writer has a message, or a story, or a cause, he or she never gets writer's block. Apply the same rule to your HTML documents, and you'll never have to worry about what you should create.

Another thing you definitely don't want to do is to put up a page that consists of nothing but huge wads of unedited, unorganized links, such as the Web site shown in Figure 2.8. (And don't mistake alphabetical order for organization!) This site is like a library where the books are stacked at random. It's almost worse than having none at all. People want useful links, but they also want to be able to find them easily.

FIG. 2.8
An unorganized list of random links is of no use to anyone. At least this site included short descriptions!

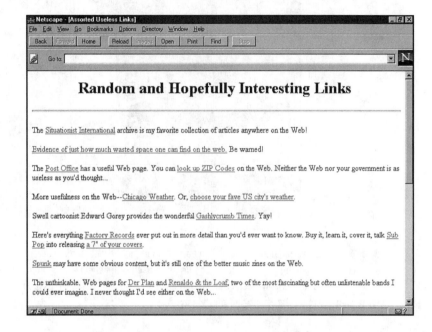

Everyone expects data in an HTML document—especially one on the Web—to be up-to-date and accurate. The worst thing you can do to your viewers is put up some purportedly useful data only to have it go stale. It's better to take your site down completely than to let it sit there with outdated, useless information.

Figure 2.9 is an example of a site past its prime. It features a graph of card prices for the collectable trading card game, "Magic: The Gathering." Prices for these cards fluctuate wildly, and when the data was current, this was a valuable service for card collectors. Unfortunately, the site is still up, and, as of this writing, the information is well over a year out of date. This is worse than useless, as someone is likely to consult this graph and not notice that the information is outdated. They could make some bad decisions based on this old data. Don't ever do this to those who visit your site. If you can't keep it current, take it down.

FIG. 2.9
The data in this graph is outdated and useless. Visitors to this site are going to be disappointed.

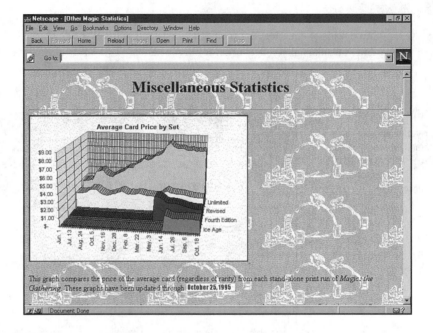

N O T E Poor grammar and poor spelling are rampant on the Web. If a document is worth doing, it's worth doing well. No one is too hurried to use a spell checker or grammar checker. People who read your documents will assume that bad English usage and misspellings mean that you don't know what you're talking about, and they'll move on. ■

Legal and Moral Issues

When you're creating a private e-mail message, closed newsgroup post, or corporate intranet, you probably don't have to worry much about possible legal problems with your HTML documents. After all, your audience is on the same team you are on, and your communications are most likely governed by company policies and guidelines. However, when you create a site on the World Wide Web you are subject to many of the same laws that govern printing, publishing, and broadcasting.

> **CAUTION**
> This section is not a legal guide. It is, rather, an overview of some of the legal issues to keep in mind when you are developing HTML documents. For advice on legal matters, consult an attorney.

Be a Legal Eagle

The first amendment to the U.S. Constitution guarantees every American the right of free speech (and, of course, most other free nations have similar laws). This does not guarantee you the right to say anything you want with impunity. People who feel that you have treated them unfairly in public have legal recourse. You can be sued for libel and slander for anything you say on the Web, just as you could if you had printed it on paper. And in this litigious society, it is probably better to err on the side of caution than to strike out boldly and without forethought.

Controversy and debate online are fine, but if you're diplomatic and noninflammatory you'll not only avoid legal battles, you'll attract more sympathizers. After all, you're on the Web to share your ideas, not to entice someone to sue you. Before you post something questionable, consider the following: Even if you're sure you'd win, do you really want to spend your time sitting in court for months on end?

The right to privacy ties in closely with libel and slander issues. If you receive private information about any of your users—through a registration form, for example—you must be very, very careful about how it is used and who has access to it. Though there is no actual law guaranteeing U.S. citizens a right to privacy, there is a long-established legal precedent that says it is a basic right implied by the U.S. Constitution. It is best to keep all such information completely private, unless you have asked for and received specific permission to use it publicly.

Perhaps no laws are more openly flaunted on the Web than those concerning copyright and plagiarism. Everyone seems to steal text, graphics, programs, hypertext link lists, HTML code, and everything else from one another pretty freely and openly. However, the most recent U.S. copyright law says that all original creative works in any medium (including electronic) are automatically assigned to their creator when created. No registration is necessary (though it is a good idea, so that ownership can be proven if challenged). Again, it's best to not "borrow" anything at all from anyone else's site, unless you have written permission to do so.

No Web-related topic has gotten more press than the issue of adult material on the Web and its accessibility by minors. It is such a hot topic that Congress included tough anti-pornography language directed at the Internet in the Telecommunications Act of 1996. Although this law was quickly challenged in the courts, it has made many ISPs very, very nervous about the content of pages posted through their sites. If you plan to post adult material on your site, you certainly should at least make people enter through a disclaimer page. And make sure you have the permission of your ISP beforehand, or you could be kicked unceremoniously offline at the first hint of controversy.

 Got you scared, now? You say you need advice? The Electronic Frontier Foundation is the champion of the rights of those online. If you have questions about copyrights, pornography, libel, or other legal issues online, the odds are good that you can find the answers on the EFF site at **http://www.eff.org** (see Figure 2.10).

Electronic Morality

Once past the legal issues, you might want to stop a moment and ponder the fine line between rights and responsibilities. Are you the guardian of society's mores? Is it up to you to try to bolster a civilization that is sagging under its own decaying weight?

FIG. 2.10

The Electronic Frontier Foundation home page features full coverage of the topic of legal issues online, including a lively discussion of the Telecommunications Act of 1996.

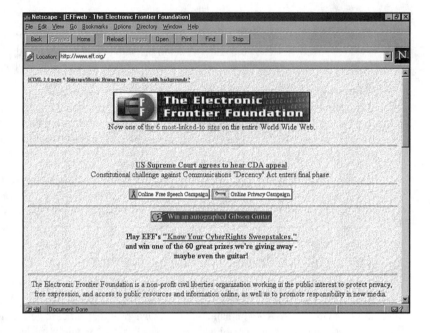

Some people consider it better to be positive than negative, to build up rather than to tear down. With a forum as wide-ranging as the World Wide Web, anyone putting up a Web site has a huge potential audience, and therefore a potential to do great good or great harm.

Nonetheless, there are legitimate issues, worthy of open discussion, that are the subjects of controversial Web sites. Take tax reform, for instance. Many sides of this issue are represented in force on the Web (see Figure 2.11), and all draw their share of criticism, harassment, and hate mail. Those who have chosen to establish these sites may consider the controversy all part of the territory. There are religious denominations, environmentalists, pro-choice and pro-life organizations, neo-Nazis, and other controversial groups on the Web that are constantly drawing fire from others. Before you establish a site that's destined to become the center of controversy, you should answer just one question: Can you take the heat? If the answer is "yes," then by all means go online with your views.

Sending Your Work Out into the World

As noted in the previous chapter, HTML isn't just for Web pages anymore. People are using HTML to create corporate intranets, flashy e-mail and news postings, and even user interfaces for applications.

So what do you do with your HTML once you've written it? As you might expect, that depends on your application.

FIG. 2.11

All sorts of controversial sites, such as this tax reform newsletter page, exist on the Web. Before you set one up, make sure you're willing to do battle for your cause.

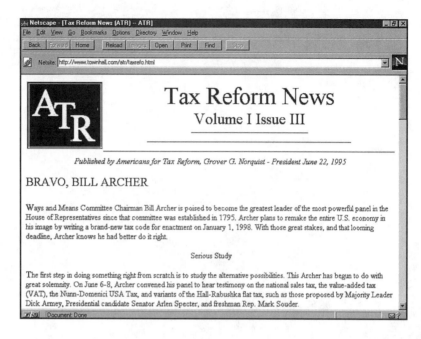

Part
I

Ch
2

If your HTML pages are destined for the World Wide Web, you'll likely upload them to your ISP (Internet service provider). Finding an ISP to host your Web pages is a relatively simple task these days. If you're on an online service like America Online, you probably already have space available to you, whether you know it or not. Most local ISPs also include a few megabytes of space for hosting your pages, all as a part of your dial-up service contract. Chapter 3, "Putting Your Web Pages Online," provides detailed information on how you can get your Web site up and running.

If you're developing for a corporate intranet, or if your Web pages will be hosted by your organization's own Web server, you need to set up the server computer to host your pages. The details will vary with different installations, and you'll need to work them out with your system administrator.

If your HTML is destined to dress up e-mail or newsgroup posts, you'll need to use an e-mail or newsgroup program that allows attaching HTML to messages. Netscape Communicator's Messenger (for e-mail) and Collabra (for news) applications include this capability, as do Internet Explorer 4.0's Outlook Express and many others.

Finally, HTML for GUI (graphical user interface) development means your HTML code will be bundled together with controls, applets, and other bits and pieces of the application for distribution as a package. If you're not the sole developer of the application itself, the project coordinator will likely be in charge of making sure all the pieces come together as needed. ●

Putting Your Web Pages Online

by Rob Falla and Mark R. Brown

In this chapter

What Are Your Options?

Before you publish your Web site to the Internet you should consider the options available; your choice depends on your individual situation. Read this section to gain a better understanding of the two Web-site publishing options—your own server versus having your site hosted by an Internet Service Provider—and select the one that best suits your needs.

The most common choice—considering the initial cash outlay required to set up and run your own server—is to let someone else worry about the equipment upkeep. Unless you're developing a complete Internet solution for a large company, one that makes use of other Internet features such as FTP (file downloading), e-mail, and possibly a database, you probably do not require your own server. Make a few phone calls, do a price and service comparison, have you site hosted by one of your local Internet Service Providers (ISPs).

The focus of this chapter is getting your Web site published on someone else's system. Considering the differences between the policies of the various ISPs, you should look for certain features before signing on with any particular ISP. In addition to a standard dial-up account with e-mail, you need a shell and an FTP account. It is only common sense that you have easy access to your Web files.

Uploading Files to an ISP

This is the easiest method if you can find an ISP that offers shell accounts and FTP (not a requirement, but makes it much easier). If you plan to make frequent modifications to the content of your site, having UNIX shell and FTP (File Transfer Protocol) access means you can quickly add and remove files, add new subdirectories, and include server-side scripts (depending on the ISP), among other benefits like using the UNIX mail to sort your e-mail.

Run Your Own Server

This option is not for everyone—it needs to be considered very carefully. The initial cash layout for the appropriate telephone line service and modem is in excess of $1,000—not a commitment to be taken lightly. In addition to purchasing the digital telephone line service and the digital modems, you also need a computer to act as the server. You do not want your accounting files and sales strategy on the same machine the world is connected to.

Both options achieve the same goal of making the data on the Web site available to anyone on the Internet with a Web-client application (*browser*). The delivery methods are the same as well. The only difference is that you are burdened with maintenance of the networked system—which can become an enormous task if any major problems arise.

Running your own server means you have total control over who sees your Web site and what kinds of content you can include with your Web site. You can make sections of the site available to anyone with a browser and restrict other parts of your Web site so only authorized users can access it. You own the Web site, and you own the space on the Internet that the Web site is occupying. This option is usually only available if you have a direct connection to the Internet.

You can run a server off your hard drive through a dial-up account, but the Web site would only be available when you are logged on. Also, you would have to make arrangements with your ISP to make sure you had the same IP address each time you log in.

Uploading to an ISP is actually like renting space in which to store your Web site files. Along with the many benefits, saving money being the biggest, there are a few drawbacks. For one, you have very little control over who can actually access the site. You can't include server-side script files unless arrangements have been made with the administrator (often requiring no more than a call to the ISP).

 Talk to your ISP if you want to use CGI Script or server-side Java and JavaScript.

The benefits to using someone else's system include not having to put out the cash to upgrade to a server grade computer, not being responsible for ensuring the system is always operating, and avoiding the monthly bill for having dedicated Internet access.

Part
I

Ch
3

Choosing an Option

It is important to determine the resources available to you (see Table 3.1).

Table 3.1   Examine the Requirements

Requirement	Own Server	ISP
Dedicated access	✓	
Dial-up access		✓
System monitoring	✓	
System maintenance	✓	

It's not that difficult to choose the appropriate publishing method once you have determined the resources available to you. Answer the following questions about your operation and Web site:

■ Do you or your firm have dedicated Internet access or the resources to set it up?

■ Do you or your firm have the resources/manpower to maintain a server?

■ Is the site a large Web application type site, using Java applets, server-side scripts, movies and audio files?

■ Do you require a secure server?

If you answered "yes" to the above questions, you probably want to run your own server. You are not required to, but it would be to your benefit. If you answered "no" to the first two questions and "yes" to the others, you may want to have a discussion with your ISP about your needs. He may have a reasonably priced solution for someone in your situation; if he can't help you, shop around. Many ISPs will try to accommodate your needs; be prepared to pay.

Do you already have the money, the equipment, and the dedicated access to the Internet? Your choice is obvious. You should look over the information about servers in the Web Servers section of this chapter and go with the one that best matches your requirements. Not much of a decision if you're already set up for it.

N O T E   Still think you need the power of running your own server, but you do not have the resources or the dedicated account? There is still a chance that you can run a server (like Microsoft's Personal Web Server) from your local computer.

Your Web site would only be accessible while you were online. The rest of the time the user would get a `File not found` error.

It is beyond the scope of this book to get into the particulars of this option. If you want to find out more, talk to your ISP. ▨

Everyone else will be uploading to the ISP. This choice still offers a range of options for dynamic content inclusions. Many ISPs will put your CGI script on their system to work with your order form, guestbook, or for whatever else you may need a CGI script.

T I P   There will most likely be a fee for putting your custom CGI script on the system. The ISP has to test the script first, to make sure it isn't going to mess up the system by inadvertently allowing someone access to the system. If it passes the test, it is put on the system. If it poses a security threat, it's not likely to be on the system until the threat is eliminated.

There's the obvious benefit of not having to worry about monitoring the system. If there are any problems, the administrator will fix it. You can concentrate on producing the Web site and let someone else worry about keeping the system alive.

Carefully consider the next two sections of this chapter when deciding which option to go with. The first, "Uploading to an ISP," takes you through the steps to publish your Web site on someone else's server. The next section, "Preparing Your Site," discusses running your own server and talks about the requirements of running it.

Uploading to an ISP

Uploading to the ISP is relatively easy. All you have to do is follow the steps outlined in this section. This section is a generic set of instructions based on a UNIX account. Check with your ISP to see if there is any special procedure that must be followed on that system.

T I P   Some ISPs require you to e-mail the HTML files to them. They place the files in a directory area designated for your Web site. These ISPs charge a fee for putting the files on, and they charge a fee for any updates to your Web site. If the ISP you are dealing with works like that, shop around. It could quickly become very expensive to keep your content fresh in such a situation.

As you progress through this section, notice the following steps:

- Preparing your UNIX shell account for a Web site
- Setting the permissions in the Web site directory
- Making any subdirectories that your site requires
- Uploading the HTML files
- Uploading any other files related to your site
- Preparing the files for presentation on the Internet

Make yourself a checklist of all the required steps. When it's time to put your files online, refer to the checklist to ensure you do not make any mistakes or forget any steps.

Preparing Your Site

The first thing you must do when putting a new Web site on the Internet is prepare the home on the networked computer in which the files will reside while they are on the Internet.

 TIP Check with your ISP before you attempt to put a Web site on their network. They may not allow UNIX Telnet sessions, or they may complete the following steps for you.

NOTE As stated at the beginning of this chapter, you should have an account with an ISP that offers shell account access. This section assumes you have the shell account. ■

You have to be online first. Once you are online, initiate a Telnet session. (If you aren't allowed to Telnet, you'll have to have your ISP do your setup for you.) The Telnet client will communicate with the remote system requesting Telnet access. The Telnet session goes like this:

1. Enter the host address in the Telnet client. Telnet establishes a connection.
2. Enter your log-in ID and password when prompted.
3. Type **pwd** at the prompt to see which directory you are in. You should be in your own area on the system. The reply message should look something like this: /user/home/userid/. That would be your directory on the system.

NOTE Microsoft Windows 95 includes a Telnet client. To use the Telnet client, click the MSDOS prompt icon. At the DOS prompt, type **telnet <host address>**. ■

Now you have initiated a Telnet session. The default directory when you Telnet into the ISP system is always your user directory.

Figure 3.1 shows what the screen looks like when you log in. Call your ISP if you are having trouble establishing a Telnet session.

On your first Telnet session you should take a few minutes to familiarize yourself with your surroundings. There are a few commands that will become useful during this and any future Telnet session.

FIG. 3.1

Here's a new Telnet connection.

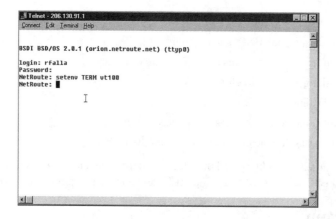

`ls`	*List.* Shows files and directories stored in the current directory that are not hidden.
`la`	*List All.* An alias for `ls -a`. Shows you all the files (including hidden files) and directories stored in the current directory (see Figure 3.2).
`mkdir`	*Make Directory.* Creates directories and subdirectories in the current directory.
`rm`	*Remove.* Deletes files stored in the current directory.
`rmdir`	*Remove Directory.* Deletes directories and subdirectories from the current directory.
`man <topic>`	*UNIX manual.* Displays the help files on the topic. `man mail` will provide the help files on the UNIX mail program.
`cd <directory>`	*Change Directory.* Change the current directory to another directory. To go up in the directory tree and simply type **'cd ..'**.

 If you want more information on the UNIX online manuals type **man man**.

Preparing the UNIX Directory

The Web site files must be placed in a subdirectory of your home directory, specified by the ISP and usually called public_html. The public_html subdirectory is the default location the browser looks in, for all Web files, when it attempts to retrieve a Web page from your account. If there is no public_html subdirectory, the complete path for the Web site files must be supplied.

In addition, the access permission level for the public_html subdirectory must be set to allow read-only access for everyone. Once the access permission for the public_html subdirectory is set, all subdirectories of public_html share the same permissions as the public_html parent directory.

FIG. 3.2

la will list all the contents of the current directory, including hidden system files, which have a dot as the first character.

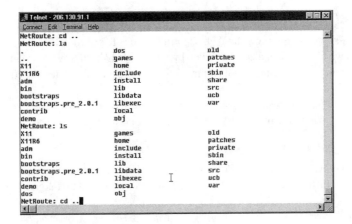

Not every BSD UNIX Operating System is the same. The steps outlined in the following list are based on the BSDI 2.0.1 Operating System. Some of the other BSDOS systems do not inherit the permissions set for the directory. The best way to determine the requirements for any system is to ask your ISP.

Follow these steps to create the public_html subdirectory and set the appropriate access permissions.

1. Type **pwd** to make sure you are in your home directory.

2. Type **mkdir public_html**. This creates the public_html subdirectory in your home directory.

3. Type **cd public_html** to make it the current directory.

TIP Steps 3 and 4 can be combined into a single step by typing **chmod 755 public_html** or **chmod 644 public_html** from the user directory.

4. Type **chmod 755** to set the access permissions of the directory to read and execute. All subdirectories of public_html have the same access permissions unless you explicitly change them. If you would prefer to set the permission to read only, type **chmod 644**.

alpha permission	numeric	for...
chmod u+rwx,go+rx public_html	chmod 755	read and execute
chmod u+rw,go+r *	chmod 644	read only

The directory is ready for your Web files. You have created the directory to store the Web files, you created subdirectories as needed, and you set the access permissions for all directories. The only thing left for your Telnet session is to end it.

To end the Telnet session, type exit or logout at the prompt. That is all there is to it—not so bad, eh?

Part

I

Ch

3

Uploading the files

The next step to getting your Web site published is to put the files in the proper directories. If you have already organized your files by type on your hard drive, you can move right into the next stage, transferring or uploading with an FTP client all the files needed by your Web site.

N O T E There are some ISPs that have accounts that do not have shell access, and everything (including creating subdirectories and giving them the correct permission) will be done using FTP. ▪

Open your FTP client and follow these instructions to connect to your ISP. As with the Telnet client, your home directory is the default directory you will be taken to with the FTP client.

N O T E The following is based on using the shareware FTP client application WS_FTP (included on the CD). If you are using another FTP client application, the steps may be slightly different. ▪

1. Create a new Profile (see Figure 3.3) in the Profile Name area. (Or choose the preset profile for your home directory, if one exists.)
2. Enter the host name *ftp.yourhost.net* (or com, org, and the like).
3. Select Automatic Detect in the Host Type area.
4. Enter your login name in the User ID area.
5. Enter your password.
6. Check the Save Password check box and click the Save button to save the new profile. When you do, the password is still there the next time you have to log in (for modifications to the Web site).
7. Leave the rest of the text areas blank and click OK. The FTP client connects to the host specified in the profile (your ISP).
8. Type the full path to and including your public_html directory in Remote Host under Default Directories.

FIG. 3.3

Setting up a new profile with WS_FTP.

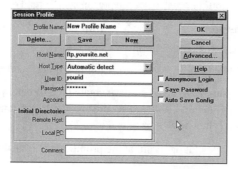

Once you are connected to the remote host, you see a split directory window. On the left side is the local (your computer) directory tree; on the right you see the remote host's directory tree.

Both directory trees are broken up into three sections. The section nearest the top contains the path of the current directory. There is a separate path on both sides, the left representing your local system, the right representing the remote host.

The midsection contains the directory tree. The current directory is the highest on the tree and any subdirectories are placed under the current directory.

The bottom section contains the files that can be found in the current directory. The one on the left shows (by default) the files in the wsftp directory on your system. The right panel should show any files present in the current directory of the remote host.

Follow these instructions to upload your Web site files to your public_html directory and the pics subdirectory on your ISP's system:

1. In the local system panel (left side), select the directory in which your Web site files are located. (Or you can click the ChgDir button and enter the exact path to the directory that contains the Web site files.)

2. In the Remote host side, double-click the appropriate directory you want. In this case it is public_html. Notice that the directory presently contains no files.

3. Using your mouse, highlight all the files that are to be transferred to the Remote directory (see Figure 3.4).

TIP Make sure the Binary radio button is selected. Although you can use ASCII for transferring text files, it is much faster to leave the setting to Binary and transfer files of all types at the same time (*bulk transfer*).

4. Click the left-pointing arrow to begin the transmission. A status box appears, indicating the progress of the transfer.

5. On the local system, go to any additional directories and transfer any relevant files to the appropriate remote directory.

While still in the FTP client, you can perform any file required management tasks. Depending on how you coded your files, you may want to change the extensions of all your files to .HTML.

TIP In most cases, there must be an index.HTML file for the Web site. If there is not, the user must specify your home page's exact name in the URL: *www.yourco.com/~yourid/pageone.html*. If there is an *index.html*, the user can simply put your Web server's domain and username, such as *www.yourco.com/~yourid*.

You're finished! Using your favorite browser, test the URL for you Web site. If it comes up properly, you can begin testing all the links on your pages to make sure your visitors don't end up clicking a dead end link.

FIG. 3.4

Select the files you want transferred and the button indicating in which direction (remote-to-host or host-to-remote) you want them to go.

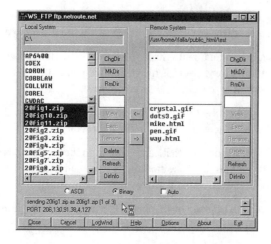

Now go out and announce your new site by using an announce service such as Yahoo!. See Chapter 40, "Listing Your Web Site in the Search Tools," for the lowdown on how to list your site effectively.

Setting MIME Types

The HyperText Transfer Protocol (HTTP) is the defined protocol for delivering Web page content over the Internet. Web server computers use HTTP to send packets of Web page data over the Internet to a user's Web browser program, which then interprets and displays that data as Web pages.

Under HTTP, each separate block of data is invisibly preceded by a text block defining its MIME type. The browser program uses this MIME-type definition to determine how to interpret the subsequent block of data. If, for example, a plug-in has been defined to handle the data type indicated in the MIME-type definition, the browser launches the appropriate plug-in before trying to display the data.

Therefore, you must configure a server to know and send the proper MIME type before it can send plug-in-compatible data. For example, if your Web site is going to include MIDI music files, you must set up your Web server to send the proper MIME-type header before delivering the actual MIDI file. Otherwise, your viewers' browser programs don't know when to launch their MIDI plug-in.

Here's a typical Web server setting for delivering MIDI content files:

```
MIME type = audio/midi or audio/x-midi or application/x-midi or
    audio/x-mid
action = binary
suffix = .mid
type = midi
```

This particular example defines four MIME types: audio/midi, audio/x-midi, application/x-midi, and audio/x-mid. The file name extension that the example defines for MIDI files is MID. Whenever a Web page this server delivers embeds a file type with the filename extension MID, the Web server sends a MIME type header that contains the four MIME types defined for MIDI files. The browser on the other end must use this MIME type header to determine which plug-in that it must use to play the data that the associated MID file contains.

You have to include this information in your Web server software's setup file for MIME-type information. How you do so depends on the specific server software you are using.

N O T E When the user installs a plug-in, the browser program automatically determines which plug-in is associated with which MIME type. If you choose <u>H</u>elp, About <u>P</u>lug-Ins from the Netscape Navigator menu, for example, you see a page that shows you which MIME types are set up to launch which plug-ins. ▪

When you set up your Web site—whether through an Internet service provider (ISP) or on your own server—you must tell your server software that you want to deliver content of a certain type or types. To do this, you provide a MIME configuration file for the Web server.

If your company or institution runs its own server, you must contact your system administrator to set up the MIME types for you. If you run your own Web server, you must set them up yourself. Netscape Communications Corporation offers extensive online documentation to assist you in setting MIME types for their servers. You can find this documentation at **http://home.netscape.com/comprod/server_central/support/index.html**.

Consider the real-world example of setting up the MIME type in the Netscape Communications Server to deliver RealAudio files. First, you would edit Netscape Communications Server's MIME.TYPES file by adding the following line:

```
type=audio/x-pn-realaudio    exts=ra,ram
```

To the Communications Server's main configuration file (MAGNUS.CONF in the examples provided in the Netscape Communication Server's documentation), you add the following line:

```
Init fn=load-types mime-types=mime.types
```

After changing both files, you reinitialize the Web server to activate the changes.

In any case, each plug-in includes documentation that specifies the MIME-type definition for the type of content with which it deals. You must define that MIME type for your Web server software.

The procedure for defining MIME types for any particular Web server is explained in the server's documentation. Specific information on the steps involved in setting up MIME types for every available server is beyond this book's scope. Refer to your Web server documentation for an explanation of how to set up specific MIME types for your particular brand of Web server software.

Microsoft Web Publishing Wizard

Microsoft's Web Publishing Wizard (see Figure 3.5) represents an effort by Microsoft to make uploading your pages to an Internet service provider quicker and easier. It's free and you can download it from their Web site at **http://www.microsoft.com/windows/software/webpost/**.

FIG. 3.5
Microsoft's Web Publishing Wizard can make the process of uploading your Web pages to an ISP quite painless.

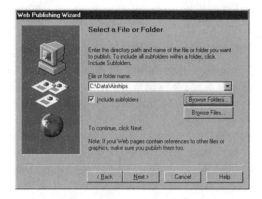

For Windows NT and Windows 95, the Web Publishing Wizard (formerly WebPost) works with most Web servers. It comes preconfigured to work with many of the big services like CompuServe, GNN, and Sprynet. If your ISP has installed a special configuration file, the Wizard is guaranteed to work smoothly. The odds are good, however, that the Web Publishing Wizard will work with your ISP whether they have or not. The program can also be used to upload your pages from your computer to an intranet.

To use the Web Publishing Wizard, you create your pages using the tools of your choice and organize them into folders just as they'll be organized online. If you can load and view your pages trouble-free from your own computer, the Web Publishing Wizard should be able to transfer them to your ISP without a hitch.

If your ISP's server can handle FrontPage Extended Web, FTP, HTTP Post, or Microsoft Content Replication System data transfers, your upload should work.

The actual process consists of just a few simple steps. You launch the Web Publishing Wizard, find the file or folder you want to post, and find your ISP's name on the program's built-in list. If your ISP isn't listed, you answer a short series of questions about your ISP (URL, file transfer method, and the like); then you give the program your Web server's name, click the Finish button, and everything is transferred automatically. Your folder structure is intact—what's on your ISP's server should be a mirror image of what's on your local drive.

Running Your Own Server

If you are in a situation where you need to run your own server and you have the resources to do it, then you need to choose the right server for your operating system. You should also take your unique situation into consideration.

The Right Server

Selecting the right server for your corporate or organizational Web is extremely important. You do not want one that is too complicated or doesn't perform your requirements.

Take a few minutes to draw up a requirements outline. It should contain information about capacity and speed expectations, whether or not you need a secure server, script language requirements, and so on.

You should visit the Web sites of the various server manufacturers discussed in this chapter and read all the relevant Web pages to determine if the server meets the minimum set of requirements you have outlined.

Change the outline as often as is required until it describes your server requirements in a clear and concise manner. As you read the product information pages, you may come across something that you hadn't thought of. You should most definitely add those items to your requirements outline.

Once you have narrowed the candidates to two or three possible servers, find out if you can download a trial version to test evaluate. Run each server through a vigorous evaluation procedure to see how well it performs in certain areas.

Your evaluation should include, in addition to anything you consider important for your circumstances, the following:

- Installation procedures—How easy or difficult are the installation procedures for the server?
- Technical support—What kind of technical support package is offered with the purchase of the server?
- HTML tools—Does the server come with HTML authoring tools?
- Speed test—How well does the server handle at different speed benchmarks?

If you invest the time finding the right server, you will avoid many of the problems associated with getting the wrong server. A few days to a week spent investigating servers is worth many days, or even weeks, worth of headaches in the future.

> **N O T E** For more information about server software, refer to one of the following Que books: *Running a Perfect Netscape Site*, *Special Edition Using Microsoft Internet Information Server 2*, and *Special Edition Using Netscape LiveWire Pro*. ■

Putting Your Site Online

When you are running your own Web server, the steps for publishing the Web site are slightly different. The biggest difference is you don't make a Telnet or FTP connection because the server is the local host. The following takes you through the steps of publishing your Web site on your own UNIX server.

Part

I

Ch

3

1. Create a root directory on your hard drive.

2. From the root directory create directories user/home/, which allow you to add as many Web accounts as you want or need.

3. Create a Web account for your site in the user/home subdirectory. Typically, your user ID is the account name.

4. Create the public_html directory in the Web account directory.

5. Assign the proper permissions (see the section "Preparing the UNIX Directory" for details).

6. Move the Web site files to the appropriate directories.

7. Change file names if required.

8. Test the links. Once again you are in the position where you must test the links on your site to ensure the user/visitor has an unobstructed visit on your site. Test the links at least monthly. Find and fix broken links.

When you are running your own server you have a few additional options to consider:

■ Should access to the site be restricted?

■ Will it be a secure server site?

■ What Web applications (if any) do you want to include?

Each of the three items in the list consist of many additional steps and procedures that must be followed. Don't be fooled by the brevity of the steps in publishing a Web site on your own server.

There are also maintenance procedures that are required on a Web server monthly, as well as many other (log report analysis, visitor count analysis, and so on) functions a server administrator must perform.

In the next section, you'll take a look at some of the Web servers that are presently available. This gives you a good starting point for finding and running the server that most meets your individual requirements.

Web Servers

Use the following section to help narrow your search for an appropriate Web server. Each Web server is presented with an introductory paragraph.

Microsoft Internet Information Server

Microsoft IIS is the Web server that comes bundled with the Windows NT operating system (see Table 3.2). IIS has been reviewed favorably by many Internet trade mags. If Windows NT is your operating system then you should give this server serious consideration. It's free anyway.

Table 3.2 Microsoft Internet Information Server

Item	Description
Product	Microsoft Internet Information Server
Web Address	**http://www.microsoft.com/iis/default.asp**
Platform	Windows NT
Address	One Microsoft Way, Redmond, WA 98052-6399
Telephone	(206) 882-8080

Microsoft Internet Information Server (MIIS) is a fairly complete Web server suite. There are no installation problems with this server, in part because you can choose to have it automatically installed when you install Windows NT 4.0.

Although it performs superbly on the Windows NT platform, that is the only platform it is available on, at present. This platform limitation automatically eliminates many potential customers for Microsoft.

The MIIS comes bundled with an FTP server, WWW server, Gopher server, and the WAIS server. In addition, MIIS also includes an HTML editor to assist authoring of HTML documents, a slew of APIs, and SSL security support.

Another feature of the MIIS package is the inclusion of the FrontPage HTML authoring application. FrontPage is an excellent authoring application for all Web developers, either new to the Net or veteran Web developers. You will have a Web site up and running in only a few short hours using FrontPage.

Luckman Web Commander

The people from Luckman are not new to the Internet. In fact, they have developed an array of Internet-related applications (see Table 3.3), many of which are included in this package.

Table 3.3 Web Commander Server

Item	Description
Company	Luckman Interactive
Web Address	**http://www.luckman.com**
Platform	Windows NT & Windows 95
Address	1055 W. 7th Street, Suite 2580, Los Angeles, CA 90017
Telephone	(213) 614-0966

Web Commander provides a complete Internet server solution package. From the time you remove the shrink-wrap to having the package fully installed on your system takes about an hour. There is helpful documentation included with the package to help you get everything running without a hitch.

The Server software is only one component of the Web Commander package. Also included in the package are HTML authoring tools, secure-server applications, ODBC database support, WAIS Toolkit, Netscape Navigator, and Perl 5.

Where MIIS is limited to operating on Windows NT, Web Commander works with both Windows NT and 95, making it accessible to a wider group of information providers than MIIS. In addition to working on both operating systems, Web Commander has a much better monitoring and logging program than MIIS.

WebSite Professional

In keeping with their reputation for providing high-quality products, O'Reilly has produced the WebSite Professional (see Table 3.4).

Table 3.4   WebSite Professional Server

Item	Description
Company	O'Reilly & Associates
Web Address	**http://www.ora.com**
Platform	Windows NT & Windows 95
Address	101 Morris Street, Sebastopol, CA 95472
Telephone	(707) 829-0515

Is security important to you? How about database connectivity? WebSite Professional provides excellent support for both, as well as a complete, GUI-based diagnostics application.

The documentation and manuals included with WebSite Professional are well written and easy to use, making installation and administration of your new server as easy as possible. There are no quick solutions to the problem of not understanding the technology.

Like MIIS and Web Commander, WebSite Professional is loaded with additional components. HTML authoring tools include SSIs, Hot Dog, WSAPI, and the Netscape Gold browser/editor.

FastTrack Server

Netscape's SuiteSpot servers are comprehensive, powerful, complex, and expensive. Sure, SuiteSpot provides a complete set of servers and tools for managing a large site, but what if you're an individual or small company that doesn't need (or can't afford) all that horsepower? Well, that's why Netscape created the FastTrack Server. An all-in-one Web server, FastTrack Server is available for Win95, NT, or UNIX for only $295, complete. You can even download a free 60-day trial version from Netscape's site at **http://home.netscape.com/comprod/ mirror/server_download.html**.

As the only Netscape server that can run under Windows 95, it's pretty obvious that Netscape had the individual and small business owner in mind when this was designed. It's also easy to use, with a graphical user interface that controls all its setup and functions.

FastTrack is an HTML document server intended primarily for use as a Web server, though it could certainly handle a small intranet, as well. It's fully compatible with Enterprise Server, so you can start small and grow as needs dictate.

An Installation Wizard makes installing FastTrack a simple process of answering a few setup questions and pressing a few buttons. A configuration agent automatically detects network settings and configures FastTrack to work properly with them. If you get stuck in the installation process or any time during future system administration, built-in context-sensitive help is just a keystroke away.

SSL security, full reporting capabilities for Web stats, and performance optimization mean that FastTrack is suitable for real-world Web applications. There's even support for server-side Java, JavaScript, and CGI applications, as well as the ability to run applications created using Netscape ONE tools. Remote management means you can administer the server from anywhere on the network.

ON THE WEB

http://home.netscape.com/comprod/server_central/product/fast_track/index.html You can find out more about FastTrack at this site.

Part

I

Ch

3

Creating Basic Web Pages with HTML 4.0

## CHAPTER 4

Creating Basic HTML Documents

by Robert Meegan and Mark R. Brown

In this chapter

Starting with the Basics

It is important to realize that an HTML document must be built on a very specific framework. This framework, in its simplest form, consists of three sets of matched *container tags*.

A tag is a simple markup element, and always takes the form <TAG>. A container is a pair of HTML tags of the form <TAG> </TAG>. You can think of the <TAG> element as turning something on, while the </TAG> turns that same thing off. For example, consider this line of HTML:

```
<I>This is in Italics.</I> But this isn't.
```

The first HTML tag, <I>, turns on italics. The second tag, </I>, turns them off. When displayed on-screen, this line of text would look like this:

> *This is in Italics.* But this isn't.

The tags themselves don't appear on-screen. They just tell the browser program how to display the elements they contain.

The simplest possible HTML document is given in Listing 4.1. The entire document is enclosed in the <HTML></HTML> container tags. The first part of the document is encapsulated in the <HEAD></HEAD> container, which itself contains a <TITLE></TITLE> container. Finally, the body of the page is contained in a <BODY></BODY> container.

Listing 4.1   The Simplest HTML Document

```
<HTML>
<HEAD>
<TITLE>A Very Basic HTML Document</TITLE>
</HEAD>
<BODY>
This is where the text of the document would be.
</BODY>
</HTML>
```

The most fundamental of all the tags used to create an HTML document is, not surprisingly, the <HTML> tag. This tag should be the first item in your document and the corresponding end tag, </HTML>, should be the last. Together, these tags indicate that the material contained between them represents a single HTML document (refer to Listing 4.1). This is important because an HTML document is a plain text ASCII file. Without these tags, a browser or other program isn't able to identify the document format and interpret it correctly.

N O T E   While most of the recent browsers properly interpret a document that is not contained within the <HTML> start and </HTML> end tags, it is still very important to use them. Many of the new uses for HTML documents, such as e-mail and Usenet postings, do not necessarily involve browsers, and the other programs are more likely to interpret an ASCII document as plain text without the hint that the <HTML> tag provides. ▪

The </HTML> end tag is just as important as the start tag. It is becoming possible to include HTML documents within e-mail messages and news postings. Without the </HTML>, the viewer does not know when to stop interpreting the text as HTML code.

The Document Heading

The document head container is not a required element, but a proper head can greatly increase the usefulness of a document. The purpose of the head is to provide information to the application that is interpreting the document. With the exception of the TITLE element, the elements within the head element are not seen by the reader of the document.

Elements within the head element do the following:

- Provide a title for the document.
- Lay out the relationships between multiple documents.
- Tell a browser to create a search form.
- Provide a method for sending special messages to a specific browser or other viewer.

Listing 4.2 shows an example of an HTML document with a proper HEAD element.

Part

II

Ch

4

Listing 4.2   A Fairly Detailed *HEAD* Element

```
<HTML>
<HEAD>
<TITLE>General Officers of the US Army in the Civil War</TITLE>
<LINK HREF="mailto:rmeegan@ia.net" REV="made">
<BASE HREF="http://www.ia.net/~rmeegan/civil">
<ISINDEX PROMPT="Enter the desired name">
<META HTTP-EQUIV="EXPIRES" CONTENT="31 Dec 1997">
<META NAME="Last Modified" CONTENT="16 Dec 1996">
<META NAME="Keywords" CONTENT="Yankee, Grand Army of the Republic,
 War Between the States">
<META NAME="Description" CONTENT="A listing of the general officers of the US
 Army in the Civil WAR">
</HEAD>
<BODY BGCOLOR="NAVY" TEXT="WHITE" LINK="RED" VLINK="BLUE" ALINK="GREEN">
<BASEFONT SIZE=3 FONT="Georgia, Century Schoolbook, Times New Roman">
<H1><FONT COLOR="YELLOW">Union Generals of the American Civil War</FONT>
</H1><BR>
This listing contains the names of the general officers of the Regular Army
  and of the Volunteer Army, as well as the date of their appointment to the
  rank.<BR><BR>
 The names are taken from<BR>
<CITE>
Statistical Record by Frederick Phisterer<BR>
Published 1883, New York<BR><BR>
</CITE>
In all cases only the full rank is given. Many officers had a <EM>brevet</EM>
  (or temporary) rank that was often one or two ranks higher than the full rank.
```

continues

Listing 4.2   Continued

```
Remember also, that it was possible for an officer to have rank in a state
militia, the Volunteer Army, and the Regular Army; all at the same time. With
brevet ranks taken into account, it was possible for an individual to have as
many as six ranks simultaneously, depending upon who he was dealing with.
</BODY>
</HTML>
```

The HEAD element is opened by the start tag, <HEAD>. This tag normally should immediately follow the <HTML> start tag. The end tag, </HEAD>, is used to close the element. The rest of the head element tags are located within this container.

Naming Your Document

The TITLE element is the only required element of the heading. It is used to give your document a name. This title is generally displayed in the title bar of the browser. The TITLE should not be confused with the file name of the document; instead, it is a text string that is completely independent of the name and location of the file. This makes it highly useful, the file name is generally constrained by the operating system of the computer that the file is located on.

The TITLE element is delimited by a <TITLE> start tag and a </TITLE> end tag. The actual title is located between these tags. Do not enclose the title in quotation marks unless you want it to appear with the quotes. It is most common for the TITLE element to be all on one line.

The title text is a string of unlimited length that can include any text except for the few special characters that are restricted in HTML. In practice, it is a good idea to keep the length of the title fairly short so that it fits on the title bar. Another thought to keep in mind when making up a title is that many browsers use the title as the caption for the icon when the browser is minimized. Try to make the first few characters particularly meaningful.

N O T E   The TITLE is normally used as the default name when a user creates a bookmark or Favorites link to the document. To make this default as useful as possible, avoid having a title like Home Page or Index. Entries like this are nearly useless in a bookmark list. ▪

Listing 4.3 is an example of a document TITLE. Figure 4.1 shows how Microsoft Internet Explorer uses the document TITLE as the title of the browser window.

Listing 4.3   An Example of the *TITLE* Element

```
<HTML>
<HEAD>
<TITLE>General Officers of the US Army in the Civil War</TITLE>
</HEAD>
<BODY>
</BODY>
</HTML>
```

FIG. 4.1

Titles provide your readers with a way to identify your documents.

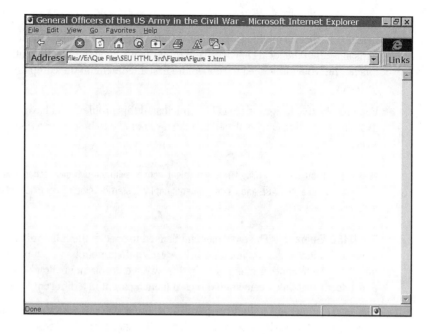

Creating a Document Hierarchy

HTML documents often have a relationship with other documents. This relationship is most frequently in terms of a link to another document. Links to other documents can be relative or absolute (see Listing 4.4). Each of these links poses its own problems. Absolute links can be long, cumbersome, and prone to breakage when the child document is moved. Relative links are easier to type and update, but they break when the parent document is moved.

Listing 4.4   Absolute and Relative Links

```
<HTML>
<HEAD>
<TITLE>News Links</TITLE>
</HEAD>
<BODY>
<IMG SRC=/gifs/news.gif ALT="News">          <-- Relative Link -->
<UL>
<BR><A HREF=http://www.cnn.com>CNN Interactive</A>
<BR><A HREF=http://www.usatoday.com>USA Today</A>
</UL>
<P>
<IMG SRC=//www.ia.net/~rmeegan/gifs/mags.gif ALT="mags">   <-- Absolute Link -->
<UL>
<BR><A HREF=http://www.infoworld.com>Infoworld Magazine</A>
<BR><A HREF=http://www.zdnet.com>Ziff-Davis Publications</A>
</UL>
<P>
</BODY>
</HTML>
```

Part
II

Ch

4

This might sound unlikely, but consider that a long document might be downloaded to a user's machine so that he might read it when offline. Any links, such as a bibliography, would be unusable when the local copy was viewed. If the user wanted to link to other documents or images, he would first need to reopen the first document on the computer where it normally resides.

Fortunately, the designers of HTML anticipated this problem and have added two elements, BASE and LINK, that can be placed in a document head to help keep a document relationship straight.

N O T E   If you're just learning HTML, you might want to skim through this section. It isn't necessary to use the BASE and LINK elements until you start developing complicated documents that require many pages. ∎

The *BASE* Element   The BASE element is used to specify the full original URL of the document. This allows relative links to work, even if a document has been moved to another directory (or even to another machine!). In this way, a BASE element allows the viewing software to find a document link, even when directed from a parent in a different location.

The BASE element has a single required attribute which provides the full URL of the document: HREF. Listing 4.5 provides an example of how the <BASE> tag is used.

Listing 4.5   Using the <*BASE*> Tag

```
<HTML>
<HEAD>
<TITLE>News Links</TITLE>
<BASE HREF="//www.ia.net/~rmeegan">
</HEAD>
<BODY>
<IMG SRC=/gifs/news.gif ALT="News">
<UL>
<BR><A HREF=http://www.cnn.com>CNN Interactive</A>
<BR><A HREF=http://www.usatoday.com>USA Today</A>
</UL>
<P>
<IMG SRC=/gifs/mags.gif ALT="mags">
<UL>
<BR><A HREF=http://www.infoworld.com>Infoworld Magazine</A>
<BR><A HREF=http://www.zdnet.com>Ziff-Davis Publications</A>
</UL>
<P>
</BODY>
</HTML>
```

Notice that the BASE element directs the viewer software where to look for the files. Even if a person has downloaded the file to his local machine, the little images for *News* and *Mags* can still be found, assuming that the reader's machine has access to the Internet.

The *LINK* Element   If the BASE element allows a browser to locate a document, there still exists the question of what the relationship between two documents might be. This becomes even more important as the complexity of your HTML document increases. To connect documents together logically, HTML includes the LINK element.

The LINK element indicates the relationship between the document that contains the <LINK> tag and another document (or other object). It consists of an URL that points to the reference object and an attribute that serves as a description of the relationship. In other words, if a parent HTML document provided a link to the current child HTML document, the current document could provide a <LINK> tag back to the parent to indicate that relationship. A document can contain as many LINK elements as needed to describe all of the relationships. Table 4.1 lists all of the attributes and their functions.

Table 4.1   *LINK* Attributes and Their Functions

Attribute	Function
HREF	Points to the URL of the other document.
REL	Defines the relationship between the current document and persons who have contributed to its existence.
REV	Defines the relationship between another HTML document and the current document.
TYPE	Specifies the type and parameters for a linked style sheet.

Part

II

Ch

4

There are many different relationships possible, and the list is not well defined in the HTML specification. The most common REV relationship is "made", which provides a link for e-mailing a document's author, as shown in the following example:

```
<LINK HREF="mailto:nul@utexas.edu" REV="made">
```

This gives the URL for communicating with the document author. The URL in this instance is the instruction to open an e-mail message addressed to nul@utexas.edu. Sandia National Laboratories, which is on the forefront of HTML document publishing, also recommends the following REV relationships to individuals with a connection with an HTML document: "author", "editor", "publisher", and "owner".

Some examples of relationships to other HTML documents that can be indicated with the REL attribute are "bookmark", "copyright", "glossary", "help", "home", "index", and "toc".

There are also two relationships that are most commonly used in ordered documents: "next" and "previous". These are particularly useful relationships. Listing 4.6 shows the HEAD element for a document that is a chapter in an online manual.

Listing 4.6   Using the *<LINK>* Tag

```
<HTML>
<HEAD>
<TITLE>Using the Satellite Identification and Tracking System (SITS)</TITLE>
<LINK REV="made" HREF="mailto:rmeegan@ia.net">
<LINK REL="toc"  HREF="contents.htm">
<LINK REL="index"  HREF="index.htm">
<LINK REL="copyright"  HREF="copyright.htm">
<META NAME="Description" CONTENT="An on-line manual for the SITS">
</HEAD>
<BODY>
</BODY>
</HTML>
```

Customized Heading Information

Although it might seem that the elements that can be placed in a document heading already cover every imaginable possibility, the truth is that they barely begin to scratch the surface. Because the procedure for the development and approval of a new HTML specification is rather slow, the companies that produce browser software often create several releases in the time between specification versions. To provide additional functionality, one final element is provided for the heading.

The META element allows a document author to define information that is outside of HTML. This *meta-information* can be used by the browser software to perform activities that are not yet supported by the official HTML specification. As a rule, META elements are not needed for a basic HTML document, but you should keep these elements in mind as you gain experience and as your pages become more sophisticated.

Figure 4.2 is an example of how the META element can be used to have the browser perform an action.

Looking at the example, you can see the following line:

```
<META HTTP-EQUIV=refresh" CONTENT="60" URL="www.fdline.org/homepage.html">
```

This is interpreted by Netscape Navigator and Microsoft Internet Explorer as the instruction to wait 60 seconds and then load a new document. This kind of instruction is often used when a document is moved from one location to another. A small document can be left at the previous location to serve as an automatic pointer to the new location.

A similar command line

```
<META HTTP-EQUIV=refresh" CONTENT="60">
```

can be used to have the browser reload the page every 60 seconds. This is useful for a page that has frequently updated information, such as a stock price ticker.

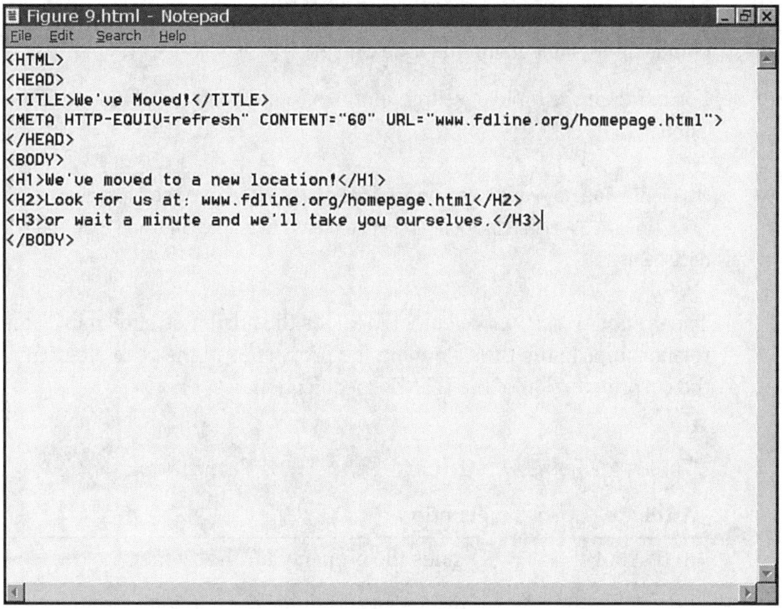

FIG. 4.2
A browser can interpret
commands in the META
element to perform
actions such as
loading a new page
automatically.

```
 Figure 9.html - Notepad
File   Edit   Search   Help
<HTML>
<HEAD>
<TITLE>We've Moved!</TITLE>
<META HTTP-EQUIV=refresh" CONTENT="60" URL="www.fdline.org/homepage.html">
</HEAD>
<BODY>
<H1>We've moved to a new location!</H1>
<H2>Look for us at: www.fdline.org/homepage.html</H2>
<H3>or wait a minute and we'll take you ourselves.</H3>
</BODY>
```

Part
II

Ch
4

N O T E   Both of these techniques are known as *client pull* because the client, your browser,
requests the new document from the server. These are advanced techniques, and you don't
need to use them except in circumstances when data is changing or the page needs to be
reloaded.

Finally, the most popular use of a META element at the present is to use the Keywords property.
Many search engines preferentially use the words defined in this element to index the document. This can be used to provide additional keys to an index that might not actually appear in
the document verbatim. Listing 4.7 shows how this works.

Listing 4.7   Using *META* Elements

```
<HTML>
<HEAD>
<TITLE>General Officers of the US Army in the Civil War</TITLE>
<META NAME="Keywords" CONTENT="Yankee, Grand Army of the Republic,
 War Between the States">
<META NAME="Description" CONTENT="A listing of the general officers of the US
 Army in the Civil WAR">
</HEAD>
<BODY BGCOLOR="NAVY" TEXT="WHITE" LINK="RED" VLINK="BLUE" ALINK="GREEN">
</BODY>
</HTML>
```

When designing a document that will be indexed by a search engine, it is also a good idea to
use the Description property. Most indexes use this description for your page, if it is present.

If no description is present, the index uses the first text available on the page, which can be confusing to some using the index.

For more on the topic of search engines, see Chapter 40, "Listing Your Web Site in the Search Tools."

N O T E The Keywords and Description properties are good first choices when you start to use META elements. Both of them are easy to understand, and they add a lot of value to your documents. ■

The syntax for the META element includes the attributes shown in Table 4.2. Much like the relationships in the LINK element, the properties of the META element are not clearly defined in the current version of the HTML specification.

Table 4.2 *META* **Attributes and Their Functions**

Attribute	Function
HTTP-EQUIV	Defines the property for the element.
NAME	Provides an additional description of the element. If this attribute is missing, it is assumed to be the same as HTTP-EQUIV.
URL	Defines a target document for the property.
CONTENT	Provides the response value for the property.

Other Heading Elements

There are two additional elements that can be found in the document heading. The first is the SCRIPT element and the second is the STYLE element. The former is used to add interactive control scripts to pages, while the latter adds various styles to page content.

The Document Body

Although the nature of the World Wide Web appears to be changing in the direction of increasing active content, most people who view your documents will still be interested in your text. This will be especially true for documents that are created for corporate intranets and for documents that serve as online manuals and texts. Because of this, whether you are converting existing documents or creating new ones, you will spend much of your time working in the body.

Starting with the Required Elements

Before you can fill in your document, you need to lay out a basic working framework. HTML documents must follow a defined pattern of elements if they are to be interpreted correctly.

Rather than retype the elements that are used in every HTML document, it is a good idea for you to create a template to use for each of your pages so that you are less likely to leave out an important detail. At the end of this chapter, we build a template that you can use as a starter. Until then, we'll use the example presented in Listing 4.8.

Listing 4.8   A Basic HTML Document

```
<HTML>
<HEAD>
<TITLE>This is an example document</TITLE>
</HEAD>
<BODY>
Enter body text here.
</BODY>
</HTML>
```

This example begins with the <HTML> tag, which, as you have read, is necessary for every HTML document. Next is the <HEAD> tag, which opens up the heading part of the document. This contains the TITLE element. We've titled the document "This is an example document." The heading is closed with the </HEAD> tag. Finally, the <BODY> element follows. This is where you place the bulk of the material in your document. Remember to close the body element with the </BODY> tag and finish the page with the </HTML> tag.

Because HTML is a markup language, the body of your document is turned on with the start tag, <BODY>. Everything that follows this tag is interpreted according to a strict set of rules that tell the browser about the contents. The body element is closed with the end tag, </BODY>.

N O T E   Strictly speaking, it isn't absolutely necessary to use the <BODY> start and end tags; HTML allows you to skip a tag if it is obvious from the context. (In this case, <BODY> would be implied after the ending </HEAD> tag, and </BODY> would be implied before the ending </HMTL> tag or the end of the document.) However, it's still a good idea to use them. Some older browsers and other HTML programs can become confused without them and may not display the document correctly. ■

In the preceding basic document, the body text is a single line. In your document, you replace this line with the main text of your document. Unless you are using a special HTML editor, you must enter your text using a strict ASCII format. This limits you to a common set of characters that can be interpreted by computers throughout the world.

▶ **See** "Creating Special Characters," **p. 104**

N O T E   Most browsers consider all nonblank white space (tabs, end-of-line characters, and so on) as a single blank. Multiple white spaces are normally condensed to a single blank. ■

Attributes of the *BODY* Element

The BODY element supports a large number of attributes. These are all important for determining the general appearance of your document. Table 4.3 lists these attributes and their functions for your convenience, but we cover each of them in more detail.

Table 4.3   *BODY* Attributes and Their Functions

Attribute	Function
ALINK	Defines the color of an active link.
BACKGROUND	Points to the URL of an image to use for the document background.
BGCOLOR	Defines the color of the document background.
BGPROPERTIES	If this is set to FIXED, the background image does not scroll.
LEFTMARGIN	Sets the width of the left margin in pixels.
LINK	Defines the color of an unvisited link.
TEXT	Defines the color of the text.
TOPMARGIN	Sets the width of the top margin in pixels.
VLINK	Defines the color of an already visited link.

Coloring Your Documents

The first small step toward creating a document is to define the colors that will be used for the various text components. If you do not specify any colors, the default colors are used. These are normally set by the reader on her viewer.

Cascading Style Sheets, which are discussed in Chapter 17, "Applying Cascading Style Sheets," are the latest and greatest way to adjust a page's colors and other styles. However, there are easy-to-use <BODY> tag attributes that can also give you elementary control over the colors of your page elements.

N O T E   Because you have no way of knowing which colors have been selected as defaults by the reader, it is considered good HTML practice to set all of the colors, if you set any. This way, the same color isn't used for more than one component. ■

There is no simple rule that can be used to define a well-balanced palette, but remember that your readers must actually *read* your document. Try to maintain a high contrast between the text and the background and don't make the color differences too subtle.

Color Definitions   Colors are defined in HTML using a hexadecimal coding system. The system is based upon the three components—Red, Green, and Blue—which leads to the common name of RGB. Each of the components is assigned a hexadecimal value between 00 and

FF (0 and 255 in decimal numbers). These three values are then concatenated into a single value that is preceded by a pound sign (#). An example of such a value is #800080, which is purple. Because few people can visualize colors based solely on a hexadecimal value, HTML defines 16 standard color names, which are listed along with their hexadecimal values, in Table 4.4.

Yahoo! maintains an extensive list of Web sites which feature color table information at **http:// www.yahoo.com/Computers_and_Internet/Internet/World_Wide_Web/ Page_Design_and_Layout/Color_Information/**.

Table 4.4   Standard Colors and Their Values

Color	Value
Black	#000000
Maroon	#800000
Green	#008000
Olive	#808000
Navy	#000080
Purple	#800080
Teal	#008080
Gray	#808080
Silver	#C0C0C0
Red	#FF0000
Lime	#00FF00
Yellow	#FFFF00
Blue	#0000FF
Fuchsia	#FF00FF
Aqua	#00FFFF
White	#FFFFFF

Part
II

Ch
4

You can use either these color names or their values when defining colors for HTML document elements. For example, the following lines are equivalent:

```
<BODY BGCOLOR="#FFFFFF">

<BODY BGCOLOR="WHITE">
```

The Body Color Attributes   The BGCOLOR attribute is used for the document background color. If your document has a background image, the BGCOLOR should be as close the primary color of the image as possible. This allows readers who may not be downloading images to see your text clearly. Many authors make this common mistake, which is particularly bad if the background image is primarily black and the text color that you selected was white. In this case, the reader of your document is greeted by the sight of what is apparently a blank page!

For example, if you are using a background graphic that is mostly black, you should also add the BGCOLOR="black" attribute to your page's <BODY> tag.

The TEXT attribute is the color used for the text in the document. Because most of your text appears in this color, it should be chosen to provide the reader with sufficient contrast. If you have elected to set the font, be aware that fonts with fine detail are often easier to read when they are dark against a bright background.

The LINK attribute is used by the browser for links that have not yet been followed. This color should be obviously different from the TEXT color, so that readers can identify links.

The VLINK attribute is used to identify links that have already been visited. A common choice for VLINK is to use a darker version of the LINK color.

The ALINK attribute marks links that are currently active. This is a relatively recent development and is normally used for documents that have multiple frames. Quite frankly, choose your other colors first; the reader is least likely to see this color than any of the others. See Chapter 12, "Framing Your Web Site," for more information about frames.

Having seen all of the things that can be colored in an HTML document, you might wonder if the results justify the effort. If you are creating a static document—such as a manual or a text-book—you might be best off to let the reader set the colors that she wishes to use. On the other hand, if your document is a high-energy page with a lot of graphics, then it is certainly worth the time to find the right blend of colors.

Filling in the Background

One popular way to dress up an HTML document is to add a background image. A background image is a graphics file that is visible under the document text. Using a background can help provide continuity to a document, or it can also serve to differentiate the various pages.

Most background images are small and are tiled across the viewer window like wallpaper. Images of textures are particularly popular for this purpose; bricks, marble, and cloth are often seen on HTML documents. Most of these serve only to fill in the blank space on the document, though. More interesting documents have a background that fits the theme of the page. Figure 4.3 shows an example of an astronomy page that uses a pattern of stars as the wallpaper.

Other types of wallpaper that can make a document look good include a corporate logo or other image. These should be very subdued, almost monochrome, so as not to interfere with the foreground text or distract from your document's message. One way to accomplish this is to emboss an existing image using a graphics program. Chapter 22, "Graphics," discusses some of the tools available for creating these images. Figure 4.4 is an example of how this can be used.

FIG. 4.3
Using a background image that fits your document is a nice, professional touch.

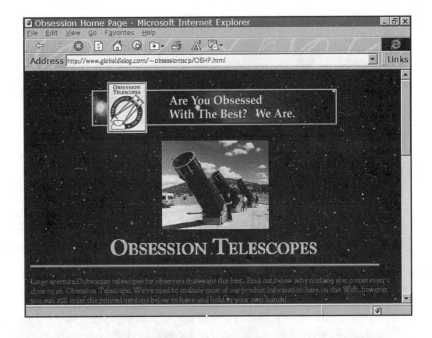

FIG. 4.4
A company logo, embossed into a monochrome background, can give continuity to a collection of documents.

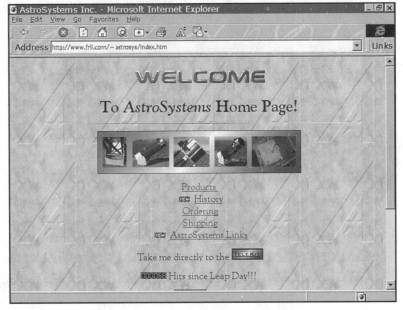

A background can also be created to watermark a document. This type of background can be used for an official seal or for a text message such as Draft or Confidential.

Background images look good, but they won't be seen by someone who's turned off the automatic loading of images. Remember the advice in the BGCOLOR section and set the background color to match the primary color of the image, so that your page is readable even if the reader doesn't get to see the background.

N O T E   The BGPROPERTIES attribute is unique to Microsoft Internet Explorer. The only acceptable value for this attribute is FIXED. If BGPROPERTIES=FIXED, the background image does not scroll with the text. This is a nice effect with a wallpaper background and is useful if you've created a watermark background. ■

Commenting Your HTML Documents

It is possible to add comments to your HTML document that aren't seen by a reader. The syntax for this is to begin your comment with the `<!--` tag and to end it with the `-->` tag. Anything located between the two tags is not displayed in the browser. This is a convenient way to leave notes for yourself or others. For example, you can enter a comment when new material is added to a document that shows the date of the new addition.

> **CAUTION**
>
> Don't assume your comments can't be seen by your readers. Most browsers allow the source of your document to be viewed directly, including any comments that you have added.

On the other hand, don't try to use comments to "comment out" any HTML elements in production documents. Some browsers interpret any > as the end of the comment. In any case, the chances of an older browser becoming confused are pretty good, resulting in the rest of your document being badly scrambled. If you are going to use comments to cut out HTML elements while you are testing the document, you should remove them in the final release.

The Address Element

One of the most important elements for your documents is the ADDRESS element. This is where you identify yourself as the author of the document and (optionally) let people know how they can get in touch with you. Any copyright information for the material in the page can be placed here as well. The address element is normally placed at either the top or bottom of a document.

The ADDRESS element consists of text enclosed by an `<ADDRESS>` start tag and an `</ADDRESS>` end tag. The text within an ADDRESS element is normally displayed in italics.

Listing 4.9 is an example of one such address element, and Figure 4.5 shows how it looks.

Listing 4.9   Using the *ADDRESS* Element

```
<HTML>
<HEAD>
<TITLE>Amateur Astronomy on the World Wide Web</TITLE>
<META NAME="Keywords" CONTENT="Astronomy, Telescope, Stargazing">
```

```
<META NAME="Description" CONTENT="Amateur Astronomy resources available on the
Web">
</HEAD>
<BODY BGCOLOR="WHITE" TEXT="BLACK" LINK="RED" VLINK="GREEN" ALINK="YELLOW" >
</HEAD>
<BODY>
<FONT SIZE=3 FACE="Verdana, Arial, Helvetica">
<BR>
<H1>Amateur Astronomy on the World Wide Web</H1>
<HR>
<H2>Magazines</H2>
<OL>
<LI><A HREF=http://www.astronomy-mall.com/Astronomy-Mall/?190,54>The Astronomy
Mall</A> - A place to find many amateur astronomy companies.
<LI><A HREF=http://www.skypub.com>Sky On-line</A> - Publishers of <I>Sky and
Telescope</I> and <I>CCD</I> magazines.
</OL>
<HR>
<ADDRESS>
Created by Robert Meegan<BR>
Last Modified on 16 Dec 1996
</ADDRESS>
</BODY>
</HTML>
```

N O T E A very important addition to the address is to indicate the date you created the document and the date of the last revision. This helps people determine if they have already seen the most up-to-date version of the document. ▪

Part

II

Ch

4

FIG. 4.5

The ADDRESS element is used to identify the author or maintainer of the document.

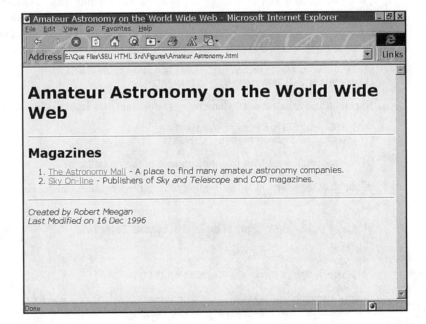

Creating a Document Template

Now, let's build a basic document template that you can use with your documents. This template allows you to start converting some of your existing documents to HTML. In the following chapters, you will see how to expand upon this template.

Let's begin with the required tags: <HTML>, <HEAD>, </HEAD>, <BODY>, </BODY>, and </HTML>. You also need to include the TITLE element, as this is a required element in HTML. Finally, put in a dummy line of text to remind yourself where to put the text. This gives you Listing 4.10.

Listing 4.10   A First Pass at a Basic Document Template

```
<HTML>
<HEAD>
<TITLE> A Basic Document Template </TITLE>
<HEAD>
<BODY>
Put the body text in here.
</BODY>
</HTML>
```

This would certainly suffice for a basic document, but you can do a lot better without much effort. First, let's add a simple gray textured background to the document, which changes the <BODY> tag to:

```
<BODY BACKGROUND="greybg.jpg">
```

Earlier in the chapter you read that if you add a background image to a document, you should set the colors so that the reader can see your text. First, set the BGCOLOR attribute to GRAY. This is the closest match to the background. We'll also set the TEXT to BLACK, and LINK, ALINK, and VLINK to BLUE, GREEN, and RED, respectively. These additions change the <BODY> tag to

```
<BODY BACKGROUND="greybg.jpg" BGCOLOR="GRAY", TEXT="BLACK",
 LINK="BLUE", ALINK="GREEN", VLINK="RED">
```

You should have an ADDRESS element for the document, so add the following:

```
<ADDRESS>Created by Robert Meegan<BR>
Created on 16 December 1996</ADDRESS>
```

Of course, you'll want to put your own name in the ADDRESS.

When all of these are added to the first pass of the template, you get Listing 4.11.

Listing 4.11   Your Final Basic Document Template

```
<HTML>
<HEAD>
<TITLE> A Basic Document Template </TITLE>
<HEAD>
<BODY BACKGROUND="greybg.jpg" BGCOLOR="GRAY", TEXT="BLACK",
 LINK="BLUE", ALINK="GREEN", VLINK="RED">
```

```
Put the body text in here.
<ADDRESS>Created by Robert Meegan<BR>
Created on 16 December 1996</ADDRESS>
</BODY>
</HTML>
```

The results of this template can be seen in Figure 4.6.

FIG. 4.6

The results of the basic document template opened in Netscape Navigator.

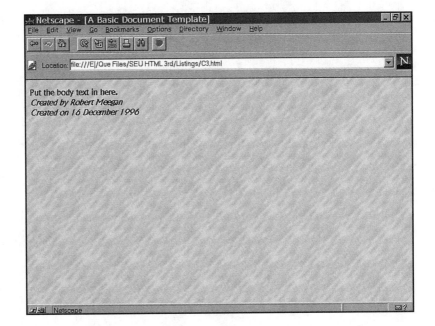

As you learn more about HTML, your template will grow and become more sophisticated. Until then, this simple document should prove to be sufficient for most purposes. ●

Part
II
Ch
4

## CHAPTER 5

Formatting Text as Paragraphs

By Mark R. Brown and Robert Meegan

In this chapter

Breaking Text into Paragraphs

Your old English teacher taught you to break your writing up into paragraphs that expressed complete thoughts, and an HTML document shouldn't be an exception. Unfortunately, line and paragraph breaks are a little more complicated in HTML than you might expect.

As a markup language, HTML requires that you make no assumptions about your reader's machine. Your document's readers can set whatever margins and fonts they want to use. This means that text wrapping must be determined by the viewer software, as it is the only part of the system that knows about the reader's setup. Line feeds in the original document are ignored by the viewer, which then reformats the text to fit the context. This means that a document that's perfectly legible in your editor (see Figure 5.1) is badly mashed together in the viewer, as shown in Figure 5.2.

FIG. 5.1

Line feeds separate the paragraphs in the editor.

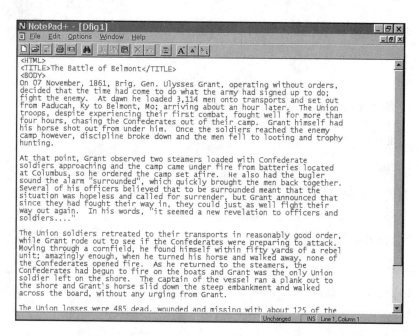

N O T E Different viewers display the same pages in different ways, depending on their default settings and user options. In this chapter, we've used examples from different browsers to mix things up a bit. ▪

The proper way to break text into paragraphs is by using paragraph elements. Place a paragraph start tag, `<P>`, at the beginning of each new paragraph, and the viewer knows to separate the paragraphs. Adding a paragraph end tag, `</P>`, is optional, as it is normally implied by the next start tag that comes along. Still, adding the `</P>` tag at the end of a paragraph can help to protect your documents against viewers that don't precisely follow the HTML standard.

FIG. 5.2

The viewer ignores the line feeds and runs the text together.

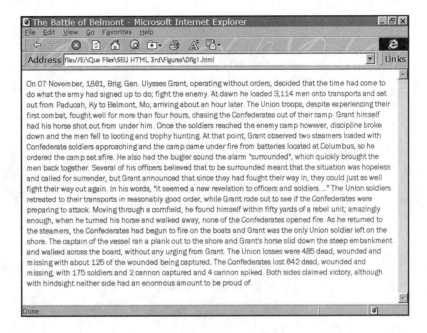

N O T E Seriously consider using the beginning and ending paragraph tags. As style elements, which give you more control over the <P> tag, become more prevalent, this syntax becomes more important.

Figure 5.3 shows what the document looks like in the editor after the paragraph tags have been added. You can see the tags were added to the start of each paragraph and that the line feeds are still in the document. Because the viewer ignores the line feeds anyway, it is best to keep them in the source document to make it easier to edit later.

When you look at the document in Figure 5.4, you can see the viewer separated the paragraphs correctly by adding a double-spaced line between them.

N O T E In some HTML documents, you see a paragraph start tag, <P>, used repeatedly to create additional white space. This is not supported in HTML, and most current viewers will ignore all of the <P> tags after the first one.

The paragraph element has one attribute that is supported by both Netscape Navigator and Microsoft Internet Explorer. This is the ALIGN attribute. The possible values for the ALIGN attribute and their functions are listed in Table 5.1. The default value, if the ALIGN attribute is not used, is for left alignment.

N O T E The ALIGN attribute can also be used with many other HTML tags to align graphics, table contents, and other page elements. Its use in these contexts will be discussed in following chapters.

Part

II

Ch

5

FIG. 5.3

If you want to separate paragraphs, use the <P> tag.

Paragraph Tags

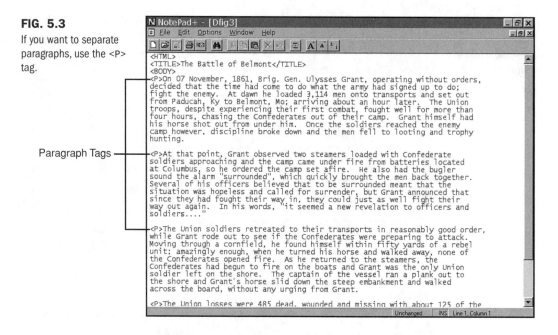

FIG. 5.4

With paragraph elements, the text becomes much easier to read.

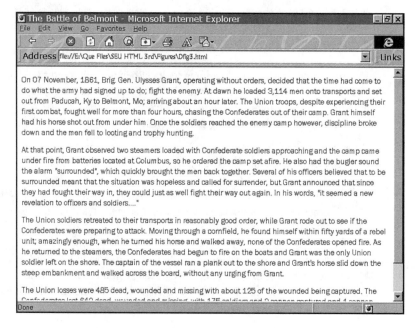

Table 5.1 ALIGN Values and Their Functions	
Attribute	**Function**
LEFT	Aligns the text with the left margin of the viewer. The right edge is ragged.
CENTER	Centers the text between the viewer margins.
RIGHT	Aligns the text with the right margin of the viewer. The left edge is ragged.

Adding and Preventing Line Breaks

As you have seen, HTML does all of the formatting at the viewing software rather than at the source. This has the advantage of device independence. But what do you do if you have a reason to break up a line of text at a certain point?

Use the line break tag, <BR>, to end a line where you want. This forces the viewer to start a new line, regardless of the position in the current line. Unlike the paragraph element, the line break does not double space the text. Because the line break element is not a container, it does not have an end tag.

One reason you might want to force line breaks is to show off your poetic muse, as shown in Listing 5.1.

**Listing 5.1   A Limerick Showing the Use of the *
* Tag**

```
<HTML>
<HEAD>
<TITLE>Creating an HTML Document</TITLE>
</HEAD>
<BODY>
<P>A very intelligent turtle<BR>
Found programming UNIX a hurdle<BR>
The system, you see,<BR>
Ran as slow as did he,<BR>
And that's not saying much for the turtle.<BR>
<CITE>Mercifully anonymous</CITE>
</BODY>
</HTML>
```

Part

II

Ch

5

When this source is viewed in Figure 5.5, you can see how the line break element works.

CAUTION

You might think you can use multiple line breaks to provide extra white space in your document. Some browsers condense multiple line breaks (multiple <BR> or <P> tags) to a single line break, however.

FIG. 5.5

Use line breaks to force a new line in the viewer.

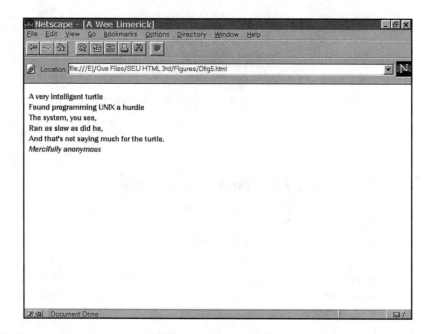

You need to be careful when using line breaks; if the line has already wrapped in the viewer, your break may appear after only a couple of words in the next line. This is particularly the case if the viewer you test your documents on has wider margins than your reader's viewer. Figure 5.6 shows an example in which the author saw that the break was occurring in the middle of the quotation, so she added a <BR>. Unfortunately, when displayed on a screen with different margins, the word "actually" ends up on a line by itself.

Just as there are instances in which it is convenient to break a line at a specified point, there are also times when you would like to avoid breaking a line at a certain point. Any text between a <NOBR> start tag and the associated end tag is guaranteed not to break across lines.

N O T E   This can be very useful for items such as addresses, where an unfortunate line break can cause unexpected results. Don't overuse the <NOBR> element, however. Text can look very strange when the natural line breaks have been changed. ▨

T I P   If you think you might need a break inside a <NOBR> element, you can suggest a breaking point with a <WBR> tag (soft line break). The viewer will only use the <WBR> if it needs it.

FIG. 5.6
Careless use of line breaks can produce an unexpected result.

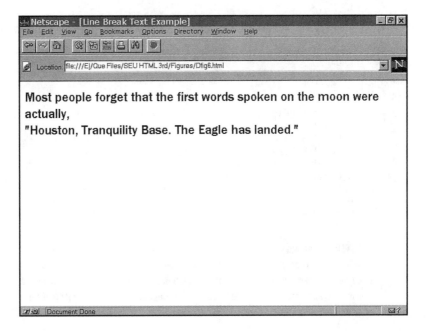

Netscape - [Line Break Text Example]
File Edit View Go Bookmarks Options Directory Window Help

Location: file:///E|/Que Files/SEU HTML 3rd/Figures/Dfig6.html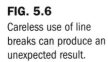

Most people forget that the first words spoken on the moon were actually,
"Houston, Tranquility Base. The Eagle has landed."

Document Done

Creating a Text Outline

So far, your HTML document probably looks a little dull. To make it more interesting, the first thing you need to do is add a little more structure to it. Web users want to be able to quickly scan a document to determine whether or not it has the information they are looking for. The way to make this scanning easier is to break the document up into logical sections, each covering a single topic.

After you have broken up the document, the next step is to add meaningful headers to each section, enabling your reader to quickly jump to the material of interest.

Adding Headings

Headings in HTML provide an outline of the text that forms the body of the document. As such, they direct the reader through the document and make your information more interesting and usable. They are probably the most commonly used formatting tag found in HTML documents.

The heading element is a *container* and must have a start tag (<H1>) and an end tag (</H1>). HTML has six levels of headings: H1 (the most important), H2, H3, H4, H5, H6 (the least important). Each of these levels has its own appearance in the reader's viewer, but you have no direct control over what that appearance is. This is part of the HTML philosophy: You, as the document writer, have the responsibility for the content, while the viewer has the responsibility for the appearance. See the example in Listing 5.2. (See Chapter 17, "Applying Cascading Style Sheets," to learn more about using style sheets to change text properties for tags such as <H1>.)

Part
II

Ch
5

Listing 5.2 An HTML Document Showing the Use of Headings

```
<HTML>
<HEAD>
<TITLE>Creating an HTML Document</TITLE>
</HEAD>
<BODY>
<H1>Level 1 Heading</H1>
<H2>Level 2 Heading</H2>
<H3>Level 3 Heading</H3>
<H4>Level 4 Heading</H4>
<H5>Level 5 Heading</H5>
<H6>Level 6 Heading</H6>
</BODY>
</HTML>
```

N O T E Although it is not absolutely necessary to use each of the heading levels, as a matter of good practice you should not skip levels because it may cause problems with automatic document converters. In particular, as new Web indexes come online, they will be able to search Web documents and create retrievable outlines. These outlines may be confusing if heading levels are missing. ■

Figure 5.7 shows how these headings look when they are displayed in Microsoft Internet Explorer.

FIG. 5.7

Here are the six heading levels as they appear in Internet Explorer.

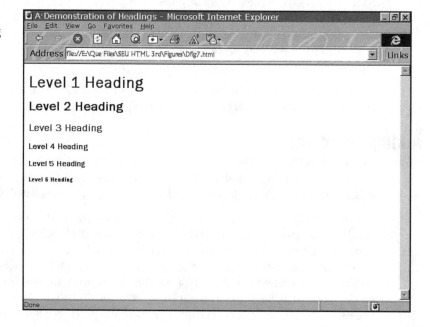

N O T E Remember that forgetting to add an end tag definitely messes up the appearance of your
document. Headings are containers and require both start and end tags. Another thing to
remember is that headings also have an implied paragraph break before and after each one. You can't
apply a heading to text in the middle of a paragraph to change the size or font. The result is a
paragraph broken into three separate pieces, with the middle paragraph in a heading format. ■

The best way to use headings is to consider them the outline for your document. Figure 5.8
shows a document in which each level of heading represents a new level of detail. Generally, it
is good practice to use a new level whenever you have two to four items of equal importance. If
more than four items are of the same importance under a parent heading, however, try breaking them into two different parent headings.

FIG. 5.8

Headings provide a
document outline.

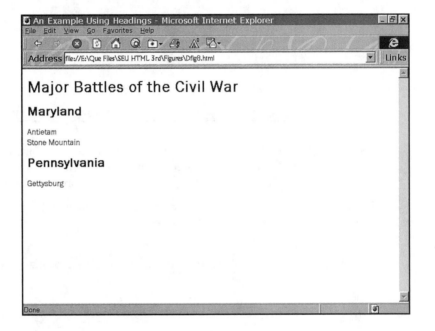

Headings can use the ALIGN attribute, just as the <P> tag does. This is important to remember,
because not all viewers show all headings left-aligned. Figure 5.9 shows the use of the ALIGN
attribute in a heading.

Adding Horizontal Lines

Another method for adding divisions to your documents is the use of horizontal lines. These
provide a strong visual break between sections and are especially useful for separating the
various parts of your document. Many viewers use an etched line that presents a crisp look
and adds visual depth to the document.

Part
II

Ch
5

FIG. 5.9
Headings can be aligned on the left, right, or in the center.

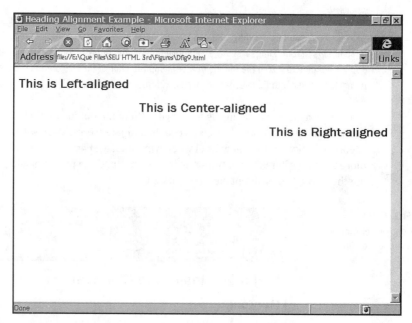

You can create a horizontal line using the horizontal rule element, <HR>. This tag draws a shaded, horizontal line across the viewer's display. The <HR> tag is not a container and does not require an end tag. There is an implied paragraph break before and after a horizontal rule.

Listing 5.3 shows how horizontal rule tags are used, and Figure 5.10 demonstrates their appearance in the Netscape Navigator viewer.

Listing 5.3   An HTML Document Showing the Use of Horizontal Rules

```
<HTML>
<HEAD>
<TITLE>Manned Space Craft</TITLE>
</HEAD>
<BODY>
<H1 ALIGN=CENTER>Manned Space Craft</H1>
<BR>
<H2 ALIGN=LEFT>Soviet</H2>
Vostok<BR>
Voskhod<BR>
Soyuz<BR>
<HR>
<H2 ALIGN=LEFT>American</H2>
Mercury<BR>
Gemini<BR>
Apollo<BR>
Shuttle<BR>
<HR >
</BODY>
</HTML>
```

FIG. 5.10

Most viewers interpret the <HR> tag as an etched line.

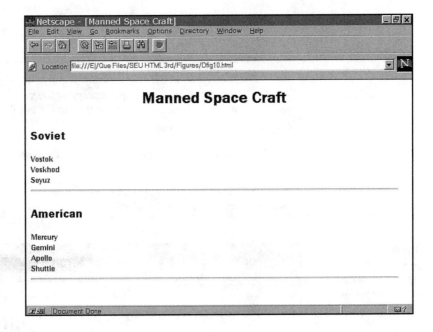

Table 5.2 lists the attributes of the <HR> tag. Listing 5.4 is similar to Listing 5.3, but shows how some of the attributes are used. Figure 5.11 shows the results as seen in Internet Explorer.

Listing 5.4   The Use of Attributes in Horizontal Rules

```
<HTML>
<HEAD>
<TITLE>Manned Space Craft</TITLE>
</HEAD>
<BODY>
<H1 ALIGN=CENTER>Manned Space Craft</H1>
<BR>
<H2 ALIGN=LEFT>Soviet</H2>
Vostok<BR>
Voskhod<BR>
Soyuz<BR>
<HR WIDTH=50% SIZE=6 ALIGN=LEFT COLOR=RED>
<H2 ALIGN=LEFT>American</H2>
Mercury<BR>
Gemini<BR>
Apollo<BR>
Shuttle<BR>
<HR WIDTH=50% SIZE=6 ALIGN=LEFT COLOR=NAVY>
</BODY>
</HTML>
```

Part
II

Ch
5

Table 5.2 **<HR> Attributes and Their Functions**

Attribute	Function
ALIGN	Can be set to LEFT, CENTER, or RIGHT.
WIDTH	Can be entered in pixels or as a percentage of the viewer window width. If a percentage is desired, add a percent time to the number.
SIZE	The height of the ruled line in pixels.
NOSHADE	If this attribute is present, the viewer does not use a three-dimensional effect.
COLOR	Specifies the color of the ruled line. An RGB hexadecimal value or a standard color name can be used.

FIG. 5.11

The attributes of the <HR> tag can make the rules more attractive.

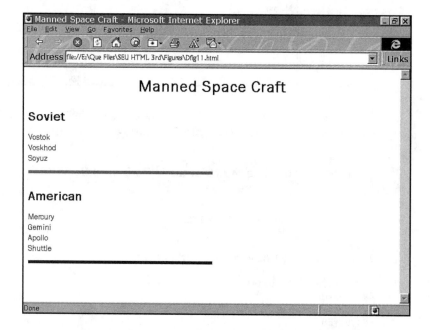

Documents created using early versions of HTML often used a graphic image to provide a more colorful and obvious break. Of course, these would not appear in viewers that had image loading turned off. Even if the viewer were loading images, a color bar was another file that had to be copied and maintained. The new <HR> attributes allow you much more flexibility in the creation of your documents at virtually no loss of speed or ease of maintenance.

Horizontal rules should be reserved for instances when you want to represent a strong break in the flow of the text. Some basic guidelines for adding rules is that they should never come between a heading and the text that follows the heading. They should also not be used to create *white space* in your document. White space—places where no content appears—is important to controlling the look and feel of your pages. Too much white space and your pages appear barren; too little and they appear crowded.

Using Preformatted Text

Is it absolutely necessary to use paragraph and line break elements for formatting text? Well, not really; HTML provides a container that can hold preformatted text. This is text that gives you, the author, much more control over how the viewer displays your document. The trade-off for this control is a loss of flexibility.

The most common and useful preformatting tag is the <PRE> container. Text in a <PRE> container is basically free-form with line feeds causing the line to break at the beginning of the next clear line. Line break tags and paragraph tags are also supported. This versatility enables you to create such items as tables and precise columns of text. Another common use of the <PRE> element is to display large blocks of computer code (C, C++, and so on) that would otherwise be difficult to read if the browser reformatted it.

Text in a <PRE> container can use any of the physical or logical text formatting elements. You can use this feature to create tables that have bold headers or italicized values. However, the use of paragraph-formatting elements such as <Address> or any of the heading elements is not permitted. Anchor elements can be included within a <PRE> container.

The biggest drawback to the <PRE> container is that any text within it is displayed in a monospaced font in the reader's viewer. This tends to make long stretches of preformatted text look clunky and out of place.

Figure 5.12 shows an example of some preformatted text in an editor. You can use the editor to line up the columns neatly before adding the character-formatting tags. The result of this document is shown in Figure 5.13.

TIP

If you are not converting existing documents, the HTML tables are much more attractive than are those you can create by using the <PRE> element. See Chapter 11, "Formatting Content with Tables," for more information on this topic.

CAUTION

Tab characters move the cursor to the next position, which is an integer multiple of eight. The official HTML specification recommends that tab characters not be used in preformatted text because they are not supported in the same way by all viewers. Spaces should be used for aligning columns.

FIG. 5.12
Preformatted text can be used to line up columns of numbers.

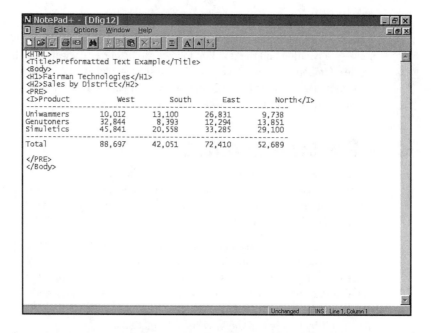

FIG. 5.13
A preformatted table can be used in a document.

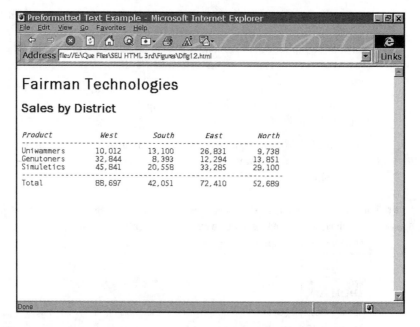

N O T E There are other preformatted container classes, but these have been declared as obsolete. The <XMP> and <LISTING> elements give you the capability to create text that is already laid out. There are some disadvantages to these in that other HTML elements are not permitted inside of them. Viewers are not allowed to recognize any markup tags except the end tag. Unfortunately, many viewers don't comply with this standard properly, and the results can be unpleasant.

The difference between the two elements are that <XMP> text must be rendered in a font size that permits at least 80 characters on a line and <LISTING> requires a font that permits 132 characters.

You should avoid using the <XMP> and <LISTING> elements unless it is absolutely necessary. Because they have been declared obsolete, viewers are not required to support them any longer. You will be more certain of what your readers are seeing if you use the <PRE> element instead.

N O T E If you want to show actual HTML code in a preformatted section, or you want to use the < or > characters, you need to use the &lt and &gt entity codes, like this:

&ltPRE&gt.

The *<DIV>* Tag

The <DIV></DIV> container (DIV stands for division) can be used to enclose and define the alignment for an entire block of page elements. It supports the ALIGN attribute, so you could use it to align a block of text and graphics to CENTER, as in this example:

```
<DIV ALIGN=CENTER>
<H1>This header is centered.</H1>
<IMG SOURCE="somepic.gif"><BR>
So are the images above and this line of text.<BR>
<P ALIGN=RIGHT>But this text is right-aligned.</P>
</DIV>
```

Note that all the elements between the <DIV> and </DIV> tags are aligned according to the definition given by the <DIV> tag, except for any elements which have their own alignments defined. As is always the case with the ALIGN attribute, it can assume the values LEFT, CENTER, or RIGHT.

You can also use inline styles with the <DIV> tag to set the style for an entire block of HTML within your document. This works because of the concept of inheritance. For example, if you want to change the text color of an entire block of tags to blue, you can put those tags in the DIV container and define a style for the <DIV> tag that sets the text color to blue. It looks like this:

```
<DIV STYLE="color: blue">
<H1>This is a heading</H1>
<P>This is a paragraph. It will look blue in the user's browser</P>
</DIV>
```

The DIV tag is also an important part of advanced page layout using Cascading Style Sheets, and will be discussed in that context in Chapters 17 and 18.

Part

II

Ch

5

Layout Tips

Understanding the HTML tags that you can use is a different matter than understanding how to use them effectively. Thus, here are a few tips that you should consider when using the tags you learned about in this chapter:

- *Use equal spacing.* Try to keep the spacing between elements consistent. That is, make sure the same amount of space is above and below each of your paragraphs. Readers perceive uneven spacing as sloppiness on your part.

- *Avoid right- and center justification.* Don't right or center-justify the main body of text. Right- and center-justified text is harder to read than left-justified text.

- *Don't go overboard with indents.* Proper indentation depends on the size of the font you're using. A larger font requires a deeper indent and vice versa.

- *Use <NOBR> with <WBR> to maintain control of line breaks.* Sometimes you want to control exactly where the browser breaks a line if it needs to. <NOBR> turns off line breaks while <WBR> provides hints to the browser that suggests a spot for a line break if necessary.

- *Consider dividing a page that uses <HR>.* If you find yourself using rules to divide a Web page into individual topics, consider splitting that Web page into individual pages so each page remains focused on a single topic.

- *Give plenty of space to artwork.* The images and tables in your HTML document should have enough white space around them so that they're set apart from the text. You don't want them to appear cramped.

- *Use headings to organize your text.* Headings give readers a visual road map that helps them locate the information in which they're interested. Use them liberally.

A Specialized Template

Using what you've learned in this chapter, you can create a more sophisticated template. Now you can use some of this chapter's features to build a template that can be used for glossaries and related documents.

The first step is to bring the existing template into your editor. Once you've loaded it, you can make the appropriate changes to the elements that are already present. These can be seen in Listing 5.5.

Listing 5.5 The Glossary Template with the First Changes

```
<HTML>
<HEAD>
<TITLE>Glossary</TITLE>
<HEAD>
<BODY BACKGROUND="greybg.jpg" BGCOLOR="GRAY", TEXT="BLACK",
LINK="BLUE", ALINK="GREEN", VLINK="RED">
<ADDRESS>Created by Author<BR>
Created on Date</ADDRESS>
</BODY>
</HTML>
```

Now you can add a title to the page and bracket the text with some horizontal rules. The terms are defined as level-two headings, left-aligned, and that the definitions themselves will be normal text. These decisions lead to Listing 5.6, which is a template that can now be saved and used anytime you need a glossary document. This same template would also work for a phone list or a catalog.

Listing 5.6 The Final Glossary Template

```
<HTML>
<HEAD>
<TITLE>Glossary</TITLE>
<HEAD>
<BODY BACKGROUND="greybg.jpg" BGCOLOR="GRAY", TEXT="BLACK",
LINK="BLUE", ALINK="GREEN", VLINK="RED">
<H1 ALIGN=CENTER>Glossary</H1>
<HR ALIGN=CENTER WIDTH=50% SIZE=5 COLOR=NAVY>
<H2 ALIGN=LEFT>Term 1</H2>
Type the definition for term 1 here.
<H2 ALIGN=LEFT>Term 2</H2>
Type the definition for term 2 here. And so on…
<HR ALIGN=CENTER WIDTH=50% SIZE=5 COLOR=NAVY>
<ADDRESS>Created by Author<BR>
Created on Date</ADDRESS>
</BODY>
</HTML>
```

Part

II

Ch

5

An example of how this template could be used is shown in Figure 5.14.

FIG. 5.14

This is an example using the glossary template.

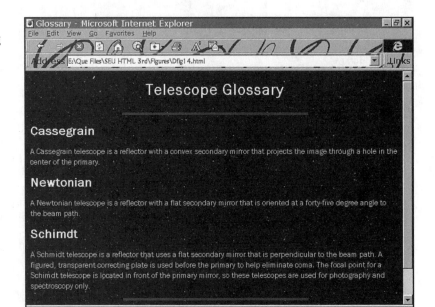

## CHAPTER 6

Applying Charcter Formatting

by Robert Meegan and Mark R. Brown

In this chapter

Text Formatting

Once you've created your document, much of the hard work is done. The text that you've written is neatly broken into paragraphs, headings are in place, and the miscellaneous items such as the title and the author information have been added. At this point you could walk away satisfied, but something still seems to be missing.

One of the primary things that separates documents created on a word processor from those produced on a typewriter is the idea of text formatting. Word processors give the author control over how her text will look. She can chose the font that she likes in the appropriate size, and she can apply one or more of a myriad of options to the text. In HTML, you have this same capability. Your only real restrictions involve the importance of viewer independence.

Logical Formatting

One of the ideas behind HTML is that documents should be laid out in a logical and structured manner. This gives the users of the documents as much flexibility as possible. With this in mind, the designers of HTML created a number of formatting elements that are labeled according to the purpose they serve rather than by their appearance. The advantage of this approach is that documents are not limited to a certain platform. Although they may look different on various platforms, the content and context will remain the same.

These logical format elements are as follows:

- <CITE>   The citation element is used to indicate the citation of a quotation. It can also be used to indicate the title of a book or article. An italic font is normally used to display citations.

  `<CITE>Tom Sawyer</CITE> remains one of the classics of American literature.`

- <CODE>   The code element is used to indicate a small amount of computer code. It is generally reserved for short sections, with longer sections noted by using the <PRE> tag described later. Code normally appears in a monospaced font.

  ```
  One of the first lines that every C programmer learns is:<BR>
  <CODE>puts("Hello World!");</CODE>
  ```

- <EM>   The emphasis element is used to indicate a section of text that the author wants to identify as significant. Emphasis is generally shown in an italic font.

  ```
  The actual line reads, "Alas, poor Yorick. I knew him, EM>Horatio</EM>."
  ```

- <KBD>   The keyboard element is used to indicate a user entry response. A monospaced typewriter font is normally used to display keyboard text.

  ```
  To run the decoder, type <KBD>Restore</KBD> followed by your password.
  ```

- <SAMP> The sample element is used to indicate literal characters. These normally are a few characters that are intended to be precisely identified. Sample element text normally is shown in a monospaced font.

  `The letters SAMP>AEIOU</SAMP> are the vowels of the English language.`

- <STRONG> The strong element is used to emphasize a particularly important section of text. Text using strong emphasis is normally set in a bold font.

  `The most important rule to remember is <STRONG>Don't panic</STRONG>!`

- <VAR> The variable element is used to indicate a dummy variable name. Variables are normally viewed in an italic font.

  `The sort routine rotates on the <VAR>I</VAR>th element.`

- <DFN> The defining instance element is used to create a sub-definition in a defining list. Variables are normally viewed in an italic font.

  `<DFN>The aardvark is an ant-eating animal.</DFN>`

Note that all of these elements are containers, and as such, they require an end tag. Figure 6.1 shows how these logical elements look when seen in the Netscape viewer.

FIG. 6.1
Samples of the logical format elements are displayed in Netscape.

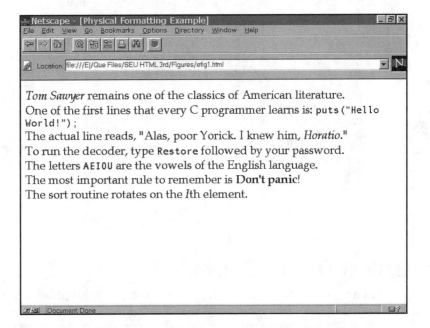

You have probably noticed that a lot of these format styles use the same rendering. The most obvious question to ask is why use them if they all look alike?

The answer is these elements are logical styles. They indicate what the intention of the author was, not how the material should look. This is important because future uses of HTML may include programs that search the Web to find citations, for example, or the next generation of

Part
II

Ch
6

Web viewers may be able to read a document aloud. A program that can identify emphasis would be able to avoid the deadly monotone of current text-to-speech processors.

The <*BLOCKQUOTE*> Element

You may have the opportunity to quote a long piece of work from another source in your document. To indicate that this quotation is different from the rest of your text, HTML provides the <BLOCKQUOTE> element. This container functions as a body element within the body element and can contain any of the formatting or break tags. As a container, the <BLOCKQUOTE> element is turned off by using the end tag.

The normal method used by most viewers to indicate a <BLOCKQUOTE> element is to indent the text away from the left margin. Some text-only viewers may indicate a <BLOCKQUOTE> by using a character, such as the "greater than" sign, in the leftmost column on the screen. Because most viewers are now graphical in nature, the <BLOCKQUOTE> element provides an additional service by enabling you to indent normal text from the left margin. This can add some visual interest to the document.

Listing 6.1 shows how a <BLOCKQUOTE> is constructed, including some of the formatting available in the container. The results of this document when read into Netscape can be seen in Figure 6.2.

Listing 6.1   Construction of a <*BLOCKQUOTE*>

```
<HTML>
<TITLE>BLOCKQUOTE Example</TITLE>
<BODY>
<BLOCKQUOTE>
Wit is the sudden marriage of ideas which before their union were not
perceived to have any relation.
</BLOCKQUOTE>
<CITE>Mark Twain</CITE>
</BODY>
</HTML>
```

Physical Format Elements

Having said that HTML is intended to leave the appearance of the document up to the viewer, I will now show you how you can have limited control over what the reader sees. In addition to the logical formatting elements, it is possible to use physical formatting elements that will change the appearance of the text in the viewer. These physical elements are as follows:

- <B>   The bold element uses a bold font to display the text.

    `This is in <B>bold</B> text.`

- <I>   The italic element renders text using an italic font.

    `This is in <I>italic</I> text.`

- ■ <TT>   The teletype element displays the contents with a monospaced typewriter font.
  `This is in TT>teletype</TT> text.`

- ■ <U>   The underline element causes text to be underlined in the viewer.
  `This text is <U>underlined</U>.`

- ■ <STRIKE>   The strikethrough element draws a horizontal line through the middle of the text.
  `This is a <STRIKE>strikethough</STRIKE> example.`

- ■ <BIG>   The big print element uses a larger font size to display the text.
  `This is <BIG>big</BIG> text.`

- ■ <SMALL>   The small print element displays the text in a smaller font size.
  `This is <SMALL>small</SMALL> text.`

- ■ <SUB>   The subscript element moves the text lower than the surrounding text and (if possible) displays the text in a smaller size font.
  `This is a  SUB>subscript</SUB>.`

- ■ <SUP>   The superscript element moves the text higher than the surrounding text and (if possible) displays the text in a smaller size font.
  `This is a <SUP>superscript</SUP>.`

FIG. 6.2

This is the appearance of the document in Netscape.

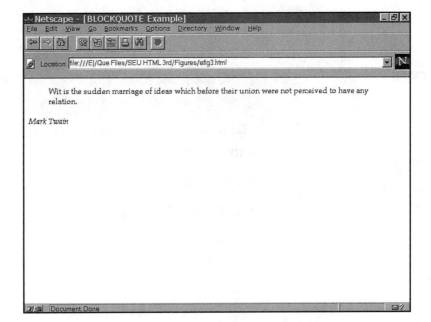

If the proper font isn't available, the reader's viewer must render the text in the closest possible manner. Once again, each of these is a container element and requires the use of an end tag. Figure 6.3 shows how these elements look in the Internet Explorer.

Part
II

Ch
6

FIG. 6.3

Samples of the physical format elements are shown in the Internet Explorer.

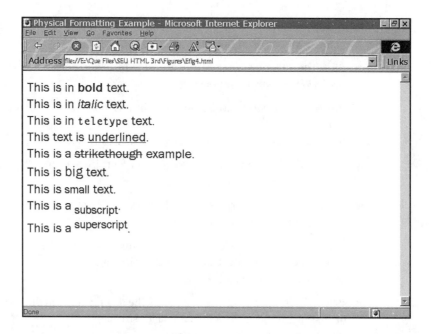

These elements can be nested, with one element contained entirely within another. On the other hand, overlapping elements are not permitted and can produce unpredictable results. Figure 6.4 gives some examples of nested elements and how they can be used to create special effects.

FIG. 6.4

Logical and physical format elements can be nested to create additional format styles. In line three of this example, the <I> and <B> tags have been combined to create bold italic text.

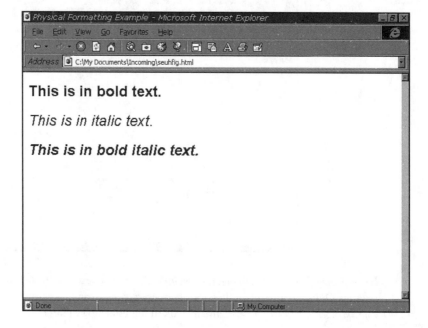

T I P There is a tag available only in Netscape Navigator that has acquired a particularly bad reputation: the `<BLINK>` tag is notorious in HTML circles. Unless you want people to speak ill of your documents, it's best to avoid this tag. If you do use it, make absolutely sure you remember to use a `</BLINK>` tag in the proper place. There's nothing more annoying than a whole page of blinking text.

Fonts

You, as document author, have the ability to control the appearance of the text in your documents. This capability was restricted entirely to the reader in versions of HTML previous to 3.2. The problem with this ability is that you can only use fonts that exist on you readers' machines. So how do you know what your user might have available?

Unfortunately, you don't. If you are building documents to be used on an intranet, your organization should set standards as to which fonts should be found on every machine. As long as this is a reasonable set, it will be easy to maintain and you will be able to choose any of the standard fonts for your document. If you are developing for the Web, however, you have a more serious problem. In practice, you really don't know what fonts your readers might have. Even the most basic selection depends greatly upon the hardware that your readers are using. There are no really graceful ways around this problem at the present, although several companies are looking into ways of distributing font information with a document.

N O T E If you are developing for the Web and you would like to use some different fonts, you should be aware that Microsoft has several fonts available for free download on their Web site. These fonts are available in both Windows and Macintosh formats. If you decide to use any of these fonts in your documents, you might want to put a link to the Web page where your readers can download the fonts, if they don't already have them.

http://www.microsoft.com/truetype/fontpack/default.htm

The *FONT* Element

The method that HTML uses for providing control over the appearance of the text is the FONT element. The FONT element is a container that is opened with the `<FONT>` start tag and closed with the `</FONT>` end tag. Unless attributes are assigned in the start tag, there is no effect of using a FONT element.

The FONT element can be used inside of any other text container and it will modify the text based upon the appearance of the text within the parent container. Using the FACE, SIZE, and COLOR attributes, you can use FONT to drastically modify the appearance of text in your documents.

The *FACE* Attribute

The FACE attribute allows you to specify the font that you would like the viewing software to use when displaying your document. The parameter for the this attribute is the name of the desired font. This name must be an exact match for a font name on the reader's machine, or the viewer will ignore the request and use the default font as set by the reader. Capitalization is ignored in the name, but spaces are required. Listing 6.2 shows an example of how a font face is specified and Figure 6.5 shows the page in Microsoft Internet Explorer.

Listing 6.2 An Example of Font Face Selection

```
<HTML>
<HEAD>
<TITLE>Font Selection Example</TITLE>
</HEAD>
<BODY>
<FONT FACE="Tolkien">
This is an example of font selection. </FONT>
</BODY>
</HTML>
```

FIG. 6.5

The FACE attribute of the FONT element lets you select the font in which the text will be displayed.

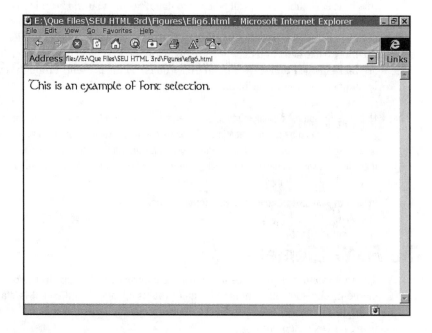

Since you don't know for certain what fonts the user might have on his system, the face attribute allows you to list more than one font, with the names separated by commas. This is especially useful, since nearly identical fonts often have different names on Windows and Macintoshes. The font list will be parsed from left to right and the first matching font will be used. Listing 6.3 shows an example where the author wanted to use a sans-serif font for his text.

Listing 6.3   Font Face Selection can use a List of Acceptable Choices

```
<HTML>
<HEAD>
<TITLE>Font Selection Example</TITLE>
</HEAD>
<BODY>
<FONT FACE="Verdana", "Arial", "Helvetica">
This is an example of font selection. </FONT>
</BODY>
</HTML>
```

In this example, the author wanted to use Verdana as his first choice, but listed Arial and Helvetica as alternatives.

The *SIZE* Attribute

The SIZE attribute of the FONT element allows the document author to specify character height for the text. Font size is a relative scale from 1 though 7 and is based upon the "normal" font size being 3. The SIZE attribute can be used in either of two different ways: the size can be stated absolutely, with a statement like SIZE=5, or it can be relative, as in SIZE=+2. The second method is more commonly used when a BASEFONT size has been specified.

Listing 6.4 shows how the font sizes are specified and Figure 6.6 shows how they would look.

Listing 6.4   An Example of Font Size Selection

```
<HTML>
<HEAD>
<TITLE>Font Size Example</TITLE>
</HEAD>
<BODY>
<FONT SIZE=1>Size 1</FONT><BR>
<FONT SIZE=-1>Size 2</FONT><BR>
<FONT SIZE=3>Size 3</FONT><BR>
<FONT SIZE=4>Size 4</FONT><BR>
<FONT SIZE=+2>Size 5</FONT><BR>
<FONT SIZE=6>Size 6</FONT><BR>
<FONT SIZE=+4>Size 7</FONT><BR>
</BODY>
</HTML>
```

Part

II

Ch

6

The *COLOR* Attribute

Text color can be specified in the same manner as the face or the size. The COLOR attribute accepts either a hexadecimal RGB value or one of the standard color names. Listing 6.5 is an example of how colors can be specified.

▶ **See** "Color Definitions," **p. 66**

FIG. 6.6

Text size can be specified with the SIZE attribute of the FONT element.

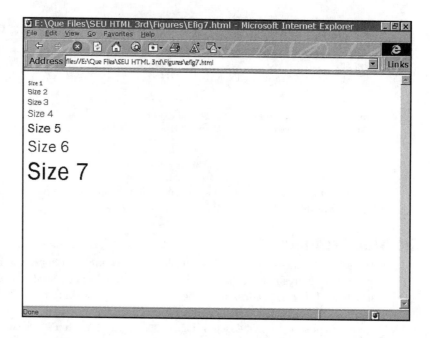

Listing 6.5   An Example of Font Color Selection

```
<HTML>
<HEAD>
<TITLE>Font Color Example</TITLE>
</HEAD>
<BODY>
<FONT COLOR="#FF0000">This text is red</FONT><BR>
<FONT COLOR="GREEN">This text is green</FONT><BR>
</BODY>
</HTML>
```

The <BASEFONT> Tag

The <BASEFONT> tag is used to establish the standard font size, face, and color for the text in the document. The choices made in the <BASEFONT> tag remain in place for the rest of the document, unless they are overridden by a FONT element. When the FONT element is closed, the BASEFONT characteristics are returned. BASEFONT attributes can be changed by another <BASEFONT> tag at any time in the document. Note that BASEFONT is a tag and not a container. There is no </BASEFONT> end tag.

BASEFONT uses the FACE, SIZE, and COLOR attributes just as the FONT element does.

Listing 6.6 is an example of the <BASEFONT> tag. Figure 6.7 shows how the example looks in Internet Explorer.

Listing 6.6 An Example of the <*BASEFONT*> Tag

```
<HTML>
<HEAD>
<TITLE>BASEFont Example</TITLE>
</HEAD>
<BODY>
This text is before the BASEFONT tag.<BR>
<BASEFONT SIZE=6 FACE="GEORGIA">
This text is after the BASEFONT tag.<BR>
Size changes are relative to the BASEFONT <FONT SIZE=-3>SIZE</FONT>.<BR>
</BODY>
</HTML>
```

FIG. 6.7

The <BASEFONT> tag can be used to control the text characteristics for the entire document.

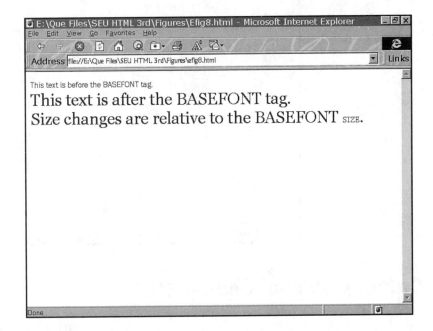

Text Formatting Tips

Now that you have all of the tools to format your text, you need to decide how you are going to use them. It is possible to use so many different fonts, sizes, and formats that your document will be unpleasant to read. Figure 6.8 is a bad example of how a document can use too many formats.

The following are general tips to keep in mind as you format your documents:

- Most documents should use only two or three different font faces.
- In general, if the body text is in a serif font, such as Times New Roman, the headings should be a sans-serif font, such as Arial.

Part
II

Ch
6

■ Italics are much less intrusive than are bold characters, which should be reserved for very important points.

■ Don't overuse underlining. When long strings of text are underlined, the user's eyes easily get confused.

■ The size of headings should decrease with the decreasing importance of the heading. This provides your readers with a quick and easy way to scan your documents.

FIG. 6.8
The ability to select formats should not be overused.

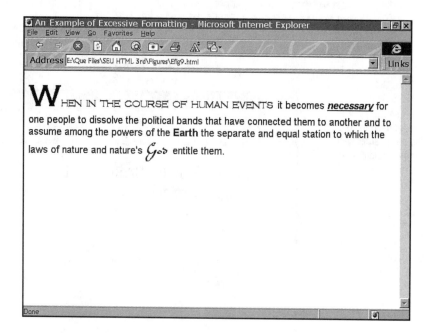

Creating Special Characters

It's bound to happen sooner or later—you'll need to include some weird character on your Web page like a copyright sign or trademark symbol. Fortunately, HTML provides an easy way to do this. For example, if you need a trademark symbol, you use the substitute `&trade`. A Web browser program will interpret this properly as ™.

HTML 4.0 adds a whole list of new "entities", or special symbols. They fall roughly into three categories.

First is a set of international typography symbols that are necessary for creating Web sites that are truly world-wide. Though we don't use them in English, most Western languages couldn't get along without the "o" with an umlaut.

The second set of new entities are mathematical symbols. Long demanded by scientists and engineers, these new symbols allow them to put complex formulas inline with regular text. An integral equation is now almost as easy to create and display elegantly as a Shakespeare quote.

NOTE Though Greek characters are included among the mathematical entities, the set is not adequate for creating documents in Greek. These symbols are intended for use in mathematical formulas only. ■

The final set of new characters included in the HTML 4.0 specification is a set of special characters that are included in Adobe's Symbol font, like daggers and fancy quotation marks.

Though entities are easy to use, the list of available characters is quite long. The full list is on the Web at **http://www.w3.org/TR/WD-entities**, but Table 6.1 lists a few popular characters to get you started:

Table 6.1   Some Symbols Defined in HTML 4.0

Entity	Symbols
&cent, &pound, &yen	¢, #, ¥
&copy, &reg	©, ®
&deg	°
&frac14, &frac12, &frac34	$\frac{1}{2}$, $\frac{1}{3}$, $\frac{3}{4}$
&divide	÷
&pi	Π
&le, &ge	< >
&amp	&
&dagger	†
&spades, &clubs, &hearts, &diams	♠, ♣, ♥, ♦

To use one of these entities in an HTML document, just include it inline with text, as in this example:

```
I like bread &amp butter, and for dessert I like &pi.
```

The &amp will be displayed as an ampersand ("&") and the &pi will show up as the mathematical symbol for pi. ●

Adding Graphics to a Web Page

by Mark R. Brown, Jerry Honeycutt,
and Robert Meegan

In this chapter

Why Graphics?

Images can make your HTML document more compelling than text alone. Imagine an HTML document that contains some fairly dry material. The specification for the techno-widget that you invented, for example. If you only put text in this document, the document would seem quite dull. On the other hand, a few well-placed graphics can break up the text, making it seem more readable, and make the document more visually appealing.

Images can often convey your message better than text alone. Can you picture this book without any figures? It wouldn't convey its message as well. Remember the old cliché, "a picture is worth a thousand words?" Beyond that, without figures you probably would have put this book right back onto the shelf because it wouldn't look very appealing.

Up to this point, you've learned about the basic HTML required to add text to your document and how to format that text. This chapter stuffs your toolkit with another tool—inline images— that lets you convey your message better and create a more visually attractive Web page. In this chapter, you learn how to add those images to your HTML documents. You also learn several tips and tricks that you need to know when using images in HTML.

Understanding the Issues

You need to carefully consider each image that you add to your HTML documents. Yes, you should carefully consider the design and contents of each image, but, in this section, you learn about other issues. For example:

- Does the image add enough value to the Web page?
- Can I borrow an image? What about copyrights?
- What about offensive or pornographic images?

What Should I Know When Using Images?

Before adding images to your HTML documents, you need to understand the issues. That doesn't mean you should avoid using images—you shouldn't. If you understand the issues, however, you're better able to choose appropriate images. Just keep these points in mind as you add each image to your document:

- *Graphics files are slow to download.* The average user with a 14.4KBps modem can wait several seconds or even several minutes while a graphics file downloads.
- *Search engines don't know what to do with images.* Search engines such as AltaVista and Excite can't index your images. Thus, if you depend heavily on images, your Web page isn't as likely to be hit upon by these search engines' users.
- *Many users don't have graphical browsers.* Thousands of folks are still using Lynx, for example, which is a UNIX-based, text-only browser. In addition, Internet Explorer and Netscape users might disable inline images in order to open Web pages faster.

■ *Images aren't always internationalized.* Such a big word, internationalized. Because HTML documents published on the Web have a worldwide audience, internationalized images might be important.

■ *Color images aren't always portable.* A color image that looks good on your computer might not look quite as good on another user's computer. Thus, you need to pay particular attention to how you use colors in an image.

Do I Have to Worry About an Image's Copyright?

The growth in electronic publishing has given rise to a startling new crime wave. Many people who are perfectly honest in all of their day-to-day dealings think nothing of using a clever graphic found on the Web. After all, once they download it, the image has lost all its ties to the original author. Regardless, copyright laws apply to electronic images just as much as they do to works like this book. If you use an image that has been copyrighted, the author can sue for damages.

How can you tell if a graphic has been copyrighted? It's not as easy as looking for a little copyright symbol in the image. Here are some tips to help you determine if an image is copyrighted:

■ Look at the original document that contained the image for a copyright notice.

■ If you borrowed the image from clip art or an image library, look in the library's document for a copyright notice.

■ If you scanned the image from a magazine or book, you can bet the image is copyrighted.

■ If you downloaded an image from a commercial site, such as an online magazine, the image is probably copyrighted.

NOTE Images that are obviously commercially oriented are usually copyrighted. These include images of people, logos, cartoon characters, and other unique images. Interesting decorations such as bullets or horizontal rules probably come from a clip-art library, which grants rights to use those images only to the purchaser of the library. ■

Can you plead ignorance if you're busted using a copyrighted image? No. You have the total responsibility for determining whether an image is copyrighted. Because this is not always practical, the best advise is to only use images that either you're completely certain are not copyrighted, those that you have been granted the right to use, or those for which you hold the copyright.

CAUTION

Changing a copyrighted work does not revoke the copyright. The copyright holder has rights to all derived works. This means that you cannot download an image, change it in some fashion, and then freely use the new version.

Part

II

Ch

7

As you can see, copyright law is a tricky thing. Your best bet is to assume that all images are copyrighted unless proven otherwise. If you have any questions or if you're developing a high-profile Web site, you should probably contact an attorney who specializes in copyright law.

Can I Get into Trouble for Pornographic Images?

Maybe. A simple rule of thumb is that you should avoid pornographic images. From a practical point of view, a Web site that has pornographic images on it is likely to be overwhelmed with traffic. As a result you may run afoul of your Internet service provider, who is almost certainly not going to be pleased with hundreds of megabytes of downloads from a single Web page.

There are a couple of legal aspects to this issue, as well:

- Most pornography has been scanned from published sources and is in violation of the copyright laws. These publishers are among the most aggressive plaintiffs in pursuit of legal damages.
- A variety of states and countries have laws regarding what is obscene. Since the Web is a world-wide medium, you might violate laws that you don't even know exist.

CAUTION

The information you read in this section is common sense. This information doesn't replace your legal counsel, however, in cases where you have real questions about pornographic images.

Picking the Right Graphics File Format

You'll find dozens of graphics file formats that you can use to store images—GIF, JPEG, PCX, PNG, WMF, and so on. When creating images for use in an HTML document, however, you're better off sticking with those file formats that most browsers understand: GIF or JPEG.

Each file format has certain trade offs. While one file format downloads faster, for example, the other format maintains more image detail. This section helps you pick the right file format by describing these trade offs. First, it briefly describes each file format, and then it compares the speed, color depth, definition, and browser support of each file format.

N O T E If you want to get right to the bottom line, use GIF. It's widely supported by most Web browsers (whereas PNG is not). It can be interlaced, which lets users view an image before it's finished downloading. It does transparency, too, so you can create great looking imagemaps with transparent backgrounds. And you can even use it to create simple animations.

▶ **See** "Graphic," **p.441**

N O T E When choosing a graphics file format, the most important issue to keep in mind is download speed versus image quality. If you're going to use an image in your Web page, you obviously want to store that image in a format that downloads as quickly as possible. On the other hand, you trade image quality for faster download speeds.

The best possible choices are GIF, PNG, or JPEG. BMP files aren't compressed at all, thus it is the slowest of all file formats to download. GIF, PNG, and JPEG all provide an acceptable experience when compared to the variety of other formats available on the Web. GIF and PNG files are larger than JPEG files, but GIF and PNG files decode faster and maintain more image detail. ■

T I P GIF does an extremely good job compressing images that contain only a handful of colors. Thus, with an image that uses only a few colors, GIF compresses better than JPEG.

Colors

GIF supports 256 colors. JPEG supports 16.7 million colors. Thus, if color depth is not important or you're using a limited number of colors in an image, you can be comfortable using GIF. On the other hand, if you want to maintain a photographic-quality color depth, then you might consider using JPEG.

Loss

Lossy compression schemes cause an image to lose detail when the graphics program saves it. That is how these schemes compress the file so much. *Lossless compression schemes*, on the other hand, don't cause an image to lose any detail at all. Table 7.1 describes each file format's compression scheme.

Table 7.1   Compression Schemes

Format	Scheme	Description
GIF	Lossless	GIF compresses without losing any detail. Thus, if you're concerned more with maintaining detail than download speed, use GIF.
PNG	Lossless	PNG also compresses without losing any detail. PNG is a good alternative to GIF, except that it's not directly supported by most Web browsers.
JPEG	Lossy	JPEG causes an image to lose detail when saved. If you're concerned more with file size than with detail, however, use JPEG.

Part
II

Ch
7

Browser Support

You really don't want readers to have to install a helper application to view the images in your HTML documents. Thus, you should stick with those file formats that are directly supported by the most popular browsers. These formats include GIF and JPEG. PNG is not yet supported by a majority of the Web browsers, so you should shy away from this format for now.

Adding Inline Images to Your HTML Document

Putting an image in an HTML document is incredibly easy—simply use the <IMG> tag with its SRC attribute, which points to the URL of the graphic file to be displayed (see Figure 7.1). Add the following tag to your HTML document at the location in which you want to display the image. Then, replace *filename* with the URL of the image you want to display.

```
<IMG SRC="filename">
```

By default, the browser displays the image inline. Thus, the browser displays it immediately to the right of any text or any other object that immediately precedes the image. Take a look at Listing 7.1, for example. It shows the same image three different times. Each time, the image is shown inline. That is, the browser displays the image immediately to the right of any text preceding it as seen below.

Listing 7.1 Using the *<IMG>* Tag

```
<HTML>
<HEAD>
  <TITLE>Using the IMG tag</TITLE>
</HEAD>
<BODY>
  <P>
    <IMG SRC="book.gif">
    This text immediately follows the image.
  </P>
  <P>
    This text is interrupted
    <IMG SRC="book.gif">
    by the image.
  </P>
  <P>
    In this case, the image appears inline after this text.
    <IMG SRC="book.gif">
  </P>
</BODY>
</HTML>
```

 TIP Consider storing all your images in a single directory off your Web site's root folder. Then, you can use relative paths in combination with the <BASE> tag (see Chapter 8, "Linking Documents Together") to access your images without specifying a full URL.

FIG. 7.1

You can insert an image anywhere in an HTML document that you like.

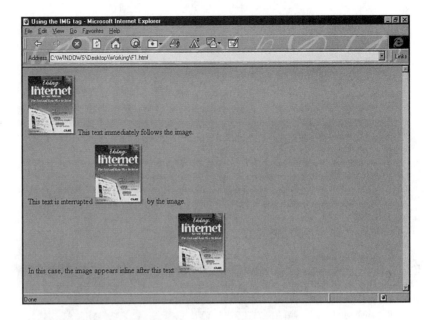

Aligning Text with an Inline Image

By default, when you insert an image inline with text, the text is aligned with the bottom of the image. Chances are good that you won't like this default alignment—it leaves a great deal of white space on the page. You can change it, though, using the <IMG> tag's ALIGN attribute. Table 7.2 describes each value you can assign to this attribute.

Table 7.2   Values for the *ALIGN* Attribute

Value	Description
TOP	Aligns the text with the top of the image
MIDDLE	Aligns the text with the middle of the image
BOTTOM	Aligns the text with the bottom of the image

Listing 7.2 shows an HTML document that inserts three images, each of which uses one of the alignment values shown in Table 7.2. Figure 7.2 shows the resulting Web page.

Listing 7.2   Using the *<IMG>* Tag's *ALIGN* Attribute

```
<HTML>
<HEAD>
  <TITLE>Using the IMG tag's ALIGN attribute</TITLE>
</HEAD>
```

Part

II

Ch

7

continues

Listing 7.2   Continued

```
<BODY>
  <P>
    <IMG SRC="book.gif" ALIGN=TOP>
    This text is aligned with the top of the image.
  </P>
  <P>
    <IMG SRC="book.gif" ALIGN=MIDDLE>
    This text is aligned with the middle of the image.
  </P>
  <P>
    <IMG SRC="book.gif" ALIGN=BOTTOM>
    This text is aligned with the bottom of the image.
  </P>
</BODY>
</HTML>
```

FIG. 7.2

By default, the baseline of the text is aligned with the bottom of an inline image.

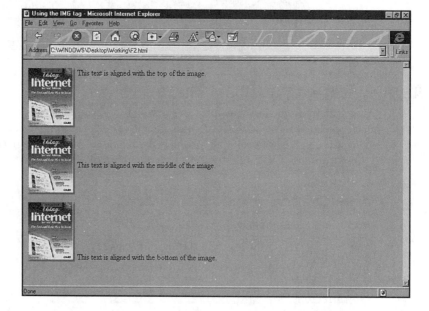

Positioning an Image on the Web Page

By default, the browser displays images inline. That is, it displays an image immediately to the right of the previous content. Text does not wrap around it. You can display an image on the left or right side of the Web page, however, allowing the surrounding content to flow around the image. This type of image is called a *floating* image.

You create a floating image by using the <IMG> tag's ALIGN attribute. This is the same attribute you use to align the surrounding text with an image. Table 7.3 describes each value you can assign to this attribute.

Table 7.3   Values for the *ALIGN* Attribute

Value	Description.
LEFT	Displays image on left side and surrounding content flows around the image
RIGHT	Displays image on the right side of the window and surrounding content flows around the image

Listing 7.3 shows an HTML document that inserts two images, each of which uses one of the alignment values shown in Table 7.3. Figure 7.3 shows the resulting Web page.

Listing 7.3   Using the *<IMG>* Tag's *ALIGN* Attribute

```
<HTML>
<HEAD>
  <TITLE>Using the IMG tag's ALIGN attribute</TITLE>
</HEAD>
<BODY>
  <P>
    <IMG SRC="book.gif" ALIGN=LEFT>
    This text will wrap around the right-hand and bottom of the image.
    This text will wrap around the right-hand and bottom of the image.
    This text will wrap around the right-hand and bottom of the image.
    This text will wrap around the right-hand and bottom of the image.
    This text will wrap around the right-hand and bottom of the image.
    This text will wrap around the right-hand and bottom of the image.
    This text will wrap around the right-hand and bottom of the image.
    This text will wrap around the right-hand and bottom of the image.
    This text will wrap around the right-hand and bottom of the image.
    This text will wrap around the right-hand and bottom of the image.
    This text will wrap around the right-hand and bottom of the image.
    This text will wrap around the right-hand and bottom of the image.
  </P>
  <P>
    <IMG SRC="book.gif" ALIGN=RIGHT>
    This text will wrap around the left-hand and bottom of the image.
    This text will wrap around the left-hand and bottom of the image.
    This text will wrap around the left-hand and bottom of the image.
    This text will wrap around the left-hand and bottom of the image.
    This text will wrap around the left-hand and bottom of the image.
    This text will wrap around the left-hand and bottom of the image.
    This text will wrap around the left-hand and bottom of the image.
    This text will wrap around the left-hand and bottom of the image.
    This text will wrap around the left-hand and bottom of the image.
    This text will wrap around the left-hand and bottom of the image.
    This text will wrap around the left-hand and bottom of the image.
    This text will wrap around the left-hand and bottom of the image.
    This text will wrap around the left-hand and bottom of the image.
    This text will wrap around the left-hand and bottom of the image.
  </P>
</BODY>
</HTML>
```

Part

II

Ch

7

FIG. 7.3

By default, the baseline of the text is aligned with the bottom of an inline image.

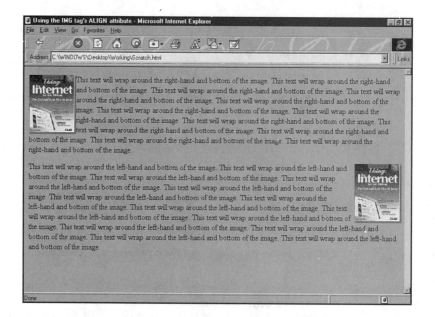

Giving the Browser Size Hints

Providing the browser a *size hint* means that you explicitly state the height and width of the image within the <IMG> tag. This has two benefits that make this a must:

- *Size hints help users who've disabled inline image.* If a user has disabled inline images and you're not using size hints, he or she sees a small icon in place of the image. Thus, the Web page is not formatted quite like you expect. Size hints cause the browser to display an empty box that is the same size as the image.

- *Size hints make the Web page render faster.* A browser displays the HTML document first, then displays the image. If you provide size hints for your inline images, the browser can display the formatted HTML document while it finishes downloading the images. Thus, the user sees the Web page faster.

You use the <IMG> tag's HEIGHT and WIDTH attributes to provide size hints to the browser. You set the HEIGHT attribute to the exact height and the WIDTH attribute to the exact width in pixels that you want to reserve for the image. Listing 7.4 shows what an HTML document that sets the height and width of an image looks like. Figure 7.4 shows what this HTML document looks like when inline images are disabled.

Listing 7.4   Using *HEIGHT* and *WIDTH* to Give Size Hints

```
<HTML>
<HEAD>
  <TITLE>Using HEIGHT and WIDTH to give size hints</TITLE>
</HEAD>
```

```
<BODY>
<IMG SRC="book.gif" WIDTH=320 HEIGHT=240>
</BODY>
</HTML>
```

FIG. 7.4
Without size hints, all you'd see in this image is a small box with an icon in it.

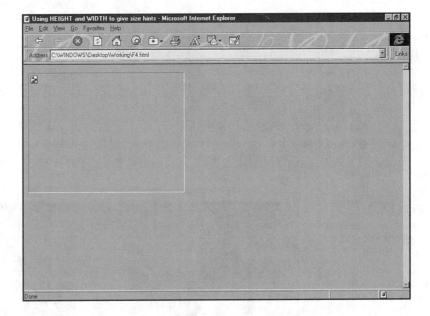

If the size you specify by using the HEIGHT and WIDTH attributes isn't the same as the actual size of the image as determined in your favorite graphics editor, the browser scales the image. The following sections describe the result of scaling the image down or up.

Scaling an Image Down   Scaling the image down means the actual image is larger than the space you reserved for it by using the HEIGHT and WIDTH attributes. In this case, the browser shrinks the image so that it fits in the reserved space.

You can easily distort an image if you're not careful specifying its size. For example, if you decrease the image's height by 50 percent and the width by 25 percent, the image will look funny in the browser (see Figure 7.5).

FIG. 7.5
Equally scaling an image's height and width is also known as maintaining the image's aspect ratio.

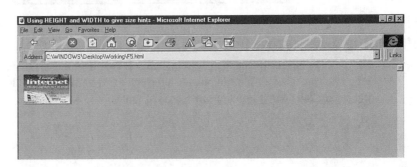

Part

II

Ch

7

> **CAUTION**
>
> Specifying a height and width that's smaller than the actual image's height and width doesn't save any download time. The browser still downloads the entire image before it scales it to fit the reserved area.

Scaling an Image Up Scaling the image up means the actual image is smaller than the space you reserved for it by using the HEIGHT and WIDTH attributes. In this case, the browser enlarges the image so it fits in the reserved space.

Just as when scaling an image down, you have to be concerned with maintaining an image's aspect ratio when you scale it up.

Unlike scaling an image down, however, you also have to worry with *pixelation*. That is, when you enlarge an image, the image's contents are expanded to fill the area. The browser makes each pixel bigger so that it fills more space. This effect is sometimes very unattractive, as shown in Figure 7.6.

FIG. 7.6
You can sometimes use pixelation to create special effects.

Providing Alternative Text

So, you've dumped a bunch of images into your HTML document. What about those users who aren't viewing images? You can provide alternative text to them that, at least, tells them about the image. You do that with the <IMG> tag's ALT attribute, like this:

```
<IMG SRC="filename" ALT="Description">
```

If the user's browser isn't displaying images, he or she sees the alternative text in the image's place. For the user whose browser is displaying images, he or she sees the alternative text until the browser is ready to display the image. Better yet, if you combine alternative text with size hints, users see a box that's correctly sized with the alternative text within its borders.

Listing 7.5 is an HTML document that uses alternative text to provide a description of the image. Figure 7.7 shows you what this document looks like in a browser that's not displaying inline images.

Listing 7.5   Using the *ALT* Attribute

```
<HTML>
<HEAD>
  <TITLE>Using the ALT attribute</TITLE>
</HEAD>
<BODY>
<IMG SRC="book.gif" WIDTH=320 HEIGHT=240 ALT="A picture of my latest book's
cover">
</BODY>
</HTML>
```

FIG. 7.7
Internet Explorer displays the image's alternative text in a pop-up window when the mouse pointer lingers over the image for more than a few seconds.

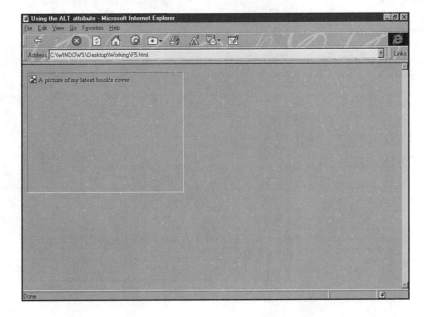

Framing an Image with a Border

By default, the user's browser displays a border around each inline image that you're using as an anchor. You have a lot of control over that border and the white space around the image.

You set the <IMG> tag's BORDER attribute to the width of the border in pixels. If you want the border to be 10 pixels in width, set this attribute to 10. Listing 7.6 shows an HTML document with three images, each of which has a different border width. Figure 7.8 shows the result in the browser.

Listing 7.6 Using the *BORDER* Attribute

```
<HTML>
<HEAD>
  <TITLE>Using the BORDER attribute</TITLE>
</HEAD>
<BODY>
<A HREF=""><IMG SRC="book.gif" BORDER=0></A>
<BR>
<A HREF=""><IMG SRC="book.gif" BORDER=5></A>
<BR>
<A HREF=""><IMG SRC="book.gif" BORDER=10></A>
</BODY>
</HTML>
```

FIG. 7.8

If you don't want the browser to draw a border around an image, set the BORDER attribute to 0.

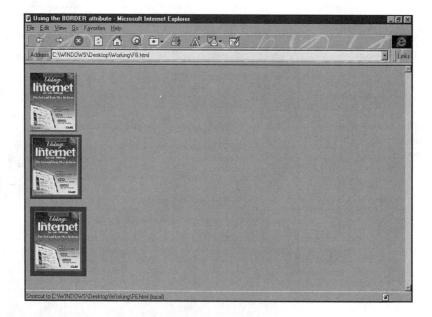

Giving an Image Space

You might not like how the text surrounding an image crowds the image. If that is the case, use the VSPACE and HSPACE attributes to add vertical and horizontal space around the image, respectively. You set each of these attributes to the amount of space, in pixels, you want to allow between the surrounding content and the image. Listing 7.7 shows an example of an image that adds additional space around the image to separate it from the text. Figure 7.9 shows you the result.

Listing 7.7   Using the *VSPACE* and *HSPACE* Attributes

```
<HTML>
<HEAD>
  <TITLE>Using the BORDER attribute</TITLE>
</HEAD>
<BODY>
<IMG SRC="book.gif" VSPACE=20 HSPACE=20 ALIGN=LEFT>
This text will wrap around the image.
This text will wrap around the image.
This text will wrap around the image.
This text will wrap around the image.
This text will wrap around the image.
This text will wrap around the image.
This text will wrap around the image.
This text will wrap around the image.
This text will wrap around the image.
This text will wrap around the image.
This text will wrap around the image.
This text will wrap around the image.
This text will wrap around the image.
This text will wrap around the image.
This text will wrap around the image.
This text will wrap around the image.
This text will wrap around the image.
This text will wrap around the image.
This text will wrap around the image.
This text will wrap around the image.
This text will wrap around the image.
This text will wrap around the image.
This text will wrap around the image.
This text will wrap around the image.
This text will wrap around the image.
This text will wrap around the image.
This text will wrap around the image.
This text will wrap around the image.
This text will wrap around the image.
This text will wrap around the image.
This text will wrap around the image.
</BODY>
</HTML>
```

Using an Image as an Anchor

Chapter 8, "Linking Documents Together," describes how to use an image as a link to another resource. It's easy. You enclose an image within the <A> tag as shown here:

```
<A HREF="http://www.mysite.com"><IMG SRC="image.gif"></A>
```

Part
II

Ch
7

FIG. 7.9
Adding white space around an image keeps it from looking too cramped.

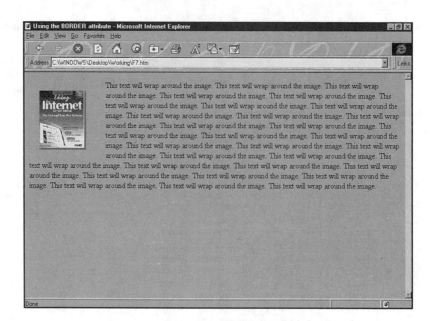

Linking Documents Together

by Mark R. Brown, Jerry Honeycutt, and John Jung

In this chapter

Understanding Hypertext and Hypermedia

Hypertext is a term you'll frequently hear associated with the Web. A *hypertext document* is a document that contains links to other documents, allowing you to jump between them by clicking the links. It's also a term associated with help files and other types of documents that are linked together. For example, if you've published a report that cites several sources, you can link the references of those sources to related works. Likewise, if you're discussing the migratory habits of the nerd-bird, you can provide links to Web pages where nerd-birds are known to frequent.

Hypermedia is based upon hypertext but contains more than text. It contains multimedia such as pictures, videos, and audio. In hypermedia documents, pictures are frequently used as links to other documents. You can link a picture of Edinburgh to a Web site in Edinburgh, for example. There are countless types of multimedia you can include on a Web page, and some of those can serve as links to other Internet documents and resources. Figure 8.1 shows you an example of a hypermedia document.

FIG. 8.1
Hypermedia documents contain much more than just text. They contain graphics, sounds, and video, too.

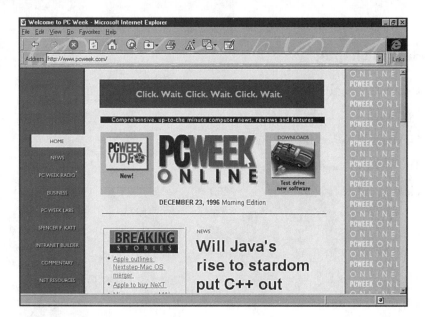

Understanding Links

A link really has two different parts. First, there's the part you see on the Web page called an *anchor.* There's also the part—the *URL reference*—that tells the browser what to do if you click that link. When you click a link's anchor, the browser loads the file or document given by the link's corresponding URL reference. You learn about both parts of a link in this chapter's following sections.

Anchors

A link's anchor can be a word, a group of words, or a picture. Exactly how an anchor looks in the browser depends largely on what type of anchor it is, how the user has configured the browser to display links, and how you created it. There are only two types of anchors: text and graphical.

Text Anchors Most text anchors look somewhat the same. A text anchor is one or more words the browser underlines to indicate the fact that it represents a link. The browser also displays a text anchor using a different color than the rest of the surrounding text (the color and appearance of links are under the author's and user's control).

Figure 8.2 shows a Web page that contains three text anchors. In particular, notice how the text anchors on this Web page are embedded in the text. That is, they aren't set apart from the text, like the references in this book, but are actually an integral part of it. Clicking one of these links loads a Web page that is related to the link. Many text anchors are used this way. The HTML for the first text link looks a bit like this (the <A> tag is discussed in "Linking to Documents and Files," later in this chapter):

```
<A HREF="vero.html">Vogon Earth Reconnaissance Office</A>
```

FIG. 8.2

You'll find Vogon's Hitch-Hiker's Guide to the Galaxy Page at **http:// www.metronet.com/ ~vogon/hhgttg.html**.

Text anchors

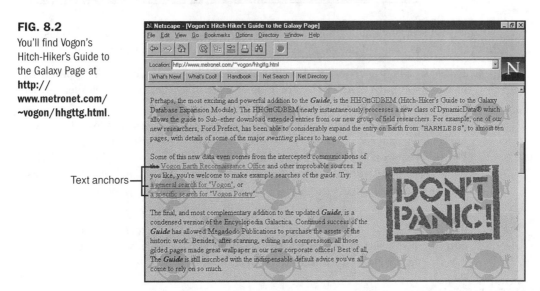

Figure 8.3 shows another Web page with a lot of text anchors. These anchors aren't embedded in the text, but are presented as a list or index of links from which you can choose. Web page authors frequently use this method to present collections of related links.

Graphical Anchors A graphical anchor is similar to a text anchor. When you click a link's graphical anchor, the browser loads the Web page that the link references. Graphical anchors aren't underlined or displayed in a different color, but can be displayed with a border. No two graphical anchors need to look the same, either. It depends entirely on the picture that you choose to use.

FIG. 8.3
List your Web site in Yahoo!.

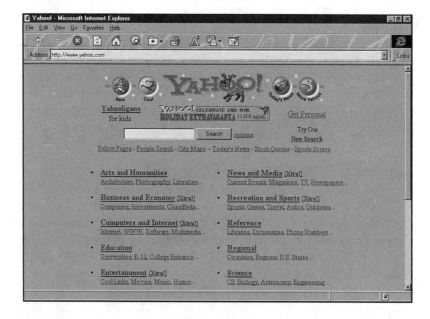

Versatility is the strong suit of graphical anchors. You can use them for a variety of reasons. Here are some examples of the ways you find graphical anchors used on a Web page:

- *Bullets.* Graphical anchors are frequently used as list bullets. You can click the picture to go to the Web page described by that list item. Frequently, the text in the list item is also a link. You can click either the picture or the text.

- *Icons.* Many Web sites use graphical anchors in a similar manner to Windows 95. They are common on home pages, and represent a variety of Web pages available at that site. Figure 8.4 shows a Web site that uses graphical anchors in this manner. The HTML for the icon on the left side of this Web page that says What's New might look a bit look this:

```
<A HREF="whatsnew.htm"><IMG SRC="whatsnew.gif" BORDER=0></A>
```

- *Advertisements.* Many Web sites have sponsors that pay to advertise on the site. This makes the Web site free to you while the site continues to make money. You usually find advertisements, such as the one shown in Figure 8.5, at the top of a Web page. Click the advertisement and the browser loads the sponsor's Web page.

URL References

The other part of a link is the URL reference. This is the address of the Web page the browser loads if you click the link. Every type of link, whether it uses a text or graphical anchor, uses either a relative or absolute reference.

Relative References   An URL reference to a file on the same computer is also known as a *relative reference.* That means that the URL is relative to the computer and directory from which the browser originally loaded the Web page. If the browser loads a page at *http://www.mysite.com/page*, for example, then a relative reference to */picture* would actually refer to the URL *http://www.mysite.com/page/picture*. Relative references are commonly used to refer to Web pages on the same computer.

FIG. 8.4
GolfWeb's home page uses graphical anchors to represent a variety of its pages you can load.

Graphical anchors used as icons

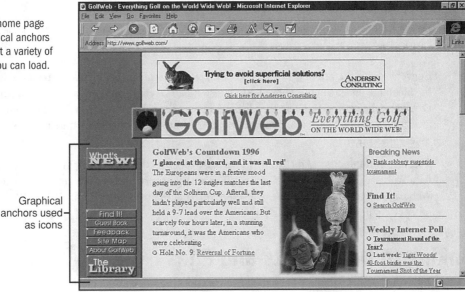

FIG. 8.5
HomeArts is an online magazine that uses sponsors to pay the bills so that the service remains free.

Graphical anchor used as an advertisement

N O T E Relative references work differently if you use the <BASE> tag in your HTML file. If you do use the <BASE> tag, relative references are always relative to the URL given in the tag. They're not relative to the URL page on which the reference appears. For example:

```
<BASE HREF="http://www.tuna.com/~mypages">
<A HREF="index.htm">
```

The link in the second line would refer to http://www.tuna.com/~mypages/index.htm, no matter where the page itself was physically located. ■

Convenience is the primary reason you use a relative reference. It's much simpler to just type the file name instead of the entire URL. It also makes it easier for you to move Web pages around on the server. Because the URL references are relative to the Web page's computer and directory, you don't have to change all the links in the Web page every time the files move to a different location.

Absolute References   An URL reference that specifies the exact computer, directory, and file for a Web page is an *absolute reference*. Whereas relative references are common for links to Web pages on the same computer, absolute references are necessary for links to Web pages on other computers.

Linking to Documents and Files

Now that you have the terminology down (anchors, links, relative references, and so on), you're ready to start adding links to your own Web pages. It's very simple. You have to tell the browser what element in the HTML file is the anchor and the address of the Internet document or resource to which you're linking. You do both things with one tag: <A>.

The following example shows you what the <A> tag looks like. This is its simplest form used for linking to another Web page on the Internet. Its only attribute is HREF, which specifies the URL to which you're linking. The URL can be any valid absolute or relative reference, such as *http://www.server.com/home/index.htm*. Since the <A> tag is a container, you must put the closing </A> tag on the other side of the anchor. That is, the opening <A> tag tells the browser where the anchor (text or graphical) starts and the closing </A> tag tells the browser where the anchor ends. This is an example:

```
<A HREF=URL>Anchor</A>
```

The following bit of HTML shows you how to add a text anchor to your HTML file. In this example, HREF references Jerry Honeycutt's home page on the Internet. The anchor, which is underlined in the Web browser, is Jerry Honeycutt's. The text before and after the <A> container isn't part of the anchor and is therefore not underlined. For that matter, nothing happens when the user clicks the text outside the container. On the other hand, when the user clicks Jerry Honeycutt's, the browser loads the home page in the browser. Figure 8.6 shows what this anchor looks like in Internet Explorer.

```
While you're here, why don't you visit
<A HREF="http://rampages.onramp.net/~jerry">Jerry Honeycutt's</A> homepage
```

FIG. 8.6

You can control the appearance of links by using the <BODY> tag.

N O T E The examples you've seen thus far use absolute references. You can also use relative references. Relative references can get a bit out of hand, however, if you store different Web pages in different directories. You'll have a difficult time remembering exactly in which directory an HTML file is stored, and thus, how to formulate the relative reference.

To remedy this problem, you can add the <BASE> tag to the top of your HTML file. In the absence of the <BASE> tag, all relative references are based upon the URL of the current HTML file. Adding the <BASE> tag provides an URL on which all relative references in the HTML file are based. It affects relative references in every HTML tag, including the <A> tag, <IMG> tag, and so on.

Thus, if you add

<BASE HREF="http://www.server.com">

to your HTML file, all relative references are based upon that address, instead of the address of the current HTML file. In this case, the relative reference, *images/face.gif*, would resolve to *http://www.server.com/images/face.gif*.

Note that the <BASE> tag's original intention was to provide the URL of the document in which it's found. This allows folks who are viewing the document out of context to locate the document on the Internet. It works perfectly well for the purpose of dereferencing relative URLs, however, and is documented by W3C in this manner. ■

 T I P Some browsers support ToolTip-style help for links. That is, when the user holds the mouse over a link for a certain period of time, the browser displays the contents of the <A> tag's TITLE attribute in a small pop-up window. Thus, if you want to provide additional information about the link to the user, assign it to the TITLE attribute, like this: <A HREF="page.html" TITLE="Go to page.html">.

The previous example showed you how to create a text anchor. Creating a graphical anchor isn't much different. Instead of enclosing text in the <A> container, you enclose an image. Consider the following HTML, which is similar to the previous example. Figure 8.7 shows what it looks like. The HREF references Jerry Honeycutt's home page, but instead of using a text anchor, it uses the <IMG> tag to create a graphical anchor. When the user clicks anywhere on the picture, the browser opens the Web page referred to by the <A> tag.

<A HREF="http://rampages.onramp.net/~jerry"><IMG SRC="photo.gif"></A>

N O T E Imagemaps are becoming much more common. They let you map certain portions of an image to different URLs. ■

FIG. 8.7

If you don't want to display a border around the image, you can add the BORDER attribute to the <IMG> tag, and set its value to 0.

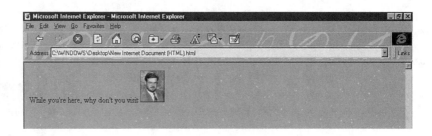

Internal Links

As well as providing links to other HTML files, you can link to an anchor within the current document. For example, you can provide a table of contents for the current Web page at the top of the page. You can then link each entry to a different section within the current Web page.

There are two steps to this. First, you must create an anchor in the HTML file that indicates the location to which you're linking. For example, if you want to provide a link to the middle portion of your Web page, you'd create an anchor in the middle and give it a name using the NAME attribute. You name the anchor so that you can refer to that name in your link. Note that because you're only naming an anchor, instead of creating a link, you don't set the HREF attribute. You still have to use the opening and closing <A> tags, but the browser doesn't highlight the contents of the <A> tag because you're not using it as a link. Here's what the named anchor looks like:

```
<A NAME=MIDDLE>Middle Section in Web Page</A>
```

After you've created the named anchor, you create a link to it. You use a special notation to link to that anchor. Instead of setting the HREF attribute to the URL of another Web page, set it to the anchor's name, prefixing the anchor's name with a pound sign (#). Consider the following example. The HREF attribute refers to the named anchor shown in the previous example. The name is prefixed with the pound sign to indicate to the browser that you're making an internal link. When the user clicks Jump to the middle, the browser aligns the anchor in the previous example to the top of the browser window.

```
<A HREF="#MIDDLE">Jump to the middle</A>
```

N O T E Some browsers do not move the named anchor to the top of the browser window if the anchor is already displayed in the window. That is, if your internal link is at the top of the Web page, and the named anchor is displayed somewhere in the middle of the Web page, when the user clicks the internal link, the browser will do nothing. ■

You can also add a name to most elements using the ID attribute. For example, you can add a name to a Header element like this:

```
<H2 id=JumpHere>You Can Jump Right To This Header!</H2>
```

You could then link directly to the name assigned by the ID attribute with this link:

```
<A HREF="JumpHere">Click Here to Jump to That Header!</A>
```

Files, Plug-In Content, and So On

When the user clicks a link to another Web page, the browser opens that Web page in the browser window. On the other hand, if the user clicks a link to a different type of document, it downloads the document to the user's computer and then decides what to do with it. One of two things happen as a result:

■ The browser knows how to handle the file, which is the case with many graphics formats, and displays the file in the browser window. For example, if you create a link to a GIF file and the user clicks that link, the browser downloads the GIF file, clears the current Web page from the browser window, and displays the GIF file in the window, as shown in Figure 8.8. In some cases, however, the browser can use a plug-in to display the file in the browser window without actually opening a separate window, even though the browser itself doesn't know what to do with the file.

FIG. 8.8

Linking to a file, GIF, for example, is not the same thing as inserting or embedding that file in your Web page.

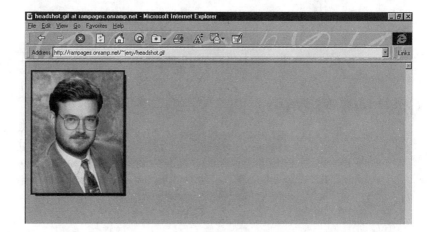

■ The browser does not know how to handle the file, which is the case for a variety of documents and many types of plug-in content. In this case, the browser downloads the file and looks for a helper application that knows what to do with it. If it finds one, it launches the helper application and passes it the downloaded file. For example, if the user clicks a link to an AVI video, the browser downloads the file, finds a helper application to play AVI files, and launches that file in the application. In most cases, the application displays the file in a separate window, as shown in Figure 8.9.

  T I P Digital Infoworks sells a product called Cyberlinks that you can use to create links in any OLE-enabled product, such as Wordpad. This means you can create hypertext links in your documents just like you can in your Web pages. For more information, see **http://www.pioneersys.com**.

FIG. 8.9
You can cause the browser to play AVI files inline by embedding them, instead of linking to them.

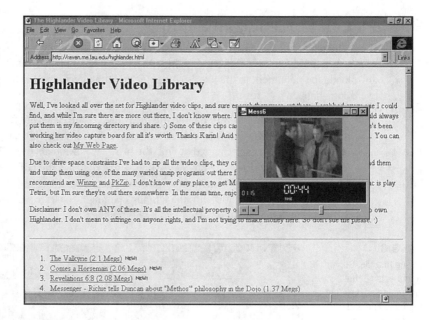

The *LINK* Element

Whereas the <A> tag is used to create hyperlinks that a user can follow when he or she wants to, the LINK element is used to connect various resources to an HTML document. Style sheets, color palettes, international versions of the document, scripts, indexes, notices—all can be tied to an HTML document using the <LINK> tag. One simple way to look at it is to think of the <A> tag as a link for readers of an HTML document, whereas the LINK tag is a resource for creators of that document.

One basic application for the <LINK> tag is to link a document to a style sheet, like this:

```
<LINK REL=stylesheet MEDIA=screen HREF="OurStyle.css">
```

This line would link the document to the style sheet "OurStyle.css" for display on a monitor screen. You can find out more about style sheets in Chapter 17, "Applying Cascading Style Sheets."

The <LINK> tag can also be used to define a document's relationship to another document. For example, if your document was a section of Chapter 4 in an HTML hyperbook, that might be indicated with this line of code:

```
<LINK REL=PARENT HREF="Chapter4TOC.html">
```

The document "Chapter4TOC.html" would be the table of contents that linked to the current document, and the LINK tag indicates that it is the parent document to the one you're reading. Note that the <LINK> element doesn't display anything in the browser window—it's simply there as a reference tool for you and for search engines and Webcrawler robots.

The `"Chapter4TOC.html"` file used in the previous example would contain the following line:

```
<LINK REV=Chapter HREF="OurDoc.html">
```

The REV attribute indicates the reverse relationship from the REL attribute. That is, it shows that a page is "superior" to the referenced document.

REV and REL attributes can take just about any value, though there is some ongoing effort to create some standardized values to make relationships between documents clearer. Here are some of the proposed values for REV and REL:

Value	Indicates
Parent	Parent document
Index	Index document
Previous	Previous page
Next	Next page
Contents	Contents page
Alternate	Alternate version
Begin	Beginning page

A value of Alternate indicates that the referenced document is an alternate version of the current page. This can be for a version for print, for example, or even a page in an alternate language. In this case, you'd add an additional attribute, LANG, to show the language of the linked version. For example, the following would indicate an alternate page in French:

```
<LINK REL=alternate HREF=FrenchDoc.html LANG=fr TITLE="Paris">
```

The initial example a few paragraphs back used the value MEDIA=screen to indicate that the stylesheet being linked to was for display on a video screen. It could have just as easily said MEDIA=print to indicate a print version.

Linking to Other Net Resources

The World Wide Web is a popular part of the entire Internet, but many others resources are available. Most of them were around long before the Web was even born and, as a result, they have a lot of stuff on them. Also as a result of the Web's newness, the other resources sometimes have a much wider audience base. Whether you're designing a home page for yourself or for your company, you may want to know how to link to those resources.

These resources can take various shapes, from the peanut gallery that is Usenet news, to personal e-mail, to the capability to access other computers through Telnet. Although you can create your own versions of these resources using forms, most of the time you wouldn't want to do so. For example, you could easily create a page with many HTML form tags, text elements, and a submit button for e-mail, but simply creating a link to e-mail with a particular address would be easier. This way, you can more easily update the page because you don't have to worry about which forms to read. Also, sometimes browsers have built-in support for some of the other resources, giving the user faster response time.

You especially want to create links to other resources on the Net if you're already using a resource. If you already have a Gopher site with information that's updated automatically, why rebuild it to fit the Web? Just adding a hyperlink to your Gopher site makes more sense. Similarly, if you're running a BBS that's on the Internet, putting in a Telnet link to it makes more sense. There's no reason for recreating, or even mirroring, your BBS through forms for the Web.

Creating a Link to E-Mail

The single most popular activity on the Internet is sending e-mail. More people use e-mail than any other resource on the Net. The reason is quite simple: If you're on the Internet, you have an e-mail address. The provider that gives you access to the Net often has at least one e-mail program available for your use. Most modern e-mail programs offer a friendly interface, with no complex commands to learn.

You'll most likely want to put in an e-mail link when you want people to give you feedback on a particular topic. Whatever it is you want comments on—be it your home page or your company's product—if you want to know what people think, use an e-mail link. E-mail links are also useful for reporting problems, such as a problematic or missing link. Typically, the Webmaster of a particular site should put these types of links to him or herself. You really have no reason not to put in a link to your e-mail address.

Creating a link to an e-mail address is similar to creating a link to another home page. The only difference is the reference for your anchor element. Normally, you put a link to a home page around some text as in the following:

```
<A HREF="http://www.mycom.com/myhome.html">Go to my home page</A>.
```

Linking to e-mail is just as simple. Instead of entering http:, which specifies a Web address, use **mailto:** to specify an e-mail address. Instead of specifying an URL, put in your full e-mail address. The preceding example now looks like this:

```
<A HREF="mailto:me@mycom.com">Send me E-mail</A>.
```

The link created with the preceding HTML looks like any other hypertext link. You can easily mix and match hyperlinks to different resources, and they'll all look the same (see Figure 8.10). When this link is selected, the browser opens its own e-mail interface for the user. Each interface is different, but most of them automatically get your e-mail address and real name, and prompt you for a subject.

Because the e-mail link is a standard URL and easily implemented, many browsers have built-in support for it. As a result, when people click an e-mail link, the Web browser will put up a primitive mail program. A few companies offer a full set of Internet applications, from an e-mail program, to a newsreader, to a Web browser. Oftentimes, these work in conjunction with each other. Consequently, when you click an e-mail link, these Internet packages start up their own e-mail programs (see Figure 8.11).

FIG. 8.10

E-mail links look just like regular hypertext links.

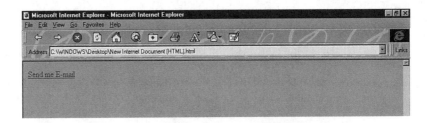

FIG. 8.11

Internet Explorer launches its own full-featured e-mail program when you click an e-mail link.

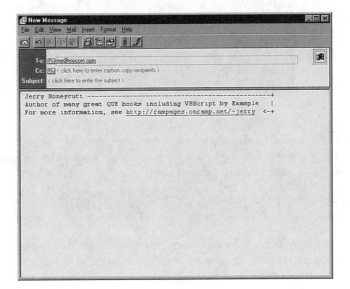

Creating a Link to Usenet News

Usenet is one of the best—or worst—resources on the Net, depending on whom you ask. Anybody with an opinion can tell you what he or she thinks. They may not know what they're talking about, but they'll let you know their opinion. Usenet is the ultimate embodiment of the freedom of speech, letting everybody say anything they want.

The opportunity for anybody, anywhere on the Net to have a voice could be an asset to your home page. Often, you may want to put in a link to Usenet when you want people to read for more information. If your home page has some information about HTML authoring, for example, you might want readers to go to a particular newsgroup for more help. You can also include such a link so people can see what the differing opinions are. If you have a certain political view and want others to see what the opposition is, a Usenet news link would be helpful.

Creating a link to a Usenet newsgroup is pretty simple; this kind of link is also just a derivative of the basic hypertext link. As you did with the e-mail link, you need to modify two parts in the anchor reference. When you're creating a Usenet link, enter **news:** instead of http:. Likewise, instead of specifying a particular URL, put in a specific newsgroup, as follows:

```
For more information, see
<A HREF="news:news.newusers.questions">news.newusers.questions</A>.
```

As you can see in Figure 8.12, the Usenet news hyperlink looks identical to other links. When a user selects such a link, the browser tries to access the user's Usenet news server. If the news server is available to that person, the browser goes to the specified newsgroup. The user can then read as much as he or she likes in that particular group.

FIG. 8.12

Usenet news links allow you to make a point to people interested in your topic.

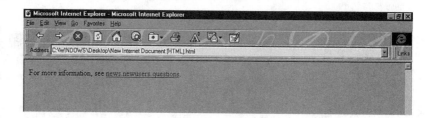

CAUTION

When a user clicks a Usenet news link, his or her browser tries to access the newsgroup in question. Because it's this user's browser and environment, he or she might not have access to the group you specified. Not all Internet providers have access to the same newsgroups. When you're creating such links, be mindful that not everybody will necessarily be able to access them.

How a Usenet hyperlink is handled is left entirely up to the Web browser the person is using. Many of them treat each article in a newsgroup as an individual hyperlink. Often, there's little in the way of sophisticated newsreading features. Some companies such as Netscape and Microsoft offer an entire suite of programs, including a Usenet newsreader (see Figure 8.13). In these cases, the newsreader of that suite is started.

Making FTP Available on Your Site

Another popular activity is accessing an FTP site. FTP, or File Transfer Protocol, allows users to copy files from other computers (the FTP site) onto their own computers. This popular method allows companies to distribute their demonstration software or patches to their products.

Putting in a link to an FTP site allows users to get a specific file from a particular location. This capability is useful for companies and shareware authors in making their products available. This type of link is also great for people who review software, allowing them to let users get the files being reviewed. People who have files (such as FAQs and interesting pictures) that they want others to get to easily might want to put in a link to an FTP site.

You create a link to an FTP site the same way you create other links, and they look the same, too (see Figure 8.14). Enter **ftp:** instead of the usual http:, and change the URL address to //*sitename/path*. Simply put, the site name looks the same as the URL address. You need to

Part

II

Ch

8

make sure the site name you specify points to a machine that accepts anonymous FTP connections. FTP links are almost always supported by the browser natively. You can create a typical FTP link as follows:

```
You can get the FAQ <A HREF="ftp://ftp.mysite.com/pub/FAQ">here</A>.
```

FIG. 8.13
When a Usenet link is accessed, some sophisticated Web browsers start up their own newsreader.

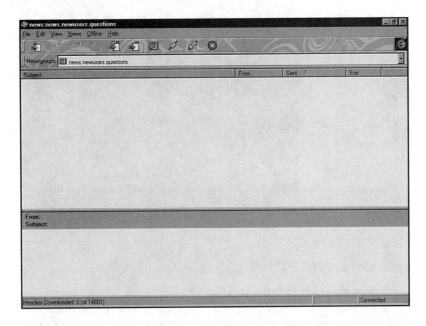

FIG. 8.14
An FTP link allows many people to access a particular file.

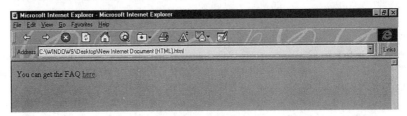

If you don't specify a particular file name, the browser lists the files in the directory you specified. This is particularly useful if you want the user to have access to multiple files. Programs available on multiple machines, or large files broken up into several chunks, typically fall into this category.

Technically speaking, there isn't too much of a difference between FTP and the Web. As a result, Web browsers support FTP links without needing another program. The browsers gives you a list of the files in the current directory, and indicates which are directories and which are files (see Figure 8.15). If you click a directory, it changes into that directory. If you click a file, the browser directly downloads the file.

FIG. 8.15

Web browsers have no problems handling FTP links by themselves.

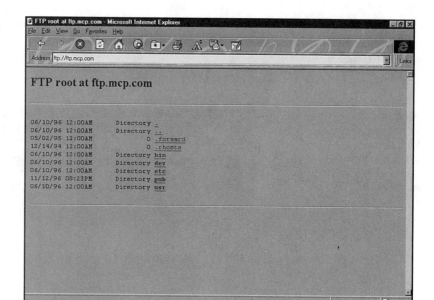

TROUBLESHOOTING

Some people can't access some of my FTP links. If a lot of people are reporting inaccessibility to some of your FTP links, try finding other sites. This error usually comes up when you have an FTP link to a particularly busy FTP site. You should try to locate other (less busy) FTP sites that have the same file to which you're pointing.

N O T E   By default, when FTP links are activated, the FTP connection that's made is known as anonymous FTP. This means that the FTP site the user is trying to access doesn't care who the user is. All the anonymous FTP site cares about is sending and receiving files to anybody who logs in with the username "anonymous." The password is often the user's e-mail address, but this isn't necessary. Anonymous FTP allows software companies and the like to distribute their products to a very wide audience.

A nonanonymous FTP is where the FTP site is very particular about who can access it. To get access to a nonanonymous FTP site, you must have an account on the FTP site itself. Basically, you can't get into a nonanonymous FTP site unless you're already in. This is probably the most widely used FTP site around, as many companies allow employees to FTP into their own accounts. ■

N O T E   You can easily change an anonymous FTP link into a nonanonymous one. Simply put a username and an at symbol (@) sign before the site name. This causes most Web browsers to automatically attempt to log in as username. The browser then prompts the user for the password for the login ID. ■

Linking Your Home Page to a Gopher Site

Before there was the World Wide Web, there was something known as Gopher. It was originally designed by the University of Minnesota (the Golden Gophers) as a way of making information that was spread out easily available. Gopher has probably been the Internet resource most affected by the Web, often being superseded by it. The biggest difference between Gopher and the Web is that it is very difficult for individual people to create their own Gopher sites or *holes*.

Although Gopher sites are not as prevalent as they once were, they still have a strong following. You can typically find Gopher sites at places that dispense a lot of automated information. Although the site could have easily been converted to HTML, it simply hasn't bothered. This conversion of Gopher data into usable HTML code is typically the work of a programmer, and often not worth the effort. Putting in an HTML link to a Gopher site allows people browsing your page easy access to a great deal of information.

You can create a link to a Gopher hole by modifying the same two elements of the anchor reference. Change the http: to **gopher:**, and change the URL to //*sitename*. The site name must be a valid Internet host name address. The link created looks like every other type of hypertext link, and built-in support is provided by most Web browsers. A Gopher hole link usually looks something like the following:

```
For more information, go <A HREF="gopher://gopher.mysite.com">here</A>.
```

Just like FTP, Gopher is a Net resource that is built into HTML. Consequently, most Web browsers support any links to a Gopher site internally. That is, you don't need a Gopher-specific application to go to a Gopher site, the browser takes care of it for you. But also just like FTP, the built-in support for Gopher is often very bland (see Figure 8.16).

FIG. 8.16

There's only so much a Web browser can do to liven up the text-based Gopher resource.

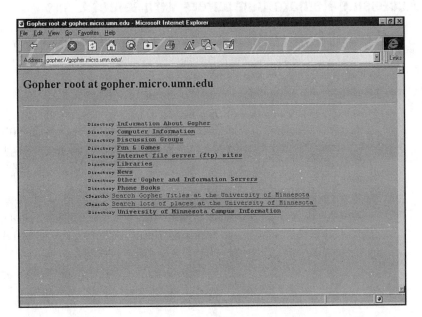

Providing Access to a Large Database with a WAIS Link

WAIS stands for Wide Area Information System, which basically means "lots of large databases you can search through." WAIS was specially designed by WAIS Corporation as a way of accessing large amounts of information. This capability is very different from what Gopher and the Web do in that WAIS was intended to cover very large chunks of information. Typically, databases that contained several million entries were considered appropriate for WAIS.

WAIS is typically accessed through a search engine because most people don't want to plod through such large stores of information. When WAIS was first introduced, custom front ends allowed easy access to a WAIS database. With the advent of the Web, however, most WAIS databases now have HTML front ends to their databases. Now you can simply fill out a Web form and click a button, and the WAIS search is underway.

You can create a link in your home page to a WAIS database as easily as you do with all the other links. You have to modify the same two anchor reference elements to hold the correct information. Instead of using http:, enter the prefix **wais:**, and change the URL location to the address of a WAIS database:

```
To search for a number in your area, click
<A HREF="wais://wais.mysite.com">here</A>.
```

N O T E Most browsers don't have built-in support of WAIS database searches. If you put in a link to one of these databases, be sure to include some sort of reference to where users can get a WAIS client. Of course, if the WAIS database you're pointing to has HTML forms support, you don't need to worry about including such information. ■

Accessing Remote Computers with Telnet Links

The capability to access other computers is not something new to the Web; it's been around for a long time. This access has always been achieved with a UNIX program called Telnet, which doesn't stand for anything in particular. Telnet allowed people to try to log into a remote machine, much the same way some people access their Internet providers. The Web allows for support of accessing remote machines through a Telnet link to a remote computer.

Usually, people trying to get on a secure system are the people for whom you want to provide a Telnet link. People who provide access to a private, Internet-accessible BBS will most likely want to put in a Telnet link. Also, companies that offer a BBS for customer support may want to make use of link to a Telnet site. Generally speaking, for most home pages, you have little or no reason to include a link to a remote site.

As you might have guessed, creating a Telnet link to a remote site requires modifying the anchor reference element. You change the http: to **telnet:**. You also need to change the URL part of the anchor reference to hostname. Hypertext links that refer to Telnet sites look the same as other links. A typical Telnet link takes the following form:

```
Click <A HREF="wais://wais.mysite.com">here</A> to access our BBS.
```

N O T E Web browsers do not support Telnet activity natively. They typically depend on an external application to talk correctly to the remote machine. If you put in a link to Telnet to another site, be sure to also include some reference to a Telnet client. ▩

N O T E There are a few operating systems that have built-in Telnet capability. Among the OSs that have this are Windows 95, Windows NT, and UNIX. ▩

Even though Telnet is a rather simple Net resource, it also has some problems. Among the many problems are issues of how to display the remote session and how to interpret keypresses. As simple as these problems may appear, they're hard to implement in a Web browser. For these reasons, most Web browsers don't have support for Telnet. Rather, they leave it up to the individual to find a Telnet program and set it up (see Figure 8.17).

FIG. 8.17
Most Web browsers don't support the Telnet links internally, so you need another program to access these links.

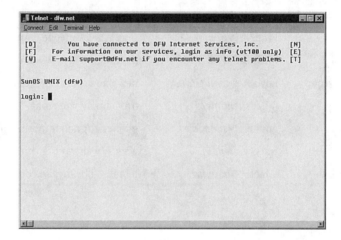

 Some Web browsers allow something extra in the anchor reference. Simply add the username you want the person to log on as, followed by the @ symbol, before the site name. Instead of

```
Access my <A HREF="telnet://mysite.com/">system!</A>
```

you can have

```
Access my <A HREF="telnet://john@mysite.com/">system!</A>
```

On those browsers that support this, the Web browser pops up a little notice. This notice tells the user what login name should be used to access the system.

How Links Work Together

You may be wondering how well these hypertext links work with each other. The answer is "Very well." Even though the links are different, they all look and behave the same. This common behavior exists because of the anchor reference that all hyperlinks use. Some may need client programs not built into a Web browser, but that's not a big deal. This identical look and feel of various hypertext links allows home pages to have a consistent feel. Consistency in a home page is important because it allows people to intuitively know they're in your home page without looking at the current URL.

The best thing you can do is to treat all hypertext links in the same manner, with slightly different formats. Just take the same basic anchors, add a reference, and put in the correct pointer to that reference (see Table 8.1). As a Web author, you must always remember that each person looking at your home page could be using any browser available. No hard and fast rules about what resources all browsers will support even exists. Whatever resource you want to link to, though, try to include a link to a location where the user can get a client.

Table 8.1   Sample Formats for Creating Links

Link To	What to Use	Sample Link
Web page	http://*sitename*/	http://www.mysite.com/
E-mail	mailto:*address*	mailto:me@mysite.com
Newsgroup	news:*newsgroupname*	news:news.newusers.questions
FTP	ftp://*sitename*/	ftp://ftp.mysite.com/
Gopher	gopher://*sitename*/	gopher://gopher.mysite.com/
WAIS	wais://*sitename*/	wais://wais.mysite.com/
Telnet	telnet://*sitename*/	telnet://bbs.mysite.com/

## CHAPTER 9

Adding Lists to a Web Page

by Mark R. Brown, Jerry Honeycutt, and Jim O'Donnell

In this chapter

Creating an Ordered List

A basic list in HTML consists of a list-identifier container plus the standard list items tag. (In HTML, all list items use one tag, `<LI>`, while the lists themselves are differentiated by their container tags.) An ordered list, also called a numbered list, is used to create a sequential list of items or steps. When a Web browser sees the tag for an ordered list, it sequentially numbers each list item by using standard numbers (1, 2, 3, and so on).

Using the *<OL>* Tag

Ordered (or numbered) lists begin with the `<OL>` tag, and each item uses the standard `<LI>` tag. If needed, you can create a list heading by using the `<LH>` tag. Close the list with the `</OL>` tag to signal the end of the list. List containers provide both a beginning and ending line break to isolate the list from the surrounding text; it's not necessary (except for effect) to precede or follow the list with the paragraph `<P>` tag.

N O T E Lists support internal HTML elements. One of the most useful elements is the paragraph tag (`<P>`), which enables you to separate text in a list item. Other useful tags include both logical and physical style tags (such as `<EM>` and `<I>`) and HTML entities. Headings are not appropriate for use in lists; although they're interpreted correctly, their forced line breaks make for an ugly display. SGML purists also object to them because heading tags are meant to define relationships in paragraphs, not lists. ■

Listing 9.1 shows how you can use the OL list container. Pay particular attention to closing tags, especially in nested lists. You can use leading blanks and extra lines to make your list code easier to read, but Web browsers ignore them. Figure 9.1 shows how Netscape Navigator interprets this HTML code.

Listing 9.1   Ordered List Example

```
<HTML>
<HEAD>
<TITLE>ordered List Example</TITLE>
</HEAD>
<BODY>
<OL>
      <LH><EM>Colors of the Spectrum:</EM><BR>
      <LI>Red
      <LI>Orange
      <LI>Yellow
      <LI>Green
      <LI>Blue
      <LI>Indigo
      <LI>Violet
</OL>
</BODY>
</HTML>
```

FIG. 9.1
Web browsers display internal HTML elements according to their defined usage.

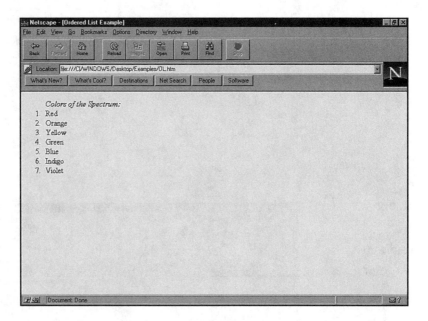

Part

II

Ch

9

It is also possible to nest ordered lists, creating a document that looks more like an outline. Listing 9.2 shows the HTML code for such a list, which is rendered in Figure 9.2.

Listing 9.2 Nested Ordered List Example

```
<HTML>
<HEAD>
<TITLE>Nested Ordered List Example</TITLE>
</HEAD>
<BODY>
<OL>
        <LH><EM>Planets of the Solar System:</EM><BR>
        <LI>Mercury
        <OL>
                <LI>57.9 million kilometers from the sun
                <LI>no satellites
        </OL>
        <LI>Venus
        <OL >
                <LI>108 million kilometers from the sun
                <LI>No satellites
        </OL>
        <LI>Earth
        <OL>
                <LI>149.6 million kilometers from the sun
                <LI>one satellite: The Moon
        </OL>
        <LI>Mars
        <OL>
```

continues

Listing 9.2   Continued

```
                <LI>227.9 million kilometers from the sun
                <LI>two satellites
                <OL>
                        <LI>Phobos
                        <LI>Deimos
                </OL
        </OL>
</OL>
</BODY>
</HTML>
```

FIG. 9.2
Sublists are automatically indented to create an outline effect.

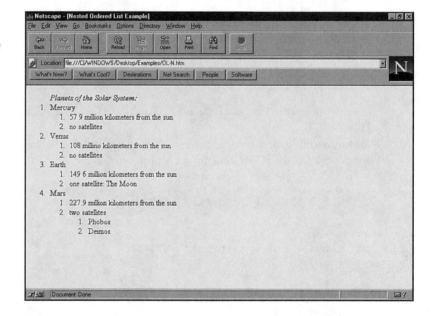

Use indentations and blank lines to organize your data when creating HTML documents. Web browsers don't care how the text is aligned or run together, but you will appreciate the extra effort when rereading and editing the HTML code.

Additional <OL> Attributes

HTML 4.0 defines a handful of attributes for the <OL> tag, which began as a Netscape extension. Now that these attributes have gained acceptance, they're part of the HTML specification.

These attributes give you control over the appearance of the item markers and the beginning marker number. Table 9.1 lists these attributes and their functions.

Table 9.1   Additional Attributes for *<OL>*

Attribute	Description
COMPACT	Renders the list in a more compact form
TYPE=A	Sets markers to uppercase letters
TYPE=a	Sets markers to lowercase letters
TYPE=I	Sets markers to uppercase Roman numerals
TYPE=i	Sets markers to lowercase Roman numerals
TYPE=1	Sets markers to numbers
START=n	Sets beginning value of item markers in the current list

Varying the marker style enables you to create distinctions between numbered lists in the same document. Listing 9.3 shows how an HTML document incorporates these attributes, and Figure 9.3 shows how these attributes can enhance a document.

Listing 9.3   Nested Ordered List Example Using *TYPE*

```
<HTML>
<HEAD>
<TITLE>Nested Ordered List Example Using Type</TITLE>
</HEAD>
<BODY>
<OL>
        <LH><EM>Planets of the Solar System:</EM><BR>
        <LI>Mercury
        <OL TYPE=A>
                <LI>57.9 million kilometers from the sun
                <LI>no satellites
        </OL>
        <LI>Venus
        <OL TYPE=A>
                <LI>108 million kilometers from the sun
                <LI>No satellites
        </OL>
        <LI>Earth
        <OL TYPE=A>
                <LI>149.6 million kilometers from the sun
                <LI>one satellite: The Moon
        </OL>
        <LI>Mars
        <OL TYPE=A>
                <LI>227.9 million kilometers from the sun
                <LI>two satellites
                <OL>
                        <LI>Phobos
                        <LI>Deimos
```

continues

Listing 9.3   Continued

```
            </OL
        </OL>
    </OL>
    </BODY>
    </HTML>
```

FIG. 9.3
Controlling the
appearance of lists
is useful for both
functional and aesthetic
purposes.

Ordered list uses
uppercase Roman
numerals

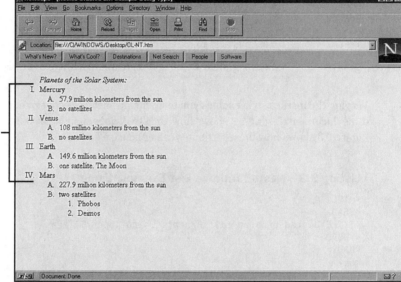

TROUBLESHOOTING

I'm creating a list of items and I need to interrupt the list for a regular paragraph of text. How can I make the list pick up where it left off and continue numbering the items sequentially? The HTML specification includes an attribute for the <OL> tag called START. Ideally then, you could pick up, say, at item 7 by specifying <OL START=7>. The number 7 is just an example. Put whatever value you want the numbering to start with.

Creating an Unordered List

HTML also supports the unordered or bulleted list, which is a list of items that does not define a specific structure or relationship among the data.

Using the *<UL>* Tag

Unordered lists (bulleted lists) use the <UL> container tag. Just like ordered lists, bulleted lists provide beginning and ending line breaks and support internal HTML elements and sublists. Also, like ordered lists, they require closing tags; include the </UL> tag to signal the end of the list. Web browsers support and automatically indent sublists, and some also vary the bullet icon based on the relative level of the list. These icons vary depending on the client software viewing the HTML document.

Listing 9.4 shows how to use the <UL> list container. Again, to make the HTML document easier to read, you can include leading blanks and extra lines, but Web browsers ignore them. Figure 9.4 shows how Netscape Navigator renders this HTML code.

Part

II

Ch

9

Listing 9.4   Nested Unordered List Example

```
<HTML>
<HEAD>
<TITLE>Nested Unordered List Example</TITLE>
</HEAD>
<BODY>
<UL>
      <LH><EM>Planets of the Solar System:</EM><BR>
      <LI>Mercury
      <UL >
           <LI>108 million kilometers from the sun
           <LI>no satellites
      </UL>
      <LI>Venus
      <UL >
           <LI>108 million kilometers from the sun
           <LI>No satellites
      </UL>
      <LI>Earth
      <UL>
           <LI>149.6 million kilometers from the sun
           <LI>one satellite: The Moon
      </UL>
      <LI>Mars
      <UL>
           <LI>227.9 million kilometers from the sun
           <LI>two satellites
           <UL>
                <LI>Phobos
                <LI>Deimos
           </UL
      </UL>
</UL>
</BODY>
</HTML>
```

FIG. 9.4
Web browsers automatically indent sublists and apply the corresponding markers.

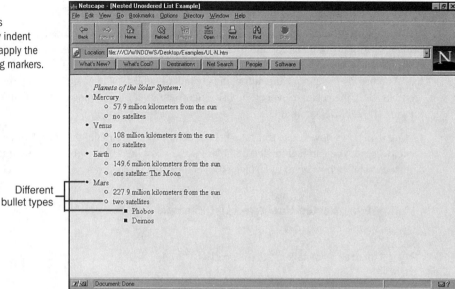

Different bullet types

Additional *<UL>* Attributes

Like the <OL> tag, the HTML specification adopted some of Netscape's extensions for the <UL> tag. You can manually control the appearance of item markers as either circles, squares, or discs. This feature is meant to give you more control over the look of bulleted lists.

You use the TYPE attribute to change the bullet used in the list. Its value can be one of disc, square, or circle. Listing 9.5 demonstrates its use in an HTML document, which is rendered by Netscape Navigator in Figure 9.5.

Listing 9.5   Nested Unordered List Example Using *TYPE*

```
<HTML>
<HEAD>
<TITLE>Nested Unordered List Example Using Type</TITLE>
</HEAD>
<BODY>
<UL TYPE=SQUARE>
        <LH><EM>Planets of the Solar System:</EM><BR>
        <LI>Mercury
        <UL TYPE=CIRCLE>
                <LI>108 million kilometers from the sun
                <LI>no satellites
        </UL>
        <LI>Venus
        <UL TYPE=CIRCLE>
                <LI>108 million kilometers from the sun
                <LI>No satellites
        </UL>
```

```
              <LI>Earth
              <UL TYPE=CIRCLE>
                     <LI>149.6 million kilometers from the sun
                     <LI>one satellite: The Moon
              </UL>
              <LI>Mars
              <UL TYPE=CIRCLE>
                     <LI>227.9 million kilometers from the sun
                     <LI>two satellites
                     <UL TYPE=DISC>
                            <LI>Phobos
                            <LI>Deimos
                     </UL
              </UL>
       </UL>
       </BODY>
       </HTML>
```

Part

II

Ch

9

FIG. 9.5

It's easy to control the display of bullet markers for your Netscape Navigator audience.

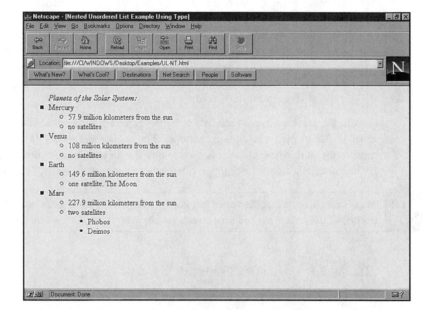

N O T E Besides attributes for the <OL> and <UL> elements, HTML 4.0 also provides extensions for individual list items. The extensions are based on those available to the list container that the item is in (ordered or unordered). Ordered lists pass on the capability to change the current TYPE of list items and also the VALUE they begin with—by using the <VALUE> tag, you can either begin a list with a value other than one, or change the numbering within a list. This would be another good way to continue a list that has been interrupted by some other type of HTML object. (All subsequent items adopt the extension changes until the list closes.) You can modify unordered list items with the TYPE extension; all subsequent items in the container use the item marker. ■

Like the <OL> tag, <UL> also supports the COMPACT attribute, which causes the browser to render the list in a more compact form.

Creating Menu Lists

You can create menu lists with another list type supported by HTML and Web browsers. The distinction here is primarily for HTML identification; most browsers' default display for the <MENU> container is very similar to the font and style used for the unordered list container. The value of this element is enhanced if you select a distinct screen format for the menu paragraph in a Web browser's preferences. The container might also be more functional in future versions of HTML and its client software, enabling browsers and other applications to identify the menu sections in your documents.

As with the previous lists, menu lists provide beginning and ending line breaks and can include other HTML elements in a menu container. The anchor element is the most likely HTML element to use in this type of list; it is used to link the menu listings to other document resources or Internet applications. Listing 9.6 shows typical uses for the <MENU> container.

 T I P Just because HTML has specific names for these list types doesn't mean you're limited in how you can use them. Experiment to see how each list delivers your information and use what works best.

Listing 9.6   Menu List Example

```
<HTML>
<HEAD>
<TITLE>Menu Listing Example</TITLE>
</HEAD>
<BODY>
<MENU>
       <LH><EM>Planets of the Solar System:</EM><BR>
       <LI><A HREF="mercury.htm">Mercury</A>
       <LI><A HREF="venus.htm"> Venus </A>
       <LI><A HREF="earth.htm"> Earth </A>
       <LI><A HREF="mars.htm"> Mars </A>
       <LI><A HREF="jupiter.htm"> Jupiter </A>
       <LI><A HREF="saturn.htm"> Saturn </A>
```

```
      <LI><A HREF="uranus.htm"> Uranus </A>
      <LI><A HREF="neptune.htm"> Neptune </A>
      <LI><A HREF="pluto.htm"> Pluto </A>
  </MENU>
  </BODY>
  </HTML>
```

Again, the current implementation of <MENU> by most Web browsers doesn't provide a visual distinction between menu and unordered lists. Netscape Navigator displays menu lists and unordered lists identically (see Figure 9.6), while Microsoft Internet Explorer displays them identically except for the omission of bullets in the latter.

Part

II

Ch

9

N O T E Menu items (and other list types) can contain hypertext links to other documents or Internet resources. Use the <A> container to create the links, as follows:

```
<A HREF="home.htm">Jump to My Home Page</A>
```

Click the text Jump to My Home Page, and the browser retrieves the document HOME.HTM. ∎

FIG. 9.6
The <MENU> tag hasn't changed much since it was incorporated into HTML 2.0.

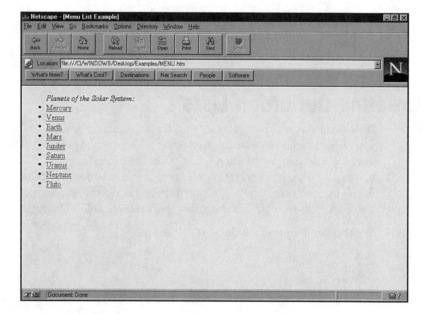

Creating Directory Lists

The <DIR> element functions much like the <MENU> element; it provides HTML identification to the section of text that has more potential usefulness than real functional value. Similar to <MENU>, <DIR> containers display with the same default settings as unordered lists.

The intended use for the <DIR> container limits items to 24 characters and displays the items in rows (like file directories in UNIX, or in DOS using the /W parameter). Current browsers don't support this interpretation. The \<DIR\> element also isn't intended to include other HTML elements; browsers interpret them correctly. When using \<DIR\>, remember to close the container with the ending \</DIR\> tag. Listing 9.7 shows typical uses of the \<DIR\> container.

Listing 9.7   *\<DIR\>* List Example

```
<HTML>
<HEAD>
<TITLE>Dir List Example</TITLE>
</HEAD>
<BODY>
<DIR>
      <LH><EM>Colors of the Spectrum:</EM><BR>
      <LI>Red
      <LI>Orange
      <LI>Yellow
      <LI>Green
      <LI>Blue
      <LI>Indigo
      <LI>Violet
</DIR>
</BODY>
</HTML>
```

Creating Definition Lists

Definition lists, also called glossary lists, are a special type of list in HTML. They provide a format like a dictionary entry, with an identifiable term and indented definition paragraph. This format is especially useful when listing items with extensive descriptions, such as catalog items or company departments. The \<DL\> element provides both a beginning and ending line break. In the \<DL\> container, the \<DT\> tag marks the term and the \<DD\> tag defines the paragraph. These are both open tags, meaning they don't require a closing tag to contain text.

The standard format of a definition list is as follows:

```
<DL>
<DT>Term
<DD>Definition of term
</DL>
```

The \<DT\> tag's text should fit on a single line, but it wraps to the next line without indenting if it runs beyond the boundary of the browser window. The \<DD\> tag displays a single paragraph, continuously indented one or two spaces beneath the term element's text (depending on how the browser interprets a definition list).

The HTML 4.0 specification provides an important optional attribute for \<DL\>: COMPACT. This attribute is supposed to be interpreted as a list with a different style, presumably with a smaller font size or more compact character spacing. This could be useful for embedded definition lists (those inside other definition, numbered, or bulleted lists), or for graphic effect. Most browsers, however, ignore the attribute, displaying the definition list to the standard format.

Definition lists can include other HTML elements. The most common are physical and logical styles and other list containers. Although Web browsers can correctly interpret elements such as headings, this is bad HTML; their forced line breaks are not pretty and heading tags are usually meant to define relationships in paragraphs, not within lists. Listing 9.8 shows examples of how you can create definition lists.

Figure 9.7 shows how this document displays in Netscape Navigator. Other browsers may format this text differently.

 T I P In Netscape Navigator, use a horizontal rule, <HR>, on a <DD> tagged line in a definition list. The rule indents with the rest of the <DD> lines, providing an easy-to-read separator for your definition text.

Listing 9.8   Definition List Example

```
<HTML>
<HEAD>
<TITLE>Definition List Example</TITLE>
</HEAD>
<BODY>
<DL>
      <DT>Mercury
      <DD>The smallest of the planets and the one nearest the sun,
      having a sidereal period of revolution about the sun of 88.0
      days at a mean distance of 58.3 million kilometers (36.2
      million miles) and a mean radius of approximately 2,414
              kilometers (1,500 miles).

      <DT>Venus
      <DD>The second planet from the sun, having an average radius
      of 6,052 kilometers (3,760 miles), a mass 0.815 times that of
      Earth, and a sidereal period of revolution about the sun of
      224.7 days at a mean distance of approximately 100.1 million
      kilometers (67.2 million miles).

      <DT>Earth
      <DD>The third planet from the sun, having a sidereal period
      of revolution about the sun of 365.26 days at a mean distance
      of approximately 149 million kilometers (92.96 million miles),
      an axial rotation period of 23 hours 56.07 minutes, an average
      radios of 6,374 kilometers (3,959 miles), and a mass of
      approximately 29.11 x 10^24 kilograms (13.17 x 10^24 pounds).
</DL>
</BODY>
</HTML>
```

Combining List Types

There are times when it's necessary to use sublists of more than one type within a single list. For instance, you may have a numbered list that includes a list as one of the numbered elements. Instead of just creating an ordered sublist, which numbers each of its items, you might prefer to display an unordered list to differentiate the sublist (while avoiding ordering the information as well). HTML supports embedded combinations of all list types. Listing 9.9 shows a sample of combined lists.

FIG. 9.7

Definition lists appear much the same as dictionary entries and enable easy reading of each term.

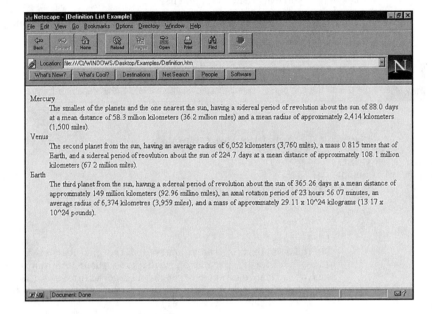

Listing 9.9 Combined List Example

```
<HTML>
<HEAD>
<TITLE>Combined List Example</TITLE>
</HEAD>
<BODY>
<OL>
        <LH><EM>Planets of the Solar System:</EM><BR>
        <LI>Mercury
        <UL>
                <UL>
                        <LI>Roman god of commerce, travel, and thievery
                        <LI>Dictionary Definition
                        <DL>
                                <DT>Mercury
                                <DD>The smallest of the planets and the one
                                nearest the sun, having a sidereal period of
                                revolution about the sun of 88.0 days at a
                                mean distance of 58.3 million kilometers (36.2
                                million miles) and a mean radius of approximately
                                2,414 kilometers (1,500 miles).
                        </DL>
                </UL>
```

```
        </UL>
        <LI>Venus
        <UL>
            <UL>
                <LI>Roman goddess of sexual love and physical beauty
                <LI>Dictionary Definition
                <DL>
                    <DT>Venus
                    <DD>The second planet from the sun, having an
                    average radius of 6,052 kilometers (3,760 miles),
                    a mass 0.815 times that of Earth, and a sidereal
                    period of revolution about the sun of 224.7 days
                    at a mean distance of approximately 100.1 million
                    kilometers (67.2 million miles).
                </DL>
            </UL>
        </UL>
    </OL>
    </BODY>
    </HTML>
```

Three list types are used in Listing 9.9: numbered, bulleted, and definition. The primary list is a numbered list of planets. Each planet has a bulleted sublist indicating the Roman god after whom it was named, followed by its dictionary definition. The users' browsers are being relied on to indent embedded lists; if more indentation were desired, the lists can be embedded inside additional, empty lists. For instance, instead of

```
<OL>
    <LI>Small example list
    <LI>That I want to indent more
</OL>
```

you can force more indentation by using

```
<OL><OL>
    <LI>Small example list
    <LI>That I want to indent more
</OL></OL>
```

Because the primary difference between list types involves either the list item markers or the format of the elements—and not the actual text representation itself—combined lists tend to display very well. Figure 9.8 shows how the samples in Listing 9.9 display in a typical Web browser.

Manually Formatting Lists

It is possible to create custom bullets with a little manual effort in your HTML code. Consider the HTML code shown in Listing 9.10.

The <UL> and </UL> tags are used to instruct the Web browser to set up the formatting and indentation to support an unordered list. However, no <LI> tags are used: Because you don't want the standard bullets, you can't use the standard list-item tag. Instead, each item in the list is specified similar to this example:

```
<IMG SRC="cube.gif" ALIGN=TOP>Red<BR>
```

FIG. 9.8
Embedded list types inherit certain formatting characteristics from the original list styles.

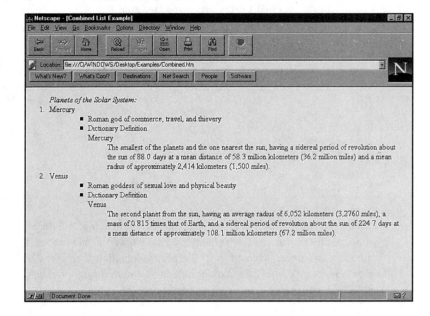

The `<IMG>` tag is used to specify and align the graphic you want to use as your bullet, followed by the list item. Because you're not using the standard `<LI>` tag to set off each item, you need to use the `<BR>` tag to insert a line break after each one. This HTML code is rendered as shown in Figure 9.9.

Listing 9.10   Manual List Example

```
<HTML>
<HEAD>
<TITLE>Manual List Example</TITLE>
</HEAD>
<BODY>
<IMG SRC="BulletSquiggle.gif" ALIGN=TOP><em>Colors of the Spectrum:</EM><BR>
<UL>
      <IMG SRC="BulletCheck.gif" ALIGN=TOP>Red<BR>
      <IMG SRC="BulletCheck.gif" ALIGN=TOP>Orange<BR>
      <IMG SRC="BulletCheck.gif" ALIGN=TOP>Yellow<BR>
      <IMG SRC="BulletCheck.gif" ALIGN=TOP>Green<BR>
      <IMG SRC="BulletCheck.gif" ALIGN=TOP>Blue<BR>
      <IMG SRC="BulletCheck.gif" ALIGN=TOP>Indigo<BR>
      <IMG SRC="BulletCheck.gif" ALIGN=TOP>Violet<BR>
</UL>
</BODY>
</HTML>
```

FIG. 9.9
With a little added work, nonstandard formatting and bullets can be used on your Web pages.

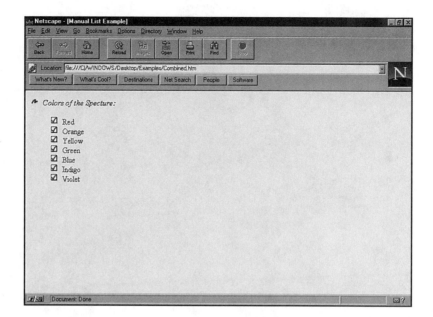

## CHAPTER 10

Building Navigational Imagemaps

by Jerry Honeycutt, John Jung, and Mark R. Brown

In this chapter

Introducing Imagemaps

Because imagemaps make use of pictures, they let users navigate content-related links in a friendly fashion. The Web uses the first Internet standard (HTML) that allows for the easy display of graphics. This is in sharp contrast to past standards, which were all text-based, such as Gopher, WAIS, and FTP. Although these older standards could transport images, this capability was never designed into them (see Figure 10.1).

FIG. 10.1

Using imagemaps is easier than text links because most folks relate to pictures better than words.

N O T E   In the wide world of HTML, you also see imagemaps referred to as *area maps* or *clickable maps*. ■

Different parts of an imagemap's graphic point to different URLs. Because the user has to know where these clickable regions are in the imagemap, you'll often find borders around each region, as shown in Figure 10.2. Note these borders are part of the graphic itself and are not created by the Web server.

You can use two different types of imagemaps: server-side and client-side. Here's how each type of imagemap works:

Server side   The browser sends the mouse pointer's coordinates to the Web server when the user clicks somewhere on the imagemap. Then the server looks up the coordinates and determines the region on which the user clicked. With this information, the server looks up the corresponding URL and returns it to the browser. As a result, the browser opens the URL.

FIG. 10.2
For imagemaps to be useful, the user must be able to easily distinguish each region in the imagemap.

Regions ──────

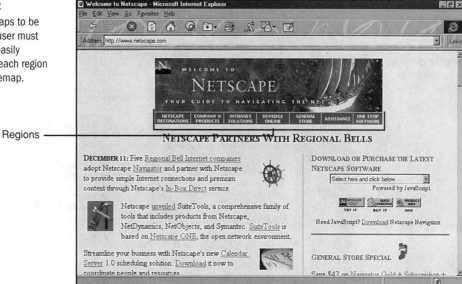

Client side   You define an imagemap's region within the Web page. When the user clicks somewhere on the imagemap, the browser looks up the region in the HTML file, determines the associated URL, and opens that URL. The browser doesn't communicate with the Web server at all.

When to Use Imagemaps

In many situations, you should consider using imagemaps instead of hypertext links. Here's a short list of some instances when using imagemaps is appropriate:

■ *When you want to represent links that have a physical relation to each other.* For example, clicking a map of the world is easier than picking from a list of countries.

■ *When you want to enable users to go to important points on your site at any time.* You can even make imagemaps a consistent feature in every page on your Web site—like a toolbar.

■ *When you want to give your Web site a sense of consistency.* Whenever you add new pages to your Web site, you'll probably want to add the navigation imagemap graphic to them (see Figure 10.3).

FIG. 10.3
By using imagemaps as a navigational tool for the user, you make getting around your home page easier.

Imagemap used as a toolbar

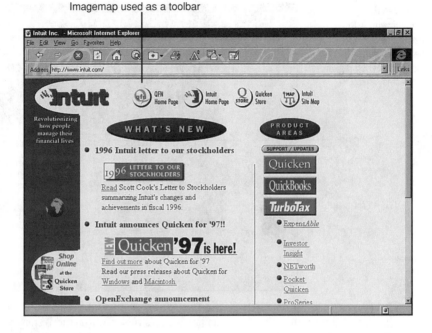

When Not to Use Imagemaps

Although imagemaps might be useful in most situations, sometimes you shouldn't use them—for example,

ON THE WEB

Server-side imagemaps require a Web server capable of handling them properly. You can get a free copy of Microsoft's Personal Web Server at Microsoft's Web site: **http://www.microsoft.com**.

- *Server-side imagemaps can't be tested without a Web server.* This means that while you're designing your imagemaps, you can't test them easily. You either have to get Web server software loaded on your own computer, or put the imagemap files on your server.

- *You should consider nongraphical browsers when designing your Web pages.* Many people still use text-based browsers when surfing the Web. Still more folks disable images in their browser so they can open Web pages faster. You should provide a textual alternative to your imagemaps, as shown in Figure 10.4.

- *If you're concerned about your Web site's performance, you should avoid using imagemaps* (or consider using text alternatives). Because imagemaps can be rather large, they can take awhile to download (particularly if the user has a 14.4K modem). Also, network traffic can sometimes make large graphics take longer than normal to download.

FIG. 10.4

Making textual alternatives for your imagemaps is essential for users with text-based browsers or users who have disabled graphics in their graphical browser.

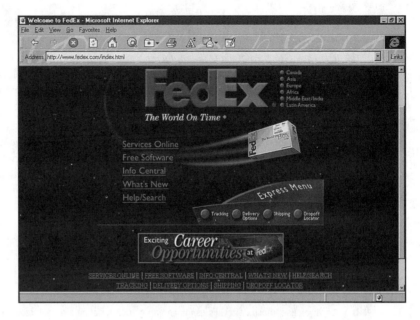

As their names imply, the differences between server-side and client-side imagemaps lie in whether the control logic is implemented on the Web server, or in the browser client. We'll cover how to use both in this chapter.

Using Server-Side Imagemaps

In order to add a server-side imagemap to your Web page, you need four things:

- The imagemap graphic
- The imagemap definition file
- The imagemap program or script
- HTML tags

Creating the Imagemap Graphic

The first thing you want to look at when building an imagemap is the imagemap graphics. If you're building a company Web site, for example, you might want to duplicate the look and feel of your corporate stationery. Chapter 22, "Graphics," has some good information if you're planning to create fresh, new graphics or modify existing ones.

In choosing your imagemap graphic, you have many considerations:

- *Store the imagemap graphic in the GIF or JPG graphics format.* Because you want as many people as possible to see your imagemap, you should make it as basic as possible. All Web browsers support GIF, and most support JPEG. If your imagemap is simple, use GIF format; if it's more detailed, uses more colors, or is a photographic image, use JPG.

■ *If you use GIF format, save the imagemap graphic as an interlaced GIF.* This format allows an image to be displayed progressively. As the image file is downloaded, more detail is added on the screen. By using this format, you let users see where the larger clickable regions are. By using interlaced GIFs as your imagemap graphic, you also help people who have slower modems.

■ *Keep the resolution of your imagemap graphic small.* Try to keep your image from being more than 600 pixels wide by 400 pixels tall. Many different computers will be accessing your page, each with a different configuration. The lowest resolution for most modern computers is 640×480. With the 600×400 resolution recommendation, you make sure almost everybody can see your image without having to scroll.

■ *Try to reduce the number of colors each of your imagemap graphics uses.* Using fewer colors makes the size of the file smaller. The smaller file size translates into a faster download for each user.

▶ **See** "Useful Graphics Tools," **p. 454**

N O T E   If you use transparent GIFs as imagemap graphics, define a default region type, as described later in this chapter. When you use Transparent GIFs (see Chapter 22) as imagemap graphics, users might be confused because the imagemap doesn't have any borders (see Figure 10.5). ■

Transparent GIF used as an imagemap

FIG. 10.5
Yahoo!'s masthead is a transparent GIF, and the main navigational interface for the user. It's not always obvious when you're in the imagemap and when you're not.

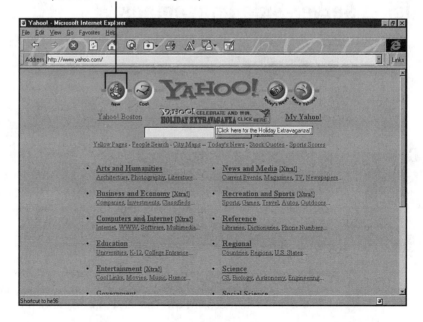

Understanding Imagemap Definition Files

To create a server-side imagemap, you're going to need more than just a pretty picture. You're going to need an imagemap definition file, which identifies where each specific region is within the imagemap.

An imagemap definition file can come in two forms: CERN and NCSA. Both contain the same basic information for the clickable regions within an imagemap. Both of them also use the same region types. The coordinates used to define the regions are also the same. The only difference between the two is the manner in which the information is presented. Because of this incompatibility, you must find out from your system administrator which format your Web server supports.

All entries in a imagemap definition file must include the URL to be accessed (see Listing 10.1). The URL can be either an absolute path or a relative path. If you're using relative paths to specify a URL, be sure to make them relative to the directory where the imagemap definition file resides, not where the imagemap resides.

▶ **See** "Understanding Links," **p. 124**

See "Understanding Links," **p. 124**

Part
II

Ch
10

Listing 10.1   Imagemap Definition File

```
#
# Sample Imagemap Definition File
# File Format: NCSA
#

# Define the default region
default http://www.myserver.com/mypage/index.htm

# Define a rectangle region
rect http://www.myserver.com/mypage/rectangle.htm 50,40 100,120

# Define a circle region
circle http://www.myserver.com/mypage/rectangle.htm 50,40 100,60

# Define a polygon region
poly http://www.myserver.com/mypage/rectangle.htm 10,20 24,70 84,45 07,11 10,20
```

The CERN Format   Originally, CERN (Conséil Européen pour la Recherche Nucléaire) was founded as a research group of European physicists. The group slowly expanded its research into the field of computers. Because they were the ones who thought of the idea, they rightfully claim the honor of being "the birthplace of the Web." When imagemaps were deemed necessary, CERN developed its format for the imagemap definition file. On Web servers that follow the CERN format, you can find files that look like this:

```
region_type (x1,y1) (x2,y2) ... URL
```

The horizontal ($x1$ and $x2$) and vertical ($y1$ and $y2$) coordinates must be in parentheses and separated by a comma. Each pair of coordinates means something different for each region type. The . . . specifies additional coordinates, such as for the `poly` region type (see "Working with Imagemap Region Types" later in the chapter). Here's an example of a CERN imagemap definition:

```
rect (60,40) (340,280) http://www.rectangle.com/
```

The NCSA Format The first wildly popular browser, Mosaic, came from the University of Illinois' National Center for Supercomputing Applications (NCSA). When this group heard of the demand for imagemaps, it came up with its own imagemap definition file format. A typical entry in one of its files would look like this:

```
region_type URL x1,y1 x2,y2 ...
```

Subtle (but significant) differences distinguish the CERN and NCSA formats. The URL for the region type comes before the coordinates with NCSA, not after, as with CERN. The coordinates defining the region need to be separated by commas, but they don't need the parentheses around them. Here's an example of an NCSA imagemap definition:

```
rect http://www.rectangle.com/ 60,40 340,280
```

N O T E You can put comments to yourself in an imagemap definition file. Simply put a pound character (#) at the beginning of any line. Everything else on the same line after the pound sign will be ignored by the Web server. Comments are useful for putting in bits of information to yourself about the referenced URL, the imagemap graphic, or anything else. For corporate Web pages, comments are particularly useful for telling others when the file was last modified, who did it, and why it was changed.

The pound sign at the beginning of the line is different than the pound sign in the middle of a URL. When a pound sign is in the middle of a URL, it specifies an internal destination point. ■

Working with Imagemap Region Types

Each entry in the definition file specifies a region type. It also tells the exact points that define the region for that type. The coordinates used by each region type are an offset, in pixels, from the upper-left corner of the imagemap graphic. The available region types are mostly geometric (see Figure 10.6).

N O T E Each imagemap depends on its own imagemap definition file to hold the information about clickable regions. This means that if your Web site has many different imagemaps, you need an imagemap definition file for each of them. ■

The Rectangle Region To get a clickable rectangle in your imagemap, use the `rect` region type. This element takes in two coordinates, the upper-left and lower-right corners of the rectangle. Any mouse clicks inside the rectangle that are within these corners activate the region. Here's an example using the NCSA format:

```
rect http://www.rectangle.com/ 100,100 120,120
```

FIG. 10.6
Excepting the default
type, you can use any
combination of these
region types.

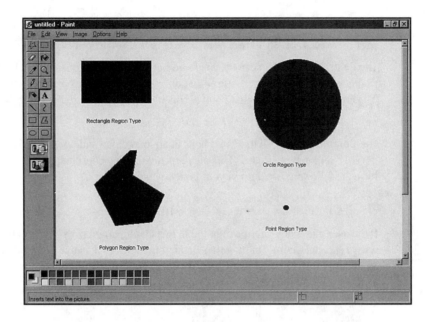

If your Web server is a CERN imagemap server, the previous example will look like this:

```
rect (100,100) (120,120) http://www.rectangle.com/
```

> **T I P** Whenever multiple region types overlap, the first one with an entry in the imagemap definition file is used.

The Polygon Region   To specify a geometric shape of an arbitrary number of sides, use the `poly` region type. This element looks for up to 100 coordinates, each referring to a vertex of the polygon. The active region is the area within the polygon. Note that you should close the polygon. That is, the first and last set of coordinates should be the same. Here's an example using the NCSA format:

```
poly http://www.polygon.com/ 0,0 100,100 120,120 80,60 40,50 10,10 0,0
```

If your Web server is a CERN imagemap server, the previous example will look like this:

```
poly (0,0) (100,100) (120,120) (80,60) (40,50) (10,10) (0,0) http://
www.polygon.com/
```

The Circle Region   To get a hot spot in the shape of a circle, you should use the `circle` region type. This element takes in two coordinates, but they are different values for different Web servers. If your Web server is an NCSA imagemap server, the two coordinates specify the coordinates for the center of the circle and a point on that circle, like this:

```
circle http://www.circle.com/ 100,100 150,150
```

If your Web server is a CERN imagemap server, you really need only one coordinate and one value. The coordinates specify the center of the circle, whereas the value defines its radius.

The clickable region of this type is everything enclosed within the circle. Here's an example:

```
circle (100,100) 50 http://www.circle.com/
```

The Point Region You can easily create hot spots the size of small circles with the `point` region type. This element requires just one set of coordinates to specify the center of the circle. The area enclosed within that point is considered the active region—for example,

```
point http://www.point.com/ 88,65
```

The Default Region If the user clicks in an imagemap and doesn't activate any region, the `default` region type is used. This element requires no coordinates. For example, assume you have the following two lines in your imagemap definition file:

```
rect http://www.rectangle.com/ 0,0 100,100
default http://www.rectangle.com/helpme
```

If the user clicks anywhere within the first rectangle, the browser opens **http://www.rectangle.com**. On the other hand, if the user clicks anywhere outside of the first rectangle, the browser opens **http://www.rectangle.com/helpme** because this URL is associated with the default region.

> **CAUTION**
>
> Whenever possible, try to avoid putting in a point alone with a `default` region type. Because the point region is so small, a user can easily miss it. As a result, the default region will be accessed instead. The user will be frustrated by not getting to the URL he or she wants. Try using small circles instead.

An imagemap definition file should, whenever possible, be configured with a default region. The default region opens a specified URL when the user clicks outside of any region. This URL can provide the user with feedback or helpful information about using that particular imagemap.

Creating Imagemap Definition Files

Creating the imagemap definition file can be a tiring part of creating the imagemap for your Web site. You can create this file in two ways: the easy way and the hard way. The easy way is to use an imagemap creation program. This type of program lets you draw imagemap region types on top of an imagemap graphic of your choice and specify the appropriate URL. You learn more about these programs in the section "Working with Mapping Programs," later in this chapter.

The hard way of creating the file is to do it by hand. Creating the file this way really isn't as difficult as you might think, but it is dull and repetitive. You need two programs to create an imagemap definition file by hand: a graphics program and a text editor. Here's how:

1. Print a hard copy of the image you're using as an imagemap and mark where you want each clickable region.

2. Load the image in a graphics program. (The program should display the coordinates of the mouse.)

3. Create a new text file for your imagemap and open it in your favorite text editor (Notepad). Consider using the MAP file extension as this is standard across the Internet.

4. For each region in your sketch, add an entry to the imagemap definition file. Use the graphics program to locate the coordinates required for each region. For example, if you are creating a region for the rectangle in Figure 10.6, place your mouse pointer at the upper-left corner of the rectangle and note the coordinates (30,20); place the mouse pointer at the lower-right corner of the rectangle and note the coordinates (130, 80); and add the following entry to your imagemap definition file:

```
rect http://www.myserver.com/mypage/rectangle.htm 30,20 130,80
```

5. Save your imagemap definition file.

Part

II

Ch

10

CAUTION

When using a graphics program to get coordinates for use in an imagemap, be careful not to actually change the image.

 If you choose to have multiple imagemaps using different imagemap graphics, you should organize everything. A good way to do this is to create a separate directory for each group of files for each imagemap. Another way of keeping multiple imagemap files distinct from each other is to keep the same file name for each imagemap component, where each will have the appropriate extension.

Using a CGI Program to Look Up Mouse Clicks

As noted earlier in this chapter, you must use a CGI program to translate a user's mouse click into a URL. The user's browser invokes your CGI program, passing to it the coordinates of the mouse click. Then, within your imagemap definition file, your program finds the region in which the user clicks. If the program finds a matching region, it returns the corresponding URL; otherwise, it returns an error.

Chapter 34, "CGI Scripting," shows you how to create CGI programs. In most cases, however, your ISP already provides a CGI program that you can use to look up URLs in an imagemap definition file.

Invoking the CGI Program   By now you might have asked yourself how you invoke the CGI script from within the Web page. You learn more about the HTML you use to create imagemaps in the next section. For now, however, imagemaps within your HTML look a bit like the following example:

```
<A HREF="http://www.myserver.com/cgi-bin/mapfile.map">
<IMG SRC=imagemap.gif ISMAP></A>
```

The HREF in the example anchor specifies a link, not to another Web page or Internet resource, but to an imagemap. Depending on how you create your imagemap and how your ISP works with imagemaps, you may also link to the actual CGI program. When the user clicks on the imagemap, the browser attempts to open this URL, passing to it the coordinates of the mouse pointer as a parameter. The server then replies by returning the URL that the CGI program determined is associated with those coordinates.

Working with an ISP　Most *Internet service providers* (ISPs) work alike, right down to the tilde (~) that many ISPs prefix to your username when creating the directory for your home page. Thus, if you're creating a personal home page on an ISP's Web server, you can bet that you'll use a format similar to the following when invoking an imagemap:

```
<a href="/cgi-bin/imagemap/~username/image.map">
<img src="myimage.gif"></a>
```

The HREF points to /cgi-bin/imagemap/~username/image.map. You simply substitute your username for *username* and the name of your imagemap file for *image.map*. Also note that most ISPs have requirements for how you store your map files. For example, my ISP requires that I store all imagemap files in the root directory of my home page, called /PUBLIC_HTML, regardless of the directory structure that my Web site uses. Your ISP may have different requirements.

Putting the HTML on the Web Page

Now that you have all the elements in place for an imagemap, you're ready to actually put it in your Web page. You do so by building from what you learn in Chapter 22. There, you can see how to make an image clickable and go to a certain URL. All you have to do is enclose the <IMG SRC> tag within an anchor element and have the anchor reference point to the appropriate Web page.

Two steps are needed to make an imagemap an integral part of a Web page on your site. First, you need to change the anchor element reference from an HTML document to point to your imagemap definition file. Second, you must add the attribute ISMAP to the <IMG SRC> tag. For example, say that you've created an imagemap definition file called MAPFILE.MAP, and its graphic is called IMAGEMAP.GIF. To put an imagemap in an HTML document, you use the following HTML code:

```
<A HREF="http://www.myserver.com/cgi-bin/mapfile.map">
<IMG SRC=imagemap.gif ISMAP></A>
```

When the imagemap is selected, the Web server runs the imagemap CGI program. The program then takes over and translates the mouse-click coordinates into a corresponding URL.

N O T E　Be sure to ask your Web master where the imagemap definition file will be stored. These file locations are determined by the configuration of your Web server. ▪

N O T E You can use the ISMAP attribute with any other image attributes. Just because you're specifying an imagemap doesn't restrict your ability to control the graphic. You can still use any other image-controlling attributes you want. ■

Putting Your Imagemap Through a Dry Run

After you've created the files for your imagemap, the only thing left to do is to test it. Even though some map-editing programs let you try the region types within the program, this built-in facility is often imperfect. The programmers have made certain assumptions with the imagemap process. The best way to test the imagemap is to put it on your Web server and act like an average user.

By testing the imagemap in this fashion, you can see different aspects that you might have overlooked. If the imagemap graphic file is too large and takes a long time to download, you'll see it. You'll also be able to see if the imagemap regions are distinct enough for the average person. Finally, you can see if the URLs for each region actually work as they should. If you're using relative links, testing the imagemap on the server is especially important.

  T I P Keep your FTP client open and ready. Then, you can quickly change and test your imagemap by flipping back and forth between the text editor, FTP client, and Web browser (don't forget to reload the Web page if you're changing the graphic).

Before releasing your imagemap for everyone's perusal, find someone else to try it. Get a friend with a different Internet service provider to access your new imagemap. He or she can give you a (somewhat) unbiased opinion of the imagemap graphic and region types.

Building Client-Side Imagemaps

Until HTML 3.2, the client-side imagemap was an extension limited to Netscape Navigator and Internet Explorer. Now, client-side imagemaps are no longer an extension; they are part of the standard.

Client-side imagemaps are similar to server-side imagemaps. The only difference is that instead of using an imagemap file and CGI script on the server, you use an imagemap that you store right in the HTML file. The greatest benefit is in the reduced network traffic. That is, instead of hitting the Web server to look up a URL, the browser handles the imagemap itself.

Defining a Client-Side Imagemap

Remember the formats of the NCSA and CERN imagemap definition files? The HTML format for an imagemap definition contains the same types of information, but it uses HTML tags. Here's what the syntax of an imagemap definition in HTML looks like:

```
<MAP NAME="mapname">
<AREA [SHAPE="shape"] COORDS="x,y,..." [HREF="URL"][NOHREF]>
</MAP>
```

The imagemap definition starts with the <MAP> tag and ends with the </MAP> tag. It's a container. So that you can refer to the imagemap definition later, you give it a name by using the NAME attribute.

You define each region, or hot spot, by using the AREA tag. The coordinate system starts from the upper-left corner of the imagemap. Table 10.1 describes each of the AREA tag's attributes.

Table 10.1   The *<AREA>* Tag's Attributes

Attribute	Description
SHAPE	Defines the shape of the region. Just like the server-side imagemap definition files, you can use rect, poly, circle, or default. If this attribute is missing, the browser assumes rect. When two regions overlap, the browser uses the first one in the list.
COORDS	Defines a comma-separated list of coordinates. Note there is a comma between each set of coordinates.
HREF	Defines the URL of the Internet resource to which the region is linked. All relative links are relative to the document containing the MAP tag, not the one containing the USEMAP attribute, if different. If you use a BASE tag in the HTML file containing the MAP tag, that URL is used.
NOHREF	Specifies the region is a dead area within the imagemap. That is, that area is not linked to any Internet resource. Note HREF and NOHREF are mutually exclusive.

Listing 10.2 shows you a complete example of an imagemap definition in HTML. Figure 10.7 shows the Web page created by this HTML code.

Listing 10.2   A Client-Side Imagemap

```
<MAP NAME=mymap>
<AREA SHAPE=RECT COORDS="0,0,100,100" HREF=item1.html>
<AREA SHAPE=RECT COORDS="101,0,200,100" HREF=item2.html>
<AREA SHAPE=RECT COORDS="201,0,300,100" HREF=item3.html>
</MAP>
<IMG SRC=mymap.gif USEMAP=#mymap>
```

Referencing the Client-Side Imagemap Definition

The final line of the previous example shows how to reference an imagemap after it's built:

```
<IMG SRC=mymap.gif USEMAP=#mymap>
```

This <IMG> tag loads the image called MYMAP.GIF. The USEMAP attribute specifies the name of the imagemap definition, which you define elsewhere in the HTML file using the <MAP> tag.

FIG. 10.7
The client-side imagemap produced by the example HTML code.

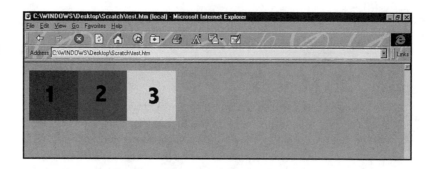

Combining Client-Side and Server-Side Imagemaps

If you want to take care of those folks with browsers that don't support client-side imagemaps while reducing network traffic for those folks with browsers that do support client-side imagemaps, you can combine the best of both worlds. You can define an imagemap that works with both client-side and server-side imagemaps. Combine both definitions within the <IMG> tag, like this:

```
<A HREF="http://www.myserver.com/cgi-bin/mymap.map">
<IMG SRC=mymap.gif USEMAP=#mymap ISMAP>
</A>
```

If the browser supports client-side imagemaps, it will use the map from the USEMAP attribute. Otherwise, the browser will use the map on the server.

N O T E   If you want to use client-side imagemaps but don't want to or can't create a server-side imagemap, you can create an alternative, like this:

```
<A HREF=textmenu.html><IMG SRC=mymap.gif USEMAP=mymap></A>
```

The user will see the image whether or not the his browser supports imagemaps. If a user clicks the image and his browser doesn't support imagemaps, he'll see a text menu from which he can choose an URL. ■

Working with Mapping Programs

As mentioned previously, you can create the imagemap definition file the easy way or the hard way. The easy way is to use one of the many programs that will create the file for you. These programs are called *mapping tools*, and they let you draw various imagemap region types on top of a specified image.

Many map-editing programs are available for both Windows and Macintosh. Generally speaking, most map-editing programs have the same basic features. They all support the three basic geometric region types: rect, poly, and circle. Some of the more advanced map-editing programs support the point and default region types. The only thing you should look for in imagemap-editing programs is how the user interface feels. Because such a wide variety is available, you don't have to use one if it doesn't feel right to you.

Part
II

Ch
10

> **TIP** Even though a map-editing program might not support every region type, you can still add other region types by editing the imagemap definition file after you have saved it.

Working with Mapedit

Mapedit 2.24 is a shareware, no-frills, map-editing program for Windows 95 and UNIX. You can get Mapedit from **http://www.boutell.com/mapedit**. It was written by Thomas Boutell, maintainer of the FAQ (frequently asked questions) for the World Wide Web. This program allows you to create imagemap definition files in either CERN or NCSA format. Mapedit provides support for the basic geometric shapes, although the point region type isn't supported.

> **N O T E** Other popular imagemap editors include CrossEye 1.0 (**http://www.sausage.com**), LiveImage 1.0 (**http://www.mediatec.com**), Map This 1.31 (**http:// www.ecaetc.ohio-state.edu/tc/mt**), and Web Hotspots 2.01 (**http:// www.concentric.net/~automata/hotspots.shtml**).
>
> Imagemap editors are also included with most commercial Web page creation programs, such as FrontPage, Pagemill, and Backstage.

Navigating Mapedit is pretty straightforward. To create a new imagemap definition file for your imagemap graphic, simply choose File and then choose Open/Create. Mapedit's Open dialog box then appears. You must have an existing imagemap graphic, which you can find by using the Browse button under the Image Filename heading. Mapedit supports GIF, JPEG, and the little-used PNG (Portable Network Graphics) image format for imagemap graphics.

> **N O T E** PNG (Portable Network Graphics) is a new graphics file format that's similar to GIF. It's *lossless*—that is, it doesn't throw away information just to compress an image, like JPEG does. So you don't lose colors when it's compressed and portable across multiple platforms. The biggest advantage of PNG over GIF is that you're not stepping on anyone's patents when you use it. In addition, PNG provides many technological benefits, such as interlaced images that appear on the screen quicker than GIF's interlaced images.

To edit an existing imagemap definition file, you can use the Browse button under the Map or HTML File heading (see Figure 10.8). To create a new imagemap definition file, simply type in the file name you want to use. Be sure to also specify whether you want a CERN or NCSA imagemap definition file, using the appropriate option buttons. Mapedit then asks you to confirm that you want to create a new imagemap.

After you click OK, the shareware notification appears. After the graphic is loaded, the shareware dialog box is dismissed, and the whole image is loaded into Mapedit. If the image is bigger than the current screen resolution, you can use the scroll bars to see different parts of the picture.

FIG. 10.8

When you want to create or edit an imagemap file with Mapedit, you have to fill in the information for this dialog box.

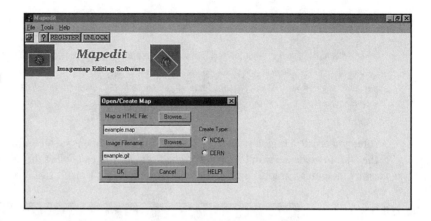

NOTE If the colors on the imagemap graphic you specified look a little weird, don't worry. Mapedit isn't concerned with the way the picture looks; it's more concerned with the imagemap region types.

You can create any number of imagemap region types by choosing options from the Tools menu. You can create circle, polygon, or rectangle region types. For people accustomed to many paint programs or other imagemap creation programs, the region-creation interface may not make immediate sense (see Table 10.2). Generally speaking, you can create shapes in other programs by clicking and holding the right mouse button, dragging the shape, and then releasing the mouse button. Unfortunately, in Mapedit it's a matter of clicking and releasing the mouse button, dragging the shape, and then reclicking and rereleasing the mouse button. After you have created a region type on the imagemap graphic, you can't delete it by using Mapedit.

Table 10.2   Creating Region Types by Using Mapedit

Region Type	How to Create
Circle	Click the left mouse button to specify the center of the desired circle and the size of the circle. Click the right mouse button when the circle is the desired size.
Rectangle	Click the left mouse button to specify one corner of the rectangle and the size of the rectangle. Click the right mouse button to specify the diagonally-opposite corner of the first corner.
Polygon	Click the left mouse button to specify a corner of the polygon. Move the mouse to the next corner you want to specify. Repeat these steps for each corner of the polygon. When you're back to the first corner, click the right mouse button.

CAUTION

Mapedit works in very distinct *modes*. That is, whatever option you last selected from the Tools menu is still active. If, for example, you just specified an URL for a rectangle region type, the next region type you'll create is a rectangle. If you just selected the Test+Edit menu item, you remain in Test+Edit mode until you specify a region type.

After you create a region type, the Object URL window opens (see Figure 10.9). Simply type in the URL to associate with the newly created region. You can define the default URL for the entire imagemap graphic by choosing File and then Edit Default URL.

FIG. 10.9

After you create a region type, Mapedit asks for the URL to which that region should refer.

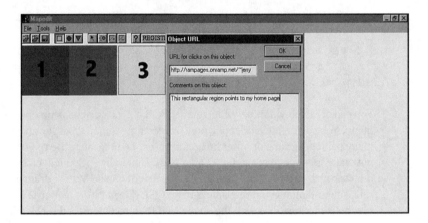

If you can't see the outline of the region type as you're creating it, don't worry. Mapedit doesn't care about the appearance of the image in its window. To change each region type's outline colors, choose File, Edit Hotspot Color.

TIP   If you make a mistake in the location of the region type, you can cancel its creation in two ways. You can either press Esc while you're specifying the size of the region, or you can click the Cancel button in the Object URL dialog box.

Using Mapedit, you can test the regions you've created. You choose Tools and then Test+Edit. When you press the left mouse button while moving the mouse over an imagemap, the URL for the corresponding region appears. This testing capability is a function of Mapedit and doesn't require a Web browser or server to use.

You can save your current imagemap definition file by choosing File and then either Save or Save As.

NOTE   Mapedit doesn't force any file-name extensions on you. As a result, when you're creating a new imagemap definition file, you need to specify the extension yourself. Most imagemap servers look for a file with the MAP extension. ■

Mapedit also allows you to easily change the position of hotspot regions. To move any clickable region, simply select the Tools menu heading, followed by the Move menu item. Next click the region you want to move, and a number of *control points* will appear. By clicking and dragging any of the control points that bound the region, you can reshape or resize it. If you click and drag the control point in the middle of the region, you'll move the entire region. Because Mapedit will still be in the Move mode, you can fine-tune the position of the clickable region.

Polygon regions can also be reshaped by adding or removing points in Mapedit. Just click the Tools menu heading and choose either the Add Points or Remove Points menu items. These two options work only on polygon region types, and do as their name implies. With the Add Points option, click the polygon you want to add a point to and then put your mouse roughly where you want the new point to appear. Similarly, for Remove Points, you click the polygon from which you want to remove a point and then select the point to remove.

Mapedit can also be used to create client-side imagemaps. Instead of loading in a MAP file, you specify an HTML file. Mapedit will look for any HTML that includes a graphic. It will present a dialog box with whatever images were found (see Figure 10.10). Select the picture you want to create a client-side imagemap for and click OK. The file name for the image is automatically filled in Mapedit's Select Inline Image dialog box. Once you click OK, you'll be taken into Mapedit as usual. After you've created all the shapes you want, saving the changes will update the HTML file.

FIG. 10.10
To create client-side imagemaps, just select the picture you want to make an imagemap for.

Part
II

Ch
10

Using Alternatives to Imagemaps

For whatever reason, you may not want to use HTML 4 imagemaps in your Web page. Maybe your audience is a group of text-only folks. Maybe your service provider doesn't support CGI scripts, and thus doesn't support server-side imagemaps, and you're afraid of abandoning those folks with older browsers. This section presents you with three alternatives to imagemaps:

Image chunks

Scripting

Textual alternatives

Image Chunks

Instead of defining rectangular regions within a larger image, you can divide the image into smaller images by using your favorite paint program. Then, you can insert each image into your Web page, causing it to appear to the user as a single image. Of course, you'll link each image to a different URL.

For example, if you divide a 100×100 image into four square chunks, each 50×50, you can combine them on the Web page like that shown in Listing 10.3.

Listing 10.3   An Imagemap Created from Individual Images

```
<A HREF=item1.html><IMG SRC=item1.gif WIDTH=50 HEIGHT=50 BORDER=0></A>
<A HREF=item2.html><IMG SRC=item2.gif WIDTH=50 HEIGHT=50 BORDER=0></A>
<BR>
<A HREF=item3.html><IMG SRC=item3.gif WIDTH=50 HEIGHT=50 BORDER=0></A>
<A HREF=item4.html><IMG SRC=item4.gif WIDTH=50 HEIGHT=50 BORDER=0></A>
```

To the user, these four chunks will appear as one larger image. However, each chunk is linked to a different URL. Note that you must specify the exact height and width of the image and turn off borders.

 T I P You can also use tables to assemble each portion of the imagemap.

Scripting

You can use VBScript or JavaScript to create client-side imagemaps. That is, you can associate a script with the mouse-click event of an image. Then, when the user clicks the mouse on that image, you can open a different URL depending on the area of the image the user clicked.

Textual Alternatives

Imagemaps and graphics in general don't translate particularly well into text. In fact, they don't translate at all. For this reason, you should provide some alternatives for people who don't have graphical browsers. Also bear in mind that some people have configured their browsers so they don't automatically load pictures. People who access the Web through UNIX's command-line mode and people with slow modems fall into these categories. Because they are a strong minority, you should provide some support for them.

You can let nongraphics users access the various points on your imagemap in a number of ways. You can provide a separate home page for these people and mention it in your graphics-intensive page. You also can put in regular hypertext links at the top or bottom of all your home pages. These links can point to the same links accessible through the imagemaps. Whichever approach you like, you should take one of them. If you ignore the text-only crowd, you're alienating a large group of people.

Building an Imagemap

You've learned a lot of general information about creating imagemaps, but you'll benefit more from walking through an example, beginning to end. The example in this section is a simple imagemap that you can use as a toolbar. The image is straightforward. When creating your own imagemap, however, you can substitute images from your own favorite clip-art library or images you create by hand. The following instructions show you how to create an imagemap:

1. Decide what links you want in your imagemap and how you want to communicate those links to the user. Then, sketch out a rough idea of what you want the imagemap to look like before you start drawing it. In this example, I'm creating regions for the following links: **http://rampages.onramp.net/~jerry**, **http://www.microsoft.com**, **http://www.netscape.com**, and **http://www.quecorp.com**.

2. Open your graphics program (Micrografx Picture Publisher) and, in this example, create a new image that's 320 pixels in width and 80 pixels in height.

3. Add each graphic—which represents each link you're putting in the toolbar—to the image. Position the graphics so that they're spread evenly across the imagemap, as shown in Figure 10.11.

Part
II

Ch
10

FIG. 10.11
An alternative to creating a transparent GIF is to fill the background with the same color as the Web pages' background color—white in this case.

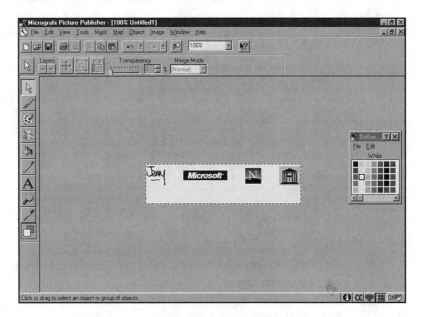

4. Add text labels underneath each graphic so the user can easily discern what each image does (see Figure 10.12).

5. Save the image as a GIF file called **IMAGEMAP.GIF**.

6. Open IMAGEMAP.GIF in either Mapedit or your favorite imagemap editor.

FIG. 10.12

In imagemaps used as toolbars, text labels help the user understand what each icon represents.

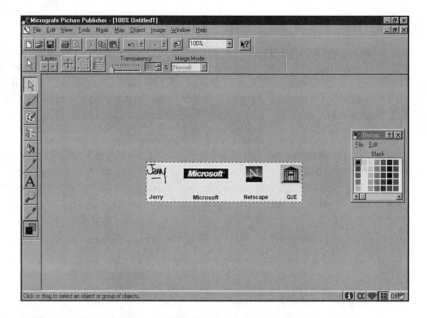

7. Create a rectangular region around each graphic in the toolbar. Don't forget to include the text label that you added underneath each graphic in the region.

8. Save the imagemap definition to a file called **IMAGEMAP.MAP**. Listing 10.4 shows you what the imagemap definition file for this example looks like.

Listing 10.4   IMAGEMAP.MAP—Imagemap Definition File

```
rect http://rampages.onramp.net/~jerry 1,0 39,77
rect http://www.microsoft.com 75,8 169,79
rect http://www.netscape.com 199,4 251,79
rect http://www.mcp.com 273,4 323,82
```

9. Add the following line of code to your HTML file. You'll replace *www.myserver.com/cgi-bin* with the path that's appropriate for your Web server. Ask your Web server administrator if you're not sure what path to use. Alternatively, you can create a client-side imagemap by using the Mapedit as described earlier in this chapter. Figure 10.13 shows you what the completed example looks like.

```
<A HREF="http://www.myserver.com/cgi-bin/imagemap.map">
<IMG SRC=imagemap.gif ISMAP></A>
```

FIG. 10.13

You can position the toolbar at the top and bottom of the Web page to make it more accessible to the user.

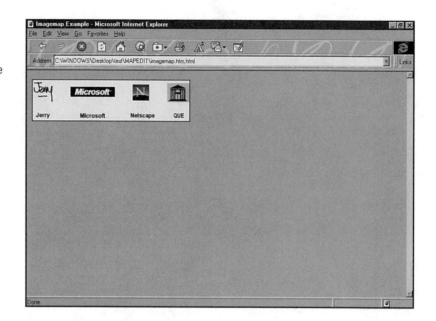

## CHAPTER 11

Formatting Content with Tables

by Jerry Honeycutt, Jim O'Donnell, and Mark R. Brown

In this chapter

Introducing Tables

As a tool for government, commercial, educational, and personal Web applications, HTML has many needs and expectations to meet. It's the language behind the most popular resource on the Internet and, as such, is required to support a greater range of uses today than perhaps its original creators had first imagined. For example, you might design a corporate Web site similar to a marketing brochure, while you'd design a government publication to present static data in tabular form. In most cases, you can use tables to better present these types of Web pages (my technical writing professor would be proud).

In print publications, tables are a basic design element. They're used to present data in rows and columns. They make comparative analysis more understandable. They're also used (albeit invisibly) to divide the printed page into sections for layout purposes. Tables should be a basic design element in your Web pages, too.

On the Web, tables have been used for a while now, thanks to Netscape and subsequently Microsoft, but they were not an official part of the HTML standard until HTML 3.2. This chapter shows you how to use HTML tables to organize content on your Web page or even to help lay out your Web page.

HTML defines tables in much the same way it defines list containers. The <TABLE> element is the container for the table's data and layout.

HTML tables are composed row by row: you indicate a new row with the <TR> (table row) tag, and you separate the data with either the <TH> (table header) or <TD> (table data) tags. Think of the <TR> tag as a line break, signaling that the following data starts a new table row. Table headers are generally shown in bold and centered by WWW browsers, and table data is shown in the standard body-text format. Whereas you can think of a row as a line in a table, a cell represents each box within the table.

▶ **See** "Adding Lists to a Web Page," **p. 143**

Understanding the Basic Tags

The HTML for a basic table is shown in Listing 11.1. All of the HTML table elements used are supported by the latest versions of the most popular Web browsers: Netscape Navigator, Microsoft Internet Explorer, and NCSA Mosaic. This table, as rendered by Internet Explorer, is shown in Figure 11.1.

Listing 11.1   A Basic Table

```
<HTML>
<HEAD>
<TITLE>Basic Table Examples</TITLE>
</HEAD>
<BODY>
<TABLE BORDER>
  <TR>
<TH>Colors</TH><TH>Of</TH><TH>The Rainbow</TH>
  <TR>
```

```
<TD>Red</TD><TD>Orange</TD><TD>Yellow</TD>
</TR>
<TR>
<TD>Green</TD><TD>Blue</TD><TD>Violet</TD>
</TR>
</TABLE>
<HR>
<TABLE BORDER>
  <CAPTION>My Favorite Groups</CAPTION>
  <TR><TH>Rock</TH><TD>Pink Floyd</TD>
<TD>Led Zepplin</TD>
<TD>The Dobbie Brothers</TD></TR>
  <TR><TH>Soft</TH><TD>Simon and Garfunkel</TD>
<TD>Peter, Paul, & Mary</TD>
<TD>Neil Young</TD></TR>
  <TR><TH>New Age</TH><TD>Enya</TD>
<TD>Clannad</TD>
<TD>Steamroller</TD></TR>
</TABLE>
</BODY>
</HTML>
```

FIG. 11.1

Most of the HTML table tags are supported by the most popular Web browsers.

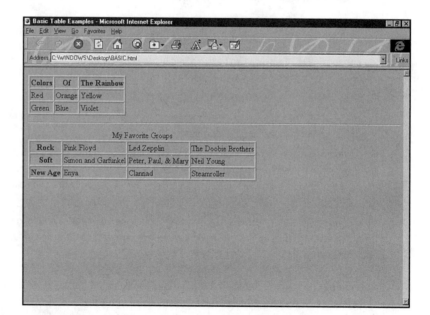

The basic HTML table tags shown in Figure 11.1 and Figure 11.2 are as follows:

- **<TABLE></TABLE>**—These HTML tags are the containers for the rest of the table data.

- **<TR></TR>**—Each row in the table is contained by these tags. You can optionally leave off the closing </TR> tag.

- **<TD></TD>**—Defines a cell. Table data is contained within these tags. You can also nest additional tables within a single cell. You can optionally leave off the closing </TD> tag.

Part

II

Ch

11

- **<TH></TH>**—These table header tags are used to define headers, usually in the first row or column of the table. You can optionally leave off the closing </TH> tag.

In addition to the basic tags shown here, some other characteristics should be noted from the example shown in Figures 11.1 and 11.2:

- **BORDER attribute**—By using the BORDER attribute of the <TABLE> tag, borders are put around the table. You set the value of this attribute to the number of pixels wide you want the border, like this: BORDER=1. If you set this attribute to 0, the browser will not display a border.
- **ALIGN attribute**—The ALIGN attribute can be specified in the <TABLE> tag with possible values of LEFT, RIGHT, and CENTER (the default is LEFT). HTML 4.0 specifies a new value for ALIGN of CHAR, which implements alignment on a specified character, such as a decimal point.
- **Table heads**—In most browsers, table heads enclosed by the <TH></TH> tags are emphasized and centered.
- **Table data**—In most browsers, table data enclosed by the <TD></TD> tags are shown in the normal font and are left-justified.

N O T E   If you're concerned about browsers displaying your header text correctly (as emphasized text, preferably in a bold font), you can use style tags to force the issue. Be careful what you wish for, though; if you want an italicized font but the browser automatically formats the text bold, you can wind up with bold italicized headers. ▧

N O T E   HTML 4.0 adds several new attributes to many table tags that are meant to improve access for international and disabled users.

For example, the AXIS="name" attribute for the <TH> tag lets you specify a spoken name for a table head, which can be used by a text-to-speech synthesizer. A similar attribute, AXES="row,column", has been added to the <TD>, or table data, tag to allow for speaking the row and column references for a table cell.

Almost every table-element defining tag also now includes the ID, CLASS, LANG, and DIR attributes. These define a named label, class definition, natural language, and text direction for table elements, respectively. ▧

Cells do not necessarily have to contain data. To create a blank cell, either create an empty cell (for instance, <TD></TD>) or create a cell containing nothing visible (<TD> </TD>). Note that   is an HTML entity, or special character, for a nonbreaking space. Though you would think these two methods would produce the same result, as you will see later in this chapter, in the section "Empty Cells and Table Appearance," different browsers treat them differently.

It's not really necessary to create blank cells if the rest of the cells on the row are going to be blank; the <TR> element signals the start of a new row, so the Web browsers automatically fill in blank cells to even out the row with the rest of the table.

> **T I P** Tables are necessarily uniform with equal numbers of cells in each row and in each column. No "L-shaped" tables (or worse!) allowed.

Aligning Table Elements

It is possible, through the use of the ALIGN and VALIGN attributes, to align table elements within their cells in many different ways. These attributes can be applied in various combinations to the <CAPTION>, <TR>, <TH>, and <TD> table elements. The possible attribute values for each of these elements are as follows:

- **<CAPTION>**—The ALIGN attribute can be specified for this element with possible values of TOP and BOTTOM (the default is TOP); this places the table caption above or below the table.

- **<TR>**—The ALIGN attribute can be specified for this element with possible values of LEFT, RIGHT, and CENTER (the default is LEFT for table data elements and CENTER for table header elements), and the VALIGN attribute can be specified with possible values of TOP, BOTTOM, MIDDLE, and BASELINE (the default is MIDDLE). If specified, this will give the default alignment for all the table elements in the given row, which can be overridden in each individual element. The BASELINE element applies to all elements in the row and aligns them to a common baseline.

- **<TH>**—The ALIGN attribute can be specified for this element with possible values of LEFT, RIGHT, and CENTER (the default is CENTER), and the VALIGN attribute can be specified with possible values of TOP, BOTTOM, and MIDDLE (the default is MIDDLE).

- **<TD>**—The ALIGN attribute can be specified for this element with possible values of LEFT, RIGHT, and CENTER (the default is LEFT), and the VALIGN attribute can be specified with possible values of TOP, BOTTOM, and MIDDLE (the default is MIDDLE).

These alignments are illustrated by the HTML document shown in Listing 11.2 and rendered by Netscape Navigator in Figure 11.2.

Part
II

Ch
11

Listing 11.2   Table Alignments

```
<HTML>
<HEAD>
<TITLE>Table Alignments</TITLE>
</HEAD>
<BODY>
<TABLE BORDER>
  <CAPTION ALIGN=BOTTOM>A Really Ugly Table</CAPTION>
  <TR>
<TH></TH><TH>##########</TH><TH>##########</TH>
<TH>##########</TH>
  </TR>
  <TR ALIGN=RIGHT>
<TH>Row 1</TH><TD>XX<BR>XX</TD><TD ALIGN=CENTER>X
</TD><TD>XXX</TD>
  </TR>
  <TR VALIGN=BASELINE>
```

continues

Listing 11.2   Continued

```
<TH ALIGN=LEFT>Second Row</TH><TD>XXX<BR>XXX</TD><TD>XXX</TD>
<TD>XXX<BR>XXXXX<BR>XXX</TD>
  </TR>
  <TR ALIGN=LEFT>
<TH>This Is<BR>The Bottom Row of <BR>The Table</TH>
<TD VALIGN=BOTTOM>XXXXX</TD>
<TD VALIGN=TOP>XXX<BR>XXXXX</TD>
<TD VALIGN=MIDDLE>XXXXX</TD>
  </TR>
</TABLE>
</BODY>
</HTML>
```

FIG. 11.2

Table element alignment can be specified row by row or for each individual element in the table.

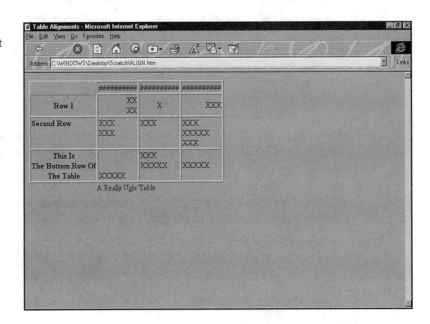

Although this table is pretty ugly, it illustrates the capabilities of the different ALIGN and VALIGN attributes, as follows:

- **Table Caption:** <CAPTION ALIGN=BOTTOM> places the caption underneath the table—overriding the default value, which would put the caption on top.

- **"Row 1":**
    - The <TR ALIGN=RIGHT> sets a default horizontal alignment to the right margin for each element in the row.
    - The <TD ALIGN=CENTER> in the third column overrides the default set in the <TR> element for just this table element.

- ■ **"Second Row":**
  - The `<TR VALIGN=BASELINE>` aligns all of the cells in the row vertically so that their baselines match.
  - The `<TH ALIGN=LEFT>` in the first column overrides the default table header alignment and aligns the table header along the left side.
- ■ **"This Is The Bottom Row of The Table":**
  - The `<TR ALIGN=LEFT>` sets a default horizontal alignment to the left margin for each element in the row.
  - The `<TD VALIGN=BOTTOM>` in the second column vertically aligns the element on the bottom of the row.
  - The `<TD VALIGN=TOP>` in the third column vertically aligns the element on the top of the row.
  - The `<TD VALIGN=MIDDLE>` in the fourth column vertically aligns the element in the middle of the row. Because this is the default behavior (and hasn't been overridden in the `<TR>` element for this row), this attribute isn't necessary.

N O T E Sitting down with your favorite text editor and hacking out the HTML for a table isn't always the best way to do it. There comes a time when a piece of paper and a no. 2 pencil are the best design tools you can use.

Take a look at Figure 11.3. It shows a sketch for a table that has two rows and four columns. The first two columns of the first row are joined, and the last two columns of the last row are joined. ■

FIG. 11.3

Laying out your table before you start writing the HTML code is the easiest way to design your tables.

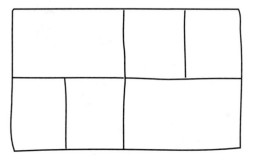

N O T E To make your HTML coding job easier, you can handwrite a `<TABLE>` tag above the table and a `</TABLE>` tag below the figure. Then, handwrite a `<TR>` at the beginning of each row, and a `</TR>` tag at the end of each row. Last, handwrite a `<TD>` and `</TD>` within each cell. If a cell is spanned, then write the number of cells it spans next to the `<TD>` tag and indicate if it spans rows or columns. Figure 11.4 shows you an example of such a sketch. ■

FIG. 11.4

After you mark up your sketch with tags, start at the top and work your way to the bottom, left to right.

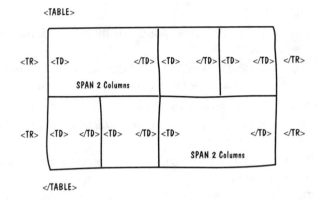

N O T E   With your marked-up sketch in hand, you're ready to write the HTML. Start at the top and work towards the bottom of the sketch in a left to right fashion. Type each tag as you encounter it. If you noted that a cell is spanned, be sure to add the ROWSPAN or COLSPAN attribute to the <TD> tag. The following listing shows you the HTML that results from the previous sketch. (Note that indenting the code can help clarify the row and column breaks.)

```
<TABLE>
<TR>
<TD COLSPAN=2> </TD>
<TD> </TD>
<TD> </TD>
</TR>
<TR>
<TD> </TD>
<TD> </TD>
<TD COLSPAN=2> </TD>
</TR>
</TABLE>
```

CHAR Alignment

HTML 4.0 specifies a new value for the ALIGN attribute called CHAR, or character alignment. This implements a much-requested feature for tables: the ability to align content on a decimal point, colon, or other common character. It is used in conjunction with a new CHAR attribute. Here's a sample of its use:

```
<TR ALIGN=CHAR CHAR=".">…table data here…</TR>
```

The TR tag in this sample uses ALIGN=CHAR to specify that data in the cells in this row should be aligned by decimal point. CHAR="." sets the alignment character as a decimal point, although it could be any ASCII character.

The CHAR value for ALIGN can be used with the COL, COLGROUP, THEAD, TBODY, TFOOT, TR, TH, and TD tags.

A new CHAROFF attribute can also be used to specify the character offset within a cell. For example, CHAROFF="30%" would tell the browser to place the character specified by the CHAR= attribute at an offset of 30% from the start of the cell.

Standard Units for Widths

Several HTML tag attributes allow you to specify the width for a frame, cell, or other page element. When you specify a width, you can use a percentage or specify an absolute width in one of several predefined units. In the preceding text, we used an example of CHAROFF="30%" to specify a character alignment offset, but we could have easily just said CHAROFF="20". This would have meant "20 screen pixels". A number in a width definition without a suffix is always assumed to be in pixels.

CHAROFF="20px" means the same thing but uses the actual suffix to specifically denote pixels, "px". You can also use "pt" to define a width in points, like this: CHAROFF="50pt". However, point widths are generally useful only in documents that are being formatted for print output on paper, since they have no absolute meaning on a monitor screen, which can be of any size.

Table 11.1 lists the acceptable suffixes for width definitions in HTML and shows their values.

Table 11.1 HTML Width Definition Values

Suffix	Value
px, [none]	pixels
pt	points
pi	picas
in	inches
cm	centimeters
mm	millimeters
em	em units
%	percent of screen width

Working with Advanced Tables

There are more sophisticated things that you can do with tables, both by using additional table attributes and by different uses of some of the ones you already know about.

HTML 4.0 *RULES* and *FRAME* Attributes

Within the TABLE element, HTML 4.0 now gives you a broad degree of control over where rules and frames are drawn within a table.

The FRAME attribute specifies which sides of a frame to render. It has the following possible values:

- VOID — No Frame
- ABOVE — Top Side
- BELOW — Bottom Side
- HSIDES — Horizontal Sides
- LHS — Left-Hand Side
- RHS — Right-Hand Side
- VSIDES — Vertical Sides
- BOX or BORDER — All Four Sides

The value BORDER is included for backwards-compatibility with HTML 3.2. <TABLE FRAME=BORDER> is the same as the older <TABLE BORDER>.

In addition to the new FRAME attribute for TABLE, there is also a new RULES attribute. The RULES attribute is used to specify additional rulings in the table interior. For example, it can turn on rulings between all columns, or between groups of rows.

Here are the values for RULES, and their meanings:

- NONE — No rules
- GROUPS — Horizontal rule between all row groups and a vertical rule between all column groups
- ROWS — GROUPS rulings, plus horizontal rules between all rows
- COLS — GROUPS rulings, plus vertical rules between all columns
- ALLRules — between all rows and all columns

> **CAUTION**
>
> At the time of this writing, neither Microsoft Internet Explorer nor Netscape Communicator supported the HTML 4.0 additions of RULES and FRAME. Before adding these attributes to your tables, make sure that support for them has been added to the major browsers.

Creating Borderless Tables

As mentioned previously, the BORDER attribute to the <TABLE> element was the HTML 3.2 element that created borders around table elements, and it has been retained in HTML 4.0 for backwards-compatibility. Even though this attribute is off by default, for most conventional tables—those used to organize information in a tabular format—borders are usually used to accentuate the organization of the information. Consider the HTML document shown in Listing 11.3 and rendered in Figure 11.5. In this case, the organization of the information is much easier to see in the version that includes borders.

Listing 11.3 Table Borders

```
<HTML>
<HEAD>
<TITLE>Table Borders</TITLE>
</HEAD>
<BODY>
<TABLE BORDER>
  <TR><TH>FRUITS</TH><TH>VEGETABLES</TH><TH>WHOLE GRAINS</TH></TR>
  <TR><TD>Apple</TD><TD>Broccoli</TD><TD>Barley</TD></TR>
  <TR><TD>Orange</TD><TD>Cauliflower</TD><TD>Weat Berries</TD></TR>
  <TR><TD>Kiwi</TD><TD>Sugar Snap Pea</TD><TD>Millet</TD></TR>
  <TR><TD>Pineapple</TD><TD>Bell pepper</TD><TD>Quinoa</TD></TR>
</TABLE>
<HR>
<TABLE>
  <TR><TH>FRUITS</TH><TH>VEGETABLES</TH><TH>WHOLE GRAINS</TH></TR>
  <TR><TD>Apple</TD><TD>Broccoli</TD><TD>Barley</TD></TR>
  <TR><TD>Orange</TD><TD>Cauliflower</TD><TD>Weat Berries</TD></TR>
  <TR><TD>Kiwi</TD><TD>Sugar Snap Pea</TD><TD>Millet</TD></TR>
  <TR><TD>Pineapple</TD><TD>Bell Pepper</TD><TD>Quinoa</TD></TR>
</TABLE>
</BODY>
</HTML>
```

Part
II

Ch
11

FIG. 11.5

In many cases, borders accentuate the organization of the information.

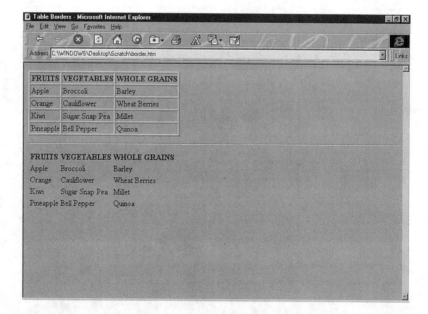

However, HTML tables can be used in other ways, rather than for the simple tabular display of data. They give an HTML author great flexibility in presenting information, grouping it, and formatting it along with other information. Consider the HTML document shown in Listing 11.4 and rendered in Figure 11.6. In this case, the use of a borderless table allows the descriptive text of the image to be displayed alongside the image.

Listing 11.4   Table Borders

```
<HTML>
<HEAD>
<TITLE>Table Borders</TITLE>
</HEAD>
<BODY>
<TABLE>
  <TR>
<TD><IMG SRC="lion.gif"></TD>
<TD>
The rampant lion is a symbol from Scottish heraldy. It symbolizes
a duty and willingness to defend one's ideals and values, such as
aret&ecirc. The color of the lion, White, is for the purity of the
brotherhood of PEZ, void of the negativity associated with some
fraternities. This White symbolizes how PEZ is a practice of the
pure theory of brotherhood. This brotherhood has its roots in common
ties and support rather than hazing and the like.
</TD>
  </TR>
</TABLE>
</BODY>
</HTML>
```

FIG. 11.6

Side-by-side presentation of information elements can be achieved by using HTML tables.

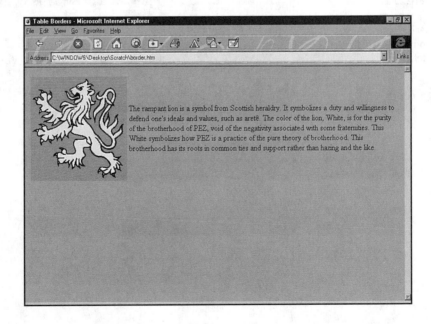

Spanning Rows and Columns

Rows and columns can be spanned—combined with adjacent cells to create larger cells for the data. For instance, in a table with five rows and five columns, the first row could be spanned across all five columns to create a banner header for the whole table. In the same table, each of the columns could have elements that spanned multiple rows. It would be possible, through spanning, to create rectangular table elements that span both multiple rows and columns, up to the full size of the table.

To span two adjacent cells on a row, use the ROWSPAN attribute with <TH> or <TD>, as follows:

```
<TD ROWSPAN=2>
```

To span two adjacent cells in a column, use the COLSPAN attribute with <TH> or <TD>, as follows:

```
<TD COLSPAN=2>
```

 TIP Don't forget to close your table data with the </TABLE> closing tag.

HTML 4.0 adds an additional attribute to TD, NOWRAP. If NOWRAP is present, cell contents disables automatic text wrapping for that cell. However, this attribute has been defined only for backwards-compatibility with current browsers and is functionally superseded by style sheets.

Listings 11.5 and 11.6 show an HTML document that makes use of row and column spanning. This example is shown in Figure 11.7, which shows some of the trouble you can get yourself into with row and column spanning. The table shown on the left is formatted correctly. However, HTML will allow you to overlap rows and columns if you aren't careful with your spanning, and the results of this can (and usually will) be unpredictable.

Part
II

Ch
11

Listing 11.5 Row and Column Spanning

```
<HTML>
<HEAD>
<TITLE>Row and Column Spanning</TITLE>
</HEAD>
<BODY>
<TABLE BORDER>
  <TR><TH COLSPAN=3>DC nationals</TH><TR>
  <TR><TH>Offense</TH><TH>Defense</TH><TH>Goalie</TH></TR>
  <TR>
<TD>Husmann</TD><TD>O'Donnell</TD><TD ROWSPAN=5>Weinberg</TD>
  </TR>
  <TR>
<TD COLSPAN=2>Popplewell</TD>
  </TR>
  <TR>
<TD>McGilly</TD><TD>Longo</TD>
  </TR>
  <TR>
<TD>Donahue</TD><TD>Seymour</TD>
```

continues

Listing 11.5 Continued

```
  </TR>
  <TR>
<TD>Camillo</TD><TD>Walsh</TD>
  </TR>
</TABLE>
</BODY>
<HTML>
```

Listing 11.6 Row and Column Spanning

```
<HTML>
<HEAD>
<TITLE>Row and Column Spanning</TITLE>
</HEAD>
<BODY>
<TABLE BORDER>
  <TR><TH COLSPAN=3>DC nationals</TH><TR>
  <TR><TH>Offense</TH><TH>Defense</TH><TH>Goalie</TH></TR>
  <TR>
<TD>Husmann</TD><TD>O'Donnell</TD>
<TD ROWSPAN=5>
Weinberg<BR>Weinberg<BR>Weinberg<BR>
Weinberg<BR>Weinberg<BR>Weinberg<BR>
</TD>
  </TR>
  <TR>
<TD COLSPAN=2>Popplewell</TD>
  </TR>
  <TR>
<TD>McGilly</TD><TD>Longo</TD>
  </TR>
  <TR>
<TD>Donahue</TD><TD>Seymour</TD>
  </TR>
  <TR>
<TD>Camillo</TD><TD COLSPAN=2>Walsh Walsh Walsh</TD>
  </TR>
</TABLE>
</BODY>
<HTML>
```

N O T E When you create larger cells in an HTML table, you might find your cell data acts a bit unruly: not breaking properly, wrapping text when it shouldn't, and crowding too close to the cell divisions. Like other HTML documents, tables support internal HTML elements, such as
 (to create a line break in the data), hypertext link anchors, inline images, and even forms.

Use an HTML table in the same manner you would a spreadsheet: for data display, for creating data layouts (such as inventory lists or business invoices), and for calculation tables (when combined with a CGI script that can take your form input and generate output data that's displayed in your HTML table). The uses for tables are limited only by your data and your creativity. ■

FIG. 11.7
If you aren't careful, you can overlap rows and columns when using spanning, which tends to give ugly results.

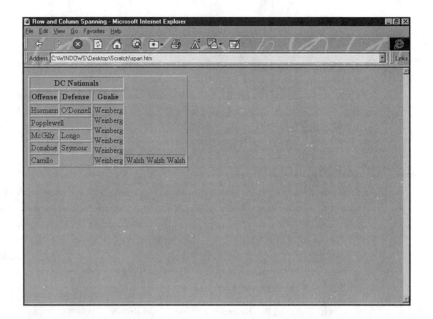

Grouping Rows and Columns

HTML 4.0 adds several tags for grouping rows and columns for the purpose of specifying common attributes for those groups.

COLGROUP assigns width and alignment attributes for a group of columns. For example, if you had a table with six columns and you wanted each of the first three columns to be 50 pixels wide and left-aligned, each of the second two columns to be 100 pixels wide and character-aligned on a decimal point, and the last column to take up the remainder of the screen width and right-aligned, you could accomplish all of this formatting with just the following three lines of HTML:

```
<COLGROUP WIDTH="50px" ALIGN=LEFT SPAN=3>
<COLGROUP WIDTH="100px" ALIGN=CHAR CHAR="." SPAN=2>
<COLGROUP WIDTH="100%" ALIGN=RIGHT>
```

Note that the SPAN attribute defines how many contiguous columns are in a COLGROUP group. If it's left out, the value defaults to SPAN=1, or a single column.

TBODY, THEAD, and TFOOT perform functions similar to COLGROUP, but they group rows instead of columns. THEAD and TFOOT define a group of rows to form a header or footer for a table, respectively. TBODY is used to group rows in the body of the table. Each is a container—that is, it is made up of corresponding begin and end tags, as in <TBODY></TBODY>—but the end tags for THEAD and TFOOT are optional, as long as a TBODY tag immediately follows. This was done for compatibility with older HTML tables.

Each row grouping container set must contain at least one TR, or table row, element.

A TFOOT block should actually *precede* the TBODY block, as browsers will logically insert the footer when needed in breaking pages.

Each row grouping element uses the same attributes and values as the COLGROUP tag.

NOTE At the time of this writing, neither Microsoft Internet Explorer nor Netscape Communicator supported the HTML 4.0 additions of COLGROUP, THEAD, TFOOT, or TBODY. Before adding these attributes to your tables, make sure support for them has been added to the major browsers. ▪

Understanding Empty Cells

As mentioned earlier, there is sometimes a difference between an empty cell in a table and one with nothing visible in it. This is particularly true with Netscape Navigator and Internet Explorer, which will display the two differently. Consider the HTML document shown in Listing 11.7, which shows two tables. In the top table, there are several empty table cells—cells with only white space in them, which Netscape Navigator will not treat as data. In the lower table, these same cells have something in them: the HTML entity , which is a nonbreaking space (an invisible character).

As shown in Figure 11.8, Internet Explorer will display these two tables differently. As you can see here, now it is mainly an aesthetic difference.

Listing 11.7 Table Example: Empty Cells

```
<HTML>
<HEAD>
<TITLE>Table Example: Empty Cells</TITLE>
</HEAD>
<BODY>
<TABLE BORDER>
  <TR><TD>Amaranth</TD><TD>  </TD><TD>Buckwheat</TD></TR>
  <TR><TD>Barley  </TD><TD>Rye  </TD><TD></TD></TR>
  <TR><TD>Quinoa  </TD><TD>Wheat</TD><TD></TD></TR>
</TABLE>
<HR>
<TABLE BORDER>
  <TR><TD>Amaranth</TD><TD> </TD><TD>Buckwheat</TD></TR>
  <TR><TD>Barley  </TD><TD>Rye  </TD><TD>  </TD></TR>
  <TR><TD>Quinoa  </TD><TD>Wheat</TD><TD>  </TD></TR>
</TABLE>
<BODY>
<HTML>
```

Controlling Table Layout

HTML introduces several attributes that you can use to increase the degree of control you have over how tables are displayed. These attributes were once Netscape enhancements, supported by Internet Explorer, but are now a part of the HTML standard. Listing 11.8 shows the HTML document for these attributes, which are rendered by Internet Explorer in Figure 11.9.

FIG. 11.8
Netscape Navigator will display tables with empty cells differently from those that contain invisible characters.

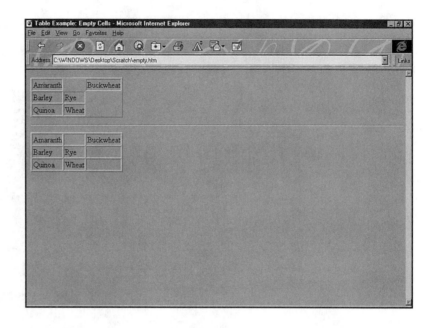

Listing 11.8   Formatting Example

```html
<HTML>
<HEAD>
<TITLE>Formatting Example></TITLE>
</HEAD>
<BODY>
<TABLE BORDER=10 CELLPADDING=10 CELLSPACING=10 WIDTH=100%>
  <TR>
<TD>Width 100%</TD>
<TD>Border<BR>CellPadding = 10<BR>CellSpacing</TD>
  </TR>
  <TR>
<TD>
<TABLE BORDER=5 CELLPADDING=5 CELLSPACING=5 WIDTH=75%>
<TR>
<TD>Width 75%</TD>
<TD>Border<BR>CellPadding = 5<BR>CellSpacing</TD>
</TR>
</TABLE>
</TD>
<TD>Have a nice day!</TD>
  </TR>
</TABLE>
<BODY>
</HTML>
```

FIG. 11.9

HTML gives you complete control over the appearance of HTML tables.

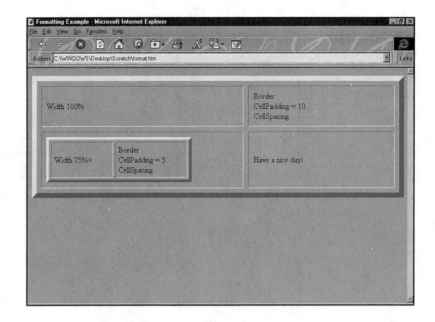

The attributes shown in Figure 11.9 are as follows:

- **WIDTH attribute**—This enables you to specify the width of the table, either in pixels or as a percentage of the width of the browser window. You can also use this attribute with individual cells.

- **HEIGHT attribute**—This enables you to specify the height of the table, either in pixels or as a percentage of the height of the browser window. You can also use this attribute with individual cells.

- **BORDER attribute**—This attribute puts a border around the table. You specify the width of the border in pixels, like this: BORDER=2.

- **CELLPADDING and CELLSPACING attributes**—These numerical attributes include extra space within each cell in the table and/or within the borders of the table. If the border is not being displayed, they are equivalent.

Using Color in Tables

HTML makes no provision for setting a table or cell's color. However, both Netscape and Internet Explorer provide extensions that let you change the color of cells and borders. You use the BGCOLOR attribute to change the color of a cell's background, before any text or images are placed into the cell. You use the BORDERCOLOR attribute to change the color of the border around the cell. Both Netscape and Internet Explorer support these attributes.

The <TABLE>, <TD>, <TH>, and <TR> tags all support BGCOLOR and BORDERCOLOR attributes. Thus, you can apply colors to the entire table, an individual cell, or an individual row of the table. The example in Listing 11.9 shows you the HTML for three tables, which show you an example of each case. Figure 11.10 shows you how these tables are rendered in Internet Explorer.

Listing 11.9 Formatting Example

```
<HTML>
<HEAD>
<TITLE>Foramtting Example</TITLE>
<HEAD>
<BODY>
<TABLE BORDER BORDERCOLOR=BLACK BGCOLOR=WHITE>
   <TR><TD>1-one</TD><TD>2-two</TD><TD>3-three</TD></TR>
   <TR><TD>4-four</TD><TD>5-five</TD><TD>6-six</TD></TR>
   <TR><TD>7-seven</TD><TD>8-eight</TD><TD>9-nine</TD></TR>
</TABLE>
Changing the entire table's color
<HR>
<TABLE BORDER>
   <TR BORDERCOLOR=BLACK BGCOLOR=WHITE><TD>1-one</TD>
<TD>2-two</TD><TD>3-three</TD></TR>
   <TR><TD>4-four</TD><TD>5-five</TD><TD>6-six</TD></TR>
   <TR><TD>7-seven</TD><TD>8-eight</TD><TD>9-nine</TD></TR>
</TABLE>
Changing a single row's color
<HR>
<TABLE BORDER>
   <TR><TD BORDERCOLOR=BLACK BGCOLOR=WHITE>1-one</TD><TD>2-two</TD>
<TD>3-three</TD></TR>
   <TR><TD>4-four</TD><TD>5-five</TD><TD>6-six</TD></TR>
   <TR><TD>7-seven</TD><TD>8-eight</TD><TD>9-nine</TD></TR>
</TABLE>
Changing a single cell's color
</BODY>
</HTML>
```

Part

II

Ch

11

FIG. 11.10

Changing the color of a cell without changing the color of the surrounding border looks very odd.

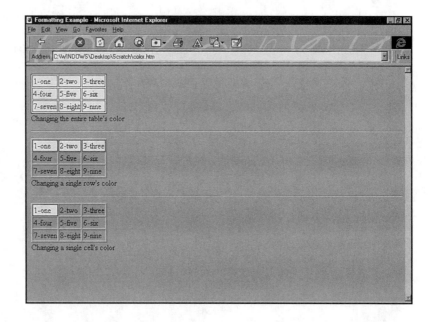

NOTE HTML defines the following color names. For your convenience, you'll also find the equivalent hexadecimal RGB values next to each color.

BLACK	#000000
SILVER	#C0C0C0
GRAY	#808080
WHITE	#FFFFFF
MAROON	#800000
RED	#FF0000
PURPLE	#800080
FUCHSIA	#FF00FF
GREEN	#008000
LIME	#00FF00
OLIVE	#808000
YELLOW	#FFFF00
NAVY	#000080
BLUE	#0000FF
TEAL	#008080
AQUA	#00FFFF ■

Using a Table Alternative

Table support has become widespread with most of the popular Web browsers, so there is less reason to avoid using tables. Still, there are folks out on the Web, either because of their Internet service provider or because of the type of connection to the Internet they have, who are forced to use Web browsers that do not have table support. If you are worried about missing such people, there are some alternatives that you can use, either instead of or in addition to using tables themselves.

Listing 11.10 shows an HTML document for a fairly simple table shown in Figure 11.11.

Listing 11.10 Row and Column Spanning

```
<HTML>
<HEAD>
<TITLE>Row and Column Spanning</TITLE>
</HEAD>
<BODY>
<TABLE BORDER>
  <TR><TH COLSPAN=3>DC nationals</TH><TR>
  <TR><TH>Offense</TH><TH>Defense</TH><TH>Goalie</TH></TR>
  <TR>
<TD>Husmann</TD><TD>O'Donnell</TD>
```

```
<TD VALIGN=TOP ROWSPAN=5>Weinberg</TD>
  </TR>
  <TR>
<TD COLSPAN=2>Popplewell</TD>
  </TR>
  <TR>
<TD>McGilly</TD><TD>Longo</TD>
  </TR>
  <TR>
<TD>Donahue</TD><TD>Seymour</TD>
  </TR>
  <TR>
<TD>Camillo</TD><TD>Walsh</TD>
  </TR>
</TABLE>
</BODY>
<HTML>
```

FIG. 11.11
A sample table showing a fairly straightforward organization of information.

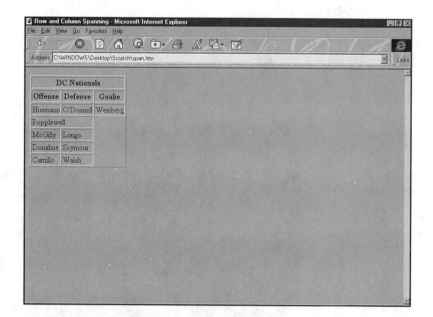

Part
II

Ch
11

Some other ways of displaying this information, not using tables, are as follows:

- Use a list. Information that is relatively straightforward can be displayed instead as a list. This information can be displayed just as well as a list, as coded in Listing 11.11 and rendered by Internet Explorer in Figure 11.12.

Listing 11.11   Row and Column Spanning

```
<HTML>
<HEAD>
<TITLE>Row and Column Spanning</TITLE>
```

continues

Listing 11.11 Continued

```
</HEAD>
<BODY>
  <STRONG>DC Nationals</STRONG>
  <UL>
<LI><EM>Offense</EM>
<UL>
<LI>Husmann
<LI>Popplewell
<LI>McGilly
<LI>Donahue
<LI>Camillo
</UL>
<LI><EM>Defense</EM>
<UL>
<LI>O'Donnell
<LI>Popplewell
<LI>Longo
<LI>Seymour
<LI>Walsh
</UL>
<LI><EM>Goalie</EM>
<UL>
<LI>Weinberg
</UL>
  <UL>
<BODY>
</HTML>
```

FIG. 11.12

Because support for lists is more widespread than for tables, using lists can sometimes be a good alternative.

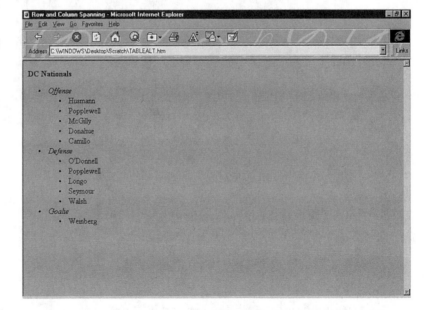

■ Use an image instead. By creating the table in a word processor, or even in your own copy of a Web browser such as Netscape Navigator, and then taking a screen shot and cropping it down to the size of the displayed table, you can include the table in your HTML document as an image. This may not be the best alternative, however, as Web browsers that do not support tables may not support images either.

▶ **See** "Adding Lists to a Web Page Displaying Text in Lists," **p. 143**

■ Use preformatted text. This will give you a table that is aesthetically unappealing, but it has the advantage of being displayed correctly in just about every Web browser, including text-only browsers such as Lynx. An example of this is shown in Listing 11.12 and Figure 11.13.

Listing 11.12   Row and Column Spanning

```
<HTML>
<HEAD>
<TITLE>row and Column Spanning</TITLE>
</HEAD>
<BODY>
<PRE>
+ — — — — — — —+— — — — — — — — — —+— — — — — — —+
¦ Offense  ¦ Defense¦ Goalie  ¦
+ — — — — — — —+— — — — — — — — — —+— — — — — — —+
¦ Husmann  ¦ O'Donnell ¦¦
¦ Popplewell  ¦¦
¦ McGilly  ¦ Longo  ¦ Weinberg¦
¦ Donahue  ¦ Seymour¦¦
¦ Camillo  ¦ Walsh  ¦¦
+ — — — — — — —+— — — — — — — — — —+— — — — — — —+
</PRE>
</BODY>
</HTML>
```

Table Examples

The use of tables to display tabular information is, by definition, pretty obvious. Tables can also come in handy when using HTML forms, as they give you the capability to create a very well-organized form for entering information. Tables can be used in other ways as well, as mentioned briefly earlier. Because they give you the ability to group text and graphics in many different ways, they can be used to enhance the way a page is displayed.

Using Tables as a Layout Tool

Consider the HTML document shown in Listing 11.13. This document includes graphics and text information, and is meant to display it as a sort-of business card. This document is shown, as rendered by Internet Explorer, in Figure 11.14.

FIG. 11.13

A preformatted table isn't very pretty, but it will be displayed correctly in just about any Web browser.

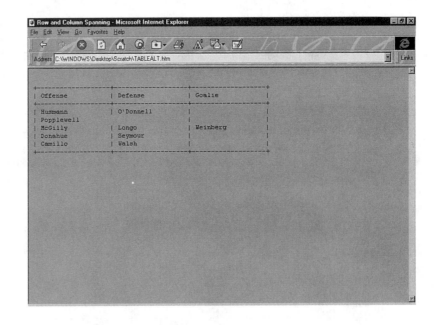

Listing 11.13   Using Tables to Display Information

```
<HTML>
<HEAD>
<TITLE>Using Tables to Display Information</TITLE>
</HEAD>
<BODY>
<TABLE>
  <TR>
<TD ROWSPAN=4 VALIGN=BOTTOM><IMG SRC="init.gif"><TD>
<TH VALIGN=TOP>Jerry Honeycutt</TH>
  </TR>
  <TR>
<TD VALIGN=TOP><EM><Books:</EM><BR>
Using the Internet with Windows 95<BR>
Windows 95 Registry and Customization Handbook<BR>
Special Edition Using the Windows 95 Registry<BR>
VBScript by Example<BR>
Using the Internet 2E<BR>
Special Edition Using the Internet 3E<BR>
</TD>
  </TR>
  <TR><HR></TR>
  <TR>
<TD ALIGN=CENTER VALIGN=BOTTOM>Send e-mail to <EM>
jerry@honeycutt.com</EM></TD>
  </TR>
</TABLE>
<BODY>
</HTML>
```

FIG. 11.14
Though at first glance this does not look like a "table," the use of an HTML table to organize the information has made the display more effective.

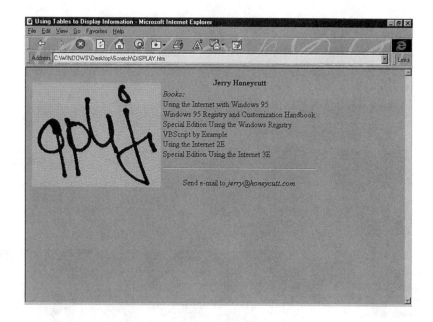

Combining Text and Lists

To refine this Web page further, some of the information presented within it can be displayed differently—in this case, by using an HTML list (an unordered list, but any other kind of list could be used just as easily). The HTML code for this is shown in Listing 11.14; it makes sense to group lists of data by using HTML list elements, and the ability to include these within a table allows the information to be conveyed more clearly. The revised Web page is shown in Figure 11.15.

Listing 11.14   Using Tables to Display Information

```
<HTML>
<HEAD>
<TITLE>Using Tables to Display Information</TITLE>
</HEAD>
<BODY>
<TABLE>
   <TR>
<TD ROWSPAN=4 VALIGN=BOTTOM><IMG SRC="init.gif"><TD>
<TH VALIGN=TOP>Jerry Honeycutt</TH>
   </TR>
   <TR>
<TD VALIGN=TOP><EM><Books:</EM><BR>
<UL>
<LI>Using the Internet with Windows 95
<LI>Windows 95 Registry and Customization Handbook
<LI>Special Edition Using the Windows 95 Registry
```

continues

Listing 11.14   Continued

```
<LI>VBScript by Example
<LI>Using the Internet 2E
<LI>Special Edition Using the Internet 3E
</UL>
</TD>
   </TR>
   <TR><HR></TR>
   <TR>
<TD ALIGN=CENTER VALIGN=BOTTOM>Send e-mail to <EM>
jerry@honeycutt.com</EM></TD>
   </TR>
</TABLE>
<BODY>
</HTML>
```

FIG. 11.15
Combining lists and tables gives you powerful means for organizing and displaying information within your Web pages.

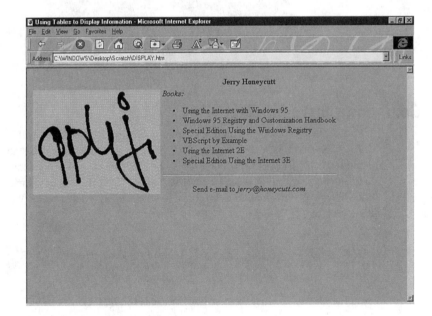

Nesting HTML Tables

Another way to display this information is to use tables within a larger table. The list items are composed of both a team name and a year (or range of years). Couldn't this information also be displayed in a table? In HTML, you can nest tables within other tables.

Listing 11.15 shows the HTML code for the business-card Web page using nested tables. It is displayed in Figure 11.16. Notice the nested tables are displayed with borders (and with cell spacing and padding reduced to make them more compact), while the outer table used to structure the whole page is not.

Listing 11.15   Using Tables to Display Information

```
<HTML>
<HEAD>
<TITLE>Using Tables to Display Information</TITLE>
</HEAD>
<BODY>
<TABLE>
  <TR>
<TD ROWSPAN=4 VALIGN=BOTTOM><IMG SRC="init.gif"><TD>
<TH VALIGN=TOP>Jerry Honeycutt</TH>
  </TR>
  <TR>
<TD VALIGN=TOP><EM><Books:</EM><BR>
<TABLE BORDER CELLSPACING=1 CELLPADDING=1>
<TR><TH>Book</TH><TH>Year</TH><TR>
<TR><TD>Using the Internet with Windows 95</TD>
<TD>1995</TD></TR>
<TR><TD>Windows 95 Registry and Customization Handbook
</TD><TD>1996</TD></TR>
<TR><TD>Special Edition Using the Windows 95 Registry
</TD><TD>1996</TD></TR>
<TR><TD>VBScript by Example</TD><TD>1996</TD></TR>
<TR><TD>Using the Internet 2E</TD><TD>1996</TD></TR>
<TR><TD>Special Edition Using the Internet 3E</TD>
<TD>1996</TD></TR>
</TABLE>
</TD>
  </TR>
  <TR><HR></TR>
  <TR>
<TD ALIGN=CENTER VALIGN=BOTTOM>Send e-mail to <EM>jerry@honeycutt.com
</EM></TD>
  </TR>
</TABLE>
<BODY>
</HTML>
```

Using an Image as a Table Header

You can easily spruce up a table by using an image as the table's header. That is, instead of displaying a plain-text heading for the table, create a snazzy image and use that instead. Listing 11.16 shows you the HTML for such a table, and Figure 11.17 shows you this table rendered in Internet Explorer. There are a couple of things you should note about this example:

- The width of the table is specified to be exactly the width of the image by using the WIDTH attribute, like this: <TABLE WIDTH=500>.

- In the <TABLE> tag, CELLSPACING is set to 0 in order to make sure the image lines up with the table correctly.

- The table heading is spanned across all columns in order to accommodate the image. In this case, the tag <TH COLSPAN=2> spans across the top two columns of the table.

Part

II

Ch

11

■ The <IMG> tag is used to insert the image into the spanned columns. Note that the border is disabled by using BORDER=0 and the height and width are set to the exact dimensions of the image by using the HEIGHT and WIDTH attributes.

FIG. 11.16
Nested tables are another way to organize information effectively within a Web page.

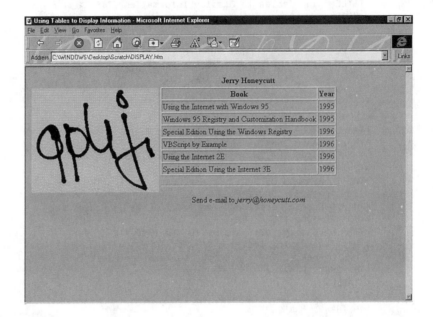

Listing 11.16   Pictures in Headings

```
<HTML>
<HEAD>
<TITLE>Pictures in Headings</TITLE>
</HEAD>
<BODY BGCOLOR=WHITE>
<TABLE WIDTH=500 CELLSPACING=0 CELLPADDING=2 BORDER=0>
  <TR>
<TH COLSPAN=2>
<IMG SRC="head.gif" BORDER=0 HEIGHT=25 WIDTH=500>
</TH>
  </TR>
  <TR>
<TD VALIGN=TOP>
<IMG SRC="internet.gif">
</TD>
<TD VALIGN=TOP>
This book will show you how to get the most out of the
Internet. You won't find intimidating, technical language
here. You'll find no-nonsense instructions for using e-mail,
Usenet, FTP, and the World Wide Web. You'll also learn how
to find your way around the World Wide Web, read the Usenet
newsgroups, and more.
```

```
    </TD>
      </TR>
    </TABLE>
    </BODY>
    </HTML>
```

FIG. 11.17
When using an image for a table heading, use your favorite paint program to fade the image before adding headings.

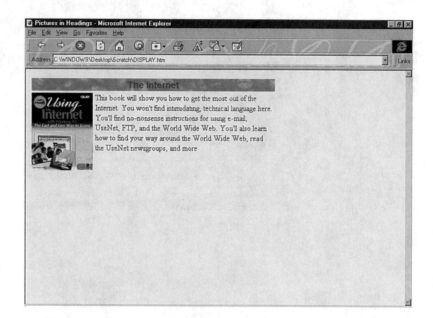

Using a Table to Lay Out a Home Page

Figure 11.18 shows you an example of a home page that uses tables extensively for layout purposes. This happens to be Microsoft's home page. Note that the toolbar at the top of the page is actually defined as a table. As well, each layout region on this page is actually a cell within the table.

Part
II

Ch
11

FIG. 11.18

Use tables to split an HTML document into individual regions in which you put your elements.

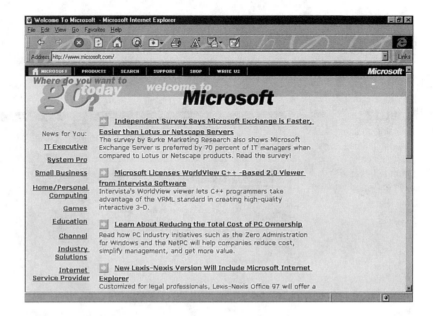

## CHAPTER 12

Framing Your Web Site

by Mark R. Brown

In this chapter

The Frames Concept

First introduced in Netscape Navigator 2.0, HTML frames create independently changeable and (sometimes) scrollable windows that tile together to break up and organize a display so that it's not only more visually appealing, but easier to work with.

Frames are similar in many ways to HTML tables. If you understand how tables work, you'll have a jump start on how to work with frames. If you want to check out how tables work before starting with frames, see Chapter 11, "Formatting Content with Tables."

However, unlike tables, frames not only organize data, they organize your browser's display window. In fact, they break up the window into individual, independent panes or frames. Each frame holds its own HTML file as content, and the content of each frame can be scrolled or changed independently of the others. In a way, it's almost as though each frame becomes its own mini-browser.

Perhaps the best way to get a feel for what you can do with frames is to look at a few real-world examples.

Netscape's DevEdge Site

As you might expect, Netscape—the inventor of frames—has some excellent examples of frames on its Web sites. Figure 12.1 is taken from Netscape's DevEdge developer's site and shows a window that is broken into four separate frames.

FIG. 12.1

Netscape's DevEdge site at **http://developer. netscape.com** showcases excellent examples of using frames to separate information from navigation.

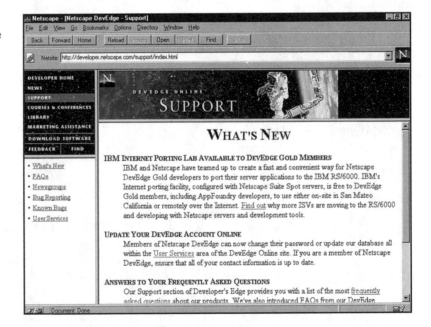

The frames on this page show how Netscape has split information display into the two frames on the right, while reserving navigation functions for the two frames on the left.

The top-right frame—which occupies about 80 percent of the width of the screen, but only about 20 percent of its height—holds a title graphic, which serves as a landmark to help you remember where you are. This is an important function, as HTML documents created using frames can get very complex very quickly. Road signs like the header graphic in this frame can help you get your bearings.

The top-left frame—which takes up about 20 percent of the horizontal real estate and approximately 30 percent of the screen height—contains a top-level navigation menu, which stays in place wherever you go on the DevEdge site. Making a selection from this menu moves you to a new information category, such as the support area or library. This graphic menu also serves as a placeholder, because it shows the currently selected area as highlighted.

The bottom-left frame—about 20 percent of the screen width and 70 percent of its height—is a list of text-based hyperlinks that make up the information menu for the currently selected category. A new text menu is displayed in this frame whenever the user selects a new category from the graphic category menu in the frame above it.

 Netscape has saved itself a great deal of time and development work by making only the category-level menus graphic, while using easier-to-create, text-only lists of links for the more numerous subcategory menus.

Finally, the bottom-right frame—which occupies the majority of the screen area, about 80 percent of its width and 70 percent of its height—contains all of the actual information displayed on this site. The information in this window is selected from the category-specific text link menu in the frame to its left.

This site can definitely serve as a template for good frames-based HTML document design for any information that is hierarchically organized by category.

The CyberDungeon

Frames aren't just for business documents. Take a look at Figure 12.2, which depicts the online CyberDungeon adventure game at **http://www.cyberdungeon.com**.

You will probably never find 10 frames used as gracefully as those on this site. (Usually it's bad practice to use more than four to six frames at a time.) This artfully done Web site anticipates the recent mantra of both Microsoft and Netscape, who are now encouraging developers to use HTML to create graphical user interfaces for application programming.

The CyberDungeon site uses a set of frames down the left side of the screen to hold graphical icons of objects you (the resident adventurer) pick up in your explorations. The top frame of the center set of three displays the text description of your current location, while the larger frame below it shows a picture of the same scene. The bottom frame gives you choices to make along the way.

FIG. 12.2
The CyberDungeon game uses a set of 10 frames to create a familiar and friendly adventure game interface.

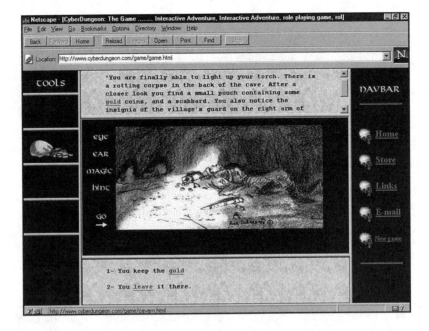

Finally, the tall, right frame keeps the CyberDungeon site's navigational menu handy as you play.

This site provides a wonderful example of how a well-designed HTML document using frames can replicate applications that previously had to be written in high-level languages like C or C++.

The Mondrian Machine

A final example is a wonderful lampoon of the too-ambitious use of frames. The Mondrian Machine site (**http://www.desires.com/2.1/Toys/Mondrian/mond-fr.html**) takes the overuse of frames—normally an ugly and heinous practice—and turns it into an art form. See Figure 12.3.

Clicking a selection in the table shown in Figure 12.3 brings up one of several different Mondrian Machines. Each, in its own unique way, creates an HTML document composed of a wild collection of frames that rapidly take over the entire screen. Each frame has no content except a background color, so the end effect is that of a painting by Mondrian, who became famous for dividing his canvases into so many colored rectangles.

The effect, though humorous and somehow compelling, shows just how much trouble you can get into if you overdo the use of frames on your own pages.

That warning having been sounded, you'll now see how frames are created.

FIG. 12.3

The Mondrian Machine serves as both a fun Web toy and a graphic illustration of what can happen if you go too crazy with frames!

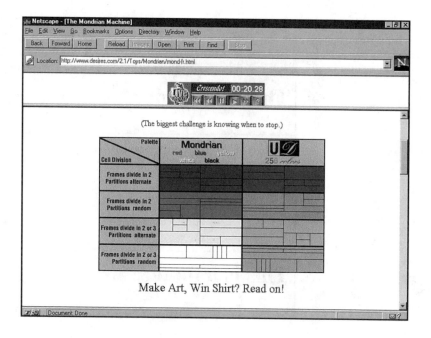

Frame Creation Basics

Diving in head first, take a look at an entire block of HTML markup code that creates a frame document of medium complexity:

```
<HTML>
<HEAD>
</HEAD>
<FRAMESET ROWS="25%,50%,25%">
      <FRAME SRC="header.htm">
      <FRAMESET COLS="25%,75%">
            <FRAME SRC="label.htm">
            <FRAME SRC="info.htm">
      </FRAMESET>
      <FRAME SRC="footer.htm">
</FRAMESET>
<NOFRAMES>
Your browser cannot display frames.
</NOFRAMES>
</HTML>
```

This example (Frames1.HTM) produces the frames page shown in Figure 12.4. As you can see, this HTML code produces four frames. The top frame spans the page and includes a header. There are two central frames, one for a label on the left, which takes up 25 percent of the screen width, and one for information on the right, which takes up the remaining space. Another frame fills the entire width of the bottom of the screen and contains a footer.

Part

II

Ch

12

FIG. 12.4

This is the frame document produced by the preceding HTML code, as displayed by Netscape.

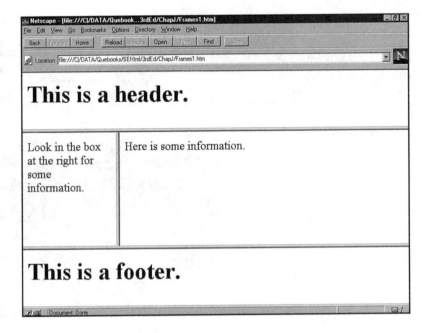

Though you won't get into the details for a couple more pages, it's important to note that this document calls four other HTML documents—header.HTM, label.HTM, info.HTM, and footer.HTM—containing the actual information displayed in each of the individual frames.

The *FRAMESET* Container

Frames are contained in a structure called a FRAMESET, which takes the place of the BODY container on a frames-formatted page. An HTML document that contains a FRAMESET definition has no BODY section in its HTML code, and a page with a BODY section cannot use the <FRAMESET> tag.

> **CAUTION**
>
> If you define a BODY section for a page that you compose with FRAMESET and FRAME commands, the frame structure is completely ignored by browser programs and none of the content contained in the frames is displayed. Instead, you only see the content contained in the BODY section.
>
> Because there is no BODY container, FRAMESET pages can't have background images and background colors associated with them. (Remember, these are defined by the BACKGROUND and BGCOLOR attributes of the BODY tag, respectively.) However, the HTML files that contain the content for the individual frames can use background colors and images, since they do use the <BODY> tag.
>
> Make sure you don't accidentally use BODY and FRAMESET within the same HTML document.

N O T E There is a proposal before the HTML standards body to implement a new type of frame container called an IFRAME, or inline frame. (It is currently implemented only in the Microsoft Internet Explorer 4.0 browser and FrontPage 98 page composition programs.) This container defines a named box inside the BODY of a regular HTML page (not a frameset). An IFRAME would float and be positionable within a page just like a graphic or other object, but its content could be changed by clicking links, like a frame. Here's an example of how it would look:

```
<HTML>

<HEAD><TITLE>IFRAME Example</TITLE></HEAD>

<BODY>

Here's an inline frame <IFRAME name="iframe" width=400 height=500></IFRAME>
which can display either of two text files:

<A target="iframe" href="HiThere.htm">Hi There!</A>

<A target="iframe" href="Hello.htm">Hello.</A>

</BODY>

</HTML>
```

Clicking the "Hi There." link would display the HiThere.HTM file in the inline frame; clicking the "Hello." link would display Hello.HTM instead, all without reloading the whole page. ■

The <FRAMESET></FRAMESET> container surrounds each block of frame definitions. Within the FRAMESET container you can only have FRAME tags or nested FRAMESET containers.

Defining *ROWS* and *COLS*

The <FRAMESET> tag has two major attributes: ROWS and COLS (columns). Here's a fully decked-out (but empty), generic FRAMESET container:

```
<FRAMESET ROWS="value_list" COLS="value_list">
</FRAMESET>
```

You can define any reasonable number of ROWS or COLS, or both, but you have to define something for at least one of them.

CAUTION

If you don't define more than one row or column, browser programs ignore your FRAMES completely. Your screen is left totally blank. In other words, you can't have a FRAMESET of just one row and one column—which would just be a single window, anyway. If you've defined at least two of either ROWS or COLS, however, you can safely omit the other attribute, and a value of 100 percent is assumed for it.

The value_list in your generic FRAMESET line is a comma-separated list of values that can be expressed as pixels, percentages, or relative scale values. The number of rows or columns is set by the number of values in their respective value lists. For example,

```
<FRAMESET ROWS="100,240,140">
```

Part
II

Ch
12

defines a frameset with three rows. These values are in absolute number of pixels. In other words, the first row is 100 pixels high, the second is 240 pixels high, and the last is 140 pixels high.

Setting row and column height by absolute number of pixels is bad practice, however. It doesn't allow for the fact that browsers run on all kinds of systems on all sizes of screens. While you might want to define absolute pixel values for a few limited uses—such as displaying a small image of known dimensions—it is usually a better practice to define your rows and columns using percentage or relative values, like this:

```
<FRAMESET ROWS="25%,50%,25%">
```

This example would create three frames arranged as rows, the top row taking up 25 percent of the available screen height, the middle row 50 percent, and the bottom row 25 percent.

TIP Don't worry about having to do the math just right—if the percentages you give for the ROWS or COLS attribute don't add up to 100 percent, they will be scaled up or down proportionally to equal 100 percent.

Proportional values look like this:

```
<FRAMESET COLS="*, 2*, 3*">
```

The asterisk (*) is used to define a proportional division of space. Each asterisk represents one piece of the overall pie. You get the denominator of the fraction by adding up all the asterisk values (if there is no number specified, 1 is assumed). In this example, with an overall pie that has six slices, the first column would get 1/6 of the total width of the window, the second column would get 2/6 (or 1/3), and the final column would get 3/6 (or 1/2).

Remember that bare numeric values assign an absolute number of pixels to a row or column, values with a percent symbol assign a percentage of the total width (for COLS) or height (for ROWS) of the display window, and values with an asterisk assign a proportional amount of the remaining space.

Here's an example using all three in a single definition:

```
<FRAMESET COLS="100, 25%, *, 2*">
```

This example assigns the first column an absolute width of 100 pixels. The second column gets 25 percent of the width of the entire display window, whatever that is. The third column gets 1/3 of what's left, and the final column gets the other 2/3.

So what are the space-allocation priorities? Absolute pixel values are always assigned space first, in order from left to right. These are followed by percentage values of the total space. Finally, proportional values are divided based upon what space is left.

CAUTION

Remember, if you do use absolute pixel values in a COLS or ROWS definition, keep them small so you are sure they'll fit in any browser window, and balance them with at least one percentage or relative definition to fill the remainder of the space gracefully.

If you use a `FRAMESET` with both `COLS` and `ROWS` attributes, it creates a grid of frames. Here's an example:

```
<FRAMESET ROWS="*, 2*, *" COLS="2*, *">
```

This line of HTML creates a frame grid with three rows and two columns. The first and last rows each take up 1/4 of the screen height, and the middle row takes up half. The first column is 2/3 as wide as the screen, and the second is 1/3 the width.

`<FRAMESET></FRAMESET>` sections can be nested inside one another, as shown in your initial example, but don't get ahead of yourself. You need to look at the `<FRAME>` tag first.

The *<FRAME>* Tag

The `<FRAME>` tag defines a single frame. It must sit inside a `FRAMESET` container, like this:

```
<FRAMESET ROWS="*, 2*">
<FRAME>
<FRAME>
</FRAMESET>
```

Note that the `<FRAME>` tag is not a container so, unlike `FRAMESET`, it has no matching end tag. An entire `FRAME` definition takes place within a single line of HTML code.

You should have as many `<FRAME>` tags as there are spaces defined for them in the `FRAMESET` definition. In this example, the `FRAMESET` established two rows, so you needed two `<FRAME>` tags. However, this example is very, very boring, since neither of your frames has anything in it! (Frames like these are displayed as blank space.)

The `<FRAME>` tag has six associated attributes: `SRC`, `NAME`, `MARGINWIDTH`, `MARGINHEIGHT`, `SCROLLING`, and `NORESIZE`. Here's a complete generic `FRAME`:

```
<FRAME SRC="url" NAME="window_name" SCROLLING=YES|NO|AUTO MARGINWIDTH="value"
MARGINHEIGHT="value" NORESIZE>
```

Fortunately, frames hardly ever actually use all of these options.

Going to the Source

The most important `FRAME` attribute is `SRC` (source). You can (and quite often, do) have a complete `FRAME` definition using nothing but the `SRC` attribute, like this:

```
<FRAME SRC="url">
```

`SRC` defines the frame content's URL. This is usually an HTML format file on the same system (paths are relative to the page containing the `FRAMESET`), so it usually looks something like:

```
<FRAME SRC="sample.htm">
```

Note that any HTML file called by the `SRC` attribute in a `FRAME` definition must be a complete HTML document, not a fragment. This means it must have `HTML`, `HEAD`, and `BODY` containers, and so on. For example, the file called by the `SRC` attribute in this example, sample.HTM, might look like this:

```
<HTML>
<HEAD>
<TITLE>
</TITLE>
</HEAD>
<BODY>
This is some Sample Text.
</BODY>
</HTML>
```

Of course, SRC can point to any valid URL. If, for example, you wanted your frame to display a GIF image that was located somewhere in Timbuktu, your FRAME might look like this:

```
<FRAME SRC="http://www.timbuktu.com/budda.gif">
```

If you specify an URL the browser can't find, space is allocated for the frame, but it won't be displayed and you get a nasty error message from your browser. Note the effect is quite different than simply specifying a FRAME with no SRC at all. <FRAME> is always created, but left blank; <FRAME SRC="unknown URL"> is not created at all—the space is allocated and left completely empty. The former fills with background color, while the latter remains the browser's border color.

> **CAUTION**
>
> Plain text, headers, graphics, and other elements cannot be used directly in a FRAME document. All the content must come from the URL defined by the SRC attribute of the <FRAME> tags. If any other content appears on a FRAMESET page, it is displayed and the entire set of frames is ignored.

Providing Alternate Content

"All of this is well and good," you say, "and I really, really want to use frames in my HTML documents. But I can't help feeling guilty about all those users who don't have frames-capable browsers. They won't be able to see my beautiful pages!"

Don't worry. Here's where you can provide for them, too.

The <NOFRAMES></NOFRAMES> container saves the day. By defining a NOFRAMES section and marking it up with normal HTML tags, you can provide alternate information for those without frames-capable browsers. This is how it works:

```
<NOFRAMES>
All your alternate HTML goes here.
</NOFRAMES>
```

You can safely think of this as an alternative to the BODY structure of a normal HTML page. Whatever you place between the <NOFRAMES> and </NOFRAMES> tags appears on browsers without frames capability. Browsers with frames throw away everything between these two tags.

N O T E If you want to include background graphics or images, you can add the <BODY> tag to your alternate content like this:

```
<NOFRAMES>
<BODY BGCOLOR="red" BACKGROUND="bgimage.gif">
content…
</BODY>
</NOFRAMES
```

As long as the BODY container is kept within the bounds of the NOFRAMES container, your document works just fine. But there's no need to use the <BODY> tag within the NOFRAMES container unless you want to take advantage of its special attributes. ▨

A Few Simple Frame Examples

Frames are very flexible, which means they can become complicated quickly. Now that you understand the basics, take a look at a few frame examples so you can get your bearings.

A Simple Page with Two Frames

The simplest possible frame setup is one with two frames, like this:

```
<HTML>
<HEAD>
</HEAD>
<FRAMESET COLS="*, 2*">
      <FRAME SRC="label.htm">
      <FRAME SRC="info.htm">
</FRAMESET>
</HTML>
```

This HTML code (2Frames.HTM) defines a page with two frames, organized as two columns. The first column takes up 1/3 of the width of the screen and contains the HTML document label.HTM, and the second takes up the other 2/3 and contains the document info.HTM. Figure 12.5 shows how Netscape Navigator displays this page.

Part II

Ch 12

You could just as easily create 10 or more columns, or use the same syntax, substituting the ROWS attribute to create 2 (or 10) rows. However, 10 columns or rows is way too many for any browser to handle gracefully. Your pages should probably never have more than three or four rows or columns.

N O T E If you want to display more information than three or four rows or columns, you should probably be using tables rather than frames. Remember, frames are most useful when you want to add an element of control in addition to formatting the display, or if you need to update displayed data dynamically. Tables are best if all you want to do is format static data into rows and columns.

Too many frames can actually crash your browser. For a real-world example (if you don't mind your browser program crashing) check out **http://www.newdream.net/crash/** (see Figure 12.6). ▨

FIG. 12.5

Netscape displays the simple two-column FRAMESET defined by the HTML code above.

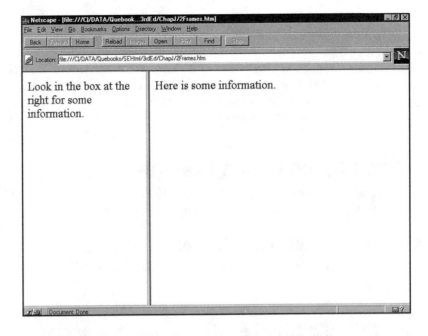

FIG. 12.6

This Web site sets out to deliberately crash your browser by creating too many frames—and succeeds! Don't cause the same problem for your viewers.

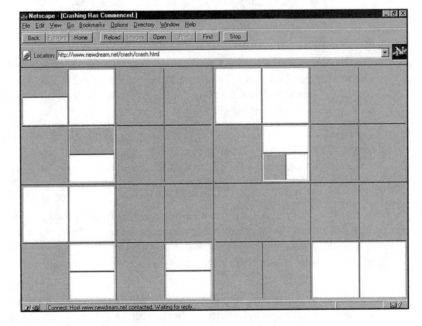

A Simple Rectangular Grid of Frames

A regular rectangular grid of rows and columns is just about as easy to implement as a rows-only or columns-only arrangement:

```
<HTML>
<HEAD>
</HEAD>
<FRAMESET ROWS="*, 2*" COLS="20%, 30%, 40%">
        <FRAME SRC="labela.htm">
        <FRAME SRC="labelb.htm">
        <FRAME SRC="labelc.htm">
        <FRAME SRC="infoa.htm">
        <FRAME SRC="infob.htm">
        <FRAME SRC="infoc.htm">
</FRAMESET>
</HTML>
```

This example (2by3Grid.HTM) creates a grid with two rows and three columns (see Figure 12.7). Because you defined a set of six frames, you've provided six FRAME definitions. Note that they fill in by rows. That is, the first FRAME goes in the first defined column in the first row, the second frame follows across in the second column, and the third finishes out the last column in the first row. The last three frames then fill in the columns of the second row going across.

Also, note that the math didn't work out very well, since the percentage values in the COLS definition only add up to 90 percent. No problem, because the browser has adjusted all the columns proportionally to make up the difference.

FIG. 12.7

This two-by-three grid of frames was created by the preceding HTML example.

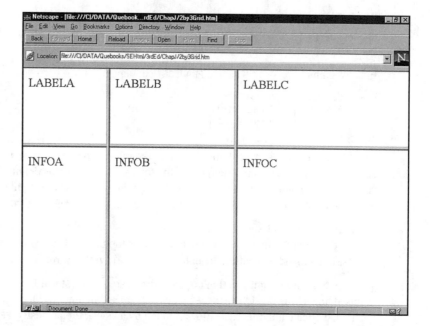

Part
II

Ch
12

Creating a Complex Grid of Frames

A bit tougher is the problem of creating a more complex grid of frames. For that, return to the example that opened this discussion (see Figure 12.4):

```
<HTML>
<HEAD>
</HEAD>
<FRAMESET ROWS="25%,50%,25%">
        <FRAME SRC="header.htm">
        <FRAMESET COLS="25%,75%">
        <FRAME SRC="label.htm">
        <FRAME SRC="info.htm">
        </FRAMESET>
        <FRAME SRC="footer.htm">
</FRAMESET>
<NOFRAMES>
Your browser cannot display frames.
</NOFRAMES>
</HTML>
```

This example (Frames1.HTM) makes use of nested FRAMESET containers. The outside set creates three rows, with 25 percent, 50 percent, and 25 percent of the window height, respectively:

```
<FRAMESET ROWS="25%,50%,25%">
```

Within this definition, the first and last rows are simple frames:

```
<FRAME SRC="header.htm">
<FRAME SRC="footer.htm">
```

Each of these rows runs the entire width of the screen. The first row at the top of the screen takes up 25 percent of the screen height, and the third row at the bottom of the screen also takes up 25 percent of the screen height.

In between however, is this nested FRAMESET container:

```
<FRAMESET COLS="25%,75%">
        <FRAME SRC="label.htm">
        <FRAME SRC="info.htm">
</FRAMESET>
```

This FRAMESET defines two columns that split the middle row of the screen. The row these two columns reside in takes up 50 percent of the total screen height, as defined in the middle row value for the outside FRAMESET container. The left column uses 25 percent of the screen width, while the right column occupies the other 75 percent of the screen width.

The frames for the columns are defined within the set of FRAMESET tags, which include the column definitions, while the frame definitions for the first and last rows are outside the nested FRAMESET command, but within the exterior FRAMESET, in their proper order.

This is not as confusing if you think of an entire nested FRAMESET block as a single <FRAME> tag. In this example, the outside FRAMESET block sets up a situation in which you have three rows. Each must be filled. In this case, they are filled by a FRAME, then a nested FRAMESET two columns wide, then another FRAME.

By now (if you are a perverse programming-type person) you may be asking yourself, "I wonder if it is possible for a FRAME to use as its SRC a document that is, itself, a FRAMESET?" The answer is "Yes." In this case, you simply use the <FRAME> tag to point to an HTML document that is the FRAMESET you would have otherwise used in place of the FRAME.

Redefine the previous example (which used nested FRAMESETs) in terms of referenced FRAME documents instead. All you're doing is moving the nested FRAMESET to its own document. Here's the first (outside) file (Frames2.HTM):

```
<HTML>
<HEAD>
</HEAD>
<FRAMESET ROWS="25%,50%,25%">
       <FRAME SRC="header.htm">
       <FRAME SRC="nested.htm">
       <FRAME SRC="footer.htm">
</FRAMESET>
<NOFRAMES>
Your browser cannot display frames.
</NOFRAMES>
</HTML>
```

And here's the second (inside) file (Nested.HTM):

```
<HTML>
<HEAD>
</HEAD>
<FRAMESET COLS="25%,75%">
       <FRAME SRC="label.htm">
       <FRAME SRC="info.htm">
</FRAMESET>
</HTML>
```

In this case, the top and bottom rows behave as before. But the second row in the "outside" file is now just a simple FRAME definition like the others. However, the "inside" file that its SRC points to is Frameset.HTM, which you created with a FRAMESET all its own. When inserted into the original FRAMESET, it behaves just as if it appeared there verbatim. The resulting screen is identical to the original example (compare Figure 12.8 to Figure 12.4).

> **CAUTION**
>
> Though it's possible to create nested FRAMESETs by using <FRAME> tags that call the same URL, it certainly isn't a good idea. This is called *infinite recursion*, which creates an infinite loop in a computer that consumes all memory and crashes the machine. Fortunately, frames-aware browsers check for this—if an SRC URL is the same as any of its ancestors it's ignored, just as if there were no SRC attribute at all.

By using nested FRAMESET containers in clever combinations, it is possible to create just about any grid of frames you can dream up. But remember that you're trying to create a friendly, useful interface, not show off how clever you can be with frames.

N O T E In Netscape Navigator 2.0, the toolbar's Back button didn't back you out of a frame, it backed you out of the whole FRAMESET to the previous page.

With versions 3.0 and above—as well as within Internet Explorer—pressing the Back button returns you to the previous state of the currently selected frame.

To navigate forward or backward within a frame, make sure you make the frame active first by clicking in it somewhere, then use the Forward or Back buttons or menu selections to navigate within that frame. ■

Part

II

Ch

12

FIG. 12.8
FRAMESET containers
can be nested or can
call other documents
containing their own
FRAMESETs. The end
result is the same.

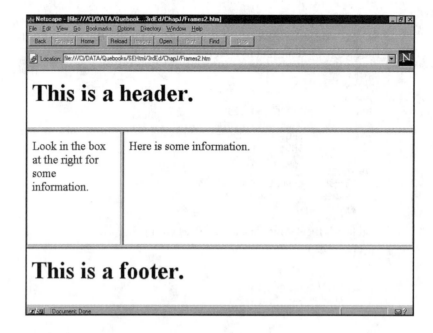

Modifying a Frame's Look and Feel

Now that you understand how framesets are used to create various grids of frames, take a look
at some of the attributes that modify how frames look and feel.

Frame Margins

The FRAME attributes MARGINWIDTH and MARGINHEIGHT give you control over the width of the
frame's interior margins. They both look like this:

```
MARGINWIDTH="value"
```

value is always a number, and always represents an absolute value in pixels. For example:

```
<FRAME MARGINHEIGHT="5" MARGINWIDTH="7">
```

would create a frame with top and bottom interior margins five pixels wide, and left and right
margins seven pixels wide. Remember, you're talking interior margins here, not borders.
MARGINWIDTH and MARGINHEIGHT define a space within the frame within which content will not
appear. Border widths are set automatically by the browser, or by the BORDER attribute, which is
discussed later in this chapter in the "Frame Borders" section.

Frame Scrollbars

Your frames will automatically have scrollbars if the content you've specified for them is too big
to fit the frame. Sometimes this ruins your page's aesthetics, so you need a way to control
them. That's what the SCROLLING attribute of the <FRAME> tag is for. Here's the format:

```
<FRAME SCROLLING="yes|no|auto">
```

There are three valid values for SCROLLING: Yes, No, and Auto. Auto is assumed if there is no SCROLLING attribute in your FRAME definition. Yes forces the appearance of a scrollbar. No keeps a scrollbar away at all costs. For example, this FRAME definition turns on scrollbars:

```
<FRAME SCROLLING=YES>
```

Frame Resizing

Frames are normally resizable by the user, but if you let the user drag your frames around, it can quickly muck the look and feel of your beautifully designed frames. Therefore, you almost always want to use the NORESIZE attribute of the <FRAME> tag to keep users from resizing your frames. Here's how:

```
<FRAME NORESIZE>
```

That's it. No values. Of course, when you set NORESIZE for one frame, none of the adjacent frames can be resized, either. Depending on your layout, using NORESIZE in a single frame will often be enough to keep users from resizing all the frames on the screen.

When you move over a resizable frame border with the mouse cursor, it changes to a double-arrow (see Figure 12.9), indicating that the frame can be resized. If you don't get the double-arrow, it means that resizing has been turned off with the NORESIZE attribute. To resize a resizable frame, grab the frame border by clicking and dragging it with your mouse to a new position.

TROUBLESHOOTING

I've created a frame using the NORESIZE attribute. What do I do about users who are using small screens on which the entire contents of the frame may not fit? Your best bet is to make sure the frame will hold all of its content at lower screen resolutions. That is, redesign the frame. Otherwise, consider reenabling, resizing, or adding scrollbars to the frame.

Part
II
Ch
12

Figure 12.9 shows an example of a frames page in which the lower-left frame has had its MARGINHEIGHT set to 50, MARGINWIDTH set to 100, and SCROLLING set to Yes. The NORESIZE attribute has not been used, so you can see what the resizing cursor looks like.

Frame Borders

You use the BORDER, FRAMEBORDER, and BORDERCOLOR attributes to set the look and feel of the borders for your frameset.

The BORDER attribute is used only with the <FRAMESET> tag, and sets the width of all the borders in the frameset. It is assigned a value in pixels, like this:

```
<FRAMESET BORDER="5">
```

This example would set the width of the frame borders to 5 pixels. BORDER can be assigned a value of 0, in which case all the frames in your frameset will be borderless.

FIG. 12.9
The HTML source for this FRAMESET is shown in the upper frame.

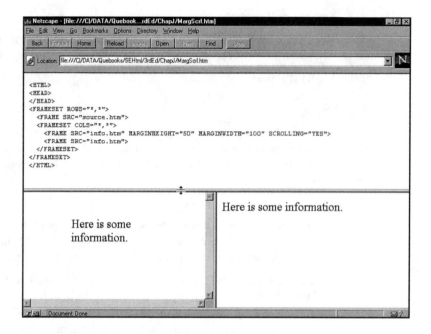

```
<HTML>
<HEAD>
</HEAD>
<FRAMESET ROWS="*,*">
  <FRAME SRC="source.htm">
  <FRAMESET COLS="*,*">
    <FRAME SRC="info.htm" MARGINHEIGHT="50" MARGINWIDTH="100" SCROLLING="YES">
    <FRAME SRC="info.htm">
  </FRAMESET>
</FRAMESET>
</HTML>
```

Here is some information.

Here is some information.

TIP The default value of BORDER (that is, the value it assumes if there is no BORDER="n" attribute specified for a given FRAMESET) is 5.

The FRAMEBORDER attribute can be used with either the <FRAMESET> or <FRAME> tag. It has two legitimate values, YES and NO. If FRAMEBORDER="YES", then frame borders are drawn with a 3-D look. If FRAMEBORDER="NO", frame borders are *invisible*, which really means that they are drawn in the default background color of the browser.

The default value of FRAMEBORDER is YES, which means that browser programs generally display 3-D frame borders.

The border for a frame will be invisible (not 3-D) only if FRAMEBORDER="NO" is set for all surrounding frames.

TIP To create a page with entirely borderless frames, set FRAMEBORDER="NO" and BORDER="0" in the top FRAMESET definition.

The BORDERCOLOR attribute can be used with the FRAMESET tag or with the FRAME tag. BORDERCOLOR can be assigned a named color value, or a hexadecimal RGB color value. Here's an example:

```
<FRAMESET BORDERCOLOR="red" ROWS="*,*">
    <FRAME SRC="info.htm" BORDERCOLOR="#FF00FF">
    <FRAME SRC="info.htm">
</FRAMESET>
```

In this example, the outer <FRAMESET> tag sets the BORDERCOLOR to red, one of the named colors for most browsers. But the following <FRAME> tag sets BORDERCOLOR to the hexadecimal value #FF00FF (which happens to be purple). The lowest level definition takes precedence. Though the FRAMESET BORDERCOLOR is defined as red, the border color of the first frame is instead set to the hexadecimal RGB value #FF00FF. The adjacent frame, which has no BORDERCOLOR definition, has a border of #FF00FF on the edge it shares with the other frame, but a color of red on borders it does not share with that frame.

NOTE RGB hexadecimal color values are precise, but obscure. (Exactly what color *is* #FA10D7?) Named colors are easier to comprehend, but not all browsers support the same color names. In general, if you stick with the sixteen common color names listed here, you'll be safe: aqua, black, blue, fuchsia, gray, green, lime, maroon, navy, olive, purple, red, silver, teal, white, yellow. ■

 TIP If two adjacent frames of the same priority attempt to define their own BORDERCOLOR, neither takes effect. They revert to the BORDERCOLOR defined at the next higher FRAMESET level.

Figure 12.10 shows an example of using the BORDER, FRAMEBORDER, and BORDERCOLOR attributes to control the look and feel of your frame borders. Note that the only frame to maintain the BORDERCOLOR defined in the outside FRAMESET definition is the one in the upper-right, the only frame that doesn't share a border with the leftmost center frame, which redefines the BORDERCOLOR. Actually, the rightmost center frame would have also had a red border on the left, but it has had its left border turned off by the FRAMEBORDER="NO" attribute it shares with the central frame. Note this complex interplay of attributes carefully. If you use them often, their interrelationships are sure to throw you for a loop more often than they make sense.

FIG. 12.10
The HTML source for this border-manipulating example is shown in the top frame.

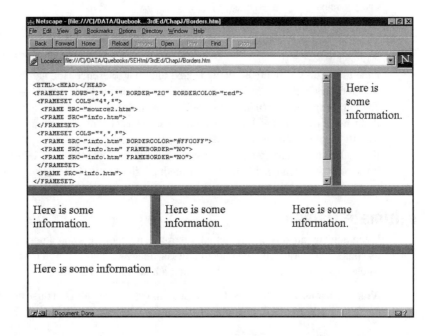

CAUTION

Microsoft Internet Explorer supports one more attribute for FRAMESET, called FRAMESPACING. It is intended to define the space between frames, and can assume pixel values. However, because Netscape Navigator and other browser programs don't support the FRAMESPACING attribute, you are strongly advised against using it unless you are creating content for an audience that uses Internet Explorer exclusively, and you have a good reason for having to specify the spacing between frames.

N O T E There are two more attributes for the <FRAME> tag: ONLOAD and ONUNLOAD. These are used with scripting languages like VBScript and JavaScript to specify a script to run when a frame is loaded or unloaded from a frameset. Scripting is covered in detail in Chapter 16, "Adding JavaScript and VBScript to HTML." ▦

Targeted Hyperlinks

Though you've examined in-depth how to create and nest framesets, and how to control the look and feel of frames, you have yet to understand how to use frames to control navigation, which is its major application. To use frames to their full advantage, you need to know how to name and target frames.

Naming and Targeting Frames

The NAME attribute assigns a name to a frame that can be used to link to the frame, usually from other frames in the same display. This example,

```
<FRAME SRC="info.htm" NAME="Joe">
```

creates a frame named "Joe," which can be referenced via a hyperlink like this:

```
<A HREF="moreinfo.htm" TARGET="Joe">Click Here to Jump to Joe</A>
```

Note the TARGET attribute in the hypertext link that references the name of your frame. When selected, this hyperlink replaces the content of the named frame "Joe"—which was given the content file info.HTM when it was created—with the content in the file moreinfo.HTM. Note that while a hyperlink without a named TARGET replaces the content in its own window or frame with the content named in the HREF attribute, a hyperlink with a named TARGET instead replaces the content in the targeted frame or window with the content named in the HREF attribute. This is the only trick you need to know for creating killer frames-based navigational systems. Of course, there are some fine points.

Legitimate Names

If you don't create an explicit name for a frame, it simply has no name, and you won't be able to use links in one frame to open documents or images in another. You'll want to name all frames whose content will be changed by clicking a link in a different frame.

All frame names must begin with an alphanumeric character. Don't use an underscore (_) as the first character in a frame name. Other than that, you're pretty much on your own.

However, there are four reserved implicit names built into HTML, and all of them do start with an underscore. These are listed in Table 12.1. All other names starting with an underscore are ignored.

Table 12.1   Reserved Implicit Frame Names

Name	Purpose
_blank	Load content directed to this name into a new, unnamed window. This name is used to completely wipe out the current frameset and start with a new, blank window.
_self	Load content directed to this name into the calling frame.
_parent	Load content directed to this link to the calling frame's parent frameset window. If it has no parent frameset, this is the same as using the name _self.
_top	Load content directed to this link to the top level frameset related to the calling frame. If the calling frame is already the top level, this is the same as using the name _self.

Here are a few examples to help clarify how these reserved names work.

If a frame contains the following link, then clicking the link launches a new, unnamed browser display window that contains the content defined in stuff.HTM. This can be a simple HTML document, or an entirely new FRAMESET definition. Whichever, this call wipes the slate clean and starts completely over.

```
<A HREF="stuff.htm" TARGET="_blank">
```

If a frame contains the following link, then clicking the link will simply cause the frame which contains the link to clear, and its content will be replaced with whatever is in stuff.htm.

```
<A HREF="stuff.htm" TARGET="_self">
```

If a frame contains the following link, the frameset that contains the frame that contains this link will be replaced by stuff.HTM.

```
<A HREF="stuff.htm" TARGET="_parent">
```

Finally, if a frame contains the following link, clicking the link replaces the entire browser window with the contents of stuff.HTM.

```
<A HREF="stuff.htm" TARGET="_top">
```

Part II

Ch 12

N O T E Hyperlinks using the <A> or anchor tag aren't the only tags that can make use of the TARGET attribute. The <AREA>, <FORM>, and <BASE> tags also use the TARGET attribute, and can be used effectively to extend and expand the utility of named frames.

Remember, too, that windows can also be named by using the TARGET attribute within the <A> tag; using named windows in conjunction with named frames adds a whole new dimension to HTML document navigation.

Updating More than One Frame at a Time

You've seen that you can click a link in one frame to change the content in another. First you name the target frame using the NAME attribute of the <FRAME> tag when creating the target frame. You then use the TARGET attribute of the <A> hyperlink tag when defining the link, as in this example:

```
<FRAME SRC="info.htm" NAME="Joe">
<A HREF="moreinfo.htm" TARGET="Joe">Click Here to Jump to Joe</A>
```

The first line of HTML is used in the frame definition document, and the second line is used in the document that links to the first.

You've also seen that you can use special implicit names to target some frames and framesets, depending on their relationship to the frame that contains the calling link.

But what if you want to update more than one frame by clicking a single link? This is possible if you set up your document correctly. The key is to update a frameset, not a single frame.

To do this, create a subframeset that is contained in its own file, as was done earlier in the example shown in Figure 12.8. If you recall, you began with an HTML document that included one frameset nested inside another:

```
<HTML>
<HEAD>
</HEAD>
<FRAMESET ROWS="25%,50%,25%">
       <FRAME SRC="header.htm">
       <FRAMESET COLS="25%,75%">
              <FRAME SRC="label.htm">
              <FRAME SRC="info.htm">
       </FRAMESET>
       <FRAME SRC="footer.htm">
</FRAMESET>
</HTML>
```

Then you took the nested frameset out and put it into its own file.

Here's the original file, with the nested frameset replaced by the FRAME definition pointing to the second file, nested.HTM. Note that you named this frame this time using the NAME attribute, calling it "Inner":

```
<HTML>
<HEAD>
</HEAD>
<FRAMESET ROWS="25%,50%,25%">
       <FRAME SRC="header.htm">
       <FRAME SRC="nested.htm" NAME="Inner">
       <FRAME SRC="TestLink.htm">
</FRAMESET>
</HTML>
```

Also note the last FRAME SRC file has been renamed TestLink.HTM—this file contains the targeted link you want to test. Call this modified file NameTest.HTM. Now here's the file (nested.HTM) that the frame named Inner calls:

```
<HTML>
<HEAD>
</HEAD>
<FRAMESET COLS="25%,75%">
     <FRAME SRC="label.htm">
     <FRAME SRC="info.htm">
</FRAMESET>
</HTML>
```

The file that occupies the bottom frame contains the file TestLink.HTM, which is listed here:

```
<HTML>
<HEAD>
<TITLE>
</TITLE>
</HEAD>
<BODY>
<A HREF="NewStuff.htm" TARGET="Inner">Click me</A>
to put new stuff into the upper center frameset.
</BODY>
</HTML>
```

The frameset created by these two files (and their associated content files) is shown in Figure 12.11.

FIG. 12.11

Here's your test page, all set to change two frames with one mouse click.

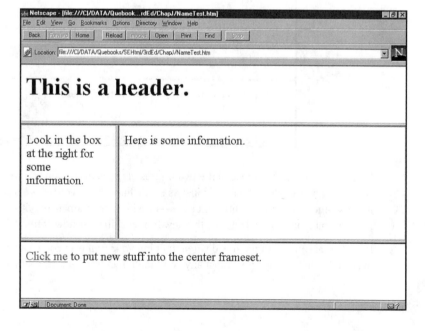

When the link Click me in the bottom window is clicked, it replaces the two frames in the center frameset (which was defined in the file nested.HTM) with new information from the document NewStuff.HTM. Say this is the content of NewStuff.HTM:

```
<HTML>
<HEAD>
<TITLE>
</TITLE>
</HEAD>
<BODY>
Here is some NEW STUFF!
</BODY>
</HTML>
```

When you click the link in the bottom window, you get the result shown in Figure 12.12.

FIG. 12.12

Clicking the hyperlink in the bottom window has replaced the two-frame central frameset with the single frame of content from a different file.

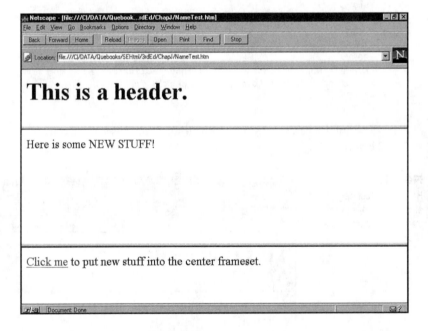

With one click, you've replaced the two frames of the central frameset with a single frame containing new content. You could just as easily have replaced the two frames with two new frames—the same size, or different sizes—or with three frames, or with a whole new frameset. All you would have to do is define the new frameset in your new content file, NewStuff.HTM.

If you're careful and think ahead when defining your framesets, you can easily create hyperlinks that can update almost any combination of frames with a single mouse click.

TROUBLESHOOTING

I have two frames that don't have the same parent frameset. Can I update both of them with one hyperlink? Yes. You have to write a JavaScript or VBScript application to handle them. In fact, this is how Netscape Communications has done multiframe updates from single hyperlinks on its own Web site.

Part

II

Ch

12

## CHAPTER 13

Collecting Input with Forms

by Jerry Honeycutt, Jim O'Donnell, and Mark R. Brown

Introducing HTML Forms

Forms are one of the most popular, interactive features on the World Wide Web (WWW). They enable users to interact with the text and graphics that are displayed on your machine. You can make forms with simple yes or no questions; you can make highly complex order forms; or you can make forms for people to send you comments.

You create forms by providing a number of fields in which a user can enter information or choose an option. Then, when the user submits the form, the information is returned to a server-side script. A script is a short program that is written specifically for each form. You can create scripts to do any number of things. You can also handle the contents of a form by using a client-side script, which you learn about in Part VI, "Scripting on the Web Server."

HTML forms give you the opportunity to gather information from people reading your Web page. Just as HTML provides many mechanisms for outputting information, the use of HTML forms enables input. These forms can be used to solicit free-form text information, get answers to yes or no questions, and get answers from a set of options.

You can add forms to your Web page with many different results in mind. You can do something simple, like asking visitors to sign a guest book or comment about your Web site. You can also use forms to gather input for a discussion group or, when combined with a secure method of transmission, take online orders for your $10 widgets. These and many other results can be achieved with HTML forms.

Working with HTML Forms Tags

The HTML tags you use to display forms are straightforward. There are three types of tags for creating fields: <TEXTAREA>, <SELECT>, and <INPUT>. You can put any number of these tags between the <FORM> and </FORM> container tags. The following is a brief description of each tag (you'll learn more about each a bit later in this chapter):

<TEXTAREA>	This tag defines a field in which the end user can type multiple lines of text.
<SELECT>	This tag enables the end user to choose among a number of options in either a scroll box or pop-up menu.
<INPUT>	This tag provides all of the other types of input: single lines of text, radio buttons, check boxes, and the buttons to submit or clear the form.

<FORM>

The <FORM> tag comes at the beginning of any form. When you create a <FORM> tag, you also define the script it uses and how it sends data using the ACTION and METHOD attributes:

ACTION	This attribute points the form to an URL that will accept the form's information and do something with it. If you don't specify an ACTION, it sends the information back to the same URL the page came from.
METHOD	This attribute tells the form how to send its information back to the script. The most common method is POST, which sends all the

information from the form separately from the URL. The other option for METHOD is GET, which attaches the information from the form to the end of the URL.

The following is an example of a `<FORM>` tag:

```
<FORM METHOD="POST" ACTION="/cgi-bin/comment_script">
...
</FORM>
```

This example says that you want the browser to send the completed form to the script `comment_script` in the `cgi-bin` directory on your server and to use the POST method to send it.

> **CAUTION**
>
> You can put any number of forms on the same HTML page, but be careful not to nest one form inside another. If you put in a `<FORM>` tag before finishing the last one, that line is ignored and all the inputs for your second form are assumed to go with the first one.

<TEXTAREA>

With `<TEXTAREA>`, you can provide a field for someone to enter multiple lines of information. By default, a `<TEXTAREA>` form shows a blank field four rows long and 40 characters wide. You can make it any size you want by using the ROWS and COLS attributes in the tag. You can also specify some default text by simply entering it between the `<TEXTAREA>` and `</TEXTAREA>` tags.

 TIP `<TEXTAREA>` fields are ideal for having users enter comments or lengthy information because they can type as much as they want in the field.

The options for the `<TEXTAREA>` tag are as follows:

NAME	This is required. It defines the name for the data.
ROWS	This sets the number of rows in the field.
COLS	This sets the width of the field in characters.
Default text	Any text between the `<TEXTAREA>` and `</TEXTAREA>` tags is used as default text and shows up inside the field.

While the ROWS and COLS attributes are not required, there is no default value for these that you are guaranteed to get on every Web browser, so it's always a good idea to set them. Listing 13.1 shows you an example using the `<TEXTAREA>` tag. Figure 13.1 shows you what this example looks like.

 TIP All input fields in a form—`<TEXTAREA>`, `<SELECT>`, and `<INPUT>`—must each have a NAME defined for its information.

Listing 13.1   TEXTAREA.HTM—*<TEXTAREA>* Default Text

```
<HTML>
<HEAD>
<TITLE>TEXTAREA.HTM</TITLE>
</HEAD>
<BODY>
<FORM>
<TEXTAREA NAME="comments" ROWS=4 COLS=40>Default text
1 2 3 ...
</TEXTAREA>
</FORM>
</BODY>
</HTML>
```

FIG. 13.1

The default text is shown as preformatted text in the <TEXTAREA> element.

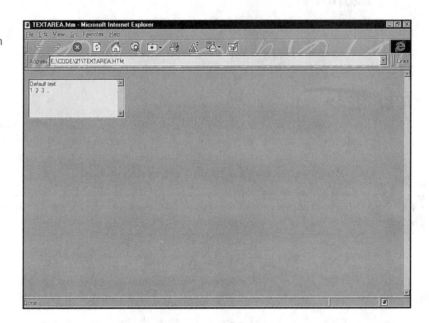

<SELECT>

The <SELECT> element shows a list of choices in either a pop-up menu or a scrolling list. It's set up as an opening and closing tag with a number of choices listed in between. Just like the <TEXTAREA> element, the <SELECT> tag requires you to define a name. You can specify how many choices to show at once by using the SIZE attribute.

The options for the <SELECT> element are as follows:

NAME   This is required. It defines the name for the data.

SIZE   This attribute determines how many choices to show. If you omit SIZE or set it to 1, the choices are shown as a drop-down list. If you set it to 2 or higher, it shows the choices in a scroll box. If you set SIZE larger than the number of choices you have within <SELECT>, a nothing choice is added. When the end user chooses this, it's returned as an empty field.

MULTIPLE   This allows multiple selections. If you specify multiple, a scrolling window displays—regardless of the number of choices or the setting of SIZE.

 TIP   Some WWW browsers don't properly display a scrolling window if the SIZE is 2 or 3. In that case, leave it as a drop-down list or think about using the <INPUT> field's radio buttons.

You present the choices the end user can make within the <SELECT> and </SELECT> tags. The choices are listed inside the <OPTION> tag and don't allow any other HTML markup.

The options for the <OPTION> tag are the following:

VALUE   This is the value to be assigned for the choice, which is what is sent back to the script, and doesn't have to be the same as what is presented to the end user.

SELECTED   If you want one of the choices to be a default, use the SELECTED option in the <OPTION> tag.

Consider Listing 13.2, the results of which are shown in Figures 13.2 and 13.3. This HTML adds a list called network to the document that contains four options: ethernet, token16, token5, and localtalk.

Listing 13.2   SELECT1.HTM—Selection via Drop-Down List

```
<HTML>
<HEAD>
<TITLE>SELECT1.HTM</TITLE>
</HEAD>
<BODY>
What type of connection:
<FORM>
<SELECT NAME="network">
      <OPTION SELECTED VALUE="ethernet"> Ethernet
      <OPTION VALUE="token16"> Token Ring - 16MB
      <OPTION VALUE="token4"> Token Ring - 4MB
      <OPTION VALUE="localtalk"> LocalTalk
</SELECT>
</FORM>
</BODY>
</HTML>
```

Part
II

Ch
13

FIG. 13.2

The `<SELECT>` tag uses the default of a drop-down list (size=1).

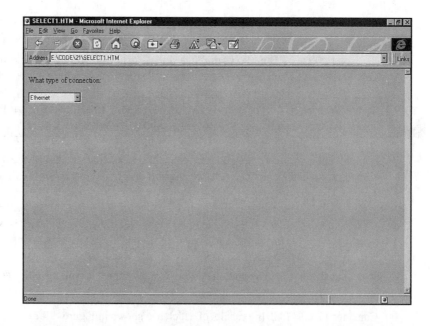

FIG. 13.3

The width of the drop-down list is determined by the size of the entries listed with the `<OPTION>` tags.

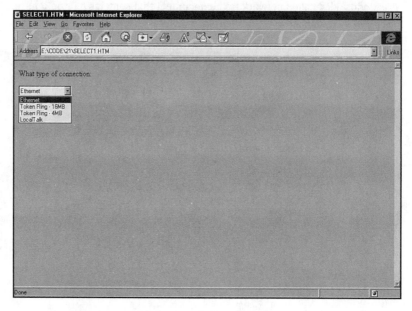

Suppose you set the tag as shown in Listing 13.3, the result of which is shown in Figure 13.4.

Listing 13.3 SELECT2.HTM—Selection via Scrollable List

```
<HTML>
<HEAD>
<TITLE>SELECT2.HTM</TITLE>
</HEAD>
<BODY>
<FORM>
What type of Connection:
<SELECT MULTIPLE NAME="network">
      <OPTION SELECTED VALUE="ethernet"> Ethernet
      <OPTION VALUE="token16"> Token Ring - 16MB
      <OPTION VALUE="token4"> Token Ring - 4MB
      <OPTION VALUE="localtalk"> LocalTalk
</SELECT>
</FORM>
</BODY>
</HTML>
```

FIG. 13.4

If you use MULTIPLE within the <SELECT> tag, then the field becomes a list of choices.

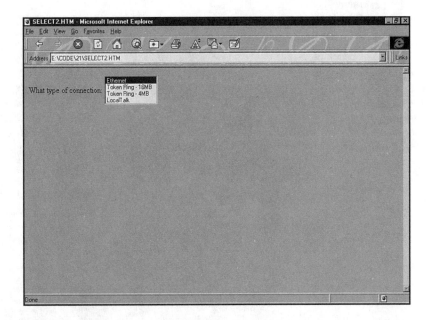

 TROUBLESHOOTING

I know the most common choices I want to present, but I want to allow people to enter their own value if they want to. How can I do that? Your best bet is to display the common choices in a <SELECT> box or pop-up menu, with one of the options set to Other. Then include an <INPUT> text field or a <TEXTAREA> field right after the list of choices (see Listing 13.4).

Part

II

Ch

13

Listing 13.4   SELECT3.HTM—Selection with Other Option

```
<HTML>
<HEAD>
<TITLE>SELECT3.HTM</TITLE>
</HEAD>
<BODY>
<FORM>
What type of Connection:
<SELECT MULTIPLE NAME="network">
      <OPTION SELECTED VALUE="ethernet"> Ethernet
      <OPTION VALUE="token16"> Token Ring - 16MB
      <OPTION VALUE="token4"> Token Ring - 4MB
      <OPTION VALUE="localtalk"> LocalTalk
      <OPTION VALUE="other"> Other...
</SELECT>
<BR>
If other, please specify:<INPUT TYPE="text" NAME="network_other">
</FORM>
</BODY>
</HTML>
```

The result of Listing 13.4 is shown in Figure 13.5.

FIG. 13.5

This type of form layout provides both a common list and a place for exceptions.

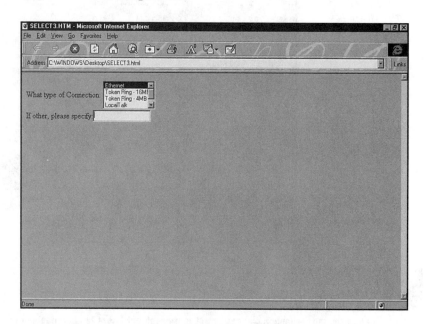

 T I P   You can use the <SELECT> tag as a navigational aid in your Web pages. You can provide a number of URLs in a list. The user can then choose one, click a Submit button, and have the server-side or client-side script jump to the URL indicated by that choice. Microsoft uses this method to direct users to different international Web sites (see **http://www.micorosoft.com**).

<INPUT>

<INPUT>, unlike <TEXTAREA> and <SELECT>, is a single tag option for gathering information. <INPUT> contains all of the other options for acquiring information, including simple text fields, password fields, radio buttons, check boxes, and the buttons to submit and reset the form.

The attributes for the <INPUT> tag are the following:

NAME
: This defines the name for the data. This field is required for all the types of input except Submit and Clear.

SIZE
: This is the size of the input field in number of characters for text or password.

MAXLENGTH
: This specifies the maximum number of characters to be allowed for a text or password field.

VALUE
: For a text or password field, it defines the default text displayed. For a check box or radio button, it specifies the value that is returned to the server if the box or button is selected. For the Submit and Reset buttons, it defines the text inside the button.

CHECKED
: This sets a check box or radio button to on. It has no meaning for any other type of <INPUT> tag.

TYPE
: This sets the type of input field you want to display. (See the types in the following section.)

Setting the *<INPUT>* Tag's *TYPE*

This section describes the possible values for the INPUT tag's TYPE attribute.

TEXT TEXT, the default input type, gathers a simple line of text. You can use the attributes NAME (this is required), SIZE, MAXLENGTH, and VALUE with TEXT. For example, consider Listing 13.5, the result of which is shown in Figure 13.6.

Listing 13.5 INPUT1.HTM—Text Input Box

```
<HTML>
<HEAD>
<TITLE>INPUT1.HTM</TITLE>
</HEAD>
<BODY>
<FORM>
A Phone Number: <INPUT TYPE="text" NAME="Phone" SIZE="15" MAXLENGTH="12">
</FORM>
</BODY>
</HTML>
```

Part
II

Ch
13

FIG. 13.6

The TEXT input type provides a very flexible input field.

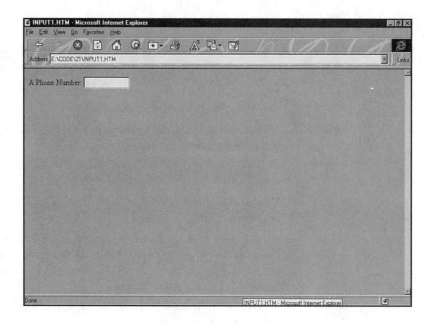

TROUBLESHOOTING

I want to let someone put in a very long URL, but the screen is not wide enough. How do I do that? A good way to enable someone to put in an extremely long text line is to simply set the size to 60 or 80 characters and not set a maximum length. This allows a user to put in a very long string, even if you can't see it all at once.

PASSWORD   PASSWORD, a modified TEXT field, displays typed characters as bullets instead of the characters actually typed. Possible attributes to include with the type PASSWORD include NAME (required), SIZE, MAXLENGTH, and VALUE. Consider Listing 13.6, the result of which is shown in Figure 13.7.

Listing 13.6   INPUT2.HTM—Text Input Box with No Echo

```
<HTML>
<HEAD>
<TITLE>INPUT2.HTM</TITLE>
</HEAD>
<BODY>
<FORM>
Enter the secret word: <INPUT TYPE="password" NAME="secret_word" Size="30"
 MAXLENGTH="30">
</FORM>
</BODY>
</HTML>
```

FIG. 13.7
Although it will look different in different browsers, the PASSWORD element hides the text that is typed.

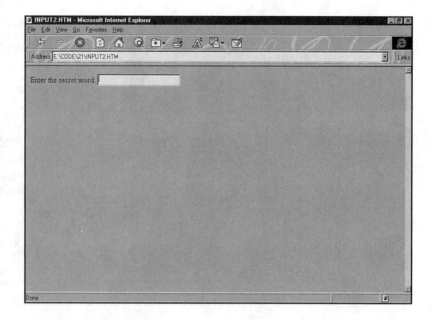

CHECKBOX CHECKBOX displays a simple check box that can be checked or left empty; use a check box when the choice is yes or no and doesn't depend on anything else. Possible attributes to include with the TYPE text include NAME (required), VALUE, and CHECKED (which defaults the check box as checked). Consider Listing 13.7, the result of which is shown in Figure 13.8. Check boxes are useful when you have a list of options, more than one of which can be selected at a time.

Listing 13.7 CHECK BOX.HTM—Check Box Form Input

```
<HTML>
<HEAD>
<TITLE>CHECKBOX.HTM</TITLE>
</HEAD>
<BODY>
<FORM>
<INPUT TYPE="checkbox" NAME="checkbox1" VALUE="checkbox_value1">
A checkbox
<INPUT TYPE="checkbox" NAME="checkbox2" VALUE="checkbox_value2"
CHECKED>A pre-selected checkbox
</FORM>
</BODY>
</HTML>
```

Part
II
Ch
13

CAUTION

You want to be especially careful when using check boxes and radio buttons in HTML documents with custom backgrounds or background colors. Depending on the Web browser used, check boxes and radio buttons sometimes do not show up with dark backgrounds.

FIG. 13.8

Select the check boxes that are commonly checked to make the form easier to use.

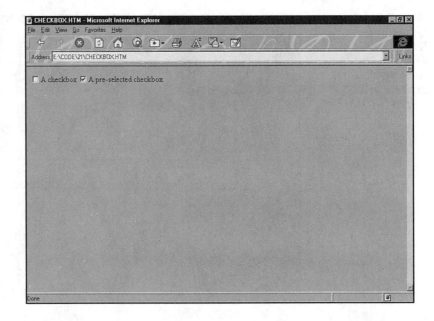

RADIO RADIO is a more complex version of a check box, allowing only one of a related set to be chosen. You can group radio buttons together by using the NAME attribute; this keeps all buttons in the same group under one NAME. Possible attributes to include with the TYPE text include NAME (required), VALUE, and CHECKED. Consider Listing 13.8, the result of which is shown in Figure 13.9.

Listing 13.8   RADIO1.HTM—Radio Button Form Input

```
<HTML>
<HEAD>
<TITLE>RADIO1.HTM</TITLE>
</HEAD>
<BODY>
Form #1:
<FORM>
      <INPUT TYPE="radio" NAME="choice" VALUE="choice1"> Yes.
      <INPUT TYPE="radio" NAME="choice" VALUE="choice2"> No.
</FORM>
<HR>
Form #2:
<FORM>
      <INPUT TYPE="radio" NAME="choice" VALUE="choice1" CHECKED> Yes.
      <INPUT TYPE="radio" NAME="choice" VALUE="choice2"> No.
</FORM>
</BODY>
</HTML>
```

Listing 13.9 is a variation on Listing 13.8. The result is shown in Figure 13.10.

FIG. 13.9

In the top form, without selecting yes or no, the end user can send back a "blank" value for this selection because none of the boxes were preselected with the CHECKED field.

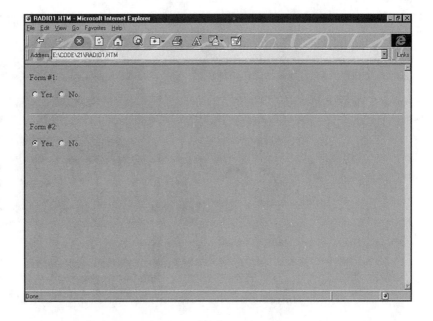

Listing 13.9   RADIO2.HTM—Radio Button Form Input with More Choices

```
<HTML>
<HEAD>
<TITLE>RADIO2.HTM</TITLE>
</HEAD>
<BODY>
<FORM>
One Choice:<BR>
     <INPUT TYPE="radio" NAME="choice1" VALUE="choice1" CHECKED>(1)
     <INPUT TYPE="radio" NAME="choice1" VALUE="choice2">(2)
     <INPUT TYPE="radio" NAME="choice1" VALUE="choice3">(3)
<BR>
One Choice:<BR>
     <INPUT TYPE="radio" NAME="choice2" VALUE="choice1" CHECKED>(1)
     <INPUT TYPE="radio" NAME="choice2" VALUE="choice2">(2)
     <INPUT TYPE="radio" NAME="choice2" VALUE="choice3">(3)
     <INPUT TYPE="radio" NAME="choice2" VALUE="choice4">(4)
     <INPUT TYPE="radio" NAME="choice2" VALUE="choice5">(5)
</FORM>
</BODY>
</HTML>
```

Part
II

Ch
13

FIG. 13.10

The end user has more choices in this variation. The first choice was the default in each list; this choice has been overridden in the second list.

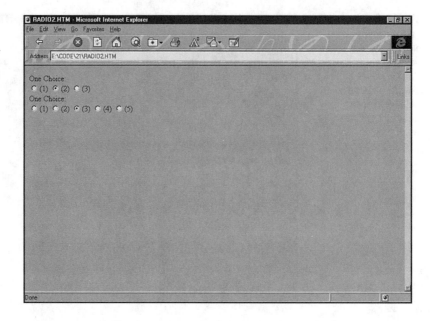

T I P   If you want to provide a long list of choices, use the <SELECT> tag so the choice doesn't take up as much space on the page.

> **CAUTION**
> If you don't specify a set of radio buttons or check boxes with one of the values as CHECKED, then you could receive an empty field for that <INPUT> name.

RESET   RESET displays a push button with the preset function of clearing all the data in the form to its original value. You can use the VALUE attribute with the RESET tag to provide text other than Reset (the default) for the button. For example, consider Listing 13.10. The result is shown in Figure 13.11.

Listing 13.10   RESET.HTM—Form Reset Button

```
<HTML>
<HEAD>
<TITLE>RESET.HTM</TITLE>
</HEAD>
<BODY>
<FORM>
     <INPUT TYPE="reset">
     <BR>
     <INPUT TYPE="reset" VALUE="Clear that form!">
</FORM>
</BODY>
</HTML>
```

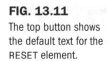

FIG. 13.11
The top button shows
the default text for the
RESET element.

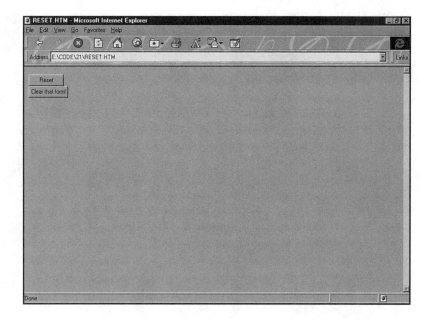

SUBMIT   SUBMIT displays a push button with the preset function of sending the data in the form to the server to be processed by a server-side script. You can use the VALUE attribute with SUBMIT to provide text other than Submit Query (the default) for the button. Consider, for example, Listing 13.11. The result is shown in Figure 13.12.

Listing 13.11   SUBMIT.HTM—Form Submit Button

```
<HTML>
<HEAD>
<TITLE>SUBMIT.HTM</TITLE>
</HEAD>
<BODY>
<FORM>
      <INPUT TYPE="submit">
      <BR>
      <INPUT TYPE="submit" VALUE="Send in the data!">
</FORM>
</BODY>
</HTML>
```

Part
II

Ch
13

Formatting and Designing Forms

Forms can be easy to read, simple one- or two-entry affairs with little to display; they can also be terrifically complex devices. As your forms get more complex, you need to carefully consider their layout. Think about how to make it obvious that certain titles are connected to certain fields and think about how to make your forms easy for anyone to use. People are often put off by complex forms that are hard to understand, so it's in your best interest to make them easy and fun to use—regardless of their complexity.

FIG. 13.12
The top button shows the default text for the SUBMIT element.

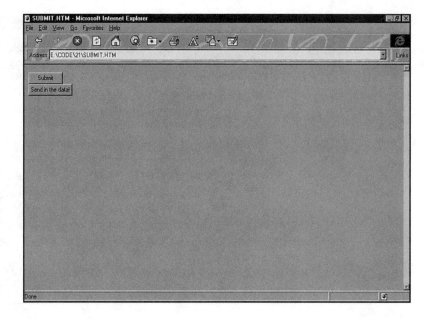

Using Line Break Tags

When you markup HTML documents, you usually just let the words wrap across the screen. Although this flexibility is wonderful to have for segments of text, it can make reading a form incredibly difficult. A quick and simple solution is to include the line break tag, <BR>, to move something to the next line.

Forcing Fields onto Separate Lines   If you want to have two fields, Name and E-Mail Address, for example, you can simply mark them up as shown in Listing 13.12.

Listing 13.12   LB1.HTM—Forms Without Line Breaks

```
<HTML>
<HEAD>
<TITLE>Form Layout and Design</TITLE>
</HEAD>
<BODY>
<H1>Line Break Tags</H1>
<FORM>
     Name: <INPUT NAME="name" SIZE="30">
     E-Mail Address: <INPUT NAME="email" SIZE="40">
</FORM>
</BODY>
</HTML>
```

Although this might look great now, it can wrap strangely on some WWW browsers and look shabby when displayed (see Figure 13.13).

FIG. 13.13
Without some type of organization, your forms can be very hard to read.

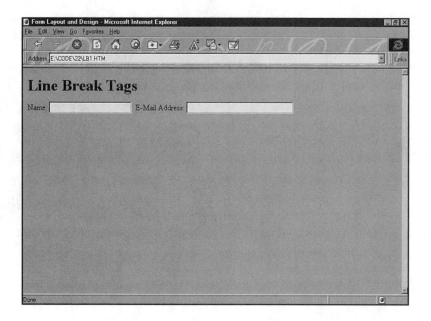

To split these lines and make them more readable, you need to include the line break tag, <BR>, between them, as shown in Listing 13.13.

Listing 13.13   LB2.HTM—Line Breaks Within Forms

```
<HTML>
<HEAD>
<TITLE>Form Layout and Design</TITLE>
</HEAD>
<BODY>
<H1>Line Break Tags</H1>
<FORM>
      Name: <INPUT NAME="name" SIZE="30">
      <BR>
      E-Mail Address: <INPUT NAME="email" SIZE="40">
</FORM>
</BODY>
</HTML>
```

Part
II

Ch
13

Adding the <BR> tag between the two fields forces the browser to wrap the field to the next line, regardless of the width of the screen. The result of Listing 13.13 is shown in Figure 13.14.

N O T E The wrapping feature of HTML can work for you to help keep a form small in size. If you have several multiple-choice items that could take up huge amounts of space on your form, you can try to keep them small and let them wrap closely together on the page.

If you're using the <SELECT> tag, the width of the pop-up menu on the screen is directly related to the words in the options to be selected. If you keep all the words small, you can provide a relatively large number of choices in a small area. ■

FIG. 13.14

The <BR> tag enables you to control the placement of form text.

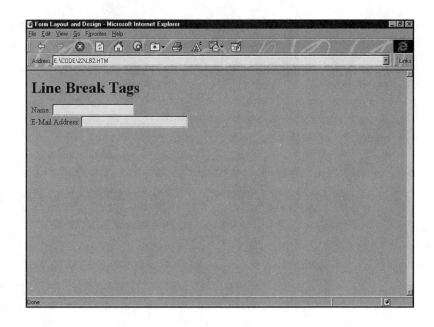

Working with Large Entry Fields   If you're working with long text entry fields or perhaps with a <TEXTAREA> field, it's often easier to put the text just above the field and then separate the different areas with paragraph breaks.

For example, if you have a text input line that is very long or a long field description, it doesn't work well to put them side by side. Also, if you want to leave a space for comments, it's easier—and looks nicer—to have the field description just above the comment area. This makes it appear that there's more space to write in. Listing 13.14 is an example of this sort of design. The result of this code is shown in Figure 13.15.

Listing 13.14   LARGE.HTM—Large Fields for Text Input

```
<HTML>
<HEAD>
<TITLE>Form Layout and Design</TITLE>
</HEAD>
<BODY>
<H1>Line Break Tags</H1>
<FORM>
      Please enter the new title for the message:<BR>
      <INPUT NAME="name" SIZE="40">
      <HR>
      Your comments:<BR>
      <TEXTAREA ROWS="6" COLS="70"></TEXTAREA>
</FORM>
</BODY>
</HTML>
```

FIG. 13.15
Using the line break tags enables you to put a label just above the field.

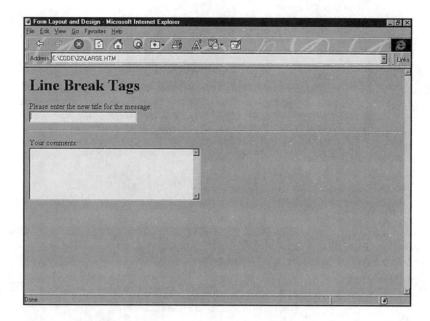

N O T E Most browsers automatically wrap a large field to the next line, treating it like an image. Because you don't know how wide (or narrow!) the client screen is, take steps to ensure the form will look as you want. If, for example, you want the field to be on the next line, put in a <BR> tag to make sure it will be! ■

Using the Preformatted Text Tag to Line Up Forms A common sight on many forms is simple text entry fields aligned haphazardly. A great trick for aligning text fields is to use the <PRE> tag. This ensures that some spaces appear before the field.

> **CAUTION**
> If you're using the <PRE> tags to line up fields, don't use any other HTML tags inside that area. Although the tags won't show up, they'll ruin the effect of lining everything up perfectly.

Listing 13.15 is an example of an entry form that uses line breaks only. The result of this code is displayed in Figure 13.16.

Listing 13.15   PRE1.HTM—Form Fields Not Aligned by Default

```
<HTML>
<HEAD>
<TITLE>Form Layout and Design</TITLE>
</HEAD>
<BODY>
```

continues

Part
II

Ch
13

Listing 13.15   Continued

```
<H1>Using PRE tags</H1>
<FORM>
      Name: <INPUT TYPE="text" NAME="name" SIZE="50"><BR>
      E-Mail: <INPUT TYPE="text" NAME="email" SIZE="50"><BR>
      Street Address: <INPUT TYPE="text" NAME="street1" SIZE="30"><BR>
      <INPUT TYPE="text" NAME="street2" SIZE="30"><BR>
      City: <INPUT TYPE="text" NAME="city" SIZE="50"><BR>
      State: <INPUT TYPE="text" NAME="state" SIZE="2"><BR>
      Zip: <INPUT TYPE="text" NAME="zip" SIZE="10">
</FORM>
</BODY>
</HTML>
```

FIG. 13.16

These fields were organized with line breaks only, so they align haphazardly.

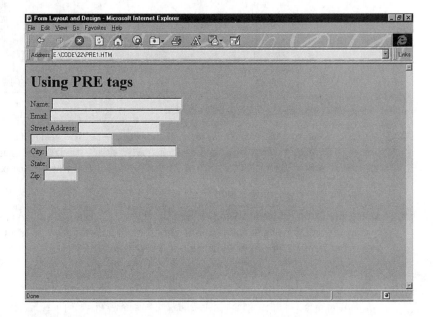

If you space things out and use the tags for preformatted text, you can create a very nice looking form. Listing 13.16 is an example of aligning fields by using the <PRE> tag, which produces the layout shown in Figure 13.17.

Listing 13.16   PRE2.HTM—Aligning Form Fields with Preformatted Text

```
<HTML>
<HEAD>
<TITLE>Form Layout and Design</TITLE>
</HEAD>
<BODY>
<H1>Using PRE tags</H1>
<FORM>
```

```
                  <PRE>
                  Name:              <INPUT TYPE="text" NAME="name" SIZE="50">
                  E-Mail:            <INPUT TYPE="text" NAME="email" SIZE="50">
                  Street Address:    <INPUT TYPE="text" NAME="street1" SIZE="30">
                                     <INPUT TYPE="text" NAME="street2" SIZE="30">
                  City:              <INPUT TYPE="text" NAME="city" SIZE="50">
                  State:             <INPUT TYPE="text" NAME="state" SIZE="2">
                  Zip:               <INPUT TYPE="text" NAME="zip" SIZE="10">
                  </PRE>
          </FORM>
          </BODY>
          </HTML>
```

CAUTION

Make sure you keep the size of the fields smaller than the general browser, or your lines will wrap off the screen. If an input field has to be large, you can use a line break to put the field on its own line.

FIG. 13.17
The layout of the preformatted text is organized and easy to follow.

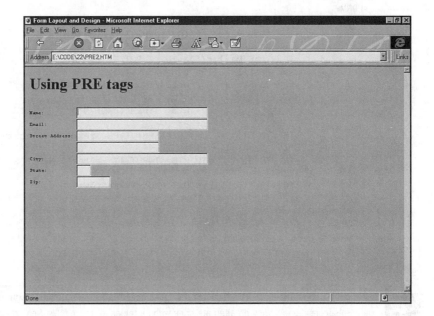

TROUBLESHOOTING

When I set up the preformatted text, it doesn't come out aligned in my HTML document! Why doesn't it match up? In some text editors, the width of each letter on the screen isn't the same. If you're creating HTML documents with a text editor or word processor, make sure you use a monospaced font such as Courier New (each character, including spaces, takes up exactly the same amount of space). That should solve the problem.

Using HTML Tables to Line Up Forms   Another way to line up form fields is to place them in an HTML table. This can produce an effect similar to using preformatted text but, because you are using regular HTML rather than preformatted text, you can also include other HTML constructs within the form. So, by using a table rather than preformatted text to align your form, you're also able to include images, hypertext links, or other HTML elements as part of the form.

Listing 13.17 is an example of the entry form shown in Figures 13.16 and 13.17, formatted using an HTML table. The result of this code is displayed in Figure 13.18.

Listing 13.17   TABLE.HTM—Aligning Form Fields with Tables

```
<HTML>
<HEAD>
<TITLE>Form Layout and Design</TITLE>
</HEAD>
<BODY>
<H1>Using HTML Tables</H1>
<FORM>
      <TABLE>
            <TR><TD>Name:</TD><TD><INPUT TYPE="text"
            NAME="name" SIZE="50"></TD></TR>
            <TR><TD>E-Mail:</TD><TD><INPUT TYPE="text"
            NAME="email" SIZE="50"></TD></TR>
            <TR><TD>Street Address:</TD><TD><INPUT TYPE="text"
            NAME="street1" SIZE="30"></TD></TR>
            <TR><TD></TD><TD><INPUT TYPE="text" NAME="street2"
            SIZE="30"></TD></TR>
            <TR><TD>City:</TD><TD><INPUT TYPE="text" NAME="city"
            SIZE="50"></TD></TR>
            <TR><TD>State:</TD><TD><INPUT TYPE="text" NAME="state"
            SIZE="2"></TD></TR>
            <TR><TD>Zip:</TD><TD><INPUT TYPE="text" NAME="zip"
            SIZE="10"></TD></TR>
      </TABLE>
</FORM>
</BODY>
</HTML>
```

TIP   Some people use browsers, particularly text-only ones, that don't support tables. If you use tables with your forms, consider including an alternate page without tables for these folks. See Chapter 11, "Formatting Content with Tables," for alternatives for browsers that don't support tables.

Using Paragraph Marks to Separate Form Sections   If you have a large form with different sections, it's handy to separate those sections. The paragraph container tag, <P>…</P>, provides a way of adding some space without making the delineation so hard that it appears to be another form. Note that Web browsers also allow you to use the <P> opening tag without the </P> closing tag to give identical results.

FIG. 13.18

HTML tables text can be combined with forms to enable the alignment of different form fields.

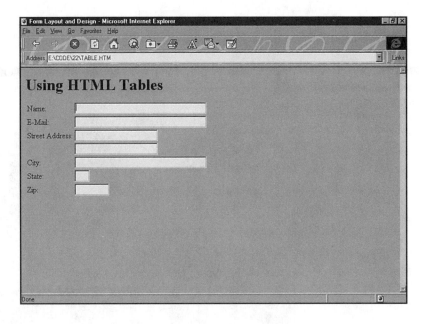

For example, a simple comment form might have places for a name and an e-mail address, but these might not be a required part of the form. In this case, separate the comment part of the form from the area that's optional. It's also possible to make it more obvious by simply making some comments in the form, such as a small heading titled Optional. A simple comment form with optional Name and E-Mail fields can have the code shown in Listing 13.18.

Listing 13.18 P.HTM—Using Paragraphs to Improve Spacing

```
<HTML>
<HEAD>
<TITLE>Form Layout and Design</TITLE>
</HEAD>
<BODY>
<H1>Using &lt;P&gt; tags</H1>
<FORM>
     <PRE>
     <I><B>Optional:</B></I>
     Name:   <INPUT TYPE="text" NAME="name" SIZE="50">
     E-Mail: <INPUT TYPE="text" NAME="email" SIZE="50">
     </PRE>
     <P>
     Your comments:<BR>
     <TEXTAREA ROWS="6" COLS="70"></TEXTAREA>
</FORM>
</BODY>
</HTML>
```

Part

II

Ch

13

Listing 13.18, using both <PRE> tags and line break tags, produces the layout shown in Figure 13.19. A similar effect can be achieved by using a table instead of preformatted text.

FIG. 13.19
Combining preformatted and wrapped areas can make your form very easy to use.

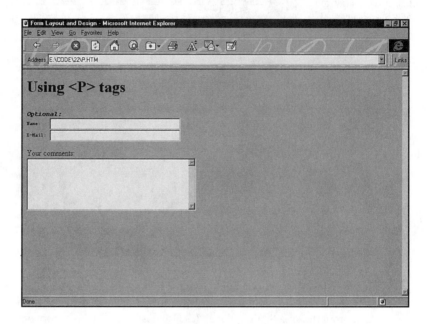

Using List Tags

There are a few occasions when line breaks and paragraph tags can't set up the form exactly as you'd like. At these times, list tags can provide just the right look! The best use of list tags is for indenting and numbering text.

Indenting Form Entries with Descriptive Lists   On the WWW, it's common to see order forms for merchandise. Finding the method of payment is a perfect use for descriptive list tags to lay out the choices. Indenting some items more than others makes the options obvious and easy to read.

N O T E   When you lay out lists, consider indenting the areas in your HTML documents that will be indented on-screen. This makes it easier to remember to finish with the descriptive list tag, </DL>. ■

For example, Listing 13.19 shows how to separate a section of credit cards from the rest of the payment methods. The result of this code is shown in Figure 13.20.

Listing 13.19   LIST1.HTM—Organizing Forms Using a Descriptive List

```
<HTML>
<HEAD>
<TITLE>Form Layout and Design</TITLE>
```

```
</HEAD>
<BODY>
<H1>Descriptive List Tags</H1>
<FORM>
      <DL>
      <DT>How would you like to pay for this?
      <DD><INPUT NAME="pay" TYPE="radio" VALUE="cash" CHECKED>Cash
      <DD><INPUT NAME="pay" TYPE="radio" VALUE="check">Check
      <DD><INPUT NAME="pay" TYPE="radio" VALUE="debit">Debit Card
          <DL>
          <DT>Credit Card
          <DD><INPUT NAME="pay" TYPE="radio" VALUE="mc">Mastercard
          <DD><INPUT NAME="pay" TYPE="radio" VALUE="visa">Visa
          <DD><INPUT NAME="pay" TYPE="radio" VALUE="disc">Discover
          <DD><INPUT NAME="pay" TYPE="radio" VALUE="ae">American Express
          </DL>
      </DL>
</FORM>
</BODY>
</HTML>
```

FIG. 13.20
Descriptive lists make the breakdown of choices obvious.

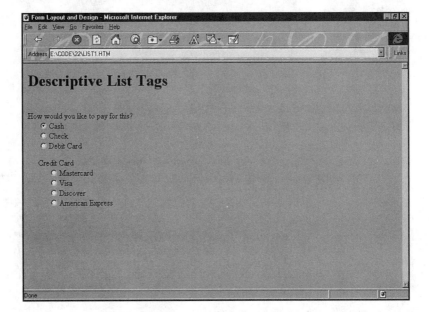

Using Ordered Lists to Number Fields It's easy to display a numbered list if you use the ordered list tag, <OL>. Listing 13.20 uses the <OL> tag to automatically number the fields. The result of this code is shown in Figure 13.21.

Part
II

Ch
13

Listing 13.20   LIST2.HTM—Organizing Forms by Using an Ordered List

```
<HTML>
<HEAD>
<TITLE>Form Layout and Design</TITLE>
</HEAD>
<BODY>
<H1>Ordered List Tags</H1>
<FORM>
        What are your three favorite books?
        <OL>
        <LI><INPUT NAME="1st" SIZE="20">
        <LI><INPUT NAME="2nd" SIZE="20">
        <LI><INPUT NAME="3rd" SIZE="20">
        </OL>
</FORM>
</BODY>
</HTML>
```

FIG. 13.21

Using ordered lists, you can reorder fields without retyping all those numbers!

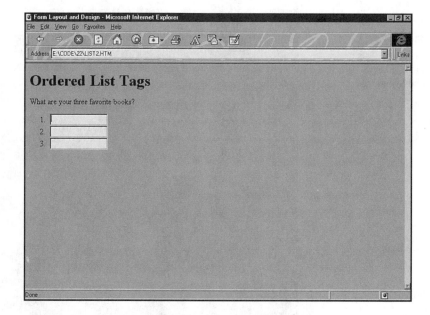

Check Box and Radio Button Layouts

Check boxes and radio buttons can provide a great deal of simple yes or no input. They can also be some of the hardest parts of a form to understand if they're not laid out correctly. There are three straightforward methods of layout: setting up the check boxes and radio buttons in a line horizontally, using a list to order them vertically, or setting them up in a grid pattern.

Setting Up Check Boxes or Radio Buttons in a Line   Probably the easiest method of layout is listing the check boxes in a line horizontally (see Listing 13.21). It has the benefits of being very simple to set up, relatively compact on the browser, and easy to understand. The only caution is to make sure there aren't too many items for one line. The intent of the form might not be obvious if you let check boxes wrap unintentionally. The result of Listing 13.21, which specifies a horizontal line of radio buttons, is shown in Figure 13.22.

Listing 13.21   BUTTON1.HTM—Organizing Forms, Check Boxes, and Radio Buttons

```
<HTML>
<HEAD>
<TITLE>Form Layout and Design</TITLE>
</HEAD>
<BODY>
<H1>Checkboxes and Radio Buttons</H1>
<FORM>
      What size would you like?<BR>
      <INPUT NAME="size" TYPE="radio" VALUE="sm">Small
      <INPUT NAME="size" TYPE="radio" VALUE="md">Medium
      <INPUT NAME="size" TYPE="radio" VALUE="lg">Large
      <INPUT NAME="size" TYPE="radio" VALUE="x">X-Large
      <INPUT NAME="size" TYPE="radio" VALUE="xx">XX-Large
</FORM>
</BODY>
</HTML>
```

FIG. 13.22
This method works well for check boxes too!

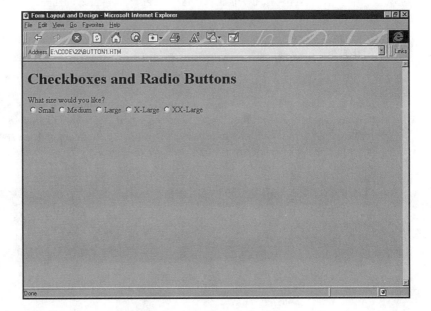

TIP When creating a Web page with a line of buttons, check it with your Web browser set to the width of a 640×480 screen to make sure your line doesn't wrap.

Lists of Check Boxes When the choices get more complex than a simple line selection, it's best to forgo compactness and spread out the choices in a list, as specified in Listing 13.22. The result of using a descriptive list in this code is shown in Figure 13.23.

Listing 13.22 BUTTON2.HTM—Organizing Forms Buttons by Using Lists

```
<HTML>
<HEAD>
<TITLE>Form Layout and Design</TITLE>
</HEAD>
<BODY>
<H1>Checkboxes and Radio Buttons</H1>
<FORM>
      <DL>
      <DT>What machines do you work on?
      <DD><INPUT NAME="mac" TYPE="checkbox">Macintosh
      <DD><INPUT NAME="pc" TYPE="checkbox">IBM Compatible PC
          <DL>
          <DT>UNIX Workstation
          <DD><INPUT NAME="sun" TYPE="checkbox">Sun
          <DD><INPUT NAME="sgi" TYPE="checkbox">SGI
          <DD><INPUT NAME="next" TYPE="checkbox">NeXT
          <DD><INPUT NAME="aix" TYPE="checkbox">AIX
          <DD><INPUT NAME="lin" TYPE="checkbox">Linux
          <DD><INPUT NAME="other" TYPE="checkbox">Other...
          </DL>
      </DL>
</FORM>
</BODY>
</HTML>
```

Making a Grid The most complex method for displaying check boxes is in a grid. Using tables, you can space out the display to create a grid effect (see Listing 13.23). You can also create a grid of radio buttons by substituting radio for checkbox in the <INPUT> tags. The result of setting up the grid in Listing 13.23 is shown in Figure 13.24.

Listing 13.23 GRID.HTM—Creating a Grid of Buttons by Using Tables

```
<HTML>
<HEAD>
<TITLE>Form Layout and Design</TITLE>
</HEAD>
<BODY>
<H1>Checkboxes and Radio Buttons</H1>
<FORM>
      What combinations?
      <TABLE>
```

```
              <TR><TD></TD><TD>Red</TD><TD>Blue</TD></TR>
              <TR><TD>Small</TD><TD><INPUT NAME="sr" TYPE="checkbox"></TD>
                           <TD><INPUT NAME="sb" TYPE="checkbox"></TD></TR>
              <TR><TD>Medium</TD><TD><INPUT NAME="mr" TYPE="checkbox"></TD>
                           <TD><INPUT NAME="mb" TYPE="checkbox"></TD></TR>
              <TR><TD>Large</TD><TD><INPUT NAME="lr" TYPE="checkbox"></TD>
                           <TD><INPUT NAME="lb" TYPE="checkbox"></TD></TR>
           </TABLE>
        </FORM>
        </BODY>
        </HTML>
```

FIG. 13.23
Complex choices are often easier to understand in a list format.

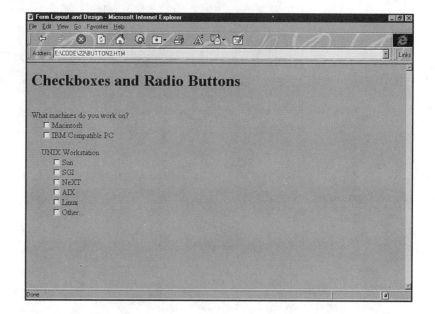

Multiple Forms in a Document

It's quite possible to put multiple forms in a single document; it often makes the document more concise and easier to understand. An example of using multiple forms is a document with a number of different methods for searching. From one form, you can choose to do a search from any of a number of locations by having each <FORM> point to a different search method.

 Also consider using multiple forms when your form is too large to fit on one or two screens; this makes it easier for your readers to use the form.

When including multiple forms in a document, visibly separate them to make them easier to understand. A common way to break up a form is to use the horizontal rule tag, <HR>, or a wide image that looks like a horizontal rule in an <IMG> tag. Put line breaks before and after the tags. For example, Listing 13.24 shows how to separate three forms by using <HR> tags to break them up. The result of this code is shown in Figure 13.25.

Part
II

Ch
13

FIG. 13.24

Grids provide a very intuitive method of making a choice.

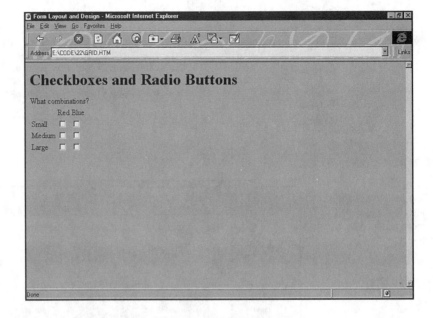

Listing 13.24 MULTIPLE.HTM—Using Multiple Forms in a Single HTML Document

```
<HTML>
<HEAD>
<TITLE>Form Layout and Design</TITLE>
</HEAD>
<BODY>
<H1>Multiple Forms in a Document</H1>
<FORM>
     What size would you like?<BR>
     <INPUT NAME="size" TYPE="radio" VALUE="sm">:Small
     <INPUT NAME="size" TYPE="radio" VALUE="md">:Medium
     <INPUT NAME="size" TYPE="radio" VALUE="lg">:Large
     <INPUT NAME="size" TYPE="radio" VALUE="x">:X-Large
     <INPUT NAME="size" TYPE="radio" VALUE="xx">:XX-Large
     <P>
     <INPUT TYPE="submit">
</FORM>
<HR>
<FORM>
     <TABLE>
          <TR><TD>Name:</TD><TD><INPUT TYPE="text" NAME="name"
          SIZE="50"></TD></TR>
          <TR><TD>E-Mail:</TD><TD><INPUT TYPE="text" NAME="email"
          SIZE="50"></TD></TR>
          <TR><TD>Street Address:</TD><TD><INPUT TYPE="text"
          NAME="street1" SIZE="30"></TD></TR>
          <TR><TD></TD><TD><INPUT TYPE="text" NAME="street2"
          SIZE="30"></TD></TR>
```

```
                <TR><TD>City:</TD><TD><INPUT TYPE="text" NAME="city"
                SIZE="50"></TD></TR>
                <TR><TD>State:</TD><TD><INPUT TYPE="text" NAME="state"
                SIZE="2"></TD></TR>
                <TR><TD>Zip:</TD><TD><INPUT TYPE="text" NAME="zip"
                SIZE="10"></TD></TR>
        </TABLE>
<P>
<INPUT TYPE="submit">
</FORM>
<HR>
<FORM>
        <DL>
        <DT>How would you like to pay for this?
        <DD><INPUT NAME="pay" TYPE="radio" VALUE="cash" CHECKED>Cash
        <DD><INPUT NAME="pay" TYPE="radio" VALUE="check">Check
        <DD><INPUT NAME="pay" TYPE="radio" VALUE="debit">Debit Card
            <DL>
            <DT>Credit Card
            <DD><INPUT NAME="pay" TYPE="radio" VALUE="mc">Mastercard
            <DD><INPUT NAME="pay" TYPE="radio" VALUE="visa">Visa
            <DD><INPUT NAME="pay" TYPE="radio" VALUE="disc">Discover
            <DD><INPUT NAME="pay" TYPE="radio" VALUE="ae">American Express
            </DL>
        </DL>
        <P>
        <INPUT TYPE="submit">
</FORM>
</BODY>
</HTML>
```

FIG. 13.25

By using horizontal rules to break up the multiple forms in this document, the intent of the form is easily apparent.

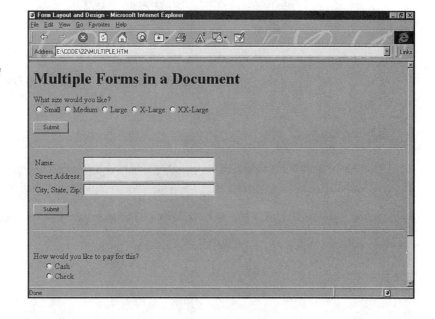

TROUBLESHOOTING

I put two forms in one document, but I only see one. Why aren't both showing up? Check to make sure you finished one form before beginning another. If you didn't include the </FORM> tag to stop the first form, the second <FORM> tag is just ignored.

Combining Forms with Tables

As discussed earlier in this section, forms can be used very effectively with HTML tables, allowing more control of the positioning of different fields. Listing 13.25 shows an address entry form that uses a table to align the different fields. The resulting Web page is shown in Figure 13.26.

Listing 13.25   TABLE2.HTM—Combining Forms and Tables

```
<HTML>
<HEAD>
<TITLE>Form Layout and Design</TITLE>
</HEAD>
<BODY>
<H1>More HTML Tables and Forms</H1>
<FORM>
     <TABLE>
          <TR><TD ALIGN=RIGHT>Name:</TD>
             <TD COLSPAN=4><INPUT TYPE="text" NAME="name" SIZE="40">
          </TD></TR>
          <TR><TD ALIGN=RIGHT>Street Address:</TD>
             <TD COLSPAN=4><INPUT TYPE="text" NAME="street1" SIZE="40">
          </TD></TR>
          <TR><TD ALIGN=RIGHT>City, State, Zip:</TD>
             <TD><INPUT TYPE="text" NAME="city" SIZE="30"></TD><TD>,</TD>
             <TD><INPUT TYPE="text" NAME="state" SIZE="2"></TD>
             <TD><INPUT TYPE="text" NAME="zip" SIZE="15"></TD></TR>
     </TABLE>
</FORM>
</BODY>
</HTML>
```

This idea can be taken even further, including other form elements such as check boxes or radio buttons, to allow the user more input options. A further refinement of the address entry form, allowing the user to input both a home and business address and specify which is preferred, is shown in Listing 13.26—the corresponding Web page is shown in Figure 13.26.

FIG. 13.26

The capability of tables to position items side by side and align them in many different ways makes them a natural for use with forms.

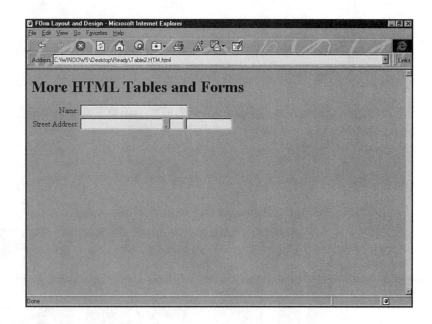

Listing 13.26   TABLE3.HTM—More on Combining Forms and Tables

```
<HTML>
<HEAD>
<TITLE>Form Layout and Design</TITLE>
</HEAD>
<BODY>
<H1>More HTML Tables and Forms</H1>
<FORM>
      <TABLE>
            <TR><TH ALIGN=LEFT COLSPAN=5>HOME ADDRESS</TH><TD><EM>Preferred?
            </EM></TR>
            <TR><TD ALIGN=RIGHT>Name:</TD>
               <TD COLSPAN=4><INPUT TYPE="text" NAME="name" SIZE="40"></TD>
               <TD ALIGN=CENTER><INPUT TYPE="radio" NAME="pref" VALUE="home">
               </TD></TR>
            <TR><TD ALIGN=RIGHT>Street Address:</TD>
               <TD COLSPAN=4><INPUT TYPE="text" NAME="street1" SIZE="40"></TD>
            </TR>
            <TR><TD ALIGN=RIGHT>City, State, Zip:</TD>
               <TD><INPUT TYPE="text" NAME="city" SIZE="25"></TD><TD>,</TD>
               <TD><INPUT TYPE="text" NAME="state" SIZE="2"></TD>
               <TD><INPUT TYPE="text" NAME="zip" SIZE="15"></TD></TR>
            <TR><TD COLSPAN=6><HR></TD></TR>
            <TR><TH ALIGN=LEFT COLSPAN=5>BUSINESS ADDRESS</
            TH><TD><EM>Preferred?</EM></TR>
            <TR><TD ALIGN=RIGHT>Name:</TD>
               <TD COLSPAN=4><INPUT TYPE="text" NAME="name" SIZE="40"></TD>
               <TD ALIGN=CENTER><INPUT TYPE="radio" NAME="pref" VALUE="bus">
```

Part

II

Ch

13

continues

Listing 13.26   Continued

```
</TD></TR>
            <TR><TD ALIGN=RIGHT>Street Address:</TD>
                <TD COLSPAN=4><INPUT TYPE="text" NAME="street1" SIZE="40"></TD>
                </TR>
            <TR><TD ALIGN=RIGHT>City, State, Zip:</TD>
                <TD><INPUT TYPE="text" NAME="city" SIZE="25"></TD><TD>,</TD>
                <TD><INPUT TYPE="text" NAME="state" SIZE="2"></TD>
                <TD><INPUT TYPE="text" NAME="zip" SIZE="15"></TD></TR>
        </TABLE>
    </FORM>
    </BODY>
    </HTML>
```

FIG. 13.27

HTML tables allow you to combine many different form fields and position them logically.

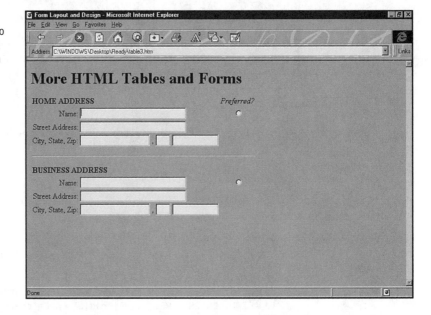

One final refinement of the address entry form (see Figure 13.28) substitutes different submit buttons for the radio buttons, shown in Figures 13.26 and 13.27. This allows the user to enter the information on the form and then specify which is the preferred address by his choice of submit button. Specifying a NAME attribute for the submit button enables the choice of button to be determined, as shown in Listing 13.27.

Listing 13.27   TABLE4.HTM—Another Example of Forms and Tables

```
<HTML>
<HEAD>
<TITLE>Form Layout and Design</TITLE>
</HEAD>
<BODY>
```

```
<H1>More HTML Tables and Forms</H1>
<FORM>
     <TABLE>
          <TR><TH ALIGN=LEFT COLSPAN=5>HOME ADDRESS</TH>
               <TD ALIGN=CENTER><EM>Preferred?</EM></TR>
          <TR><TD ALIGN=RIGHT>Name:</TD>
               <TD COLSPAN=4><INPUT TYPE="text" NAME="name" SIZE="40"></TD>
               <TD ALIGN=CENTER><INPUT TYPE="submit" NAME="home" VALUE="Home">
          </TD></TR>
          <TR><TD ALIGN=RIGHT>Street Address:</TD>
               <TD COLSPAN=4><INPUT TYPE="text" NAME="street1" SIZE="40">
          </TD></TR>
          <TR><TD ALIGN=RIGHT>City, State, Zip:</TD>
               <TD><INPUT TYPE="text" NAME="city" SIZE="25"></TD><TD>,</TD>
               <TD><INPUT TYPE="text" NAME="state" SIZE="2"></TD>
               <TD><INPUT TYPE="text" NAME="zip" SIZE="15"></TD></TR>
          <TR><TD COLSPAN=6><HR></TD></TR>
          <TR><TH ALIGN=LEFT COLSPAN=5>BUSINESS ADDRESS</TH>
               <TD ALIGN=CENTER><EM>Preferred?</EM></TR>
          <TR><TD ALIGN=RIGHT>Name:</TD>
               <TD COLSPAN=4><INPUT TYPE="text" NAME="name" SIZE="40"></TD>
               <TD ALIGN=CENTER><INPUT TYPE="submit" NAME="bus"
VALUE="Business"></TD></TR>
          <TR><TD ALIGN=RIGHT>Street Address:</TD>
               <TD COLSPAN=4><INPUT TYPE="text" NAME="street1" SIZE="40">
          </TD></TR>
          <TR><TD ALIGN=RIGHT>City, State, Zip:</TD>
               <TD><INPUT TYPE="text" NAME="city" SIZE="25"></TD><TD>,
          </TD>
               <TD><INPUT TYPE="text" NAME="state" SIZE="2"></TD>
               <TD><INPUT TYPE="text" NAME="zip" SIZE="15"></TD></TR>
     </TABLE>
</FORM>
</BODY>
</HTML>
```

Final Notes on Form Layouts

When you're creating forms, it's always a good idea to keep the form on a single page. Further, because you can't control what browser someone uses to look at your pages, you need to observe some general guidelines, as follows:

- If your form is very short, keep it under 14 lines. This ensures that it will fit on one page in most browsers. It doesn't always work, but it does create a compact page that's easy for most people to see. A good trick for keeping the pages compact is using <SELECT> tags with the size set to 1 (to show a pop-up menu) or 3 or 4 (for a small scrolling window for multiple choices) instead of having large numbers of check boxes and radio buttons.

- If your form is large (more than two pages on any browser), don't put the Submit or Reset buttons in the middle of the form. If you do, someone reading the form might not continue beyond those buttons and miss an important part of the form.

■ Put the fields on your form in a logical order. This sounds obvious, but it's easy to forget.

■ Think about your forms well before you start creating them. If you know what choices you want to provide, it makes your final layout much easier.

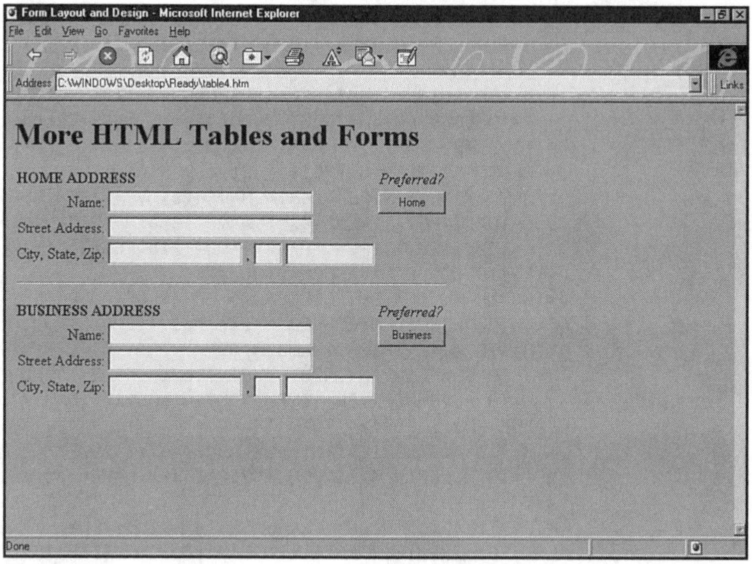

FIG. 13.28
The options available for using forms with HTML tables are limited only by your imagination.

HTML 4.0 Forms Additions

As useful as HTML forms have been, they have suffered from a variety of shortcomings and limitations, ranging from a lack of hotkey support to their reliance on only two control buttons. With the release of the HTML 4.0 specification, all that has changed. Just about every feature requested by a feature-hungry public has been added to HTML 4.0 forms.

N O T E As of this writing, the HTML 4.0 specification is brand new and neither Netscape Communicator nor Microsoft Internet Explorer support the all-new forms tags or attributes discussed
in this section. So not only can't we show you example screens, we're also passing along a caution not
to use these new tags and attributes until these browser programs add support for them. ■

New Tag Attributes

ACCESSKEY is a new attribute for use with the LABEL, A, and CAPTION tags. With it, you can define a single case-insensitive hotkey for activating a forms element. For example,

```
<LABEL ACCESSKEY="N">Name<INPUT TYPE="TEXT" NAME=USER></LABEL>
```

would create a text input field for inputting a name. When the page containing this form element is displayed, pressing the Alt+N key combination on the keyboard (Cmd+N on the

Macintosh) would change the focus immediately to this field. The user could input her name without having to first select the field by clicking it with the mouse or stepping to it using the Tab key. As an indicator to the user, the "N" in the label "Name" is underlined.

The new DISABLED attribute for INPUT, TEXTAREA, SELECT, OPTION, OBJECT, LABEL, and BUTTON turns off an element and grays it out on the screen. (The element is also skipped when tabbing between elements.) It should be used when a form element is currently inappropriate or if you want to skip a field for some reason. Once DISABLED, the only way to turn an element back on is by using an associated script, such as JavaScript.

N O T E It is not immediately clear in the HTML 4.0 specification just exactly what you need to do to make such changes dynamically via a script. Hopefully this will become known as HTML 4.0 is implemented in the major browsers.

The TEXTAREA tag and the INPUT tag's TEXT and PASSWORD types have a new READONLY attribute that can be used to prohibit user input in those fields. If you want to pass back some data that you've preset for a user, this is one way to do it. At the same time, you're making sure that data is known to the end user but is not modifiable by him. Again, you can use a script to change this state dynamically if you wish.

ONCLICK, ONFOCUS, ONBLUR, ONSELECT, and ONCHANGE are new attributes that function as place-holders for scripts that run when each of the indicated events occurs. The ONCLICK script runs when a mouse click occurs over an element, ONFOCUS when it becomes the input focus, ONBLUR when the focus moves away from the element, ONSELECT when chosen, and ONCHANGE when data in the field has changed. These exciting new attributes open up a world of new possibilities. Again, the specifics of their implementation await browsers that can interpret these new attributes.

Ever wanted to add those nifty pop-up ToolTips to your online forms? Now you'll be able to, thanks to the new TITLE attribute, which is available for use with all form input elements. Just specify TITLE="ToolTip Here" for any element.

Under HTML 3.2, there was no specified order for tabbing through elements. You hit the Tab key and the form's input focus advanced to whatever element was next in line by virtue of where it appeared in the HTML source. Unfortunately, that didn't always correspond to how those elements were arranged on the page. Now, thanks to the new HTML 4.0 TABINDEX attribute, that's going to change. It's easy to add—just add TABINDEX=n to each element, where n is equal to its place in the tabbing sequence. n must be an integer, but it can also have a negative value, which indicates that the element should be left out of the tabbing sequence. If two elements have the same TABINDEX value, they are assigned a tabbing sequence based on their order in the HTML source. Likewise, elements without a TABINDEX value are inserted into the sequence based on their source positions. As with HTML 3.2 forms, Shift+Tab moves the focus backwards through the order. Also, the Enter key is still used to activate an element that has the current focus.

Part
II

Ch

13

New HTML 4.0 Forms Tags

In addition to the new attributes discussed in the previous section, HTML 4.0 also adds several new forms-related tags.

The new LABEL tag is used to associate a label with a form element. It is useful for creating a user interface for selecting a form control. For example,

```
<LABEL FOR=NAME>Name</LABEL>
Lots of stuff goes here…
<INPUT TYPE=TEXT NAME=YOURNAME ID=NAME>
```

Clicking the NAME link in the LABEL will jump the end user to the text input field with the ID of NAME, as indicated by the FOR=NAME attribute of the LABEL tag, and will shift the focus to that field.

The LABEL element supports the use of the ID, CLASS, LANG, and DIR attributes for internationalization and access for those with disabilities, and also makes use of the STYLE attribute for accessing style sheets. The new TITLE, DISABLED, ACCESSKEY, ONCLICK, ONFOCUS, and ONBLUR attributes discussed in the previous section are also all supported by LABEL.

HTML 3.2 forms supported only the Submit and Reset buttons. HTML 4.0 forms improve on this with a user-definable BUTTON element. The BUTTON tag works in conjunction with the new ONCLICK attribute, which associates clicking the button with executing a script. The DISABLED, TABINDEX, ONFOCUS, and ONBLUR attributes are also supported by BUTTON. <BUTTON> is a container, so it must be used with an associated </BUTTON> tag. In between, you can include any HTML to define the button contents, as in this example:

```
<BUTTON ONCLICK="script.scp">
<IMG SRC="ButtonImage.gif">
Click this button to do something great!
</BUTTON>
```

Finally, the new FIELDSET container is used in conjunction with a new CAPTION container to group form elements, as in this example:

```
<FIELDSET>
  <CAPTION ACCESSKEY=N TABINDEX=1>Name Fields</CAPTION>
  <LABEL ACCESSKEY=F><INPUT TYPE=TEXT NAME=FirstName>First Name</LABEL><BR>
  <LABEL ACCESSKEY=L><INPUT TYPE=TEXT NAME=LastName>Last Name</LABEL>
</FIELDSET>
```

Note that the CAPTION container is used to define a tab order (via the TABINDEX attribute) for the entire FIELDSET group. Likewise, the FIELDSET gets a separate ACCESSKEY than that given to each of the individual elements.

FIELDSET containers are nestable, but each should contain only a single CAPTION field.

FIELDSET also supports use of the new TITLE attribute. ●

## CHAPTER 14

Inserting Objects into a Web Page

by Jerry Honeycutt and Mark R. Brown

In this chapter

Three Ways to Go

There are three ways to put multimedia objects into your pages: browser plug-ins, ActiveX controls, and Java applets. You'll briefly examine each in this chapter.

You'll also learn how to use HTML tags to insert any of these three kinds of multimedia "players" into your HTML documents. Let's start by looking at browser plug-ins.

Getting to Know Plug-ins

When a user starts a Web browser—Netscape Communicator, for example—on her desktop, it checks the appropriate folder (see Table 14.1) to see what plug-ins are installed. Communicator makes a note of each plug-in and its MIME type, which indicates the type of file with which the plug-in is associated.

Table 14.1 Netscape Plug-in Folders	
Platform	**Folder**
MAC	Plug-ins, directly under the Netscape folder
Windows	Plugins, directly under the Netscape folder.
UNIX	/usr/local/netscape/plugins

When the user opens a Web page that embeds a multimedia file, Communicator notes the MIME type of the file, finds a plug-in that can open that type of file (if available), and loads the plug-in, passing it the file. The drawing in Figure 14.1 illustrates this concept for you. The most important concept for you to understand is that you, as the HTML author, embed a multimedia file into your Web page, while a plug-in on the user's computer actually displays that file in the Web browser.

FIG. 14.1
You provide the data, and the user provides the plug-in.

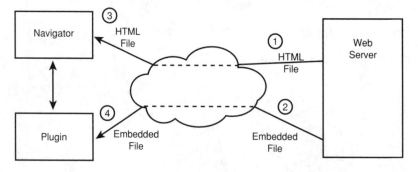

1. Web page
2. Multimedia (or Embedded) file
3. Communicator
4. Plug-in

TIP The information contained in this section is valid for all plug-ins, whether you use the <EMBED> tag or <OBJECT> tag to insert them.

Embedded Plug-ins

Embedded plug-ins are visible on the Web page and display inline with the rest of the Web page's content. Embedded plug-ins always occupy a rectangular area on the Web page (see Figure 14.2). You, as the HTML author, embed the multimedia file in the Web page, and the plug-in, on the user's computer, displays that file inside the Web page.

Embedded plug-ins can be hidden. That is, the HTML author can designate that the plug-in is not to display anything on the Web page. For example, you might not want to display anything on the Web page if you're embedding a sound file.

FIG. 14.2
Live3D is a Netscape plug-in for displaying VRML worlds that comes with Netscape Communicator.

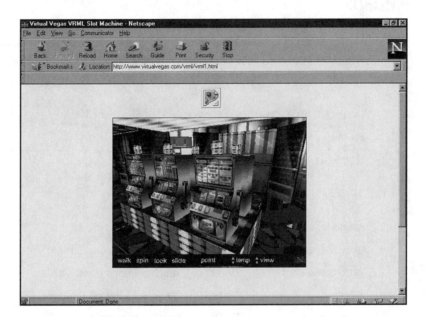

Full-Page Plug-ins

Other plug-ins are full page; they don't occupy space in the Web page itself, but occupy the entire browser window. After the user has finished interacting with the plug-in, she can click Back on Communicator's Navigation toolbar to return to the original Web page.

Inserting Plug-ins into Your Web Page

With the latest Web browsers, and thanks to the efforts of the World Wide Web Consortium (W3C), you have two different ways to embed plug-ins into your Web page. You can use the old

Part
II

Ch
14

sturdy <EMBED> tag, or you can use the new HTML 4.0 standard <OBJECT> tag. Making this choice is a lot harder than actually writing the HTML for either. Here are some thoughts on the subject, though, that might help you:

- Use the <EMBED> tag if you're concerned with compatibility across a variety of Web browsers. This Netscape extension has been in place since Navigator 2.0 and thus many other Web browsers have adopted its use.

- Use the <OBJECT> tag if (1) you want to be hip to the latest HTML technology, (2) you want to conform to the HTML 4.0 standard, or (3) you want to use the <OBJECT> tag's apology section to supply content for those browser's that don't support plug-ins. The simple truth of the matter is that both Microsoft and Netscape are adopting the use of the <OBJECT> tag for this kind of work, so you might want to start doing it yourself.

<EMBED>

You have a fair amount of control over any plug-in that you embed into your Web page using the <EMBED> tag. You can control its size, for example, or whether or not the browser actually displays the plug-in. Many plug-ins also allow you to set additional attributes that control them. Table 14.2 describes each attribute of this tag.

Table 14.2   <EMBED> Attributes

Attribute	Description
ALIGN=value	LEFT—align text flush left RIGHT—align text flush right TOP—align text with top BOTTOM—align text with bottom
BORDER=num	Width of frame's border in pixels
FRAMEBORDER=value	NO—do not draw border around frame
HEIGHT=num	Height of frame as defined by UNITS
HIDDEN	Makes the plug-in invisible on the page
HSPACE=num	Width of left and right margin in pixels
NAME=name	Name of the embedded object
PALETTE=value	FOREGROUND—foreground colors BACKGROUND—background colors
PLUGINSPAGE=URL	URL of the Web page that contains instructions for installing the plug-in if the user does not have it installed
SRC=URL	URL that indicates the location of the embedded multimedia data file; if you don't use this attribute, use TYPE
TYPE=type	MIME type of the embedded object, which determines the plug-in that loads; use TYPE for plug-ins that require no data

Attribute	Description
UNITS=*value*	PIXELS—use pixels as a unit of measurement, while EN—use half the normal display font point size
VSPACE=*num*	Width of top and bottom margin in pixels
WIDTH=*num*	Width of frame as defined by UNITS

Many plug-ins also have *private attributes*. Communicator looks for all of the attributes described in Table 14.2 when it parses the <EMBED> tag, but it ignores other attributes. When Communicator loads the associated plug-in, it passes the plug-in all of the attributes it found. For example, many audio plug-ins have a private attribute called AUTOSTART, which indicates whether or not you want the plug-in to immediately start playing the sound file when it loads.

<OBJECT>

W3C has made the <OBJECT> tag an official part of HTML 4.0. Many vendors, however, including Microsoft and Netscape, had already adopted the <OBJECT> tag before the specification was finished. You can get the full details on this tag at W3C's Web site: **http://www.w3.org/pub/WWW/TR/WD-object**.

Using the <OBJECT> tag is just a bit more complicated than using the <EMBED> tag. You have to form the <OBJECT> tag as described in Table 14.3, specify any required parameters using the <PARAM> tag, and provide content for those users who have browsers with no <OBJECT> support or who don't have the required plug-in. This topic is covered in depth later in this chapter, in the ActiveX section.

Table 14.3   *<OBJECT>* Attributes for Plug-ins

Attribute	Description
BORDER=*num*	Width of frame's border in pixels
CLASSID=*URL*	URL of the plug-in, on the Internet, for installing the plug-in if the user does not have it installed
DATA=*URL*	URL of the object's data file
HEIGHT=*num*	Height of frame as defined by UNITS
HSPACE=*num*	Width of left and right margin in pixels
ID=*name*	Name of the embedded object
TYPE=*type*	MIME type of the embedded object, which determines the plug-in that loads; use TYPE for plug-ins that require no data
TYPE=*type*	MIME type of the object's data file
VSPACE=*num*	Width of top and bottom margin in pixels
WIDTH=*num*	Width of frame as defined by UNITS

Part
II

Ch
14

Sandwiching <PARAM> Tags   You can provide additional properties to the plug-in, if the plug-in supports them, using the <PARAM> tag. You embed a <PARAM> tag between the beginning and ending <OBJECT> tags for each property you want to provide to the plug-in, like this:

```
<OBJECT definition>
  <PARAM NAME="LOOP" VALUE="TRUE">
</OBJECT>
```

Using the <PARAM> tag is similar to using private properties with the <EMBED> tag. The NAME attribute is the name of the property and the VALUE attribute is the actual value that you want to assign to that name. Thus, the following PARAM tag is equivalent to the AUTOSTART attribute in the <EMBED> tag you see just below it:

```
<PARAM NAME=AUTOSTART VALUE=TRUE>

<EMBED blah-blah-blah AUTOSTART=TRUE>
```

Providing Alternate Content (Apology)   Not all browsers or users are created equal. Some browsers won't know what in the world to do with the <OBJECT> tag. Still, some users won't have access to a plug-in that you've embedded into your Web page. The authors of the <OBJECT> tag working draft have created a way for you to handle this situation, however: alternative content. Some folks also call the alternative content the apology section. Here's how it works:

- If the browser can handle the <OBJECT> tag and it has a plug-in available for the specified data type, the browser parses the <OBJECT> tag and any <PARAM> tags contained within it. It ignores everything else, though.

- If the browser can handle the <OBJECT> tag, but it doesn't have a plug-in available for the specified data type, the browser ignores the <OBJECT> tag and the <PARAM> tags contained within it. The browser does parse any other content contained within the <OBJECT> tag, however.

- If the browser can't handle the <OBJECT> tag, it won't be able to handle the <PARAM> tag either. By design, the browser will not parse those tags, but will parse anything else in its path, including content inside the <OBJECT> tag.

Consider Listing 14.1, for example, which is an example of inserting a multimedia file into a Web page. If the browser doesn't do the <OBJECT> tag, all it's going to parse is the <A>, <IMG>, and </A> tags. If the browser does support the <OBJECT> tag, but it doesn't have a plug-in for MOX files, it ignores the <OBJECT> and <PARAM> tags, parsing the same tags as in the previous case. Last, if the browser does support the <OBJECT> tag and it has a plug-in for MOX files, it parses the <OBJECT> and <PARAM> tags, ignoring everything else.

Listing 14.1   Alternative Content

```
<OBJECT DATA=MYFILE.MOX WIDTH=100 HEIGHT=100>
  <PARAM NAME=AUTOSTART VALUE=TRUE>
  <A HREF="get-mox.htm">
    <IMG SRC=need-mox.gif WIDTH=100 HEIGHT=100>
  </A>
</OBJECT>
```

Some Real-World Plug-In Examples

A Word with Our Lawyer, Please?

Copyright laws protect the author of a work from other folks making illegal copies of it. You can't photocopy a magazine article or make a duplicate of a musical CD, for example, without violating the copyright law. If you do, the organization that owns the copyright can pursue the matter in court (translation: sue the pants off of you).

The copyright laws apply to electronic expression as much as they do to other forms. Thus, the Web pages and multimedia files you find on the Internet can have copyrights with just as much weight as the copyright on this book. Ignorance isn't an excuse, either. Just because you didn't know that a file was copyrighted doesn't protect you when the copyright hits the fan.

So, having scared you a bit, how do you know if an image is indeed copyrighted? It's not quite as cut-and-dry as looking for a copyright symbol (audio clips don't have one). In fact, there is no requirement that work contain a copyright symbol in order to be protected by the copyright laws. You can check a few other places for a file's copyright status, however:

- Look for a copyright notice in the document that originally contained the file. This is the most likely place to find such a notice.

- If you're using a video from a library, check the library's license agreement to see what kind of rights you have for redistribution.

- Look for any comments embedded within the file that might include a copyright notice. Most audio and video editors allow you to edit and view embedded comments.

Before you can jazz up your Web page with multimedia, you have to make or find it. Making your own multimedia content isn't always practical, especially for a novice. You have to work within a third-party authoring environment such as a video editor and sometimes have to purchase additional hardware such as a video camera. You can learn more about creating your own multimedia content in Part IV, "Serving Multimedia Content."

Using free or store-bought multimedia libraries is the quickest route to multimedia bliss. Most multimedia libraries come with a combination of graphical images, sound clips, and video clips. Some libraries do include a handful of Shockwave files, too. While you can find a whole host of different plug-ins, you'll mostly use audio and video in your Web page. It's a reality for most HTML authors, and that's good for two reasons:

- Netscape Communicator, and most other Web browsers, have the built-in capability to play audio and display video files. Netscape has LiveAudio and LiveVideo, for example. Microsoft has ActiveMovie.

- Audio and video files are relatively easy to come by. You can download files from the Internet, or you can purchase CD-ROMs from your local computer retailer that contain a selection of both file types. Yes, you can also make these files on your own, which you learn how to do in Part IV, "Serving Multimedia Content."

Part
II

Ch
14

NOTE To see a list of those types of plug-ins that come with Communicator, choose Help, About Plug-ins from Communicator's main menu. You'll see a list similar to that shown in Figure 14.3. ■

FIG. 14.3
Click click here, at the top of this page, to see a list of plug-ins available at Netscape's Web site.

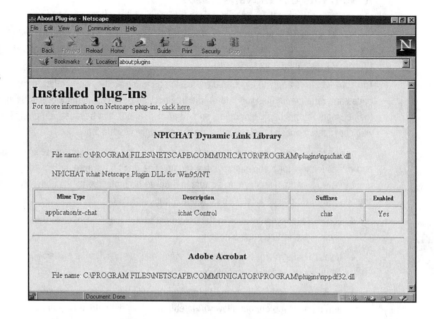

Audio

Netscape Communicator comes with an audio plug-in called LiveAudio. As shown in Figure 14.4, LiveAudio has a very simple user interface that the user can interact with to stop, play, and pause the audio clip, as well as adjust the volume. LiveAudio handles a majority of the sound files you'll find on the Internet. It definitely handles WAV and MIDI files, which takes care of most of the audio content you'll embed into your Web page.

FIG. 14.4
LiveAudio sports controls that anyone who has ever used a tape deck can understand.

N O T E A user must have a sound card and speakers installed in her computer in order to hear any audio clips embedded in your Web page. Chances are good that most users do have a sound card these days, though. ■

You can use either the <EMBED> or the <OBJECT> tag to embed an audio file into your Web page. Listing 14.2 shows you an example of a Web page that uses <EMBED>. The SRC, WIDTH, and HEIGHT attributes are the same ones you learned about earlier in this chapter. If you want the user to see the audio controls, you must use the WIDTH and HEIGHT attributes. The best size for the controls is 144 pixels wide and 60 pixels high.

Listing 14.2   Embedding Audio Using *<EMBED>*

```
<HTML>
  <HEAD>
    <TITLE>Embedding audio using EMBED</TITLE>
  </HEAD>
  <BODY>
    <EMBED SRC=EXAMPLE.WAV HEIGHT=60 WIDTH=144>
  </BODY>
</HTML>
```

Listing 14.3 shows you the same example using the <OBJECT> tag. The parameters are the same as those for the <EMBED> tag, except that you use the DATA attribute instead of the SRC attribute to specify the source file.

Listing 14.3   Embedding Audio Using *<OBJECT>*

```
<HTML>
  <HEAD>
    <TITLE>Embedding audio using OBJECT</TITLE>
  </HEAD>
  <BODY>
    <OBJECT DATA=EXAMPLE.WAV WIDTH=144 HEIGHT=60>
    </OBJECT>
  </BODY>
</HTML>
```

LiveAudio supports several private attributes, each described in Table 14.4.

Part
II

Ch
14

Table 14.4   LiveAudio's Private Attributes

Attribute	Description
AUTOSTART=*value*	TRUE—plays automatically FALSE—doesn't play automatically
AUTOLOAD=*value*	TRUE—load clip automatically FALSE—don't load clip automatically
STARTTIME="*mm:ss*"	Start time from beginning of clip
ENDTIME="*mm:ss*"	End time from beginning of clip
VOLUME=*num*	Initial value as a percentage
CONTROLS=*value*	CONSOLE—display the console SMALLCONSOLE—display small console PLAYBUTTON—display play button PAUSEBUTTON—display pause button STOPBUTTON—display stop button VOLUMELEVER—display volume slider

TIP   Choose MIDI files over WAV files every chance you get. For the same file size, you can get a much longer audio clip from a MIDI file than you can from a WAV file. It's more economical.

Video

Like audio, you can use the <EMBED> or <OBJECT> tag to embed a video into your Web page. Listing 14.4 shows you an example of a Web page that uses the <EMBED> tag to embed an AVI file into a Web page. The SRC, WIDTH, and HEIGHT attributes are the same ones you learned about earlier in this chapter.

Listing 14.4   Embedding a Video Using *<EMBED>*

```
<HTML>
  <HEAD>
    <TITLE>Embedding a video using EMBED</TITLE>
  </HEAD>
  <BODY>
    <EMBED SRC=EXAMPLE.AVI WIDTH=150 HEIGHT=100>
  </BODY>
</HTML>
```

Listing 14.5 shows you the same example using the <OBJECT> tag. Note that the parameters are the same as those for the <EMBED> tag, except that you use the DATA attribute instead of the SRC attribute to specify the source file. In this example, you see the <IMG> tag sandwiched in the object, which provides alternative content for users who can't display videos. Figure 14.5 shows what this video looks like in Communicator.

Listing 14.5   Embedding a Video Using *<OBJECT>*

```
<HTML>
  <HEAD>
    <TITLE>Embedding a video using OBJECT</TITLE>
  </HEAD>
  <BODY>
    <OBJECT DATA=EXAMPLE.AVI WIDTH=150 HEIGHT=100>
      <IMG SRC=EXAMPLE.GIF WIDTH=150 HEIGHT=100>
    </OBJECT>
  </BODY>
</HTML>
```

FIG. 14.5
To access the controls when they're not visible on the Web page, right-click the video.

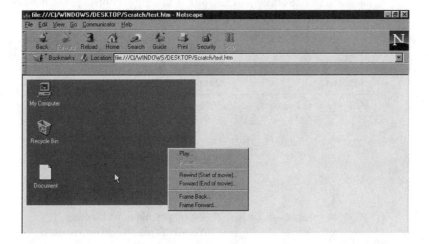

AVI Files (LiveVideo)   LiveVideo, which is the plug-in for AVI files, has some additional private attributes that you can use to better control how the plug-in displays in the browser. You see those attributes in Table 14.5.

Part
II

Ch
14

Table 14.5 LiveVideo's Private Attributes

Attribute	Description
AUTOSTART=*value*	TRUE— video starts automatically FALSE—video doesn't start automatically
LOOP=*value*	TRUE—video plays repeatedly FALSE—video plays one time
CONTROLS=*value*	TRUE—plug-in shows video controls FALSE—plug-in doesn't show video controls

TIP Turn your favorite AVI video into an animated GIF. Download the GIF Construction Set from Ziff-Davis (**http://www.hotfiles.com**), which converts an AVI file into an animated GIF frame by frame. It cuts the size of the file in half, and allows the user to see the animation as the file loads from the Web server.

MOV Files (QuickTime)   The QuickTime plug-in included with Netscape Communicator also has some private attributes that you can specify to control how it displays in the browser. You see those attributes in Table 14.6.

Table 14.6 QuickTime's Private Attributes

Attribute	Description
AUTOPLAY=*value*	TRUE—automatically start FALSE—don't automatically start
CONTROLLER=*value*	TRUE—display a toolbar FALSE—don't display a toolbar
LOOP=*value*	TRUE—play video repeatedly FALSE—play video a single time
PLAYEVERYFRAME=*value*	TRUE—play while downloading FALSE—don't play while downloading
HREF=*URL*	URL to which the video is linked
TARGET=*FRAME*	Targeted link for the video

Rewarding the User (Bandwidth)

Be considerate of those users who have slow connections to the Internet. A user who has a 28.8K connection to the Internet, which is very common, will wait over four minutes for a 1M video to download. A 1M video, on the other hand, plays only for a few seconds; thus, you're asking a user to wait four minutes to view a few seconds of video—blah. The user will feel cheated unless it's a pretty spectacular video clip. Mark Brown calls this the *wait/reward ratio*. Think of it this way: if the only reward you get after waiting seven hours for Thanksgiving dinner is Kentucky Fried Chicken, you'd feel a bit cheated.

The solution? Provide a link on your Web page to the video clip. If a user wants to see the video clip, she can click on the link—it's her choice. For example, you might add a link to your Web page, with a warning, that looks something like this:

```
Take a look at this AVI video of my new Yorkie.

This video is 1M in size. At 14.4K, it'll take over nine minutes to down-
load. At 28.8K it'll take over four minutes.
```

Finding Other Useful Plug-ins

You'll need to use a third-party plug-in if you want to embed multimedia content into your Web page other than video, audio, and VRML—for example, Shockwave.

Netscape maintains a fairly comprehensive list of plug-ins. You'll find this list at http:// home.netscape.com/comprod/products/navigator/version_2.0/plugins. Click one of the categories (there are six: 3D and Animation; Business and Utilities; Presentations; Audio/ Video; Image Viewers; and What's New), and you'll see a list of plug-ins. For each plug-in, you'll see a description and links to the vendor and example Web pages.

However, the ultimate resource for plug-ins is BrowserWatch (**http://browserwatch. iworld.com/plug-in.html**, shown in Figure 14.6). You can view the list by different categories: multimedia, graphics, sound, document, productivity, or VRML. You can also view the list of plug-ins by platform: Macintosh, OS/2, UNIX, and Windows.

FIG. 14.6
The BrowserWatch Web site provides links to each plug-in's vendor, as well as links to example Web pages.

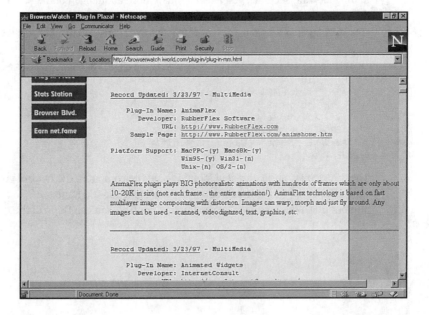

Part
II

Ch
14

TIP If you use a plug-in that the user isn't likely to already have installed, use the PLUGINSPAGE attribute to point Communicator to the download page for that plug-in. Doing so will help Communicator install the plug-in more or less automatically.

Inserting ActiveX Controls

ActiveX controls are small applications that run only on Windows platforms and only in Microsoft Internet Explorer (IE).

That's a bit of an oversimplification, actually. There is a plug-in that lets ActiveX controls run in Netscape Navigator, if you really want to use them. However, it's best to assume if you use ActiveX controls that your target audience will be using IE on a Windows platform.

That having been said, it should be noted that there is one very good reason for using ActiveX controls in your HTML documents: if you know they're going to be viewed on a Windows system in Internet Explorer, ActiveX controls are the fastest, most efficient objects you can use for multimedia and interactive controls. Why? Because ActiveX controls are written to run natively on those machines. Where plug-ins are often big and unwieldy, and Java applets must be interpreted before they are run, ActiveX controls download automatically, reside on your system, and run efficiently under Windows.

You use the <OBJECT> tag to insert ActiveX objects into an HTML document. With regard to ActiveX controls, the <OBJECT> tag identifies the control you're using. That is, the <OBJECT> tag identifies which control on the user's computer you want to use and gives that instance of the control a name, which you can use in scripts. That's all.

In the following sections, you'll learn much more about each of the <OBJECT> tag's attributes as they relate to ActiveX controls. Before doing that, however, take a look at how you use the <OBJECT> tag in a Web page. In its simplest form, the <OBJECT> tag looks something like this:

```
<OBJECT
        classid="clsid:1A771020-A28E-11CF-8510-00AA003B6C7E"
        id=Track1
        width=400
        height=2
        align=left>
<IMG SRC="noobject.gif">
<PARAM NAME="Image" VALUE="image.gif">
</OBJECT>
```

The CLASSID attribute uniquely identifies, on the computer, the control you're using. Every control installed on the user's computer is installed in the Registry. The control's CLASSID is the number that Windows uses to identify that control. You can think of the CLASSID as a name that is guaranteed to be unique. You'll learn more about this attribute later. In this case, we're using the View Tracker control. You use the ID attribute to identify the control to the scripts in your Web page. WIDTH, HEIGHT, and ALIGN work the same as with other types of tags; they specify the size and location of the control on the Web page.

ON THE WEB

You can get a good idea as to what types of ActiveX controls are available by going to **http://www.microsoft.com/activex/gallery**. If you're running Internet Explorer, several useful ActiveX controls were already installed along with IE.

Setting a Control's Properties with the *PARAM* Tag

You will need to set the properties of the ActiveX controls you put on the Web page in order to control its appearance or function. For example, you need to give the Stock Ticker control the URL of the text file it should use for data. You need to provide the Label control with the text it should display. The only way to know for sure which properties each control requires is to check the control's documentation. You can also use the ActiveX Control Pad to set a control's properties.

ON THE WEB

The ActiveX Control Pad is a free tool available for downloading from the Microsoft site at **http://www.microsoft.com**.

So, how do you set these properties? You use the <PARAM> tag to assign a value to a named property within the control. This works very much like Visual Basic property sheets. Note the <PARAM> tag has no closing </PARAM> tag. Table 21.2 describes the attributes you use with the <PARAM> tag. You frequently need to use only the NAME and VALUE attributes.

Table 14.2   Attributes of the *PARAM* Tag

Attribute	Description
NAME	Defines the name of the property. An ActiveX control can treat the name as case-sensitive.
VALUE	Specifies the value of the property identified in NAME.
VALUETYPE	Can be one of REF, OBJECT, or DATA.
TYPE	Refers to Internet Media Type (RFC 1590) of the item referred to in the VALUE field when VALUETYPE = REF.

Part
II

Ch
14

NAME, VALUE, and TYPE are self-explanatory. Table 21.3 describes the settings you can use with VALUETYPE.

Table 14.3   Values for *VALUETYPE* Attribute

Value	Meaning
REF	VALUE contains an URL.
OBJECT	VALUE contains URL of another OBJECT.
DATA	VALUE contains string data.

The following is an example of inserting an ActiveX control by using the <OBJECT>tag. The CLASSID attribute specifies the Popup Menu control, and each <PARAM> tag adds a menu item to the menu.

```
<OBJECT
        id=iemenu1
        classid="clsid:0482B100-739C-11CF-A3A9-00A0C9034920"
        width=1
        height=1
        align=left
        hspace=0
        vspace=0
    >
    <PARAM NAME="Menuitem[0]" VALUE="First Choice">
    <PARAM NAME="Menuitem[1]" VALUE="Second Choice">
    <PARAM NAME="Menuitem[2]" VALUE="Third Choice">
    <PARAM NAME="Menuitem[3]" VALUE="Fourth Choice">
    <PARAM NAME="Menuitem[4]" VALUE="Firth Choice">
</OBJECT>
```

More About the *<OBJECT>* Tag

The <OBJECT> tag has a number of attributes you can use. The sections that follow describe each attribute. In reality, however, you'll find yourself using only a few: CLASSID, ID, HEIGHT, WIDTH, ALIGN, and, possibly, CODEBASE.

ALIGN   You use the ALIGN attribute to specify where to place the object. You can position an object relative to the text line or on its own on the left, right, or center of the page. Table 20.4 describes the settings you can use to align the object with the text line. Table 21.5 also describes the settings you can use to align the object with the page.

Table 14.4   Aligning the Object with the Text Line

Setting	Description
TEXTTOP	The top of the object is aligned with the top of the current font.
MIDDLE	The middle of the object is aligned with the baseline of the text line.
TEXTMIDDLE	The middle of the object is aligned with the middle of the text line.
BASELINE	The bottom of the object is aligned with the baseline of the text line.
TEXTBOTTOM	The bottom of the object is aligned with the bottom of the current font.

Table 14.5   Aligning the Object with the Web Page

Setting	Description
LEFT	The object is aligned with the left side of the Web page and text flows around the right side of the object.
CENTER	The object is aligned in the center of the Web page and the text starts on the line following the object.
RIGHT	The object is aligned with the right side of the Web page and text flows around the left side of the object.

BORDER   When you use an object as part of a hypertext link, you can specify whether or not the object has a border. The BORDER attribute specifies the width of the border around the object. If you don't want a border around the object, set this attribute to 0, like this: BORDER=0.

CLASSID* and *CODEBASE   You use CLASSID to refer to the ActiveX control to be placed within the object's borders. There are several different ways to indicate the object to be inserted here. ActiveX uses the clsid: URL scheme to specify the ActiveX class identifier.

ON THE WEB

For further information on the clsid: URL scheme, see **http://www.w3.org/pub/WWW/Addressing/clsid-scheme**.

The best way to obtain the CLSID for an ActiveX control is to look at the control's documentation. You can look up Microsoft's ActiveX controls at Microsoft's ActiveX Gallery. Alternatively, use the ActiveX Control Pad to insert an ActiveX control in your Web page so you don't have to

Part

II

Ch

14

worry about the CLSID. If the CLASSID attribute is missing, ActiveX data streams will include a class identifier that can be used by the ActiveX loader to find the appropriate control.

The CODEBASE attribute can be used to provide an URL from which the control can be obtained. If the control is already installed on the user's computer, the browser will do nothing with this attribute. If the control isn't installed on the user's computer, however, the browser will try to download the control from the URL in CODEBASE and install it.

N O T E You can also get the CLASSID for an ActiveX control from the Windows Registry, like this:

1. Open the Registry Editor. Choose Run from the Start menu, type **regedit**, and press Enter.

2. Locate a control under HKEY_CLASSES_ROOT, such as Internet.Gradient or Internet.Label.

3. Note the default value of the clsid subkey for that control. This is the string you use in the CLASSID attribute.

You can learn more about clsids in *Special Edition Using the Windows 95 Registry* or *Windows 95 Registry and Customization Handbook* by Que. ■

CODETYPE The CODETYPE attribute is used to specify the Internet Media Type for the code pointed to by the CLASSID attribute. Browsers use this value to check the type of code before downloading it from the server. Thus, the browser can avoid a lengthy download for those objects that it doesn't support.

Currently, the CODETYPE attribute is supported in a limited fashion in Internet Explorer 3.0. Microsoft has indicated that TYPE will be implemented for all relevant MIME types.

DATA The DATA attribute contains an URL that points to data required by the object, for instance, a GIF file for an image. Internet Explorer currently supports the DATA attribute.

DECLARE You'll use the DECLARE attribute to tell the browser whether to instantiate the object or not. If the DECLARE attribute is present, it indicates the object should not be instantiated until something references it. That is, the browser will note the declaration of the object, but won't actually load it until you reference it.

HEIGHT The HEIGHT attribute defines the height, in pixels, to make available to the ActiveX control when rendered by the browser. The Web browser may (or may not) use this value to scale an object to the requested height.

HSPACE The HSPACE attribute defines the amount of space, in pixels, to keep as white space on the left and right as a buffer between the ActiveX control and surrounding page elements. The Web browser may (or may not) use this value to allocate white space.

ID The ID attribute defines a document-wide identifier. This can be used for naming positions within documents. You also use the control's ID to reference it in scripts.

NAME   You use the NAME attribute to indicate whether an object wrapped in a <FORM> tag will be submitted as part of the form. If you specify NAME, the Web browser submits the VALUE property of the object to the host. If you don't specify NAME, the ActiveX control is assumed to be decorative and not functional in the form.

STANDBY   STANDY is a short string of text the browser displays while it loads the ActiveX control.

TYPE   The TYPE attribute is used to specify the Internet Media Type for the data specified by the DATA attribute.

ON THE WEB

You can learn more about Internet Media Types by referring to RFC 1590. You can get RFC 1590 from the Internet at **ftp://ds.internic.net/rfc/rfc1590.txt**.

USEMAP   The value in USEMAP specifies an URL for a client-side imagemap.

VSPACE   The VSPACE attribute defines the amount of space in pixels to keep as white space on the top and bottom as a buffer between the ActiveX control and surrounding page elements. The Web browser may (or may not) use this value to allocate the requested white space.

WIDTH   The WIDTH attribute defines the width, in pixels, to make available to the ActiveX control when rendered by the browser. The Web browser may (or may not) use this value to scale an object to the requested width.

Connecting Controls to Scripts

Now, we're getting to the meat of the matter. You've learned how to insert ActiveX controls into your Web page by using the <OBJECT> tag. Now, you need to learn how to interact with those controls by using a scripting language. In the sections that follow, you'll learn how to handle the events that are fired by a control. You'll also learn how to get and set a control's properties from your scripts. Incidentally, my scripting language of choice is VBScript, so that's what I'm using in these examples. The JavaScript versions of these examples aren't much different, however.

▶ **See** "Adding JavaScript and VBScript to HTML," **p.337**

ActiveX controls act like and quack like the elements on a form. That is, you interact with each ActiveX control's properties, methods, and events in exactly the same way in which you interact with a form's element. You handle a control's events when the control needs attention; you call a control's methods, and you get and set the control's properties.

Handling an Event

You can use a couple of different methods of handling events for forms and elements (event-procedures, inline event handlers, and so on). One such method is to use the FOR/EVENT attributes of the SCRIPT tag.

Part

II

Ch

14

The FOR and EVENT attributes let you associate a script with any named object in the HTML file and any event for that object. Take a look at the following:

```
<SCRIPT LANGUAGE="VBScript" FOR="btnButton" EVENT="Click">
<!--
 window.alert( "Ouch! You clicked on me." )
-->
</SCRIPT>
<OBJECT ID="btnButton" WIDTH=96 HEIGHT=32
        CLASSID="CLSID:D7053240-CE69-11CD-A777-00DD01143C57">
        <PARAM NAME="Caption" VALUE="Click Me">
        <PARAM NAME="Size" VALUE="2540;847">
</OBJECT>
```

You can add this code to an HTML file, and you'll see a button (with an ID of btnButton) that executes the script when you click it. Take a look at the <SCRIPT> tag. It contains the FOR and EVENT attributes that define the object and event associated with that script. FOR="btnButton" EVENT="Click" says that when an object named btnButton fires the Click event, every statement in this script is executed.

Some events pass arguments to the event handlers. How do you handle arguments when you're handling the event by using the FOR/EVENT syntax? Like the following:

```
<SCRIPT LANGUAGE="JavaScript" FOR="btnButton" EVENT=
"MouseMove(shift, button, x, y)">
```

The enclosed script can then use any of the parameters passed to it by the MouseMove event.

 Once you've specified a language in your HTML file, you don't need to do it again. Your browser defaults to the most recently used language in the HTML file. You can put <SCRIPT LANGUAGE="VBScript"> </SCRIPT> at the very beginning of your HTML file one time and forget about it. The rest of the scripts in your file will use VBScript.

You just saw the Click event. ActiveX controls support a wide variety of other events. The best way to know for sure which events a control supports is to consult the control's documentation or the ActiveX Control Pad's documentation. For your convenience, however, the following list describes the most prevalent and useful events:

- BeforeUpdate occurs before data in a control changes.
- Change occurs when the value property in a control changes.
- Click occurs when the user either clicks the control with the left mouse button or selects a single value from a list of possible values.
- DblClick occurs when the user clicks twice rapidly with the left mouse button.
- DropButtonClick occurs when a drop-down list appears or disappears.
- KeyDown occurs when a user presses a key.
- KeyUp occurs when a user releases a key.
- KeyPress occurs when the user presses an ANSI key.

- MouseDown occurs when the user holds down a mouse button.
- MouseUp occurs when the user releases a mouse button.
- MouseMove occurs when the user moves the mouse pointer over a control.
- Scroll occurs when the user changes a scroll bar.

N O T E Often, the easiest way to see the events, properties, and methods that an ActiveX control supports is to insert it into a Web page by using the ActiveX Control Pad and pop open the Script Wizard. The Script Wizard lists all of the control's events in the left-hand pane. It lists all of the control's properties and methods in the right-hand pane. ■

Changing an Object's Properties

Many objects let the user input data. For example, the user can choose an item from a list, type text into an edit box, or click a check box. What good are those objects if you can't get and set their value? Not much. You read the value of most elements by using the object's value property in an assignment or logical expression. The following example assigns the text the user typed into the txtTextBox control to a variable called str. The next example compares the text the user typed into the txtTextBox with the word "Howdy".

```
str = txtTextBox.value

If txtTextBox.value = "Howdy" Then
```

You can also set the value of an element from within a script by assigning a string to the element's value, as follows:

```
txtTextBox.value = "New Contents of the Text Box"
```

The value property is the default property for most ActiveX controls that accept user input. Thus, you can use them in an expression without explicitly using the value property, like this:

```
alert txtTextBox
txtTextBox = "New Contents of the Text Box"
```

Adding Java Applets to Your Pages

Sun Microsystems's object-oriented programming language Java is creating a lot of interest on the Web. You can use Java to create dynamic, interactive Web pages. You don't have to be a Java programmer to use Java applets—many are available on the Web for free.

▶ **See** "Finding Java Applets to Borrow," **p. 529**

The Java language is object-oriented and very similar to C++. It was designed to take many of the best features of C++ while simplifying it to make writing programs easier.

Programs are normally created to run on only one type of operating system. Windows 95 programs have been specifically created to run on systems running the Windows 95 operating system and will not run on the Macintosh or on a UNIX system. Java programs, however, are intended to be platform independent. Java programs are compiled into a series of *bytecodes* that

Part
II

Ch
14

are interpreted by a Java interpreter. After a Java program has been compiled, it can run on any system with a Java interpreter. You do not need to recompile it.

This capability makes Java an ideal language for programs on the Web. With so many different systems on the Web, creating programs that will work with all of them is very difficult. Because Java programs are platform independent, programs are no longer restricted to running on one platform. They can run on any platform to which Java has been ported.

Java has been ported to many different platforms. Sun has ported Java to Solaris, Windows NT, Windows 95, and the Macintosh. Other companies have ported Java to Silicon Graphics IRIX, IBM OS/2, IBM AIX, and Linux.

Using the *<APPLET>* Tag

Java programs that can be embedded into WWW pages are called Java *applets*. To run applets from Web pages, you must have a browser that supports Java, such as HotJava, Netscape, or Internet Explorer.

If you want to write your own Java applets, you should download the Java Development Kit from Javasoft or purchase Microsoft's Visual J++. Javasoft is available for free on the Web. You can download it from the Javasoft Home page at **http://www.javasoft.com**.

Microsoft Visual J++ is relatively inexpensive. You can purchase it at most computer retailers such as CompUSA or Computer City.

Now take a look at a few examples. Listing 14.1 shows the code for a simple Java applet.

Listing 14.1   A "Hello World" Java Applet

```
import java.applet.*;
import java.awt.*;

class HelloWorld extends Applet {
    public void paint(Graphics g) {
        g.drawString("Hello World!",20,20);
    }
}
```

When you place this applet into a page and run it, it prints Hello World!. But, before you can use it in a page, you must compile the applet using javac, the Java compiler. The files that Javac creates are called Java class files. A class file is the platform-independent object file that the browser retrieves when downloading a Java applet.

To use this applet on an HTML page, you have to describe it using the <APPLET> tag. Listing 14.2 shows an HTML page that loads this example applet.

Listing 14.2   HTML for Hello World Applet

```
<HTML>
<HEAD>
<TITLE>HelloWorld Applet</TITLE>
<BODY>
<APPLET CODE=HelloWorld HEIGHT=100 WIDTH=150>
</APPLET>
</BODY>
</HTML>
```

The <APPLET> and </APPLET> tags act as a container for the Java applet definition. They indicate to the browser that a Java applet should be loaded. The CODE attribute tells the browser which Java applet should be downloaded. The browser reserves space in the page by using the WIDTH and HEIGHT attributes, just as it reserves space for the IMG element. Then the browser downloads the Java class specified in the CODE attribute and begins running the applet.

In this case, the applet being downloaded is HelloWorld, and it reserves a space 150 pixels high and 200 pixels wide in the page. Figure 14.7 shows what the page looks like when the browser loads it.

FIG. 14.7

A simple Java applet.

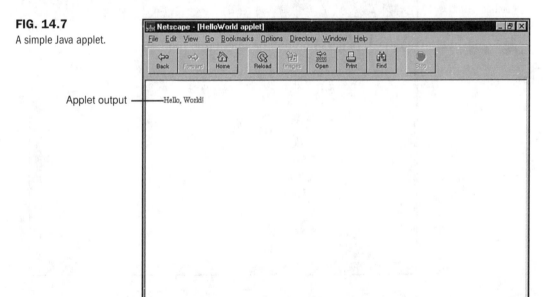

Applet output ———

Browsers that can't display Java applets don't display anything when this page is loaded. To prevent this situation from happening, you can place HTML markup or text between the <APPLET> and </APPLET> tags. Browsers that can't display Java applets display the HTML markup instead. You can use this approach to tell visitors to your pages what they would have seen if the applet had loaded.

Browsers that can display applets don't display any of this HTML markup. Listing 14.3 shows an HTML page with alternative HTML markup.

Listing 14.3   HTML for Hello World Applet

```
<HTML>
<HEAD>
<TITLE>HelloWorld Applet</TITLE>
<BODY>
<APPLET CODE=HelloWorld HEIGHT=100 WIDTH=150>
<H1>WARNING!</H1>
The browser you are using is unable to load Java Applets!
</APPLET>
</BODY>
</HTML>
```

Figure 14.8 shows how this page looks in a browser that doesn't support Java applets.

FIG. 14.8
Instead of showing the Java applet, the HTML text is displayed. This way, you can alert visitors to your page about what they're missing.

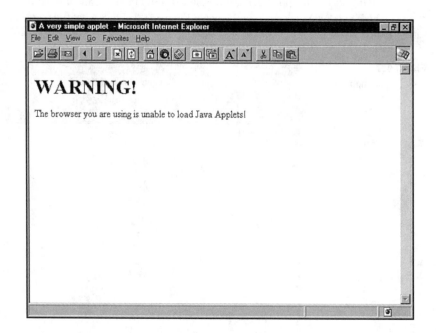

TIP You aren't restricted to writing Web applets with Java. You can write full applications with it as well. The HotJava browser and the Java compiler are both written in Java.

The CODE, WIDTH, and HEIGHT attributes of the <APPLET> tag are all required. You also can use other attributes in the <APPLET> tag. Table 14.1 shows the attributes available and their functions.

Table 14.1   APPLET Attributes and Their Functions

Attribute	Function
CODE	Defines the applet class to load. (required).
WIDTH	Defines the width in pixels of the area in the HTML page to reserve for the applet. (required).
HEIGHT	Defines the height in pixels of the area in the HTML page to reserve for the applet. (required).
ALT	Defines the alternate text to display if the applet tag is understood, but applet loading is turned off or not supported.
CODEBASE	Defines the directory where the classes for the applet are stored. If this attribute is not specified, the directory of the HTML page is searched.
NAME	Defines the name of this instance of an applet. This attribute can be used by an applet to find another applet on the same page.
ALIGN	Defines how this applet is aligned in the HTML page. Any of the ALIGN options discussed in previous chapters are legal here.
VSPACE	Defines how many pixels of space are reserved above and below the applet.
HSPACE	Defines how many pixels of space are reserved on either side of the applet.

Using the *<OBJECT>* Tag to Insert Java Applets

As of HTML 4.0, the <OBJECT> tag is actually the "preferred" method of inserting plug-ins, ActiveX controls, and Java applets into HTML documents. However, the <EMBED> and <APPLET> tags will be supported for backwards compatibility.

Using the <OBJECT> tag to insert a Java applet is actually quite similar to using the <APPLET> tag method. Many of the same attributes are supported. Here's a simple example:

```
<OBJECT CLASSID="java:program.start" HEIGHT=100 WIDTH=100></OBJECT>
```

This example adds the CODETYPE and CODEBASE attributes, and includes an added PARAM element:

```
<OBJECT CODETYPE="application:java-vm" CODEBASE="http://hostname/pathname/"
CLASSID="java:program.start" HEIGHT=100 WIDTH=100>
<PARAM NAME="options" VALUE="abc">
</OBJECT>
```

In short, using the <OBJECT> tag with Java applets isn't much different from using it with ActiveX objects or plug-ins. ●

Part
II

Ch
14

Creating Advanced Web Pages with Dynamic HTML

## CHAPTER 15

Making Your Web Sites Accessible to Impaired and International Users

by Mike Morgan

In this chapter

Understanding the Needs of the Visually Impaired

A variety of laws, as well as common courtesy, require architects to make provisions for people with handicaps when they design buildings. Most of us work in buildings with ramps for wheelchairs and Braille on the elevator buttons. When we design Web pages, we need to think about similar needs. A red text against a deep green background may become invisible to someone with red-green color-blindness (the most common form of color-blindness). The tiny fonts commonly used with "Best experienced with" and "Best viewed with" browser buttons are useless to people with limited vision. People with text-only browsers, including speech-based browsers popular with those who have lost their sight, cannot benefit from highly graphical designs.

This section provides guidelines for Web designers who want to ensure that their site is accessible to all users.

N O T E   Some users have other disabilities that interfere with their use of the Web. A user with a neuromuscular disorder may find the mouse difficult to use—he or she may prefer to tab from link to link. A user with certain neurological disorders may be adversely affected by blinking text or by certain animated GIFs.

While the information in this section is primarily aimed at making Web pages accessible to those with visual impairments, application of these guidelines will help people with other needs as well. ■

While many different disabilities can interfere with a person's use of the Web, the principal limitations are those associated with vision. For our purposes as Web site designers, we need to make our sites accessible to people who may have any of three types of vision impairments:

- *Color-blindness.* An inability to distinguish two or more colors. The most common form of color blindness is an inability to distinguish red and green. This form of color-blindness occurs almost exclusively in men.

- *Low or limited vision.* A variety of disorders in which the user has some residual sight but may need the text and images enlarged, the fonts changed, or the contrast between text and background improved.

- *Blindness.* A loss of vision so profound that the user has to switch to other ways of obtaining information, such as audio or tactile paths. The most common way for blind people to access the Web is through a screen reader—a software application that translates the text placed on the screen by the browser into spoken words.

In addition to the visually impaired, accessibility guidelines contain recommendations for improving the Web experience for the deaf and the hard of hearing. Persons who have some residual hearing are often able to use Web audio by turning up the volume or by using headphones to block background noise. Persons who are deaf need to have information presented in visual form. For example, an audio clip may be accompanied by a transcript or captions.

By following the recommendations applicable to those with visual or auditory disabilities, persons with cognitive or language disabilities are often able to use the Web. A clean, straightforward design with numbered lists and plenty of visual cues will help these individuals find the information on your site.

Some persons with physical disabilities find it difficult to use the mouse. At the operating system level, both Apple and Microsoft include utilities to aid in operating the mouse and keyboard. Check your site with popular browsers to make sure these utilities work correctly. (For example, some Java Virtual Machines override the system's built-in accessibility utilities, such as StickyKeys, MouseKeys, and ToggleKeys.)

ON THE WEB

http://www.boston.com/wgbh/pages/ncam/symbolwinner.html   If you follow the guidelines from this section, you may want to mark your site with the keyhole symbol (shown in Figure 15.1). This symbol was chosen by the National Center for Accessible Media (NCAM) to denote Web sites that contain accessibility features to accommodate the needs of disabled users.

FIG. 15.1
If you follow the guidelines for online accessibility, add this symbol to your Web site.

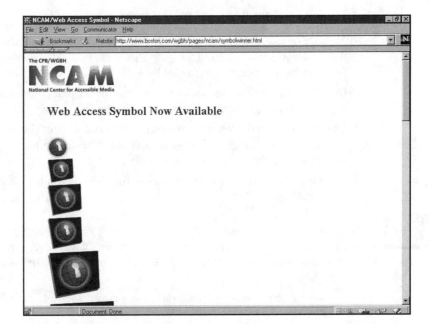

Access for Those Who Are Color-Blind

Phyllis Rae of the Anitec Imaging Corporation (**http://www.anitec.com/**) reports that nearly nine percent of the population suffers from some form of color vision deficiency, also known as color-blindness. The perception of color depends upon the health of the cones on the retina. Each cone has one of three types of photopigments, commonly called red, green, and blue. Disease, age, fatigue, and general health can interfere with these cones, distorting the perception of color.

If you don't take care to make sure your site is accessible to people with limited color vision, you risk turning away nearly one out of ten people.

ON THE WEB

http://www.anitec.com/faithful/intro_to_color/7_Physio/index.html This page on the Anitec site describes the physiological causes and effects of color-blindness.

Jane Berliss, Lewis Kraus, and Susan Stoddard, in their Web paper, "Design of Accessible Web Pages," provide several guidelines on the use of color and pattern.

ON THE WEB

http://www.infouse.com/disabilitydata/guidelines.text.html If you're serious about designing for accessibility, read "Design of Accessible Web Pages" online.

Here are a few of Berliss, Kraus, and Stoddard's recommendations:

- Make color coding redundant with other means of conveying information. For example, if special words that appear in the glossary are colored red, they should also be set in a distinguishable typeface, such as bold.

- Check your design on a monochrome monitor (or set your color monitor to a 1-bit color depth). If your page becomes unreadable, change the design.

- Use black or dark shades of blue or purple for text. Use light shades of blue-green, green, yellow, or orange for background. Avoid using similar hues together (for example, blue-green lettering on a blue background).

- Don't use textured backgrounds. Compare the difference in legibility between Figure 15.2 and Figure 15.3.

 T I P The latest browsers support Cascading Style Sheets (CSS) so that you can separate content from appearance. Use a style sheet to apply your design decisions. Then, if you find you need to change your design to better accommodate the needs of your audience, you only need to make the change in one place.

For more information about Cascading Style Sheets, be sure to read Chapter 17, "Applying Cascading Style Sheets."

 N O T E According to the World Wide Web Consortium (W3C), browsers may eventually allow the end user to turn off your style sheet or apply one designed by the end user. That way, an end user could develop a style sheet that meets his or her special needs and apply that style sheet to improve the usability of your pages. While the current generation of browsers have been slow to adopt this recommendation, it should be available in the near future. To learn more about the W3C's recommended user interface, see **www.w3.org/TR/WD-style#ui**. ◾

FIG. 15.2
When seen in
monochrome, the text
of this page is difficult
to distinguish from the
background.

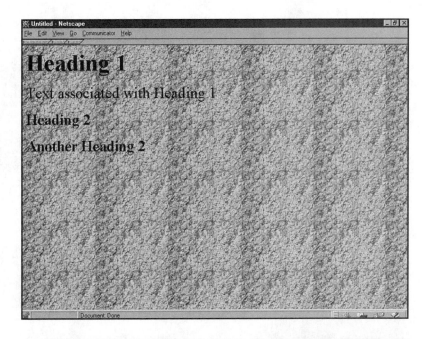

FIG. 15.3
This page uses an
attractive background
graphic, but the text is
positioned over the
solid part of the
graphic.

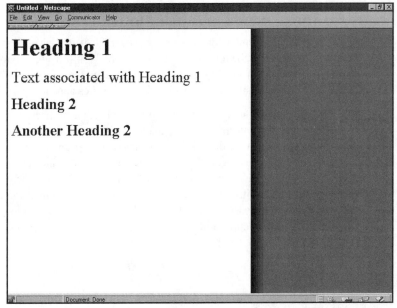

 TIP Not only are designs with clean backgrounds more accessible to people with limited vision, they generally load faster. The background graphic shown in Figure 15.3 was found on the site of the Bandwidth Conservation Society (**www.infohiway.com/faster/**). Figure 15.4 shows their page on background design—not only is it highly accessible, but it is a model of a fast-loading page.

FIG. 15.4
The Bandwidth
Conservation Society
uses a small back-
ground graphic to
produce a stunning
(and highly accessible)
Web page.

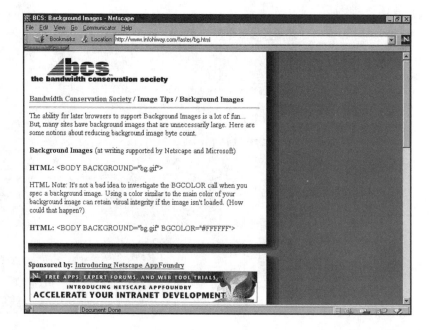

Access for Those with Limited Vision

A search of a popular online database reveals over 3,000 articles on "disability," but only four matching "disability AND Internet." A search of the Web (through **search.com**) finds nearly 162,000 pages that address "disability," and 449 that match "disability AND Internet." Of those, 29 also mention accessibility. About a third of those sites appear to be relevant.

All of this information suggests that designing Web pages for accessibility is an emerging technology. Plenty of information is available to help you make your pages more accessible. If you're looking for a way to distinguish your site, consider giving it a clean, accessible design. You don't have to review all of the sites and papers that describe accessibility. Staff at the Trace R&D center at the University of Wisconsin (**http://www.trace.wisc.edu/text/guidelns/ htmlgide/htmlgide.htm**) have reviewed the guidelines from many sources and listed the "Unified Web Site Accessibility Guidelines." This section, on access for persons with limited vision, and the next section, addressing those who use screen readers, is based on these unified guidelines.

ON THE WEB

http://www.microsoft.com/enable/dev/guidelines.htm   If you're developing a product that will participate in the Windows 95 or Windows NT logo programs, pay attention to the accessibility guidelines here on the Microsoft site. You must comply with them in order to win your logo.

Designing Text for Accessibility   Before the introduction of the <FONT> tag and Cascading Style Sheets, some Web designers used bitmapped text to get the precise effect they wanted.

This approach was of dubious benefit to sighted users, and it can cause serious problems for persons with limited vision. If the visitor wants to increase the size of the text, the graphic doesn't scale. If the visitor is using a screen reader, he or she is told only that there's a graphic present.

Today, the best way to manage the appearance of your pages is through style sheets. Let the end user override the style sheet if he or she needs to increase the text size. If you must include a graphic, be sure to provide usable ALT text, or a text-only version of the page.

Take a look at Figure 15.5. The code for that graphical link is:

```
<A HREF="http://housecall.antivirus.com/"><IMG SRC="Ambu.gif"
ALT="Run anti-virus scan" HEIGHT=104 WIDTH=104></A>
```

FIG. 15.5
Use ALT text to provide cues to text-only readers.

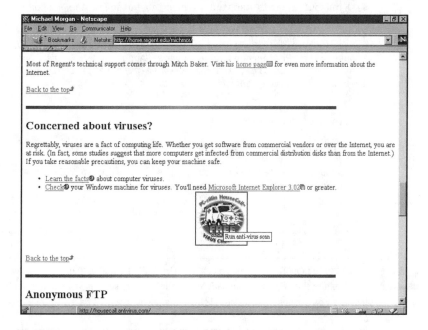

Browsers like Netscape Communicator 4.0 display the ALT text when the user moves the cursor over the image. If the user has turned off image autoloading, most browsers will display the ALT text in lieu of the graphic. If the user's graphic is text-only, such as Lynx, the user sees only the ALT text.

ON THE WEB

http://ugweb.cs.ualberta.ca/~gerald/lynx-me.cgi   If you don't have access to Lynx, use this CGI script to get a feel for what text-only visitors see.

Be sure that visitors to your site know how to change the font size on your page. You may want to use some JavaScript to detect the type and version of browser and then provide a link to a page of instructions that tell the user how to control the appearance of the page. Listing 15.1 shows how to detect a particular browser and version.

Listing 15.1   appVer.js—Use JavaScript to detect the type of browser the user is running.

```
var theNavigatorResult = navigator.appVersion.indexOf("\(Win");
var theExplorerResult = navigator.appVersion.indexOf("Windows");

// Find out if this machine is running Netscape and Windows
if (theNavigatorResult != -1)
{
  document.write("<P>To change the font size in Netscape Navigator,
choose Edit, Preferences. Then choose Appearance, Fonts. Set the
font sizes as desired, and check \"Use my default fonts,
overriding document-specified fonts.\"</P>");
}
else
if (theExplorerResult != -1)
{
  if (navigator.appVersion.indexOf("MSIE 4") == -1)
  {
    document.write("<P>To change the font size in MSIE, choose
View, Fonts, and choose a font size.</P>");
  }
  ...
}
```

 Be sure to use proportional markup such as <H1> and <H2> rather than fixed font sizes so that user can adjust the size of the font. Similarly, use logical markup such as <EM> and <STRONG> rather than physical styles such as <I> and <B>. Learn more about styles in Chapter 6, "Applying Character Formatting."

If a user's browser allows him to set his own style sheet, you can encourage him to use settings that meet his particular needs. For example, the user could apply a rule such as the following:

```
BODY {font-size: xx-large}
```

Just be sure you don't lock the size attribute in your style sheet by writing this:

```
BODY {font-size: medium | important}
```

▶ **See** "Understanding the Cascade," **p.358**

Preformatted Documents   Many Web sites include documents with complete formatting information, such as those written in Adobe's Portable Document Format (PDF). Adobe offers an online server (called Access) and a Windows plug-in (at **http://www.adobe.com/ prodindex/acrobat/accessplugin.html**) that allows users to convert PDF files to HTML offline.

ON THE WEB

http://access.adobe.com/   Use the forms available from this site to convert PDF files to HTML. The resulting HTML can be read by increasing the font size or using a screen reader.

For example, **http://www.adobe.com/prodindex/PDFS/sourcebooksp97.pdf** contains a 40-page color catalog of Adobe's products. (The file is approximately 5.8M.) Figure 15. 6 shows the result of converting the first two pages with Adobe's access server.

FIG. 15.6
Use the advanced form to specify which pages should be converted.

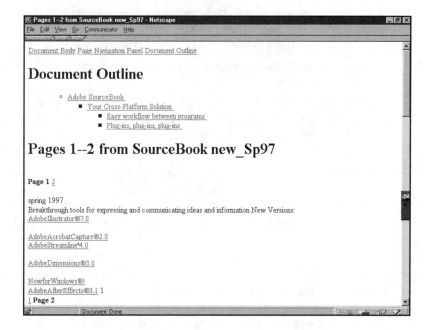

 TIP   If you include PDFs in your site, provide a link to one or both forms at **access.adobe.com**. Adobe encourages users to convert PDF documents online, through their server. Users should only need to use the Access plug-in if they're working with PDFs that are not available from the Internet.

Graphics   Site visitors with limited vision may find it difficult to use imagemaps. If you're providing a text-only version of your page, just replace the imagemap with conventional anchors. If you are serving one version of the page for all users, be sure to include ALT text. If the user is using a browser that supports client-side imagemaps, he or she will be able to use the ALT text as a navigational aid. Listing 15.2 shows one way to code a client-side imagemap.

Listing 15.2   imagemap.html—Include *ALT* Text in Your Client-Side Imagemaps

```
<IMG SRC="virginia.gif" ALT="Image Map of the State of Virginia"
USEMAP="#map1" BORDER=0>
<MAP NAME="map1">
<AREA COORDS="0,0,30,30" HREF="northva.html" ALT="Northern Virginia">
<AREA COORDS="34,34,100,100" HREF="hamproad.html" ALT="Hampton Roads">
</MAP>
```

▶ **See** "Building Client-Side Imagemaps," **p.173**

CAUTION

If you set the colors in a style sheet, your visitors may be stuck with them. In some browsers, the browser colors don't override the colors specified in the style sheet.

For example, Navigator 4.01 allows the user to choose Edit, Preferences, Appearance, Colors, and then check Always Use My Colors, Overriding Document. Unfortunately, this option does not override colors specified by a style sheet.

In IE 4.0, users can override style sheet colors by choosing View, Internet Options. Then, in the General tab, choose Accessibility and check Ignore Colors Specified on Web Pages. The end user can also specify a personal style sheet from this dialog box.

Multimedia   If you include audio or video in your site, you need to ensure that the information is accessible in alternate forms. You may want to provide a transcript of the audio clip or stream for the benefit of people who are hard of hearing or deaf. People who are using a search engine to locate a particular part of an audio or multimedia clip will also benefit from a transcript.

ON THE WEB

http://library.whitehouse.gov/?request=audio   When the President prepares his weekly radio address, he releases a written transcript as well as the audio broadcast. The White House staff indexes the audio clip to the Web site—you can search for a particular word or phrase and then hear the President's comments on that topic. Figure 15.7 shows this design in action.

You can use Netscape's Media Server to build a site that presents synchronized audio and Web pages. This design allows you to present textual information synchronized to an audio stream. You can also add a "closed-caption" track to a QuickTime video.

To synchronize a multimedia presentation with a Netscape Media Server audio narration, you add a `[Timeline]` section to the LiveAudio Metafile (also known as a .LAM file).

User Interaction   Web developers tend to use Java applets to build complex user interfaces that cannot be easily implemented in HTML. Users with limited vision may find the complexity of these applets difficult to navigate.

FIG. 15.7
Search for a word such as "Bosnia," and follow the links to hear the President address the subject.

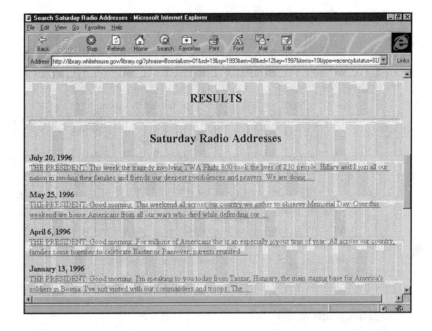

The Trace R&D Center at the University of Wisconsin (the same folks who prepared the unified guidelines for accessibility) prepared a set of recommendations for Sun Microsystems. While most of the recommendations apply to the language developers, Section II D of their report applies to applet programmers:

- Provide important information in more than one modality. For example, an applet programmer can attach a label to an image, or use the `Image.getProperties()` method to read the description field from a PNG graphic.

- Trigger events by user input rather than user actions. This design allows a user to freeze the event while he or she is processing the information. For example, don't trigger an event based on `mouseEnter()`. Use `mouseUp()` or `keyDown()` instead.

- Allow user modification of application/applet appearance and presentation modality. The programmer can use methods such as `setFont()` to allow end users to modify the appearance of the applet. Likewise, the programmer can use `java.awt.SystemColor()` to ensure that the applet uses colors set at the system level by the user. That way, if the user needs to modify the screen to increase contrast, the applet also uses the new color scheme.

- Provide semantic information about the application/applet, its objects, and their actions. Provide help files. If the applet includes a custom control, use a conventional dialog box to walk the end user through each element associated with the control.

- Provide mouseless navigation. If the applet programmer develops custom controls, he or she should implement the `isFocusTraversable()` and `isTabbable()` methods. That way, the Java FocusManager will allow the user to interact with the controls from the keyboard. (Programming note: catch both the `mouseDown()` event and `keyDown()` event for the Tab key; when you get either event, call `requestFocus()`. Once you have focus, change the control visually so the user can tell that the mouse-click or keypress worked.)

■ Notify the user of important changes in the semantics of the display. Avoid using the font, font size, or text color to communicate information. Instead, pop up an alert, change a ToolTip, or play a sound. Better yet, let the user choose one of these solutions at runtime.

■ Provide menu access to commands. Version 1.1 of the Java Development Kit (JDK) includes several new methods for menu access. Check your JDK 1.1 documentation for `java.awt.MenuShortcut`, `MenuItem`, and `MenuBar`.

While these recommendations can be carried out by using version 1.1 or higher of the Java Development Kit, even a cursory review of the available applets shows that most programmers have not followed these recommendations. If you want to ensure accessibility, you must either avoid most Java applets or have them written to your specifications.

Java programmers can take advantage of accessibility features built into the latest version of the Java Foundation Classes. For more information, visit **http://java.sun.com/products/jfc/index.html#access**.

ON THE WEB

http://trace.wisc.edu/java/report.htm   Read Trace's report to Sun about ways to add accessibility to Java applets.

T I P   Not all browsers support Java, and not all users enable Java in their browsers. If you add an applet to your site, be sure to include code to accommodate non-Java users:

```
<APPLET CODE="geosearch.class" WIDTH=100 WIDTH=50
ALT="This applet allows the user to perform database searches,
with the results displayed on maps.">
<IMG SRC="geosearch.gif">
<P>If you were using Java, an applet would appear here that allows you
to search the database and view the results on a map.</P>
</APPLET>
```

N O T E   The <APPLET> tag has been deprecated in HTML 4.0, meaning that it is still supported, but new pages should use the <OBJECT> tag. The <OBJECT> tag allows you to install applets with powerful new features. See **http://developer.netscape.com/library/wpapers/beanconnect/index.html** to learn how to use the <OBJECT> tag to install BeanConnect components—Java applets that communicate with each other and with HTML forms and JavaScript. ■

While Trace did not specifically address ActiveX controls, the recommendations it makes to applet programmers are equally relevant to ActiveX developers. Like most applet programmers, most ActiveX developers have not addressed accessibility. If you want to use ActiveX controls on your site, consider having them written to your specifications.

ON THE WEB

http://www.microsoft.com/enable/products/java.htm   Microsoft has announced that its implementation of the Java Virtual Machine explicitly supports features to aid accessibility.

Testing   Some of the best tools for testing the accessibility of your site are the ones you're already using: validators, WebLint, and Doctor HTML.

Learn about validators and related tools in Chapter 39, "Verifying and Testing HTML Documents."

ON THE WEB

http://www.cast.org/bobby/   To ensure that your HTML is accessible, add Bobby to your list of HTML checkers. Bobby includes checks for a number of accessibility rules, including the ones given in this section. It will show you where the problems are and give recommendations on how to fix them.

Access for Those Who Use Screen Readers

People with some residual vision may be able to get information from a Web page by increasing the contrast and enlarging the text and images. For persons who are blind, however, the tool of choice is the screen reader. A *screen reader* is a software application, often operated in conjunction with a hardware speech synthesizer, that translates the text on the screen to spoken words. This task is a difficult one, particularly in light of complex Web pages with multiple interacting frames, bitmapped text, and now, push technology.

A typical screen reader begins in the upper-left corner of each window—HTML frames are often treated as separate windows—and works from left to right and then top to bottom (just the way we read). When it finds text—not a graphic shaped like text—it passes that text to the speech synthesizer.

Like most PC accessories, speech synthesizers can be internal or external and may be implemented in hardware or software. The most popular speech synthesizers are external hardware devices connected to the computer through the serial port. The speech synthesizer has a table that helps it determine how to pronounce English words. It also has a table of "exception words." Using these rules and tables, the speech synthesizer produces sound that, hopefully, resembles the way a human would pronounce the word. Speech synthesis results are mixed. Like most products, you get what you pay for. Many blind people are limited by inexpensive and unsophisticated speech synthesizers and have had to learn to be creative when interpreting the sounds their synthesizers make.

ON THE WEB

http://www.prairienet.org/benchmark/   Jim Fay has made it his business to provide descriptions and recommendations on all sorts of technology that assists people with disabilities. Visit his site to read about screen readers.

ON THE WEB

http://www.austin.ibm.com/sns/index.html   IBM offers a comprehensive set of accessibility tools called the Special Needs System. Its screen reader is described at **www.austin.ibm.com/sns/snssrd.html**.

N O T E   If a user needs access to a page in a language other than English, they need to have a screen reader and a synthesizer that support that language. Many screen readers and synthesizers support common European languages such as French, Spanish, and German, but the user must be sure to switch both the screen reader and the synthesizer when he or she opens the non-English page.

T I P   Screen readers are primarily designed for the blind community. Some sighted dyslexic users—particularly stroke victims—have reported that screen readers aid them in understanding Web pages. If you're a Web developer, be aware that some users may use their screen reader on single words. If you're dyslexic, check with your health care professional to see if such a device might be useful in your case.

Screen readers will work with any Windows application—they are as useful with Microsoft Word as they are with Netscape Navigator. There's another class of software—speech browsers—that support the direct transformation of HTML to speech. For example, Productivity Works, Inc. (**www.prodworks.com**) makes a browser—pwWebSpeak—that drives a speech synthesizer directly from HTML.

NetPhonic (**www.netphonic.com**) has developed a system—Web-On-Call—that provides access to Web pages via telephone. As a Web publisher, you need to install its server as well as hardware to connect your system to the telephone lines. It supports up to eight lines with off-the-shelf configurations and can scale beyond that number with custom configurations.

T I P   NetPhonic is not aiming its product at the market of visually disabled people. It is selling its system as a telephone-based interactive voice response system. If you design your Web site for screen readers and add a Web-On-Call server, you could have your Web site double as a set of telephone menus. Visit **http://www.netphonic.com/demo/contact.htm** to get access to a demonstration.

In addition, most conventional browsers offer accessibility enhancements, either through operating system utilities or through built-in capabilities.

ON THE WEB

http://www.microsoft.com/ie/most/howto/?/ie/most/howto/access.htm   Learn how to
operate Microsoft Internet Explorer without a mouse. For best results, open this page while you're in
MSIE 3.0 or above—the server will install an ActiveX accessibility utility.

Designing Text for Accessibility   Many screen readers are like the text-based Lynx Web
browser—the user uses the Tab key to advance from link to link. Unlike Lynx, the user hears
only the text of the link itself. Thus, a link like

```
<A HREF="http://www.trace.wisc.edu/">Click here</A>
to visit the Trace site.
```

will give the user only the words "Click here." A better design might be

```
<A HREF="http://www.trace.wisc.edu/">Visit the Trace site</A>.
```

With this approach, the user is encouraged to "Visit the Trace site," a much more interesting
prompt.

TIP

If you have a series of links, place them in a list or separate them by <BR> tags. Some screen readers
become confused if there's more than one link on a line and run them together.

Likewise, be careful about text in tables. Screen readers read one line at a time, while the human eye
will often read down the column. Either design your tables so that they can be read a line at a time, or
rethink your design to avoid the table. (For example, you might offer a text-only version of the page that
provides the information in paragraphs instead of a table.

Screen readers usually ignore (or sometimes mispronounce) punctuation marks. Don't use
nonstandard punctuation such as emoticons (for example, :-)) in any material that may pass
through a screen reader.

Screen readers have a particularly difficult time moving or changing text. Text surrounded by
the <BLINK> or <MARQUEE> tags, or scrolling text displayed by Java applets or JavaScript, will
cause the screen reader to misspeak and may even crash the program. For best accessibility,
provide a text-only equivalent of any pages that use these special features.

ON THE WEB

http://www.trace.wisc.edu/world/java/java.htm   For tips on the use of both Java and JavaScript
on your accessible Web site, visit this page on the Trace R&D Center's Web site.

Page Layout   Many modern Web pages display multiple columns, sometimes implemented
through frames. Figure 15.8, for example, shows the CNET channel in Netcaster. The screen is
loaded with content, but a screen reader may present this content in a confusing way.

FIG. 15.8
Multiple columns of information can be confusing when read by a screen reader.

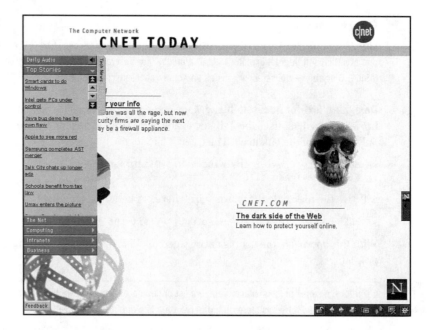

Netscaster and the various channels are described in Chapter 32, "Building Netscape Netcaster Channels."

If you need to present information in multiple columns, consider offering a text-only page for the benefit of low-bandwidth users and visitors with screen readers. Another nice design is to use icons (with ALT text) in each cell of the table. Figure 15.9 shows the U.S. Postal Service's WINGS site, which uses this design.

 TIP   If your site is generated directly from a spreadsheet or a database, you may not want to invest the time to build a text-only version of each page. Consider providing a phone number or e-mail address; encourage someone who needs help interpreting the data to contact you directly.

Most Web designers feel comfortable dropping an unordered list (<UL>) onto any page. Users with a screen reader may find it difficult to tell where the list begins and ends. The screen reader may run adjacent list items together or separate into two or more items those items that need multiple lines. Consider switching to ordered lists (<OL>) and cueing the reader by announcing the number of items on the list. For example, the list in Listing 15.3 is considered a more accessible design than the one in Listing 15.4.

Listing 15.3   ordered.html—Ordered Lists Put Numbers on Each List Element

```
<P>Our solar system has nine major planets.</P>
<OL>
<LI>Mercury</LI>
```

```
<LI>Venus</LI>
<LI>Earth</LI>
<LI>Mars</LI>
<LI>Jupiter</LI>
<LI>Saturn</LI>
<LI>Uranus</LI>
<LI>Neptune</LI>
<LI>Pluto</LI>
</OL>
```

FIG. 15.9
The U.S. Postal Service operates the Web Interactive Network of Government Services (WINGS), considered by many to be a model of accessibility.

Listing 15.4   unordered.html—An Unordered List Shows only Bullets

```
<P>Let's review the planets in our solar system.<P>
<UL>
<LI>Mercury</LI>
<LI>Venus</LI>
<LI>Earth</LI>
<LI>Mars</LI>
<LI>Jupiter</LI>
<LI>Saturn</LI>
<LI>Uranus</LI>
<LI>Neptune</LI>
<LI>Pluto</LI>
</UL>
```

N O T E   Numbering lists can also help people with certain cognitive disabilities by providing them with cues about where they are in the list. ■

 ## ON THE WEB

http://trace.wisc.edu/wings/   Visit this page for good examples of HTML lists. One such list is shown in Figure 15.10. Continue on into the links on this page for even more information about how to design for high accessibility.

FIG. 15.10
This page from the Trace R&D Center at the University of Wisconsin shows how to ensure that lists work well with screen readers.

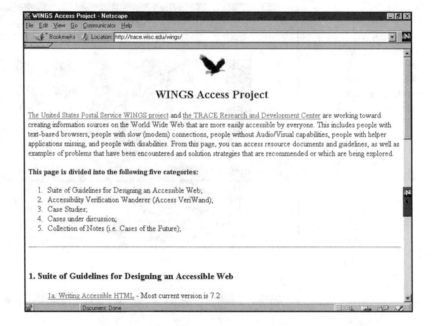

Learn more about lists in Chapter 9, "Adding Lists to a Web Page."

TIP   If your style guide requires bullet lists when no particular order is required, but you're content to allow visitors to see numbered lists when they need them, encourage those visitors to apply their own Cascading Style Sheet (CSS). Here's a rule that will switch all of their lists to numbered lists:

```
UL LI {list-style-type: decimal}
```

In general, frames wreak havoc with screen readers. If you choose to use frames, use the <NOFRAMES> tag to display a text-only version of each page. Users with small monitors will appreciate the ability to reduce the screen clutter as well. Learn more about frames in Chapter 12, "Framing Your Web Site."

Graphics   It's not just the blind who are unable to see graphics. Users with slow modem connections often choose to disable image autoloading in order to improve performance. Many users, particularly those on college campuses, access the Internet though a text-only browser: Lynx. In order to satisfy the needs of these users, you must ensure that information is presented in a textual form as well as graphically.

For example, if you provide an imagemap, be sure to include conventional links. If the image has meaning for nongraphical users, include ALT text so they know what the graphic was.

 TIP Site visitors with certain cognitive disabilities may find it easier to work with graphics than with text. Similarly, people with neuromuscular disorders often find imagemaps with large clickable targets to be easier to use than small text links. For maximum accessibility, provide both text and graphics and let the user choose how they want to interact with your site.

When you design your ALT text, be sure to keep it simple. Some screen readers have problems if the text wraps inside the rectangle reserved for the graphic. Be sure to include punctuation at the end of the ALT text so that the screen reader inserts a pause. That way the ALT text doesn't run together with the other text on that page.

 TIP If you use horizontal lines to separate sections of your page, use an <IMG> tag rather than an <HR> tag. That way you can attach text like ALT="Horizontal line." so that the text-only user is aware that you are starting a new section. If the nature of the new section is not clear from the text, you might even have the ALT text of the horizontal line introduce the section. For example, you could write

<IMG SRC="graphics/blueline.gif"

ALT="--------------Section 3. Computer Viruses------------------"

HEIGHT="8" WIDTH="480">

The dashes in the ALT text help the sighted text-only user see that a new section is coming up.

Sometimes a graphic is purely decorative, and no ALT text is appropriate. If you leave the ALT text off, many screen readers and text-only browsers will tell the user that a graphic exists, leaving the user to wonder what they are missing. Just set ALT="" to tell the text-only visitor that they can safely ignore the graphic.

 TIP If you have some graphics that need more explanation than you can put in an <ALT> tag, consider placing a small transparent GIF after the graphic. (GIFs are image files based on the Graphical Interface Format. Transparent GIFs have one color set to be "transparent," so that the background color appears through the image.) Make the image a link to explanatory material, perhaps in a footnote at the bottom of the page. Because the GIF is transparent, it will be invisible to sighted readers who have graphics enabled. Text-only readers will see the GIF's ALT text. If they follow the link they'll get a textual description of the graphic that they couldn't see. Figure 15.11 shows an example of this technique, as viewed from Lynx.

FIG. 15.11

Use an invisible GIF to cue text-only readers that a description is available.

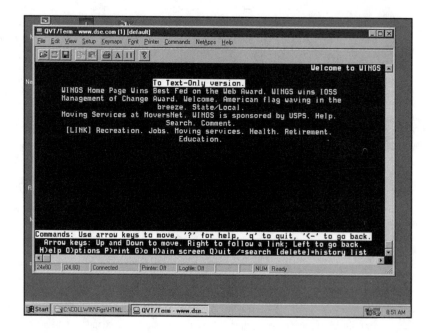

If you find that your pages have so many graphics that the ALT text and links to descriptions become tedious, consider developing a text-only version of your site. You can also build a hybrid site—ask the user if he or she prefers a graphics-rich version of the site or a faster, mostly text version. Use JavaScript to store his or her answer in a cookie, as shown in Listing 15.5. Then build your pages with a server-side script such as Netscape LiveWire, Microsoft's Active Server Pages, or CGI. Each page should examine the contents of the user's cookie and return an appropriate version of the page. For many pages, they will be only a few graphics. You could serve those pages to all users and build only two versions of the page when necessary.

Listing 15.5 cookies.js—Use Cookies to Save a Form's State

```
<SCRIPT LANGUAGE="JavaScript">

// These functions are designed to integrate with an HTML form
// named "FEEDBACK," which has text fields Mail and Memo and
// checkboxes Speed, Content, and Graphic.

// Modify WriteCookies() and GetCookies() to work with your
// own forms.

function GetValue( Offset )
{
// Extract the value from the cookie at the given offset
  var End = document.cookie.indexOf(";", Offset);
  if ( End == -1 )
    End = document.cookie.length;
```

```
// Return the portion of the cookie beginning with the offset
// and ending with ';'.
  return unescape( document.cookie.substring( Offset, End) );
}

function GetCookie( Name)
{
// Return the value of a cookie by name.
  var Len = Name.length;

// Look at each substring that's the same length as the cookie name
// for a match. If found, look up the value and return it.
  var i = 0;
  while (i < document.cookie.length )
  {
    var j = i + Len + 1;
    if ( document.cookie.substring( i, j ) == (Name + "=") )
      return GetValue( j );
    i = document.cookie.indexOf( " ", i ) + 1;
    if ( i == 0 )
      break;
  }
  return null;
}

function SetCookie( Name, Value, Expire )
{
// Make or change a cookie given its name and value. The name and value
// are required, but the expiration date isn't. Note that if you don't
// specify an expiration date, the cookie only exists for the current session.
  document.cookie = Name + "=" + escape( Value ) + ";expires=" + Expire;
}

function WriteCookies()
{
// Write all the cookies for the FEEDBACK form
  var Expire = "Friday,25-Feb-2000 12:00:00 GMT";
  with ( document.FEEDBACK )
  {
    SetCookie( "Mail", FEEDBACK_MAIL.value, Expire );
    SetCookie( "How", FEEDBACK_HOW.selectedIndex, Expire );
    SetCookie( "Memo", FEEDBACK_MEMO.value, Expire );
    SetCookie( "Speed", FEEDBACK_SPEED[0].checked ? "1" : "0", Expire );
    SetCookie( "Content", FEEDBACK_CONTENT[0].checked ? "1" : "0", Expire );
    SetCookie( "Graphic", FEEDBACK_GRAPHIC[0].checked ? "1" : "0", Expire );
  }
}

function GetCookies()
{
// Load the form with the values in the cookie
  with ( document.FEEDBACK )
  {
```

continues

Listing 15.5   Continued

```
        FEEDBACK_MAIL.value = GetCookie( "Mail" );
        FEEDBACK_HOW.selectedIndex = GetCookie( "How" );
        FEEDBACK_MEMO.value = GetCookie( "Memo" );
        FEEDBACK_SPEED[0].checked = GetCookie( "Speed" ) == "1";
        FEEDBACK_SPEED[1].checked = GetCookie( "Speed" ) == "0";
        FEEDBACK_CONTENT[0].checked = GetCookie( "Content" ) == "1";
        FEEDBACK_CONTENT[1].checked = GetCookie( "Content" ) == "0";
        FEEDBACK_GRAPHIC[0].checked = GetCookie( "Graphic" ) == "1";
        FEEDBACK_GRAPHIC[1].checked = GetCookie( "Graphic" ) == "0";
    }
}
</SCRIPT>
```

N O T E   The Portable Network Graphic (PNG) allows you to embed a text description in the graphic itself. PNG is gradually taking its place along side GIF and JPEG graphics. Look for browsers to give users access to PNG's built-in text. ■

Multimedia   Many sites include complex media types such as large images or video clips that are displayed using browser plug-ins or ActiveX controls. Users with a slow network connection may choose to skip these embedded files. Users without the proper plug-ins have to take extra steps to access the information. Visually impaired users may not be able to see the data at all. For more information about embedded objects see Chapter 14, "Inserting Objects into a Web Page."

For all these reasons, be sure to include a link to a description of each embedded file. You should describe the contents of the file. You may also want to tell the user how to configure his or her browser so the sighted user can view the file. Be sure to give the user some idea of how large the file is so that he or she can make a decision whether to invest the download time.

Michael Herrick of Matterform Media has designed a collection of tiny icons called QBullets. In general, you can place a QBullet after a link to tell the site visitor what that link does (for example, opens a form, leads to a list of links, or initiates a file download). Herrick includes a series of thermometer icons in his collection so that you can tell the visitor the approximate size of the downloadable file.

ON THE WEB

http://www.matterform.com/qbullets/   Download the latest set of QBullets from Matterform's site.

If a graphic is central to the point of your Web page, consider leaving a link to it on the text-only version of the page. That way, the visually impaired user can open the link and show it to a sighted colleague.

User Interaction   Most screen readers work well with the major browsers to read HTML forms. If you want to be sure that everyone has the opportunity to fill out your form, allow the user to request a form by e-mail so they can print it out, or supply a phone number so they can supply the information over the phone.

Information about how to build HTML forms is found in Chapter 13, "Collecting Input with Forms."

N O T E Some screen reader users report that occasionally they will not hear the screen reader report an edit box if that box is empty. The solution is to add a space to the box:

```
<INPUT TYPE=Text NAME="AnEditBox" VALUE=" " SIZE=20>
```

ON THE WEB

http://web.mit.edu/wwwdev/cgiemail/ This site provides a CGI script for e-mailing forms.

Testing As a simple test of any Web page, place a piece of paper against the screen and slowly move it down. As you reveal text, read it—you'll get a pretty good idea of how most screen readers will render your document. Most screen readers will treat each frame like a separate document, so process one frame at a time. If you don't like the effect, include a <NOFRAMES> version.

ON THE WEB

http://www.wwwebit.com/magical-mist/ribbon.htm Once your page is ready for final testing, submit it to **mist@cdepot.net**. They'll give you recommendations on how to ensure that your page is compatible with most screen readers. Once you have their seal of approval, you can display the "Speech Friendly Site" ribbon.

ON THE WEB

http://www.w3.org/TR/WD-acss If you're already using Cascading Style Sheets (CSS) get ready for Audio CSS, or ACSS (pronounced "access"). If adopted, this standard could allow you to add audio markup to your documents in much the same way you now use CSS for visual markup. While you're on the W3C site, read **www.w3.org/TR/WD-print** to see how to use style sheets to tune your pages for good appearance in print.

Understanding the Needs of the International Audience

Twice every year the Graphics, Visualization & Usability Center (GVU) at Georgia Tech (**www.gvu.gatech.edu/user_surveys/**) conducts a survey of Web users. For the past year the percentage of users who live in the U.S. has been dropping—in the 7th Survey, conducted in April 1997, that percentage had fallen to just over 80 percent (**http://www.gvu.gatech.edu/user_surveys/survey-1997-04/graphs/general/Major_Geographical_Location.html**). That same survey found that almost 92 percent of Web users used English as their primary language, but in Europe, both German and French had increased dramatically.

N O T E The Georgia Tech surveys are conducted twice a year, in April-May and in October-November. To participate, visit **http://www.gvu.gatech.edu/user_surveys/** during the survey months and follow the link to the current survey forms. ■

The import is clear—there really is a World Wide Web. If you want to develop a site that has truly global impact, you need to think about making your site accessible to people who do not speak English, or at least to people who are more comfortable in a different language.

In order to support a language, you must combine three components:

- Content in the target language
- The ability to display the characters of the target language
- The ability to give the user the content upon request

To develop the content, you'll need a translator. Be aware that some computer concepts, such as the wording on buttons or other controls, need to change to match the target culture (a concept variously known as internationalization and localization). Be sure to get a translator who has experience with Web sites.

ON THE WEB

http://www.yahoo.com/Social_Science/Linguistics_and_Human_Languages/ Translators_and_Interpreters/ Visit this Yahoo! category to learn more about translators. From here you can find commercial translators as well as a few free services. You'll also want to visit **www.yahoo.com/Business_and_Economy/Companies/Computers/Software/Localization/** for ideas on localization. You'll find a FAQ on internationalization at **http://www.vlsivie.tuwien.ac.at/ mike/i18n.html**.

The remainder of this section addresses encoding issues and methods for seamlessly serving the right translation when the user requests the document.

ON THE WEB

http://www.javasoft.com/docs/books/tutorial/intl/concepts/features.html Java 1.1 supports several new features, including a `Locale` class, `ResourceBundles`, and `Format` classes, which aid in developing localized versions of a Java applet or application.

Understanding Encodings

Before a Web client can display a Web page, the client must know how the page designer intended each character to be displayed. The first question for the client is, "How many bits correspond to each character?" Since the number of symbols in a character set is limited to two to the number of bits, the size of the character "package" limits the number of characters. For most European languages, 256 characters is plenty. For some Asian languages, even 65,535 may not be enough. (In China, people are inventing new characters every day, principally for use in personal names.)

This section describes the three major types of encoding: 7-bit ASCII, 8-bit ISO-8859, and 16-bit Unicode.

Simple ASCII   The earliest computers shared much in common with the teletype industry. Characters were encoded in 7 bits. Since 2^7 is 128, these first codes could represent 128 characters—enough for the upper- and lowercase letters, the numbers, and a few dozen punctuation and control characters.

Someone has to decide which of the numbers from 0 to 127 should stand for a *k*, and which for an *A*, and so on. The two leading contenders for a standardized encoding were IBM's Extended Binary Coded Decimal Interchange Code, or EBCDIC, and the American Standard Code for Information Interchange (ASCII). While IBM still uses EBCDIC in some of its larger computers, ASCII has come to dominate the industry. There is an ASCII standard that specifies which characters correspond to which number. (For example, K is 107 and A is 65.)

As time wore on, it became clear that computer data was easier to manipulate when it was stored in containers with a width equal to a power of two. It has become common to store characters in bytes—containers that are 8 bits wide. Since 2^8 is 256, there's room for 128 more characters beyond the ASCII standard. In the desktop computer industry, each manufacturer chose symbols as they saw fit. (For example, Apple filled the upper 128 characters with some mathematical symbols and some international currency symbols such as the pound sterling and the yen. IBM's PC has smiley faces and the symbols for the four suits of cards.)

ISO-8859 Encodings   After a few years of sibling rivalry among the desktop computer manufacturers, the international standards community defined a series of encodings that take advantage of the upper 128 characters.

If your Web pages were prepared by an editor such as Netscape Composer, you may find a line at the top of the file that specifies the encoding:

```
<META HTTP-EQUIV="Content-Type" CONTENT="text/html; charset="iso-8859-1">
```

ISO-8859-1 is the Latin character set that native English speakers recognize. Many European languages use character sets that are similar to English but have a few special characters of their own. For example, ISO-8859-2 supports central European languages. Other languages, such as Russian, have an alphabet that is based more on Greek than on Latin. ISO-8859-5 supports the Cyrillic encoding. Similarly, ISO-8859-7 supports Greek and ISO-8859-9 supports Turkish.

ON THE WEB

http://www.utoronto.ca/webdocs/HTMLdocs/NewHTML/iso_table.html   You can get a complete listing of the ISO-8859-1 characters online. For a list and character set of all of the ISO-8859 standards, see **www.wbs.cs.tu-berlin.de/~czyborra/charsets/**. Remember, the first 128 characters of each ISO-8859 standard are simply the ASCII characters.

You can change the encoding your browser uses from the menu. In Microsoft Internet Explorer 4.0, for example, choose <u>V</u>iew, Internet <u>O</u>ptions. Click the Fonts button on the General tab, and set the desired Character Set. You'll see the change only if you're looking at a page that uses the "upper 128," since most English pages only use standard ASCII.

For example, visit **www-koi.kulichki.com/ostrova/bera/Folklor/index.html**. This page is in Russian and is encoded in Cyrillic. Set your encoding to ISO-8859-5 (Cyrillic) to see the page shown in Figure 15.12.

FIG. 15.12

Be sure to set your encoding to match the language of the site you're visiting.

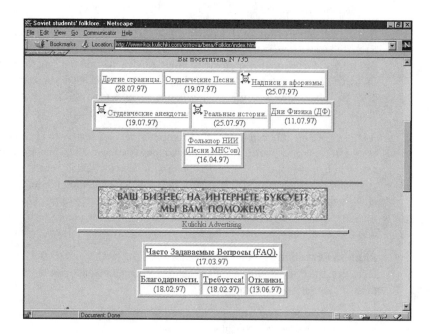

Beyond 8 Bits: Unicode Many languages, such as the languages of Eastern Asia, require far more than 256 symbols. The latest entry to the encoding field is Unicode, which supports 65,536 discrete symbols by making the package for a character 16 bits wide.

N O T E The World Wide Web Consortium (W3C) has committed to the internationalization of the Web. To that end, they have specified that Unicode, rather than ASCII, is the base character set of HTML, beginning with HTML 4.0. Look for more sites to start using Unicode (ISO 10646-1). ■

ON THE WEB

http://www.unicode.org/ Unicode has a home page! Learn everything you want to know about this encoding standard.

Offering Alternative Languages

If you're serious about internationalization, sooner or later you have to deliver the contents of your Web site in the target language(s). If you have the latest server, and if your visitors are using a late-model browser, you can automate the process. Otherwise, provide links to each target language and let the user choose.

Using HTTP/1.1 to Offer Language Variants   When a Web browser contacts a Web server to request a resource such as a Web page, the two software applications communicate by using a protocol called HTTP—the HyperText Transfer Protocol. In January, 1997, version 1.1 of that protocol was formally adopted as a "standards-track" specification. That fact means that Request For Comments (RFC) 2068 is now undergoing final review. Unless someone finds a serious flaw at the last minute, HTTP 1.1 will become the standard for Web browsers and servers. The major browser and server vendors are already adding HTTP 1.1 features to their products.

What does all of this standards activity have to do with international accessibility? Just this: beginning with HTTP 1.1, an end user can list his or her preferred languages, and the browser and the server can negotiate to find a suitable version of the document. Here's an example of how that negotiation works:

```
Client to Server:

I'd like a copy of the Product Catalog. I have a PDF reader and an HTML browser.
I'd prefer a version in German, but can accept English.

Equivalent HTTP headers:

ACCEPT text/pdf; q=0.9, text/html; q=0.1
ACCEPT-LANGUAGE de; q=0.8, en; q=0.2
GET prodcat HTTP/1.1

Server to Client:

Here it is.

Equivalent HTTP headers:

HTTP/1.1 200 OK
VARY ACCEPT, ACCEPT-LANGUAGE
Content-type: text/pdf prodcat.en
```

The client, a Web browser, tells the server that the user prefers to receive the document in Adobe's Portable Document Format (PDF) but will accept HTML. He also prefers a German version but will accept English.

The Web server replies by sending the PDF version of the document. Since it doesn't have a German copy, it sends the English version.

TIP   If you'd like to offer your documents in more than one language, check with your Webmaster to see if your server supports HTTP/1.1. Read your server's documentation or follow your Webmaster's instructions about how to name your documents so that the server can recognize the language of each document.

Setting Up the Browser for Language Variants   The newest browsers now allow you to specify the languages you want them to request. For example, in Netscape Communicator, choose Edit, Preferences and choose Navigator, Languages. Figure 15.13 shows the resulting dialog. Use the Add button and the up and down arrows to list the languages you will accept, in the order you prefer them. For example, the figure shows that the user prefers any type of German but will accept any type of English. (German is available in Austrian and Swiss variations, in addition to German as spoken in Germany; English is available in both British and U.S. varieties.)

FIG. 15.13

Use the Languages preference to specify which languages you will accept.

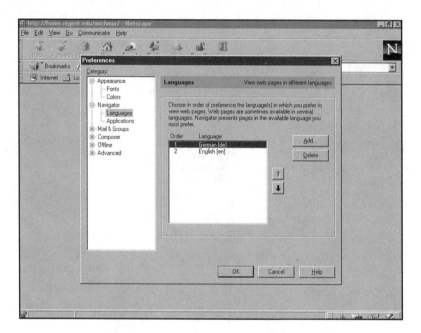

Older Ways to Offer Translations   If your server, or your user's browsers, aren't ready for HTTP/1.1 yet, but you want to offer your information in more than one language, follow the time-tested method of listing all of the available languages on the first page of your site. (Many developers also include a small flag representing the home nation of each language.) The new visitor reads down the list until she sees an offer she can understand, then follows that link to the first page of the site in her preferred language. Figure 15.14 shows such a site.

NOTE   If you connect to SavvySearch from outside the U.S., you may see the site displayed in your native language. Dreilinger has programmed his CGI script to do a reverse lookup on your IP address to get the country of your domain. Then, he looks at a table to determine what your native language (most likely) is and sets his language parameter to match your language (if he has an appropriate translation on file).

This approach isn't perfect, but it's a nice touch.

FIG. 15.14
Daniel Dreilinger,
developer of
SavvySearch, has lots
of friends fluent in
different languages.

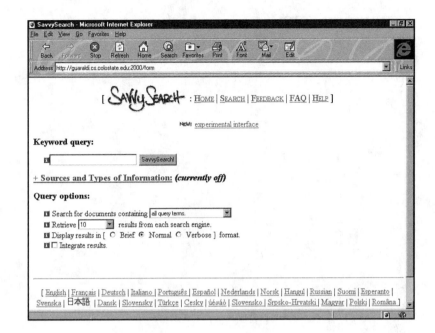

## CHAPTER 16

Adding JavaScript and VBScript to HTML

by Jerry Honeycutt

In this chapter

Introducing Scripts

Scripts are important to an HTML author. I'm of the strong opinion that in the future you'll focus more on writing scripts than HTML tags. Whereas to create a document's content you'll use an HTML editor, which works like any popular desktop publishing program, you'll write scripts to make those documents interactive. Think of it this way: You use a word-processor to create documents, but you still must write the occasional macro to make a document interactive or solve special problems.

You're not going to learn how to write good scripts after reading this one chapter. Though it is a good basic introduction to scripting, particularly to the mechanics of adding scripts to HTML, you can't rely on it to teach you how to program. For that, take a look at Que's *Special Edition Using JavaScript* or *Special Edition Using VBScript*. If you're already familiar with the basic programming concepts, however, you can rely on Appendixes C, "JavaScript Keyword Reference," and D, "VBScript Keyword Reference," to show you all of the keywords supported by both scripting languages.

Choosing Between Server- or Client-Side Scripts

Server-side (see Part VI, "Scripting on the Web Server") scripts execute on the Web server, feeding HTML to the browser as a product of their computations. Write a server-side script for each circumstance if any of the following statements is true:

- You're serving customized content based on information you know about the user.
- You need to include output from a legacy application or database in your HTML documents.
- You're writing a client-side script just to generate HTML as the user opens the Web page.
- You have to process a user's form input on the server (transaction or search processing, for example).

N O T E   Writing a server-side script isn't always possible, particularly if the service hosting your Web pages doesn't support server-side scripts. In such cases, you have no choice but to write a client-side script or relocate your Web pages to a service that does support scripts. ■

Client-side scripts interact with the HTML while the user is viewing it. Write a client-side script if any of these statements is true:

- Your script must interact with the user's environment, creating a canvas window that doesn't have toolbars or menus, for example.
- You want to change the appearance of the Web page as the user interacts with it.
- You want to prevent frequent round-trips to the server by validating form input before submitting it.
- Writing a server-side script would require frequent round-trips to the server to change the document's content.

Choosing Between JavaScript and VBScript

JavaScript is loosely based on C++ and has gained worldwide acceptance on the Internet. You can use JavaScript to interact with the user's environment, change the appearance of the content while the user interacts with it, and even make embedded objects cooperate with each other. Both Netscape Navigator and Internet Explorer support JavaScript.

VBScript is based on Microsoft's Visual Basic. You also use it to create client-side scripts that interact with the user's environment, change content dynamically, and glue together objects. VBScript's biggest advantage is that you can leverage your existing knowledge about Visual Basic onto the Web page. Currently, Internet Explorer is the only Web browser that supports VBScript directly—a pretty big weakness.

When choosing between each of these languages, consider the following criteria for making your decision:

- Do your scripts have to run on both Internet Explorer and Netscape Navigator? If so, use JavaScript.

- If you don't yet know how to program and you want to get up-to-speed quickly, start with VBScript because it's the easier language to learn—particularly if you already know Visual Basic.

- Do you need the flexibility of creating complex scripts involving advanced data structures and programming constructs? If so, your best bet is JavaScript because it's more versatile than VBScript.

 You can mix both JavaScript and VBScript within the same HTML file, so you're not forced to make a black-or-white decision. Do remember that Internet Explorer is the only browser supporting VBScript at this time.

Understanding How Browsers Interpret Scripts

JavaScript and VBScript are *interpreted languages* as opposed to *compiled languages*. Developers create programs using a compiled language such as C++. A *compiler* actually translates each instruction into *machine code* that the computer executes directly. A program called an *interpreter* interprets and executes a script line by line, however.

An interpreted language is slower than a compiled language, but, considering the usage of an interpreted language, that's not really an issue. Your scripts are interpreted by the Web browser and are usually very small. As well, they probably only execute in response to something that the user does (clicking the mouse), instead of executing continuously as compiled programs sometimes do.

When a Browser Executes Scripts

When a user opens a Web page, the browser makes note of every script in the HTML document. It translates the scripts into intermediate code that represents the keywords in the script as tokens (binary values representing the keywords), which are more efficient to interpret because they're smaller than the original keywords. It also creates a table called a *symbol table* that contains the name of each script function (scripts that are called by name from other scripts). The browser looks up functions in this symbol table as they are invoked.

The user's Web browser executes different types of script code at different times. The browser typically doesn't execute functions as the Web page loads; it waits for an event that you associate with a function to execute them instead. When an object on the Web page fires an event, the browser looks up the function associated with that event in the symbol table; then the browser executes it. Also, anytime a script invokes a function, the browser looks it up in the symbol table to find the code. The browser executes *inline* scripts as it loads the Web page, however. Inline scripts are code you embed that's not actually inside a function. You use inline scripts to affect how the browser draws the Web page.

In Listing 16.1, for example, the last line in the script executes as the browser loads the Web page, which creates the Web page shown in Figure 16.1. The remaining lines don't execute until some event causes the function called AddSeries to execute.

Listing 16.1   Sample Script

```
function AddSeries( Last )
{
  intTotal = 0;
  for( i = 1; i <= Last; i++ )
  {
    intTotal += i;
    alert( intTotal );
  }
}

document.write( "Howdy" );
```

How a Browser Handles Events

With scripting, you embed instructions into your Web pages that describe how you want the browser to handle certain events. Events are things that happen on the Web page. Mouse actions such as clicking and moving cause most events, but many other types of events can occur on a Web page such as a timer finishing its countdown. Regardless, most events are caused by some action.

Figure 16.2 illustrates this *event-driven* concept. Figure 16.2 has three key parts: an object, the event itself, and the event handler. The following list describes the three parts:

- An *object* can be anything on the Web page—a button will do nicely, but any HTML tag can also generate events.

- Objects raise *events* in response to something the user does to an object. For example, if the user clicks a button, the button raises a click event.

- *Event handlers* take action on the event. To create an event handler, you associate a function with the event. Then the browser executes that function whenever that event occurs.

FIG. 16.1

document.write writes content to the Web page as the browser loads the HTML file.

Result of document. write("Howdy");

FIG. 16.2

Events signal to the browser that an object on the Web page needs attention by a script. The browser determines which function to use.

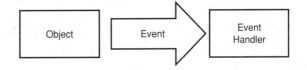

Benefits of Event-Driven Programming

Events have many benefits over the old style of programming. The biggest benefit is the fact that you stay in control of the computer. Here are the highlights:

- *You determine the order in which a program executes.* Clicking different parts of the screen, such as buttons, menus, and windows, causes different bits of code to execute. Contrast that to a procedural application that determines the order in which the code executes: starts at the beginning, expects to see certain inputs at certain times, and stops when it hits the last line of code.

- *When an event-driven program is waiting for an event, it's not using much of the computer's resources.* This lets the computer do other tasks, such as run other programs. Event-driven programs have a message loop that checks for messages. If no messages are waiting, the program returns control back to the operating system to give another program a shot.

- *Events simplify programming.* Instead of a program constantly checking each input device, the program sits back and waits for the operating system to send it an event. The program

continues

continued

doesn't miss out on input when it's not looking, either, because every input event is queued and waiting for the program.

● *Events allow programs to work with objects that define their own behavior.* The operating system simply forwards events to an object, and the object's event handlers determine how to handle it. The program doesn't need to know how the object works internally; it just needs to know how to talk to it.

Learning to Program: Writing Scripts

You can write scripts in two ways. The first way is by using a wizard such as the Scripting Wizard that comes with Microsoft FrontPage and FrontPage Express. These wizards allow you to write very simple scripts and associate them with events and objects using a intuitive mouse-driven interface. If you're interested in approaching scripts this way, you don't need to learn how to program. You can learn more about using Microsoft's Scripting Wizard in "Writing Scripts with the ActiveX Control Pad," later in this chapter.

You can also write scripts the old-fashioned way: using a text editor. Doing so requires that you have an intimate understanding of the script language you're using. You can type your scripts directly into a file using your HTML editor, or you can type them into a plain text file that you link to your HTML file. You need to understand a few concepts about programming before you start writing scripts, however. If you already have basic programming skills, you can skip the rest of this section. If not, you need a quick overview of programming concepts such as variables and expressions.

Variables

Variables are names for a small chunk of memory in which you store a value. Variables can store a number or any bit of text. You don't need to worry about where in the computer's memory the script stores the variable's value because you use the variable's name to change or read its value.

Mathematical Expressions

Mathematical expressions return the result of a calculation. Two things make up a mathematical expression: *operands* (numbers, strings, or variables) and *operators*. When you add two numbers using a calculator, the numbers are the operands, and the plus sign (+) is the operator. Likewise, the minus (-), multiplication (*), and division signs (/) are operators. In most cases, you assign the result of a mathematical expression to a variable so that you can recall the result later. Examples of mathematical expressions written in JavaScript include the following:

8 + 4   Adds 8 and 4, returning 12 as a result.

2 * 3 + 1   Multiplies 2 by 3 and adds 1, returning 7 as a result.

`3 + 2 * 5`	Multiplies 2 by 5 because the multiplication operator has a higher order of precedence and adds 3, returning 13 as a result.
`(3 + 2) * 5`	Adds 3 to 2 because they're grouped together in parentheses and multiplies by 5, returning 25 as a result.
`x = 1 + 2`	Adds 1 and 2, storing the results in a variable called x.
`x = y + 2`	Adds 2 to the value stored in y and assigns the result to a variable called x.

NOTE An operator's level of precedence determines the order in which the interpreter evaluates each operator in an expression. A multiplication operator has a higher order of precedence than an addition operator, so the interpreter evaluates the multiplication operator first.

The exception to this rule is when you put a portion of the expression inside parentheses. The interpreter evaluates anything you place inside parentheses before it evaluates the rest of the expression. If you have one set of parentheses with another, the interpreter evaluates the innermost set before evaluating the outermost set. ▪

Boolean Expressions

Boolean expressions let you make decisions. They always evaluate to one of two values: `True` or `False`. You can assign the result of a Boolean expression to a variable, use it to control a loop, or use it to make a decision.

A simple Boolean expression contains any two values combined with a Boolean operator. *Comparison operators* are the heart and soul of Boolean expressions. You use them to determine the relationship between two values (greater-than, less-than, equal, and so on) and return `True` if the comparison is true or `False` if the comparison is false. For example, `1 < 2` returns `True` because one is less than two. On the other hand, `1 > 2` returns `False` because one is not greater than 2. Table 16.1 describes the most common comparison operators.

Table 16.1   Comparison Operators

Symbol	Description	Syntax
=	Equality	*Expression1 = Expression2*
<> (!=)	Inequality	*Expression1 <> Expression2*
<	Less than	*Expression1 < Expression2*
>	Greater than	*Expression1 > Expression2*
<=	Less than or equal	*Expression1 <= Expression2*
>=	Greater than or equal	*Expression1 >= Expression2*

Part
III

Ch
16

The following are some examples that use comparison operators:

2 < 3	The result is True because 2 is indeed less than 3.
4 > 5	The result is False because 4 is not greater than 5.
4 <= 4	The result is True because 4 is less than or equal to 4.
x < 10	The result is True if x is any value less than 10; otherwise, the result is False.
y = x	The result is True if y and x contain the same value; otherwise, the result is False.

Logical operators let you combine multiple comparison operators in a single expression. They're very simple to use; you plug in a couple of values and get a predictable result in return. For example, A And B is always True if both values are True. It's always False if either value is False. The following list describes the most important logical operators that JavaScript and VBScript support:

Not	The Not operator negates a Boolean value. Not True returns False, for example, and Not False returns True.
And	The And operator compares two Boolean values and returns True if both values are True. Otherwise, it returns False. Table 16.2 shows you the result for each combination of *Boolean1* and *Boolean2*.

Table 16.2 *And* Operator

Boolean1	*Boolean2*	Result
True	True	True
True	False	False
False	True	False
False	False	False

Or	The Or operator compares two Boolean values and returns True if either value is True. Otherwise, it returns False. Table 16.3 shows you the result for each combination of *Boolean1* and *Boolean2*.

Table 16.3 *Or* Operator

Boolean1	*Boolean2*	Result
True	True	True
True	False	True
False	True	True
False	False	False

Xor The Xor operator compares two Boolean values and returns True if both values are different. Otherwise, it returns False. Table 16.4 shows you the result for each combination of *Boolean1* and *Boolean2*.

Table 16.4 *Xor* Operator

Boolean1	Boolean2	Result
True	True	False
True	False	True
False	True	True
False	False	False

The following are some examples of Boolean expressions that rely on logical operators:

2 < 3 And 4 > 5 Returns False because this expression evaluates to True And False.

1 > 0 And 4 < 5 Returns True because this expression evaluates to True And True.

2 < 3 Or 4 > 5 Returns True because this expression evaluates to True Or False.

x < 0 And y > 0 Returns True if x is negative and y is positive.

x Or y Returns True if either variable contains a True value.

Decisions

VBScript and JavaScript contain a variety of statements you can use to control how your script flows. The syntax is different in each language, but both languages have roughly the same form.

The most basic type of decision making statement you'll use is the If...Then...Else statement. This statement evaluates a decision and conditionally executes a block of statements depending on the result. The statement has many different forms, but in general it looks like this:

```
If Condition Then
    Statements
Else
    Statements
End If
```

The first line is the heart of the If...Then...Else statement. It begins with the keyword If and ends with the keyword Then. *Condition*, the middle part, is the criteria. This is a Boolean expression that evaluates to either True or False. You learned to write Boolean expressions earlier in this chapter. If the condition is True, the script executes the first block of statements; otherwise, the script executes the second block of statements.

The following example shows you an `If...Then..Else` statement written in JavaScript. The condition is x < 3. If that condition is `True`, the interpreter executes the first `alert` statement. If that condition is `False`, the interpreter executes the second `alert` statement.

```
if( x < 3 )
  alert( "x was less than 3" );
else
  alert( "x was equal to 3 or greater" );
```

Loops

You can write a script that repeatedly executes the same statements until some condition is met or, alternatively, until some condition is not met. This is called *looping*. The primary reason to write a loop is so that you don't have to repeat a bunch of statements, like this:

```
Add the first number to sum
Add the second number to sum
Add the third number to sum
Add the fourth number to sum
Add the fifth number to sum
```

You can put these statements in a loop, instead, and let the script repeat them for you:

```
repeat the following line five times
  assign the next number to sum
```

Both VBScript and JavaScript support a variety of looping mechanisms, each with its own syntax. In general, though, a loop looks like this:

```
Loop Condition
    Statements
```

`Statements` is called the *body* of the loop. The interpreter iterates the loop over and over until `Condition` becomes `True`. Each time the interpreter does so, it executes the statements in the body of the loop.

The following example shows you a `while` loop in JavaScript. As long as i is less than 10, the interpreter executes the two statements contained in the body of the loop. The first statement simply displays the current value of i. The second statement adds 1 to i. The number of times that this loop executes depends entirely on the value of i as the interpreter enters the loop; if i started at 0, the loop executes 10 times.

```
while( i < 10 )
{
  alert( i );
  i = i + 1;
}
```

Functions

Functions (and subprocedures in VBScript) let you divide your scripts into chunks you call from any other script. Invoking a function in your script is called *calling* a function. You give a function a name and a list of arguments. You call the function by its name and pass arguments by their position. In general, a function looks like this:

```
Name( Arguments )
    Statements
End
```

Name is the name of the function, which you use to invoke the function from a script or associate the function with an object's event. *Arguments* is a list of parameters that you pass to the function as variables. *Statements* is all the code you want the interpreter to execute each time it invokes the function. A function can also return a value to the calling script; thus, you can use a function on the right side of an equal sign, like this:

```
Result = MyFunction( Variable1, Variable2 )
```

The whole process works as follows:

1. You call a function by name to invoke it, passing any values on which you want it to operate as arguments.

2. The interpreter executes the function, setting each variable in the argument list to the values you passed.

3. When the function finishes, it specifies a return value to the interpreter, which returns the result in the expression that invoked the function.

Adding Scripts to Your HTML File

You embed scripts in an HTML file using tags, much like any other content you put in a Web page. Scripts are put between the <SCRIPT> and </SCRIPT> container tags, as shown in Listing 16.2. You specify the language you're using by assigning the MIME type of the language to the TYPE attribute: text/vbscript for VBScript or text/javascript for JavaScript.

Listing 16.2   A Sample Script

```
<SCRIPT TYPE="text/vbscript">
<!--
    ' The following line is executed when the page is loaded
    Alert "Howdy from Texas"

    ' The following function is executed online when invoked
    Sub Pause
        MsgBox "Click on OK to Continue"
    End Sub
' -->
</SCRIPT>
```

When your browser loads a Web page that includes scripts (*parse time*), it immediately evaluates each <SCRIPT> block it encounters. The browser grabs everything in a <SCRIPT> block and passes the content off to the scripting engine. The scripting engine looks at the <SCRIPT> block the browser gave it and looks for any functions and global variables (variables outside a function). The scripting engine compiles the functions and global variables and stashes their names in the symbol table for later use. The scripting engine immediately executes statements it finds outside a function, though. This is called *immediate execution*. Scripts that the browser executes immediately are called *inline scripts*.

N O T E Prior to HTML 4.0, you might have used the LANGUAGE attribute to specify the scripting language you're using. W3C encourages you to use TYPE instead of the LANGUAGE attribute because its values are not standardized. Note that Internet Explorer and Navigator don't support the TYPE attribute as of this writing. Until both browsers do, you can safely use the LANGUAGE attribute to specify the scripting language by assigning either JAVASCRIPT or VBSCRIPT to it, like this:

```
<SCRIPT LANGUAGE=JAVASCRIPT>
<SCRIPT LANGUAGE=VBSCRIPT>
```

Specifying a Default Scripting Language

You can specify a default scripting language for an HTML file and forget about specifying it within each <SCRIPT> tag. You use the <META> tag at the beginning of your HTML file. Set HTTP-EQUIV to Content-Script-Type and set CONTENT to the MIME type of the scripting language you're using. The following example sets the default language for the HTML document to JavaScript:

```
<META http-equiv="Content-Script-Type" content="text/javascript">
```

You can also set the default scripting language using an HTTP header as shown in this example for VBScript:

```
Content-Script-Type: text/vbscript
```

> **CAUTION**
>
> Failing to specify the scripting language you're using is not only incorrect but also can cause problems for you in the future. Either define your choice globally or within each <SCRIPT> tag, but don't rely on the browser's default scripting language to always be JavaScript or VBScript.

Linking to Scripts Instead of Embedding Them

You can link to a script that's stored in a separate text file instead of embedding the script into the HTML document. To do so, assign the URL of the file containing your scripts to the <SCRIPT> tag's SRC attribute:

```
<SCRIPT SRC=script.vbs TYPE="text/vbscript">
```

Because you must still specify the language using the TYPE attribute, you can use only a single language within each text file. To help identify the types of scripts stored in each file, use an appropriate file extension. Consider using the following conventions:

- Use the VBS file extension for files containing VBScript scripts.
- Use the JS file extension for files containing JavaScript scripts.

Hiding Scripts from Older Browsers

Many browsers can't interpret scripts. When one such browser encounters a script, it ignores the <SCRIPT> and </SCRIPT> tags because it doesn't know how to interpret them (this behavior is by design). Then the browser displays everything between those two tags as content, which is not exactly what you had in mind. Figure 16.3 shows an example of what this looks like.

FIG. 16.3

You can see this example for yourself by mistyping SCRIPT in the <SCRIPT> tag and opening the Web page in Navigator or Internet Explorer.

Part

III

Ch

16

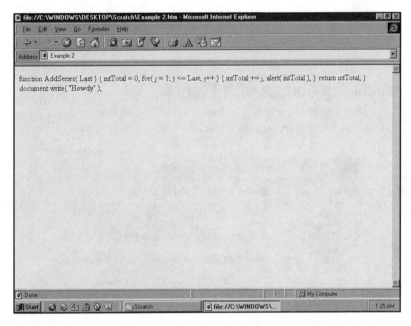

You use an HTML comment to hide scripts from browsers that don't support scripting, however. Make the opening HTML comment the first line within the script. The closing HTML comment should be the last line in the script block. Note that when using JavaScript you begin this line with a JavaScript comment (//) because after JavaScript starts interpreting code, it thinks that everything else in the script is actual JavaScript code. VBScript users begin the same line with a VBScript comment ('). Script-enabled browsers ignore the comments and interpret the scripts, whereas other browsers ignore all the content between the comments. Listing 16.3 shows you a JavaScript example.

Listing 16.3   Hiding Scripts

```
<SCRIPT TYPE="text/javascript">
<!--
  function AddSeries( Last )
  {
    intTotal = 0;
    for( j = 1; j <= Last; j++ )
    {
```

continues

Listing 16.3   Continued

```
        intTotal += j;
        alert( intTotal );
    }
    return intTotal;
 }

  document.write( "Howdy" );
//-->
</SCRIPT>
```

Associating Scripts with Events

Most objects on a Web page have events. That includes each HTML tag, control, or form element. Some events to which you attach scripts include those listed in Table 16.5.

Table 16.5   Events Defined in HTML 4.0

Name	Event Is Raised When
OnLoad	The browser finishes opening the HTML document.
OnUnload	The browser unloads the HTML document.
OnClick	The user clicks the mouse on an element.
OnDblClick	The user double-clicks an element.
OnMouseDown	The user presses the mouse button.
OnMouseOver	The user moves the mouse over an element.
OnMouseMove	The user moves the mouse over an element.
OnMouseOut	The user moves the mouse out of an element.
OnFocus	An element receives keyboard focus.
OnBlur	An element loses keyboard focus.
OnKeyPress	The user presses and releases a key.
OnKeyDown	The user presses a key over an element.
OnKeyUp	The user releases a key over an element.
OnSubmit	A form is submitted to the Web server.
OnReset	A form is reset.
OnSelect	The user selects text in a text field.
OnChange	An element loses focus and has changed.

Recall from Figure 16.2 that objects, events, and event handlers all work together. You have to associate an object with an event handler via that object's event. You do that by adding the event's attribute to the object's HTML tag and setting its value to a single statement that executes the function. For example, to associate a JavaScript function called MyFunction() with the onClick event of a button, you write the button's <INPUT> tag as follows:

```
<INPUT TYPE=BUTTON NAME=BUTTON onClick="MyFunction()">
```

You can just as easily associate an event handler with any other event in Table 16.5. In this case, the event attribute is onClick. Add another event attribute from the first column of Table 16.5 to the tag in the preceding example to associate an event handler with that event, like this:

```
<INPUT TYPE=BUTTON NAME=BUTTON onClick="MyFunction()" MouseOut="ByeMouse()">
```

You can also use the FOR and EVENT attributes, which let you associate a script with any named object in the HTML file and any event for that object. Take a look at the following:

```
<SCRIPT FOR="Button" EVENT="Click" TYPE="text/javascript">
<!--
 window.alert( "Ouch! You clicked on me." )
-->
</SCRIPT>
<INPUT TYPE=BUTTON NAME=Button>
```

This defines a button (with a NAME of Button) that executes the script when the user clicks it. The <SCRIPT> tag contains the FOR and EVENT attributes that define the object and event associated with that script. FOR="Button" EVENT="Click" says that when an object named Button triggers the Click event, every statement in this script is executed.

Writing Scripts with the ActiveX Control Pad

There is certainly a better way to add scripts to your HTML documents. The *ActiveX Control Pad* is a free product from Microsoft that makes short work of this. You get it through Microsoft's Site Builder Workshop at **http://www.microsoft.com/workshop/author/cpad**. Figure 16.4 shows you the Control Pad's HTML editor with an HTML file in it.

TIP   The Control Pad uses VBScript by default. If you want to use JavaScript, you need to set it to do so. Choose Tools, Options, Script from the main menu and select JavaScript. The Script Wizard now generates JavaScript language scripts rather than VBScript.

The Script Wizard provides two different ways you can edit scripts: List view and Code view. List view is a bit easier to use. Click the Script Wizard button in the toolbar to open the Script Wizard. Then click the List View button at the bottom of the window. See the window shown in Figure 16.5.

FIG. 16.4
The Editor window shows you only the contents of your HTML. Save the file to disk and open it in your Web browser to preview what the Web page looks like.

Object icon

Script icon

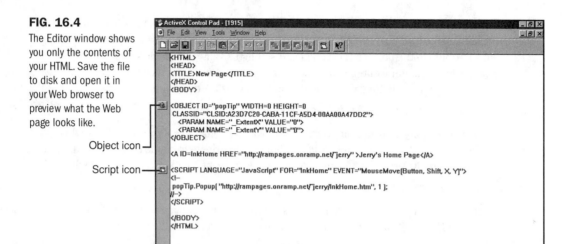

FIG. 16.5
In most cases, the List view is all you ever need to create exciting Web pages.

You associate an object's event with another object's methods and properties. Select an event on the left pane of the wizard. Choose a method or property in the right pane. When you click the Insert Action button, the Script Wizard prompts you for the value of the property or for any parameters you want to pass to a method. You can rearrange the order of the actions in the bottom pane of the Script Wizard. Close the Script Wizard, and it'll add your script to the HTML file.

If you're more comfortable with the traditional programmer view of life, use the Script Wizard's Code view (see Figure 16.6). This works just like the List view, except that you don't see a list of associated events and actions in the bottom pane. You see the actual code the Script Wizard creates instead. Click the Script Wizard button in the toolbar to open the Script Wizard. Then click the Code View button at the bottom of the window, add your script, and close the Script Wizard.

Part

III

Ch

16

FIG. 16.6
You must use Code view if you want to use compound statements such as If in your scripts.

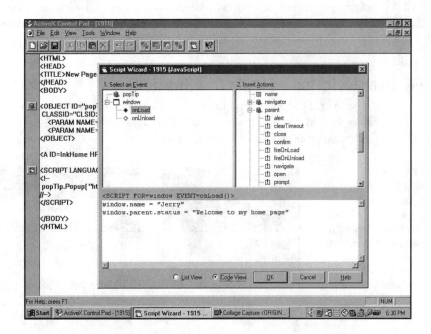

 TIP Keep your Web browser running with the Web page on which you're working in it. Then you can save the changes, flip to the browser, and refresh the Web page to see your changes while you're working in Control Pad.

Using Scripts from Other People

The quickest way to add scripts to your Web page is by using a script that you download from a gallery or library. For example, the Template Studio (**http://tstudio.usa.net**) is a comprehensive gallery that contains numerous scripts you can use in your Web page. The scripts you find on this site include scripts for detecting the user's browser, dynamically replacing an image, controlling a window, displaying messages, and setting cookies.

Gamelan (**http://javascript.developer.com**) also has a comprehensive site that you can use to find good scripts for your Web page. Tutorial examples, games, and other miscellaneous scripts are featured on this Web site. You can use modify them to suite your own purposes and use them to learn more about scripting. As a bonus, you'll find documentation that helps a new JavaScript developer get up-to-speed fast.

If you want even more immediate gratification, however, you can try out the scripts described in the following sections. These scripts help you add fly-over help for the links on your Web page.

T I P Netscape provides more than a dozen, real-world example JavaScript Web pages that you can use. Open **http://developer.netscape.com/library/examples/examples.html#javascript** in your Web page.

Fly-Over Help for a Link's Destination

Take a look at Communicator's status line when you hold the mouse pointer over a link. It shows the URL to which the link points. You can provide a more useful description of the link's destination by using a script (see Figure 16.7).

FIG. 16.7
Providing a more thorough description of a link can prevent the user from visiting Web pages in which she isn't interested. Thus, you're saving Internet bandwidth.

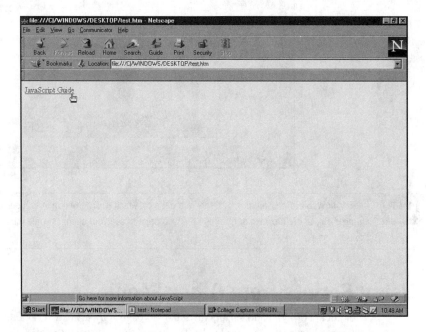

You use the <A> tag's onMouseOver event to display the help text and its onMouseOut event to remove the text. For every link on your Web page, add the following onMouseOver attribute to its <A> tag. Each time the user moves the mouse over the link's anchor, the two statements assigned to this event execute. The first statement, self.status='The help text'; displays the text contained within the single quotes on the browser's status line. Change this text to a brief description of the link. The following shows the second statement, `return true;`, which prevents the browser from displaying the link's URL reference on the status line:

```
onMouseOver="self.status='The help text'; return true;"
```

Also add the `onMouseOut` event attribute to each `<A>` tag as you see in the following example. This works just like the `onMouseOver` attribute you just read about except that it clears the status line when the user moves the mouse out of the link. The effect is that the user sees the help text as long as she holds the mouse over the link; but when she moves the mouse away from the link, the status line clears.

```
onMouseOut="self.status=''; return true;"
```

Using Forms and JavaScript for Navigation

If you've visited Microsoft's site recently, you've seen forms used for navigation. Here's how it works: you select an item from the drop-down list and click a button. The browser opens the URL associated with that list item (see Figure 16.8).

FIG. 16.8
Alternatively, you can create a server-side script that processes the user's choice on the server. This approach is more efficient, however, because it's done on the client.

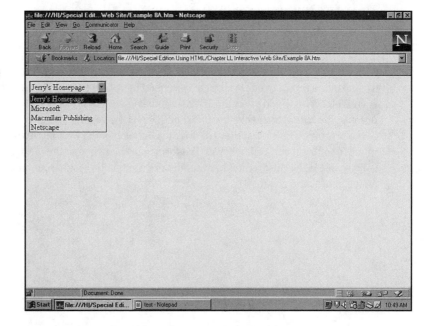

Listing 16.4 shows the HTML for a form with a single drop-down list. It opens the Web page that the user chooses from the list. The function `OpenURL()` is associated with the `<SELECT>` tag's `OnChange` event. When the user selects an item from the form's list, `OpenURL()` sets `window.location` to the associated URL.

Listing 16.4   Form and Script for Navigation

```
<HTML>

<SCRIPT LANGUAGE=JAVASCRIPT>
<!--
  function OpenURL( Index )
  {
    if( Index == 0 ) window.location = "http://rampages.onramp.net/~jerry";
    if( Index == 1 ) window.location = "http://www.microsoft.com";
    if( Index == 2 ) window.location = "http://www.mcp.com";
    if( Index == 3 ) window.location = "http://www.netscape.com";
  }
//-->
</SCRIPT>

<FORM NAME=NAVIGATE>
  <SELECT NAME=LIST SIZE=1 OnChange="OpenURL(
document.NAVIGATE.LIST.selectedIndex )">
  <OPTION NAME=JERRY>Jerry's Homepage
  <OPTION NAME=MS>Microsoft
  <OPTION NAME=QUE>Macmillan Publishing
  <OPTION NAME=NETSCAPE>Netscape
  </SELECT>
</FORM>
</HTML>
```

To make this work in your Web page, you need to update the form's list to contain an entry for each Web site to which you want the user to navigate. Then you need to add a line to the OpenURL function that checks the index of the user's selection and opens the appropriate URL in the browser. The easiest thing to do is to copy one of the existing lines, change the index number so that it corresponds with the form, and then change the URL assigned to window.location. Just remember that the first item in the list has an index of 0, the second has an index of 1, and so on. ●

## CHAPTER 17

Applying Cascading Style Sheets

by Jerry Honeycutt

In this chapter

Understanding Style Sheets

A critical portion of W3C's HTML 4.0 recommendation is style sheets, particularly if you're interested in dynamic HTML. Style sheets let you separate the content of your HTML documents from their presentation. And by associating scripts with HTML elements, you can change the document's format as the user interacts with the it.

The two major Web browsers, Internet Explorer 4.0 and Netscape Communicator, support style sheets defined by HTML 4.0: *Cascading Style Sheets Level 1* (CSS1). They both support CSS1 to varying degrees, though.

W3C treats the style sheet mechanism (the HTML used to associate styles with a document) separately from the style sheet language (the statements that specify formatting). CSS1 is the most prevalent style sheet language, however, so I'll show you how to write CSS1 rules in this chapter in addition to how to associate style sheets with an HTML document. Appendix B, "Style Sheet Property Reference," covers CSS1 in more depth.

Attaching a Style Sheet to Your HTML Document

HTML 4.0 provides the mechanism to associate a style sheet with a document, but it doesn't care what style sheet language you're using—CSS1 or even a more complex language that's yet to be invented. Regardless, you must specify the style sheet language to the browser so that it knows how to parse it. You do so by using the <META> tag:

```
<META http-equiv="Content-Style-Type" content="text/css">
```

You can also define the style sheet language using the following HTTP header:

```
Content-Style-Type: text/css
```

If you don't specify a style sheet language using the <META> tag or an HTTP header, the default is CSS1. Even though the default is CSS1, make a point of explicitly defining the language you're using so that you don't rely on this default behavior.

Linking a Style Sheet

You can create a style sheet in a separate file and then apply that style sheet to all the pages on your Web site. I recommend this method because it makes creating a consistent Web site much easier. In fact, you can create a corporate style sheet and have all members of your organization use it with their Web sites.

You store a linked style sheet in a text file with the CSS file extension. It's a plain text file that you can create with your favorite text editor (Notepad, for example). The format of the text file is readable and easy to understand. Thus, you won't have any trouble creating your style sheets by hand.

To link to a style sheet stored in a separate file, store all your styles in the CSS file and link your HTML files to it using the <LINK> tag, like this:

```
<LINK REL=STYLESHEET HREF="http://www.myserver.com/mysheet.css" TYPE="text/css">
```

Assign the URL of the style sheet to the HREF attribute. Set TYPE to the MIME type of the style sheet language, "text/css" for CSS1.

 Store your corporate style sheets in a common location on the Web server and then have everyone who is creating Web pages reference that style sheet from his or her HTML files. Everyone can even use the same <LINK> tag. In this way, you can have a more consistent look across all the Web pages on the server.

Embedding a Style Sheet

You don't have to store your style sheet in a separate file. You can embed the style sheet inside each HTML file. Note that the styles within an embedded style sheet only affect the HTML within that file; thus, you can't embed a style sheet in an HTML file and expect to use that across multiple HTML files without copying it into each file.

You use the <STYLE> container to embed a style sheet in your HTML file. Put this container between the <HTML> and <BODY> tags of your file, like this:

```
<HTML>
<HEAD>
</HEAD>
<STYLE TYPE="text/css">
  Style definitions go here
</STYLE>
<BODY>
</BODY>
</HTML>
```

The <STYLE> tag's most important attribute, called TYPE, specifies the MIME type. It identifies the style sheet language so that browsers that don't support style sheets or the specified language won't display the contents of the <STYLE> container. For CSS1, set it to "text/css". The <STYLE> tag has three other attributes that you learn about later in this chapter: MEDIA, LANG, and DIR.

Defining Styles Inline

Inline styles are simple styles that you define on-the-fly. You can use inline styles to quickly change the appearance of a single tag, for example. You can also use inline styles to override a style for a particular tag. For example, if you've defined a style that sets the color of the <H1> tag to blue, you can set the color of a specific element using the <H1> tag to red.

With inline styles, you define a tag's style within the tag itself. You do this by using the STYLE attribute, which is supported by all the child tags of the BODY tag. To define an inline style, add the STYLE attribute to the tag for which you want to change the style and set its value to the string representing the style definition, like this:

```
<H1 STYLE="color: blue">
```

N O T E   If an inline style conflicts with an embedded or linked style, the inline style wins. If in a
linked style sheet you define the color of an <H1> tag to be blue and you also define the
color of a particular <H1> tag within your HTML file to be red, the browser will display that particular
occurrence of the <H1> tag using the color red. ▪

You can use inline styles with the <DIV> tag to set the style for an entire block of HTML within
your document. This works because of the concept of inheritance, which you learn about later
in this chapter. For example, if you want to change the text color of an entire block of tags to
blue, you can put those tags in the <DIV> container and define a style for the <DIV> tag that sets
the text color to blue. It looks like this:

```
<DIV STYLE="color: blue">
  <H1>This is a heading</H1>
    <P>This is a paragraph. It will look blue in the user's browser</P>
</DIV>
```

You can also use inline style sheets with the <SPAN> tag to change the formatting for a few
words or even just a few letters. For example:

```
This is a <SPAN STYLE="color: blue">simple</SPAN> block of text.
```

CAUTION

Don't abuse inline styles. They'll quickly clutter your HTML file so that it's more difficult to read and much
more difficult to maintain. This obviously diminishes the greatest advantage of style sheets: separating
format from content.

Importing Style Sheets

You learned about linking to a style sheet earlier in this chapter. You can also use the @import
keyword to import a style sheet into your HTML file; however, many browsers don't support
@import yet. Remember that you're just importing the text file, thus you have to insert it in the
<STYLE> container. In this manner, importing a style sheet works just like embedding a style
sheet into your HTML file. For example:

```
<STYLE TYPE="text/css">
@import url(http://www.myserver.com/style.css);
</STYLE>
```

Matters of Style

Style sheets can help you create a great-looking site. Other style matters, however, contribute as
greatly, if not more, to the impact your site has on its users:

- Put navigational aids at the top and bottom of each Web page so that the user can easily
  move around your site.

- Limit your graphics. Many folks are still using slow connections, so keep graphics down to 50K
  or less.

- Indicate to the user that a particular link leaves your Web site. You can use a special icon next to the link.

- If you're using frames on your site, provide an alternative to the user who has a frameless browser.

- Design your Web pages for 640×480 resolution. Yes, people still use monitors at that resolution.

Naming and Combining Style Sheets

The <LINK> tag's TITLE attribute allows you to name the style sheet. If you don't assign a value to TITLE, the style sheet is *persistent*, and the user can't disable it (unless he disables style sheets altogether). Assigning a value to TITLE changes the style sheet to *default*, and the user can choose from any number of named style sheets.

The browser combines any style sheets with the same title that have the alternate keyword attached to the REL attribute. In the following example, the browser applies the styles in both FIRST.CSS and SECOND.CSS because both <LINK> tags assign alternate to REL and have the same title.

```
<LINK TYPE="text/css" REL="alternate stylesheet" TITLE="Example" HREF=first.css>
<LINK TYPE="text/css" REL="alternate stylesheet" TITLE="Example" HREF=second.css>
```

Understanding the Cascade

You can use multiple styles to control how your Web page looks; the browser follows a certain set of rules to determine the precedence and resolves conflicts between styles (cascading order). For example, you can define a style sheet for your Web site, and the reader can have her own style sheet. The cascading rules determine who wins if both style sheets define a style for a particular type of text.

Each rule is assigned a weight by the browser. When the browser is working with the occurrence of a particular tag, it finds all the rules that apply to it. The browser then sorts those rules by their weight, applying the style with the greatest weight. In general, there are just a few rules that you need to be aware of when dealing with competing style sheets:

- The author's style sheet overrides the user's style sheet, whereas the user's style sheet overrides the browser's default values.

- Inline styles take precedence over embedded style sheets, whereas embedded style sheets take precedence over linked style sheets.

You can also override the precedence for a rule by using the important keyword. In the following example, the assignment of red to the property color and the assignment of sans-serif to the property font-family are marked as important. Thus, the browser will not override these styles. If two competing style sheets mark the same property as important, however, the rules in the previous list apply.

```
H1 {color: red ! important font-weight: bold font-family: sans-serif !
important}
```

Creating Style Sheets for Each Type of Media

HTML 4.0 style sheets give you the opportunity to specify the type of media for which a style sheet is intended. The browser uses the style sheet that's associated with the media on which the user is viewing the document. For example, you can associate three style sheets with an HTML document. The browser uses the first one if a user views the document on the screen, the second one for printing, and the third one for speech.

To associate a style sheet with a media type, you use the `<STYLE>` tag's `MEDIA` attribute. In the following example, you see two different style sheets. The browser uses the first one for the screen and the second for printing.

```
<STYLE TYPE="text/css" media="screen">
  style definitions
</STYLE>

<STYLE TYPE="text/css" media="print">
  style definitions
</STYLE>
```

Table 17.1 describes the media types that HTML 4.0 supports.

Table 17.1	HTML 4.0 Media Types
Type	**Description**
Screen	Style sheet intended for a computer screen
Print	Style sheet intended for a printer
Projection	Style sheet intended for overheads
Braille	Style sheet intended for Braille devices
Speech	Style sheet intended for speech synthesizer
All	Style sheet intended for all devices

Adding Rules to a Style Sheet

Linked and embedded style sheets allow you to define styles for one or more individual tags. For example, you can create a style sheet that defines styles for the `<H1>`, `<H2>`, `<P>`, and `<EM>` tags. Each style definition is called a *rule*. A rule contains a *selector* (the HTML tag), followed by the declaration (the definition of the style). The rule's selector ties the style's definition to tags you use in the HTML file. The following is an example of what a rule that defines a style for each occurrence of the `<H1>` tag looks like:

```
H1 {color: blue}
```

The declaration is enclosed in curly braces ({}). Each item in the declaration has two parts: the property name and the value you're assigning to the property, separated by a colon (:). In the previous example, `color` is the property name, and `blue` is the value you're assigning to it. HTML predefines dozens of property names (`font-size`, `font-style`, `color`, `margin-right`, and so on), which you'll learn about in Appendix B. Each property also accepts a predefined type and range of values.

The following example shows you a few rules contained within an embedded style sheet:

```
<STYLE TYPE="text/css">
  H1 {color: blue}
  P {font-size: 10pt}
</STYLE>
```

Setting Multiple Properties in a Single Rule

You can set multiple properties within a single declaration. You do this by separating each assignment with a semicolon (;):

```
H1 {color: blue; font-size: 12pt; text-line: center}
```

In this example, the browser displays each occurrence of the `<H1>` tag using the color blue, font size of 12 points, and centered in the browser window. For all other properties, the browser uses its default values. For example, it sets the `font-style` property to `normal`.

Grouping Selectors Together in a Single Rule

If you want to define a similar style for several tags, you can list them individually in your style sheet, like this:

```
P {font-size: 12pt}
UL {font-size: 12pt}
LI {font-size: 12pt}
```

You can group the selectors together, however, and define a rule for them as a group. The following example groups the selectors in the previous example on one line and defines a rule that sets the `font-size` property to `12pt`:

```
P, UL, LI {font-size: 12pt}
```

Note the comma between each selector in the list. Omitting this comma means a totally different thing (see the following section, "Defining Parent-Child Relationships in Rules," later in this chapter).

Defining Parent-Child Relationships in Rules

With HTML style sheets, you can be very specific about when a style is applied to a tag. For example, you may want to define two styles for the `<LI>` tag: one that's applied when it's a child of the `<UL>` tag and another when it's a child of the `<OL>` tag. You do this with contextual selectors.

Contextual selectors define the exact sequence of tags for which a style will be applied. In other words, you can specify that a style applies to a particular tag, such as `<LI>` only if it's a child of the `<OL>` tag, like this:

```
OL LI {list-style-type: decimal}
```

You can also specify that a particular style applies to the <LI> tag only if it's a child of the <UL> tag, like this:

```
UL LI {list-style-type: square}
```

Note the list of selectors is not comma separated. Separating each selector with a comma would cause all the tags in the list to be assigned the rule.

Understanding Inheritance

In HTML, tags inherit certain properties from their parents. For example, all the tags within the <BODY> tag (<P> and <UL>) inherit certain properties from the <BODY> tag. Likewise, the <LI> tag inherits properties from the <UL> tag that contains it.

Consider the following bit of HTML:

```
<STYLE TYPE="text/css">
P {color: blue}
</STYLE>
<BODY>
<P>Hello. This is a paragraph of text. <EM>This text is emphasized</EM>
</P>
</BODY>
```

The style sheet for this example sets the color for the <P> tag to blue. There is no definition for the <EM> tag. You might expect the text in the <EM> tag to change back to the default color: black. That's not the case. Because the <EM> is within the container tag <P> (it's a child, in other words), the <EM> tag inherits the color property from the <P> tag.

Working with Classes in Your Style Sheets

A class defines a variation of style, which you refer to in a specific occurrence of a tag using the CLASS attribute. For example, you can define three variations of the H1 style and then use each one in the appropriate context. You define a class much like you normally define a style, only you add an arbitrary class name to the end of the tag, separating them with a period, as in the following example:

```
H1.blue {color: blue}
H1.red {color: red}
H1.black {color: black}
```

Then, when adding the <H1> tag to your HTML document, you set the CLASS attribute to indicate exactly which style you're using:

```
<H1 CLASS=red>Red Heading</H1>
```

T I P You can address all the tags within a particular class by omitting the tag name from the selector, like this: `.red {color: red}`. After defining this style, any tag that you associate with the `red` class, will be displayed using the color red.

Defining a Style for a Specific Element

You can use an inline style to define how a particular element looks by assigning the style to the element's STYLE attribute. You can make your HTML document easier to read, however, by giving an element an ID; then you associate a style with that element using its ID.

For example, the following <P> tag assigns `test` to the ID attribute:

```
<P ID=test>This is a test paragraph</P>
```

You can define a rule that affects only that element by using the its ID as the selector for the rule, prefixed with a pound sign (#), like this:

```
#test {color: red}
```

Part

III

Ch

17

Working with Special Elements such as Anchors

CSS defines a concept called *pseudo-classes*, which are special selectors that define how certain HTML elements look at certain times. For example, CSS defines a pseudo-class that defines how an anchor looks when the user clicks on it or how the first line of a paragraph looks. In general, pseudo-classes look like the following example.

```
selector:pseudo-class { property: value }
```

CSS1 defines three pseudo-classes for anchors: `link`, `active`, and `visited`. When you use these pseudo-classes with the A selector in a style rule, you're defining how a normal, active, and already visited link looks on the Web page. For instance, the following example defines unvisited links as blue, active links as red, and visited links as yellow:

```
A:link {color: blue}
A:active {color: red}
A:visited {color: yellow}
```

CSS1 defines a pseudo-class for the first line of a paragraph. Any style rule you assign to the selector called `first-line` applies to the first line of that element. If you use the `first-line` pseudo-class with the <P> tag, for example, the first line of each paragraph uses the formatting you specified in the rule. The following example causes the first line of every paragraph to be bold:

```
P:first-line {font-weight: bold}
```

Similarly, you can change the formatting for the first letter in an element using the `first-letter` pseudo-class. This is handy to create special effects such as drop-caps:

```
P:first-letter {font-size: 400%; float: left}
```

Adding Comments to Your Style Sheet

If your style sheet gets complicated or you need to explain why you've made a particular design decision, you can add a comment to the style sheet. Comments only serve to document your style sheet; they don't have any impact on how the browser displays the HTML document.

Enclose your comments between /* and */. The following example shows you what a one-line comment looks like:

```
BODY {margin-left: 1in}          /* Create space for sliders */
H1 {font-size: 16; margin-left: -1in}     /* Out one inch */
H2 {font-size: 14; margin-left: -1in}     /* Out one inch */
```

You can also use the /* and */ characters to create block comments. This is useful to explain an entire portion of your style sheet. Like this:

```
/*------------------------------------------------------------
   The margin-left property is set to one inch for the BODY tag.
   Since all of its enclosed tags will inherit this setting, the
   entire page will appear to be indented by one inch. The first-
   and second-level headings are indented to the left by one inch
   so that they slide out into the margin.
   ----------------------------------------------------------*/

BODY {margin-left: 1in}          /* Create space for sliders */
H1 {font-size: 16; margin-left: -1in}     /* Out one inch */
H2 {font-size: 14; margin-left: -1in}     /* Out one inch */
```

Hiding Style Sheets from Older Browsers

HTML style sheets are new. Internet Explorer and Netscape are the first browsers to support them. You need to worry about all those browsers that don't support style sheets, however.

Most browsers are designed to simply ignore the tags and attributes they don't understand. Thus, they'll ignore the <STYLE> tag, for example. They won't necessarily ignore what you put in the <STYLE> tag, though, and will display its contents as text on the Web page. To get around this problem, you can use an HTML comment within the <STYLE> tag to hide the style definitions, like this:

```
<STYLE TYPE="text/css">
<!--
H1 {color: red}
-->
</STYLE>
```

Browsers that don't support style sheets display the HTML files with their default styles. They'll ignore the style definitions.

TIP Open each HTML document in browsers that don't support style sheets so that you can verify how your Web pages look.

Building Style Sheets Using a Program

Building a style sheet by hand is easy; building a large style sheet by hand is tedious and error prone. Recently, several programs have been introduced to make building style sheets rather simple:

- *Sheet Stylist*. Sheet Stylist is a first-rate program that lets you take advantage of every feature found in CSS1, even though most browsers don't yet support them. Figure 17.1 shows you what its Style Editor looks like.

  http://www.tcp.co.uk/~drarh/Stylist

FIG. 17.1
Sheet Stylist's user interface is intuitive, with most work being done via this tabbed dialog box.

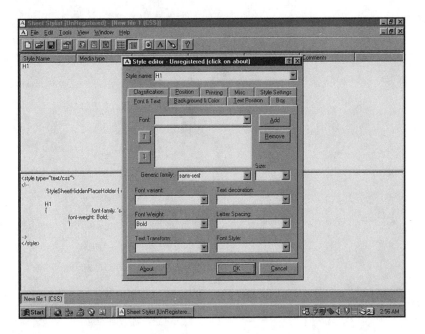

- *Cascade*. Cascade is a complete CSS1 editor for the Macintosh.

  http://interaction.in-progress.com/Cascade

- *StyleMaker*. StyleMaker is one of the better CSS1 editors available for Windows 95. It provides complete access to the CSS1 features. It's strongest point is that it allows you to preview each change in a dummy Web page as you make it; thus, you get instant feedback.

  http://danere.com/StyleMaker

Aside from style sheet editors, many of the popular HTML editors you learn about in Chapter 42, "Using HTML and Site Tools," support CSS1. For example, HotDog and HotMetaL both support CSS1.

T I P

To see style sheets in action, visit Microsoft's Web site at **http://www.microsoft.com**, and view the home page's source.

Positioning HTML Elements

by Jerry Honeycutt

In this chapter

Understanding CSS Positioning

In the desktop publishing world, layers are rectangular blocks of text and artwork that you can position anywhere on the page. You can also overlap layers so that one is hidden behind another or so that one bleeds through another. Publishers use layers to create some pretty awesome layouts. Take a look at any print advertisements or brochures, for example. Chances are, the publisher used layers.

While desktop publishers might take layering for granted (even the simplest of desktop publishing programs allow you to create and overlap layers), HTML designers don't. Because HTML is streaming, they've never had the capability to overlap blocks of text and artwork. That is, each preceding HTML element is displayed before the next—in order. HTML has never provided for the positioning of an HTML element, much less for overlapping HTML elements.

Until now—HTML 4.0 introduces the CSS positioning. If you're unsure of how to use style sheets, you should review Chapter 17, "Applying Cascading Style Sheets."

Positioning an HTML Element

You define an element's position using a style. Within a style's rule, you assign either RELATIVE or ABSOLUTE to the POSITION property. If you assign RELATIVE, the browser positions the element relative to its normal position (the location at which it would naturally appear). If you assign ABSOLUTE to POSITION, the browser positions the element relative to the parent container, whether it be the document or some other element, such as a <DIV> tag. In most cases, you use ABSOLUTE to place an element at an exact location relative to its parent. Use RELATIVE if you want to nudge an element slightly out of its normal location.

You position an element using a style's TOP and LEFT properties, like this:

```
#element {position: absolute; top: 100; left: 20}
```

When you assign the example style to an element, the browser positions it 100 pixels down and 20 pixels to the right of document's top, left-hand corner.

LEFT and TOP are represented in pixels, by default, and are relative to the top, left corner of the containing area within the HTML document. For example, to position an element 10 pixels from the left edge of the browser window and 40 pixels from the top edge, use LEFT=10 and TOP=40. The browser draws the HTML document as though the positioned element does not exist, and then the element is overlapped with the Web page at the given offset. You can also assign percentages to LEFT and TOP, which represent a percentage of the parent container's width and height, respectively. Listing 18.1 positions an element in the middle of the Web page. As shown in Figure 18.1, the contents of the HTML document bleed through the contents of the positioned element because it's transparent.

Listing 18.1   Positioning an Element in the Middle of the Page

```
<HTML>
<HEAD>
<TITLE>Listing CC.1</TITLE>
```

```
</HEAD>
<STYLE TYPE="text/css">
  #example {position: absolute; top: 40; left: 100}
</STYLE>
<BODY>

<IMG ID=example SRC=init.gif>

<P>You can position an element anywhere you like.</P>
<P>This element is positioned, however, so that it overlaps
the HTML document below it. Notice how this text displays
through the image's transparent background.</P>

<P>This element is positioned, however, so that it overlaps
the HTML document below it. Notice how this text displays
through the image's transparent background.</P>

<P>This element is positioned, however, so that it overlaps
the HTML document below it. Notice how this text displays
through the image's transparent background.</P>

<P>This element is positioned, however, so that it overlaps
the HTML document below it. Notice how this text displays
through the image's transparent background.</P>

</BODY>
</HTML>
```

FIG. 18.1
You can position the
element wherever you
want on the browser
window.

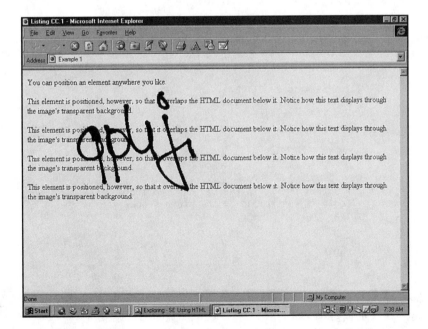

Changing the Size of an Element

You can change the height and width of the rectangular area occupied by an element. You use the WIDTH and HEIGHT properties. Like TOP and LEFT, you can assign a length or percentage to either of these properties. You can also assign AUTO to them and the browser automatically determines the appropriate width and height.

```
#element {position: absolute; top: 20; left: 20; width: 100; height: 100}
```

You don't use the WIDTH attribute to define the element's absolute width. This property suggests a width for purposes of wrapping the text contained within the element. If the text doesn't completely fill the element, however, the element is not actually as wide as the specified value. If you're inserting an image (or another element the browser can't wrap) inside an element, and the image is wider than the suggested width, the element's actual width is bigger than the suggested value.

T I P The OVERFLOW property determines what the browser does in the case that an element's contents are larger than the element's size. Assign NONE, and the contents are not clipped. Assign CLIP, and the browser chops off the content to fit in the rectangular area. Assign SCROLL, and the browser allows you to scroll the window so you can see more of it.

Listing 18.2 shows an example of an element that is 160 pixels wide and positioned 80 pixels from the top. As shown in Figure 18.2, the text wraps within the element, just like it would wrap within a table cell that's 160 pixels wide.

Listing 18.2   Specifying the Width of an Element

```
<HTML>
<HEAD>
<TITLE>Example 2</TITLE>
</HEAD>
<STYLE TYPE="text/css">
  #example {position: absolute; top: 80; left: 40; width: 160}
</STYLE>
<BODY>

<DIV ID=example>
  This text is within the DIV tag. Notice how its
  length is controlled by the width property.
</DIV>

</BODY>
</HTML>
```

T I P You can use positioned elements to perform many of the same formatting tricks you've learned to do with the <TABLE> tag.

FIG. 18.2
You can leave either the TOP or LEFT attributes out, and the browser positions the element as though the omitted attribute is 0.

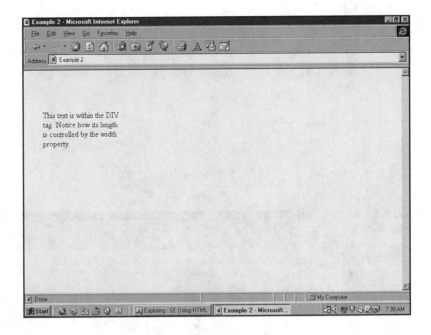

Overlapping Multiple Elements

You can cause elements to overlap by setting each element's TOP and LEFT attributes so that one appears on top of another. Figure 18.3 shows two elements. The first contains a handful of text and has a background image. The second element contains an image with a transparent background. The second element is positioned so that it overlaps the first (see Listing 18.3).

Listing 18.3 Overlapping Elements

```
<HTML>
<HEAD>
<TITLE>Example 3</TITLE>
</HEAD>
<STYLE TYPE="text/css">
  #example {position: absolute; top: 40; left: 60}
  #another {position: absolute; top: 80; left: 200}
</STYLE>
<BODY>

<DIV ID=example>
  <B>This is the first layer. It's behind the second layer.</B><BR>
  <B>This is the first layer. It's behind the second layer.</B><BR>
  <B>This is the first layer. It's behind the second layer.</B><BR>
  <B>This is the first layer. It's behind the second layer.</B><BR>
  <B>This is the first layer. It's behind the second layer.</B><BR>
```

continues

Part
III

Ch
18

Listing 18.3   Continued

```
    <B>This is the first layer. It's behind the second layer.</B><BR>
    <B>This is the first layer. It's behind the second layer.</B><BR>
    <B>This is the first layer. It's behind the second layer.</B><BR>
    </DIV>


    <IMG ID=another SRC=init.gif>


    </BODY>
    </HTML>
```

FIG. 18.3

Because the image in
the second element has
transparent areas, the
content behind this
element bleeds through.

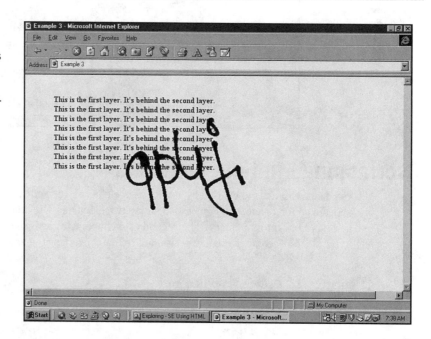

N O T E   By default, the browser draws overlapped elements in the order it encounters them. That is,
it draws the first element, overlaps that with the next element, and so on. ■

If you don't like the order in which the browser overlaps elements, you can change it. The most
straightforward way is by using the Z-INDEX property, which defines the stacking order for
elements:

```
#example {position: absolute; top: 100; left: 100; z-index: 1}
```

You set this attribute to any positive integer value. An element with a stacking order larger than
another draws over the other element. For example, an element with a stacking order of 10
overlaps an element with a stacking order of five. On the other hand, an element with a stacking order of three is overlapped by an element with a stacking order of five.

Listing 18.4 is an example of three elements, each of which uses the Z-INDEX attribute to define its stacking order. The first has a stacking order of two; the second has a stacking order of one, and the third has a stacking order of three. Thus, the browser draws the second element first, the first element second, and the third element last, as shown in Figure 18.4.

Listing 18.4   Using *Z-INDEX*

```
<HTML>
<HEAD>
<TITLE>Example 4</TITLE>
</HEAD>
<STYLE TYPE="text/css">
  #ex1 {position: absolute; top: 40; left: 60; z-index: 2}
  #ex2 {position: absolute; top: 80; left: 200; z-index: 1}
  #ex3 {position: absolute; top:100; left: 80; z-index: 3}
</STYLE>
<BODY>

<DIV ID=ex1>
<B>This is the first element. It's in the middle.</B><BR>
<B>This is the first element. It's in the middle.</B><BR>
<B>This is the first element. It's in the middle.</B><BR>
<B>This is the first element. It's in the middle.</B><BR>
<B>This is the first element. It's in the middle.</B><BR>
<B>This is the first element. It's in the middle.</B><BR>
<B>This is the first element. It's in the middle.</B><BR>
<B>This is the first element. It's in the middle.</B><BR>
</DIV>

<DIV ID=ex2>
<B>This is the second layer. It's behind the first layer.</B><BR>
<B>This is the second layer. It's behind the first layer.</B><BR>
<B>This is the second layer. It's behind the first layer.</B><BR>
<B>This is the second layer. It's behind the first layer.</B><BR>
<B>This is the second layer. It's behind the first layer.</B><BR>
<B>This is the second layer. It's behind the first layer.</B><BR>
<B>This is the second layer. It's behind the first layer.</B><BR>
<B>This is the second layer. It's behind the first layer.</B><BR>
</DIV>

<IMG ID=ex3 SRC=init.gif>
</LAYER>

</BODY>
</HTML>
```

Part
III

Ch
18

FIG. 18.4
The Z-INDEX property essentially defines the order in which each element is drawn.

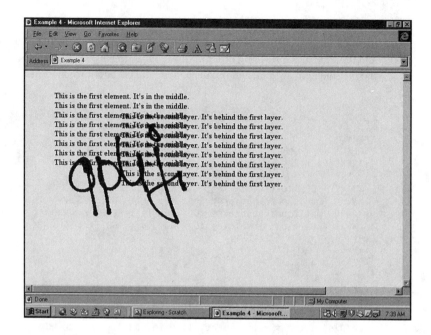

 TIP You can overlap several elements at the same position, define each element's stacking order in sequence, and then peel away the elements one at a time (using a script) to create a simple animation.

Nesting Positioned Elements

So far, you've only seen cases in which a handful of elements were added to the HTML document. They were siblings in that one was not contained within another. You can insert one element inside another, however, to create a parent-child relationship. In that case, the child (inside) is relative to the parent (outside). Thus, if you position an element called PARENT and locate it at 10, 10; and nest an element inside of PARENT called CHILD located at 5, 5; the child element actually displays at 15, 15 on the HTML document. If you move the parent element to 20, 20, the child element moves right along with it to 25, 25.

Listing 18.5 shows you an example of nested elements. The parent element contains an image of a rough Christmas tree. It contains a number of nested elements that represent bulbs. The coordinates of each nested element are relative to the upper-left corner of the parent. If you moved the Christmas tree to another location on the Web page, the bulbs would move right along with it (see Figure 18.5).

Listing 18.5 Nesting Elements

```
<HTML>
<HEAD>
<TITLE>Example 5</TITLE>
```

```
</HEAD>
<BODY>

<DIV STYLE="position: absolute; top: 100; left: 100">
<IMG SRC=xtree.gif>

  <IMG STYLE="position: absolute; top: 140; left: 60" SRC=ball1.gif>
  <IMG STYLE="position: absolute; top: 20; left: 100" SRC=ball2.gif>
  <IMG STYLE="position: absolute; top: 130; left: 120" SRC=ball1.gif>
  <IMG STYLE="position: absolute; top: 170; left: 140" SRC=ball2.gif>
  <IMG STYLE="position: absolute; top: 200; left: 120" SRC=ball2.gif>
  <IMG STYLE="position: absolute; top: 80; left: 80" SRC=ball3.gif>
  <IMG STYLE="position: absolute; top: 90; left: 125" SRC=ball3.gif>
  <IMG STYLE="position: absolute; top: 200; left: 60" SRC=ball3.gif>
  <IMG STYLE="position: absolute; top: 200; left: 180" SRC=ball3.gif>

</DIV>
</BODY>
</HTML>
```

FIG. 18.5

By capturing the mouse events for each bulb, you can allow the user to move the bulbs around on the Christmas tree.

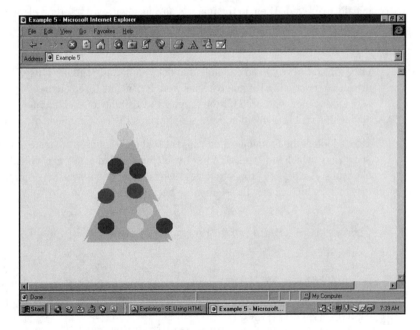

Part

III

Ch

18

Positioning Elements with Scripts

You get a lot of publishing capabilities just from being able to position an element anywhere on an HTML document and overlap it with others. You can create a variety of special effects, however, by attaching a script to an element and using that script to hide or show it—you can even move it around the browser window.

Given an element's ID, you reference it using the object model (see Chapter 19, "Scripting the Object Model"), like this:

```
document.all.item(id, 0)
```

id is the element's ID. The 0 indicates that you want the first occurrence of any element with that particular ID.

To access one of the styles, use the `style` object by appending `.style` to the object representing the element; then append the name of the style you're accessing to the end of that. Here's an example:

```
document.all.item(id, 0).style.property
```

Using a Script to Hide or Show an Element

You can use a script to hide and show elements on the HTML document. For example, you can create an element that you only want to display when the user moves the mouse across an image. In that case, you'd set the element's VISIBILITY property to "hidden" so that it's not initially displayed. Then, in the image's OnMouseOver event, set the element's visibility property to "", like this:

```
document.all.item(id, 0).style.property = "";
```

Listing 18.6 shows you an example that does something similar. It uses JavaScript, but you can use another scripting language just as well. It contains three elements and three buttons. The script associated with each button toggles the visibility of each element. Click a button associated with a visible element and the script makes the element invisible (see Figure 18.6).

Take a look at the function called ToggleFirst(). It toggles the state of the flag called ShowFirst, which indicates whether the element called FIRST is visible. It then sets the element's visibility property to "hidden" if ShowFirst is false; otherwise, it sets the property to "", which causes the element to become visible.

Listing 18.6 Hiding and Showing Elements

```
<HTML>
<HEAD>
<TITLE>Example 6</TITLE>
</HEAD>

<STYLE TYPE="text/css">
  #first {position: absolute; top: 80; left: 60}
  #second {position: absolute; top: 120; left: 200}
  #third {position: absolute; top: 140; left: 180}
</STYLE>

<SCRIPT LANGUAGE=JAVASCRIPT>
  ShowFirst = true;
  ShowSecond=false;
  ShowThird=true;
  function ToggleFirst()
  {
```

```
      ShowFirst = !ShowFirst;
      document.all.item("first", 0).style.visibility = ShowFirst ? "" :
          "hidden";
   }

   function ToggleSecond()
   {
      ShowSecond = !ShowSecond;
      document.all.item("second", 0).style.visibility = ShowSecond ? "" : "hid-
den";
   }

   function ToggleThird()
   {
      ShowThird = !ShowThird;
      document.all.item("third", 0).style.visibility = ShowThird ? "" :
          "hidden";
   }

</SCRIPT>

<BODY>
<DIV ID=first>
<B>This is the first layer. It's in the middle.</B><BR>
<B>This is the first layer. It's in the middle.</B><BR>
<B>This is the first layer. It's in the middle.</B><BR>
<B>This is the first layer. It's in the middle.</B><BR>
<B>This is the first layer. It's in the middle.</B><BR>
<B>This is the first layer. It's in the middle.</B><BR>
<B>This is the first layer. It's in the middle.</B><BR>
<B>This is the first layer. It's in the middle.</B><BR>
</DIV>

<DIV ID=second STYLE="visibility: hidden">
<B>This is the second layer. It's behind the first layer.</B><BR>
<B>This is the second layer. It's behind the first layer.</B><BR>
<B>This is the second layer. It's behind the first layer.</B><BR>
<B>This is the second layer. It's behind the first layer.</B><BR>
<B>This is the second layer. It's behind the first layer.</B><BR>
<B>This is the second layer. It's behind the first layer.</B><BR>
<B>This is the second layer. It's behind the first layer.</B><BR>
<B>This is the second layer. It's behind the first layer.</B><BR>
</DIV>

<IMG ID=third SRC=init.gif>

<FORM NAME=TOGGLE>
  <TABLE ALIGN=CENTER>
    <TD>
      <INPUT NAME=FIRST TYPE=BUTTON VALUE="Toggle First Layer "
      onclick="ToggleFirst();">
    </TD>
    <TD>
      <INPUT NAME=SECOND TYPE=BUTTON VALUE="Toggle Second Layer"
```

Part
III

Ch
18

continues

Listing 18.6   Continued

```
      onclick="ToggleSecond();">
    </TD>
    <TD>
      <INPUT NAME=THIRD TYPE=BUTTON VALUE="Toggle Third Layer "
      onclick="ToggleThird();">
    </TD>
  </TABLE>
</FORM>

</BODY>
</HTML>
```

FIG. 18.6

As you click buttons to hide an element, the browser peels that layer away, unveiling what's underneath.

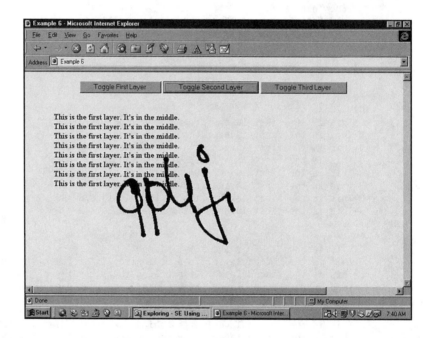

 T I P   In Windows, you've seen dialog boxes that contain a button with the text More>>. When you click that button, additional fields are presented. You can achieve the same effect in an HTML form by attaching a script to a form's button that shows another form hidden within a <DIV> tag.

Moving an Element with a Script

Besides showing and hiding an element, you can also move it around on the Web page. You can use this to create some pretty fancy animation, such as a curtain that appears to open, unveiling the contents of the page. Moving an element around is easy. You set the value of the left and top properties (using posLeft and posTop so that you don't have to change the length as a string with units), as shown in Listing 18.7 and Figure 18.7.

This example contains two elements. It also contains four buttons, label Up, Down, Left, and Right. Each button is associated with a function that moves the second element in the appropriate direction. For example, the Up function subtracts 10 from the second element's top property, which has the effect of moving the element up 10 pixels. The Right function adds 10 to the second element's left property, which has the effect of moving the element right 10 pixels.

Listing 18.7 Moving an Element with a Script

```
<HTML>
<HEAD>
<TITLE>Example 7</TITLE>

<SCRIPT LANGUAGE=JAVASCRIPT>
  function Up()
  {
    document.all.item("second", 0).style.posTop -= 10;
  }

  function Down()
  {
    document.all.item("second", 0).style.posTop += 10;
  }

  function Left()
  {
    document.all.item("second", 0).style.posLeft -= 10;
  }

  function Right()
  {
    document.all.item("second", 0).style.posLeft += 10;
  }

</SCRIPT>
</HEAD>
<BODY>

<DIV STYLE="position: absolute; top: 200; left: 300"; z-order: 2">
<B>This is the first layer. It's always on top.</B><BR>
<B>This is the first layer. It's always on top.</B><BR>
<B>This is the first layer. It's always on top.</B><BR>
<B>This is the first layer. It's always on top.</B><BR>
<B>This is the first layer. It's always on top.</B><BR>
<B>This is the first layer. It's always on top.</B><BR>
<B>This is the first layer. It's always on top.</B><BR>
<B>This is the first layer. It's always on top.</B><BR>
<B>This is the first layer. It's always on top.</B><BR>
</DIV>

<IMG ID=second STYLE="position: absolute; top: 180; left: 0; z-order: 1"
SRC=init.gif>
```

Part

III

Ch

18

continues

Listing 18.7 Continued

```
<FORM NAME=BUTTONS>
<TABLE>
<TR>
<TD></TD>
<TD ALIGN=CENTER>
<INPUT WIDTH=100% NAME=UP TYPE=BUTTON VALUE="Up" onclick="Up();">
</TD>
<TD></TD>
</TR>

<TR>
<TD ALIGN=CENTER>
<INPUT NAME=LEFT TYPE=BUTTON VALUE="Left " onclick="Left();">
</TD>
<TD></TD>
<TD ALIGN=CENTER>
<INPUT WIDTH=100 NAME=RIGHT TYPE=BUTTON VALUE="Right" onclick="Right();">
</TD>
</TR>

<TR>
<TD></TD>
<TD ALIGN=CENTER>
<INPUT WIDTH=100 NAME=DOWN TYPE=BUTTON VALUE="Down " onclick="Down();">
</TD>
<TD></TD>
</TR>

</TABLE>
</FORM>

</BODY>
</HTML>
```

Expanding Forms: An Example

There are two types of users in this world: basic and advanced. With forms, you find many cases in which a basic user needs to fill in only a few of the simpler fields, while the advanced user needs to fill in all of the fields, including the more advanced fields.

You can display all of the form's fields at one time and let the basic user ignore the advanced fields or you can hide the advanced fields and let the advanced user get to them by clicking a special button. The latter is the approach that Windows 95 and Windows NT 4.0 take in many cases. Have you ever seen a dialog box in Windows with a button labeled Advanced or More? When the user clicks one of these buttons, the dialog box unfolds to show more fields.

With CSS positioning, hiding a portion of a form until a user clicks a button is easy. Listing 18.8 is just such an example. At the bottom of this HTML document, you see a portion of the form sandwiched in a <DIV> tag. The <DIV> tag's visibility property is initially set to "hidden". The function OpenMore toggles the visibility of the hidden portion of the form and changes the text displayed in the button to reflect the state of the form.

FIG. 18.7

As you move the second element by the first, it disappears under the first element, because the second element has a larger z-order.

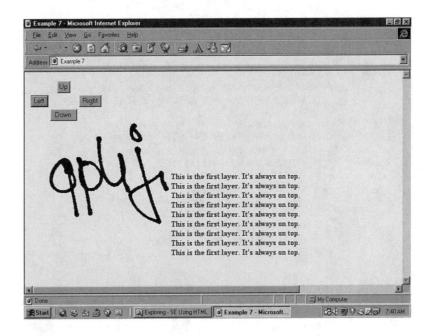

Listing 18.8 Expanding a Form

```
<HTML>
<HEAD>
<TITLE>Example 8</TITLE>

<SCRIPT LANGUAGE=JAVASCRIPT>

blnMoreIsUp = false;

// Display the hidden form if it's not already displayed. Otherwise, hide it.
// Also, change the text in the button to reflect the current state of the
hidden form.

function OpenMore()
{
  blnMoreIsUp = !blnMoreIsUp;
  document.all.item("MORE", 0).style.visibility = blnMoreIsUp ? "" : "hidden";
  document.FEEDBACK.FEEDBACK_MORE.value = blnMoreIsUp ? "Less<<" : "More>>";
}

</SCRIPT>
```

continues

Listing 18.8   Continued

```
</HEAD>
<BODY>

<FORM NAME=FEEDBACK METHOD=GET ACTION="mailto:jerry@honeycutt.com"
OnSubmit="return IsValid()">
  <TABLE CELLPADDING=10>
   <TR>
      <TD VALIGN=TOP>
         <B>Please provide your e-mail address:</B><BR>
         <INPUT NAME=FEEDBACK_MAIL TYPE=TEXT SIZE=40>
      </TD>
      <TD VALIGN=TOP>
        <B>How did you find our site:</B><BR>
        <SELECT NAME=FEEDBACK_HOW SIZE=1>
           <OPTION VALUE=1>AltaVista
           <OPTION VALUE=2>Excite
           <OPTION VALUE=3>Lycos
           <OPTION VALUE=4>Yahoo!
           <OPTION VALUE=5>WebCrawler
           <OPTION VALUE=6>Friend
           <OPTION VALUE=7>Other Link
      </SELECT>
      </TD>
   <TR>
      <TD VALIGN=TOP ROWSPAN=2>
        <B>Tell us what you think about our Web site:</B><BR>
        <TEXTAREA NAME=FEEDBACK_MEMO COLS=45 ROWS=8>
        </TEXTAREA>
      </TD>
      <TD VALIGN=TOP>
        <B>How did we rate?</B><BR>
        <TABLE BORDER=1>
          <TR ALIGN=CENTER>
            <TH></TH><TH>Yes</TH><TH>No</TH>
          </TR>
          <TR ALIGN=CENTER>
            <TD ALIGN=LEFT>
              Did this site load fast enough?
            </TD>
            <TD>
              <INPUT NAME=FEEDBACK_SPEED TYPE=RADIO>
            </TD>
            <TD>
              <INPUT NAME=FEEDBACK_SPEED TYPE=RADIO>
            </TD>
          </TR>
          <TR ALIGN=CENTER>
            <TD ALIGN=LEFT>
              Did you find the graphics interesting?
            </TD>
            <TD>
              <INPUT NAME=FEEDBACK_GRAPHIC TYPE=RADIO>
            </TD>
            <TD>
              <INPUT NAME=FEEDBACK_GRAPHIC TYPE=RADIO>
```

```
            </TD>
          </TR>
          <TR ALIGN=CENTER>
            <TD ALIGN=LEFT>
                Was the content suitable?
            </TD>
            <TD>
              <INPUT NAME=FEEDBACK_CONTENT TYPE=RADIO>
            </TD>
            <TD>
              <INPUT NAME=FEEDBACK_CONTENT TYPE=RADIO>
            </TD>
          </TR>
        </TABLE>
      </TD>
    </TR>
    <TR ALIGN=RIGHT>
      <TD>
        <TABLE WIDTH=100%>
          <TD ALIGN=LEFT>
            <INPUT NAME=FEEDBACK_MORE TYPE=BUTTON VALUE="More>>"
            OnClick="OpenMore()">
          </TD>
          <TD>
            <INPUT NAME=FEEDBACK_RESET TYPE=RESET VALUE=Clear>
            <INPUT NAME=FEEDBACK_SUBMIT TYPE=SUBMIT VALUE=Submit>
          </TD>
        </TABLE>
      </TD>
    </TR>
</TABLE>

<!-- This DIV contains the hidden part of the form that the user sees when
     they click on More>>. The event-handler at the top of this file shows
     the layer. -->

<DIV ID=MORE STYLE="visibility: hidden">
  <TABLE CELLPADDING=10>
    <TR>
      <TD>
        <B>Type the URL of your home page:</B><BR>
        <INPUT NAME=FEEDBACK_URL TYPE=TEXT SIZE=60>
      </TD>
      <TD>
        <B>Type your phone number:</B><BR>
        <INPUT NAME=FEEDBACK_PHONE TYPE=TEXT SIZE=32>
      </TD>
    </TR>
  </TABLE>
</DIV>

</FORM>

</BODY>
</HTML>
```

Part
III

Ch
18

Figure 18.8 shows the resulting form with the hidden form expanded.

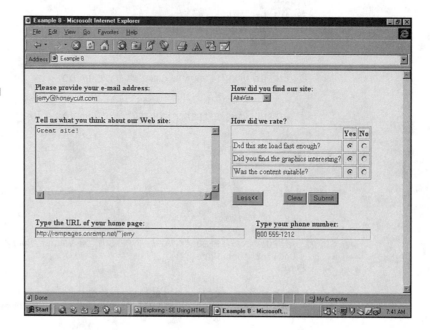

## CHAPTER 19

Scripting the Object Model

by Jerry Honeycutt

In this chapter

Introducing Dynamic HTML

Dynamic HTML is the next great Web wave. For the uninitiated, it includes a combination HTML, styles, and the scripts used to manipulate both.

The differences between Microsoft's and Netscape's dynamic HTML are enormous. So much so that writing a dynamic HTML Web page that's cross-platform compatible is almost impossible. The biggest difference between both versions of dynamic HTML is the object model. Microsoft's object model goes much farther than Netscape's. It exposes every single element on the page, supporting a variety of properties, elements, events, and collections for each. Microsoft's object model comes closer to what I expect W3C to define as a recommendation later. Thus, all the examples in this book work with Internet Explorer, but some don't work with Communicator.

 You can learn more about each company's object model at its respective Web site. You can also learn more about W3C's impending document object model recommendation on its Web site. Here are the URLs for your convenience:

> **http://www.microsoft.com/msdn/sdk/inetsdk/help/dhtml/ref_objects/ objects.htm#om40_objects**
>
> **http://home.netscape.com/eng/mozilla/3.0/handbook/javascript/navobj.htm**
>
> **http://www.w3.org/Press/DOM-core.html**

Working with Elements on the Web Page

Dynamic HTML is about interacting with the Web page; thus, you must be able to gain access to the elements on the page (note that Internet Explorer is currently the only browser that exposes every page element).

The most explicit method to access an element is to use the `all` object, which you can index using an ordinal number, element name, or element ID. For example, the following JavaScript line sets e to the object representation of the element whose ID is `Example`. You can just as easily use the element's name or index it by its position in the `all` collection.

```
e = document.all( "Example" );
```

The document object model provides two alternatives for gaining access to a page element. Either of the following forms works. Note that you can simply write the ID of the element as the object, shown in the second example, as long as the ID is unique across the entire Web page and does not conflict with names found in the object model or JavaScript.

```
e = document.all.Example
```

```
e = Example
```

N O T E *Collections* (Microsoft speak) and *arrays* (Netscape speak) provide access to a group of related items. For example, the `forms` collection is an array that contains a single element for each form on the Web page. Because `forms` is a child object of `document`, you access it like this:

document.forms. You can index the forms collection by number, or you can use an element's ID or name, like this: document.forms("MyForm"). After you've created a reference to an object using a collection, you can access any of that object's properties, methods, events, or collections. ▪

Accessing Multiple Elements in a Collection

In the previous examples, you assigned to e the element with the ID Example. If the Web page contains only one element with that ID, you can access any of its properties like this: e.property. What happens if the Web page contains more than one element with that ID, though? In that case, e is a collection, with each item in the collection pointing to one of the matching elements.

As shown in Listing 19.1, you can test the variable to see whether it contains a single value or is a collection. If the variable's length property is null, the variable contains a single value. If it's not null, the variable contains an array of values that you index using an ordinal number. You can visit each value in the collection, shown in the for loop, and access each value's properties.

Listing 19.1   Working with Collections

```
<HTML>
  <P ID=Test>Hello</P>
  <P ID=Test>Goodbye</P>

  <SCRIPT LANGUAGE=JAVASCRIPT>
    var i, e;

    e = document.all( "Test" );
    if( e.length == null )
      alert( "There is one element in the collection" );
    else
      for( i = 0; i < e.length; i++ )
        alert( i.toString() + ": " + e[i].innerText );
  </SCRIPT>
</HTML>
```

Part
III

Ch

19

Changing the Content of an Element On-the-Fly

You probably already realize that you can dynamically write HTML to the Web page as the browser opens it. You do so using the document.write method. The problem is that you can't use this method to change the Web page's content after the browser finishes opening it. In Internet Explorer's object model, every element contains two interesting properties that allow you to do this (this doesn't work with Communicator):

- ▪ innerText contains the text content of a container tag without the HTML.
- ▪ innerHTML contains the complete content of a container tag including the HTML.

Listing 19.2 shows an example that modifies the text you see on the Web page after it's open. At the top of the file, you see a <P> tag with the ID Test. When the user clicks the button, the browser calls the event handler ChangeText(). The first line of ChangeText() sets innerText to a value, which causes the browser to completely replace the text in the <P> tag with the new value. The third line sets innerHTML to a value that contains raw HTML, which the browser neatly inserts into the <P> container. Using both innerText and innerHTML, you can change the Web page's content without making a round-trip to the server.

Listing 19.2 Dynamically Changing the Web Page's Content

```
<HTML>
  <P ID=Test>Example Text</P>

  <FORM>
    <INPUT ID=Click TYPE=BUTTON VALUE="Click" onClick="ChangeText();">
  </FORM>

  <SCRIPT LANGUAGE=JAVASCRIPT>
    function ChangeText()
    {
      Test.innerText = "Dynamically Built Text";
      window.alert( "See the new text" );

      Test.innerHTML = "Dynamically Built <STRONG>HTML</STRONG>";
      window.alert( "See the new HTML" );
    }
  </SCRIPT>
</HTML>
```

Handling Events Generated by the Object Model

You, as a JavaScript programmer, are already familiar with creating event handlers. There are a few things you should know about Internet Explorer's and Communicator's event models, however, which relate specifically to events generated by the document object model:

- Internet Explorer supports the concept called *event bubbling*, which means that an event bubbles up through the page's hierarchy until it reaches the top. If the user clicks the word here in Listing 19.3, the event goes to the <A> tag first; then it bubbles up to the <P> tag. The last two objects to see the event are the document and the window. Listing 19.4 is an example that you can use with Internet Explorer to help you better understand bubbling; open this file in Internet Explorer, and watch each message as it pops up.

- Communicator supports the concept called *event capturing*, which is the opposite of event bubbling in that the event starts at the top of the page's hierarchy and filters its way down. If the user clicks the word here, the event goes to the document and window objects first; then it goes to the <A> tag. Note that Communicator skips the <P> tag because it doesn't expose any events.

Listing 19.3 Event Bubbling versus Event Capturing

```
<HTML>
  <BODY>
    <SCRIPT LANGUAGE=JAVASCRIPT>
      function Hello()
      {
        window.alert( "You clicked the heading" );
      }
    </SCRIPT>

    <P>Click <A onClick="Hello();" HREF="">here</A>, and you see a message</P>
  <BODY>
</HTML>
```

These two differences are extremely important to you if you're building cross-platform Web pages. Event bubbling and event capturing are techniques that you can use to write a single event handler to handle events for a group of objects. It's a great convenience. You learn about this topic in the following sections.

> **CAUTION**
>
> If you're writing cross-platform Web pages, don't rely on event bubbling or capturing at all. Each method is incompatible with the other, so your page won't work in both browsers.

Listing 19.4 Understanding Event Bubbling

```
<HTML>
  <BODY onclick="alert( 'Click!' );">

  <DIV onClick="alert('Outside');">
    <DIV onClick="alert('Middle');">
      <SPAN onClick="alert('Inside');">Click Me</SPAN>
    </DIV>
  </DIV>

  </BODY>
</HTML>
```

Part
III

Ch
19

Getting More Information About an Event

Both Internet Explorer and Communicator provide additional information to your event handlers in the form of the event object. This object is only available within an event handler. event is implemented differently in Internet Explorer and Communicator. Table 19.1 shows some of the most useful properties for the event object in both browsers.

Table 19.1 The *event* Object

Property	Description
Internet Explorer	
cancelBubble	Set `true` to cancel the bubble
keycode	ASCII keycode of the key that was pressed
returnValue	Set `false` to cancel action (that is, form post)
srcElement	HTML object that caused the event
x	Mouse x position when event was raised
y	Mouse y position when event was raised
Netscape Communicator 4	
target	HTML object that caused the event
type	The type of event that was raised
pageX	Mouse x position when the event was raised
pageY	Mouse y position when the event was raised
which	Mouse button number or ASCII keycode

Canceling an Event's Bubble in Internet Explorer

You can't always let an event bubble all the way to the top of the page's hierarchy. For example, if you have a handler for onClick in both <BODY> and <P> tags, Internet Explorer is going to invoke both of them—probably not what you intended.

In Listing 19.5, for example, when the user clicks Click Here, the event first goes to the <P> tag, which displays the message You clicked the paragraph. Then the event automatically bubbles up to the <BODY> tag, which displays the message You clicked elsewhere in the body. To prevent the event from bubbling up past a certain point, set event.cancelBubble to true in your event handler. In Listing 19.5, simply uncomment the last line in the script. This prevents the browser from sending the event any farther up the document's hierarchy.

Listing 19.5 Canceling an Event's Bubble

```
<HTML>
  <BODY onClick="alert('You clicked elsewhere in the body');">

  <P onClick="ClickMessage();">Click Here</P>

  <SCRIPT LANGUAGE=JAVASCRIPT>
    function ClickMessage()
    {
```

```
        alert( "You clicked the paragraph" );
        // window.event.cancelBubble = true;
      }
    </SCRIPT>
  </BODY>

</HTML>
```

Handling an Event for a Group of Objects

As noted earlier, event bubbling makes it possible to handle an event for a group of related objects. For example, if you want to create a rollover effect for five blocks of text, you can write an event handler for each block, or you can close all five blocks within a <DIV> tag and write a single event handler for the <DIV> tag. Remember that the event object tells you exactly which object generated the event using the srcElement property. You test this property to determine which object in a group caused the event; then you handle it appropriately.

Listing 19.6 shows an example that uses a single event handler to handle the onClick event for a group of related objects. Note that all the <SPAN> tags have unique IDs and are enclosed within a single <DIV> tag. The <DIV> tag associates the function called LinkClick() with the onClick event. Within LinkClick(), you see an If statement that tests srcElement.id to match the appropriate code to the appropriate object. If the source element's ID is 1, the event handler displays You clicked the first item; if the ID is 2, the event handler displays You clicked the second item, and so on.

Listing 19.6 Handling Multiple Objects with a Single Event Handler

```
<HTML>
  <BODY onclick="alert( 'Click!' );">
    <SCRIPT LANGUAGE=JAVASCRIPT>

      function LinkClick()
      {
        if( window.event.srcElement.id == "1" )
        {
          window.alert( "You clicked the first item" );
          window.event.cancelBubble = true;
        }
        else
          if( window.event.srcElement.id == "2" )
          {
            window.alert( "You clicked the second item" );
            window.event.cancelBubble = true;
          }
          else
            if( window.event.srcElement.id == "3" )
            {
              window.alert( "You clicked the third link" );
              window.event.cancelBubble = true;
```

continues

Listing 19.6   Continued

```
            }
        }
    </SCRIPT>

    <DIV onClick="LinkClick();">
        <SPAN ID="1">First Item</SPAN><BR>
        <SPAN ID="2">Second Item</SPAN><BR>
        <SPAN ID="3">Third Item</SPAN>
    </DIV>

    </BODY>
</HTML>
```

Connecting Scripts to Styles and Classes

A growing part of dynamic HTML is the capability to change the style of an element within a script. Internet Explorer 4.0 is currently the only browser that provides this capability, but after W3C has a document object model recommendation, Communicator will quickly follow suit.

Internet Explorer's document object model exposes all the styles for every element on the Web page. You access an element's style using the style property, as shown in the following line of code. Test.style is the style object for the element called Test; color is the property that reflects the CSS color attribute.

```
Test.style.color = "red";
```

Appendix B, "Style Sheet Property Reference," shows you all the possible CSS attributes. The document object model exposes all of them. You must know a few rules about naming CSS attributes in your scripts, though, because CSS uses dashes in attribute names, and that's not valid in JavaScript:

- ■ Capitalize the first letter immediately to the right of each dash.
- ■ Remove each dash from the style name.

Listing 19.7 shows an example of a Web page that changes a <P> tag's background and foreground colors on-the-fly. The user types the proper name of the background and foreground and then clicks Change. The event handler ChangeColor() sets the backgroundColor and color properties for the Test element's style to the values supplied by the user.

Listing 19.7   Changing an Element's Style

```
<HTML>

    <P ID="Test">This is a regular HTML element</P>
    <HR>
    <FORM>
        Type a color name for the background:
        <INPUT ID=Background TYPE=TEXT SIZE=20 VALUE="White"><BR>
```

```
      Type a color name for the foreground:
      <INPUT ID=Color TYPE=TEXT SIZE=20 VALUE="Black">
      <INPUT TYPE=BUTTON VALUE="Change" onClick="ChangeColor( Background.value,
Color.value );">
   <FORM>

   <SCRIPT LANGUAGE=JAVASCRIPT>

      function ChangeColor( Background, Color )
      {
        Test.style.backgroundColor = Background;
        Test.style.color = Color;
      }

   </SCRIPT>

</HTML>
```

Changing an element's individual style properties isn't always the most efficient way to change how an element looks. If you're changing a number of properties during an event handler, define two different classes for the element; then swap the classes during the event handler using the element's className property. Listing 19.8 shows such an example. Each time the user clicks Change, the browser calls the event handler ChangeColor(). ChangeColor() tests the Test element's className attribute to see which style is assigned to it. If it's currently set to Normal, the event handler changes it to Reverse, and vice versa. Note that the <P> tag initially sets the CLASS attribute to Normal.

Listing 19.8   Changing an Element's Class

```
<HTML>

  <STYLE>
    .Normal {background-color: white; color: black}
    .Reverse {background-color: black; color: white}
  </STYLE>

  <P ID="Test" CLASS="Normal">This is a regular HTML element</P>
  <HR>
  <FORM>
    Click button to change styles:
    <INPUT TYPE=BUTTON VALUE="Change" onClick="ChangeColor();">
  <FORM>

  <SCRIPT LANGUAGE=JAVASCRIPT>

    function ChangeColor()
    {
      if( Test.className == "Normal" )
        Test.className = "Reverse";
      else
        Test.className = "Normal";
```

Part

III

Ch

19

continues

Listing 19.8   Continued

```
    }

  </SCRIPT>

</HTML>
```

Redefining How Links Behave

With events and now styles under your belt, you are ready to put together a more complete example. The one shown in Listing 19.9 changes how links look and work on the Web page. When the user moves his mouse over an anchor, the anchor changes color. When he moves his mouse off the anchor, it changes back to its original color. Here's more information about this example:

■ This example defines two styles: A and A.LitUP. A becomes the default style used for all <A> tags in the Web page. A.LitUp is the style used to change how links look when the user rolls his mouse over the anchor.

■ Two event handlers are defined for the <BODY> tag: RollOn(), which handles the onMouseOver event, and RollOff(), which handles the onMouseOut event. Because these event handlers are defined in the <BODY> tag, they'll capture any onmouseover or onmouseout events for the document that weren't canceled.

■ RollOn() checks the source of the onMouseOver event. If the event is not generated from an <A> tag, it returns. Otherwise, it changes the style class for the source element to A.LitUp. This has the effect of changing the color of the anchor when the user moves his mouse over it.

■ RollOff() also checks the source of the onMouseOut event. If the event was generated by an <A> tag, it changes the style class for the source element to A. This returns the color to the original color for the anchor.

Listing 19.9   Redefining How Links Behave

```
<HTML>
  <BODY onmouseover="RollOn();" onmouseout="RollOff();">

  <STYLE>
    A { color: blue; font-size: smaller; font-family: arial;
        font-weight: bold; text-decoration: none }
    A.LitUp  { color: red; font-size: smaller; font-family: arial;
               font-weight: bold; text-decoration: underline }
  </STYLE>

  <SCRIPT LANGUAGE=JAVASCRIPT>
    function RollOn()
    {
      if( window.event.srcElement.tagName != "A" ) return;
```

```
        if( window.event.srcElement.className == "" )
          window.event.srcElement.className = "LitUp";
    }

    function RollOff()
    {
      if( window.event.srcElement.className == "LitUp" )
        window.event.srcElement.className = "";
    }
  </SCRIPT>

  Visit <A HREF="http://rampages.onramp.net/~jerry">Jerry Honeycutt's</A>
  homepage.
  Alternatively, you can visit some of my favorite Web sites:
  <UL>
    <LI><A HREF="http://www.microsoft.com">Microsoft Corporation</A>
    <LI><A HREF="http://www.netscape.com">Netscape Corproation</A>
  </UL>
  </BODY>
</HTML>
```

Creating Rollover Effects for Toolbars and Menus

Listing 19.10 is to Listing 19.9 (it only works with Internet Explorer 4.0). You use it to create menus or toolbars that change as the user moves her mouse over them. Here's how it works:

- Two styles are defined for the rollover effect: Normal and LitUp. The first just changes the cursor to a hand so that the user knows she is over something that's clickable. The second reverses the color of the object.

- Each item in the toolbar is enclosed within a <SPAN> tag. Each tag has a unique ID. All the items in the toolbar are enclosed within a single <DIV> tag that defines event handlers for onMouseOver and onMouseOut. Events generated in the <SPAN> tags bubble up to the <DIV> tag.

- The event handlers RollOn() and RollOff() toggles the style for the object that generated the event so that the object appears to reverse colors when the user moves her mouse over it, as shown in Figure 19.1.

Part

III

Ch

19

Listing 19.10   Creating Rollover Effects for Toolbars and Menus

```
<HTML>
  <BODY>

  <SCRIPT LANGUAGE=JAVASCRIPT>
    function RollOn()
    {
      if( window.event.srcElement.className == "Normal" )
        window.event.srcElement.className = "LitUp";
    }
```

continues

Listing 19.10   Continued

```
      function RollOff()
      {
        if( window.event.srcElement.className == "LitUp" )
          window.event.srcElement.className = "Normal";
      }
  </SCRIPT>

  <STYLE>
    .Normal { cursor: hand }
    .LitUp  { cursor: hand; color: white; background-color: black }
  </STYLE>

  <DIV onMouseOut="RollOff();" onMouseOver="RollOn();">
    <SPAN CLASS="Normal">First Item </SPAN>
    <SPAN CLASS="Normal">Second Item</SPAN>
    <SPAN CLASS="Normal">Third Item </SPAN>
  </DIV>

  </BODY>
</HTML>
```

FIG. 19.1

When the user moves
the mouse pointer over
one of the items in the
<DIV> tag, the item
changes colors.

Use the cursor property
to set pointer to a hand.

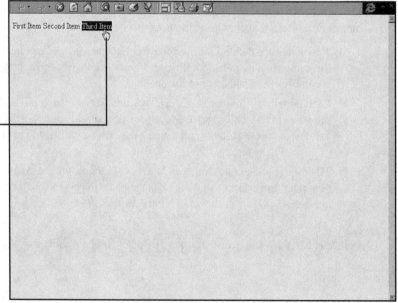

Controlling an Object's Visibility

You can make certain elements on the Web page visible or invisible using the style object's
display property. Set this property to none, and the browser hides the object, like this:

```
element.style.display = "none";
```

Set this property to an empty string, as shown in the following line of code, and the browser shows the element.

```
element.style.display = "";
```

Hiding an element also causes the browser to reflow the Web page so that there isn't a huge hole where the invisible element exists. Figure 19.2 shows a page before and after the item was hidden.

FIG. 19.2
When the element is hidden, the browser reflows the Web page as if the element isn't there at all.

Document reflows when this text is hidden.

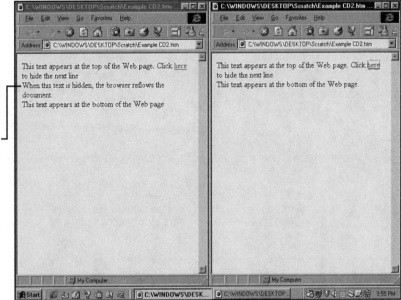

Showing and Hiding Portions of a Form

You can hide the advanced fields of a form from a beginning user and let an advanced user get to them by clicking a special button. The latter is the approach that Windows 95 and Windows NT 4.0 takes in many cases. Have you ever seen a dialog box in Windows with a button labeled Advanced or More? When the user clicks one of these buttons, the dialog box unfolds to show more fields.

Listing 19.11 is an example of such a form on a Web page. The last part of the form defined in this example contains a <DIV> tag with the ID More. It contains a number of fields that aren't displayed initially because the <DIV> tag is hidden. The onClick event handler for the FEEDBACK_MORE button you see in the form is OpenMore(). This function toggles a Boolean flag called MoreIsUp, which tracks the status of the hidden area in the form, and sets the <DIV> tag's display property accordingly. Note that it also changes the label on the button to reflect the status of MoreIsUp.

Listing 19.11   Showing and Hiding Portions of the Web Page

```
<HTML>
<SCRIPT LANGUAGE=JAVASCRIPT>

MoreIsUp = false;

// Display the hidden form if it's not already displayed. Otherwise, hide it.
// Also, change the text in the button to reflect the current state of the
hidden form.

function OpenMore()
{
  MoreIsUp = !MoreIsUp;
  More.style.display = MoreIsUp ? "" : "none";
  FEEDBACK.FEEDBACK_MORE.value = MoreIsUp ? "Less<<" : "More>>";
}
</SCRIPT>

</HEAD>
<BODY>

<FORM NAME=FEEDBACK METHOD=POST ACTION="mailto:jerry@honeycutt.com">
  <TABLE CELLPADDING=10>
   <TR>
      <TD VALIGN=TOP>
         <B>Please provide your e-mail address:</B><BR>
         <INPUT NAME=FEEDBACK_MAIL TYPE=TEXT SIZE=40>
      </TD>
      <TD VALIGN=TOP>
        <B>How did you find our site:</B><BR>
        <SELECT NAME=FEEDBACK_HOW SIZE=1>
           <OPTION VALUE=1>AltaVista
           <OPTION VALUE=2>Excite
           <OPTION VALUE=3>Lycos
           <OPTION VALUE=4>Yahoo!
           <OPTION VALUE=5>WebCrawler
           <OPTION VALUE=6>Friend
           <OPTION VALUE=7>Other Link
      </SELECT>
      </TD>
    <TR>
      <TD VALIGN=TOP ROWSPAN=2>
         <B>Tell us what you think about our Web site:</B><BR>
         <TEXTAREA NAME=FEEDBACK_MEMO COLS=45 ROWS=8>
         </TEXTAREA>
      </TD>
      <TD VALIGN=TOP>
         <B>How did we rate?</B><BR>
         <TABLE BORDER=1>
           <TR ALIGN=CENTER>
             <TH></TH><TH>Yes</TH><TH>No</TH>
           </TR>
           <TR ALIGN=CENTER>
             <TD ALIGN=LEFT>
```

```
              Did this site load fast enough?
          </TD>
          <TD>
            <INPUT NAME=FEEDBACK_SPEED TYPE=RADIO>
          </TD>
          <TD>
            <INPUT NAME=FEEDBACK_SPEED TYPE=RADIO>
          </TD>
        </TR>
        <TR ALIGN=CENTER>
          <TD ALIGN=LEFT>
            Did you find the graphics interesting?
          </TD>
          <TD>
            <INPUT NAME=FEEDBACK_GRAPHIC TYPE=RADIO>
          </TD>
          <TD>
            <INPUT NAME=FEEDBACK_GRAPHIC TYPE=RADIO>
          </TD>
        </TR>
        <TR ALIGN=CENTER>
          <TD ALIGN=LEFT>
              Was the content suitable?
          </TD>
          <TD>
            <INPUT NAME=FEEDBACK_CONTENT TYPE=RADIO>
          </TD>
          <TD>
            <INPUT NAME=FEEDBACK_CONTENT TYPE=RADIO>
          </TD>
        </TR>
      </TABLE>
    </TD>
  </TR>
  <TR ALIGN=RIGHT>
    <TD>
      <TABLE WIDTH=100%>
        <TD ALIGN=LEFT>
          <INPUT NAME=FEEDBACK_MORE TYPE=BUTTON VALUE="More>>"
          OnClick="OpenMore()">
        </TD>
        <TD>
          <INPUT NAME=FEEDBACK_RESET TYPE=RESET VALUE=Clear>
          <INPUT NAME=FEEDBACK_SUBMIT TYPE=SUBMIT VALUE=Submit>
        </TD>
      </TABLE>
    </TD>
  </TR>
</TABLE>

<!-- This division contains the hidden part of the form that the user sees
when they click on More>>. The event handler at the top of this file shows the
layer. -->
```

continues

Listing 19.11 Continued

```
<DIV ID=More STYLE="display: none">
  <TABLE CELLPADDING=10>
    <TR>
      <TD>
        <B>Type the URL of your home page:</B><BR>
        <INPUT NAME=FEEDBACK_URL TYPE=TEXT SIZE=60>
      </TD>
      <TD>
        <B>Type your phone number:</B><BR>
        <INPUT NAME=FEEDBACK_PHONE TYPE=TEXT SIZE=32>
      </TD>
    </TR>
  </TABLE>
</DIV>

</FORM>

</BODY>
</HTML>
```

Creating an Expanding/Collapsible Outline

Listing 19.12 uses the `display` property to build a collapsible outline. Initially, the top-level topics are showing. If the user clicks a topic heading that is collapsed, the browser expands the next level of the outline under that topic. If the user clicks a topic heading that is expanded, the browser collapses all the content under it.

You can build your outline using any HTML tags you want, as long as you nest tags for subtopics within the tags of parent topics. In this example, I used the `<UL>` tag because it automatically indents each outline level. The only thing you absolutely must do for the scripts to work is to give each tag an appropriate ID. The top level of the outline can have any ID you want; OL in this case. Each subtopic would then append a serial number to it indicating its position in the outline: 1, 2, 3, and so on. Any third-level topics would again append a serial number to the parent's ID. Here's what the IDs would look like for a simple outline that has one main topic, two under that, and three third-level topics:

> **Outline**
>> Outline1
>>> Outline11
>>> Outline12
>>> Outline13
>> Outline2
>>> Outline21
>>> Outline22
>>> Outline23

To identify the elements that belong to the outline, you assign the Outline class to the CLASS attribute of each element. You must also set the display property of each subitem to none so that it doesn't show initially. Here's what a typical line in an outline might look like:

```
<P ID="Outline12" CLASS="Outline" STYLE="display: none">Outline Item</P>
```

The last thing you must do is surround the entire outline with a <DIV> tag. The tag must associate the OutlineClick() function with the onClick event. Because events bubble up from each outline element to the <DIV> tag, a single script is all that's required to handle every outline level.

The script contains three functions that make the outline work:

- OutlineClick(). This function is the event handler for the <DIV> tag that surrounds the entire outline. This function first makes sure that the object raising the event is the Outline class assigned to it. Then it checks to make sure that the topic has children using the children collection. If the object does have children and the children are not currently displayed, it calls Expand(), passing its own ID as a parameter, to show all the children.

- Expand(). This function starts with a counter set to 1 and appends the counter to the ID given as a parameter. If an element with that combined ID exists, the function hides it. The function then increments the counter by 1 and repeats the process until it doesn't find any more subitems for that topic.

- Collapse(). This function is a bit more difficult to understand. Because it must collapse an arbitrary number of outline levels, it's a recursive function. It accepts the ID of the level to collapse as a parameter. If the level has no children, it simply returns. If the level does have children, it hides each child. To make sure that any items appearing below each child are also hidden, it recursively calls itself with the ID of the child item.

Part III
Ch 19

Listing 19.12   Creating an Expanding/Collapsible Outline

```
<HTML>

<SCRIPT LANGUAGE=JAVASCRIPT>
  function OutlineClick()
  {
    var Source, Targets, i;

    Source = window.event.srcElement;
    if( Source.className == "Outline" )
    {
      Targets = document.all(Source.id).children;
      if( Targets.length != 0 && Targets[0].style.display == "none")
        Expand( Source.id );
      else
        Collapse( Source.id );

      window.event.cancelBubble = true;
```

continues

Listing 19.12 Continued

```
      }
    }

    function Expand( Level )
    {
      var i, Target;

      i = 1;
      Target = document.all( Level + i.toString() );
      while( Target != null )
      {
        Target.style.display = "";
        i++;
        Target = document.all( Level + i.toString() );
      }
    }

    function Collapse( Level )
    {
      var i, Target;

      if( document.all( Level ).children.length == 0 )
        return false;
      else
      {
        i = 1;
        Target = document.all( Level + i.toString() );
        while( Target != null )
        {
          Collapse( Target.id );
          Target.style.display = "none";
          i++;
          Target = document.all( Level + i.toString() );
        }
      }
    }
  }
</SCRIPT>

<STYLE>
  .Outline { cursor: hand }
</STYLE>

<DIV onClick="OutlineClick();">
  <UL ID="OL" CLASS="Outline" >
    Outline (click to expand outline)
    <UL ID="OL1" CLASS="Outline" STYLE="display: none">
      First Outline Item
        <P ID="OL11" CLASS="Outline" STYLE="display: none">
        You can nest content as deep as you like within the outline.<BR>
        As long as you use the appropriate IDs and assign each outline<BR>
        element to the Outline class, the outline will work automatically.<BR>
        Just copy the scripts in this example to your HTML file.<BR>
        Note that you can use this outline script with any HTML tags.<BR>
        I've used the UL tag here, though, so that the outline would<BR>
```

```
          be automatically indented at each level.
          </P>
        <UL ID="OL12" CLASS="Outline" STYLE="display: none">
          A Sub-item underneath the first outline item
        </UL>
        <UL ID="OL13" CLASS="Outline" STYLE="display: none">
          Another sub-item underneath the first outline item
          <UL ID="OL131" CLASS="Outline" STYLE="display: none">Test 1</UL>
        </UL>
      </UL>
    </UL>
  </DIV>

  </HTML>
```

Positioning HTML Elements on the Web Page

Both Internet Explorer and Communicator use CSS positioning, which you learned about in Chapter 18, "Positioning HTML Elements." You can script the position of an element using the `style` object. You use the `left`, `posLeft`, `top`, `posTop`, and `zIndex` properties to affect the position of elements from within your scripts.

For example, use the following code to change an element's position to an absolute position of 30, 45:

```
element.style.left = 30;
element.style.top = 45;
```

 TIP Shun Netscape layers in favor of Cascading Style Sheet positioning. They work roughly the same and are compatible across both Internet Explorer and Communicator.

The examples in the following sections show you how to use positioning to create some astonishing effects for your Web page. Note that a recurring theme in these and most positioning examples is the timer. In the document object model, you can set a timer that raises an event at the end of the allotted time. The following line of code shows you how to set a timer. The first parameter to `setTimeout()` is the function call that the timer should make when the timer expires, `Ding()` in this case. The second parameter is the number of milliseconds for which to set the timer. Remember that there are 1,000 milliseconds in one second. The third parameter is the language used by the function listed in the first parameter.

```
Timer = window.setTimeout( "Ding()", 500, "JAVASCRIPT" );
```

Creating a Simple Animation

Listing 19.13 shows how to build simple animations using a combination of CSS positioning and the document object model's timer. The object that we're animating in this example is the `<DIV>` tag shown at the end of the listing. This tag has the ID `Ani`, and the `position` property is set to `absolute`.

Part
III

Ch
19

At each timer event, the event handler Ding(), which is associated with the timer, moves the <DIV> tag just a bit farther. The variables Hdir and Vdir indicate the horizontal and vertical directions that the object moves. To calculate the horizontal offset, for example, Hdir is multiplied by 10, and the result added to the current left-hand position as an offset. The event handler has to set the timer again because the timer only goes off once after it's set.

This example has an additional feature. The function ChangeDirection() is associated with the document's onClick event. When the user clicks the desktop, ChangeDirection() checks the event object to see where the user clicked. ChangeDirection() changes Hdir and Vdir to indicate the direction relative to the object's current position on which the user clicked.

Listing 19.13   Creating a Simple Animation

```
<HTML>
<BODY onClick="ChangeDirection()">
  <SCRIPT LANGUAGE=JAVASCRIPT>

    var Timer;
    var Hdir = 1;
    var Vdir = 1;

    function Ding()
    {
      Ani.style.posTop += Vdir * 10;
      Ani.style.posLeft += Hdir * 10;
      Timer = window.setTimeout( "Ding()", 500, "JAVASCRIPT" );
    }

    Timer = window.setTimeout( "Ding()", 500, "JAVASCRIPT" );

    function ChangeDirection()
    {
      if( window.event.clientX < Ani.style.posLeft )
        Hdir = -1;
      else
        Hdir = 1;

      if( window.event.clientY < Ani.style.posTop )
        Vdir = -1;
      else
        Vdir = 1;;
    }
  </SCRIPT>

  <DIV ID=Ani STYLE="position: absolute; left: 0; top: 0">
    This content is going to move across the screen.
  </DIV>

</BODY>
</HTML>
```

You can create much more advanced animations than the one shown in this example. To do so, fill an array with a "storyboard" that indicates the position and time at that position. Then the Ding() function can set the position and time according to the storyboard. This gives you complete control over how an object moves across the screen.

Implementing Fly-Over Help for Your Links

You can give the user ToolTip-style help for the links on your Web page (or any element on your Web page actually). Here's how it works:

- When the user hovers the mouse pointer over a link for about a second, the help window for that item opens next to the pointer.
- The help window disappears immediately when the user moves the mouse pointer off the link.
- If the mouse pointer hovers over the link for longer than about ten seconds, the help window disappears of its own accord.

Listing 19.14 implements these features as shown in Figure 19.3. The only style defined in this example is Help, which describes how the help window looks. In this case, it has a yellow background and black text. It also puts a frame around the item. The <DIV> tag you see at the top of the listing is an absolutely positioned element that is used as the help window. It doesn't cause the Web page to reflow, so it looks more like a pop-up window.

Each link on the Web page defines the onMouseOver and onMouseOut events. The onMouseOver event is associated with the FlyOver() function, which accepts as its only parameter the text to display in the help window. The onMouseOut event is associated with the ClearFlyOver() function, which hides the help window. Here's how these functions work together to display the fly-over help:

- FlyOver(). This function sets a timer for one second that calls DoFlyOver() when the timer expires. It also stashes the help text and mouse coordinates in global variables because these values are not available outside the onMouseOver event.
- DoFlyOver(). This function sets the text in the help's <DIV> tag, sets the position of the <DIV> tag to a small offset from the mouse pointer, and displays it by setting display to an empty string. Last, it sets a timer that calls ClearFlyOver() after about ten seconds.
- ClearFlyOver(). This function simply hides the help window by setting its display property to none.

Part
III

Ch
19

Listing 19.14   Implementing Fly-Over Help for Your Links

```
<HTML>

  <STYLE>
    .Help {
```

continues

Listing 19.14 Continued

```
                position: absolute; posTop: 0; posLeft: 0;
                border-width: thin; border-style: solid;
                background-color: yellow; color: black;
                height=20; width=240;
            }
</STYLE>

<DIV ID=FOArea CLASS="Help" STYLE="display: none">
</DIV>

<SCRIPT LANGUAGE=JAVASCRIPT>
  var HelpX, HelpY, HelpText;
  var ToShow, ToClear;

  function DoFlyOver()
  {
    if( ToClear != -1 ) window.clearTimeout( ToClear );

    FOArea.innerText = HelpText;
    FOArea.style.posLeft = HelpX + 8;
    FOArea.style.posTop = HelpY + 8;
    FOArea.style.display = "";

    ToClear = setTimeout( "ClearFlyOver()", 10000, "JAVASCRIPT" );
  }

  function ClearFlyOver()
  {
    FOArea.style.display = "none";
  }

  function FlyOver( Text )
  {
    HelpText = Text;
    HelpX = window.event.clientX;
    HelpY = window.event.clientY;
    ToShow = setTimeout( "DoFlyOver()", 1000, "JAVASCRIPT" );
  }
</SCRIPT>


<A onMouseOut="ClearFlyOver();"
   onMouseOver="FlyOver( 'Open Jerrys home page' );"
   HREF="http://rampages.onramp.net/~jerry">Jerry Honeycutt</A><BR>

<A onMouseOut="ClearFlyOver();"
   onMouseOver="FlyOver( 'Open Microsoft Web Page' );"
   HREF="http://www.microsoft.com">Microsoft</A>

</HTML>
```

FIG. 19.3
You can associate fly-over help with any HTML tag that you put on your Web page.

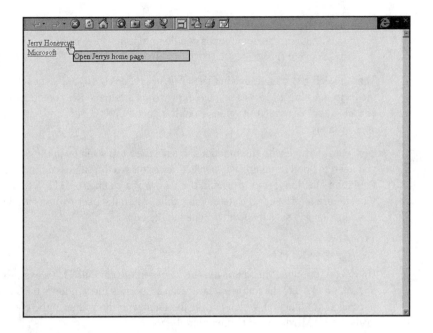

Reading and Writing Cookies Using the Object Model

Most applications you run on your desktop remember your last settings and recall those settings each time you open the appropriate dialog box. Unfortunately, HTML forms don't follow this behavior. Some browsers will remember your settings during the current session; however, when you close and reopen the browser, those settings are lost.

You can emulate this behavior using cookies. You use cookies to save information on the user's computer that you can recall and use during a later session (this causes some users great consternation). The browser's built-in objects don't provide all the functions you need to use cookies, though. You need to define functions to save and parse cookies. The script shown in Listing 19.15 contains all the functions you need to use cookies in your own HTML documents:

- `SetCookie()`. This function saves a value to the document's cookie by the given *Name* with the value contained in *Value*. It sets the expiration date to the date contained in *Expire*. If you don't provide an expiration date, the value lasts as long as the current session. Note that the date must be formatted like this:

  `Day,DD-MMM-YYYY HH:MM:SS GMT`

- `GetCookie()`. This function looks for a value called *Name* and returns its value. It looks at each value in the document's cookie until it finds the right one. Then it uses `GetValue()` to parse out the value.

Part
III

Ch
19

■ GetValue(). This function looks for a value called *Name* and returns its value. It looks at each value in the document's cookie until it finds the right one. Then it uses GetValue() to parse out the value.

The remaining two functions in this script, WriteCookies() and GetCookies(), are specific to the form in listing 19.15. WriteCookies() writes a value to the cookie for each field in the form. GetCookies() reads all the values from the document's cookie and sets each field in the form appropriately.

You're now armed with the functions to save the form's values to the document's cookie. Now you need to hook them up. The perfect place to save the values to the cookie is in the form's validation function: IsValid(). Add the following two lines of HTML to the end of this function (just before the last return statement); then, when the user submits a valid form, the validation function will save the form's values to the cookie.

```
if( blnValid )
    WriteCookies();
```

How about prefilling the form with the values in the cookie? That's easy. Change the <BODY> tag so that it looks like the following line. This associates the window's OnLoad event with the GetCookies() function, which prefills the form with the values in the cookie each time the user loads the HTML document containing the form.

```
<BODY OnLoad="GetCookies()">
```

Listing 19.15 Reading and Writing Cookies Using the Object Model

```
<HTML>
<SCRIPT LANGUAGE=JAVASCRIPT>

MoreIsUp = false;

// Display the hidden form if it's not already displayed. Otherwise, hide it.
// Also, change the text in the button to reflect the current state of the
hidden form.

function OpenMore()
{
  MoreIsUp = !MoreIsUp;
  More.style.display = MoreIsUp ? "" : "none";
  FEEDBACK.FEEDBACK_MORE.value = MoreIsUp ? "Less<<" : "More>>";
}
</SCRIPT>

<SCRIPT LANGUAGE=JAVASCRIPT>

// Extract the value from the cookie at the given offset.

function GetValue( Offset )
{
  var End = document.cookie.indexOf (";", Offset);
  if( End == -1 )
    End = document.cookie.length;
```

```
  // Return the portion of the cookie beginning with the offset
  // and ending with the ";".

  return unescape( document.cookie.substring( Offset, End) );
}

// Return the value of a cookie by name.

function GetCookie( Name )
{
  var Len = Name.length;

  // Look at each substring that's the same length as the cookie name
  // for a match. If found, look up the value and return it.

  var i = 0;
  while( i < document.cookie.length )
  {
    var j = i + Len + 1;
    if( document.cookie.substring( i, j) == (Name + "=") )
      return GetValue( j );
    i = document.cookie.indexOf( " ", i ) + 1;
    if( i == 0 )
      break;
  }
  return null;
}

// Create or change a cookie given it's name and value. The name and value
// are required, but the expiration date isn't. Note that if you don't specify
// an expiration date, the cookie only exists for the current session.

function SetCookie( Name, Value, Expire )
{
  document.cookie = Name + "=" + escape( Value ) + ";expires=" + Expire;
}

// Write all the cookies for the FEEDBACK form.

function WriteCookies()
{
  var Expire = "Friday,25-Feb-2000 12:00:00 GMT";

  with( document.FEEDBACK )
  {
    SetCookie( "Mail", FEEDBACK_MAIL.value, Expire );
    SetCookie( "How", FEEDBACK_HOW.selectedIndex, Expire );
    SetCookie( "Memo", FEEDBACK_MEMO.value, Expire );
    SetCookie( "Speed", FEEDBACK_SPEED[0].checked ? "1" : "0", Expire );
    SetCookie( "Content", FEEDBACK_CONTENT[0].checked ? "1" : "0", Expire );
    SetCookie( "Graphic", FEEDBACK_GRAPHIC[0].checked ? "1" : "0", Expire );
  }
}
```

Part

III

Ch

19

continues

Listing 19.15   Continued

```
// Load the form with the values in the cookie.

function GetCookies()
{
  with( document.FEEDBACK )
  {
    FEEDBACK_MAIL.value = GetCookie( "Mail" );
    FEEDBACK_HOW.selectedIndex = GetCookie( "How" );
    FEEDBACK_MEMO.value = GetCookie( "Memo" );
    FEEDBACK_SPEED[0].checked = (GetCookie( "Speed" ) == "1");
    FEEDBACK_SPEED[1].checked = (GetCookie( "Speed" ) == "0");
    FEEDBACK_CONTENT[0].checked = (GetCookie( "Content" ) == "1");
    FEEDBACK_CONTENT[1].checked = (GetCookie( "Content" ) == "0");
    FEEDBACK_GRAPHIC[0].checked = (GetCookie( "Graphic" ) == "1");
    FEEDBACK_GRAPHIC[1].checked = (GetCookie( "Graphic" ) == "0");
  }
}

function IsValid()
{
  blnValid = true;

  with( document.FEEDBACK )
  {
    if( FEEDBACK_MAIL.value == "" )
    {
      window.alert( "You must provide a mail address" );
      blnValid = false;
    }

    if( !(FEEDBACK_SPEED[0].checked || FEEDBACK_SPEED[1].checked) ||
        !(FEEDBACK_CONTENT[0].checked || FEEDBACK_CONTENT[1].checked) ||
        !(FEEDBACK_GRAPHIC[0].checked || FEEDBACK_GRAPHIC[1].checked))
    {
      window.alert( "Please select Yes or No for each rating" );
      blnValid = false;
    }
  }

  if( blnValid )
    WriteCookies();

  return blnValid;
}

</SCRIPT>

<BODY onLoad="GetCookies();">

<FORM NAME=FEEDBACK METHOD=POST ACTION="" onSubmit="return IsValid();">
  <TABLE CELLPADDING=10>
    <TR>
      <TD VALIGN=TOP>
        <B>Please provide your e-mail address:</B><BR>
        <INPUT NAME=FEEDBACK_MAIL TYPE=TEXT SIZE=40>
```

```
        </TD>
      <TD VALIGN=TOP>
        <B>How did you find our site?:</B><BR>
<SELECT NAME=FEEDBACK_HOW SIZE=1>
            <OPTION VALUE=1>AltaVista
            <OPTION VALUE=2>Excite
            <OPTION VALUE=3>Lycos
            <OPTION VALUE=4>Yahoo!
            <OPTION VALUE=5>WebCrawler
            <OPTION VALUE=6>Friend
            <OPTION VALUE=7>Other Link
        </SELECT>
        </TD>
    <TR>
      <TD VALIGN=TOP ROWSPAN=2>
        <B>Tell us what you think about our Web site:</B><BR>
        <TEXTAREA NAME=FEEDBACK_MEMO COLS=45 ROWS=8>
        </TEXTAREA>
      </TD>
      <TD VALIGN=TOP>
        <B>How did we rate?</B><BR>
        <TABLE BORDER=1>
          <TR ALIGN=CENTER>
            <TH></TH><TH>Yes</TH><TH>No</TH>
          </TR>
          <TR ALIGN=CENTER>
            <TD ALIGN=LEFT>
              Did this site load fast enough?
            </TD>
            <TD>
              <INPUT NAME=FEEDBACK_SPEED TYPE=RADIO>
            </TD>
            <TD>
              <INPUT NAME=FEEDBACK_SPEED TYPE=RADIO>
            </TD>
          </TR>
          <TR ALIGN=CENTER>
            <TD ALIGN=LEFT>
              Did you find the graphics interesting?
            </TD>
            <TD>
              <INPUT NAME=FEEDBACK_GRAPHIC TYPE=RADIO>
            </TD>
            <TD>
              <INPUT NAME=FEEDBACK_GRAPHIC TYPE=RADIO>
            </TD>
          </TR>
          <TR ALIGN=CENTER>
            <TD ALIGN=LEFT>
              Was the content suitable?
            </TD>
            <TD>
              <INPUT NAME=FEEDBACK_CONTENT TYPE=RADIO>
            </TD>
            <TD>
```

Part
III

Ch
19

continues

Listing 19.15   Continued

```
                    <INPUT NAME=FEEDBACK_CONTENT TYPE=RADIO>
                </TD>
              </TR>
            </TABLE>
        </TD>
      </TR>
      <TR ALIGN=RIGHT>
        <TD>
            <TABLE WIDTH=100%>
              <TD ALIGN=LEFT>
                <INPUT NAME=FEEDBACK_MORE TYPE=BUTTON VALUE="More>>"
                OnClick="OpenMore()">
              </TD>
              <TD>
                <INPUT NAME=FEEDBACK_RESET TYPE=RESET VALUE=Clear>
                <INPUT NAME=FEEDBACK_SUBMIT TYPE=SUBMIT VALUE=Submit>
              </TD>
            </TABLE>
        </TD>
      </TR>
    </TABLE>

    <!-- This division contains the hidden part of the form that the user sees
    when they click on More>>. The event handler at the top of this file shows the
    layer. -->

    <DIV ID=More STYLE="display: none">
      <TABLE CELLPADDING=10>
        <TR>
          <TD>
            <B>Type the URL of your home page:</B><BR>
            <INPUT NAME=FEEDBACK_URL TYPE=TEXT SIZE=60>
          </TD>
          <TD>
            <B>Type your phone number:</B><BR>
            <INPUT NAME=FEEDBACK_PHONE TYPE=TEXT SIZE=32>
          </TD>
        </TR>
      </TABLE>
    </DIV>

</FORM>

</BODY>
</HTML>
```

Differences Between Internet Explorer and Communicator

W3C is in the process of standardizing the document object model. Today, however, you have a problem. Both Internet Explorer and Communicator use different object models, making compatibility difficult. In fact, the differences in both object models is at the heart of what each vendor calls dynamic HTML:

- *Microsoft.* The document object model exposes every element on the Web page, including style sheet properties. Also, each element exposes properties, methods, events, and collections, as appropriate.

- *Netscape.* The document object model does not go as far as Microsoft's. It exposes a limited number of elements and doesn't expose style sheet properties at all. With Communicator, then, you can't change how elements look on the Web page after it loads the page.

Both browsers expose the traditional objects: `window`, `navigator`, `document`, `history`, `location`, `anchor`, `applet`, `area`, `form`, `element`, `options`, `image`, and `link`. Communicator exposes an additional object called `layer`, though, which allows you to programmatically work with proprietary layers. Internet Explorer exposes a variety of objects that are unique to it, including `all`, `cell`, `rows`, `children`, `embeds`, `plugins`, `external`, `filters`, `rules`, `style`, `styleSheet`, `styleSheets`, `screen`, `scripts`, `TextRange`, and `userProfile`.

## CHAPTER 20

Binding Data to HTML

by Jerry Honeycutt

In this chapter

Introducing Data Binding

At the moment, the way you publish data online is to build an HTML file on the server using information collected from a database. Once the browser opens the HTML file, it can't distinguish the data from any other content on the page; thus, you aren't able to control the data with scripts once the page is open in the browser.

Data binding allows you to associate database data with HTML elements. HTML 4.0 exposes several new properties and methods for many tags that make data binding possible. These allow you to bind data from a data source to the elements on your Web page. You can treat the data separate from the content and have full control over all of it.

Understanding Data Binding

To fully understand data binding, take a look at an example. The user is provided with a table that lists some of the books I've written. To make the information more accessible, I want to allow the user to view it via publication data, category, or title. Using older methods, these options are available:

- Provide three separate tables, each of which contains rows sorted by each category.

- Create a database on the server, and use a script to generate a table sorted by the user's preferred category. If the user wants to change categories, the browser has to make a round-trip to the server.

- Bind an ActiveX control to the data that allows the user to sort the data within the control's frame. This requires the user to download the control and still requires a script on the server to produce the data.

Using data binding, the user can view the data any way he or she likes without any of those constraints. Here's how:

1. Add a data source to the Web page.
2. Bind HTML elements to the data source.
3. Write scripts that control the bound table.

Adding a Data Source Object to Your Web Page

Data Source Objects (DSO) are objects that a vendor such as Microsoft provides. DSOs serve two different functions:

- DSOs provide the method for transporting data to the browser. A DSO can use any method it chooses to specify the data source: SQL, URLs, and so on.

- DSOs provide the means to manipulate the data. For example, a DSO provides methods, properties, and events that allow you to sort or filter the data.

Microsoft provides two different DSOs with Internet Explorer 4.0. The *Advanced Data Connector* (ADC) provides access to databases through server and ODBC components. The *Tabular*

Data Control (TDC) provides access to tabular data stored in comma-delimited text files. You can output this text file from any source: a spreadsheet, DBMS, or even your favorite text editor.

In order to provide data to your Web page, you must embed a DSO in the HTML file. In the example for this chapter, you learn to embed a TDC. Then you create the data source. Once you've done both steps, the DSO is ready to provide data to your Web page.

Embedding the TDC

The TDC is an ActiveX control; thus, you embed it in your Web page using the <OBJECT> tag as shown in Listing 20.1. Chapter 14, "Inserting Objects into a Web Page," describes how to insert ActiveX controls into your Web page. Make sure you assign an ID to ID and use the correct CLASSID. Set the WIDTH and HEIGHT attributes to 0 so that this control doesn't occupy any space on the Web page.

The first <PARAM> tag sets the URL of the data file by assigning MyData.Txt to DataURL. The next <PARAM> tag tells the control that you're using a delimiter, a comma in this case, and to assume the first row in the file is a header. Note the height and width is 0 so that the control doesn't display on the Web page.

Listing 20.1   Embedding a TDC in an HTML File

```
<OBJECT ID=TDC CLASSID="clsid:333C7BC4-460F-11D0-BC04-0080C7055A83" WIDTH=0
HEIGHT=0>
   <PARAM NAME=DataURL VALUE="MyData.Txt">
   <PARAM NAME=TextQualifier VALUE=",">
   <PARAM NAME=UseHeader VALUE="True">
</OBJECT>
```

Building the Text File

The text file you create is comma-delimited. The first row indicates the column names; each column is separated by a comma. Each subsequent row represents data. Take a look at Listing 20.2 for an example. Store this file on your Web server using the name you specified in the previous listing.

Part
III

Ch
20

Listing 20.2   Example Text File

```
Category, Title, Date, Price:FLOAT
Internet, Using the Internet, 10/97, 5.99
Internet, Special Edition Using the Internet, 12/97, 99.99
Internet, Using the Internet with Windows 97, 12/95, 1.99
Windows 95, Windows 95 Registry and Customization Handbook, 3/96, 59.99
Windows NT, Platinum Edition Using NT Server 4.0, 10/97, 999.99
HTML, Special Edition Using HTML 4.0, 10/97, 9.99
```

There are a couple of important things to note about this text file:

- You can indicate the data type of a particular column by appending it to the end of the column name as shown in Listing 20.2. :FLOAT indicates that the data object should treat the column as a floating-point value when sorting or filtering it. Table 20.1 describes the other data types you can use.

- You can use HTML for any value in the table. Use this fact to associate an image with a particular column by embedding the <IMG> tag in the table. See "Specifying a Data Format," later in this chapter, to learn more about the DATAFORMATAS attribute.

Table 20.1   Data Types for Use with TDC

Type	Description
String	Text data
Date	Calendar date
Boolean	Logical data
Int	Integer number
Float	Floating-point number

 T I P   Type your data into a spreadsheet such as Excel and export it to a comma-delimited text file.

Associating HTML to a Data Source Object

HTML 4.0 contains two new attributes that allow you to bind data to elements: DATASRC and DATAFLD. Within an element, DATASRC references the data source object. You assign the ID of the data source object to it with the pound (#) prefix. Now, the <SPAN> tag shown in the following line references the DSO you embedded earlier in this chapter.

```
<SPAN DATASRC=#TDC></SPAN>
```

By itself, the preceding line doesn't do anything. You must reference a specific column by assigning the name of the column to the DATAFLD attribute. In the following example, the <SPAN> tag refers to the Title column. The browser displays the title from the currently selected record.

```
<SPAN DATASRC=#TDC DATAFLD=Title></SPAN>
```

Listing 20.3 shows you the complete example, which displays the Title field from the database you created earlier.

Listing 20.3   Data Binding Example

```
<HTML>
<HEAD>
  <TITLE>Data Binding Example</TITLE>
</HEAD>

<BODY>

<OBJECT ID=TDC CLASSID="clsid:333C7BC4-460F-11D0-BC04-0080C7055A83" WIDTH=0
HEIGHT=0>
  <PARAM NAME=DataURL VALUE="MyData.Txt">
  <PARAM NAME=TextQualifier VALUE=",">
  <PARAM NAME=UseHeader VALUE="True">
</OBJECT>

  Title: <SPAN DATASRC=#TDC DATAFLD=Title></SPAN>

</BODY>
</HTML>
```

Tags Supporting Data Binding

The following list describes the HTML tags that support data binding, providing the DATASRC, DATAFLD, and DATAFORMATAS attributes:

- DIV
- INPUT-TEXT
- INPUT-RADIO
- INPUT-CHECKBOX
- INPUT-HIDDEN
- TEXTAREA
- MARQUEE
- IMG
- SELECT
- APPLET
- OBJECT
- PARAM
- TABLE
- BUTTON
- A
- FRAME
- IFRAME
- LABEL

Part

III

Ch

20

Of particular note in this list are the following input tags: INPUT-TEXT, INPUT-RADIO, INPUT-CHECKBOX, INPUT-HIDDEN, TEXTAREA, SELECT. Whereas the remaining tags display a particular field from a record, these input tags actually allow the user to change the record. When the user changes a field, the browser feeds the changes back to the DSO, which in turn writes the changes to the database.

Binding Data to a Table

When you bind a data source to a table, the browser uses the table as a template, repeating each row for each record in the database. Within the table, you can specifically choose which fields to use in each column.

Listing 20.4 shows you a complete example that binds data to a table. The table is divided into two parts: a heading and a body. The <THEAD> tag defines the table headings and the <TBODY> tag defines the table body. The browser repeats everything appearing in the <TBODY> container once for each record in the data source. The DATASRC attribute within the <TABLE> tag indicates the DSO. Pay particular attention to how the body looks. You don't use the DATAFLD attribute with each <TD> tag. Instead, you include a <SPAN> tag within each cell and assign the name of the field to the <SPAN> tag's DATAFLD attribute. The browser repeats that table row once for each record in the database.

Listing 20.4   Binding Data to a Table

```
<HTML>
<HEAD>
  <TITLE>Data Binding Example</TITLE>
</HEAD>

<BODY>

<OBJECT ID=TDC CLASSID="clsid:333C7BC4-460F-11D0-BC04-0080C7055A83" WIDTH=0
HEIGHT=0>
  <PARAM NAME=DataURL VALUE="MyData.Txt">
  <PARAM NAME=TextQualifier VALUE=",">
  <PARAM NAME=UseHeader VALUE="True">
</OBJECT>

<TABLE ID=Table DATASRC=#TDC BORDER=1>
  <THEAD>
    <TR>
      <TH>Title</TH><TH>Date</TH>
    </TR>
  </THEAD>
  <TBODY>
    <TR>
      <TD><SPAN DATAFLD=Title></SPAN></TD>
      <TD><SPAN DATAFLD=Date></SPAN></TD>
    </TR>
  </TBODY>
</TABLE>

</BODY>
</HTML>
```

You can get pretty fancy with tables and data binding. For example, in Listing 20.5, the table body contains two rows for each record. The Category field spans across both rows, the Title field is in the top row, and the Date field is in the bottom row. Figure 20.1 shows you what this table looks like in Internet Explorer 4.0.

Listing 20.5   Binding to Fancy Tables

```
<HTML>
<HEAD>
  <TITLE>Data Binding Example</TITLE>
</HEAD>

<BODY>

<OBJECT ID=TDC CLASSID="clsid:333C7BC4-460F-11D0-BC04-0080C7055A83" WIDTH=0
HEIGHT=0>
  <PARAM NAME=DataURL VALUE="MyData.Txt">
  <PARAM NAME=TextQualifier VALUE=",">
  <PARAM NAME=UseHeader VALUE="True">
</OBJECT>

<TABLE ID=Table DATASRC=#TDC BORDER=1>
  <THEAD>
    <TR>
      <TH>Category</TH><TH>Title/Date</TH>
    </TR>
  </THEAD>
  <TBODY>
    <TR>
      <TD ROWSPAN=2><SPAN DATAFLD=Category></SPAN></TD>
      <TD><SPAN DATAFLD=Title></SPAN></TD>
    </TR>
    <TR>
      <TD><SPAN DATAFLD=Date></SPAN></TD>
    </TR>
  </TBODY>
</TABLE>

</BODY>
</HTML>
```

Specifying a Data Format

By default, the browser assumes each field in the table is raw data. You can set the DATAFORMATAS attribute for a tag to HTML, however, which indicates that the browser should render the data as actual HTML. For example, if you have a column of data called Cover containing an <image> tag, such as <IMG SRC=cover.gif>, you can render that using a tag like this:

```
<SPAN DATASRC=#TDC DATAFLD=Cover DATAFORMATAS=HTML>
```

DATAFORMATAS is valid only on the <DIV>, <SPAN>, and <MARQUEE> tags. Table 20.2 describes the other formats supported by this attribute.

FIG. 20.1

Make sure you define the body of your table using the <TBODY> container, because the browser repeats everything within it for each record.

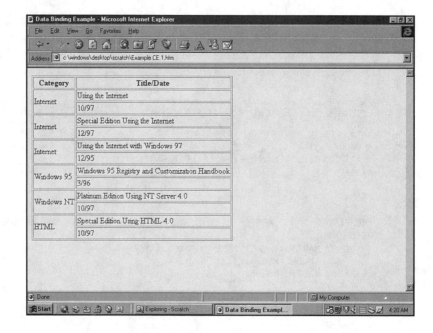

Table 20.2   Formats for Data Binding

Type	Description
HTML	Render data as HTML
TEXT	Render data as text

Scripting the Data Source Object

The DSO is responsible for providing the data and the mechanisms for working with the data. Thus, to manipulate the data in your Web page, you must use its properties and methods. The only method that the TDC supports is Reset(), which causes the TDC to refresh the data on the Web page. It supports a handful of properties, though, which are described in Table 20.3.

Table 20.3   TDC Properties

Name	Description
Properties	
AppendData	TRUE—append data to existing data set
	FALSE—don't append data to data set
CaseSensitive	TRUE—data is case-sensitive
	FALSE—data is not case-sensitive

Name	Description
Properties	
CharSet	Identifies the character set of the data file
DataURL	URL of the data file
EscapeChar	Specifies a character to use as escape character; useful for escaping quotes in the date, for example, `"Quotes \"within\" quotes`
FieldDelim	String value that specifies the field delimiter; the default is a comma
Filter	The criteria used to filter the data set; for example, `Age < 30 & Name = 'Jerry'`
Language	String specifying the language used by the data set as defined by ISO 369
RowDelim	String value that specifies the row delimiter; the default is `newline`
Sort	String list of columns by which the data is sorted, separated by semicolons; prefix a field with a minus sign to sort descending, for example, `"x; -y"`
TextQualifier	Character used to surround fields that contain special characters such as newlines, tabs, and commas; the default is a double quotation mark
UseHeader	TRUE—first line contains headers FALSE—first line contains data
Methods	
Reset	Forces the control to filter or sort the data based upon the new settings

Sorting the Database

Sorting a data source is a matter of telling it by which column you want to sort, and then executing the sort. You tell the TDC the column by which you're sorting using the SortColumn property. Assign to this property the name of the field. You assign True to the SortAscending property to sort in ascending order, False otherwise. After having told the TDC how you want to sort, execute the sort using the Reset() method as shown in Listing 20.6. The user types a column name in the field and clicks the Sort button; the script then forces the TDC to refresh the data in the Web page.

Part
III

Ch
20

Listing 20.6 Sorting a Data Source

```
<HTML>
<HEAD>
  <TITLE>Data Binding Example</TITLE>
</HEAD>

<BODY>
```

continues

Listing 20.6   Continued

```
<OBJECT ID=TDC CLASSID="clsid:333C7BC4-460F-11D0-BC04-0080C7055A83" WIDTH=0
HEIGHT=0>
  <PARAM NAME=DataURL VALUE="MyData.Txt">
  <PARAM NAME=TextQualifier VALUE=",">
  <PARAM NAME=UseHeader VALUE="True">
</OBJECT>

<SCRIPT LANGUAGE="VBSCRIPT">
  Sub SortTable()
    TDC.SortAscending=True
    TDC.SortColumn=SortFrm.Column.Value
    TDC.Reset()
  End Sub
</SCRIPT>

<FORM NAME=SORTFRM>
  <INPUT NAME=COLUMN TYPE=TEXT SIZE=10>
  <INPUT NAME=SORT TYPE=BUTTON VALUE="Sort" OnClick="Call SortTable()">
</FORM>

<TABLE ID=Table DATASRC=#TDC BORDER=1>
  <THEAD>
    <TR>
      <TH>Category</TH><TH>Title/Date</TH>
    </TR>
  </THEAD>
  <TBODY>
    <TR>
      <TD ROWSPAN=2><SPAN DATAFLD=Category></SPAN></TD>
      <TD><SPAN DATAFLD=Title></SPAN></TD>
    </TR>
    <TR>
      <TD><SPAN DATAFLD=Date></SPAN></TD>
    </TR>
  </TBODY>
</TABLE>

</BODY>
</HTML>
```

Filtering the Data That the Browser Displays

You don't have to display all of the records in the database at one time; you can carefully choose the records to include. For example, you can let the user pick a category, as shown in Listing 20.7, and then display records only in that category. You assign the field name by which you're filtering to the FilterColumn property and the value to the FilterValue property. You can define a relationship between these two by assigning a criterion to FilterCriterion. This value can be a comparison operator (<, >, <=, >=, =).

In Listing 20.7, the equivalence operator (=) is assigned to FilterCriterion. Then, the value that the user typed into the Category field is assigned to the FilterValue property and

`Category` is assigned to `FilterColumn`. When the user clicks the Refresh button, the script sets up the sort defined by the `Sort` field, sets up the filter defined by the `Category` field, and calls the `Reset()` property to refresh the data source.

Listing 20.7   Filtering a Data Source

```
<HTML>
<HEAD>
  <TITLE>Data Binding Example</TITLE>
</HEAD>

<BODY>

<OBJECT ID=TDC CLASSID="clsid:333C7BC4-460F-11D0-BC04-0080C7055A83" WIDTH=0
HEIGHT=0>
  <PARAM NAME=DataURL VALUE="MyData.Txt">
  <PARAM NAME=TextQualifier VALUE=",">
  <PARAM NAME=UseHeader VALUE="True">
</OBJECT>

<SCRIPT LANGUAGE="VBSCRIPT">
  Sub RefreshTable()

    ' Specify how to sort the table

    TDC.SortAscending=True
    TDC.SortColumn=SortFrm.Column.Value

    ' Specify how to filter the table

    If SortFrm.Category.Value = "" Then
      SortFrm.Category.Value = "*"
    End If

    TDC.FilterColumn = "Category"
    TDC.FilterValue = SortFrm.Category.Value
    TDC.FilterCriterion = "="

    ' Reset the table

    TDC.Reset()
  End Sub
</SCRIPT>

<TABLE>
  <FORM NAME=SORTFRM>
    <TR>
      <TD>Sort by:</TD><TD>Category:</TD><TD></TD>
    <TR>
    <TR>
      <TD>
        <INPUT NAME=COLUMN TYPE=TEXT SIZE=10>
      </TD>
      <TD>
```

continues

Listing 20.7 Continued

```
            <INPUT NAME=CATEGORY TYPE=TEXT SIZE=10 VALUE="*">
        </TD>
        <TD>
            <INPUT NAME=SORT TYPE=BUTTON VALUE="Refresh" OnClick="Call
RefreshTable()">
        </TD>
    </FORM>
</TABLE>

<TABLE ID=Table DATASRC=#TDC BORDER=1>
    <THEAD>
        <TR>
            <TH>Category</TH><TH>Title/Date</TH>
        </TR>
    </THEAD>
    <TBODY>
        <TR>
            <TD ROWSPAN=2><SPAN DATAFLD=Category></SPAN></TD>
            <TD><SPAN DATAFLD=Title></SPAN></TD>
        </TR>
        <TR>
            <TD><SPAN DATAFLD=Date></SPAN></TD>
        </TR>
    </TBODY>
</TABLE>

</BODY>
</HTML>
```

Figure 20.2 shows you the result of this Web page in Internet Explorer 4.0.

 You can set any of the sort and filter properties using the TDC <OBJECT> tag's <PARAM> tag. For example, to set the FilterColumn property, use a tag like this: <PARAM NAME=FilterColumn VALUE=Category>.

FIG. 20.2
When the user leaves the Category field empty, the script assigns an asterisk (*), which is a wildcard, to the field.

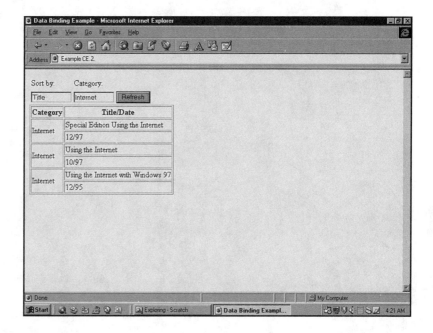

## CHAPTER 21

Embedding Web Fonts into a Web Page

by Jerry Honeycutt

Introducing Web Fonts

W3C's Web fonts working draft extends the existing CSS1 style sheet mechanism to support the @font-face at-rule, which allows you to embed fonts into the Web page. The benefit is obvious: You can package the fonts you use in your Web page with the HTML document. At this writing, Web fonts are not part of the HTML 4.0 proposal, but Web fonts might become part of it by the time the proposal becomes a recommendation. You can see W3C's working draft for Web fonts at **http://www.w3.org/Style/Group/WD-font-970710**.

Microsoft and Netscape use different terminology for Web fonts. Microsoft calls them *embedded fonts*. Netscape calls them *dynamic fonts*. In either case, the mechanisms are roughly similar, but the font formats (OpenType for Microsoft and TrueDoc for Netscape) and utilities to build font files are different. You learn about both in this chapter.

Exploring Web Fonts

Forget about Web fonts for a moment and consider the problem that HTML authors have always had: You build a dynamite Web page that depends on a fanciful font to make a certain impression. You use either a style sheet or the <FONT> tag to specify the font face by name. Then the user opens your Web page, but the browser can't find a matching font. The browser tries many alternative fonts and chooses one that doesn't quite meet your expectations. As a result, the user sees something that looks like Figure 21.1, when you intended the user to see a Web page similar to Figure 21.2.

FIG. 21.1

This problem is particularly nasty if you're using the symbols from a font, as demonstrated here.

FIG. 21.2
As intended by the author, the symbols show up when the font is available.

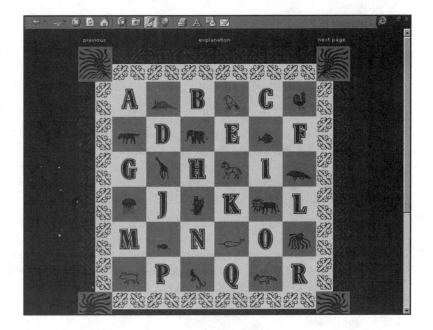

Web fonts eliminate this problem. They allow you to build a Web page that appears to the user exactly as you intended. Instead of hoping and praying that the user's browser can find a matching font, you can package the font with your Web page so that you're certain it will be available.

Embedding a Font into Your Web Page

You embed a font into a Web page via a *font description*. A font description links a style sheet's *font reference* to the font data, whether it is on the server or local machine. You use the `@font-face` at-rule, which is an extension to CSS1 style sheets (see Chapter 17, "Applying Cascading Style Sheets"), to create font descriptions. It takes the form of any other rule:

```
@font-face { property: value; property; value }
```

In the `@font-face` at-rule, you provide the name of the font using the `font-family` property. The browser looks up font descriptions for each particular style rule using this property.

You reference the location of the font using the `src` property to which you can assign an URL in the form of `URL(URL)`. For example, `URL(./fonts/mine)` specifies the location of a font file called `mine` in a folder called `fonts`. `URL` can be a relative or absolute path. The `src` property also provides a means to specify the format of the font data: `TrueDoc` or `OpenType`, for example. You append `format(font-format)` to the value you assign to `src`, like this:

```
src: URL(./fonts/mine) format(opentype)
```

Part
III

Ch
21

In the following example, the @font-face at-rule downloads the font called Old World from the relative URL fonts/oldworld. Any time the P style is applied to the Web page, the browser searches all the font descriptions to find font data for the Old World font.

```
<STYLE TYPE="text/css">
  @font-face { font-family: "Old World"; src: url(fonts/oldworld) }
  P { font-family: "Old World" }
</STYLE
```

You can also assign an adorned font name to src. An *adorned font name* is the name of the font as a user sees it on a menu or font selection dialog box. This indicates that you're referencing a font that exists on the user's computer as opposed to downloading the font from the server. To use an adorned font name, you assign a value that looks like local(name) to src, where name is the name of a font such as Gloucester MT Extra Condensed.

Because you can assign more than one value to src, you can assign an adorned font name to it, followed by a downloadable font. This forces the browser to look for a particular font on the user's computer, and if it can't find the font, it downloads the font from the server. In the following example, the browser tries to find Old World Light on the user's computer; failing that, it downloads fonts/oldworld from the server:

```
<STYLE TYPE="text/css">
  @font-face
  {
    font-family: "Old World";
    src: local(Old World Light), url(fonts/oldworld);
  }
</STYLE
```

Describing the Font's Characteristics

The @font-face at-rule supports several properties that you use to describe the font's characteristics. You can provide multiple font descriptions for a single font family. When the browser applies a style that references that font family, it finds the font description whose properties match the style. Here's a brief description of each property and the values you can assign to it (the first value for each property is the default):

Property	Possible Values	Description
font-family	Family name	Describes the family name of the font.
font-style	normal, italic, oblique	oblique indicates a slanted face, and italic indicates a cursive face.
font-variant	normal, small-caps	small-caps indicates a small-caps variant of the face.
font-weight	all, normal, bold, 100, 200, 300, 400, 500, 600, 700, 800	This descriptor indicates the weight of the face relative to other faces in the same family.
font-size	all, length	This descriptor indicates the sizes provided in the font file.

The @font-face properties are the same that you use in normal style rules; the difference is that with @font-face, you can assign multiple values to each property using a comma-delimited list of values. Here's how Web fonts match styles to font descriptions:

- If you specify a single value for a property, the same property within the style rule must match exactly in order for the browser to choose the font description.
- If you specify multiple values for a property, the property within the style rule must match any one of the values in the list in order for the browser to choose the font description.
- If you don't specify a property at all, the property within the style rule must match the default value in order for the browser to choose the font description.

Given the example in Listing 21.1, a style rule that sets font-family to Texas and font-weight to 200, 300, or 400 will match the first font description, which refers to the font stored in ./fonts/texas-bold. A style rule that uses the Texas font family and formats the text as italic will use the second font description, however, which refers to the font stored in ./fonts/texas-italic.

Listing 21.1 Sample Font Descriptions

```
<STYLE TYPE="text/css">
  @font-face
  {
    src: URL(./fonts/texas-bold) format(OpenType);
    font-family: Texas;
    font-weight: 200, 300, 400;
  }

  @font-face
  {
    src: URL(./fonts/texas-italic) format(OpenType);
    font-family: Texas;
    font-weight: normal;
font-style: italic, oblique;
  }
</STYLE>
```

 TIP You can use the <STYLE> tag's MEDIA property to limit an embedded font to a particular output media such as the screen or printer. See Chapter 17, "Applying Cascading Style Sheets," for more information.

Progressively Rendering Embedded Fonts

The user's Web browser won't render the HTML until it's downloaded all the embedded fonts. If the font you're embedding is quite large, the user must wait several moments before he or she sees the content of your Web page. This is in contrast to the more immediate gratification that a user gets now as the browser displays the Web page's text quickly.

You can force the browser to display the Web page's contents before downloading the font, however. You do that by embedding the font in an external style sheet. You link to that style sheet after the browser opens the Web page by using a script to assign the URL of the style sheet to the stylesheets collection. Assuming that you've stored a style sheet with an embedded font in a file called mystyle.css, the script in Listing 21.2 causes the browser to download that font only after it's finished loading the Web page.

Listing 21.2 Linking to a Style Sheet

```
<SCRIPT TYPE="text/vbscript">
  Sub Window_OnLoad
    document.stylesheets(0).href = "mystyle.css';
  End Sub
</SCRIPT>
```

In the third line of the listing, the URL of the style sheet is assigned to document.stylesheets(0).href. This assumes that there is at least one style sheet in the Web page and that it's being overwritten. You'd replace that index with an appropriate index if you were using multiple style sheets. Alternatively, you can dimension a new style sheet object and assign the URL of your style sheet file to it. This requires you to add the following HTML at the top of your document:

```
<LINK REL="stylesheet" HREF="null">
```

Embedding *OpenType* Fonts into Your Web Page

Microsoft's provides a tool called WEFT (Web Embedding Fonts Tool) that you use to embed fonts in your Web page. You can download WEFT for free from **http://www.microsoft.com/typography/web/embedding/weft/default.htm**.

WEFT analyzes each page in your site, noting how you use fonts in each. It then builds compressed font objects that it automatically links to each Web page.

Downloading Free Fonts from Microsoft

Microsoft provides a number of free fonts that you can embed in your Web page. Open **http://www.microsoft.com/typography/web/fonts/default.htm**, and you can pick from any of the following:

- Arial
- Comic Sans MS
- Courier New
- Georgia

- Impact
- Times New Roman
- Trebuchet MS
- Verdanda
- Webdings

Checking the Copyright Status of a Font

You can get into serious trouble if you embed a copyrighted font in your Web page without permission. You can check a font to see if you're free to distribute it using Microsoft's Font Properties Extension. Download this utility from **http://www.microsoft.com/typography/property/property.htm** and follow the instructions you see on the screen to install it.

After you install the Font Properties Extension, right-click a font file (look in C:\Windows\Fonts), choose Properties, and you see the dialog box shown in Figure 21.3. The Embedding tab tells you what you can and cannot do with the font. For example, you might see a message that says Installable embedding allowed. You also see the font's copyright on the Names tab.

FIG. 21.3

The Font Properties Extension adds several new tabs to the existing Font Properties dialog box.

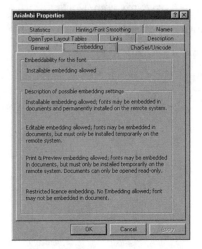

Embedding *TrueDoc* Fonts into Your Web Page

To create and embed TrueDoc fonts into your Web page, you must have author tools. At the time of this writing, these tools were not yet available, but Table 21.1 points you to the vendors that have promised to add TrueDoc support to their authoring tools.

Table 21.1 TrueDoc Authoring Tools

Vendor	URL
Astrobyte	http://www.astrobyte.com
Bare Bones Software	http://www.barebones.com
Boomerang Software	http://www.mosaiccom.com
Corel Corporation	http://www.corel.com
Digiflyer	http://www.digiflyer.com
FutureTense	http://www.futuretense.com
HexMac	http://www.hexmac.com
InfoAccess, Inc.	http://www.infoaccess.com
Macromedia, Inc.	http://www.macromedia.com
MySoftware Company	http://www.mysoftware.com
Network Computer, Inc.	http://www.nc.com
RMX Technologies, Inc.	http://www.rmx.com/world
Sausage Software Ltd.	http://www.sausage.com
SoftQuad	http://www.softquad.com
TextCenter AB	http://www.textcenter.se
TLCO Software	http://www.tlco.com

## PART IV

Serving Multimedia Content

## CHAPTER 22

Graphics

by Eric Ladd and Mark R. Brown

In this chapter

How Graphic Information Is Stored

When you see a graphic on your computer screen, what you're really seeing is a collection of colored screen pixels that, taken together, produce a meaningful image. An image file, therefore, has to contain information on how to reproduce that collection of pixels on-screen. This is accomplished by describing the pixels' properties mathematically and storing these descriptions in the file.

The catch in this situation is that there's not a unique way to mathematically describe image data. Given time, you can come up with your own way and, thus, your own storage format. Because you can express image data many ways, there are many possible image file formats—on the order of several dozen!

Fortunately, each of these formats can be classified as one of two types: a bitmapped graphic or a vector graphic. The next two sections examine the specifics of each type.

Bitmapped Graphics

With a bitmapped graphic, information about each pixel is stored as a sequence of bits in the file. Depending on the storage formats, these bits could represent colors, saturation levels, brightness, or some other visual characteristic of the pixel. What's important is that each sequence of bits tells the computer how to paint the pixel on the screen.

Bitmaps are something of a natural format because they store information in exactly the same way the computer displays it on a monitor. This means the program that renders the image has to do very little processing. It just reads in the data and passes that information along to the screen drivers, which, in turn, display the pixels.

N O T E   The above is not entirely true if the bitmapped image is compressed. Compression reduces the size of an image file by reducing the amount of information needed to replicate the image. A compressed file will download more quickly, because of its smaller size, but it needs to be decompressed before the image can be displayed. This decompression step means additional processing effort. ■

Vector Graphics

A vector graphic file contains mathematical information that is used to redraw the image on the screen. When a computer displays a vector image file, it reads in the redrawing instructions and follows them. This might sound like a lot of unnecessary processing, but there is an important advantage to this approach: You can rescale the image to new sizes without loss of resolution because there's no fixed relationship between how its defined in the file and the pixel-by-pixel image on the screen. When you try to resize a bitmapped file, you often get a loss of resolution that detracts from the image.

Vector graphic formats are typically used for images with distinct geometric shapes. Computer Aided Design (CAD) drawings are examples of this type of image.

N O T E   Some file formats combine the best of both bitmapped and vector graphics into what's
called a metafile format. Windows metafiles (.WMF) are frequently used to store clip-art
images that need to be resized often. ■

Web Graphic Formats

When you focus your attention on Web graphics, the vast number of usable graphic storage
formats quickly reduces to two. The Graphics Interchange Format, or GIF, was developed by
CompuServe in 1987 to store graphics used over its network. The other format came about
more recently and is named for the group that developed it: the Joint Picture Experts Group, or
JPEG. Both formats are bitmapped formats. Currently, there is virtually no support for vector
storage formats, except by means of browser plug-ins.

The specifics of each of these formats, and instances when you would want to use one over the
other, are discussed in the following sections.

GIF

CompuServe released the GIF standard in 1987 and updated it in 1989 and 1990. The current
standard is 89a, and it supports 8-bit color. That is, a GIF image can contain up to 2^8, or 256
colors.

How GIF Works   Image data in a GIF file is organized into related blocks and subblocks that
provide information on how to paint screen pixels to reproduce the image. When transmitting a
GIF image, a program called an encoder is used to produce a GIF data stream of control and
data blocks that are sent along to the destination machine. There, a program called a decoder
parses the data stream and assembles the image.

GIF is a compressed format as well. GIF files employ the LZW compression scheme to reduce
the amount of information needed to completely describe the image. The LZW scheme is best
suited to simple images like line drawings or images with just a few unique colors. As the number of colors grows, LZW compression becomes less efficient, providing compression ratios of
2:1 or less.

N O T E   The LZW compression used with GIFs was actually conceived by the Unisys Corporation
and not by CompuServe. CompuServe and Unisys were entangled in patent disputes for a
while. The end result was CompuServe's licensing of the GIF format—a move that had Internet
developers worried that they would have to pay for a license. Fortunately for them, the license
agreement pertained only to software that was primarily used for accessing CompuServe. The
downside was these developers still had to worry about licensing with Unisys as well. Unisys has yet to
pursue this with any vigor though, and the GIF format continues to be one of the most popular formats
on the Internet. ■

Transparent GIFs   GIF supports many effects that are desirable on Web pages. Chief among
these is transparency. In a transparent GIF, you can designate one color to be the transparent

color. Then, whenever the GIF is rendered on screen, pixels painted with the transparent color will actually be painted with the color of the page background. This gives the illusion of the pixels being transparent, since they allow what's behind them to show through.

The advantage of transparent GIFs is that they make a graphic appear to float freely on a page. To see what this means, take a look at Figure 22.1. The image at the top is nontransparent. The words you see are sitting inside of a rectangular bounding box, and both the words and the bounding box are visible. The bottom image is a transparent GIF in which the color of the bounding box was designated as the transparent color. The result is that the bounding box disappears and the words seem to sit on the background with no particular boundary around them.

FIG. 22.1
You can make images float on a page by using a transparent GIF.

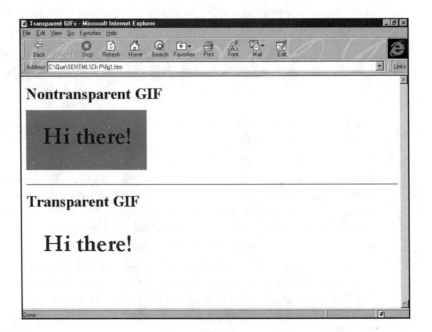

Many graphics programs available today come with support for creating transparent GIFs. Lview Pro, a graphic utility discussed later in this chapter, makes it very easy to designate a transparent color in a GIF.

Interlaced GIFs   When you store a GIF in an interlaced format, nonadjacent parts of the image are stored together. As the GIF is decoded, pixels from all over the image are filled in rather than being filled in row by row. The result is that the image appears to "fade on" to the page, as if it were being revealed from behind Venetian blinds. This permits the user to get a sense of the entire image right away instead of having to wait for the whole thing to be read in from top to bottom.

It usually takes several passes for the image to fade in completely. Figure 22.2 shows an interlaced GIF on the Discovery Channel site in the process of being read in. The complete image is shown in Figure 22.3.

FIG. 22.2
An interlaced GIF appears fuzzy as it is read in.

Interlaced GIF (partially decoded)

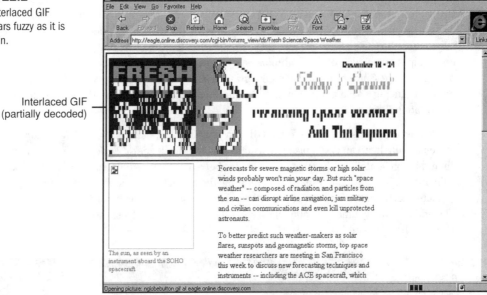

FIG. 22.3
As the last pieces of image data are read in, the interlaced GIF comes into sharper focus.

Interlaced GIF (fully decoded)

Just as with transparency, most good graphics programs give you the option of saving a GIF as interlaced. All three programs discussed in this chapter support interlaced GIFs.

Animated GIFs   The first animations that appeared on the Web required a great deal of effort. Using an approach introduced by Netscape called *server push*, you could create an animation by having a server literally push several images down an open HTTP connection. When presented in sequence on the browser screen, these images created the illusion of animation. Setting this up required knowledge of the Common Gateway Interface (CGI) and some type of programming language. Since most digital media graphic artists don't have knowledge of CGI programming, producing a Web animation often required collaboration between the artists and the server administrator.

Then it occurred to someone that the GIF 89a standard supports multiple images stored in the same file. Further, you could place instructions in the file header that describe how the images should be presented. In short, the 89a standard gives you everything you need to produce an animation! The individual frames that comprise the animation can all be stored in one file, and you can specify in the file header parameters like how much delay before starting the animation and how many times the animation should repeat. Figure 22.4 shows several animated GIFs on the 7-Up site.

FIG. 22.4
Animated GIFs let you place animations on a page without knowledge of programming.

Animated GIFs—

Creating animated GIFs has become fairly easy with the advent of software tools like the GIF Construction Set, available at **http://www.mindworkshop.com**. In this program, you can specify the individual GIF files that make up the animation and presentation instructions in a set of dialog boxes. When you're finished with the setup, the program will create the animated GIF file using the information you specified.

> **CAUTION**
>
> Like many popular Web page components, a number of animated GIFs have been made publicly available for download at many sites. The result is that these GIFs quickly become overused. Placing such a GIF on your pages does nothing to distinguish them. If you really need an animated GIF on your page, create your own unique animation. Don't put a trite animated GIF on a page just for the sake of having one there.

JPEG

JPEG actually refers to a set of formats that supports full-color and grayscale images and stores them in compressed form. JPEG stores color information at 24 bits per pixel, allowing an image to contain 2^{24} or over 16.7 million colors! This makes it the format of choice for photographs, especially nature photographs, where a continuum of colors is in play (see Figure 22.5).

FIG. 22.5
Photographs of naturally occurring objects are prime candidates for being stored as JPEGs.

JPEG image ——

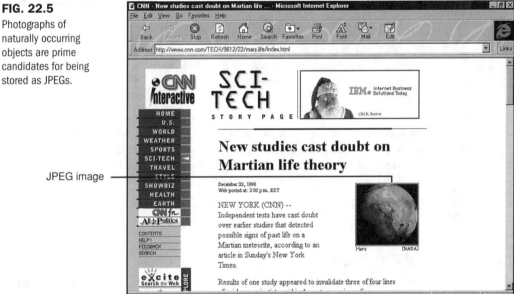

How JPEG Works JPEG can handle so many colors while still keeping file sizes reasonable because it compresses the image data. You even have some control over how big or small the file ultimately is. You can specify a high level of compression to get a very small file, but the quality of the image on-screen will be reduced.

When you decompress a JPEG image, there is always some amount of loss, meaning that the image will not look the way it did originally. Fortunately, JPEG's compression/decompression scheme is such that the lost image data tends to be in the higher color frequencies, where it is harder for the human eye to detect the differences. In spite of this loss, you can still use JPEG to achieve compression ratios between 10:1 and 20:1 without appreciable change in the image. This means you've essentially reduced the amount of storage space per pixel from 24 bits to 1 or 2 bits—quite a savings! You can take the compression ratios even higher, but as noted above, the loss will become more detectable and image quality will suffer.

TIP Always do the conversion to JPEG as your very last step in creating a Web image. Resaving as a JPEG after each change can increase the amount of loss, since the image is recompressed each time.

Progressive JPEGs JPEG isn't as versatile a format as GIF when it comes to supporting desirable Web page effects. However, a relatively new type of JPEG, called a progressive JPEG or p-JPEG, provides an analogy to the interlaced GIF. A p-JPEG is stored as a series of scans that together comprise the entire image. When the first scan is read in, users see a blocky approximation of the whole image, so they can quickly get an idea of what they're ultimately going to see. As subsequent scans are read in, the image comes into sharper focus.

N O T E People often ask if there will ever be transparent JPEGs. Unfortunately, the answer to this question is no. To understand why, recall that there is always some loss during JPEG compression/decompression. This means that some pixels are not colored with the same color they originally were.

Now suppose you've specified a transparent color for the JPEG. If a pixel originally colored with the transparent color is assigned a new color due to the loss, then that pixel will no longer be transparent. Similarly, nontransparent pixels could be colored with the transparent color after compression/decompression, meaning that they will end up being transparent. Either way, you get the opposite of what you wanted and the on-screen results would be disastrous.

Unless JPEG is changed to become a lossless format, there is little hope of there ever being transparent JPEGs. ■

When to Use GIF or JPEG

Given that you have the choice between two formats for Web graphics, you may find yourself wondering when to use one or the other. To help you answer that question, review some guidelines below.

You have to use a GIF if you want transparency or animation, since it's the only format that supports them. Beyond that, you should consider GIF for the following types of images:

- Black-and-white line art and text
- Images with a limited number of distinct colors
- Graphics with sharp or distinct edges (most menus, buttons, and graphs fit this category)
- Graphics that are overlaid with text

JPEG is better suited for the following situations:

- Scanned photographs and ray-traced renderings
- Images that contain a complex mixture of colors
- Any image that requires a palette of more than 256 colors

Because the compression computations work better with a continuum of color, the JPEG format is not well suited to images that have very sharp color changes.

Up and Coming: PNG

GIF and JPEG are currently the two principal Web formats, but there's a new kid on the block that shows a great deal of promise. The Portable Network Graphics (PNG) format has been defined as a network standard by the World Wide Web Consortium (W3C).

PNG is described as "an extensible file format for the lossless, portable, well-compressed storage of raster (bitmapped) images. PNG provides a patent-free replacement for the GIF format and can also replace many common uses of the older TIFF format. Indexed-color, grayscale, and true color images are supported. PNG is designed to work well in online viewing applications, such as the World Wide Web, and so it is fully streamable with a progressive display option." Look for PNG graphics to become more prevalent on the Web as this new standard is adopted. It is already supported by Internet Explorer 4.0 and Netscape Communicator 4.0.

ON THE WEB

You can find out more about the PNG graphics format on the W3C Web site at **http://www.w3.org/ Graphics/PNG/**.

Making Good Use of Images

While it is true that a properly designed image can enhance a document, a poorly designed image can detract from it. Graphic images certainly have their place in Web documents, and in fact, they are expected in many places by users. The next few sections look at the types of graphics commonly found on the Web and give you some tips on how to maximize the effectiveness of each kind.

Main Page Graphics

If you've visited many Web sites, you've very likely noticed the tendency to put a large graphic on the main page of a site that lets a visitor navigate to all of the major sections of the site. Such a graphic is a good idea for many reasons. It lets the user know right away what major content sections are available. Additionally, it lets the site designer establish a visual look for each section, which can be helpful to users later as they navigate through the site. But there are pitfalls to this type of image. Here are some things to think about:

- *Keep the file size small*. Forcing users to wait a long time for a large image to load can prompt them to interrupt the loading and move on to another site. Make sure that your main-page graphics are a reasonable size—somewhere between 50K and 100K, if possible.

- *Be consistent.* Use the graphics elements (color, icons, headings) that you associate with each content section consistently throughout the site. This gives visitors a better chance of figuring out where they are and how to get to where they want to go.

- *Provide a text-based alternative.* Users with text-only browsers, or who have image loading turned off, won't be able to see your main-page graphic at all. Be sure to include a set of hypertext links that these users can use to navigate to the major areas of your site.

Your main-page graphic is the first thing users will see when visiting your site and sets the tone for the rest of their time there. The best rule of thumb for this kind of graphics is to make sure it is eye-catching and distinctive, without falling prey to one of the issues above.

Icons

Icons are small graphics that are meant to represent a certain content section or piece of information on your site. Commonly used icons include a question mark for Help and Frequently Asked Questions (FAQ) sections or a magnifying glass for a search engine.

Because icons are small, file size is usually not a problem. Icons download quickly and, once they are in a user's cache, can be reused again and again without further downloading. But an icon's smallness can also be a disadvantage because you have to pack a very specific concept into a fairly small part of the screen. For this reason, your chief concern when designing icons is *intuitiveness*. Users should be able to look at an icon and almost immediately discern what it means.

The best way to see if your icons are intuitive is to test them with a group of users as you're designing the site. A commonly used test involves presenting users with a set of potential icons and asking them to write down what they think each icon represents. If you find that most users interpret an icon the same way, you can feel pretty good about using that icon to represent the idea they say it does. If there's no clear interpretation of an icon, you should scrap it or send it back to the drawing board.

Once you have chosen your icons, be sure to use them consistently. This helps to reinforce their meaning with the user and makes navigating your site much less stressful.

N O T E If you expect a global audience to visit your site, you also need to consider how your icons will be interpreted by users from cultures different from your own. This typically requires trying out your icons on users from those cultures, if at all possible. ▪

Navigation Bars

Very large sites have to support the user with some kind of navigation aid. Navigation image-maps are frequently found at the top or bottom (and sometimes both) of a document and give the user single click access to the major content areas of the site and other useful resources like a table of contents or a search engine. You may also include some navigation options that point to places within a given section of a site, particularly if the user has had to drill down several levels to get to a document.

Navigation graphics present some of the same design issues as main-page graphics. These include the following:

- *Being consistent.* Consistency is much more important at this level, since the user may have forgotten what the main-page graphic looks like. Be sure to incorporate the visual cues you built into your main-page graphic when you design navigation graphics, and also make use of your icons. If you have an iconographic representation of each section of your site, you can line them up in a row to produce a simple navigation bar that the user should be able to use easily.

  Consistency also applies to where you place the navigation graphic in a document. If users see navigation options at the bottom of the first few pages they see, they'll come to expect it to be there on every page.

- *Providing a text-based alternative.* Again, you can't forget about users who can't see graphics or who have shut them off. Make sure there is always a set of hypertext links available that duplicates the links found in the navigation graphic.

Backgrounds

A well-chosen background image can make a page look very distinctive. Many corporate sites have a faded version of the company logo in the background. This approach reinforces the company's corporate identity, while not being so obtrusive that it obscures the primary content of the document.

Another popular approach to background images is to use a very small pattern that is tiled to fill the browser window. Typically these files are very small and load quickly. However, if the tiling isn't smooth, it can produce seams on the page that can distract a user. Fortunately, more and more graphics programs are including a tessellating function that allows you to produce seamless tiling in all directions when using a tiled background pattern. Both Paint Shop Pro and Adobe Photoshop come with this useful feature.

 Whether you're using a large image or tiling a small image in your background, you can use the BGCOLOR attribute of the <BODY> tag to immediately paint the background with a color that approximates the dominant color of your background image. This smoothes over the transition to the image, and if the image fails to load, the user can at least have a sense of what color your background was supposed to be.

The worst thing you can do is use a background image that is so busy that it detracts from content in the foreground. If you're not using a solid color or a pattern, make sure that the visual elements in you background image are sufficiently muted so that they don't interfere with the user's ability to read and understand the content of your document.

Finding Graphics Online

Not everyone is lucky enough to have a team of digital graphic artists on staff to support a Web site. If your role as a Webmaster is "jack-of-all-trades," that most likely means you're responsible for graphic content as well. Fortunately, there are many sites on the Web that provide royalty-free graphics that you can download and use on your own site.

One particularly good public repository of graphics is Microsoft's Multimedia Gallery at **http://www.microsoft.com/workshop/design/mmgallry/**. Not only can you find icons, background patterns, and navigation graphics in the Gallery but you can also download audio clips as well!

One caution about using graphics from a public download site: other people might be using them too. This robs your site of a truly distinctive look and, in cases where the graphics are overused, can make your pages seem trite. Do you remember the little colored balls people used as bullets in a bulleted list? This is a classic example of an overused graphic. The colored balls even made a comeback as animated GIFs where the color of the ball cycles through many different colors!

Don't let your pages be common—try to customize the graphics you download to set them apart. One easy way to do this is to repaint the graphics in the color scheme of your site. This makes them seem more like they were designed just for your site.

Bandwidth Issues

As popular as graphics are with users, they can become immensely unpopular when they take forever to download. By keeping file sizes small, you minimize the time your users spend waiting to see your pages. A good rule of thumb is to keep each large image to between 50K and 100K. Icons should be even smaller—between 5K and 10K.

Think of Your Audience

Even with small file sizes, different users may have to wait different lengths of time for an image to download. A 50K image may transfer in just a few seconds over a T1 connection, but dial-up users who are limited to 14.4Kbps or 28.8Kbps may have to wait several minutes. Be sure to remember your users with slower connections when you design your graphics. You may even ask a few of them to test your image files to see if they require a long time to download.

 TIP   Don't forget to use the ALT attribute in your <IMG> tags so that the user can see a description of your image in case it fails to load.

Corporate intranet designers tend to be a little more fortunate in this department. Most intranet users are on a high-speed connection over the company's Wide Area Network (WAN). With such a homogeneous group, it's usually possible to design higher-end graphics and still have reasonable download times. You should still have some coworkers test your images though, especially those who are located a great distance from your server.

Tips for Reducing File Size

If you think you have an image file that's too big, don't despair! There are plenty of techniques for bringing the size down. Depending on the makeup of the image and the format you saved it in, you may want to try one of the following:

- *Resize the image.* Larger images take up more disk space because there are more pixels and, hence, more color information that has to be stored. By shrinking the height and width of an image to the smallest they can be, you take a big step toward making the file as small as it can be.

> **CAUTION**
>
> Always resize an image in a graphics program, keeping the aspect ratio the same. If you try to use the WIDTH and HEIGHT attributes of the <IMG> tag to resize the image, you're relying on the browser to do the resizing and you're likely to be disappointed with the results. Additionally, resizing with the browser doesn't save you download time because the original image file still has to be downloaded.
>
> ▶ **See** "Adding Inline Images to Your HTML Document," **p. 112**

- *Use thumbnails.* Thumbnails are very small versions of an image, usually a photograph. Because they're smaller, their file sizes are smaller too.
- *Store GIFs as JPEGs.* JPEG compression works best on images with lots of color gradation. If you have a GIF file that fits this description, try saving it as a JPEG to see if that makes the file any smaller.
- *Increase the compression ratio.* If you're working with a JPEG, you can resave it at a higher compression ratio to shrink the file size. But don't forget the trade-off: higher compression reduces the quality of the image.
- *Reduce the color depth.* Color depth is another way to express how many colors can be stored by a format. A GIF image has a color depth of 8 bits (256 colors)—but what if there are fewer than 256 colors in the image? In this case, you can reduce the color depth to a smaller number of bits per pixel. With less information to store per pixel, the resulting file will be smaller.
- *Adjust contrast levels in the image.* Contrast refers to the brightness of objects in the image relative to one another. Most popular graphics programs offer retouching options like gamma correction and highlight/midtone/shadow that change contrast within an image. By tweaking these values, you can usually bring down your file size.
- *Suppress dithering.* Dithering refers to the use of colors in an existing color palette to approximate colors that are not in the palette. Dithering tends to increase file size in GIFs because the GIF compression scheme is less efficient when adjacent pixels are painted with different colors. Disabling dithering will make more adjacent pixels have the same color so the compression can better shrink the file.

Working with Scanned Images

It's not always necessary to create your own graphics. In fact, it's very often convenient to scan something in (if you have access to a scanner) or use an image that someone else has already scanned in. Either approach is perfectly valid. No one will ever expect you to create all of your own images. When you do use a scanned image though, you should make sure that it really contributes to the message you're trying to convey in your document and that you're not just using it for the sake of using it.

> **CAUTION**
>
> Some people will let you use images that they scanned as long as you give them credit in your document. Make sure you acknowledge the sources of your scanned images.

When to Use Them and Where to Get Them

If you do have a flatbed scanner, making your own scanned images is a simple task. You can use the software that came with the scanner, or you can use a program like Photoshop or Paint Shop Pro.

If you're looking for existing scanned images, you can try any of the following sources:

- *Graphics service bureaus.* A graphics service house may have existing images you can use on a royalty basis. It can also probably scan images at a higher quality that you could on a desktop scanner.

- *Stock photo and clip art CD-ROMs.* Many companies sell CD-ROMs with stock photos and/or simple line art you can use. You usually have to acknowledge the producer of the CD in your document as the source of the images.

Manipulating Scanned Images

Scanned images invariably need some kind of touch-up done on them so they are a truer representation of the original. By zooming in on the scanned image in an editor, you can usually see imperfections along the edges of objects and in the coloring of pixels. Be sure to give your scan a good "once over" in this way so it can look its best in your document. (Most scanners come with some kind of image touchup software, like Adobe Photoshop.)

Useful Graphics Tools

Throughout this chapter, reference has been made to many different manipulations and edits you can make to an image. Now it's time to look at some of the programs you can use to make these modifications. The next five sections introduce you to the following image editing programs:

- Lview Pro
- Paint Shop Pro

- Adobe Photoshop
- Microsoft Image Composer
- GIF Construction Set

Each of these is a great graphics program in its own right. You should consider each one and then select the one that meets your needs and is within your budget.

This section concludes with a look at the GIF Construction Set, a shareware program you can use to create animated GIFs.

LView Pro

Lview Pro is a great shareware program you can use to edit existing graphics or to convert them to GIF or JPEG format. It offers many of the common manipulation features found in most paint programs plus several other options that give you very fine control over image appearance.

N O T E The information on LView Pro presented here is based on the evaluation copy of version 1.D2. You can download the latest version of LView Pro by pointing your browser to **http:// www.lview.com/**. A license costs $30 U.S. plus $5 U.S. for shipping and handling. ■

Figure 22.6 shows the LView Pro window along with its extensive tool palette. Almost every tool in the palette corresponds directly to one of LView Pro's menu options.

FIG. 22.6
LView Pro's tool palette enables you to make modifications to most aspects of an image.

The only LView Pro tool for creating anything is the Add Text tool. It stands to reason that you'll probably have to use a different program to create your graphics. But, what LView Pro lacks in ability to create, it makes up for with its ability to make very particular changes to an image. These program features are found under the Edit and Retouch menus.

The Edit Menu   LView Pro's Edit menu provides options for many of the basic manipulations that Paint can perform, including horizontal and vertical flips and rotations by 90 degrees to the right or left. The Add Text option, discussed above, is also found under the Edit menu.

The Resize and Redimension options can create some confusion for the user who is unfamiliar with them. Resize changes the dimensions of an image, with the option to retain the image's aspect ratio (the ratio of the width and height). When you resize, you can choose from a standard set of sizes or you can enter your own size. Redimension lets you choose from only the standard set of sizes and doesn't permit you to keep the same aspect ratio.

The Capture option under the Edit menu does a screen capture of either the Desktop, the Window, or the Client Area. When you invoke one of the screen capture options, LView Pro will minimize itself and capture the region that you requested on-screen.

The Retouch Menu   The options under LView Pro's Retouch menu really expand the program beyond a simple graphics manipulator. One option of note is Gamma Correction, a parameter that can impact the contrast in an image (and therefore the size of the image file). Gamma correction is used to increase or decrease the brightness of pixels in the image. You can set gamma correction values for Red, Green, and Blue color components separately by moving the scrollbar next to each color. A gamma correction value greater than zero will brighten the color, and values less than zero will darken the color. If you want to adjust the gamma correction for all three colors simultaneously, check the Lock RGB Scrollbars check box. This moves all three scrollbars whenever you move any one of them. To reduce the size of an image file, you can reduce the contrast in the image. This means you want a negative value for gamma correction.

Another useful option under the Retouch menu is Palette Entry. Choosing this option calls up the Select Color Palette Entry dialog box, shown in Figure 22.7. From this dialog box, you can select one of the colors in the current image's palette and change its RGB color specification. You can also select the image's transparent color from this dialog box.

FIG. 22.7

Changing a particular palette color is easy with the Palette Entry option of the Retouch menu.

A final Retouch option of interest is Color Depth (see Figure 22.8). This option is used to select a True Color image (24 bits per pixel, 16.7 million colors) or a Palette image (up to 8 bits per pixel and 256 colors). Palette images can be two colors (black and white), 16 colors (like the default Windows palette), 256 colors (as with a GIF image), or a custom number of colors. If you're decreasing your color depth, you may want to activate Floyd-Steinberg dithering, a process that uses combinations of colors in the palette to approximate colors that are not in the palette.

FIG. 22.8
If you need to reduce your color depth to make an image file smaller, you can do it in Lview Pro from the Color Depth dialog box.

LView Pro Properties Settings   The Properties dialog box (choose File, Properties) lets you do much more than set up retouch instructions. There are 11 different tabs on the panel that enable you to configure LView Pro to run according to your own image editing preferences.

Two of the tabs deserve special attention because of their relevance to creating Web graphics. The GIF tab, shown in Figure 22.9, has two check boxes that can be used to instruct LView Pro to save a GIF file as either interlaced or transparent.

FIG. 22.9
LView Pro can make interlaced and transparent GIFs if you tell it to do so.

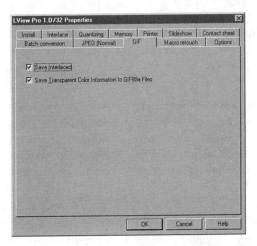

N O T E   To designate the transparent color in LView Pro, choose Retouch, Background Color and select the color you want to be the background color from the palette you see. When you save the image as a transparent GIF, the background color will become the transparent color. ■

The other noteworthy tab is the JPEG tab, shown in Normal mode in Figure 22.10. From this tab you can choose compression and decompression options, including progressive decompression for making a progressive JPEG.

FIG. 22.10

LView Pro can also make a progressive JPEG once you activate progressive compression.

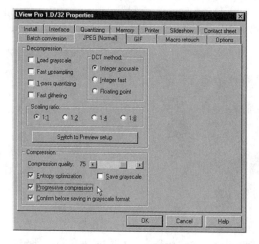

Paint Shop Pro

Another good shareware program for graphics work is Paint Shop Pro from JASC, Inc. Paint Shop Pro handles many types of image storage formats, enables you to do the most common image manipulations, and even comes with a screen capture facility.

Figure 22.11 shows an image loaded into Paint Shop Pro, along with the many available tool panels that give you single-click access to Paint Shop Pro's functions. The Zoom panel lets you zoom in to magnifications as high as 16:1 and out to magnifications as low as 1:16. Tools located on the Select panel allow you to sample colors, move the image around in the window, define a custom area of the image to clone or resize, and change the foreground and background colors.

The Paint panel is a welcome addition that was not available in earlier versions of Paint Shop Pro. It supports 22 different tools you can use to make your own graphics. These tools enable you to create brush, pen, pencil, marker, and chalk effects; draw lines, rectangles, and circles; fill a closed region with color; add text; and sharpen or soften part of an image. The Histogram window displays a graphic representation of the luminance of all colors in the image, measured with respect to the brightest color.

 You can toggle any of the tool panels on or off by using the options found under the View menu.

Paint Shop Pro's versatility enables you to open images stored in 25 bitmapped formats, including GIF and JPEG, and 9 meta/vector formats (image components stored as geometric shapes that combine to produce the entire image), including CorelDRAW!, Micrografx, and Ventura.

However, it can save in only one of the raster formats. Nevertheless, Paint Shop Pro is still handy for converting to bitmapped formats. The Batch Conversion option under the File menu lets you select any number of files to convert to a new storage format (see Figure 22.12).

FIG. 22.11
Paint Shop Pro's tool panels give you easy access to common painting and image manipulation.

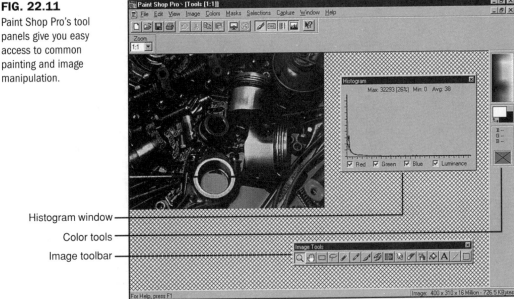

Histogram window —
Color tools —
Image toolbar —

FIG. 22.12
Have a bunch of files to convert? Paint Shop Pro can be set up to handle them all at once.

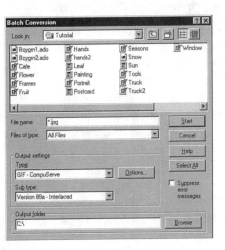

TWAIN refers to a set of industry standards that allows graphics programs to work with image acquisition hardware like scanners. If you have a TWAIN-compliant scanner attached to your computer, you can use the File, Acquire option to scan in a new image. The Select Source option, also under the File menu, lets you choose which device you want to use for the acquisition.

The Image menu includes the options used to do many of the standard manipulations like flipping the image upside down, creating a mirror image of an image, and rotating the images. The Image, Resample option is used to change the size of an image, without the jagged edges caused by standard resizing. You'll also find several effect filters under the Image menu that let you add or remove noise, enhance darker or lighter colors, and blur (sharpen or soften) the image. You can even define effect filters of your own.

The Colors menu is host to many of the advanced image manipulations you read about in the LView Pro section, including adjustment of brightness, gamma correction, RGB values, and conversion to grayscale or photographic negative versions of an image. You can also load, modify, and save color palettes from the Colors menu. The Increase and Decrease Color Depth options allow you to change the number of colors being used to render the image.

Paint Shop Pro adds some color editing functionality that LView Pro doesn't have. The Highlight/Midtone/Shadow option under the Adjust pop-up list lets you skew an image's contrast to emphasize highlights, shadows, or mid-range colors. The posterizing effect (choose Colors, Posterize) makes the image look more like a poster by reducing the number of bits used per RGB color channel. You can also use the Colors, Solarize option to invert colors that are above a luminance level you specify.

One very useful feature of Paint Shop Pro is its screen and window capture facility. Options in the Capture, Setup dialog box are used to capture the whole screen, a single window on the screen, the client area inside a window, or a user-defined area. You can also choose whether the mouse pointer should be included in the capture and which hotkey will activate the capture.

The current release of Paint Shop Pro comes bundled with many more special effects filters than in previous versions. These include the following effects:

- *Add Drop Shadow.* Drop shadows are a great way to make your graphics appear to float over the document. The Add Drop Shadow function makes it simple to add drop shadows to your images. Just make sure that you use a common light source for images that will be placed on the same page.

- *Create Seamless Pattern.* Earlier in this chapter, it was noted that background images are often small files that are read in and tiled to fill the browser window. To avoid seams between tiled copies of the same image, you need to tessellate the edges of the image so that they come together smoothly. Paint Shop Pro has automated this procedure with the Create Seamless Pattern function.

- *Cutout.* The Cutout function allows you to remove a section of an image, allowing you to see through it to what lies behind it.

- *Chisel.* Applying the Chisel function to a selected area of an image transforms it to make it appear as if it were chiseled out of stone.

- *Buttonize.* You can use the Buttonize function to apply a three-dimensional border to a selected portion of an image to make it appear raised. This is especially useful in creating clickable buttons that readers can use to select different navigation options.

- *Hot Wax Coating.* Rather than holding a burning candle over an image on your computer monitor, you can avail yourself of the Hot Wax Coating effect to make it look like you did.

Additionally, you can install Adobe Photoshop-compatible plug-ins and define your own effect filters.

When it comes to saving an image as a GIF or JPEG, Paint Shop Pro can handle the basic format, as well as most of the associated effects. About all that Paint Shop Pro won't do is allow you to save a progressive JPEG.

Paint Shop Pro is a very capable image editing program. You can also purchase it bundled with Kai's Power Tools SE for added functionality. To order this combination package, contact JASC sales at 1-800-622-2793. For more information about Kai's Power Tools, consult **http://www.metatools.com/**. To learn more about Paint Shop Pro, direct your browser to **http://www.jasc.com/**.

Adobe Photoshop

Adobe promotes Photoshop as the "camera for your mind," but it's really much more—it's the premier software package for doing graphical manipulations. You can use Photoshop to create your own original artwork, scan in an image, or make edits to an existing image. Photoshop can read in files stored in over a dozen formats and save them in just as many formats, including GIF and JPEG.

Making Your Own Artwork   Photoshop supports you in graphics creation with an extensive toolbar, located on the left side of the window (see Figure 22.13). You can choose tools for placing text, filling regions, drawing lines, airbrushing, painting, freehand drawing, smudging, blurring, and lightening.

FIG. 22.13
Many of the drawing options found in other image creation programs are available in Photoshop as well.

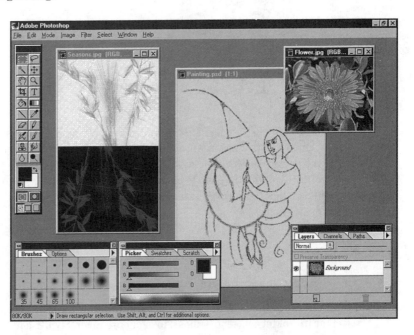

Many toolbar tools have special options available in the dialog box at the bottom left of the Photoshop window.

Layers and Channels   One of Photoshop's nicest features is image layers—different levels of the image you can overlay to produce the entire image. Figure 22.14 shows an image that uses layers. The sun is on a separate layer from the checkered background, but when the two are superimposed, they produce the desired image.

FIG. 22.14

Layers separate the different components of an image into their own separate entities so you can work on them individually.

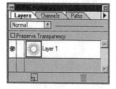

A graphic element in a given layer can be painted with RGB color, and Photoshop will provide access to each component color through color channels. Figure 22.15 shows the channels for the sun layer from the graphic in Figure 22.14. The sun is painted yellow, which is formed by a combination of green and blue. Notice in Figure 22.15 that there is no contribution from the red channel—only from the green and blue channels.

FIG. 22.15

Color channels split a color into its individual red, green, and blue components.

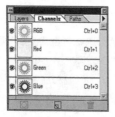

Web Graphics Effects   Photoshop can help you apply a number of desirable effects to Web graphics. One important one is anti-aliasing, a process that softens the jagged edges that often occur at a boundary between two different colors. Anti-aliasing an edge is fairly easy to do. You just select the item with the edge to be anti-aliased by using the Lasso tool (freehand region selection) and then check the Anti-aliased box on the Options tab in the dialog box at the bottom-left of the window.

N O T E   Anti-aliasing is available when using the magic wand, fill, and line tools as well. ■

Embossing is an effect that makes an image look "raised," just as lettering on an engraved invitation is raised. Photoshop has an embossing filter that is easy to apply to an image. You select the part of the image to emboss, then choose Filter, Stylize, and then select the Emboss option from the pop-up list that appears. An image and its embossed equivalent are shown in Figure 22.16.

FIG. 22.16

Embossing "raises" parts of an image and gives your pages the illusion of depth.

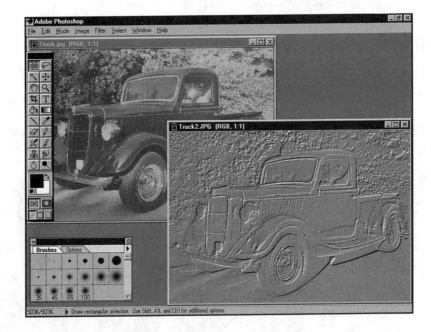

Photoshop also supports saving files in GIF, interlaced GIF, transparent GIF, JPEG, and progressive JPEG formats, although plug-in programs are required to accomplish this. Two of the most popular plug-ins are PhotoGIF and ProJPEG from BoxTop Software, Inc. You can download the latest versions from BoxTop's Web site at **http://www.boxtopsoft.com/**.

So Much More!   Trite as it may sound, Photoshop is much more than what has been noted here. Some of the program's other handy features include the following:

- Numerous built-in effects filters and many more available from plug-in programs (Kai's Power Tools is one set of utilities that is particularly well integrated into Photoshop.)
- Options for dithering to lower color depths and different color palettes
- Highly efficient memory management
- A flawless interface with other Adobe products like Illustrator and PageMaker

Photoshop is a powerful image creation and modification tool that makes a worthy addition to your software library. For many folks, the limiting factor is often price, since Photoshop can cost between $500 and $1,000 per license, depending on which platform you're running it. Students can obtain a "light" version of Photoshop at a substantial discount. If you're running a highly graphical Web site and you can afford Photoshop, you should seriously consider purchasing it as your graphics tool of choice.

N O T E   For a fuller treatment of Photoshop and its many features, consult Que's *Special Edition Using Photoshop 3 for Macintosh*. The Windows version of Photoshop 3 has the same functionality, although the interface may be different in places. ■

Microsoft Image Composer

Microsoft continues to expand its software offerings that support Internet publishing by producing Microsoft Image Composer (see Figure 22.17), which is a feature-rich, image-editing program that works with Microsoft FrontPage and the Microsoft GIF Animator.

FIG. 22.17

Microsoft Image Composer comes bundled with either Microsoft FrontPage or Microsoft's Visual InterDev.

Image Composer breaks new ground in developing graphics for Web documents by introducing *sprite technology*. Put simply, a sprite is an image whose shape is not necessarily rectangular (like it would be in any other image program). Instead, a sprite's shape is exactly the shape of the object in the image. Microsoft provides a good example on one of its Image Composer Web pages (see Figure 22.18). The image on the left is a sprite. It does have a rectangular bounding box, but the image's shape is that of the bunch of flowers. The image on the right would be done in a traditional image editor. You could make the black background transparent to achieve the same effect you get in the sprite, but this would require extra steps that aren't needed with Image Composer.

> **CAUTION**
> Macromedia Director users should not confuse Image Composer sprites with Director sprites. Although they share the same name, they are not the same thing.

FIG. 22.18

A sprite is an image that takes on the shape of the object in it, instead of just being rectangular.

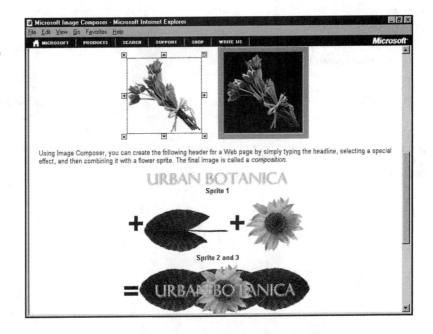

Sprites are made possible by an Image Composer feature called the *alpha channel*. Every sprite has a built-in, 8-bit (256 color) alpha channel that stores transparency information. This means you can have up to 256 levels of transparency—much more flexible than the single transparent color you get in a transparent GIF! You can use the levels of transparency to seamlessly overlay sprites (refer to Figure 22.18) and create eye-catching effects. When you've finished your composition, you can export the whole thing as a GIF and place it in any of your Web documents.

Beyond sprite technology, Image Composer offers many of the things you'd want in a graphics editing program. It saves images in both the GIF (including transparent GIF) and JPEG formats. You get all of the standard image creation tools like paint, fill, text, and shapes. Further, you get over 500 different special effects filters that include the following:

- Angled strokes
- Dry brush
- Fresco
- Halftone screen
- Neon glow
- Pencil sketch
- Stained glass

Those are just a few. Image Composer can also work with Adobe-compatible plug-ins like Kai's Power Tools 3.0, KPT Convolver, and Andromeda Series 1 Photography. The Impressionist plug-in package is shipped with Image Composer, and the effects found in Adobe Gallery Effects 1.51 are resident in Image Composer already.

ON THE WEB

For more information about Microsoft Image Composer, point your Web browser to **http://www.microsoft.com/imagecomposer/**.

N O T E   Don't forget about Alchemy Mindworks' excellent program GIF Construction Set, which is covered in detail in Chapter 25, "Animation." ■

T I P   Macintosh users should check out GifBuilder for creating animated GIFs.

## CHAPTER 23

Audio

by Mark R. Brown

In this chapter

Playing Audio Files

There are three different kinds of audio files your computer can play: digitized audio, music files, and text-to-speech. Text-to-speech is a technique for converting text files into (somewhat) recognizable speech by replacing the letters with phonemes. The Macintosh is particularly adept at this. Music files are like sheet music—they specify a sequence of notes and the "instruments" to play them. MIDI music files are the most popular format in this category. Digitized audio is sound that has been run through an analog-to-digital converter to turn it into data. Your PC's system sounds are WAV format files that are digitized audio.

> **N O T E** Audio CD tracks are also digitized audio files, but they are decoded and played directly by your CD player's circuitry. As you may have found out at one time or another, your computer can crash and potentially leave an audio CD playing happily away, blithely unaware of your system failure. ■

Audio plug-ins are available for all varieties of digitized sound files, as well as MIDI music and speech. When you want to add audio to an HTML document, you'll likely rely on one of these plug-ins to play your sounds. This chapter steps through many of the most popular audio plug-ins for browser programs, and tells you how to add plug-in–compatible sounds to your HTML documents.

Audio Hardware: What You Need

Back in the "good old days" of personal computing—when "PC" was always followed by "XT", processor numbers were only four digits long, and software ran directly off floppy disks—every PC shipped with a tinny little AM-radio quality speaker that beeped nastily at you any time you did something wrong. Some masochists (the kind who like to scrape their fingernails on blackboards) even wrote a few annoying DOS programs that played what they claimed to be digitized sounds on that little speaker. But no normal human being ever heard a single recognizable sound in the cacophonous din that emanated from a PC when those programs ran.

Now that we're in the high-tech age of multimedia computers—complete with 24-bit True Color animations, 16-bit stereo music soundtracks, and digitized CD-ROM voice-overs by the likes of Star Trek's Patrick Stewart—all PCs still ship with that same nasty, tinny little speaker.

To get real audio out of your PC, you need a sound card. If you bought your computer recently, or if you've spent a few bucks upgrading, the odds are good you already have a sound card. If you don't, you can pick one up for anywhere between $30 and $800, depending on what you want it to do.

A good 16-bit stereo Sound Blaster Pro (or compatible) sound card does just about everything the average person needs done audio-wise, and does it for under $100. If you haven't invested in a sound card yet, drop this book right now, scan a few computer magazine reviews and ads, run to your local computer store, buy a sound card, and plug it in. You'll need one for any sound player plug-in you might choose to use.

LiveAudio

Because it ships with Netscape Navigator 3.0 and beyond, the LiveAudio plug-in is essentially the "official" Netscape audio player. Unlike many other audio plug-ins, LiveAudio doesn't use a proprietary sound-file format, but instead plays industry standard AIFF, .AU, MIDI, and .WAV files. LiveAudio features an easy-to-use console with play, pause, stop, and volume controls.

N O T E Over 70 percent of the people surfing into your site will be using Netscape Navigator as their Web browser. About 25 percent will be using Microsoft Internet Explorer. Both handle most audio in the same way, via an audio player plug-in. "Netscape" plug-ins are 99.99 percent compatible with Internet Explorer, so what we say here about them applies to IE, as well. ■

As long as your system is equipped with a sound card, LiveAudio enables you to listen to audio tracks, sound effects, music, and voice files embedded in Web pages. You can also use LiveAudio to listen to stand-alone sound files on the Web, on a local area network, and on your own computer system.

LiveAudio is a huge improvement over the NAPlayer audio helper application that Netscape shipped with versions of Netscape Navigator prior to version 3.0. Where NAPlayer played only Sun/NeXT (.AU and .SND) and Mac/SGI (.AIF and .AIFF) sound files, LiveAudio automatically identifies and plays four of the most popular standard sound formats:

- .AIFF, the Macintosh/SGI sound format
- .AU, the Sun/NeXT sound format
- MIDI, the Musical Instrument Digital Interface music format
- .WAV, the Microsoft Windows sound format

.AU files were once the Internet standard file format; .AIFF files are the Macintosh standard; and .WAV files are the Windows standard file; so LiveAudio can play a good percentage of the nonproprietary sound files that you're likely to encounter on the Web. Add its capability to play MIDI music, and LiveAudio proves itself a very good "Swiss Army Knife" plug-in for Web audio.

LiveAudio Controls

When you encounter a LiveAudio-compatible sound file embedded or linked into a Web page, LiveAudio creates the on-screen control console shown in Figure 23.1.

The LiveAudio plug-in works with both embedded sound files, like the two it encountered in Figure 23.1, and with stand-alone sound files. In the case of stand-alone files, a blank Netscape window displays only a LiveAudio console.

N O T E An embedded file is one that appears inline in an HTML document. A stand-alone file is one you load by itself, either from the Internet or from your own system. ■

FIG. 23.1

The LiveAudio plug-in appears as a minimalist inline audio-player control console.

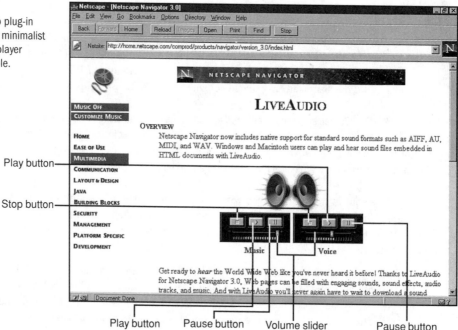

The LiveAudio console controls are intuitive and easy to use (see Figure 23.1). The Stop, Play, and Pause buttons work just as they do on a tape or CD player. You click the Play button to play the sound, the Stop button to stop it, and the Pause button to pause audio playback. If you click the Pause button a second time, play resumes from the point at which you paused the sound.

Click to the right or left of the Volume slider knob to increase or decrease volume. The volume can be jumped only in increments of 20 percent—you can't slide the volume smoothly from 0 percent to 100 percent. The light-emitting diode (LED) bar graph below the Volume slider indicates the current volume level. The dark green LEDs are for the 0–40 percent range; light green LEDs take over for 40–100 percent.

Right-clicking the LiveAudio console displays the pop-up menu shown in Figure 23.1. This menu includes selections that duplicate the Play, Stop, and Pause buttons. The menu also provides a selection to display the program's About dialog box and a final nonselectable menu item that tells you the volume level as a percentage of the maximum.

The LiveAudio player has a single keyboard hot key: the spacebar. Pressing the spacebar reactivates whichever button you pressed last (Stop, Play, or Pause). Restopping an already stopped playback is of limited use, but if you last pressed Pause, the spacebar becomes an unpause/repause toggle. If you last pressed Play, the spacebar becomes a handy replay key.

Using the *<EMBED>* Tag with LiveAudio

The <EMBED> tag is used to embed plug-in content on an HTML page, and the way in which a page designer uses the <EMBED> tag often determines how plug-in content is displayed.

For example, the <EMBED> tag's attributes control several different aspects of the LiveAudio plug-in's functionality. Here's a typical example:

```
<EMBED SRC="audio.aif" WIDTH=144 HEIGHT=60 AUTOSTART=false VOLUME=100
    CONTROLS=Console>
```

This example plays the Macintosh format sound file AUDIO.AIF (SRC="audio.aif") only when the user presses the Play button (AUTOSTART=false). The LiveAudio control window is 144 pixels wide (WIDTH=144) and 60 pixels high (HEIGHT=60) and contains a complete control console (CONTROLS=Console).

Table 23.1 lists all the attributes associated with the <EMBED> tag for the LiveAudio plug-in, as well as their legal values. All attributes are optional except for SRC, WIDTH, and HEIGHT, which are generally required when embedding plug-in content.

Table 23.1 *<EMBED>* Tag Attributes for the LiveAudio Plug-In

Attribute	Values
SRC="*filename*"	A file name with an extension associated with a MIME type assigned to be played by LiveAudio (.AU, .AIFF, .AIF, .WAV, .MIDI, or .MID). Required.
WIDTH=*integer*	The control console width in pixels. Required.
HEIGHT=*integer*	The control console height in pixels. Required.
AUTOSTART=TRUE|FALSE	If True, the sound clip plays automatically. The default is False.
AUTOLOAD=TRUE|FALSE	If False, the sound clip does not automatically load. The default is True.
STARTTIME="*mm:ss*"	The start time in minutes and seconds from the start of the clip. The default is 00:00.
ENDTIME="*mm:ss*"	The end time in minutes and seconds from the start of the clip. The default is the end of the clip.
VOLUME=*percentage*	Playback volume expressed as a percentage of the maximum. The default is the last previously set volume.
ALIGN="*value*"	The point at which to align the control panel with respect to adjoining text. The possible values are CENTER, BASELINE, TOP, LEFT, and RIGHT. BASELINE is the default.

continues

Part

IV

Ch

23

Table 23.1 Continued

Attribute	Values
CONTROLS="*value*"	The controls to include on the control panel. The values can be CONSOLE, SMALLCONSOLE, PLAYBUTTON, PAUSEBUTTON, STOPBUTTON, or VOLUMELEVER. The remainder of this table describes the sets of controls associated with each of these values. The default is CONSOLE.
CONSOLE	A full set of controls: Play, Pause, Stop, and Volume.
SMALLCONSOLE	A reduced set of controls consisting of Play, Stop, and Volume. AUTOSTART defaults to True.
PLAYBUTTON	The Play button only.
PAUSEBUTTON	The Pause button only.
STOPBUTTON	The Stop button. Also, the sound file unloads.
VOLUMELEVER	The Volume control only.
CONSOLE="*name*"	A combination of controls that enables you to include multiple sound clips on a page. For example, you could specify CONSOLE="MySetup" as an attribute on two <EMBED> lines on a single HTML page; then each line would use the controls defined by the other as well as its own.

N O T E If you specify the settings CONTROLS="VolumeLever" and CONSOLE="_MASTERVOLUME", the user changes the system's master volume (not just the sound clip's volume) by manipulating the volume slider. ■

If you need to set up a Web server to deliver LiveAudio-compatible content, you first must set up the proper MIME types. How you do so varies with the specific server software; check your server documentation or ask your system administrator to set up the following MIME types, shown in Table 23.2, with associated filename extensions:

Table 23.2 MIME Types for LiveAudio

MIME Type	Extensions
audio/basic	.AU
audio/x-aiff	.AIF, .AIFF
audio/aiff	.AIF, .AIFF
audio/x-wav	.WAV
audio/wav	.WAV

MIME Type	Extensions
audio/x-midi	.MID, .MIDI
audio/midi	.MID, .MIDI

The <EMBED> tag works similarly with other plug-ins, though they may specify their own attributes.

Other Audio Plug-Ins

Though LiveAudio is bundled with Netscape Navigator, there are many, many more audio plug-ins available for delivering audio content in your HTML documents. This section takes a quick look at a few of the most popular.

N O T E   The latest version of Macromedia's Shockwave for Director plug-in—originally just for playing multimedia presentations—now includes the ability to play streaming audio in real time—that is, you don't have to download an audio file completely before beginning to play it. Macromedia is now enthusiastically promoting Shockwave as a viable alternative to an audio-only delivery medium. You might want to check it out, especially if you intend on delivering multimedia content in your documents, as well as audio. Macromedia's Web site is at

http://www.macromedia.com/ ▓

TrueSpeech

If nothing else, TrueSpeech is convenient. If you're using Windows 3.1 or Windows 95, the supplied Sound Recorder program can digitize sound files and convert them to TrueSpeech format. You can then use the TrueSpeech player to listen to them on the Web in real time. Despite its name, TrueSpeech can be used for any type of audio file. You don't need a special server. You can download TrueSpeech players for Windows 3.1, Windows 95, Windows NT, Macintosh, and PowerMac from the DSP Group's home page at **http://www.dspg.com**.

Crescendo and Crescendo Plus

Most sound cards go a step beyond merely digitizing and playing back sounds. They can also generate their own sounds. If your sound card is MIDI-compatible (as most are), you have more than a passive record-and-playback system—you have a full-fledged music synthesizer. With a MIDI plug-in, you can experience Web sites with a full music soundtrack.

LiveUpdate's Crescendo plug-in enables Navigator to play inline MIDI music embedded in Web pages. With a MIDI-capable browser, you can create Web pages that have their own background music soundtracks. Because MIDI instruments can be sampled sounds, you can also create sound-effects tracks.

Crescendo requires an MPC (MIDI-capable) sound card and Navigator version 2.0 or above. The plug-in launches automatically and invisibly and is a fun addition to Web browsing.

 Crescendo is available for Windows 95 and Windows NT, Windows 3.1, and Macintosh. You can download Crescendo at **http://www.liveupdate.com/midi.html**.

An enhanced version, Crescendo Plus, adds on-screen controls and live streaming. With the live streaming feature, you don't have to wait for a MIDI file to download completely before it starts playing. You can purchase Crescendo Plus also from LiveUpdate's Web site.

ToolVox

If all you need is speech, three kinds of speech plug-ins are available for Navigator:

- Players for digitized audio that is of less-than-music quality.
- Text-to-speech converters, currently available only for the Macintosh.
- Speech recognition plug-ins, which are also for the Macintosh only

ToolVox provides audio compression ratios of up to 53:1, which creates very small files that transfer quickly over the Internet. Speech can be delivered in real time even over 9,600-baud modems. One unique feature is you can slow down playback to improve comprehension, or speed it up to shorten listening times without changing voice pitch.

Like the higher-fidelity RealAudio (which is discussed in the Chapter 27, "Streaming Audio"), ToolVox streams audio in real time, so you don't have to wait for a file to download before you can listen to it.

ToolVox doesn't need special server software to deliver audio content from your Web server. The player, in the form of a Navigator plug-in, controls buffering and playback. As a result, any standard HTML server can act as a streaming media server. Even the encoder is free. It compresses a speech file from .WAV format to an 8kHz, 2,400 bits-per-second (bps) VOX file.

Voxware has also announced plans to release ToolVox Gold, an enhanced version of ToolVox.

 ToolVox Navigator plug-ins are available for Windows 3.1 and Windows 95. Voxware also promises Macintosh and PowerMac versions. You can download these plug-ins from the Voxware site at **http://www.voxware.com/download.htm**.

EchoSpeech

EchoSpeech compresses speech at a ratio of 18.5:1. Therefore, 16-bit speech sampled at 11,025Hz is compressed to 9,600bps. Even users with 14.4kbps modems can listen to real-time EchoSpeech audio streams. Because EchoSpeech is designed to code speech sampled at 1,1025Hz rather than 8,000Hz, EchoSpeech files sound better than ToolVox.

Real-time decoding of 11kHz speech requires only 30 percent of a 486SX-33 CPU's time. EchoSpeech plug-ins are also small—40–50K when decompressed.

No server software is required to deliver EchoSpeech content; your Internet service provider (ISP) or server administrator need only declare a new MIME type and pay a one-time $99 license fee. To add EchoSpeech files to your Web pages, you compress them with the EchoSpeech Speech Coder (available for evaluation with free downloading) and then use the HTML <EMBED> tag to include the files in your documents.

EchoSpeech is available for Windows 3.1, Windows 95, and Macintosh. You can get EchoSpeech at **http://www.echospeech.com**.

Talker and Other Macintosh Speech Plug-Ins

MVP Solutions' Talker plug-in is just for the Macintosh. The plug-in uses the Macintosh's built-in PlainTalk speech-synthesis technology to create text-to-speech voice messages—in other words, Talker reads text files to you out loud. This plug-in uses much less bandwidth than recorded audio, and you can change the words that your Web page speaks by editing a text file.

Speech capability is one area in which Macintosh owners can claim a considerable edge over Windows and Windows 95 Navigator users—this plug-in will simply never work on those platforms because they lack the speech-synthesis technology of the Macintosh. You can find Talker at **http://www.mvpsolutions.com/PlugInSite/Talker.html**.

If you haven't yet installed Apple's English Text-to-Speech software on your Macintosh, you can download a copy of the software's installer from Apple's site at **ftp://ftp.info.apple.com/ Apple.Support.Area/Apple.Software.Updates/US/Macintosh/System/Speech/ PlainTalk_1.4.1/**.

William H. Tudor's Speech Plug-In for the Macintosh and PowerMac does essentially the same thing as Talker. You can get Tudor's plug-in at **http://www.albany.net/~wtudor/**.

Macintosh plug-ins aren't limited only to talking to you—they can also listen to you and understand what you're saying!

Bill Noon's ListenUp is for the Power Macintosh running System 7.5 or above. The plug-in also requires the PlainTalk Speech Recognition v1.5 program. You can find out all the details and download the plug-in at **http://snow.cit.cornell.edu/noon/ListenUp.html**.

Digital Dream's ShockTalk speech recognition plug-in isn't a Navigator plug-in at all; it's a plug-in for the Shockwave for Director plug-in. ShockTalk is available for Macintosh and PowerMac. You can find the plug-in at **http://www.surftalk.com/**.

More Sound Plug-Ins

If you can't get enough of listening to sound, this section describes a few more Navigator sound plug-ins.

 Arnaud Masson's MIDI plug-in is for the Macintosh and PowerMac only. You can get it at **http://www.planete.net/~amasson/**

Another Macintosh-only plug-in for MIDI files is GRAME's MidiShare. You can find this plug-in at **http://www.grame.fr/english/MidiShare.html**

Do you prefer the sound of the orient? Sseyo's Koan might better suite your taste. It plays real-time, computer-generated Japanese Koan music on Windows 3.1 and Windows 95 versions of Navigator. You can find Koan at **http://www.sseyo.com/**

DBA from Delta Beta (**http://www.deltabeta.com**) for Windows 95 is a player for audio files compressed in Delta Beta's .DBA format. (The compressor is freely downloadable.)

DSM Plug-in by Dmitry Boldyrev (**http://www.spilk.org/dsm/**) for Mac Power PC lets you play ScreamTracker 3 (S3M), Oktalyzer, ProTracker, FastTracker (MOD), TakeTracker, MultiTracker (MTM), Farandole Tracker (FAR), Composer 669 (669), MIDI, and other computer music files.

Pixound from Hologramophone Research (**http://www.pixound.com/**) for Mac Power PC, Macintosh, and Windows 95 is truly strange; it translates pictures into sound as you move the mouse cursor over an image on a Pixound-enabled Web page.

Virtual Sound Canvas from Roland (**http://www.rolandcorp.com/vsc/vscd.html**) for Mac Power PC, Macintosh, Windows 95, Windows 3.1, and UNIX, is a software emulation of a Roland SC77 sound module. Ultra-cool.

Yamaha XG MIDPlug from Yamaha (**http://www.yamaha.co.jp/english/xg/html/ midhm.html**) for Mac Power PC, Windows 95, and Windows 3.1 is a software Yamaha synthesizer. ●

## CHAPTER 24

Video

by Mark R. Brown

In this chapter

Presenting Multimedia

Video, animation, and interactive multimedia presentations can really liven up your Web pages. They pull in and involve your audience in a way that simple text and static graphics can't. Of course, presenting inline multimedia elements means creating and delivering a whole new kind of page content that can't be viewed by using browser programs that only understand HTML. Only plug-in capable browsers can display such a wide variety of multimedia content.

Although plug-in compatible content integrates almost seamlessly into your pages, developing and delivering that content involves steps that are quite different from those involved in creating straight HTML pages. Each type of content—video, animation, and multimedia—must be created using a different program specifically designed to create that type of content. Each must then be displayed by using a different browser plug-in.

Limitations on Multimedia Content

Many real-world factors place a practical limit on what kinds of plug-in compatible content you can use on your site. File size (mainly a concern in regards to throughput over dialup connections) and browser compatibility are certainly two primary considerations. There is also the issue of good content versus good looks and how that helps determine what plug-ins are best for your site. Finally, there's the issue of the sheer number of plug-ins available and how you quickly run into the problem of pure practicality.

N O T E   Most of the plug-ins that you read about in this chapter work equally well in Microsoft Internet Explorer and Netscape Navigator. However, you'll likely find comparable ActiveX controls for each of the plug-ins discussed in this chapter at the publisher's Web site that are intended specifically for Internet Explorer. ▨

File Size and Dialup Connections

When developing plug-in compatible content for delivery over the World Wide Web, a prime consideration is *bandwidth*, or how much data can be delivered to your audience in a given amount of time.

Users with fast, direct-dedicated T1 or T3 landline connections will, under ideal conditions, have no problem viewing real-time videos or listening to real-time audio broadcasts. Even interactive multimedia presentations will be up and ready to be displayed in a reasonable amount of time.

Those connecting to your Web site via dialup connections will have problems viewing huge files of any type. Over a standard 14.4Kbps (kilobit per second) or 28.8Kbps dialup connection, even large GIF and JPEG graphics can take several minutes to load. Pages that are extremely graphics-rich can take 15 minutes or more to download over such slow connections.

Multiply the problem by a factor of 10, or even 100, for video and multimedia content, and you begin to see that plug-in compatible content is not generally a realistic option for those who are connecting to the Web via a dialup connection.

However, remember that the real issue is file size, not content type. A MIDI music file might be only a couple of kilobytes in size and is a good candidate for delivery even over dialup lines. Videos and multimedia presentations are not totally out of the question, either, as long as your viewers are willing to wait for them to download first—you won't be able to stream them for viewing in real-time. The issue here is whether the content is worth waiting for.

If you consider who your audience is, it's easy to determine what types of content you can provide. If your viewers are likely to be connecting from university, corporate, or government sites with direct Internet links, then bandwidth is not generally an issue, and almost any type of content can be incorporated into your pages. On the other hand, if most of your viewers are likely to be connecting to the Internet via dialup lines from home or through online services, your pages should be sparser, with smaller files that can be viewed in a reasonable amount of time over a slow dialup connection.

A good rule of thumb is to remember that a 14.4Kbps dialup can read a maximum of about 1.7K (kilobytes) of data per second from the Net. Thus, a 25K file will take about 15 seconds to download (if everything goes well). A 250K file will take two and a half minutes. If that 250K file is a 10-second animation, your viewer is likely to feel cheated that she had to wait so long for such a short display. Keep this wait/reward ratio in mind whenever you develop any plug-in compatible content for your pages, and you should be able to keep your site under control and your audience happy.

Browser Compatibility

Many companies promote their own proprietary formats on the Web for everything from video and audio to compressed graphics and animation.

The problem with proprietary formats on the World Wide Web is that they can quickly prevent the Web from being worldwide at all. Each new proprietary format leads to further Balkanization of the Web—that is, to its division into ever smaller, more proprietary pieces.

Not that innovation is bad. It has become painfully obvious that older technologies—WAV audio files, for example—just aren't robust enough for future use on the Web. The files are too big for the information they hold. Compression is the key to the future expansion of the Web; it's certainly the key to emerging multimedia and 3-D technology.

How can we reconcile this issue? Clearly, we need to continue to experiment with new formats but without scattering them throughout the Web without compunction. Any experiments should be localized. Discussion should be encouraged. Then new standards should be proposed for adoption throughout the Web.

The latest HTML standard incorporates many of Netscape Communication Corporation's and Microsoft's innovative extensions and will see many more changes in the future. Graphics, audio, video, and multimedia standards should be pursued as well.

In the meantime, plug-ins provide an excellent way to experiment with new and different types of page content, hopefully without dividing Web users into drastically opposing camps. If you keep your content *optional*, you'll go a long way towards promoting feelings of cooperation and good will among all Web users.

How can you do this? Keep your home page generic. Use only HTML-formatted text and standard GIF and JPEG graphics on your home page; then use links to jump to pages that contain your plug-in compatible content files. For example, you might use a GIF image of a still from a video on your home page as a link to a separate page that includes the entire video.

It's also good form to include text-only, or at least text-and-GIF-graphics versions of your pages for viewing by those who can't or won't use plug-ins to experience the full thrust of your highly glorified pages. After all, HTML is about communication, and you can't communicate if there are those who can't or won't view your pages.

Listing 24.1 shows the HTML code for a courteous page that provides only text and graphics up front, with a link to both enhanced and unenhanced pages:

Listing 24.1 Linking to Enhanced and Unenhanced Pages

```
<HTML>
<HEAD>
<TITLE>The Wonderful World of Weebles</TITLE>
</HEAD>
<BODY>
<H1>The Wonderful World of Weebles</H1>
<HR>
Weebles are cool! I've been into those rockin', sockin'
little Playschool Weebles since I was a kid, and think
there must be a lot of people out there on the Web who
share my interest. That's why I've created the Wonderful
World of Weebles!<P>
<A HREF="Animated.htm"><IMG SRC="weebles2.gif" ALT="[LINK]"></A>
Click here for Multimedia...
<A HREF="Standard.htm"><IMG SRC="weebles3.gif" ALT="[LINK]"></A>
or here for standard Weebles.<P>
</BODY>
</HTML>
```

This page loads fast over even slow dialup lines and displays just fine in any graphical browser program (see Figure 24.1). It then provides links to pages both with and without multimedia content. The fancy stuff can come on page two, and if people want to bookmark your fancy page rather than your home page, that's fine.

The key is courtesy. Your home page should be generic; fancy multimedia content should be optional. That way, everyone can view your site.

Of course, compatibility is less of an issue over corporate intranets where everyone is likely to be issued the same browser and plug-ins, and file type standards are likely to be firmly established. Still, there may be situations where staff on the road or at satellite sites dial into the intranet via potentially slow connections, so keep those poor souls in mind when you consider multimedia content.

FIG. 24.1

This does what a courteous page should do: it presents its case right up front, it loads fast, and it provides links to more user-friendly pages.

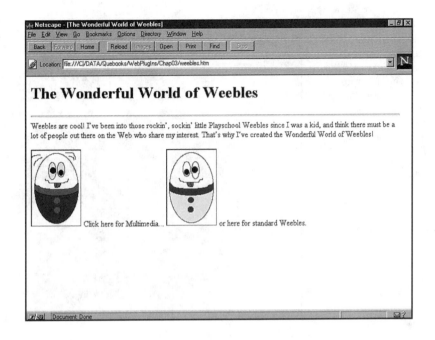

What Are Plug-Ins Best Used For?

So what use are plug-ins? Plug-ins can deliver content that is more vibrant, interactive, and involving than straight HTML text or GIF graphics. They are best used to deliver content that goes beyond what text and graphics can do.

For example, Figure 24.2 shows an interactive concentration-style game on the *Toy Story* site. Its purpose is to involve the viewer with the story's characters and make them familiar in a fun way. By making the experience interactive and hands-on, the creators of the *Toy Story* site have done at least three positive things:

- By virtue of its uniqueness (that is, it's a game, not just static text and images), the experience is memorable.
- The game involves memorizing images of the characters from the movie. This makes them familiar and comfortable, which means that Web surfers who play this game will likely want to see more of them.
- Interactivity means that the viewer has to hang around long enough to finish the game, which allows time for the message "*Toy Story* is fun!" to become imprinted.

All these things help the creators of the *Toy Story* site to achieve their primary goal, which is to increase interest in the movie *Toy Story*, thus selling more videos and licensed merchandise.

It all sounds rather mercenary when put into these terms, but it's not all that bad—the user was looking for entertainment and enjoyment when she came into the *Toy Story* site, and this game certainly provides that. It's a classic win-win situation.

FIG. 24.2

This Shockwave multimedia game on the *Toy Story* movie Web site is more than just cool—it involves the viewer with the story's characters and gets her interested in seeing the movie.

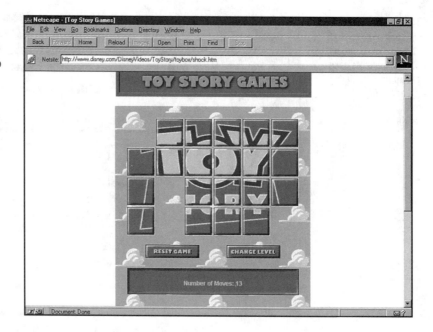

If your plug-in content provides the same kind of experience on *your* site, you've done things the right way. Your viewer should go away with a positive impression, a sense of having experienced something good, and a clear idea of what it is you were trying to communicate.

Before you include any plug-in compatible content on your pages, ask yourself the following questions:

- What is my message?
- How does this content help me deliver my message?
- Will viewing this content be a pleasing experience to my viewers?
- Will my viewers get the message better by interacting with this content than they would without it? Keep in mind the wait/reward ration you learned about earlier.

If you can answer these questions in the positive, you can justify using at least some plug-in compatible content on your pages.

Plug-in Content Creation Programs

Every plug-in delivers content created by its own unique content creation program. That's a fact of life. Just as you must use a paint program to create GIF graphics, you must use the proper audio digitizing, video grabbing, spreadsheet creating, or other type of program to create each type of plug-in content.

And each content creation program is unique, with its own user interface, controls, quirks, and capabilities. The sad truth is you have to install and learn to use a whole new program for every type of content you want to create.

From a real-world point of view, this is going to limit the amount and types of content you can provide on your pages. Although it might sound appealing to have a site that includes audio, video, multimedia, interactive games, spreadsheets, ad nauseum, the truth is that you simply don't have time to learn how to create and deliver every single kind of plug-in content in existence. You have to be selective.

NOTE Don't forget your audience, too. For every plug-in you use, that's one more plug-in your viewers are going to have to install. If they need to download and install a half-dozen plug-ins before they can view your page, the odds are good that they'll just move on to a more user-friendly site!

That means sifting through the chaff to find the kernels of wheat. And, of course, one person's chaff is another person's wheat. Animation might be what you want to present on your personal Looney Toons Web site, whereas in your day job as an investment analyst, you might be more interested in putting spreadsheets on the corporate intranet.

Keep It Small

As mentioned earlier, bandwidth is the primary consideration for delivery on the World Wide Web. That makes nonreal-time plug-ins most appropriate for Web pages. Video in real-time is a practical impossibility on dialup connections. It's best to avoid real-time video on your Web pages, but nonreal-time (that is, download-then-view) files are okay, as long as you include a warning for your audience on your Web page that long download times are involved.

In general, try to keep your files as small as possible. Multimedia games are fine if they download quickly. Remember that much of a plug-in compatible file's capabilities come from the plug-in itself. Data files can be relatively small while incorporating a lot of flashy content. Watch your file sizes and don't worry about how much the file is doing. A file doing a lot but doing it efficiently is the key to successful plug-in use over the Internet.

Plug-Ins and Intranets

Although plug-ins open up many new possibilities when browsing the World Wide Web, they really shine on intranets. Why? Because organizations can really benefit from the file standardization that intranets impose, and intranets don't suffer from the bandwidth problems that can hound sites on the Internet.

As a corporation grows, it sometimes Balkanizes—that is, departments and groups drift apart in the way they work and even in what tools they use to do that work. For example, your company's accounting department might use Lotus 1-2-3 as its spreadsheet program, whereas engineering uses Microsoft Excel. The secretarial pool might use WordPerfect, whereas R&D uses Word. Worse, the secretaries might all be on Macs, and engineering uses UNIX workstations. If this sort of situation prevails at your organization, communication among departments might be spotty, at best.

Part

IV

Ch

24

However, a corporate intranet can help smooth over these communication problems. With exceptions, Mac, Windows, and UNIX computers running HTML browser programs can all view the same documents. A report created in HTML by the accounting department on a Windows 95 machine can easily be read by engineering on a UNIX workstation or by the HR department on its Macintoshes. Plug-ins are now more widely available across platforms, so they can also be used to view MPEG movies, listen to RealAudio sound clips, and view Word documents that are included in intranet pages. If nothing else, HTML makes it easy to include alternate content for machines that can't read proprietary formats, so everyone can access the same information, regardless of format.

Because corporate intranets run over fast computer networks, streaming video, real-time audio, and other bandwidth-intensive data can also easily be included on intranet sites. This makes video-based in-house training, interactive multimedia, and other data-intensive applications naturals for inclusion on an intranet (see Figure 24.3). Plug-ins geared to displaying multimedia are likely to see much more use on corporate intranets than on the Web.

FIG. 24.3
By publishing multimedia files on its intranet, HBO is saving thousands of dollars previously incurred for printing, duplication of videocassettes, and distribution of marketing campaign materials among 200 to 300 sales representatives.

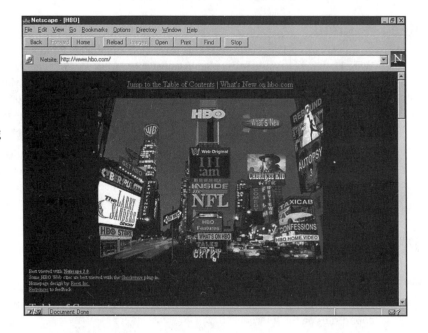

Video and Animation Plug-Ins

Pictures that move—that's the magic of video and animation. With only sound and graphics, HTML documents are static. But with video and animation, pages come alive with television-like action.

Of course, all this motion comes at a price—even a few seconds of video or animation can come in a package of several megabytes, and with the time involved in transmitting data over the Internet, that can mean sluggish response and jerky images.

When to Use Video Content

Suppose that you have a stunningly cute VHS video recording of your little niece Gloria spitting up her first mouthful of strained peas, and you have a hunch it would make a wonderful addition to your personal Web page.

Uh…probably not. Unless you have a million relatives browsing the Web, the odds are good that nobody wants to wait the dozens of minutes it takes his dialup connection to download 15 seconds of video that shows dear little Gloria at her worst. Not only that, it's probably going to take you a few hours—or at least a couple of hundred dollars—to get that short video clip onto your site.

Video Speed

As with all HTML document content, when considering when to use video or animation content, keep in mind the effort/payoff ratio. And with video and animation, that ratio is often low.

If your audience is mostly connecting to the Internet via a dialup connection, your use of video should be sparse. Not only that, you should give your viewers ample warning. Don't put a video on your home page. Instead, put a link to your video content and include a warning next to the link that tells them how long they can expect the download to take and how long a video clip they're going to experience for their trouble.

A 14.4Kbps connection can deliver, at best, 1,800 bytes of information per second; a 28.8 dialup twice as much (3,600). Divide the size of your file (in bytes) by these numbers and put those figures in the warning on your Web page, like this:

```
Click here to see the AVI video of Lindberg Landing.

This video is 1M in size. On a 14.4 connection, it will take approximately
9¹/₂ minutes to download. On a 28.8 connection, it will download in
approximately 4¹/₂ minutes.
```

If you are delivering information mostly to those who connect directly to the Internet via commercial, university, or government sites, then you can be more generous in your use of video. Users on a 56Kbps direct line will be able to download a 1M video in just over two minutes. Still, two minutes is a good chunk of time. If you are using a video plug-in capable of *streaming* its content (so that the video can be viewed as it's coming down the line), you have a much better chance of keeping viewers with you. However, you also stand a chance, even on a fast direct line, of having your video content not keep up with real-time. In other words, your viewers might experience skips and jumps. Some of the latest streaming video software can help alleviate these problems—see Chapter 28, "Streaming Video," for more on these programs.

On a corporate intranet, all such worries vanish. You should be able to deliver video content at will. However, if your corporate intranet includes remote sites connected via the Internet, remember their special needs.

Content Considerations

As always, after the technical details are worked out, your major consideration should be this: does the content add to the value of your site? Is it relevant? Does it fit your theme and topic? If the answer to any of these questions is no, you should probably ask yourself whether something else would do the job better.

Videos and animations are especially suited to the following tasks:

- *Training.* Many people learn better by watching someone else do something before trying it out for themselves.

- *Education.* Historical film clips, entertaining animations, and other visual aids can be extremely useful in helping to emphasize and illustrate important concepts.

- *Entertainment.* If your site is mostly devoted to entertaining your viewer, video clips and fun animations are some of the best entertainment around (see Figure 24.4).

- *News.* People are used to getting their news on TV, and if you are in the business of delivering news to your viewers, clips of important events connote an immediacy and sense of involvement you just can't get from text and still images.

FIG. 24.4
The site promoting the blockbuster film *Independence Day* is the perfect place for a few exciting video clips. Even so, the authors place each clip on its own page and link to them from a menu that warns of large file sizes.

Pages where video and animation should be used sparingly or not at all include the following:

- *Lengthy presentations.* If your presentation goes on for many pages, using too many video or animation clips slows down your presentation to the point that only the most dogged viewer will ever get through it all.

- *Index pages.* Pages of links should be used as reference points, not sources of entertainment. If your link pages include videos, it's a sure bet that people won't be willing to suffer through the long load times again and again just to use your links. They'll go elsewhere.

- *Reference material.* If the main purpose of your site is to serve as a reference source, at least have the courtesy to link to any videos or animations—or big graphics, as far as that goes. If people are going to come back to your site on a regular basis, they will not want to have to load in video data every time.

Consider not only the time your viewers will put into downloading and watching your videos and animations, but also the time you'll invest in creating it.

Creating Video Content

When you get down to it, videos and animations are the same thing—a series of still images presented one after the other to give the illusion of motion. The only real difference is the source. Videos are generally a series of digitized, real-world images, whereas animations are usually hand-drawn (or at least hand-assembled).

Using a PC to digitize video from a live source can be surprisingly complex and expensive. Just as you need a sound card to digitize audio, you need a video digitizer card to digitize video. These generally aren't cheap. You can buy a card (or external box) to digitize a single image for around $200. But to capture live video streams requires a card that could cost well in excess of $1,000, though recently a few lower-cost alternatives have been introduced. You also need a fast system with a lot of memory and a huge amount of online storage. A computer system set up to do professional quality real-time video digitizing can set you back $6,000 to $10,000, and we're not even talking VCRs, video mixers, and other esoteric add-ons.

For example, the Salient Video Capture Subsystem model VCS89 (**http:// www.salientsys.com/**) offers real-time video digitization, image processing, data compression, high-resolution graphics display, and mass storage of captured images. It comes with 8M of video buffer memory and up to 128M of program memory. It can capture images at up to 1280×1024 resolution, at up to 16 million colors using its on-board Texas Instruments DSP (Digital Signal Processor) chip, the TMS320C80-40. It includes a fast, wide SCSI-2 interface and is a PCI format card. The VCS board with 0M of program RAM and 8M display RAM retails for $5,000. Of course, to use this card, you also need a fast Pentium PCI bus computer with a lot of RAM of its own, as well as several gigabytes of hard drive storage space.

Other high-end video capture cards include the Targa 1000, DPS Perception, Quadrant Q-Motion 250, and MiroVideo DC-20. All are high-priced with similar requirements. Popular video capture software you can use with these cards includes Adobe Premiere 4.0, Ulead Media Studio Pro 2.5, and Asymetrix Digital Video Studio.

A few lower-cost video digitizing solutions have come to market lately in the under-$1,000 range. The Avid Cinema card for the Macintosh costs under $500, for example, but it still requires a high-end Mac with a lot of system resources. Toshiba's $399 JK-VC1 PC Card is designed for use with its high-end laptops, which comply with the new Zoom Video standard. Winnov's Videum capture card for PCs is under $300 but can only capture AVI videos in an extremely low-resolution 160×120 pixel format. The under-$200 Motion Picture capture card suffers from the same problem.

Each of these cards comes with its own proprietary video capture software. But the industry software standard for capturing, editing, and producing high-quality computer video is set by Adobe Premiere. With a price of $795-$995 (depending on your platform), you might argue that it should be excellent. But we're talking top-notch professional features, here. Truthfully, Adobe Premiere—and most of the high-end capture boards now on the market—are overkill (and overpriced) for Web work, unless you're working with a corporate budget.

If you have the budget to investigate this avenue further, you can find more information by checking out the Yahoo! index for video frame grabbers at **http://www.yahoo.com/ Business_and_Economy/Companies/Computers/Peripherals/Graphics_Cards/ Frame_Grabbers/**.

But there are cheaper and easier solutions. Unfortunately, they involve that annoying equation you seem to run into everywhere in life:

> Time = Money

People are always looking for ways to turn a quick buck with their computers, and the odds are good that living close to you is someone who has already shelled out for one of the mondo-expensive frame grabbing systems just described. The odds are also good that he's dying to recoup some of his investment by digitizing video clips for people like you. Check your local phone book for Video Digitizing services. Prices vary greatly, but you can probably get a rate comparable to $40/minute. (That's per minute of video time, not per minute of conversion time.) There are, of course, companies that offer these services over the Web, too. You'll find some listed at **http://www.yahoo.com/Computers_and_Internet/Multimedia/Video/**.

A less expensive, though more time consuming, method of creating video clips is to employ an animation technique: digitize individual frames using an inexpensive frame capture device, and then assemble them using an animation program.

Video Frame Digitizers

A handful of devices on the market lets you digitize a single frame at a time from a video source such as a VCR or camcorder, which you can then assemble into a video frame animation. One of the most popular and least expensive of these devices is the Snappy Video Snapshot. (If you want to capture single live video images, you need a device with a built-in camera, like the Connectix QuickCam or WinCam.One.)

Snappy

The Snappy video frame capture device is a self-contained palm-sized unit that plugs into your computer's printer port. You run a cable from the video out port of your VCR or other video source into a jack on the Snappy, install the software, and start digitizing.

As you play a video, you preview it on-screen in the Snappy window (see Figure 24.5). Clicking a button instantly freezes and captures a digital image up to 1500×1125 in 16.8 million colors, which can then be enhanced or saved in one of several common file formats. The Snappy software is even Twain-compliant (a standard used for scanning), so you can digitize images from within many software programs that support scanners.

FIG. 24.5
The Snappy video digitizing software lets you adjust brightness, contrast, and other image characteristics.

For more information on the Snappy, check out Play Incorporated's site at **http://www.play.com**.

Connectix QuickCam

The second way to digitize video images is to use a video camera designed to interface directly with a computer. The most famous, inexpensive, computer-interfaced, digital video camera is the Connectix QuickCam (see Figure 24.6). A tiny ball-shaped video camera that connects to your computer's serial and keyboard ports, the $99 fixed-focus QuickCam can digitize gray scale video clips and still images up to 340×240 resolution. It's a great way to get bitmap pictures into your computer, if you can live with digitizing images of things that are close by. A $299 version can do the same thing in color and has a focusable lens.

The Connectix QuickCam comes with two programs, one for digitizing still images and one for creating short video clips. The video creation program can even assemble animations from a series of still video snaps. If you want to create videos from live images rather than videotape or a TV image, then the QuickCam might be a good choice for you.

You can get more information at the Connectix site at **http://www.connectix.com**.

FIG. 24.6

The Connectix QuickCam is tiny and easy to hook up and use. This is the black-and-white version, though an almost identical color version is also available.

WinCam.One

WinCam.One is a similar (if slightly larger) $199 video still camera. Like the Color QuickCam, WinCam.One uses an inexpensive CCD (Charge Coupled Device) array and a focusable plastic lens in a combination that is the video camera equivalent of an inexpensive film camera. It's a lot like having a nonportable electronic digital camera like those currently marketed by Nikon, Canon, Sony, and others. (These also can provide you with the images you need to create animated sequences, by the way.) The digitizing software included with WinCam.One (see Figure 24.7) gives you a great deal of control over brightness and so on, but it's mostly an easy-to-use point-and-shoot setup.

WinCam.One digitizes in high-quality, 24-bit True Color at 640×480 resolution. However, it doesn't do video streams—just single image still capture. It does have one impressive trick up its sleeve though—its serial interface cable can be up to 250 feet long, and WinCam.One can even be run from a remote site by using only a modem and a telephone line! More information can be found online at **http://www.wincam.com**.

Both QuickCam and WinCam.One are totally digital—they deliver their image to the computer without ever using an analog signal. Both do most of the work in the computer software, not camera circuitry, so they are ridiculously cheap. Each is targeted to a slightly different audience, but either can be used to create digital images for use on your pages.

FIG. 24.7
The WinCam.One digitizing software features a control panel that allows minute control over image quality.

Video for Windows Plug-Ins

The three standard video formats are Video for Windows, QuickTime, and MPEG. Video for Windows is the standard for PC platforms; QuickTime is used extensively on the Macintosh; and MPEG is the standard for high-end video. This chapter discusses plug-ins for each.

A Video for Windows driver is built into the Windows 3.1, Windows 95, and Windows NT operating systems. Windows' Media Player is the system-supplied, stand-alone application for playing Video for Windows movies, which are identified by the file name extension AVI (which stands for Audio Video Interleave). Not surprisingly, AVI format movies have also become popular on the Web. With the right plug-in, you have no problem viewing them inline in HTML pages.

TROUBLESHOOTING

When I try to play an online AVI file using a plug-in, I get a message saying `Cannot find` `"vids:msvc" decompressor`. What's wrong? Your Windows 95 MS Video 1 video compressor might not be loaded. It's required for playing any AVI file. Go to the Win95 Control Panel, select Add/ Remove Programs, Windows Setup, and Multimedia. Scroll down to Video Compression and make sure that there is a check mark in the box. If you have to add one, you are prompted to insert your Windows 95 system CD-ROM or disks.

Part
IV

Ch
24

VDOLive

Before Netscape came up with its own video plug-in, VDOLive enabled inline Video for Windows clips to be included in HTML pages and played back in real-time.

Unlike the other AVI video plug-ins discussed in this chapter, VDOLive requires a separate VDOLive Personal Server program to deliver video from your server computer. The VDOLive Personal Server and Tools software package enables you to deliver up to two streams of video; capture, compress, and serve up to one minute of video and audio; and will scale up to 256Kbps connections. But the server and plug-in work as a team. You need the server, and your viewers need the plug-in to view your content.

What's the advantage? Well, if your viewers are operating over a slow connection, VDOLive intelligently downloads a video file, skipping over enough information to retain real-time playback. The percentage of actual reception is displayed in the lower-right corner of the VDOLive display window. In cases of severe bandwidth shortage, such as 14.4Kbps connections, you get a low frame rate (approximately one frame each one to three seconds), but you are still able to view videos. In other cases, the VDOLive Player and the VDOLive Server try to converge at the best possible bandwidth, which can sometimes result in blurry display and/or low frame rate. Although this can result in jerky playback, especially over a slow modem connection, it makes for adequate viewing rather than intolerable viewing.

VDOLive is available for Power Macintosh, Windows 3.1, and Windows 95/NT from VDONet's site at **http://www.vdolive.com/download/**.

Other AVI Video Plug-Ins

Several more plug-ins are available for displaying AVI video in your HTML pages.

Iterated Systems' CoolFusion plays inline Video for Windows (AVI) movies. It lets you view videos at any size all the way up to full-screen, and you can stop, replay, and save them using a full set of controls. Using optional EMBED tag attributes, CoolFusion can even play video when the user drags the mouse pointer over it, or it can provide an alternate audio track (perhaps another language) that plays on a double-click. Like LiveVideo, CoolFusion needs no special server software. A future version will support playback of QuickTime MOV movies as well as AVI movies. For Windows 95 or Windows NT, CoolFusion requires a 256-color graphics card, though a 24-bit or high-color graphics adapter is recommended. You can download CoolFusion at **http://webber.iterated.com/coolfusn/download**.

Vosaic, or Video Mosaic, has been developed as a joint venture between the University of Illinois and Digital Video Communications. Plug-ins are available for both Netscape and Spyglass Mosaic. Features include embedded hyperlinks allowed within the video stream, and moving objects in the video stream are clickable and can lead to other documents. Mac, PowerPC, and Windows versions can be downloaded from **http://vosaic.com/html/video.html**.

The VivoActive Player is a streaming AVI video plug-in that uses Video for Windows AVI files that have been compressed up to 250:1 into a new VIV file format, which can be transmitted by using standard HTTP protocol; so you don't need special server software to use them on your pages. The VivoActive Player plug-in is available for Windows 95 and Windows NT from **http://www.vivo.com**.

QuickTime Plug-Ins

QuickTime is the video format used on the Apple Macintosh. However, because it was one of the first movie formats and because it is so widely used by the art community that favors the Mac, QuickTime MOV movie files are in ample supply on the Web.

The Apple QuickTime Plug-In

Apple's QuickTime plug-in (see Figure 24.8) lets you view QuickTime content directly in the browser window. The QuickTime plug-in works with existing QuickTime movies, as well as with movies prepared to take advantage of the plug-in's fast-start feature. The fast-start feature presents the first frame of the movie almost immediately and can begin playing even before the movie has been completely downloaded.

Part

IV

Ch

24

FIG. 24.8
The Apple QuickTime plug-in features an integral control toolbar and a right mouse button pop-up menu.

If you didn't get it with a copy of Netscape Navigator, you can download the latest versions of the QuickTime plug-in for the Mac, PowerMac, Windows 3.1, or Windows 95/NT from **http://quicktime.apple.com/sw**. After you have it up and running, check out the QuickTime Plug-in Sample Site at **http://www.mediacity.com/~erweb**.

All flavors of the Apple Macintosh ship QuickTime-enabled, but if you want to play QuickTime movies on your Windows computer, you need the proper version of QuickTime for Windows, in addition to the QuickTime plug-in. You can download versions for Windows 3.1 and Windows 95/NT from **http://quicktime.apple.com**.

The plug-in can play many kinds of QuickTime movies (MOV files) including movies with text, MIDI, and other kinds of data. The QuickTime plug-in supports a wide set of embedded commands allowing changes in user interface and background playing of content, such as music. If you have downloaded and installed the QuickTime VR component, it also lets you interact with QuickTime VR Panoramas and Objects.

QuickTime VR stitches together a series of images into a panorama or scene (see Figure 24.9). To view VR scenes, you also need to get the QuickTime VR Component from the QuickTime Software page and drop it into your Netscape plug-in folder. It's available at **http://quicktime.apple.com/sw**.

FIG. 24.9
To view a QuickTime VR
panorama, you just click
and drag the mouse.

If you're interested in creating QuickTime movies to play back on your site, you can find tools for Webmasters (like the Internet Movie Tool for the Mac) at **http://quicktime.apple.com/ sw.** You can also check into **http://quicktime.apple.com/dev** for more information on how to use QuickTime in HTML documents.

To use QuickTime movies on your site, you have to associate the MIME type video/quicktime with the file name extension MOV on your server. Then you must use the EMBED tag, complete with the required SRC, HEIGHT, and WIDTH attributes.

In addition, you can use the following optional attributes:

 TIP If you want to display the movie's controller, you need to add 24 pixels to the HEIGHT.

- HIDDEN. Hides the movie. Appropriate only for sound-only QuickTime files.
- AUTOPLAY=TRUE | FALSE. If TRUE, plays the movie automatically. Default is FALSE.
- CONTROLLER=TRUE | FALSE. If TRUE, displays the control toolbar. Default is TRUE. If you display the toolbar, the HEIGHT parameter should be 24 pixels greater than the actual height of the movie, to make room for the toolbar. (Do not use CONTROLLER=TRUE with QuickTime VR files.)
- LOOP=TRUE | FALSE | PALINDROME. Defaults to FALSE. If TRUE, plays the video over and over. PALINDROME plays the movie forward, then backward, and then repeats in an infinite loop. (Not used with VR files.)
- PLAYEVERYFRAME=TRUE | FALSE. If TRUE, plays every frame as it is received, even if this means playing at a slow rate. Defaults to FALSE. (Automatically turns off audio.)
- HREF="URL". Provides a link for the movie object.
- TARGET="FRAME". Provides a targeted link for the movie.

- `PAN=integer`. For VR movies only. Specifies initial pan angle, from 0.0 to 360.0 degrees.
- `TILT=integer`. For VR movies only. Specifies initial tilt angle, from –42.5 to 42.5 degrees.
- `FOV=integer`. For VR movies only. Specifies initial field of view angle, from 5.0 to 85.0 degrees.
- `NODE=integer`. For VR movies only. Specifies initial node for a multi-node VR movie.
- `CORRECTION=NONE|PARTIAL|FULL`. Optional VR movie parameter.

Other QuickTime Plug-Ins

Many QuickTime movie plug-ins are available on the Web. This section discusses a few more you might want to try.

Knowledge Engineering's MacZilla is a Mac-only plug-in that's sort of the Swiss Army knife of plug-ins. Besides QuickTime movies, it plays or displays: MIDI background music; WAV, AU, and AIFF audio; and MPEG and AVI movies. Using its own plug-in component architecture, MacZilla can extend and update itself over the Net with the click of a button. You even get a built-in MacZilla game! Download it from Knowledge Engineering at **http://maczilla.com**.

MovieStar by Intelligence at Large is less ambitious—it's only for QuickTime movie playback. Using the MovieStar Maker, a multimedia editing application also available for download, Webmasters can optimize QuickTime movies so that Navigator users can view them while they download. You can also use autoplay, looping, and many other settings. This one is available for Windows, Windows 95, and Macintosh at **http://www.beingthere.com/**.

Need more choices? At least three more QuickTime player plug-ins are available for Netscape: Iván Cavero Belaúnde's ViewMovie for Windows 95 and Macintosh at **http://www.well.com/ ~ivanski/**; TEC Solutions' TEC Player, also for Windows 95 and Mac, at **http:// www.tecs.com/TECPlayer_docs**; and Kevin McMurtrie's Mac-only Multimedia Plugin at **ftp://ftp.wco.com/users/mcmurtri/MySoftware/**.

MPEG Plug-Ins

MPEG is the standard video compression method developed by the Motion Picture Experts Group. MPEG video delivers excellent quality with better compression than other methods. The MPEG-1 standard is used for computer-based video on the Internet and CD-ROMs, whereas MPEG-2 is designed for commercial broadcast applications.

MPEG works best with a video board capable of doing hardware decompression. But even running in software on fast Pentium systems, MPEG works pretty well.

InterVU MPEG Plug-In

InterVU's MPEG plug-in plays streaming MPEG video without specialized MPEG hardware or a proprietary video server. It gives you a first-frame view inline, streams viewing while down-loading, and supports full-speed cached playback off your hard drive. InterVU is available for

PowerMac and Windows 95/NT. It can be downloaded from **http://www.intervu.com/download.html**.

InterVU has no pop-up menu, but it does have an integral control toolbar (see Figure 24.10).

FIG. 24.10
The InterVU MPEG player plug-in has minimalist controls but offers full streaming playback.

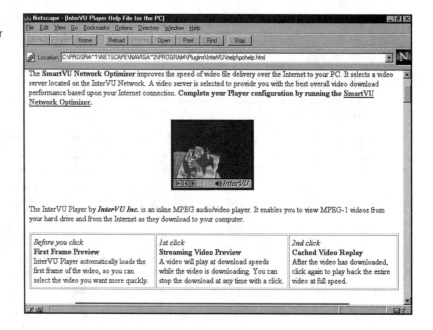

You click the Play button to start a video playing. While a video is playing, the Play button is replaced by a Stop button. Clicking the left mouse button anywhere on the video also starts and stops the video.

As you download the file, a speaker symbol appears if the file has sound, and a crossed out speaker symbol appears if the file is silent.

After the MPEG file has played to completion, a disk button appears on the control bar next to the Play button. If you want to save the file, left-click this disk button, and a Save As dialog box appears.

To replay an MPEG video, click the Play button again.

Clicking the InterVU logo in the lower-right corner connects you to the InterVU Web site.

To embed MPEG videos into your pages for viewing with InterVU, you first need to make the following MIME type associations in your server software:

video/mpeg	mpg
	*.mpe
	*.mpv
	*.mpeg

```
                         *.mp1
                         *.mp2
   video/x-mpeg          mpg
                         *.mpe
                         *.mpv
                         *.mpeg
                         *.mp1
                         *.mp2
```

Next, you use the EMBED tag, including the standard SRC, WIDTH, and HEIGHT attributes, as well as these optional attributes:

- AUTOPLAY=NO | YES. If YES, the clip is automatically played. NO is the default. (It's unfortunate that this plug-in doesn't use TRUE and FALSE with AUTOSTART, which is the standard usage.)

- FRAMERATE=integer. Legitimate values are from 1 to 25, representing frames per second. (This attribute automatically disables sound.)

- LOOP=Integer. Enter the number of times you want the video to play. Each time the Start button is pressed, the video plays the specified number of times.

- DOUBLESIZE=YES | NO. Default is NO. If YES, the video is shown at double the encoded size.

- HALFSIZE=YES | NO. As DOUBLESIZE, but half the size.

- CONBAR=YES | NO. If NO, the control toolbar is not displayed. Default is YES.

- FRAMES=YES | NO. If YES, autoplays the video on a Mac when Netscape Framesets are used.

- PALETTE=FOREGROUND | BACKGROUND. If FOREGROUND, specifies that the video's palette be used as the standard palette on a 256-color screen.

Part
IV

Ch
24

## CHAPTER 25

Animation

by Mark R. Brown

In this chapter

Animation Online

In Chapter 24, "Video," you learned that you can create a "video" by assembling individual digitized images into an animated sequence. You can, of course, also draw animations frame by frame. Even at a slow playback rate such as 11 frames per second (considered the absolute minimum even by today's cheap Saturday-morning cartoon production houses), you can see that drawing takes time (see Figure 25.1)—a great argument for using video and animation sparingly. If you've got talent and all the time in the world, however, you can use tools such as Pixar's RenderMan (a close cousin to the software used by Pixar to create the movie *Toy Story*) to create your own animation masterpieces.

FIG. 25.1

Even a short animated cartoon such as this one at the official Pinky & the Brain Web site can be composed of hundreds of individual drawings.

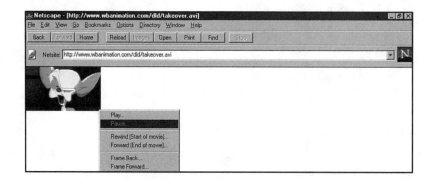

RenderMan (**http://www.pixar.com**) is an expensive product; its price and high-end features make it overkill for all but the most professional animators. For most of us—especially those of us interested only in delivering short animations for playback on our Web pages—it makes more sense to use a combination of simpler (and cheaper) tools. Enliven and Emblaze are examples of less expensive tools, and they're optimized for the Web as well. But it's "89a" animated GIF images that have taken the Web by storm. We'll cover all of these formats in this chapter.

ON THE WEB

For links to many publishers of animation programs, check Yahoo!'s list of animation links at **http://www.yahoo.com/Computers_and_Internet/Graphics/Computer_Animation/**.

Creating Your Own Animations

Everybody loves a good cartoon. A simple animation can add a lot to your Web page. Although animations are essentially the same as videos—that is, they are a series of still frames displayed sequentially—there can be a great difference in scale.

Videos take up a lot of memory, storage space, and transfer bandwidth because videos images are usually complex, real-world images composed of a lot of pixels in a wide variety of colors.

Animations, on the other hand, are often simple images comprising only a few colors. Because of this, they compress extremely well in comparison to video. If they are put into a proprietary format that is optimized for the delivery of simple animation, they can be even smaller.

Compression is one good reason to consider animations when adding life to your pages. If you pick a good format, you can deliver animations hundreds of times faster than you can deliver video clips.

Whether you're creating an animation based on digitized images from the real world or one comprising hand-drawn images, the process consists of the same two steps:

1. Create the art for the individual frames of the animation, either by digitizing them or drawing them.
2. Assemble the individual frames into an animated sequence.

Creating Animation Frames

If your animation will consist of a series of digitized images, you need to start by digitizing those images. The preceding chapter discussed some products you can use to digitize individual frames from a VCR or other video source, as well as some products that allow you to digitize video still frames directly from a camera connected to your computer.

▶ **See** "Video Frame Digitizers," **p. 488**

Part

IV

Ch

25

You can also use a scanner to create individual animation frames. You can scan photos or illustrations, or you can draw your own images on paper and scan them. If you're more of a "hands-on" artist than a "digital" artist, this can be a more comfortable way to go. Just remember to make small changes from one frame to the next, or your efforts won't play back smoothly.

> **CAUTION**
>
> Scanned images and digitized image files can be huge—much too large to use in creating an animation. Scan or digitize your images in 256 colors and keep the image size small—320×200 at the absolute maximum, much smaller if possible. Otherwise your animations take forever to assemble and even longer to download and view.

Finally, you can use a paint program to create your images directly. This doesn't have to mean that you draw every image by hand. You can also load a digitized image and modify it. In fact, that's what you're going to do in the following example.

First of all, you need to load a paint program. I've chosen Paint Shop Pro because it's capable of performing many special effects that don't require any artistic ability whatsoever. To start, load a previously digitized picture of yours truly (see Figure 25.2). After all, I wouldn't want to massacre anybody else's picture; would you?

▶ **See** "Paint Shop Pro," **p. 458**

FIG. 25.2

Step one in creating the sample animation is to load the image on which you want to base the animation.

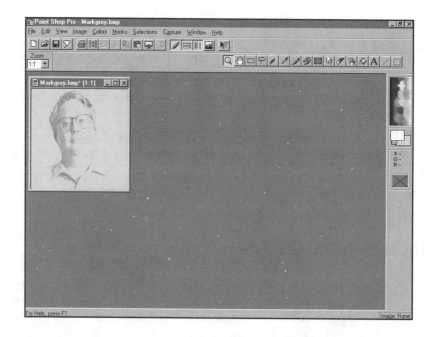

Use Paint Shop Pro's Deformation feature to add motion blur to this image and create a six-frame animation of my face getting fuzzy. To do this, you first create six individual pictures. Select Edit, Copy from the menu bar and then Edit, Paste, As New Image (Ctrl+V) five times (see Figure 25.3).

FIG. 25.3

Copying the original image five times creates the six frames you need for the animation.

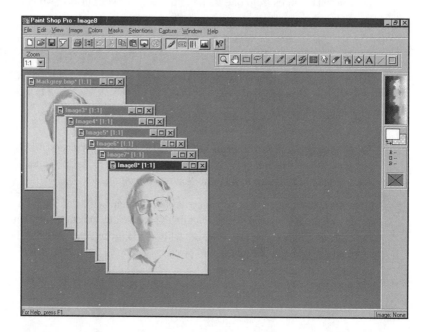

> **TIP** Because you are using copies of the same GIF image, you avoid some of the major hassles involved in creating animations from multiple images. Otherwise, you'd have to spend a lot of time matching color palettes and color depth, resizing images to the same size, and saving them all in the same form at (GIF).

Leave the original image alone. That one forms the base frame of the animation. Select the second frame and choose Image, Deformations, Motion Blur from the menu, and you see the dialog shown in Figure 25.4.

FIG. 25.4
Motion blur is one of dozens of special effects available in Paint Shop Pro.

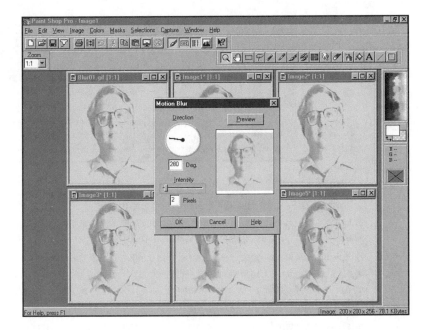

Blur the first image to an intensity of two pixels. The second, blur to four pixels; continue until the last image is blurred by ten pixels. Each image is subsequently more blurry than the previous by two pixels (see Figure 25.5).

The final step in the frame creation process is to save each of the images as an individual GIF format file.

Assembling an Animation

At this point, you could choose to create an animation in a proprietary animation format using a commercial animation program, but there's a better choice for use on the Web: a GIF animation. GIF animations require no special playback plug-ins or programs—both Microsoft Internet Explorer and Netscape Navigator play GIF animations all by themselves.

Part
IV

Ch
25

FIG. 25.5

You now have a sequence of progressively blurry images that you can assemble into an animation.

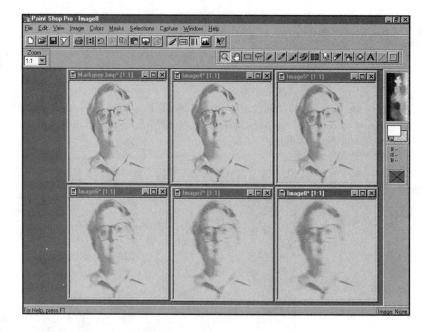

Animated GIFs and the GIF89a Specification

GIF format bitmap images have been around practically forever. One indication of the durability of the GIF image format is that the latest specification (89a) was written in 1989.

This specification included two important features that have made GIF images a mainstay of Web page design. The first is transparency. By declaring a GIF image's background color as transparent, you can create logos that allow your Web page's background to show through, which makes a pleasing effect.

The second important feature built into the GIF89a specification is the capability to create animated GIF images. By combining a string of separate GIF images into a single file along with control instructions, you can turn a set of individual GIF images into an animation. When you include this animation on your Web page, both Microsoft Internet Explorer and Netscape Navigator play the animation in place.

It is now therefore relatively painless to create animated icons, short animated presentations, and even "videos" put together from digitized frames that the majority of the Web browsers can play without requiring the use of a plug-in. (If you don't find this exciting, you haven't been paying attention!)

The best tool, bar none, for assembling animated GIFs on Windows-based computers is Alchemy Mindworks' GIF Construction Set (see Figure 25.6). This program is shareware (registration fee: $20 + $5 shpg.) and can be downloaded from **http://www.mindworkshop.com**.

TIP Both Paint Shop Pro and GIF Construction Set let you create GIFs with transparent backgrounds.

FIG. 25.6
GIF Construction Set
is a must-have tool
for creating GIF
animations.

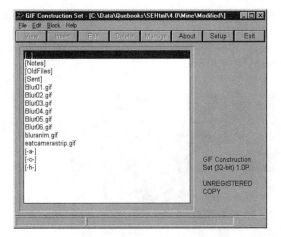

Although you can use GIF Construction Set for doing more than creating animated GIFs, and although you can use it to create animated GIFs by hand, this example employs its built-in Animation Wizard to create the animation. The beauty of this method is that you don't have to tweak a lot of settings to build the animation. Later, if you want, you can adjust anything that seems not quite right.

NOTE If you're a Mac user, you can build GIF animations using GifBuilder by Yves Piguet of Switzerland. It can assemble PICT, GIF, TIFF, or Photoshop images into GIF animations, and it can also convert QuickTime movies, FilmStrip, or PICS files. You can find out more about it (and download it) from **http://iawww.epfl.ch/Staff/Yves.Piguet/clip2gif-home/GifBuilder.html**.

To begin, select File, Animation Wizard (Ctrl+ A) from the menu; you see the Animation Wizard dialog shown in Figure 25.7.

FIG. 25.7
GIF Construction Set's
Animation Wizard
provides a painless
way to create GIF
animations.

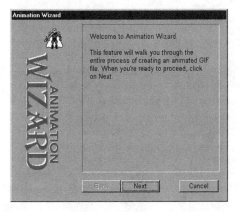

From here, it's just a matter of following the instructions in the dialog. The first step asks whether the animation is for a Web page (see Figure 25.8). It is, so click the appropriate radio

Part
IV

Ch
25

button. The Animation Wizard uses the choice here to determine how many colors to use when it creates the animation. When you indicate that you're creating an animation for a Web page, the wizard automatically optimizes the color palette for viewing in a Web browser. Finally, select the Next button.

FIG. 25.8

Animation Wizard wants to know whether it should optimize the animation for viewing on the World Wide Web.

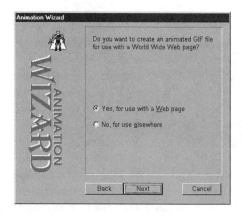

The second step asks whether you want the animation to loop indefinitely (see Figure 25.9). Indicate that you do. You want to make sure that you don't include too many infinitely looping GIF animations on the same page, however, because they consume valuable computer time and can be very annoying to your viewers. If your animation is simply an introduction, you want it to play only once.

FIG. 25.9

To loop or not to loop? That is the question.

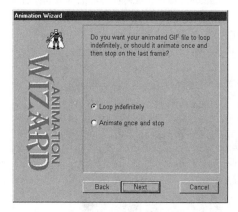

T I P   Have you ever seen an annoying looping animated GIF on a Web page? You can stop them at any time by clicking your browser's Stop button. Make sure you wait until the rest of the page elements are finished loading.

Step three asks whether the individual images are hand-drawn or "photorealistic" (see Figure 25.10).

FIG. 25.10

Here's where you tell the Animation Wizard what kinds of images it's working with.

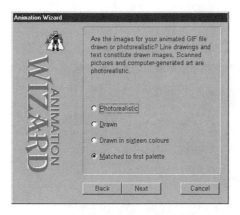

For your images, you could answer Photorealistic, which is GIF Construction Set's term for a digitized image. However, because all the images have the same color palette, you can choose Matched to First Palette. The Animation Wizard uses the answer to this question to determine how to match the colors among all of the pictures you give it. Because your pictures all use the same colors, you can save some processing time by choosing this answer. If you answer Photorealistic, Animation Wizard spends time matching and dithering colors, which is unnecessary for this example. If your images are hand-drawn, text images, or other simple graphics, you check the Drawn or Drawn in Sixteen Colours option, whichever is appropriate. (Note the spelling of "Colours." Can you tell that Alchemy Mindworks is based in Canada?)

The next step is to define how fast the animation will play (see Figure 25.11). The default is 100/100ths of a second (or a whole second) per frame. You probably want the animation to play a bit faster, so choose 50/100ths of a second between frames. If that's too fast or too slow, you can change it by later editing the file manually.

FIG. 25.11

Playback speed is an important determining factor in what kind of impression your animation makes.

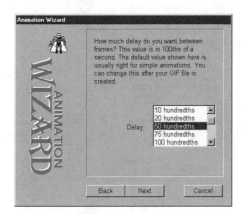

GIF Construction Set lets you specify a different delay for each frame in manual mode. This is great if, for example, you are creating an animated slide show and you want to display some slides longer than others.

Part
IV

Ch
25

Now that you've taken care of the mechanics, it's time to load the individual frames (see Figure 25.12).

FIG. 25.12

Open a file requester to load your animation frames.

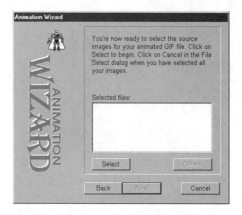

Clicking the Select button opens a file selection dialog (see Figure 25.13). Note that GIF Construction Set can load several different file formats besides GIFs: BMP, JPG, TGA, PCX, and PNG files are all supported.

FIG. 25.13

Loading a series of frames in GIF Construction Set.

Click a filename to load a frame and then the next and so on. Click Cancel to finish. When done, you see a list of the files you've loaded in the wizard dialog (see Figure 25.14). That's the final step.

Now that you're done, the wizard tells you what you need to do next (see Figure 25.15).

At this point, you click the Done button to finish the wizard. Then, you need to select File, Save As from the menu to save the finished animation.

You can take a look at your animation by clicking the View button in the GIF Construction Set toolbar (see Figure 25.16). The animation displays in its own screen, and you hit the Escape key to exit.

FIG. 25.14
You can highlight a file and click the Delete button to remove a file from the list.

FIG. 25.15
The wizard's done and there's only one more step.

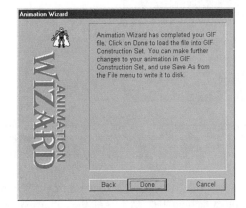

FIG. 25.16
GIF Construction Set's main window lists the component parts of the animated GIF.

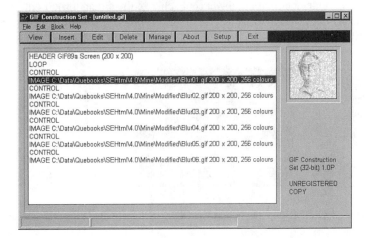

You can see from the list in the window that the animated GIF file is composed of a HEADER, a LOOP definition, and a sequence of alternating CONTROL and IMAGE functions. Although the Animation Wizard set the values for all these elements, you can change any of them manually by double-clicking an element in the list. For example, double-clicking an IMAGE entry opens the Edit Image dialog shown in Figure 25.17.

FIG. 25.17
GIF Construction Set lets you manually edit all the elements that compose an animation.

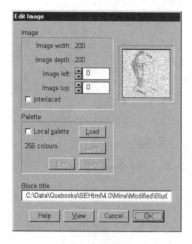

 TIP If you want your animation to loop back and forth—for example, if you want my picture to get fuzzy and then unfuzzy in steps—you can reuse the frames in reverse order in the last half of the animation.

You probably don't want to mess with the animation right now, but if you do, a quick click on the Help button invokes contextual help that explains all the options you can change.

Do you remember that I said you could change the timing if you want? You do that by double-clicking the CONTROL element immediately preceding the IMAGE you want to change the timing for. This opens the Edit Control Block dialog (see Figure 25.18).

FIG. 25.18
This dialog lets you change the timing of your animation.

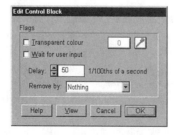

From this dialog, you can adjust the Delay setting to change the delay timing for the selected frame.

If you want to delete an element, all you have to do is highlight it with the mouse and click the Delete button. To insert an element, you click the Insert button and select the type of element you want to insert from the Insert Object menu that pops up (see Figure 25.19).

FIG. 25.19
You can easily add elements to an existing animation using this handy control.

Converting a Video to an Animation

Suppose you approached the problem from another point of view. What if you have an existing Video-for-Windows animation or video clip that you want to convert to an animated GIF? Obviously, I wouldn't have brought it up unless GIF Animation Studio could make the conversion for you automatically. Select the command File, Movie to GIF from the menu and you are prompted to select an AVI file to load. Then you see the Movie Options dialog shown in Figure 25.20.

FIG. 25.20
Converting an AVI file to an animated GIF is a piece of cake.

From here, you can select the color mapping you want the program to apply to the file. (I suggest you select the Help button first to find out what all the options mean.)

Once your AVI file is converted, you see the main window again, displaying your new GIF animation file (see Figure 25.21). You can fiddle with all the individual elements as though you had created an animation from scratch.

Part
IV

Ch
25

FIG. 25.21

Not satisfied with your automatic movie-to-GIF conversion? Play with the pieces yourself.

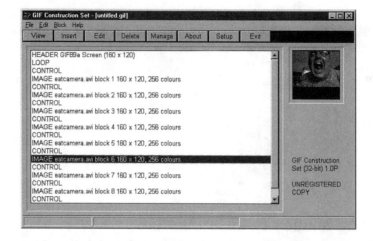

One thing you can do is select Block, Extract from the menu to select and save individual frames or blocks of frames as separate files. This option is great if you want to clean up a frame or two in a paint program and then insert them back into your animation.

Even more fun is to choose Block, Image Strip. You see the dialog box shown in Figure 25.22, which you can use to create a horizontal or vertical strip composed of all the images in your animations.

FIG. 25.22

This dialog lets you build a sort of film strip based on your animation.

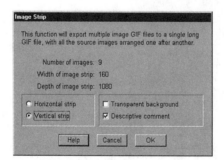

Figure 25.23 shows what such an image strip looks like. Although they are interesting in and of themselves, such image strips are also useful as data structures for creating Java-based animations.

 T I P Although Microsoft Internet Explorer and Netscape Navigator display GIF animations just fine, most graphic programs display only the first frame of a GIF animation.

GIF Construction Set is capable of much, much more, but you've got the animation you wanted, so I end the discussion here. You can use this same series of steps to create your own GIF animations for your Web site.

FIG. 25.23
Paint Shop Pro displays an image strip of an animation that was created by GIF Construction Set's Movie to GIF function.

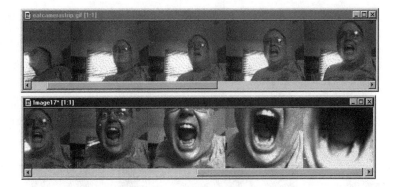

Animated GIFs are relatively small, they play in the most popular Web browsers without the use of plug-ins, and they are relatively easy to create with inexpensive shareware tools. However, if you're serious about creating more complex animations for delivery over the Web or a corporate intranet, you might want to check out one of the more popular proprietary-format animation systems.

Other Animation Formats

Animation always requires at least two proprietary programs, one to create animations and save them in a special format and a second to play those special format files. Because you can't create animations unless you use a proprietary animation-creation product, you won't have any material to embed unless you download or buy the programs anyway. These animation creation programs all contain extensive information on how to include the final result in your pages.

Enliven

Enliven provides an excellent example of how yesterday's solution just isn't good enough for today's problems on the Web. Version 1.0 of the Enliven suite was composed of three distinct software components: Enliven Viewer, a browser plug-in; Enliven Server, software for Windows NT Web servers to feed multiple streams of animation to browsers; and Enliven Producer, a post-production environment to prepare content for online delivery.

Today, that arrangement has changed. There's no longer an Enliven Viewer plug-in; it's been replaced by a small, quick Java applet that loads and runs quickly without the hassle of downloading, unzipping, and installing a separate browser plug-in. When you run into a site that uses an Enliven animation now, it looks like any other Java applet. Enliven Server was totally revamped. Like its predecessor, it delivers streaming animation content in real time, but the content has changed. There is no longer an Enliven Producer program to create yet another proprietary animation format. Instead—thanks to an agreement between Enliven's parent company Narrative and multimedia giant Macromedia—Enliven now uses Macromedia Director animations.

In short, the end user has it easy because she doesn't have to install yet another plug-in to view Enliven animations; they load and play streaming animations quickly. Web site developers don't have to buy and use yet another proprietary animation program to create content; they use Macromedia Director, a well-established industry standard. Enliven makes its money selling fast, real-time, streaming content server software.

Figure 25.24 shows Narrative's demo page from which you can play a handful of Macromedia Director pseudo-ads. The speed with which they download and play, even over my poky 28.8Kbps modem connection, is truly impressive.

FIG. 25.24
Click a link on this page to view streaming Macromedia Director animations courtesy of the new Enliven 2.0 server.

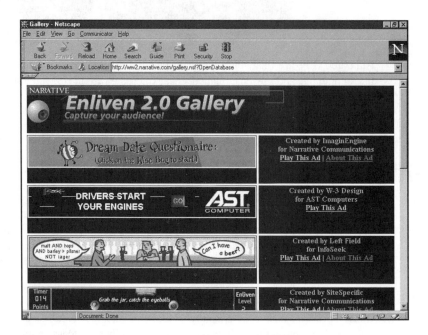

You can find out more about Enliven at Narrative's Web site at **http://www.narrative.com**.

Other Animation Options

GEO Interactive Media Group's Emblaze was formerly plug-in-based, but now it is a real-time, Java-based animation player applet that plays a proprietary animation format. GEO says the animation format needs only 3MB to 4MB of disk space for approximately 30 minutes of play time. The animations can display at a rate of 12 to 24 frames per second in 256 colors in real time over a 14.4Kbps connection. Animations are created using the commercial Emblaze Creator program, which can integrate animation with sound. The end result is an animation that plays quickly over the Web, even over slow 14.4Kbps dial-up connections. The latest version also allows you to combine video and interactive elements for multimedia presentations. Emblaze files require no special server program. You can find Windows 3.1, Macintosh, PowerMac, and Windows 95 versions of the Creator program at **http://www.emblaze.com/atlantis/frameset.htm**.

Totally Hip Software is another company that is in the process of moving from its own proprietary format to something standard. Its Sizzler plug-in and its special animation creator are still available, but Totally Hip seems to be actively promoting a program called WebPainter 2.0, which helps you create Web-standard GIF animations. WebPainter 2.0 includes a built-in graphics editor as well as an animation tool, and includes advanced features such as onion skinning, foreground and background layers, a cel strip window, multiple cel editing, and enhanced transformation tools. The Windows version imports and exports AVI files, and the Macintosh version does the same for QuickTime movies. You can download a free demo of either version (as well as the Sizzler plug-in and Sizzler animation Editor) from Totally Hip Software's Web site at **http://www.totallyhip.com/**.

Deltapoint's Web Animator 1.1 combines animation, sound, and live interaction. The latest version is available for Windows as well as the Macintosh and can save GIF animations as well as its own proprietary, plug-in–driven format. (Are you noticing a trend here?) The authoring tool for creating animations to add to your own site is also available from Deltapoint's Web site at **http://www.deltapoint.com/animate/index.htm**. ●

Part

IV

Ch

25

## CHAPTER 26

Multimedia Applets

by Mark R. Brown

In this chapter

Adding Multimedia

Among the dozens of available multimedia authoring systems, it seems as though every one of them has a plug-in for delivering its particular brand of multimedia file inline in HTML documents. Is all this extra delivery really necessary?

In the context of the "big picture," it probably isn't. Java and JavaScript are turning out to be the tools of choice for application, animation, and multimedia applications in HTML documents, mostly because the major browser programs—Netscape Navigator and Microsoft Internet Explorer—support embedded Java applets. (Java and multimedia are discussed later in this chapter.)

That development means you have to be a programmer to develop multimedia content for your pages, and not all of us are programmers. Thanks to multimedia plug-ins, we don't have to be. If your users are willing to download and install a plug-in, you can use any of the multimedia programs discussed in this chapter to bring multimedia content to your site. You can pick the tool that's most appropriate to your requirements.

Over corporate intranets, the solution is even simpler. If you've been using one of the programs to create presentations, training materials, or other multimedia content for your company, you can instantly make that content available to your entire organization by installing the right plug-in on all your desktop systems. You get another advantage from the fact that anyone can develop multimedia for your intranet using end-user development programs. You don't have to rely on your programmers to do it for you.

ASAP WebShow

Software Publishing Corporation's ASAP WebShow 2.0 is a plug-in for viewing, downloading, and printing ASAP WordPower presentations or for participating in real-time ActivePresenter presentations. Similar to PowerPoint presentations, WordPower and Active Presenter presentations can contain tables, organization charts, bullet lists, and other graphic and text elements in a slide show format. Because the files are compressed, they can be transmitted very quickly.

You can embed presentations and reports as icons or live thumbnails or in a window on a page. Each slide can be viewed in a small area window, enlarged to fill the current page or zoomed to full screen. You can select one slide at a time or watch a continuously running show. The latest version even allows attached RealAudio sound.

Windows 95 and Windows 3.1 versions are available (see Figure 26.1), and you can even download a fully functional copy of ASAP WordPower for a free 30-day trial for creating your own WebShow-compatible presentations. All are available at **http://www.spco.com/PRODUCTS/ WSMAIN.htm**.

FIG. 26.1

The ASAP WebShow toolbar and right mouse button pop-up menu give you complete control when viewing its PowerPoint-style slide show presentations with your browser.

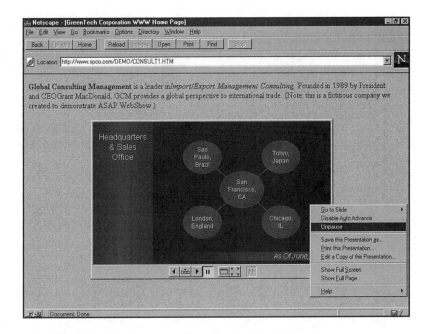

You use ASAP WordPower to create the slide shows for your pages. It can import PowerPoint 7.0 files and convert them to ASAP WordPower format. You can even drag and drop individual slides from the PowerPoint slide viewer into WordPower. ASAP WordPower also imports graphics files in PCX, BMP, WMF, TIF, and GIF formats. Built-in transition effects, dozens of border styles, and a set of startup templates simplify the creation of compelling slide shows. The suggested retail price for ASAP WebShow is $99.

Slide show sound is handled through integration with RealAudio.

The ASAP WebShow Presentation Kit contains everything you need to create, view, and hear a presentation in your HTML documents. For $129, you get both Windows 95 and Windows 3.1 versions of the ASAP WordPower presentation creation program, the ASAP Viewer plug-in, the ASAP Image Compressor, the RealAudio Player program, a two-stream RealAudio Server (Windows 95/NT only), and the RealAudio Encoder (which creates RealAudio files).

The ASAP Image Compressor is an add-on for ASAP WordPower and lets you save presentations in a compact format. The Compressor allows you to adjust the balance of image quality and file size in a compressed presentation. (Only the bitmap images in a presentation are compressed.) The ASAP Image Compressor is also available for download from the ASAP Web site.

To use ASAP WebShow presentations in your own pages, you must set the MIME type `application/x-asap` to the file name extension ASP on your server.

ASAP WebShow content is embedded on HTML pages using the `<EMBED>` tag, along with the required `SRC`, `HEIGHT`, and `WIDTH` parameters.

Part
IV

Ch
26

In addition, WebShow supports a wide range of additional <EMBED> tag parameters. If you don't use any of the optional parameters, default settings result in a display that puts the presentation in an embedded window, includes a navigation bar, and provides the capability to save, print, and edit the presentation. Following are some of the most important WebShow optional parameters; for a full list, consult the WebShow documentation or refer to the help pages on the ASAP Web site:

AUTOADVANCE= ON|OFF

If ON, automatically advances to each slide. To temporarily stop autoadvance, click the Pause button on the navigation bar or right-click in the ASAP WebShow window and select Pause from the pop-up menu. To completely turn off autoadvance, right-click in the ASAP WebShow window and then click Disable Auto Advance. To turn on autoadvance from the current slide, select Enable Auto Advance from the pop-up menu.

BORDER= RAISED|RECESSED|SLIDE| SHADOWED|SIMPLE|NONE

Changes the border type.

DELAYTIME= <INTEGER>

In seconds, indicates the delay before advancing to next slide when in autoadvance mode.

DITHERING= EMBED|PAGE|SCREEN|NONE

For 256-color screen display only, specifies dithering method.

EFFECT= <EFFECTNAME, DIRECTION>

Transition effect between slides. Transitions include:

Effect Name	Direction
BLINDS	LEFT|RIGHT
BLINDS	UP|DOWN
CLOSE	HORIZONTAL|VERTICAL
FADE	
DEFAULT	
IRIS	IN|OUT
NONE	
OPEN	HORIZONTAL|VERTICAL
RAIN	UP|DOWN
REPLACE	
SCROLL	UP|DOWN
SCROLL	RIGHT|LEFT
WIPE	UP|DOWN

Effect Name	Direction
WIPE	RIGHT|LEFT
PEEL	UPPERRIGHT|LOWERLEFT
PEEL	UPPERLEFT|LOWERRIGHT

LOOPBACK= ON|OFF	If ON, presentation loops on playback.
MENU= ON|OFF	If ON, enables the right mouse button pop-up menu.
NAVBAR= ON|OFF	If ON, displays the navigation bar.
NAVBUTTONS= ON|OFF	If ON, displays the Next Slide, Previous Slide, and Go to Slide buttons on the navigation bar.
ORIENTATION= LANDSCAPE|PORTRAIT| N:M|FREEFORM	Specifies how the presentation slide page fits in the window. LANDSCAPE or PORTRAIT maintains the aspect ratio by displaying the slide show in letter-box format. N:M uses the custom aspect ratio specified, where N and M represent the proportion between width and height. With FREEFORM (default), the slide fills the available window space.
PALETTE= FOREGROUND|BACKGROUND	If FOREGROUND, uses the embedded object's palette as the palette for the display window.
PAUSE= ON|OFF	If ON, autoadvance slide shows pause before playing.
PAUSEBUTTON= ON|OFF	If ON, includes the Pause button on the navigation bar.
PRINTING= ENABLED|DISABLED	If ENABLED, the Print This Presentation menu item appears on the pop-up menu.
SAVEAS= ENABLED|DISABLED	If ENABLED, the Save This Presentation As menu item appears on the pop-up menu.
SOUND= <URL OF A SOUND CONFIGURATION FILE>	Specifies a sound configuration file to play.
ZOOMBUTTONS= ON|OFF	If ON, Zoom buttons for full page and full screen appear on the navigation bar.

Part
IV

Ch
26

ASAP WebShow supports sound by invoking the RealAudio server. Because RealAudio uses a special server program, WebShow presentations can't embed RealAudio RA files directly. Instead, you use the SOUND attribute of the EMBED command to specify the URL of a sound configuration file, which is simply a text file that contains the URL of the actual RealAudio file.

You can create a sound configuration file using a text editor. Here's the syntax:

```
<slide#>=<URL of the RealAudio sound file on the RealAudio server>
```

Here's a real-world example:

```
1=pnm://audio20.prognet.com/test/jupiter/slide1.ra
2=pnm://audio20.prognet.com/test/jupiter/slide2.ra
3=pnm://audio20.prognet.com/test/jupiter/slide3.ra
```

You can include as many RA files in a sound configuration file as you want. However, the URL you put in the SOUND attribute definition with the <EMBED> tag must be absolute, not relative. In other words, it must be a complete URL. Here's an example:

```
<EMBED SRC="DEMO2.ASP" Width="300" Height="170" sound="http://www.spco.com/
asap/presents/rasound.txt">
```

ASAP WebShow is a powerful tool for creating business slide show-style presentations, and its <EMBED> tag attributes let you control most of the plug-in's behavior through HTML.

TIP If you want to publish your Microsoft PowerPoint presentation on the Web, you can use the PowerPoint Animation Player that you find at **http://www.microsoft.com/powerpoint/internet/ player/default.htm**.

Shockwave for Macromedia Director

Shockwave for Director is a plug-in that lets you play multimedia movies created with the most popular multimedia creation tool available today—Macromedia Director. In this section, you take a close look at the process involved in using the Shockwave plug-in for Netscape Navigator—and the Shockwave ActiveX control built into Microsoft Internet Explorer 4.0—to deliver Director content on your pages.

Director versus Java and JavaScript

The Shockwave for Director plug-in came before Java; it was introduced at about the same time as Netscape Navigator 2.0, which added plug-in capability. Hundreds of developers began using Macromedia Director—literally overnight—to add animation and interactive multimedia content to their Web sites. Many of them already had Director movies on hand that they had created for other applications. All they had to do was run them through the new Afterburner Xtra module and place the converted movies on their Web pages using the <EMBED> tag.

Suddenly, Web pages included inline animations, games, and button-rich interactive multimedia presentations. It was clear the Web would never be the same again.

Then Netscape added support for Java and JavaScript. Shockwave didn't go away, but suddenly, Java was the new darling of Web site developers. Animations, presentations, and even interactive multimedia sites multiplied by the thousands. Now it seems as though Java and JavaScript are all you hear about.

Did Java and JavaScript kill Shockwave? Did they completely take over the multimedia and animation niche that the Shockwave for Director plug-in had created? Hardly. With a quarter of a million copies of Director in use, Macromedia is still doing quite well. Java and JavaScript jumped into a niche that was expanding so rapidly that there was plenty of room. Shockwave could hold its own and also keep expanding its influence, even as Java and JavaScript carved out their own territories.

In truth, Java and Director appeal to two inherently different types of people. You develop content with Macromedia Director in a friendly point-and-click environment that uses a stage metaphor. You bring in *casts* composed of *actors*, who strut their stuff on a *stage*. The end result is even referred to as a *movie*. Director includes painting and animation tools with menus, dialog boxes, and buttons. People who are used to creating content with end-user applications such as Word and Paint are those who are most comfortable developing multimedia content using Director.

N O T E Don't confuse Director movies with digitized video movies such as Video for Windows or QuickTime files. Although they share a common name, Director movies are much more than a simple sequence of images; they are multimedia scripts. ▪

On the other hand, Java and JavaScript are programming languages. They resemble the C programming language, which is the most popular language for developing applications, so they appeal mostly to programmers. People who think in terms of code and programs are more likely to develop their multimedia content with Java and JavaScript.

N O T E Although you use a user-friendly program to create Director movies, the end result is actually a script or set of scripts in a language called Lingo. You can edit these scripts or even write your own from scratch. Director really offers the best of both worlds. ▪

What You Can Do with Shockwave for Director

The Shockwave for Macromedia Director plug-in (see Figure 26.2) can integrate animation, bitmap, video, and sound and can bundle all of them with an interactive interface, complete with control buttons and graphic hot spots. Its playback compatibility with a variety of computer platforms including Windows, Macintosh, OS/2, and SGI has helped make Director the most widely used professional multimedia authoring tool.

Using Shockwave for Director, a Director movie run over the Internet can support the same sort of features as a Director movie run off a CD-ROM, including animated sequences, sophisticated scripted interactivity, user text input, sound playback, and much more. You can even add hot links to URL addresses.

You can download the Shockwave for Director plug-in from Macromedia's Web site at Shockwave, **http://www.macromedia.com**.

Before the mechanics of Director are discussed, consider what you can do on your site with the Shockwave plug-in for Director.

Part
IV

Ch
26

FIG. 26.2

The Shockwave for Director plug-in features no controls or menus of its own. Any such controls must be provided as part of the Director movie.

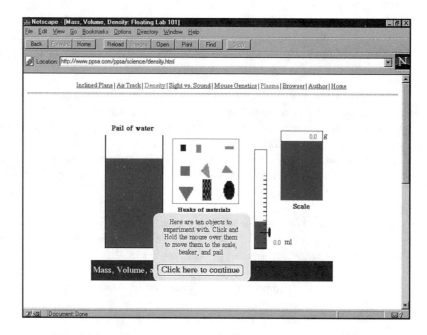

Although you are only limited by your imagination (and network download times), there are several categories that lend themselves well to Director solutions:

- **Animation**—You can use Director to create frame animations (including audio, if you want) that are second to none.

- **Games**—Director games can be as fast and fun as those written in high-level programming languages.

- **Entertainment**—You can tie together video and audio content and deliver it as a unified package.

- **Training**—Interactivity through on-screen buttons and graphic hot spots means student-guided training is a snap.

- **Education**—The capability to tie together myriad components means you can compose excellent educational materials.

- **Presentations**—With a variety of built-in transitions and the capability to link text and graphics with voice-overs, Director presentations are a step above conventional slide shows.

- **Applications**—Everything from user navigational interfaces to out-and-out application programs are candidates for creation with Director.

Creating Director Movies for Shockwave

How do you actually create Director movies? The simple answer is with Macromedia Director. The creation process involves many steps and a bit of a learning curve. Although Director is an excellent tool, multimedia files are content-rich, which is another way of saying they are complex. Even a relatively unambitious file can include still graphics, animation sequences, digitized audio or video, and interactive components. Creating all of that content and tying it together is a significant challenge, even if you've got the right tools.

To start with, you need a copy of Macromedia Director. At $850 retail, it's not cheap, but it's worth every penny if you plan to create much in the way of multimedia.

Director 6.0 (the latest version) is available for Windows 95/NT, Windows 3.1, Power Macintosh, and Macintosh.

Director is based on a theater metaphor. You have a stage where you can view your Director movie. Behind the scene, you have a cast window that stores all your media objects. These media objects can be sounds, 2-D and 3-D graphics, animations, digital video, text, and even database objects. To organize your media elements on the stage, you use the score. The score window allows you to precisely sync your media elements and provide different layers of elements on the screen.

Figure 26.3 shows the main Director screen.

FIG. 26.3

The Director screen consists of many elements that can be invoked when needed.

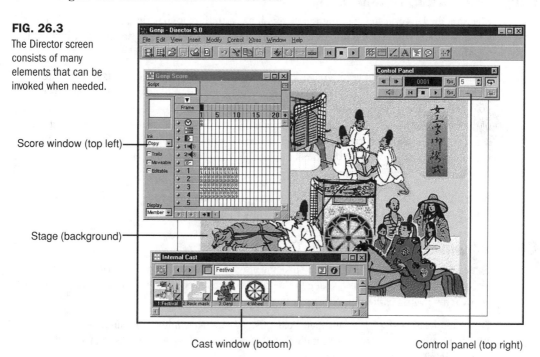

Score window (top left)

Stage (background)

Cast window (bottom)

Control panel (top right)

Part
IV

Ch
26

Director movies are composed of cast members, which are media elements such as images or sounds. You insert the cast members into the score window, which sequences all the file's elements. (Director also includes a full set of paint and other tools for creating these media elements in the first place.) After you create and coordinate all a movie's elements, you save the result as a Director movie file.

To use a Director movie in your HTML documents, you must first run it through Afterburner, a post-processor application that compresses and converts your Director movies for faster playback. The Afterburner application doesn't alter the way a Director movie appears or behaves but merely preps it by compressing it and changing its file format. Afterburner is available for download from the Macromedia Web site at **http://www.macromedia.com.** After you download and install it, Afterburner runs when you select it from the Director Xtras menu. Compressed (or *shocked*) Director movies have the file name extension DXR, rather than DIR.

Before serving up Shocked Director movies, you must configure your server computer to recognize and handle them by associating the file name extensions DIR, DXR, and DCR with the MIME type `application/x-director`.

The final step in the process is, of course, to `EMBED` your Director movie files on your pages. You use the ubiquitous `<EMBED>` tag and the required `SRC`, `WIDTH`, and `HEIGHT` parameters. You can also elect to use the `PALETTE` attribute. If `PALETTE=FOREGROUND`, the Director movie's palette is loaded and used as the palette for the entire page. Default is `PALETTE=BACKGROUND`.

Lingo Network Extensions

Macromedia Director ties together all its elements with the Lingo scripting language. Lingo is a rich language with many complex commands, and it's documented in the Director box with two thick manuals, plus comprehensive online help.

Many new extensions to the Lingo language are specifically designed to work in the context of delivering multimedia content in HTML documents. For example, new Lingo commands allow your Director movie to continue displaying an animation while it's streaming the next segment of the movie from a network. Most of the new network Lingo commands allow you to set some sort of process in motion, check back later to see if it's finished, and then act after the process is complete. This is different from most non-network Lingo commands that execute a process and then immediately give you a result.

Even if you're an old Lingo wrangler, make sure you familiarize yourself with these new Lingo commands before you attempt to create content for plug-in delivery.

Director Limitations on HTML Pages

Some special limitations for Shocked Director movies do not apply to standard Director movies. Most of these limitations are due to the fact that the Director movie must be able to interact over a network (either an intranet or the Web).

For example, Shocked Director movies can't use movie-in-a-window, nor can it use any of the Wait For options in the tempo channel. The Director manual covers all these network limitations in detail.

Page Design Considerations

The majority of Web users use relatively slow 28.8Kbps dial-up connections. At these rates, the user can receive about 1KB of information a second, so it takes about one minute to transfer a

60KB file. Remember this when creating Director files for Web pages. Don't torture your viewers with overly long download times.

Here are some other things to consider when designing HTML pages with Shocked content:

- Although technically there's no limit on how many movies you can incorporate into a page, don't include more than three. Remember that when a user leaves a page containing shocked Director movies, the Shockwave plug-in frees the RAM it was using to play them.

- You might encounter technical problems when your browser sorts out the sound tracks of two movies playing simultaneously. Use automatically played sound in only one movie per page, and program the others so that the user can play the sound tracks by clicking the mouse.

- Movies programmed to loop indefinitely tie up the processor. It is strongly recommended that you program a movie to stop playing after a given number of loops or program some way for the user to stop the movie.

Optimizing Director Movies

Here are some tips and techniques that will help you create effective and efficient Director movies for your site:

- Keep each cast member as small as possible to keep file size down.

- Use small graphics and resize them to suit your needs. Use the Sprite Info dialog box to reset a cast member back to its normal size or any specific size.

- Use Lingo to add interactivity to your application. If possible, use Lingo loops and branches to sections of your movie.

- Use the Transform Bitmap dialog box to dither a graphic to a lower bit depth.

- To add spectral variety without adding size, set the background or foreground color of a black-and-white bitmap to another color with the Tools window.

- Use scaleable text in text fields instead of bitmapped text.

- Use objects from the Tools window whenever possible in place of bitmapped graphics.

- Use ink effects on graphics you already have before creating a new bitmap. Layering graphics with different ink effects can produce some interesting results.

- Use film loops to reuse cast members.

- Tile small bitmaps to produce backgrounds. Create tiles that have heights and widths of 16, 32, 64, or 128 pixels to maintain perfect tiling.

- Use small looping music clips instead of long soundtracks.

- Sample all sound to 11.025kHz.

- Try capturing and sequencing a few single frames from a video clip in lieu of playing a whole video.

- Render anti-aliased bitmaps to solid system colors, especially black or white.

Part
IV

Ch
26

More Information

The Online ShockWave Developer's Guide at **http://www.macromedia.com/support/ director/how/shock/** contains a great deal of detailed information about building sites that use Shocked content.

Other Multimedia Plug-Ins

At least a dozen more multimedia plug-ins are available, and more are coming all the time. You can keep up-to-date on multimedia plug-ins development by checking the Plug-Ins Plaza Web site at **http://browserwatch.iworld.com/plug-in/plug-in-mm.html**.

Shockwave for Authorware   Macromedia's latest Shockwave plug-in—Shockwave for Authorware—lets you view Authorware 4 interactive multimedia *courses* and *pieces* right in the browser window. Intended for the delivery of large, content-rich multimedia presentations such as courseware and training materials, Authorware can also write viewer data back to a server computer using FTP, so it's useful for creating market surveys, tests and quizzes, and customer service applications. If you don't already have the Shockwave plug-in, you can download Windows 95/NT, Windows 3.1, and Macintosh versions of Shockwave for Authorware from the Macromedia Web site at **http://www.macromedia.com/**.

Astound Web Player   The Astound Web Player plug-in displays multimedia documents created with the Astound or Studio M programs. These presentations can include sound, animation, graphics, video, and even interactive elements. The Astound Web Player is available for Windows 95 and Windows 3.1. If you plan to include movies in your presentations, you need QuickTime for Windows, which is also available from the Astound site at **http:// www.astoundinc.com/products/astound/webplayer.html**.

mBED   The mBED plug-in plays multimedia *mbedlets*, small applets that are intended as interesting interactive on-the-page components. mBED is not intended for big, killer multimedia applications. It's intended to create interactive multimedia buttons and spot animations. The MBD file format and the built-in mBED players are license-free. You need the mBED Interactor program to actually create your own animations. mBED is available for Windows 95/ NT, Windows 3.1, Macintosh, and PowerMac. You can find out more and download these plug-ins from **http://www.mbed.com**.

ToolBook II   Asymetrix's ToolBook II is one of the top multimedia authoring tools. With the Neuron plug-in, you can deliver ToolBook II multimedia titles over the Net. The Neuron plug-in supports external multimedia files, so you can access either complete courseware or multimedia titles or just the relevant portions of titles in real time. Content that is not requested is not downloaded, saving download time and making the application more responsive. The Neuron plug-in and a 30-day trial version of the ToolBook II program are both available for free download at Asymetrix's Web site at **http://www.asymetrix.com/toolbook2/neuron/ index.htm**.

PowerMedia   RadMedia (**http://www.radmedia.com**) has a plug-in to play multimedia applications built in RAD PowerMedia 3.0. Designed for corporate communicators and Web designers, PowerMedia provides authoring and viewing of interactive content, presentations, training, kiosks, and demos. It's available for Windows 95/NT and several UNIX platforms. The download file for this plug-in is 9MB, and the sample PowerMedia applications on the RadMedia site are also in the multi-megabyte range. If your multimedia needs are serious—especially if you are running over a fast T1 or intranet connection—you should check out this solution. Free demonstration CD-ROMs for PowerMedia are available for qualified users.

mPire   The mFactory *mPire* plug-in plays multimedia files created using its mTropolis program. Check out **http://www.mfactory.com/** for information and download availability.

SCREAM   Finally, the SCREAM inline multimedia player for Windows 3.1, Windows 95, and Macintosh is also worth a look, if only to check out a site and a program created by a company with the cool name—Saved by Technology. It's at **http://www.savedbytech.com/Scream/GetScream.htm**.

Java and Multimedia

Web page designers frequently turn to Java for multimedia. Why? Because it's fast, Java applets are small and download quickly, and they don't require the user to install a plug-in before he or she can view them.

A good programmer can churn out an effective multimedia Java applet just about as quickly as a designer can create a Shockwave file. The trick is, of course, that you need a programmer, not a designer, to do it. That's the downside.

The upside is that most Java applets are smaller than comparable Shockwave or other multimedia files. That means they download and run more quickly, and in these early days of Web development, that's what Web features ultimately want to achieve—efficient use of bandwidth.

Add in the fact that the two most popular Web browsers—Microsoft Internet Explorer and Netscape Communicator—both run Java applets right out of the box, without the need for bulky plug-ins, and you've got a compelling reason to develop your online multimedia presentations using Java.

Part
IV

Ch
26

Finding Java Applets to Borrow

Most of us aren't Java programmers. Are we left behind? Not necessarily. You see, thousands of Java applet developers out there are more than willing to share their work. Some of the Java applets on the Web are commercial works; you have to pay to use them. Some are shareware; you can try them for free, but you have to pay if you use them on your site. A surprising number of Java applet creators are more than happy to let you appropriate their work for display on your Web site.

A word of caution: Make absolutely, positively sure that any applets you "borrow" for your own site have really been released for free public use. If you run into a Java applet online that you think would look cool on your site, and it's not immediately apparent that it's up for grabs, e-mail the Webmaster and make sure you can use it before just blithely sticking it on your page.

Take a look at a few of the applets that are available for public use. You can go to several good sites on the Web to browse through bundles of accessible Java applets. A good place to start is Yahoo!'s list of sites at **http://www.yahoo.com/Computers_and_Internet/ Programming_Languages/Java/Applets/**.

If you want to find the applets themselves, you might check out the Java Applet Rating Service (JARS) at **http://www.jars.com** (see Figure 26.4).

FIG. 26.4

The JARS site not only lists Java applets; it also rates them.

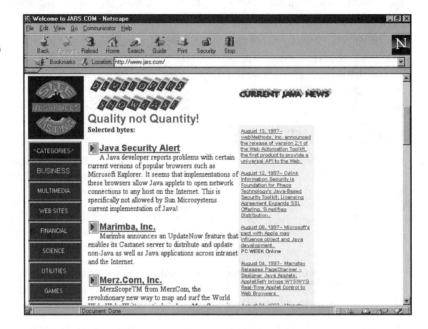

JARS rates Java applets and awards them Top 1 percent, Top 5 percent, and so on, so it's easy to see which applets are the best (at least in the opinion of JARS's independent judges). The JARS site also lists applets by category. For example, by sifting through the listings, you can see the URL for Yuri Alkin's Fractal Explorer applet (see Figure 26.5). Fractal Explorer displays beautiful images, and it lets you tweak them to your liking. It's freeware, so you can lift and use it on your own site.

Along practical lines is David Jameson's Shared Whiteboard applet (see Figure 26.6). It lets several people sketch on the same screen. Everyone can see what the others are drawing. This applet is also freeware.

Another excellent source of Java applets is the Gamelan site at **http://www.gamelan.com** (see Figure 26.7).

Scan through the lists at Gamelan and you're bound to come up with some interesting applets. One great example is the film strip animator shown in Figure 26.8.

This Java applet takes a GIF filmstrip image, breaks it into animation frames, and then presents these frames as an inline animation.

FIG. 26.5

This Java applet lets you view colorful fractal graphics.

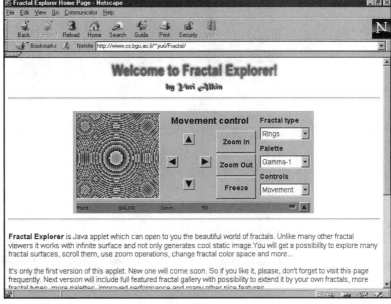

FIG. 26.6

Share sketches online with this Java applet.

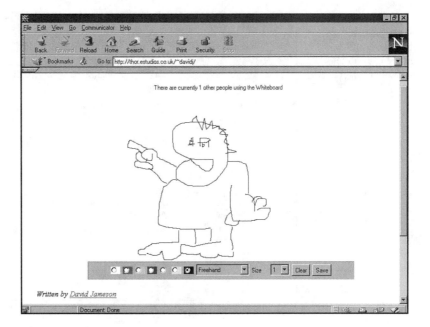

Once you find a Java applet you like at JARS or Gamelan, how do you get it onto your own Web page? Easy. Each applet is accompanied by download instructions. Once you download an applet, you find a file that explains how to use it in your own pages.

FIG. 26.7

The Gamelan site offers hundreds of Java applets listed in categories. This page links to several hundred multimedia applets.

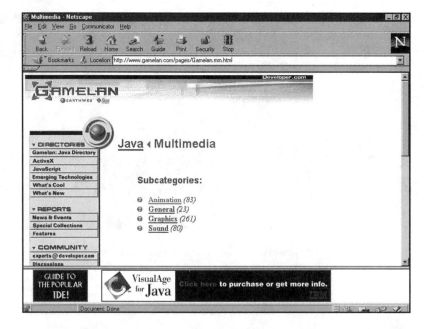

FIG. 26.8

This site provides you with a free animation applet and then shows you how to use it!

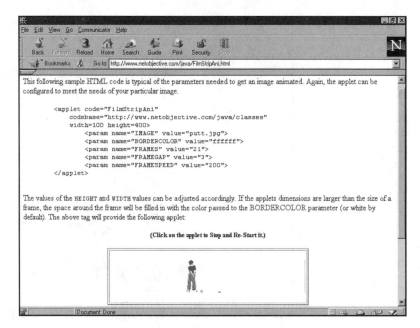

Dynamic HTML

One more way to create interactive, animated, multimedia Web pages is with Dynamic HTML. Dynamic HTML is a new set of HTML tools and standards supported in both Microsoft Internet Explorer and Netscape Communicator. Using Dynamic HTML techniques, you can create layered, animated pages with graphics that move, change, appear, and disappear, all in response to user actions. This is interactive multimedia in the truest sense of the word.

Part III, "Creating Advanced Web Pages with Dynamic HTML," covers Dynamic HTML in depth. If you're interested in creating truly dynamic Web pages using nothing but HTML, check it out. ●

Part

IV

Ch

26

## CHAPTER 27

Streaming Audio

by Mark R. Brown and Mike Morgan

In this chapter

RealAudio

With any emerging technology, being first presents a tremendous advantage. RealSystems (formerly Progressive Networks) (**www.real.com**) was the first company to deliver real-time streaming audio over the World Wide Web. Because it is being used by so many professionals, their product, RealAudio, illustrates the process of adding streaming audio to your HTML documents. Other plug-ins have different requirements—for example, many do not require special server software—but you'll find the process is more similar than it is different for embedding different audio formats into your HTML documents.

N O T E   Real System's latest product, RealPlayer, combines their streaming audio and streaming video protocols. We'll talk about streaming video in Chapter 28, "Streaming Video." Although we'll use RealAudio as the example in this chapter, chances are you may opt to handle streaming audio by installing RealPlayer on your computer.

You can get more information about RealPlayer at **http://www.real.com/products/player/index.html**. You can learn more about RealNetworks at **http://www.real.com/corporate/index.html**. ■

Since its introduction, thousands of Web sites have begun to deliver RealAudio content over the Internet. Today, it is undoubtedly the most popular streaming audio application on the Net, with more than 8 million RealAudio Players downloaded from the RealNetworks Web site.

N O T E   Netscape has introduced their Netscape Media Server and Netscape Media Player programs, which will compete heartily for the niche currently occupied by RealAudio. In addition to real-time, high-quality streaming audio, these programs also allow synchronized multimedia content. These programs provide high-quality audio even with 14.4Kbps modem connections, and automatic bandwidth-optimized streaming for the best possible audio quality at various connection speeds. Audio can be synchronized with HTML documents, Java applets, and JavaScript for a multimedia experience. Players are available for Macintosh Power Mac, all versions of Windows, and UNIX systems. More information and download files are available at the following address:

http://search.netscape.com/download/mplayer.html. ■

How RealAudio Works

RealAudio files are digitized audio; that is, they start out as analog sound, which is fed through a sound card and digitized into a stream of digital bits.

RealAudio is actually a suite of three programs that work together. The RealAudio Encoder encodes preexisting sound files or live audio streams into the RealAudio format. The RealAudio Server delivers these encoded RealAudio streams over the Internet or your company intranet. (A RealAudio Server and a Web server are often run simultaneously on the same server computer.) Finally, the RealAudio Player plays these streams when they are received by your computer. Versions of all are available from the RealNetworks Web site at **http://www.real.com/** (see Figure 27.1).

FIG. 27.1

The RealNetworks RealAudio site is a treasure trove of downloadable software, technical information, and audio streams.

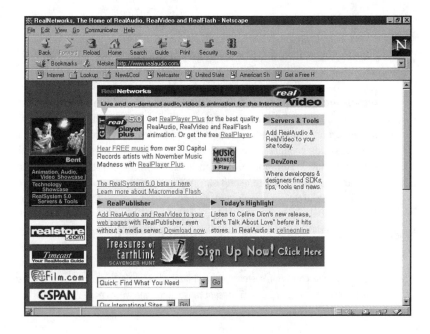

If you're just planning to listen to RealAudio on the Web or on your company's intranet, all you need is the RealAudio Player. If you want to publish RealAudio content for your Web server to deliver, you also need the RealAudio Encoder. If you run your own Web server, you need the RealAudio Server, as well.

N O T E   RealNetworks supports the LiveMedia Real-time Transport Protocol (RTP) and Microsoft's ActiveMovie Streaming Format (ASF) in all their RealAudio products. ▪

RealAudio streams are compressed and encoded from either a preexisting sound file or live audio. The RealAudio codecs can output files that are optimized for 14.4Kbps or 28.8Kbps modem delivery, or delivery over a higher speed line such as the Integrated Services Digital Network (ISDN). (If a file is intended for delivery over a fast direct Internet or intranet connection, use the high-bandwidth ISDN codec.) The resulting file is always much smaller than the original. For example, a one-minute monaural .WAV file (sampled at 22 kHz) takes up about 2.6 megabytes; the RealAudio 4.0 version, encoded with a 6.5Kbps codec, is only 42 kilobytes in size, whereas the ISDN version is about 296 kilobytes. These numbers represent compression ratios of about 62:1 and 8:1, respectively. The resulting low-bandwidth RealAudio file has a quality comparable to an AM radio broadcast and is best for speech only, whereas the quality of the high-bandwidth codec approaches CD-ROM quality and is adequate for stereo music.

The compression routines in the RealAudio Encoder leave out some sound file information; that's the nature of compression. You give up a little quality for a great gain in transmission speed. These omissions appear in the resulting audio stream as a sort of "graininess" or loss of depth and tone quality.

Part

IV

Ch

27

If you're familiar with the technical aspects of the World Wide Web, you know that the HyperText Transfer Protocol (the protocol of the Web) uses a connection-oriented communications method called the Transmission Control Protocol (TCP). The RealAudio Server delivers audio streams in a different manner. The TCP protocol, upon which the Web is based, emphasizes reliability. TCP ensures that accurate data packets are always received, even if that means retransmitting some of them to overcome errors. A different protocol, the UDP protocol, emphasizes speed, sometimes at the cost of reliability. Sacrificing reliability is bad when you're talking about sending a Java applet, for which every bit counts. Inaccurate or incomplete audio transmissions are interpreted by your ears as just a little noise, like a skip or static in a radio station signal. Much more important to audio is the uninterrupted transmission of the signal so that large blocks of audio aren't skipped and transmission continues in real time. For that reason, RealAudio uses a special server program to deliver RealAudio data packets by using the UDP protocol. Though using this program may mean an occasional skipped "sound byte," it means the data stream continues on, uninterrupted, in real time.

N O T E   To get around the problem of occasional packet loss, the RealAudio Server incorporates a loss correction system that minimizes the impact of lost packets. This system works well when packet loss is in the 2 to 5 percent range, and even works acceptably when packet loss is as high as 8 to 10 percent. ■

A RealAudio Server connection is actually a two-channel, two-way communication system: UDP is used for sound-data transmission, and TCP is used to negotiate the proper bandwidth based on the codec as well as to communicate pause, fast forward, play, and rewind commands. Because of this two-channel communication, you can listen to a RealAudio stream just as you would an audio tape. Because the stream is delivered to your computer on demand, in real time, the RealAudio Player's commands to the RealAudio Server can jump you back and forth to different spots in the audio stream. (Of course, this feature works only for prerecorded audio; live audio broadcasts are like listening to the radio.)

N O T E   RealNetworks developed RealAudio as an open architecture application and encourages RealAudio development by third parties.

The Playback Engine Application Programming Interface (API) provides software developers with direct access to the functionality of the RealAudio Player so that commercial Web authoring tools and other applications can incorporate RealAudio streams.

The Encoder API allows developers to use a variety of audio compression algorithms with RealAudio. For example, you can use Macromedia's SoundEdit 16 on the Macintosh to save sound files directly into the RealAudio format. Visit **http://www.macromedia.com/software/sound/** to learn more about this product.

The RealAudio APIs are available as part of the RealMedia Software Development Kit, available from the RealNetworks Web site at **http://www.real.com/devzone/sdks/index.html**. ■

The RealAudio Player

When you download the RealAudio Player for Windows 3.1, Windows 95/NT, Macintosh, or UNIX, you tell the server what connection speed you use. The server uses this information to choose the codecs that are appropriate for your machine. You get two versions of the RealAudio Player: one is a stand-alone program that can also be used as a browser helper application, and the other is a browser plug-in, with versions available for both Netscape Navigator and Microsoft Internet Explorer.

The RealAudio stand-alone application (shown in Figure 27.2) is a fully functional program that you can use to play RealAudio files from any source, including your own hard drive, a corporate intranet, or the World Wide Web. It's one of a growing number of applications that can access the Web independently of a browser program.

FIG. 27.2

The stand-alone RealAudio player can be used as a browser helper application or can play sound files from any source.

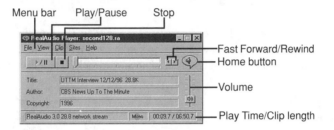

Whether you listen to a prerecorded or live-audio stream, and whether it comes from your own hard drive, a local network, or the Web, a RealAudio stream will begin playing as soon as the Player has latched onto a few packets. You don't have to wait for the whole stream to load before it starts playing. Because it's a stand-alone application, you can even go on to browse other Web pages and the RealAudio file will continue to play in the background.

The Netscape plug-in is also installed automatically when you install RealAudio. It automatically plays inline RealAudio files that have been included on Web pages using the <EMBED> tag. It manifests itself as controls that appear inline in the Web page. How many controls you see depends on how the RealAudio file has been embedded. This topic will be covered in detail later in this chapter, in the section titled "Using RealAudio Content on Your Web Pages."

NOTE If a Web page includes RealAudio content using a standard link, you'll have to click the link to hear the audio stream, and your browser will launch the stand-alone RealAudio Player as a helper application. You'll then need to close the Player after the clip is done playing.

However, if the RealAudio content is included using the <EMBED> tag, your browser will automatically use the RealAudio plug-in, and any activated controls will appear inline in the Web page. Depending on the page design, the clip may even begin playing automatically. The plug-in will remain in place until you leave the associated Web page.

Learn more about embedding multimedia content in your Web pages by reading Chapter 14, "Inserting Objects into a Web Page." ■

Part
IV

Ch
27

Installation and Setup

You can download the latest version of the RealPlayer setup program (which includes both RealAudio and RealVideo) from the RealNetworks Web page at **http://www.real.com/ products/player/index.html**. Choose either RealPlayer (which is free) or RealPlayer Plus (which includes one-button scanning as well as free technical support). Select the proper version from the online form for your computer and connection speed.

N O T E   You can run RealPlayer (with both audio and video capabilities) on Windows 95 and NT systems as well as the PowerPC Macintosh. RealNetworks is also developing versions of RealPlayer for various versions of UNIX.

The older RealAudio Player runs on Windows 3.1 machines, as well as OS/2. The Macintosh version runs on 68040 Macs with a Floating Point Unit (FPU). RealNetworks has versions of the RealAudio Player for most popular versions of UNIX. ■

After you have a copy of the RealAudio Player (or RealPlayer) setup program on your hard drive, double-click the file you downloaded to run the setup program. After you successfully install the RealAudio player, the player automatically launches and plays a welcome message.

ON THE WEB

You can get full instructions for setting up the UNIX version of RealAudio from the RealNetworks site at **http://www.real.com/help/player/unix3.0/**.

ON THE WEB

If you're having trouble playing RealAudio streams through your local area network's firewalls, check out the instructions in Real Systems Tech Support Library at **http://www.real.com/help/library/**. You can find the documents on firewalls at **http://www.real.com/help/firewall/index.html**.

Controls and Menus

The RealAudio Player controls are elementary.

The Toolbar includes Play/Pause, Stop, and a Time Into Clip Indicator. It also includes Fast Forward/Rewind buttons, which work in 10-second increments, and a Home Button. The Home Button shows a spinning speaker when the Player is receiving a file and a lightning bolt when it is encountering a high data loss. Clicking the Home Button takes you to the RealAudio home page at **http://www.realaudio.com/**.

The Volume slider is at the right side of the Player window. Title, author, and copyright information is displayed to the left of the Volume slider in the Clip Info window. The current state of the Player is displayed in the Status Bar at the bottom of the Player window, with the play time and clip length shown in the lower-right corner.

If you're listening to a Web page with embedded RealAudio content, you may see inline versions of any or all of these controls inside the Web page, depending on how the Web page has been set up.

TROUBLESHOOTING

Why don't I hear any sound from very short sound clips? The file may be too short. Current versions of the RealAudio Player will not play files shorter than one second.

N O T E Play, Pause, and Stop are also available from a right-mouse-button, pop-up shortcut menu, and the RealAudio Player menus are also pretty simple. ■

The RealAudio File menu lets you open a RealAudio file from a drive on your system or network, or from a server on an intranet or the World Wide Web. Open File (Ctrl+O) is the option for loading an .RA or .RAM file from disk or network; Open Location (Ctrl+L) lets you specify the URL of a file located on an intranet or Web site. If you use Open Recent, you'll find a list of recently played RealAudio files.

N O T E A RealAudio URL has this format:

```
pnm://Server:Port#/pathname
```

pnm:// indicates the file is located on a RealAudio Server system. Server:Port# is the address of the RealAudio Server. pathname is the complete directory path and file name. Here's a real-world example:

```
pnm://audio.realaudio.com/welcome.ra
```
■

From the View menu, you can turn on or off the display of the Player Info and Volume window or Status Bar. Choosing Preferences (Ctrl+P) brings up the Preferences dialog box, in which you can set Network, Proxy, and other advanced options. The Statistics item pops up a dialog box containing information about the current connection. (The Preferences and Statistics dialog boxes are also available from the right-mouse-button, pop-up menu.) Finally, Always on Top keeps the RealAudio Player window on top of all other open windows.

The Clip menu (or the right-mouse-button, pop-up menu) lets you choose to play the Previous (PageUp) or Next (PageDown) clip. The Sites menu takes you directly to the RealAudio Home Page, RealAudio Guide, or RealAudio Help Page. The last menu, Help, has two choices: Contents (F1) and About.

Part

IV

Ch

27

ON THE WEB

You can locate plenty of cool RealAudio sites on the Internet. Want to find some practical RealAudio sound sites? Check out Timecast (shown in Figure 27.3) at **http://www.timecast.com/**. Continually up-to-date, Timecast is the definitive guide to live RealAudio broadcasts and the best prerecorded RealAudio content on the Web. It's all there, from ABC News and PBS specials to live FM radio and real-time sports broadcasts. You can even customize your own daily news broadcast with time-sensitive, audio content delivered live.

FIG. 27.3
Timecast is the ultimate
Web guide to RealAudio
sites.

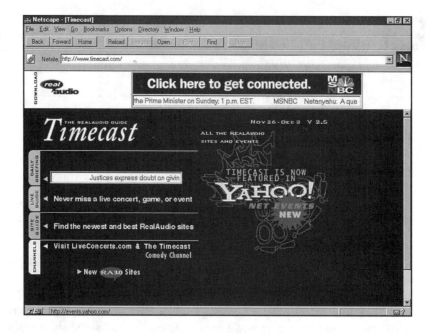

The RealAudio Encoder

You use the RealAudio Encoder (see Figure 27.4) to translate audio-format files into RealAudio
files. This encoded RealAudio material can then be played over an intranet or the Internet in
real time, using the RealAudio Server to send and the RealAudio Player to receive.

FIG. 27.4
The RealAudio Encoder
lets you specify a
Source file and a
Destination file, and you
can set Description
elements. You can also
choose the Compression
Type in the Options
window.

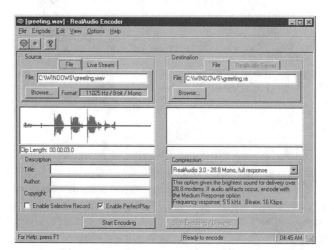

The RealAudio Encoder 3.0 (**http://www.real.com/encoder/realaudio.html**) is available for
Microsoft Windows 95/NT, Microsoft Windows 3.1, Macintosh, and several versions of UNIX.

The RealAudio Encoder supports the input file formats listed in Table 27.1.

Table 27.1   Input File Formats Supported by RealAudio Encoder

Type	Sampling Rate	Resolution
.WAV audio	8, 11, 22, 44 kHz	8- or 16-bit, monophonic
.AU audio	8, 22, 44 kHz	monophonic
raw .PCM data	8, 11, 22, 44 kHz	8- or 16-bit, monophonic

The RealAudio Encoder does not support compressed files. If you need to encode a compressed file, convert that file to one of the supported formats by using a sound-editing utility, such as Macromedia's SoundEdit 16.

Installing the RealAudio Encoder

You can download the RealAudio Encoder from the RealNetworks site at **http://www.real.com/encoder/realaudio.html.** Installation and setup are similar to that of the RealAudio Player described earlier in this chapter.

Because audio encoding is more demanding than simply playing back encoded files, you should be aware that RealNetworks recommends a minimum of a 486/66 CPU with 8M of RAM and 1M of hard drive space for installation of the Encoder program, plus an additional 1 to 2K of hard drive space per second of audio you plan to encode and store. You'll also need a 16-bit sound card capable of recording an 8kHz signal or higher. For a table showing the sampling rate required for each codec, see **http://www.real.com/encoder/rasysreq.html**.

Encoding

You need to start with a sound file in .WAV, .AU, or .PCM format. The Web is a great source of a wide variety of sound files, of course. We suggest prospecting at **http://www.yahoo.com/Computers_and_Internet/Multimedia/Sound/Archives/**. If you want to record your own sound files, you'll need an audio-digitizing program. Most sound cards come with such a program. You can record audio from tape or other external audio sources by using your sound card's line input, or you can record live audio by using its microphone input. For the specifics of how to record sound with your particular sound card, check your sound card manual.

Part
IV

Ch
27

> **CAUTION**
>
> As you do with any other content on the Web, be sure you get permission before adopting the material for your site. Plenty of material is free online, but many sound files are subject to copyright.

N O T E The RealAudio Encoder does not support compressed files or files of a format other than
.WAV, .AU, or .PCM. If your file is in a different format, you can convert it to a compatible
format by using an audio-file editing program. Several commercial products are available, or you may
want to experiment with shareware. To find a shareware editor, visit **shareware.com**, pick your platform,
and search for "sound edit."

You can sometimes get better results when encoding a sound file if you perform some adjustments to
the file before you encode it. Almost any adjustment that makes the file sound cleaner and clearer will
make the final encoded version sound better, too. Most audio-digitizing programs are capable of
performing at least a few basic adjustments like equalization or noise gating. Check out **http://
www.real.com/help/content/audiohints.html** for specific audio-editing tips. ◼

Follow these steps to encode audio files for RealAudio. (Refer back to Figure 27.4.)

1. In the RealAudio Encoder Source panel, select the File tab. Then click Browse and
    choose the source file. A default file name automatically appears in the Destination panel.

2. Either use the default file name in the Destination panel, or select a different destination.

3. In the Options panel, select the desired Compression Type. High-bandwidth codecs
    provide higher fidelity but require an ISDN (or faster) Internet connection. Low-
    bandwidth codecs are optimized for 14.4Kbps modem connections, whereas medium-
    bandwidth codecs are suitable for 28.8Kbps connections.

4. In the Description panel, enter the title, author, and copyright information for the clip.
    You can leave these fields blank.

5. If you want to listen to the audio file as it is being encoded, check the Play While
    Encoding box under Options, and choose to play the original audio file or the .RA file
    that is being created.

6. Choose Start Encoding from the Encode menu, or click the leftmost toolbar button.

N O T E The RealAudio Encoder 3.0 can encode live audio input directly from your PC's sound card.
However, only the version of the Encoder provided with the RealAudio Server 3.0 can send
the RealAudio output directly to the Server for live broadcast on the Internet. A special server utility
called the Live Transfer Agent (LTA) acts as a bridge between the RealAudio Live Encoder and the
Server. The LTA transfers encoded RealAudio from the Live Encoder to the Server in real time to allow
for live feeds.

You can encode any sound data delivered to your sound card, including CD audio. The downloadable
trial version of the Encoder has this feature disabled. ◼

If Show Audio Signal is selected under the Options menu, you'll see amplitude graphs of the
source and destination files.

A minimal set of controls is available via the Encoder menus. All these controls are intuitive,
and are explained via the Help, Contents menu selection.

N O T E The RealAudio Encoder will automatically encode a .WAV or .AU file when you drag an icon of the file to the RealAudio Encoder shortcut on your desktop.

You also can run the Encoder from the command line to encode multiple audio files automatically with options from a setting file. Complete instructions are located on RealNetworks's Web site at **http://www.real.com/help/encoder/win3.0/settings.html**. ∎

After you have an .RA format file, you need to create an associated .RAM metafile. The metafile is a text file that contains a single line containing the full URL for the .RA file. A typical .RAM file might look like this:

```
pnm://audio.realaudio.com/welcome.ra
```

The .RAM file containing this line would probably be called `welcome.ram`, to make its association with the encoded RealAudio file it calls, `welcome.ra`, clear. Why use an intermediary .RAM file to play an .RA file? Well, for one thing, .RAM files can contain a list of URLs for .RA files, which will be played in sequence. (Just make sure .RAM files that contain lists of .RA file URLs don't contain any blank lines!) For another, .RAM metafiles can contain timing instructions that will start an .RA file playing at some time into the file rather than at the beginning.

To add timing instructions to a .RAM file, you append the starting time to the end of the URL preceded by a dollar sign, like this:

```
pnm://audio.realaudio.com/welcome.ra$0:30
```

This file would begin playing 30 seconds into the .RA file. The complete format is this:

```
$dd:hh:mm:ss.t
```

`dd` signifies days, `hh` hours, `mm` minutes, `ss` seconds, and `t` is tenths of a second (note the decimal point before the `t`).

Using RealAudio Content on Your Web Pages

If you are content with having viewers of your site launching the stand-alone RealAudio player as a browser helper application, you can use a standard HTML link to play RealAudio files on your Web page, as in this example:

```
<A HREF="pnm://audio.realaudio.com/duck.ram">Duck Quacking</A>
```

This line of HTML code produces a text link labeled `Duck Quacking` that, when clicked, launches the stand-alone RealAudio Player. The viewer must click the Play button to hear the duck.RAM file and then exit the RealAudio Player program.

Part
IV

Ch
27

CAUTION

In general, you must have the RealAudio Server software installed and properly configured on a server host before you can use RealAudio content on your Web pages. For a different approach, read the comments on pseudostreaming in the section "The RealAudio Servers," later in this chapter.

Embedding Audio on Your Web Page

A more elegant solution is to use the <EMBED> tag to incorporate an inline RealAudio file, like this:

```
<EMBED SRC=" pnm://audio.realaudio.com/duck.rpm" WIDTH=300 HEIGHT=134>
```

The SRC attribute specifies the URL of the RealAudio file to play. Note that, to avoid backward compatibility conflicts with the stand-alone RealAudio Player, URLs for use with the <EMBED> tag—which invokes the RealAudio plug-in—use an .RPM extension instead of the .RAM extension. In all other ways, however, files with an .RPM extension are identical to .RAM files; they differ only in the file-name extension.

The WIDTH and HEIGHT attributes specify the size of the embedded component. Unlike images, plug-ins do not size automatically. The WIDTH and HEIGHT can be specified in pixels (the default) or percentages of screen width (for example, WIDTH=100 percent).

Here's the generic syntax for using the <EMBED> tag with RealAudio files:

```
<EMBED SRC=source_URL WIDTH=width_value HEIGHT=height_value
[CONTROLS=option] [AUTOSTART=True] [CONSOLE=value] [NOLABELS=True]>
```

The CONTROLS, AUTOSTART, CONSOLE, and NOLABELS attributes are specific to RealAudio, and are all optional.

The CONTROLS attribute defines which RealAudio Player controls appear embedded on the Web page. Table 27.2 lists all the valid values for the CONTROLS attribute.

Table 27.2   Values for the *CONTROLS* Attribute

Value	Description
CONTROLS = All	Embeds a full Player view including the ControlPanel, InfoVolumePanel, and StatusBar. (This value is the default if CONTROLS is not specified.)
CONTROLS = ControlPanel	Embeds the Play/Pause button, the Stop button, and the Position slider. (Same as the stand-alone Player application with none of the options on the View menu checked.)
CONTROLS = InfoVolumePanel	Embeds the information area showing title, author, and copyright with a Volume slider on the right side. (Same as the panel displayed by the stand-alone Player application when the Info and Volume option on the View menu is checked.)
CONTROLS = InfoPanel	Similar to InfoVolumePanel, but this value embeds the information area showing title, author, and copyright without the Volume slider.
CONTROLS = StatusBar	Embeds the Status Bar showing informational messages, current time position, and clip length. (Same as the panel displayed by the stand-alone Player application when the Status Bar option on the View menu is checked.)

Value	Description
CONTROLS = PlayButton	Embeds the Play/Pause button only.
CONTROLS = StopButton	Embeds the Stop button only.
CONTROLS = VolumeSlider	Embeds the Volume slider only.
CONTROLS = PositionSlider	Embeds the Position slider (scroll bar) only.
CONTROLS = PositionField	Embeds the field of the Status Bar that shows Position and Length.
CONTROLS = StatusField	Embeds the field of the Status Bar that displays message text and progress indicators.

If you set AUTOSTART=TRUE, the plug-in automatically begins playing the RealAudio file when the page is visited. Use this feature to begin a narration or play background music automatically. Because only one RealAudio clip can play at a time, if you specify AUTOSTART for more than one <EMBED> tag, only the last one to load will play automatically. (The order in which the source files arrive is dependent on the Web server and Netscape's cache.)

The CONSOLE attribute lets you relate any number of clips that appear on the same Web page together. Normally, each is independent; but the clips that are related by the CONSOLE attribute are controlled by the same controls. To relate two RealAudio clips on the same page, you simply give them each a CONSOLE attribute with the same name. Here's an example:

```
<EMBED SRC="sample1.rpm" WIDTH=30 HEIGHT=33 CONTROLS="PlayButton"
CONSOLE="Clip1">
<EMBED SRC="empty1.rpm" WIDTH=300 HEIGHT=33 CONTROLS="PositionSlider"
CONSOLE="Clip1">
```

Normally, the first clip would have an associated Play Button, and the second would have a Position slider. However, because these clips both have the attribute CONSOLE="Clip1", the Play Button and Position slider work for both clips.

You can specify a CONSOLE value of "_master" to link one clip to all the others on a Web page. Use this value when you want a control such as a StatusBar to display information for all your audio clips.

If your clip includes controls (such as InfoPanel and InfoVolumePanel) that display the title, author, and copyright information, you can suppress this information by using the attribute NOLABELS=TRUE.

If you're concerned about people who use browsers that don't support the <EMBED> tag, don't worry; just use the <NOEMBED> tag to include alternative content. Follow the EMBED line with a line like this:

```
<NOEMBED> Content for non-capable browsers </NOEMBED>
```

For example, including a line that would launch the RealAudio helper application automatically if a browser doesn't support plug-ins would be nice, as shown here:

```
<EMBED SRC="sample1.rpm" WIDTH=300 HEIGHT=134>
<NOEMBED><A SRC="sample1.ram"> Use the RealAudio helper app! </A></NOEMBED>
```

> **CAUTION**
>
> Don't accidentally use an .RPM file when you mean to use an .RAM file to launch the stand-alone RealAudio
> Player as a helper application! If you do, you'll get a full-screen instance of the RealAudio plug-in instead!
>
> Here's what not to do:
>
> `<A HREF="sample1.rpm">Play sample clip full-screen!</A>`

The HTML code in Listing 27.1 implements three instances of RealAudio clips on the same
Web page. The results are shown in Figure 27.5.

Listing 27.1   Implementing Three RealAudio Clips on a Page

```
<HTML>
<HEAD>
<TITLE>RealAudio EMBED Examples</TITLE>
</HEAD>

<BODY>
<H1>Examples</H1>
<P>Here are three examples of the RealAudio Plug-in.</P>
<P>These examples require the RealAudio Player 2.0 or greater.</P>
<H2>(1) Play and Stop buttons only</H2>
<EMBED SRC="audio/jazz.rpm" ALIGN=BASELINE WIDTH=40 HEIGHT=20
CONTROLS=PlayButton CONSOLE="jazz2">
<EMBED SRC="audio/jazz.rpm" ALIGN=BASELINE WIDTH=40 HEIGHT=20
CONTROLS=StopButton CONSOLE="jazz2">
The "CONTROL" command specifies which attributes of the plug-in you want
displayed.<P>
The "CONSOLE" command allows the two elements to affect the same music clip.
<H2>(2) Control Panel only</H2>
<EMBED SRC="audio/tchai.rpm" WIDTH=200 HEIGHT=35 CONTROLS=ControlPanel>
<H2>(3) Entire Plugin</H2>
<EMBED SRC="audio/pace.rpm" WIDTH=300 HEIGHT=135 CONTROLS=All>
</BODY>
</HTML>
```

Using ActiveX to Add RealAudio Content

If the visitors to your Web site are prepared to handle ActiveX controls, you can use the
<OBJECT> tag to install the proper control:

```
<OBJECT
  ID=RAOCX
  CLASSID="clsid:CFCDAA003-8BE4-11cf-B84B-0020AFBBCCFA"
  HEIGHT=140
  WIDTH=312>
<PARAM NAME="SRC" VALUE="pnm://audio.realaudio.com/file.ra">
<PARAM NAME="CONTROLS" VALUE="all">
</OBJECT>
```

FIG. 27.5

This page uses the RealAudio plug-in three different ways.

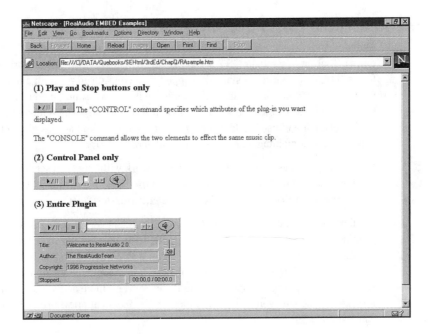

The value of the parameters such as CONTROLS, CONSOLE, and AUTOSTART are identical to those used with the Navigator plug-in.

 TIP Set HEIGHT and WIDTH to 0 to make the ActiveX control invisible.

The RealAudio Servers

The RealAudio Server is available in two versions: the RealAudio Basic Server and the Real Server families. Both incarnations send RealAudio audio streams over a network (intranet or Internet) to users of the RealAudio Player (or Real Player). The Basic Server is intended for light duty, and typically runs on the same host as your Web server. The RealServer family is RealNetwork's high-end product; it is designed to support large commercial and intranet sites. Note, too, that there are some support and licensing restrictions on the Basic Server. Check the licensing agreement for details.

Part
IV

Ch
27

 TIP If your needs are modest, you might not need a RealAudio Server at all. RealNetworks supports a "pseudostreaming" protocol based on HTTP and TCP. To learn how to serve a streaming audio file directly from your Web server, see **http://www.realaudio.com/help/content/httpstream.html**. You may also want to read the white paper at **http://www.real.com/help/content/http_vs_ra.html**.

The RealAudio Basic Server

The RealAudio Basic Server runs on a 486 or Pentium system running Windows 95 or Windows NT, or on Macintosh OS 7.5.x or higher. It is also available on a variety of UNIX platforms. The Basic Server is started, stopped, and configured through a user-friendly graphical interface. In a typical installation, the server delivers two simultaneous audio streams. Each stream requires 10Kbits per second of network bandwidth, which means you'll need a 56Kbps or T1 leased line to use it effectively. It supports full-random access for each stream and generates a log file containing usage statistics and error information.

 Generally, you can set up the Basic Server to work with any Web server that supports configurable MIME types. You can download the Basic Server directly from the Web. See **http://www.real.com/server/basic/index.html/** for details.

You'll probably want to install the RealAudio Basic Server on the same computer that's running your Web server. You can run it on a separate machine, but because it takes up so little in the way of resources, you really don't need to run it this way. To install the server, all you have to do is double-click the server setup file icon. When installation is complete, the RealAudio Basic Server Control Panel will open and the Basic Server will be activated. Before setting up your RealAudio Web site, you will need to identify the file location where you want to store your audio and log files.

Setting MIME Types

One task you must perform before either version of the RealAudio Server can deliver RealAudio content is to configure your Web server to recognize the MIME types listed in Table 27.3.

Table 27.3 RealAudio MIME Types	
Extension	**MIME Type Definition**
.RA, .RAM	`audio/x-pn-realaudio`
.RPM	`audio/x-pn-realaudio/plugin`

The process for setting MIME types varies from Web server to Web server; check your server documentation for details on how to set MIME types for your particular server. But don't forget to do so. If you don't set these types, viewers will be prompted to save the file to disk.

Real Servers

RealNetworks distributes three packages based on their "RealSystem."

- *An Internet package.* This family of high-end servers can support 100 simultaneous connections from a properly configured host.
- *Intranet Systems.* The intranet version of Real System's server products comes with a training bundle that will help you get your intranet up and running quickly.

■ *The "commerce" package.* Pick and choose the features you need to satisfy your customers.

ON THE WEB

http://www.real.com/server/   Start on this page to learn about the range of RealNetworks servers available.

CAUTION

Streaming audio can require 10 to 20Kbps or higher per connection, depending on the codec you choose and the bandwidth negotiated. You can easily install a server that will saturate several 56Kbps leased lines. Talk to RealNetworks about your plans; you may need to budget for several T1s to support the load on your site.

N O T E   The Real Servers support Bandwidth Negotiation. This feature allows a RealAudio Player to select the best version of the audio clip automatically, based on the throughput of the available connection.

To use this feature, you must use the RealAudio Encoder to create two or more stream files. In the directory you have set up as your source for .RA files, for each sound you want to deliver you create a subdirectory that contains all versions of the encoded file. The 14.4 encoded file should be called 14_4.18, and the 28.8 file should be named 28_8.36. You should reference the subdirectory—which should be named to include the .RA extension—rather than a specific file in the URL listed in the associated .RAM or .RPM file. A utility called raconv, which is included with the RealAudio Server 3.0, automates this process. See **http://www.real.com/help/server/server2.0/contman.html** for full details. ■

You can configure the RealAudio Server to work with any Web server that supports configurable MIME types. It works with all popular servers, including Netscape Enterprise and Microsoft Internet Information Server.

Synchronized Multimedia

The most advanced feature of the Real Server is its capability to synchronize RealAudio clips to serve as elements in a multimedia presentation. The process is straightforward but involves three distinct steps.

Synchronized multimedia "shows" should take place only on pages that include frames. One frame is reserved for the RealAudio plug-in with its associated controls, and at least one frame is needed to display the multimedia content. This design is necessary because loading a new page would otherwise replace the page containing the plug-in, which stops the plug-in from playing. By using frames, you keep the plug-in active.

▶   **See** "Framing Your Web Site," **p. 215**

Part

IV

Ch

27

First, build a text file listing the times that the frame content should change and the URLs that should be loaded at those times. The format is:

```
u starttime endtime URL
```

The starting `u` is required for each line. The `starttime` and `endtime` elements have the format `dd:hh:mm:ss.t`, where `dd` is days, `hh` is hours, `mm` is minutes, `ss` is seconds, and `t` is tenths of a second. (This same format is used for delayed play in .RAM files.) These times refer to the time in the clip at which the frame should begin and end playing. You must include the number of seconds; you can omit finer- or coarser-grained times as desired. `URL` is the URL of the frame to be displayed at the indicated time. You should have no blank lines between lines in the list. However, the input file can contain comment lines beginning with the # symbol. A real-world example might look like this:

```
u 00:00:10.0 00:00:59.9 http://www.RealAudio.com/
u 00:01:00.0 00:02:00.0 http://www.mysite.com/page2/
```

This input file tells the Player to send the Web browser to the RealAudio home page at 10 seconds into the audio clip. At one minute into the audio clip, the Web browser will display a page from `www.mysite.com`.

After you build this text file, you must compile it into a binary by using the `cevents` command-line tool supplied with the server. The syntax is:

```
cevents source.txt audiofilename.rae
```

The resulting .RAE file (which should have the same base name as the associated .RA audio file) is then placed in the same directory as the .RA audio file. This file is automatically located by the RealAudio Server when the listener opens the associated .RA file. The RealAudio Server streams audio and event information to the Player. As the event information is streamed to the RealAudio Player, the RealAudio Player then sends requests to the Web browser telling it when to update the page's content.

ON THE WEB

Detailed information on creating RealAudio Synchronized Multimedia files is available at **http://www.real.com/reate/synchmm.html**.

Netscape Media Player and Server

Netscape has targeted its SuiteSpot family of servers (which includes the Netscape Media Server) for intranet users. The media server can accommodate audio clips (after the manner of Real Systems' servers). It also supports live events. Because many live events will quickly outstrip even the 100-plus simultaneous connections that can be supported by high-end servers, Netscape recommends that live events be placed on the Net by using multicasting. Figure 27.6 shows the Media Server being configured for such an event.

FIG. 27.6
Use multicasting to reduce bandwidth demands during a live feed.

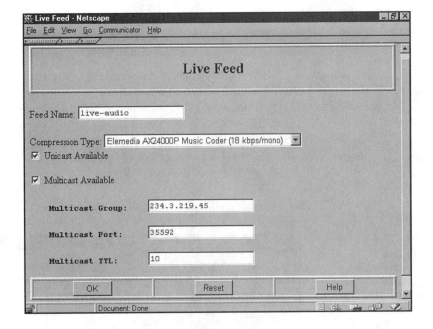

Understanding Multicasting

In conventional Internet Protocol transmissions (known as *unicasting*), each packet has a designated destination. If two users connect to the same source, two connections are set up. Identical data is sent to each end user. Each connection consumes processor power and, more importantly, bandwidth.

A better approach is to assign a Class D (multicasting) address and port as the "destination" of each packet from the live feed. Then each user who wants to listen to the feed "tunes in" to that address and port. Because the server needs only one real-time connection, the load on the server and the network is modest, and the number of listeners is virtually unlimited.

 T I P If you're producing a live event for consumption inside your organization, set the packet Time-To-Live low so that the multicasted packets won't pass beyond your firewall.

Integrating Netscape's Media Player into Your Web Site

Netscape uses the Internet standard Real-Time Streaming Protocol (RTSP) as the basis for communications between the Media Server and the Media Player. After you set up a Media Server and place content on it, the easiest way to add that content to a Web page is to use an rtsp:// URL.

N O T E Netscape worked with RealNetworks to develop the RTSP. You'll notice many similarities between the Netscape media products and RealNetworks' software. ∎

Part
IV

Ch
27

As you do with RealNetworks' line of products, you add Netscape's streaming audio to a Web page by writing a metafile and then referencing the metafile in an <EMBED> tag. Netscape's version of the metafile is called .LAM, for Live Audio Metafile.

Also as you do with RealNetwork's products, you need to run a utility to encode your audio in streaming format (here called LiveAudio format). Netscape's utility is called the Media Converter. Not only will this converter build LiveAudio out of non-streaming formats, it will also write the .LAM file and the <EMBED> tag for you. A typical <EMBED> tag might read as follows:

```
<EMBED SRC="http://www.xyz.com/Media/test.lam" OPTIONS=TRUE
PLAYBUTTON=TRUE STOPBUTTON=TRUE VOLUME=TRUE SEEK=TRUE
HEIGHT=29 WIDTH=325 LOOP=TRUE AUTOSTART=TRUE>
</EMBED>
```

Figure 27.7 shows the resulting instance of the Media Player plug-in.

FIG. 27.7
If you specify
OPTIONS=TRUE
PLAYBUTTON=TRUE
STOPBUTTON=TRUE
VOLUME=TRUE
SEEK=TRUE, you'll get
this set of controls.

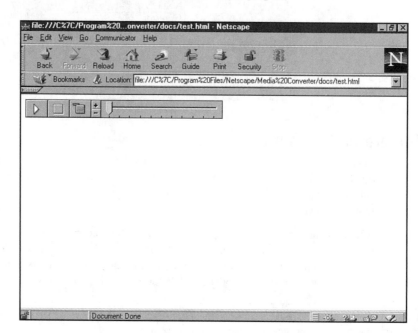

 T I P If you want to provide end users with a different set of controls than the ones built into the Media Player, you can use Netscape's LiveConnect technology and the Java language to build a different interface.

Xing's StreamWorks

Xing Technology has built their streaming audio solution (as well as a streaming video solution) around the industry standard, MPEG, also known as ISO CD 11172. MPEG, developed by the Moving Pictures Experts Group, includes standards for highly compressed video as well as audio. The third part of the MPEG I standard, ISO CD 11172-3, addresses audio compression.

MPEG's audio standard is based on perceptual codecs, which take advantage of the fact that certain sounds cannot be detected by the human ear even when they are present in the signal. MPEG audio is defined in three layers; each layer offers higher performance (and increased complexity) than the one before it. Each layer is also compatible with the one before it; a layer-2 decoder can decode a bit stream encoded in layer-1.

Perceptual codecs can be tested only by live human evaluators. Table 27.4 shows the scale used in MPEG listening tests, in which human listeners compare the encoded sound with the original sound.

Table 27.4   Human Listeners Evaluate Sound Sources on a Scale of 1 to 5

Score	Meaning
5.0	Transparent (encoded signal is indistinguishable from the original)
4.0	Perceptible difference but not annoying
3.0	Slightly annoying
2.0	Annoying
1.0	Very annoying

Table 27.5 summarizes the quality and target bit rate for the three MPEG audio layers.

Table 27.5   For Moderate Bit Rates, Layer-3 Scores Appreciably Better Than Layer-2

Layer	Quality	Target Bit Rate
Layer-1	N/A	192Kbps
Layer-2	2.1 to 2.6	128Kbps
Layer-3	3.6 to 3.8	64Kbps

The quality figures in this table are for bit rates of around 60 to 64Kbps—roughly comparable to a 56Kbps dial-up connection or a single B-channel ISDN line. At bit rates of 120Kbps, layer-2 and layer-3 performed about the same; listeners found it difficult to distinguish the encoded signals from the originals.

XingMPEG Encoder

Use the XingMPEG Encoder to convert audio files such as .WAV and MPEG 2 audio files, as well as QuickTime and AVI movies, to the industry-standard MPEG format.

N O T E   The XingMPEG Encoder is optimized for Intel's MMX technology. If you want to convert files quickly, be sure to use an MMX-enhanced Pentium. ■

StreamWorks Server and Player

After you convert your files to MPEG audio format, use Xing's StreamWorks Server to make your files available to the Web. (You can use the same software to send MPEG video, as well.)

When an end user connects to your .XDM file, the user's browser will invoke the StreamWorks Player program, as shown in Figure 27.8.

FIG. 27.8

Xing Technology's StreamWorks player can play audio or display video clips.

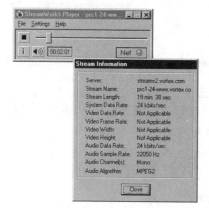

## CHAPTER 28

Streaming Video

by Mike Morgan

In this chapter

Adding Streaming Video—Why Your Connection Must Change

Currently, streaming video is the most demanding content you can add to your Web page. Despite tremendous advances in the technology, streaming video places demands on your server and its connection to the Internet, and on your users' machines and *their* connection to the Net.

The following sections describe the requirements of full-speed video transmission—the kind you get on your television—and then shows how the latest technology enables you to send video over the Internet.

> **N O T E**   Some technology forecasters predict that, by the year 2000, your television, your computer, and your telephone will all be combined into a single appliance. They predict that the integration of streaming video into the Internet is one of the most important technical changes in this century. ▨

ON THE WEB

http://www.hypertech.co.uk/video/digvid.htm   Visit this "Guide to Digital Video" for the latest information on digital and desktop video. The focus is on local networks and CD-ROMs, but you also can find links to sites that describe various aspects of Web-based streaming video.

Broadcast Video

When you turn on your television, you receive a video signal that refreshes at a rate of about 30 frames per second. (The reality is a bit more complex; a single frame of broadcast video consists of two interlaced fields, plus a brief period between frames. U.S. television sends 60 fields per second with 525 lines per frame, whereas European television sends 50 fields per second with 650 lines per frame.) The complete picture contains about 600,000 dots of information—200,000 in each of the three primary colors, red, green, and blue.

Along with this information, the broadcaster sends information about the brightness (called *luminance*) and chroma at each dot. (*Chroma* is the degree to which a color is diluted with white.) The broadcaster also sends synchronizing information so that the receiver knows when to start a new field, and one or two channels of audio. In conventional broadcasting, the finished color television signal occupies a band 6 MHz wide.

To pack this enormous amount of information onto an Internet dial-up connection, changes have to be made. The next two sections describe the ways in which engineers have transformed both the video signal and the Internet itself to make streaming video possible.

Squeezing the Signal

One of the easiest ways to improve the quality of streaming video is to resolve to send less content. You can reduce the size of video content by using some of the same techniques popular with still images: reduce the size of the image and reduce its color depth. With still images, you often experiment by encoding the image as a GIF or a JPEG to see which format gives you the best quality for the smallest size. Likewise, you can choose from a variety of coding techniques (represented by *codecs*) to compress your video data.

The next section describes each of these techniques for reducing the bandwidth required by the video.

Codecs   The first engineering technique used to support streaming video is to take advantage of the large amounts of redundancy in the signal. Most television signals actually change very little from frame to frame. Compressors/decompressors, or codecs, compress the signal by a factor of 26:1 or more.

ON THE WEB

http://www.microsoft.com/netshow/codecs.htm   You'll find a nice tutorial on codec technology on the Microsoft site. You should also visit **www.codeccentral.com** for one-stop information on multimedia codecs.

Much of the dramatic capability the newest codecs have comes from the fact that they change their sampling rate as they run. If you see a codec that advertises itself as "fixed rate," it comes from an earlier generation; it may still be useful, but it won't have the compression capability of a variable-rate codec.

T I P   If you're adding streaming video to your site, you should compare codecs carefully. Your choice of codec is the single biggest factor that determines how much bandwidth you need for connecting your server and how much bandwidth an end user needs to receive your content.

Note, too, that some bandwidth is required for network overhead. If you're designing content for a 28.8Kbps dial-up connection, make sure the total bandwidth of your video and audio content stays below about 22Kbps to leave room for the overhead.

Many of the codecs available in streaming video products follow international standards. For example, H.261 and H.263 are the video coding standards developed by the International Tele-communication Union/Telecommunication Standardization Sector (ITU-T). H.261 is designed for videoconferencing and videophones. It supports bitrates of 64Kbps to 1,920Kbps. H.263 is designed for low-bitrate video; the basic configuration of the video source coding is based on H.261.

N O T E   You'll sometimes hear H.261 referred to as "P*64" because its bitrate is defined as the number p, which ranges from 1 to 30, times 64Kbps. ▪

ON THE WEB

http://rice.ecs.soton.ac.uk/peter/h261/h261.html   You can compare H.261 codecs at various settings by viewing the video available here. You'll find a similar page for H.263 at **http://rice.ecs. soton.ac.uk/peter/h263/h263.html**.

Part

IV

Ch

28

When developing streaming video, some experts expressed concern that the H.261-based codecs lacked the power to deal with the full range of video sequences. After all, they said, H.261 was developed for teleconferencing, in which every frame is much like every other frame—a talking head moving slightly from frame to frame. A clip of a football game, on the other hand, is characterized by high spatio-temporal complexity—the image changes dramatically within a short time span.

The Moving Pictures Expert Group (MPEG) has released an encoding standard for both audio and video content. The formal name of the standard is ISO/IEC JTC1 SC29 WG11, which says that it is the product of Work Group 11 of Subcommittee 29 of Joint Technical Committee 1 of the International Organization for Standardization/International Electro-technical Commission; everyone calls it MPEG. Much of the recent activity in streaming video has been based on MPEG-4, the MPEG initiative for very low bitrate coding. Loosely defined, the target range for MPEG-4 is 176×144 pixel images, with a frame rate of 10 frames per second, coded for a bitrate of 4,800 to 64,000 bps—precisely the range covered by today's dial-up connections.

ON THE WEB

http://www.crs4.it/HTML/LUIGI/MPEG/mpegfaq.html   Although this page is becoming dated, it gives a good overview of the MPEG standard.

TIP   If you're serving an audience that has a variety of connection speeds—some users with 28.8Kbps dial-up connections and others with high-speed intranets—encode the content with several different codecs, one for each speed.

Be sure to choose codecs that will be available to your end users—preferably ones that come with the player application. That way, you'll be sure that end users can play back your encoded content.

To find out what audio and video codecs are installed on a Windows 95 or Windows NT machine, open the Multimedia control panel and choose the Devices tab, as shown in Figure 28.1. Here you'll see a list of your codecs.

FIG. 28.1

Use the Multimedia control panel to see which codecs are already installed on your machine.

Smaller Images   The second engineering technique is that most streaming video technologies are designed for an image that's not much larger than a postage stamp. Unlike with television, in which the user sits across the room looking at a screen that's 19 inches or more across, most computer users sit within a foot or two of their screens. An image that's two inches across on your computer screen appears to the user to be about the same size as a 19-inch image viewed from across the room.

Fewer Colors   Third, many streaming video technologies sacrifice color depth. A typical television image can contain many thousands of different shades and hues, but the image may still be usable with as few as 8 or 16 colors.

Slower Frame Rate   Finally, most streaming video technologies slow the frame rate down—way down. At low bandwidths such as a 28.8Kbps dial-up link, the frame rate may drop to one frame every two or three seconds.

> **N O T E**   When the pace of a video is relatively slow, many codecs can predict much of the next frame with very little bandwidth. This capability allows the video player to buffer several frames. If the data connection becomes noisy, or the action on the video becomes fast-paced, the player may be able to supply enough frames out of its buffer that the end user cannot tell a problem occurred. Because even fast-paced video clips usually are not fast-paced all the time, a streaming video product that falls a bit behind real time is likely to have a chance to catch up before the buffer becomes empty. ■

Expanding the Pipe

The second major technology change that is making streaming video possible is the revolution in connection capacity. Although many businesses pass information around their intranets at 10Mbps or more, their connection to the Internet may be only 1.54Mbps (on a T1 link). That connection may be shared by dozens of simultaneous users.

Most home users have connections that are even slower (though they seldom have to share them). The old reliable 14.4 and 28.8Kbps modems are rapidly being replaced by 33.6Kbps and 56Kbps modems. Even faster technologies—dual-channel ISDN at 128Kbps and Asymmetrical Digital Subscriber Line (ADSL) at 1.5Mbps and faster—promise affordable high-speed connections to many users.

ON THE WEB

http://www.coe.uga.edu/resources/gsams/onramp/adsl.html   Some telephone companies are offering Asymmetrical Digital Subscriber Lines (ADSL) for around $100 per month. If this price/performance ratio sounds attractive to you, visit this site to learn more about high-speed connections. If you're in Pacific Bell's service area, learn more at **http://www.pacbell.com/products/business/fastrak/adsl/index.html**

Part
IV

Ch
28

From the point of view of the server, a popular piece of video on a Web site can be devastating. Suppose you have a Web page that receives 100,000 visits per day; the page, including graphics, is 60K. If the average user can receive the content at a rate of 30,000 bits per second, and if all the requests were distributed evenly throughout the day, you could support the load on your server by supporting about 23 simultaneous 30Kbps connections. That works out to about 694Kbps. Because the requests won't be evenly distributed, you'll probably want to provide at least twice that capacity; a 1.54Mbps-wide T1 connection could provide adequate performance.

Now suppose that you add a modest streaming video clip—say, 5 minutes at 22Kbps—to the page. If every visitor plays the clip, you need more than 90 times the original capacity. If you needed a single T1 before, you now need between 30 and 60 T3 connections. The communications cost impact is staggering, not to mention the additional computing power that would be required.

The essence of video-on-demand is *unicasting:* each user gets his or her own connection to the server. An alternative design is called *multicasting*. Instead of sending the video to each user upon request, the video clip (or live event) is played continuously to a special address (called a Class D, or multicast, address). Anyone who wants to listen in can "tune in" to that address. (You can always spot a Class D address—the first octet will be between 224 and 239. Thus, 225.1.2.3 is a Class D address.)

N O T E You can learn more about multicasting in RFC 1112, "Host Extensions for IP Multicasting." RFCs are "Requests for Comments," many of which serve to define standards on the Internet. You can download RFC 1112 from **http://ds.internic.net/rfc/rfc1112.txt** or another RFC repository closer to you.

If you replace your video clip with a multicast feed, you need only one connection in addition to those already provided for the static page content. The additional connection could be at a speed as low as 22Kbps. You can accommodate this additional load easily, with little or no change in the communications configuration.

Much of the early work on multicasting was done with the Virtual Internet Backbone for Multicast IP, or MBONE. At that time, many routers—the boxes that steer data packets around the Net—did not accommodate multicasting. The design of the MBONE was to provide multicasting in many small areas and connect these multicasting centers together with unicasting connections (known as *tunnels*).

Today many routers support multicasting, so the need for the MBONE is not as great as it once was. On the other hand, the rise of streaming video has increased the demand for bandwidth. Many of the lessons learned on the MBONE are applicable to the ways servers and networks are designed to support streaming video.

ON THE WEB

http://www.best.com/~prince/techinfo/mbone.html   Learn about MBONE applications and technical information.

Streaming Video—The Market

The combination of highly compressed video and higher bandwidth connections has made streaming video a reality. The largest players in the computing industry, including Microsoft and Oracle, are making major investments to ensure that content providers and end users adopt their particular technology. This section summarizes the leading video formats and products:

- RealNetworks—The same folks who introduced streaming audio (with RealAudio) have taken the early lead in streaming video. RealNetworks' latest servers and players support both audio and video content. See Chapter 27, "Streaming Audio," for more information about RealNetworks. (Note that RealNetworks was formerly named Progressive Networks—you'll still see that name from time to time.)

- VDOnet—VDOnet Corporation achieved fame in the videoconferencing market with VDOPhone. They have allied with Microsoft to provide streaming video, agreeing to use Microsoft's Active Streaming Format (ASF) for media storage. They are also working with Microsoft to migrate their clients from their own VDOLive products to Microsoft's NetShow.

- Vivo—One of the first players in the streaming video market, Vivo has strong ties to Microsoft and NetShow.

- VXtreme—VXtreme has been another serious player; recently Microsoft bought this company.

- Microsoft—Microsoft has entered the streaming video market largely by investing in the existing technology companies. They own 10 percent of RealNetworks, developers of RealVideo. They own VXtreme outright and have also named VDOnet as a "Premier Provider of Solutions for Broadband Video Networks." Microsoft's product, NetShow, is based on their own Active Streaming Format.

- Xing Technology—Xing has taken a different approach from RealNetworks and Microsoft, delivering efficient MPEG compressors and streaming technology.

- Apple Computer—Apple was the leader in multimedia technology, introducing their QuickTime format soon after the Macintosh came out. They have developed an experimental streaming version of QuickTime but put the project on hold during their reorganization early in 1997. Apple has announced that streaming video will be integrated into the QuickTime format in 1998.

ON THE WEB

http://www.vdo.net/cgi-bin/press?54   Learn more about the strategic alliance between Microsoft and VDOnet from this press release.

The remainder of this chapter examines each of these technologies in detail.

RealVideo

RealNetworks, the folks who first developed streaming audio, added streaming video in early 1997. Today they are combining the two protocols: the client is called RealPlayer, and the servers belong to a family known as Real Servers. RealNetworks has the lion's share of what is still a fairly small market; their competitor, Microsoft, has made a 10 percent investment in them. Microsoft has also invested heavily in other companies with similar technology; they have taken an equity position in VDOnet Corporation, and they own VXtreme outright.

The following sections describe the process of developing video content and delivering it to the desktop.

ON THE WEB

http://www.real.com/products/realvideo/index.html   Start here to visit RealNetworks' online description of RealVideo.

Before You Start: Non-Technical Considerations

Many of the issues related to producing video for the Internet have nothing to do with technology. Here's a checklist of steps you should take when getting ready to shoot your own video:

1. Develop a storyboard, showing your video scene by scene. Remember to keep your overall design simple; shorter is better.

2. Script each scene. Again, keep your design simple and short.

3. Arrange for actors, props, locations, and other resources. Use professional actors whenever possible; the quality will show through in your finished product.

4. Obtain high-quality cameras. Although you may not need professional-quality equipment, don't try to do professional work with VHS or 8mm camcorders. Invest in, or rent, a Hi8 camera, such as the Sony TR400.

5. Make sure you budget for high-quality microphones as well as a good mixer and audio capture board. Poor audio ruins more productions than poor video.

6. During filming, keep the camera steady and let the actors move. Shots in which the camera moves are based on advanced techniques and should be left to the professionals. Be sure you stay close to the action; remember that the finished product will be only an inch or so across.

7. Make sure you get plenty of light. Your video is more likely to be too dark than too light.

You'll have a choice of video formats going into your video capture system. The most common formats, shown here in order of decreasing quality, are

- Betacam-sp (also known as Beta)
- Satellite television (for example, Direct TV)
- Laserdisc
- S-VHS (Super-VHS)
- VHS

Note, too, that you'll often have a choice of S-Video or Composite output from your video hardware. S-Video generally gives somewhat higher quality.

ON THE WEB

http://www.yahoo.com/Business_and_Economy/Companies/Entertainment/VideoProduction/
If, after reviewing this section, you decide to hire a professional to produce your video, check out the listings on Yahoo!. Make sure the company you choose has prior experience producing streaming video for use on the Internet.

Video Capture Hardware

The first step in producing a RealVideo clip is to capture the video and audio to the disk. You'll need two computer components for this step (in addition to lights, camcorder, and other equipment for the actual production):

- Video Capture Card
- Seagate A/V Professional Disk Drive

N O T E If you already have your video in QuickTime or AVI format, you can skip this step and go directly to encoding.

Video Capture Card One place where you can save in your video budget is on your video card. Video cards come in a range of quality, from some low-budget cards priced at under $1,000, to professional-grade cards costing thousands of dollars. If you're producing content for use on a CD-ROM or other non-network delivery mechanism, you'll appreciate the difference in quality. Unless the video you're producing will also be used off the Web, however, you don't need to use the high-end cards. The codecs will decrease the quality of your video to the point where the end users cannot tell the difference between video captured through a top-of-the-line video capture card and video captured through a much less expensive device.

T I P Most video capture cards can output your finished video back to tape. After you edit your video and have a finished product ready for digitizing, save it to videotape as well. You can use the tape as a demo to show off your work without having to have access to the Net.

ON THE WEB

http://www.yahoo.com/Computers_and_Internet/Information_and_Documentation/
Product_Reviews/Peripherals/Video_Cards/Video_Capture/ Read the online reviews of video capture cards before choosing your product.

Like most computer equipment, any video capture card you buy runs the risk of being obsolete tomorrow. Nevertheless, the following few companies and products have been around for a while and have a good reputation:

Part
IV

Ch
28

■ Quadrant International (**http://qi.com/**)—if you're on a tight budget, check out the Q-Motion P100. It's no longer in production, but Quadrant still has a few in the warehouse. You may also find it on the used market. Their current entry level boards, the Q-Motion 200-series, are only a few hundred dollars. (Check **http://qi.com/products/retail/index.html** to find the availability and pricing of their products.)

■ Truevision (**http://www.truevision.com/**)—Truevision makes the popular Targa series. Their products are professional-grade; visit their Web site to see the features and quality available at this end of the market. Note that Truevision uses the Zoran chip, which outputs a form of AVI video called Motion-JPEG. You'll need to scale this output and convert it to Video For Windows before sending it to the RealVideo encoder.

■ FAST (**http://www.fast-multimedia.com/**)—FAST offers products that compete against both Quadrant and Truevision.

■ miro (**http://www.miro.com/**)—The miroVideo DC30 offers a technically sophisticated video capture system at an affordable price. Like Truevision, miro uses the Zoran chip, forcing you to take an extra step before encoding.

You'll find the latest list of video capture cards that have been tested by RealNetworks at **http://www.real.com/products/realvideo/reviewg/rvencoding.html**. In general, any video capture device that produces Video For Windows output is acceptable.

Seagate A/V Professional Disk Drive   Although strictly speaking the A/V Drive is optional, consider the use of a special hard drive. Video capture puts an extraordinary load on your hard drive; many products that are quite acceptable for storing other files cannot keep up with video. Seagate's A/V Professional series have been specifically designed for video capture.

N O T E   The reason most hard drives can't capture video reliably is that they must stop accepting data occasionally. From time to time, most disk drives must stop accepting data for a moment so that they can recalibrate. With most applications, this temporary downtime is unnoticeable; the application storing data to the drive stops and waits for the disk drive to catch up. With real-time video, however, the video card and its associated software can't wait; any downtime on the drive translates into dropped frames.

To learn more about configuring Seagate's A/V Professional drives to work properly in a video capture application, read **http://www.seagate.com/support/disc/AV_pro.shtml**. ■

Editing the Video

Most video professionals prefer Adobe Premiere (**http://www.adobe.com/prodindex/premiere/main.html**) for editing their video. Your video capture card probably came with an editor, too, which may be entirely satisfactory.

N O T E   Several of the leading streaming video companies, including RealNetworks, offer Adobe Premiere plug-ins, allowing you to export from Premiere directly into the encoded format. Learn more at **www.adobe.com/prodindex/premiere/streamvid.html**. ■

T I P Many amateurs over-edit, getting caught up in cross fades, dissolves, and complex transitions. Get your drama from the pacing of the cuts and from background music, not from the technical gimmicks of the editor.

Encoding Video

Earlier in this chapter, in the section "Adding Streaming Video—Why Your Connection Must Change," you learned that the process of turning a high-bandwidth video signal into a bitstream that can pass through the Internet is computationally complex. That process is called *encoding*. To do it right, you'll need plenty of computing resources.

ON THE WEB

http://205.158.7.51/docs/ccguide_rv10.pdf   Download this content developer's guide (an Adobe PDF document) from RealNetworks' site. It shows you how to build high quality video presentations and stream them economically.

Encoding a Pre-Recorded Clip   In many cases, you'll produce a digital video clip, edit it, and then send it to the RealVideo encoder. If you use this approach, you don't need the fastest hardware because the encoder isn't under the time constraints imposed by live data.

If you're a Windows user, you can get by with a 486 at 66 MHz for simple encoding tasks. If you're processing complex video images with a low-bandwidth codec, however, you'll want additional speed. For best results, get a faster processor; RealNetworks recommends a Pentium 120. Similarly, 16M of RAM is adequate, but 32M is recommended.

Mac users can get by with a PowerPC and 16M of RAM, though a PowerPC 604 with 32M is recommended.

Live Encoding   When you're encoding a live event, the encoder doesn't have an opportunity to stop and work a bit harder on a difficult sequence; the encoder must keep up with the incoming data. You'll need fast hardware to keep up with this demanding task.

If you're planning to encode at a frame rate faster than two frames per second, RealNetworks recommends that you use a dual Pentium at 200 MHz with at least 64M of RAM, running Windows NT. If you're content with a slower frame rate, you can drop down to a Pentium at 166 MHz and 32M.

Scaling and Cropping   The RealVideo encoder accepts any frame size that has a height and width that are multiples of 16; 176×144 is a nice size. (It will also accept 160×120.) Most video capture cards produce frames that are somewhat larger than these figures; for example, the smallest frame the miro DC30 and the Truevision Bravado 1000 can produce is 320×240. You'll need to scale and crop the video before sending it to the encoder. You can make these changes in your video editor.

Choosing a Codec   One of the codec's major tasks is to extract enough information from the original video to allow the video player to predict most of the pixels of the next frame. If you

Part IV Ch 28

need to produce a bitstream that can fit over a dial-up connection, this task becomes technically challenging. You can set three variables that will measurably affect the quality of your output:

- Audio codec
- Video bitrate
- Frame rate

Although end users will put up with low-quality video, they must be able to hear the audio track. Table 28.1 shows some rules of thumb for choosing the audio codec if you are designing a clip for a 28.8Kbps connection. (Better audio codecs are available if the end user has a higher speed connection.)

Table 28.1 Choose the Audio Codec First, Based on the Quality of Sound You Require

Type of Audio	Recommended Codec	Audio Bitrate in Kbps
Voice	6.5Kbps voice	6.5
Background music	RealMedia 8Kbps music	8.0
Foreground music	RealMedia 12Kbps music	12.0

A low-speed dial-up connection typically has 28.8Kbps of bandwidth available. Some of this bandwidth is required for network overhead; you should not use more than 22Kbps for your video clip. Plan for a lower figure—19Kbps. Of that 19Kbps, give the audio bitstream as much room as it needs, and force the video to work with the remainder. Table 28.2 shows RealNetworks' recommended bitrate for four different connection speeds.

Table 28.2 Choose Your Bitrate Based on the End User's Connection Speed

Connection Speed in Kbps	Target Bitrate in Kbps
28.8	19
56.0	44
64.0	56
128.0	105

After you select an audio codec and a video bitrate, the only control left is the frame rate. Here are some rules of thumb for encoding various types of video:

- Fixed camera shot with low motion—The frame rate will run between 4 and 10.
- Fixed camera shot with some motion—The frame rate may drop toward 2 fps.
- Fixed camera shot with high motion—The frame rate drops to about 1 fps.

- Zooming camera with low motion—Expect a frame rate of about 2 fps.
- Multiple shots, low motion—The frame rate approaches 1 fps.
- Multiple shots, high motion—The frame rate drops below 1 fps.

 If you have a video clip that cannot be encoded with a frame rate higher than 1 fps, consider switching to "slide show mode." Figure 28.2, part of an Elton John music video from **ramhurl.real.com/cgi-bin/ ramhurl.cgi?ram=eltonj20_12_5.rm**, shows this mode.

FIG. 28.2

If you need to put the music in the fore-ground, consider switching to slide show mode for the video.

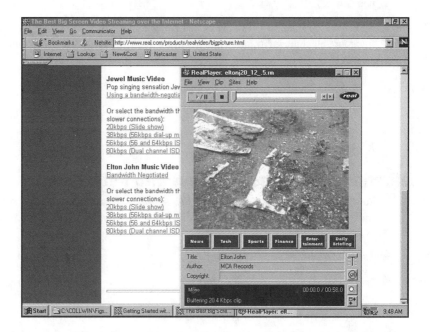

You can tell the encoder to "optimize frame rate." It will adjust the frame rate based on the spatio-temporal complexity of the video that it is encoding. If you still cannot encode your video to fit within your targeted bitrate, decrease the frame size and try again.

 You don't have to choose codecs by trial and error. Start with the templates that come with the RealVideo encoder, and find one that's a close match to your clip. If you're not happy with the results of any of the templates, switch to Advanced mode and write your own template, based on the closest matching template you can find.

You have a choice of two video codecs: standard and fractal. For low bitrates, you'll get better results from the standard codec. At higher bitrates, experiment to see which codec you prefer; most clips encode somewhat better in the standard codec.

Part
IV

Ch
28

Serving Video from Real Servers

Serving streaming video isn't as demanding as encoding it, but you'll still want a fast computer to host the server. RealNetworks recommends that you use a 486 at 66 MHz or faster; a Pentium, of course, is even better. RealNetworks offers versions of their server for most common UNIX systems, including Sun's Solaris and SunOS, Silicon Graphic's IRIS, DEC UNIX, and IBM's AIX.

For any of these operating systems, you should budget 3M of RAM plus 60K for each simultaneous user.

The RealVideo Servers employ "Smart Networking"; they will attempt to use the most efficient transport mechanism available, stepping through the following mechanisms in order:

- Multicast
- UDP
- TCP
- HTTP

▶ **See** "How RealAudio Works," **p. 536**

Delivering the Finished Product with RealPlayer

Your finished HTML page should include a link to **http://www.real.com/products/player/index.html**. There your visitors can download a free copy of RealPlayer or an evaluation copy of RealPlayer Plus.

TIP Use bandwidth negotiation (described in Chapter 27, "Streaming Audio,") to let the end user's copy of RealPlayer work with the server to determine the optimum bandwidth. Figure 28.3 shows a clip of actor John Tuturro being interviewed by Spike Lee. This 36.4Kbps clip is played through a 28.8Kbps connection, from **ramhurl.real.com/cgi-bin/ramhurl.cgi?ram=tutn.rm**.

When the RealPlayer client connects to the server, it uses a TCP/IP connection to send bandwidth information to the server. The client and the server agree on a bandwidth, and the server begins to download a version of the video encoded with the proper codec. If there's no version of the video encoded with a slow-enough codec, the client cannot receive the video clip.

Other Players

During 1997, Microsoft began taking a stake in the streaming video market. They bought 10 percent of RealNetworks, established strategic alliances with Vivo and VDOnet, and bought one major player—VXtreme—outright.

Microsoft seems convinced that streaming video is going to be an important part of the Web. By consolidating the major players around their standard (the Active Streaming Format), they may bring some degree of standardization to this emerging market. These moves also ensure that their product, NetShow, is left in a strong position.

FIG. 28.3

The server works with the client to select the best bandwidth.

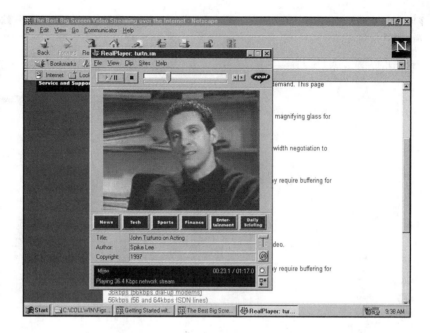

VDOLive

VDOnet's product, VDOLive, is characterized by the fact that the content needs to be encoded only once. A video file that is encoded by using VDOnet's technology will take advantage of higher bandwidth as it becomes available. This design allows you to make video content available through a single link; if a user with a 28.8Kbps modem connects, he or she will see a slow, rather fuzzy image. If the user has ADSL or another high-bandwidth connection, he or she will see near TV-quality video. (The threshold for getting clear, 30 frame-per-second video seems to be about 512Kbps.) In contrast, RealNetworks recommends that you encode the content several times—once for each bandwidth you plan to support—though they do support bandwidth negotiation so that the end user can connect through a single link.

VDOnet reports that, under ideal conditions, an end user with a 56Kbps modem can display 15 to 19 frames per second at a frame size of 320×240 pixels. Of course, this figure goes down as the available bandwidth at the server and the client decrease. Figure 28.4 shows the VDOLive player in action.

ON THE WEB

http://www.vdo.net/   Start your "VDO Experience" at VDOnet's home page. You can download the player by clicking Download Software. Then go to VDO Guide and visit the Site Gallery or the Best of VDO.

Part
IV

Ch
28

FIG. 28.4
White House Drug Czar
General Barry McCaffrey,
live through VDOLive.

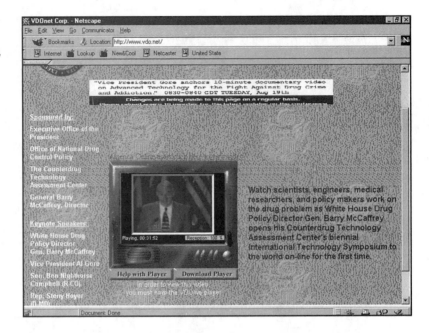

VXtreme

VXtreme's Web Theater supports low bit-rate streaming but is aimed at the 56Kbps niche. Starting with Web Theater 2.2, it can provide high-quality quarter-screen video (320×240). Figure 28.5 shows a smaller frame: 150×154.

FIG. 28.5
VXtreme's site features
a Microsoft video
describing its
approach to
streaming video.

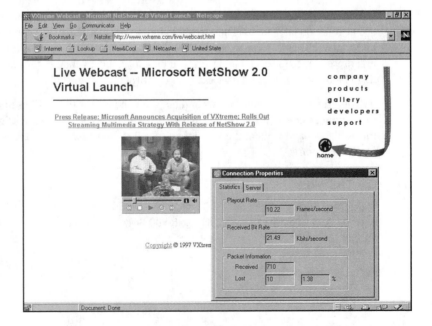

By acquiring VXtreme, Microsoft got access to their technology, their customers, and their employees. VXtreme's customers include CNN Interactive, Warner Brothers, CNNfn, and General Electric. You can see some of these sites by visiting **http://cnnfn.com/fnonair/vxtreme/index.html** and **http://www.warnerbros.com/vxtreme/**.

ON THE WEB

http://www.vxtreme.com/   For more information about VXtreme and their acquisition by Microsoft, visit their Web site.

Vivo

Vivo Software was one of the first companies to enter the streaming video market. They are working closely with Microsoft; they support Microsoft's ASF and can directly play video produced with Microsoft NetShow. Their production environment, VivoActive Producer, generates ASF files, readable from their own player or from NetShow. Figure 28.6 shows the VivoActive Player. This screen shot is from PBS's *Nova* program, produced by WGBH. For similar programs, visit **http://www.pbs.org/wgbh/pages/nova/avalanche/previews.html**. (Vivo also offers non-streaming AVI and QuickTime versions of these clips, as well as RealAudio narration.)

FIG. 28.6
Nova's program on avalanches features scientist Othmar Buser.

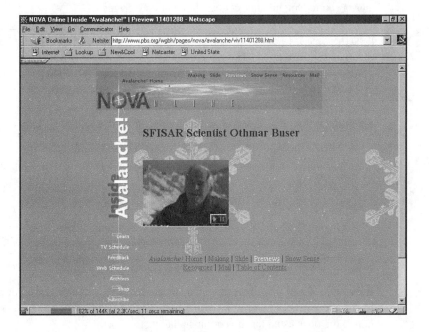

ON THE WEB

http://www.vivo.com/index.html   From here, you can download the VivoActive Player and visit Vivo Software's site gallery.

Microsoft and the Active Streaming Format

By acquiring an interest in many of the major streaming video players, Microsoft hopes to establish its Active Streaming Format (ASF) as the *de facto* standard for streaming video. From that position, Microsoft's own streaming video product, NetShow, may be able to challenge RealNetworks' RealVideo for market dominance.

N O T E   Microsoft has demonstrated a unified multimedia technology called DirectX. Look for this Microsoft standard to play an important role in Internet multimedia. Learn more about their approach at **http://directx/default.asp**. ■

ON THE WEB

http://www.microsoft.com/products/prodref/201_ov.htm   Learn about NetShow from the Microsoft site. You'll also want to visit **www.microsoft.com/netshow/** for more technical information.

Encoding Video with NetShow Tools

NetShow comes with tools that convert existing video files, including AVI and QuickTime movies, to Microsoft's Active Streaming Format (ASF). Microsoft distributes 10 codecs but allows you to plug in other codecs that you may prefer.

T I P   If you choose to use a codec that doesn't come with the NetShow player, be sure to give your site visitors a way to download it. Microsoft provides sample code for this task at **http://www.microsoft.com/netshow/codecs.htm#install**. The disadvantage of this approach is that it relies on the CODEBASE parameter of the <OBJECT> tag, which is specific to Microsoft Internet Explorer.

Selecting a Codec   Microsoft ships five codecs in the NetShow client core installation kit:

- MPEG Layer-3—Used for low- to medium-bitrate audio.
- Lernout & Hauspie CELP 4.8 kbit/s—Provides a voice-grade audio codec.
- Microsoft MPEG-4—Generates video at bitrates from 28.8Kbps to 300Kbps.
- Vivo H.263—Used for compatibility with VivoActive Producer.
- Vivo G.723.1 and Vivo Siren—Used for audio compatibility with VivoActive Producer. These codecs generate 6.4Kbps and 16Kbps bitstreams, respectively.

NetShow is also compatible with any fixed-rate ACM codec.

If the end user has opted for the full installation of the NetShow player, or if he or she has Microsoft Internet Explorer 4.0, you can count on the following codecs being present in addition to the ones listed for the core installation:

- Duck TrueMotion RT—A medium- to high-bitrate video codec.
- ClearVideo—A low- to medium-bitrate video codec provided for compatibility with the Osprey 1000 video capture card (**http://www.osprey.mmac.com/products. html#o1000**).

- VDOnet VDOwave—A low- to medium-bitrate codec that outputs 28.8Kbps to 150Kbps data with up to 15 fps.

- Voxware Metasound and Voxware Metavoice RT24—The Metasound RT24 is used for speech-only encoding; it outputs a 2.4Kbps bitstream. Four Metasound codecs are included: AC8, AC10, AC16, and AC24. The last two digits of the name indicate the bitrate. For example, the Metasound AC8 generates an 8Kbps bitstream.

End users with Internet Explorer 4.0 will also have the Intel H.263 codec, a good low- to medium-bitrate video codec.

ON THE WEB

http://www.microsoft.com/netshow/codecs.htm   Learn more about NetShow's codec-independence.

System Requirements   The system requirements for the NetShow tools (which include their encoder) are comparable to those for RealVideo: you should have at least a 486 running at 66 MHz with 16M of RAM, though a 200 MHz Pentium Pro with 32M or more is recommended.

CAUTION
Many of the examples on the Microsoft's NetShow Web site show VBScripting or other features available only in Microsoft Internet Explorer. If you intend to make your Web pages accessible to Netscape Navigator users as well, avoid these Microsoft-specific features.

The NetShow Server

Not surprisingly, the NetShow server runs on Microsoft's Windows NT 4.0 operating system. They offer both unicast and multicast connections. Recall that too many simultaneous unicast connections can saturate a server; NetShow offers a server management feature that allows you to limit the number of concurrent users or even limit the amount of data coming from one server. If you set up a server farm, you can arrange for requests to be distributed across multiple servers, to keep the load within the capabilities of any one machine.

N O T E   NetShow also offers an "illustrated audio" mode, with audio synchronized with still images. This mode corresponds with RealVideo's "slide show" mode, described earlier in this chapter in the section "RealVideo." ■

ON THE WEB

http://www.microsoft.com/netshow/provider/webcstrs.htm   If you want help developing or hosting your NetShow content, check this list of providers who are working with Microsoft.

Part
IV

Ch
28

Loading the NetShow Player

Players are available for Windows 95 and Windows NT machines. Microsoft is developing versions for the Macintosh, Windows 3.1, and various UNIX platforms. Figure 28.7 shows a Microsoft-illustrated ASF file that gives driving directions from the Seattle-Tacoma airport (SEATAC) to Microsoft's main campus in Redmond, Washington.

FIG. 28.7
Use illustrated audio when you need to emphasize audio over video content.

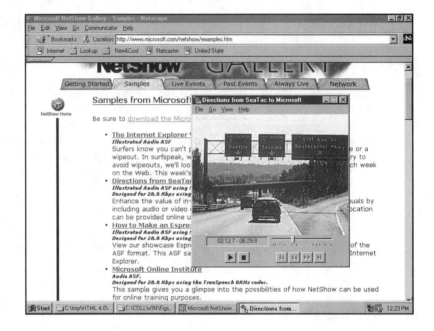

ON THE WEB

http://www.microsoft.com/netshow/download/player.htm   Direct visitors to this page so that they can download the NetShow player.

Xing StreamWorks and XingMPEG

Recall from Chapter 27, "Streaming Audio," that Xing Technology Corporation has made a strong commitment to the standards set by the Moving Pictures Experts Group (MPEG). Xing offers XingMPEG, which is an MPEG encoder and player, and StreamWorks, which allows you to download XingMPEG files as streaming video. Their gallery, at **http://www.xingtech.com/ content/sw2_content.html**, contains over 80 sites demonstrating both audio and video content. Figure 28.8, shot from **video.aquarius.eds.com/jason/j6.xdm**, demonstrates Streamwork's capability to expand the image to the full screen (with a consequent loss of resolution).

FIG. 28.8
Dr. Bob Ballard
introduces this video
clip of JASON's voyage
to Hawaii.

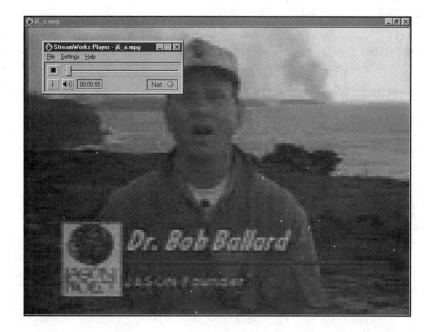

ON THE WEB

http://www.xingtech.com/   Learn more about Xing's products and download their free players.

▶ **See** "Xing's StreamWorks," **p. 554**

Apple's QuickTime

Apple introduced QuickTime technology early in the life of the Macintosh. They quickly delivered both a Macintosh and a Windows version of viewers. Not surprisingly, QuickTime became the *de facto* standard for time-based media, including video content. Market research firm Griffin Dix Research Associates found that QuickTime and the Mac OS are the platforms of choice in the digital video and multimedia markets (**http://product.info.apple.com/ press_releases/1997/q4/970805.pr.rel.griffindix.html**).

Today Apple offers several members of the QuickTime family, including the following:

- QuickTime VR, which allows you to build panoramas from a sequence of still images. Using QuickTime VR, the end user can look up and down, zoom in and out of the scene, and interact with objects by clicking and dragging.
- QuickTime IC, for image capture
- QuickTime Conferencing, for real-time audio and video
- QuickTime Live
- An optional software-based MPEG playback codec
- QuickTime 3D, which includes support for the 3D Metafile (3DMF) format. QuickTime 3D allows QuickTime to represent complex three-dimensional animation.

Part

IV

Ch

28

ON THE WEB

http://quicktime.apple.com/qtsites.html Apple calls the combination of the members of the QuickTime technology family the "QuickTime Media Layer." You can visit QuickTime-enhanced sites by following the links that start on this page.

In addition to the "tween" track for 3DMFs, QuickTime supports sampled audio tracks and a special music track (based on high-quality 16-bit MIDI).

N O T E Apple's MPEG codec allows cutting, copying, and pasting of MPEG files—rare capabilities among video players. ▨

ON THE WEB

http://quicktime.apple.com/ Learn more about Apple's QuickTime technology online. Download their PDF document, "QuickTime and the Internet Fact Sheet," to learn more about including QuickTime movies on your Web page.

Netscape bundles Apple's QuickTime plug-in with their browsers, so Web developers can embed QuickTime movies in their pages. Figure 28.9 shows a sophisticated example of QuickTime, with 16-bit color, MIDI sounds, text track overlays, and modifier track transitions. MovieWorks is a Macintosh application that allows developers to integrate text, sound, paint, and video easily.

FIG. 28.9
This QuickTime sample was built with MovieWorks Interactive.

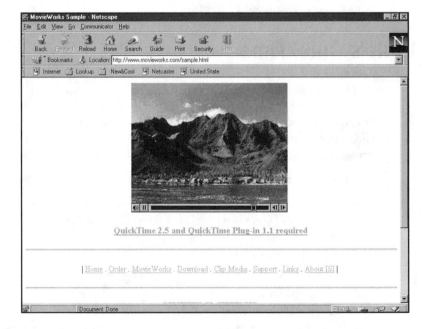

Fast-Start

Like the Windows AVI format, a QuickTime movie generally needs to be downloaded to the client computer before it can be played. To support Web users, Apple rearranged the order of the information in the QuickTime file. This rearrangement is called "fast-start." The QuickTime plug-in reads the length and size of the movie and makes a determination on how much of the file it needs before it can begin to play. Even on a dial-up connection, the QuickTime movie can begin to play within a few seconds.

ON THE WEB

http://www.digigami.com/moviescreamer/   If you want to apply fast-start to a QuickTime movie from your Windows or UNIX computer, get MovieScreamer from DigiGami. Mac users can use QuickTime 2.5 itself, available at **quicktime.apple.com/sw/sw.html**. Just click the Make movie self-contained and Make movie playable on other computers options in the Save As dialog box.

T I P   If you have QuickTime movies and want to make them available by streaming video, consider using the RealVideo encoder to convert them to RealVideo.

Streaming QuickTime and QuickTime TV

Although fast-start represents an improvement for QuickTime, QuickTime is still essentially a file-based technology. Apple wants to offer a true streaming video technology; their first version, called "streaming QuickTime," is described at **http://streaming.quicktime.apple.com**. The demo application developed with streaming QuickTime was called "QuickTime TV." QuickTime TV is a real-time–only technology—just the opposite of conventional QuickTime. To support video clips with a real-time technology, Apple developed "broadcasters" and "reflectors" to make it easy to multicast the video content.

In March 1997, Apple put the streaming QuickTime project on hold; they expect to start it again so that streaming QuickTime moves into the supported version of QuickTime in 1998. Meanwhile, all the tools, players, and sample files are available through **http://streaming. quicktime.apple.com**. Figure 28.10 shows a screen shot of a streaming QuickTime clip developed by KCAT (Channel 20), a community broadcast station in California.

FIG. 28.10
KCAT makes video
content available
over the Web.

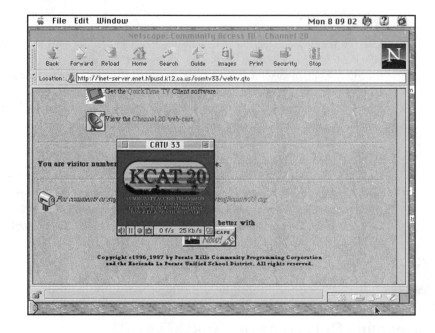

## CHAPTER 29

VRML Worlds

by Jim O'Donnell and Mark R. Brown

In this chapter

The Virtual Reality Modeling Language

The Virtual Reality Modeling Language (VRML) is a language intended for the design and use of three-dimensional, multiperson, distributed interactive simulations. To put it in simpler language, VRML's designers intend it to become the building block of cyberspace.

The World Wide Web is based on HTML (Hypertext Markup Language), which was developed from the SGML (Standard General Markup Language) standard. SGML and HTML are fundamentally designed as two-dimensional text formatting toolsets. Mark D. Pesce, Peter Kennard, and Anthony S. Parisi presented a paper called Cyberspace at the First International Conference on the Web in May 1994, in which they argued that because humans are superb visualizers and live and work in three dimensions, extending the Web with a third dimension would allow for better organization of the masses of data already on the Web. They called this idea the Virtual Reality Markup Language. The concept was welcomed, and the participants immediately began searching for a format to use as a data standard. Subsequently, the M in VRML was changed from *Markup* to *Modeling* to accentuate the difference between the text-based nature of the Web and VRML.

ON THE WEB

The paper, Cyberspace, is available over the Web at **http://www.hyperreal.com/~mpesce/www.html**.

Silicon Graphics' Open Inventor was chosen as the basis for creating the VRML 1.0 standard. Open Inventor is an object-oriented C++ developer's toolkit used for rapid development of three-dimensional graphic environments. Open Inventor has provided the basis for a number of standards, including the Keystone Interchange Format used in the entertainment industry and the ANSI/ISO's X3H3 3D Metafile specification.

The second version of VRML moved away from Open Inventor in order to achieve better performance and additional functionality.

VRML's design specifications were guided by the following three goals:

- Platform independence
- Extendability
- The capability to work over low-bandwidth connections

VRML Objects

The building blocks of VRML creations, usually called VRML worlds, are objects created in VRML. The VRML language specification contains a collection of commands, called *nodes*, for the creation of a variety of simple objects such as spheres, boxes, and cylinders, as well as objects consisting of an arbitrary collection of vertices and faces.

N O T E For a three-dimensional object, *faces* are the flat surfaces that make up the object, and *vertices* are the points where the faces meet. A cube, for instance, is made up of six square faces, each defined by four vertices. There are eight vertices needed to define a cube, since each vertex is shared by three faces. ■

VRML allows for the creation of more complex objects through the combination of simple objects. It is a hierarchical language, with *child* objects attached to their *parents* in a transformation hierarchy. For instance, if a complex object was being defined to create a model of a human body, then the lower arms would be attached to the upper arms, which would be attached to the torso, and so on. The rest of this chapter focuses on the creation of VRML objects.

VRML Worlds

The assemblage of VRML objects into a (hopefully) coherent whole defines a VRML world. There are many example VRML worlds on the Web that use the three-dimensional paradigm for different purposes. To define the placement and relationship of different objects to one another, you need to be able to specify their relative sizes and positions, using VRML's coordinate system. Additionally, VRML allows you to define what lighting sources are present in your world and what preset views are included.

Adding Motion and More to VRML

VRML 1.0 worlds are static. The only motion within them is the movement of the viewpoint representing the user as he or she uses a VRML browser to travel through the VRML world. With the definition of VRML 2.0, VRML's capabilities were extended to allow the creation of dynamic worlds.

VRML 2.0 objects can be given movement of their own, and three-dimensional sound (audio that sounds different depending on the position of the listener with respect to the source) can be added. Another capability introduced with VRML 2.0 is the ability to add behaviors to VRML objects. *Behaviors*—which can be scripted or specified in Java applets, for instance—are characteristics of objects that depend on their relationship to other objects in the VRML world, to the viewer, or to other parameters, such as time. For instance, a VRML 2.0 fish in an aquarium might swim away if you get too close to it.

Why (and How) Should You Use VRML?

As a Web author interested in VRML, you need to ask yourself what you would like to achieve with it. There are two important constraints that must be kept in mind. The first is that badly authored VRML worlds can end up being *big*. Specifying three-dimensional objects as a collection of flat surfaces can lead to very large object descriptions, particularly when trying to model a curved surface. The other important issue is that the connection speed of the majority of people on the Internet is still limited to no higher than that achieved with a 28.8KBps modem.

Complex VRML worlds can take a long time to be transmitted over the Internet, which very often limits the audience to only those people looking for cool VRML worlds. These worlds can also be extremely complicated to define and set up, requiring much more discussion than the space we have here. (Something more along the lines of Que's *Special Edition Using VRML* is needed to adequately cover the subject.)

However, a very good use for VRML (one that doesn't have the problems of requiring huge files to be downloaded) is to add special effects to HTML Web pages. Because you can embed small VRML scenes into HTML Web pages, VRML is an ideal addition to the Web author's bag of tricks.

This chapter's primary focus is to familiarize you with enough VRML that you can create small VRML scenes to achieve specific special effects within your Web pages. In the course of doing so, you will also learn enough of the VRML language and syntax to give you a good grasp on the language fundamentals so that you can move on to the creation of larger VRML worlds, if you want.

Basic VRML Syntax

VRML files are plain ASCII (though they are often gzipped—compressed by using the GNU zip, or gzip, utility—to make them easier to transmit over the Internet), which means that you can create them using ordinary text editors. It is likely that you will decide to use a VRML authoring program if you want to create a very large, complex VRML world—and even for smaller worlds, if you have an authoring program available—in which case the details of VRML syntax are hidden from you. It is a good idea to get a basic grasp of the important VRML language elements, though. Later, this knowledge will help you get the results you want.

Listing 29.1 shows a simple VRML file that displays a red cone on a white background (see Figure 29.1).

Listing 29.1 rcone.wrl—Display a Red Cone on a White Background

```
#VRML V2.0 utf8

WorldInfo {
    info "Special Edition, Using HTML, 4th Edition4th Edition"
}

Background {
    skyColor 1 1 1
}

DEF RedCone Shape {
    appearance Appearance {
        material Material {
            diffuseColor 1 0 0 # the color red
        }
    }
    geometry Cone { }
}
```

FIG. 29.1
Specifying simple objects can be done with just a few lines of VRML code.

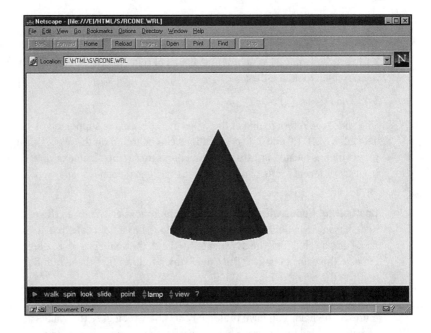

The VRML comment character is the pound sign (#); everything after a # on any line is a comment (such as `the color red`). The first line of the file begins with a #, so it is a comment. Unlike other comments in the file, this one is necessary. It identifies the file as being VRML and gives the version number of VRML used. VRML browsers require this information to be located at the start of any VRML file.

The first line of the file shown in Listing 29.1 reads `#VRML V1.0 ascii`, meaning the file conforms to version 1.0 of the VRML specification. The word `ascii` means the standard ASCII character set is used in the file. VRML 2.0 files generally have the comment `#VRML V2.0 utf8` in their first line, indicating conformance to the VRML 2.0 specification and that an international character set based on ASCII is being used.

Other than ignoring comments, the file format is entirely free form. Anywhere there is white space—tabs, spaces, or carriage returns—you can have as much or as little space as you'd like. For instance, an equivalent listing to the one shown in Listing 29.1 is:

```
#VRML V2.0 utf8

WorldInfo { info "Special Edition, Using HTML, 4th Edition4th Edition" }
Background { skyColor 1 1 1 } DEF RedCone Shape { appearance
Appearance { material Material { diffuseColor 1 0 0 # the color red
}}
geometry Cone { } }
```

 TIP As with any programming language, you should structure and comment your VRML files well enough that they can be easily read and understood.

Nodes and Fields

If you are familiar with the C, C++, or Java programming languages, you might recognize the curly braces ({ and }) which define blocks of related information. VRML files are made up of *nodes*, which look like this:

```
NodeType { fields}
```

The `NodeType` refers to one of the types of nodes that is supported by the VRML specification. The full VRML 1.0 and 2.0 specifications can be found on the Web, through the VRML Repository, which is located at **http://www.sdsc.edu/vrml/**. The example shown in Listing 29.1 uses six different kinds of nodes, `WorldInfo`, `Background`, `Shape`, `Appearance`, `Material`, and `Cone`.

Configuring Nodes with Fields   Inside the braces are *fields*. In the example, the `WorldInfo` node has an `info` field, and the `Material` node has a field called `diffuseColor`. Each field has a name and a value. For the `diffuseColor` field, the value is `1 0 0`, a set of three numbers that indicate the color to use for the Cone, which follows (the three numbers list the color's components in the order red, green, blue).

Field values can be simple numbers, groups of numbers, strings, images, Boolean values, and more. Some fields can have multiple values, in which case the values are separated by commas and surrounded by square brackets. For example, you could specify three information strings in the `WorldInfo` node:

```
WorldInfo { info [ "First line", "Second line", "Third line" ] }
```

Naming Nodes   Any node can be assigned a name by which it can be referred to later. This is done with the `DEF` prefix, as shown here and in Listing 29.1:

```
DEF RedCone Shape { ... }
```

You can assign any name to any node.

Objects, Hierarchies, Transforms

A VRML world can be thought of as a hierarchy of simple VRML objects. In VRML, the `Transform` node is used as the container for an object. Not all `Transform` nodes contain geometry (vertices and faces of VRML objects); they are used for grouping other objects into a more complex object. This is how object hierarchies are specified in VRML. The attachment information is specified by placing objects within other objects, using the `Transform` node and other grouping nodes. A node can contain a *children* field to list objects that are attached to it.

Simple VRML Objects

The VRML 2.0 specification includes ten nodes that let you specify geometric shapes. All VRML 2.0 objects are made up of one or more of these nodes. These nodes consist of four for geometric shapes, one for text, three for the creation of points, lines, and polygon-based objects, and two special nodes for creating terrain and extruded shapes.

Geometric Shapes

You already saw an example of the `Cone` node in Listing 29.1. Along with the `Cone` node, VRML allows you to directly create spheres, boxes, and cylinders. The syntax for each of these nodes is shown in the following list:

- ▓ `Cone`: The syntax for this node is:

```
Cone {
    bottomRadius    radius
    height          height
    side            TRUE or FALSE
    top             TRUE or FALSE
}
```

- ▓ `Box`: The syntax for this node is:

```
Box {
    size       width height depth
}
```

- ▓ `Cylinder`: The syntax for this node is:

```
Cylinder {
    radius      radius
    height      height
    sides       TRUE or FALSE
    top         TRUE or FALSE
    bottom      TRUE or FALSE
}
```

- ▓ `Sphere`: The syntax for this node is:

```
Sphere {
    radius          radius
}
```

Each of these nodes has default values for each of its fields. So, if you specify a sphere by simply using `Sphere{}`, you will get a sphere with a radius of one.

> **N O T E** While the `Sphere`, `Cone`, and `Cylinder` nodes seem to specify curved surfaces in VRML, when the VRML file is parsed by a VRML browser the objects are converted into vertices and faces through a process called *tessellation*. To see this for yourself, load a VRML example showing one of these curved surfaces into a VRML browser and switch the browser into flat-shading mode to see the individual faces. ▓

Text

The `Text` node allows you to create flat-text objects in VRML. Because the resulting text is flat, it is possible that it might not be visible when viewed, if looked at edge-on. The `Text` node has four fields, `string`, `fontStyle`, `MaxExtent`, and `length`, and its syntax is as follows:

```
Text {
    string          ["string(s)",...]
```

```
fontStyle        FontStyle node that gives justification, spacing, font
maxExtent        maximum size in any direction
length           lengths of the text strings in the string field
}
```

Listing 29.2 shows an example of the use of the Text node, with the results shown in Figure 29.2.

Listing 29.2   ascii2d.wrl—Two-Dimensional Text in VRML

```
4th Edition#VRML V2.0 utf8

WorldInfo {
    info "Special Edition, Using HTML, 4th Edition"
}

Background {
    skyColor 1 1 1
}

Shape {
    appearance Appearance {
        material Material {
            diffuseColor 0 0 0
        }
    }
    geometry Text {
        string [ "This Is", "A Test", "Of Text" ]
        fontStyle FontStyle { spacing 2 justify "MIDDLE" }
    }
}
```

FIG. 29.2

VRML text is two-dimensional; if you rotate it so that you view it edge-on, it is not visible.

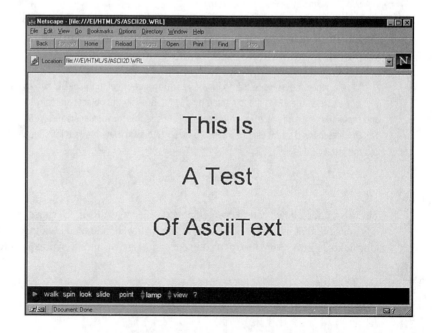

General VRML Shapes

The nodes discussed so far are useful to start, especially if you're building simple worlds by hand. Most VRML files, however, make extensive use of another node, `IndexedFaceSet`. An `IndexedFaceSet` node is a way of describing an object using a set of vertices that are joined by faces. Listing 29.3 shows an example of this, which creates a pyramid using five vertices and five faces to create the four sides and the base (see Figure 29.3).

Listing 29.3   pyrface.wrl—Building General Shapes Using IndexedFaceSet

```
4th Edition#VRML V2.0 utf8

WorldInfo {
    info "Special Edition, Using HTML, 4th Edition"
}

Background {
    skyColor 1 1 1
}

DEF Pyramid Shape {
    appearance Appearance {
        material Material {
            diffuseColor 0 0 1
        }
    }
    geometry IndexedFaceSet {
        coord Coordinate {
            point [ -1 0 -1,
                     1 0 -1,
                     1 0  1,
                    -1 0  1,
                     0 2  0 ]
        }
        coordIndex [ 0, 4, 1, -1
                     1, 4, 2, -1,
                     2, 4, 3, -1,
                     3, 4, 0, -1,
                     0, 1, 2, 3, -1 ]
    }
}
```

The array of vertex coordinates is specified by using the `Coordinate` node and its own field, `point`. The `point` field takes multiple values, each of which is a triplet of numbers giving the X, Y, and Z coordinates of one vertex. There can be as many vertices as you need. Keep in mind, though, that each vertex only needs to be specified once, no matter how many faces it is used in, because vertices define single points that may be shared by multiple faces.

The `IndexedFaceSet` node contains a field called `coordIndex` that stores a list of faces, as specified by the indices of vertices in the order they are used for each face. For instance, the sequence `0, 4, 1, -1` is used to create one face from the 0th, 4th, and 1st vertices (vertices are numbered from 0). The `-1` signifies the end of the current face; the next face begins with the next number.

FIG. 29.3
VRML indexed face sets can be used to construct arbitrary three-dimensional solids.

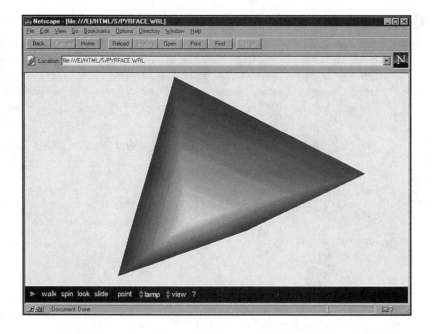

N O T E   Although IndexedFaceSet is a very powerful tool, there are some things to watch out for when you are using it.

Make sure all the vertices in a given face are *coplanar*, meaning that the face is flat. If one or more of the vertices are not in the same plane, then the object will look very strange when viewed from certain angles.

Avoid T-intersections. Two faces should always meet at a shared edge. If you have a face that touches another face without sharing common vertices, the round-off errors in the VRML browser will cause viewing problems.

Avoid using too many faces, when possible, because using too many will slow down rendering more than any other factor.

VRML includes two other nodes that work much the same as IndexedFaceSet, called IndexedLineSet and PointSet. Each is used similarly to IndexedFaceSet, except that IndexedLineSet is used to construct a general set of lines between a set of vertices, and PointSet creates a field of dots at the vertices.

Adding Color and Texture to VRML Objects

VRML offers several different ways of changing the appearance of its objects. One of these, the Material node, shown previously in Listing 29.1, is used to create a red cone. Two nodes in particular can be used to affect the color, texture, and general appearance of VRML objects: the Material and ImageTexture nodes.

Material

The most common use of the `Material` node is that shown in Listing 29.1—using its `diffuseColor` field to specify the color of an object. The `Material` node supports other fields for achieving different effects.

ImageTexture

With the `ImageTexture` node, it is possible to achieve a much wider variety of effects. The `ImageTexture` node maps an image file to a VRML object. Listing 29.4 shows an example with my picture mapped onto a VRML cube (see Figure 29.4).

Listing 29.4   cubejod.wrl—Map Images to VRML Objects Using Texture2

```
4th Edition#VRML V2.0 utf8

WorldInfo {
    info "Special Edition, Using HTML, 4th Edition"
}

Background {
    skyColor 1 1 1
}

DEF Pyramid Shape {
    appearance Appearance {
        material Material {
            diffuseColor 0 0 1
        }
        texture ImageTexture {
            url "bernie.gif"
        }
    }
    geometry Box { }
}
```

Because the faces are all flat in the preceding example, the image used isn't noticeably distorted. That isn't the case when images are mapped to curved surfaces, such as those created by `Sphere`, `Cone`, or `Cylinder` nodes. In these nodes, images are distorted as they are mapped to the curved surfaces. Note that different graphics formats can be used as textures; which formats are supported is VRML browser-specific.

Creating VRML Worlds and Inline VRML Scenes

In the context of this discussion, a VRML world refers to a VRML file that is designed to be stand-alone, and will be loaded into a VRML-compatible Web browser on its own, without being embedded in an HTML-based Web page. Though there is no lower or upper limit on the size and complexity of a VRML world, these worlds tend to be fairly large. The three-dimensional VRML paradigm is often used to allow the user to "move through" the VRML world, visiting the parts of interest to him.

FIG. 29.4
Images can be mapped
to the faces of VRML
objects.

One example of good use of VRML worlds is demonstrated through sites that model an actual three-dimensional object, building, or geographic location, allowing remote users from all over the world to actually "see" what that object looks like, perhaps even to travel through it. The University of Essex, in Britain, maintains such a site at **http://esewww.essex.ac.uk/campus-model.wrl**. This VRML world consists of a three-dimensional model of their campus. Users can move around the campus and see it from any conceivable angle. In addition, each building on the campus contains a hyperlink to an HTML Web page with information about that building.

Inline VRML scenes are best used to achieve a given special effect within an HTML Web page. By creating a very small, very specialized VRML scene and displaying it inline, you can achieve a variety of special effects. This is particularly true if you add some of the animation and movement extensions possible with VRML 2.0, as discussed later in this chapter. An inline VRML scene can be used to achieve a similar effect to an animated GIF; depending on the desired effect, this can be done with a VRML file smaller than the GIF.

Design Considerations

After you come up with an idea for your VRML environment, you need to consider a number of other factors that influence the final design. As well as deciding what objects you want to put in the VRML environment and where they are with respect to each other, there are other factors that might limit what you can achieve. How big a VRML environment should you create? How detailed should it be? How should it be shaped? How should everything be laid out? How should you create it?

Size and Detail

The first thing you should consider before drafting your environment is size—not in terms of the space it takes up in the virtual world, but the final size of your WRL file. In a perfect world, everyone has a high-powered graphics workstation and a T1 line connecting them to the Internet, and you don't have to worry about how big your VRML file is, how long it takes to transmit over the Internet, or how long it takes to render after it arrives at the client machine.

In reality, however, things are quite different. Most people are running 486 and Pentium PCs over 14.4Kbps and 28.8Kbps modems. If you come up with a VRML world that is 10M, you severely limit your audience because of the hour and a half download time and the time it takes for the client computer to render it. No matter why you are interested in providing VRML environments on the Web, no one will look at it if it takes that long.

Therefore, you need to consider how big you are going to make your VRML environment and how detailed it should be. It is a question of compromise. You can have a very large environment, but then you cannot add a great amount of small detail. Or, if you have only a few objects in your environment, they can probably be displayed with a great deal of detail. It becomes a trade-off between size and detail.

That is why it is important to start the process with a purpose for your VRML environment. If you are trying to sell something and you want your customers to understand what they are getting, you should probably opt for multiple VRML environments, each of which displays a few objects—or even just one—in great detail. However, if you want to give your users a sense of what it's like to stand next to the Pyramids in Egypt, texturing each pyramid brick by brick isn't necessary. If you want to let your users tour a model of your entire electronics workshop, you might not need to include every oscilloscope and soldering iron. But, if you want them to see the tools used, you can limit your environment to a single workbench.

Design and Layout

After you have decided how big your environment will be and what to include in it, the next step is to decide how it will look. A VRML environment is like any other space, virtual or not. If it looks cluttered and unkempt, people won't want to look at it. You need to decide how you want things to be laid out and how you want people to navigate through your environment. Is it a scene that they will be looking at from a distance? Or do you want them to jump in and poke around?

Again, the important factor in answering these questions is your environment's purpose. For example, if you are creating a VRML world that requires users to follow a particular sequence, then you need to find ways to direct their travels through your world. On the other hand, if you want people to be able to freely explore through your VRML world, you might want to have a more open environment. Even if you are recreating a space that exists in the "real world," you need to consider what is necessary and not necessary.

VRML World Design Steps

We will now go through the steps required to design a very simple VRML world. First, we go through the process of initial layout, building VRML objects together into compound objects and placing them in our world. Then, we find out about some of the ways to add realism to our VRML world, through the use of textures, lighting, and the addition of multiple camera viewpoints. Finally, we find out how to link our VRML world to other VRML worlds, HTML pages, or anything with an URL.

While the process of building this VRML world might be easier with a VRML authoring or three-dimensional modeling software package, this chapter instead shows how it is done by hand. By performing the steps of VRML world-building manually, you get a much better grasp of the fundamentals of the VRML language, and if you subsequently want to use a VRML authoring tool, this foundation makes it much easier.

ON THE WEB

Yahoo! lists a plethora of VRML authoring tools at **http://www.yahoo.com/Computers_and_Internet/ Internet/World_Wide_Web/Virtual_Reality_Modeling_Language__VRML_/Authoring/**.

Mapping Your VRML Environment

Rather than charging off and starting to throw together VRML objects that you might need in your world, the first step in the design process should be to sketch out what you want your world to look like. An important tool at this point of the design process is a simple sheet of graph paper. By using graph paper, including both a top view and a side view of what you would like to put in your world, you get a very good first idea of the following important points:

- What simple VRML objects do you need?
- What compound objects do you need, and how should they be created from the simple ones?
- How much space do you need in your environment?
- Where should the VRML objects be placed in that environment?
- Where can you add lighting and camera views for the best effects?

VRML Coordinate Systems   While it is important to have a visual way of thinking to design your VRML environment, the way it is stored is as a set of coordinates and mathematical transformations. You need to convert your visual design into these coordinates and transformations—this is one of the reasons that sketching out your world on graph paper is a good idea. To fully understand how to accomplish this, you need to know a bit about the coordinate systems that VRML uses, as well as the vectors and transformations it employs.

Cartesian coordinates, those used in VRML, are named after the geometry developed by René Descartes. They are basically the standard way of describing the two- or three-dimensional geometry of something. By default, when you begin looking at a VRML scene, the positive direction of the x-axis goes from left to right, the positive direction of the y-axis goes from down to up, and the positive direction of the z-axis goes from the back of the environment toward the front. This is called a right-handed coordinate system because if you curl the fingers of your right hand from the x- towards the y-axis, your thumb will point along the z-axis.

The right-handedness of the coordinate system also comes into play when you discuss rotations. The direction of a positive rotation about an axis is determined by the *right-hand rule*. For instance, to determine the direction of a positive rotation about the z-axis, point your right thumb along the z-axis in its positive direction. The way your fingers curl defines a positive rotation. Figure 29.5 shows the Cartesian coordinate system used within VRML.

FIG. 29.5
VRML uses the Cartesian coordinate system shown to create objects and define where objects are placed with respect to one another.

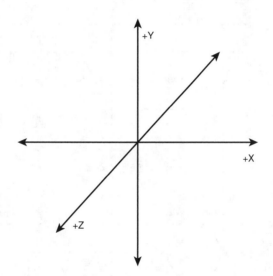

Vectors A point in the Cartesian coordinate system is called a *vertex*. A vertex is simply a location in space represented by three numbers: x, y, and z. A *vector* is related to a vertex, in that it is also represented by x, y, and z coordinates. Whereas a vertex represents a point in space, a vector represents a direction. So, the vertex (1,0,1) represents the point x=1, y=0, and z=1. The vector (1,0,1) represents the direction you would be traveling in going from the origin, the point (0,0,0), to the vertex (1,0,1).

VRML Units When specifying coordinates and rotation angles in VRML, you need to remember the measure of distance is a *meter*, and the measure of rotation angle is a *radian*.

N O T E A *radian* is a unit used to measure angles and rotations. There are 2π radians in 360°, so you can determine the number of radians from a given number of degrees by multiplying by π/180, about 0.00175. ▨

Putting Your Design on Paper

The first step in the design of a VRML world is to sketch what you want it to look like. By putting this down on graph paper, you are already a long way toward defining the coordinates, size, and position of the things in the world.

Figures 29.6 and 29.7 show a top and side view of the VRML world you will try to put together throughout the rest of this chapter. Figure 29.6 shows a "front" view of the world, with the z-axis pointing straight out of the paper. The two drawings define what the world should look like pretty well; you might find it helpful to include another side view, however, looking down the x-axis, for example.

FIG. 29.6

Top view of your planned VRML world.

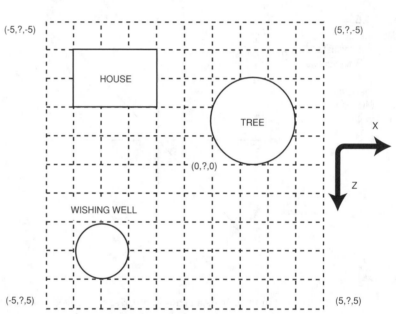

Now that you have your VRML world sketched out, go back and see if these sketches answer the questions asked about the design:

- **What simple VRML objects do you need?**

  It looks like you need a flat plane for the ground, a cube and a solid made from an indexed face set for the house, a sphere and a cylinder for the tree, and a cylinder or two for the wishing well.

- **What compound objects do you need, and how should they be created from the simple ones?**

  The compound objects that need to be formed are the house and its roof, the treetop and its trunk, and the parts of the wishing well.

- **How much space do you need in your environment?**

  The virtual environment needs to be a 10-meter cube.

■ **Where should the VRML objects be placed in that environment?**

The coordinates shown on the graph paper sketches define exactly where each object needs to go in three-dimensional space (three-space).

FIG. 29.7
Here is a side view of your planned VRML world.

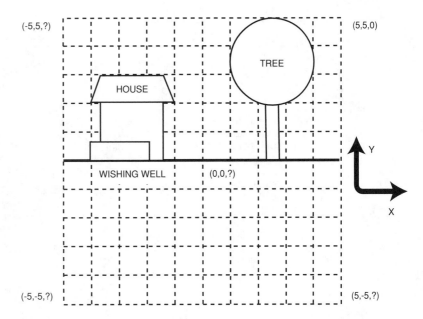

Moving Things Around

Creating the objects needed for our example shouldn't be very difficult. However, we now need to be able to move them around within the VRML environment. Without the capability to do this, all created objects will be lumped together at the origin of the VRML coordinate system. This moving is done using VRML's Transform node, whose syntax is:

```
Transform{
    translation        x y z
    rotation           rx ry rz ra
    scale              x y z
    scaleOrientation   rx ry rz ra
    center             x y z
    children           [ ]
}
```

The Transform node is used to move, scale, and rotate all the objects in its *children* field. Listing 29.5 shows the beginnings of our VRML world, showing the ground and the house, after the house has been moved to its correct position (see Figure 29.8).

Listing 29.5   world1.wrl—The Transform Node Is Used to Move Objects

```
4th Edition#VRML V2.0 utf8

WorldInfo {
    info "Special Edition, Using HTML, 4th Edition"
}

Background {
    skyColor 1 1 1
}

Shape {
    appearance Appearance {
        material Material {
            diffuseColor 0 0.75 0
        }
    }
    geometry IndexedFaceSet {
        coord Coordinate {
            point [ -5 0  5,
                     5 0  5,
                     5 0 -5,
                    -5 0 -5 ]
        }
        coordIndex [ 0, 1, 2, 3, -1 ]
    }
}

Transform {
    translation -2.5 1 -3
    children [
        Shape {
            appearance Appearance {
                material Material {
                    diffuseColor 0 0 0
                }
            }
            geometry Box { size 2.3333 2 1.3333 }
        }
    ]
}
```

Creating Object Hierarchies

Unless your VRML world is very simple—even simpler than our example—you might find yourself very often building up more complex VRML objects from simpler ones. While it is possible to treat each of the objects separately—and move and scale each individually—it's a lot easier to create the compound object from the individual ones and then manipulate that object with one operation. The VRML Transform node is used to create compound objects by enclosing other nodes. An object hierarchy is created by defining simpler objects and specifying their positions with respect to one another using a Transform node. Then, the entire hierarchy can be manipulated at once.

FIG. 29.8
The Transform node allows simple and compound VRML objects to be moved around the VRML environment, as well as rotated and scaled.

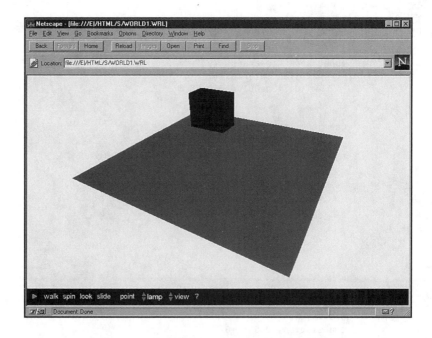

Listing 29.6 shows the next addition to our VRML world, the addition of the roof to our house. Note that the roof is created with an IndexedFaceSet and positioned on top of the bottom part of the house using a Transform node. Then, the compound object representing the complete house is moved into the correct position within the VRML environment (see Figure 29.9).

N O T E In this listing, differences between it and the previous one are shown in italic. For further listings, as we build up this example, we will show only the new elements. ■

Listing 29.6   world2.wrl—Creating Compound Objects with the *Transform* Node

```
#VRML V2.0 utf8

WorldInfo {
    info "Special Edition, Using HTML, 4th Edition"
}

Background {
    skyColor 1 1 1
}

#
# The Ground
#
```

continues

Listing 29.6   Continued

```
Shape {
    appearance Appearance {
        material Material {
            diffuseColor 0 0.75 0
        }
    }
    geometry IndexedFaceSet {
        coord Coordinate {
            point [ -5 0  5,
                     5 0  5,
                     5 0 -5,
                    -5 0 -5 ]
        }
        coordIndex [ 0, 1, 2, 3, -1 ]
    }
}


#
# The House
#

Transform {
    translation -2.5 1 -3
    children [
        Shape {
            appearance Appearance {
                material Material {
                    diffuseColor 0 0 0
                }
            }
            geometry Box { size 2.3333 2 1.3333 }
        }
        Transform {
            translation 0 1 0
            children [
                Shape {
                    appearance Appearance {
                        material Material {
                            diffuseColor 0 0 1
                        }
                    }
                    geometry IndexedFaceSet {
                        solid FALSE
                        coord Coordinate {
                            point [
                                -1.5 0 -1,
                                -1.1667 1 -0.6667,
                                1.5 0 -1,
                                1.1667 1 -0.6667,
                                1.5 0 1,
                                1.1667 1 0.6667,
                                -1.5 0 1,
                                -1.1667 1 0.6667
                            ]
```

```
                }
                coordIndex [
                    0, 2, 4, 6, -1,
                    1, 3, 5, 7, -1,
                    0, 2, 3, 1, -1,
                    2, 4, 5, 3, -1,
                    4, 6, 7, 5, -1,
                    6, 0, 1, 7, -1
                ]
            }
        }
    ]
}
]
}
```

FIG. 29.9
Creating compound
objects in VRML makes
it much easier to create
and manipulate
complex scenes.

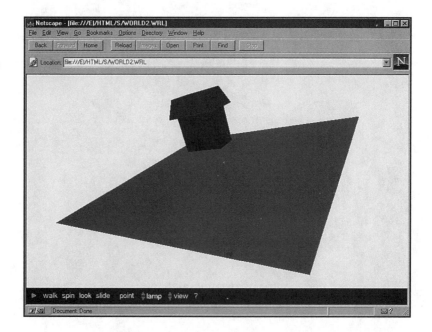

With the ability to create compound objects, we can add the rest of the elements to our VRML world—a tree made up of a sphere and a cylinder, and the wishing well made up of two cylinders. Listing 29.7 shows the new VRML code to produce these objects, and the resulting scene is shown in Figure 29.10.

Listing 29.7 world3.wrl (excerpt)—Completing the VRML World

```
#VRML V2.0 utf8

WorldInfo {
    info "Special Edition, Using HTML, 4th Edition"
```

continues

Listing 29.7 Continued

```
}

Background {
    skyColor 1 1 1
}

#
# The Ground
#

Shape {
    appearance Appearance {
        material Material {
            diffuseColor 0 0.75 0
        }
    }
    geometry IndexedFaceSet {
        coord Coordinate {
            point [ -5 0  5,
                     5 0  5,
                     5 0 -5,
                    -5 0 -5 ]
        }
        coordIndex [ 0, 1, 2, 3, -1 ]
    }
}

#
# The House
#

Transform {
    translation -2.5 1 -3
    children [
        Shape {
            appearance Appearance {
                material Material {
                    diffuseColor 0 0 0
                }
            }
            geometry Box { size 2.3333 2 1.3333 }
        }
        Transform {
            translation 0 1 0
            children [
                Shape {
                    appearance Appearance {
                        material Material {
                            diffuseColor 0 0 1
                        }
                    }
                    geometry IndexedFaceSet {
                        solid FALSE
                        coord Coordinate {
```

```
                        point [
                            -1.5 0 -1,
                            -1.1667 1 -0.6667,
                            1.5 0 -1,
                            1.1667 1 -0.6667,
                            1.5 0 1,
                            1.1667 1 0.6667,
                            -1.5 0 1,
                            -1.1667 1 0.6667
                        ]
                    }
                    coordIndex [
                        0, 2, 4, 6, -1,
                        1, 3, 5, 7, -1,
                        0, 2, 3, 1, -1,
                        2, 4, 5, 3, -1,
                        4, 6, 7, 5, -1,
                        6, 0, 1, 7, -1
                    ]
                }
            }
        ]
    }
    ]
}

#
# The Tree
#

Transform {
    translation 2.5 1.5 -1.5
    children [
        Shape {
            appearance Appearance {
                material Material {
                    diffuseColor 0.5 0.25 0
                }
            }
            geometry Cylinder {
                radius 0.1667
                height 3
            }
        }
        Transform {
            translation 0 1.5 0
            children [
                Shape {
                    appearance Appearance {
                        material Material {
                            diffuseColor 0 1 0
                        }
                    }
                    geometry Sphere {
                        radius 1.5
```

continues

Listing 29.7   Continued

```
                    }
                }
            ]
        }
    ]
}

#
# The Wishing Well
#

Transform {
    translation -3 0.3333 3
    children [
        Shape {
            appearance Appearance {
                material Material {
                    diffuseColor 1 1 1
                }
            }
            geometry Cylinder {
                radius 1
                height 0.6667
            }
        }
        Shape {
            appearance Appearance {
                material Material {
                    diffuseColor 0 0 0
                }
            }
            geometry Cylinder {
                radius 0.8
                height 0.7
            }
        }
    ]
}
```

Adding Realism with Textures

Earlier you learned a little about how to use the ImageTexture node to add realism to an object through the addition of image file textures. By default, VRML maps the image file specified by ImageTexture to each entire face of the solid in question—the six faces of a cube or the top, bottom, and curved surface of a cylinder, for instance. When mapping a texture to a surface to make it more realistic, it is best to tile small images repeatedly over the different faces. This can be done by using the TextureTransform node. Its syntax is

```
TextureTransform {
    translation    x y
    rotation       angle
    scale     x y
    center         x y
}
```

FIG. 29.10
All of your objects have
been placed in the
VRML world.

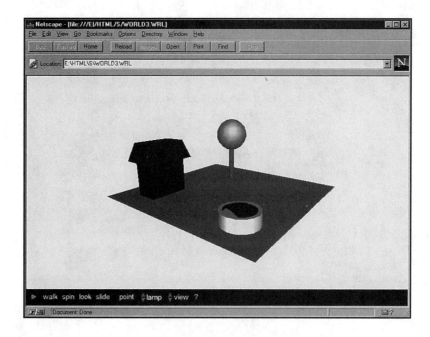

These fields allow you to move, rotate, scale, and center the image on the solid to determine how it is applied. To make a tiled texture more realistic looking, the most important field is `scale`, which determines how many times the image will be tiled. Note that `scale` refers to how the coordinates of the object to which the texture is being mapped will be scaled, so scale factors that are greater than one result in the image appearing smaller on the object and tiled more times.

Listing 29.8 shows an example of the texturing applied to our VRML world (the full listing on the CD shows the textures applied to all of the objects). In this case, a rocky appearance is given to the wishing well, and other, more realistic appearances are given to the other objects in the VRML world.

Listing 29.8   world4.wrl (excerpt)—Using Textures to Add Realism

```
#
# The Wishing Well
#

Transform {
    translation -3 0.3333 3
    children [
        Shape {
            appearance Appearance {
                material Material {
                    diffuseColor 1 1 1
```

continues

Listing 29.8 Continued

```
            }
            texture ImageTexture {
                url "bernie.gif"
            }
            textureTransform TextureTransform {
                scale 8 1
            }
        }
        geometry Cylinder {
            radius 1
            height 0.6667
        }
    }
    Shape {
        appearance Appearance {
            material Material {
                diffuseColor 0 0 0
            }
        }
        geometry Cylinder {
            radius 0.8
            height 0.7
        }
    }
  ]
}
```

FIG. 29.11
While textures certainly lend a more realistic appearance to a VRML world, they do slow down the file transmission and rendering, so use them only when needed.

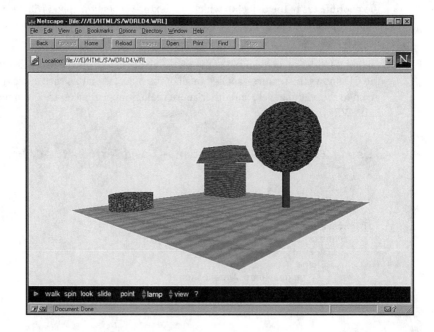

Linking to the Web

VRML, like HTML, is a language meant to be used on the Internet and the Web. An essential element for this is the hyperlink. This allows VRML worlds to be linked to other VRML worlds. And, if the VRML browser supports it, URLs can also be followed to HTML Web pages and other Internet resources.

Inline   One use of VRML's capability to link to the Web is through the `Inline` node. This node allows you to include VRML objects in your VRML worlds from any local VRML file or any VRML world on the Web. The syntax of the `Inline` node is

```
WWWInline {
   url "path of local file or URL"
}
```

The VRML object, objects, and VRML world defined by that file or URL are placed into your VRML world as if the code for them was entered in the same place in your VRML code.

Anchor   Hyperlinks are implemented in VRML by using the `Anchor` node. The important fields for this node are the `url` field, which is used to specify the URL hyperlink, and the `description` field, which gives a text description of the link. Objects that are defined within the `Anchor` node are the objects to which the hyperlink is attached. Like `Transform`, `Anchor` is a container node; the other VRML nodes that it contains become the anchors for the hyperlink defined by the node. The syntax of the `Anchor` node is

```
WWWAnchor {
    url          "url of some VRML world"
    description "description of that world
    children other VRML node(s)...
}
```

Features of VRML 2.0

The VRML 1.0 language specification allows for the creation, presentation, and viewing of static three-dimensional scenes and worlds. VRML 2.0 was designed to build on that standard to provide much more. The goal of the VRML 2.0 standard is to provide the tools to create three-dimensional worlds that include movement and sound and allow the objects within the world to be programmed with behaviors that allow them to react to your presence. VRML fish can be programmed to swim away from you if you get to close, for instance.

A second goal of VRML 2.0 is to create a foundation for Web-based three-dimensional content that can continue to evolve and grow. As computers continue to grow more and more powerful, the Internet continues to develop, and high-bandwidth, high-speed connections become more commonplace, the VRML standard will continue to be developed to take advantage of the new capabilities.

The capabilities of VRML 2.0 over VRML 1.0 fall into the five general categories of static world enhancements, interaction, animation, scripting, and prototyping. These are discussed in the VRML 2.0 specification, available at **http://vrml.sgi.com/moving-worlds/**. They are summarized in the following sections.

Enhanced Static Worlds

VRML 2.0 supports several new nodes and fields that allow the static geometry of VRML worlds to be made more realistic. You can create separate backdrops for the ground and the sky, using colors or images. Objects such as clouds and mountains can be put in the distance, and fog can be used to obscure distant objects. Irregular terrain can be created, rather than using flat planes for your surface. VRML 2.0 also provides three-dimensional sound to further enhance realism.

Interaction

VRML 2.0 includes a new class of nodes, called sensor nodes, that are able to set off events in response to different inputs. Touch and proximity sensors react to the presence of the viewer either touching or coming close to an object. A time sensor is capable of keeping track of the passage of time, allowing time-correlated events to be added to your VRML world. And VRML 2.0 supports realistic collision detection and terrain following to ensure that your viewers bounce off of (or at least stop at) your walls and solid objects and are able to travel through your world while easily following things like steps and inclines.

Animation

VRML 2.0 interpolator nodes allow you to create predefined animations for any of the objects in your VRML world. These animations can be programmed to occur automatically or in response to some other factor, either an action of your viewer or at a given time. With these interpolators, you can create moving objects, objects such as the sun or the moon that change color as they move, or objects that change shape. The viewpoint can also be animated to create an automatic guided tour of your VRML world.

Scripting

The key to many of VRML 2.0's other features—particularly the movement of VRML 2.0 objects—is its support of scripting. Scripting is used to program objects' behaviors, not only allowing them to move but also giving them the capability to react realistically to objects around them. A script is the link that is used to take an event—generated by a sensor node, for instance—and generate the appropriate action.

Prototyping

The final category of enhancement to VRML 2.0 is the capability for prototyping. What this allows you to do is to create your own nodes. By grouping a set of nodes to achieve a specific purpose, within a new prototype node, that node becomes available for reuse.

 N O T E For more information, tutorials, and examples of VRML 2.0, as well as VRML 1.0 and other VRML implementations, take a look at the excellent Web site provided by Vijay Mukhi at **http://www.neca.com/~vmis/vrml.htm**. ■

VRML Resources

 Probably the central clearinghouse of all things VRML, appropriately called the VRML Repository, is located at **http://www.sdsc.edu/vrml/**. This Web site contains a vast array of information about VRML, links to sites containing VRML browser and authoring software, and just about anything else you can think of that has to do with VRML.

VRML Software

A wide range of software is available on the Web, most of it listed on the VRML Repository. The general categories of software available include the following:

- VRML browsers and plug-ins
- VRML and other 3-D authoring programs
- VRML applications

VRML Object Libraries

If you are interested in creating VRML objects for use in a VRML world or with an embedded VRML special effect in a Web page, you should probably take a look around on the Web before starting from scratch. There are many places to get three-dimensional objects that you can use for your purposes, both in VRML files and in other formats that can be converted to VRML.

The best place to start, predictably, is the VRML Repository. This site maintains a library of example applications, categorized by topic, that can be examined through the Web page at **http://www.sdsc.edu/vrml/**.

 Among the many other sites featuring VRML examples, applications, and objects, one is the VRML Models site located at **http://www.ocnus.com/models/models.html**. This site, like the VRML Repository library, features an indexed list of VRML objects and worlds. A unique feature of the VRML Models site is its VRML Mall, which is an actual three-dimensional gallery through which you can view all of their VRML objects.

 Finally, the Mesh Mart, located at **http://www.meshmart.org/**, was set up as a source of three-dimensional objects. While most of these objects are not in VRML format, they are available in formats that can be easily converted to VRML. Through the Mesh Mart, a program called wcvt2pov.exe is available that can convert between many different three-dimensional formats. It can read in files with the following formats:

- AOFF (GEO) files
- AutoCAD (DXF) files
- 3D Studio (3DS) files
- Neutral File Format (NFF)
- RAW (RAW) files
- TPOLY (TPOLY) files
- TrueType fonts (TTF) files
- Wavefront (OBJ) files

In addition, it can write out files in the following formats:

- AutoCAD (DXF)
- 3D Studio (ASC)
- Neutral File Format (NFF)
- OpenGL
- POVRay V2.2 (POV, INC)
- PovSB (PSB)
- RAW (RAW)
- TPOLY (TPOLY)
- VRML V1.0 (WRL)
- Wavefront (OBJ)

P A R T

V

Pushing Content

Building Channels with CDF

by Jerry Honeycutt

In this chapter

Introducing Webcasting

Webcasting is the capability to broadcast content to the user on a regular schedule. You decide how much content to download and how often to update it using a *Channel Definition File* (CDF). Microsoft's incarnation of this standard, which you can learn more about at W3C's Web site, is called *Active Channels*.

A user subscribes to your channel using his Web browser, which allows him to monitor the channel for changes and browse its content offline. The browser notifies the user when content is added to or changed on your channel by displaying a starburst (a *gleam* in Microsoft vernacular) next to the channel's icon. Optionally, if the user enables the mail notification for the subscription, the browser sends an Internet mail message to the user.

Broadcasting a channel requires three steps on your part, each of which you learn about in this chapter: designing the channel, building the CDF file, and posting your channel to the Internet. You can get really fancy and add your channel to Internet Explorer Channel Guide as well, which advertises your content to everyone using Internet Explorer.

Designing Channels

A channel is nothing more than Web pages; still, users have very different expectations. They expect much more panache with a channel. For starters, keep these notes in mind when organizing your channel:

- *Keep the top level simple.* You organize channels hierarchically, with the top level being what the user sees as the logo in the Channel Bar. Don't put more than seven items under the first level of the channel. The user sees these items in the channel's submenu; putting more than eight items makes choosing one from the menu more difficult.

- *Use a flat organization for other levels.* Keep the organization of each level relatively flat so that the user doesn't have to work as hard to find the information for which he's looking. (You use the CDF tags <CHANNEL> and <ITEM> to create your channel's hierarchy.)

- *Help the user identify items in the top level.* Provide icons for each first-level item in the channel and a logo to be used in the Channel Bar. Don't provide icons for levels below the first, however, as the browser provides them.

You can deliver that extra punch if you follow these recommendations:

- *Use Dynamic HTML in your channel.* The sure-fire way to make your channel shine is to use Dynamic HTML. You can make every item on the Web page respond to user interaction; for example, you can create a list of headlines that pops up the full story as the user moves the mouse over each headline.

- *Allow the user to browse offline.* Many Java applets and ActiveX controls don't work correctly when the user is browsing the Web page offline. If you dynamically load images, the browser might not download the images referred to in the script. Test your channel before posting it so you know it works offline.

- *Display small chunks of information on each page.* The closest analogy most people make to Webcasting is TV programming. Users are accustomed to seeing small, focused bits of information on the screen. Keep your content simple and small so that you don't overwhelm the user.

- *Build slim Web pages that load with a snap.* The user doesn't expect to wait for your page to draw, even if he's reading it from the cache. Design the first level of Web pages so that they seem to snap instantly onto the screen. You can provide links to content that is a bit more sluggish.

- *Use cascading style sheets and Web fonts.* Style sheets and downloadable fonts give you complete control over how you present your content. Build a style sheet that you use across all of the pages in your channel.

- *Add pizzazz to your Web pages with multimedia.* Users expect to see much more than text and pictures on a channel. Include media that make your Web pages more interesting. Multimedia doesn't automatically diminish your ability to make your channel snappy, though, as long as you carefully pick what you use.

Part

V

Ch

30

 TIP You can learn how to build great channels by learning from the publishing professionals. Look at your favorite magazines to see how they lay out pages for advertisements, editorials, and so on. Visit some of the more popular channels on the Internet to see how they design their content.

Creating a CDF File

A CDF file is an index of HTML files that make up your channel. In it, you specify the update schedule, channel hierarchy, page titles, abstracts, and more. You can download only the CDF to the user's computer, which causes the user to have to go online to browse the channel's content, or you can download the CDF file and all the updated content. Keep in mind that in many cases, the user can override your settings in the CDF file so that more or less content is downloaded.

CDF is an application of XML. As with HTML, you store CDF tags in a text file—only you give it the CDF file extension. The syntax is even similar to HTML tags. You begin and end each tag with brackets, for example. Some tags are containers, requiring a start and end pair, while other tags are empty tags. With CDF, you put a slash before the closing bracket of empty tags. Here's an overview of each type of syntax (empty tag, container tag, and child tags):

Empty tag with attributes:
```
<TAG ATTR="VALUE" ATTR="VALUE" />
```

Container tag with attributes:
```
<TAG ATTR="VALUE">This is the content</TAG>
```

Container tag with child tags:
```
<TAG ATTR="VALUE">
    <CHILD1>This is the content</CHILD1>
    <CHILD2 ATTR>
</TAG>
```

N O T E In HTML, you don't have to quote the value that you assign to an attribute as long as that value doesn't contain spaces. For example, HREF=./html/file.htm is valid. With CDF, you have to quote each and every value, however, or the parser might not work. For example, HREF="./html/file.htm". ▉

Each CDF file includes at least one <CHANNEL> tag, which defines the top-level channel. You can nest <CHANNEL> tags to create a hierarchy of channels with the first <CHANNEL> tag representing the top-level and the tags nested under that representing the first level. Each <ITEM> tag points to a Web page in the channel. The most basic CDF file looks like the one shown in Listing 30.1 (you'll build upon this example throughout this chapter).

Listing 30.1 A Basic CDF File

```
<?XML version="1.0"?>
<!DOCTYPE Channel SYSTEM "http://www.w3c.org/Channel.dtd">

<CHANNEL HREF="http://www.honeycutt.com/channel.html">
</CHANNEL>
```

The first two lines describe the contents of the file as an XML implementation, pointing the browser to **http://www.w3c.org/Channel.dtd** for the Channel DTD. The last two lines show you how to specify the opening page of the channel using the <CHANNEL> tag's HREF attribute. This is the Web page the user sees when he opens your channel in the channel viewer. You can optionally include the BASE attribute to include the base URL for the channel, which the browser uses to resolve relative URLs.

Describing Your Channel's Hierarchy

You can nest one <CHANNEL> within another to create a hierarchy of channels—the outside tag presents the top level, the tags nested in that represent the first level, and so on. For example, if you nest three of these tags, one within another, the user would see the first-level subchannel when he clicks on the top level. When the user clicks the first level, he'd see the second level. Figure 30.1 illustrates this by showing you a typical channel in Internet Explorer's Channel Bar.

The <CHANNEL> tag describes a channel hierarchy, but the <ITEM> tag refers to the Web pages that make up the content of your channel. When the user clicks a channel containing <ITEM> tags, he sees a list of Web pages. While you can nest <CHANNEL> tags within each other, you can't nest <CHANNEL> or <ITEM> tags within another <ITEM> tag. HREF is a required attribute that you set to the URL of the Web page for that item. Optionally, set LASTMODE to the date the item was last changed in the form *YYYY-MM-DD:THHMM+HHMM* and LEVEL to the number of levels below the item to download to the user's cache.

FIG. 30.1
The user can also browse a channel's hierarchy in Internet Explorer's Favorites menu.

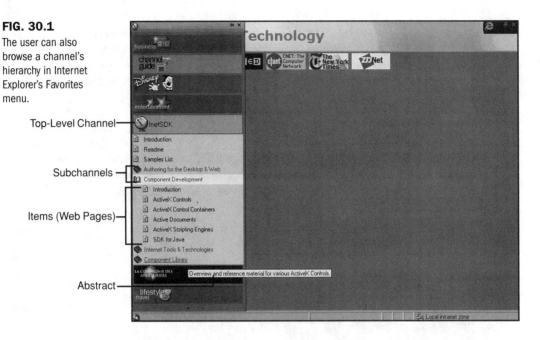

Listing 30.2 shows you an example of a channel with a complex hierarchy. When the user opens the top level, he sees the Web page indicated by HREF in the browser; the subchannels and items indicated by this tag's child tags will appear in the Channel Bar. If the user opens the second subchannel, he'd see two items and an additional channel he can click. Note the use of relative URLs, which are resolved against the topmost container tag in this case.

Listing 30.2   A Complex CDF File

```
<?XML version="1.0"?>
<!DOCTYPE Channel SYSTEM "http://www.w3c.org/Channel.dtd">

<CHANNEL HREF="http://www.honeycutt.com/channel.html" BASE="http://
www.honeycutt.com">
    <ITEM HREF="intro.html"></ITEM>
    <CHANNEL HREF="more/stuff.html">
        <ITEM HREF="books.html"></ITEM>
        <ITEM HREF="bio.html"></ITEM>
        <ITEM HREF="tips.html"></ITEM>
    </CHANNEL>
    <CHANNEL HREF="other/stuff.html">
        <ITEM HREF="games.html"></ITEM>
        <ITEM HREF="tricks.html"></ITEM>
        <CHANNEL HREF="deep/stuff.html">
            <ITEM HREF="cdf.html"></ITEM>
        </CHANNEL>
    </CHANNEL>
</CHANNEL>
```

N O T E Using the `<ITEM>` tag has little to do with the browser's crawler, the software that downloads the channel to the user's computer. The crawler actually analyzes the links in each Web page to determine what it should download. The `<CHANNEL>` and `<ITEM>` tags express the relationships between Web pages so that the browser can display that relationship in the Channel Bar. ◼

Nesting CDF Tags

CDF allows you to nest tags in interesting ways. By doing this, you can build interesting hierarchies for your channel. The following table describes how you can nest the CDF tags described. For example, you can put an `<ABSTRACT>` tag within a `<CHANNEL>` and an `<ITEM>` tag.

Tag	Child Tags	Parent Tags
`<ABSTRACT>`		`<CHANNEL>`
		`<ITEM>`
`<CHANNEL>`	`<ABSTRACT>`	
	`<CHANNEL>`	
	`<ITEM>`	
	`<LOG>`	
	`<LOGIN>`	
	`<LOGO>`	
	`<LOGTARGET>`	
	`<SCHEDULE>`	
	`<TITLE>`	
`<EARLIESTTIME>`		`<SCHEDULE>`
`<INTERVALTIME>`		`<SCHEDULE>`
`<ITEM>`	`<ABSTRACT>`	`<CHANNEL>`
	`<LOG>`	
	`<LOGO>`	
	`<TITLE>`	
	`<USAGE>`	
`<LATESTTIME>`		`<SCHEDULE>`
`<LOG>`		`<ITEM>`
`<LOGIN>`		`<CHANNEL>`
`<LOGO>`		`<CHANNEL>`
		`<ITEM>`
`<LOGTARGET>`	`<PURGETIME>`	`<CHANNEL>`
`<PURGETIME>`		`<LOGTARGET>`
`<SCHEDULE>`	`<EARLIESTTIME>`	`<CHANNEL>`
	`<INTERVALTIME>`	`<ITEM>`
	`<LATESTTIME>`	

Tag	Child Tags	Parent Tags
<TITLE>		<CHANNEL>
		<ITEM>
<USAGE>		<ITEM>

Scheduling Updates to Your Channel

You can create a default schedule that determines the frequency at which the browser checks for changes, updating the user's computer with fresh content. You specify a range of times, and the browser randomly picks a time within that schedule. Doing so, the browser avoids overwhelming the server because the load is spread out across the entire time range. A user who connects to the Internet via a dial-up connection updates his channels manually, though, so the server will get hits throughout the day.

To schedule your channel, you must first specify how much content to download to the user's computer. Set the <CHANNEL> tag's LEVEL attribute to the number of levels you want to download to the user's computer. For example:

```
<CHANNEL HREF="http://www.honeycutt.com/channel.html" LEVEL="3">
```

Then, you specify the schedule using the <SCHEDULE> tag. This tag has two attributes, STARTDATE and ENDDATE, that indicate the range of dates that the schedule applies. The format for these attributes is *YYYY-MM-DD*—for example, 1998-02-14. If you omit these attributes, the schedule starts with the current day. You specify the interval at which to update the content using the <INTERVALTIME> child tag. You set DAY to the number of days over which the schedule repeats, HOUR to the number hours, and MIN to the number of minutes. Thus, to update the content every day and a half, you'd write an <INTERVALTIME> tag that looks like this: <INTERVALTIME DAYS=1 HOUR=12>.

Listing 30.3 shows you an example that schedules a channel to be updated once every six hours beginning on 10/1/97 and ending on 11/1/97.

Listing 30.3   Scheduling the Download

```
<?XML version="1.0"?>
<!DOCTYPE Channel SYSTEM "http://www.w3c.org/Channel.dtd">

<CHANNEL HREF="http://www.honeycutt.com/channel.html" LEVEL="3">
    <SCHEDULE STARTDATE="1997-10-01" ENDDATE="1997-11-1">
        <INTERVALTIME HOUR="6" />
    </SCHEDULE>
</CHANNEL>
```

You can optionally specify a range of time, occurring at each interval, for which the browser will download updated content. For example, if you only want the browser to download content starting one hour after the interval and ending five hours after the interval, you'd set the <EARLIESTTIME> and <LATESTTIME> tags as shown in Listing 30.4. Both of these tags accept the same attributes as the <INTERVALTIME> tag.

Listing 30.4   Using <*EARLIESTTIME*> and <*LATESTTIME*>

```
<?XML version="1.0"?>
<!DOCTYPE Channel SYSTEM "http://www.w3c.org/Channel.dtd">

<CHANNEL HREF="http://www.honeycutt.com/channel.html" LEVEL="3">
    <SCHEDULE STARTDATE="1997-10-01" ENDDATE="1997-11-1">
        <INTERVALTIME HOUR="6" />
        <EARLIESTTIME HOUR="1" />
        <LATESTTIME HOUR="5" />
    </SCHEDULE>
</CHANNEL>
```

The schedule you add at the top level is the default schedule for the entire channel, but you can create separate schedules for each nested subchannel or item. Note in Listing 30.5, you don't see the STARTDATE or ENDDATE attributes, indicating that the schedule begins immediately and never expires. The very last schedule shows you how to schedule the update for an individual Web page. If an item's LASTMOD attribute indicates that the content hasn't changed recently, the browser will not download fresh content for the item.

Listing 30.5   Scheduling Each Subchannel and Item

```
<?XML version="1.0"?>
<!DOCTYPE Channel SYSTEM "http://www.w3c.org/Channel.dtd">

<CHANNEL HREF="http://www.honeycutt.com/channel.html" BASE="http://
www.honeycutt.com">
    <SCHEDULE>
        <INTERVALTIME DAY="1" />
    </SCHEDULE>
    <ITEM HREF="intro.html"></ITEM>
    <CHANNEL HREF="more/stuff.html">
        <SCHEDULE>
            <INTERVALTIME HOUR="3" />
        </SCHEDULE>
        <ITEM HREF="books.html"></ITEM>
        <ITEM HREF="bio.html"></ITEM>
        <ITEM HREF="tips.html"></ITEM>
    </CHANNEL>
    <CHANNEL HREF="other/stuff.html">
        <ITEM HREF="games.html"></ITEM>
        <ITEM HREF="tricks.html"></ITEM>
        <CHANNEL HREF="deep/stuff.html">
            <ITEM HREF="cdf.html">
                <SCHEDULE>
                    <INTERVALTIME HOUR="3" />
                </SCHEDULE>
            </ITEM>
        </CHANNEL>
    </CHANNEL>
</CHANNEL>
```

Describing Your Channel in the Channel Bar

When the user is browsing the Channel Bar, he can use additional help figuring out what's what. You provide a title for each channel and item using the `<TITLE>` tag. Include this tag as a child of each `<CHANNEL>` or `<ITEM>`. The user sees this title next to the channel's icon in the Channel Bar, instead of seeing the URL by default. Here's what the `<TITLE>` tag looks like:

```
<TITLE>Title of Item</TITLE>
```

You provide a brief description of each channel and item using the `<ABSTRACT>` tag. The browser displays this as a ToolTip when the user holds the mouse pointer over the item in the Channel Bar. Keep the description short, a few sentences at most, and make sure it accurately describes the content of the item. This tag can be a child of both `<CHANNEL>` and `<ITEM>`. Here's what this tag looks like:

```
<ABSTRACT>This is the description to display in a tool-tip</ABSTRACT>
```

The last tag you use to describe your channel is the `<LOGO>` tag, which describes the images used to represent an item in the Channel Bar. The browser displays the icon next the item's title. You can specify a 16×16 icon or a 32×80 image to use as a logo. The browser uses the 32×80 logo in the Channel Bar and the 16×16 icon everywhere else. You can use any standard image format including GIF or JPG, and, in some cases, you can use a Windows ICO file for the 16×16 icon. You assign the URL of the image to the `<LOGO>` tag's HREF attribute. Then, you define the type of image by assigning one of the values in Table 30.1 to the STYLE attribute. `<LOGO>` is an empty tag, as shown here:

```
<LOGO HREF="http://www.honeycutt.com/image.gif" STYLE="ICON" />
```

Table 30.1 Image Types

Type	Size	Description
ICON	16×16	Represents the channel or item and is displayed next to the title
IMAGE	32×80	Represents the channel at the top level of the Channel Bar

Listing 30.6 builds upon the example you've worked on up to this point. It adds the `<TITLE>`, `<ABSTRACT>`, and `<LOGO>` tags to each channel and item in the CDF file. Remember that I recommend you only provide icons for the top and first levels of your channel hierarchy and let the browser take care of the rest. Do include a title and abstract for each and every level, though, so you can give the reader as much information as possible while he navigates the Channel Bar.

Listing 30.6 Describing Your Channel

```
<?XML version="1.0"?>
<!DOCTYPE Channel SYSTEM "http://www.w3c.org/Channel.dtd">
```

continues

Listing 30.6   Continued

```
<CHANNEL HREF="http://www.honeycutt.com/channel.html" BASE="http://
www.honeycutt.com">
    <TITLE>Jerry's Wild and Crazy HTML Channel</TITLE>
    <ABSTRACT>I give you the latest information about HTML shenanigans.
    </ABSTRACT>
    <ICON HREF="images/channel.gif" />
    <SCHEDULE>
        <INTERVALTIME DAY="1" />
    </SCHEDULE>
    <ITEM HREF="intro.html">
        <TITLE>Introduction</TITLE>
        <ABSTRACT>A description of what you find in this channel</ABSTRACT>
        <ICON HREF="images/intro.gif" />
    </ITEM>
    <CHANNEL HREF="more/stuff.html">
        <TITLE>More Stuff</TITLE>
        <ABSTRACT>The latest and greatest stuff about HTML</ABSTRACT>
        <ICON HREF="images/stuff.gif" />
        <SCHEDULE>
            <INTERVALTIME HOUR="3" />
        </SCHEDULE>
        <ITEM HREF="books.html">
        <TITLE>Books</TITLE>
        <ABSTRACT>A list of all my books to date.</ABSTRACT>
        </ITEM>
        <ITEM HREF="bio.html">
            <TITLE>Biography</TITLE>
            <ABSTRACT>Jerry's biography</ABSTRACT>
        </ITEM>
        <ITEM HREF="tips.html">
            <TITLE>Tips for HTML authors</TITLE>
            <ABSTRACT>Check here for the latest HTML tips</ABSTRACT>
        </ITEM>
    </CHANNEL>
    <CHANNEL HREF="other/stuff.html">
        <TITLE>Other stuff about the Internet</TITLE>
        <ABSTRACT>The latest information about other Internet standards
        </ABSTRACT>
        <ICON HREF="images/other.gif" />
        <ITEM HREF="games.html"></ITEM>
        <ITEM HREF="tricks.html"></ITEM>
        <CHANNEL HREF="deep/stuff.html">
            <ITEM HREF="cdf.html">
                <SCHEDULE>
                    <INTERVALTIME HOUR="3" />
                </SCHEDULE>
            </ITEM>
        </CHANNEL>
    </CHANNEL>
</CHANNEL>
```

Logging Hits While the User Is Offline

CDF provides a mechanism for recording hits to your channel while the user is browsing it offline. This is the only way you're going to be able to track usage information for it. To enable the browser to track hits for you, you must add the `<LOG>` tag to each `<ITEM>` container in your channel. This tag's only attribute is VALUE, to which you assign the event to be logged. Currently, the only value you can assign to VALUE is document:view, which logs a hit every time the user opens the HTML file causing the document:view event. For example:

```
<LOG VALUE="document:view" />
```

You tell the browser where to log hits adding the `<LOGTARGET>` tag to each `<CHANNEL>` container. This tag works similar to HTML's `<FORM>` tag. You assign the URL of the script that accepts log data to HREF. Then, you specify the HTTP method by assigning PUT or POST to the METHOD attribute. The SCOPE attribute indicates which hits you want logged: ALL indicates every hit, OFFLINE indicates only offline hits, and ONLINE indicates only online hits. The default value is ALL. Here's what the `<LOGTARGET>` tag looks like when included as part of a `<CHANNEL>` tag:

```
<CHANNEL HREF="http://www.honeycutt.com/channel.cdf">
    <LOGTARGET HREF="http://www.honeycutt.com/cgi-bin/log" METHOD="POST">
    </LOGTARGET>
</CHANNEL>
```

Within the `<LOGTARGET>` container, you can specify the range of time for which the browser reports hits using the `<PURGETIME>` tag. Set this tag's DAY attribute to the number of prior days for which the browser reports hits. Set the HOUR attribute to the number of hours and the MIN attribute to the number of minutes. For example, if you only want the browser to report hits for the last day and a half, use `<PURGETIME>` like this:

```
<PURGETIME DAY="1" HOUR="12" />
```

Authenticating a User

If you're implementing HTTP authentication on your channel, you must ensure that the browser has the user's name and password it can log onto the channel without user intervention. You do so using the empty `<LOGIN>` tag, which causes the browser to collect the user's name and password during the subscription process. This tag's DOMAIN attribute contains the domain name of the server that's authenticating the user—honeycutt.com, for example. The METHOD attribute indicates the type of authentication as described in Table 30.2. Here's an example:

```
<LOGIN DOMAIN="honeycutt.com" METHOD="BASIC">
```

You can provide a default username and password so that the browser can pre-fill the login wizard so the user only has to dismiss the dialog box. You assign the username to USER and password to PASS. If you don't provide the username or password, the browser prompts the user for them and won't continue the subscription process without them.

 TIP After the subscription process, you no longer have to include `<LOGIN>` in your CDF file as the browser stores the authentication information in the subscription information that it keeps.

Part

V

Ch

30

Table 30.2 Authentication Types

Type	Description
BASIC	*Plain Text*. Base64 string containing the name and password.
DPA	*Distributed Password Authentication*. Challenge-response method similar to that used by the Microsoft Network.
MSN	*Microsoft Network*. Challenge-response method used by the Microsoft Network.
NTLM	*NT LAN Manager*. Challenge-response method based upon the user's name.
RPA	*Remote Passphrase Authentication*. CompuServe's authentication method.

 T I P You can use Active Server Pages to dynamically generate a CDF file based upon the user's preferences. Collect the user's preferences when he first subscribes to the channel. Then, store the preferences as HTTP cookies and dynamically build the CDF file each time the user browses your channel.

Creating a Desktop Component or Screen Saver

By default, the browser displays each item in a channel as a Web page. You can cause the browser to use an item differently, however, by including the <USAGE> tag within the <ITEM> container:

```
<ITEM HREF="http://www.honeycutt.com/intro.htm">
    <USAGE VALUE="ScreenSaver" />
</ITEM>
```

As shown in the example, the <USAGE> tag's only attribute is VALUE. This indicates how you intend for the browser to use the parent item. Table 30.3 describes each of the values you assign to this attribute.

Table 30.3 Usage Values

Value	The item is:
Channel	Displayed in the channel viewer
Email	Mailed to the user when updated
NONE	Not displayed in the Channel Bar
DesktopComponent	Displayed on the user's desktop
ScreenSaver	Displayed as a screen saver
SmartScreen	Displayed as a screen saver

N O T E You learn more about creating Active Desktop and Active Screen Saver items in Chapter 31, "Supporting the Active Desktop." ■

Posting the CDF File to Your Web Site

Your pages are ready and you've created your CDF file; now you need to post your channel on the Internet. Doing so is no different than posting your normal Web pages—copy your files to the Web server. Be sure to include your CDF file. Note that CDF files only work properly when opened from a Web server. Thus, you can't test your CDF file by opening it from your computer.

 You must provide a link to your CDF file, though, so the user can launch the subscription process. You can put this link anywhere on your Web site, but you should consider building a special Web page for this link that advertises your channel. If you're broadcasting a portion of your existing Web site, include a link on the primary Web page for that portion. You can see an example of this on Microsoft's Web site: **http://www.microsoft.com/msdn/sdk/inetsdk/ asetup/default.htm**. A text or graphical link will do the trick:

```
<A HREF="http://www.honeycutt.com/subscribe.cdf>Subscribe</A>
<A HREF="http://www.honeycutt.com/subscribe.cdf><IMG SRC=subscribe.gif></A>
```

The subscription process works something like this:

1. The user clicks the link to the channel's CDF file.
2. The browser downloads and parses the CDF file, opening a subscription window similar to the one shown in Figure 30.2.

FIG. 30.2

The user can customize the amount of content he wants and the schedule on which he wants it updated.

3. The user customizes the amount of content, the schedule, logon, and even the notification method, and dismisses the dialog box.
4. The browser adds the subscription information to the Channel Bar. The user can browse the channel by clicking its icon in the Channel Bar.
5. Per the schedule specified for the channel, the browser downloads a fresh copy of the CDF file; then, it checks for updated content on the channel and downloads it.

OSD for Distributing Applications

Up to this point, the primary way that publishers distribute software is through disks or CD-ROMs. Many publishers do post products on the Internet that the user can download, but the whole process is still initiated and steered by the user.

In combination with CDF, OSD (Open Software Description) promises to allow you to *push* software to the user's desktop in a similar way to how you use CDF to push Web content. A user subscribes to an *application channel*, which automatically updates the user's computer with the latest version of your application.

OSD is a technology that is co-developed by Microsoft and Marimba. Netscape and other vendors have backed it, though, and OSD has been submitted to W3C for acceptance as a recommendation. Many details are missing as of this writing, however, but you can learn more about OSD at **http://www.microsoft.com/standards/osd**.

Adding Your Channel to Internet Explorer's Guide

I can think of no better way to get the word out about your channel than to place it on Internet Explorer's Channel Guide. That way, everyone with a copy of Internet Explorer will see the advertisement for your channel and can subscribe to it by clicking it in the guide. Microsoft has a few rules you must follow to be listed in the channel guide:

- You must use Dynamic HTML in your channel.

- You must provide a preview page approximately 365×460 pixels in size. This is the Web page that tells the user more about your channel and is the page from which the user subscribes to your channel.

- You must provide RASCi ratings for your site.

- You must put the Add Active Channel logo on your preview page and link it to your channel's normally updated CDF file. To get this logo, you must agree to the license agreement you find at Microsoft's Web site (**http://www.microsoft.com/sbnmember/lounges/lev2/logolicense.asp**).

N O T E   To submit a channel to Microsoft for inclusion in the channel guide, you must be a member of the SiteBuilder Network. You can join at **http://www.microsoft.com/sitebuilder/default.htm**. ▨

When you're convinced that your channel follows the rules, you're ready to submit your channel for review. Open **http://www.microsoft.com/sbnmember/apply/ChannelApplication.asp** in your browser, and you are asked to submit the following items:

- A CDF file that looks like Listing 30.7. *URL* is the URL of your preview page. *CDF* is the URL of your channel's regularly updated CDF file (yes, you produce a second CDF file). You must also provide the *Title*, *Description*, *IMAGE* URL, and *ICON* URL as indicated in the listing.

- A logo image that will be placed in the channel guide. This image should be 32×80 pixels in size.
- Your RASCi ratings information.
- A description of your channel for the index.

Listing 30.7   Channel Guide CDF

```
<?XML VERSION="1.0" ENCODING="UTF-8"?>
<!DOCTYPE Channel SYSTEM "http://www.w3c.org/Channel.dtd">

<CHANNEL HREF="URL" BASE="CDF">
    <TITLE>Title</TITLE>
    <ABSTRACT>Description</ABSTRACT>
    <LOGO HREF="IMAGE" STYLE="IMAGE"/>
    <LOGO HREF="ICON" STYLE="ICON"/>
</CHANNEL>
```

TIP Microsoft provides a tool called Liburnia you can use to automatically build a CDF file. You can find more information about this product at **http://www.microsoft.com/sbnmember/download/ default.htm**. Microsoft FrontPage also helps you build CDF files quicker by providing a CDF Wizard.

Part
V

Ch

30

Supporting the Active Desktop

by Jerry Honeycutt

In this chapter

Understanding the User's Desktop

With Internet Explorer 4.0, the user's desktop becomes a primary means by which he organizes Internet-related information:

- The user places shortcuts to his most frequently visited Internet sites on the desktop.
- The user accesses his favorite Internet shortcuts from the Start button by choosing Favorites.
- The user puts shortcuts to his favorite Internet tools in a toolbar that he places in the taskbar.
- The user organizes his channel content by clicking the Channel button in the taskbar.

In the middle of all this is Active Desktop content in the form of Active Desktop Components. Desktop content is brief and concise, offering headlines or summaries that lead to stories on your channel. Desktop content is the first thing the user sees when he logs on to the computer. Upon seeing an interesting summary, the user clicks it and is presented with the entire story in Internet Explorer 4.0.

The user organizes Active Desktop content right along with his Internet shortcuts, Favorites menu, and so on. Figure 31.1 shows you an example of desktop content, which contains headlines for Microsoft's Site Builder Network. When the user clicks one of the links, Internet Explorer 4.0 opens the related channel content in the browser.

FIG. 31.1

You can suggest a size for a desktop item, but the user can move and stretch it anyway he likes.

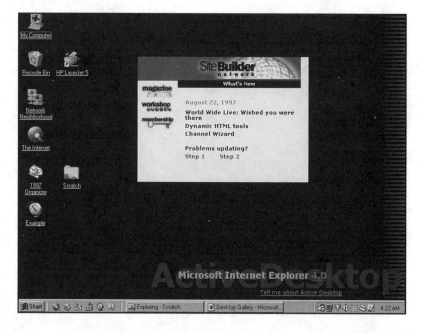

Desktop content is a perfect complement for channel content. You develop both of them using the same technologies, CDF and Dynamic HTML. Through careful design, you make your channel content more approachable, which draws more repeat visitors to it. Think of desktop content as the teaser that draws the user to your channel.

Examples of Active Desktop Content

The possibilities for desktop content are endless, and I hope the following list will inspire you with some ideas of your own:

- *Announcements*. On a corporate intranet, you can broadcast messages via desktop content. For instance, you can broadcast price updates to a field sales force.

- *Chat lists*. You can build Active Desktop content that lets the user know when his favorite people are online (such as ICQ, see **www.mirabilis.com**) or when new chat channels are available.

- *Headlines*. Active Desktop content is especially well suited to displaying headlines that lead to stories on your Web site.

- *Searches*. Build a search engine for your Web site that the user can put on his desktop.

- *Site indexes*. Build an index for your site, using an outline control, that the user can put on the desktop. Then, the user can navigate to precise Web page on your site.

- *Tickers*. You can display any kind of information in a ticker, but time-sensitive information works best: sports scores, stock quotes, and weather.

Part
V
Ch
31

What You Need to Know

Building content for the Active Desktop is not dissimilar to building Active Channel content. You specify the content of your content and schedule updates using a CDF file, as you learned in Chapter 30, "Building Channels with CDF." There are a few things you should know specifically about Active Desktop content, however:

- You must specify the shape of your content within your CDF file. This is a suggestion that the user is free to change.

- When Internet Explorer 4.0 installs an item on the desktop, it automatically adds it to the user's subscription folder.

- Active Desktop content is automatically cached so the user can browse it offline. You specify an updated schedule in the CDF file.

- Users are automatically notified when the Active Desktop content is changed on your Web server.

- The user schedules each desktop item separately.

Designing for the Active Desktop

Creating an HTML file for the Active Desktop is a bit unique. You're accustomed to building Web pages that display in a medium-size browser window and whose contents were potentially complex. Forget what you've learned; you must keep it simple. You can't go wrong if you follow these tips, though:

- *Make sure your item works offline.* Most users do not have a LAN connection to the Internet. If your content requires an online connection, the user won't see it while he's offline. Use your CDF file to make sure that Internet Explorer 4.0 downloads all the images, applets, or objects that your item requires.

- *Don't include navigation in your item.* Active Desktop items are intended to be a portal to your channel content or Web site. Don't expect the user to navigate content within the item's frame.

- *Keep your Active Desktop item small.* Most users still have small monitors at a resolution of 640×480. Don't require the user to give most of his desktop real estate to your item. Produce items that are no bigger than one-sixth of a 640×480 display.

- *Don't open pop-up windows.* You can use a variety of methods to pop open a window within your Web page: Java windows, alerts, and so on. Don't do so because this confuses the reader; he won't know from where the message comes.

- *Assume a 256 color palette.* Build your images so they use a 256 color palette because most users still use this setting in Windows 95. If you do otherwise, images in your desktop items won't look right on some computers.

- *Rate your Active Desktop content.* Include rating tags in your content that gives parents and managers control over the content displayed on a computer's desktop.

- *Use Dynamic HTML.* Dynamic HTML, used with good taste, gives your Active Desktop item a more professional appearance. You're integrating content with the user's operating environment.

N O T E   By default, Internet Explorer 4.0 arranges the desktop into a 3×2 grid. When it adds an item to the desktop, it finds an empty cell in which to add it. Thus, make sure you keep your items below 214×220. Doing so ensures that your desktop item won't overlap with any other item when Internet Explorer 4.0 adds it to the desktop.

Examining How the Active Desktop Works

The Active Desktop is a container that can host any HTML object, such as HTML files, ActiveX controls, images, and so on. With Internet Explorer 4.0, the desktop is actually two different layers:

- *Icon layer.* This layer contains all the user's desktop shortcuts, wallpaper, and so on. This layer is the traditional Windows desktop.

- *HTML layer.* This layer contains all the user's Active Desktop content. The user's wallpaper, which is stored in C:\Windows\Web\Wallpaper\wallpapr.htm by default, describes the general look of the desktop. Information about the desktop components, such as each component's URL and position, is stored in the Windows Registry.

Building an Active Desktop Item

Building an item for the Active Desktop is little different from building a channel (see Chapter 30, "Building Channels with CDF"). You build a single HTML file as shown in Listing 31.1. Note that the content is lean, providing links to the primary Web site in a compact space. It uses Dynamic HTML to highlight links as the user rolls the mouse pointer over them.

Listing 31.1 HTML for Sample Active Desktop Item

```
<html>
<head>
<title>Sample Desktop Content</title>
<style type="text/css">
  <H1>    {font-family: sans-serif; font-size: 14}
  .normal { color: blue; font-family: sans-serif; font-size: 12;
          font-weight: bold}
  .hilite { color: red; font-family: sans-serif; font-size: 12;
          font-weight: bold}
</style>
</head>

<script language="VBSCRIPT">
  Sub MouseOver()
    If window.event.srcElement.tagName = "A" Then
      window.event.srcElement.className = "hilite"
    End If
  End Sub

  Sub MouseOut()
    If window.event.srcElement.tagName = "A" Then
      window.event.srcElement.className = "normal"
    End If
  End Sub
</script>

<body>

<H1 align=right>Links to Jerry's Home Page:</H1>
<div style="border: 1px solid black" align=right
    onmouseover="call MouseOver()" onmouseout="call MouseOut()">
<p><A href="http://rampages.onramp.net\~jerry" class="normal">
      Home Page
    </A>
  <p><A http://rampages.onramp.net\~jerry\books.htm" class="normal">
      List of Books
    </A>
  <p><A http://rampages.onramp.net\~jerry\bio.htm" class="normal">
      Biographyand Resume
    </A>
  <p><A http://rampages.onramp.net\~jerry\essays.htm" class="normal">
      Index of Essays
    </A>
</div>
</body>
</html>
```

The next step is to build a CDF file for the Active Desktop item. Your CDF file should be very simple, as shown in Listing 31.2. Note that the HREF attribute in the <CHANNEL> tag points to the same Web page as the HREF attribute in the <ITEM> tag. The schedule I've set for this desktop item is every seven days because that's approximately how often I want to update my Web site and tell the user about recent changes.

The most important thing to note about the CDF file in Listing 31.2 is the <USAGE> tag under the <ITEM>. You see VALUE set to DesktopComponent, which tells the browser to install HTML file as an item on the user's desktop. You can also assign ScreenSaver to this attribute and Internet Explorer will install your content as a screen saver on the user's computer. The <WIDTH> and <HEIGHT> child tags give the browser a suggestion for the size of the item.

Listing 31.2   Sample CDF File for an Active Desktop Item

```
<?XML version="1.0"?>
 <!DOCTYPE Channel SYSTEM "http://www.w3c.org/Channel.dtd">

 <Channel HREF="http://rampages.onramp.net/~jerry/desktop.htm">
   <Schedule>
     <IntervalTime DAY="7" />
   </Schedule>

   <Item HREF=" http://rampages.onramp.net/~jerry/desktop.htm ">
     <Title>Jerry Honeycutt's Home Page</Title>
     <Usage VALUE="DesktopComponent">
       <Width VALUE="120" />
       <Height VALUE="80" />
     </Usage>
   </Item>
 </Channel>
```

T I P   You must upload both files to a Web server in order to experiment with them. Internet Explorer 4.0 does not correctly parse CDF files that are on your local disk.

Figure 31.2 shows you the result. In this case, the user subscribed to the CDF file contained in Listing 31.2, and Internet Explorer 4.0 put the content contained in Listing 31.1 on the desktop.

FIG. 31.2
This Active Desktop item uses little of the user's desktop real estate and makes it possible to announce new features on the Web site as they become available.

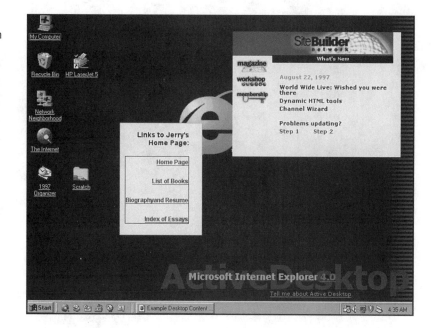

## CHAPTER 32

Building Netscape Netcaster Channels

by Jerry Honeycutt

Designing Your Channel

Most users have grown to expect a certain amount of fluctuation in the quality of the Web sites they visit. The push audience is a bit more sophisticated, however, and its expectations are much higher. They expect better information and more of an eye-popping experience. The content is totally up to you, but HTML 4.0 provides many features you can use to provide the experience:

- *Multimedia*. Use rich multimedia, particularly in your opening page, to draw the user into the site. See Part IV, "Serving Multimedia Content."
- *Dynamic HTML*. Use Dynamic HTML to give the user a lively, interactive experience. See Part III, "Creating Advanced Web Pages with Dynamic HTML."
- *CSS1 positioning*. Create multi-layered Web pages that have a magazine-type quality to them. See Chapter 17, "Applying Cascading Style Sheets."
- *Web fonts*. Use the best fonts for the job because you can download the fonts to the user. See Chapter 21, "Embedding Web Fonts into a Web Page."

 TIP Netcaster downloads fresh content in the background. You're freer to use images and other objects because the user won't perceive them as a performance problem.

Users Are Browsing Offline

As you're building your site, keep in mind that the user will not be connected to the Internet in most cases. The Netcaster crawler, which is responsible for following and downloading the links on your site, does not parse JavaScript code. If you use a script to load an image in your Web page, the crawler won't download it. To solve this problem, hide an element in your HTML document that references the image, as shown in Listing 32.1. Likewise, the crawler won't download any class files that a Java applet references. The only solution to this problem is to package all your class files in a single JAR file.

Listing 32.1 Forcing Netcaster to Load Images

```
<DIV STYLE="position: relative; visibility: hidden;">
  <IMG SRC="theimage.gif">
<DIV>
```

Special Considerations

Developing a channel is different from developing an ordinary Web site. Because your pages are viewed in Netcaster and might even be displayed for long periods of time on the user's desktop, take these considerations into mind:

- *Download your depth to a minimum*. Design your site so that it has a flatter organization. In fact, don't require the user to download any more than two levels of it in order to enjoy it.

- *Use size hints for images.* Include height and width hints for all your image tags. Doing so allows Netcaster to optimize the page layout, especially when viewing offline.

- *Don't use redirection.* Redirection causes Netcaster to open a URL other than the specified link. This can cause unpredictable behavior in Netcaster.

- *Don't depend on screen size.* Keep your site independent of the user's screen size. Take advantage of the features in JavaScript 1.2 that allow you to build resolution-independent sites, and test your site on 640×480, 800×600, and 1024×768 screens. See **http://developer.netscape.com/library/documentation/index.html** to learn more about JavaScript 1.2.

- *Avoid using scrollbars in your channel.* You want the user to be able to look at your channel's content by interacting with it. Don't splash a huge page on the screen and expect the user to scroll through it to find content.

- *Use hidden anchors.* Hidden anchors allow the Netcaster crawler to download needed files that are not within the first two levels of your site. When inserted in the channel's home page, the following anchor causes the crawler to download the given HTML file, even though it doesn't otherwise appear in the crawler's path:

```
<A HREF="myfile.htm"></A>
```

- *Maintain consistency.* Maintain the consistency of your channel's user interface. Remember that the user is going to think of your channel more as an application than a Web site.

Part
V

Ch
32

Putting the Add Channel Button on Your Site

To get people to subscribe to your channel, you need to provide an easy mechanism for them to do so. Netscape recommends you put a button on your site labeled Add Channel as shown in Figure 32.1.

You can download the graphic for this button from Netscape's Web site at **http://developer.netscape.com/one/dynhtml/images/ncnow.gif**. Then, embed it using the HTML in Listing 32.2.

Listing 32.2   The Add Channel Button

```
<A HREF="#" onClick="subscribe(); return( false );">
  <IMG NAME="ncnowimage" SRC="ncnow.gif"
    WIDTH=117 HEIGHT=55 BORDER=0 ALT="Add Channel">
</A>
```

Adding Your Channel to Netcaster with a Script

The button you added in the preceding section launches a script that adds your channel to Netcaster. You write the script using a new JavaScript 1.2 object called Channel. The function shown in Listing 32.3 is an example of the typical subscription function.

FIG. 32.1
Clicking the Add Channel button launches the script that you write in the next section.

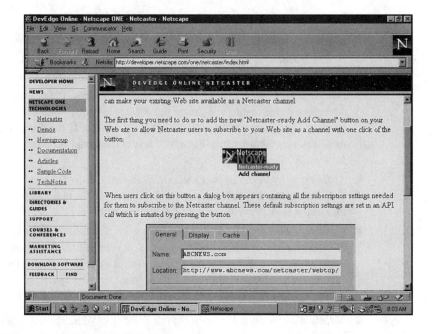

Listing 32.3   Subscription Function

```
Function subscribe()
{
  var Netcaster = components['netcaster'];
  var Channel = Netcaster.getChannelObject();

  Channel.url = "http://www.server.com/channel/home.html";
  Channel.name = "XYZ Channel";
  Channel.desc = "This channel is for people who use XYZ."

  Channel.intervalTime = 60;

  Channel.macCacheSize = 1024000;
  Channel.depth = 3;

  Channel.topHint = 0;
  Channel.leftHint = 0;
  Channel.widthHint = 400;
  Channel.heightHint = 600;
  Channel.mode = "window";

  Netcaster.addChannel( Channel );
}
```

Examine Listing 32.3 line-by-line:

■ The first two lines of the script create a new channel object in which you define your channel.

- Lines three to five set a few basic properties for your channel such as its URL, name, and description. The description that you set in line five appears to the user as tool-tip style help when the user moves the mouse over your site's button in the Channel Finder.

- The sixth line controls how often Netcaster updates the user's computer with fresh content. This value is the number of minutes between scheduled updates. If your channel changes frequently, set a shorter interval. If it changes infrequently, set a longer interval.

- Lines seven and eight let you suggest to the user how much of your site Netcaster should download. Set `maxCacheSize` to the maximum amount of cache space your site needs on the user's computer. This value is in bytes. Set `depth` to the number of levels of links that Netscape crawler will traverse.

- The next four lines suggest a size and type of window. `topHint`, `leftHint`, `widthHint`, and `heightHint` are suggestions for the shape of the window in which the user views the channel. `mode` is the type of window in which your channel appears and can be any of the values from Table 32.1.

Table 32.1   Channel Modes

Mode	Description
full	Displays in a full-screen Navigator window.
webtop	Displays in a Webtop, which has no title bar or window borders and occupies the entire desktop.
window	Displays in a normal Navigator window; you suggest a window shape using the hints.

Part
V

Ch
32

- The last line in Listing 32.3 establishes your channel in Netcaster.

Generating the Code with the Add Channel Wizard

No need to write the subscription script yourself; you can use Netscape's Netcaster Add Channel Wizard to generate all the HTML and scripts for you. Then, you copy the code into your HTML. Here's how:

1. Go to **http://developer.netscape.com/one/netcaster/index.html** and click Netcaster Add Channel Wizard.

2. Read the overview, and click Start the Add Channel Wizard. You see the first page of the Add Channel Wizard. Click Next, and you see the page shown in Figure 32.2.

3. Fill in the name of your channel and the URL. Click Next to continue, and you see the next page, which allows you to choose an update interval.

4. Select how often you want to update your channel on the user's computer: 30 minutes, 1 hour, 2 hours, 3 hours, 12 hours, day, or week. Click Next, and you see page shown in Figure 32.3.

FIG. 32.2

Don't worry too much about creating a fancy URL because the user will never see it.

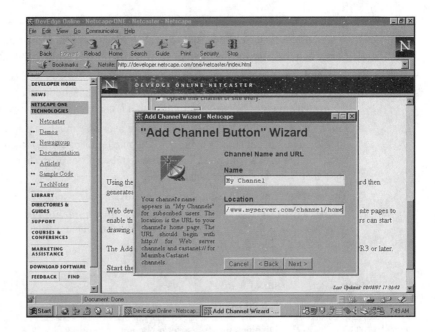

FIG. 32.3

The user is able to customize these settings.

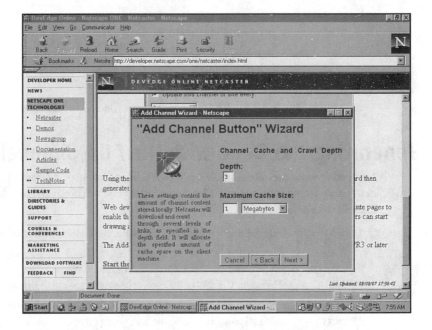

5. Type the depth to which you want Netcaster crawler to scan your site, and type the maximum cache size you recommend for it. Don't forget to specify whether the size you typed is in kilobytes or megabytes. Click Next.

6. Select a display mode: Webtop or Default Window. The Add Channel Wizard shows you an example of your selection on the left-hand side. Click Next.

7. Type the width, height, left-hand coordinate, and top coordinate in the spaces provided. You can provide any combination of these values because they are all optional. Click Next to continue.

8. In the space provided, type the text that you want to display on your Add Channel button. Click Next.

9. Click Finish, and the Add Channel Wizard opens the source for your subscription script and Add Channel button in a canvas window. It also asks you if you want to notify Netscape about your Channel; click OK if you do or Cancel if you don't.

10. Copy and paste the source from the canvas window into your HTML file. You'll find all the scripts required for your channel at the top of the file and the Add Channel button at the bottom.

CAUTION

The code shown in Listing 32.4 is an example only; don't use it for your channel. Netscape updates the Add Channel Wizard frequently, and thus the code it produces will probably vary from that shown in the listing.

The scripts that the Add Channel Wizard creates are much more complicated and thorough than what you created in the previous section. Listing 32.4 shows you the results. Here's a brief description of each function you find in the code that the Add Channel Wizard creates:

`needNetcaster`	Opens a new browser window that tells the user how to install Netcaster if he doesn't already have it.
`addChannelAPI`	Adds your channel to Netcaster. This function is very similar to the one you created in Listing 32.3.
`activateNetcaster`	Opens Netcaster.
`pollActive`	Continuously checks to see if Netcaster is currently active on the user's desktop.
`netcasterSniffer`	Checks to see if the user has installed Netcaster and, if not, calls `needNetcaster` to help him get it.

Part

V

Ch

32

Listing 32.4   Add Channel Wizard Results

```
<SCRIPT LANGUAGE="JavaScript">

function needNetcaster() {
   window.open("http://netcaster.netscape.com/finder/need_netcaster.html",
   "need_netcaster","width=500,height=400,titlebar=yes,toolbar=no,
   location=no,directories=no,status=yes,menubar=no,scrollbars=yes");
   }
```

continues

Listing 32.4   Continued

```
  function addChannelAPI() {
    needNetcaster(); }
</SCRIPT>

<SCRIPT LANGUAGE="JavaScript1.2">
    var chanURL = "http://www.myserver.com/channel/home";
    var chanName = "My Channel";
    var chanIntervalTime = 720;
    var chanMaxCacheSize = 1048576;
    var chanDepth = 3;
    var chanActive = 1;
    var chanMode = "window";
    var chanType=1;

    var getChannelObject = null;
    var addChannel = null;
    var nc = null;
    var ncActive = 0;
    var poller = null;


  function activateNetcaster() {
     nc.activate();
     }
  function pollActive() {
     if (nc.active) {
         ncActive=1;
         setTimeout(addChannelAPI,10000);
         clearInterval(poller);
         }
  }

  function netcasterSniffer() {
     if (!components["netcaster"]) {
     alert("This page requires the Netcaster component.");
     needNetcaster();
      }
      else {
         nc = components["netcaster"];
         if (nc.active == false) {
             activateNetcaster();
         poller=setInterval(pollActive,500);
         }
         else {
             ncActive = 1;
             addChannelAPI();
         }
     }
  }

  function addChannelAPI() {
      if (ncActive == 0) netcasterSniffer();
      else {
          nc = components["netcaster"];
          import nc.getChannelObject;
```

```
        import nc.addChannel;
        var chan = getChannelObject();
        chan.url = chanURL;
        chan.name = chanName;
        chan.intervalTime = chanIntervalTime;
        chan.maxCacheSize = chanMaxCacheSize;
        chan.depth = chanDepth;
        chan. active = chanActive;
        chan.mode=chanMode;
        chan.type=chanType;
        addChannel(chan);
    }
    ncActive = 0;
}

function clikImg() {}
</SCRIPT>
<TABLE><TR><TD ALIGN="CENTER">
<A HREF="#" onClick="addChannelAPI(); clikImg(); return(false);">
<IMG NAME="ncnowimage" SRC="http://home.netscape.com/inserts/images/ncnow.gif"
 WIDTH=117 HEIGHT=55 BORDER=0 ALT="Add My Channel Now!"><br>
Add My Channel Now!
</a></td></tr></table>

<SCRIPT LANGUAGE="JavaScript1.1">
// This code helps Netscape track use of button
document.ncnowimage.src=
  "http://home.netscape.com/inserts/images/ncnow.gif?"+document.location;
function clikImg() {
document.ncnowimage.src="http://home.netscape.com/inserts/
images/ncnow.gif?AddedChannelName=My%20Channel&AddedChannelURL=
http://www.myserver.com/channel/home";
}

</script>
```

N O T E Netcaster also supports Castanet channels. Developing Castanet channels is much more complex than building Netcaster channels because you have to learn a bunch of new technologies and purchase a Castanet server. You can get more information about creating Castanet channels at **http://www.marimba.com**. ■

Interacting with Netcaster via JavaScript

You can interact with Netcaster from your channel by using the JavaScript extensions Netscape introduces into JavaScript 1.2 as well as the new Channel object.

Before using Netcaster's methods, you have to import them into your document. In your script, make sure Netcaster is active, see the functions pollActive and activateNetcaster in the previous section, and then execute the following two lines:

```
import components["netcaster"].getChannelObject;
import components["netcaster"].addChannel;
```

N O T E This chapter gives you an overview of Netscape's extensions. For a complete reference on Netcaster extensions, open **http://developer.netscape.com/library/documentation/ netcast/devguide/contents.htm** in your Web browser. ■

Netcaster Component

The Netcaster component provides information about and access to Netcaster. Table 32.2 describes its properties and methods. Note that you can make your code easier to read by getting the Netcaster component first and then using that to access its properties:

```
nc = components["Netcaster"]
```

Table 32.2 *Netcaster* Properties and Methods

Name	Example	Description
Properties		
active	nc.active	Returns True if Netcaster is installed and running; otherwise, returns False.
componentVersion	nc.componentVersion	Returns the version number of Netcaster as a string: 1.0.
name	nc.name	Returns the string netcaster.
Methods		
activate();	nc.activate();	Activates Netcaster.
addChannel(*obj*)	nc.addChannel(channel);	Adds the channel represented by the channel object, *obj*, to Netcaster. Netcaster adds the channel to the My Channels container.
getChannelObject()	new = nc.getChannelObject();	Returns a new channel object that's initialized with the default values.

Channel Object

The Channel object provides access to all a channel's properties. As you saw in "Adding Your Channel to Netcaster with a Script," earlier in this chapter, you use the getChannelObject() method to create a new channel and the addChannel() method to add a channel to Netcaster. In Table 32.3, which describes the channel object's properties, assume that a new channel was created and assigned to the variable called ch.

Table 32.3 Channel Object Properties

Name	Example	Description
absoluteTime	ch.absoluteTime = 720;	Specifies the time for daily or weekly updates. You must set this property if you set the update interval daily or weekly. You calculate this value by adding a value from each column in Table 32.4.
cardURL	ch.cardURL = icon.gif	Specifies a graphical icon for the channel that is displayed in the My Channels. You can set it to the URL of any image. This property is not implemented in Netcaster 1.0.
depth	ch.depth = 2	Specifies the number of levels that the Netcaster crawler will download from your channel.
desc	ch.desc = "A really great channel"	Provides a description for the channel that appears as tool-tip style help in the My Channels.
estCachSize	ch.estCacheSize = 1024000	Describes the estimated amount of disk space that your channel will occupy on the user's computer. This value is in kilobytes. Set it to -1 if you don't your know channel's estimated size.
heightHint	ch.heightHint = 200	Specifies the preferred height for your channel's window.
intervalTime	ch.intervalTime = 60	Specifies the number of minutes to wait between each update. You can use one of the special negative numbers to represent predefined times: -2 for every 15 minutes, -3 for every 30 minutes, -4 for every hour, -5 for daily, and -6 for weekly.
leftHint	ch.leftHint = 0	Specifies the preferred coordinate of the channel window's left edge.
maxCacheSize	ch.maxCacheSize = 1024000	Describes the maximum amount of disk space required by the channel. This value is in kilobytes.
mode	ch.mode = "webtop"	Specifies the type of window in which Netcaster displays your channel. Possible values include window, full, or webtop.
name	ch.name = "my channel"	Assigns a name to your channel.

Part

V

Ch

32

continues

Table 32.3   Continued

Name	Example	Description
topHint	ch.topHint = 120	Specifies the preferred coordinate of the channel window's top edge.
url	ch.url = "http://server/mychannel"	Points to the top-level page of your channel. It must be an absolute URL.
widthHint	ch.widthHint = 240	Specifies the preferred width of the channel's window.

Table 32.4   Values for Absolute Times

Day	Hour
0 (Sunday)	0 (Midnight)
1440 (Monday)	60 (1am)
2880 (Tuesday)	120 (2am)
4320 (Wednesday)	180 (3am)
5760 (Thursday)	240 (4am)
7200 (Friday)	300 (5am)
8640 (Saturday)	360 (6am)
	420 (7am)
	480 (8am)
	540 (9am)
	600 (10am)
	660 (11am)
	720 (12am)
	800 (1pm)
	860 (2pm)
	920 (3pm)
	980 (4pm)
	1020 (5pm)
	1080 (6pm)
	1120 (7pm)
	1200 (8pm)

Day	Hour
	1260 (9pm)
	1320 (10pm)
	1380 (11pm)

TIP The values in Table 32.4 are actually the number of minutes since 12:00AM Sunday that elapses up to any point during a week. Thus, you can specify a time such as 12:15am Sunday with a value of 15 or a time such as 11:45 Wednesday with a value of 4320 + 1380 + 45 = 5745.

Understanding How the Netcaster Crawler Works

The Netcaster Crawler downloads the home page of your site. Then, it follows the links it finds down to the level you specify in `depth`. Crawler downloads all the HTML files first, and then it downloads any images and objects to which those documents are linked. It takes this approach so that the user will at least have the text content of your channel if the download fails for any reason.

As indicated earlier in the chapter, server redirection causes problems for Netcaster Crawler. Netcaster caches your channel and indexes each page by URL returned from the server instead of the URL specified in a link. Thus, if you have a link to `http://netcasteriscool` that the server redirects to `http://netcasteriscool/stuff.html`, Netcaster won't find the page in the cache. Netcaster goes online and opens the URL again. If it can't go online, Netcaster notifies the user that it can't connect to the network, even though the page is actually cached on the user's disk.

Page aliases cause similar problems for Netcaster Crawler. If you write a URL that specifies a host such as `http://netcaster`, relying on the host to open `index.html`, Netcaster will store the page in the cache as `http://netcaster/index.html` but won't find it because it looks up the page as `http://netcaster`.

If while viewing a channel, the user causes Netcaster to follow a link or open a Java class that isn't cached, Netcaster tries to connect to the Internet to download it. If Netcaster can't download the item, it notifies the user and retrieves the item the next time it updates the channel.

TIP You can use `ROBOTS.TXT`, described in Chapter 40, "Listing Your Web Site in the Search Tools," to control what the Crawler downloads from your site.

Part
V

Ch
32

Scripting on the Web Server

## CHAPTER 33

Understanding XML

by Luke Andrew Cassady-Dorion

In this chapter

A New Language for the Web

Since HTML made its smashing debut a few years ago, it has seen numerous revisions. Each revision brought more features to the specification, which may, in turn, be implemented in a given browser. More often than not, a browser implements not only most of the features defined by the specification, but also a series of its own proprietary tags. The Netscape layer tag is an example.

In looking at the revision problem that plagued HTML, it became necessary to develop a new markup language that could be implemented once and never need revisions. Instead of looking to a new mark-up language, the engineers at the W3C decided to look back to the roots of HTML.

As most of you remember, HTML is a very slimmed-down version of SGML, which is a feature-rich language for marking up data. SGML as it currently exists is a rather good language for marking up data. Unfortunately, it is not geared for deployment in a network environment. Where SGML is a good extensible language, HTML is a simple non-extensible language. As a middle point with the network-centric non-extensible HTML on one end and the non-network-centric extensible SGML on the other, the engineers at the W3C developed eXtensible Markup Language (XML).

XML as envisioned by the W3C will exist in only one form for as long as the Web exists. It is designed to allow developers to dynamically describe the information stored in a Web page. By making Web pages self-describing, it will be possible to not only have Web browsers accessing the Web, but also for developers to write custom search tools which scour the Web for specific information.

In designing XML, the W3C has taken into account ten design goals. These goals define a plan for a markup language that is better than HTML in that it fixes the evolution and compatibility problems, and is better than SGML in that it's geared for Internet deployment and is easier to use.

The W3C defines the XML's goals as follows (taken from **http://www.w3.org/TR/WD-xml-lang**):

- XML shall be straightforwardly usable over the Internet.
- XML shall support a wide variety of applications.
- XML shall be compatible with SGML.
- It shall be easy to write programs that process XML documents.
- The number of optional features shall be kept to the absolute minimum, ideally zero.
- XML documents shall be human-legible and reasonably clear.
- The XML design should be prepared quickly.
- The design of XML shall be formal and concise.
- XML documents shall be easy to create.
- Terseness in XML markup is of minimal importance.

This chapter will examine where XML as a language is heading. The chapter will give an overview of the technology, discuss its uses, and also some areas where it is not of use.

XML as a Metalanguage

XML is what is referred to as a *metalanguage*, or a language for describing other languages. In your case, XML allows you to create documents that describe themselves to their reader. While some may attempt to say that the same is true for HTML, HTML lacks an easily expandable vocabulary. In order to expand on HTML, a proposal needs to be submitted to and approved by the W3C. However, to expand on XML, one simply has to use the new descriptors in an XML file. For example, take a look at the XML fragment in Listing 33.1:

Listing 33.1   Sample XML Describing a Listing of Books

```
<heading>Great San Francisco Books</heading>
<title>Tales of the City</title>
<author>Armistead Maupin</author>
<title>The Vampire Lestat</title>
<author>Anne Rice</author>
<title>Access San Francisco Restaurants</title>
<author>Graceann Walden</author>
```

The most obvious thing in Listing 33.1 is that these tags, while HTML-like, are not in any way approved by the W3C. This could obviously create problems to applications that you want to work with the data.

Though HTML does describe to a browser the manner in which the HTML page should be displayed on screen, that is not an XML document's purpose. An XML document simply serves to describe the data contained in the files. When an XML page is sent to a browser for on-screen display, it usually arrives with a style sheet or Document Type Definition (DTD), which tells the browser how to display the text. What's important is that XML does not simply make on-screen display easier, it also simplifies the job of applications, such as search engines. Because the XML in Listing 33.1 describes to the reader the location of all authors, search engine applications can now easily index the document by author.

Creating XML

An explanation of what XML is and what needs it provides for are covered in the previous sections. In this next section, you dive in and take a look at what is required of an XML document.

In its raw form, XML looks very similar to HTML, as you can see in Listing 33.1. The languages sport a similar look because of their common ancestor, SGML. XML and HTML have many functional differences.

Part
VI

Ch
33

The first, most obvious difference is that XML tag structure is very rigid. In HTML, there are tags that always have an opening and closing tag pair (`<CENTER></CENTER>`), tags that stand alone (`<BR>`), and tags that do either (`<P></P>`, or simply `<P>`). To further confuse the tag situation, most browsers will attempt to display even incorrect HTML. For example, if you are missing a `</TABLE>` tag Navigator will usually still display the table, while Internet Explorer will not. This browser work-around may make a lot of Web pages look better, but since incorrect HTML is still displayed, sloppy HTML coding is also encouraged.

In contrast, XML requires that all tags either exist in pairs, or announce to the reader that a closing tag is not present. For example, the `<BR>` tag rendered in XML appears either as `<BR></BR>` or `<BR/>`. Note that when the `<BR/>` tag stands alone, it ends with a trailing slash, indicating the lack of a closing tag.

In addition to those requirements, XML also requires that all attribute values occur in quotation marks. For example, the following tag pair is incorrect: `<COLOR value=red></COLOR>`. Instead, opt for the slightly different: `<COLOR value="red"></COLOR>`. HTML originally asked the same of authors. However, it seems that over time, authors stopped using quotation marks and browsers stopped requiring them.

Finally, XML allows no illegal nesting of tags. This means that for every open tag, its closing tag must appear at an unambiguous location. For example, in Listing 33.2, there may be some confusion regarding which question is being closed by the first and then the second `</question>` tags.

Listing 33.2   Invalid XML tag structure

```
<title>Coversation</title>
<question>What is the average flying speed of a swallow?
<question>What kind of swallow?</question></question>
```

Listing 33.3 contains a better option.

Listing 33.3   Valid XML tag structure

```
<title>Coversation</title>
<question>What is the average flying speed of a swallow? </question>
<question>What kind of swallow?</question>
```

Creating Valid/Well-Formed Pages

One of the keys to creating XML pages is knowing the rules the reader applications use when evaluating a given page. Because these rules are strictly defined (and hopefully enforced), it is actually rather easy to create documents that follow all the required rules. In fact, at the end of this chapter there are URLs to three publicly available parsers that you can use to test your currently developing XML.

When developing an XML file, that file can be defined as either valid, well-formed, or both. Valid XML files are those that have and follow a given Document Type Definition (DTD).

N O T E   A DTD is any number of files that contain a formal definition of a given type of document. Because they have origins in SGML, there are already thousands of DTDs. However, one can easily create a new DTD if the document requires it. For examples of existing DTDs, see "More Information," in this chapter. ▣

When distributed, an XML document will provide a link to a DTD in its header. An example header (with a dummy URL) is contained in Listing 33.4.

Listing 33.4   XMO document header

```
<?XML VERSION="1.0"?>
<!doctype silly system "http://www.dtdDomain.com/file.dtd">
```

In contrast to the valid XML file, you can also create a well-formed XML file. A well-formed XML file is one that can be used without a DTD. While a DTD is not required, a well-formed XML file must use the heading shown in Listing 33.5. A well-formed file must also follow the tag and attribute rules specified earlier in the chapter.

Listing 33.5   Header for a well-formed XML document

```
<?XML VERSION="1.0" RMD="NONE">.
```

Moving from HTML to XML

Most of you have spent significant time developing HTML files. You need to know how to convert those HTML files to XML files. Since a lot of the transfer (
 to <BR/> for example) can be automated, you most likely want to incorporate the changes into some sort of script (Applescript, Sed, and the like) and perform a batch transfer of all your HTML files.

You will have little trouble converting those files to XML if you have carefully developed HTML. However, sloppy HTML needs some fixing due to XML's strong typing. The first step in converting an HTML page to an XML page is making sure the page is well-formed (see this chapter's section titled "Creating Valid/Well-Formed Pages"). After this is done, you need to add a DTD to the XML document's header and ensure that it references one of the available HTML DTDs. The HTML DTD tells the reader application how to deal with each of the tags that are part of the HTML specification. An example DTD is <!DOCTYPE HTML SYSTEM "http://www.domain.com/dtds/html.dtd">.

Part
VI

Ch
33

More Information

XML is definitely something to get excited about. In the next year—assuming all goes well—we will begin to see Web pages which actually describe themselves to their readers. To keep track of new developments regarding XML, watch the following links and mailing lists.

Parsers (or reader applications):

- Norbert Mikula's NXP at **http://www.edu.uni-klu.ac.at/~nmikula/NXP/**.
- Tim Bray's Lark at **http://www.textuality.com/Lark/**.
- Sean Russell's kernel at **http://jersey.uoregon.edu/ser/software/XML.tar.gz**.
- The Microsoft XML parser **http://www.microsoft.com/standards/xml/xmldl.htm**.

Web sites/mailing lists:

- The XML FAQ at **http://www.ucc.ie/xml**.
- The XML specification at **http://www.w3.org/pub/WWW/TR/**.
- Available SGML DTDs at **http://www.ucc.ie/cgi-bin/PUBLIC/**.
- The XML mailing list archived at **http://www.lists.ic.ac.uk/hypermail/xml-dev/**.

## CHAPTER 34

CGI Scripting

by Mark R. Brown and Melissa Niles

In this chapter

What Is the CGI?

In previous chapters you learned how to mark up content for your Web site by using the HTML standard. Now, we will begin our exploration of the CGI (Common Gateway Interface), which will greatly enhance the level of interactivity on your site. With the use of CGI scripts, you can make your Web presentations more responsive to your users' needs by allowing them to have a more powerful means of interaction with your material.

Here is the answer to the $100 question. What is the CGI anyway? Well, in order to answer that, you are going to need a little background information first.

Each time you sit down in your favorite and start surfing the WWW, you are a client from the Internet's point of view. Each time you click a link to request a new Web document, you are sending a request to the document's server. The server receives the request, then gets the document and sends it back to your browser for you to view.

The client/server relationship that is set up between your browser and a Web server works very well for serving up HTML and image files from the server's Web directories. Unfortunately, there is a large flaw with this simple system. The Web server is still not equipped to handle information from your favorite database program or from other applications that require more work than simply transmitting a static document.

One option the designers of the first Web server could have chosen was to build in an interface for each external application from which a client may want to get information. It is hard to imagine trying to program a server to interact with every known application and then trying to keep the server current on each new application as it is developed. Needless to say, it would be impossible. So they developed a better way.

These wise developers anticipated this problem and solved it by designing the Common Gateway Interface, or CGI. This gateway provides a common environment and a set of protocols for external applications to use while interfacing with the Web server. Thus, any application engineer (including yourself) can use the CGI to allow an application to interface with the server. This extends the range of functions the Web server has—including features provided by a potentially limitless number of external applications.

How the CGI Works

Now that you have read a little background, you should have a basic idea of what the CGI is and why it is needed. The next step in furthering your understanding of the CGI is to learn the basics of how it works. To help you achieve this goal, this material is broken down into the following sections:

- The process
- Characteristics
- The output Header and MIME types
- Environment variables

The Process

The CGI is the common gateway or door that is used by the server to interface—or communicate—with applications other than the browser. Thus, CGI scripts act as a link between whatever application is needed and the server, while the server is responsible for receiving information from, and sending data back to, the browser.

> **N O T E** As a technical note, you should be aware that some people like to use the term *program* to refer to longer, usually compiled, code and applications written in languages like C and C++. When this is the case, the term *script* is then used to indicate shorter, noncompiled code written with languages like SH and PERL. However, for the purpose of this and the following chapter, the terms *program* and *script* will be used interchangeably as the divisions between them are being rapidly broken down. ▨

For example, when you enter a search request at your favorite search engine, a request is made by the browser to the server to execute a CGI script. At this time, the browser passes the information that was contained in the online form, plus the current environment, to the server. From here, the server passes the information to the script. This script provides an interface with the database archive and finds the information that you have requested. Once this information is retrieved, the script processes the information entered by the visitor and sends the result to the server, which feeds it back to the visitor's browser as a list of matches to your query.

GET and POST

There are two popular methods of sending information to your scripts. The first is with the GET method. The GET method is the default method used. If no method is specified, then the default METHOD="GET" is assumed by the browser. If you are creating a form, then you can use this method by specifying this method when you insert the <FORM> tag within your document. An example would be

```
<FORM ACTION="mail.pl" METHOD="GET">
```

When using the GET method, the information entered by the visitor is sent to the server within the environment variable, QUERY_STRING. And as in the case of any environment variable, you are limited to 255 characters. This includes any space characters.

The other method commonly used is the method, POST. Using the method POST, information entered by the visitor is sent directly to your script through the server's STDOUT and your script's STDIN. The advantage of using the method POST, is that you aren't limited to 255 characters as you are when using the GET method. Here's an example of a form that uses the method POST:

```
<FORM ACTION="mail.pl" METHOD="POST">
```

ON THE WEB

There is a very nice online description of the CGI at The Common Gateway Interface, found at **http://hoohoo.ncsa.uiuc.edu/cgi/**.

Characteristics of the CGI

Another way of looking at the CGI is to see it as a socket that attaches an extra arm on your server. This new arm, the CGI script, adds new features and abilities to the server that it previously lacked.

The most common use for these new features is to give the server the ability to dynamically respond to the client. One of the most often seen examples of this is allowing the client to send a search query to a CGI script that then queries a database and returns a list of matching topics from the database. Besides information retrieval, another common reason for using CGI scripts is to customize the user interface on the Web site. This commonly takes the form of counters and animations.

 TIP If you see bin or cgi-bin in the path names of images or links, it is a good indication that the given effect was produced by a CGI script.

As you read earlier, there are two basic methods of sending information to your script. Those methods mentioned were the GET and the POST methods. Depending on which method is used, your script will parse the information differently. While this difference is small, it can create havoc if your script doesn't parse the information coming from the visitor correctly. Listing 34.1 checks which method is being used and parses the information coming from the visitor based on the method used.

Listing 34.1   PERL Script that Parses Information Depending on Method

```perl
#! /usr/bin/perl

if ($ENV{'REQUEST_METHOD'} eq 'POST')
{
read(STDIN, $buffer, $ENV{'CONTENT_LENGTH'});
@pairs = split(/&/, $buffer);
foreach $pair (@pairs)
{
($name, $value) = split(/=/, $pair);
$value =~ tr/+/ /;
$value =~ s/%([a-fA-F0-9][a-fA-F0-9])/pack("C", hex($1))/eg;
$contents{$name} = $value;

}
}

if ($ENV{'REQUEST_METHOD'} eq 'GET')
{
@pairs = split(/&/, $ENV{'QUERY_STRING'});
foreach $pair (@pairs)
{
($name, $value) = split(/=/, $pair);
$value =~ tr/+/ /;
```

```
$value =~ s/%([a-fA-F0-9][a-fA-F0-9])/pack("C", hex($1))/eg;
$contents{$name} = $value;


}
}
```

Using this basic header to all your CGI scripts written in PERL will save you a lot of headaches. The information is parsed and split automatically, with each item sent by the visitor placed into an array called @contents. Each individual item in the array can be called by using $contents{'name'}, where the name is the name assigned to the variable when you created your form.

The MIME Content-Type Output Header

It won't be long into your CGI programming career when you will want to write a script that sends information to the server for it to process. Each file that is sent to the server must contain an output header. This header contains the information the server and other applications need to transmit and handle the file properly.

The use of output headers in CGI scripts is an expansion of a system of protocols called MIME (Multipurpose Internet Mail Extensions). Its use for e-mail began in 1992 when the Network Working Group published RFC (Request For Comments) 1341, which defined this new type of e-mail system. This system greatly expanded the ability of Internet e-mail to send and receive various nontext file formats.

 N O T E Since the release of RFC 1341, a series of improvements has been made to the MIME conventions. You can find some additional information about this by looking at RFC 1521 and RFC 1522. A list of all the RFC documents can be found online at **http://ds0.internic.net/rfc/**. These documents contain a lot of useful information published by the Network Working Group relating to the function and structure of the Internet backbone. ▪

Each time you, as a client, send a request to the server, it is sent in the form of a MIME message with a specially formatted header. Most of the information in the header is part of the client's protocol for interfacing with the browser. This includes the request method, a URI (Universal Resource Identifier), the protocol version, and then a MIME message. The server then responds to this request with its own message, which usually includes the server's protocol version, a status code, and a different MIME message.

The bulk of this client/server communication process is handled automatically by the WWW client application—usually your Web browser—and the server. This makes it easier for everyone, since you don't have to know how to format each message in order to access the server and get information. You just need a WWW client. However, to write your own CGI scripts, you will need to know how to format the content-type line of the MIME header in order for the server to know what type of document your script is sending. Also, you will need to know how to access the server's environment variables so you can use that information in your CGI scripts. In the following sections, you will learn everything necessary to accomplish both of these tasks.

N O T E   If it won't be long into your CGI programming career when you decide to write your own WWW client, then you need to understand the client/server communication process before you can begin. A good place to start your search for more information about this is the World Wide Web Consortium (W3C) Reference Library at **http://www.w3.org/pub/WWW/Library/**. ▓

Using a Content-Type Output Header

Each document that is sent via a CGI script to the server, whether it was created on the fly or is simply being opened by the script, must contain a content-type output header as the first part of the document so the server can process it accordingly. In Table 34.1 you see examples of a few of the more commonly used MIME content-types and their associated extensions.

Table 34.1   Examples of MIME Types and Extensions

Content-Type	Extensions
application/octet-stream	bin exe
text/html	html htm
text/plain	txt
text/richtext	rtx
video/mpeg	mpeg mpg mpe
video/quicktime	qt mov
video/x-msvideo	avi

To help you better understand how to properly use content-types within a CGI script, let's work through an example. Suppose you have decided to write a CGI script that will display a GIF image each time it is executed by a browser.

The first line of code you need is a special comment that contains the path to the scripting language that you are using to write the program. In this case it is PERL. The comment symbol (#) must be followed by an exclamation point (!) then the path. This special combination of (#!) on the first line of the file is the standard format for letting the server know which interpreter to use to execute the script. The reason this special comment is used is that while UNIX servers use this line of code to locate the script's interpreter, other types of server systems have alternate methods of specifying the interpreter's location. However, since this line of code starts with a (#) symbol, it is still a valid PERL comment and does not cause problems on nonUNIX servers.

```
#!/usr/local/bin/perl
```

The next line you will need simply sets the variable $gif to the full path name of the image you want to display.

```
$gif = "/file/path/your.gif";
```

 TIP You should double check to make sure you include the correct path name to your language's interpreter.

Now, it is time to let the server know that it will be receiving an image file from this script to display on the client's browser. This is done by using the MIME content-type line. The print statement prints the information between the quotation marks to the server. Each set of \n characters that you see on this line adds a carriage return with a line feed. This gives you the required blank line that must occur after the content-type information. A blank line lets the server know where the MIME header stops and where the body of information, in this case the GIF, starts.

```
print "Content-type: image/gif\n\n";
```

The next line creates a file handle named IMAGE that forms a link from this script to the file contained in the variable $gif, which you set earlier.

```
open(IMAGE,$gif);
```

Now, you create a loop that sends the entire contents of the gif to the server as the body of the MIME message you began with the content-type line.

```
while(<IMAGE>) { print $_; }
```

To avoid being sloppy, close the file handle to the gif now that you are done sending the image.

```
close(IMAGE);
```

Finally, let the PERL interpreter know that the CGI script is finished running and can be stopped.

```
exit;
```

This type of script can be modified into something a little more useful. For example, you could turn it into a random image viewer. Each time someone clicks the link to the script, it executes and feeds a random GIF image to the client's browser.

Environment Variables

Hopefully, you now have a little better understanding of what is involved as the client and server communicate with each other. Along with the information discussed earlier, a host of environment variables are sent during the client/server communications. Although each server can have its own set of environment variables, for the most part, they are all subsets of a large set of standard variables described by the Internet community to help promote uniform standards (see Figure 34.1).

If you have bin access on a UNIX server, then you can use the following script to easily determine which environment variables your server supports. In addition, this script should also work on other server types such as Microsoft Windows NT server if you properly configure the server to recognize and execute PERL scripts.

Once again, this is the magic line that lets the server know which type of CGI script this is so it can launch the appropriate interpreter.

```
#!/usr/local/bin/perl
```

This next line, as was described, is the MIME output header that lets the server know to expect an HTML document to follow.

```
print "Content-type: text/html\n\n";
```

Now that the server is expecting to receive an HTML document, send it a list of each environment variable's name and current value by using a `foreach` loop.

```
foreach $key (keys(%ENV)){
print "\$ENV{$key} = \"$ENV{$key}\"<br>\n";
}
```

Finally, you need to tell the interpreter that the script is finished.

```
exit;
```

FIG. 34.1
Using the CGI script environment.pl from a browser generates a screen similar to this one.

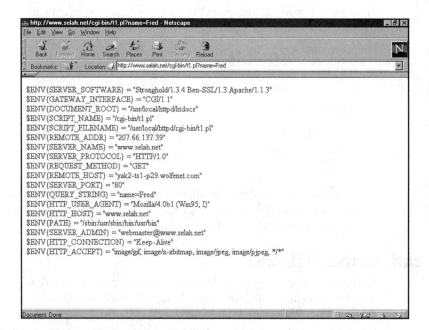

```
$ENV{SERVER_SOFTWARE} = "Stronghold/1.3.4 Ben-SSL/1.3 Apache/1.1.3"
$ENV{GATEWAY_INTERFACE} = "CGI/1.1"
$ENV{DOCUMENT_ROOT} = "/usr/local/httpd/htdocs"
$ENV{SCRIPT_NAME} = "/cgi-bin/t1.pl"
$ENV{SCRIPT_FILENAME} = "/usr/local/httpd/cgi-bin/t1.pl"
$ENV{REMOTE_ADDR} = "207.66.137.39"
$ENV{SERVER_NAME} = "www.selah.net"
$ENV{SERVER_PROTOCOL} = "HTTP/1.0"
$ENV{REQUEST_METHOD} = "GET"
$ENV{REMOTE_HOST} = "yak2-ts1-p29.wolfenet.com"
$ENV{SERVER_PORT} = "80"
$ENV{QUERY_STRING} = "name=Fred"
$ENV{HTTP_USER_AGENT} = "Mozilla/4.0b1 (Win95; I)"
$ENV{HTTP_HOST} = "www.selah.net"
$ENV{PATH} = "/sbin:/usr/sbin:/bin:/usr/bin"
$ENV{SERVER_ADMIN} = "webmaster@www.selah.net"
$ENV{HTTP_CONNECTION} = "Keep-Alive"
$ENV{HTTP_ACCEPT} = "image/gif, image/x-xbitmap, image/jpeg, image/pjpeg, */*"
```

TIP If the browser you use doesn't support an environment variable, the value of the variable is set to `null` and is left empty.

As you can see from the example, most of the variables contain protocol version information and location information such as the client's IP address and the server's domain. However, if you are creative, you can put some of these variables to good use in your CGI scripts.

One good example is the use of the environment variable HTTP_USER_AGENT. This contains the name and version number of the client application, which is usually a Web browser. As you can see from Figure 34.1, the Netscape 4.0 browser used when running this script has a HTTP_USER_AGENT value of Mozilla/4.0b1 (Win95; I).

Once you know what the values are for various browsers, it is possible to write a CGI script to serve different Web documents based on browser type. Thus, a text-only browser might receive a text version of your Web page, while image-capable browsers will receive the full version.

Can You Write CGI Scripts?

Before you can get started writing your own CGI scripts, you need to find out if your server is specially configured to allow you to use them. The best thing to do is contact your system administrator and find out if you are allowed to run CGI scripts on the server. If you can, you also need to ask what you need to do to use them and where you should put the scripts once they are written.

In some cases, system administrators do not allow clients to use CGI scripts because they feel they cannot afford the added security risks. In that case, you will have to find another means of making your site more interactive.

If you find that you can use CGI scripts and are using a UNIX server, then you will probably have to put your scripts into a specially configured directory, which is usually called cgibin or cgi-bin. If you are using Microsoft's Internet Server, then you will probably put your CGI programs in a directory called Scripts. This allows the system administrator to configure the server to recognize that the files placed in that directory are executable. If you are using a NCSA version of HTTPD on a UNIX system, then this is done by adding a ScriptAlias line to the conf/srm.conf file on the server.

NOTE It is important to remember that although CGI scripts are not necessarily complex, you need to have some basic understanding of the programming language you wish to use and the server you plan to run the scripts on. Poorly written scripts can easily become more trouble than they are worth. For example, you could delete entire directories of information or shut down your server if your script were to start launching new processes in a geometric fashion.

Before starting down the road to becoming a CGI scripter, you should do the following:

- Get a programming book on the scripting language you plan to learn.

- Ask the network administrator of your local server how to run scripts on your system and what security features she wants you to implement in them.

- Subscribe to a listserv and read the appropriate news groups on the language you plan to use. These are wonderful resources for programming information and good places to ask for help if you are stuck. You might start with the generic UseNet GCI programming newsgroup comp.infosystems.www.authoring.cgi and grow from there. ■

Part

VI

Ch

34

Which Language Should You Use?

Now that you know what a CGI script is, how it works, and what it can do, the next thing you need to consider is which language you should use. You can write a CGI script in almost any language. So, if you can program in a language already, there is a good chance you can use it to write your scripts. This is usually the best way to start learning how to write CGI scripts, since you are already familiar with the basic syntax of the language. However, you still need to know which languages your Web server is configured to support.

UNIX-based Apache and CERN Web servers are the most common. These platforms are easily configured to support most of the major scripting languages, including C, C++, PERL, and the basic shell scripting languages like SH. On the other hand, if your Web server is using the Mac server, then you might be limited to using AppleScript as your scripting language. Likewise, if you are using a Windows NT server, you might need to use Visual Basic as your scripting language. However, it is possible to configure both these systems to support other scripting languages like C and PERL, or even Pascal.

N O T E If you are interested in finding out which scripting languages your server is configured to support, you should ask your system administrator to give you a listing of what is available on your server.

Also, if you have access to a UNIX-based server and can log into a shell account, then you can find out which languages your system supports by using the UNIX command "which."

If you are using the SH shell, you should see the following:

```
$ which sh
/usr/bin/sh
$ which perl5
/usr/local/bin/perl5
```

Many scripting languages are freely distributed and fairly easy for an experienced administrator to install. As a last resort, you can always request that a new language be considered for addition to your local system. ◼

If you are lucky, you may find that your server is already configured to support several CGI scripting languages. In this case, you just need to compare the strengths and weaknesses of each language you have available with the programming tasks you anticipate writing. Once you do this, you should have a good idea of which programming language is best suited to your needs.

Common CGI Scripting Languages

When it comes to the CGI, anything goes. Of the vast numbers of programming languages out there, many more than you could possibly learn in a lifetime, most can work with the CGI. So, you will have to spend a little time sifting through the long list to find the one that will work best for you. For some, which language used will completely depend on what you are most familiar with, or what languages are available for use.

Even though there are a lot of different languages available, they tend to fall into several categories based on the way they are processed—compiled, interpreted, and compiled/interpreted—and on the logic behind how the source is written—procedural and object-oriented. A listing of the more prevalent languages is found in Table 34.2.

Table 34.2   Various Languages Used to Create CGI Applications

Language	System	Type
Shell	UNIX	Interpreted (Command Line Interface)
PERL	UNIX, Windows, Macintosh, Amiga	Interpreted
C	UNIX, Windows	Compiled
C++	UNIX, Windows	Compiled
Visual Basic	Windows	Compiled
AppleScript	Macintosh	Interpreted
TCL	UNIX	Interpreted
REXX (AREXX)	OS2, Amiga	Interpreted (some versions can be compiled)

Creating CGI Scripts

Once you have decided on a language to use, you find that various applications can be developed using the CGI. By far, e-mail, guestbook, redirection, counters, and advertisement banners are the most widely used scripts found to add interactivity to your Web pages, or to simply spice up a Web page. These scripts are covered in this section in more detail.

An E-Mail Script

E-mail scripts are just about the oldest and most used scripts in use on the World Wide Web. Interfacing the Web with e-mail just seems like a good idea. By doing so, you can give someone visiting your site the ability to communicate with you whether or not she has an e-mail account herself. All their browser needs to be able to do is allow the visitor to use forms.

Another benefit of an e-mail script is that you can create scripts that notify you if, let's say, a visitor enters information into a guestbook. You can also provide online ordering. A visitor selects items to be purchased. When they are done, the items requested can be e-mailed to you, or someone in your company, for processing.

Listing 34.2 is a form a user can fill out. The fields entered are name, an e-mail address, a subject line, and comments. Just about the same items most people fill out when sending e-mail via conventional means.

Listing 34.2   mail.html—A Simple Form that Allows the Visitor to Send E-Mail

```
<HTML>
<HEAD><TITLE>EMAIL ME!</TITLE></HEAD>
<BODY BGCOLOR=#FFFFFF>
<H1>EMAIL ME!</H1>
Please fill out the form to send me email!<P>
<FORM ACTION="mail.pl" METHOD="POST">
Realname:<INPUT TYPE="TEXT" NAME="realname"><br>
Email address:<INPUT TYPE="TEXT" NAME="email"><br>
Subject: <SELECT NAME="subject">
<OPTION>Hello!
<OPTION>Help!!
<OPTION>Reply please
</SELECT>
<P>
Enter your comments:<br>
<TEXTAREA NAME=comments ROWS=10 COLS=60>
</TEXTAREA>
<P>
<INPUT TYPE="SUBMIT">
</FORM>
</BODY>
</HTML>
```

Once the form is filled out by the visitor, the information entered is then sent to the server, which in turns sends that information to the CGI script indicated by using the ACTION attribute. In this case, the information entered by the visitor is sent to the script mail.pl.

If you take a look at Listing 34.3, you can see the full version of our mail.pl script. The first line tells the system this is a PERL script, and the full path is given to PERL, which is the program that will interpret the script.

Next, two variables are set. The first variable is the path to the sendmail program, which will actually send the e-mail to its destination. The second variable is the recipient, that is, the e-mail address that will receive the e-mail. We define this here so that the person visiting the site can't save a copy of our form and change the e-mail address to which this message is being sent.

Next, the script breaks the input stream coming from the server and places the value of each entry into the array named contents. This allows you to easily manipulate the information entered by the visitor.

Lastly, the e-mail is sent, and a Thank You page is displayed back to the visitor, letting him know that his comments were successfully sent.

Listing 34.3   mail.pl—The Visitor's Comments Are Processed and Sent to the Recipient

```perl
#!/usr/bin/perl
$mailprog = "/usr/lib/sendmail";
$recipient = "user\@foo.bar.com";


if ($ENV{'REQUEST_METHOD'} eq 'POST')
{
read(STDIN, $buffer, $ENV{'CONTENT_LENGTH'});
@pairs = split(/&/, $buffer);
foreach $pair (@pairs)
{
($name, $value) = split(/=/, $pair);
$value =~ tr/+/ /;
$value =~ s/%([a-fA-F0-9][a-fA-F0-9])/pack("C", hex($1))/eg;
$contents{$name} = $value;

}
}

# Open The Mail
open(MAIL, "|$mailprog -t") || die "Can't open $mailprog!\n";
print MAIL "To: $recipient\n";
print MAIL "From: $contents{'email'} <$contents'realname'}>\n";
print MAIL "Subject: $contents{'subject'}\n\n";
print MAIL "$contents{'comments'}\n\n";
close(MAIL);

print <<"HTML";
<HTML>
<HEAD><TITLE>Thank you!</TITLE></HEAD>
<BODY BGCOLOR=#FFFFFF>
<H1>Thank you!</H1>
Thank you for your comments!
<P>
<HR>
<CENTER>
<A HREF="http://www.selah.net/cgi.html">[Return to the main page]</A>
</CENTER>
</BODY>
</HTML>
HTML
exit;
```

By convention, one of the most important parts of a CGI script is to return something to the visitor. In the above example, you simply thanked the visitor for his comments. To send something back to the visitor is one of the basic rules of CGI scripting. Doing so tells the visitor that the information they entered was processed correctly, or at times the information returned will be results to a query they entered. Using search engines is a good example of returning information to the visitor. If a header is sent to the visitor without any content, then your browser will simply sit there or, in the case of Netscape, a dialog box will appear stating that the document contains no data.

A Simple Guestbook Script

Guestbook scripts are another popular script. I'm sure you have seen some sort of guestbook script on someone's personal home page, and even on commercial sites.

Guestbooks scripts allow the visitor to not only interact with you but also with other individuals that visit your site. By using a guestbook script, you just expanded upon how those visiting your site can interact. Guestbook scripts are used to allow the visitor to simply say "Hello" or to allow visitors to ask questions, hoping that someone visiting the site at a later date can answer that question.

The guestbook script, written by Jeffry Dwight, can be found on the CD-ROM named SGB1.EXE and contains both the HTML code, initially provided to allow visitors to enter comments, and the guestbook itself, allowing the visitor to read what others have entered. This script was written in C to run on Windows NT and Windows 95 (tested with WebSite and MS's Personal Web Server on Windows 95). The compiled binary has been provided, as well as the source code and makefile.

The script is fairly simple and heavily commented with explanations on how the CGI script works. If you take a look at Figure 34.2, you can get an idea of how it works as it stands. If you have a C compiler (a must if you are going to create CGI scripts in C), you can edit the script so the script is customized to the look and feel of your specific site.

FIG. 34.2
SGB1 is a simple CGI script written in C that allows your visitors to communicate with each other.

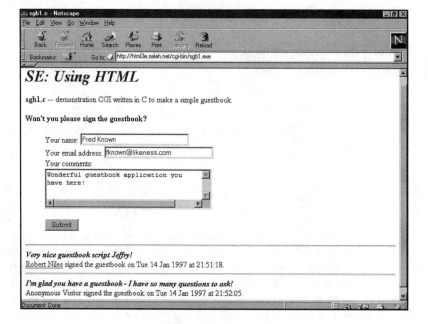

ON THE WEB

For those of you who would like to use a guestbook script that was written in PERL, Matt Wright provides a nice guestbook script that can be found at **http://www.worldwidemart.com/scripts/ guestbook.shtml**.

A Redirection Script

Another commonly requested script is the redirection script. A redirection script allows the visitor to select an item from a list and automatically send it to the site chosen.

Okay, so this is basically how links on Web pages work in the first place. Very true, but what you might, or might not, be aware of is you can log only where a visitor came from; the server doesn't have the capability to log where you go to. Redirection scripts solve this problem.

No longer are advertisers interested solely in how often their banner is displayed to the public. Advertisers want to know if their banner is having an effect on those visiting your site. Redirection scripts help you log how many times a link has been clicked.

The script redirect.pl, shown in Listing 34.4, performs this function by taking the URL that the visitor requested and logging it, and then by using the Location header, they are redirected to the site in question.

First, when the script is called, three buttons are provided for the visitor to click. Once clicked, the script logs the request to the log file specified in the variable logfile. In this instance, the log file is called redirect.log. The log file contains the date and which place the visitor wished to visit.

Listing 34.4   redirect.pl—A Simple Script that Logs the URL the Visitor Clicks

```
#!/usr/bin/perl

# Copyright 1996, Robert Niles

$logfile = "redirect.log";

if ($ENV{'REQUEST_METHOD'} eq 'POST')
{
read(STDIN, $buffer, $ENV{'CONTENT_LENGTH'});
@pairs = split(/&/, $buffer);
foreach $pair (@pairs)
{
($name, $value) = split(/=/, $pair);
$value =~ tr/+/ /;
$value =~ s/%([a-fA-F0-9][a-fA-F0-9])/pack("C", hex($1))/eg;
$contents{$name} = $value;
```

continues

Part **VI**

Ch **34**

Listing 34.4   Continued

```
}
}

chop($date = 'date');
&logit if $contents{'location'};
print "Content-type: text/html\n\n";
print <<"HTML";
<HTML>
<HEAD><TITLE>Whatever</TITLE></HEAD>
<BODY>
<H1>Whatever</H1>
<form action="/cgi-bin/redirect.pl" method="POST">
<input type="submit" name="location" value="Infoseek"><br>
<input type="submit" name="location" value="AltaVista"><br>
<input type="submit" name="location" value="WebCrawler"><br>
</form>
</body>
</html>
HTML

exit;


sub logit {

if ($contents{'location'} eq "Infoseek")
{
$location = "http://www.infoseek.com";
}
if ($contents{'location'} eq "AltaVista")
{
$location = "http://www.altavista.com";
}
if ($contents{'location'} eq "WebCrawler")
{
$location = "http://www.webcrawler.com";
}

open(LOG, ">>$logfile");
print LOG "$date User clicked on: $contents{'location'}\n";
close(LOG);
print "Location: $location\n\n";
exit;
}
```

Simple Count

Counters allow you to find out how many people have visited your page. A page with a low count could tell you the page might not be worth keeping. A page with a high count might indicate that it could use some expansion.

Counters are on just about every other page on the Net. In some instances they have been used as a way of bragging, "My dad is tougher than your dad." Some counters seem quite irritating in that they are heavily loaded with graphic images and seem to take forever just to display. Others, though, are simple counters created to inform not only the administrator of the site of how busy a site might be but also those visiting your site as to how often your page is visited—a very handy tool if you are attempting to attract potential advertisers.

The count.pl script shown in Listing 34.5 demonstrates how you can keep track of how often your site is being visited. The script is simple and displays only a small line with the number times your page has been accessed. The script can also be configured so that the access count is not displayed to those visiting your site. This allows you to know what your "hit" rate is without divulging the count to everyone visiting your page.

The script is accessed by using Server Side Includes (SSI). By using SSI to execute a script, you don't have to access the script directly, or with a form. What SSI does is return the result of a script directly within the HTML document that called the script.

Whether you can use SSI depends on your Web administrator. Some sites, for security reasons, do not allow normal users to utilize SSI. Also, some of the older Web servers don't have the ability to use SSI. If in doubt, check with your administrator.

How SSI is used varies, but with count.pl you want to use the SSI command,

```
<!--#exec cgi="count.pl"-->
```

wherever you want the page to display the count. For example, if you would like to have the access count displayed at the bottom of your page, you would have an HTML document that looks like:

```
<HTML>
<HEAD><TITLE>Counting!</TITLE></HEAD>
<BODY>
<H1>HI!</H1>
Hello visitor!<p>
You are visitor number: <!--#exec cgi="count.pl"-->
</BODY>
</HTML>
```

The count.pl script can also be used to keep track of several pages by using one script. Just make sure the path is pointing to where the script resides. In this example, the script resides in the same directory in which the script was called. If the script resides in the /cgi-bin/ directory, then the SSI command will need to reflect this.

Also, ensure that the countfile exists. This script is quite simple, and although it functions well, it doesn't create the countfile automatically.

Last, not all versions of PERL use the `flock()` function. If your version of PERL doesn't support `flock()`, then you will want to rewrite the script to use `fcntl()`.

Listing 34.5   count.pl—A Simple Hit Counter

```perl
#!/usr/bin/perl
# simplecount 1.0
# count.pl

$uri = $ENV{'DOCUMENT_URI'};

$countfile = "count";

print "Content-type: text/html\n\n";

open(COUNT, "+<$countfile") || do{
print "Can't open count file";
die; };
flock(COUNT, 2);

while (<COUNT>) {
chop;
($file, $count) = split(/:/, $_);
$counts{$file} = $count;
}

$counts{$uri}++;

seek(COUNT, 0, 0);


foreach $file (keys %counts) {
print COUNT $file, ":", $counts{$file}, "\n";
}

flock(COUNT, 8);
close(COUNT);

print $counts{$uri};

exit;
```

An Advertisement Banner

Using advertisement banners like those seen on the more popular Web pages have been mentioned in the last two sections. Advertisement banners allow a company to place a small ad on your page that is, usually, linked to its site. The nice thing about allowing advertisement banners is that companies are quite willing to pay large sums of money for you to display their banner—especially if you have a site that is heavily accessed. In fact, the busier your site, the more money you can make with advertising!

The script randpic.pl randomly picks and displays a banner like the banner shown in Figure 34.3. Each banner displayed contains the path to the banner image, the URL visitors will be sent to if they click the banner, a short line used as the graphic alternative, and a line in which a short slogan is displayed.

FIG. 34.3
Randpic.pl is a simple
script that randomly
picks and displays
an advertisement on
your page.

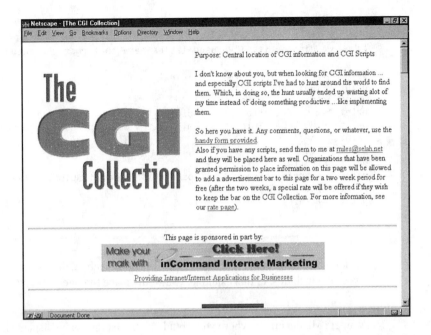

If you take a look at Listing 34.6, there are four arrays used to provide information about each
banner. The first section of the script defines each array. The next section selects a random
number using the current time as the seed. Once done, HTML is created, which is placed in
the HTML document calling the randpic.pl script.

Listing 34.6 randpic.pl— Place Advertisement Banners on Your Web Pages

```perl
#!/usr/bin/perl
# randpic.pl


@pics= ("pics/cgiad.gif",
"pics/img2.gif");

@url= ("www.selah.net/rate.html",
"www.in-command.com/");

@alt= ("The CGI Collection",
"InCommand Internet Marketing");

@comment= ("Advertise on the Web with The CGI Collection",
"Providing Intranet\/Internet Applications for Businesses");

# Now we pick a random number and assign it to $picnum
srand(time ^ $$);
$picnum = rand(@pics);
```

continues

Listing 34.6   Continued

```
# Now we display it. I've used tables here to format the output nicely.

print "Content-type: text/html\n\n";
print "<table border=0>";
print "<tr><td align=center>";
print "<a href=\"http://$url[$picnum]\">";
print "<IMG SRC=\"$pics[$picnum]\" alt=\"$alt[$picnum]\" border=0>";
print "</A>";
print "</td></tr>";
print "<tr><td align=center>";
print "<a href=\"http://$url[$picnum]\">$comment[$picnum]</a>";
print "</td></tr>";
print "</table>";
exit;
```

Just like the count.pl script discussed in the previous section, this script requires the use of Server Side Includes. In this example, you would place the line

```
<!--#exec cgi="randpic.pl"-->
```

in your HTML document where you would like the banner to be displayed.

Now that you have been introduced to CGI scripting, it's time for you to write your own scripts (or simply edit the scripts provided to suit your needs), which can be used to spice up your pages and provide a little more interactivity between you and those visiting your site. After all, allowing those visiting your site to interact with you, and others, is the main reason why the World Wide Web has become so popular.

ON THE WEB

If you would like more information on CGI scripts, and various CGI scripts available for use, visit **http://www.yahoo.com/Computers_and_Internet/Internet/World_Wide_Web/ CGI___Common_Gateway_Interface/**.

## CHAPTER 35

Active Server Pages

by Mike Morgan

In this chapter

Understanding ASP

When a Web browser contacts your server, the browser uses the HyperText Transfer Protocol (HTTP) to request some resource by name. A typical request is

```
GET /index.html HTTP/1.0
```

This request tells the server that the browser wants the Web page stored in the server's document root (/)whose name is index.html. The message also notifies the server that the client is using version 1.0 of HTTP.

In most cases the server's job is simple—it locates the requested page and sends it back to the client. If the filename ends in a special suffix, however, the server may have to perform additional processing. For example, the Webmaster may turn on server-side includes; if the filename ends in SHTML the server examines the file for special commands and then executes each command. The output of each command is inserted into the file; the finished file is then sent back to the client.

On the Microsoft Internet Information Server (IIS) and its smaller cousin, the Personal Web Server, the server checks to see if the filename ends in ASP. If it does, the server examines the file looking for scripts and then runs each script. The server inserts the output of each script into the file and sends the finished file back to the client.

> **CAUTION**
>
> Don't just change the extension of every file on your server from HTM to ASP. Every time the server has to check a file for scripts, it takes a bit of processing time. If you only use ASP when a file contains a script, the load on the server is small. If you force the server to check every page, the load adds up and can reduce the performance of your server.

N O T E The IIS supports ASP scripts written in Microsoft's language (VBScript) as well as Microsoft's version of JavaScript (JScript). You can also buy third-party modules (called "scripting engines") for your server that support other languages, such as Perl, REXX, and Python. ▪

Because ASP runs on the server, this technology does not depend on the end user's browser or platform. As long as the ASP scripts generate valid HTML, the resulting page should work as well on a Macintosh running Navigator 4.0 as it does on a Windows 95 machine running Microsoft Internet Explorer 3.02.

ON THE WEB

http://www.microsoft.com/infoservsupport/content/faq/   Microsoft has provided Frequently Asked Questions lists (FAQs) on several aspects of Active Server Pages.

This section introduces ASP scripting and shows two examples: one that reads the contents of a form, and another that retrieves data from a database.

ASP Scripts

When you write an HTML file, you put HTML tags (delimited by <...>) and plain text together. Your HTML may also contain comments, delimited by <!...>. When you add ASP scripts, you add another delimiter: <%...%>. Thus, if you write

```
<% theSequence = "first" %>
```

the server passes the string inside the delimiters to the scripting engine for its primary scripting language. By default, that language is VBScript. As a result, VBScript opens a new variable (theSequence) and assigns a string value ("first") to it.

ASP Output Directive From time to time you'll want to display the value of some expression. Most frequently, you'll do this while you're developing the script in order to check your logic. The syntax for the ASP output directive is

```
<%= expression %>
```

Thus, if you wrote

```
<% theSequence = "first" %>
<%= theSequence %>
```

you would see "first" appear in the resulting page.

ASP Processing Directive Use the syntax

```
<%@ keyword %>
```

to pass information to the server. For example, to tell the server to use VBScript as the primary scripting language, write

```
<%@ Language = VBScript %>
```

as the top line of your file. (The scripting language is VBScript by default, but it's considered "good form" to set it explicitly.)

You can set five different variables in the processing directive:

- LANGUAGE specifies the primary scripting language.
- CODEPAGE sets the character encoding.
- LCID specifies the locale identifier.
- TRANSACTION tells the server to run the script in a transaction context.
- ENABLESESSIONSTATE tells the server to keep track of the user's state within each session.

The effect of each of these keywords is explained later in this chapter.

Working with Forms

Suppose you have the HTML form shown in Listing 35.1 in your Web page:

Part

VI

Ch

35

Listing 35.1   form.htm—The Fields of This Form Will Be Read by an ASP

```
<FORM METHOD="GET" ACTION="process.asp">
<BR>First name: <INPUT TYPE="text" NAME="first">
<BR>Last name: <INPUT TYPE="text" NAME="last">
<BR><INPUT TYPE="submit" VALUE="Enter">
</FORM>
```

When a user submits this form, the contents are sent to the page named process.asp. The browser packages the fields of the form into a query string; the server makes this string available through an object called Request. You can read fields in the query string by using Request's QueryString() method. Listing 35.2 shows a simple ASP script to process the contents of form.htm.

Listing 35.2   process.asp—Use This Simple ASP Script to Process the Contents of the Form

```
<%@ Language = VBScript %>
<HTML>
<HEAD><TITLE>Welcome</TITLE></HEAD>
<BODY>
<H1>Welcome</H1>
<P>Hello, <%= Request.QueryString("first") %>
<%= Request.QueryString("last") %> </P>
<P>Welcome to my site.</P>
<P><A HREF="next.htm">Next</A></P>
</BODY>
</HTML>
```

Handling Multi-Item <SELECT>s   If you have a multi-item <SELECT> in your form, use the alternate version of QueryString() as shown in Listings 35.3 and 35.4.

Listing 35.3   multi.htm—One of the Fields of This Form May Have Multiple Values

```
<FORM METHOD="GET" ACTION="doMulti.asp">
<BR>First name: <INPUT TYPE="text" NAME="first">
<BR>Last name: <INPUT TYPE="text" NAME="last">
<BR>Occupation (select all that apply):
<SELECT NAME="Occupation" MULTIPLE SIZE=5>
<OPTION Executive>Executive
<OPTION Professional>Professional
<OPTION Engineer>Engineer
<OPTION Skilled>Skilled Labor
<OPTION Clerical>Clerical
</SELECT>
<BR><INPUT TYPE="submit" VALUE="Enter">
</FORM>
```

Listing 35.4   doMulti.asp—Use This ASP Script to Read the Values from "Occupation"

```
<%@ Language = VBScript %>
<HTML>
<HEAD><TITLE>Welcome</TITLE></HEAD>
<BODY>
<H1>Welcome</H1>
<P>Hello, <%= Request.QueryString("first") %>
<%= Request.QueryString("last") %> </P>
<P>Welcome to my site.</P>
<P>
<% theNumberOfOccupations = Request.QueryString("Occupation").Count %>
<% if theNumberOfOccupations = 0 %>
You must be unemployed
<% else if theNumberOfOccupations = 1 %>
Your occupation is
<% Request.QueryString("Occupation")(1) %>
<% else %>
Your occupations are
<% Request.QueryString("Occupation")(1) %>
<% For i = 2 to theNumberOfOccupations - 1 %>
  ,<% Request.QueryString("Occupation")(i) %>
<% Next %>
and <% Request.QueryString("Occupation")(theNumberOfOccupations) %>
<END IF>
.</P>
<P><A HREF="next.htm">Next</A></P>
</BODY>
</HTML>
```

Using *METHOD="POST"*   Many Web designers prefer to use POST rather than GET to send form data back to the server. The advantage of POST is that there is no limit to the number of characters that can be sent back, while some combinations of software truncate GET strings. If you're reading data from a <FORM> that uses POST, use Request's Form collection to read the contents of the form.

For example, if the form shown in Listing 35.3 had used POST instead of GET, we could have used the following line to retrieve the data from the field named "first":

```
<%= Request.Form("first") %>
```

Accessing a Database

One of the most useful things you can do with an ASP script is give the user access to a database. Microsoft makes this step particularly easy by allowing you to write ActiveX Data Objects (ADOs) based on Microsoft's Open Database Connectivity (ODBC) standard.

> **N O T E**   For a different approach to connecting to a database, see your server documentation's section on the "Internet Database Connector," or IDC. With the IDC you can send queries to a database (through ODBC), format the returned data, and send the resulting page to the user's browser.
>
> Microsoft recommends that users migrate to ADOs, but it will continue to support other methods into the near future. ■

Part
VI

Ch
35

What is ODBC?

ODBC is Microsoft's implementation of the X/Open and SQL Access Group (SAG) Call Level Interface (CLI) specification. By using ODBC, your program can read and write records from an idealized database by using standard Structured Query Language (SQL) statements. The ODBC drivers take care of translating the standard SQL into the exact calls necessary for each database. In the case of SQL databases such as Microsoft SQL Server, little translation is required. In the case of "databases" such as text files and Microsoft Excel spreadsheets, the drivers are more complex.

Figure 35.1 illustrates ODBC's architecture, which has five logical layers:

- *Application layer.* The "front end" that allows the user to interact with the software. For Active Server Pages, the application includes the ASP script, the server, and the user's Web browser.

- *ODBC Interface.* An Application Programming Interface that allows the application to communicate with the rest of ODBC in a standardized way, regardless of what kind of database is being used as the data source.

- *Driver Manager.* A "traffic director" that makes sure each ODBC call is routed to the correct driver and data source.

- *Driver.* The software that translates ODBC's standard SQL statements into the commands supported by a particular database product. The driver also handles network communications for data sources that are accessed through the network.

- *Data Source.* The set of files and associated software that hold the data. A data source may be as simple as a text file or Microsoft Excel spreadsheet, or it may be a sophisticated database management system distributed across several mainframes or mid-range computers.

Connecting your ASP script to the database is a three-step process:

1. Make a Data Source Name (DSN) file
2. Connect to the database
3. Retrieve data

In addition to these three steps, you should consider whether or not you need to use transactions to manage your database access. This section addresses each of these points.

Making a Data Source Name File   In order for an ODBC application to connect to a data source, the application uses a Data Source Name, or DSN. ODBC supports a variety of DSNs, many of which are stored in the system registry. Microsoft recommends that ADO developers use a file-based DSN, so that the DSN can easily be moved or shared.

To make a new DSN file, open the ODBC control panel and choose the File DSN tab, shown in Figure 35.2.

FIG. 35.1
ODBC consists of five distinct layers.

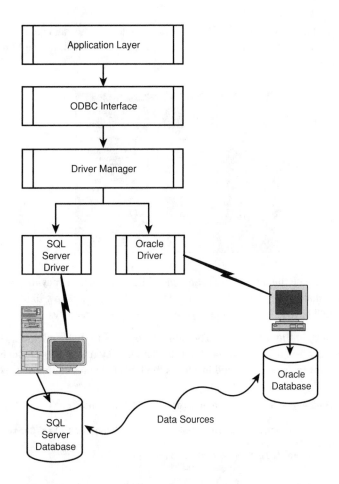

FIG. 35.2
Use the File DSN tab when you're connecting from an ADO.

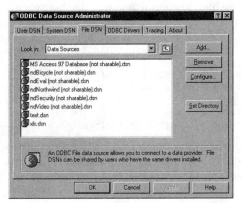

If you don't already have a file DSN that is suitable for your data source, click on Add and select the driver that's right for your data source. Figure 35.3 shows eight drivers available on this machine.

FIG. 35.3

Choose the driver that matches your data source.

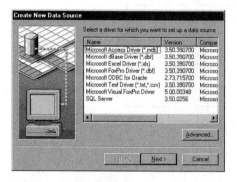

Once you name the new DSN file and click Finish, the driver may display a series of dialogs. Uses the dialogs to tell the driver where to find the data and how to interpret it. When you're done you'll have a new DSN file in your Data Sources directory.

Connecting to the Database   The ActiveX component that implements the ADO is called `Connection`. Tell the ASP script about the database by making a new `Connection` object. Then use `Connection`'s `Open` method to access the DSN file you built in the preceding step.

```
<%
  Set cnnConn = Server.CreateObject("ADODB.Connection")

  'For convenience, keep your DSN file in \Program Files\Common Files\
  '  ODBC\Data Sources
  cnnConn.Open "FILEDSN = theDatabase.dsn"
%>
```

Retrieving Data   Once you have a connection to your database open, you can send standard SQL statements through ODBC. Suppose your database includes a table called `FruitTable` with two columns: `fruitNumber` and `fruit`. To list the table, you could write the following:

```
<%
'This script assumes we have already instantiated a new Connection
'object and opened a connection to the data source through our
'DSN file.
'Now lets issue the query:
strSQL = "SELECT fruitNumber, fruit FROM FruitTable"
Set rstFruits = cnnConn.execute(strSQL)
Response.Write("<TABLE><TR><TH>Fruit Number</TH><TH>Fruit</TH></TR>")
Do Until rstFruits.EOF
  Response.Write("<TR><TD>" & rstFruits('fruitNumber') & "</TD><TR>" &
    rstFruits('fruit') & "</TD></TR>")
Loop
Response.Write("</TABLE>")
%>
```

If you're using ASP scripts to access a database, be sure to read your server's documentation on other access tools. For example, Microsoft supports a `RecordSet` object that gives you more precise control over which records are displayed, and a `Command` object that allows you to impose high-level control over the way requests to the database are managed.

> **CAUTION**
>
> Be sure to observe any licensing limits imposed by your database manager. If you are licensed for, say, 15 simultaneous connections, you may use up those connections quickly once your application is placed into service. Read your server's documentation on connection pooling to learn how to live within your database manager's limits, and be sure to close your connections once you're through with them.
>
> To learn more about connection pooling, read about it in the Microsoft KnowledgeBase at **http://www.microsoft.com/kb/articles/Q164/2/21.htm** and **http://www.microsoft.com/kb/articles/Q166/8/86.htm**.

You can release a database connection by placing the following lines in your ASP, after the `</BODY>` tag:

```
cnnConn.Close
Set cnnConn = Nothing
```

Selecting a Transaction Model   When you allow more than one user to access the same database at the same time, it's time to think about *transactions*. Transactions provide four behaviors, often summarized by the acronym ACID:

- *Atomicity*. All of the program steps inside a transaction are either committed together, or abandoned (rolled back) together. There's no such thing as a transaction that's "half-done."

- *Consistency*. The transaction must leave the database in a consistent state. For example, if a transaction deletes a record, it must delete all references to that record as well.

- *Isolation*. Each transaction is independent of all others. It doesn't matter whether you apply transaction 1, and then transaction 2, or transaction 2, and then transaction 1—the end result should be the same.

- *Durability*. Once the transaction is complete, the change should be considered to be permanently applied to the database. Many commercial database managers keep a log of all transactions; in the event of a hardware failure, they can restore the database from the log.

The following steps illustrate how an airline reservation system might work, without transactions:

1. You contact Travel Agent #1 to book a flight to Hawaii. Travel Agent #1 opens the database and reads out the available seats. She finds that there is only one seat left on the flight that you want.

2. While you are considering taking the seat, a different passenger contacts Travel Agent #2 about the same flight. Travel Agent #2 queries the database, finds out about the one open seat, and tells her prospective traveler about it.

3. Both you and the other passenger decide to take the seat. Both travel agents enter the data at about the same instant. Travel Agent #1 happens to be just a bit faster—she changes the database and tells you that you have a confirmed ticket. Then Travel Agent #2's booking goes through, changing the database so that the seat appears to have been sold to the other passenger.

4. Both you and the other passenger arrive at the airport. The other passenger's name is in the database with a reservation. To your dismay, the agent at the counter tells you the computer has no record of your reservation. Sorry about that!

Now suppose that this system had been designed with transactions:

1. You contact Travel Agent #1 to book a flight to Hawaii. Travel Agent #1 opens the database and reads out the available seats. She finds that there is only one seat left on the flight that you want.

2. While you are considering taking the seat, a different passenger contacts Travel Agent #2 about the same flight. Travel Agent #2 queries the database, finds out about the one open seat, and tells her prospective traveler about it.

3. Both you and the other passenger decide to take the seat. Both travel agents enter the data at about the same instant. Travel Agent #1 happens to be just a bit faster—she starts a transaction and changes the database. Once the transaction has committed she tells you that you have a confirmed ticket. At about the same time Travel Agent #2's booking arrives at the database; when Agent #2 attempts to acquire a write-access transaction, she is told that the database is currently being changed. When your transaction is complete, she finds that she cannot sell the seat, because you have already bought it. She works with the other passenger to find a different flight.

4. You arrive at the airport. Your name is in the computer, and your reservation is confirmed. Aloha!

If you decide that you need the protection of transactions, you need to install Microsoft Transaction Server (MTS). Follow your IIS and MTS documentation to make MTS packages. Once you have set up MTS packages, you can write your scripts so that database accesses generate new transactions. Use the MTS Explorer to register the components responsible for database access with MTS.

> **CAUTION**
>
> If you register a component with MTS that has application- or session-scope, the MTS and the script are likely to become confused. Transaction resources are deactivated when they are not in use; you cannot be assured that the component will maintain state properly.
>
> If you need to maintain state on a page that uses MTS-registered ActiveX components, give page scope to the components themselves, and then use `Application` or `Session` properties to record the scope. Pass that scope to and from the components as required.

You tell the IIS to enforce your database access with transactions by using the `Transaction` directive:

```
<%@ Transaction = value %>
```

where *value* can take one of four character strings:

- `Requires_New`—Database access starts a transaction.
- `Required`—Database access starts a transaction.
- `Supported`—Database access does not start a transaction.
- `Not_Supported`—Database access does not start a transaction.

Although a script can explicitly tell the MTS (by calling `ObjectContext.SetAbort`) that it wants to exit a transaction before the transaction has committed, in general the script cannot tell that an access failed. The failure may be associated with a network failure or a disk drive filling up. You should include two procedures in each page where transactions are used:

- `OnTransactionCommit` is called if the MTS reports that the transaction succeeded.
- `OnTransactionAbort` is called if the MTS reports that the transaction failed.

 T I P If the transaction aborts the database server will take care of restoring the database to its pre-transaction state. You should use your `OnTransactionAbort` event handler to reset any application, session, or local variables as necessary.

Using Components to Build Scripts

Both VBScript and JScript use objects to encapsulate some aspects of program behavior. If you're familiar with client-side VBScript, you know that you use `CreateObject()` to make a new instance of an object. In your ASP scripts you can use both built-in objects and ActiveX components. This section describes both kinds of objects. Once you know how to use components, you can assemble pages with ASP scripts and ActiveX components into ASP applications. ASP applications are described later in this chapter, in the section "ASP Applications."

> **CAUTION**
>
> In an ASP script, calling `CreateObject()` produces an error—use `Server.CreateObject()` instead.

In addition to using objects, you can also encapsulate behavior by using `#include` files and by writing procedures (such as VBScript subroutines or JScript functions). If you're already familiar with JavaScript, you may prefer to work in Microsoft's version of that language, JScript. You can learn more about JavaScript and its cousins in Chapter 16, "Adding JavaScript and VBScript to HTML."

You can direct the server to include another file in your ASP script by using the server-side include `#include` directive. If you write

```
<!--#include file="myFile.inc"-->
```

the server will look in the directory that includes your ASP file for the file named myFile.inc, and it will use that file as though it were actually included in your ASP file.

N O T E You should avoid exposing the actual paths on your hard drives to Web users. IIS allows you to declare *virtual directories,* which serve as roots for Web applications or other sites on your server.

If you use virtual directories on your server, use the form

<!--#include virtual="/myApp/myFile.inc"-->

to tell the server to look for the included file in the myApp virtual directory. ■

Built-In Objects We've already seen some of the objects built into the server, such as Request and Response. The full list of built-in objects includes these six objects:

■ Request—Provides access to information on the client machine, including HTML forms, cookies, and client certificates. You also use Request to read any files uploaded to the server.

■ Response—Used to send information to the client. Use the Response to set HTTP headers, send HTML, redirect the browser to another URL, or set client cookies.

■ Server—Commonly used to make new instances of objects through its CreateObject() method. The Server object can also be used to encode strings, transform virtual paths to physical paths, and set the time-out for the script.

■ Session—Used to preserve information as the user moves from one page to the next. Session is also used to set time-out for an idle session.

■ Application—Shares information between all users of a given application.

■ ObjectContext—Used to either commit or abort a transaction.

T I P To take maximum advantage of Microsoft-supplied objects, be sure to read about their methods and properties in the "Scripters Reference" section of your server's documentation.

ActiveX Components In addition to procedures and built-in objects, you can write your own objects in a programming language such as Visual Basic.

N O T E You can write ActiveX components in any language that supports the Component Object Model (COM), such as C, C++, or Java, as well as Visual Basic.

Once you have written them, you can call ActiveX components on a Microsoft server from ASP scripts, ISAPI applications, or other ActiveX components. ■

Microsoft has already supplied 12 ActiveX components that are useful in ASP scripts:

■ AdRotator—Displays several ads according to a specified schedule

■ BrowserType—Reports on the capabilities of the end user's browser

■ Database Access—Based on ActiveX Data Objects (ADOs)

- `Nextlink`—Used to build tables of contents
- `FileSystemObject`—Provides access to files through the server's operating system
- An `SMTP Mail` object—Allows ASP scripts to send and receive mail
- `Tools`—Provides utility methods on the client machine, such as `FileExists()`, `Owner()`, `PluginExists()`, `ProcessForm()`, and `Random()`
- `Status`—Reports various aspects of the server's status, including the date and time the server started, the number of unique visitors who have accessed the server, and an HTML table listing the 32 most recently visited pages
- `MyInfo`—Contains information about the owner of a Windows 95 Personal Web Server
- `Counter`—A general-purpose counter object
- `Content`—Rotates HTML content strings based on a specified schedule
- `PageCounter`—Reports the number of times a particular URL has been accessed

N O T E Microsoft does not officially support the `Content`, `PageCounter`, or `PermissionChecker` components. You can get support from other users of these components in the **microsoft.public.inetserver.iis.activeserverpages** newsgroup or through the Active Server Pages mailing list. If you don't have that newsgroup on your local news server, read it on **news:/ /msnews.microsoft.com**.

To subscribe to the Active Server Pages mailing list, send mail to

`listserv@listserv.msn.com`

with

`subscribe Denali [firstname lastname]`

in the body of the message.

Unlike supported components, the full name of these components begins with `ISSample`. Thus, to make a new instance of `PermissionChecker` in VBScript, write

`Set thePermissionChecker =`
`Server.CreateObject("IISample.PermissionChecker")`

To make a new instance of an ActiveX component, use the `Server.CreateObject()` method and specify the registered name (`PROGID`). Thus, to make a new ad rotator in VBScript, write

`<% Set theAdRotator = Server.CreateObject("MSWC.AdRotator") %>`

You can also use a special version of the `<OBJECT>` tag to make a new object:

```
<OBJECT RUNAT=Server ID=theAdRotator PROGID="MSWC.AdRotator">
</OBJECT>
```

Be sure to include the `RUNAT=Server` attribute so that the instance is made on the server, and not on the client computer.

Setting Component Scope   When you make a new instance of an ActiveX component, you can decide to make that instance accessible from any of three levels:

- *Application-scope.* The instance is shared by everyone who is using the application.
- *Session-scope.* One instance of the component exists per active session.
- *Page-scope.* The instance is deleted when the user exits the page.

Professional programmers generally avoid *global variables* such as application-scope components. Most ASP scripters prefer to use page-scope or, at most, session-scope.

By default, new instances have page-scope. You can set session-scope or application-scope with the <OBJECT> tag:

```
<OBJECT RUNAT=Server SCOPE=Session ID=MyAd PROGID="MSWC.Adrotator">
</OBJECT>
```

or

```
<OBJECT RUNAT=Server SCOPE=Application ID=MyID
CLASSID="Clsid:00000293-0000-0010-8000-00AA006D2EA4">
</OBJECT>
```

N O T E If you choose to set up application-scope instances, place the <OBJECT> tag in the file Global.asa. █

You can also use `Server.CreateObject()` to specify the scope by making the new instance a property of the session or application:

```
<% Set Session("MyAd") = Server.CreateObject("MSWC.Adrotator") %>
```

If you use `Server.CreateObject()` to make a new instance, the instance comes into existence immediately. If you use the <OBJECT> tag, the instance isn't built until it is referenced. For session-scope instances, therefore, you get better performance if you use <OBJECT> tags.

For additional performance improvements, make sure that components with application- or session-scope have their threading model set to "Objects Marked as Both." These objects will be shared among more than one user—if you use a single-threaded or free-threaded model, one user may be blocked while another user is using the instance.

ASP Applications

Once you know how to write ASP scripts and call components, you can assemble Active Server Pages and components into ASP applications. Define a directory to hold the pages; all of the ASP files inside that directory or its subdirectories are part of a single application. By using that design, you can have more than one application on your server.

When you write Web applications you must address the fact that HTTP is a *stateless protocol*. That is, the server cannot tell whether two HTTP requests come from the same user or two different users. Similarly, if a user makes a particular choice on one page, HTTP does not give the server a way to remember that choice and use it on future pages.

Recall from the previous section that Microsoft has built `Application` and `Session` objects into the ASP model. You can use these two objects to remember information from one HTTP request to the next. If you store information in the `Application` object, that information will be shared among all users of the application. If you store the information in the `Session` object, the information will be associated with a single user as he or she moves through the application.

> **N O T E** Often a user abandons an application without completing the last page. For example, an on-line shopper may fill a "shopping cart" with items and never check out. You should set the session time-out so that, after some period of inactivity, the server resources associated with the session are released. (The default time-out period is 20 minutes.) ▪

Managing Applications

You should place a file named Global.asa in your application's root directory. Here you can declare object instances that have application- or session-scope.

Starting and Ending an Application   When a user first accesses a page of the application, the server looks at the Global.asa file and calls the `Application_OnStart` procedure, if it exists. Similarly, when the server is shut down, the application stops, and the server calls `Application_OnEnd`. Listing 35.5 shows how to write an `Application_OnStart` procedure.

Listing 35.5   global.asa—Add an *Application_OnStart* Procedure to global.asa to Provide Start-Up Processing

```
<SCRIPT LANGUAGE=VBScript RUNAT=Server>
Sub Application_OnStart
...
End Sub
</SCRIPT>
```

> **N O T E** You can also use the Unload button in Internet Service Manager to stop an application. The server will call `Application_OnEnd`, just as it does when the server is shut down. ▪

Storing Data at the Application Level   One way to think of the `Application` object is as a dynamic array. You can store variables and their values in the `Application` object; such variables are available to any page of the application.

For example, suppose you want to feature a particular product in a sales application. You might place the following line in Global.asa.

```
<% Application("FeaturedProductSKU") = "1269109" %>
```

Now, on any page, you can use `Application("FeaturedProductSKU")` to find the current featured product. You might pass this number to a database, look up a product description and price, and place that information on various pages.

Part
VI

Ch
35

Managing Sessions

When a user first accesses any ASP page in an application, the server generates a unique number, called the SessionID. Then it sends that SessionID to the user's browser, asking the browser to make a cookie for the SessionID.

CAUTION

Not all browsers support cookies, and not all users accept cookies. Some users ask their browsers to warn them when they are offered a cookie—the users get a warning such as the one shown in Figure 35.4.

If a user doesn't accept the cookie, or the browser can't store it, none of the Session information will be available to the application.

To learn other methods of preserving state, see Chapter 20, "Preserving Data," of *Webmaster Expert Solutions* (Que, 1996).

FIG. 35.4

Some users prefer not to accept cookies, or want to be warned before they accept them.

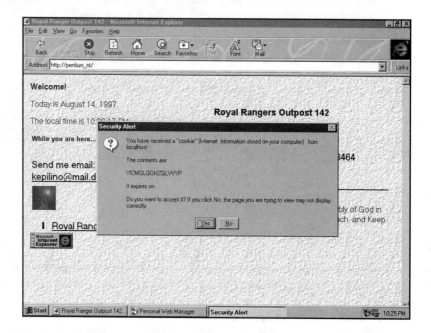

Starting and Ending a Session   As an ASP scripter, you can use the Session to maintain user state in any of three ways:

- Place a Session_OnStart procedure in the application's Global.asa file.
- Place an <OBJECT> tag with session scope in the Global.asa file.
- Store a value in the Session object.

A session will end when the session time-out expires. For example, if the time-out value is 20 minutes, the server resources associated with the session are released 20 minutes after the user last requests or refreshes a page.

You can explicitly end a session by calling `Session.Abandon`. For example, if you are writing a shopping-cart application, you may want to end the session after the user has checked out. This design prevents a user from returning to a completed order, modifying it, and checking out again.

N O T E   The cookie set by the server does not have an expiration date, so it won't be stored on the user's hard drive. If a user starts a session then exits the browser and restarts it, the `SessionID` is lost and the user must start a new session when he or she returns to the application.

If you need to store data on the user's hard drive (so that it will be available after the user has closed the browser) write a cookie with an expiration date:

```
<%
Response.Cookie("preference") = "text-only"
Response.Cookie("preference").Expires = "January 1, 1999"
%>
```

CAUTION
Browsers differ regarding whether the elements of a URL are case-sensitive. To Netscape Navigator, the intranet application http://myapp/ has a different URL from http://MyApp/. To Microsoft Internet Explorer, both URLs are the same. If you set a cookie on a page named http://myapp/page1.asp and attempt to retrieve it from http://MyApp/page2.asp, Explorer will give you the cookie, but Navigator will not.

The solution is to make sure that you use case consistently whenever you write a link in your application.

If you don't plan to use the `Session` object or its associated capabilities on a particular page, you can get a performance boost by marking a page as sessionless. Place the following line as the top line of your ASP file:

```
<%@ EnableSessionState=False %>
```

Suppose you have an application with two frames. If Frame 1 needs to use `Session` features but Frame 2 does not, mark Frame 2 as sessionless. Many browsers will then request both frames—Frame 2 may well be downloaded to the user's machine while the server is processing the scripts in Frame 1.

Storing Data at the Session Level   You can associate user-specific data with the `Session` object. Suppose you have the user fill out a form that requests the user's first and last name. You might write

```
<% Session("FirstName") = Request.QueryString("first") %>
<% Session("LastName") = Request.QueryString("last") %>
```

Then, on subsequent pages, you might write

```
<H1>Welcome, <%= Session("FirstName") %></H1>
```

Application Security

If you're operating a Microsoft Internet Information Server, you should take the time to become familiar with Windows NT security. Microsoft uses system-level security as the foundation for ASP application security when the user accesses the application locally.

In order for a user to access your application over the Web, you must set up to three access permissions:

- Any virtual directories with ASP files must have script access permission enabled.
- Any directory that has HTML files as well as ASP files must have read permission.
- If you choose to include EXE or DLL files in a directory, you must set execute permission for that directory.

If you want to restrict access to authorized users only, use your Web server to set either Basic Authentication or Windows NT Challenge/Response Authentication, and disable anonymous access.

If you choose Basic Authentication, the user is prompted for a username and password.

If you choose Windows NT Challenge/Response Authentication, the server requests an X.509 certificate from the client browser. This method is more secure than Basic Authentication, but not all browsers support it, and many users do not yet have certificates. (You can refer users to Verisign, at **http://www.verisign.com/**, to get a personal certificate, or your organization can operate its own Certificate Server.)

Internationalization

Sometimes you need to make an application accessible to people who prefer a language other than English. Some of these users can work with a variant of the Latin character set; others, such as readers of Japanese, Chinese, and Korean, need a much larger character set. In order to internationalize your application, you may need to make two changes:

- Set the code page to match the character encoding used on the page.
- Set the locale so that date, time, and other localizable characters are properly set.

▶ **See** "Understanding the Needs of the International Audience," **p. 329**

Setting the Code Page   The code page specifies the character set used on the page. Internally, Microsoft Internet Information Server uses Unicode, the 16-bit per character standard. If your page uses characters that fall outside the standard ASCII range (0-127) some characters may not be displayed properly unless the browser is set to use the same character set as the page.

N O T E   Character encodings are typically specified by the number of their international standard (for example, ISO-8859-1). Code pages are proprietary—the most common ones are specified by IBM and Microsoft. Code pages are specified by number (for example, code page 950 specifies some common Chinese characters). Table 35.1 shows common code pages and their character set (charset) equivalents. ■

Table 35.1   Charsets and Code Pages

Charset Name	Codepage Number
U.S.	437
Baltic	775
Multilingual (Latin I)	850
Slavic (Latin II)	852
Cyrillic (Russian)	855
Turkish	857
Portuguese	860
Icelandic	861
Hebrew	862
Canadian-French	863
Arabic	864
Nordic	865
Russian	866
Modern Greek	869
Thai	874
Japanese	932
Chinese (PRC, Singapore)	935
Korean (Hangul)	949
Chinese (Big 5)	950

Windows NT does all of its internal processing in Unicode. If you are working with ActiveX components that work with Unicode, and all of the visitors to your site are on systems that handle Unicode, you may never need to set the code page. On the other hand, most computers will need to switch from Unicode to some single-byte encoding for many years to come. Windows 95, for example, does not use Unicode. When Windows 95 is sold, it is typically sold with a single language pack—machines sold in the U.S. are set up to work in English, while machines sold in Brazil are loaded with Portuguese. Microsoft supports three language platforms

Part
VI

Ch
35

with Windows NT. Platform WE is associated with Western languages such as English, Spanish, French, and German. The number of characters and symbols is small—below 256—and the characters are read from left to right. Platform ME is associated with languages such as Turkish, Hebrew, and Arabic. The size of the alphabet is still small, but the text flows from right to left. Platform FE is used for Asian languages such as Chinese, Japanese, and Hangul (the major character set in Korea). There are thousands of characters. In print, the characters are read from top to bottom, though on computers a left to right ordering is culturally acceptable.

You can set the code page for a single ASP page by placing the following directive in the first line of the page:

```
<%@ CODEPAGE= 932 %>
```

Occasionally you will need to set the code page to a different value temporarily while the script is running. You can make this change by following a six-step procedure:

1. Use a `CODEPAGE` directive to set the page's default code page.

2. Store the code page as a `Session` property. For example, in VBScript you might write

   ```
   <% Session("OriginalCodePage") = Session.CodePage %>
   ```

3. Set `Session.Codepage` to a new value.

4. Work in the new code page.

5. Restore the original code page.

6. Send content back to the client.

Setting the Locale   Many elements of computer processing depend upon the country and culture where the processing is being done. Some obvious points include how dates and currency are displayed. Some less obvious changes include how items are compared and sorted into lists. The Windows operating system provides for many different *locales*; you can set the locale by specifying the Locale ID (`LCID`) in the first line of the page:

```
<%@ LCID = LCID %>
```

Tools and Techniques for Building Your Active Server Pages

Previous sections of this chapter focused on the technology used in Active Server Pages. This section describes the mechanics of writing an ASP. This section shows:

■ How to write an ASP with a simple text editor

■ How Visual InterDev improves the ASP-writing process

■ How to debug a new ASP script

Writing ASP Pages and Applications

You can learn about Active Server Pages by using the Personal Web Server (which runs on Windows 95 and Windows NT 4.0 Workstation machines). For simple pages and small applications, all you need to get started is a text editor. As your applications grow, you'll find yourself spending much of your time maintaining links, adding new features, and managing database connections. This section describes three tools you may want to use to reduce your workload:

- *Learn good development techniques*. Concentrate on good design practices and intensive testing. You'll need these skills whether you write your pages with the latest high-end tool or a simple editor.
- *Evaluate Visual InterDev*. Microsoft's development tool is tailor-made for complex applications, especially if you want to give the end user access to a database.
- *Use the Script Debugger*. Many expert programmers evaluate a development environment largely on the strength of its debugger. Microsoft supplies a debugger that lets you step your way through the script and examine values as you go.

Working on a Single Page   Begin your experience with ASPs by writing a few ASP-enhanced pages. While you may eventually write complete applications, you'll learn fastest if you work through one of Microsoft's tutorials or just build a few pages on your own.

 T I P   Use the sample ASPs that come with your server's Roadmap as a starting point for learning to script. Microsoft's documentation also includes nice tutorials on both VBScript and JScript.

After you've had enough experience to determine which language you prefer, get a comprehensive reference book on that language.

When you're writing a single Active Server Page, start by writing the page's HTML. You can use any tool you like to lay out the HTML, including a simple text editor such as WordPad. Include some "placeholder" HTML for the results of your ASP scripts. Later, when you write the scripts, you can comment out or even remove the placeholder code.

Next add any processing directives you need; make sure they appear in the top line of the file. Finally, add the ASP scripts and test the page with your browser.

Writing a Small Application   If you're building a full application, set up a virtual directory to hold the application's pages. Consider starting your implementation by writing the global.asa page. Use the techniques given for a single page to write the first page in the application. Use this page to check application-scope and session-scope variables and components. Make sure they're working as expected.

Continue building the site by adding the rest of the pages. Some of these pages will end up being Active Server Pages; others will be built with static HTML only. Build a mock-up of your application entirely out of static HTML, and show that mock-up to the people who will use the application. (If the application is for an intranet, you may be able to get input from the whole user community. If you're developing an Internet application, get input from representative users.)

Part
VI

Ch

35

Once you and your users are satisfied with the design, add ASP scripts and components, and include any database connections you need. Keep an eye on the total number of ASPs in your application. Remember, the more ASPs you have, the slower your server will run. If you're running a database server and a Microsoft Transaction Server on the same machine that hosts your IIS, your host may become overloaded. If you spread the load over multiple machines, watch the load on your network to make sure it doesn't slow your application down.

 T I P   Many professional software developers allocate 50 percent of their time on a project to requirements analysis and design, and another 25 percent or so to testing. Before you start writing VBScript or JScript, take some time to lay out the application on paper. You may even want to use index cards to represent each page, and then move them around until you and the end users are happy with the design.

 ON THE WEB

http://www.microsoft.com/frontpage/   If you want to stick with Microsoft products and need some help getting your HTML together, consider Microsoft FrontPage 98. From this page follow links to a downloadable beta copy or an on-line demo. (Mac users, learn about the Macintosh version of the product at **http://www.microsoft.com/frontpage/brochure/macpd.htm**.)

Using Visual InterDev

While a simple text editor is sufficient to get you started with Active Server Pages, you'll find that the amount of time maintaining the pages grows dramatically when you have a multi-page application, particularly if you are using the application to access databases. You can reduce the amount of maintenance time by using Microsoft's development tool, Visual InterDev.

 ON THE WEB

http://www.microsoft.com/products/prodref/177_ov.htm   Visit Visual InterDev's home page to learn more about its features, system requirements, and pricing.

You can run Visual InterDev on a Windows 95 machine or under Windows NT. To help you evaluate the product, you might want to download a 12-minute demo from **http://www.microsoft.com/vinterdev/us/download/autodemo.htm**.

Debugging ASP Scripts

Microsoft introduced the Script Debugger for client-side scripts in VBScript and JScript with MSIE 3.02. Starting with MSIE 4.0, they have offered a script debugger that will work with ASP scripts as well as client-side scripts.

Like most symbolic debuggers, you can use the Script Debugger to do the following:

- Start and stop the script
- Step through the script, one line at a time

- Set breakpoints, so the script will stop at a specified line
- Examine the values of any expression
- Examine the script's call stack

In addition, the Debugger understands HTML syntax and can show you an outline of your page. The Debugger also understands both VBScript and JScript and uses color codes to show the syntax of your scripts.

The latest pre-release of the Script Debugger understands Java and ActiveX; Microsoft promises that these capabilities will be integrated into a coming release of the Debugger.

ON THE WEB

http://www.microsoft.com/intdev/scriptie/dbgdown-f.htm   You can download a copy of the Script Debugger from Microsoft's site. Learn about the debugger in general at **http:// www.microsoft.com/workshop/prog/scriptIE/default.HTM**.

## CHAPTER 36

Developing With LiveWire Pro

by Michael Morgan and Mark R. Brown

Netscape's LiveWire Pro

Netscape Communications got its start, of course, developing browsers and servers. As a company, Netscape has as much experience as anybody in using its own products to develop Web sites. In 1995, as it began to extend its line of servers, Netscape also decided to develop application development tools. These tools are now marketed under the name LiveWire.

The very use of the term *application development* as it applies to the Web recognizes Netscape's observation that the static HTML files of older Web sites are now insufficient to sustain the growth of the Web. More and more developers were moving to the Common Gateway Interface (CGI) to enable them to add capabilities to their sites, but the complexity of CGI and the talent required to develop a new script limited the number of sites that could take advantage of this technology.

Netscape's current direction enables Webmasters who do not have extensive programming skills to reuse components built into Java and to integrate applications with JavaScript. LiveWire Pro includes the tools that enable you to integrate a database that understands the Structured Query Language, or SQL (pronounced see-quel) into their Web sites.

The "Pro" in LiveWire Pro

Increasingly, the intranet marketplace is shaping up to a battle between Netscape Communications and Microsoft Corporation. Microsoft has nearly two decades of experience marketing personal computer applications. Bill Gates has succeeded in building an impressive group of analysts, programmers, and managers who can quickly produce and maintain software products. Microsoft's Windows 95 is particularly strong among corporate users and thus is commonly used on intranets. By offering its second generation servers and LiveWire on both UNIX and Windows NT, Netscape has ensured that a corporation's choice of server machine will not prevent you from choosing a Netscape solution.

Netscape Communications, by contrast, was founded in 1994 and has a fraction of the resources of Microsoft. Unlike Microsoft, however, Netscape was born for the Net; its understanding of what works on the Net, and specifically on the Web, is its greatest asset.

During the explosive growth years of personal computers, Microsoft and others made money selling interpreters for the computer language BASIC—enabling millions of people who were not professional programmers to write applications. In the battle for intranet market share, both Microsoft and Netscape understand that the winner will be the company that markets the best visual programming environment, enabling Webmasters who are not professional programmers to develop sophisticated applications for the Web.

Microsoft is promoting Visual Basic Script (VBScript) and ActiveX Objects as its entries in this market, whereas Netscape is offering LiveWire Pro, which is bundled as a component of one of Netscape's server software packages, either Enterprise Server Pro 3.0 or SuiteSpot 3.01. The LiveWire Pro package has six components:

■ Netscape Navigator Gold—A Netscape Navigator client with integrated word processing capabilities that enable users to develop and edit live online documents in a WYSIWYG environment.

■ LiveWire Site Manager—A visual tool that enables you to see the entire site at a glance and to manage pages, links, and files using drag and drop.

■ LiveWire JavaScript Compiler—An extension to Netscape servers that enables you to build distributed applications in server-side JavaScript, with some of the functionality remaining on the client computer and some running on the server.

■ Database Connectivity Library—Software programs that provide an Application Programmer Interface (API) between JavaScript and any of several commercial relational databases.

■ Informix-Online Or Oracle7 Workgroup Database—a developer version of either INFORMIX-OnLine Workgroup, the entry-level version of Informix's OnLine Dynamic Server, or a limited-deployment copy of the Oracle7 Workgroup Server.

■ Crystal Reports Professional Version 5.0—a report-design and data-analysis tool for Windows systems is included with the Windows NT version of LiveWire Pro.

Using only the components of LiveWire Pro, you can develop an application that accesses and integrates data in an Informix database and serves it up as dynamic Web pages or as a data stream to a client-based application.

N O T E   More information about Crystal Reports is available online at **http://www.crystalinc.com/crystalreports**. ■

N O T E   LiveWire Pro includes support for database managers from Informix, Oracle, and Sybase, as well as support for the Microsoft open database connectivity (ODBC) standard. Through ODBC, a LiveWire application can access databases built using dBase, Visual FoxPro, and even such "standards" as text files.

LiveWire Pro implements its interface to the Informix, Oracle, and Sybase libraries through the vendor's API, rather than through ODBC drivers. Compared to an ODBC-based approached, LiveWire Pro's design facilitates database configuration and provides better performance. ■

LiveWire Pro is available as part of Netscape's *SuiteSpot* package of servers. SuiteSpot consists of the following tools:

■ Enterprise Server—Netscape's high-end Web server.

■ Catalog Server—A search tool that you can use to build and maintain databases of all the resources on a site.

■ Proxy Server—A tool for maintaining copies of frequently used files on a local machine.

■ Mail Server—A tool that supports the Simple Mail Transfer Protocol (SMTP) for server-to-server communications, and the Post Office Protocol (POP) for communications with mail clients.

■ LiveWire Pro—The application-development and database-connectivity tool described in this chapter.

Figure 36.1 shows the SuiteSpot architecture.

FIG. 36.1

SuiteSpot insulates you from the differences between various operating systems and hardware.

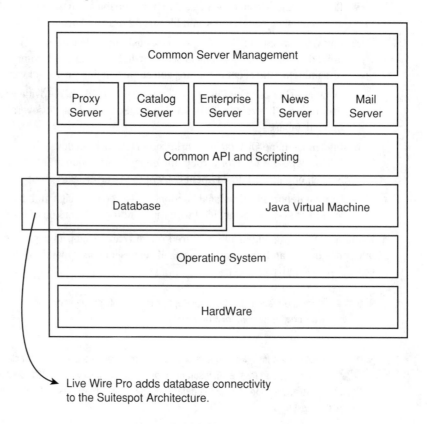

Live Wire Pro adds database connectivity to the Suitespot Architecture.

Netscape's pricing is structured so that SuiteSpot costs the same as the four servers (Enterprise, Catalog, Proxy, and Mail). If you're going to buy the four servers anyway, buy SuiteSpot and get LiveWire Pro for free. For more information, go to **http://home.netscape.com/comprod/server_central/ product/suite_spot/index.html**.

How LiveWire Works

Although you can build LiveWire applications without understanding how LiveWire works, such an understanding not only helps during the debugging process but also leads to a more efficient distribution of the work between the various computers available.

As you know, users access a Web site through their *Web browser,* for example, as Netscape Navigator. This software, known as the *client,* asks the Web server for entities such as HTML pages. The address for each such entity is a *Uniform Resource Locator*, or URL. The protocol by which requests are made and answered is the *HyperText Transfer Protocol,* or HTTP.

Most Webmasters also know that, in addition to offering static pages of HTML (which the browser renders into Web pages), they can write programs that run on the server. These programs follow the CGI protocol, which enables them to get information from the user and process it in ways that go well beyond the capabilities of HTTP. A CGI script typically finishes by returning some HTML to the client so the user sees a new page.

A Brief HTTP Tutorial

Most HTTP requests ask the server to send a specific entity (typically an HTML page) to the client. These requests contain the keyword GET. If the server is properly configured, some URLs can point to programs that are run (instead of being sent back to the client) and the output of the program is returned. Such URLs correspond to CGI scripts that are accessed using the GET method.

Other CGI scripts require more input, such as the output of an HTML form. Such scripts are written to use a different method, called POST. When the server recognizes a POST request, it starts the CGI script and then passes the data stream coming in from the client to the "standard input" file handle (also known as STDIN) of the CGI script.

CGI is a useful general-purpose mechanism—many sites use CGI successfully to e-mail the results of an HTML form to the site owner, search the site for key information requested by the user, or even query a database. However, Netscape is offering alternatives to CGI for many reasons:

- Every time a CGI program is activated, it starts, runs, and exits. The process of starting, called *forking* on many operating systems, is computationally expensive. If the CGI script is busy, the server can spend much of its time forking the same script over and over.

- Communication between the server and the CGI script is limited to streams of data in STDIN or perhaps a few characters in environment variables. The CGI script cannot ask the server any questions, so the server has to package up everything that any script might want to know and store it for every script.

- CGI scripts are generally written in Perl, Tcl, or even C and C++—general-purpose languages that have no built-in mechanisms for dealing with the CGI protocol. Many Webmasters are not comfortable writing the code necessary to implement CGI in such a language.

- CGI scripts directly call the features of the operating system, so they are not particularly portable between UNIX and Windows NT servers.

- Infiltrators can use CGI scripts to compromise the security of a site. Although you can "harden" a CGI script to make it resistant to most of these attacks, many Webmasters are not aware of these techniques or choose not to use them. Consequently, some system administrators either do not allow CGI scripts on their machines or insist on inspecting the script before it is installed. These restrictions add cost and delay to the maintenance of the site and may rule out CGI enhancements altogether.

■ CGI scripts, by definition, are run on the server, but many functions (such as validating the input of a form) require less bandwidth and return results faster if they are run on the client's machine.

You can add CGI or Netscape's server-side alternative, LiveWire, to a corporate intranet server, just as you might add CGI or LiveWire to an Internet server. CGI scripts require special configuration of the server. The LiveWire application must be installed using the Application Manager.

 T I P Even in the relatively benign environment of an intranet, do not ignore the security concerns about CGI. Many scripts provide access to critical corporate resources and should be hardened against infiltrators from *inside* the company.

What Options Does Netscape Offer?

Netscape offers two kinds of choices to Webmasters who want to extend a site beyond the capabilities of HTTP:

■ Choice of language in which to write the application

■ Choice of machine on which to run the application

Webmasters using the high-end Enterprise server can serve applications (called *applets*) written in Java, an object-oriented language developed specifically for the Web by Sun Microsystems. They can also write programs in JavaScript, a simplified language loosely based on Java. JavaScript is designed to be embedded in an HTML file and run on the client machine. The Netscape browser understands JavaScript and can execute these programs.

Java applets are stored on the server but are downloaded and run on the client machine. JavaScript scripts are usually run on the client. If LiveWire is installed on the server, Java applets can be compiled and run on that machine as well.

N O T E Although client-side JavaScript and server-side JavaScript (that is, LiveWire applications) use the same language, LiveWire provides several runtime objects on the server that are crucial in building a LiveWire application. The section "Server-Side JavaScript" later in this chapter describes these objects in more detail. ■

A programmer can also write an application for a specific platform (such as a Windows computer or a Macintosh) that integrates with the Netscape browser. These applications, called *plug-ins,* are activated when the server sends a specific MIME media type that the plug-in is designed to handle. Plug-ins are usually written in C++.

The predecessors of plug-ins, called *helper applications*, are available on all browsers, whereas plug-ins work on just a few browsers other than Netscape Navigator. Helper applications open a separate window and run as a separate process; plug-ins are integrated into the client and can send messages back and forth to the Netscape browser. This tight integration allows programmers to do more with plug-ins than they can with helper applications.

Figure 36.2 illustrates the variety of options available to the programmer in a Netscape environment.

FIG. 36.2

If the site uses Netscape servers and the user runs Netscape Navigator, you have many choices of where to place programs.

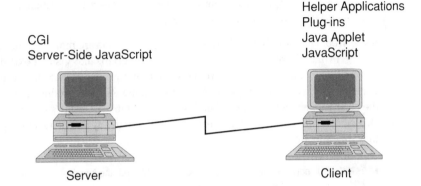

CGI
Server-Side JavaScript

Helper Applications
Plug-ins
Java Applet
JavaScript

Server

Client

N O T E JavaScript was once called "LiveScript." That name still appears in some literature, and the JavaScript compilers and interpreters still support it. Only the name has changed—the language remains the same. ■

Many people, particularly those who are not professional programmers, say that programming in JavaScript is easier than programming in Java. Using LiveWire, you can embed JavaScript on a page but have it run on the server. Then the results of that script are sent to the client software.

What Does LiveWire Do with a Request?

To understand the role LiveWire plays, you must first understand how LiveWire handles JavaScript on the server. The LiveWire Server Extension Engine includes a script compiler for JavaScript. When a developer finishes writing a page that includes server-side JavaScript, he or she submits it to the compiler. The compiler attaches the compiled image (a set of bytecodes) to the page.

Recall that a Web server usually handles a GET request by finding the requested entity and sending it back to the client. When LiveWire is installed on a Netscape server, an extra step is inserted in this process. LiveWire registers an interest in certain URLs, and when one of those URLs is requested, the server turns control over to the JavaScript runtime interpreter in the LiveWire Server Extensions. That interpreter runs the code that bytecodes attached to the page represent. The finished result, which includes both static HTML and dynamic program output, goes back to the client.

N O T E Netscape likes to use the term *live* in its literature. As Netscape uses the term, it is a synonym for *dynamic* as that term is used by most Webmasters. Thus *live online document* and *dynamic Web page* mean the same thing. ■

Understanding SQL

Recall that the single difference between LiveWire and LiveWire Pro is that LiveWire Pro provides access to relational databases. This section describes relational database management systems (RDBMSs) and their language, SQL.

Some Webmasters with a background in PC applications are more comfortable with database managers like dBase than they are with newer programs like Visual FoxPro or Microsoft SQL Server. Many of the newer or more powerful programs use SQL. SQL was one of the languages that emerged from early work on RDBMSs. Among RDBMS products, SQL has emerged as the clear winner. Nonrelational databases such as Object Design's object-oriented database, ObjectStore, often offer a SQL interface in addition to any native data manipulation language they may support.

N O T E SQL began as an IBM language, but by 1988 both the American National Standards Institute (ANSI) and the International Organization for Standardization (ISO) had standardized the language as ISO-ANSI SQL. The 1988 ISO-ANSI standard described a well-defined language, but no commercial implementation exactly matched the standard. For example, the 1988 standard did not provide a mechanism for creating or dropping indexes—a feature that every commercial implementation requires.

The 1989 version of the ANSI-ISO standard was more complete but still not rich enough for commercial vendors. Netscape recommends that LiveWire Pro developers use the query format from the 1989 standard. Most commercial vendors now support the 1989 standard.

The 1992 ANSI standard is much richer than the previous versions. Its page count is four times that of the 1989 standard—building a commercial implementation is a serious undertaking. To help bridge the gap, ANSI has declared the 1989 standard as the ANSI 92 Entry Level standard (often called ANSI 92-compliant SQL in marketing material). The U.S. National Institute of Standards and Technology (NIST) has certified most database vendors to be compliant to the ANSI 92 Entry Level. ■

The Relational Model

Most industrial-strength database managers use the *relational model* of data. The relational model is characterized by one or more "relations," more commonly known as *tables*, as illustrated in Figure 36.3. LiveWire provides direct access to tables through the Database Connectivity Library.

In a well-defined database, each table represents a single concept. For example, a book wholesaler might need to model the concept of a book. Each row holds one record—information about a single title. The columns represent the fields of the record—things that the application needs to know about the book, such as the title, the publication year, and the retail price. Every table must have some combination of columns (typically just one) that uniquely identifies each row; this set of columns is called the *primary key*. For the book table, this column could be the book's ISBN.

FIG. 36.3

A single table is defined by its columns and keys; the table holds the data in rows.

ISBN	Title	Publication Year	Retail Price	Publisher ID
0-7897-0801-9	Webmaster Expert Solutions	1996	59.99	7897
1-57521-070-3	Creating Web Applets with Java	1996	39.99	57521
0-7897-0790-X	Enhancing Webscape Web Pages	1996	34.99	7897
1-56205-473-2	Webmasters' Professional Reference	1996	55.00	56205
1-57576-354-0	An Interactive Guide to the Internet	1996	75.00	57576
1-57521-016-9	Bots & Other Internet Beasties	1996	49.99	57521
1-56205-573-9	Building Internet Database Servers/CGI	1996	45.00	56205
1-57521-049-5	Java Unleashed	1996	49.99	57521
0-7897-0758-6	Special Edition Using HTML, Second Edition	1996	49.99	7897
0-7897-0604-0	Special Edition Using Java	1996	49.99	7897
1-57521-073-8	Teach Yourself JavaScript in a Week	1996	39.99	57521
0-7897-0753-5	The Big Basic Book of the Internet	1996	19.99	7897
1-56205-521-6	Flying Through the Web: VRML	1996	30.00	56205

Each table may also contain "pointers"—called *foreign keys*—to other tables by storing the primary key from the other table in its own columns. For example, in Figure 36.4 each book is associated with a publisher by storing the publisher's key in the book record. In the book table the publisher ID is a foreign key. In the publisher table the publisher ID is the primary key.

FIG. 36.4

A foreign key links two relations.

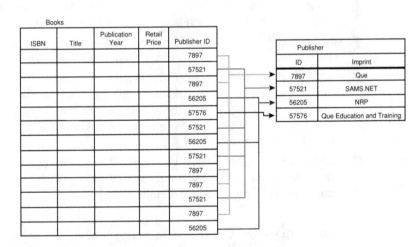

Database design is a specialty area in computer science. If you are setting up a new database and do not have experience in database design, consider hiring a specialist to help. Relational databases are pulled in two competing directions. If redundancy exists between the tables, the tables may become inconsistent. For example, if the books table included the address of the publisher as well as the publisher ID, the application could update the publisher's address in the publisher table but fail to update the address in the book table.

An easy way to ensure consistency is to divide a database into many small tables, thereby avoiding redundancy. But if the database is large, a design with many small tables may require many queries to search through tables looking for foreign keys. Large databases with little or no redundancy can be inefficient both in terms of space and performance.

Database designers talk about five levels of *normalization*—standards to ensure database consistency. The normal forms are hierarchical; a database in third normal form satisfies the guidelines for first, second, and third normal forms. Here are the guidelines that define the five normal forms:

- First normal form—Each row-column intersection must have one and only one value. For example, a database in which all of the books published by a given publisher in 1996 are stored in a single row-column intersection violates the rule for first normal form.

- Second normal form—Every nonkey column must depend on the entire primary key. If the primary key is *composite*—made up of more than one component—no nonkey column can be a fact about a subset of the primary key. A practical way to achieve second normal form is to require each primary key span to be just one column.

  For example, an ISBN is a number that uniquely identifies a book. (There's one on the back cover of this book.) The ISBN contains several internal fields, including one for the publisher and one for the individual book title. If a table included the ISBN as a composite primary key (for example, one column for the publisher ID and another for the book ID), and the table also included a column PublisherAddress, which depended on the publisher ID *only*, that table would violate second normal form.

- Third normal form—A nonkey column can depend on another nonkey field. Each column must be a fact about the entity identified by the primary key.

- Fourth normal form—Independent one-to-many relationships between primary key columns and non-key columns cannot occur. For example, a table like the one shown in Table 36.1 would violate the fourth normal form rule because Cities Toured and Children are independent facts. An author who has no children and has toured no cities could have a blank row.

- Fifth normal form—Break tables into the smallest possible pieces to eliminate all redundancy within a table. In extreme cases tables in fifth normal form may consist of a primary key and a single nonkey column.

Table 36.1 Numerous Blanks Characterize Tables That are Not in Fourth Normal Form

Author	Children	Cities Toured
Brady	Greg	Seattle
Brady	Cindy	Los Angeles
Brady	Bobby	
Clinton	Chelsea	Washington
Clinton		Los Angeles
Clinton		St. Louis

Databases should not be indiscriminately put into fifth normal form. Such databases are likely to have high integrity, but they may take up too much space on the disk (because many tables will have many foreign keys). They are also likely to have poor performance because even simple queries require searches (called *joins*) across many tables. The best design is a trade-off between consistency and efficiency.

An empty row-column intersection is called a *null*. The specification of each table shows which columns are allowed to have null values.

A SQL Primer

A typical life cycle of a database proceeds like this:

1. The database is created with the SQL CREATE DATABASE command:

   ```
   CREATE DATABASE bookWholesale
   ```

2. Tables are created with the CREATE TABLE command:

   ```
   CREATE TABLE books
   (isbn char(10) not null,
   title char(20) not null,
   publicationYear datetime null,
   retailPrice money null))
   ```

3. One or more indexes is created:

   ```
   CREATE INDEX booksByYear ON books (publicationYear)
   ```

   Many RDBMSs support *clustered* indexes. In a clustered index the data is physically stored on the disk sorted in accordance with the index. A clustered index incurs some overhead when items are added or removed but can give exceptional performance if the number of reads is large compared to the number of updates. Because a disk has only one physical arrangement, the maximum number of clustered indexes on each table is one.

   SQL also supports the UNIQUE keyword, in which the RDBMS enforces a rule that says that no two rows can have the same index value.

4. Data is inserted into the tables:

   ```
   INSERT INTO books VALUES ('0789708019', 'Webmasters Expert Solutions', 1996,
   69.95)
   ```

   Depending on the application, new rows may be inserted often, or the database, once set up, may stay fairly stable.

5. Queries are run against the database:

   ```
   SELECT title, publicationYear WHERE retailPrice < 40.00
   ```

   For most applications, queries are the principal reason for the existence of the application.

6. Data may be changed:

   ```
   UPDATE books
   SET retailPrice = 59.95
   WHERE ISBN='0789708019'
   ```

7. Data may be deleted from the tables:

```
DELETE FROM books
WHERE publicationYear < 1990
```

8. The tables and even the database itself may be deleted when you no longer have a need for them.

```
DROP TABLE books
DROP DATABASE bookWholesale
```

If the number of queries is high compared to the number of inserts, deletes, and updates, indexes are likely to improve performance. As the rate at which database changes climb, the overhead of maintaining the indexes begins to dominate the application.

When a table is created, the designer specifies the data type of each column. All RDBMSs provide character and integer types. Most commercial RDBMSs also support multiple character types; floating-point (also known as decimal type); money; various date and time types; and even special binary types for storing sounds, images, and other large binary objects.

The Database Connectivity Library of LiveWire provides mappings from a vendor-neutral set of data types to the vendor-specific data types of the RDBMS.

Understanding Transactions

In many applications, the user needs a way to group several commands into a single unit of work. This unit is called a *transaction*. This example shows why transactions are necessary:

1. Suppose you call the airline and ask for a ticket to Honolulu. The ticket agent queries the database, looking for available seats, and finds one on tonight's flight. It's the last available seat. You take a minute to decide whether you want to leave so soon.

2. While you are thinking, another customer calls the airline, asks the same question, and gets the same answer. Now two customers have been offered the same seat.

3. You make your decision—you'll fly tonight. Your ticket agent updates the database to reflect the fact that the last seat has been sold.

4. The other customer now decides to take the seat. That ticket agent updates the database, selling the ticket to the other customer. The record showing that the seat was sold to you is overwritten and lost.

5. You arrive at the airport and find that no one has ever heard of you. The other customer is flying in your seat.

This sequence is a classic database problem, called the *lost update*. A skilled SQL programmer would solve the lost-update problem by beginning a transaction before processing the query. The database gives the ticket agent a "read lock" on the data, but the ticket agent cannot update the database with only a read lock. When the ticket agent starts to sell the seat, the application requests an exclusive write lock. As long as that agent has the write lock, no one else can read or write that data. After the agent gets the write lock, the application queries the database to verify that the seat is still available. If the seat is open, the application updates the database, marking the seat as sold. Then the transaction ends, committing the changes to the database. Here's what the lost-update scenario looks like when transactions are used:

1. You call the airline and ask for a ticket to Honolulu. The ticket agent gets a read lock and queries the database, looking for available seats. One is available on tonight's flight. It's the last available seat. You take a minute to decide whether you want to leave so soon.

2. While you are thinking, another customer calls the airline, asks the same question, and gets the same answer. Now two customers have been offered the same seat.

3. You make your decision—you'll fly tonight. Your ticket agent gets an exclusive write lock on the data, rereads the database to verify that the seat is still available, updates the database, and releases the lock.

4. The other customer now decides to take the seat. That ticket agent gets a write lock and reruns the query. The database reports that the seat is no longer available. The ticket agent informs the customer, and they work to find a different seat for that customer.

5. You arrive at the airport and take your seat on the airplane. Aloha.

Transactions are also useful in system recovery. Because writing to the hard drive, often over a network, is time-consuming, many database implementations store updates in local buffers for a while. If the system fails before the RDBMS can actually update the database, the system could lose some of those updates. The solution used in most commercial products is to write a record of every change to the database in a special place on the hard drive called the *transaction log*. If a failure occurs before the update is actually made in the database, the transaction log can be replayed during recovery to complete the update.

Understanding Cursors

Webmasters whose experience is mostly with PC-based database engines are used to queries that return a single record. For example, dBase III had the concept of a *pointer*. The programmer could say

```
GOTO 3
DISPLAY
```

and dBase would return all of the fields of the third record. The programmer could next enter

```
DISPLAY NEXT 1
```

and the program would advance the pointer and display record 4.

Many SQL programmers find this single-record notation a bit awkward. In SQL, you are more likely to say

```
SELECT * WHERE publicationYear = 1996
```

This query may return zero, one, or many records. Even if the programmer "knows" that exactly one record will be returned, such as a query on the key field like

```
SELECT * WHERE ISBN='0789708019'
```

the nature of the language is such that the program still "thinks" it got back a set of records.

Many commercial SQL implementations support the concept of a *cursor*. A cursor is like the dBase pointer—it indicates one record at a time and can be moved back and forth across a set of records. LiveWire Pro supports a cursor-based construct to retrieve data. To set up a cursor, you say

```
myCursor = database.cursor (selectStatement, updateFlag);
```

where *selectStatement* is an ANSI 89-compliant SQL SELECT statement and *updateFlag* (which takes on values TRUE and FALSE) controls whether the particular cursor can update the database.

N O T E In the object-oriented language C++, an object's methods are accessed using dot notation. If the programmer has allocated a new aircraft object and wants it to climb to 10,000 feet, she or he might say

```
theAircraft.climb(10000);
```

The more common C++ technique is to have a variable hold the address of the aircraft object. Such a variable is called a *pointer* (no relation to the pointers in dBase). To call an object's method through a pointer, the programmer uses an arrow notation, like this:

```
theAircraftPointer->climb(10000);
```

Pointers (in the C and C++ sense) are powerful tools, but direct access memory locations opens a security risk that the designers of Java and JavaScript were not willing to take. Unlike C++, Java and JavaScript allocate new objects, not pointers to objects, so the programmer uses the dot notation rather than the arrow notation. ▪

After the cursor exists, the programmer can move it around the rows that the SELECT statement retrieved. For example,

```
myCursor.next()
```

loads the cursor with the next retrieved row.

Introduction to Crystal Reports

Many Webmasters find the day-to-day task of building ad hoc SQL queries time-consuming and even a bit daunting. However, if you run LiveWire on a Windows NT server, you can use Crystal Reports, bundled with LiveWire Pro, to prepare ad hoc queries. Crystal Reports has five major benefits:

- Multiple-detail section reports and subreports—A single report can contain multiple sections. Alternatively, the developer can write complete stand-alone reports and then embed them as subreports in a master document.

- Conditional reports—Sections of a multiple-detail section report, or text objects, may be set to vary according to data conditions. For example, a customer record might have a language flag, enabling the user to print a report in either English or Spanish.

- Distribution of reports over the Web—Reports can go out over the Web by exporting the report to HTML.

- Form-style reports—Text and objects may be placed on the page with the help of grids, guidelines, and rulers.
- Cross-tab reports—Reports can present summary information in a concise two-dimensional format.

The latest version of Crystal Reports treats all fields, texts, and other elements as objects, which the user can place graphically on the page in the Crystal Reports Report Designer application.

The Database Connectivity Library

The section entitled "A SQL Primer" earlier in this chapter showed the typical sequence of events in the life cycle of a database. Most Web sites that are integrated with databases enable Web users to query the database and possibly to insert or delete data. Seldom would you add or drop tables or indexes or create or delete databases.

On those occasions when the built-in API is not powerful enough to handle the application, the programmer can use *passthrough SQL*—a mechanism for sending any SQL to the target database. For example, the programmer could use

```
database.execute ("CREATE TABLE books
   (isbn char(10) not null,
   title char(20) not null,
   publicationYear datetime null,
   retailPrice money null)");
```

> **CAUTION**
>
> As its name implies, passthrough SQL does not attempt to interpret the SQL—it sends it straight to the target RDBMS. This approach might require the programmer to write slightly different code, depending on whether the site has Informix, Oracle, Sybase, or one of the other supported databases installed.
>
> Passthrough SQL is useful for building new databases, but it cannot bypass the cursor mechanism and return rows as a set. When retrieving data, the built-in cursor mechanism should be used, rather than a native call via passthrough SQL.

Opening and Closing the Connection

Recall that CGI scripts are started (forked) for every HTTP request. This process is computationally expensive. Unlike CGI scripts, LiveWire applications remain running until you explicitly shut them down. A side benefit to this design approach is that a LiveWire Pro application can open a connection to the database when it is started and leave that connection open almost forever.

One of the first things a LiveWire Pro application usually does when it is installed is open a connection to the database. The syntax is

```
database.connect(dbType, servername, username, password, databaseName);
```

where *dbType* is one of the following databases:

- ORACLE
- SYBASE
- INFORMIX
- ILLUSTRA
- ODBC

and *servername*, *username*, *password*, and *databaseName* are the usual pieces of information needed to access a database.

Other requests to this application—whether from the same client but for different pages or from other clients—use the same connection to the database. Figure 36.5 shows several applications and clients interacting with databases. Not having to relaunch the application for each request improves performance on subsequent requests to the application.

FIG. 36.5
When the system reaches steady state, you don't waste any time starting applications or establishing database connections.

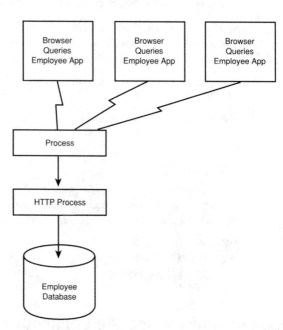

An application can test its connection with the connected() method. The following code shows how to start a connection and verify that the database was found and the login was successful:

```
database.connect (INFORMIX, theServer, mmorgan, mySecretWord, demoDB);
if (!database.connected())
  write("Error in connecting to database.");
else
  .
  .
  .
```

The system stores information about the connections between applications and databases on the server in shared memory. Over time, the connection spreads to the various copies of the Netscape Server process. Figure 36.6 illustrates this mechanism, which is known as *diffusion*. At any time the programmer can have the application disconnect from the database—this step causes all copies of the server to disconnect from the database. You might call for a disconnect for two reasons:

- An application can have only one connection open at a time, and you may want to switch the application to a different database.
- RDBMSs are usually licensed for some maximum number of concurrent connections. Disconnecting an application that no longer needs a connection frees that connection for use by another application.

FIG. 36.6

Database connections spread throughout the server until every server process is connected to the database.

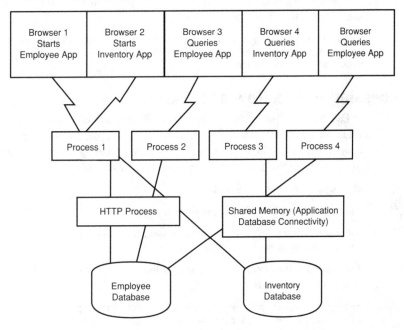

Diffusion of Database Connections

Whatever the reason for calling for disconnection, it is easy to do. The call

```
database.disconnect();
```

disconnects all application processes from the database.

 TIP The copy of the Informix RDBMS bundled with LiveWire Pro is limited to a single connection. Although this database engine is entirely satisfactory for development, most Webmasters prefer to license a database with more connections for live use.

Inserting Data into Tables

All updates must be done through updatable cursors. Here's a fragment of JavaScript that makes a new, updatable cursor and inserts a new row.

```
myCursor = database.cursor("SELECT isbn, title, publicationYear, retailPrice
 FROM books", TRUE);
myCursor.isbn= "078970255x9";
myCursor.title = "Running a Perfect Netscape Site";
myCursor.publicationYear = 1996;
myCursor.retailPrice = 49.99;
myCursor.insertRow (books);
```

Deleting Rows

Deleting rows is easy. Start with an updatable cursor and point it to the row to be deleted. Now call the cursor's deleteRow method. For example, to delete a row that corresponds to a discontinued book, the programmer might write

```
myCursor = database.cursor ("SELECT * FROM books WHERE isbn =
 request.discontinuedBookISBN", TRUE);
myCursor.deleteRow(books);
```

Accessing Data a Row at a Time

In LiveWire Pro you can use cursors to make data available one row at a time and to get to the value stored at a row-column intersection. For example, the bookWholesale database has a table called books; the books table has a column called retailPrice. Given a cursor that points to some row of that table, the programmer could write

```
thePrice = myCursor.retailPrice;
```

Cursors can also be set up to provide an implicit sort order:

```
myCursor = database.cursor(SELECT MAX(retailPrice) FROM books);
mostExpensiveBook = myCursor[0];
```

The names of the columns in the SELECT list can be accessed by an index. For example, the programmer can write

```
myCursor = database.cursor( SELECT * FROM books);
firstColumnName = myCursor.columnName(0);
secondColumnName = myCursor.columnName(1);
```

Updatable cursors can be used to insert and delete records or to change the fields of a record. For example, to set a new price for a book in the books table, the programmer could write

```
myCursor = database.cursor ("SELECT * FROM books WHERE isbn =
 '0789708019',updatable);
myCursor.retailPrice = 59.95;
myCursor.updateRow(books);
```

Accessing Data as a Set

Sometimes the programmer needs to show all the data in a table as a list. The programmer could make a cursor and loop through all the rows in the retrieved data. As a convenience, however, LiveWire Pro offers the SQLTable function.

When the programmer calls

```
database.SQLTable(selectStatement);
```

the Database Connectivity Library displays the result of the SELECT statement in an HTML table, along with column names in the header.

Often the application design calls for a list of records like the one shown in Figure 36.7, with each record being hyperlinked to a more detailed single-record page such as the one in Figure 36.8. Because cursors cannot span HTML pages of an application, the best way to satisfy this requirement is to build one cursor on the list page to select all the relevant records and format each field into HTML. The single-record page would take a primary key and use it to make a new cursor, whose select statement looks up all of the fields of the record associated with that key.

FIG. 36.7

The designer intends for the user to choose a record from this list.

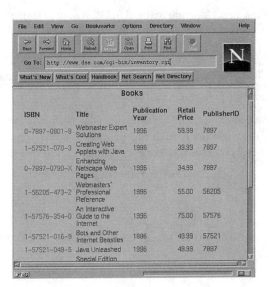

Using BLObs

In the content-oriented applications characteristic of the Web, you often want to store images, software, or audio or video clips in the database. A new database type, called the *Binary Large Object (BLOb)*, was introduced into SQL by commercial vendors to meet these kinds of needs. For example, suppose the book wholesaler wants to store an image of the cover of the book in the database. The general syntax for retrieving an image from a BLOb and outputting it with an HTML image tag is

```
myCursor.blobFieldName.blobImage (imageFormat, ALTstring, ALIGNstring, ISMAP);
```

FIG. 36.8

Each selection on the list brings the user to a single-record page like this one.

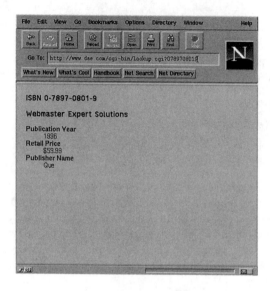

ISBN 0-7897-0801-9

Webmaster Expert Solutions

Publication Year
1996
Retail Price
$59.99
Publisher Name
Que

`ALTstring`, `ALIGNstring`, and `ISMAP` are optional fields. If they are supplied, they are used in the HTML image tag. Thus the programmer of the bookWholesale application could say

```
myCursor.cover.blobImage("gif", "The cover of the book", "Left", ISMAP);
```

BLObs can be hyperlinked so they are read by helper applications and plug-ins, like this:

```
blobFieldName.blobLink(mimeType, linkText);
```

This construct is most commonly used with large BLObs, such as an audio clip. The Netscape server keeps the BLOb in memory until the user clicks on another link or until a 60-second timer runs out, whichever comes first. Here's an example of how to send a BLOb to the client:

```
myCursor = database.cursor ("SELECT * FROM blobbedBooks");
while (myCursor.next())
{
  write (myCursor.isbn);
  write (myCursor.cover.blobImage("gif"));
  write (myCursor.authorReading.blobLink("audio/x-wav", "Selected highlights
  from" + myCursor.title);
  write ("<BR>");
}
```

This code puts up the GIF of the book cover. When the link is selected, the client downloads and plays the audio selection—a few seconds of the author naming the highlights of the book.

BLObs are inserted into records in much the same way as other data is inserted. For example:

```
myCursor = database.cursor("SELECT * FROM blobbedBooks, TRUE);
myCursor.isbn="X0789708019";
myCursor.cover = blob("CoverOfWebmasters.gif");
myCursor.insertRow("blobbedBooks");
```

Transactions in LiveWire Pro

Three database methods support transaction control:

- ▪ beginTransaction()
- ▪ commitTransaction()
- ▪ rollbackTransaction()

These three constructs can be used to build code like this:

```
database.BeginTransaction();
int db_error = 0;
dbError = database.execute ("INSERT INTO books(isbn, title) VALUES (request.isbn,
request.title);
if (!dbError)
{
dbError = database.execute ("INSERT INTO authors VALUES (request.isbn,
request.author1));
if (dbError)
  database.rollbackTransaction();
else
  database.commitTransaction();
}
else
// Error occurred while processing book itself
database.rollbackTransaction();
```

Error Handling

LiveWire Pro provides a degree of insulation between the programmer and the RDBMS. However, if something goes wrong, most programmers want to get the most specific error messages available—the ones generated by the RDBMS. To satisfy this need, the Database Connectivity Library returns two different levels of error message.

Every API call returns an error code. The programmer can test the return code—if it is false, no error occurred. TRUE returns codes that indicate the type of error (for example, server error, library error, lost connection, no memory).

If the error comes from the server or the library, the programmer can call four functions to get more specific information:

- ▪ database.majorErrorCode returns the SQL error code.
- ▪ database.majorErrorMessage returns the text message that corresponds to the major error code.
- ▪ database.minorErrorCode returns any secondary code sent by the RDBMS vendor's library, such as a severity level.
- ▪ database.minorErrorMessage returns any secondary message returned by the vendor library.

When the programmer is running the JavaScript `trace` utility, all error codes and messages are displayed.

JavaScript and the Second-Generation Netscape Servers

Java and JavaScript play a key role in the new FastTrack and Enterprise servers, and even in the non-HTTP servers like Mail, News, Catalog, and Proxy. Each server implements a virtual Java machine and understands JavaScript. Furthermore, each server has hooks into the Database Connectivity Library. Consequently, a programmer can tell the server to store information about itself and its work in a database and can then serve that information to the Net via LiveWire Pro.

Understanding Java and JavaScript

Java is a Web-oriented language. Like traditional languages such as C and C++, it must be compiled before the program will run. Like C++, it is object-oriented. The programmer builds objects at runtime based on object descriptions written by the programmer or inherited from the language's class libraries.

Unlike traditional languages, Java is not compiled into the target machine's native instruction set. It is instead compiled into hardware-independent bytecodes. Netscape implements an interpreter for these bytecodes in its products (for example, Netscape Navigator).

When the programmer completes an application (called an *applet*), HTML page designers can embed the applet in their pages. At runtime the applet is downloaded and executed and runs on the server.

JavaScript is an interpreted language loosely based on Java. JavaScript programs are stored in source form in the HTML page. At runtime the page, with its JavaScript, is downloaded to the Netscape client, and the JavaScript is interpreted and run.

Server-Side JavaScript

If LiveWire is installed on the server, the programmer can invoke the LiveWire compiler like this:

```
lwcomp [-cvd] -o binaryFile file
```

where `binaryFile` is the name of the output file (which typically has a file suffix of WEB) and `file` is the name of input file. If the input file consists of a mix of HTML and JavaScript, it has a suffix of HTML (or HTM in a DOS/Windows environment). If the input file is pure JavaScript, it has a suffix of JS.

Table 36.2 shows the five command-line options available with the LiveWire compiler.

Table 36.2   The Programmer Uses Command-line Options to Issue Broad Directives to the Compiler

Option	Meaning
-c	Check only; do not generate binary file.
-v	Verbose output; provide details during compilation.
-d	Debug output; the resulting file output shows the generated JavaScript.
-o	*binaryFile* name; give the output file this name.
-h	Help; display this help message.

TIP The -v (verbose) option provides so much useful information that it is almost always worth including. Get in the habit of always calling the compiler with the -v option set.

You can run the resulting binary file under the trace utility (to see each function call and its result codes). In trace, calls to the debug function in the code are activated. Some programmers prefer to insert calls to the write function in their code to check the value of variables or verify the program logic.

When JavaScript is run under LiveWire, the runtime environment creates several objects that are available to the programmer. The request object contains access methods to the components of the HTTP request, including members that, in CGI programming, are passed by environment variables. Examples include request.ip and request.agent. The request object also includes fields for each of a form's fields and from URLs.

The predefined object server contains other members that replace CGI environment variables, such as hostname, host, and port.

LiveWire uses the client object to maintain user state between requests. The application can be written to preserve user choices across requests using Netscape cookies or other state preservation mechanisms. LiveWire offers the method client.expiration(*seconds*) to tell the system to destroy the client after a certain number of seconds of inactivity.

The Virtual Java Machine

In order to provide cross-platform portability, each of the new Netscape servers includes a virtual Java machine in its architecture. Instead of writing CGI for, say, a UNIX machine, and later having to port it to NT, the Netscape design enables you to write just one version of the program—in JavaScript. That program will run on the virtual Java machine regardless of whether the underlying hardware and operating system is UNIX, Windows NT, or Windows 95.

Putting It All Together—a Database Example

This section shows a simple example application using LiveWire Pro. The application is intended to be set up with start.htm (in Listing 36.1) as its initial page and with home.htm (in Listing 36.2) as the default page.

Listing 36.1   *start.htm*—JavaScript connects to the database.

```
<html>
<head>
   <title> Start Book Wholesalers Application </title>
</head>
<body>
<server>
if(!database.connected())
  database.connect("INFORMIX", "myserver",
          "mmorgan", "ASecretWord", "booksDemo")
if (!database.connected())
  write("Error: Unable to connect to database.")
else {
   redirect("home.htm")
}
</server>
</body>
</html>
```

Listing 36.2   *home.htm*—A central point giving the user access to the application's functions.

```
<html>
<head>
   <title>Book Wholesalers Application</title>
   <meta name="GENERATOR" content="Mozilla/2.01Gold (Win32)">
</head>
<body>
<hr>
<h1>Administrative Functions</h1>

<ul>
<li><a href="invent.htm">Show Inventory</a> </li>

<li><a href="addTitle.htm">Add a Title</a></li>

<li><a href="delTitle.htm">Delete a Title</a></li>

<li><a href="sales.htm">Make a Sale </a></li>
</ul>

</body>
</html>
```

Figure 36.9 shows the application's home page.

FIG. 36.9
The Book Wholesalers application enables the merchant to add and delete titles, list the inventory, and sell books.

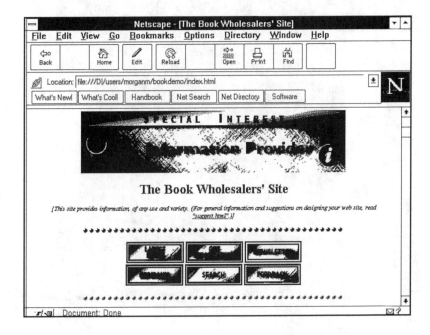

One option given to the user is to list the titles in the database. Listing 36.3 shows how to implement this option. Figure 36.10 shows the result.

Listing 36.3 *invent.htm*—Show the active inventory.

```html
<html>
<head>
   <title> Inventory List </title>
   <meta name="GENERATOR" content="Mozilla/2.01Gold (Win32)">
</head>
<body>
<server>
database.SQLTable("SELECT isbn,title, author,publishers.pubName,quantity On Hand
FROM books, publishers WHERE books.publisherID = publishers.publisherID");
</server>
<p>
<a href="home.htm">Home</a>
</p>
</body>
</html>
```

The user selects the `Addtitle.htm` page, shown in Listing 36.4, and fills out the form to enter a new title. Note that this page builds a `<SELECT>` list on the fly from the database, as shown in Figure 36.11.

FIG. 36.10

The invent.htm page puts up a list of all books in the database.

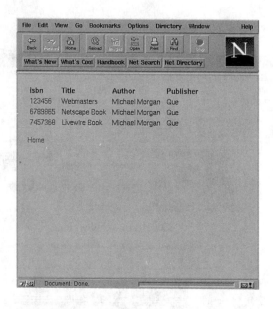

Listing 36.4   *Addtitle.htm*—Add a new title to the inventory.

```html
<html>
<head>
   <title> Add New Title </title>
   <meta name="GENERATOR" content="Mozilla/2.01Gold (Win32)">
</head>
<body>
<h1>Add a New Title</h1>
<p>Note: <b>All</b> fields are required for the new title to be accepted.
<form method="post" action="add.htm"></p>
<br>Title:
<br><input type="text" name="title" size="50">
<br>ISBN:
<br><input type="text" name="isbn" size="10">
<br>Retail Price:
<br><INPUT TYPE="text" name="retailPrice" size="6">
<br>Publisher
<SELECT NAME="publisherID">
<SERVER>
publisherCursor = database.cursor("SELECT id, name FROM publishers ORDER BY
name");
while (publisherCursor.next())
{
   write ("<OPTION Value="+publisherCursor.id+">"+publisherCursor.name);
}
</SERVER>
</SELECT>
<BR>
<input type="submit" value="Enter">
<input type="reset" value="Clear">
```

```
</form>
<p><a href="home.htm">Home</a> </p>
</body>
</html>
```

FIG. 36.11

Addtitle.htm asks the user about the new title.

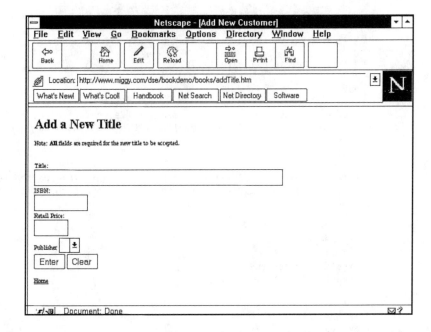

When the user submits `Addtitle.htm`, control passes to `Add.htm` (shown in Listing 36.5), which actually does the insert into the database. Control then returns to `Addtitle.htm`.

Listing 36.5   *Add.htm*—Complete the process of adding a title.

```
<html>
<head>
   <title> Title Added </title>
   <meta name="GENERATOR" content="Mozilla/2.01Gold (Win32)">
</head>
<body>
<server>
 cursor = database.cursor("SELECT * FROM books",TRUE);
 cursor.isbn = request.isbn;
 cursor.title = request.title;
 cursor.retailPrice = request.retailPrice;
 cursor.publisherID = request.publisherID;
 cursor.quantity_on_hand = 0;
cursor.updateRow(books);
   redirect("addTitle.htm")
</server>
</body>
</html>
```

When you follow the link to `Deltitle.htm`, you see a list (generated from the database at runtime) of all the available titles. You click on an ISBN to remove that book from the database. Listing 36.6 shows the page, and Figure 36.12 shows what the user sees.

Listing 36.6   *Deltitle.htm*—The user prepares to delete a title.

```
<html>
<head>
   <title> Delete A Title</title>
</head>
<body>
<server>
cursor = database.cursor("SELECT isbn, title, retailPrice, publishers.name FROM
books, publishers WHERE books.publisherID = publishers.ID ORDER BY isbn");
</server>
<table border>
<caption>
<center><p><b><font SIZE=+1>Titles by ISBN</font></b></p></center>
<center><p><b><font SIZE=+1>Click on ISBN to remove the title</font></b></p></
center>
</caption>
<tr>
<th>ISBN</th>
<th>Title</th>
<th>Retail Price</th>
<th>Publisher</th>
</tr>
<caption>
<center><p>
<server>
while(cursor.next())
{
  write("<TR><TD><A HREF='remove.htm?isbn='"+cursor.isbn+"</A></
  TD><TD>"+cursor.title+
     "</TD><TD>"+cursor.retailPrice+"</TD><TD>"+
     cursor.name+"</TD></TR>");
}
</table>
</body>
</html>
```

The `remove.htm` page actually updates the database. Listing 36.7 shows the code for this page.

Listing 36.7   *Remove.htm*— Remove the title from the database.

```
<html>
<head>
<title> Customer Removal </title>
</head>
<server>
if(request.isbn != null)
{
```

```
    cursor = database.cursor ("SELECT * FROM books WHERE isbn =" +
    request.isbn,TRUE);
    cursor.deleteRow(books)
}
redirect("delTitle.htm");
</server>
</body>
</html>
```

FIG. 36.12

The user selects a title to delete; the list is generated in server-side JavaScript from the database.

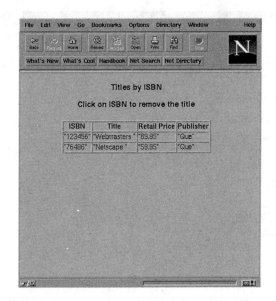

To sell books from inventory, the store employee goes to Sales.htm. Listing 36.8 shows the code for the page, which is displayed in Figure 36.13.

Listing 36.8   *Sales.htm*—Enable the store to sell books.

```
<html>
<head>
    <title> Sell Copies </title>
</head>
<body>
<h1>Sell Copies</h1>
<p>Note: <b>All</b> fields are required for the title to be sold.
<form method="post" action="sell.htm"></p>
<br>ISBN:
<br><input type="text" name="isbn" size="10">
<br>Number of Copies:
<br><INPUT TYPE="text" name="copies" size="6">
<BR>
<input type="submit" value="Enter">
```

continues

Listing 36.8   Continued

```
<input type="reset" value="Clear">
</form>
<p><a href="home.htm">Home</a> </p>
</body>
</html>
```

FIG. 36.13

Use this page to sell books from inventory.

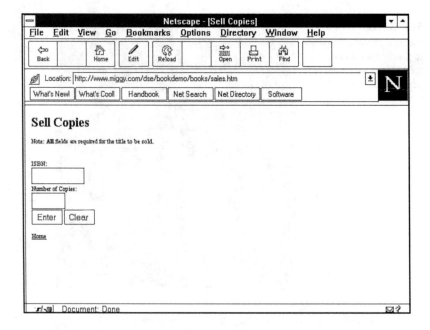

Listing 36.9 shows how to confirm a transaction. Figure 36.14 shows the page.

Listing 36.9   *sell.htm*—Confirm the transaction <HTML>.

```
<HEAD>
<TITLE>Selling Copies</TITLE>
</HEAD>
<BODY>
cursor = database.cursor("SELECT title, isbn, retailPrice,
          publishers.name, quantityOnHand FROM books, publishers
          WHERE isbn=" + request.isbn +" AND
          publishers.ID = books.publisherID");
if (cursor.next())
{
  if (cursor.quantityOnHand > request.quantity)
  {
    write ("<FORM ACTION=sold.htm METHOD=GET>");
    write ("<P>Confirm sale of <STRONG>" + request.copies +
       </STRONG> of<BR>" + cursor.title + "<BR>ISBN " +
```

```
            cursor.isbn + "<BR>Retail Price " +
            cursor.retailPrice + "<BR>Publisher " +
            cursor.name</P>");
        write ("<INPUT TYPE=submit NAME=submit VALUE=Yes>");
        write ("<INPUT TYPE=button NAME=home VALUE=No
            onClick='redirect("home.htm");'>");
        write ("<INPUT TYPE=hidden NAME=isbn VALUE=" +
            request.isbn + ">");
        write ("<INPUT TYPE=hidden NAME=quantity VALUE=" +
            request.quantity + ">");
        write ("</FORM>");
    }
    else
        write ("<P>There are only " + cursor.quantityOnHand +
            " copies on hand.</P>");
}
else
{
    write ("<P>ISBN " + request.isbn + " not on file.</P>");
</BODY>
</HTML>
```

FIG. 36.14

You should confirm
user-initiated changes
in the database.

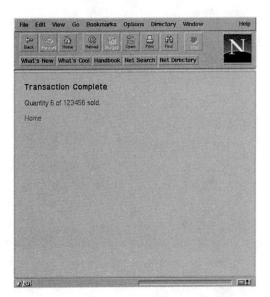

The sold.htm page actually does the database update. Listing 36.10 shows the code.

Listing 36.10   *sold.htm*—**Complete the sale.**

```
<HTML>
<HEAD>
<TITLE>Sold Copies</TITLE>
</HEAD>
<BODY>
<SERVER>
cursor = database.cursor("SELECT * FROM BOOKS WHERE isbn=" + request.isbn,TRUE);

// move onto selected row
cursor.next();
cursor.quantityOnHand = cursor.quantityOnHand - request.quantity;
cursor.updateRow(books);
</SERVER>
<P>
<H1>Transaction Complete</H1>
<P>
<server>
write ("Quantity " + request.quantity + " of " + request.isbn + " sold.");
<server>
</P>
<A HREF="home.htm">Home</A>
</BODY>
</HTML>
```

## CHAPTER 37

Databases

by Melissa Niles

In this chapter

Why Use Databases?

Almost every organization, no matter the organization's size, uses a database for one reason or another. An untold amount of information is stored in a database, whether that information is about people (employment information, personal information, performance issues) or news-making events (bad weather, deaths, birth, marriages, or social events). That information may be your company's inventory of products, how your company is doing in sales, or who your most prominent customers are. Whatever the case, individuals and organizations alike want or need to store information—most of which is kept in some sort of database. Now comes the World Wide Web and, as you can tell, just about every company wants some sort of presence on the Web. You can easily see this by all the www-dot-whatever-dot-coms placed in just about every commercial on television!

If your organization, or the organization you are developing a Web presence for, has information in a database it would like to provide on the World Wide Web, it can be done one of two ways. The first is to simply take a look at the information in the databases and place relevant information in an HTML document. If any of the information changes they not only have to edit the contents of the database, they also have to edit the HTML document.

The second way is to simply develop applications that query the database and generate a document, returning the latest information available. If database information changes, the Web documents automatically reflects those changes.

Databases Available

A multitude of databases can be used with your Web application to provide dynamic information to site visitors. What you end up using depends mostly on what your organization is currently using, or what fits into your organization's budget. This section lists some of the more common database solutions that are widely used on the Web.

Oracle

Oracle is the largest database developer in the world, providing databases for Windows NT and various UNIX flavors. Oracle has created its own set of tools (mainly PL/SQL, in conjunction with the Oracle Web Agent). These tools, coupled with the Oracle Webserver, allow you to create Web pages with little effort using information stored in the database. PL/SQL allows you to form stored procedures that help speed the database query. The Oracle database engine is a good choice for large businesses that handle large amounts of information but, of course, you're going to pay for that. Today's price range for Oracle 7 and the Oracle Web server together is over $5,000.

ON THE WEB

http://www.oracle.com/products/tools/WDS/ Visit Oracle's Web page for more product information and how you can use Oracle with the World Wide Web.

Sybase

Sybase System 11 is a SQL database product that has tools for a dynamic Web page production. A product by Powersoft, the NetImpact Studio, integrates with Sybase to provide a rich set of tools to help anyone create dynamic HTML documents. The NetImpact Studio consists of an HTML browser/editor accompanied by a personal web server. They allow you to create pages using a WYSIWYG interface. The Studio also comes with a Web database, support for JavaScript, and support for connecting to application servers.

NetImpact can be used in conjunction with PowerBuilder, an application used to create plug-ins and ActiveX components. It also can be used to complement Optima++, which is used to create plug-ins and supports Java applet creation.

Sybase can also be used with web.sql to create CGI and NSAPI (Netscape Server Application Programming Interface) applications that access the Sybase database server using Perl. Sybase is available for Windows NT, and UNIX.

ON THE WEB

http://www.sybase.com/   For more information on Sybase, see their Web page.

mSQL

mSQL is a middle-sized SQL database server for UNIX that is much more affordable than the commercial SQL servers available on the market. Written by David Hughes, it was created to allow users to experiment with SQL and SQL databases. Version 1.0.16 is free for non-commercial use, but you have to pay for individual and commercial use. The price is quite fair—about $170. Version 2.0 has just been released with new tools and even more powerful queries.

For additional information on mSQL, along with documentation and a vast array of user-contributed software, see **http://Hughes.com.au/** or **http://AusWeb.com.au/computer/Hughes/**.

Illustra

Illustra, owned by Informix, is the commercial version of the Berkeley's Postgres. Available for both Windows NT and UNIX, Illustra uses an ORDBMS, or Object-Relational Database Management System. By using ORDBMS, queries are performed at very quick speeds. Illustra also uses DataBlade modules that help perform and speed queries. The Web Datablade module version 2.2 allows the incorporation of your data on the Web with reduced effort. For more information see **http://www.informix.com/**, which contains detailed information on Illustra, along with additional information on how you can use Illustra with your Web-based applications.

Microsoft SQL

Microsoft released its own SQL database server as a part of its Windows NT Back Office Suite. Microsoft is trying to compete with Oracle and Sybase. It has released the server for

Part
VI

Ch
37

about $1,000 (at the time of this writing), but you must also buy the SQL Server Internet Connector, which costs about $3,000. These two products allow you to provide unlimited access to the server from the Web.

 For additional information on Microsoft's SQL Server and how you can use Microsoft's SQL Server in conjunction with the World Wide Web, see **http://www.microsoft.com/sql/**.

Postgres95

Postgres95 is a SQL database server developed by the University of California at Berkeley for use on UNIX systems. Older versions of Postgres are also available but no longer supported. The site, at **http://s2k-ftp.CS.Berkeley.EDU:8000/postgres/**, provides additional information about Postgres95, along with the source code, which is available for download.

Ingres

Ingres (Interactive Graphics Retrieval System) comes in both a commercial and public domain version. Berkeley originally developed Ingres to work with graphics in a database environment, but the school no longer supports the public domain version. You can still find it on the university's Web site.

 Ingres uses the QUEL query language as well as SQL. QUEL is a superset of the original SQL, making Ingres even more powerful. The public domain version is available for UNIX systems at **ftp://s2k-ftp.cs.berkeley.edu/pub/ingres/**.

 Computer Associates owns the commercial version of Ingres, called OpenIngres. This version is quite robust and capable of managing virtually any database application. The commercial version is available for UNIX, VMS, and Windows NT. For more information about the commercial version, visit **http://www.cai.com/products/ingr.htm**.

 For more information about both the commercial and public domain versions of Ingres, visit the North American Ingres Users Association at **http://www.naiua.org/**.

FoxPro

Microsoft's Visual FoxPro has been a favorite for Web programmers, mostly because of its long-time standing in the database community, as well as its third-party support. Foxpro is an Xbase database system that is widely used for smaller business and personal database applications. Foxpro is also available for most Windows platforms.

 For more information on FoxPro, see **http://www.microsoft.com/catalog/products/visfoxp/** and visit Neil's Foxpro database page at **http://adams.patriot.net/~johnson/neil/fox.html**.

Microsoft Access

Microsoft Access is a relational database management system that is part of the Microsoft Office suite. Microsoft Access can be used to create HTML documents based on the information stored in the Access database with the help of Microsoft's Internet Assistant or with the use of Microsoft's Active Server Pages (ASP). Microsoft's Internet Assistant is an add-on available free of charge for Access users. Using Microsoft's ASP technology requires the use of MS Information Server with ASP installed. Microsoft Access can also support ActiveX controls, which make Access even more powerful when used with the Microsoft Internet Explorer.

 A job forum page was created to allow you to see how Access can be used in conjunction with the World Wide Web. For more information on Microsoft Access and the job forum, see **http://www.microsoft.com/Access/Internet/JobForum/**.

 If for some reason the database your organization uses isn't listed here, don't worry. Most likely someone out there has created an interface in which you can use your database on the World Wide Web. The best way to find out is to perform a search using one of the many search engines available. For a starting point, take a look at **http://www.yahoo.com/Computers_and_Internet/World_Wide_Web/Databases_and_Searching**.

Part
VI
Ch
37

Side-by-Side Comparison

Choosing a database to suit your organization's needs is difficult, and should be carefully planned. It's quite difficult to tell you which database would best suit your needs without spending a bit of time with a company and seeing how that company operates. The person who would know which database is best for your organization is you. Even so, Table 37.1 might help you narrow down your choices.

Table 37.1 A Comparison of Some of the Most Widely Used Databases on the Web

Database	Platforms	Suggested Use
Oracle	UNIX, NT	Large business
Sybase	UNIX, NT	Large business
mSQL	UNIX	Personal, small business
Illustra	UNIX, NT	Medium to large business
MS SQL	NT	Medium to large business
Postgres95	UNIX	Personal and small to medium business
Ingres	UNIX, NT	Small to large business
Foxpro	Windows Macintosh	Small to medium business
MS Access	Windows	Personal and small to medium business

Database Tools

Just as there are multiple databases available, there are also multiple methods of integrating your database with the World Wide Web. What tools you should use depends heavily on what platform your database resides, your knowledge of programming, and your programming language skills. In the following sections, you take a look at a few of the most common tools that make accessing databases easy for Web developers.

PHP/FI

PHP/FI was developed by Rasmus Lerdorf, who needed to create a script that enabled him to log visitors on to his page. The script replaced a few smaller ones that were creating a load on Lerdorf's system. This script became PHP, which is an initialization for Rasmus' Personal Home Page tools. Lerdorf later wrote a script that enabled him to embed commands within an HTML document to access a SQL database. This script acted as a forms interpreter (hence the name FI), which made it easier to create forms using a database. These two scripts have since been combined into one complete package called PHP/FI.

PHP/FI grew into a small language that enables developers to add commands within their HTML pages instead of running multiple smaller scripts to do the same thing. PHP/FI is actually a CGI program written in C that can be compiled to work on any UNIX system. The embedded commands are parsed by the PHP/FI script, which then prints the results through another HTML document. Unlike using JavaScript to access a database, PHP/FI is browser-independent because the script is processed through the PHP/FI executable on the server.

PHP/FI can be used to integrate mSQL, along with Postgres95, to create dynamic HTML documents. It's fairly easy to use and quite versatile. You can visit **http://www.vex.net/php/** for more information on PHP/FI, along with examples of how PHP/FI can be used.

Cold Fusion

Allaire created Cold Fusion as a system that enables you to write scripts within an HTML. Cold Fusion, a database interface, processes the scripts and then returns information within the HTML text in the script. Cold Fusion currently costs anywhere from $89 to $995, depending on your needs. The product is definitely worth the price. Allaire wrote Cold Fusion to work with just about every Web server available for Windows NT and integrates with just about every SQL engine—including those database servers available on UNIX machines (if a 32-bit ODBC driver exists). A version for Sun Solaris has also been recently released.

Cold Fusion works by processing a form, created by you, that sends a request to the Web server. The server starts Cold Fusion and sends the information the visitor entered to Cold Fusion engine, which is used to call a *template file*. After reading the information the visitor entered, Cold Fusion processes that information according to the template's instructions. Next, it returns an automatically generated HTML document to the visitor. For more information on Cold Fusion visit the Allaire Web site at **http://www.allaire.com/**.

w3-mSQL

w3-mSQL was created by David Hughes, the creator of mSQL, to simplify accessing an mSQL database from within your Web pages. w3-mSQL works as a CGI script which is used to parse your Web pages. The script reads your HTML document, performs any queries required, and sends the result to the server and then on to your site's visitor. w3-mSQL is much like a smaller-scale PHP/FI; it makes it easy for you to create Web documents that contain information based on what is in your database.

A sample bookmarks script and database dump is included within the w3-mSQL archive. For more information see **http://hughes.com.au/software/w3-msql.htm**.

MsqlPerl

MsqlPerl is a Perl interface to the mSQL database server. Written by Andreas Koenig, it utilizes the mSQL API and allows you to create CGI scripts in Perl, complete with all the SQL commands available to mSQL. You can download MsqlPerl at **ftp://Bond.edu.au/pub/Minerva/msql/Contrib/**.

MsqlJava

MsqlJava is an API that allows you to create applets that can access an mSQL database server. The package has been compiled with the Java Developer's Kit version 1.0 and tested using Netscape 3.0. Additional information on MsqlJava can be found on the following Web site. You can also download the latest version and view the online documentation, as well as see examples of MsqlJava in action at **http://mama.minmet.uq.oz.au/msqljava/**.

WDB

WDB is a suite of Perl scripts that helps you create applications that allow you to integrate SQL databases with the World Wide Web. WDB provides support for Sybase, Informix, and mSQL databases, but has been used with other database products as well.

WDB uses what author Bo Frese Rasmussen calls "form definition files," which describes how the information retrieved from the database should be displayed on the visitor's web browser. WDL automatically creates forms on-the-fly that allow the visitor to query the database. This saves you a lot of the work preparing a script to query a database. The user submits the query and WDB performs a set of conversions, or *links*, so the visitor can perform additional queries by clicking one of the links. Visit the WDB home page for further information on WDB: **http://arch-http.hq.eso.org/wdb/html/wdb.html**.

Web/Genera

Web/Genera is a software toolset used to integrate Sybase databases with HTML documents. Web/Genera can be used to retrofit a Web front end to an existing Sybase database, or it can be used to create a new one. When using Web/Genera, you are required to write a schema for the Sybase database indicating what fields are to be displayed, what type of data they contain, what column they are stored in, and how you want the output of a query formatted. Next, Web/Genera processes the specifications, queries the database, and formats an HTML document. Web/Genera also supports form-based queries and whole-database formatting that turns into text and HTML.

Web/Genera's main component is a program called symfmt, which extracts objects from Sybase databases based on your schema. After the schema is written, compile the schema by using a program, called sch2sql, which creates the SQL procedures that extract the objects from the database.

After you have compiled the schema, you can retrieve information from the database using URLs. When you click a link, the object requested is dynamically loaded from the Sybase database, formatted as HTML, and then displayed to the visitor.

Web/Genera was written by Stanley Letovsky and others for UNIX. The Web/Genera site contains additional information. Along with downloading the latest version, this site talks about Web/Genera's history and how it can be used today. You can find the Web site at **http://gdbdoc.gdb.org/letovsky/genera/**.

MORE

MORE is an acronym for Multimedia Oriented Repository Environment and was developed by the Repository Based Software Engineering Program (RBSE). MORE is a set of application programs that operate in conjunction with a Web server to provide access to a relational database. It was designed to allow a visitor access to the database using a set of CGI scripts written in C. It was also designed so that a consistent user interface can be used to work with a large number of servers, allowing a query to check information on multiple machines. This expands the query and gathers a large amount of information. Visit the MORE Web site for additional information on both MORE and RBSE at **http://rbse.jsc.nasa.gov:81/DEMO/**.

DBI

DBI's founder, Tim Bunce, wanted to provide a consistent programming interface to a wide variety of databases using Perl. Since the beginning, others have joined in to help build DBI so that it can support a wide variety of databases through the use of a Database Driver, or DBD. The DBD is simply the driver that works as a translator between the database server and DBI. A programmer only has to deal with one specification, and the drivers use the appropriate method to access any given database.

The following databases are a few that have database drivers. Most are still in testing phases, although they are stable enough to use for experimenting.

Oracle	mSQL
Ingres	Informix
Sybase	Empress
Fulcrum	C-ISAM
DB2	Quickbase
Interbase	Postgres

Visit the DBI Web page for the latest developments on DBI and various Database Drivers. Authors continue to develop this interface where DBDs are being built for additional databases. You can find this site at **http://www.hermetica.com/technologia/DBI/**.

DBGateway

DBGateway is a 32-bit Visual Basic WinCGI application that runs on a Windows NT machine as a service that provides World Wide Web access to Microsoft Access and FoxPro databases. It is being developed as part of the Flexible Computer Integrated Manufacturing (FCIM) project. DBGateway is a gateway between your CGI applications and the database servers. Because your CGI scripts only communicate with the Database Gateway, you only need to be concerned with programming for the gateway instead of each individual database server. This provides two advantages—programming a query is much easier because the gateway handles the communication with the database, and scripts can be easily ported to different database systems.

The gateway allows a visitor to your site to submit a form that is sent to the server. The server hands the request to the gateway, which decodes the information and builds a query forming the result based on a template, or it can send the query's result raw.

 Visit **http://fcim1.csdc.com/** to view the DBGateway's user manual, view the online FAQ, and see how DBGateway has been used.

Microsoft's Visual InterDev

 Visual InterDev is a visual interface in which you can create web applications that easily integrate with various databases. Visual InterDev is a graphical environment that allows you to create Active Server Pages (ASP). It comes with a full set of tools to add a whole range of HTML tags and attributes while allowing you to do so with VBScript or Jscript. For more information, see **http://www.microsoft.com/vinterdev/**.

Databases for Everyone

As you see, there are many options available, both in which database you might consider and what tools are available. Even so, most of these options are expensive and some of the databases and tools discussed might not be practical for small businesses.

For the smaller organization you can still provide dynamic content using less expensive options. Two of these are flat file and dbm databases, which cost no more than the convenience of having a machine that already provides Web services. Whether you have your own Web server or are hosting your pages on an ISP's Web server, flat file and dbm databases are an option to consider. If the databases are relatively small, no visitor will be the wiser.

Flat File Databases

Other than being cheap, flat file databases are just about the easiest you can create. Beyond the necessary programming language, there is nothing else needed to create a small ASCII text database.

A flat file database consists mainly of lines of text where each line is its own entry. There is no special technique to indexing the database. Because of this, flat file databases are usually relatively small. The larger the database, the longer it takes to perform queries to the database.

A Simple Flat File Example   With any database there are three important factors in designing Web-based database applications. First, you need to be able to read from the database. Second, you need to search the database. Last, if you want visitors to order products, or even if you want to easily manage the information in your database, you want to be able to write to the database.

With these factors in mind, you want to design a simple phonebook database which allows you to write, read, and search a database for information. With the ability to perform these three functions, you can easily design your own database to suit your specific needs, or simply change these examples, customizing each one. With minor changes, these scripts can be used for inventory management, storing personnel information, or whatever suits your fancy.

Designing the HTML Pages   For your phonebook, the first thing that you need is an HTML page, which allows someone to enter information into, or read from, the database. You must first decide what you want the visitor to enter.

In this example, the HTML document consists of three forms. The first form allows the visitor to enter information into the phonebook database. The second form allows the visitor to display the contents of the database, and the third form allows the visitor to perform a keyword search on the database.

You can expand on this later, but right now you simply want the visitor to be able to enter a first name, a last name, and a telephone number, all of which are stored in your flat file database.

The first form assigns the input from the visitor into three names: fname, lname, and phone. A hidden input type (see Listing 37.1), named act (for action), is created, which tells your script which action it is expected to perform.

Listing 37.1   *Pbook.html*—HTML Code that Allows Visitors to Query a Phonebook Database

```
<HTML>
<HEAD><TITLE>Flat file Phonebook</TITLE></HEAD>
<BODY>
<H1>Your Flat file Phonebook</H1>
<HR>
<H2>Insert Information</H2>
<FORM ACTION="/cgi-bin/pbook.pl" METHOD="POST">
<PRE>
  First Name: <INPUT TYPE="text" NAME="fname">
   Last Name: <INPUT TYPE="text" NAME="lname">
Phone Number: <INPUT TYPE="text" NAME="phone">
</PRE>
<INPUT TYPE="hidden" NAME="act" VALUE="add">
<INPUT TYPE="submit" value="Add to Phonebook">
</FORM>
```

```
<HR><P>
<H2>Display Information</H2>
<FORM ACTION="/cgi-bin/pbook.bat" METHOD="POST">
<INPUT TYPE="hidden" NAME="act" VALUE="display">
Click on <INPUT TYPE="submit" value="Display">
to view all entries in the phonebook
</FORM>
<HR><P>
<H2>Search the Phonebook</H2>
<FORM ACTION="/cgi-bin/pbook.bat" METHOD="POST">
Enter a keyword to search for: <INPUT TYPE="text" NAME="keyword">
<INPUT TYPE="hidden" NAME="act" VALUE="search">
<INPUT TYPE="submit" VALUE="Start Search">
</FORM>
</BODY>
</HTML>
```

Writing to a Flat File Database   The first section of your script (see Listing 37.2) separates the information coming from the form that your visitor filled out. After that, the script checks to see if the action requested was to add information to the database. If so, the database file is opened and the information from the visitor is placed in the database file on a single line.

Listing 37.2   *Pbook.pl*—The Script Reads *STDIN* and Separates Its Contents

```perl
if ($ENV{'REQUEST_METHOD'} eq 'POST')
{
    read(STDIN, $buffer, $ENV{'CONTENT_LENGTH'});
    @pairs = split(/&/, $buffer);
    foreach $pair (@pairs)
    {
        ($name, $value) = split(/=/, $pair);
        $value =~ tr/+/ /;
        $value =~ s/%([a-fA-F0-9][a-fA-F0-9])/pack("C", hex($1))/eg;
        $contents{$name} = $value;

    }
}
print "Content-type: text/html\n\n";
$phonebook = "phonebk.txt";
if ($contents{'act'} eq "add") {
open(BOOK, ">>$phonebook") || do {&no_open;};
print BOOK "$contents{'fname'}:$contents{'lname'}:$contents{'phone'}\n";
close(BOOK);
print <<"HTML";
<HTML>
<HEAD><TITLE>Information added</TITLE></HEAD>
<BODY>
<H1>Information added</H1>
The information entered has been added to the phonebook.
<HR>
<CENTER>
```

continues

Listing 37.2   Continued

```
<A HREF="/pbook.html">[Return to the Phonebook]</A>
</CENTER>
</BODY>
</HTML>
HTML
exit;
}
sub no_open {

print <<"HTML";
<HTML>
<HEAD><TITLE>Error!</TITLE></HEAD>
<BODY>
<H1> Error! Could not open the database!</H1>
<CENTER>
<A HREF="/pbook.htm">[Return to the Phonebook]</A>
</CENTER>
</BODY>
</HTML>
HTML

exit;
}
```

At this time, the information entered by the visitor has been placed in the database. If you were to take a look at the text file holding the information provided by the visitor, it would look something like:

```
John:Doe:555-5555
```

This format is called *colon delimited*, meaning that each field is separated by a colon. Any character can be used to delimit each field in a flat file database, and it is best to use a character that is not present in a field. Using the colon, for example, would not be wise if you wanted to include an URL in the database. In that case, a comma might be more suitable.

Reading from a Flat File Database   If the visitor clicked Display, the information from the database is retrieved and simply appears to the visitor in a table. By using a table, the contents of the phonebook can easily be formatted into something that is easy to view.

As you can see in Listing 37.3, you check to see if the value of act is equal to display; if so, a page is created and the contents of your database appear, where each line of information is broken into its respective part. To accomplish this, use Perl's split function. The value of $line is split and assigned to the array entry. By splitting each line, you can control how you want the information to appear to the visitor (see Figure 37.1).

FIG. 37.1

You can control how the information is displayed by separating the contents of the database.

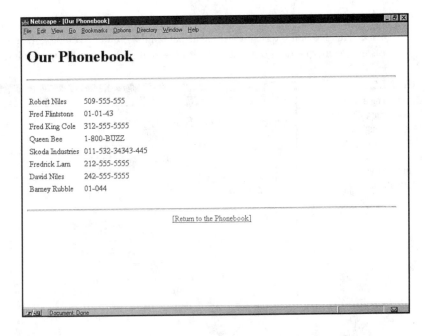

Listing 37.3   All Entries Are Displayed to the Visitor

```
if ($contents{'act'} eq "display") {

...

open (BOOK, $phonebook) || do {&no_open;};
until (eof(BOOK))
{
  $line = <BOOK>;
  @entry = split(/:/, $line);
  print "<TR><TD>$entry[0] $entry[1]</TD><TD> $entry[2]</TD></TR>";
}

close(BOOK);

...
```

Once the information from the database is displayed, finish the HTML document and exit the script.

Searching a Flat File Database   Last, you want to see if the visitor requested to perform a keyword search (see Listing 37.4). If so, you need to open the database and check each line against the keyword entered by the visitor.

First, the database is opened and the top portion of the results page is created. Next, you have a counter, which is initially set to zero (more on this in a moment). Now, each line is read and checked against the value contained in the variable $contents{'keyword'}. If so, the count is incremented and the result printed as part of the created Web page (see Figure 37.2). Use the same technique here that you did earlier—split each line to be printed into an array.

FIG. 37.2

By providing a method in which the visitor can search through a database, you remove the need to weed through excess information.

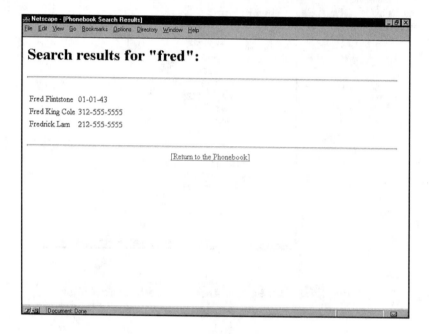

Once you exit the loop, you check the count. If the count is equal to zero, you know there were no entries in the database that matched the keyword search, and you inform the visitor that their search produced no results. Listing 37.4 gives you an idea of how this can be accomplished.

Listing 37.4 Each Line Is Checked and only Matching Results Are Returned

```
if ($contents{'act'} eq "search") {

open (BOOK, "$phonebook") || do {&no_open;};


$count=0;

 until (eof (BOOK))
 {
   $line = <BOOK>;
   chop($line);
   if ($line =~ /$contents{'keyword'}/gi)
    {
     $count++;
     @entry = split(/:/, $line);
     print "<TR><TD>$entry[0] $entry[1]</TD><TD> $entry[2]</TD></TR>";
    }
```

```
    }

if ($count==0)
    {
      print "No Matches";
    }

close(BOOK);
```

Once the script has checked each line against the keyword, the database is closed; the script finishes the Web page and exits the script.

For the script in its entirety, see the CD-ROM accompanying this book. A version for those using Perl on a Windows NT or Windows 95 platform is available as well.

On the CD

dbm Databases

Most UNIX systems have some sort of dbm database. dbm is a set of library routines that manage data files consisting of key and value pairs. The dbm routines control how users enter and retrieve information from the database. Although not the most powerful mechanism for storing information, using dbm is a faster method of retrieving information than using a flat file. Because most UNIX sites use one of the dbm libraries, the tools you need to store your information to a dbm database are readily available.

There are almost as many flavors of dbm libraries as there are UNIX systems. Although most of these libraries are incompatible with one another, all basically work the same way. You'll first explore each of the dbm flavors to give you a good understanding of their differences. Afterward, you are shown how to create an address book script, which should give you a better idea of how dbm databases work.

The following list describes the most common dbm libraries available and explains some of the differences between each of the dbm libraries.

- dbm—The library routines for dbm are simple but can handle most jobs without problem. The library contains the most functions allowing you to create databases, store, retrieve, and delete information, as well as a few functions that help you move around within the database. dbm stores the database in two files. The first has the extension PAG and contains the bitmap. The second, which has the extension DIR, contains the data.

- ndbm—Much like dbm with a few additional features, ndbm was written to provide better, and hence, faster storage and retrieval methods. Also, dbm can only have one database open while, with ndbm, you can open many databases. Like dbm, ndbm stores its information in two files, using the extensions PAG and DIR.

- sdbm—If you have installed Perl, you most likely have sdbm installed. sdbm comes with the Perl archive, which has been ported to many platforms. This means you are able to use dbm databases, as long as there is a version of Perl for your computer. sdbm was written to match the functions provided with ndbm, so code portability shouldn't be a problem, either. For more information on sdbm and Perl, see the Perl language home page at **http://www.perl.com/perl/**.

■ gdbm—The GNU version of the dbm family of database routines. This library does its own file locking to ensure that two or more users cannot write to the database simultaneously. gdbm has the same functions as ndbm, as well as the capability to reorganize the database and cache data. The database has no size limit, depending only on your system's resources. gdbm databases create only one file, having the extension DB.

■ Berkeley db 1.85—This significantly expands on the original dbm routines. As well as creating hashed tables, the library can also create databases based on a sorted balanced binary tree (BTREE) and store information with a record line number (RECNO). The method you use depends completely on how you want to store and retrieve the information from a database. Berkeley's db creates only one file, which has no extension.

If for some reason you can't find a particular dbm database on your system, do a search on the Web for dbm databases. With the exception of dbm, the other interfaces are freely available. You will likely want at least one of the dbm interfaces on your favorite FTP site.

dbm databases are relatively easy to use. Unfortunately, the use of dbm is poorly documented. Even so, you can find some additional information at **http://www.polaris.net/docs/gdbm/**.

A dbm Example   Now that the preceding section has briefly introduced the various dbm interfaces, this section demonstrates how you can use them. As mentioned earlier, dbm databases can decrease the amount of time it takes to insert and retrieve information to and from a database. When your database starts growing, and using one of the larger database engines is still overkill (especially on your pocketbook), you might want to look into using dbm.

Inserting Information into a dbm Database   dbm databases have two fields: a key and the data (sometimes called the *value*). The *key* is simply a string that points to the data. The string within the key must be unique within a database. Note the following example:

Key	Data
Robert Niles	rniles@selah.net
Jason Lenny	jason@yakima.net
Ken Davis	kdavis@your.com
John Doe	jdoe@imtired.selah.net
Santa Claus	sclaus@north.pole.com
Bert	rniles@selah.net

The data, on the other hand, can contain any type of information. The data might contain an URL, an e-mail address, or even a binary file. Examine the following script, DBBOOKADD.PL, which adds information to a dbm database. This script is available on this book's companion CD-ROM.

The main components for using dbm are the Perl module, DB_FILE.PM, and the file control module, FCNTL.PM (see Listing 37.5). DB_FILE.PM acts as an interface to the dbm routines. The FCNTL.PM module provides functions that enable you to control access to the database so that two or more people cannot write to the database at the same time.

Listing 37.5   The Information from the Form Is Parsed in Order to Perform the Appropriate Function

```perl
#!/usr/bin/perl

use DB_File;
use Fcntl;

if ($ENV{'REQUEST_METHOD'} eq 'POST')
{
        read(STDIN, $buffer, $ENV{'CONTENT_LENGTH'});
        @pairs = split(/&/, $buffer);
        foreach $pair (@pairs)
        {
                ($name, $value) = split(/=/, $pair);
                $value =~ tr/+/ /;
                $value =~ s/%([a-fA-F0-9][a-fA-F0-9])/pack("C",
        hex($1))/eg;
                $form{$name} = $value;

        }
}
$file="addresses";
```

To connect to the database, you use the `tie()` function. The syntax for `tie()` is as follows:

```perl
tie(%hashname, DB_File, filename, flags, mode)
```

You can assign any `hashname`, although the name must start with the percent sign (%). Because you are using the DB_FILE.PM module, you must specify the filename. The `filename` identifies the file in which you are storing the data. You next specify the `flags`, which vary depending on which dbm routines you are using. In this example, you use the flags that enable you to read from and write to files (`O_RDWR`) or, if the file doesn't exist, to create files (`O_CREAT`). The `mode` sets the database file's permissions. The mode 0660 specifies that the owner can read from and write to the database file, and that the group can only read from the file.

```perl
$database=tie(%db, 'DB_File', $file, O_RDWR|O_CREAT, 0660);
```

This next, very simple line, is what magically adds the information to the database. You use the hash variable to enter the information into the database. The syntax for this line is as follows:

```perl
$hashname{key}=value
```

The following line places `$form{'name'}` into the database as the key, and assigns `$form{'email'}` to that key as its value:

```perl
$db{$form{'name'}}=$form{'email'};
```

Now you use the `untie()` function, which releases control of the database, and then `undef()`, which undefines the variable `$database`:

```
untie(%db);
undef($database);
```

Although a dbm database can contain only the key and a pair, you can trick the database into adding more fields. For example, if you want to include a telephone number, you have to add it to the value; by inserting some sort of separator, you can later identify the two separate entries. The following example uses the `join()` function, which joins separate strings together with a colon:

```
$db{$form{'name'}}=join(":",$form{'email'},$form{'phone'});
```

For example, if `$form{'email'}` contains the string `jdoe@selah.net`, and `$form{'phone'}` contains the string `555-5555`, the `join()` function produces the following string:

```
jdoe@selah.net:555-5555
```

Because e-mail addresses and telephone numbers do not include colons, the colon is probably the best choice for separating each entry. Of course, what you use to delimit each entry depends on what kind of data you need to store.

What happens if a user tries to enter a name already stored in a key? As your script currently stands, it would simply continue as if nothing happened. However, because each key must be unique, the script does not add the information to the database. To tell the visitor that the entry failed, you have to add a line that checks whether the name entered matches an existing key.

```
&error if $db{"$form{'name'}"};
```

Your `error` subroutine tells the visitor what happened and gives the visitor a chance to try again:

```
sub error {
print <<"HTML";
<HTML>
<HEAD><TITLE>Error!</TITLE></HEAD>
<BODY>
<H1>Error! -Name exists</H1>
I'm sorry, but the name you entered already exists.
If you wish to try again, click
<A HREF="/dbbook.html">here</A>.
</BODY>
</HTML>
HTML

exit;
}
```

Retrieving Information from a dbm Database   Now that you have entered information into the database, you want to enable your site's visitors to retrieve the information. Listing 37.6 starts this process by accessing the database and generates the top portion of the Web page.

Listing 37.6 The Database Is Accessed, and the Top Portion of the Web Page Is Generated

```perl
#!/usr/bin/perl
# dbbook.pl
use DB_File;
use Fcntl;
print "Content-type: text/html\n\n";
$file="addresses";
$database=tie(%db, 'DB_File', $file, O_READ, 0660) || die "can't";
print <<"HTML";
<HTML>
<HEAD><TITLE>Simple dbm address book</TITLE></HEAD>
<BODY>
<CENTER>
<H1>A Simple Address Book</H1>
<TABLE BORDER=1>
HTML
```

Because you've entered the phone number and e-mail address into the value separated by a colon, you now must separate the phone number and e-mail address. The easiest way to do so is with the split() function. After you split this information, you pass the contents to the array @part:

```perl
while (($key,$value)= each(%db)) {
 @part = split(/:/,$value);
```

You can use an if statement to check whether the visitor entered an e-mail address. If the visitor did so, you print a link, using the HREF anchor. Otherwise, you simply print the key, then use the array to print the e-mail address and phone number:

```perl
if ($part[0]) {
   print "<TR><TD><A HREF=\"mailto:$part[0]\">$key</A></TD>";
   }
 else {
print "<TR><TD>$key</TD>";
   }

 print "<TD>$part[0]</TD><TD>$part[1]</TD></TR>\n";
}
```

Finally, you finish the Web page, closing the table, body, and HTML file. You need to use untie() to release control of the database, undefine the $database variable, and exit the script.

```perl
print <<"HTML";
</TABLE>
<P>
<A HREF="/dbbook.html">[Add to address book]</A>
</BODY>
</HTML>
HTML
untie(%db);
undef($database);
exit;
```

Searching a dbm Database You have learned how to enter information into the database and also how to retrieve information from the database. What would happen if the database starts to become extremely large? If you have 100 entries in the database, it could make for an extremely large Web page if you were to display everything within the database. Also, looking for a single name in the database could be a pain.

To solve this problem, you can enable the visitor to search through the database (see Listing 37.7). For example, a visitor could enter the last name Doe, thus narrowing down the number of names the visitor has to weed through.

Listing 37.7   Input from the User Is Parsed, and the Database Is Accessed

```perl
#!/usr/bin/perl
# dbbooksearch.pl

use DB_File;
use Fcntl;
if ($ENV{'REQUEST_METHOD'} eq 'POST')
{
        read(STDIN, $buffer, $ENV{'CONTENT_LENGTH'});
        @pairs = split(/&/, $buffer);
        foreach $pair (@pairs)
        {
                ($name, $value) = split(/=/, $pair);
                $value =~ tr/+/ /;
                $value =~ s/%([a-fA-F0-9][a-fA-F0-9])/pack("C",
        hex($1))/eg;
                $form{$name} = $value;

        }
}
print "Content-type: text/html\n\n";

$file="addresses";
$database=tie(%db, 'DB_File', $file, O_READ, 0660)
   || die "can't";
print <<"HTML";
<HTML>
<HEAD><TITLE>Simple dbm address book results</TITLE></HEAD>
<BODY>
<CENTER>
<H1>A Simple Address Book Results</H1>
<TABLE BORDER=1>
HTML
```

As each key/value pair loads from the database, each key is checked to see whether the key matches the string that the visitor entered:

```perl
while (($key,$value)= each(%db)) {
if ($key =~ /$form{'name'}/i) {
```

N O T E The /i switch, using Perl, allows for case-insensitive matching. Therefore, if the user enters Bert, bErT, or bert, the entry would match Bert, bert, Robert, or Bertman. ■

If you find a match, you print it.

```
@part = split(/:/,$value);
 if ($part[0]) {
    print "<TR><TD><A HREF=\"mailto:$part[0]\">$key</A></TD>";
    }
 else {
    print "<TR><TD>$key</TD>";
    }
 print "<TD>$part[0]</TD><TD>$part[1]</TD></TR>\n";
 }
}
```

Part
VI
Ch
37

Then you complete the Web document, untie the database, undefine the variable, and exit the script.

```
print <<"HTML";
</TABLE>
<P>
<A HREF="/dbbook.html">[Add to address book]</A>
</BODY>
</HTML>
HTML

untie(%db);
undef($database);

exit;
```

You could also search the value. Such a search gives you even more flexibility on what information is returned.

The script in its entirety is located on the CD-ROM that accompanies this book. As well, there is a version for Windows NT and Windows 95 (pbook.zip) on the CD-ROM, which performs the same functions using the sdbm database that is distributed with Perl.

Using SQL Databases

Most SQL database servers consist of a set of programs that manage large amounts of data. These programs offer a rich set of query commands that help manage the power behind the SQL server. The programs also control the storage, retrieval, and organization of the information within the database. Thus, you can change, update, and remove the information within the database—after the support programs or scripts are in place.

A relational database doesn't link records together physically, like a dbm database does with the key and value pair. Instead, a relational database simply provides a field that can match information and returns the results as though the information were organized that way.

Relational databases store information in tables. A table is like a miniature database stored within a main database that groups the information together. For instance, you can have one database that contains one or more tables.

Each table consists of columns and rows. The columns identify the data by name, as in the following example:

Name	Home Phone	E-Mail
Fred Barns	555-5555	fbarns@somewhere.net
Melissa Devons	555-5556	missy@thisplace.com
John Doe	555-5557	jdoe@whatcha.want.com

The name, phone number, and e-mail address are the columns, and each entry set is the row.

Although this book's purpose isn't to explain how relational databases work, you need a basic understanding of the concept. Suppose you stored the preceding information in a table called Personal. You can join information from two or more tables within your query. Suppose that the following table is called Work:

Name	Work Phone	Department
Fred Barns	555-5558	sysadmin
Melissa Devons	555-5559	programmer
John Doe	555-5560	janitor

Within your query, you can have something like the following:

```
select * from personal,work where personal.name=work.name
```

This query would print information about individuals from both tables. Keep in mind that this example is a very simple one. Queries from relational databases can get extremely complex. In fact, there are professionals whose sole job is to manage multiple databases with multiple tables, and ensure that when this information is queried from a database the results are intelligible.

SQL is a query language that has become standardized. The simple language contains commands that query a database for information. The SQL language was written to be easily understandable. If you were to read a query, the query's syntax would sound much the same as if you were explaining the query to another person. Examine the following example:

```
select personal.name,personal.home_phone,personal.email,
work.work_phone, work.department from personal,work
where personal.name=work.name
```

Even the following example would work on most systems:

```
select * from personal,work where personal.name=work.name
```

where the asterisk is a wild card that matches everything.

To insert information into a database, use a query as follows:

```
insert into table (name, home_phone, email) VALUES ('rniles',
'555-5555','rniles@selah.net')
```

You can easily determine what these queries do just by examining them.

Using Microsoft's Active Server Pages

Active Server Pages (ASPs) is Microsoft's answer to CGI scripting. Using Microsoft's ASP technology, you can create scripts using Visual Basic Script, Java, Jscript, or even PerlScript without a need to compile your code beforehand.

ASP technology works only with Microsoft's Internet Information Server (IIS) and is part of Microsoft's ActiveX technology. Each script as it is requested by the visitor is compiled and executed on the server at runtime. This creates a very flexible atmosphere in which you can easily develop and test scripts.

One of the most useful functions is the ability to access information from a database. Along with ASP technology, Microsoft provides a component called the Active Database Object (ADO). The ADO provides you with access to any OLE/DB or ODBC-compatible data source for use within your scripts.

If you're at all familiar with how Microsoft's Internet Database Connector (IDC) and the HTML extension (HTX) works, creating ASP scripts will be a piece of cake. ASP scripts work much the same way, where all scripting is contained within a document and inside the <% … %> tags. For example, take a look at the following code:

```
<%
if err.number > 0 then
 response.write("An error occured while adding this name")
end if
%>
```

Within the tags we have a short snippit of VBScript which checks a condition, and if an error occurs, the script sends a message to the visitor, informing them of this error. We close the condition and then close the tag.

Outside of the <% … %> tag, you can write any HTML code you prefer without doing anything special. For example:

```
<H1>Add to Phone book</H1>
<%
if err.number > 0 then
 response.write("An error occured while adding this name")
end if
%>
</BODY>
</HTML>
```

Only the information within the <% … %> tag is compiled and executed by the server! If you look at Listing 37.8, we have provided a short VBScript which takes information from the visitor and enters that information into a database. If no information was entered, an HTML document is displayed, in which they can fill out each available form field.

Listing 37.8   aspexample.asp—A small example on how easy it is to enter information onto a database using ASPs.

```
<%
datasource = "PBOOK"
tblNames = "NAMES"
tblAddr = "ADDRESSES"
if request("ACT")="add" and request("OK") <> "" then
on error resume next
sql ="INSERT INTO NAMES (FNAME,LNAME) VALUES ('" + request ("FNAME") + "','" +
request ("LNAME") + "')"
set conn = Server.CreateObject("ADODB.Connection")
set rs = Server.CreateObject("ADODB.RecordSet")
conn.Open datasource
rs.Open sql, conn

if err.number =0 then response.redirect("pbook.asp")
quit
end if
if request("CANCEL") <> "" then
  response.redirect("pbook.asp")
end if
%>
<HTML>
<HEAD>
<META NAME="GENERATOR" Content="InCommand Interactive">
<TITLE>Template</TITLE>
</HEAD>
<BODY>

<H1>Add Job</H1>

<%
if err.number > 0 then
  response.write("An error occured while adding this name")
end if
%>
<FORM METHOD="POST" ACTION="addname.asp">
<INPUT TYPE="HIDDEN" NAME="ACT" VALUE="add">
<TABLE>
<TR BGCOLOR="#CCCCCC"><TD ID=fname>First Name #: </TD><TD><INPUT NAME="FNAME"
VALUE="<%=request("FNAME")%>"></TD></TR>
<TR><TD ID=fname1 VALIGN=TOP>Last Name: </TD><TD><INPUT NAME="LNAME"
VALUE="<%=request("LNAME")%>"></TD></TR>
<TR><TD></TD><TD><INPUT TYPE="SUBMIT" NAME="OK" VALUE="OK"> <INPUT
TYPE="SUBMIT" NAME="CANCEL" VALUE="Cancel"></TD></TR>
</TABLE>
</FORM>
<HR>
<A HREF="main.asp">Main Menu</A>
</BODY>
</HTML>
```

Even though Listing 37.8 is a simple example, you should have a good idea of how you can create your own ASP scripts. If you have ever felt that VBScript is your cup of tea, but were concerned about whether your scripts will run on all web browsers, ASP relieves you of this concern since everything is compiled on the server. The only thing the browser sees is a document full of HTML.

Using Oracle

Oracle, the industry's database heavyweight, provides a collection of tools that allow an administrator to easily provide web content using information within an Oracle database. Easily might be a relative term here, since all the lingo Oracle provides makes you feel like you're back in school learning long division. Even so, once the generic terms provided by Oracle are understood, connecting to a database through the Web and displaying the results of a query to those visiting your site should seem like a breeze.

Web Listener

Oracle utilizes what is called a Web Listener. Simply put, a *Web Listener* is a Web server that recognizes various methods in which the Web Listener may be accessed. To find out whether a request will be for an HTML document or a CGI script, Oracle's Web Listener detects what kind of document the visitor is requesting. The document might be a simple HTML document, or a script used to access the database.

For example, if the Web Listener detects the string owa and is properly placed with the HTTP request, the Web server knows that it's supposed to activate the *Oracle Web Agent* (often referred to as OWA—more on this in a moment), and process the request using information stored in the Database Connection Descriptor (DCD). The DCD tells the Web Agent both the database access privileges the PL/SQL agent has when executing a request, and the schema used for accessing the database.

As stated, the terminology can be a bit confusing. In order to clear things up a bit, take a look at this example URL: **http://www.justanexample.com/owabin/owa/sample_empinfo**.

This example URL can be broken into three parts, which are important to the Web Listener.

The first section, `http://www.foobar.com/owa-bin`, defines the path to the Oracle Web Agent. The *owa* portion tells the Web Listener that the Oracle Web Agent will be used. The last section, *sample_empinfo*, contains information on connecting to the database using PL/SQL. This URL can even be used within a HTML form. For example:

```
<FORM ACTION="http://www.foobar.com/owa-bin/owa/sample_empinfo"
METHOD="POST">
```

PL/SQL

PL/SQL is the language for connecting to an Oracle database. PL/SQL is a programming language that contains a superset of the structured query language (SQL) and is used to access the Oracle database. Where SQL is a language to simply query a database, PL/SQL allows you to create functions, use flow control and loops, assign variables, constants, datatypes, and various other statements that help you program applications that submit data to a database, and allows you to format the output of a query.

Another feature of PL/SQL is that you are allowed to store compiled PL/SQL code directly in the database. By doing so, you can call programs you created directly from the database which can be shared by other individuals (even at the same time!), removing the need for having multiple applications that do the same thing.

Unfortunately, PL/SQL is not an industry standard. PL/SQL can currently only be used with Oracle. This creates a problem with portability of code where you might want to have one interface that can be used to access various databases.

If you have installed the PL/SQL Web Toolkit with Oracle, you can use PL/SQL to format the output of queries into HTML format. The toolkit provides a full range of commands that are converted to HTML tags that include information from a query. For example, if you had an employee database which contained the name, ID number of an individual, a phone number, and the e-mail address of each of these employees, the following DCD would provide a HTML document like that in Figure 37.3.

FIG. 37.3

Using Oracle's Web Toolkit enables the administrator to create HTML documents created based on information in an Oracle database.

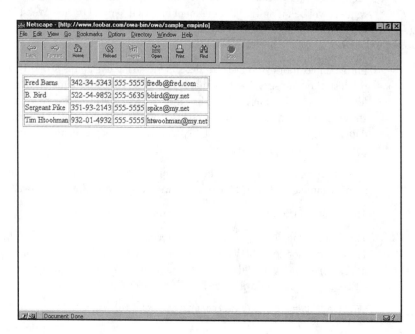

The following PL/SQL query provides the visitor with this information.

```
Create or replace procedure emplist is
employees boolean;
```

```
begin
employees := htp.tablePrint('emp', 'BORDER=1');
end;
```

Additional Information

Complete coverage of Oracle's Web tools would require a book on its own; details on PL/SQL alone would likely fill an entire book. Unfortunately, this book can't go too deeply into every aspect of Oracle's abilities. The information here should whet your appetite, though, and if you have more questions about Oracle, visit the following Web sites. Together with the information contained herein, you should be able to decide if Oracle is the best solution for you.

Part
VI

Ch
37

 Thomas Dunbar has taken the time to provide information on how PL/SQL works with the World Wide Web. This page contains a couple of examples that should give you a better understanding of how PL/SQL and Oracle work. You can visit his page at **http://gserver.grads.vt.edu/**. For more information on PL/SQL itself, see **http://www.inf.bme.hu/~gaszi/plsql/plsql_manual.html**.

Managing Your Web Site

Managing and Staging Files

by Jerry Honeycutt and Mark R. Brown

Managing Your Source Files

If you're working with a fairly complex Web site, you might start pulling your hair out trying to manage all those HTML files—not to mention graphics, sounds, videos, ActiveX controls, plug-ins, and so on. The tools you learn about in this chapter will help you better manage all those files. Here's a list of the tools discussed in the chapter.

- ■ *Visual SourceSafe*. Visual SourceSafe is Microsoft's version control system. Originally designed to manage programming source files (C++ and so on), Visual SourceSafe is a natural tool to use for managing your Web site's source files.

- ■ *Spidersoft WebGal*. WebGallery is a tool that manages small bits of HTML, scripts, and so on. You don't use it to manage your entire Web site, but you use it to manage reusable bits of HTML code.

- ■ *Microsoft FrontPage*. FrontPage is Microsoft's graphical HTML editor. You can use FrontPage Explorer to graphically manage all of the files in your Web site.

- ■ *NetObjects Fusion*. Fusion is similar to Microsoft FrontPage 98 in that you can use it to graphically manage the files in your Web site.

- ■ *Other Techniques*. This section shows you additional techniques you can use to manage your source files, such as organizing them into a logical directory structure.

Visual SourceSafe

Microsoft Visual SourceSafe (see Figure 38.1) is a product that developers traditionally use for version control. It allows a developer to maintain each version of a file as the developer makes changes to it. For example, a developer might create a source file and check it into the SourceSafe. Then, when the developer is ready to make changes to the file, he checks out of SourceSafe, makes any required changes, and checks it back into SourceSafe. SourceSafe keeps both versions of the file so that the developer can backtrack if necessary. Not only that, SourceSafe makes it easy to report on the history of a file, merges changes from multiple developers, and so on.

Visual SourceSafe has features that a Web developer will find useful, too. Since you work with many source files on a daily basis, SourceSafe is an ideal solution to help you keep track of the changes you make. You can organize all of your HTML and graphics files into projects that represent a Web site. Then, the Visual SourceSafe Administrator can designate your project as a Web site project. Once that's done, you can use three special SourceSafe features to help manage your site:

- ■ *Check hyperlinks*. Double-checks the links stored in your HTML files.
- ■ *Create a site map*. Creates a map of the HTML files stored in your project.
- ■ *Deploy*. Deploys the files stored in the project to your Web server.

For more information about how you can use Visual SourceSafe to manage your Web site, take a look at Microsoft's Visual SourceSafe Web site at **http://www.microsoft.com/ssafe**.

FIG. 38.1

Visual SourceSafe organizes your projects like file folders.

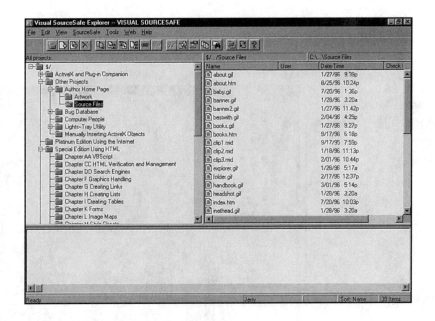

Spidersoft WebGal

As your Web site becomes more complex and more people work on the site, reusable code will become much more valuable. You'll want to reuse and share style sheets, for example. You'll also want to reuse small bits of HTML that generate forms, frames, and tables. What about scripts? Scripts are a perfect thing to reuse in your Web site.

You can't find a better tool that you can use to manage reusable HTML than Spidersoft's WebGal. First, WebGal is a well-built, world-class program. Its quality rivals many products that Microsoft builds. You can get your own copy of WebGal at Spidersoft's Web site (**http://www.spidersoft.com**). Click Download to download the install file. Figure 38.2 shows you what WebGal looks like with the sample gallery file loaded.

WebGal has features that are especially designed for managing reusable bits of HTML and other objects. For example:

- *Store and organize any text resource.* You can use WebGal to store and organize bits of HTML such as forms, scripts, and style sheets.

- *Copy and paste text resources into your favorite HTML editor.* You can easily copy any item in the gallery to your favorite HTML editor.

- *View Web related files.* WebGal includes viewers that let you view a variety of files, including GIF, JPEG, PNG, WAV, MID, HTML, OCX, CLASS, JAVA, and so on.

- *Preview resources by using the built-in browser.* WebGal includes a built-in browser (Internet Explorer) you can use to preview reusable resources, including controls, HTML, sounds, Java applets, pictures, and so on. When you've found just the right resource, you paste it into your HTML document.

■ *Store file dependencies along with HTML fragments.* Frequently, a reusable bit of HTML refers to images, sounds, controls, and so on. You store the HTML along with all of the files it uses as a single object.

FIG. 38.2

WebGal has an Explorer-like interface.

WebGal organization

WebGal item viewer

View and change properties for item

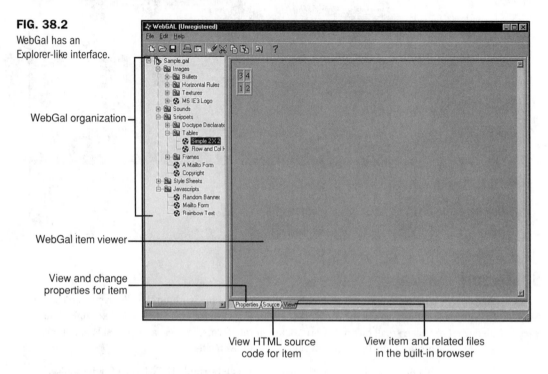

View HTML source code for item

View item and related files in the built-in browser

Using Microsoft FrontPage 98

Microsoft FrontPage 98 is one of the hottest HTML editors on the market. If the only thing that FrontPage 98 provided was a WYSIWYG HTML editor, that would be enough. But FrontPage 98 also provides a graphical tool you can use to manage the organization all of the files on your Web site. Take a look at Figure 38.3. Chapter 42, "Using HTML and Site Tools," shows you how to install and use FrontPage 98. You can download a trial version from Microsoft's Web site at **http://www.microsoft.com/frontpage**.

With FrontPage 98, you don't have to worry about how the files are organized within your Web site. FrontPage Explorer manages the organization of your files behind the scenes. That is, instead of dealing with directories and files, you work with documents in FrontPage Explorer. So what else can you do with FrontPage Explorer? Plenty, as noted here:

■ *Use wizards to quickly create an entire Web site.* FrontPage Explorer comes with several wizards you can use to create a complete Web site in minutes. All you have to do is answer a few simple questions.

■ *View the relationships between Web pages.* FrontPage Explorer graphically displays the relationship between each Web page. You can easily see how all the Web pages are linked together.

■ *Maintain your links.* FrontPage Explorer automatically notifies you when a link goes bad. In addition, if you rename a file, FrontPage Explorer automatically fixes each reference to that file.

▶ **See** "Microsoft FrontPage 98," **p. 883**

FIG. 38.3
You must let FrontPage 98 manage the directory structure itself. You view the organization of your files through FrontPage Explorer.

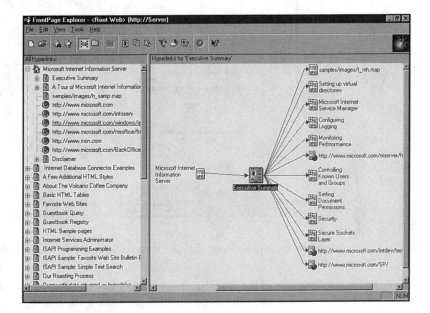

Part
VII

Ch
38

Using NetObjects Fusion

NetObjects Fusion is a product with very similar features to Microsoft FrontPage. It's a complete Web site manager and HTML editor rolled into a single product. Whereas FrontPage Explorer displays a Web site as a group of pages with lines connecting them (a directed graph), Fusion displays a Web site as a strict hierarchy that you can view as a structure chart (see Figure 38.4) or an outline.

You can download an evaluation copy of NetObjects Fusion from the NetObjects Web site at **http://www.netobjects.com**. Click Software Download and follow the instructions you see on the Web page.

 Since FrontPage's site management features are a bit stronger than Fusion's, and Fusion's site wizards are stronger than FrontPage's, many folks start their Web site using Fusion and then manage it using FrontPage.

Working Directly with Files

Microsoft FrontPage and NetObjects Fusion are tools that automatically manage your HTML files for you. You're not actually aware of how those files are stored on the disk. If you're still hand editing and organizing HTML files, however, you need to come up with a scheme that helps you keep everything straight.

FIG. 38.4

Double-click one of the boxes representing a Web page to open it in Fusion's HTML editor.

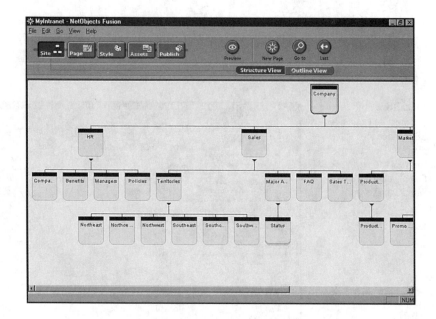

The following sections describe things you should consider when organizing your Web site in this manner.

Using the Structure of the File System   Use the hierarchical structure of the file system. If you think about your Web site for a moment, you'll realize that it probably has a very hierarchical structure, like an outline. Create a directory structure on your disk that reflects this organization.

For example, if your Web site is organized similar to Figure 38.5, you might create a directory structure that looks like Figure 38.6. Note how the home page is in the root directory, while each Web page to which the home page is linked has a directory directly underneath the home page. All of the files required by a Web page (graphics, sounds, controls, and so on) are stored in the directory with the home page so you can keep an accurate inventory of the files on which the Web page is dependent.

Mirroring Your Web Site Locally   If you're not using one of the Web site management programs such as Microsoft FrontPage or Visual SourceSafe, you'll want to keep a copy of your Web site on your local hard drive—regardless of your Web site's directory structure. In fact, you should edit those files locally, and then upload them to the Web site when they're ready. Doing so, you always know that the files on your local disk are the one-and-only master copy of your Web site.

When working with the files on your local disk, you can use one of the Windows built-in file utilities to organize them:

- Explorer—Windows 95 and Windows NT provide Explorer, which is very similar to File Manager but works more closely with the files on your disk.

- File Manager—All versions of Windows, including Windows 95, provide File Manager. In Windows 95, choose <u>R</u>un from the Start menu, type **FILEMAN.EXE**, and press Enter.

FIG. 38.5

Keep your Web pages simple and organized hierarchically so that users can more easily navigate your Web site.

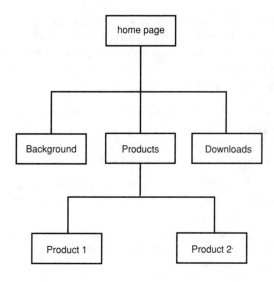

FIG. 38.6

If you link to a Web page from multiple places, don't duplicate the directory for that Web page; just refer to the first occurrence of it.

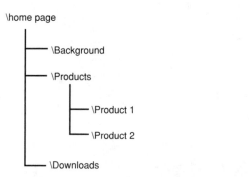

CAUTION

In order to mirror your Web site locally, you must use directory names and filenames that are valid on both your workstation and the Web server. Note that you can use WS_FTP (the popular Windows 95 file transfer program, available from most Internet download sites, such as **http://www.shareware.com**) to automatically convert file extensions from one form to another when you upload your HTML files. For example, WS_FTP will automatically convert files with the HTM extension to the HTML extension when you upload them.

Creating Relative References   Relative references are URLs that are relative to the URL of the containing HTML document. For example, next/page.htm is a relative reference, whereas http://www.myserver.com/next/page.htm is an absolute reference.

You should always use relative references when linking to a resource on your own Web site. The reason is simple. If you change servers, or you move your Web site to another directory, you have to change all of the absolute references. If you're using a tool such as FrontPage, these would be fixed for you automatically. Since you're managing your files manually, you have to actually change each reference within each file. Relative references assure that if you simply move the entire directory structure of your Web site from one location to another, you don't have to change each reference.

▶ **See** "Understanding Links," **p. 124**

Launching Related Files   Make sure you have the appropriate programs associated with the files to which a Web page is dependent. By doing so, you can easily launch those files while you're exploring the Web site's files. For example, if you're exploring your Web site, you might want to take a look at a graphics file or play a sound file.

Windows 95 users have it made. You can view most graphics formats using QuickView, which is provided with Windows 95. You can also launch most video and sound files using the Media Player.

 TIP   If you don't have a program associated with a particular type of file, such as JPG, you can probably view that type of file in your Web browser.

## CHAPTER 39

Verifying and Testing HTML Documents

by Jerry Honeycutt and Mark R. Brown

Validating Your HTML Documents

In the world of software development, programs are built in essentially three phases: design, programming, and testing. The purpose of each phase is self-explanatory.

When building HTML documents, you probably work with the same sort of phases. You design your HTML document, even if you just make a mental note of the document's general layout, before you begin working on it. Then you implement the HTML document by writing individual lines of HTML code. Finally, you test your Web pages to make sure they work as you planned and that they're syntactically correct.

Using tools that make that last phase, testing and verification, more productive is the topic of this section. You can find various tools on the Internet to help you test your HTML files. Some of the tools you learn about in this section verify the syntax (form) of your HTML files. Other tools in this section just verify the links in your HTML files. Regardless of their function, these tools enable you to verify that Web browsers can understand your HTML files and that your files provide a positive experience to the user.

Doctor HTML

Doctor HTML is a verification service that analyzes the contents of a Web page. For example, you can use it to spell-check a Web page, verify the syntax of the HTML in a Web page, or even check a Web page for broken links. You can also use Doctor HTML to verify your entire Web site, but site verification is a commercial service to which you must subscribe.

Doctor HTML isn't a program that you download onto your computer before using. It's a service (implemented as a CGI script) that you access on the Web at **http://www2.imagiware. com/rRxHTML/**. Click Single Page Analysis in the left frame to see the Web page shown in Figure 39.1. Table 39.1 describes each test shown in the figure.

Table 39.1   Doctor HTML Tests

Test	Description
Spelling	Removes the tags and accented text from the HTML file and scans it for spelling errors.
Image Analysis	Loads all the images to which the HTML file is linked, then determines the bandwidth required by each image and reports any images that require excessive download time. In addition, Doctor HTML reports the size of each image, as well as the number of colors.
Document Structure	Tests the structure of the HTML file, including unclosed HTML tags.
Image Syntax	Makes sure you're using the HEIGHT, WIDTH, and ALT attributes within the IMG tag. These attributes give the browser hints that help it load the HTML document faster.

Test	Description
Table Structure	Checks the structure of each table in the HTML document and looks for any unclosed TR, TH, and TD tags.
Verify Hyperlinks	Reports each invalid link that your HTML file contains. Just because Doctor HTML reports a link as being "dead" doesn't mean that the link is invalid; the server may be running slowly.
Form Structure	Verifies the structure of each form in the HTML file. It looks only at INPUT tags.
Show Commands	Displays an indented list of HTML commands that shows the structure of your HTML document.

FIG. 39.1
You can order all tests by selecting Do All Tests or order individual tests by selecting Select From List Below.

Click to start test
Type the URL

Select to order individual tests

Select the tests you want to order

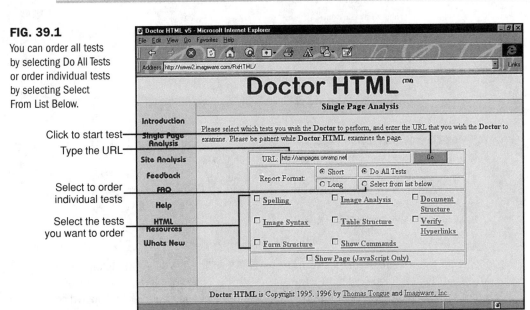

Using Doctor HTML is straightforward. Type the URL of the Web page you want to verify in the URL field. To specify the individual tests you want to run, choose Select From List Below, select each test, and then click Go. Figure 39.2 shows the results of the tests I performed on my home page.

N O T E Doctor HTML looks only at Web pages. You provide the URL of a Web page or site that you want Doctor HTML to check, and it analyzes the files it finds. You can't use Doctor HTML to verify small bits of HTML that you type in a form or HTML files contained in your local file system. ■

FIG. 39.2
Doctor HTML's output is
easy to read.

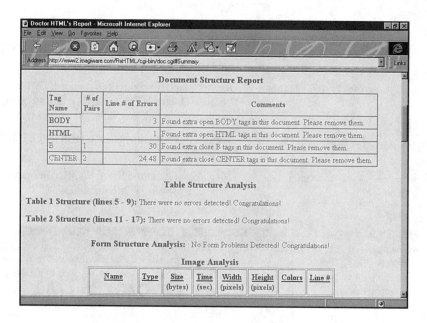

Document Structure Report

Tag Name	# of Pairs	Line # of Errors	Comments
BODY		3	Found extra open BODY tags in this document. Please remove them.
HTML		1	Found extra open HTML tags in this document. Please remove them.
B	1	30	Found extra close B tags in this document. Please remove them.
CENTER	2	24 48	Found extra close CENTER tags in this document. Please remove them.

Table Structure Analysis

Table 1 Structure (lines 5 - 9): There were no errors detected! Congratulations!

Table 2 Structure (lines 11 - 17): There were no errors detected! Congratulations!

Form Structure Analysis: No Form Problems Detected! Congratulations!

Image Analysis

Name	Type	Size (bytes)	Time (sec)	Width (pixels)	Height (pixels)	Colors	Line #

Verifying Links Within a Web Page   One of the best uses for Doctor HTML is to verify the links that your Web page contains. Here's how to perform the test:

1. Type the URL of your Web page in the URL text box.
2. Choose Long.
3. Choose Select From List Below.
4. Select Verify Hyperlinks from the list of tests to run.

Figure 39.3 shows sample output from Doctor HTML. The table lists each link found in the Web page. For each link it identifies the link's URL; the type, size, and change date of the file to which the link points; the line numbers on which the link is used; and any additional comments regarding the link.

N O T E   Doctor HTML doesn't verify the links contained within image maps.

Checking the Performance of Your Images   One of the biggest user complaints is the time required to download Web pages that contain many images. You can get a realistic view of how long a typical user will spend downloading your Web page by using Doctor HTML to check the download time for each image on the page. Here's how:

1. Type the URL of your Web page in the URL text box.
2. Choose Long.
3. Choose Select From List Below.
4. Select Image Analysis from the list of tests to run.

FIG. 39.3
Doctor HTML lists only those links for which it finds warnings or errors.

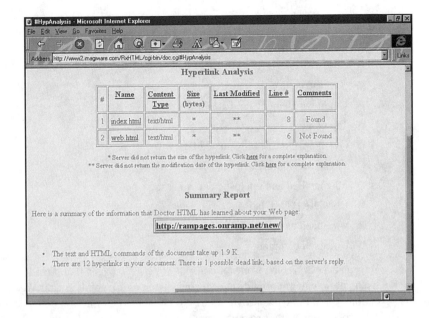

FIG. 39.4
The summary indicates the total download time for all of the images on the Web page.

You'll see results similar to Figure 39.4. The most important column to note is the Time column, which indicates how long the image takes to download using a 14.4K modem.

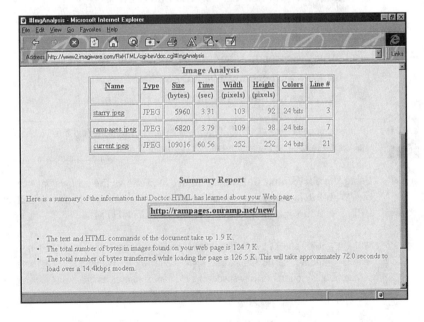

Weblint

Like Doctor HTML, Weblint is a Web-based HTML verification service. It checks the syntax and style of the Web page to which you point it. Some of the things that Weblint checks are:

- Basic structure
- Unknown elements and attributes
- Tag context
- Overlapped or illegally nested tags
- IMG tags that don't use ALT
- Mismatched and unclosed container tags
- Obsolete HTML tags
- Here used as anchor text
- Unclosed comments

You can access Weblint from various gateways (Web pages that provide access to Weblint). Each gateway might provide a form you use to point Weblint to your Web page and set the options you want to use with Weblint. Note that the gateways do not necessarily provide identical forms; some forms are quite complex, whereas others ask only for the Web page's URL. Here's a list of Weblint gateways:

> **http://www.fal.de/cgi-bin/WeblintGateway**
>
> **http://online.anu.edu.au/CNIP/weblint/weblint.html**
>
> **http://www.cen.uiuc.edu/cgi-bin/weblint**
>
> **http://www.ts.umu.se/~grape/weblint.html**
>
> **http://www.netspot.unisa.edu.au/weblint/**
>
> **http://www.unipress.com/cgi-bin/WWWeblint**

TIP The most comprehensive Weblint gateway is at **http://www.fal.de/cgi-bin/WeblintGateway**. This site enables you to configure Weblint exactly as you want.

Using the Fal Weblint Gateway   Figure 39.5 shows the gateway at **http://www.gal.de/cgi-bin/WeblintGateway**, known as the *Fal Weblint gateway*. Type the URL of the Web page in URL, select the options you want, and click Check HTML.

N O T E   If you specify the path to the root of a home page when you open it in your Web browser, the Web server automatically opens an HTML file named INDEX.HTM. The validation services require you to explicitly specify the filename, however, as they won't look for INDEX.HTM on their own. ■

Using the UniPress WWWeblint Gateway   Figure 39.6 shows a much simpler gateway. The UniPress WWWeblint gateway (Unipress is the author of Weblint) at **http://www.unipress.com/cgi-bin/WWWeblint** is a very simple form that only collects the URL of the Web page. After providing the URL, click Check It to verify the Web page.

FIG. 39.5
Click Simple if you want to use a version of the Fal Weblint gateway that provides fewer options.

Type the URL

Click to start

Options

Warnings

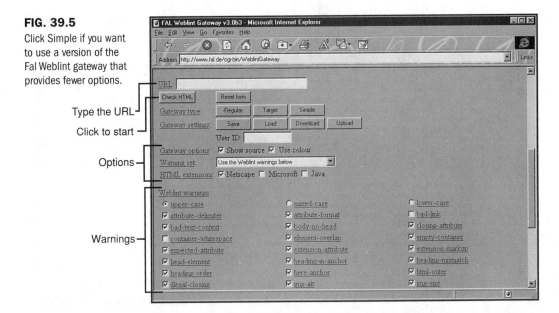

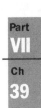

FIG. 39.6
In contrast to the Fal Weblint gateway, the UniPress WWWeblint gateway doesn't support Internet Explorer extensions.

Type

Warnings

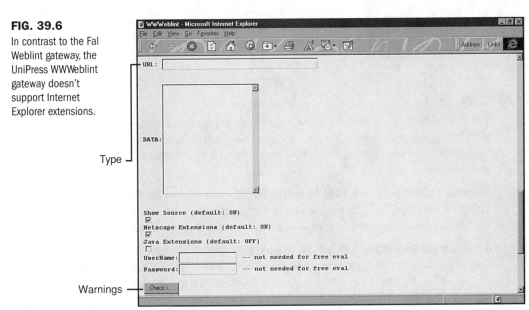

Figure 39.7 shows sample output from Weblint. The top portion of the output lists any warnings and errors Weblint found in the Web page. The bottom portion is a formatted listing of the HTML. The listing is formatted so that the structure of the HTML and the URLs in the HTML are easy to identify.

FIG. 39.7
In addition to listing
warnings and errors
separately, Weblint
embeds them within the
formatted listing.

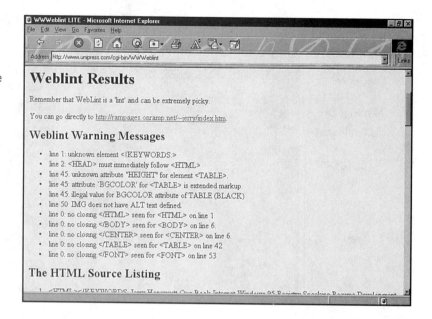

 You can use Netscape's source viewer to get a better view of the format of an HTML document. Choose View, Source from Netscape's main menu. The viewer will highlight the tags and attributes, as well as each URL, contained in the HTML file.

WebTechs

The WebTechs Validation Service checks the conformance of one or more Web pages to the HTML standards you choose. You can also give WebTechs a fragment of HTML to validate by typing it directly into the form. You'll find WebTechs at **http://www.webtechs.com/html-val-svc/** (see Figure 39.8).

Manually Submitting a Web Page to WebTechs   To submit your Web pages to WebTechs for validation, select the level of conformance at the top of the form, type a list of URLs in the space provided, and click Submit URLs for Validation. Figure 39.9 shows some sample output.

Automatically Submitting a Web Page to WebTechs   You don't have to visit the WebTechs Web site to submit a Web page for validation. You can add a button to the bottom of a Web page that automatically submits that Web page for validation. This approach is particularly handy if you're working on a Web site and frequently submitting it for validation. Add the form (see Listing 39.1) to the end of your Web page. Then anytime you want to validate the page, click Submit for Validation. Note that you must change the URL pointed to by the URL's input element to point to the Web page that contains it. You might also change the value of the `level` field to that of your browser.

FIG. 39.8
While visiting this site, check out *Web Apps Magazine,* an online magazine for Web professionals.

Select conformance

Select types

Type list

Click to start

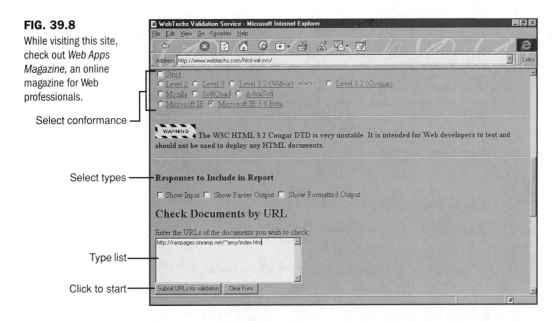

FIG. 39.9
For a better understanding of the WebTechs output, see the FAQ at **http://www.cs.duke.edu/~dsb/wt-faq.html**.

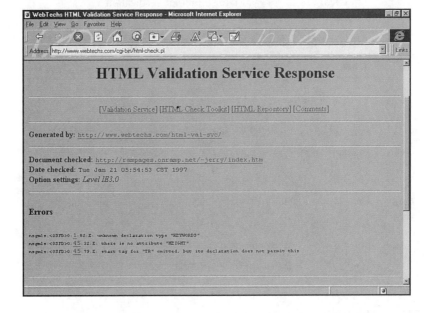

Listing 39.1   Form to automatically submit a URL to WebTechs.

```
<FORM METHOD=POST ACTION="http://www.webtechs.com/cgi-bin/html-check.pl">
<INPUT TYPE=HIDDEN NAME="recommended" VALUE=0>
<INPUT TYPE=HIDDEN NAME="level" VALUE="IE3.0">
<INPUT TYPE=HIDDEN NAME="input" VALUE=1>
<INPUT TYPE=HIDDEN NAME="esis" VALUE=0>
<INPUT TYPE=HIDDEN NAME="render" VALUE=0>
<INPUT TYPE=HIDDEN NAME="URLs"
 VALUE="http://rampages.onramp.net/~jerry/index.htm">
<INPUT TYPE=SUBMIT VALUE="Validate this URL">
</FORM>
```

Here's what each input value contains:

recommended	0 = standard; 1 = strict
level	See Table 39.2
input	1 = show input; 0 = don't show input
esis	1 = show parser input; 0 = don't show parser output
render	1 = render HTML; 0 = don't render HTML
URLs	URL to submit for verification

Table 39.2   Values for the Level Input Element

Value	Description
2	Level 2
3	Level 3
Wilbur	Level 3.2 Wilbur
Cougar	Level 3.2 Cougar
Mozilla	Mozilla (Netscape)
SQ	SoftQuad
AdvaSoft	AdvaSoft
IE	Microsoft IE
IE3.0	Microsoft IE 3.0 Beta

Other Verification Services

You'll also find a handful of other useful verification services on the Web. None of the services described in this section are as comprehensive as the services you learned about earlier. Nevertheless, each provides some sort of unique or useful verification service.

For example, you can use URL-Minder to catch changes to URLs that your Web page references. In addition, the Slovenian HTMLchek is a decent alternative to the other validation services if you're having trouble connecting to them.

Slovenian HTMLchek HTMLchek is a verification service created at the University of Texas at Austin. The online version is available on the Web at **http://www.ijs.si/cgi-bin/htmlchek** (see Figure 39.10). HTMLchek does just about the same thing as Weblint, but its output is considerably harder to read and understand.

FIG. 39.10

HTMLchek hasn't been updated in a while; it doesn't provide support for HTML 3.2 or other browser extensions.

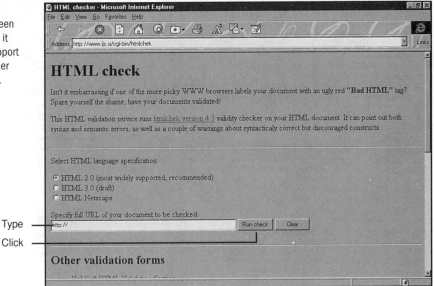

U.S.M.A. (West Point) Figure 39.11 shows the U.S. Military Academy's verification service, called HTMLverify (**http://cgi.usma.edu/cgi-bin/HTMLverify**). You can specify an URL for HTMLverify to test, or you can type some HTML in HTML Source. Click Verify to start the test.

Harbinger Harbinger is a Web site that contains the WebTechs verification service. You can find it at **http://www.harbinger.net/html-val-svc**. The interface is very similar to the WebTechs interface described earlier in the chapter. If you can't access WebTechs, try this site instead.

URL-Minder URL-Minder is a Web-based service that notifies you when the Web page at an URL changes. You give it your e-mail address and a list of URLs. The service then notifies you when the content of one of the URLs you specified has changed. The address for URL-Minder is **http://www.netmind.com/html/url-minder.html**.

N O T E You can also embed a form in your Web page that enables your users to receive e-mail notification when your Web site changes. See the URL-Minder Web site for an example.

FIG. 39.11

HTMLverify is a modified version of Weblint.

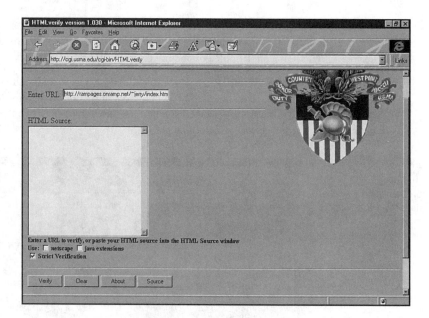

## CHAPTER 40

Listing Your Web Site in the Search Tools

by Jerry Honeycutt, Robert Meegan, and Mark R. Brown

In this chapter

Promoting Your Pages

Current estimates show that the Web has more than 20 million pages. Even using the fastest connection and taking just seconds to glance at each page would take a reader the better part of a decade to see them all, by which time perhaps 10 times as many new pages would have appeared. Because the Web is so huge, it is very unlikely that many people will find your page by pure chance. In fact, if your page has no links leading to it from other pages, chances are good that no one will ever find it.

Because the reason to create a Web page in the first place is to publish information, you want to encourage other people to visit your page. The best way to bring people to your page is to make the job of finding it as easy as possible. This chapter not only shows you how to list your site with the best search tools on the Internet but also explains other methods you can use to get your site noticed.

Understanding the Kind of Advertising You Need

The type of advertising that you do depends greatly on the nature of your page. If you are doing a page as a hobby, spending a thousand dollars to get a week's worth of exposure on one of the popular sites probably isn't worth the cost to you. On the other hand, if your site is the home page of a major multinational corporation, the attention that a professionally designed advertisement can bring more than justifies the expense.

N O T E   Although the term *advertising* is used extensively in this chapter, most of the methods listed here are free. A better term might be *Web page promotion*. ■

With this point in mind, you should take the first step toward advertising on the Web, which is to answer the following questions about your site:

- How much traffic do I want at my site?
- Does my site have a broad appeal, or is it for a more specialized audience?
- How much of a budget do I have to advertise my site?
- How much time can I devote to advertising my site?
- How important is it to the success of my business (or hobby or organization) that my site become well-known?

If your page is an extension of your favorite hobby or interest and your primary intention is to share information with other enthusiasts, you can mount a low-key advertising campaign. Most of the people who find your page will do so through links with other pages that cover the same topics. Think hard about the sites that you like to visit, and you'll probably find that most of your visitors like the same sites.

N O T E   Even if you are starting a page just as a hobby, it doesn't need to end there. Many of the most successful aspects of the Web began as part-time activities. ■

Nonprofit organizations can achieve tremendous exposure on the Web, far out of proportion to the amount of money invested. These organizations often have enough volunteer manpower to find a large number of free locations to advertise the site.

For a small business, the Web can be an excellent place to advertise. On the Web, unlike most other forms of advertising, even a small company can display itself in a way that is as impressive as that of a huge conglomerate. Unlike the print world, the Web gives everyone access to full-color images and advertising regardless of budget. In the democratic world of the Web, all addresses are equally impressive, giving your company real estate that is just as valuable as that of your larger competitors.

If your company is a mail-order or service business that can support customers around the country, or even the world, investing a greater proportion of money and energy in Web advertising may well be worthwhile. If you work at one of these companies, you may want to consider using a commercial marketing service.

Listing with WWW Search Engines

Most people find what they're looking for on the Web by using one of the many available search tools. These systems are huge databases containing as many as 20 million Web pages, coupled with powerful indexing software that can conduct quick searches. Many of the search engines are run on mainframe computers or large parallel processors that can handle hundreds of searches simultaneously. Other search engines run on arrays of Windows NT servers.

In the beginning of the Web, universities ran the first search servers, but now private companies have taken over most of these early efforts. What benefit do these companies get in return for providing free searches on their expensive computers? Advertising! The index sites are some of the most frequently visited on the Web, and those who maintain these sites can charge high rates to the companies that advertise on these pages. That doesn't mean that they charge you to list your site, though. Many search companies—Yahoo!, AltaVista, InfoSeek, and Excite, for example—have become so successful that they're now publicly traded on the stock exchange or have been bought by larger companies.

Part
VII

Ch
40

N O T E   WebTrack's study of Web advertising discovered that 5 of the top 10 sites in terms of revenues from advertising were search tools. ■

In addition to the older sites, more than a hundred newer indexes are available. Some of them are restricted to a specific topic, and others are still very small, but all offer the opportunity to get your site noticed.

As you explore the Web, you soon discover that it possesses its own collection of fauna. The wildlife of the Web consists of autonomous programs that work their way across the millions of links that connect the sites, gathering information along the way.

These programs are known by such colorful names as *robots, crawlers, walkers, spiders* (a generic term), *worms,* and (in the case of one Australian program) *wombats.* What do these spiders do? Almost without exception, they arrive at a page, index it, and search it for any links to other pages. These new links are recorded and followed in turn. When all the links on a particular chain have been followed, the next path is restored from the database and the process continues. Examples of these engines are Lycos and WebCrawler, which you learn more about later in this chapter. A large number of special-purpose spiders are also used to generate statistics regarding the Web. These programs do not generate databases that can be used for text searching, though.

> **N O T E**   Most spiders index the title and content of each Web page they visit. Some search tools—
> AltaVista and Infoseek—also index the `<META>` tag if it's included on the page. (You learn about the `<META>` tag later in this chapter.) ■

The alternatives to these spiders are the *structured systems*. Whereas spiders don't organize links hierarchically, structured systems store Web pages indexed against a series of categories and subcategories. You browse or search through the categories looking for entries. The hierarchical nature of these structured systems appeals to many people who are more comfortable using an index where they can see all the categories. For example, Yahoo! is a very popular index that almost looks more like an online service than a search tool.

The type of system on which you perform your searches is entirely a matter of personal taste. From the standpoint of advertising your site, you need to be aware of the differences. Some of the structured systems restrict you to a limited number of index entries. This limitation can mean that people who are looking for just the things that you offer may not find you because they are looking in the wrong place.

The Major Search Engines

A complete listing of indexes would be out of date as soon as it was finished. New sites are added monthly, and even sites that are maintained by large corporations have disappeared. I have listed a few of the main sites in this section, but you should take the time to do some of your own searching when you decide to publish your pages.

In the big league is the handful of sites that claim to have indexed a sizable portion of the Web. These sites are the most popular systems, used by most Web surfers. You need to register with these servers first to maximize your exposure. Table 40.1 lists the major search engines on which I recommend you list your Web site. The sections that follow describe each search tool in more detail.

Table 40.1   Major Search Engines

Name	URL
AltaVista	http://www.altavista.digital.com
Excite	http://www.excite.com
Infoseek	http://www.infoseek.com
Lycos	http://www.lycos.com

Name	URL
WebCrawler	**http://www.webcrawler.com**
Yahoo!	**http://www.yahoo.com**

All of the sites in Table 40.1 are free to the user. They're sponsored by advertisers. Your listings are also free.

> **CAUTION**
>
> Some of the earliest robots were poorly written and could swamp a server with hundreds of requests within seconds of each other. Fortunately, most recent robots are courteous enough not to overload their hosts. If your server does crash, check the logs for a single site that retrieved many documents within a short period of time. If such a site exists, try to contact the postmaster at the site that made the requests and let him or her know about the problems you saw.

AltaVista   AltaVista (see Figure 40.1) is a search engine that's owned and operated by Digital. It started indexing the Web in the summer of 1995 and went public with 16 million indexed pages in December of 1995. AltaVista gets about 30 million hits per day.

FIG. 40.1
Click Add URL to add your site to AltaVista.

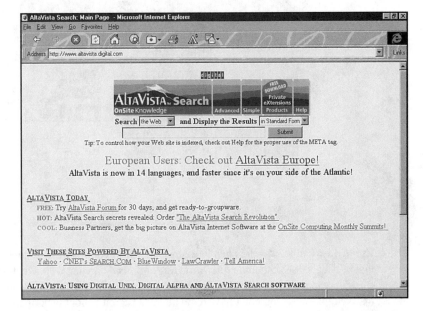

AltaVista scours the Web looking for sites to index. When it finds a site, it indexes the site three levels deep. That is, it indexes the home page, any pages to which the home page is linked, and any pages to which the second-level pages are linked. When AltaVista indexes a page, it indexes the full text of the page. It stores the results in its database, on which a user's search is performed.

N O T E If your Web site changes, you don't need to relist it with AltaVista or most of the other search engines. AltaVista visits its sites periodically, reindexing the contents of the site that have changed. AltaVista is unique in that it notes how often a site changes, and adjusts the frequency of its visits to a given site based on the frequency of its changes. ▓

To list your site with AltaVista, open AltaVista (**http://www.altavista.digital.com**) in your Web browser and click the Add/Remove URL link at the bottom of the page. Follow the instructions you see on the next page. To remove your site from AltaVista, follow the instructions you find at this Web site.

Excite   Excite (see Figure 40.2) started in 1993. It currently indexes more than 50 million Web pages, making it one of the largest databases on the Web. What makes Excite unique among the search engines is that it also contains over 60,000 reviews of individual Web sites. Thus you can get a third-party perspective on the type and quality of information at a particular Web site before you visit.

FIG. 40.2
Click Add URL to add
your site to Excite.

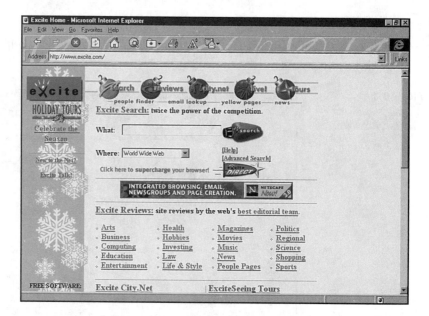

Excite does a full-text index, just like AltaVista. However, Excite also does a concept-based index. That is, if Excite finds the words *Dog* and *Food* on your Web site, those words will match a user's search if he or she uses the terms *Pet* and *Food*. A user is more likely to find your site on Excite because you don't have to be nearly as careful about picking just the right words.

Like AltaVista, Excite indexes a site three levels deep: the home page, its links, and the next level of links. Excite reindexes its site about every two weeks.

To list your site with Excite, open Excite in your Web browser (**http://www.excite.com**) and click Add URL link at the bottom of the page. Follow the instructions on the subsequent Web page. To remove your site from AltaVista, follow the instructions you find at this Web site.

Robot Spiders

If a spider wants to visit your site, there's really nothing you can do to prevent it. Your site is on the Internet, and the pages are available for the spider to access. On the other hand, if you want to keep spiders off your Web site so that they don't affect its performance, most spiders will honor your request if you add a file called ROBOTS.TXT to the root directory of your Web server.

Creating this file is easy. Create a new text file in your root directory called ROBOTS.TXT. Add a line that begins with the field name User-agent. This field must then contain the name of the robot that you want to restrain. You can have multiple User-agent fields, or you can exclude all agents not specifically mentioned in a User-agent field by using a field value of *. The line following each User-agent field should begin with the field name Disallow:. This field should contain an URL path. The robot named in the User-agent field will ignore any URL that begins with the path specified in the Disallow field.

Here are some examples you can use:

```
# Any text that begins with a pound-sign is treated as a comment
User-agent: Webcrawler # Applies to the robot named Webcrawler
Disallow: /webpages/data/ # Webcrawler will skip URLs in this path


# This example is the universal "do not disturb" sign
User-agent: * # All robots
Disallow: / # Every URL begins with a / in the path
```

Infoseek   Infoseek started as a very meager search tool in January 1994, but it's all grown up now (see Figure 40.3). Infoseek indexes more than 50 million Web pages and is a major contender for the best search tool on the Internet.

FIG. 40.3

Click Add Site to add your site to Infoseek.

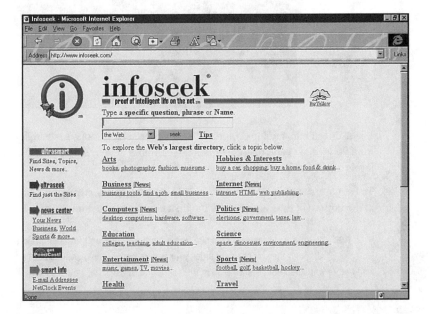

Like the other tools, Infoseek does a full-text index. However, its indexes are only two levels deep, and it only visits your site every three weeks, instead of every two weeks.

To list your site with Infoseek, open Infoseek (**http://www.infoseek.com**) in your Web browser. Then click the Add URL link at the bottom of the page. Follow the instructions you see on the next page. To remove your site from Infoseek, follow the instructions you find at this Web site.

T I P   When submitting your Web site to a spider, only submit the top-level page (home page). The spider will traverse your site to find other pages linked to the home page.

Lycos   Lycos (see Figure 40.4) is one of the granddaddies of the Internet and has gone through some huge changes during its lifetime. Its user interface is greatly improved, its index is larger, and its hierarchical database is better organized than before.

FIG. 40.4

Click Add Your Site to Lycos to add your site to Lycos.

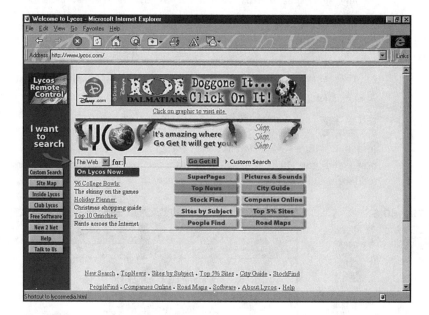

Lycos doesn't do a full text index like the other search tools. Instead, it creates an abstract from your home page that describes the contents of your site. Lycos indexes your site three levels deep, and it revisits sites about every two weeks.

To list your site with Lycos, open it (**http://www.lycos.com**) and click Add Your Site to Lycos at the bottom of the page. Follow the instructions you see on the subsequent Web page.

N O T E   When you submit your Web site to a search engine, don't expect immediate results. Although the spider might index your site immediately, you can expect a two-to-four week wait before your site actually shows up in the search database. ■

WebCrawler   WebCrawler (see Figure 40.5) started as an educational project in 1994. America Online purchased it in 1995. Today, WebCrawler gets about three million hits per day.

FIG. 40.5
Click Add URL to add your site to WebCrawler.

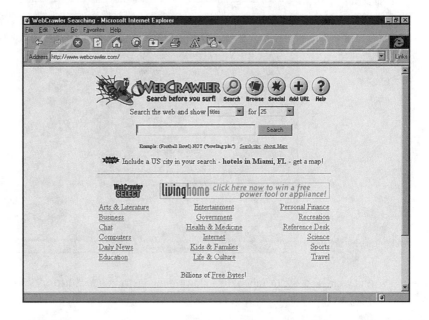

WebCrawler does a full-text index. It only indexes your site one level deep, however, so it only takes information from your home page. In addition, WebCrawler visits its sites about once a month. Consequently, WebCrawler has taken a beating in the press. *PC Magazine* recently gave WebCrawler a failing grade. You should not ignore WebCrawler, however, because it has a very large following given that it's owned by America Online.

To list your site with WebCrawler, open WebCrawler's Add URL page at **http:// www.webcrawler.com/Help/GetListed/AddURLS.html**. You might also want to check out their search engine tips at **http://www.webcrawler.com/Help/GetListed/ HelpAddURL.html**.

Yahoo!   Yahoo! (started in 1994 as a hobby of its creators) is my favorite search tool. Unlike the other tools, Yahoo! is not a worm. It categorizes Web sites that users submit into a hierarchical index. You find what you're looking for by either searching the hierarchy or traversing down each category until you find a Web site in which you're interested.

Yahoo! (see Figure 40.6) is one of the best-organized hierarchical indexes on the Internet. Beyond indexing Web sites, however, Yahoo! provides dozens of other services. For example, Yahoo! categorizes Web sites by their regional areas, such as my hometown of Frisco, Texas. It also provides telephone books (white and yellow pages) in which you can look up a phone number and maps so that you can find a restaurant near you or get directions to your favorite computer store.

Part
VII

Ch
40

FIG. 40.6

You'll find Yahoo! on the Internet at **http:// www.yahoo.com**.

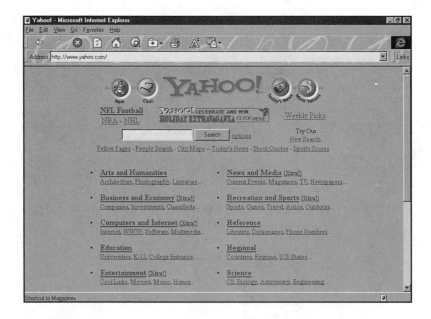

Add your Web site to Yahoo! by following the instructions at **http://www.yahoo.com/docs/ info/include.html**.

Using Submission Services

You do not always have to do all the work yourself. Several good services submit your pages to the major search systems for you. Many of these services charge for this function, but a few services perform the work for free.

 Submit It! is a nice forms-based system. You provide all the relevant data for your page, and Submit It! registers you with your choices of more than a dozen popular search tools (see Figure 40.7). This service is free and can help you hit most of the major search sites. You can found Submit It! at **http://www.submit-it.com**.

Many other submission services are also available on the Web. Table 40.2 lists a few to get you started.

Table 40.2   Submission Services

Name	Free?	URL
AAA Internet Promotions	No	**http://www.websitepromote.com**
Ace Basic	No	**http://sffa/acebase.html**
1 2 3 Add Masters	Yes	**http://www.netfit.com/123-add-masters/index.shtml**

FIG. 40.7
You can use Submit It!
to register with multiple
search engines.

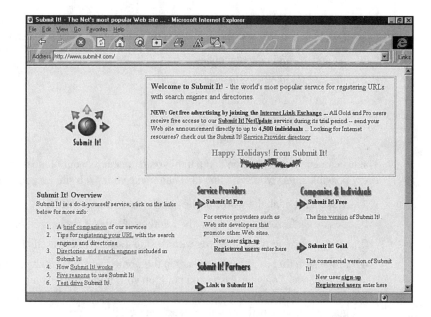

Just as with the search tools, any list of services on the Web is obsolete almost as fast as it is generated. Your best bet is to do a little checking on your own to see what else is out there. A good place to start is the Web Announcements topic on Yahoo!.

The big advantage of a submission service is that it cuts down on the amount of work that you have to do. The disadvantage is that your submissions are made automatically, using the same categories and keywords for each database. This approach is probably sufficient if your page is personal or is intended for a specific audience.

If your page is the Web presence for your company or your organization, you should spend the time to learn about each of the databases. That way you can ensure that your listing ends up under the right headings. After all, the time required to submit your page is nothing compared to the effort you've put into making it as good as it is.

Putting Your Site at the Top of the List

Listing your Web site with a search engine is one thing. Making sure that it appears at the top of the list when a user does a search is a whole different matter. I've seen a lot of folks try their hardest to pick the right set of keywords only to be disappointed when their site didn't make it to the top of the list.

Good Planning Gets You on Top

The best way to make sure your site appears at the top of the list is to do a bit of planning. Sit down with a piece of paper and a few of your colleagues and brainstorm on all the types of queries you think users will use to find your site. Try to anticipate them. Are you selling pet food? If so, people might use the following combination of queries to locate your site:

> pet and grooming and supplies
>
> dog and (food or supplies)
>
> dog and (flea or pest) and treatment
>
> pet and (leash or collar)
>
> dog and (toy or ball or bed)

The list can go on and on. Don't stop until you're absolutely out of ideas and have covered every possible query you can think of. Then make your Web site responsive to those queries.

1. Make a list of all the words in the queries you came up with.
2. Beside each word, write down the number of times it appears in your list of queries.
3. Sort the list, putting the words with the most occurrences at the top of the list.
4. Make sure that each word appears in the home page of your site at least one time. Check off each word on your list as you put it on your home page. You can also use the <META> tag to list your keywords for search engines that catalog the <META> tag. (See " Categorize Your Site with the <META> Tag" on pg. 797)

Other Tips for Getting on Top

Here are some additional ideas to make sure people find your site:

- Use good keywords in your Web page—Make sure to use words that your prospective audience would choose to use, not words that your technical staff would use. For example, your engineers might call it a "super-duper widget," but your customers will probably call it a "thingy."

- Use the <META> tag to embed keywords into your home page—This approach works only for AltaVista and Infoseek. The next section describes how to use the <META> tag.

- Don't rely solely on graphics in your HTML file—In particular, a home page that contains nothing more than an imagemap is disastrous when it comes to listing with the search engines because you haven't given the searching engine anything to index.

- Keep your scripts, VBScript or JavaScript, away from the top portion of your Web page— The search engines that create abstracts will display your scripts instead of a good abstract of your Web site.

- Keep each Web page on your site focused on a particular topic—That is, don't include information about pets on a Web page that contains information about Windows NT Server. This mix will severely confuse concept-based search engines such as Excite. If each Web page is narrowly focused on particular topic, you have a better chance of that page bubbling to the top of the list.

> **CAUTION**
>
> Some folks will tell you that the way to get your site to the top of the list is to repeat the appropriate keywords. For example, if you want users to find your site when they search for the keyword Windows 95, then you might repeatedly fill an HTML comment tag with those keywords. Don't do this. Many of the search engines are now catching on to this little trick and will knock your listing out of the index.

Categorize Your Site with the *<META>* Tag

You can use the HTML <META> tag to tell the search engine a bit more about how to categorize your site. This method doesn't work with all the search engines, however, as the concept- and abstract-based search engines don't necessarily use keywords to categorize a Web site.

The <META> tag is simple. It enables you to create pseudotags within your HTML file. Here's what it looks like:

```
<META NAME=name CONTENT=content>
```

You set the NAME attribute to the name of the tag you are creating and the CONTENT attribute to the content of that tag. This technique is useful only if something on the Internet, for example, client or search tool, is expecting to find a <META> tag by a certain name.

To help along some of the search engines that do look for the <META> tag, you can create two tags called <KEYWORDS> and <DESCRIPTION>. The <KEYWORDS META> tag provides a list of key-words separated by commas for the search engine . You can use this type of <META> tag to specify keywords that don't occur within the text of your HTML file. The <DESCRIPTION META> tag contains a description of your Web site that the search engine will display to the user when it includes your site in a list. Here's what both tags look like:

```
<META NAME="KEYWORDS" CONTENT="pet, dog, cat, food, toys, grooming">
<META NAME="DESCRIPTION" CONTENT="My online pet store provides
 all of your pet supplies."
```

 TIP If your home page uses an image map with little text, at least use a <META> tag for those search engines that parse the <META> tag.

If you are using HTML 4.0, you should add the LANG attribute to the <META> tag, along with NAME and CONTENT information, to specify the human language that a document is written in. For example,

```
<META NAME="KEYWORDS" LAND=en-us CONTENT="pet, dog, cat, food, toys, grooming">
```

indicates that the page is written in U.S. English. You can also use the LINK element to specify links to translations of the document in other languages or formats.

Part

VII

Ch

40

Other Ways to Get Noticed

The Web provides many ways other than search tools to get noticed, including listings, links on other sites, index pages, and newsgroups. Some methods require a bit of work or expense on your part, but others are free.

Best of the Web Listings

One of the more amazing things to come out of the Web has been the tremendous proliferation of "Best of the Web" sites. These systems generate listings under various names, such as What's Cool, What's Hot, Top 5%, Best of the Web, Hot Picks, and so on (see Figure 40.8). In practice, of course, the selection of pages for these lists is completely arbitrary. With the rapid growth of the Web, it is unlikely that anyone has ever even visited five percent of the sites currently available, let alone enough to make a reasonable judgment of which are the very best.

FIG. 40.8

Several organizations present "Best of the Web" awards.

So how are these lists maintained? In most cases you can submit your site's URL to the list administrator, and he or she visits your site and reviews it. If your site meets that list's selection criteria, you get added to the list.

Some of these lists provide you with a small graphic to display on your page to indicate that you have been awarded the honor, and virtually all the lists include links to your page after you have been accepted.

What is the real value of these lists? In the cosmic scheme of things, very little. But some of these lists are well-known, and many people use them as launching points for random surfing. If you have a general interest site, getting it listed on a couple of these pages can really boost your traffic.

Some examples of these sites are:

- Cool Site of the Day—This strange and quirky site is located at **http://cool.infi.net**.
- Macmillan Winner's Circle—This site recognizes excellence in personal home pages; go to **http://www.mcp.com/general/workshop/winner**.
- What's Cool—If you can manage to get yourself onto Netscape's What's Cool Page, you'll have to beat back the visitors with a stick. You can find this index of pages at **http://home.netscape.com/home/whats-cool.html**.

Links from Other Web Sites

Even more than the Web crawlers and structured systems, the primary method for traversing the Web is by using links found on other pages (see Figure 40.9). To expose your page to the maximum number of potential visitors, you should make an effort to get as many sites as possible to include links to your site.

FIG. 40.9
Many sites have long lists of links to other related sites.

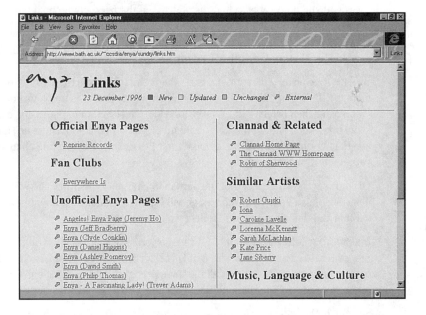

Part
VII

Ch
40

Most sites that cover a specific topic are more than pleased to include links to other sites that cover the same topic. By including as many links as possible, they make themselves more useful and, hence, more popular. To encourage people to link to your page, you need to identify sites that might be interested in linking to yours and then contact the site administrator.

Finding Sites from Which to Link   The best way to find sites to contact about linking to your site is to surf the Web. Find sites that are of interest to you, and you'll probably find the sites that are of interest to people who would visit your site. Where should you start surfing? The same places that your visitors would.

Start with the indexes and see what's out there. Try several of the more popular ones and be sure to try both structured systems and Web crawlers. If one of indexes is particularly useful, you know that it is a good place to register your site. The ones that aren't useful can wait before you submit to them.

After you find some sites, visit them and see what they have to offer. You're looking for sites that have a theme that is similar to yours, without being identical. For example, if your page contains links to everything that a person might ever want to know about hog farming, pages that might make good links to your page include general farming pages, pages that cover animal husbandry, and pages for companies that do business with hog farmers, including both suppliers and consumers. Other pages that also cover aspects of hog farming but are not duplicates of yours would also be worth linking to.

Convincing Sites to Link to Your Site   The best way to get a link to your Web page is to simply contact the owner of the page that you'd like to be linked from and ask him or her to create the link. You can most easily accomplish this task by sending e-mail to the page author. In most cases you should be able to find the address of the person who maintains the link on one of the pages at the site. Failing this, try sending e-mail to the address Webmaster at the site that interests you. Finally, if all else fails, you can examine the HTML source for the site's main page to see whether the author's address is included in a comment field.

Be sure to explain what your site is all about and to include the URL of the home page in your message. If the page that you want the other site to link to is not your home page, tell the Webmaster the correct URL. A brief (one line) description of your page can save him or her some time when adding the link. Remember that other Webmasters are just as busy as you are and that anything you can do to make their life easier increases the chance that they will link to your page.

Of course, you can expect that the person in charge of the other site will check out your page before adding a link. The Webmaster will want to make sure that your page actually is what you say it is and that its quality will reflect well on his or her site.

Making Your Site Worth a Link   To make your site more worthwhile for others to link to, the first step is to ensure that it is free of HTML errors and that it loads correctly. Ask people from outside your site to check that all the images are available and that all the tags display in the proper format. No one wants to be associated with a site that is filled with sloppy work.

Second, include useful, current, and interesting information and images. No one wants to spend time downloading a site just to find that it contains a mess of outdated or boring gibberish. Links to shareware programs can also make your page more popular.

CAUTION

Before adding a link to download any program, be sure that the program explicitly states that it is for freeware or shareware distribution, particularly if it is not stored on your server.

Finally, make your site attractive. Ask yourself if the page makes you want to read it; then get the opinions of some people you can trust.

An important step toward making your site successful is to include a number of links to other sites that might be of interest to visitors to your site. The entire concept of the Web revolves around the interconnection of millions of sites. Don't make your page a dead end.

TIP Check occasionally that all the links on your page still lead somewhere. Pages maintained by other people may disappear, often without notice. See Chapter 39, "Verifying and Testing HTML Documents," for more information.

If your site is a personal page, include connections to pages of your friends and colleagues. A hobby site should include as many links to other sites with similar interests as you can find. Check the links to make sure that they point to pages that you want to be associated with; then include them.

N O T E Although you can certainly add a link to a page without the prior consent of the owner of the page, letting him or her know of the new link is courteous. The owner may also have a preference as to which page you establish the link. ■

Business and organization pages can include links to other sources of information related to their site. Including links to your competitors is not necessary, but having links that point to your suppliers and customers might be very effective. Encourage them to include reciprocal links back to your page. Remember that the most effective form of advertising is networking and that a link to your page is an implicit recommendation.

Specialized Index Pages

If your pages are focused on a specific topic, registering with any specialized index pages that cover your area of interest is well worth the time.

At present, you can find many sites for business-related topics. This fact isn't surprising, but what is amazing is the incredible variety of index pages available for other interests as well. A search of the Web turns up many specialized pages that contain dozens of links. Here are a few examples of these pages:

- Art Planet—A professionally run site that supports searches based on companies, keywords, or artists (see Figure 40.10). It is located at **http://www.artplanet.com/ index.html**.

- The Hamster Page—This is the definitive hamster resource page, and you can find it at **http://www.tela.bc.ca/hamster**.

- Special Needs Education Network—A site that provides a number of links to resources for people with special needs and parents of children with special needs. You can find it at **http://schoolnet2.carleton.ca/~kwellar/snewww.html**.

FIG. 40.10

You can use specialized search tools such as Art Planet to promote your page.

- Chess Space—A comprehensive index to everything in the chess world. It is located at **http://www.redweb.com/chess**.

- Points of Pediatric Interest—More than 650 links dedicated to pediatric medicine and child care. You can find it at **http://www.med.jhu.edu/peds/neonatology/poi.html**.

- Church Online—A worldwide list of Christian churches. It is located at **http://www.churchonline.com/index.html**.

In the business world, pages exist for many different types of companies. You can see some of the tremendous variety in the following pages:

- TruckNet—A site specializing in just about everything that you might ever want to know about the trucking industry. It is located at **http://www.truck.net**.

- Petro-Links—This site has links to oil companies, suppliers, petroleum industry magazines, and applicable government agencies. It is located at **http://www.findlinks.com/petrolinks.html**.

- Fashion Net—A service with hundreds of links to companies that are involved in the fashion and clothing industries. Not all these companies have Web sites, but many do. You can find Fashion Net at **http://www.fashion.net**.

- Thomas Register—A site run by the company that publishes the famous *Thomas Register of Manufacturers*. If you work for a manufacturing company or if you supply manufacturing companies, you really should submit your site at **http://www.thomasregister.com**.

Using Newsgroups Effectively

A Web site is very difficult to find in the vast reaches of the Internet. Fortunately, you can use public bulletin boards to broadcast information to many people simultaneously. These public areas are known as newsgroups, and they serve as public forums for communications and debate.

Much like everything else on the Internet, these groups have their own rules and customs. Very broadly, they fall into two categories: open and moderated groups. *Open groups* are pretty much what the name implies, in that anyone can post a message. Unfortunately, this freedom often leads to a very low signal-to-noise ratio. In *moderated groups*, all postings pass through a moderator (or group of moderators) who screens the messages and removes off-topic messages. This process greatly improves the proportion of postings that are relevant to the subject of the newsgroup.

Regardless of the type of newsgroup, proper use can greatly increase the traffic at your Web site. By the same token, however, improper use can cause ill feelings and will not attract the visitors that you are looking for.

The Announcement Groups   The first newsgroups to use when spreading the word about your new Web site are the announcement groups. These groups are dedicated to the purpose of broadcasting messages dealing with new sites and services (see Figure 40.11). Most of these groups are moderated and do an excellent job of keeping messages on-topic.

FIG. 40.11
comp.infosystems.
www.announce is the
number one site for
posting new sites.

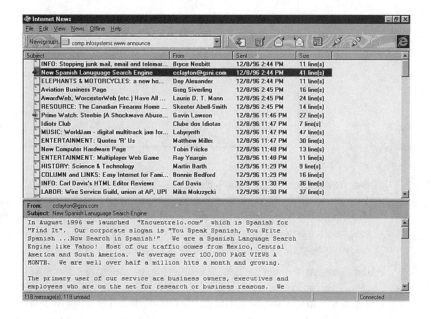

comp.infosystems.www.announce lists virtually every site that is submitted to it. The rules of this group are standard for many of the announcement groups. Postings should be relevant to the purpose of the group and should not have a commercial purpose other than the announcement of a Web site that provides further information about a commercial product or service. The announcement message should clearly list the URL of the new page, preferably on a separate line. The message should also include a clear but brief description of the nature of the site. Finally, the subject of the message should be clear and precise. The subject should begin with a word or two that clearly defines your site, as shown in the example in Figure 40.12.

Other good groups to announce in are **comp.internet.net-happenings** and **misc.entrepreneurs** (for business sites).

FIG. 40.12

This announcement is clear and concise, and it tells prospective visitors what they can expect.

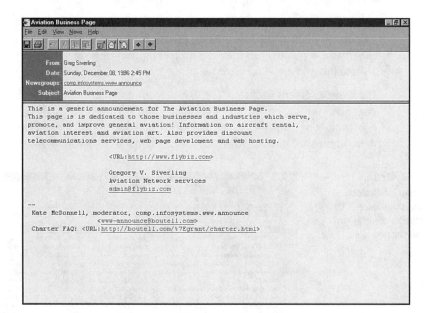

Other Newsgroups   After you have posted on the announcement newsgroups, you should take some time to find any other groups that may involve topics covered in your Web site. Far more than 20,000 newsgroups are operating right now, although your Internet provider may cache only a fraction of this number. With this kind of diversity, finding the groups that most closely match your interests is normally not difficult.

After you narrow down the field to a small handful of groups, the next step is to read the various messages that are posted. Try to identify people who are regular posters and look for threads that have a long life. The practice of reading messages on a group without posting is known as *lurking*. You lurk in a group to become more familiar with it before you post.

One of the features of many groups is the occasional posting of what is called a FAQ. This message is a list of Frequently Asked Questions, and reading it carefully can help you avoid asking any questions that might have been answered repeatedly in the past.

The primary benefit to lurking is that when you are ready to post messages, you can do so in a manner that is perceived as highly competent and professional.

After you do start posting, you should make a special effort to ensure that your posts are well written and on-topic. Remember that you are not just carrying on a friendly conversation, but rather you are advertising your page. Avoid mentioning your Web site in the body of your posting, but include your signature at the end of the message. If your postings are worth reading, people will make an effort to visit your pages, too.

One form of message posting is not recommended: Sending messages to post on multiple newsgroups, regardless of the group's topic, is known as *spamming* (see Figure 40.13). This kind of posting is a tremendous waste of bandwidth, and many people, particularly those who pay for their access based on time spent logged in, do not appreciate your postings.

FIG. 40.13
The message about saving on long-distance charges is off-topic for this group and is an example of spamming.

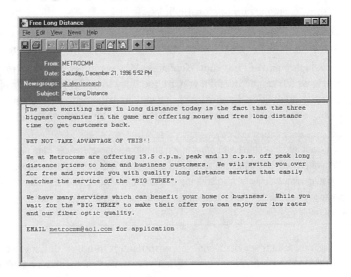

An unfortunate side effect of spamming is that it tends to attract retaliation from residents of the Internet. This retaliation can begin at the annoyance level and rapidly escalate. To avoid any unpleasantness, you should follow the rules and act in a responsible manner.

N O T E The primary offense caused by spamming is the waste of huge amounts of storage space on computers around the world. To help curb the problem, many newsgroups have programs that can excise spamming messages automatically from the group, often before most people even see the message. One side effect of spamming is that you may become blacklisted, which can expose you to remarkable levels of harassment from cybervigilantes. ▦

Using a Publicity Consultant

Developing an effective Web advertising campaign can clearly take a lot of work. For a hobbyist, this time might not "cost" much, but for a busy professional who is trying to build up

Part
VII

Ch
40

business through the Web, the time required may be more than he or she can afford. One solution to this problem is to hire a publicity consultant to get your site noticed.

Some of the functions that a publicity consultant should perform follow.

- Submitting your site to all the major search engines and to any others that may be appropriate—Every submission should be followed up to make certain that the database actually added your site and that it can be located under the correct headings.

- Locating appropriate newsgroups—Some agents also identify threads that are relevant to your site and then post messages that subtly promote your site. This task is rather delicate, so you should ask to see examples of the agent's work before hiring someone for this job.

- Identifying pages for reciprocal links—An agent should also take care of contacting the other sites and arranging for the links.

- Locating and purchasing advertising space on commercial Web pages—An agent with many contacts and clients may be able to arrange lower rates than you could by yourself.

- Developing and editing your Web site—Most agencies also do Web site development work, which can be useful if you are too busy to develop your own site or if you have no artistic capabilities. Even if you are a skilled artist or writer, having a professional critique your work and make suggestions may be productive.

TIP Before you enter into a contract with anyone, you should ask for references from previous clients. Contact the references and ask if the agent was aggressive in promoting their sites and prompt in communicating with the clients. Also take the time to look at the client sites themselves. Are they professional in appearance? Well-designed pages indicate that the client's recommendation should carry a solid weight.

The cost of consultant services can range from a few hundred dollars to tens of thousands, depending on the scope of the work. When you do contract with a consultant, consider the possibility of basing the fee on the amount of traffic that your site receives. This approach requires the agent to put his or her money on the line and increases the incentive to provide good service. Be aware that this tactic may increase the cost of services to you because the consultant is now sharing some of the risk.

Advertise Your Site in Print

In this chapter you've examined a number of ways to advertise your site on the Internet. However, you can also increase your exposure through other methods. Indeed, if you don't use these other techniques, you may miss out on many opportunities.

The simplest of all advertising tools is to include your site's URL in the signature on all your e-mail. Including your URL costs nothing and has the advantage of appearing before an audience that is (or at least should be) receptive to your message already.

You should also add your Web site URL to your business cards and stationery. In effect, your Web site is your office in cyberspace, and you should include its address alongside your physical office. Before you do so, however, remember to walk through your site carefully to check for a professional and finished appearance. You wouldn't invite potential clients into a half-finished office covered with graffiti, and you shouldn't show them your work in progress on the Web, either.

Finally, include your URL on any ads you place in magazines, newspapers, or trade journals. For many people the discovery of a Web site in an advertisement is an illicit thrill. It's a way of letting people with access to the Web feel that they're an exclusive group and that you're catering especially to them. Take advantage of the cachet that comes with being on the Web whenever you can.

Internet Ratings and PICS

One distinction you do not want is to have your pages marked to be blocked for access. Many parents, schools, libraries, religious institutions, and even businesses are concerned that children or employees might be accessing pornographic (or at the very least, unproductive) sites while they're browsing the Web.

In the last two years, several new software products have sought to address this problem by creating lists of sites from which a browser is blocked. These programs create lists of URLs that a browser is forbidden to access. The problem with this system is that every publisher has its own list of what should and shouldn't be blocked. Standards were needed.

The industry now has an independent method for indicating site content, called the Platform for Internet Content Selection (PICS). Simply put, PICS lets you label the appropriateness of your own site. Blocking programs can then simply strip out your own rating material and use it to determine whether to block your site. (As a side benefit, the PICS standard also supports other types of labeling, code signing, privacy, and copyright management.)

The PICS format uses a META declaration to label a page, as in this example taken from the W3C site:

```
<HEAD>
  <META http-equiv="PICS-Label"
  content='(PICS-1.1 "http://www.gcf.org/v2.5"
  labels on "1994.11.05T08:15-0500"
  until "1995.12.31T23:59-0000"
  for "http://w3.org/PICS/Overview.html"
  ratings (suds 0.5 density 0 color/hue 1))
  '>
<TITLE>Page Title</TITLE>
</HEAD>
<BODY>
Body of Document.
</BODY>
```

Part

VII

Ch

40

The RATINGS value is taken from any of a number of ratings vocabularies supplied by various vendors or organizations. You can choose any one vocabulary, or, because you can have more than one <META> tag, you can supply ratings using several different vocabularies. This approach enables you to support blocking software from many companies.

N O T E Three of the most popular sources for rating vocabularies are:

- SafeSurf Internet Rating Specifications: **http://www.safesurf.com/ssplan.htm**
- Recreational Software Advisory Council on the Internet (RSACi) Specificationshttp: **http://www.rsac.org/ratingsv01.html**
- CyberNOT Rating Service: **http://www.microsys.com/pics/pics_msi.htm**. ▓

PICS offers a wide range of options and is an evolving standard. You can find out more about PICS from the W3C Web site at **http://www.w3.org/PICS**.

Here's a list of various blocking programs that are PICS-compatible, their vendors, and their Web sites:

- Cyber Patrol and Cyber Sentry
  Microsystems Software Inc.
  http://www.microsys.com/cyber/default.htm
- Internet Explorer 3.0
  Microsoft Corporation
  http://www.microsoft.com/ie/
- Net Shepherd
  Net Shepherd
  http://www.shepherd.net
- Specs for Kids
  NewView
  http://www.newview.com
- SurfWatch
  Spyglass
  http://www.surfwatch.com
- Cyber Snoop
  Pearl Software
  http://www.pond.com/~pearlsft/snoop.htm

N O T E PICS labels can be used to label just about anything with a URL, not just Web sites. The list includes FTP and Gopher, but not e-mail. ▓

Building a Secure Web Site

by Mark R. Brown

Security on the Internet

Even the big boys get their noses tweaked now and then. In the summer of 1996, both the U.S. Central Intelligence Agency and the U.S. Department of Justice—organizations that one would think would have pretty tight security—had their Web sites vandalized. The CIA became the "Central Stupidity Agency" and DOJ became the "Department of Injustice." Both sites had their pages populated with diatribes against the Communications Decency Act, as well as Nazi images and pornographic pictures. Both organizations lost much face over the incidents.

Certain aspects of your Web site cannot be protected. Your HTML source will always be publicly viewable—and stealable. Any graphics you have embedded in Web pages will be stealable, as will any VBScript and JavaScript code. Java source code can be kept secure, but compiled .class files are stealable.

The fact is, no one is immune to Internet treachery. You need to be aware of the risks and the ways in which you can protect your network resources.

Play at Your Own Risk

If you connect a computer to a network, you expose that computer and the data it contains to security threats. That is the unavoidable truth.

Recall the 1996 movie *Mission: Impossible*. In that movie, the Impossible Missions squad had to steal information from a supersecure computer at CIA headquarters. Why was that computer so secure? Because it was kept in a locked room and connected to no network. To steal data from the machine, the squad had to break into the room and copy information onto a disk. Though they succeeded (naturally, for the sake of the plot), their efforts went far beyond what most wired evildoers are willing to undertake.

The advantages of having Internet-connected employees far outweigh the risks associated with exposing private information to unwelcome prying eyes. You shouldn't shun Internet connectivity because you fear security breaks. But sometimes the bad guys win. You can't beat them all the time. It's part of doing business online. However, you need to protect yourself as much as possible.

Safe Serving

When you start connecting computers to a network, particularly the Internet, you should be aware of the bad things that can befall your system and the data it holds. Security breaches fall into four general categories:

- Theft of data that's making its way along the data pathways of the Internet
- Theft of private data stored on a networked computer
- Modification of public data, including Web page vandalism
- Hijacking of a server so that server can be used as a base for other attacks, hiding the true identity of the responsible people

In planning your protection, you should decide what level of security you want to achieve. This should depend upon several factors, including:

- *The sensitivity and value of what you have to protect.* No one cares about your e-mail to your mother. No one cares about your contributions to the JavaScript mailing list or your recipe file. People do, however, want information with monetary value. If you have plans and reports on your machine that your competitors would pay money to see, those plans and reports merit protection.

- *The attractiveness of you or your organization as a target.* If you run the network presence of some small-time software developer, you probably don't have to worry too much about vandalism-motivated attacks. On the other hand, if you run a site for a prominent organization (Microsoft, say, or an abortion-rights group), people may break into your site just to mess it up. And never deliver a direct challenge to hackers to get them to "test" your security. You might get more than you bargained for.

- *The amount of money you want to spend on security.* Security requires time, expertise, and equipment, all of which come with price tags. You have to decide how much you're willing to spend on protecting data. Clearly, you should spend less on protecting a given piece of data than the data itself is worth.

- *The amount of time you have to build and maintain a security system.* Organizations usually don't hire security experts. Most of the time, they dump responsibility for network security on the network administrator or Webmaster, who most likely already is pretty overworked. Organizations have to decide how to budget the technical people's time to achieve the best results.

Once you've decided what you have to protect and the resources available for protecting it, you have to decide upon a target degree of security—again keeping in mind that you can't win all the battles all the time.

Most people are content to keep their sensitive information isolated from the Internet through the use of a firewall (covered later in this chapter), some password protection, and intelligent use of their server's standard security software. Others take a more extreme approach—using multiple layers of cryptography and advanced protection schemes like proxy servers. Still others rely on the good nature of human beings and take practically no precautions. The decision is up to you.

Viruses

Since the Michaelangelo virus scare of 1993, computer viruses have been the subject of popular and technical news reports. They sound terrifying—malicious little programs replicating themselves all over the place, wreaking havoc on hard drives, and playing hob with Windows. The Internet has provided viruses with a whole new way to spread.

In truth, viruses are scary and they really can shut down a system in a hurry, destroying critical data in the process. But they're not as widespread as the popular and industry media might lead you to believe. Like any other security threat, you need to be informed about what viruses are and how they work in order to protect your data from them.

What Are They?

Viruses are computer programs gone wrong. Usually, they do some kind of malicious deed, such as deleting files or displaying an annoying message, without anyone's assistance and without the knowledge of the victim, until it is too late.

There are several kinds of viruses:

■ *Viruses with their own files*. These viruses have their own executable files that copy themselves onto a target computer's hard disk. Viruses of this kind are easiest to detect.

■ *Viruses that attach themselves to other files*. These viruses cling to other files as a form of camouflage. Frequently, viruses of this kind will attach themselves to operating system files.

■ *Trojan horses*. Just like the Trojan horse of mythology, Trojan horse viruses pretend to be one thing when in fact they're something else. Typically, Trojan horses take the form of a game that deletes files while the user plays.

How to Protect Your System

Viruses are bad news, but they're not an insurmountable problem. There are a couple of things you can do to protect yourself from them, and neither of these preventatives are especially difficult to implement.

Common Sense   Protecting your computer from viruses is like protecting yourself from colds. A little bit of common sense goes a long way toward limiting your machine's exposure. Just like you shouldn't shake hands with someone who is sneezing frequently, don't install unknown software on your computer, and particularly not on your Web server. Try to limit the software you install to shrink-wrapped programs straight from a software retailer (though once in a while, they too will carry viruses). Freeware and shareware often carry viruses, so be sure to scan such programs with anti-virus programs before putting them to work.

This goes double for games and other entertainment software packages, which sometimes are fronts for Trojan horses and other malicious software.

Anti-Virus Software   The virus-protection industry is a huge one. Equip your server with one of the commercially available virus-protection software packages (Symantec Norton Anti-Virus is the top seller) and keep your chosen package updated by installing the manufacturer's update modules regularly (usually once every quarter).

General Security Precautions

Much of what you can do to prevent unwanted intrusions into your systems is quite simple. In just an hour or two, you can implement these changes and make your system significantly less attractive to casual electronic vandals.

Taking these security precautions is like putting a security system on your car. Sure, an enterprising criminal could defeat your computer security precautions, just as an ambitious thief could break into your car despite your security system. It's an issue of the ease with which a bad guy could get at your stuff—an electronic vandal might move on to easier targets if he saw your site was protected, even a little bit. The following are some of the most cost- and time-effective security precautions you can take.

If It's Not There, They Can't Steal It

Don't make a stupid mistake and leave sensitive files in locations where they might be happened upon by the wrong people. Don't laugh—it happens.

Keep all your sensitive files in private folders, preferably on a computer protected by a firewall. You'll learn more about firewalls later in this chapter.

Get Rid of Guest Accounts

Many server operating systems, including Windows NT 4.0 Server, come from the factory with a preconfigured Guest account. That is, they have a username defined as Guest (often with no password) that gives certain access to anyone who wants it. Though Guest privileges usually are extremely limited, they sometimes are enough to provide a toehold for people looking to get other privileges for nefarious purposes.

Delete your server's Guest account. If someone wants limited access for a short time, make them contact you and ask for a special account. If you must have a generic account for all temporary users, at least make the username something other than "Guest." That way, you'll keep the bad guys guessing and maybe inspire them to move on to easier targets.

Figure 41.1 shows the warning you get when you delete the Guest account on a Windows NT 4.0 system.

FIG. 41.1
Deleting the Guest account in Windows NT 4.0 brings up this dialog.

Rename the Administrator Account

Similarly, most operating systems for networked computers include a preconfigured account for the person in charge of maintaining that system. Almost without variation, this account has the username "Administrator."

This is bad, because when a bad guy is breaking into a system, he or she is supposed to have to guess at least two things: a username and a password. By leaving your computer configured with an all-powerful user with the username Administrator, you're giving away half of the secret.

So, you should rename your Administrator account. Make it "BorisSpider0175" or some name that only you know. Just don't make it something obvious (your name or your electronic mail address) and don't leave it as Administrator. Changing the account name in any operating system takes five minutes, if that long.

Figure 41.2 shows the dialog box used to configure usernames and passwords in Windows NT 4.0.

FIG. 41.2
Configuring usernames and passwords in Windows NT 4.0 is done from within this dialog box.

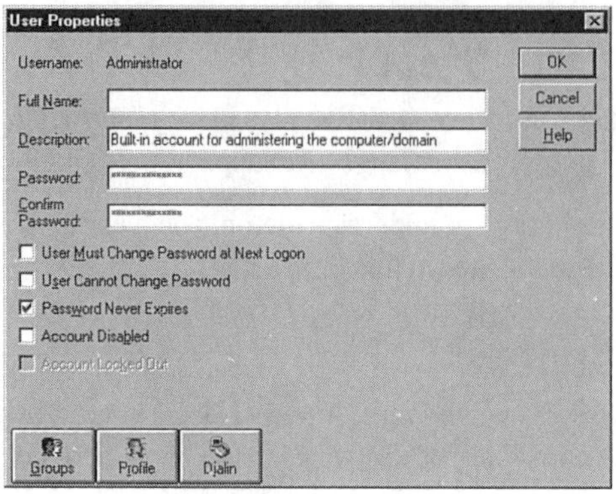

Choose Passwords Intelligently

You've probably heard this advice before, but its importance is magnified on a Web server and it bears repeating. Do not allow users to have obvious passwords. Don't let them use any of the following as their passwords:

- Their names
- The names of anyone in their family
- Their Social Security or employee numbers
- Their car's license plate sequence
- Their ZIP code
- Their telephone number
- Passwords they use on other systems
- Anything else that is either public information or easily guessable

It's also a good idea to disallow any standard word in any language as a password. Doing this prevents potential intruders from running through a dictionary (automatically, very fast) in search of a password.

A better way to choose a password is to choose a sequence of letters, numbers, and symbols that appears random but in fact is easily memorable. Don't forget to mix upper- and lowercase letters, too. For example, a password might be based on the sentence, "My second child, Judy, weighs 40 pounds." That could be translated into the seemingly inscrutable password "m2cJw40#." No one would ever guess that, and it would take a long time to figure it out by brute force. However, make sure that you choose a password that you can remember, or your system administrator will learn to hate you.

Also, make sure passwords get changed frequently—every month at least, and more frequently if you suspect that someone is trying to intrude. Many systems have an option,

Force User to Change Password that you should use. However, don't adopt a simple password changing scheme, such as simply adding one to your password every month.

Finally, never, ever write your password down, especially in an insecure location. Bottom line— make sure your password is kept as securely as the system it is supposed to protect.

Disable Unneeded Protocols

You can't break into a computer via Telnet if that computer doesn't support the Telnet protocols. If you have no use for a particular Internet service on a particular machine, disable that service. You can reenable it if you ever need to use it, and meanwhile, you're preventing intruders from using that service to their advantage.

Keep track of which services people are using on which computers and disable the unused services promptly.

Be Miserly with Write Privileges

System administrators have the ability to define which users can do what with the system. Among the most valuable privileges is the Write privilege—the ability to save information on the hard disk. Any user lacking this privilege may be able to read information (look at Web documents, for example) but is not able to write anything.

This prevents several problems, including:

- People copying viruses onto your server's hard drive
- People deleting, replacing, or modifying Web pages (as happened at the CIA and DOJ sites)
- People creating illegal usernames and passwords for their own future use

Figure 41.3 shows an administrator configuring access privileges in Windows NT 4.0.

FIG. 41.3
Configuring access privileges in Windows NT 4.0.

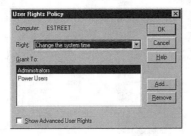

Disable Your Server's Directory Browsing Feature

Most Web server software packages allow you, the administrator, to enable and disable a feature that allows Web surfers to browse through folders on your server's hard disk, as if your Web server were an FTP server. When this feature is disabled, surfers are limited to viewing pages and cannot see the contents of directories.

Always keep your server software's directory browsing feature turned off. Doing so makes it that much harder for outsiders to see things you don't want them to see.

Also your system's root directory and the root URL of your Web site should never be the same. Keep all private files in nonpublic server directories.

Watch Your System Logs

Every operating system suitable for use on a server keeps a log of system events. Usually, system logs make note of who logs on and when, who tries to log on and fails, and who tries to access which pieces of data on the system. System logs also record errors and other technical failures.

You should review your system log regularly—every other day at least. Look for indications that someone is trying to gain access or privileges illegally. You'll often have time to pick up on these goings-on because the process of breaking into a computer is a time-consuming one and may require efforts spread over several days. Figure 41.4 shows a typical system log, this one from Windows NT 4.0.

N O T E You can always tell where your pages and images are being accessed from by looking at the referrer log of your Web server. If there are requests for images that didn't come from your domain, it usually means that someone at the requesting domain has a URL link to one of your images on their Web page. ■

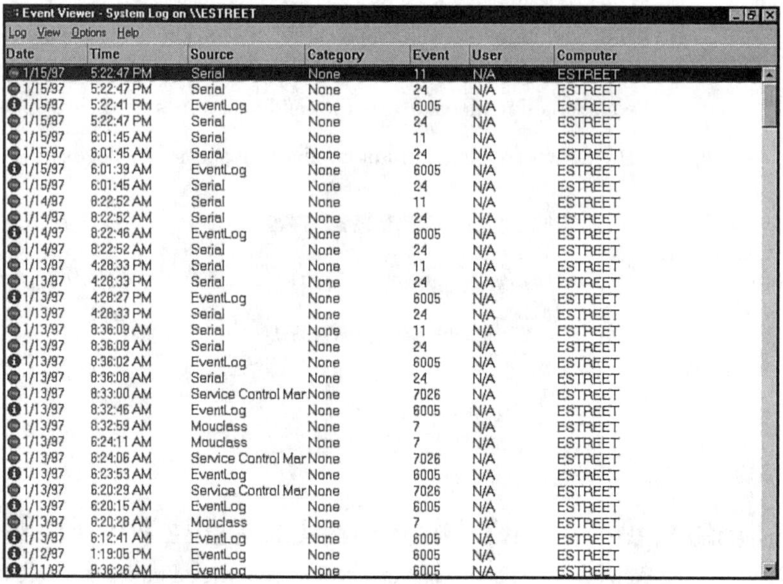

FIG. 41.4

This is a Windows NT 4.0 event log.

Date	Time	Source	Category	Event	User	Computer
1/15/97	5:22:47 PM	Serial	None	11	N/A	ESTREET
1/15/97	5:22:47 PM	Serial	None	24	N/A	ESTREET
1/15/97	5:22:41 PM	EventLog	None	6005	N/A	ESTREET
1/15/97	5:22:47 PM	Serial	None	24	N/A	ESTREET
1/15/97	6:01:45 AM	Serial	None	11	N/A	ESTREET
1/15/97	6:01:45 AM	Serial	None	24	N/A	ESTREET
1/15/97	6:01:39 AM	EventLog	None	6005	N/A	ESTREET
1/15/97	6:01:45 AM	Serial	None	24	N/A	ESTREET
1/14/97	8:22:52 AM	Serial	None	11	N/A	ESTREET
1/14/97	8:22:52 AM	Serial	None	24	N/A	ESTREET
1/14/97	8:22:46 AM	EventLog	None	6005	N/A	ESTREET
1/14/97	8:22:52 AM	Serial	None	24	N/A	ESTREET
1/13/97	4:28:33 PM	Serial	None	11	N/A	ESTREET
1/13/97	4:28:33 PM	Serial	None	24	N/A	ESTREET
1/13/97	4:28:27 PM	EventLog	None	6005	N/A	ESTREET
1/13/97	4:28:33 PM	Serial	None	24	N/A	ESTREET
1/13/97	8:36:09 AM	Serial	None	11	N/A	ESTREET
1/13/97	8:36:09 AM	Serial	None	24	N/A	ESTREET
1/13/97	8:36:02 AM	EventLog	None	6005	N/A	ESTREET
1/13/97	8:36:08 AM	Serial	None	24	N/A	ESTREET
1/13/97	8:33:00 AM	Service Control Mar	None	7026	N/A	ESTREET
1/13/97	8:32:46 AM	EventLog	None	6005	N/A	ESTREET
1/13/97	8:32:59 AM	Mouclass	None	7	N/A	ESTREET
1/13/97	6:24:11 AM	Mouclass	None	7	N/A	ESTREET
1/13/97	6:24:06 AM	Service Control Mar	None	7026	N/A	ESTREET
1/13/97	6:23:53 AM	EventLog	None	6005	N/A	ESTREET
1/13/97	6:20:29 AM	Service Control Mar	None	7026	N/A	ESTREET
1/13/97	6:20:15 AM	EventLog	None	6005	N/A	ESTREET
1/13/97	6:20:28 AM	Mouclass	None	7	N/A	ESTREET
1/13/97	6:12:41 AM	EventLog	None	6005	N/A	ESTREET
1/12/97	1:19:05 PM	EventLog	None	6005	N/A	ESTREET
1/11/97	9:36:26 AM	EventLog	None	6005	N/A	ESTREET

If you recognize a pattern that indicates someone is trying to do something they shouldn't be doing (look for repeated login failures and overly long Telnet sessions), you need to take preemptive action. Block all access from the offending domain, if the attacks are coming from outside. Send the user a note that says you're aware of what's going on and that you'll revoke privileges if the misbehavior continues, if he or she is from your system. Lots of administrators will pull the plug on a user first and then tell him or her why. Disabling the user's account prevents damage from occurring after you reprimand the user. It also illustrates a certain willingness to play hardball.

Scripting, Programming, and Security

As interactivity grows in the online world, the activity on our networks is becoming increasingly complex. As a rule, it's tougher to secure a complex system than a simple one. So, as the Web gets more complex with the addition of programming and scripting languages, the opportunities for ne'er-do-wells to take advantage of flaws in the system proliferate.

Generally, language designers have done an excellent job of putting together network-aware languages with security in mind. Java, the most popular programming language for Internet applications, is apparently bulletproof. JavaScript and VBScript are limited in their vulnerability to security breaches by their limited scope of operation.

Other network programming languages, however, present some real opportunities for dastardly deeds to be done. ActiveX Controls are so complex as to be only minimally secure. Common Gateway Interface (CGI) routines have been around a while, but since they offer access to the server's processor, they have the potential to do harm.

This section gives you an overview of the security inherent in several of the most popular network programming and scripting languages.

Java

The people who designed Java at Sun Microsystems did so with security in mind. They wanted to make it impossible to write a virus in Java and impossible for any Java program to do harmful things to a computer on which it was running.

They succeeded. Java lacks many of the low-level memory-management routines that characterize other object-oriented programming languages, such as C++. The absence of these routines has two main effects—one of which is to make it impossible for bad guys to use low-level memory-management tricks to break into programs. The other effect is that Java programs are much simpler to write than C++ programs.

Recently, Java has come out of its sandbox. With the latest versions of Netscape Navigator and Microsoft Internet Explorer, you can give Java permission to write to your disk drive or network. This has already given rise to security questions regarding Java applets on the Web. There are a number of active forums on the Web which discuss Java security issues. The Princeton University Web site at **http://pantheon.yale.edu/~dff/java.html** provides links to many of the best.

JavaScript and VBScript

 These scripting languages, used to add automation and limited intelligence to HTML documents, once had such limited power that they couldn't really do much harm. However, JavaScript has recently been used to copy the contents of a surfer's Autoexec.BAT file without the surfer's knowledge. Take a look at **http://www.scoopy.com/secure.htm** to see how.

CGI

Common Gateway Interface (CGI) routines are programs that run on the server to provide interactivity and intelligence to Web surfers. Because they use the server's CPU to perform operations, there is the possibility that a person could fool the CPU into thinking that a certain stream of data was a CGI request, when in fact it was a virus or other unauthorized program being sent in for processing.

The easiest and most popular way to defeat CGI attacks is to configure your processor to terminate all CGI activity that continues for more than three seconds or so. This way, legitimate users have CGI access to the processor, while the people trying to break in, whose routines likely will require extra time, will be cut off. You may also want to keep CGI scripts in nonpublic folders or use CGI wrappers (programs that encrypt CGI data streams) to protect against intrusions.

Plug-Ins and ActiveX Controls

Plug-ins and ActiveX controls do most of their stuff on the client side, so any harm they do likely will be there.

But the concern for client-side harm is real, since plug-ins and especially ActiveX Controls are very complicated and very difficult to secure.

The best way to protect against plug-in and ActiveX Control harm on the client side is to remind people to use the same precautions in selecting ActiveX Controls and plug-ins that they would use in selecting other software. Remind them to use plug-ins and ActiveX Controls only from reputable sources and to always use anti-virus software.

Secure Transactions

Encryption in and of itself is interesting, but its application to Internet transactions makes it relevant to this discussion. There are two leading protocols for conducting secure transactions on the Internet, both of which can use RSA encryption. They are Secure Sockets Layer (SSL), developed by Netscape, and Secure HTTP (SHTTP), developed by Enterprise Integration Technology (EIT). These two protocols are usually referenced with respect to online commerce, but they are really just mechanisms for secure communication and could also be put to use for transmitting other sensitive information. SSL is a separate protocol from HTTP, the communications protocol of the Web, while SHTTP is an extension of the HTTP protocol. Let's look at the two in turn and see what they do and how they work.

Secure Sockets Layer (SSL)

SSL is the most common Web security protocol. It was developed by Netscape, and it is supported by all major browsers, including Netscape Navigator and Microsoft Internet Explorer. SSL allows for various methods of encryption to be used, with various levels of strength. The encryption algorithm used is negotiated by a client and server at the time of a transaction.

Currently, Netscape Navigator implements several types of SSL encryption with several encryption key sizes, from a relatively weak 40-bit encryption key to a practically unbreakable 192-bit encryption key.

Most commercial Web server software supports SSL. Check your server documentation for information on how it works in your setup. Most noticeably, URLs for accessing a document securely begin with https://, rather than http://.

Secure HTTP (SHTTP)

Secure HTTP (SHTTP) is identical to SSL from the surfer's standpoint. The browser and server establish the encryption algorithms that they will use to make the transaction, and information is transmitted securely using those algorithms.

SHTTP differs from SSL in that it is an extension of the HTTP protocol, as opposed to an entirely separate protocol running concurrently with HTTP.

SHTTP isn't used a lot, since SSL technology was out first and thereby collected a large share of the transaction-security market. Though many servers and browsers support SHTTP, its popularity is steadily dwindling.

N O T E   Yes, once, a man in Europe decrypted a single message that had been encoded with 40-bit SSL (the weakest kind of SSL) as part of a contest sponsored by Netscape Communications. Here are some facts about what he pulled off:

- He had 120 workstations and two parallel supercomputers running nonstop for eight days. The computer time he used cost about $10,000.

- He did not crack SSL itself, only the one message. Since SSL uses a different encryption algorithm for every encrypted message, theoretically one would need another eight days with 120 workstations and two parallel supercomputers to crack just one more message.

If this had been real life and not a contest, the information he decrypted would have to have been worth more than $10,000 in order for the decryption process to have been cost-effective. I don't know what your credit limit is, but it's clear from this example that going through the hassle of decrypting an SSL transmission is just not worth it to get a credit card number.

Remember, the encryption that was broken in the contest was 40-bit SSL. It would have taken over 1,000,000,000,000 (one trillion) times more computing power to solve a message encrypted with 128-bit SSL. ▪

Part

VII

Ch

41

Certificates

Authentication, which is essential to secure transactions, is the process of making sure people really are who they claim to be. User names and passwords serve authentication purposes for system-access purposes, but certificates serve to ensure authentication when two machines or sites try to communicate with one another. That's important when online transactions are going on.

Certificates are electronic documents that contain digitally signed pieces of information that authenticate a secure server by verifying the connection between a server's encryption scheme and the server's identification. Cryptographic checks, using digital signatures, ensure that the validity of certificates can be absolutely trusted.

 Certificates are issued by third parties called certificate authorities. To obtain a certificate for your site, you must contact a certificate authority and register with it. The authority will verify that you are who you claim to be and then will create a digital certificate that is unique to you. There is usually a fee associated with this for businesses. For more information on certificates, check out the VeriSign Web site at **http://www.verisign.com**.

Pretty Good Privacy (PGP)

 A public-domain encryption scheme, Pretty Good Privacy, developed by Phil Zimmerman of the Massachusetts Institute of Technology is, as the name implies, good enough for most personal online data-encryption needs, including encrypted electronic mail. To date, PGP has been used mainly for encrypted electronic mail, but its use may expand now that a conflict between the U.S. government and Zimmerman (the government claimed that PGP is so powerful, it could be used by subversive foreign powers without the knowledge of the U.S. authorities) has finally been straightened out. You can get more information and PGP software at **http://www.pgp.com/**.

Firewalls

Like the carpet-defending mother who made you take your shoes off outside after playing in the mud, *firewalls* protect your network from the dangers of tracked-in data. Named for the fireproof barrier between the engine compartment and passenger cabin of an automobile or airplane, network firewalls form a barrier that's supposed to be (and is, if you do it right) impervious to attempts to get through it.

How Firewalls Work

A firewall is a computer through which all data entering or leaving a local area network (LAN) en route to or from the Internet must pass. In their role as gatekeepers, firewalls work like two-way filters, allowing certain data to pass out of the LAN and allowing other data (usually much more restricted) to pass from the Internet into the LAN.

For example, a firewall might be set up to protect an intranet. People logged on to the intranet could do whatever they wanted on the Internet—their Web requests would pass out through the firewall and data could come into the intranet in response to those requests. Users could send Internet electronic mail out through the firewall. They also could send out Gopher, Telnet, and FTP requests through the firewall and receive data in response to those requests.

But the firewall's filter is much less porous in the other direction. In most cases, firewalls are configured to allow nothing but electronic mail to come inside the firewall unsolicited. Everything else, such as Telnet and Web data, must enter in response to a request that went out from a legitimate user inside the network.

In cases in which an organization's public Web server is protected by a firewall, the firewall needs to be configured to allow Web data requests to pass from the Internet to the public Web server.

ON THE WEB

For more information about firewalls, look at the Firewalls FAQ at **http://faq.sph.umich.edu/faq/ files/firewalls-faq,** or at Kathy Fulmer's list of firewall tools developers at **http://www.greatcircle. com/firewalls/vendors.html**.

Implementing a Firewall

The key to implementing a firewall lies in the configuration files of the computer (usually a packet router) that functions as the physical firewall.

So, to set up a firewall, you need to install a dedicated router between the network you're protecting and the potentially hostile network (the Internet, most often) so all data passing between the two networks must pass through the router. This is a physical process—make sure all the wires coming into your network bearing Internet data pass through the router first.

Second, you need to set the router's configuration files to correspond to the rules you've set up for data exchange. A typical set of data-exchange rules looks like this:

- Don't allow any source-routed packets into the protected network. Spoofers like to use source-routed packets to bluff their way onto protected networks.

- Drop any packets from the outside that claim to be from the local network. These clearly aren't up to anything beneficial.

- Allow all packets that are part of established connections (such as those involved in a Web-document exchange) to pass unmolested. This allows you to place your Web server behind the firewall and allows the users of the defended network to use the Web without hassle.

- Block connections to low port numbers, except for those associated with DNS requests and SMTP mail transfers.

Part
VII

Ch
41

Checking Your Security

Forewarned is forearmed—an old saw that holds true for computer networks more than in any other field. Once you've installed a security system, don't sit back and assume your information is safe. The bad guys aren't getting any dumber. Instead, constantly test and refine your security system to make sure it will stand up against the latest break-in techniques.

There are several techniques for testing the security of a site. Some of the most popular are described in this section.

SATAN

On the logic that the best way to get site administrators to improve their sites' security is to make their security weaknesses blindingly obvious to everyone, SATAN (Security Administrator's Tool for Analyzing Networks) was released to the public.

SATAN looks at any UNIX-based network site and points out ways in which evil-minded people could circumvent security and illegally exploit system resources. SATAN derives its knowledge from publicized information of bugs in systems and so will refer you to fixes for any troubles it detects, if any fixes are available to you. SATAN features a friendly interface, giving output as HTML documents that are viewable with practically any Web browser.

Incidentally, Dan Farmer, the author of SATAN, did an informal security survey of about 2,200 Web sites in January 1997. He found that about three-quarters of the surveyed sites—many of them bank sites and other high-profile sites—had "serious security flaws."

ON THE WEB

http://www.interaus.net/1995/6/satan.html   You can read more about SATAN here.

Cracking Consultants

SATAN is a useful tool for administrators trying to flush out security weaknesses, but it detects only fairly well-known security flaws. What happens when your site is crackable, but only by a very skilled operator with highly specialized and current information? Generally, you won't find out about a security breach until it's too late.

That's why many organizations, mainly those with lots of valuable information to protect, hire people to try to break into their systems and, when they succeed (and they usually do), tell the organizations how to head off similar attacks in the future. The "Tiger Teams"—ultra-secret, cracking squads employed by the National Security Agency and Department of Defense—regularly challenge Pentagon computers.

If you have sufficiently valuable information on your network, there's no more certain way to test its safety than with a trained break-in artist. ●

## CHAPTER 42

Using HTML and Site Tools

by Eric Ladd, Todd Stauffer, and Pamela Rice Hahn

In this chapter

The Purpose of an HTML Editor

When you author an HTML document, all you're really doing is creating a plain text file. In the early days of HTML authoring, a simple text editor like vi (for UNIX) or Notepad (for Windows) was all document authors had to assist them. Later came add-on templates and libraries for existing word-processing packages. These allowed users to stick with a familiar interface while giving them special functions to handle the more common authoring tasks. As the HTML standard grew to include more tags, dedicated tag editor programs emerged. These programs have interfaces that are similar to most word-processing programs, but are loaded with special options to help set up not only the HTML tags, but the many attributes you can use with the tags to alter their effects.

The latest stage in this evolution is the what-you-see-is-what-you-get (WYSIWYG) HTML editor. This is something of a misnomer because with these programs you rarely see any HTML code. Rather, you compose the page as you would have it look on a browser screen, and the program writes the corresponding HTML. This type of program promises to revolutionize Internet publishing because now all you need to know is how to format text and drag-and-drop objects on a page. The editor takes care of knowing the HTML.

This chapter takes an in-depth look at some of the features of the three most prominent WYSIWYG HTML editors available today. In this chapter, you will learn the basics of how to use the following:

- Netscape Communicator
- Microsoft FrontPage 98
- Adobe PageMill

By considering your own authoring needs and the capabilities of each of these programs, you should be able to make a solid decision on which one to use in your publishing efforts.

A Word About WYSIWYG HTML Editors

For people who don't want to learn HTML or for those who abhor the thought of typing out of all those tags longhand, WYSIWYG editors are a blessing. But there's another group that would have you believe that WYSIWYG editors are the scourge of the Internet publishing community. Members of this group are typically folks who have been doing HTML authoring for a (relatively) long time and who are accustomed to coding by hand in a simple text editor.

While lamenting the rapid, forward surge in technology is questionable, part of their argument is valid. WYSIWYG editors are tools that allow anyone, regardless of their HTML proficiency and their knowledge of what constitutes suitable content, to publish a document online. What this means is that you're much more likely to see documents that are poorly designed, that have lewd or self-indulgent content, or that generally have no business being on the Internet. WYSIWYG editors empower everyone to place information on the Internet, and it's important to realize that when everyone gets into the act, the information you see will be less homogeneous than what was there before.

In spite of this, WYSIWYG editors are here to stay, and you're very likely to find yourself using one. If you do, you should not treat it as an excuse to not learn HTML. Indeed, as you work with such an editor, you might find your knowledge of HTML helping you to better use the program. For example, you might look at a dialog box showing the properties of an image on your page and recognize how the controls in the dialog box relate to the different attributes of the <IMG> tag. After you see the relationships between the program features and HTML, you'll become a smarter and faster user of WYSIWYG software.

Netscape Communicator

Netscape's latest entry in the feverish competition for your Internet desktop is Netscape Communicator—a suite of software that includes the following:

- Netscape Collabra—Collabra allows you to create and participate in online forums that are much like UseNet newsgroups.

- Netscape Composer—An extended version of Netscape Navigator Gold, Composer lets you author documents for a corporate intranet, the World Wide Web, and even for electronic mail.

- Netscape Conference—Similar to Microsoft's NetMeeting, Conference supports real-time interaction between users through shared documents, a common whiteboard, and chat channels.

- Netscape Messenger—Messenger is Netscape's new e-mail client that is completely compatible with open standards while being tightly integrated with Composer, allowing you to create HTML-based e-mail.

- Netscape Navigator 4.0—Netscape's popular browser, updated with a highly customizable interface and even stronger support for Java, JavaScript, and embedded objects.

When you fire up Netscape Communicator, you'll see the screen shown in Figure 42.1. Note the floating toolbar you see in the figure. Using this toolbar, you can switch quickly from your browser to your inbox (Messenger), your discussion groups (Collabra), or your WYSIWYG editor (Composer). If you find that the toolbar is getting in your way, click the Netscape logo on the toolbar to minimize it. The minimized toolbar will still be available to you at the bottom of whatever Netscape window you have open.

 TIP You can move the floating toolbar by clicking the ridged bottom-left corner of the toolbar and dragging it to where you want it to be. You can also right-click this corner to reveal a context-sensitive menu that lets you change the orientation (horizontal or vertical) of the toolbar and whether or not the toolbar is always in front of your Netscape window.

Part

VII

Ch

42

The balance of this section focuses on Netscape Composer—the WYSIWYG tool you can use to create and publish Internet documents.

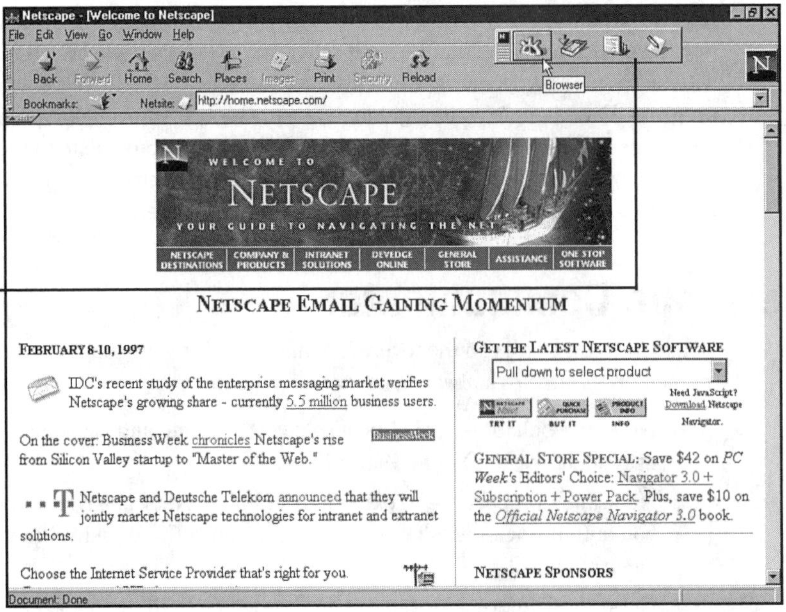

FIG. 42.1
Netscape Communicator opens up the Navigator 4.0 browser by default.

Floating toolbar ——

Getting Started

You have a number of different ways to get started with Netscape Composer. From the File menu, you can choose the New Page or Open Page options. Holding your mouse pointer over New Page reveals a drop-down list of three different ways to start a new document. These are:

- Start with a blank page (Blank)
- Create a new page from an existing template (From Template)
- Create a new page using a Page Wizard (From Wizard)

Selecting the blank page opens up the Composer window with nothing in it. Choosing the template option causes new window in Navigator to open up a templates page on Netscape's Web site. If you opt for the Page Wizard, you also get sent to Netscape's site—this time to Netscape's online Page Wizard that walks you through the creation of a page.

N O T E When you choose the Page Wizard, a new window in Netscape Navigator does not open like it does with the Templates option. ■

CAUTION

To make proper use of the Templates and Page Wizard options, you need to have a PPP connection running so that you can access Netscape's site.

Also, under the File menu is the Open Page option. When you select this, you'll see the dialog box shown in Figure 42.2. Here you can enter the URL of an online document you want to edit or the directory path and file name of a local document. If you want to edit the document, and not just view it, be sure you've clicked the radio button next to the word Editor.

FIG. 42.2
You can open a remote or local document in either your Netscape browser or editor.

Another way you can start your editing session with Composer is to choose the Composer option from under the Window menu. When you do, you'll see the choices shown in Figure 42.3. These options essentially replicate the ones available to you under the File menu.

FIG. 42.3
Before the Composer window opens, the Create New Page dialog box prompts you for what kind of document you want to start with.

Your final option for getting started is to click the Web Page Composer button on the floating toolbar. This launches the Composer with a blank page, as shown in Figure 42.4.

Building Your Document

With the Composer open, you're ready to author your document. Composer supports you in this activity in a host of different ways. The next several sections show you how to take care of the following authoring tasks:

- Formatting text, both at the character and paragraph levels
- Placing graphics in your document
- Linking text and images to other documents
- Creating HTML tables
- Calling up a document's basic properties

Formatting Text Placing and formatting text with Composer is as easy as it is with just about any word processor. To get some text in the Composer window, click your mouse pointer at the position you want the text to begin and type away. The words you see will be in the default type size, face, and color.

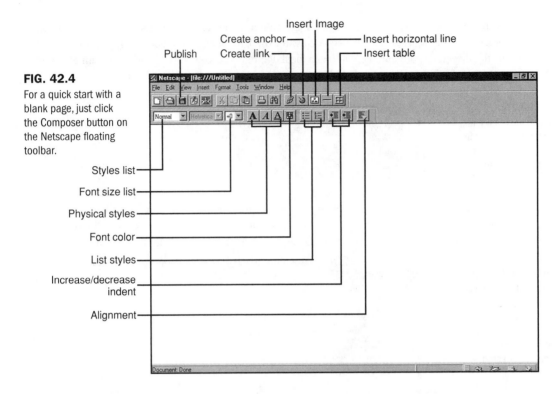

FIG. 42.4

For a quick start with a blank page, just click the Composer button on the Netscape floating toolbar.

Modifying text you type in is just a matter of highlighting it (passing the cursor over the text while holding down the left mouse button) and applying the effect you want. You can apply text effects in many ways. Referring to Figure 42.4, note the Composer Format toolbar. The first drop-down list on the toolbar contains the six heading levels, preformatted text, address, list item, and description text styles. The Normal+ style adds some extra line spacing to the Normal style, creating a little extra white space above and below the text.

Following the styles drop-down list is the font drop-down list, from which you can choose which typeface the highlighted text should appear in. The small drop-down list to the right of the font drop-down list is for changing the font size. Selecting positive values increases the size, while selecting negative values decreases it.

The next three buttons on the Format toolbar apply bold, italics, and underline styles, respectively, to highlighted text. The button immediately to the right of the underline style button lets you change the color of highlighted text from its default black. When you click this button, you get the Color dialog box, from which you can choose one of the available colors in the palette or define a custom color for your text.

Formatting at the paragraph level also happens from the Format toolbar. You can format a block of text as a bulleted or numbered list, increase or decrease indent levels, and set left, right, or center alignment with the rightmost buttons on the toolbar. All of these formatting options are available to you from the Format menu as well. In fact, if you choose Format, Paragraph, you'll get a few extra styles—Title and Block Quote—that aren't available anywhere on the toolbar.

Placing Graphics   Graphic elements help break up your page and prevent it from becoming an unattractive sea of text. Even a simple horizontal line can go a long way toward making a document more readable. To add a horizontal line, just place your cursor where you want the line to go and either click the Insert Horizontal Line button on Composer's upper toolbar (the Compose toolbar) or choose Insert, Horizontal Line. By default, a horizontal line will reach all the way across the page, be two pixels high, and have a three-dimensional shading effect. You can change any of these attributes of the line by right-clicking your mouse pointer on the line and selecting the Horizontal Line Properties option from the context-sensitive menu. In the resulting dialog box, you can adjust the line's height, width, and shading. Also, if you reduce the line's width, so that it no longer reaches all the way across the screen, you can change the alignment so that the line appears either flush left or flush right.

Graphics also include images, of course, and Composer makes it almost as easy to place an image as it is to place a horizontal line. By clicking the Insert Image button on the Compose toolbar or by choosing Insert, Image, you get the dialog box shown in Figure 42.5. Here you specify the location of the image, as well as a low resolution version of the image, a text alternative to the image, how the image should be aligned, how much space to leave around the image, whether or not the image should have a border and how big that border should be, and the height and width of the image. You can also choose to edit the image if you've set up a default image-editing program in the Composer preferences.

N O T E   If you choose to make the image float in the left or right margin with text wrapping around it, you'll have to view the page in the browser window because Composer's display does not support this feature.

N O T E   Including a text alternative for every image is an important service to users whose browsers don't support images or to those with images turned off.

T I P   It's a good idea to click the Original Size button and check the box next to Lock width/height. This way the browser won't try to change the size of the image—something that browsers don't do very well. If you need an image to be bigger or smaller, your best bet is to make the change in an image editor.

If you ever need to change the attributes of an image after you've placed it, just right-click the image and select the Image properties option from the pop-up menu. This returns you to the Properties dialog box in Figure 42.5, where you can make the desired changes.

Setting Up Hyperlinks   Linked documents are a hallmark of the Web, and Netscape Composer makes it easy for you to set up links on both words (hypertext) and images (hypergraphics). If the text you want to convert to hypertext is already on the page, simply highlight it and click the Make Link button on the Compose toolbar or choose Insert, Link. What you'll see next is the dialog box shown in Figure 42.6. The text you highlighted is shown in the Link Source section of the box. All you need to do to complete the link is furnish the URL of the document you're linking to and any anchors you're targeting within that document.

FIG. 42.5
The Image Properties
dialog box gives you
very fine control over
placement and
appearance of images.

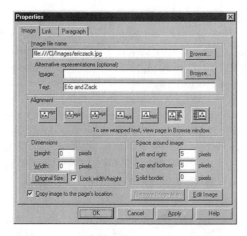

N O T E   If you just click the Make Link button or choose Insert, Link without selecting any text, there will be an empty field in the dialog box where you can type in the link text. ▨

FIG. 42.6
The Link Properties
dialog box shows the
text or image that
you're linking and
the document you're
linking to.

Highlighted text⏤

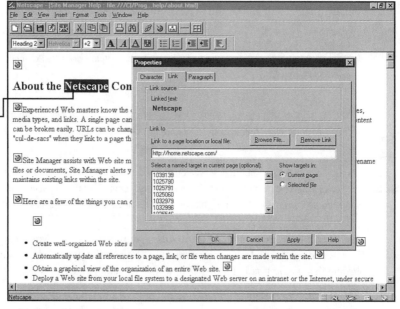

Setting up a link on an image is just as simple. First, click the image to select it and then click the Make Link button or choose Insert, Link. This time you'll see the path to the image file in place of the text you're linking. Again, all you need to supply is the URL of the target document and any named anchors you might be using.

TIP Set the border around a linked image to zero pixels if you don't want a colored border around a linked graphic.

Using Tables It used to be that coding HTML tables was one of the most tedious jobs an author could encounter. But now with WYSIWYG tools, composing tables becomes an easy matter because you can do it right on screen, and the editor writes out all of the tags for each cell and row. To insert a table with Netscape Composer, click the Insert Table button on the Compose toolbar or choose Insert, Table. You'll then see the Table Properties dialog box shown in Figure 42.7. On the Table tab of this box, you can set up the basic configuration of the table—the number of rows and columns, how wide and tall it should be, whether or not it should have a caption, and how it is aligned on the page. After you choose the parameters you want, clicking OK puts a skeleton of the table you designed up on the page.

FIG. 42.7
You begin an HTML table in Composer by specifying the global attributes of the table.

After you have all of your data entered into the table, you can go to work on getting row and cell properties the way you want them. To change the attributes of a row, right-click anywhere in the row, choose the Table Properties option, and select the Row tab. From here you can set vertical and horizontal alignment and the background color of cells in the row. Similarly, you can right-click a cell, choose Table Properties, and select the Cell tab to change vertical and horizontal alignment, background color, text wrapping, use of the column heading style, spanning characteristics, and the height and width of the cell (see Figure 42.8).

FIG. 42.8
You have full control over how a table looks right down to the cell level.

Part
VII

Ch
42

Setting Page Properties All of the discussion thus far has focused on setting up different elements on a page. However, it's important to realize that you can use Composer to set up characteristics of the page itself. By choosing Format, Page, you call up the dialog box you see in Figure 42.9. From here, you can select from the following tabs:

- General—This tab contains fields for specifying the document's title, author, description, keywords, and classification. The title information you supply is what appears between the <TITLE> and </TITLE> tags. The rest of the information is stored in <META> tags and can be used by Web robots to index your document.

- Appearance—Background colors and images and link colors are specified on this tab. You can configure your own color scheme or choose from several predefined color schemes.

- Advanced—If you need to set up your own <META> tags, or if you want to specify Netscape system variables (<META> tag with HTTP-EQUIV attribute), you can do so from this tab.

FIG. 42.9

Don't forget to title your document! It's an important service to readers and to programs trying to index your page.

Publishing Your Document

When you're satisfied with your document and it's time to publish it, Composer can help you with that, too—even if you're publishing to a remote server!

NOTE Composer prompts you to save your document before publishing it. This way, you can be assured that you're publishing your most recent changes. ▓

Setting Publishing Options If you're going to be publishing a lot of documents to a remote machine, you should take a moment to set up Composer publishing preferences. To do this, choose Edit, Preferences, Editor Preferences to call up the dialog box you see in Figure 42.10. The tab you're interested in is the Publish tab.

The tab is divided into two parts. The upper part deals with how links and images are treated during the transfer. Checking the Maintain links box tells Composer to change the HTML code

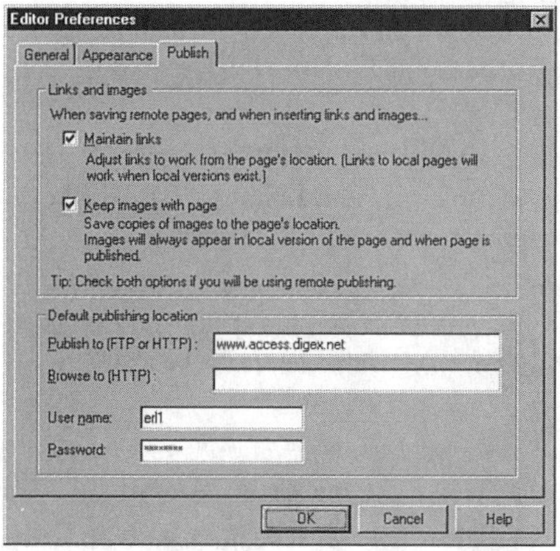

FIG. 42.10
Composer supports remote publishing via FTP and can automatically change your pages to work on the remote machine.

as it publishes it so that the links you created work on the remote machine. The Keep Images With Page option sends copies of all images on the page to the same directory that you save the page in. A good rule of thumb is to keep both of these checked. Otherwise, you might end up doing a lot of extra work yourself to make links work and to make images show up where they're supposed to be.

The lower half is where you set up your remote login session. Most users choose the Publish to FTP or HTTP option, in which case you need to give the server name or IP address of the remote machine and your login ID and password on that machine.

Sending Your Document to a Remote Server   To perform the actual transfer to the remote machine, click the Publish button on the Compose toolbar or choose File, Publish to reveal the Publish Files dialog box. You can choose to send just the file or file together with other files in the same folder. You can also change the default publishing location if you happen to be publishing to a different machine than the one you set up in your editor preferences. After you've decided what to publish and to where, click OK to initiate the transfer.

N O T E   The preceding sections provide a very basic introduction to Composer. Indeed, we could probably write an entire book on Composer alone! If you want to learn more about Composer, you should visit Netscape's Web site, **http://home.netscape.com/**. In addition to reading the online documentation, you can download Composer from the site, install it on your machine, and experiment with it yourself—perhaps the best learning experience of all! ■

Microsoft FrontPage 98

The Microsoft updates to its Web development collection FrontPage 98 makes it compatible with its Office suite of products and the upcoming Windows 98. Together with Internet Explorer, FrontPage 98 provides a total Web site creation solution that includes the following components:

Part
VII

Ch
42

- FrontPage Explorer—With the Explorer you can set up a structure for a site (called a Web in FrontPage vernacular) and use the Explorer's different views to get complete information about the site.

- FrontPage Editor—The Editor is the WYSIWYG part of FrontPage. New tab features allow you to select your choice of view: Editor, HTML, or Preview—the true WYSIWYG Web view of your document.

- Microsoft Image Composer—New to the FrontPage family with FrontPage 97, Microsoft continues to improve Image Composer, the utility you can use to manipulate graphics and images in a number of ways with such features as the newly added GIF animator and WordArt.

- TCP/IP Test Utility—If you're unsure of your network connection, the FrontPage TCP/IP test can run a quick check to let you know if everything is working correctly.

- FrontPage Web Server—FrontPage's CGI-compliant Web server lets you test your site locally before you make it live. FrontPage 98 also includes the Microsoft Personal Web Server as well as improved intranet-creation integration between Office 97 and the Windows NT server.

This section of the chapter will focus mainly on the FrontPage Explorer and Editor, because these are the components you'll use to set up sites and create documents. Other FrontPage components are considered briefly.

The FrontPage Explorer

When you start up the FrontPage Explorer and select your view, you see the screen shown in Figure 42.11. The two major areas of the window provide two very different ways of looking at a Web. With no Web loaded, the Explorer window is largely empty, so your first step is to give yourself something to work with.

> **CAUTION**
>
> Before you start working on a Web, make sure you have a Web server program running. The Web server that comes bundled with FrontPage is fine for this purpose.

There are appearance changes in the FrontPage 98 Explorer as well. Note the View options along the left side of the Explorer screen, which include:

- Folders—Organize files and folders
- All Files—View information about all files
- Navigation—Design the Web's structure for navigation bars
- Hyperlink Status—Test and repair all hyperlinks
- Themes—Choose a new look for your FrontPage Web
- Tasks—Create and manage tasks

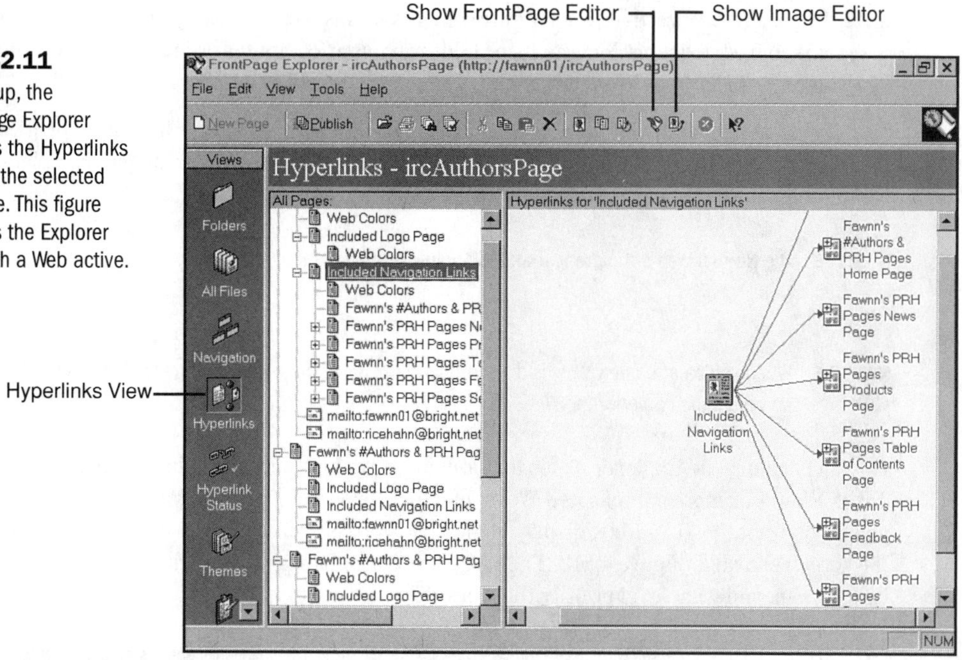

Show FrontPage Editor ─┐   ┌─ Show Image Editor

FIG. 42.11
At startup, the
FrontPage Explorer
displays the Hyperlinks
View of the selected
Web site. This figure
displays the Explorer
view with a Web active.

Hyperlinks View ─────

Creating a New Web   On starting FrontPage 98, the program gives you the option of selecting a current Web or beginning a new one.

To start a new Web from within Explorer, choose File, New, FrontPage Web or click the New FrontPage Web toolbar button. You will then see the New FrontPage Web dialog box, from which you can choose one of six Web templates or one of three Web wizards. These include:

- Corporate Presence Wizard—By walking you through several dialog boxes, this Wizard collects information that is typically found on a corporate Web site and builds a Web with the responses you provide.

- Customer Support Web—If you're planning to provide customer support over the Internet, you may wish to investigate this Web, which is especially useful for companies supporting software products.

- Discussion Web Wizard—This wizard also takes you through a series of dialog boxes that create a Web to support threaded discussions and a full-text search.

- Empty Web—Choose this option to start completely from scratch. An Empty Web is useful if you have a preexisting page done in the Editor or in another authoring program and want to incorporate it into a Web.

- Project Web—Corporate intranet users can put project management online with the Project Web. The Web helps to track individual tasks and progress toward the goals of the project.

Part
VII

Ch
42

■ Import Web Wizard—Added improvements to this wizard mean you can use it to create a Web from existing documents or folders on your computer or local network, from another FrontPage Web, or from an URL on the World Wide Web.

If you're creating a Web with a purpose that's consistent with one of the templates or wizards, then you should choose the appropriate one. To begin with a blank page an you can place content on, select the Normal Web option.

N O T E The Normal Web template is the default choice when creating a new Web. ■

N O T E When you create a new Web, you are required to supply the network address of your server and a unique name for the Web. ■

One nice feature the Explorer has is the built-in To Do List, accessible in FrontPage 98 as the Tasks View. For more complicated Webs, like the Corporate Presence Web, the wizard asks you if you want the To Do List displayed after the Web is created. If you choose Yes, you'll see the screen shown in Figure 42.12. The List tracks what pages need work, who had responsibility for them, and what level priority the work is.

FIG. 42.12

Previously known as The Explorer To Do List in FrontPage 97, the Tasks View tracks unfinished tasks and who is responsible for completing them.

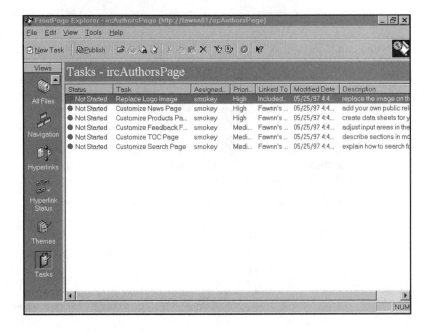

 You're not limited to using the Tasks for Webs that you create using a FrontPage wizard. You can invoke the Tasks selection at any time by clicking the Tasks button on the Explorer Views bar. After you call it up, you can add and update tasks on the list as needed.

Viewing a Web   After you have loaded a Web into the Explorer, you can look at it in one of the five following ways:

■ Hyperlink View—The Hyperlink View is the default Explorer view (see Figure 42.13). In this view, you see a hierarchical rendition of your Web site on the left side of the window—much the same way as the left side of the Windows Explorer shows you the hierarchical folder structure on your hard drive. If you click a plus sign (+), it expands the hierarchy found below the object with the plus sign. Clicking a minus sign (-) collapses an expanded hierarchy.

On the right side, you see a more graphic portrayal of your site—illustrating with arrows links to other pages within the site and off the site. You can click items whose icons have a plus (+) sign to expand the view further.

FIG. 42.13

The Hyperlinks view gives the hierarchical rendition of your Web site on the left with a graphic portrayal of that site on the right.

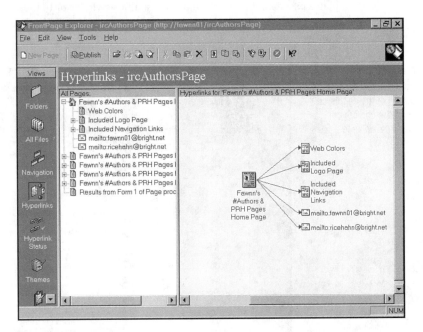

The Hyperlink View makes it easy to see how your documents are linked together, and where you might be missing some critical links. Also, if you're looking for broken links pointed out by the Explorer link checker, this is the view you want to use.

If you're using a "drill-down" kind of design for your site, the Hyperlink View gives you the best way to look at it. If you're looking for a certain page, you can follow the hierarchy right to it. The outline structure also makes it easy to see the most logical places to insert new pages.

■ Folders—You can switch to the Folder View by clicking the Folder View button on the Explorer View bar or by selecting View, Folders. This view more closely resembles that of Windows Explorer, showing the folder hierarchy in the left side of the window and document-specific information such as titles, file names and sizes, and modification dates on the right side (see Figure 42.14).

Part

VII

Ch

42

The Folder View can be handy in a number of situations. The last change date information can tell you how "fresh" information is on a page or whether a person responsible for an update has made the necessary changes. File size information is important for graphics and multimedia files and the Folder View can help you identify files that are too big to be part of your Web.

- All Files View—This view gives you the information on all the files in your selected Web, similar to how that information is displayed in Windows Explorer's Details view.

- Navigation View—This view displays a split screen that allows you to drag files from the Windows Explorer-style display at the bottom onto the Navigation set-up area at the top of the page. FrontPage then adds Navigation bars to each page moved to that view.

- Graphical Themes—FrontPage 98 comes with a series of fully-coordinated page templates based on themes ranging from a fifties-style flavor to those with a corporate presence; each them includes the graphics images for the background, divider, and task buttons.

FIG. 42.14
The Folders View gives you all of the details on all of the component files in a Web site.

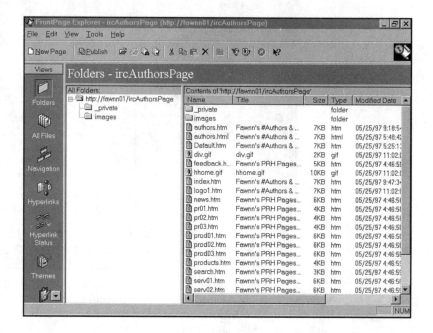

Link Tools   Visiting a Web site that has broken or outdated links can be one of a Web surfer's most frustrating experiences. It's frustrating for the site administrator, too. Keeping track of all links on a large site requires incredible attention to detail.

Keeping track of links to other sites is all but impossible without checking each link individually on a regular basis. Fortunately for both parties, the FrontPage Explorer comes with the following link utilities that help to alleviate these problems:

■ Hyperlink Status View—Select Hyperlink Status from the View bar or choose Tools, Verify Hyperlinks to instruct the Explorer to perform a check on all of the links in your Web, including links to pages that are not on your Web. The Explorer reports its findings back to you in a window like the one you see in Figure 42.15. Links to pages within your site are shown with a red circle and the word Broken if they are broken, or are not shown at all if they are working. Links that couldn't be checked are shown with a yellow circle and a question mark in front of them. To verify these links, click the Verify button you see in the dialog box.

You can verify each external link by selecting it in the window and clicking the Verify button. If an external link is verified, the Explorer places a green circle with the word OK in front of the link. If an external link is broken, it gets a red circle with the word Broken.

FIG. 42.15
You can generate a report on the integrity of all internal and external links by choosing either the Hyperlinks Status view or Tools, Verify Hyperlinks. This simplifies the steps necessary should you need to move a Web to a new location.

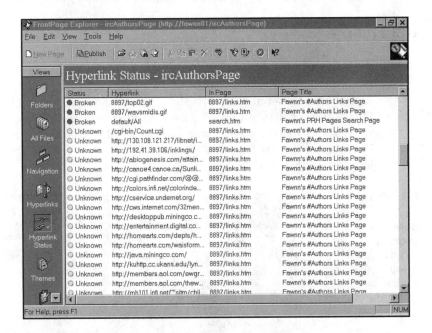

■ Recalculate Hyperlinks—The Recalculate Hyperlinks command (choose Tools, Recalculate Hyperlinks) updates the displays in each of the three views to reflect any changes made by you or other authors. It also regenerates all dependencies in the open Web. Dependencies are items that are read into a page like the FrontPage Components discussed below.

Other Useful Explorer Features   The FrontPage Explorer comes with some other handy features that can make your life as a Web site author much easier. These include the following:

■ Proxy Server Setup—Security is a critical issue to most Webmasters. Consider the recent case of the Central Intelligence Agency Web site that was hacked and modified to contain very offensive content. Because of events like this, many Webmasters choose to set up a proxy server (or firewall) to act as an intermediary between their servers and

Part
VII

Ch
42

the rest of the Internet. Choosing Tools, Options opens a dialog box with a Proxies tab where you can specify a proxy server for your Web server.

■ Import/Export of Individual Documents—You can import an existing document into the Web you're working on by selecting File, Import. This is what you want to use if you start with an Empty Web and want to incorporate an existing page into it. Likewise, choose File, Export to export a selected document so that you have a standalone version of it. Be careful when importing documents though, as some page-element properties might need to be manually edited for FrontPage to recognize them. This is particularly true for images.

With your Web created, it's time to put some content on its component pages. You do this by using the FrontPage Editor—a full-featured, WYSIWYG page composition program.

The FrontPage Editor

When you fire up the FrontPage Editor, you see a WYSIWYG environment in which you can create your Web documents—all without even typing an HTML tag (see Figure 42.16). You can choose to either start with a blank page by selecting the New button, typing Ctrl+N, or selecting File, New. To edit an existing HTML document, choose the Open (file folder) button, Ctrl+O, or select File, Open. The Tabs on the bottom left make it easy to switch between how you view your Web document in progress. The HTML tab shows you your source code (see Figure 42.17) while the Preview tab displays how your document will appear in most newer browsers (see Figure 42.18).

FIG. 42.16

The FrontPage 98 Editor is where you add content to the documents you set up in the Explorer. This view also offers the option to either show or hide the Format Marks.

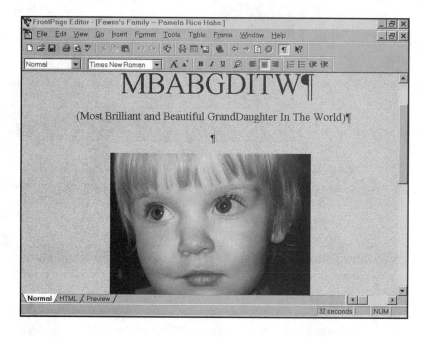

FIG. 42.17
In the HTML view, you can directly edit the source code.

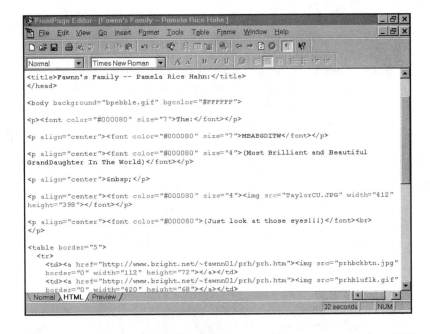

FIG. 42.18
Web Preview is the third view. It shows how your Web page will appear on most browsers. All three views are now just a tab choice away.

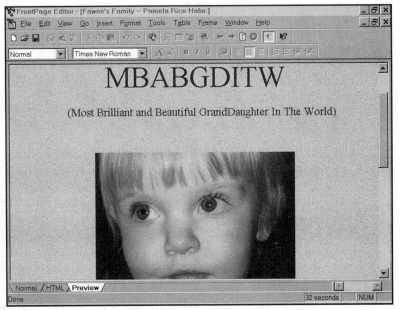

Some features new to the FrontPage 98 Editor include:

■ WYSIWYG frames—WYSIWYG Frame Set Editing in FrontPage 98 makes it easy to customize frames from templates or create your own. Resizing them is simple because you can drag the border to alter a frame. Pages and frame sets can be edited directly on the screen now, too.

- Table Drawing Tool and Drag & Drop Table Editing—In FrontPage 98, changes that once were done within a dialog box can now be completed on-screen. The user can either create a customized table by drawing it or by editing it using drag and drop to move or copy table rows and columns; tables can be resized in by simply dragging rows and column borders with the mouse.

- Forms that send e-mail—FrontPage 98 includes the ability to use the new Form Save Results FrontPage Component to create a form that sends submissions directly to an e-mail address.

- Cascading Style Sheets—FrontPage 98 includes the ability to incorporate Cascading Style Sheets (CSS) that conform to the open specification endorsed by the World Wide Web Consortium. This means Web page developers can format creative page layout settings using CSS-defined complex styles for the titles, paragraphs, and headers.

- Dynamic HTML support—FrontPage 98's Dynamic HTML support provides the ability to create expanding and collapsing outlines, the ability to define the tab order and "ALT+" key shortcuts for all your form fields, page transitions with stunning visual effects, and create text animations such as revealing words letter by letter or text flying in from off of the screen.

CAUTION

In an online conversation with author Pamela Rice Hahn, fellow Web page developer C. S. Wyatt recently defined Dynamic HTML as "a standard that changes dynamically every two weeks." Therefore, keep in mind that until the W3C determines the final Dynamic HTML standard and the browser developers comply with that final standard, introducing Dynamic HTML on your Web page may mean that some users won't be able to properly display your page.

- One Button Publishing—The Web Publishing Wizard is for users publishing their webs to servers that do not contain the FrontPage Server Extensions. Version 1.5 takes advantage of the FrontPage 98 one-button-publishing feature to forestall the most common errors that can occur when publishing a Web using FTP.

- Auto-thumbnail, Text on Images, Washout, and other Image Editing Tools—In addition to the expanded graphics editing features, FrontPage 98 provides a shortcut button in the Clip Art Gallery that takes the user to Microsoft ClipGallery Live, an Internet site from which a user can automatically add selections to the Clip Art Gallery.

- Microsoft Internet Explorer and Netscape Communication Integration—This Edit feature lets the Web page author transfer work from either browser directly to FrontPage 98, edit your work, and then save the changes back to the server.

N O T E Veteran HTML authors will be happy to learn that FrontPage 98 allows you to edit HTML code directly. You can simply select the HTML view, rather than having to open the file in a separate text editor.

Starting a New Document   When you select File, New to start a new document, you don't just get a blank screen to work in. Rather, you are given the option to activate one of the Editor's many templates and page creation wizards. Templates give you a structured document with several informational "holes" that you can fill in with appropriate text (see Figure 42.19). Page creation wizards collect information from you through a series of dialog boxes and then use the information you supply to author a page.

FIG. 42.19
The Table of Contents template gives you a structure into which you can enter page information for other areas of interest on your site.

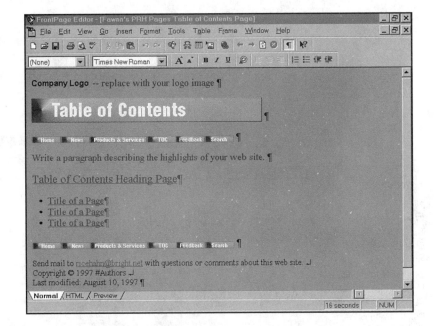

Figure 42.20 shows a dialog box from the Frames Wizard—a useful feature for developing framed pages without having to worry about all of those confusing <FRAMESET> tags. There are a number of standard framed layouts from which to choose that are prepackaged in FrontPage 98. However, should you need layout other than one of those provided, you can set it up yourself by choosing the Make a Custom Grid option in the wizard's first dialog box.

The FrontPage Editor also comes with a Forms Page Wizard and one for Database Connector.

You can set up an interface to an Open Database Connectivity (ODBC) compliant database by using the Database Connector Wizard (see Figure 42.21). Over a series of dialog boxes, you are prompted for the ODBC data source, the template file for the results, and what Structured Query Language (SQL) queries you want to make against the database.

The Forms Wizard is available as an option from the New Page selections. It can spare you much of the drudgery of coding a form. Many common form fields come prepackaged, and all you need to do is place them on your form. If the prepackaged form fields don't include the types of fields you need, FrontPage also lets you build a customized form from the ground up. You can pass the form results to a CGI script, or you can use the FrontPage Save Results box to write the form data to a file. Results can be saved in HTML, plain text, or rich text formats.

Part
VII

Ch
42

FIG. 42.20
Frames can be simple
when you use the
FrontPage Editor's
Frames Wizard because
of the variety of
standard frames layouts.

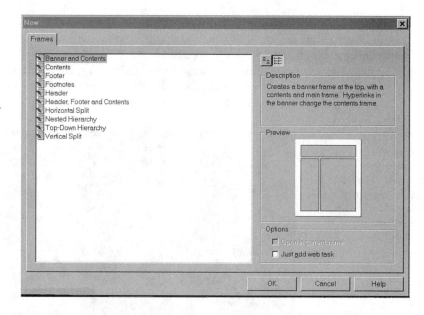

FIG. 42.21
The Internet Database
Connector Wizard
simplifies the steps
necessary to configure
the ODBC connection.
ODBC (Open Database
Connectivity) is the
acronym for the
standard for accessing
different database
systems.

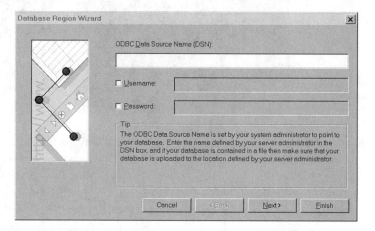

In addition to the wizards, FrontPage can get you started with more than 20 standard page
templates, including the following:

- Bibliography
- Feedback Form
- Frequently Asked Questions
- Guest Book
- Search Page
- Table of Contents (see Figure 42.19)
- User Registration

Web site designers can make good use of a number of these templates. Specifically, the wide assortment of columned page layouts (with or without sidebars) makes for an effective presentation appearance for press releases and press release directories, and What's New pages are frequently found on corporate sites. Almost any organization's page can benefit from a Frequently Asked Questions addition to their site. The ability to create those pages with the use of these templates simplifies the Web author's job considerably.

N O T E If you are creating corporate sites, make certain you determine as part of your agreement who is responsible for editing page content. Don't assume your job is done after you place the appropriate supplied text onto the page. As Webmaster, you'll hear about every grammatical error and overlooked typo. The savvy Web author provides for such client error occurrences by establishing a Web page content change provision in the contract, with a set fee schedule for doing those corrections. ■

The Editor Toolbars After you have a document started, or have loaded one in from an existing Web, you can make use of the Editor's many features to create or change the page. Figure 42.22 shows the Editor with all of its toolbars active. Many are just like the toolbar buttons you would see in other Microsoft Office applications. Others that are more specific to HTML authoring are labeled with callouts in the figure.

FrontPage 98 Editor toolbars available from the View menu are:

- Standard Toolbar
- Format Toolbar
- Image Toolbar
- Forms Toolbar
- Advanced Toolbar
- Table Toolbar
- Status Bar
- Format Marks

N O T E You can toggle the display of any of the toolbars under the Editor View menu. ■

Of particular note are the Image toolbar, the Forms toolbar, and the Advanced toolbar. When you select an image on the page, the Image toolbar becomes active and allows you to trace hot regions for imagemaps, or make a color in the image transparent. The Forms toolbar places form controls at the cursor's position on your page. Using buttons on the Advanced toolbar, you can place ActiveX controls, scripts, embedded objects, a Java applet, or an HTML tag not supported by one of the Editor's menus.

N O T E The Image toolbar default location is across the bottom of the screen as shown in Figure 42.22; however, you can drag and drop that toolbar to other locations should you find that more convenient. If you prefer to not always display this toolbar, it will come into view automatically anytime you select an image. Otherwise, if you display it at all times, it remains inactive until you select an image. ■

FIG. 42.22
FrontPage's Editor
supports document
authoring with eight
different toolbars.

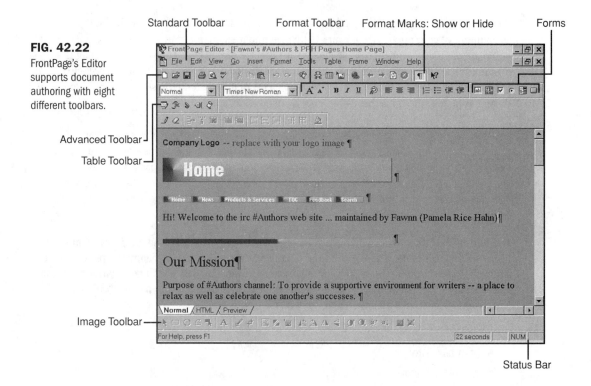

Standard Toolbar — Format Toolbar — Format Marks: Show or Hide — Forms

Advanced Toolbar

Table Toolbar

Image Toolbar

Status Bar

Formatting Text You can apply styles to text in a variety of ways. The physical styles (bold, italics, underline) are available on the toolbar. All you need to do is highlight the text to format and click the appropriate button. The Style drop-down box works similarly and gives you access to a much greater range of styles, including heading and list styles.

To either side of the physical style toolbar buttons are the Increase/Decrease Text Size buttons and the Text Color button, which lets you paint highlighted text with a different color.

For several formatting options at once, select Format, Font and then select the Special Styles tab to reveal a dialog box in which you can click different styles to apply them to highlighted text.

When you want to insert vertical space between page elements and you use the Enter key to do it, it is interpreted as a paragraph break (or tag) in your HTML code. If you just want a line break (or <BR> tag), you can use Shift+Enter or insert it manually by choosing Insert, Line Break, and then selecting Normal Line Break.

Some text elements are best handled outside of the Editor. If you have text elements that are common to each page, such as copyright information or a Webmaster e-mail address, you might want to consider copying and pasting these items into your pages using a plain-text editor like Notepad. The FrontPage Editor can take a long time to load an entire page because it also loads images. A plain-text editor just loads the HTML code and is therefore much faster.

Inserting Images   To place an image on your page when you use the FrontPage Editor while working on a Web, choose Insert, Image to open the dialog box you see in Figure 42.23; Figure 42.24 shows the subsequent dialog box when you use the FrontPage editor as a stand-alone program. In the box, you get the option to load the file from the current Web, a local drive, a remote machine, or from a clip art collection.

FIG. 42.23
You can place images from local or remote sources in your FrontPage Editor document.

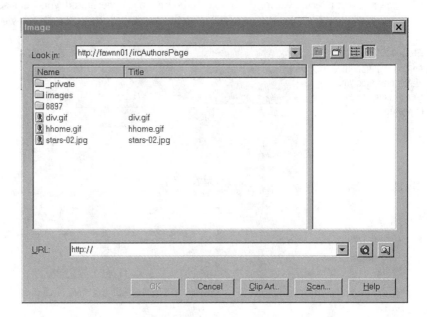

FIG. 42.24
You get this image box from which to make your image selection when you use the FrontPage Editor as a stand-alone program— that is, when not working within a Web.

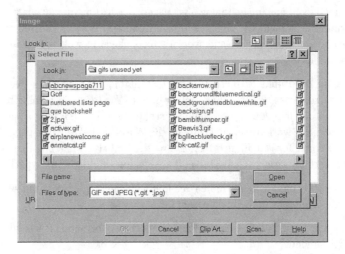

Part
VII

Ch
42

By default, the image is placed at the current cursor location and is left-justified with an ALIGN value of BOTTOM (the text next to the image will line up with the bottom of the image). You can exercise greater control over the placement of the image in the image's Properties box.

To reveal the image's properties, double-click the image or right-click the image and select the Properties option you see in the context-sensitive pop-up menu. If you have the image already selected, you can also choose the Properties view from the Edit Image Properties menu or by using Alt+I. The various tabs in the Image Properties dialog box, shown in Figure 42.25, allow you to specify image alignment, border size, horizontal and vertical spacing, low resolution, and text alternatives for the image. If the image is hyperlinked, you can also specify what URL it is linked to. There's even a Video tab in case you're placing an AVI movie via the <IMG> tag.

FIG. 42.25

An Image's Properties dialog box gives you greater control over image attributes.

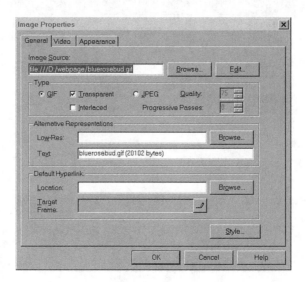

If you need to edit an image that you've placed in a document, you can fire up Microsoft's Image Composer to make the changes. Image Composer is a full-featured graphics editor with support for scanning devices and special effects filters, as well as the more common graphic manipulations.

Setting Up Hyperlinks   To create hypertext, highlight the text to serve as the anchor and click the Create or Edit Hyperlink toolbar button. You then see a dialog box. In this dialog box, you can choose to link to a page that is currently open in the Editor, a page that is part of the Web that you're working on, any page on the World Wide Web, or a page that you ask the Editor to create for you. Figure 42.26 shows the Edit Hyperlink box that appears when you select Insert, Hyperlink (Ctrl+K) to edit an existing (highlighted) hyperlink.

If you need to change the attributes of a link, you can right-click it and select the Hyperlink Properties option from the pop-up menu.

As shown in Figure 42.27, General Page Properties information is available from the File, Page Properties menu.

FIG. 42.26

The Edit Hyperlink dialog box lets you link to files on your site, files out on the Web, or files you have yet to create, or you can manually edit an existing hyperlink URL.

To color your links, right-click anywhere on the page and select the Page Properties option to reveal the dialog box you see in Figure 42.28. Options on the Background tab enable you to paint your visited, unvisited, and active links with whatever color you choose. Figures 42.29 and 42.30 show two features new to FrontPage 98—the Custom and Language options.

FIG. 42.27

Items in the Page Properties dialog box correspond to tags in the document head and attributes of the <BODY> tag.

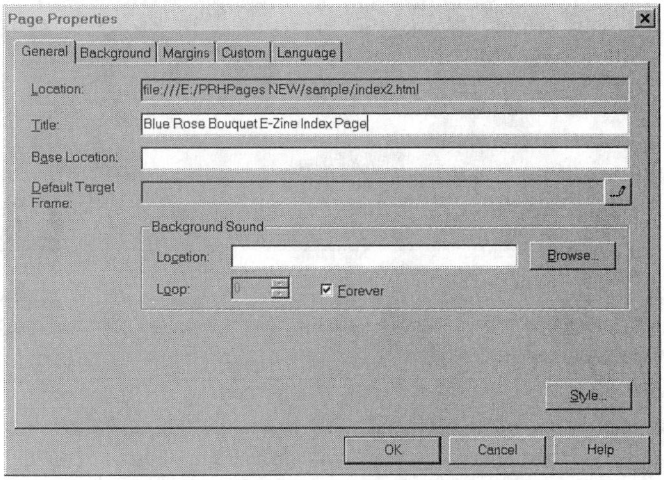

FIG. 42.28
From this dialog box, the Web page author sets such <BODY> tag attributes as background and text color as well as coordinated hyperlink colors.

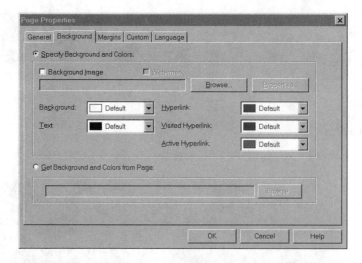

FIG. 42.29
The Custom option is new to the Page Properties dialog box selections in FrontPage 98; it provides page generator information.

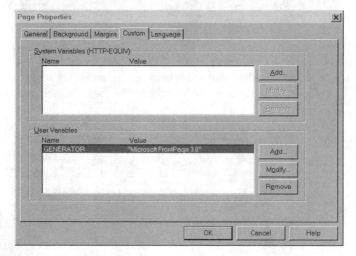

 TIP You can also set up titles, page margins, base URLs and targets, text color, and <META> tags from the Page Properties dialog box.

Setting up a linked image is virtually the same as setting up linked text. Simply click the image you want to link and then click the Create or Edit Link button to open the dialog box. If you're setting up an imagemap, click the image once to select it and then use the tools on the Image toolbar to set up the different hot regions. After you trace out a hot region, the Editor displays the same dialog box you saw in Figure 42.26, so you can enter the URL to associate with the hot region.

FIG. 42.30
The new Language
option allows the
choice of English versus
the Multilingual HTML
encoding style for
saving and loading
your page.

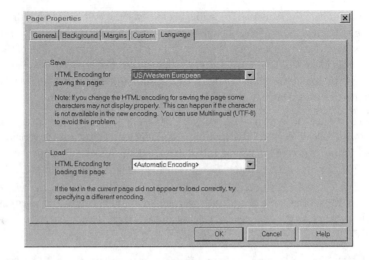

N O T E The FrontPage Editor uses client-side imagemaps. If you need to implement a server-side imagemap, look at the HTML source code to get the hot-region coordinates, and then type out your map file by hand. ▨

Creating Tables To insert a table, choose Table, Insert Table or click the Insert Table toolbar button. When you do, you see a dialog box like the one in Figure 42.31. After entering the table size and border, alignment, padding, and spacing attributes, the Editor places a blank table in your document, and you can fill in the cells with text, images, form fields, and even other tables.

FIG. 42.31
You set up a table in
your document by filling
out the Insert Table
dialog box.

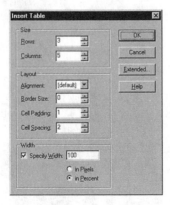

N O T E Most of the options under the Table menu are grayed out unless the cursor is in a table cell. ▨

Part
VII

Ch
42

You can delete the content of individual cells of a table by highlighting them and pressing Delete, but it is more of a challenge to delete an entire table. Even if you remove all cell contents, FrontPage still leaves you with an empty table on-screen and all of the related table tags in the HTML code. To remove the entire table, double-click your mouse just to the left of the table to highlight the whole thing. After it's highlighted, you can press Delete or Backspace to remove the entire table from both your screen and your HTML code.

You can color the individual cells in your tables, thanks to HTML extensions now supported by Netscape and Microsoft browser products. To color a cell, right-click inside the cell and choose Cell Properties from the pop-up menu that appears. You can then choose your background color (or image) in the Custom Background section of the dialog box.

 TIP Coloring the individual cells can overstate the block-like nature of the cells. To reduce this effect, you might want to color your table cells with the same color you use to color your page background.

N O T E Although FrontPage 98 has made strides toward browser compatibility integration, the manner in which it displays a table might not be exactly the same as the way Netscape Navigator or Microsoft Internet Explorer displays it. Therefore, it is always a good idea to look at your Web document in those browsers to determine if you've achieved the desired effect.

Saving Your Document   To save your document for the first time, select File, Save As to open the dialog box shown in Figure 42.32. Notice that in this box you can save the document as a normal file or as a document template. Clicking OK saves the file to your current Web.

FIG. 42.32
When saving it for the first time, you can make your document into a template for reuse at a later time.

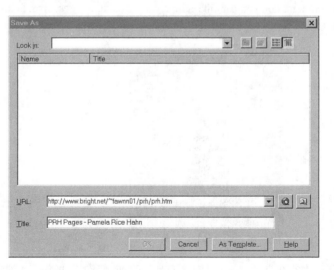

Using FrontPage Components

FrontPage Components (known as WebBots in FrontPage 97) are preprogrammed dynamic objects that run when you save a file or when a user views your file online. The FrontPage

Editor comes with several components that you can build into your pages. Some (such as Timestamp and Table of Contents) are available from the Insert menu; others are incorporated into your page from the Insert, FrontPage Component menu selection. These dynamic objects include:

- *Comment*. Formerly known as the Annotation bot, the Comment FrontPage Component places what is essentially a page description text for your use only into your HTML code. Site visitors can't see an annotation, but other people editing the annotated document can see it. Comments are displayed in purple in the font size and style of the current paragraph.

- *Confirmation Field*. To confirm the contents of a key form field, you can build a Confirmation Field FrontPage Component into the confirmation page.

- *HTML Markup*. As more and more HTML extensions are introduced, you can use the Insert HTML option from the Insert, FrontPage Component menu command to add nonstandard tags to your documents. (The View, Advanced Toolbar menu command displays this option as the icon of a page with a pencil beside of it.) FrontPage does not check this HTML for validity, so it's up to you to make sure the HTML code you insert uses proper syntax. The inserted HTML code appears on the FrontPage Editor screen as a question mark in angle brackets (<?>) that is colored in yellow.

- *Include Page*. The Include Page FrontPage Component reads in the contents of another file and displays them on the page. This is useful if you're including a standard element on every page, like a mailto link to your Webmaster or a navigation bar. By using the Include Page FrontPage Component to place standard items on pages, you can keep these items in one file, and changes made to that file are enough to make changes throughout your entire site.

- *Scheduled Image*. If you want an image to appear on a page, but only for a certain amount of time, you can use the Scheduled Image FrontPage Component. You tell that FrontPage Component what image to use, when to start displaying it, when to stop displaying it, and what it should display outside of the scheduled period.

- *Scheduled Include Page*. The Scheduled Include FrontPage Component works the same way as the Schedule Image one, except it displays the contents of another file during the scheduled period.

- *Search Form*. The very useful Search Form FrontPage Component (formerly known as the Search bot) gives you a simple way to set up full-text searching capabilities on your Web. The component generates a query form and then does the search based on the user's input. FrontPage lets you specify the prompting text, the width of the input field, and the labels on the submit and reset buttons. You can also customize the search output with a given match's search score, file date, and file size. When the user submits such a form, the results display the hyperlinks of pages within your Web that match that criteria.

- *Substitution*. A Substitution FrontPage component is replaced with the value of a selected page or Web variable such as Author, Modified By Description, or Page-URL.

Part
VII

Ch
42

■ *Table of Contents.* The Table of Contents FrontPage Component prepares a table of contents for your site, starting from any page you choose. It even recalculates the table when pages are edited, if you tell it to do so while setting it up.

■ *Timestamp.* The Timestamp FrontPage Component is particularly useful if you intend to note the time and date of the most recent changes to a page. It gives you the choice between the date the page was last updated or the date that the page was last automatically updated.

FrontPage Components are unique in that their functionality is built right into FrontPage. This is very different from programming that supports similar functions, as these programs are typically written separate from the coding of the HTML. FrontPage integrates these two activities into one.

N O T E Much of the power of the FrontPage suite is derived from its set of standard FrontPage Components. Additionally, you can write your own components (formerly known as bots) by using the FrontPage Software Developer's Kit included with FrontPage 98. More information is available on this at **http://eu.microsoft.com/FrontPage/ProductInfo/faqs.htm**. ■

Adobe PageMill

When you think of documents, it's logical to also think of the Adobe Corporation—the folks who brought us programs like PageMaker and the Internet document format PDF (Portable Document Format). It shouldn't surprise you then that Adobe has an entry in the WYSIWYG Web document editor field. Adobe PageMill is an easy-to-use document authoring tool with many neat features, including the capability to manipulate images without using a separate utility program.

The PageMill Window

With PageMill, you have a point-and-click, drag-and-drop, mousing-about interface to help you in your document authoring—much like you have with a word processor (see Figure 42.33).

The PageMill window is the heart of the program—it's where you type all your text (or paste it in from another program) and position your multimedia elements. The window is very drag-and-drop aware, so you can simply drag text or graphics from their original program into the PageMill window. In certain cases, you can even drop the icon of a document or graphic file into the PageMill window, and the image or text will appear in the PageMill window (see Figure 42.34).

For the most part, however, you use the PageMill document window in nearly the same way you use a word processor. You can use the mouse to place your insertion point (cursor) on the page, highlight text for some action or to pick up graphics, and move them around on the page.

You might have noticed the PageMill window looks a little like a Web browser. That was done on purpose. The document window is actually two windows in one. To change between these windows in PageMill, you click the Toggle Preview Mode button on the PageMill toolbar.

Menu items   Buttonbar controls   Edit/Preview mode button   Attribute Inspector

FIG. 42.33
All HTML coding is accomplished through the PageMill interface elements.

The main document window

Pasteboard

The Link Location Bar

FIG. 42.34
Drag and drop is a big improvement over the raw HTML method of entering graphics.

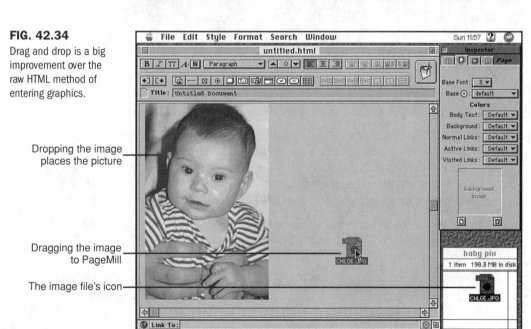

Dropping the image places the picture

Dragging the image to PageMill

The image file's icon

The two windows represent two different modes that really alter PageMill's functionality drastically:

- Edit mode—When the toggle mode button looks like a pen and paper, you're in edit mode. This is the mode that PageMill needs to be in so you can enter text by using the keyboard, make changes to text appearance, and add graphics.

- Preview mode—Now the toggle button looks like a 3-D globe. In this mode, PageMill acts more like a browser, allowing you to see how your pages will look on the Web while giving you an opportunity to test your hypertext and hypermedia links.

N O T E If you use the File, Open command in PageMill to open an existing HTML document, PageMill starts out in Preview mode. Click the toggle mode button to edit the document. New documents start in Edit mode. ■

The PageMill Toolbar

The toolbar is where you find a lot of the common tools that you need to use in creating your Web page. Not everything that's possible with HTML is available from the toolbar—many commands are buried in the menus—but you'll find a lot of everyday stuff is right up front, just like in your favorite word-processing program (see Figure 42.35).

FIG. 42.35

The PageMill toolbar can be used to accomplish many common Web authoring tasks.

One important toolbar button deserves special mention. More than one PageMill-experienced Web author has missed something fairly obvious at the bottom of the toolbar…the Title field.

Giving your Web documents a title is an important part of creating the page. Titles appear in the bar at the top of a user's Web browser window. They are also used as entries in bookmark lists and are scanned by robots that index your pages. Unfortunately, for some reason, a lot of folks skip over the title when creating pages in PageMill. Don't forget that the title text box is there. All you have to do to give your page a title is click in the text box and type away.

The toolbar has one other special feature worth mentioning. At the bottom-left corner of the toolbars, right next to the title text box, is the page icon. It doesn't look like much, but it's at the heart of creating links in your PageMill documents.

In edit mode, move the mouse pointer up to the page icon, click it and drag (holding down the mouse button). Notice the page icon comes along for the ride. What you're holding with the mouse is a hyperlink to this particular document.

If you are working in another document, you can drag this page icon directly to the other document, drop it in that document window and create a link to this page. It's that simple.

N O T E Actually, it's not quite that simple. There's one other factor—the page represented by the page icon needs to be saved before the page icon is active. ■

The Link Location Bar

Down at the bottom of the page is the heart of PageMill's hyperlink capabilities...the link loca-tion bar. It's here that you enter URLs for your hyperlinks.

N O T E You need to be in Edit mode to place a hyperlink. ■

The link location bar actually performs two different functions, depending on the current mode:

- Edit mode—In edit mode, you use the link location bar to enter URLs for hyperlinks. To create a link, you usually highlight text (or select an image) with the mouse, then enter the URL for the link by typing it in the link location bar.
- Preview mode—In preview mode, the link location bar is primarily used to show you the URLs for the links on the page. Notice the link location bar changes to show you the associated URL when you move the mouse pointer over a hyperlink.

The Attribute Inspector

If you can't get something done with PageMill's toolbar, chances are that you can do it in the Attribute Inspector. The Inspector is easily the most powerful element of the PageMill inter-face, allowing you to do everything from change typefaces to add background images to your Web pages to manage the HTML forms you create for user feedback (see Figure 42.36).

 T I P You can toggle the Attribute Inspector on and off by pressing command (Apple) + ; (plus semicolon) or by choosing the command Show Attribute Inspector or Hide Attribute Inspector in the Window menu.

FIG. 42.36
The Attribute Inspector uses different modes to change its options based on the type of element you need to alter—the Web page itself, text on the page, graphics, or form data.

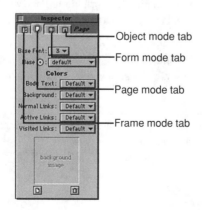

Object mode tab
Form mode tab
Page mode tab
Frame mode tab

Part
VII

Ch
42

The Attribute Inspector is a small floating window that's based on the idea that you'll use it in different modes depending on the elements you need to change. Those modes are:

- Page attributes—Clicking the Page mode button gives you a variety of options that relate to how the overall Web page will appear to viewers. Options include things like adding a background graphic to your page and changing the text color.

- Text attributes—Click the Text mode button and your given the choice of changing highlighted text into nearly any conceivable HTML format.

- Graphic/Form (Object) attributes—This mode button is only available if you've selected a graphic or form element (like a text box) in the document window. Then, pressing the button gives you options based on what you selected. For graphics, you can alter the height and width, enter ALT text, or add a border (see Figure 42.37). For form elements, you can give the field a variable name, choose the size for the element, or enter other form-related attributes.

FIG. 42.37
Most HTML options for images are available right from the Attribute Inspector.

The Image Viewer

Adobe's experience with graphics comes shining through in the PageMill Image Viewer. From within your document, you can view images, choose a transparent color in a GIF, and even create clickable imagemaps.

There's only one question: how do you find the Image Viewer? The answer is simple: If you've placed an image in the document window, make sure you're in Edit mode and then just double-click the image (see Figure 42.38).

On a PC, you can use the File, Open command to open an image directly into the Image Viewer, without placing it in the document. On a Macintosh, File/Open is Command+O.

FIG. 42.38

It's not exactly an image-editing program, but the Image Viewer does let you create important Web-related effects in your images.

Graphic icon┘
Image mapping label┘
Interlacing toggle┘
Zoom controls┘

Selector tool
Image mapping tools
Transparency tool
Shuffle hotspot
Hotspot color
Link location icon

We could fill an entire chapter with information on how to use the Image Viewer, but space constraints compel us to just look quickly at an overview of the Image Viewer's capabilities:

■ Creating imagemaps—Imagemaps are graphics that are mapped with different hot regions, which are mapped to different URLs. Click a certain part of a graphic, and you head off towards one Web page; click another and you load a multimedia file or a help page. This is the technology used on a lot of Web sites to create clickable interfaces.

■ Transparency—The Image Viewer has the capability (when dealing with GIF files) to turn a particular color of the image transparent (usually the background color). This gives the impression the graphic is sitting directly on the page—a popular effect on most Web documents.

■ Image linking—In contrast to imagemaps, it's also possible to make an entire image point at just one URL. The image becomes a hyperlinked button of sorts.

■ Interlacing—The GIF file format is also capable of being saved in a special way, called *interlacing*. This allows many Web browsers to gradually display the image as it is transferred across the Internet. An interlaced GIF appears to fade onto a page over the course of several passes.

Another of the Image Viewer's special features is the image icon located at the top-left of the viewer window. It's another neat little tool that you can use to drag and drop to your HTML pages.

If you've loaded a graphic directly into the Image Viewer and you'd like to place that graphic on a Web page you're creating in PageMill, click the Arrow tool in the Image Viewer. Then, click and drag the image icon into the document window of the destination page. Drop the image on the page, and it should appear now as part of the new Web page.

The Pasteboard

One final key interface element is the Pasteboard, which you can access on a PC by choosing Window, Show Pasteboard; on a Macintosh, choose Command+/. Basically, the Pasteboard works like the Clipboard in Windows or Mac—it's designed to aid in cut-and-paste. But, it's also something that the Clipboard never has been. It's easy to use with multiple images, clips of text, and HTML elements (see Figure 42.39).

Part
VII

Ch

42

FIG. 42.39

The Pasteboard gives you the freedom to keep common elements, graphics, or text clips handy for quick drag-and-drop operations.

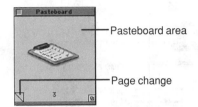

Pasteboard area

Page change

Aside from drag-and-drop support and the capability to store different types of elements on the same page, the Pasteboard also features five different pages for you to work with. Clicking the page controls at the bottom of the Pasteboard window lets you change pages.

 TIP Get to know the Pasteboard. You'll be amazed how quickly things go when you don't have to open a new image or retype text when you're authoring multiple Web pages.

You've probably gathered from the discussion of the PageMill interface that many common document authoring tasks—like formatting text or placing an image—are pretty easy with PageMill. You are correct! PageMill's word processor-like interface and drag-and-drop capabilities make authoring a snap. For this reason, we'll focus on the more advanced document components—tables, forms, and frames— for the rest of the chapter.

Creating Tables

Creating the initial table in PageMill is the easy part. First, place the insertion point (cursor) at the point in your document where you want the table to appear. Then, from PageMill's toolbar, click and hold the Insert Table icon. While you hold down the mouse button, drag down and to the right. You should see an expanding grid that appears to grow out of the Insert Table icon. When the table reaches the dimensions you desire, let go of the mouse button. PageMill creates the table and places it in your document window (see Figure 42.40).

After you have the table available to you in the document window, there are two things you should notice. First, clicking once on the border of the table selects it as an object and (assuming you have the Attribute Inspector visible) changes the Object tools to those that are relevant for a table.

Second, clicking the interior of a table makes the table active, which allows you to enter data and change the attributes of rows, columns, and individual cells. Once again, you might notice that the Attribute Inspector changes Object tools to reflect this (see Figures 42.41 and 42.42).

FIG. 42.40
PageMill's Insert Table command makes it simple to create a table of nearly any size.

Insert table icon —
Grow the grid —

PageMill creates and places the table —

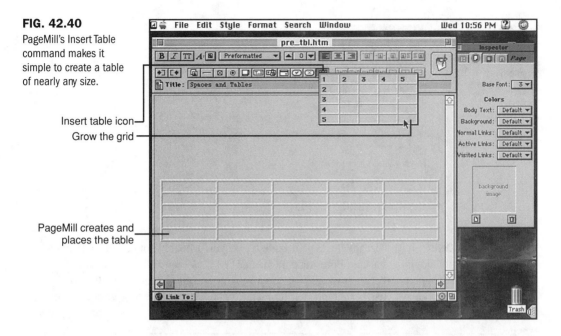

FIG. 42.41
The Inspector tools for table-as-object.

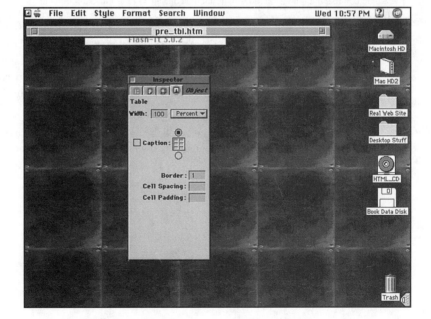

FIG. 42.42

Inspector tools for an
active table (with cells
highlighted).

Filling in Cells   If you already made your table active, you probably noticed that one of the cells has a blinking cursor in it. Entering data for this cell is as easy as typing. Anything alpha-numeric is free game (that is, anything you enter on your keyboard should look fine in a cell), and you can even use text-emphasis commands to add some spice to your entries (see Figure 42.42).

 You can use the Tab key to move right one cell or Shift+Tab to move left one cell.

As you read in the Chapter 11, "Formatting Content with Tables," a cell can be either a header cell or a data cell. To create a header cell, you begin by clicking the cell to select it. If you like, you can click in one cell, then drag to select a number of cells across a particular row or down a column. When you have the range selected for your header cells, use the Attribute Inspector to select the Make Header option.

Data that appears in these header cells will, by default, appear bold in your user's browser window (assuming the browser supports tables). Otherwise, the cell acts the same as any other data cell.

FIG. 42.43
Entering and emphasizing text in a table cell.

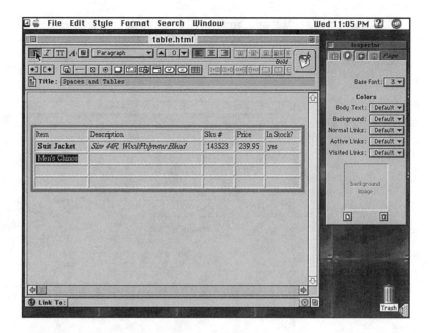

Adding (or Deleting) Rows and Columns   Adding rows and columns is easy enough to do in PageMill, provided you're already working in an active table. (And, even if you're not, activating the table is just a matter of double-clicking, as you've already seen.)

Start by selecting the column directly to the left of the area where you want the new column to appear. To do this, begin by clicking in the top cell of the column, then drag the mouse pointer to the bottom cell. When you release the mouse button, you should see that the entire column has been highlighted. (With rows, highlight the row directly above the point at which you want to insert the new row.) Now, click the Insert Row/Column button. It's that simple!

Deleting columns and rows is a similar process, only this time you get to highlight the actual column or row in question. Drag to select the offending column or row, then click the Delete Column/Row button once. It should disappear right away. The other columns or rows squeeze together—almost as if the now departed cells in your table had never even existed.

Adding a Table Caption   You can give your table a title or footer with the table caption option. With the table selected as an object (but not active), use the Attributes Inspector to activate the Caption option by clicking its check box. When checked, a caption appears at the top of your table (see Figure 42.44).

FIG. 42.44

Adding a table caption with the Attributes Inspector.

Click to add a caption

Space for caption appears in table

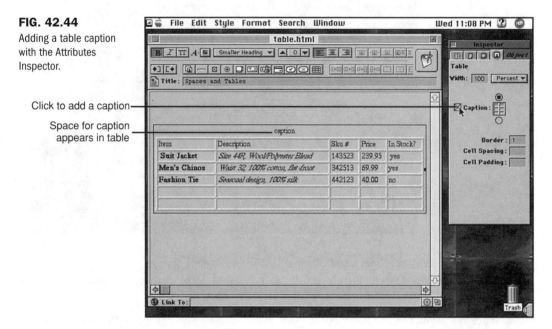

Next to the caption text box you have two options: top or bottom. By default, your caption will appear at the top of the table. If you prefer to have it at the bottom, change that option by using the pull-down menu.

To edit the caption, make the table active by double-clicking it. Now you can place the cursor in the caption box (if it isn't already there) and type a new caption or title for your table. When you're done, use the standard movement keys to continue on to other cells within the table.

Changing Alignment   After you've got some data in your table, you might quickly decide that it needs to be formatted in some way that's different from the default. When you first enter data, everything is aligned to the left of the cell, and in between the top and bottom borders. If you want to change this, all you have to do is highlight and click.

To do the highlighting, click and hold the top-left corner of the cell's border and slowly drag the mouse pointer into the cell. When the entire cell highlights (and just that cell), you're ready to change alignment attributes (see Figure 42.45).

FIG. 42.45
Highlighting a single
cell in your table.

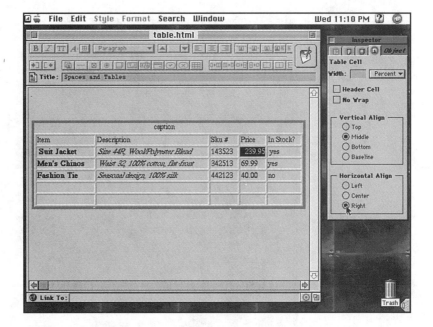

Next, look at the Attribute Inspector, where you see a number of cell parameters you can configure. Among these is alignment—both vertical and horizontal. Click the radio button next to the option you want to change, and then select the new alignment type you want to apply.

N O T E Aligning entire rows or columns of cells is similar to aligning individual cells, except that you have to highlight the entire row or column. ▣

Another ability you have in PageMill is the option of adding space around your data or between your cells, or making the visible border larger or smaller. To use the cellpadding, cellspacing, and border features, you need to have selected the table as an object (it should be inactive). Then move over to the Attribute Inspector and play around with the numbers. If you want a larger border, for instance, enter **5** instead of **1**. You can create a borderless table (a table with no visible lines) by entering **0** for the border. Remember to press Return or Enter after changing one of these numbers. The results appear immediately in the document window.

Creating Forms

PageMill also makes the composition of online forms much easier than coding them by hand. To get started, go into the Attribute Inspector and specify an ACTION URL and a METHOD for your form. After you've got these basic form attributes in place, your next step is to concentrate on the actual form elements. PageMill makes this easy, because each of the major elements has its own button in the toolbar (see Figure 42.46).

Part
VII

Ch
42

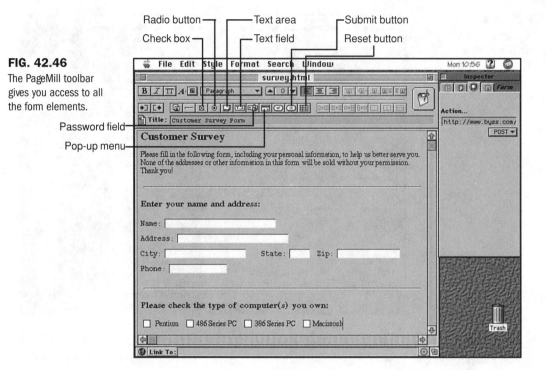

Radio button — Text area — Submit button
Check box — Text field — Reset button

FIG. 42.46
The PageMill toolbar gives you access to all the form elements.

Password field
Pop-up menu

One of the more common uses for forms is to accept multiple lines of text from a user, perhaps for feedback, bug reports, or other uses. We'll look at how to place a text area in PageMill as a prototypical example of how to place a form element. Placing other form controls on a page is done almost the same way.

TIP Don't forget that an important part of every form is the descriptive text you use to introduce each element.

To add a text area to your document, place the insertion point (cursor) at the point in the document where you want the text area to appear, then click the Insert Text Area button in PageMill's toolbar (see Figure 42.47).

Now, you need to click once on the text area (to select it as an object) and head over to the Attribute Inspector.

The Inspector needs three things from you: a name for this form element, the number of rows you want displayed on the screen, and the number of columns you want displayed. The name can really be just about anything you want it to be—although it will eventually have to be a name recognized by the CGI script that deals with this information.

TIP If someone else is creating your form's script, discuss the names of your form elements with them beforehand.

FIG. 42.47

Adding a text area to
your document.

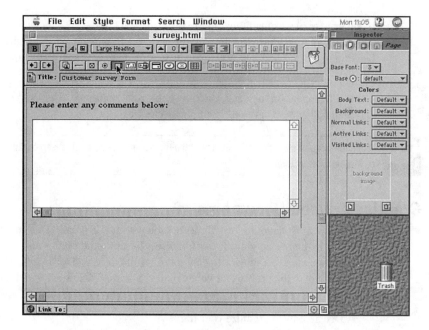

Notice that you can also use the mouse to set the rows and columns for your text area by clicking and dragging the drag boxes that surround the text area (see Figure 42.48).

FIG. 42.48

Putting your finishing
touches on the text
area.

Give the text area a name

Default text

Use grab boxes to resize

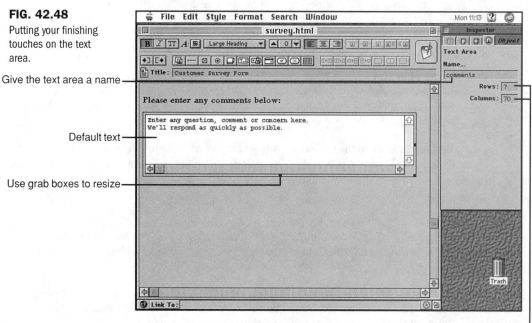

Choose dimensions

If you want to place default text in the text area (text that your users will see before they enter something themselves), double-click the text area to make it active. A cursor should begin blinking inside the text box. Then just type away and your default text appears.

Placing other form elements follows a similar process. Just select where you want the form element to appear on the page, click the appropriate button on the toolbar to place the element, and then polish it off in the Attribute Inspector.

 TIP Your knowledge of the different attributes of the form-related tags is immensely helpful when working in the Attribute Inspector.

Creating Framed Documents

Perhaps the most daunting task for a document author is creating a framed document. It's easy to get lost in the mire of doing your framesets to set up the frames and then doing even more work to populate the frames with content. As with tables and forms, PageMill is a useful tool that can simplify the process for you. Creating a framed document in PageMill is basically a three-step process. Specifically, you need to:

- Decide how to organize your frameset
- Tweak the framed layout to meet any special requirements
- Place content in each frame and save the document

After you're comfortable with frames, you can move on to creating them in PageMill. The first thing you need to decide is how you want to organize the frameset interface. Then you need to use the Inspector to alter or fine-tune some of the frames-oriented options. Finally, you create the pages for each pane and save the whole mess.

Creating the Frameset The way you create your frameset is somewhat dependent on what you want to do. For instance, if your sole reason for creating a frame document is to have a nonscrolling logo at the top of the page, you need two different frames in your document—two rows.

To do that, you hold down the Option key while pointing and clicking the top edge of the document window (see Figure 42.49). Hold down the mouse button and drag the mouse down into the document. Release the button and you create a divider that splits the window into two frames.

You can also create your frames in columns—in fact, you can do both. Let's say that you not only want part of your frameset to include a nonscrolling logo, but you also want to add a list of hyperlinks to serve as a table of contents for your site. You do that by adding a column to the bottom row.

Below that first dividing line, click and drag the left border of the document window while holding down the Option key. You should be pulling a new divider across the screen to the right. The divider only appears in the second row (see Figure 42.50).

FIG. 42.49
Hold down Option and
drag the top of the
document window
down to create two
rows of frames.

Click and drag here—

Divider is created—

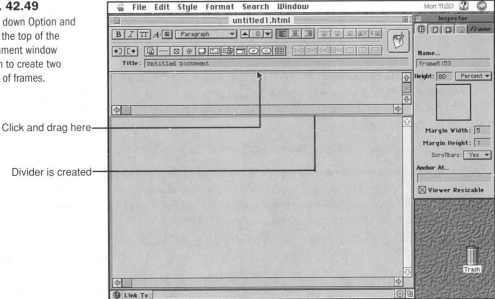

FIG. 42.50
Creating a column
frame divider gives our
example three different
panes for loading Web
documents.

Click and drag
left border

Column frame
divider is created

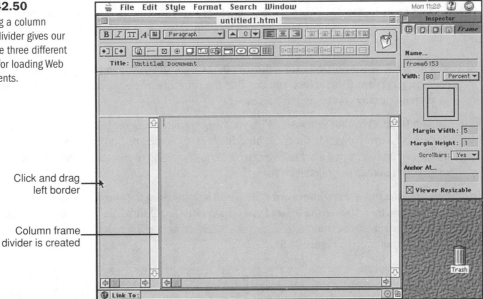

Now you have empty frames for each of the different documents you want to load. The top
frame is for your logo page, the left column is for the table of contents, and the right column
(the largest pane) holds any of the other content.

N O T E   If you need to delete one of the frames, just drag the frame divider back to its window border. Drop it on the border (or as close as possible), and PageMill asks you if you're trying to remove the frame from the document. ▨

Frame Options and Attributes   With the empty frames created, you can move on to make adjustments to the frames' appearance and behavior. To do this, you turn your attention to the Attribute Inspector. It's here, as always, that you can tweak your frames and make your framed layout more to your liking.

In particular, you can set the following attributes in the Inspector:

- ▨ Name   The Name attribute gives the selected frame a name. This is the internal name used by PageMill for targeting purposes. It isn't necessary for you to change the name, but it might be useful if you plan to edit any of the HTML by hand, because PageMill makes up really creative names like Frame345298.

- ▨ Width   In the Width field, you enter a number and the units to associate with the width of a frame. Generally, it's best to stick with percentages, but, if you really want things fixed on the screen, you can choose pixels.

- ▨ Scroll bars   You can also choose whether or not each of your frames will have scroll bars. The Auto setting is used when you want scroll bars if there's something to scroll, but you want them to disappear when everything fits in the frame.

- ▨ Viewer Resizable   Most frames-capable browsers permit users to resize a frame by dragging one of its borders to a new location. If you want to suppress this capability, turn off the Viewer Resizable option.

You're by no means obliged to any changes to the frameset parameters. If you're happy with them as you created them, then you can skip the Attribute Inspector and move right on to the next step—placing content in the frames.

Adding Content to Your Frames   With your empty frames all prepped and ready to go, it's time to put some content in them. So how do you get documents into their respective frames? There are two ways: just start typing in a frame to create the document, or use the File menu to load a document in the selected frame.

The first method is straightforward enough, so let's focus on the second. Select one of your frame areas, then choose the Insert Page option from PageMill's File menu. In the dialog box, find the document you want to load, then click OK. Now that frame has a default document associated with it (see Figure 42.51).

CAUTION

You might be asked if you'd like to save Frame345256 or something similar when you choose to load a new page in your frame. If you've done any work in that frame, you'll lose it if you don't save it at this point. If you haven't done anything in that frame, though, it's okay to go ahead and click Don't Save.

FIG. 42.51

After inserting an existing document in the frame, it becomes the default document associated with that part of the frameset document.

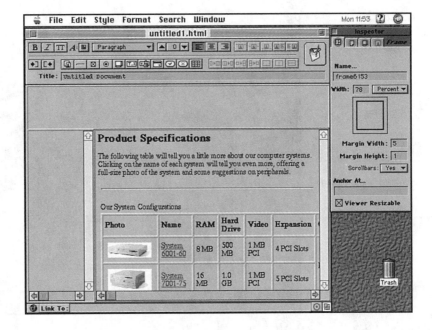

So what does it mean to be the default document associated with a frame? When the user loads the frameset into his browser, the default documents come along for the ride. They're the first documents that automatically appear in their frames when the frameset is loaded.

Creating Targets

The point of frames is eventually to replace those default documents with new ones—at least in one of the panes of the frameset. To do that, you have to create links with targets.

In PageMill, that's pretty simple. You start by creating a link in any of the ways described earlier in the chapter. Then, highlight the link again (if it isn't already) and click and hold the mouse on the Target icon at the bottom of the document window. You can also click and hold the mouse button on the highlighted link (see Figure 42.52).

 TIP You can triple-click a hyperlink to quickly highlight all its text.

In the Target pop-up menu, select the text or part of the page that you want to appear as your link. Notice that the Target menu is actually a little representation of your page; you can simply highlight the frame you want to select as a target, then release the mouse button. Now, when the user clicks that link, the resulting Web document is loaded in the targeted frame.

Part
VII

Ch

42

FIG. 42.52
Choosing a target for
your hyperlink.

Choose the frame
where you want the—
selected link to display

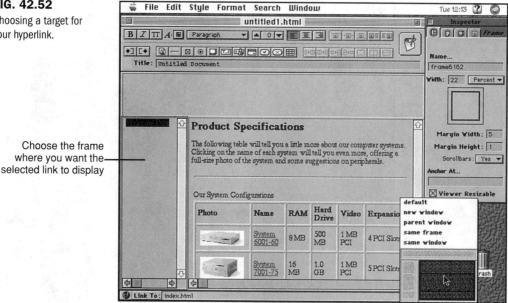

So what are all those words doing? In a nutshell, here's what happens if you choose them instead of one of the frames:

- default—The target is whatever is the current default—usually the frame in which the link originates.

- new window—When this link is clicked, the resulting document is displayed in a new browser window created specifically for that purpose.

- parent frameset—The resulting document is displayed in the current frame, after any other frames on the current level are removed.

NOTE Consider our three-paned scenario—two rows, and, in the second row, two columns. A link that appears in one of the columns in that second row is targeted to the parent frameset. When the user clicks that link, the two column frames disappear, and the new document is displayed in the parent of those columns frames—the entire second row frame. ■

- same frame—The resulting document is displayed in the same frame as the hypertext link (and the document holding the hypertext link is unloaded).

- same window—The resulting document is displayed in the current browser window, after the frameset is unloaded. The new document will no longer be using a frames interface.

Saving All This Stuff

It's very important to remember to save everything when you're working in a frameset document. After all, even though you are working in one PageMill document window, you're actually editing two, three, or more documents at one time. And, they all need to be saved.

> **CAUTION**
>
> Pay close attention when PageMill prompts you to save something—even in Preview mode. If you don't save the file that's in one of your frames, you'll have to recreate it from scratch.

Take a quick look at the File menu when you're working with frames. See anything different? You've suddenly got a bunch of options for saving your frames documents (see Figure 42.53).

FIG. 42.53
There's a ton of saving you have to do when you edit framed documents.

Save frame commands

Save frameset commands

Save it all

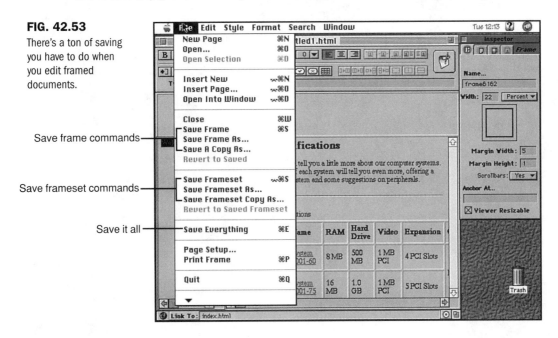

What do all these different options do for you? Well, there are three to concentrate on; the rest are useful, too, but most of them are just Save As... options that let you rename the files in question. Here are the big ones:

- *Save Frame*. The currently selected frame (outlined in blue) is saved by using its current file name. This is for default documents that you've edited on-screen.

- *Save Frameset*. The frameset document—the container that describes where the frame dividers are supposed to be—is saved under the current file name. (If it's still Untitled, you are given an opportunity to name it.)

- *Save All*. This option saves the frameset and all the default documents currently being displayed in the different panes. Probably the safest choice.

Learning by Example

Creating a Personal Web Site

by Mike Morgan

Designing a Personal Web Site

A personal Web site differs from a corporate or intranet site in that it is smaller and typically built on a tight budget. A business can afford to hire a professional HTML writer. A person writing his own page is often learning HTML as he goes. His site is not likely to use JavaScript, CGI, or other advanced features.

While the code may be less sophisticated than a professionally developed site, there's no reason the personal Web site cannot be developed with professionalism. Start by deciding why you even want a Web site, and what you hope it will accomplish. Then outline a site that will meet those objectives.

This section describes the steps in designing a Web site:

1. Identify your objectives.
2. Outline your overall site.
3. Design each page.

Once you've accomplished these three steps, you're ready to write HTML. The remainder of the chapter shows how to write HTML by using a variety of commercial and shareware tools.

A Personal Web Site? Who Needs One?

Even a cursory look at the World Wide Web reveals that many sites are operated by businesses who are providing information about their products, either for marketing or technical support purposes. Many people are surprised at the concept of a "personal Web site." While too many personal sites are poorly focused and not useful, there are at least three good reasons to place a personal site on the Web:

- As part of a commercial site, to add credibility to a company.
- To promote an idea or program that the author finds personally interesting, even without a commercial tie-in.
- To serve as a personal introduction—sort of an extended business card.

For an example of the first type of personal site, see **www.dse.com/Company/mike.html**, shown in Figure 43.1. This page, part of the personal Web site of the author of this chapter, is part of a site operated by DSE, Inc.

Mark R. Brown, who wrote this chapter in an earlier edition of this book, operates **www2.giant.net/people/mbrown/**, a site on his favorite topic, airships. Figure 43.2 shows the home page of Mark's personal site.

Gerald Oskoboiny, who developed one of the most popular HTML validation sites on the Web, introduces himself at **ugweb.cs.ualberta.ca/~gerald/**. Click on his name on any page of his validation site (**ugweb.cs.ualberta.ca/~gerald/validate/**) and you'll go to his personal page, shown in Figure 43.3. Here you'll find his resume, a list of his Web projects, and a list of future projects he'd like to undertake. You'll also find links to other pages of the Web that represent

Oskoboiny's interests. As the developer of one of the most popular validators, Oskoboiny is one of the more influential members of the HTML development community; this page helps you get to know him as a person.

FIG. 43.1

This page showcases the author of this chapter, in his role as a company employee.

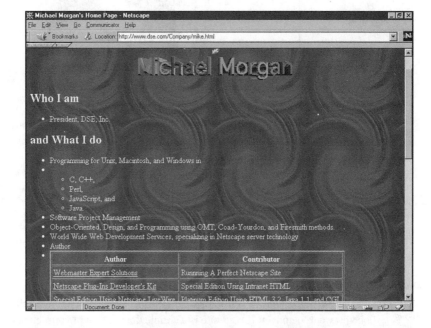

FIG. 43.2

There's enough interesting information on this site to hold an airship fan's attention.

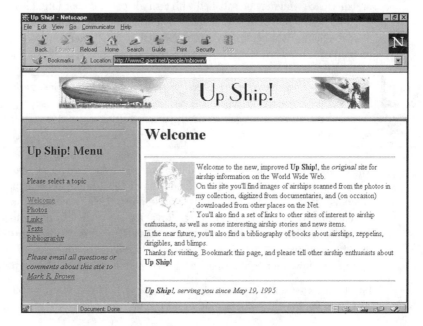

FIG. 43.3

If you've used Gerald Oskoboiny's excellent validator, you've probably been curious about Gerald himself.

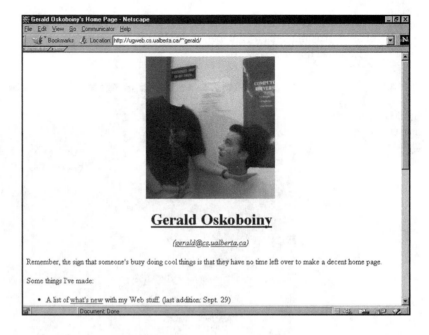

Building an Outline

Once you've decided why you want a personal Web site, you need to think about the information you want to convey. If your site is a simple description of yourself and your background or experience, you may be satisfied with a single page. If your intent is to promote an idea, you'll need a bit more content. Some people will want more than one personal site—one to describe themselves personally, and one for each major interest area or topic they want to put on the Web.

TIP Each of us has many different interests. Don't fall into the trap of putting more than one topic into your personal site. Focus each site on one topic, and use each page to develop a single part of that topic. The search engines will do a better job indexing your pages, and your readers will find it easier to retrieve the information they want.

The example in this chapter is drawn from one of Chris Kepilino's personal pages. Chris has many interests. He's a NASCAR fan (and a fan of Ricky Rudd, in particular). He's the Webmaster for his company's site (**www.dse.com**). He's also a leader of his church's outreach ministry to boys—a program known as Royal Rangers. The example site for this chapter is Chris's Royal Ranger site (**www.dse.com/Chris/Rangers/home.html**). This chapter uses this site to showcase several development tools and methodologies. The finished site is a good example of how you might develop a page related to a personal project or interest.

Royal Rangers is a world-wide program. The boys in Chris's church participate in local events, sectional events (which cover southeast Virginia), and district events (which draw boys from

Virginia and the neighboring states). Chris's primary objective for his site is to provide information about upcoming events to the boys and their parents in his local outpost. His secondary objective is provide on-line information about sectional and district events for use by leaders in other churches.

Figure 43.4 shows the outline of Chris's Royal Rangers site.

FIG. 43.4

Use an outlining tool such as SmartDraw to prepare an outline of your proposed site.

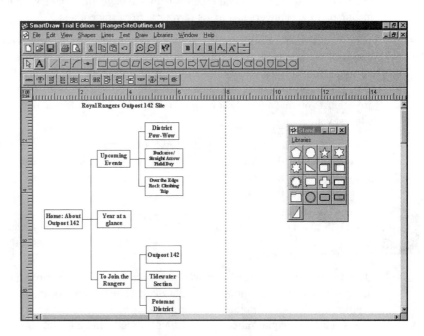

ON THE WEB

ftp://ftp.simtel.net/pub/simtelnet/win95/graphics/sd95-311.zip The graphic in Figure 43.4 was built by SmartDraw, a flowcharting tool for Windows 95 and Windows NT. Similar tools are available for all major platforms. Check www.shareware.com for specifics. (For example, Macintosh users may want to look at Public Works, available from ftp://ftp.amug.org/pub/amug/bbs-in-a-box/files/publish/o-p/publicworks-0.9.9.sit.hqx.)

N O T E   One of the features of SmartDraw that makes it attractive for building outlines of Web sites is that it supports a range of graphical templates. If you're building a large site, you can use smaller graphics. You may also choose to use graphics to represent the *type* of page. For example, you might give pages of links one shape, and downloadable files a different shape. That way you (or a client) could tell something about the design of your site without having to read the outline in detail. ■

Choosing a Focused Topic   Surprisingly enough, the first step in setting up a personal Web site is often the most difficult—choosing a topic for each page. It's important that each page have a single topic. This approach will help you bring visitors to your Web site. Suppose you're interested in auto racing. If your site is indexed by the search engines under keywords like "NASCAR" and "auto racing," you'll draw visitors with those interests. If the same page also addresses, say, Royal Rangers, the effect in the search engines is to dilute the auto racing keywords. Your page will appear to be less relevant to auto racing, so you'll draw fewer visitors. Many of the visitors who do find their way to that page may not be willing to scroll past information on Royal Rangers just to get to your auto racing content.

The World Wide Web is a unique medium in that just about anyone can put up a site and sit back and see who visits. The problem is, that's just what happens. Most Web sites—especially personal Web sites—aren't well thought out. Many people put up a site that includes everything they're interested in: their family, hobbies, line of work, and so on. Let's face it, the odds are against you that anybody surfing into your site will be interested in all of the things that interest you.

The first thing you need to do is pick a topic. If you want to cover more than one topic, set up two or more Web sites. You can even make a tasteful "Table of Contents" page that directs people to your various topics. Keep the topics separated, or you'll lose your audience by making a bad first impression.

 TIP On the Web, all you have is a first impression. With millions of sites on the Web, nobody's going to stick around your site long if you don't impress them. They'll surf off to a more appealing site.

Once you have your topic, it's important to narrow it down even more. Run your topic past the major search engines to see who else has done a site on the subject, as shown in Figure 43.5. If your interest is rock climbing, you might want to concentrate on a particular geographical area, or a specific technique. Yahoo lists 323 sites on rock climbing, and you've got to attract a specific group if you're going to make a name for yourself. If you're going to focus on Yosemite, you're competing with nine other sites. You may stand a better chance of becoming a Web legend (at least among local climbers) if you concentrate on the mountain in your own back yard. There are only two sites on climbing in Virginia, and one of those is a climbing gym 100 miles from the nearest mountain.

The topic chosen for the site shown in this chapter is narrow enough to virtually guarantee uniqueness: the activities of a single Royal Ranger outpost. This site is of immediate interest to around 100 people. Much of the material, however, describes activities at the section and district level, so Chris can reasonably expect visits from Rangers and their leaders throughout the mid-Atlantic region. Furthermore, many leaders visit other outpost's sites to get ideas for activities, so the site may be of benefit to anyone associated with Royal Rangers.

N O T E If you're building a personal Web site for your own enjoyment more than as a resource for other users, you don't need to think as much about keeping your pages focused. Just have fun and experiment.

FIG. 43.5
When choosing a topic for your Web site, check out search engines like Yahoo! (**www.yahoo. com**) to see who else has addressed your topic, and find out what they've already done.

Storyboarding the Pages

After selecting a focused topic, with a subtopic for each page, the next step is to choose the types of content you'll provide on your site. Depending upon your subject matter, you may want to include video clips, audio files, graphics, lists of hyperlinks, text files, or database information.

 T I P It's best to go with what you have access to that's unique. If a particular graphic or video clip is already available on the Web, don't copy it—link to it. Aside from copyright restrictions, hyperlinking helps you avoid reinventing the wheel. Just be sure to check your site regularly to keep the links up-to-date.

In the case of the Royal Ranger site, Chris has an extensive library of photographs he's taken at Ranger events over the years. He also has some interesting text articles he can include or link to.

 T I P Make sure all of the material you put on-line is in the public domain, or get permission from the copyright holder to use it. Though there's a lot of "borrowing" on the Web, there's no need to violate copyright laws when you're putting up your Web site. Make sure you have permission before you make the copy.

 ON THE WEB

http://www.hwg.org/resources/business/copyright.html   Learn more about copyright issues and the Web from the HTML Writers Guild. This unique resource is free. You'll get even more info if you join the guild. The only "cost" is the on-line e-mail list you're asked to subscribe to.

Page Design

While you don't need to be a professional HTML writer to put up a personal page, you will benefit from a few professional pointers. Consider joining the HTML Writers Guild (**www.hwg.org**)—there's no charge. At least review their Web site and search the archives of their mailing lists to find any messages that might be useful.

Choosing an HTML Level   One of your first decisions should be which level of HTML to use. As a general rule, use the latest released version. Check **www.w3.org/MarkUp/** to see whether a particular level (for example, 3.2, 4.0) is officially released, or still in draft.

If the level is released, then all of the major browsers (for example, Microsoft Internet Explorer and Netscape Communicator) typically support the tags. Visit **www.hwg.org/resources/html/demos.html** to see more browser testers and lists of which features are supported by which browsers. BrowserCaps (**www.pragmaticainc.com/bc/**) is a particularly useful site in this regard.

Be sure that each page gets the `<!DOCTYPE>` line at the top that reflects the level of HTML you've chosen. If your HTML editor doesn't add it, you should add that line by hand.

> **N O T E**   When you validate HTML, you validate against a specific level of the language. The specifications for each level are provided in computer-readable form in a file called a Document Type Definition, or DTD. Use the `<!DOCTYPE>` line to tell validators where to find the DTD you want to use when your code is tested. For example, if you're using HTML 4.0, you might write
>
> `<!DOCTYPE HTML PUBLIC "-//W3C//DTD HTML 4.0//EN">`
>
> You can find a comprehensive list of DTDs at **http://ugweb.cs.ualberta.ca/~gerald/validate/lib/catalog**. ■

ON THE WEB

http://www.pineapplesoft.com/reports/sgml/index.html—DTDs are part of a larger language, the Standard Generalized Markup Language, or SGML. SGML is the language in which other Internet-related languages, including HTML, are defined. Learn more about SGML from Benôit Marchal's site, "SGML in Plain English."

Thinking About Bandwidth   You should plan to include some graphics on your page, if only to make it more interesting. Too many graphics can slow the download of your page, especially if your visitors have a dial-up connection. Here are some rules of thumb that will improve the performance of your graphics:

- ■ Be sure to set the height and width tags on every graphic. Many browsers will use this information to lay out the page, allowing the graphic to load later.

- ■ Keep the graphic as small as possible—not just in height and width, but in color depth as well. Visit the Bandwidth Conservation Society's Web site (**www.infohiway.com/faster/index.html**) to learn how to tighten your graphics.

- Keep your background graphics small. Better still, use a background color.
- Make sure you set the ALT attribute on every image, so users can turn the graphics autoload off without losing information.
- Consider supplying a low-resolution version of the graphic with the LOWSRC attribute; many browsers will display the low-resolution version first, and then will bring in the larger high-resolution version.

Getting it Right: Checking the HTML

Whether you choose to write your HTML by hand (in a text editor), or with a tool such as Hot Metal Pro (**www.softquad.com**), Microsoft FrontPage (**www.microsoft.com/frontpage/**), or Netscape Composer (a component of Netscape Communicator, described at **home.netscape.com/comprod/products/communicator/composer.html**) you should be sure to submit your finished pages to a validator. Validators look for the <!DOCTYPE> line at the top of each page—be sure you or your tool have supplied it.

▶ **See** "Verification and File Management," **p. 773**

Once you've verified that your HTML is valid, use other tools such as Weblint and Doctor HTML to ensure that your HTML is good. The example shown in this chapter is tested against all three of these tools.

Promoting Your Site

After your site is published and has passed all of the HTML tests, it's time to tell the world about your site. Begin by listing your site with the major search engines. Then find similar sites and ask them to list your site on their list of links. (You will, of course, return the favor.) Finally, don't hesitate to use non-electronic means to promote your URL. If your personal site addresses a topic of widespread interest, then newsletters, word of mouth, and fan or enthusiasts clubs are appropriate ways to spread the word about your personal site.

▶ **See** "Listing Your Web Site in the Search Tools," **p. 785**

Building a Personal Page with Microsoft's Personal Web Manager

If you're using Microsoft Windows 95 or Windows NT 4.0 Workstation (with Service Pack 3 or higher) as your desktop machine, you can put together a simple personal Web page and publish it with Microsoft's peer Web service. Figure 43.6 shows the Personal Web Manager, the component of the Personal Web Server that allows you to actually set up your personal page.

To set up a personal page, start by clicking the About Me icon in the left frame. Figure 43.7 shows the About Me form. We can approximate the first of the Royal Rangers page we want by selecting My Organization in the "This Site is for" menu.

FIG. 43.6

If you're using one of the newer Microsoft operating systems, you may be able to run the Personal Web Server on your desktop.

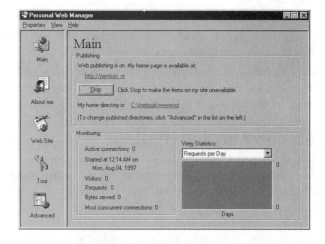

FIG. 43.7

Choose an appropriate "This Site is for" item to customize the personal page.

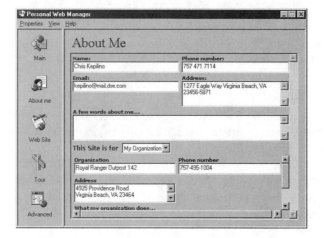

Once you've filled out the form, click the Web Site icon in the left frame. The first time you choose this icon you'll start a wizard that prompts you for a page type, style, background, title and a list of favorite hyperlinks. You may also select whether you want to have a guest book and private message area on the page.

When you're done configuring your page, click on the Main icon and follow the link to your finished page. Figure 43.8 shows the page generated by the Personal Web Manager, as viewed in Microsoft Internet Explorer.

We get our first indication that the HTML of this page is not what it should be by viewing the page in Netscape Communicator. Figure 43.9 shows the Personal Web Manager's generated HTML in Netscape's browser. Note that the entire left column, with the date, time, and list of favorite links, is missing. Either there's a serious problem with Navigator 4.0 (the browser in Communicator) or there's a problem with this HTML.

FIG. 43.8
By default, the Personal Web Manager uses Internet Explorer to show you your page.

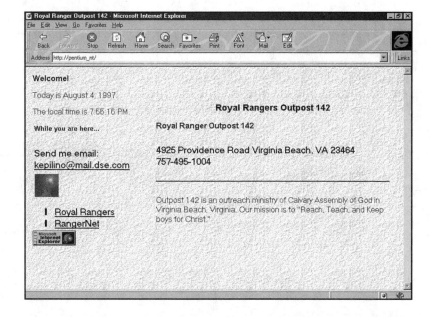

FIG. 43.9
The code generated by the Personal Web Manager does not work correctly in Netscape's browser.

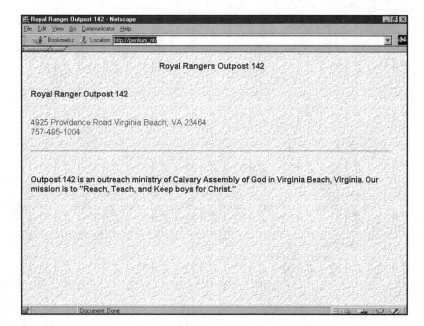

The Personal Web Manager does not write HTML—it writes an Active Server Page, or ASP. Microsoft's server uses the ASP to generate HTML at runtime. To check the quality of the HTML, publish the generated page to a server that is accessible from the Internet, and run Gerald Oskoboiny's Kinder, Gentler Validator (KGV), located at **http://ugweb. cs.ualberta.ca/~gerald/validate/**. You'll need to add an HTML 4.0 <!DOCTYPE> line to the top of the file:

```
<!DOCTYPE HTML PUBLIC "-//W3C//DTD HTML 4.0 //EN">
```

The validator uses that line to know which level of HTML to use when checking the code. With the <!DOCTYPE> in place, the finished code is shown in Listing 43.1.

Listing 43.1   home.htm—This code was generated by Microsoft's Personal Web Manager.

```
<!DOCTYPE HTML PUBLIC "-//W3C//DTD HTML 4.0 //EN">
<html>
<head>
<title>Royal Ranger Outpost 142</title><LINK REL=StyleSheet HREF='modern.css'
TYPE='text/css' MEDIA=screen>
</head>
<body

         Background="/bg10.gif"

 topmargin="5" leftmargin="5">

       <TABLE border="0" cellpadding=8 width="100%">
       <tr>
       <td valign=top

        rowspan=2

        nowrap>

       <h2>Welcome!</h2>


<p>Today is August 4, 1997.<p>
The local time is 7:55:16 PM.<br>
<p>
<TABLE border=0><TR><TD><h4>While you are here...</h4></TD></TR>  
            <TR><TD>Send me email:<BR>
            <a href="mailto:kepilino@mail.dse.com">kepilino@mail.dse.com</a></
TD></TR>
       </TABLE><TABLE border='0'>
            <TR><TD>
            <IMG SRC="4favlink.gif" width="50" height="50" align="left">
            </TD>
            </TR>

       <TR><TD><ul>
       <li><A HREF='http://www.royalrangers.org/'>Royal Rangers</A><BR><li><A
HREF='http://www.rangernet.org'>RangerNet</A><BR>
       </ul></TD></TR>
       </TABLE>
```

```
        <a href="http://www.microsoft.com/ie/default.asp"><img src="/ie.gif"
        border=0 height=31 width=88></a>


        </TD>
        <TD width="18" VALIGN="top"> <!-- SPACER CELL --></TD>
        <TABLE border="0" cellpadding=8 width="100%">
                <TR>
                <TD align=center valign=top >

                <H1>Royal Rangers Outpost 142</H1>
                </TD>
                </TR>


                <TR>


                <TD VAlign="top"> <!-- PAGE TYPE CONTENTS --><!-- IF NO Pagetype
picture, then colspan=1 -->
                        <h2>Royal Ranger Outpost 142</h2><BR>
                4925 Providence Road Virginia Beach, VA 23464                <br>
                757-495-1004<br>


                        <h2>
                        <HR>

                        </H2><br>
                        <H3>Outpost 142 is an outreach ministry of Calvary
Assembly of God in Virginia Beach, Virginia. Our mission is to "Reach, Teach,
and Keep boys for Christ."</h3>


                </TD>
                </TR>
                <!-- ADDITIONAL PERSONAL CONTENTS -->
        </TABLE>
        <!-- END ADDITIONAL PERSONAL CONTENTS -->
        </TD>
        </tr>
        </table>

</body>
</html>
```

The HTML validator shows that the Personal Web Manager's code has several serious defects:

- The Personal Web Manager has attempted to place a `topmargin` attribute and a `leftmargin` attribute in the `<BODY>`.

- home.htm has two non-breaking spaces (` `) between the end of the last row of the table and the `</TABLE>` tag. (Characters are not permitted in that location.)

- The Personal Web Manager has set a 100% `width` attribute on a `<TD>` tag.

- The Personal Web Manager has set a `width` attribute on a `<TABLE>` tag.

- In line 61, the wizard placed an `<HR>` inside an `<H2>` header.

- In line 71 there's a spurious `</TD>`.

As a user of Personal Web Manager, there is nothing you can do to prevent these defects—they represent a problem with Microsoft's product. If you want to correct them, you need to use a text editor to make the corrections one at a time.

Weblint, which takes a pickier view of the code, has found an additional 18 defects.

If you want a quick page that looks OK in Internet Explorer, Personal Web Manger produces such a page. Unfortunately the quality of the code is quite poor—Chris opts not to use this page in his finished Royal Rangers site.

▶ **See** "Active Server Pages," **p. 679**

Building a Personal Page with Netscape Composer

If you've chosen Netscape Naviagtor 4.0 as your Web browser, you already have Netscape Composer. Both are components of Netscape Communicator. Launch Netscape Communicator and choose <u>P</u>age Composer from the <u>C</u>ommunicator menu.

Starting from a Template

You can build a page from scratch in Composer, or you can use a template. Templates are available online. Once you've started Composer, choose <u>F</u>ile, <u>N</u>ew, Page From <u>T</u>emplate. Then click on the Netscape <u>T</u>emplates button in the resulting dialog. Figure 43.10 shows a portion of the list of available templates.

FIG. 43.10

To build a personal page quickly, start with one of Netscape's on-line templates.

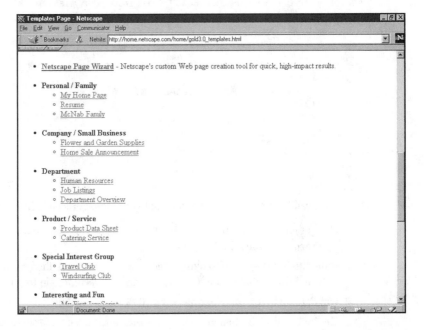

Both the Travel Club page and the Windsurfing Club page are reasonable approximations to the home page of Chris's Royal Rangers home page. Once you've chosen a page template, choose File, Edit Page, and then choose File, Save to have the browser save a copy of the page on your hard drive.

Using the Netscape Page Wizard

You can also build a new page by using the Netscape Page Wizard. Once you've started Composer, choose File, New, Page From Wizard. Your browser will connect to Netscape's site and put up a three-frame page. Click the Start button—you may have to scroll down to see it—in the upper-right pane.

Follow the instructions in the upper-left pane, and enter the information requested in the bottom pane. The upper-right pane shows a preview of the page. Figure 43.11 shows a the page part-way through the building process.

FIG. 43.11

Click on the links in the upper-left pane, and fill in the information at the bottom of the page.

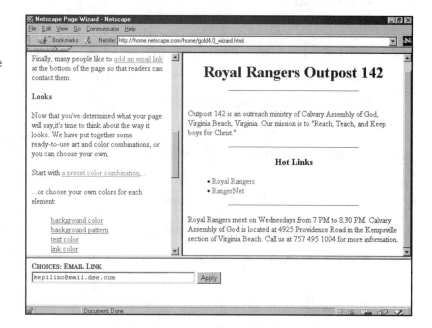

When you're done, click the Build button in the upper-left frame. Netscape's CGI script generates the page and returns it in a full browser window. Be sure so choose File, Edit Page, and then choose File, Save to have the browser save a copy of the page on your hard drive.

Editing with Composer

Whether you started your page from a template or from the Page Wizard, you can now use Composer to put the finishing touches on your page. Composer is a WYSIWYG (What You See Is What You Get) editor. Make changes using the tools on the toolbar, and Composer will write the HTML to get the desired effect.

Listing 43.2 shows the code produced by the Page Wizard. Figure 43.12 shows the corresponding page.

Listing 43.2 home.html—This page was built by the Netscape Page Wizard.

```
<HTML>

<HEAD>

   <META HTTP-EQUIV="Content-Type" CONTENT="text/html; charset=iso-8859-1">

   <META NAME="GENERATOR" CONTENT="Mozilla/4.01   (WinNT; I) [Netscape]">

   <TITLE>Royal Rangers Output 142</TITLE>

</HEAD>

<BODY TEXT="#CCCCCC" BGCOLOR="#333333" LINK="#FF6666" VLINK="#CCCC66"
ALINK="#CCCC66">


<CENTER>

<H1>

Royal Rangers Output 142</H1></CENTER>


<CENTER><IMG SRC="rule12.gif" ></CENTER>



<P>Outpost 142 is an outreach ministry of Calvary Assembly of God in Virginia

Beach, Virginia. Our mission is to "Reach, Teach, and Keep boys for Christ."


<P> 

<CENTER><IMG SRC="rule12.gif" ></CENTER>


<CENTER>

<H3>

Hot Links</H3></CENTER>


<DL>

<DD>
```

```
<IMG SRC="bullet4.gif" > <A HREF="http://www.royalrangers.org">Official

Royal Rangers page</A></DD>


<DL><IMG SRC="bullet4.gif" > <A HREF="http://www.rangernet.org/">RangerNet</A></
DL>

</DL>



<CENTER><IMG SRC="rule12.gif" ></CENTER>



<P>Royal Rangers meet on Wednesday evenings from 7 PM to 8:30 PM. Calvary

Assembly of God is located at 4925 Providence Road, in the Kempsville section

of Virginia Beach. Call us at 757 495 1004 for more information.


<P> 
<CENTER>If you have comments or suggestions, email me at <I><A
HREF="mailto:kepilino@mail.dse.com">kepilino@mail.dse.com</A></I></CENTER>


<CENTER></CENTER>


<CENTER><A HREF="http://home.netscape.com/comprod/mirror/index.html"><IMG
SRC="netnow3.gif" BORDER=1 ></A></CENTER>


<CENTER></CENTER>


<CENTER><B>This page created with Netscape Navigator Gold</B></CENTER>


</BODY>

</HTML>
```

FIG. 43.12

This page is produced from the HTML in Listing 43.2

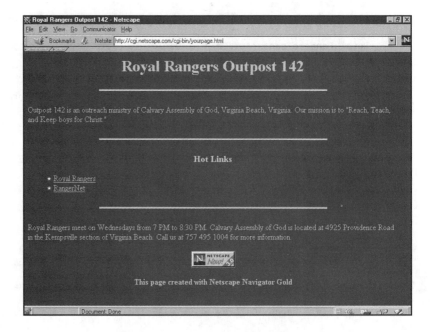

Clearly this code could stand to be cleaned up a bit—the formatting leaves something to be desired. Of more immediate concern is the lack of a `<!DOCTYPE>` tag. Let's add an HTML 4.0 `<!DOCTYPE>` tag, publish the page, and check out the quality of the HTML.

Adding a `<!DOCTYPE>` Tag   `<!DOCTYPE>` is, of course, essentially a comment. To add a comment in Composer write it as an HTML tag. Choose Insert, HTML Tag. Enter the HTML 4.0 `<!DOCTYPE>` tag in the resulting dialog box, as shown in Figure 43.13.

Publishing From Composer   The easiest way to check the quality of the HTML in a document is to place the document on the Web, where KGV, Weblint, and Doctor HTML can all reach the file. From the Composer menu, choose File, Publish. Fill in the resulting dialog. If you use a Netscape server you can publish directly to the HTTP server, otherwise you'll need to use FTP. Figure 43.14 shows the finished dialog for the first page of Chris's site.

When you choose one-button publishing via FTP, Composer logs into the specified FTP server, changes to the specified directory, and copies the specified files to that directory using binary transfer. (If you select an HTTP URL, it does the same thing via the HTTP PUT command. Note that not all HTTP servers can accept files in this way.)

Checking the HTML   Once the page is on the Web, you can easily check the HTML. Go to Gerald Oskoboiny's Kinder, Gentler Validator (KGV) at **http://ugweb.cs.ualberta.ca/~gerald/validate/** and fill in the URL of the page to check.

 While you're setting up KGV, check "Include Weblint results" and "run Weblint in 'pedantic' mode." Pedantic mode makes Weblint especially picky—just what you want in a code-checking program.

FIG. 43.13
If you don't use a
`<!DOCTYPE>` tag,
validators and other
tools assume your page
is intended to be HTML
2.0-compliant.

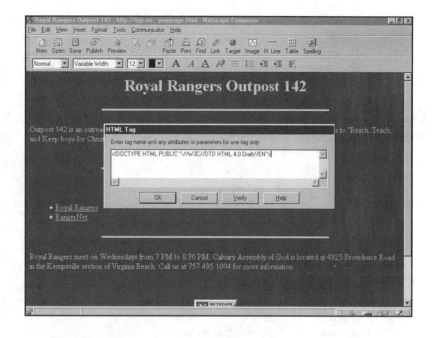

FIG. 43.14
Netscape Composer
offers one-button
publishing via HTTP's
PUT method, or by FTP.

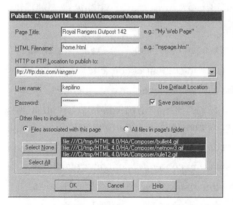

When you're ready, click "Submit this URL for validation." KGV will process the page and return the results of its analysis.

For Chris's page, built with Page Wizard, the validator reports several problems with the `<DL>` that is used to display the bullets. Close examination reveals that the Page Wizard has written code that follows the following outline:

```
<DL>
<DD></DD>
<DL></DL>
</DL>
```

Clearly the third line of this construct should be

```
<DD></DD>
```

Once we make this change, this code flies through the validator. You can stop and add the code sample Gerald provides, so that a "Valid HTML 4.0" icon appears on the page.

 T I P   Add the URL of the page to the HREF attribute in the Valid HTML 4.0 icon's anchor tag. That way, clicking on the icon will rerun the validator—a convenience to you and your visitors. For Chris's home page, the finished code reads:

```
<A HREF="http://ugweb.cs.ualberta.ca/~gerald/validate/?
url=http://www.dse.com/Chris/Rangers/home.html"><IMG SRC=
"http://ugweb.cs.ualberta.ca/~gerald/validate/valid_html4.0.gif"
ALT="HTML 4.0 Checked!"></A>
```

Note, too, that the Valid HTML icon doesn't show up well against a black background. You may want to consider using a light background in the finished version, in order to solve this problem.

Now that you know your code is valid HTML 4.0, let's see if it's any good. Scroll down the KGV Validation Results page to the "Weblint Results" section. This section lists more than 40 recommendations that will improve the quality of the code. If you disregard the "… is extended markup" comments—Weblint is stuck in HTML 2.0 thinking—you still have eight solid recommendations:

- line 7: did not see `<LINK REV=MADE HREF="mailto…">` in HEAD
- line 11: leading whitespace in content of container element H1
- lines 15, 22, 30, 33, 35, 45: IMG does not have ALT defined
- lines 15, 22, 30, 33, 35, 45, 50: setting WIDTH and HEIGHT attributes on an IMG tag can improve rendering performance on some browsers
- line 25: bad style—heading `<H3>` follows `<H1>` on line 11
- line 25: leading whitespace in content of container element H3
- line 43: `<I>` is physical font markup—use logical (such as EM)
- line 47: `<B>` is physical font markup—use logical (such as STRONG)

Adding a `<LINK REF=MADE HREF="mailto…">` line in the file's HEAD allows some users of certain browsers (notably Lynx) to easily send e-mail back to the page's author.

You should remove the whitespace in the headers; some browsers will display a garbage character in place of the whitespace.

Once Chris has made these changes, his resulting code passes both the KGV validator and Weblint (in pedantic mode). This code is shown in Listing 43.3.

Listing 43.3   home2.html—With a few modifications this code is ready for both an HTML 4.0 validator and Weblink (in pedantic mode).

```html
<!DOCTYPE HTML PUBLIC "-//W3C//DTD HTML 4.0 //EN">
<HTML>
<HEAD>
   <META HTTP-EQUIV="Content-Type" CONTENT="text/html; charset=iso-8859-1">
   <META NAME="GENERATOR" CONTENT="Mozilla/4.01   (WinNT; I) [Netscape]">
   <TITLE>Royal Rangers Output 142</TITLE>
   <LINK REV=MADE HREF="mailto:kepilino@mail.dse.com">
</HEAD>
<BODY TEXT="#CCCCCC" BGCOLOR="#333333" LINK="#FF6666" VLINK="#CCCC66" ALINK="#CC
CC66">

<CENTER>
<H1>Royal Rangers Output 142</H1></CENTER>

<CENTER><IMG SRC="rule12.gif" ALT="" HEIGHT=22 WIDTH=468></CENTER>


<P>Outpost 142 is an outreach ministry of Calvary Assembly of God in Virginia
Beach, Virginia. Our mission is to "Reach, Teach, and Keep boys for Christ."

<P> 
<CENTER><IMG SRC="rule12.gif" HEIGHT=22 WIDTH=468 ALT=""></CENTER>

<CENTER>
<H2>Hot Links</H2></CENTER>

<DL>
<DD>
<IMG SRC="bullet4.gif" ALT="-" HEIGHT=9 WIDTH=9>
<A HREF="http://www.royalrangers.org">Official
Royal Rangers page</A></DD>

<DD>
<IMG SRC="bullet4.gif" ALT="-" HEIGHT=9 WIDTH=9>
<A HREF="http://www.rangernet.org/">RangerNet</A></DD>
</DL>

<CENTER><IMG SRC="rule12.gif" HEIGHT=22 WIDTH=468 ALT=""></CENTER>


<P>Royal Rangers meet on Wednesday evenings from 7 PM to 8:30 PM. Calvary
Assembly of God is located at 4925 Providence Road, in the Kempsville section
of Virginia Beach. Call us at 757 495 1004 for more information.

<P> 
<CENTER>If you have comments or suggestions, email me at <EM><A HREF="mailto:kep
ilino@mail.dse.com">kepilino@mail.dse.com</A></EM></CENTER>
```

continues

Listing 43.3   Continued

```
<CENTER><A HREF="http://home.netscape.com/comprod/mirror/index.html"><IMG SRC="n
etnow3.gif" ALT="Download Netscape Communicator" BORDER=1 HEIGHT=31 WIDTH=88></A
></CENTER>

<CENTER><STRONG>This page created with Netscape Navigator Gold</STRONG></CENTER>


<P><A HREF="http://ugweb.cs.ualberta.ca/~gerald/validate/?url=http://www.dse.com
/Chris/Rangers/home.html"><IMG SRC="valid_html4_0.gif"
ALT="HTML 4.0 Checked!" HEIGHT=32 WIDTH=48></A>
</BODY>
</HTML>
```

Imagiware, makers of Doctor HTML (**www2.imagiware.com/RxHTML/**), offer two versions of their on-line HTML checker. The first is free; the second is a for-fee service. Figure 43.15 shows the results of running Doctor HTML on the code in Listing 43.3. While no new problems were discovered, Doctor HTML adds some interesting new information:

- If a visitor has a 14.4 Kbps connection, the entire page will load in about 2.5 seconds.

- There are two potential spelling errors. (The words Doctor HTML found, "RangerNet" and "Kempsville," are both spelled correctly.)

- All four of the hyperlinks in the document are currently valid.

FIG. 43.15

If your page passes Weblint, Doctor HTML is not likely to find too many more problems.

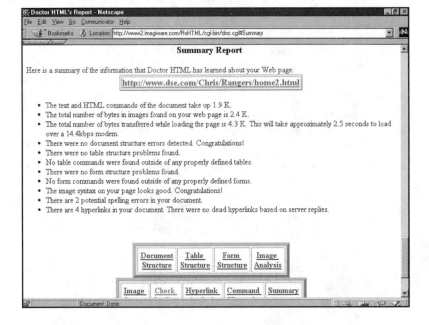

CAUTION

You should always check the Hyperlinks Analysis section. If Doctor HTML claims that a link is valid, but the size is unusually small, the remote server may have returned a "This page has moved" message. Check those links yourself.

Using an HTML Editor

If you want to be sure you're writing good HTML, there's no substitute for learning HTML and writing the code yourself.

An HTML editor can help, since tags can be dropped into place, rather than being typed by hand. HotMetal Pro (**http://www.softquad.com/**) is one of the better HTML editors. Figure 43.16 shows the personal page template from HotMetal Pro.

FIG. 43.16
HotMetal Pro's default personal page is a good starting point for Chris's Royal Ranger page.

Listing 43.4 shows the code for Figure 43.15.

Listing 43.4   hotmetal1.htm—HotMetal Pro's personal page template is close to perfect HTML 4.0.

```
<!DOCTYPE HTML PUBLIC "-//SQ//DTD HTML 2.0 + all extensions//EN" "hmpro3.dtd">
<HTML>
```

continues

Listing 43.4   Continued

```
<HEAD>
<TITLE>{Your Name Here}'s Home Page [animation] [Theme 1]</TITLE></HEAD>
<BODY BACKGROUND="grassbkg.gif" BGCOLOR="D0D0D0" TEXT="FFFFFF">
<CENTER>
<H2><!--You may substitute any image for this one.--><IMG
SRC="IMAGE/home.gif" ALT="Home on the Web" ALIGN="BOTTOM"><BR>{Your Name
Here}'s Homepage<BR><!--You may change this bar to any of the sample bars in
the bar directory.--><IMG
ALIGN="BOTTOM" SRC="IMAGE/grassani.gif"
ALT="/\/\/\/\/\/\/\/\/\/\/\/\/\/\/\/\/\/\/\/\/\/\/\/\/\/\/\/\/\/\/\/\/\/\/\/\/\/\/\/
\/\/\/\/\/\/" WIDTH="100%" HEIGHT="63"></H2></CENTER>
<CENTER>
<P><A HREF="My Resume [Theme 1]"><IMG
ALIGN="BOTTOM" SRC="IMAGE/rsme_btn.gif"
ALT="Resume"><!--CHOOSE EDIT URL FROM
THE LINKS MENU TO SET THIS LINK TO YOUR RESUME--></A><A
HREF="My Hobbies [Theme 1]"><IMG
ALIGN="BOTTOM" SRC="IMAGE/hoby_btn.gif" ALT="Hobbies"><!--CHOOSE EDIT URL FROM
THE LINKS MENU TO SET THIS LINK TO YOUR HOBBIES PAGE--></A><A
HREF="My Biography [Theme 1]"><IMG
ALIGN="BOTTOM" SRC="IMAGE/bio_btn.gif" ALT="Biography"><!--CHOOSE EDIT URL FROM
THE LINKS MENU TO SET THIS LINK TO YOUR BIOGRAPHY--></A><A
HREF="My Favorite Web Sites [Theme 1]"><IMG
ALIGN="BOTTOM" SRC="IMAGE/web_btn.gif" ALT="Web Sites"><!--CHOOSE EDIT URL FROM
THE LINKS MENU TO SET THIS LINK TO YOUR WEB SITES PAGE--></A><A
HREF="mailto:YOUR_USERID@YOUR_SERVER"><IMG
SRC="IMAGE/mail_btn.gif" ALT="Email Me" ALIGN="BOTTOM"><!--CHOOSE EDIT URL FROM
THE LINKS MENU TO SET THIS LINK TO YOUR EMAIL ADDRESS: see the HOW TO on MAILTO
for more information--></A></P></CENTER>
<P>{INTRODUCE YOUR PAGE -- For example: &quot;Welcome to my own little plot of
cyberland on the net.  I'm glad you dropped by.  Please feel free to wander
around.&quot;}</P>
<P>If you have any questions, or would just like to drop me a line, please send
email to:
<A HREF="mailto:YOUR_USERID@YOUR_SERVER">{INSERT YOUR EMAIL ADDRESS HERE}<!--
CHOOSE
EDIT URL FROM THE LINKS MENU TO SET THIS LINK TO YOUR EMAIL ADDRESS: see the HOW
TO on MAILTO for more information--></A>.</P>
<CENTER>This page was created, of course, using
<IMG SRC="IMAGE/html.gif" ALIGN="ABSMIDDLE"></CENTER></BODY></HTML>
```

Unlike most HTML editors, HotMetal Pro includes a built-in validator. Choose Special, Validate Document to run this tool. Not surprisingly, the personal page template validates with the internal validator.

Copy the template to the Web and run KGV (with Weblint in pedantic mode). You'll need to change the <!DOCTYPE>—the one supplied specifies SoftQuad's own variant of HTML. The default template shows only one error: on line 38, the ALIGN attribute is set to ABSMIDDLE. Legal values for this attribute are MIDDLE, BOTTOM, LEFT, and RIGHT.

Once you've made that one change, hotmetal1.htm passes the KGV. Weblint has 11 recommendations (not counting the usual warnings about extended markup). Eight of these recommendations have to do with setting ALT, WIDTH, and HEIGHT in IMG tags.

All in all, you can generate a personal page with acceptable HTML by using Netscape Composer; you can generate quite good HTML with HotMetal Pro and similar editors.

ON THE WEB

http://www.dse.com/Chris/Rangers/home.html   Visit the finished results of Chris's development online, at the Output 142 site.

Publishing a Corporate Web Site

by Mike Morgan

Objectives, Methods, and Resources

If you've drawn the task of designing your organization's Web site, your first question should be, "Why do we want a Web site?" Some organizations are putting up Web sites just because everyone else is doing it. The most successful organizations, however, are following a three-step process:

1. Identify the objective for the site and at least one specific goal.
2. Develop at least three different methods that can reasonably accomplish those goals.
3. Allocate the resources needed to implement the best methods, where "best" is defined as the plan that promises the largest payback for the resources expended.

This approach is called *OMR* for the three key components: Objectives, Methods, and Resources. The key to OMR's success is to deal with these three components in the order given.

OMR in Action

Here's an example of OMR: suppose you are designing a Web site for a residential real estate broker. As you talk with the broker and her agents, you find that they have plenty of buyers. In their market, the limiting factor in their company's growth is the number of homes available for sale. You determine that a reasonable objective is to locate people who want to sell their homes and persuade them to consider listing their homes with the broker.

Objectives and Goals   Before you begin to design the site, you need to make the objective more specific. Once the site is up, you'll need to determine whether the objective has been met. You'll want to continually place fresh material on the site—choose material that continues to support the objective, so that the performance of the site gets better and better.

A goal is a measurable objective. It should include a time and a level of performance. For the real estate broker's site, for example, the objective may be "locate people who want to sell their homes." One goal might be, "Within six months of being published, the site will generate four leads a month."

Most businesses define their objectives and goals in terms that translate into sales. Their objectives and goals may take one of several forms. Here are some ideas:

- Direct Sales—Some businesses have a product that can actually be sold over the Web. For example, Nikka Galleria (**http://www.dse.com/nikka/**) sells high-quality paintings and sculptures online.

- Lead Development—Many firms use the Web to develop qualified sales leads. First Jefferson Mortgage (**http://www.firstjefferson.com/**) uses its site to present a wide range of mortgage products. Visitors to the site can fill out a form to prequalify for a loan. The final steps, such as employment and earnings verification, are taken by the company's loan officers over the phone or in person.

- Technical Support—Satellite Systems Corporation (SSC) sells beacon receivers and antenna tracking systems to businesses that operate satellite Earth stations. Its customers include television stations, telecommunications operators, and manufacturers of mobile satellite stations—not home users putting a dish on their roof. A firm with a technically sophisticated product such as SSC (**http://www.satsyscorp.com/**) can use its Web site in conjunction with an FTP site to deliver technical documentation about its products.

N O T E The HTML and graphics for the Nikka Galleria site are on the CD-ROM that accompanies this book, in `chap44/nikka/`.

Nonbusiness organizations do not measure their success in sales, *per se*. For example, a political organization might define its goals in terms of funds raised or votes cast. A nonprofit organization might use its site to communicate with its volunteers and to encourage other people to volunteer their time.

Methods Once the site owner has identified an objective and one or more goals, it's time to design the site. The design depends upon the goals, the audience, and the industry. The best designs are developed by a team whose members understand all three aspects of site design.

Here's one approach to developing a site design:

1. Identify the decision you want the visitor to make. For example, if you're a business you may want the visitor to buy your product. The decision is often identical to the site objective.

2. Figure out how close you can bring the visitor to that decision on the Web site. For example, if you're a real estate broker or a mortgage broker you know you can't close the sale online. You should use a form to allow the qualified visitor to identify himself or herself—use the form to follow up and close the sale using traditional means.

3. Talk to your sales force about the questions and objections they commonly find among prospects. Be sure these issues are addressed on the site.

4. Talk to the marketing staff about the audience they want to reach. Real estate and mortgage brokers, for example, may want to reach an upscale, mobile audience in a specific geographic area.

Use each of these four steps to design a different part of the Web site and its associated business processes. While you should follow these four steps in the order given, you should use them as the basis for design in *reverse* order:

1. **Who's the audience?** Use the answer to this question to identify how you want to promote the site's address (also known as the Uniform Resource Locator, or URL).

2. **What information and motivation does the prospect need?** Use this answer to identify the site's content. You'll also need to decide how to present the content (for example, text, graphics, streaming audio or video)

3. **What online decision do I want the customer to make?** Often the answer is to have the customer fill out a form. Allow them to contact you in as many ways as possible, including online forms, e-mail, fax, and toll-free telephone.

4. **What ultimate decision do I want the customer to make?** Use this answer to design the business processes that support the Web site. For example, do you need a bank of operators staffing a toll-free number? Does the Web site allow customers to place an order online that goes directly to a fulfillment center? Can the product itself be delivered electronically (such as a subscription to an online magazine)?

Using the real estate broker as an example, here's how you might answer those four questions:

1. **Who's the audience?** Homeowners in the Hampton Roads, Virginia, area who are considering selling. They may sell because they are being transferred out of the area, because their family is growing, or because their family is grown (that is, "empty-nest" families). Many of these homeowners are considering selling their homes themselves, or are already listed For Sale By Owner and are becoming frustrated with that approach.

2. **What information and motivation does the prospect need?** How quickly can this broker sell my home? What are his or her qualifications? What is his or her track record? Is the difference between using this broker and selling the home myself really worth the cost of the broker's commission?

3. **What online decision do I want the customer to make?** The homeowner should fill out a form, giving the broker information about the property and the homeowner's circumstances. The immediate result of this decision will be follow-up by a Realtor to help the homeowner assess the market potential of his or her home. If the site is successful, the broker will get four qualified leads per month through the site.

4. **What ultimate decision do I want the customer to make?** The broker sets up business processes to convert qualified leads into signed listing agreements and, ultimately, a Sold sign on the homeowner's property. These business processes might include another section to the Web site: homes for sale.

Use the answers to these questions to develop several different designs. Often you'll get the most variation in the second question: What information and motivation does the prospect need? It's easy to add multimedia "sizzle" to the site. You're more likely to reach your goals, however, if you develop solid content first and then use the presentation (such as multimedia) to make the content more effective.

N O T E   Many companies choose a design that is loaded with content. They then place their offer and their form deep within the site and provide "ads" at strategic places on the content pages. For example, if you are a mortgage broker, consider using your site to educate the visitors about the range of mortgages available and letting them see for themselves which product might be best for their needs. Then provide forms on which they can request additional information, or even prequalify for a mortgage.

Most Web experts agree that a content-rich site can be quite effective even if the presentation is limited to text and simple graphics, while a sensational multimedia site with little content is more likely to generate awards than leads. ■

For each design, use your own experience on other sites and your company and industry's experience to estimate how effective the design will be. This information may be difficult to come by, particularly if your company or industry is new to the Web. You may want to start with a simple site that's strong in content and then add dynamic HTML and multimedia a little at a time and see how the change in the presentation affects the response. For more information about measuring the effectiveness of the site, see the comments in "Measuring the Results," later in this section.

For each design, you should also develop a budget. The budget should include:

- One-time costs, such as the cost of hardware, software, and development labor
- Ongoing costs, including connection charges and maintenance labor
- Per-response costs, including the cost of processing a customer's request for information

Resources   Suppose you've followed the recommendations given and have developed the design alternatives shown in Table 44.1. Here the "high-speed" design might represent a high-speed connection to the Internet with lots of graphics and multimedia.

ON THE WEB

http://cnn.com/   This site, shown in Figure 44.1, represents a typical "high-speed" site. No expense was spared—the site includes dynamic content, Java applets, and, of course, QuickTime video.

FIG. 44.1
CNN spared no expense in developing its Web site.

"Low-budget" represents an attractive site with text and graphics, hosted on a virtual host by an Internet service provider.

ON THE WEB

http://www.dse.com/gsh/   This Realtor's site, shown in Figure 44.2, has none of the frills of the high-speed site but has paid for itself many times over.

FIG. 44.2

This site offers information for both home buyers and sellers. It paid for itself within 30 days of going online.

"Middle-of-the-road" is a compromise design—less bandwidth than the high-speed connection, and with a tighter graphics and multimedia budget.

ON THE WEB

http://www.familychannel.com/   The Family Channel's site, shown in Figure 44.3, is far less elaborate than CNN's but still offers a nice blend of graphics and information.

Table 44.1   Costs and Benefits of Three Different Designs

Design	Leads per Month	Costs One-Time	Monthly	Per-Response
High-speed	40	$40,000	$4,000	$50
Middle-of-the-road	30	$15,000	$2,000	$50
Low-budget	10	$ 4,000	$ 500	$50

FIG. 44.3

The family graphic in the upper-right corner is continually refreshed by a Java applet.

Part

VIII

Ch

44

Selecting the Best Alternative   Your sales and accounting staff can help you turn this information into a cost-benefit analysis. For example, the sales staff may tell you that for every 10 qualified leads you give them they'll average $10,000 in net revenue. The accounting staff may tell you that the company computes the value of an investment by using its Internal Rate of Return (IRR). Between the sales staff and the accounting staff, you should be able to prepare a cash flow projection such as the one shown in Table 44.2.

Table 44.2   Projected Cash Flow for High-Speed Design Alternative

Month	Fixed Expenses	Leads	Variable Expenses	Income	Net
1	$(40,000)	0	$ -	$ -	$(40,000)
2	$ (4,000)	0	$ -	$ -	$(4,000)
3	$ (4,000)	10	$ (500)	$10,000	$ 5,500
4	$ (4,000)	15	$ (750)	$15,000	$ 10,250
5	$ (4,000)	20	$(1,000)	$20,000	$ 15,000
6 thru 24	$ (4,000)	40	$(2,000)	$40,000	$ 34,000

The Net column in Table 44.2 represents an Internal Rate of Return of 34 percent over the first 24 months of the project.

> **T I P**   Be sure to consult your accounting staff before developing your data. Each company uses different formats and standards—you'll save yourself some work if you develop the data using your company's forms.

Following the same logic, the IRR of the middle-of-the-road alternative is 52 percent, and the IRR of the low-budget alternative is 70 percent. Based on these figures alone, you would recommend the low-budget alternative.

> **N O T E**   If you're not a financial expert, use the built-in formulas in your spreadsheet to assess the relative values of your designs. For example, in Microsoft Excel you can get an Internal Rate of Return for a block of cells by using the IRR() function. Be sure you check with your accounting staff to see that you are using the correct function.
>
> Note, too, that many organizations have a *hurdle rate*—a minimum rate of return the project must offer if it is to be considered. If your company's hurdle rate is 40 percent, you could drop the high-speed alternative from consideration, since its IRR is 34 percent. ▥

The figures in this example are illustrative only. While many organizations get an excellent rate of return from relatively simple Web sites, others easily justify the extra expense of high-speed connections, high-end servers, and multimedia Web pages. Do your own calculations and select the alternative that's right for your organization.

Sell into all Levels of the Organization

Most of the expense of developing and maintaining a Web site has to do with the cost of development. Once you've spent the company's money to bring a visitor to the site, give that visitor many different ways to satisfy your goals. For example, consider allowing the visitor to make any of the following decisions:

■ I'm ready to buy; here's my order.

■ I'm interested in your product; please contact me.

■ I'd like to know more; please send me an information packet.

■ I'm not ready right now; please keep me on your mailing list.

■ I'm not ready right now; please send me e-mail when your site is updated.

■ I don't make the decisions, but I'd like technical information.

Many marketing experts call this technique "selling into all levels of the organization." You can also use this technique to convert more visitors into customers by having a wide range of price points. Suppose your product is fine art selling for $1,000 and up. Consider offering limited edition prints for a few hundred dollars, and posters for a few dollars. Once you have converted a visitor to a customer, you can learn more about the customer and offer additional products that meet that customer's needs.

Consider placing a cookie on your visitor's machine. Use it to record the date and time of his visit. When the visitor comes back, use dynamic HTML to read the cookie and show them which pages have changed since the last visit. For example, you might place an attractive "New" graphic next to pages that have been updated since the last visit.

You can learn more about cookies in Chapter 16, "Adding Javascript and VBScript to HTML."

Measuring the Results

The Greek philosopher Socrates is credited with saying, "The unexamined life is not worth living." Modern quality experts have restated this position: "You cannot improve something you do not measure." With that thought in mind, let's look at ways to add "instrumentation" to the site to determine how well you're doing at meeting your goals.

Interpreting the Log All industrial-strength servers maintain a variety of logs that show how many requests your server handled for each page. The raw numbers from these logs are often called *hits*. For your purposes as a Webmaster, hits are a meaningless number. Suppose you have two pages, one with three graphics and one with seven. The first page will generate four hits every time someone requests it—one hit for the page itself and one for each graphic. The second page will generate twice the number of hits even if its popularity is exactly the same as the first page.

When you designed your site and estimated the number of people who would fill out the site's form each month, you probably used two figures to estimate the site's effectiveness: the number of visitors per month and the number of leads generated per hundred visitors.

Here's a simple procedure for computing the effectiveness of a Web site:

1. Determine the number of requests for the site's home page—the natural starting point of most visitors.
2. Determine the number of requests for the page that comes after the site's form—often this page is a Thank You page.
3. Track the total number of requests from Step 1 and the ratio of the requests between Step 1 and Step 2.

Suppose you find that 1 visitor in 100 fills out the form and becomes a qualified lead, and your goal is 30 qualified leads per month. You find that your site's home page, http://www.xyz.com/index.html, is being requested 1,000 times per month (leading to 10 leads per month). You may decide that, considering the size of your audience, 1,000 visitors per month is low. By promoting your site more effectively (both online and by traditional means), you may be able to increase the number of visitors. If you can generate 3,000 visitors per month, you'll reach your goal of 30 leads per month.

For more information on increasing the total number of visitors to your site, see "Making Your Site Findable," later in this chapter.

The rest of this section describes how to increase the likelihood that a visitor will become a qualified lead.

Computing Page Loss Ratios   Depending upon the design of your site, you'll often have a typical path a visitor might take through the site. Consider, for example, the simple six-page site shown in Figure 44.4. This site has been designed with content about the company (on **index.html**), the products (on **products.html**), and the staff qualifications (on **staff.html**).

FIG. 44.4

Use a graphical view of the site to identify natural paths.

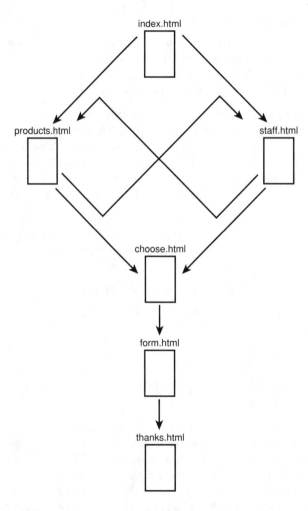

A typical visitor might start at the home page (**index.html**) and go down the product information path (**products.html**) or the people path (**staff.html**). They might also explore one path and then follow a link to the other path. Once the questions about the products and staff are answered, the visitor is encouraged to go to a page that helps them select the right product for their needs (**choose.html**). Finally, they fill out a form (**form.html**) by which they identify themselves to the sales staff. When they've successfully filled out the form, a Thank You page (**thanks.html**) appears.

NOTE You can use this model for much larger sites if the site is arranged into sections. For example, you could have 12 pages of product information and 4 pages about the staff, but still use this general model to track a visitor's progress through the site. ▪

Use the server's log to identify how many visitors came to each page. A simple examination might reveal the information in Table 44.3.

Table 44.3   A Simple Log Analysis

Page	Referrer	Count
index.html	various	1,000
products.html	index.html	300
products.html	staff.html	100
staff.html	index.html	200
staff.html	products.html	100
choose.html	products.html	70
choose.html	staff.html	30
form.html	choose.html	100
thanks.html	form.html	10

TIP If your server cannot give you the kind of figures shown in Table 44.3, use your operating system's command-line utilities. For example, in UNIX you can use `grep` and `wc -l` to quickly discover the total number of visitors to your home page in the month of April of 1998:

```
grep "Apr/1998" access.log ¦ grep "index.html" ¦ wc -l
```

You can also capture this information by using JavaScript to write it into a cookie on the user's browser and then reading the cookie as the user passes through key points on your site.

Copy this information back onto your site schematic to get a better feel for these numbers. Figure 44.5 shows these figures on our example site.

If you assume that the number of people who start their visit at an interior page (that is, not the home page) is small, then the number of visitors to this site is about 1,000. (You can examine the access and referrer logs to verify that the home page is most visitor's starting point.) Of those 1,000 people, only 10, or one in 100, made it all the way to the Thank You page that comes after the form. To improve that ratio you need to understand where these folks are dropping off.

FIG. 44.5

Annotate the site schematic with figures from the log.

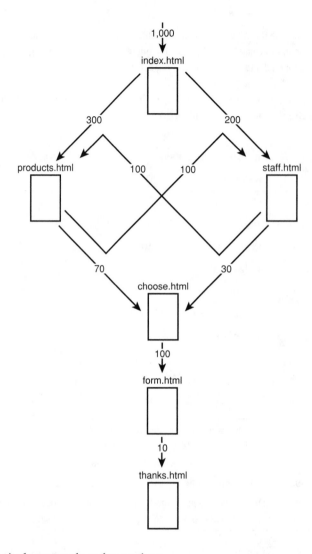

In general, a site loses people at three points:

- Home-page loss
- Internal-page loss
- Form loss

If you see large numbers of people who come to the home page and leave without further examining the site, one of two factors may be at work. First, these visitors may have gotten to your site by mistake. Perhaps they entered keywords in a search engine, and the search engine recommended your site inappropriately. For more information about search engines, see "Making Your Site Findable," later in this chapter.

Use your server's referrer log to see how people came to your site. If many of the people who left after reading the home page came from a single search engine, check that search engine to see how your home page is categorized. You may be able to change the terms that match your site in order to decrease the number of disappointed visitors.

Sometimes you'll find that visitors come to your site but are turned off by your home page and don't explore the site further. Examine your home page to see if you can find elements that are offensive or aesthetically displeasing. Consider testing your home page with focus groups or other human testers to see whether they see a problem. Examine the server's user-agent log to see if the visitors who leave your site early tend to be using a particular browser. If you're not careful to validate your site's HTML, some browsers will render your site in unpleasant colors or jumbled type. A few browsers may even crash if your HTML is particularly offensive. See Chapter 39, "Verifying and Testing HTML Documents," to learn how to write high-quality HTML.

Part VIII

Ch 44

In this example, half of the site's visitors never get beyond the home page. The Webmaster needs to take the steps recommended here to find out why the internal pages are not being visited more frequently.

If a visitor moves beyond your home page, it's likely that he came to the site he wanted to visit and the home page gave him enough information that he was willing to look inside. It's quite possible that this person represents a qualified lead—you would like to see this person fill out your form so you can follow up and help meet his needs. Look at Figure 44.5 again. Of the 500 visitors who came past the home page and went into the interior of the site, only 100 made it to the form. Four-hundred people visited products.html—300 from the home page and another 100 from staff.html. Only 70 of those, or 17.5 percent, got to choose.html and then the form. Similarly, 300 people visited staff.html, but only 30 of those, or 10 percent, eventually visited the form. Perhaps there is something on these interior pages that convinces the visitor that they do not want the product. Examine the pages carefully. Use focus groups or other human evaluators to help you determine why these pages do not motivate visitors to move further.

Finally, of the 100 visitors who actually arrived at the form, 90 percent left without filling it out. Make sure the form is visually attractive. Consider adding a free offer, or reassuring the visitor that filling out the form does not place them under any obligation to buy the product. If your form is an order form, make sure you offer a guarantee. Again, consider using human evaluators to examine your form and determine how you might improve your offer.

If you attract large numbers of qualified visitors to your site and present them with a clear, compelling description of your offer, many of them will choose to fill out your form and request follow-up.

ON THE WEB

http://www.tlc-systems.com/dir.html   Web-Scope is one of the few analyzers that reports visitors' paths through your site. Web-Scope can generate a summary report for 16 days previous to its report. It also reports an interesting statistic: "pages per visitor." See the sample report in Figure 44.6.

FIG. 44.6

Manual examination of
Web-Scope's output
shows paths, depth,
and dwell-time for
each visitor.

Computing Dwell Time   One worthwhile statistic is the amount of time a user kept the page
on the screen—a figure called *dwell time*. While you can't be sure what the user was doing, a
page that is left on the screen for a minute or more is more likely to have been read than a page
that is discarded a few seconds after it is loaded.

You can use client-side JavaScript to keep track of dwell time. Whenever you load a page, store
the current time. When the page is unloaded, compute the dwell time as the difference between the current time and the load time. Then send the URL of the current page and the
computed dwell time back to a server script.

Tracking Repeat Visitors   Often visitors will come to your site, visit for a while, and then
leave. Some of these visitors will return later, possibly to an interior page and will go on to
complete the form and become qualified leads. Store a cookie on the visitor's browser when he
or she first comes to your site. Log information such as the referrer and the date and time of
the visit. Check for that cookie on every page. If it doesn't exist, you have a first-time visitor
coming directly to an interior page, possibly as a referral from a search engine. If the cookie
does exist, store a record of this visit in the cookie and make a note of the visit on the server.

Repeat visitors have often seen something on your site that they like and are coming back for
more information. If you have a content-rich site, they may be using you as a resource. Keep
offering them fresh, high-quality content. If your content is meeting their needs, they are likely
to become customers one day.

Refining Referrers   When a Web browser contacts your server, it sends a series of lines defined by the HyperText Transfer Protocol (HTTP). One of those headers is Referer. Your Web
server can be configured to write these headers into a log (commonly called the *referrer log*). It

will also make the contents of this header available to server scripts. (For example, in CGI the variable name is REFERER.)

Use your server's referrer log or a server script to identify which page contains the link that the visitor followed to get to your site. You can use this information to:

■ find out which search engines are generating referrals.

■ find out which popular search engines are *not* generating referrals (so that you add your site to these search engines).

■ find out which directories, catalogs, and other pages contain links to your site.

■ find out which ads you may have placed are generating referrals to your site.

Making Your Site Findable

Much of the previous section, "Objectives, Methods, and Resources," describes ways to increase the rate at which visitors to your site become qualified leads and, eventually, sales. The foundation for converting visitors to leads, of course, is to have plenty of visitors. This section describes how to make your site findable by people who want to know more about your products, services, and technology.

Understanding Search Engines and Robots

Suppose an Internet user wants to learn about mortgages in southeast Virginia (a region known as Hampton Roads). The user might go to any of a dozen or more search engines and enter a search phrase such as "mortgages AND Hampton Roads Virginia." The Hampton Roads area consists of several cities—the user might also enter "mortgages AND Virginia Beach" or "mortgages AND Norfolk." If your company offers mortgages in that region, your site should be listed in response to any one of these queries.

You can explicitly submit your site to many search engines. Indeed, at least once search engine—Yahoo!—lists only sites that have been explicitly submitted. Most search engines, however, operate *robots* that explore the Web. When the robot encounters a new page, it examines the page and attempts to classify it by keywords it finds on the page. Robots are the most important way that your interior pages get indexed on the Web.

T I P   Each search engine looks at slightly different elements of the page in order to find keywords. For best results, make sure the following HTML elements accurately reflect your page's contents:

● TITLE

● Headers (H1 through H6)

● <META> tags with keywords

● The first few sentences of text in the <BODY> tag

You should examine the server's referrer log regularly. If you find that one or more of the popular search engines is not contributing many referrals, use that search engine and try to look up your site. If the page is not correctly indexed, resubmit the page to the site.

You may find that your site is correctly indexed, but appears on a list with hundreds of similar sites. Look for ways to make your site stand out from the others. Some search engines copy the first few characters from the BODY into the page's entry. Make sure the first sentence or two of each page contains an accurate summary of the page that will make sense to someone reading the page out of context.

N O T E Some search engines do not look inside FRAMESETs to index the contents of the FRAMEs. If you have important information on an interior page, consider offering it on a nonframe page as well, and make sure that page gets indexed. Place a link on the nonframe page offering the frame version of the information. ▪

Getting into Yahoo! Yahoo! (**www.yahoo.com**) is quite possibly the most popular search engine on the Web. They maintain their quality by being different from the robot-driven search engines. Yahoo! itself is a searchable catalog. Human indexers (called Yahoo! Surfers) visit each submitted site and classify it. To get your page into Yahoo!, follow these three steps:

- Look in Yahoo! to find the categories which are most descriptive of your company or products. (Make sure someone hasn't already submitted your site. If they have, you should use the Yahoo! change form at **http://add.yahoo.com/fast/change**.)

- Find the best category for your company or products. You might want to start by searching by keyword to find similar sites. Yahoo! has 14 major categories; within each one is a hierarchy of sub-categories. In general, you should choose the most specific category that applies, since you'll have fewer competing sites in the category.

- Once you've selected the best category for your site, go to that category and follow the Add URL link. Follow the instructions on the pages and forms that follow.

If your site is commercial—it sells something or describes a company that offers products or services— you should look for your category inside the Business and Economy:Companies hierarchy.

If your company offers its products or services in a specific geographic region—say, one city—submit your page in the appropriate Business and Economy:Companies category, but make sure the regional nature of your business is obvious on your home page. The Yahoo! Surfer will add a cross-reference from the Regional hierarchy.

While you're getting into Yahoo!, visit Magellan (**www.mckinley.com**). Like Yahoo! (and unlike nearly all other search engines) Magellan is oriented around categories. In general, you get into Magellan by getting listed in Excite. Follow the Add Site link from Magellan's home page to get their latest policy.

While you're exploring Yahoo! categories, take note of the Directories link that appears at the top of most category pages. This link lists category-specific or industry-specific pages of links. In many industries, it's as important to get listed in the right directory as it is to get placed in the search engines. Visit the relevant directory sites to learn how to add your company to the directory.

The Other Search Engines Except for Yahoo! and Magellan, most search engines rely on automatic classifiers to decide how to index your pages. These search engines look at the title, header tags, and <META...> tags. If you follow the guidelines given later in this chapter, in the section "Making Your Site Searchable," most robots will properly index you.

> **N O T E** Some site developers have observed that many requests are made to the search engines for pornographic sites. They then add a large number of sexually explicit keywords to their site in order to build a large number of hits.
>
> Not only is this strategy (called spamdexing) of dubious logic, but the search engines themselves will block it. If they determine that your page is full of repeated keywords, all major search engines will simply ignore your page. ■

Part

VIII

Ch

44

While there are hundreds of search engines, only a few are generally considered to be the "major" search engines. These few include:

- Alta Vista—**http://www.altavista.digital.com/**
- Excite—**http://www.excite.com/**
- HotBot—**http://www.hotbot.com/**
- Infoseek—**http://infoseek.com/**
- Lycos—**http://www.lycos.com/**
- Open Text—**http://www.opentext.com/**
- Web Crawler—**http://webcrawler.com/**

While you may choose to be listed in other search engines, you should start with these, and then move on to the less popular (but possibly more specific) search engines.

> **T I P** Once you've decided on the keywords that should represent your site, go to an integrated search tool such as SavvySearch (**http://guaraldi.cs.colostate.edu:2000/**) and submit a search based on those keywords.
>
> SavvySearch develops a search plan based on its knowledge of more than two dozen different search engines. You can navigate through all of those search engines to see who else has sites similar to yours. This information may help you decide which search engines you want to be in, and how you want to tailor your site to distinguish it from the competition.

ON THE WEB

http://www.kcpl.lib.mo.us/search/srchengines.htm—This site, developed by the Kansas City Public Library, describes seven major search engines.

It's easy to get into the search engines—the real trick is to make sure your page is so well-indexed that users who are looking for a product or service that you offer will find your site easily. When possible, you should be at the top of the list. You should certainly strive to be among the top five or ten sites listed.

Most search engines rank the sites they report by relevance, but each search engine has a slightly different idea of what aspects of a Web page make it "relevant." The more you learn about the different search engines, the easier it is to ensure that your pages score well.

ON THE WEB

http://www.searchenginewatch.com/features.htm   Learn about the search engines from the point of view of a site developer.

For some of the most specific recommendations about scoring well, visit **http://www.deadlock.com/ promote/**. This site, authored by Jim Rhodes of Deadlock Promotions, covers every detail of getting into the search engines and scoring well. Rhodes also offers an e-zine that describes his latest products and findings.

The process of getting well-placed in the search engines is not perfect. After you submit your page, wait a week or two, then check to be sure you're properly indexed. If your page doesn't appear, or if it appears but is not indexed as you would like it to be, make any changes you need to make to your site and resubmit it to the search engine.

A Public Relations Primer

Many Web experts are convinced that users find more Web sites through traditional media than they find online. It's important to get your site and its pages listed in the major search engines. You should also work with your company's public relations and advertising specialists to make sure that your site is part of the company's overall presence.

Make Your URL Memorable   If a radio announcer is to read your URL on the air or a driver is to note it on a billboard, the URL must be short and memorable. If your company's name is XYZ, Inc., clearly you should favor an URL of http://www.xyz.com/ over http://www.myServiceProvider.com/~xyz/. Of course, if your company is new or if you're just beginning to establish a Web presence, you may find that the "obvious" domain name is already taken. Look for other obvious names for your company, such as xyzonline.com or xyznet.com. If your organization's audience is primarily associated with one geographical area, consider using a geographical domain name such as xyz.va.us.

Many companies are dropping the http:// portion of the URL. Many users know enough to put it in, and modern browsers such as Netscape Communicator will default to the HTTP protocol if a user should leave it out entirely. Other companies are making the www optional. For example, CNN gives out its URL as **http://cnn.com**. You should make sure your name server is set up so that your URL works whether the user includes www or not.

Put Your URL Everywhere   Chances are, your company already has a successful program to get the company's name and products known in the marketplace. Make sure your public relations and advertising staff are aware of your Web site. Every piece of paper that leaves your offices—business cards, stationary, purchase orders, invoices—should have your URL.

TIP For years advertisers have included a "key" in their address, such as a department code, so they could tell which advertising channels were effective. Consider adding a key to your URL. For example, your TV ads could reference www.xyz.com/tv/ while your ads in a magazine for personal computer owners might reference www.xyz.com/pc/. When a user requests one of these pages, set a cookie recording the key and then redirect his or her browser to your home page. Now you can collect statistics on your visitors and sort them by advertising channel.

Get People Talking   Your public relations (PR) staff is familiar with press releases, and probably works with editors from your industry's magazines on a first-name basis. They know that these editors are deluged with press releases about new corporate Web sites. Help your PR staff find something unique about your site to promote. Do you have an online magazine or a clever demo? That information is likely to be of more interest to the trade magazine's readers than the simple fact that you're online.

ON THE WEB

http://www.compare.net/   If your product is sold to consumers and end-users, it may be appropriate for it to be compared on one of the consumer product guide sites. **Compare.net**, or its counterpart, **www.productreviewnet.com**, are good starting points.

If your site is truly unique, you may be able to get it promoted on television. CNN and the major networks often feature Web sites, particularly on their weekend or mid-day topical programs. MSNBC, the joint venture between Microsoft and NBC, is constantly looking for good material for its show, *The Site*. If you get picked up by MSNBC, you may also find your site featured on CNBC or even an NBC News broadcast. Find out from your PR staff whether getting your site featured on any of these programs is possible.

TIP Appoint someone in your organization to read the articles in UseNet newsgroups that are relevant to your company. Whenever possible they should answer questions posted to the newsgroup, or provide help. At the bottom of their response they should include a `.sig` file that mentions your company's products or services and gives the URL.

You should never spam a UseNet newsgroup, but by posting appropriate and useful information you'll get a good reputation and build name awareness. You'll also be listed in the UseNet search engine at **www.dejanews.com**, which increases the likelihood of people finding your site.

Making Your Site Searchable

If you've adopted a content-rich design, your site may actually look like many different sites. For example, the Family Channel's home page reveals six different areas of information:

- Shows—find out when each show airs and learn some of the program's background. A typical "show" page includes a list of the stars and links to the show's own home pages.
- FamFun—play games online. Fun for family members of all ages.

- Video & Sound—use RealPlayer, a streaming video plug-in, to play video clips of your favorite programs. See Figure 44.7 for an example of this part of the site.

- Learning—special information for teachers, parents, and homeschoolers.

- Home & Family—a link to **www.homeandfamily.com**, one of the Family Channel's leading programs.

- Seal Of Quality—Family Channel's collection of books, CD-ROMs, and videos that contain positive family entertainment.

FIG. 44.7

The Family Channel's site contains streaming video in RealPlayer format.

Any site with more than about 20 pages should include an index page, such as the one shown in Figure 44.8.

Larger sites cannot index every page—they should take a two-pronged approach. First, build an index of sections, such as the site index provided by Netscape and shown in Figure 44.9. Second, make the site searchable, so that a user can go directly to any relevant page, as shown in Figure 44.10.

You can make your site searchable by adding software to automatically index all pages. You can also use a catalog server (such as Netscape's Catalog Server, a component of SuiteSpot) to maintain a taxonomy of your site. The rest of this section describes these two techniques.

FIG. 44.8
Even a small site can benefit from an index of pages.

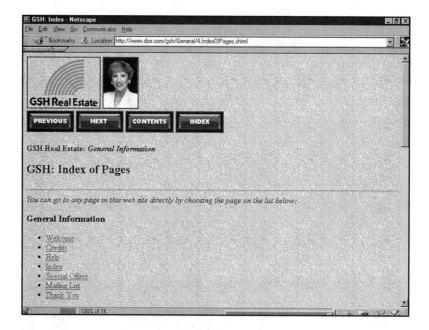

FIG. 44.9
Large sites should index their sections.

FIG. 44.10
Apple Computer's site contains 114 references to "Mac OS 8 multitasking."

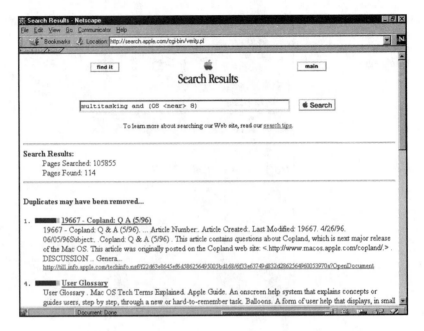

Indexing Your Site

One of the best ways to add value to your site is to make it searchable. In order for your site to be searchable, you need three components: an index, a search engine, and a presentation manager that displays the results as HTML. As shown in Table 44.4, search software can be classified by how it maintains these components.

Table 44.4—Classifications of Search Engines			
Product	**Indexing**	**Search**	**Presentation**
HTGREP	Manual	Brute-force	Filter
site-idx.pl	From <META> keywords	via ALIWEB	via ALIWEB
WAIS	Automatic	Z39.50 server	Gateway

N O T E Some HTML tools such as Microsoft FrontPage and Backstage have searching features built-in. These tools are covered in Chapter 42, "Using HTML and Site Tools." ■

HTGREP and site-idx.pl are relatively simple indexers but are quite useful for small sites. Larger sites will benefit from the Wide Area Information Server, or WAIS. WAIS servers and their HTTP gateways can be challenging to set up—many corporate Webmasters prefer to use servers such as the Netscape Enterprise server, which includes a built-in search engine.

Using HTGREP   HTGREP was developed by Oscar Nierstrasz at the University of Berne, Switzerland.

ON THE WEB

http://iamwww.unibe.ch/~scg/Src/Doc/htgrep.html   You can download HTGREP and its documentation from this Web site.

This section shows an example of HTGREP at work on the Nikka Galleria site (**http://www.dse.com/nikka/**). At any given time, several works of art are available for purchase. Visitors to the site can find something close to what they're looking for and then use HTGREP to search the site for similar works.

Working with *site-idx*   As its name suggests, site-idx.pl is an indexer, but it bases its work on keywords supplied by the Webmaster on each page. The result of running site-idx.pl is an index file that can be submitted to search engines such as ALIWEB. This section introduces a simple ALIWEB-like search engine that can read an index file and serve up pages based on the index file's contents.

ON THE WEB

http://www.ai.mit.edu/tools/site-index.html   site-idx.pl is the work of Robert S. Thau at the Massachusetts Institute of Technology. This program was written to address the indexing needs of ALIWEB (**http://www.nexor.co.uk/aliweb/doc/aliweb.html**).

Unlike most search engines, ALIWEB relies neither on human classifiers (like Yahoo! does) nor on robots. ALIWEB looks for an index file on each Web site and uses that file as the basis for its classifications.

The indexing is done by the site developer at the time the page is produced, the search is done by ALIWEB (or a local ALIWEB-like CGI script), and the results are presented by that CGI script.

The index file must be named site.idx and must contain records in the format used by IAFA-compliant FTP sites. For example, the events-list document on the server at the MIT Artificial Intelligence Laboratory produces the following entry in **http://www.ai.mit.edu/site.idx**:

```
Template-Type: DOCUMENT
Title: Events at the MIT AI Lab
URI: /events/events-list.html
Description: MIT AI Lab events, including seminars, conferences, and tours
Keywords: MIT, Artificial Intelligence, seminar, conference
```

The process of producing site.idx would be tedious if done by hand. Thau's program automates the process by scanning each file on the site, looking for keywords. The recommended way to supply these keywords is with <META> tags in the header. <META> tags have the following general syntax:

```
<META NAME="..." CONTENT="...">
```

Valid names include:

- description
- keywords
- resource-type (typically Document for files and Service for search engines)
- distribution (typically Global)

Remember that the descriptions ultimately appear in a set of search results. Each description should stand alone so that it makes sense in that context. Thau's program uses the HTML <TITLE> tag to generate the document title. Thus, a document at MIT might include the following lines in the <HEAD> section:

```
<TITLE>MIT AI lab publications index</TITLE>
<META NAME="description" CONTENT="Search the index of online and hardcopy-only
publications at the MIT Artificial Intelligence Laboratory">
<META NAME="keywords" CONTENT="Artificial Intelligence, publications">
<META NAME="resource-type" CONTENT="service">
```

By default, site-idx.pl looks for the description, keywords, and resource type in <META> tags. This behavior can be overridden so that any document with a title gets indexed, but the override undoes most of the benefits of using site-idx.pl.

Taking Advantage of WAIS   For large Web sites, the best search engines are full-index systems. The archetype of this family is the Wide Area Information Server, or WAIS. This section describes WAIS and its numerous cousins, all of which are characterized by automated indexing, powerful search tools, and a gateway between the database and the Web.

ON THE WEB

http://www.cis.ohio-state.edu/hypertext/faq/usenet/wais-faq/   Check out this Frequently Asked Questions list for an overview of WAIS. User-level information on queries is available at **http://town.hall.org/util/wais_help.html**.

WAIS is a different service than the Web. WAIS is based on ANSI Standard Z39.50, version 1 (also known as Z39.50 88). Clients exist for most platforms, but the most interesting work lies in integrating WAIS databases with the Web.

The document author(s) and you, as the installer, must agree on a document format, so that the format file can prepare a meaningful index. If the document authors routinely use <META> tag keywords in a standardized way, you can build a format file to extract the information from those lines.

Because the Web and WAIS use two different protocols (HTTP and Z39.50, respectively) there must be some program or programs between the Web user and the database to format the query and present the responses. One approach is to use a CGI front end to a WAIS server.

ON THE WEB

http://ls6-www.informatik.uni-dortmund.de/SFgate/SFgate.html   To access a freeWAIS-sf
database from the Web, use SFgate, a CGI program that uses `WAISPERL`, an adaptation of PERL linked
with the freeWAIS-sf libraries. You can find SFgate online.

The Enterprise Server's Built-In Search Engine   *Netscape took note of the fact that many
Webmasters wanted to make their sites searchable, but didn't want to deal with the complexities of WAIS. Netscape's solution was to build the Verity full-text search engine into its Enterprise Web server, beginning with version 3.0.*

Many sites benefit from full-text search, but if you wait until a user makes a request to search
your files, your server can get bogged down reading files from the hard drive. Verity, the company that supplies the full-text search engine for Netscape's Enterprise server, has designed its
search engine to work from sets of indexes called *collections*.

You build a collection over all of the files in a single directory or, optionally, a directory tree.
Figure 44.11 illustrates the two kinds of collection possible. Figure 44.11a shows a collection
based on a single directory (which may have many documents). Subdirectories are not included in this collection. Figure 44.11b shows a collection that includes all of the documents in
a directory and all of its subdirectories.

Part

VIII

Ch

44

FIG. 44.11
Collections may be
based on a single
directory or on a
directory with its
subdirectories.

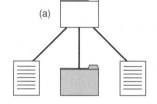
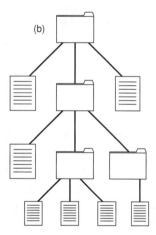

A user searches for a document in a three-step process:

1. The user enters search criteria.
2. The search engine returns results listing the matching pages.
3. The user chooses one or more documents to examine.

In general, you design an HTML page for each of these steps. (As you gain experience in setting up text search systems, you may decide to combine any two of these steps into a single
page.)

If you were writing a conventional HTML page, you could specify everything in your search, results, and documents pages with static HTML. Since the contents of these pages is based on the contents of your site, however, you need to write *pattern files* instead of static documents. In your pattern files you include pattern variables—identified by two leading dollar signs (for example, $$background).

Netscape has already defined many useful pattern variables. You can add additional pattern variables if you like.

Once you have your collections designed and built and you have selected the pattern variables you want to use, you're ready to call the search function /ns-search. You can pass pattern variables to /ns-search using GET or POST. To search the finance and manufacturing collections for the string Model 1000, you could include the following HTML on your query page:

```
<A HREF=/ns-search?NS-collection=finance&NS-collection=manufacturing&
NS-query=Model+1000>Search for finance and manufacturing
information about the Model 1000</A>
```

After you've called /ns-search, that function sets some reserved pattern variables of its own. You can use these variables in subsequent queries:

- NS-collection-list—An HTML multiple select list of all the collections in dblist.ini where NS-display-select is YES in the dblist.ini file.

- NS-collection-list-dropdown—an HTML drop-down select list version of NS-collection-list.

- NS-collections-searched—the number of collections searched for this request.

- NS-display-query—the input query to the results page. In HTML, you have to escape the < and > characters.

- NS-docs-found—the actual number of documents that the search engine found for this request.

- NS-doc-href—the HTML href tag for the document.

- NS-docs-matched—the number of documents returned from the search (up to NS-max-records) for this request.

- NS-doc-name—the document's name.

- NS-doc-number—the sequence number of the document in the results page list.

- NS-doc-path—the absolute path to the document.

- NS-doc-score—the ranked score of the document (ranges 0 to 100).

- NS-doc-score-div10—the ranked score of the document (ranges 0 to 10).

- NS-doc-score-div5—the ranked score of the document (ranges 0 to 5).

- NS-docs-searched—the number of documents searched through for this request.

Listing 44.4 shows how these variables can be used in a pattern file.

Listing 44.4   ns-query.pat—Netscape's Default Query Page

```
<HTML>
<HEAD>
<TITLE>ES3.0 TEST: $$banner</TITLE>
</HEAD>
<BODY BGCOLOR="$$background">
<TABLE WIDTH=100%>
<TR>
<TD ALIGN=LEFT><IMG $$logo></TD>
<TD ALIGN=RIGHT><H1>$$sitename</H1></TD>
</TR>
</TABLE>
<HR>
To search for an article, choose a subject, then enter a single word,
several words, or a phrase. You can get <A HREF="$$help">search tips,
</A> or perform an <A HREF="/ns-search?
NS-query-pat=/text/NS-advquery.pat">advanced search.</A><P>
<TABLE CELLPADDING=5>
<TR><TD ALIGN=RIGHT><B>Subject: </B></TD>
<FORM METHOD="POST" ACTION="/ns-search?NS-search-page=results">
<INPUT TYPE="HIDDEN" NAME="NS-search-type" VALUE="NS-boolean-query">
<INPUT TYPE="HIDDEN" NAME="NS-max-records" VALUE="$$NS-max-records">
<TD>$$NS-collection-list-dropdown</TD></TR>
<TR><TD ALIGN=RIGHT><B>Search for: </B></TD>
<TD ALIGN=LEFT><INPUT NAME="NS-query" SIZE=40 VALUE="$$NS-query">
    <INPUT TYPE="SUBMIT" VALUE="Search"></TD></TR>
</FORM>
</TABLE>
<HR>
<B><FONT SIZE=-1>$$copyright</FONT></B>
</BODY>
</HTML>
```

Figure 44.12 shows how this page looks from the browser.

Building a Catalog

Most Internet users have visited Yahoo! or one of the other catalogs of the Internet. By using the Netscape Catalog Server, you can build your own catalog—of your site, or of the Internet as a whole. This section describes the Netscape catalog server.

The Catalog server system includes a Resource Description Server, or RDS, which is responsible for exploring a designated portion of the Web and returning results to the Catalog server itself. Each RDS launches one or more robots, which summarize the Web resources (typically HTML pages) that they find based on HTML tags and <META...> tags. Figure 44.13 shows how these components work together.

FIG. 44.12

Use Netscape's default query page as a starting point for building your own queries.

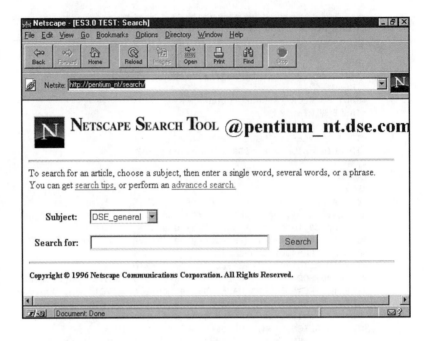

FIG. 44.13

A typical Catalog server configuration includes several RDSs, many robots, and of course, a Catalog server.

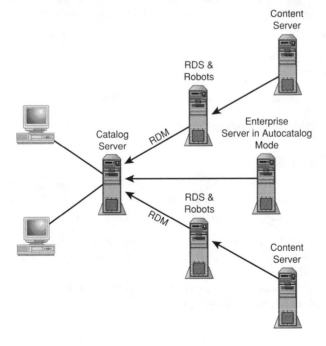

The Catalog server uses the Resource Description Format, or RDF, to store its summary objects.

Browsing   Sometimes a user doesn't know enough about a topic or the catalog to build a good query. She may want to explore the catalog first to find out what sort of information is available. You facilitate her exploration by building a *taxonomy* of the resources in the catalog. Figure 44.14 shows the top level of the sample taxonomy supplied by Netscape.

FIG. 44.14

Netscape supplies a typical corporate taxonomy.

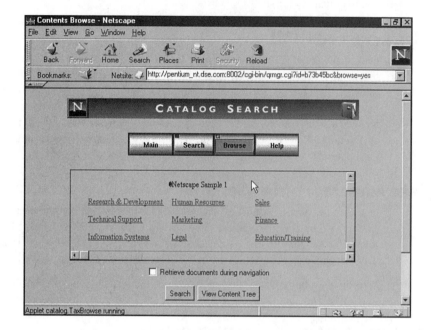

If a subcategory has further categories under it, the Catalog server makes that subcategory a link. The user can click such a link to make the subsubcategories. If the check box Retrieve Documents During Navigation is selected, the taxonomy will show documents as well as subcategories.

N O T E   Retrieving documents during navigation significantly slows down navigation. Encourage your users to use the browser to navigate to the correct category and then use Search to retrieve relevant documents. ■

If the user wants to see the entire taxonomy in one window, they can click the View Contents Tree button.

What's New and What's Popular   The user can get the equivalent of a What's New or a What's Cool button choosing New or Popular from the pop-up View menu. If you're building customized versions of these pages, consider setting the currSearchType parameter to New or Popular to provide such a link directly.

Using Dynamic HTML and Multimedia

If you've determined that the objectives and goals of your site justify the use of sophisticated packaging such as dynamic HTML and multimedia, use the techniques described in this section to enhance your site.

Use Advanced HTML

One advantage of HTML 3.2 and, now, HTML 4.0, is that the HTML standard closely matches the actual practice found in advanced browsers such as Netscape Communicator and Microsoft Internet Explorer 4.0. For example you can use Cascading Style Sheets to isolate style issues in your page, allowing you to concentrate first on content and then add stylistic embellishments. You can also use the <FRAMESET> tag to divide the browser window into frames; this practice is supported in both Netscape and Microsoft products. Learn more about Cascading Style Sheets in Chapter 17, "Applying Cascading Style Sheets."

Take Advantage of JavaScript

One of the easiest (and least expensive) ways to increase the utility of a site is to add client-side JavaScript. For example, you can use JavaScript to validate HTML forms before they are submitted. You might also use JavaScript to write dynamic HTML. You can read a cookie and display a dynamic page based on the user's previous visits to your site.

You can learn more about client-side JavaScript in Chapter 16, "Adding Javascript and VBScript to HTML," and about server-side JavaScript in Chapter 36, "Developing with LiveWire Pro."

Add Java Applets and ActiveX Objects

Many libraries of Java applets and ActiveX objects are available on the Web, and both Netscape Communicator and Microsoft Internet Explorer support these objects. HTML 4.0 provides a standard interface for including such objects in your pages. If you need a fast way to present certain content in a highly graphical way, consider using objects from one of these libraries.

Use Plug-Ins for Streaming Audio and Video

One of the most impressive ways of delivering content is to use streaming audio or even streaming video. Unlike simple graphics such as GIF and JPEG files, streaming audio and video are not native formats for Web browsers. Users need to install browser plug-ins in order to use streaming audio or video.

ON THE WEB

http://home.netscape.com/comprod/products/navigator/version_2.0/plugins/audio-video.html   You can get a current list of audio and video plug-ins for Navigator online from the Netscape site.

Much of the early work in streaming audio was done by Progressive Networks (**http:// www.real.com/**). Its product, RealAudio, supports audio at the quality of a strong AM broadcast station over a 14.4Kbps connection. Over a 28.8Kbps connection, the quality improves to that of FM stereo. ISDN and faster connections support near-CD-quality audio.

Progressive's RealVideo streaming video plug-in delivers newscast-quality video over a 28.8Kbps connection and full-motion video over ISDN or faster connections. Their latest client product, RealPlayer, can deliver both RealAudio and RealVideo in one application.

Another early entry into the streaming video market was VDONet (**http://www.vdo.net**). VDONet's VDOLive product delivers compressed video even over low-bandwidth connections. A 28.8Kbps dial-up connection can support 10 to 15 frames per second.

Learn more about multimedia in Part IV, "Serving Multimedia Content." In particular, Chapter 27 addresses streaming audio, and Chapter 28 addresses streaming video.

Netscape LiveAudio   Streaming audio is available for Netscape Navigator (a component of Netscape Communicator) through the Netscape Media Player Audio Streaming Plug-in. This plug-in handles media type "audio/x-liveaudio," which is served by the Netscape Media Server.

Apple QuickTime   For years the "gold standard" for video on both Macintosh and Windows computers has been Apple Computer's QuickTime technology. You can use Apple's QuickTime Plug-in to display QuickTime animation, music, MIDI, audio, video, and Virtual Reality inside a Web page. QuickTime's *fast-start* feature allows the content developer to send streaming content (including video).

ON THE WEB

http://quickTime.apple.com/sam/   Start on this Apple site to visit a variety of commercial sites using QuickTime technology. Visit **http://www.digigami.com/moviescreamer/demo.html** to see a side-by-side comparison of streaming and nonstreaming video.

Figure 44.15 shows QuickTime in action. MovieScreamer, featured here, is an accelerator that applies fast-start to a QuickTime movie.

FIG. 44.15

See for yourself the dramatic difference fast-start makes.

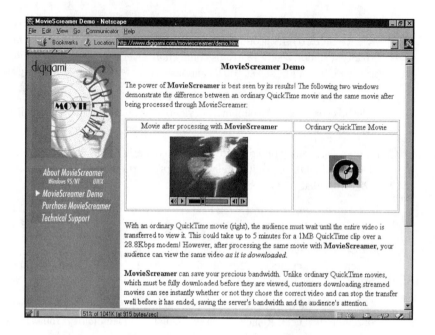

## CHAPTER 45

Building a Corporate Intranet

by Mike Morgan

In this chapter

Understanding the Intranet

An *intranet* is an internal network solution that uses the TCP/IP protocol and existing Internet technologies. These technologies range from Web servers and HTML to e-mail, network news, and multicasted live media. The essential idea of the intranet is that anything you've used on the Internet can be used inside your organization to build customized solutions.

This section describes six application areas you can address with your intranet:

- Disseminating information through internal Web sites and catalogs
- Putting your company directory online
- Collaborating through e-mail
- Collaborating through network news
- Collaborating through conferencing
- Coordinating schedules

The section "Security for Your Intranet" describes how you can turn your intranet into an extranet without leaving your network vulnerable to attack.

Setting Up an Intranet Web Server

Most intranets are started when a system administrator places a Web server on the local network. You can run a robust, secure Web server on any popular version of UNIX, or on Windows NT. The Macintosh is also popular as a host for the Web server. You can get a Web server for free (such as the popular Apache server, available at **http://www.apache.org/**) or pay to get additional features. Netscape Communications offers two Web servers: the entry-level FastTrack server, which you can set up in just a few minutes, or the powerful Enterprise server, which includes advanced features such as free-text search and user agents. If you have elected to use Microsoft's Windows NT as your server, you probably already have its Internet Information Server (IIS) software.

In its simplest form, the host of your Web server just needs a network interface card (NIC) and a connection to your local area network (LAN). If you intend to operate an extranet, you also need a connection from your LAN to the Internet. The section "Security for Your Intranet" addresses this connection. You may also want a connection to the Internet if your intranet spans more than one site. That way you can use the Internet as a low-cost way to connect the various networks in your company. Be sure to use a tunneling router, described in the section "Security for Your Intranet" to encrypt your packets as they move from one site to another.

To place your intranet Web server into operation, prepare your pages on a local computer and then copy them to the Web server's host. If you're using Netscape LiveWire (described in Chapter 36, "Developing with LiveWire Pro") or Microsoft's FrontPage (described in Chapter 42, "Using HTML and Site Tools"), the tool itself will copy your pages to the server. If you're building the pages by hand, you can run an FTP (File Transfer Protocol) server on the same machine that hosts your Web server and copy the pages from your machine to the host via FTP.

Designing the Site

A good way to start the planning process of your intranet is to make a list of your audience's needs. A great way to get ideas is to identify the company's objectives and goals and then develop one or more designs that will help the company meet its goals. Choose the design that gives you the best return on your investment.

▶ **See** "Publishing a Corporate Web Site" **p. 903**

N O T E You can use your Web server to deliver static pages of information or dynamic Web applications. Whether you're building a static site or a dynamic application, the techniques of outlining, storyboarding, and then designing individual pages are equally applicable. ▪

Many of your intranet applications will need to access corporate databases. Learn more about this technology in Chapter 37, "Databases."

Starting the Design Process You can use electronic tools to help capture your design. Microsoft PowerPoint (**www.microsoft.com**) can help you present screens of information to potential users, giving them a feel for the intranet application. Figures 45.1 and 45.2 show two screens of a PowerPoint presentation describing an intranet-based customer service application. Figure 45.1 describes the first steps of an intranet Web application for inbound telemarketing. In Figure 45.2, the developer has prepared an HTML mock-up of the first screen, and has captured a snapshot of that screen in the PowerPoint presentation. By using PowerPoint, the developer was able to add annotation to the presentation.

Part

VIII

Ch

45

FIG. 45.1
PowerPoint is an excellent tool for capturing and presenting key design decisions.

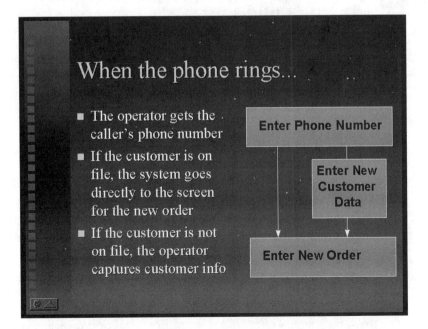

When the phone rings...

- The operator gets the caller's phone number
- If the customer is on file, the system goes directly to the screen for the new order
- If the customer is not on file, the operator captures customer info

Enter Phone Number

Enter New Customer Data

Enter New Order

FIG. 45.2

If you've built HTML mock-ups of the application's pages, embed the page in PowerPoint and use PowerPoint's text tools to provide additional information.

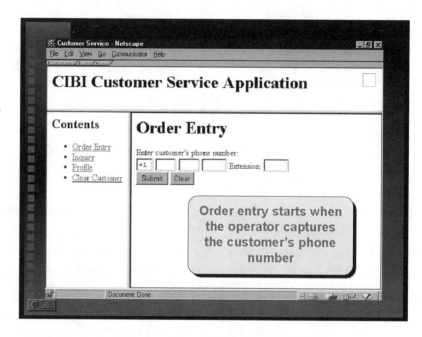

N O T E   Portions of a Web-based telemarketing application, as well as a PowerPoint presentation describing the full application, are available on the CD-ROM that accompanies this book. Look in the **chap45/telemark/** directory. ■

Charting tools such as Visio (**www.visio.com**) can help you organize and present the connections between pages. By mapping out your content, you will have an instant visual reference as to how your site will function and flow, as well as how all of the documents will be hyperlinked together. When your virtual "skeleton" is complete, you will instantly be able to tell how balanced your intranet is, and which department(s) may need to provide additional content.

You can also use site management applications such as Microsoft FrontPage or Netscape LiveWire to get an idea of how the site is designed. Figure 45.3 shows an outline of a typical site, developed in Microsoft's FrontPage.

By mapping out your content, you have an instant visual reference as to how your site will function and flow, as well as how all of the presented documents will be hyperlinked together. When your site's "skeleton" is complete, you will be able to see how balanced (or unbalanced) your intranet is. If you don't have enough material to meet your goals for one or more departments, you'll be able to see that fact instantly.

Building the Storyboard   Once you are satisfied with your site outline, the next step is to build a complete storyboard. You may have already captured screens when you were outlining your intranet's applications. Now you can "connect the dots," laying out the contents of each page. For your first efforts, a pen and paper are sufficient to capture your design. On each page, you should

■ Outline any framed contents.

■ Draw a square to represent where the graphics go.

■ Write a few sentences to describe the behavior of any client-side or server-side scripts.

■ Note any special components, such as Java applets or ActiveX controls.

■ Show links (including forward and backward links and links to related pages).

FIG. 45.3

Building a site mock-up will help you in the overall planning of your Web site.

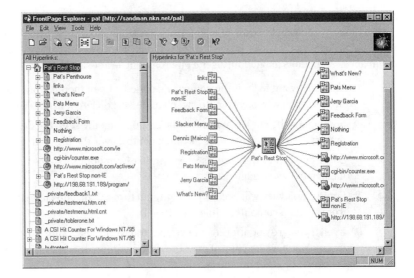

Part

VIII

Ch

45

 TIP You'll improve your site's internal consistency if you use a style guide. Choose one of the guides available online and adapt it to your specific needs. Use this guide as a checklist to make sure that each page has all the common elements you want, including links to adjacent pages, the home page, and a search or index page.

 ON THE WEB

http://www.hwg.org/resources/html/style.html This page on the HTML Writers' Guild site contains a list of HTML style guides available online.

Be sure to subject your design to human review, starting when it's just an outline. You won't be able to satisfy everyone—every element of your site must be able to meet a minimum return on the investment—but you should get as much feedback as you can.

 TIP Use a Red Team of reviewers to increase site effectiveness and save money. A *Red Team* is a group of people whose skills and interests generally match those of your target audience. They are deliberately not involved in the design process. Show them the finished design and use their feedback to hone the design into its finished form.

Understanding the User Environment

When you develop pages for a public Web site, you need to take into account the fact that your visitors will be using a wide range of browsers and connection speeds. If you design pages with frames, for example, you should also provide a nonframes version. If your pages are graphics-rich and load well over ISDN or faster connections, you should provide a text-only version for use by visitors who have a slow dial-up connection.

At first glance, you might think that you could relax all of these decisions when you start designing your intranet because the company has some control over how users connect and which browsers they use. There are several reasons, however, that you should not make too many assumptions about your user's environment—for example,

- You don't want to limit the company's options. Even though your company uses one browser today, it may want to switch and use a different browser in the future.

- Sometimes the choice of browser is left up to the division, the department, or even the employee. You may not have as much control over the browser as you think.

- Some employees may access your intranet from home, using whatever browser they happen to have installed.

- Some employees will access your intranet through dial-up connections (from home or from a laptop computer while they travel).

- Even if you are not offering an extranet today, you may want to open your intranet in the future. You have no control over the user environment chosen by your customers, suppliers, or other outsiders.

Page Design

Although your intranet may include a variety of types of servers (for example, Web, directory, and media) and your Web server may include many different applications, the core of your Web server is likely to be static HTML pages. This section gives recommendations on how to design pages for your intranet.

Choosing an HTML Level When you write for an Internet audience, you typically use the latest official level of HTML. If you're writing for an internal audience and you need to take advantage of some of the features of the newest draft release, you may choose to use those features as long as the browsers commonly used in your organization support the draft feature.

 T I P Whether you use a stable HTML level or a draft version, be sure to use the <!DOCTYPE...> tag at the beginning of the document to declare which level of HTML you're writing. When your page is ready, be sure to validate it so you know you've written syntactically correct HTML.

▶ **See** "Designing a Personal Web Site," **p. 878**

 ON THE WEB

http://www.webtechs.com/html-tk/   If your pages are not accessible from the Internet, you won't be able to use public validators such as WebTech (**http://www.webtechs.com/html-val-svc/**) or

Gerald Oskoboiny's Kinder, Gentler Validator (KGV) (**http://ugweb.cs.ualberta.ca/~gerald/validate/**). Visit this site to download a validator that you can run on your local host. Learn more about what a validator is and what it does in Chapter 39, "Verifying and Testing HTML Documents."

Opting for HTML Extensions   Advanced Web browsers such as Netscape Navigator 4.0 (a component of Netscape Communicator) and Microsoft Internet Explorer 4.0 offer various features beyond those described in the World Wide Web Consortium's HTML specifications. For example, both browsers offer the <FRAMESET> tag, which is not yet part of the HTML standard. Both browsers also support a scripting language (Netscape supports JavaScript and Microsoft supports JScript and VBScript) and external objects (Java applets, Navigator plug-ins, and ActiveX controls).

If your organization uses browsers that support extended features, you may choose to use those features in your designs. As you use them, remember the users who may call in from home, or those extranet users who access your network from outside the organization, and make sure you haven't designed a page that is unusable by those users.

Designing for Bandwidth   Many organizations run their intranet over an Ethernet-based local area network, or LAN. Users on such a LAN can count on 10Mbps raw speed, though as the load on the LAN increases, the effective throughput per user can fall appreciably. Faster technologies exist and are commonly used in larger organizations. The speed of a connection is also known as its *bandwidth*.

Some organizations have several different sites that are geographically distant from one another. They link them into a wide area network (WAN) using leased lines. Typical speeds are 56Kbps (for a leased digital line), 64 or 128Kbps (for ISDN), or even 1.5 to 5MBps (for T1 and T3 connections respectively). Higher bandwidth connections are expensive. In many parts of the U.S., a T1 connection costs over $1,000 a month. In some parts of the world that bandwidth is not available at any price. When you design your intranet pages and applications, it's nice to be able to count on high speed. Be careful, however, that a user on a busy LAN or WAN or a user on a dial-up connection doesn't find your design unusable.

Page Coding

After the storyboarding is done and your design has been reviewed, begin the actual HTML coding process. Here's a five-step process used by many Webmasters and site designers:

1. **Lay out the pages that are mostly links**. Often the home page fits this description, as will pages that introduce each major section, department, or application.

2. **Add content**. Place your text and the key graphics. Later you'll add incidental graphics such as button icons.

3. **Add links, possibly in a bullet list (<OL>…</OL>), as a placeholder for imagemaps.** Remember that some users may disable automatic loading of graphics. Consider leaving the bullet list in place in the final version. Figure 45.4 illustrates such a design.

4. **Ask for another review**. If you're using a Red Team or other review mechanism, have your site reviewed again.

5. **Add final enhancements**. Add incidental graphics. Hook up the forms. Implement scripts. Be sure to test the site, including scripts and forms, just as you would any software.

FIG. 45.4

If the user chooses not to load the graphic, he or she can still follow the links to the sections of the art gallery.

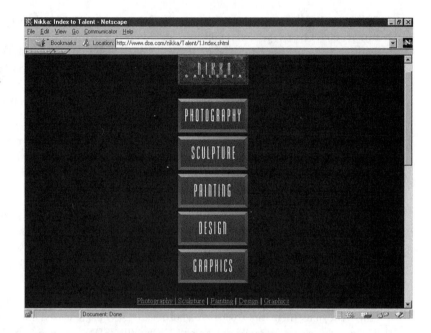

 TIP Not every file on your intranet has to be coded in HTML. You can add hyperlinks to any file type. When a Web browser encounters a file type that it cannot display or does not know how to handle, the user is prompted with a dialog box. He or she can open the file with an application (such as Microsoft Word) or save the file to the disk.

If your organization has standardized on Microsoft Office 97 products, you can have your users configure their browsers so that all PowerPoint documents are opened by Microsoft PowerPoint. Applications configured in this way are called *helper applications*.

 ON THE WEB

http://www.microsoft.com/office/viewers/default.htm If you need to make a Microsoft Office 97 document available to users who don't have Microsoft Office 97, ask them to install the viewers available at this site. Viewers are available for Word, Excel, and PowerPoint.

CAUTION

You should discourage your users from using products that have a macro language as helper applications. Some viruses are passed through macros. If the browser opens Microsoft Word whenever it sees a Word document, it may open a file with a macro virus and infect the machine.

Instead, use a viewer or a "lite" application, such as WordPad, that does not support macros. Once the user is confident that the document is not an attempt to spread a virus, he or she may choose to open it in Word.

Industrial-Strength E-Mail

If you use your intranet only to provide static Web pages and dynamic applications, you're missing much of the potential of your network. Electronic mail, or e-mail, is the most popular single application on the Internet, and you can take advantage of this technology on your intranet.

Like the Web, e-mail is a client-server technology. You'll need an SMTP (Simple Mail Transfer Protocol) server to deliver mail from one site to another. You'll also want a POP (Post Office Protocol) server or IMAP (Internet Message Access Protocol) server to store the messages until they are retrieved by the user.

An SMTP server is built into most versions of UNIX, and UNIX POP servers are freely available on the Internet. You can also buy mail servers from Microsoft and Netscape. Microsoft Exchange is part of BackOffice Server. The Netscape Messaging Server is included in Netscape's SuiteSpot.

While many users think of e-mail in terms of text, you can use the Multimedia Internet Mail Extensions (MIME) to attach all sorts of files to an e-mail message. Advanced mail clients allow you to add attachments easily and show the attachment as a clickable graphic at the end of the message (see Figure 45.5).

Part

VIII

Ch

45

FIG. 45.5

This e-mail message contains an attached Microsoft Word document.

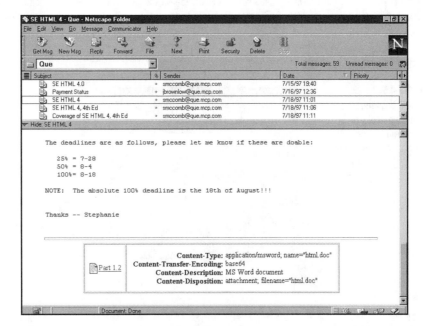

You can also include HTML in your e-mail message, allowing you to embed lists, graphics, and even Java applets in your messages (see Figure 45.6).

FIG. 45.6

This e-mail message is an HTML document.

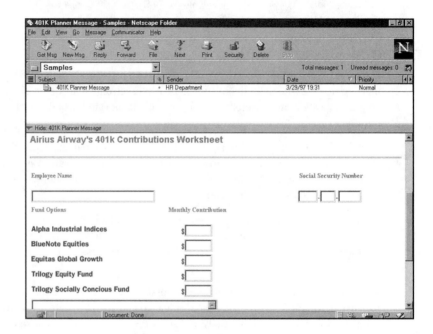

  Only advanced e-mail clients such as Netscape Messenger and Microsoft Outlook Express can display HTML-based e-mail messages. Use your address book to record whether a particular recipient can handle HTML-based messages. (See Figure 45.7 for an example of the address book in Netscape Messenger.)

FIG. 45.7

Use the address book to keep track of which recipients can handle HTML-based messages.

Your Own Newsgroups

Many Internet users are aware of Usenet, the great collection of newsgroups that are propagated from one server to another around the world. If your company has a topic of widespread interest, you can petition the Usenet community to add a newsgroup. A simpler approach is to host a newsgroup on your own server and make it available over the Internet.

On your intranet, you can set up newsgroups for every project and department. Your employees can use a newsreader to subscribe to any of these newsgroups and, with proper authority, can read and post messages. (If your company uses Netscape Communicator, you already have an excellent newsreader embedded in that product.) You can also set up *moderated newsgroups*—newsgroups in which every posting is sent to a human moderator who determines whether to allow the message to be posted.

Many of the free news servers are most appropriate for public servers and Usenet. Commercial news servers, such as the Netscape Collabra server, offer sophisticated security options as well as the capability to build "virtual newsgroups" based on text search. (Collabra is available in Netscape's SuiteSpot.)

Part
VIII

Ch
45

ON THE WEB

http://www.stairways.com/rumormill/index.html If you use a Macintosh server, you can download this shareware news server. Windows NT-based sites may prefer **ftp://ftp.agt.net/pub/coast/nt/internet/nd10a2nt.zip**. UNIX site administrators should visit **http://www.isc.org/inn.html**. InterNetNews (INN) is widely used as the UNIX news server.

Real-Time Conferencing

In most companies, the cost of overnight mail and long-distance telephone is a significant part of doing business. You can replace many overnight mail packages with e-mail (described earlier in this section). When you need a person-to-person meeting, consider using the Internet instead of the phone.

ON THE WEB

http://www.imtc.org/imtc/i/activity/i_voip.htm Learn more about Internet telephony at the Voice Over IP forum of the International Multimedia Teleconferencing Consortium, Inc. You can get a list of commercial software providers at **http://www.yahoo.com/Business_and_Economy/Companies/Computers/Software/Internet/Internet_Phone/**.

If you're using Netscape Communicator, you already have Netscape Conference. Add a microphone, and you're ready to communicate with other Conference users around the Net.

Several companies are offering video-conferencing. Shark Multimedia (**www.sharkmm.com**) has developed the SeeQuest video-conferencing kit, which includes a high-speed modem, speaker phone, and Connectix QuickCam camera. Both color and black-and-white versions of the kit are available.

Specom offers a competing system—SuiteVisions. SuiteVisions includes a 24-bit digital color camera called the VisionCAM. You can get more information on SuiteVisions from **http://www.specom.com/**.

Understanding Calendar Servers

If you're collaborating by using e-mail and newsgroups, then you don't care too much when users pick up or send their messages. If your work group is spread across many time zones, you don't have to do any calculations to figure out "If it's 3 P.M. here, are they still at work there?" You just send your message and read the reply when it arrives.

If you want to hold real-time meetings over the phone or use audio- or video-conferencing on the Internet, or in person, you need to coordinate personal calendars. Most commercial groupware products include some mechanism for sharing calendars. The Professional Edition of Netscape Communicator includes Netscape Calendar, which works with Netscape's Calendar Server (a component of Netscape SuiteSpot).

You can use Netscape Calendar to keep your own calendar. When you need to set up a meeting, you can ask the software to suggest times when all of the participants are available. "Participants" can include resources such as a conference room or special equipment. You can also put several agendas up side-by-side (as shown in Figure 45.8) and find a time that is convenient for most participants.

FIG. 45.8

Use Netscape Calendar's Group Agenda to find a time that is convenient for everyone. Look down the Combined column for free time slots.

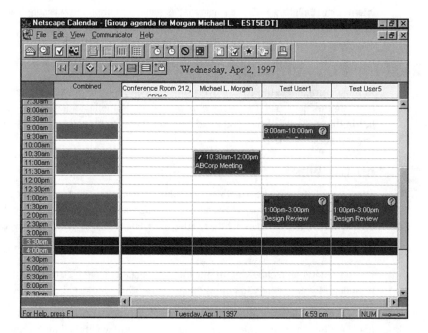

Adding a Directory Server

If you're using your intranet for collaboration, your users need to be able to find one another. In a small organization everyone may know everyone else. Everyone at least knows the names of the people with whom he or she needs to collaborate. They can use the company phone book to find the person's phone extension and, perhaps, his or her e-mail address.

As the organization grows, the task of maintaining a written phone book becomes time-consuming. You may want to explore the use of a directory server on your intranet. The international standard for online directories is OSI X.500. Most Internet experts agree that X.500 is an adequate standard for directories, but the protocols for reading and writing the directory are complex and difficult to implement on the Internet. The Internet Engineering Task Force (IETF) has released a "slimmed down" access protocol called LDAP (the Lightweight Directory Access Protocol).

Netscape has implemented a server based on X.500 and LDAP—Netscape calls the product Directory Server—and includes it in its SuiteSpot package. You can implement a gateway between the Directory Server and the Web, but if your users are using Netscape Communicator you can access a Directory Server directly, as shown in Figure 45.9.

FIG. 45.9

Use this Preferences dialog box to integrate Communicator with your Directory Server.

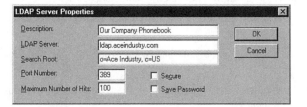

Netscape chose to use vCards, an open standard for personal data interchange, as the basis for directory entries. Once you've told your copy of Communicator which directory server(s) to use, you can look up people and resources in the directories and retrieve their vCard. If you like, you can copy the vCard to your Personal Address Book, as shown in Figure 45.10.

FIG. 45.10

Use vCards to integrate your personal address book with the Directory Server.

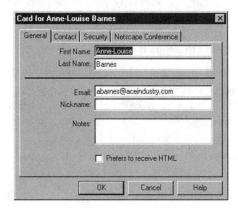

A vCard is the electronic equivalent of a business card. Once you have a person's vCard, you can easily e-mail them or connect to them by using Netscape Conference.

Security for Your Intranet

If your LAN is completely isolated from the Internet, you are primarily interested in host-level security. Your network is vulnerable to attack by your own employees. When you connect your LAN to the Internet, however, you open yourself to other kinds of attack. Only a small percentage of Internet users are likely to attack your site, compared to the number of employees who may go after your site. The sheer size of the Internet, however, means that many attackers from the Internet may be trying to break into your intranet.

For more information on Web security, see Chapter 41, "Building a Secure Web Site."

In its simplest form, an intranet is a LAN connected to the Internet. Although most Internet users are far too busy working on their own projects to have time to attack your network, there are some Internet users who will attempt to gain unauthorized access to your computers. In general, these adversaries fall into one of six categories:

- Casual users, who might inadvertently come across sensitive data.
- Curious users, who will browse sensitive data if they can get to it but will not break the law.
- Greedy users, who won't break the law but won't hesitate to sell sensitive information if they can get to it.
- Criminal users, who are willing to break the law to satisfy their curiosity but have little or no financial incentive.
- Well-financed criminals, who are willing to break the law during the attack and are well-financed enough to use sophisticated tools. This category includes the infamous *über-hacker*.
- Foreign governments, who have essentially unlimited resources.

As shown in Figure 45.11, your company's security stance represents a tradeoff between security, ease-of-use, and performance. Your security position represents a management decision based, in part, on the kind of attacker you think may come after your site and the value of the information. Here are two rules of thumb to help you decide how much you should budget for security:

- Make your security tight enough that the attacker is motivated to move on to a less secure site. One way to do this is to make the attacker pay more to break into your site than the information is worth.
- Don't pay more for security than the expected value of a loss. If you don't care if the information on your intranet is read, or even written, by an attacker, then you don't need security.

FIG. 45.11
Your company's management needs to set a security policy that balances security, performance, and usability.

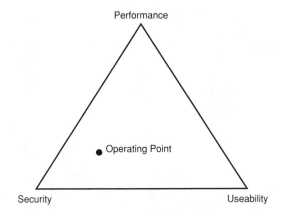

Performance

• Operating Point

Security   Useability

Many aspects of security can be controlled on a resource-by-resource basis. Thus, if you have a section of your intranet that lists company social events, you may choose not to secure that part of the site as tightly as you secure the corporate financial data.

> **CAUTION**
>
> Many sites are set up so that each server trusts the others. A successful attack on the server that hosts the company social calendar might allow an adversary to break into the server that carries accounting data.

This part of the chapter addresses two levels of intranet security. Network security pertains to the security of your data packets as they are transported across the network. Host security addresses operating-system issues—if an adversary can gain access to a command prompt on your UNIX or Windows NT host, he or she may be able to read or change information managed by the server. Finally, this section addresses server security—mechanisms by which you can reduce the likelihood of a user visiting your Web or news site and accessing sensitive information.

Network Security

Figure 45.12 illustrates a typical LAN with access to the Internet. An outside user may come from a LAN on other company site, accessing your LAN as part of the company's intranet. The user may also be an extranet user, authorized to read and write a portion of your network's data. He or she might also be an Internet user, coming onto your intranet to access a name server, mail server, or even a Web server.

Regardless of why the outsider has come to your LAN, you should take several steps to ensure that only authorized users get onto the network and that they get access only to specific data.

FIG. 45.12

Outside users may come
from the intranet,
extranet, or Internet.

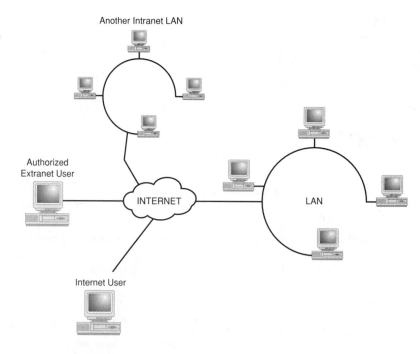

You may choose to protect your network at any of several points. Most network administrators will choose to use a combination of security techniques. Figure 45.13 shows several common security tools:

- **Firewall routers.** These hardware devices allow access only to selected outsiders, and then only to specified resources.

- **Proxy servers.** This software program checks the credentials of a user. If the user is authorized to access the requested data, the proxy server retrieves the data and sends it on to the user.

- **X.509v3 certificates.** Both servers and end-users can present X.509v3 certificates to prove their identity. The certificates serve as the basis for public-key encryption techniques.

- **Secure Sockets Layer (SSL).** Many servers offer a secure version of their protocol. For example, Netscape Web servers offer "HTTPS," a secure version of HTTP. When running a secure protocol, data is sent through the Secure Sockets Layer, a security protocol originally developed by Netscape Communications.

- **Tunnelling Routers.** If your intranet spans more than one site, you should ensure that all data is encrypted before it is sent over the Internet. Connect your sites with tunnelling routers to provide this level of encryption.

FIG. 45.13
Use network-level tools to decrease the likelihood of someone reading or changing data on the network.

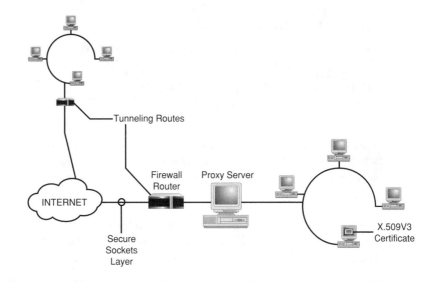

 Whoever designs your company's access control system is setting your company's access control policy. Don't leave this important responsibility to the technical staff. Management should take an active role in determining policy and then have the technical staff implement the policy. Finally, have auditors check the implementation to be sure that it matches the specified policy.

Firewall Routers   Routers are the traffic directors of the Internet. If you place a machine on the Internet and give it an IP address of 207.2.80.1, you must also provide a router that tells the rest of the network where packets for that address should be directed. When you connect a LAN to the Internet, you must place a router between the two so that packets can pass between the Internet and the LAN.

This router gives you a good place to start implementing your access control policy. Routers that deny access to unauthorized packets are called *firewall routers*. Today, most routers can be configured to offer some firewall services.

Listing 45.1 shows an example of a typical firewall router configuration. By design, most firewall routers severely restrict the packets that pass from the Internet to the intranet. In this example, packets associated with e-mail (the Simple Mail Transfer Protocol, or SMTP) and the Domain Name Service (DNS) are allowed through, as are FTP packets that go to non-privileged ports.

Listing 45.1   router.cfg—Firewall Router Blocks Most Packets from Unknown Sources

```
no ip source-route
access-list 101 deny ip 207.2.80.0.0.0.0.255
access-list 101 permit tcp any established
```

continues

Listing 45.1 Continued

```
access-list 101 permit tcp any host 207.2.80.10 eq smtp
access-list 101 permit tcp any host 207.2.80.20 eq dns
access-list 101 permit tcp any 20 any gt 1024
access-list 101 deny tcp any any range 6000 6003
access-list 2 permit 207.2.80.0 255.255.255.0
```

N O T E Listing 45.1 is intended only to give you an idea of what sort of checks can be made by a firewall router. Check the documentation that came with your router and consult a computer security expert to determine the best way to implement your company's access control policy. ▪

The first line in Listing 45.1 tells the router not to allow an outsider to force packets upon you. Source-routing allows the originating router to specify how the packet will be routed—useful as a diagnostic tool, but a deadly vulnerability on an intranet.

The second line tells the router than anyone coming from the outside world who claims to be on the local LAN (address 207.2.80.x) is a fraud. Because local users often have privileges that are inappropriate for outsiders, this line is an important safeguard. The next line,

```
access-list 101 permit tcp any established
```

tells the router not to disrupt any established TCP connection. With this rule in place, you can change the router's configuration without disturbing connections that are already in place. Since most HTTP connections are short-lived, this line does not open a significant security hole.

The next three lines deliberately open a hole in the firewall. The first of these lines allows any outsider to send packets to machine 207.2.80.10, the mail server, as long as the packet uses the Simple Mail Transfer Protocol (SMTP). This line allows outsiders to send mail to people in our organization. The next line is similar. It allows outsiders to use our nameserver to convert domain names (for example, www.xyz.com) to IP addresses (for example, 207.2.80.1). The next line in this section,

```
access-list 101 permit tcp any 20 any gt 1024
```

tells the router to permit anyone using FTP (which comes from port 20) to access the higher port numbers (greater than 1024) on our machine. This line allows your staff to transfer files via FTP, as long as they run a nonprivileged process on a nonprivileged port.

The next line explicitly denies outside access to certain high-number ports that are associated with X Window and the Network File System (NFS)—two services that no outsider has any business accessing.

The last line makes an entry to access list 2, which controls who is allowed to make changes in the router's configuration. This line says that anyone on your local network (207.2.80.x) or the local host (255.255.255.0) is authorized to make changes (assuming they can satisfy other security restrictions).

Because a firewall router is installed at the interface between the LAN and the Internet, it can only protect against attacks from the Internet. Specifically, it offers no protection against the following threats:

- Employees or others who can access the machines directly can carry files away on floppy disks.

- If an insider installs a modem on his or her computer and connects it to a phone line, anyone who dials that number has access to that computer and, perhaps, the rest of the network.

- Most computer viruses will pass through most firewalls and can wreak havoc on the computers on the network.

Firewall routers are an important first step in securing your network against attack. For best protection, however, they should be used in conjunction with other security technologies, such as proxy servers and channel security.

Proxy Servers   Most organizations will want to operate a proxy server in connection with their firewall router. The router implements general policies at a level that is low in the protocol stack, close to the hardware. A proxy server offers pin-point access control at a level much higher in the protocol stack. Figure 45.14 shows a typical firewall installation that includes a proxy server. This configuration is known as a *screened host firewall*.

Part

VIII

Ch

45

FIG. 45.14

In a screened host configuration, most packets are required to go to the bastion host.

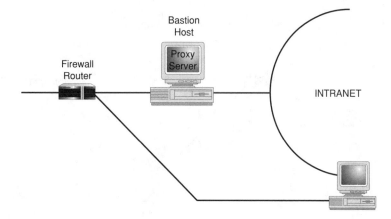

In a screened host firewall, the firewall router allows only a handful of packets to pass directly to the LAN. (Such packets might include packets destined for the mail server or nameserver, as shown in Listing 45.1 earlier.) All other packets are sent to a proxy server on the bastion host. For example, suppose the company wants to operate a Web server for use by the general public. The Web server itself is running on the LAN, on machine 207.2.80.1. Anyone attempting to access 207.2.80.1 from outside the LAN is denied access. The company offers a proxy server on the bastion host, 207.2.80.90. If an outside user queries the company's nameserver and asks for the IP address of the machine named www, the nameserver directs that user to 207.2.80.90—the proxy server. When the outside user sends a query to port 80 (the default HTTP port) of

207.2.80.90 (the proxy server), the firewall router permits it to pass. The proxy server checks its security tables to see if it is authorized to send back the requested page. If it is, then it checks its cache to see if it has a current copy. If it doesn't have a cached copy, the proxy server contacts the real Web server, fetches the page, and returns it to the requesting user.

If an adversary attacks the proxy server and is able to defeat its security, he or she has access to pages in the cache and other files on the bastion host. The adversary could use the bastion host as a launching point to attack other hosts on the LAN, but if the hosts themselves are secure, the attacker is confronted with extra work. All but the most determined adversaries will become discouraged and will move on to easier prey.

T I P

For even more security, consider using a screened subnet, in which several servers—Web, mail, and DNS—are set up on bastion hosts that are isolated from the LAN by yet another router. The region between the two routers is called the Demilitarized Zone, or DMZ. Because all the services an outsider might legitimately want are in the DMZ, the firewall router doesn't have to leave any security holes open to the LAN itself. Figure 45.15 shows a screened subnet firewall.

FIG. 45.15
With a screened subnet, the firewall router blocks all outside attempts to access the LAN itself.

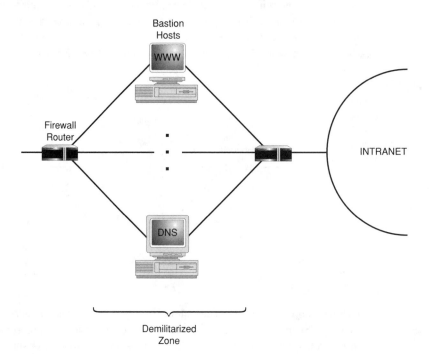

ON THE WEB

http://home.netscape.com/comprod/server_central/product/proxy/index.html/   You can learn more about Netscape's Proxy Server (a member of the SuiteSpot family) online. You might also want to learn about SOCKS, a popular free proxy server, at ftp://ftp.nec.com/pub/security/socks.cstc, and the Microsoft Proxy Server (http://www.microsoft.com/proxy/default.asp).

N O T E The Netscape Proxy Server comes bundled with virus-scanning software. While the odds of your machines contracting a virus from the Internet are relatively low, there's no reason to take a chance. If your proxy server includes a virus scanner, enable it and subscribe to the updates so you're protected from the latest viruses. ▨

Sniffers and X.509v3 Certificates   IP packets passing over an Ethernet contain a hardware address. In general, each network interface card (NIC) can "hear" all of the packets, but only "listens to" the packets whose address match the card's address. Special hardware called a network analyzer or, colloquially, a "sniffer," can be hooked to a network that will listen to every packet. Furthermore, many NICs can be placed in a special mode, called *promiscuous mode*, in which they listen to every packet.

A network technician can use a *sniffer* or, equivalently, a PC with its NIC in promiscuous mode, to troubleshoot an Ethernet segment. An attacker can use the same technology to read the contents of every packet, hunting for sensitive information that has been sent in the clear (unencrypted).

If you're sending and receiving packets over the Internet, you should consider all packets vulnerable. If your intranet asks for or sends sensitive information, you should use an encrypted channel for that information. The easiest way to get an encrypted channel is to use Netscape's Secure Sockets Layer, or SSL, in concert with an existing protocol.

In order to implement SSL, at least one party on the connection needs to have a public encryption key that has been certified by a Certification Authority. You can get these certificates (known as X.509v3 certificates) from your organization's own Certificate Server, or from a public Certification Authority such as Verisign (**www.verisign.com**).

If your intranet consists of several sites joined by the Internet, you should consier protecting your intranet by encrypting all packets that go from one site to another. You can accomplish this level of encryption by using special routers (called *tunnelling routers*) that apply an encryption algorithm to all packets that they send out and a decryption algorithm to all incoming packets. The next two sections describe SSL and tunnelling routers.

SSL   While the Secure Sockets Layer (SSL) was developed by Netscape, the details have been made available by Netscape and the technology has been widely implemented. For example, there is a secure version of Apache, the free Web server for UNIX.

Most of Netscape's products support an SSL option. You can turn on SSL in Netscape's Web servers (both FastTrack and Enterprise), Directory Server, and Collabra (news) Server. You can also enable SSL on either side of the proxy server. You can also use X.509v3 certificates to encrypt e-mail, by using the S/MIME protocol.

If an end user has an X.509v3 certificate, you can use certificates as the basis for access control. You might tell your Web server that only members of the Accounting department have access to the financial data and then provide a list of the members of the Accounting department. How can the server verify that a user really is who they say they are? By asking the user's client software to present an X.509v3 certificate.

If the user doesn't have a certificate, you'll have to use usernames and passwords as the basis for access control. This mechanism is inferior to X.509v3 certificates for two reasons: First, if the password is ever sent over a nonsecure channel, it can be compromised by an adversary with a sniffer, and second, the user has to remember many different passwords. The user may be tempted to write the password down or use the same password on more than one system. Either way, the likelihood of the password being discovered increases.

Tunnelling Routers If your intranet spans more than one LAN, you should connect them with tunnelling routers. Tunnelling technology, built into many firewall routers, encrypts packets leaving one router destined for another router on your intranet. This solution allows you to build a virtual intranet, connecting your LANs over the Internet instead of using dedicated lines.

ON THE WEB

http://gregorio.stanford.edu/papers/firewall/firewall.html This paper, "Designing an Academic Firewall: Policy, Practice, and Experience with SURF," describes Stanford University's experience with building a virtual intranet. It contains a relevant section (**http://gregorio.stanford.edu/papers/ firewall/node12.html#SECTION00051000000000000000**) on secure IP tunnelling.

Server Security

Most servers allow you to specify access control by IP address, host name, or user ID. You can also restrict the type of access (for example, read, write, delete). For example, the Access Control entry shown in Figure 45.16 restricts the access to the resources in the sensitive directory.

FIG. 45.16

Use the Enterprise Server's Access Control page to specify the resource to restrict.

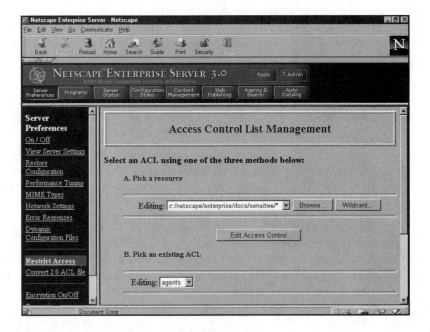

Figure 45.17 shows the Access Control List (ACL) being set up. This ACL reads

■ First, deny all access to anyone, from anywhere, but continue checking rules.

■ Second, allow all access to people in the `admin` group if they come from a host in the 207.2.80.*x* network. (Continue checking rules.)

■ Finally, allow read access only to anyone if they come from a host in the 207.2.80.*x* network. (There are no more rules to check.)

FIG. 45.17
Use the Enterprise
Server's Access Control
Lists to specify pinpoint
access control for each
resource.

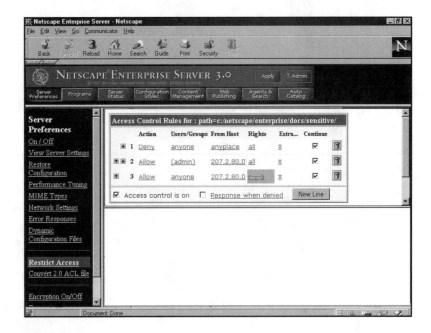

You can apply access control to nearly all servers, including Web servers, proxy servers, news servers, calendar servers, and directory servers.

Host Security

The best server security in the world is worthless if an adversary can gain access to the host's command prompt. Depending upon the operating system, you may be vulnerable to attack through a mail server, an FTP server, or other network software. You may also be attacked from a trusted host, or by an insider who has access to Telnet or to the machine itself.

Much of the advice on host security is operating system specific. Be sure to read any security notices issued by your operating system vendor and make recommended changes that apply to your configuration.

ON THE WEB

http://www.cert.org/   Keep up with the latest security notices online, both here and at **http://ciac.llnl.gov/**.

N O T E Learn more about protecting a UNIX machine in Chapter 40, "Site Security," of *Webmaster Expert Solutions* (Que, 1996). Many of the principles in this chapter are also applicable to other operating systems, such as Windows NT. ■

## CHAPTER 46

Publishing an Online Magazine

by Clayton Walnum

In this chapter

What Is an Online Magazine?

Webster's *New World Dictionary* defines "*magazine*" as "a publication, usually with a paper back and sometimes illustrated, that appears at regular intervals and contains stories, articles, and so on by various writers and, usually, advertisements." The definition of an online magazine is almost the same; just drop the paper back and add animations, sound effects, videos, dynamic (changing) page layouts, and interactive elements that are impossible to include in a print magazine.

So, how is a regular Web site different from an online magazine? After all, most large Web sites are collections of written works and illustrations, these works having been written and created by several authors and artists. Many modern sites even include advertisements. Does that make these sites online magazines? Not necessarily. There are actually three additional attributes that differentiate a successful online magazine from a conventional Web site:

- An online magazine's entire content is updated at scheduled intervals.
- An online magazine exists only for its own sake.
- An online magazine usually has strictly thematic content.

In the following sections, you explore these three attributes and see exactly how they apply to an online magazine.

Updating at Scheduled Intervals

When Tuesday comes around, I expect to find the next issue of *Time* magazine in my mailbox. I expect it each and every Tuesday, and when it doesn't arrive on time, I wonder why. Likewise, Web users expect a well run online magazine to publish new issues on a regular basis.

Moreover, Web users expect to find new material when the next issue is published. This is one of the things that separates a sophisticated non-magazine Web site like Microsoft's from a well run online magazine. Sure, Microsoft updates its Web pages regularly. In fact, many of Microsoft's pages are updated daily. However, Microsoft doesn't replace the bulk of its content on a regular schedule. Instead, Microsoft updates only those pages that have become out of date, leaving the rest as they were previously published.

Existing for Its Own Sake

An online magazine publisher usually has only one main goal: to get people to access and read the magazine. That is, the magazine *is* the product. The magazine usually doesn't act as a front for some other business (unless that other business is the selling of advertising, which is definitely part of the magazine business).

Yes, it's true that some companies publish "magazines" on a regular basis, such magazines being filled with articles that hawk the company's wares and offer glowing reviews of products that just happen to be for sale by the publisher. I submit that these aren't really magazines at all, but rather a snappy form of catalog.

Creating Strictly Thematic Content

Virtually all magazines are designed to attract a specific audience interested in a specific topic. *Time* magazine online (**http://www.pathfinder.com/time/index.html**) attracts people who want to read in-depth articles about current events; *People* Online (**http://www.pathfinder. com/people/index.html**) attracts people who want to read about celebrities' lives; *PC Magazine* Online (**http://www.pcmag.com**) attracts people who want to read about IBM-compatible computers.

The problem with thematic content is that it's not always so easily defined. While it's obvious that *PC Magazine Online* is aimed at computer buffs, who reads *RollingStone.com (***http:// www.rollingstone.com***)*? Is it people who want to read music reviews? Folks who want to know the best movie to see this weekend? Do people read *Rolling Stone* for its political commentary or for the interviews with famous musicians? *Rolling Stone*'s theme isn't dictated so much by the type of articles it publishes, but rather by the attitude with which it approaches those articles. Whether *Rolling Stone* is publishing an article on Bill Clinton's legal troubles or on Aerosmith's latest concert tour, they approach the topic in a manner that'll attract a hip audience.

Breaking the Rules

Of course, none of the previously discussed magazine attributes are carved in stone. Magazines, especially the online variety, bend the rules often and with impunity. Because a specific magazine happens to be behind schedule with new issues doesn't mean the publication is no longer a magazine. Similarly, if a magazine's articles don't always seem to fit in with a theme, that doesn't mean the magazine should be shut down for misrepresentation. But one thing's for sure: If all of the previously discussed attributes are missing from a Web site, the site in question is decidedly not an online magazine. And, it's safe to say that the more an online magazine sticks to the rules, the more readers it will attract.

Part
VIII

Ch
46

Online Magazine Design

This chapter is about the nuts and bolts of publishing an online magazine. That is, you learn some handy tricks to help you assemble all the stuff you get from your artists and writers into a well organized publication. As you assemble your online magazine, you need to draw upon all the Web skills you've developed. You need to take advantage of the latest technology. Only the most dazzling and captivating online magazines capture the interest of the Web community.

This brings you to the biggest difference between online magazine and conventional print magazines. As mentioned previously, online magazines can contain animations, sound effects, videos, dynamic page layouts, and interactive elements that are impossible to include in a print magazine. In the sections that follow, you see how to incorporate these types of elements into a simple online magazine.

The Magazine in Question

In this section, you explore the small online magazine that's included on this book's CD-ROM. The sample magazine is based on my Web site, which just happens to use a magazine as a design metaphor. That is, although my Web site looks like a magazine, it isn't updated on a regular schedule. In fact, there are many pages that haven't changed at all since the site was first published. Moreover, my Web site exists to sell and support my books, which doesn't fit in well with the goal of an online magazine. However, because much of the work of designing an online magazine has already been done with my Web site, I decided to select some of the site's pages and refine them for this chapter's sample magazine.

> **CAUTION**
>
> To get the most out of the sample online magazine, you must have Microsoft Internet Explorer 4.0 installed on your computer. This is because the magazine takes advantage of new HTML technology that's currently supported only by Internet Explorer 4.0.

N O T E The bulk of my Web site was designed by my good friend, Maurice Molyneaux, who is an artist, a writer, and a game designer. Maurice currently works for the computer game company, Psygnosis. ▪

Installing the Online Magazine

To get the most out of the Clayton Walnum online magazine, you need to copy its files to your hard drive. You can find the magazine files in the Magazine folder of this book's CD-ROM. Just copy the folder to your hard drive's root directory. Of course, if this were a real online magazine, it would need to be placed on the Internet. Luckily, it's not necessary to have a running Web site to demonstrate how to create a simple online magazine.

N O T E You must be sure to copy the Online Magazine folder to your hard drive's root directory because, as you discover later, a couple of the URLs used to implement channels refer to the c:\Online Magazine directory. The other URLs are all relative to the HTML pages and should work fine no matter where the magazine is installed. ▪

Browsing the Magazine

After you have the Clayton Walnum magazine installed on your hard drive, find the Default.htm file and give it a double-click. The magazine's cover page appears in your Web browser, as shown in Figure 46.1.

N O T E For best results when viewing the sample online magazine, you should set your desktop to the 800×600 resolution using at least 256 colors. If you want to see the photographs in all their glory, set your system to True Color. ▪

FIG. 46.1

Just like most print magazines, the Clayton Walnum online magazine features a snazzy cover.

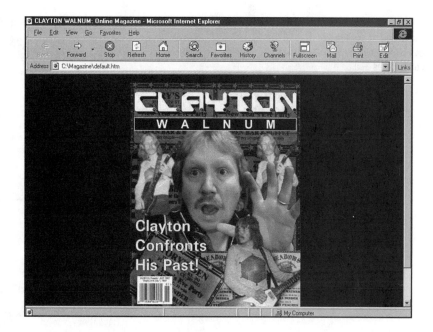

Thanks to audio streaming, when the cover appears you hear a very short theme song, at which point you can click the cover to open the magazine. If you like, you can admire the cover and wait for the page's timer to open the magazine for you. (It takes about 20 seconds.)

The first magazine page is a complete table of contents (see Figure 46.2). This page, like all the other magazine pages, is set up using HTML frames. A navigation bar on the left gives you access to any page in the magazine, whereas the Table of Contents page is a more complete, magazine-like table of contents.

You can find a lot of cool stuff on the Table of Contents page. For example, thanks to Dynamic HTML (DHTML), the magazine's issue date flickers between red and black. DHTML also makes clickable links change as the mouse passes over them. Text links change color (from blue to red), whereas image links shrink when in contact with the mouse, as you can see by looking at the Next button at the top of the page in Figure 46.2. Other cool stuff includes the button for subscribing to the site using Microsoft's CDF technology and the way you can make the photo disappear from the navigation bar by clicking the text under the picture—another example of DHTML.

Each of the links in the navigation bar or on the full table of contents lead to the magazine's various articles, each of which is featured in its own Web page. For example, clicking Current Releases brings you to the HTML page that describes some of my latest books. You can see this page in Figure 46.3, which follows the general layout used throughout the magazine. This layout includes navigation buttons at the top and bottom of the page, as well as the use of nested (but invisible) tables to control the layout of page elements.

FIG. 46.2

The magazine features a complete table of contents, as well as a navigation bar that always shows an abbreviated table of contents.

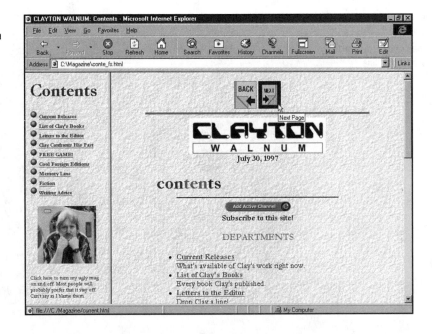

FIG. 46.3

This is the Current Releases page, which illustrates the basic design theme used throughout the magazine.

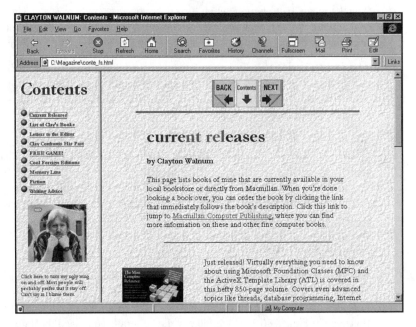

The navigation buttons at the top and bottom of each page enable the reader to browse through the magazine page-by-page. If you click the Back button, you don't go back to the page you previously viewed, but rather to the previous page in the magazine. In other words, the buttons enable you to turn the pages of the magazine. They don't work like the Back and

Forward buttons in the Internet Explorer's toolbar. If you want to jump immediately to the full Table of Contents page, just click the Contents button.

If you want to see something really cool, click the FREE GAME! link in the navigation bar, which instantly gets you to the Download a Free Game page. If you look near the bottom of the page, you see two links, Installing Poker Squares and Playing Poker Squares (see Figure 46.4). Click either of these links and text magically appears in the page. For example, Figure 46.5 shows the result when you click the Installing Poker Squares link. A paragraph of text appears after the link, with the page automatically adjusting itself to accommodate the addition. This is more DHTML magic, along with some JavaScript.

FIG. 46.4

The Installing Poker Squares and Playing Poker Squares links hide a DHTML surprise.

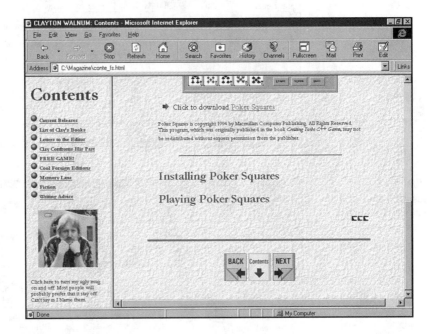

If you click the Installing Poker Squares link again, the text disappears, leaving the page as it was when it first displayed. If you click the Playing Poker Squares link, not only does a lot of new text appear, but images and a table also appear, as shown in Figure 46.6. These links show how DHTML can add dynamic layouts to your Web pages, layouts that include various types of elements.

Another item of interest is the Clay in the Morning page, which can be accessed only from the bottom of the main table of contents, as shown in Figure 46.7. Click the See Clay First Thing in the Morning link to get to the page. I won't spoil the surprise (go ahead and click, but be ready for a nasty sight), except to say that the Clay in the Morning page is an example of video streaming.

Part
VIII

Ch

46

FIG. 46.5
Click the link and text appears from nowhere.

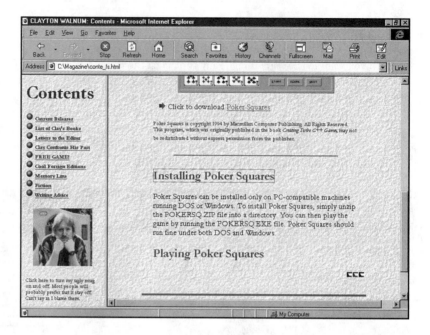

FIG. 46.6
Another click reveals new text, images, and even a table.

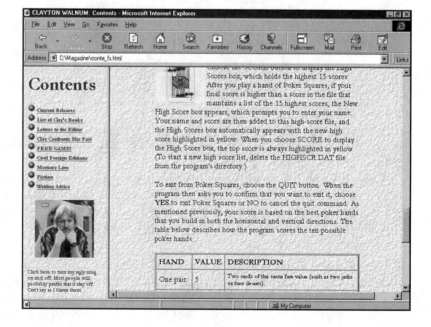

Finally, the Clayton Walnum online magazine supports simple channels, which are used with Microsoft Internet Explorer 4.0. You can subscribe to the magazine by clicking the Add Active Channel button at the top of the Table of Contents page. When you do, you see the dialog box shown in Figure 46.8. Just click the OK button to complete the subscription.

FIG. 46.7
The See Clay First Thing in the Morning link is available only in the main table of contents.

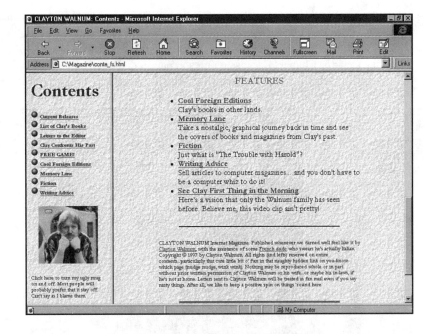

FIG. 46.8
When you subscribe to the magazine, you see this dialog box.

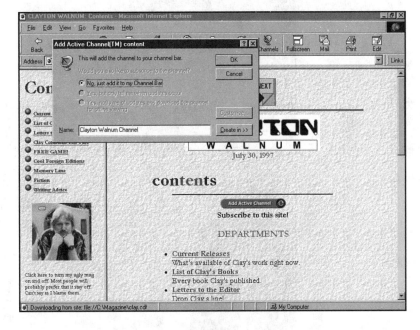

N O T E The subscription dialog box shown in Figure 46.8 has most of its options disabled because those options aren't available for a disk-based magazine. If you want to get the full subscription experience, log onto my Web site at **http://www.connix.com/~cwalnum**, and click the Add Active Channel button on the title page. ∎

When you complete the subscription, Internet Explorer displays the Channel Explorer Bar and the site to which you just subscribed. If you look at the channel bar (see Figure 46.9), you can see the 194×32 image that represents the Clayton Walnum online magazine. And, if you look at the Desktop Channel Bar (assuming you have it displayed on your desktop), you can see the Clayton Walnum online magazine 80×32 image in with the other channels (see Figure 46.10).

FIG. 46.9

After you subscribe, the Clayton Walnum channel's 194×32 image appears in the Channel Explorer Bar.

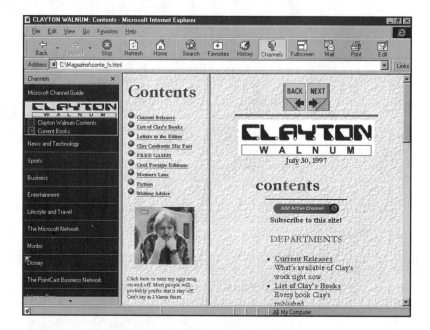

FIG. 46.10

The new subscription also appears in the Desktop Channel Bar.

Now that you've explored some of the more interesting sights in the Clayton Walnum online magazine, go ahead and explore on your own. Get a feel for the magazine's design and layout. And watch for a few surprises along the way.

The Sample Magazine Design

There are, of course, a billion ways to design and lay out an online magazine. Although the Clayton Walnum sample magazine sticks to a typical magazine structure, you can do just about anything you want with your own creations. However, remember that nothing's more frustrating than being unable to find your way around a Web site. I'm sure you've been to Web sites that were so convoluted you didn't think you'd ever find your way out. For this reason, the Clayton Walnum site limits itself to a simple two-layer hierarchy, as shown in Figure 46.11.

FIG. 46.11

A simple link hierarchy keeps readers from getting lost.

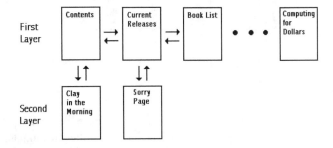

The first layer consists of the main table of contents and the magazine pages themselves. The second layer consists of a few odd-ball pages, such as the Clay in the Morning page, that are not part of the magazine's regular page sequence. When you get to one of these pages (see Figure 46.12), you'll see that the only available links either return you to the page you came from or take you to the main table of contents. This organization keeps the reader from getting lost in the site.

To keep things even more organized, all the main pages are arranged in a sequential order. By using the Back and Next buttons at the top and bottom of the pages, the reader can move through the magazine page-by-page, which is a layout metaphor based on print magazines, something with which everyone's familiar. The navigation bar on the left of every page (except the cover) enables the reader to jump to any page in the magazine without having to follow the sequential links, just as if they flipped to the middle of a conventional print magazine. Because the navigation bar is always available—not to mention the Contents buttons on every main page—it's virtually impossible for the reader to get lost in the site.

While the structure of the magazine keeps the reader from getting lost, the visual layout of each page sticks to a simple design that's attractive, as well as utilitarian. The top of each page looks essentially the same, being comprised of a set of navigation buttons, followed by the article name, by-line, and description enclosed in horizontal rules. This header is followed by the body text, after which another set of navigation controls at the bottom of the page lets the reader navigate to another page without having to scroll back up the top of the current page.

FIG. 46.12

At the second level, you can only return to the page you came from or to the main table of contents.

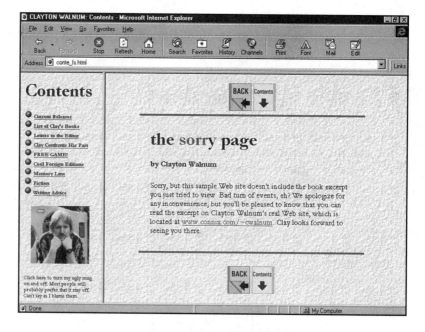

Each page (except one) uses a paper-like background image that provides texture to the page. And, as you will see, each page uses HTML tables to lock the most important page layout elements from resizing and reorganizing themselves as the reader enlarges or shrinks his browser window. The downside of this layout locking is that the pages don't look their best at resolutions under 800×600. Every time you gain something, you have to give something else up!

The Magazine's HTML Files

In this section, you examine the magazine more closely, by exploring the HTML files that create each page. Along the way, you learn about powerful HTML techniques, including DHTML, CSS, frames and tables, and audio and video streaming. Because you should by now have a good background in HTML, only new techniques in the following sections are explained in detail. If there are parts of the HTML that you don't understand, look up the associated topic in this book's index and reread the appropriate sections of the book.

Exploring the Cover Page

The magazine's cover page is implemented by a small HTML file (default.htm) that includes some interesting features. For example, if the reader doesn't click the cover within 20 seconds, the magazine automatically opens to the table of contents. This is accomplished by the HTML shown in Listing 46.1.

Listing 46.1 Isthe_01.txt—Automatically Flipping the Page

```
<head>
  <title>CLAYTON WALNUM: Online Magazine</title>
  <meta http-equiv=Refresh content="20; url=conte_fs.html">
</head>
```

The HTML line of interest here is the <META> tag. This line instructs the browser to display the conte_fs.html page in 20 seconds. The conte_fs.html file sets up the magazine's frames.

Next in default.htm is the line that defines the page's background and text colors, as well as begins the body portion of the document:

```
<body bgcolor=00000000 text=ffffffff>
```

Following the <BODY> tag are the lines that display the cover image and set the image up as a link to the magazine's contents. Listing 46.2 shows these lines.

Listing 46.2 Isthe_02.txt—Displaying the Cover Link

```
<center>

    <a href=conte_fs.html>
        <img width=350 height=455 src=images\cover-2.jpg align=center border=0
            alt="Clayton Walnum -- Click here to continue">
    </a>

    <p><b>Click cover to turn the page</b>

</center>
```

Last but not least are the lines that play the cover's theme song. These lines, shown in Listing 46.3, embed Microsoft's ActiveMovie control into the page. The ActiveMovie control is handy to have around, because it can stream both audio and video from your Web server to the magazine's reader. The control comes with Microsoft Internet Explorer 4.0, as well as with the Internet Client SDK, both of which you can download from Microsoft's Web site (**www.microsoft.com**).

Listing 46.3 Isthe_03.txt—Streaming Audio Using the ActiveMovie Control

```
<OBJECT CLASSID="CLSID:05589FA1-C356-11CE-BF01-00AA0055595A">
  <PARAM NAME="FileName" VALUE="sounds\jetsnbel.wav">
  <PARAM NAME="ShowDisplay" VALUE="0">
  <PARAM NAME="ShowControls" VALUE="0">
  <PARAM NAME="AutoStart" VALUE="-1">
  <PARAM NAME="PlayCount" VALUE="1">
</OBJECT>
```

Part VIII
Ch 46

As you can see, Listing 46.3 uses the `<OBJECT>` tag to embed the control into the page. By setting several of the control's parameters, the page can force the control to hide its interface, as well as to automatically play the WAV file that contains the theme song. You can read more about the ActiveMovie control in the Internet Client SDK, which I strongly suggest that you download if you want to develop sophisticated Web sites. (See the section "Keeping Up with DHTML" later in this chapter for more information on obtaining the Internet Client SDK.)

Exploring the Frames Page

When you move to the magazine's first page, which is the table of contents, your browser window divides into two frames. The frame on the left always displays an abbreviated table of contents, so that the reader can jump instantly to any article in the magazine. The frame on the right displays the current magazine page. The conte_fs.html file, shown in Listing 46.4, sets up the frames.

Listing 46.4   lsthe_04.txt—Setting Up the Frames

```
<html>
<head>
  <title>CLAYTON WALNUM: Contents</title>
</head>
<frameset cols="175,*">
  <frame src=contentsf.html noresize scrolling=no>
  <frame src=contents.html name=rightframe>
</frameset>
</html>
```

As you can see in the listing, `conte_fs.html` creates a frameset in which the first frame is 175 pixels wide, with the second frame consuming the remaining space in the browser window. The left hand frame cannot be resized or scrolled. The contentsf.html file, which is the source file for the left frame, defines the abbreviated table of contents, whereas the contents.html file defines the contents for the right frame. The contents.html file contains the full Table of Contents page. However, the right frame's contents changes as the reader browses the magazine.

Exploring the Abbreviated Contents Page

The contentsf.html file defines the abbreviated table of contents. The magazine always displays this page in the left frame, giving the reader instant access to any part of the magazine. Listing 46.5 shows how this file implements the page's `<HEAD>` tag.

Listing 46.5   lsthe_05.txt—Linking to a Style Sheet

```
<head>
  <title>Contents Frame</title>
  <link rel=stylesheet href=styles.css type=text/css>
</head>
```

Notice that the <HEAD> tag links the page to the magazine's style sheet, which is contained in the styles.css file. Every page in the magazine links to the styles.css style sheet, which makes it easy to change a specific style throughout the entire magazine. For example, if you want to change the style used by the body text, you only need to change the BODY style definition in the styles.css file. Then, the body text in the entire magazine automatically changes to reflect the new style.

Listing 46.6 shows the magazine's style sheet. This style sheet probably isn't as complete as it should be for an online magazine, but it's enough to demonstrate the concept. When you create your online magazine, you'll probably want to create a style in the style sheet for every style used throughout your magazine. Then it's a snap to restyle a magazine's contents.

Listing 46.6 styles.css—The Magazine's Style Sheet

```
/****************************************************
 * Style sheet for the Clayton Walnum magazine
 * sample Web site.
 ****************************************************/

/* General styles */
body {font: 12pt garamond, times; color: black;}
li {font: 12pt garamond, times; color: black;}

/* Page titles */
.red {font: bold 28pt garamond, times; color: #800000;}
.green {font: bold 28pt garamond, times; color: #008000;}
.blue {font: bold 28pt garamond, times; color: #000080;}

/* Anchor styles */
a.normal {font: 12pt garamond, times; color: blue;}
a.small {font: 8pt garamond, times; color: blue;}
a.large {font: bold 18pt garamond, times; color: blue;
  text-decoration: none;}

/* Contents page subheads */
.conheads {font-size: 14pt; font-weight: bold; color: red;}

/* Legal paragraphs */
.legaltext {font-size: 8pt; color: #800000;}
a.legal {font: 8pt garamond, times; color: blue;}

/* By-lines */
.byline {font: bold 12pt garamond, times; color: black;}
.whitebyline {font: bold 12pt garamond, times; color: white;}

/* Special body text */
body.white {font: bold 12pt garamond, times;
   color: white; background=black}

/* Caption text */
.caption {font: bold italic 10pt garamond, times;
  color: red; background=black}
```

Part
VIII

Ch
46

Getting back to the contentsf.html file, after the <HEAD> tag, the HTML tells the browser what to display as the page's background image, like this:

```
<body background=images\bg10.gif>
```

Then, a <SPAN> tag assigns the custom red style class to the page's title:

```
<span class=red>Contents</span>
```

Next come the links to each of the magazine's pages. These links are implemented using DHTML to change a link's style when the reader's mouse passes over the link. Listing 46.7, for example, shows how the page defines the first link, which leads the reader to the Current Releases page.

Listing 46.7 lsthe_07.txt—Defining a Link with DHTML

```
<img src=images\harvbull.gif width=15 height=15 border=0>
<a class=small href=current.html target=rightframe
  onmouseover=this.style.color='red';
  onmouseout=this.style.color='blue';>
  <b>Current Releases</b></a><br>
```

The first line defines the image that's displayed next to the link, whereas the second line specifies the style class for the link, the source page, and the target page. If you remember what you've learned about frames, the target page is the frame in which the source HTML appears—in this case, the right frame.

The third and fourth lines are where things get interesting. DHTML defines a number of events to which page elements can respond. Two of those events are onmouseover, which occurs when the mouse pointer passes over the area consumed by an element, and onmouseout, which occurs when the mouse pointer moves out of the area consumed by the element. Table 46.1 lists element events you can use with DHTML.

Table 46.1 Events Generated by HTML Elements

Event	Description
onclick	Generated by a left mouse click on an element
ondblclick	Generated by a double left mouse click on an element
onkeydown	Generated by pressing a key down
onkeypress	Generated by a key press and release
onkeyup	Generated by releasing a pressed key
onmousedown	Generated by any mouse click on the element
onmousemove	Generated when the mouse pointer moves over an element
onmouseout	Generated when the mouse pointer moves off the element

| onmouseover | Generated when the mouse pointer moves over the element |
| onmouseup | Generated by a mouse-button release over an element |

In Listing 46.7, when the onmouseover event occurs on a text link, the text's color style changes to red. When the onmouseout event occurs, the text's color style returns to blue. Other text links on the page work the same way.

At the bottom of the page, the reader can toggle the photo on and off by clicking the text below the photo. The first step in preparing this effect is to display the image and give it an ID that enables the document to refer to and manipulate the photo:

```
<div align=center>
  <img id=photo src=images\clay1.jpg width=122 height=115 border=0>
</div>
```

After displaying the photo, the page must display the text that controls the photo, which it does as shown in Listing 46.8.

Listing 46.8 lsthe_08.txt—Displaying the Text That Controls the Photo

```
<span class=legaltext style=cursor:hand
  onclick="togglePhoto(document.all.photo);"
  onmouseover=this.style.color='red';
  onmouseout=this.style.color='blue';>

  <p>Click here to turn my ugly mug on and off. Most people will
     probably prefer that it stay off. Can't say as I blame them.
</span>
```

This text block, like other text links on the page, responds to the onmouseover and onmouseout events to highlight the text when the mouse pointer passes over it. In addition, the text block handles the onclick event by calling the togglePhoto() function, which is defined in the JavaScript code later in the HTML file. The call passes the photo element, which is accessed through its ID, into the function so that the function can manipulate the photo. Listing 46.9 shows the script that contains the togglePhoto() function.

Listing 46.9 lsthe_09.txt—The *togglePhoto()* Function

```
<script language=JAVASCRIPT>

function togglePhoto(element)
{
  if (element.style.visibility == "hidden")
    element.style.visibility = "visible"
  else
    element.style.visibility = "hidden"
}

</script>
```

Part VIII
Ch
46

The `togglePhoto()` function simply checks the status of the photo's `visibility` style and turns the photo on or off depending on the style's current setting.

Exploring the Full Contents Page

When you open the Clayton Walnum online magazine, the first page you see is the table of contents. Unlike the abbreviated contents shown in the left frame, the full table of contents gives not only links to each article, but also describes each article, as well as provides other information, including the current issue's date and the legal paragraph at the end of the page. The full table of contents also includes a button the reader can click to add the magazine to his or her channel list. This full table of contents is defined in the contents.html file.

Listing 46.10 shows the `<HEAD>` tag for the file, which links the styles.css style sheet to the page. All the pages in the magazine link to the style sheet.

Listing 46.10   lsthe_10.txt—Linking to the Style Sheet

```
<head>
  <title>CLAYTON WALNUM: Table of Contents</title>
  <link rel=stylesheet href=styles.css type=text/css>
</head>
```

The `<BODY>` tag, shown in Listing 46.11, sets a timer that controls the blinking date at the top of the page.

Listing 46.11   lsthe_11.txt—Responding to Events in the *<Body>* Tag

```
<body background=images\bg10.gif
  onload="window.tm=setTimeout('changeColor()',500)"
  onunload="clearTimeout(window.tm)">
```

In the first line, the tag sets the page's background image to bg10.gif. In the second line, the tag creates a timer that runs for 500 milliseconds, at which point the browser calls the `changeColor()` script function, which is shown in Listing 46.12. The page creates the timer in response to the `onload` event. The third line tells the browser to clear the timer when the `onunload` event occurs.

Listing 46.12   lsthe_12.txt—The *changeColor()* Function

```
<script language="JAVASCRIPT">

  function changeColor()
  {
    var color = document.all.blinkText.style.color;

    if (color == "red")
      color = "black";
```

```
    else
      color = "red";

    document.all.blinkText.style.color = color;
    window.tm=setTimeout('changeColor()',500);
  }

</script>
```

The `changeColor()` function first retrieves the current color of the text element, which has the ID `blinkText`. The function then determines whether to set the text color to red or black, after which the function resets the timer and exits. The text that the function controls is displayed near the top of the HTML file, like this:

```
<b><span id=blinkText>July 30, 1997</b></span>
```

This `<SPAN>` tag assigns the `blinkText` ID to the magazine's date text, as well as displays the date in its position at the top of the table of contents.

Also at the top of the Table of Contents page are the buttons that enable the reader to scan through the magazine one page at a time. These buttons are images that work just like text links, including responding to the `onmouseover` and `onmouseout` events. In the case of the buttons, though, the color of the images doesn't change. Instead, the HTML instructs the browser to load and display a new image when the mouse passes over the button. Listing 46.13 shows the lines that accomplish this feat. Notice that all the `onmouseover` and `onmouseout` events do is assign a new image file to the button's `src` property. This creates an interesting animated button effect that signals to the reader that the button is an interactive part of the page.

Part
VIII

Ch
46

Listing 46.13   lsthe_13.txt—Handling the Events Generated by the Buttons

```
<a href=default.htm target=_top><img src=images\prevpage.gif align=center
   width=46 height=55 border=0 alt="Contents Page"
   onmouseover="this.src = 'images/prevpage2.gif';"
   onmouseout="this.src = 'images/prevpage.gif';"></a>
<a href=current.html><img src=images\nextpage.gif align=center
   width=46 height=55 border=0 alt="Next Page"
   onmouseover="this.src = 'images/nextpag2.gif';"
   onmouseout="this.src = 'images/nextpage.gif';"></a>
```

Another element of special interest on the Table of Contents page is the Add Active Channel button. As you learned previously in this book, Internet Explorer 4.0 brings a new type of push technology to the browser called channels. Using channels, you can subscribe to a Web site and be notified automatically of changes to the site. To create a simple channel, you must write a CDF (channel definition format) file that describes the channel, and create a 194×32 image to represent the channel in the Channel Explorer Bar, an 80×32 image to represent the channel in the Desktop Channel Bar, and a 16×16 icon to represent the channel in Internet Explorer's Favorites menu. When the reader clicks the Add Active Channel button, the browser reads the associated CDF file and sets up the subscription. Listing 46.14 shows the Clayton Walnum channel's CDF file. As you can see, the file defines a channel with two pages that will be tracked by the subscription.

Listing 46.14 Isthe_14.txt—The Channel's CDF File

```
<?XML version="1.0"?>

<CHANNEL HREF="default.htm" BASE="c:/Magazine/">

    <TITLE>Clayton Walnum Channel</TITLE>
    <ABSTRACT>Clayton Walnum Web Site</ABSTRACT>
    <LOGO HREF="images/claywide.gif" STYLE="IMAGE-WIDE"/>
    <LOGO HREF="images/clay.gif" STYLE="IMAGE"/>
    <LOGO HREF="images/clayicon.gif" STYLE="ICON"/>

    <SCHEDULE STARTDATE="1997.11.01" ENDDATE="1999.12.31">
      <INTERVALTIME DAY="1"/>
      <EARLIESTTIME HOUR="1"/>
      <LATESTTIME HOUR="12"/>
    </SCHEDULE>

    <ITEM HREF="contents.html" LASTMOD="1997.11.05T16:00">
      <TITLE>Clayton Walnum Contents</TITLE>
      <ABSTRACT>Table of contents for the Clayton Walnum Web site</ABSTRACT>
      <LOGO HREF="images/contents.gif" STYLE="ICON"/>
    </ITEM>

    <ITEM HREF="current.html" LASTMOD="1997.11.05T16:00">
      <TITLE>Current Books</TITLE>
      <ABSTRACT>Currently available books by Clayton Walnum</ABSTRACT>
      <LOGO HREF="images/books.gif" STYLE="ICON"/>
    </ITEM>

</CHANNEL>
```

N O T E In order to use the Add Active Channel button in your Web sites, you must register with Microsoft and agree to their terms. Point your browser to **http://www.microsoft.com/ sbnmember/ielogo/default.asp** for more information. ▪

Finally, notice how the HTML for the Table of Contents page uses tables to keep the page elements from changing size and position when the reader resizes his browser window. All of these layout tables, which are set to an explicit pixel width, have their border attribute set to 0 so that the tables are invisible on the page. You might want to go through the HTML for the page and set all the table borders to 1 so that you can see how the layout works. For example, Figure 46.13 shows the Table of Contents page's table with a visible border. This is the only table on this page.

FIG. 46.13
A table with an explicit width forces all elements of the page to stay in place, regardless of the browser window's size.

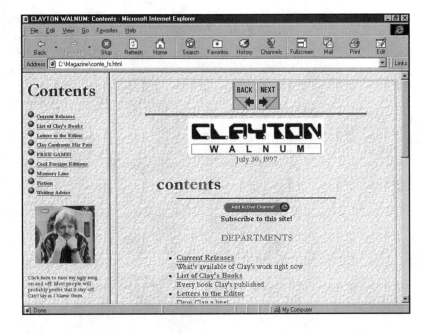

Other magazine pages use multiple, or even nested, tables to better control the positioning of page sections. For example, The Current Releases page places each page section into its own table. Figure 46.14 shows how the page's header elements have their own table, whereas Figure 46.15 shows how each book entry has its own table.

FIG. 46.14
The elements at the top of the page are organized into a single table.

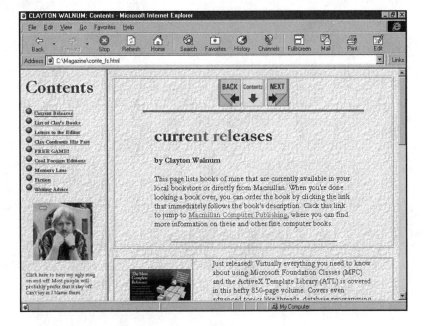

FIG. 46.15
Each book description also gets its own table.

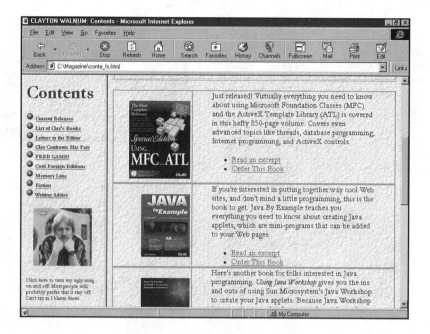

You can easily manipulate these different tables to create special layouts. Figure 46.16, for example, shows how you can stagger the width of the tables to vary the layouts for each book entry on the page. You can even add a cell to the table to display another image to the right of the book description. Because each table is independent of the others, you have a lot of design freedom, while still being assured that the design will not change when viewed in different sized browser windows.

Exploring the Free Game Page

The Free Game page has another good example of DHTML. Here, you can click text links to make whole sections of the page appear and disappear. This effect is again accomplished by linking element events with JavaScript functions. The page first associates the `onclick` event with the `toggleText()` function, like this:

```
<body background=images\bg10.gif onclick="toggleText()">
```

Now, whenever the reader clicks anywhere on the Web page, the browser calls the `toggleText()` function, which determines how to handle the click.

Listing 46.15 shows the HTML lines that display the first text link in question.

Listing 46.15   lsthe_15.txt—Defining the Controlling Link

```
h2><a class=ex href=# title="Learn to install Poker Squares" id=Install
  onmouseover=this.style.color='red'
  onmouseout=this.style.color='blue'>
  Installing Poker Squares</a></h2>
```

FIG. 46.16

You can change any individual table to vary the page layout.

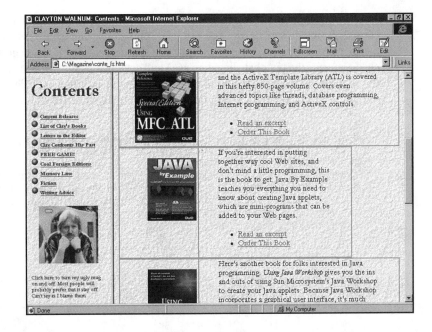

This text link is given the ID Install so that the JavaScript function can refer back to it. Thanks to the onmouseover and onmouseout events, this text link acts like the others in the magazine, highlighting when the user's mouse passes over it. However, when the user clicks the link, the browser generates an onclick message, which results in a call to the toggleText() script function. Listing 46.16 shows the toggleText() function.

Listing 46.16 Isthe_16.txt—The *toggleText()* Function

```
<script language="JAVASCRIPT">

  function toggleText()
  {
    if (event.srcElement.id != "")
    {
      var child = event.srcElement.id + "Text"
      var element = document.all[child]
      if (element != null)
        if (element.style.display == "none")
          element.style.display = ""
        else
          element.style.display = "none"
      event.returnValue=false
    }
  }

</script>
```

Part
VIII

Ch
46

The function first checks whether the element associated with the event has an ID. If the clicked element has no ID, the function has nothing to do and simply returns. If there is an ID, the user probably clicked one of the text links. In this case, the function gets a reference to the child element (the text that should appear) and sets the element's `display` style appropriately, toggling the element on or off. In the case of the Install link, the child element is the paragraph with the `InstallText` ID. This paragraph element is shown in Listing 46.17.

Listing 46.17 Isthe_17.txt—The InstallText Page Element

```
<DIV id=InstallText style=display:none>
  <p>Poker Squares can be installed only on PC-compatible machines
  running DOS or Windows. To install Poker Squares, simply unzip
  the POKERSQ.ZIP file into a directory. You can then play the game
  by running the POKERSQ.EXE file. Poker Squares should run fine
  under both DOS and Windows.</p>
</DIV>
```

The second text link on the Free Game page works similarly, except the element that the link toggles on and off is much larger than the `InstallText` element and includes not only text, but also images and tables.

N O T E   When you examined the abbreviated contents frame, you saw how you could toggle a photo on and off by clicking a text link. In that case, when the picture vanished, the page didn't close up to reclaim the space where the picture had been. However, on the Free Game page, when the text elements appear and disappear, the page reformats itself to accommodate the changes. That's the difference between the `visibility` style, which is used with the photo on the contents frame, and the `display` style, which is used to make text appear and disappear in the Free Game page. ■

Exploring the Clay in the Morning Page

As you saw when you explored the Clayton Walnum online magazine, the Clay in the Morning page streams a video clip from the server to the reader. You might remember that the magazine did something similar with a sound file on the cover page. A very flexible component, the ActiveMovie control, can be used to stream sound or video (or both). As you can see in Listing 46.18, the Clay in the Morning page sets exactly the same ActiveMovie properties as the cover page did. The only difference is that the `PlayCount` property is set to 10, which causes the video to repeat 10 times.

Listing 46.18 Isthe_18.txt—Streaming Video with the ActiveMovie Control

```
<OBJECT CLASSID="CLSID:05589FA1-C356-11CE-BF01-00AA0055595A">
<PARAM NAME="FileName" VALUE="video\monkey.mpg">
<PARAM NAME="ShowDisplay" VALUE="0">
<PARAM NAME="ShowControls" VALUE="0">
<PARAM NAME="AutoStart" VALUE="-1">
<PARAM NAME="PlayCount" VALUE="10">
</OBJECT>
```

A Closer Look at DHTML

As you examined the sample online magazine in the previous sections, you got a quick introduction to some of the power you gain when using Dynamic HTML. Because DHTML wasn't covered previously in this book, this section will give you a brief overview of this powerful new Web technology.

Microsoft's goal with DHTML is to create an advanced form of HTML that enables Internet developers to create Web pages as powerful and responsive as conventional multimedia applications. To do this, DHTML must transfer the bulk of processing from the server to the client browser, which can manipulate the Web page much faster. The extra speed is due to the client browser not having to wait for the server to transmit the data needed to update a page.

DHTML provides an object model that enables a Web developer to identify and manipulate any element on a Web page. For example, in the previous section, you saw how you can give a paragraph of text an ID and then use that ID to manipulate the text, just as if it were an object like an ActiveX control. By manipulating the element's properties from a script, you can dynamically change the Web page's content right on the client machine, without having to wait for slow data transmissions over the Internet.

Some of the major capabilities of DHTML are the following:

■ *Dynamic Styles*. The styles of a DHTML document can be changed in response to events generated by the mouse, the keyboard, or timers. Any script language can be used to access and manipulate styles.

■ *Dynamic Content*. A Web page's content can be changed on-the-fly by adding or deleting elements. The Web page automatically reformats itself to accommodate the changes.

■ *2-D Positioning*. Using DHTML, a Web developer can explicitly position page elements using x and y coordinates, as well as incorporate z-order positioning, which determines which objects pass over others when the objects overlap.

■ *Multimedia Controls*. DHTML includes multimedia controls that enable Web developers to display animation sequences, apply filters, perform transitions, stream audio and video, and more.

■ *Database Support*. DHTML is data-aware, meaning that Web pages now have the power to handle databases with increased efficiency and convenience. DHTML can format tables for database records, as well as enable the Web developer to create more useful data-aware forms.

In the following sections, you'll take a closer look at the capabilities of DHTML.

Part **VIII**

Ch **46**

Discovering Dynamic Styles

As you browsed the Clayton Walnum online magazine, you saw several examples of dynamic styles in action. For example, on the abbreviated contents page, you saw a photo that appears and disappears in response to your mouse clicks. When you click the text associated with the photo (see Figure 46.17), you generate an event to which the Web page can respond in various ways. In this case, the Web page toggles the photo on or off by manipulating the photo's `visibility` style. Modifying an element's styles on-the-fly is the essence of dynamic styles.

FIG. 46.17

You can use dynamic styles to make page elements that appear and disappear in response to user actions.

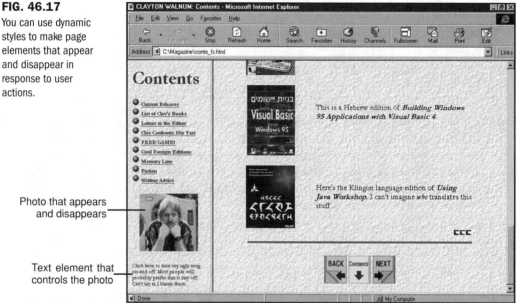

Photo that appears and disappears

Text element that controls the photo

Another example of dynamic styles in the sample magazine are the navigation buttons that change appearance when the mouse passes over them (see Figure 46.18). This effect is accomplished by modifying the images' `src` styles in response to `onmouseover` and `onmouseout` events. Finally, the magazine's text links that change color when the mouse passes over them are another example of dynamic styles.

FIG. 46.18

By changing an image's *src* style in response to events, you can create dynamic graphics.

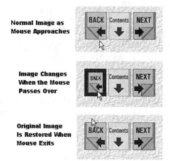

Normal Image as Mouse Approaches

Image Changes When the Mouse Passes Over

Original Image Is Restored When Mouse Exits

Discovering Dynamic Content

Dynamic content is another feature of DHTML used in the Clayton Walnum online magazine. As you learned, dynamic content enables you interactively to add or delete elements from a Web page in response to events—without having to call upon the server to deliver a new HTML document to the reader's browser.

You saw an example of this on the Free Game page. There, you clicked a text link, which caused new text, image, and table elements to appear in the Web page. When the new elements appear or disappear, the page automatically reformats itself. This is different from using dynamic styles to toggle an element. In that case, the page doesn't reformat itself, because the element is still part of the page, albeit an invisible part.

Discovering Exact Positioning

DHTML also enables Web developers to position page elements exactly, using 2D coordinates. Scripts can modify an element's coordinates, causing the element to move around the page. A good example of this technique is the Asteroids-like game (see Figure 46.19) you can find in the Internet Client SDK. This online game is implemented entirely using DHTML and JavaScript. No ActiveX controls or Java applets needed!

FIG. 46.19
Combining DHTML with a scripting language, you can create online games.

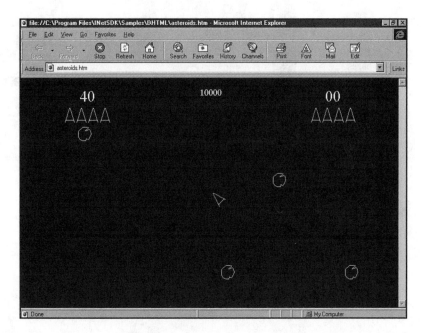

DHTML also supports *z* coordinates for page elements. The *z* coordinate determines which element appears on top when two or more elements overlap. This enables you to set up a pseudo 3D environment on a Web page, with different elements passing in front of or behind other elements.

Discovering Multimedia Controls

DHTML and Microsoft Internet Explorer include a number of standard ActiveX controls that enable you to create many types of multimedia events in your Web pages. For example, you saw examples of audio and video streaming in the Clayton Walnum online magazine. The audio and video elements were played using the ActiveMovie control.

You can read more about the ActiveMovie control, and other controls, in the Internet Client SDK, which you can download from Microsoft's Web site. (See the section "Keeping Up with DHTML" later in this chapter for more information on the Internet Client SDK and Microsoft's Site Builder Network.)

Discovering Databases with DHTML

Using DHTML, you can create data-aware Web pages. When you bind a database table to a DHTML table, the page can automatically generate the rows needed to display the data. Moreover, you can create many types of data-aware forms. Figure 46.20 shows an example on Microsoft's Site Builder Network that binds records to text boxes in a Web page form. When the user clicks the arrows, the form automatically displays previous or succeeding records from the database.

FIG. 46.20
Dynamic HTML enables you to create data-aware Web pages.

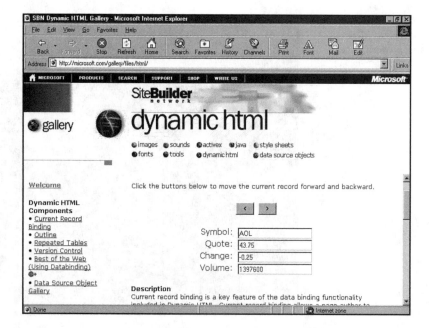

Keeping Up with DHTML

DHTML is still, as of this writing, in its formative stages. Microsoft updates its Web Developer areas with new information almost daily. To keep up with what's happening with DHTML, you should definitely log onto Microsoft's Site Builder Network often (see Figure 46.21). To do this, point your Web browser to **http://www.microsoft.com/sitebuilder/**. If you join the Site Builder Network (it's free and takes only a minute or two), you'll have access to lots of valuable files that you can download. Moreover, there are dozens of articles on just about any topic related to Web development, including DHTML and channels.

FIG. 46.21
Microsoft's Site Builder Network is the place to keep up with new Web developments.

Appendixes

What's New in HTML 4.0

by Sue Charlesworth

In this chapter

A Brief History of HTML

Interest in and use of the World Wide Web has been expanding at a phenomenal rate. As the Web grows, so must its vehicle of communication, HTML. The HTML 2.0 specification is dated November, 1995. Since then, the HTML 3.0 draft specification expired on September 28, 1995, without becoming recommended, and HTML 3.2 became a W3C (World Wide Web Consortium) Recommendation on January 14, 1997. Now we have the public draft for HTML 4.0, announced on July 8, 1997. This draft is almost certain to undergo changes before being accepted by the W3C as a Proposed Recommendation—if it does, indeed, ever become a recommendation.

In addition to this official work on HTML, the browsers have been making their own additions to HTML. Some changes were eventually adopted into W3C HTML Recommendations; others remain proprietary coding aspects that only the individual browsers recognize. The browsers' versions of HTML changed, too, in a game of marketing and programming one-upmanship, hoping to lock Web developers into using one browser or the other exclusively.

Designing for the Web can be a confusing activity, indeed.

What's Different in HTML 4.0

In order to keep up with (or try to) the rapidly changing world of HTML, we present here the changes between HTML 3.2 and HTML 4.0. HTML 4.0 introduces eight new elements, deprecates ten (more about deprecation in a bit), and makes obsolete three more. Frames, formerly only found in the browser versions of HTML, join the official fold. Tables provide better tabular presentation; forms more readily respond to the needs of the disabled; style sheets provide for better formatting and presentation; and multimedia, scripting, and printing are improved. And, as if that weren't enough, HTML 4.0 uses a different character-encoding format that expands the number of alphabets and languages able to implement Web documents.

Let's start with the changes to single tags first, then move on to the topics, like tables, that encompass more than an individual tag.

New Tags in HTML 4.0

The W3C document "Changes between HTML 3.2 and HTML 4.0" lists eight new tags in HTML 4.0. A brief description of these tags follows.

<Q>...</Q>   The `<Q>…</Q>` tag acts much the same as the `<BLOCKQUOTE>` tag, but applies to shorter quoted sections, ones that don't need paragraph breaks.

Example:

```
According to the W3C, <Q>BLOCKQUOTE is for long quotations and
Q is intended for short quotations that don't require paragraph breaks.</Q>
```

HTML 4.0 requires both the start tag and the end tag for `<Q>`.

<ACRONYM>...</ACRONYM>   The `<ACRONYM>…</ACRONYM>` tag indicates an acronym in the text. `<ACRONYM>` is a "phrasal" tag, meaning that it helps define the structure of a text phrase.

Make sure to use `<ACRONYM>` for the acronym itself, not the title that the letters stand for. `<ACRONYM>` behaves like `<EM>`, `<STRONG>`, and `<CODE>`.

Example:

```
Working with the World Wide Web requires a good head for acronyms.
<ACRONYM>HTML</ACRONYM>, <ACRONYM>WWW</ACRONYM>, and <ACRONYM>HTTP</ACRONYM>
are but a few of the acronyms found around the Web.
```

HTML 4.0 requires both the start tag and the end tag for `<ACRONYM>`.

`<INS>...</INS>` and `<DEL>...</DEL>` Use `<INS>...</INS>` to mark parts of a document that have been added since the document's last version. `<DEL>...</DEL>`, similarly, marks document text that has been deleted since a previous version.

Example:

```
Welcome to our online personnel policy guide. <INS>In the spirit of relaxed
living, our dress code now requires only that you meet TV's decency standard.</
INS> <DEL>In the spirit of conservative virtues, we require every employee to
wear a suit to work every day.</DEL>
```

HTML 4.0 requires both the start tag and the end tag for both `<INS>` and `<DEL>`.

`<COLGROUP>...</COLGROUP>` `<COLGROUP>...</COLGROUP>` allows you finer control over the formatting of tables by specifying groups of columns that share width and alignment properties. Every table must have at least one `<COLGROUP>`; without any specific `<COLGROUP>` definition, HTML 4.0 assumes the table consists of a single column group that contains all the columns of the table.

If you wanted, for example, to create a table that had a single, wide description column followed by a series of small check boxes, you would code:

```
<TABLE>
<COLGROUP span="10" width="30">
<COLGROUP span="1" width="0*">
<THEAD>
<TR>…
</TABLE>
```

This way, the first `<COLGROUP>` tag formats all ten check boxes, much nicer than typing in ten identical specifications—for each row!

The start tag for `<COLGROUP>` is required; the end tag is optional.

`<FIELDSET>...</FIELDSET>` With the `<FIELDSET>...</FIELDSET>` tag, you can group related form fields, making your form easier to read and use. Human brains like to be able to classify information, and `<FIELDSET>` helps do just that.

When you enclose a group of form elements in the `<FIELDSET>` tags, the browser will group the elements so you can easily tell they belong together. Figure A.1 shows how Internet Explorer 4.0 displays Listing A.1.

HTML 4.0 requires both the start tag and the end tag for `<FIELDSET>`.

App

A

FIG. A.1

<FIELDSET> groupings
in Internet Explorer 4.0.

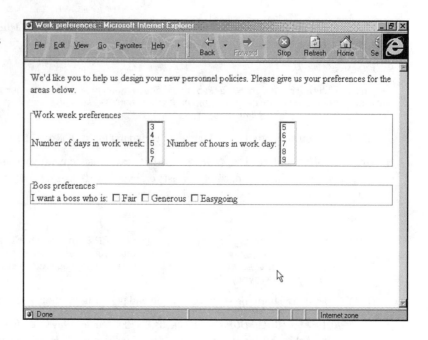

Listing A.1   Grouping form information using _<FIELDSET>_

```
<HTML>
<HEAD>
<TITLE>Work preferences</TITLE>
</HEAD>
<BODY>
We'd like you to help us design your new personnel policies.
Please give us your preferences for the areas below.

<FORM action="..." method="post">
   <FIELDSET>
      <LEGEND align="top">Work week preferences</LEGEND>

      Number of days in work week:
      <SELECT NAME="WorkWeek" SIZE="5">
      <OPTION VALUE="3day">3
      <OPTION VALUE="4day">4
      <OPTION VALUE="5day">5
      <OPTION VALUE="6day">6
      <OPTION VALUE="7day">7</SELECT>

      Number of hours in work day:
      <SELECT NAME="WorkDay" SIZE="5">
      <OPTION VALUE="3day">5
      <OPTION VALUE="4day">6
      <OPTION VALUE="5day">7
      <OPTION VALUE="6day">8
      <OPTION VALUE="7day">9</SELECT>
```

```
      </FIELDSET>
   <P>
      <FIELDSET>
         <LEGEND>Boss preferences</LEGEND>
         I want a boss who is:
         <INPUT NAME="BossValues" TYPE="checkbox" VALUE="Fair">Fair</INPUT>
         <INPUT NAME="BossValues" TYPE="checkbox" VALUE="Generous">Generous</INPUT>
         <INPUT NAME="BossValues" TYPE="checkbox" VALUE="Easy">Easygoing</INPUT>
      </FIELDSET>
   </FORM>
   </BODY>
   </HTML>
```

<LABEL>...</LABEL>   If you looked at the code for the <FIELDSET> example above, you saw the <LABEL>...</LABEL> tags in action. Use <LABEL> with <FIELDSET> to attach a label to the form grouping. Figure A.2 is the same as the <FIELDSET> example, except that the first <LABEL> has been removed.

HTML 4.0 requires both the start tag and the end tag for <LEGEND>.

FIG. A.2

The <FIELDSET> example with the first <LABEL> removed.

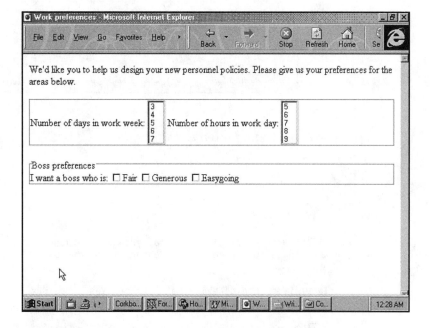

<BUTTON>...</BUTTON>   The <BUTTON>...</BUTTON> tag, another addition to forms, allows you to have push buttons on forms that more closely resemble push buttons available in Windows and other applications. Many aspects of <BUTTON> are similar to those of <INPUT> elements of types submit and reset, but <BUTTON>, in the words of the W3C, "allows richer presentational possibilities."

One example of a "richer presentational possibility" is the fact that a <BUTTON> has beveled, shadowed edges, looking 3-D rather than flat, and "moves" when clicked, giving the impression of being pushed in, then released. Listing A.2 and Figure A.3 show buttons at work.

FIG. A.3

The <BUTTON> tag at work.

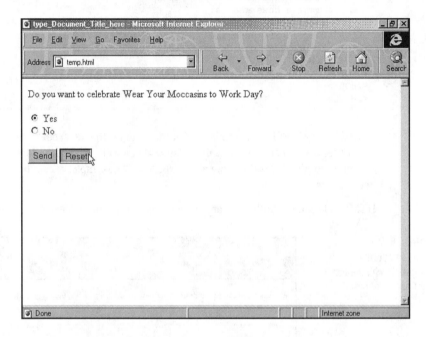

Listing A.2   Adding a Button to a Form

```
<HTML>
<HEAD>
<TITLE> Moccasin Day </TITLE>

</HEAD>
<BODY>

<FORM action="http://somesite.com/prog/adduser" method="post">
Do you want to celebrate Wear Your Moccasins to Work Day?

<P>
    <INPUT type="radio" name="vote" value="Yes"> Yes<BR>
    <INPUT type="radio" name="vote" value="No"> No<BR>
    <P>
    <BUTTON name="submit" value="submit" type="submit">
    Send</BUTTON>
    <BUTTON name="reset" type="reset">
    Reset</BUTTON>
  </FORM>

</BODY>
</HTML>
```

HTML 4.0 requires both the start tag and the end tag for <BUTTON>.

Deprecated Tags in HTML 4.0

Deprecated tags and attributes are those that have been replaced by other, newer, HTML constructs. Deprecated tags are still included in the HTML draft or recommendation but are clearly marked as deprecated. Once deprecated, tags may well become obsolete. The draft "strongly urges" the nonuse of deprecated tags.

<ISINDEX>...</ISINDEX>   <ISINDEX> allowed a form to contain a simple string search. This action should be replaced by an <INPUT> form element.

<APPLET>...</APPLET>   The <APPLET>...</APPLET> tag enabled the running of a Java applet. This tag has been replaced by the more encompassing <OBJECT>...</OBJECT> tag.

<CENTER>...</CENTER>   The <CENTER>...</CENTER> tag, oddly enough, centered text or graphics. <CENTER> is deprecated in favor of <DIV> tag with the align attribute set to "center."

<FONT>...</FONT>   <FONT>...</FONT> allowed the specification of font sizes, colors, and faces. Style sheets, rather than HTML code, have taken over character formatting duties.

> **N O T E**   Based as it is on SGML, HTML purists have never been happy using markup—the description of a document's structure—to define presentation, or how a document appears. With the formal (pending) adoption of style sheets, character formatting can be taken out of HTML code. ■

<BASEFONT>...</BASEFONT>   <BASEFONT>...</BASEFONT> set a base font size that could then be referenced for size increases or decreases. Use style sheets instead to set and reference relative font sizes.

<STRIKE>...</STRIKE> and <S>...</S>   Both <STRIKE>...</STRIKE> and <S>...</S> created strikethrough characters. Replace these tags with style sheets.

<U>...</U>   <U>...</U> created underlined characters. As with the tags above, use style sheets to create underlines.

<DIR>...</DIR>   Moving away from fonts, we have the <DIR>...</DIR> tag. <DIR> describes a directory list. While originally designed to output elements in horizontal columns like UNIX directory listings, browsers formatted <DIR> lists like unordered lists. As there is no difference between the two, use a <UL>...</UL> list instead of a <DIR>...</DIR> list.

<MENU>...</MENU>   <MENU>...</MENU> lists have also fallen by the wayside. The <MENU> tag described single-column menu lists. As with <DIR> lists, browsers made no distinction between <MENU> and <UL> lists. Use <UL>...</UL> lists instead of <MENU> ones.

Obsolete Tags in HTML 4.0

Obsolete tags have been removed from the HTML specification. While browsers may still support obsolete tags, there is no guarantee that this support will continue.

The three tags that become obsolete in HTML 4.0 are <XMP>, <PLAINTEXT>, and <LISTING>. In all cases, replace these tags with <PRE>.

N O T E   Despite the fact that the HTML 4.0 draft doesn't specifically mention frames as new, and despite the fact that you may have seen them in use for some time now, frames are new to the official HTML specification. ▨

Internationalization

Despite its name, the World Wide Web has had some difficulty reaching out past the Western languages and alphabets. In general, character representation in HTML was largely confined to the use of the ISO 8859-1 (Latin-1) character set. This character set contains letters for English, French, Spanish, German, and the Scandinavian languages, but no Greek, Hebrew, Arabic, or Cyrillic characters, among others, and few scientific and mathematical symbols. Also, the Latin-1 character set contains no provisions for marking reading direction.

Part of the problem with Latin-1 is that it simply doesn't have room to handle all the alphabets and languages of the world. It is an 8-bit, single-byte coded graphic character set and, as such, can represent only up to 256 characters.

Enter Unicode. Unicode is a character-encoding standard that uses a 16-bit set, thereby increasing the number of encoded characters to more than 65,000 characters.

HTML 4.0 uses the Universal Character Set (UCS) as its character set. UCS is a character-by-character equivalent to Unicode 2.0 ●

Style Sheet Property Reference

by Jerry Honeycutt

In this chapter

Background Properties

HTML style sheets provide you the capability to decorate the background of an element by using color and images. Note that using the properties described in the following sections doesn't define the background for the Web page as a whole. These properties set the background of an element on the Web page. For example, if you define a background for the <UL> tag, as in the following example, then the background only appears within each occurrence of that tag on the Web page.

```
UL {background-image: URL(http://www.myserver.com/images/watermark.gif)}
```

You can group the background properties described in the following sections using background. You specify the background color, image, repeat, attachment, and position like this:

```
background: white URL(http://www.myserver.com/images/bg.gif) repeat-x fixed top,
left
```

background-attachment

The background-attachment property determines whether the background image is fixed in the browser window or scrolls as the user scrolls the window. You can use this property to create a watermark behind your Web page that stays put regardless of which portion of the Web page the user is viewing.

You can assign two possible values to background-attachment, as described in Table B.1.

Table B.1 *background-attachment* **Values**

Value	Description
fixed	The image is fixed within the browser window.
scroll	The image scrolls as the user scrolls the window.

background-color

You can change the background color for an element by using the background-color property. You can assign one of the valid color names to background-color or an RGB value such as #808080 (white). For example, if you define a style for the <UL> tag that changes the background color to blue, then all the unordered lists in your HTML file will be displayed with a blue background.

 TIP Changing the background color for certain types of tags is useful to highlight information on the Web page.

background-image

You can display a background image in an element by setting the value of the background-image property to the URL of an image. This has the effect of a watermark displayed behind that element on the Web page (the element's content is displayed over the background image).

You set the URL by using the URL(*address*) format, like this:

```
H1 {background-image: URL(http://www.myserver.com/images/heading.gif)}
```

Units in CSS1

Most style sheet properties accept some sort of length. You can use many different units to specify a length, too. HTML supports two types of units: relative and absolute lengths. The following table describes the relative units.

Unit	Example	Description
em	0.5em	The height of the element's font, relative to the output device
ex	0.75ex	The height of the letter X, relative to the output device
px	15px	Pixels, relative to the output device

Whenever possible, use relative units so that your Web pages will scale better from one device to the next. You can also use the absolute units as described in the following table.

Unit	Example	Description
in	.5in	Inches
cm	1cm	Centimeters
mm	20mm	Millimeters
pt	12pt	Points (1pt = 1/72 inch)
pc	1pc	Pica (1pc = 12pt)

Aside from relative and absolute lengths, you can also specify most lengths in terms of percentages. With HTML style sheets, percentages are almost always relative to the parent element. For example, if you're specifying a font size of 50 percent, what you're really saying is that you want the element's font size to be half as big as the parent element's font size.

---

background-position

You change the position of the background image by using the background-position property. The position is always relative to the top-left corner of the element in which you're positioning the image. That is, if you're positioning an image for the <UL> tag, the image's position will be relative to the top-left corner of the unordered list.

The background-position property looks like

```
background-position: x y
```

where *x* is the horizontal position, and *y* is the vertical position of the image. *x* and *y* can be a percentage, which is relative to the size of the element; a fixed amount such as `1in` (one inch); or one of the keywords that indicate a relative position as described in Table B.4. For example:

```
background-position: center 20
```

Table B.2 *background-position* Positions

Keyword	Description
top	Aligns the image with the top of the containing element; only useful when substituted for *y*.
left	Aligns the image with the left side of the containing element; only useful when substituted for *x*.
right	Aligns the image with the right side of the containing element; only useful when substituted for *y*.
bottom	Aligns the image with the bottom of the containing element; only useful when substituted for *y*.
center	Centers the image within the containing element; when substituted for *x*, the image is centered horizontally; when substituted for *y*, the image is centered vertically.

background-repeat

You can cause the user's browser to tile the background image so that it fills the entire area of the containing element. The `background-repeat` property can have four values, as described in Table B.3.

Table B.3 *background-repeat* Values

Value	Description
repeat	Repeats the image both vertically and horizontally
repeat-x	Repeats the image horizontally
repeat-y	Repeats the image vertically
no-repeat	Doesn't repeat the image

color

The `color` property determines the foreground color for the element. Thus, the browser displays the element's text using this color. You can set `color` to a named color or an RGB value. Named colors include those in the following list:

black	silver	gray	white
maroon	red	purple	fuchsia
green	lime	olive	yellow
navy	blue	teal	aqua

Box Properties

W3C's style sheet recommendation provides you the capability to define the borders, margins, and padding for elements on the Web page. You can wrap a border around a heading, for example, or change the margins of the `<P>` tag so that any occurrences of this tag are indented into the page. Here's an overview of the properties that you can use to change the boxes associated with an element:

Border
: You use the border properties to set the left, right, top, and bottom borders of an element. You can set the border's width, color, and style.

Margin
: You use the margin properties to set the left, right, top, and bottom margins of an element. With these properties, you only specify the size of the margin.

Padding
: You use the padding properties to specify how much space the browser displays between the border and the content of the element. With the padding properties, you only specify the size of the margin.

Figure B.1 shows you how the border, margin, and padding properties work with the `height` and `width` properties to form the boxes around the element. The following list describe these in more detail:

- The `height` and `width` properties determine the overall size of the element's containing box.
- The margin properties determine the element's margins within its containing box.
- The border properties determine the position of the border within the element's margins.
- The padding properties determine the amount of space between the element's border and the contents of the element itself.

You can group border properties in five different ways. You can specify the properties for a particular side of the element, using `border-top`, `border-right`, `border-bottom`, or `border-left`. You can also specify all sides of the border at one time by using `border`.

With any of these attributes, you specify the width, style, and color of the border, as in the following example:

```
border-top: thin dotted black
```

FIG. B.1

Four boxes are actually around each element.

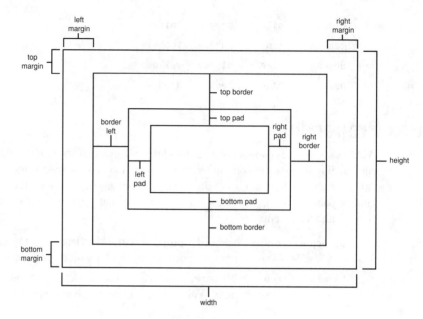

You can group the margin properties using `margin`. You specify the top, right, bottom, and left, like this:

```
margin: .5in 1in .5in 1in
```

You can also group the margin properties using `padding`. You specify the top, right, bottom, and left padding values, like this:

```
padding: .25in .25in .25in .25in
```

If you specify only one value, the browser uses that value for all sides. If you leave out one or more values, the browser takes the missing value from the opposite side. For example, if you leave off the last value (left), the browser sets the left padding to the value you specified for the right margin.

border-bottom-width

You set the width of the bottom border by using the `border-bottom-width` property. This doesn't affect the other sides of the border. You can assign any of the values described in Table B.4 to this property.

Table B.4   *border-bottom-width* Values

Value	Description
thin	Displays the border by using a thin line.
medium	Displays the border by using a medium line.

Value	Description
thick	Displays the border by using a thick line.
length	You can define the exact width of the border by using points (pt), inches (in), centimeters (cm), or pixels (px); (for example, 2in).

border-color

The border-color property sets the color of the element's border. You can use a named color, such as RED, or you can use an RGB value, such as #FF0000.

border-left-width

You set the width of the left border by using the border-left-width property. This doesn't affect the other sides of the border. You can assign any of the values described in Table B.6 to this property.

border-right-width

You set the width of the right border by using the border-right-width property. This doesn't affect the other sides of the border. You can assign any of the values described in Table B.6 to this property.

border-style

The border-style property determines the style of the border that the browser displays. You can specify from one to four values for this property:

One Value	All four borders are set to the style.
Two Values	The top and bottom borders are set to the style in the first value, and the left and right borders are set to the style in the second value.
Three Values	The top border is set to the style in the first value; the right and left borders are set to the style in the second value; and the bottom border is set to the style in the third value.
Four Values	The top border is set to the style in the first value; the right border is set to the second value; the bottom border is set to the third value; and the left border is set to the fourth value.

Table B.5 describes the values you can use for a border's style.

Table B.5 *border-style* **Values**

Value	Description
none	No border.
dotted	Dotted line drawn over the top of the element.

continues

Table B.5 Continued

Value	Description
dashed	Dashed line drawn over the top of the element.
solid	Solid line.
double	Double line drawn over the top of the element; the width of the two lines and the space between them equals the border-width value.
groove	3-D groove drawn in colors based upon color.
ridge	3-D ridge drawn in colors based upon color.
inset	3-D inset drawn in colors based upon color.
outset	3-D outset drawn in colors based upon color.

border-top-width

You set the width of the top border by using the border-top-width property. This doesn't affect the other sides of the border. You can assign any of the values described in Table B.7 to this property.

TROUBLESHOOTING

I've set the width of my border, but it still doesn't display. Setting the width of the border isn't enough. You also have to set the border style by using the border-style property because the default style for every border is none.

clear

The clear property determines whether the browser can display floating elements on the sides of an element. The property's value indicates the sides on which floating elements are not allowed. For example, clear: left means that the browser can't float elements on the left side of the element. Table B.6 describes the values you can assign to this property.

Table B.6 *clear* Values

Value	Description
none	Floating elements are allowed on all sides.
left	Floating elements are not allowed on the left.
right	Floating elements are not allowed on the right.
both	Floating elements are not allowed on either side.

float

The float property specifies that the element is floated to the left or right side, with the surrounding elements flowing around it. Table B.7 describes the values you can assign to this property.

Table B.7 *float* **Values**

Value	Description
none	Displays the element where it is
left	Move to the left and wrap text around it
right	Move to the right and wrap text around it

height

You set the total height of the element with the height property. You can set this property for text blocks or images. For example, you can use the height and width properties to create a special warning on the Web page that has a fixed size. Height is more useful with images, however. You can set this property to any length, a percentage value, or auto, which lets the browser determine the best size for the element.

margin-bottom

You set the bottom margin by using the margin-bottom property. You can specify any valid length, a percentage value (relative to the height and width) of the element, or auto, which lets the browser determine the best margins to use for the element. You can also use a negative margin size to create special effects such as hanging indents.

margin-left

You set the left margin by using the margin-left property. You can specify any valid length, a percentage value (relative to the height and width) of the element, or auto, which lets the browser determine the best margins to use for the element. You can also use a negative margin size to create special effects.

margin-right

You set the right margin by using the margin-right property. You can specify any valid length, a percentage value (relative to the height and width) of the element, or auto, which lets the browser determine the best margins to use for the element. You can also use a negative margin size to create special effects.

margin-top

You set the top margin by using the `margin-top` property. You can specify any valid length, a percentage value (relative to the `height` and `width`) of the element, or `auto`, which lets the browser determine the best margins to use for the element. You can also use a negative margin size to create special effects.

padding-bottom

The `padding-bottom` property specifies the amount of space to display between the element's bottom border and the element's contents. You can set this property to a valid length or a percentage value (relative to the `height` and `width`) of the element.

padding-left

The `padding-left` property specifies the amount of space to display between the element's left border and the element's contents. You can set this property to a valid length or a percentage value (relative to the `height` and `width`) of the element.

padding-right

The `padding-right` property specifies the amount of space to display between the element's right border and the element's contents. You can set this property to a valid length or a percentage value (relative to the `height` and `width`) of the element.

padding-top

The `padding-top` property specifies the amount of space to display between the element's top border and the element's contents. You can set this property to a valid length or a percentage value (relative to the `height` and `width`) of the element.

width

You set the total width of the element with the `width` property. You can set this property for text blocks or images. You can set this property to any length, a percentage value, or `auto`, which lets the browser determine the best size for the element.

Classification Properties

You use the list properties to specify how lists display in the browser window. You can change the position of the marker (`list-style-position`) and the style or image used for the marker (`list-style-type` and `list-style-image`). The sections that follow describe each property in more detail. Enjoy.

The list properties are inherited, so if you define a property for the `<UL>` tag, all its enclosed `<LI>` tags inherit those properties. These tags are only meaningful for HTML list tags.

You can group the list properties using `list-style`. You specify the marker type, marker image, and position, like this:

```
list-style: square URL(http://www.myserver.com/images/marker.gif) inside
```

list-style-image

You use the `list-style-image` property to specify an image that the browser will display as the marker for a list item. The property's only value is the URL, using the `URL(address)` format, of the image to use as the marker, like this:

```
list-style-image: url(http://www.myserver.com/images/marker.gif)
```

To affect all the items within a list, set this property for the list container, such as `<UL>` as opposed to the list item `<LI>`. You can override an individual list item, however, by setting this property in a single occurrence of the `<LI>` tag.

list-style-position

The `list-style-position` property determines the relative position of the marker. Table B.8 describes the possible values you can assign to this property.

Table B.8 *list-style-position* **Values**

Value	Description
Inside	The list item's text wraps to the next line underneath the marker.
Outside	The list item's text wraps to the next line underneath the start of the text on the previous line (hanging indent).

list-style-type

You use the `list-style-type` property to specify the type of marker the browser will display. Use this instead of a marker image. Table B.9 describes each of the possible values you can assign to this property.

Table B.9 *list-style-type* **Values**

Value	Description
disc	Disc
circle	Circle
square	Square
decimal	Numbered (1, 2, 3, ...)
lower-roman	Lowercase roman numerals (i, ii, iii, ...)

continues

App

B

Table B.9   Continued

Value	Description
upper-roman	Uppercase roman numerals (I, II, III, …)
lower-alpha	Lowercase alphabet (a, b, c, …)
upper-alpha	Uppercase alphabet (A, B, C, …)
none	No markers

white-space

The white-space property defines how the browser handles white space within the element. You can leave things alone and let the browser collapse all the white space, or you can specify that the browser treat white space as if you're within a <PRE> container. Table B.10 shows you the values you can assign to this property.

Table B.10   *white-space* Values

Value	Description
normal	White space is collapsed.
pre	Handle white space like the <PRE> tag.
nowrap	Wrapping is only permitted with .

Font Properties

You can group the font properties using font. You specify the weight, style, size, and family, as in the following example:

```
font: bold normal 12pt times, serif
```

font-family

font-family is a prioritized list of typefaces for the element. You can specify a single typeface or a list of alternatives, separated by commas, as in the following example:

```
font-family: Courier, Times, Serif
```

You can use a font name you expect to be on the user's computer, such as Courier or Helvetica, or you can use a generic font name. Table B.11 shows the generic font names and provides an example of a font that looks similar.

Table B.11 Generic Fonts

Name	Similar to:
serif	Times New Roman
sans-serif	Arial
cursive	Script
fantasy	Comic
monospace	Courier New

App

B

In case the user doesn't have the font you've requested, always use a generic font name as the last item in the list. In the previous example, serif is the last font in the list. If the user doesn't have courier or times, the browser will use the generic font instead.

If you're using a font name that has multiple words, enclose the font name in quotes, as in the following example:

```
font-family: "Courier New", serif
```

font-size

font-size determines the size of the text in points (pt), inches (in), centimeters (cm), or pixels (px). You can also use a percentage, which is relative to the parent element's font size. You can also use one of the values shown in Table B.12.

Table B.12 *font-size* Values

Value	Description
xx-small	50 percent smaller than the x-small font
x-small	50 percent smaller than the small font
small	50 percent smaller than the medium font
medium	A medium-sized font, probably 10 points
large	50 percent larger than the medium font
x-large	50 percent larger than the large font
xx-large	50 percent larger than the x-large font
larger	50 percent larger than the parent element's font
smaller	50 percent smaller than the parent element's font

N O T E The W3C recommendation that browser programs use a scaling factor of 50 percent is only a recommendation. Vendors are free to use any scaling factor that they want. Thus, the values in Table B.12 are only guidelines.

font-style

You can change the style of the font by using the `font-style` property. Table B.13 describes the possible values.

Table B.13 *font-style* **Values**

Value	Description
normal	Selects a normal face
oblique	Selects an oblique face
italic	Selects an italic face

font-variant

You use the `font-variant` property to display text in small caps. Setting this property to `normal` causes the browser to display the text normally. Setting this property to `small-caps` causes the browser to display the text using small caps.

font-weight

`font-weight` determines the thickness of the font. You can assign `normal`, `bold`, `bolder`, or `lighter` to this property. You can also use the series of numbers from 100, 200, ... 900 to this property, with each successive number representing a weight that is thicker than the previous number. For example, `font-weight: 700` sets a thicker font weight than does `font-weight: 400`.

 TIP A font weight of 400 is roughly equivalent to a normal font weight.

Text Properties

Text properties give you complete control over how the browser displays an element's text. You can change its color, size, font, spacing, and so on. The sections that follow describe each text property you can set.

letter-spacing

`letter-spacing` determines the spacing between each letter in a line of text. You can set this property to `normal` and let the browser worry about it, or you can set this property to any valid length, such as `1px`.

line-height

You use the `line-height` property to set the leading for an element. An element's leading is the distance between the baselines of two text lines. You can use any valid length or a percentage (which is relative to the parent element's line-height property), or you can set this property to normal. Note that the spacing is added before each line, not after.

> **CAUTION**
> This setting doesn't work well on text lines that use multiple font sizes on the same line of text.

text-align

text-align defines how text is aligned in an element. You can set this property to any of the values shown in Table B.14.

App
B

Table B.14 *text-align* **Values**

Value	Description
left	Text is left justified.
right	Text is right justified.
center	Text is centered within the element.
justify	Text is left and right justified.

text-decoration

You can add special decorations, such as underlining, to an element by using the text-decoration property. Table B.15 describes the values you can assign to this property. You can combine these values, too.

Table B.15 *text-decoration* **Values**

Value	Description
none	No decorations
underline	Underlined text
overline	Text with a line over it
line-through	Strikethrough
blink	Blinking text

text-indent

You use the text-indent property to indent the first line of an element's text. You can set this property to any valid length. For example, here's how to indent the <P> tag's text to the right by one inch:

```
P {text-indent: 1in}
```

You can create a hanging indent by setting a tag's style text-indent to a negative value and margin-left to a positive value.

text-transform

text-transform specifies that the text should be changed according to the values in Table B.16.

Table B.16 *text-transform* **Values**

Value	Description
capitalize	Capitalizes first letter of each word
uppercase	Uppercases all letters in the element
lowercase	Lowercases all letters in the element
none	No transformation

vertical-align

You use the vertical-align property to change the vertical position of the element's text within the element itself. You can use one of the keywords described in Table B.17.

Table B.17 *vertical-align* **Values**

Value	Description
baseline	Aligns the baseline of the element with the baseline of the parent
middle	Aligns the middle of the element with the middle of the parent
sub	Subscripts the element
super	Superscripts the element
text-top	Aligns the top of the element with the top of the parent element's text
text-bottom	Aligns the bottom of the element with the bottom of the parent element's text
top	Aligns the top of the element with the tallest element on the line
bottom	Aligns the bottom of the element with the lowest element on the line

word-spacing

word-spacing determines the spacing between each word in a line of text. You can set this property to normal and let the browser worry about it, or you can set this property to any valid length, such as 1px.

Internet Explorer 4.0, Netscape Communicator, and CSS1

Table B.18 describes the CSS1 properties that Internet Explorer 4.0 and Netscape Communicator support as of this writing. The first column is the name of the property. You see a check mark in the second column beside features that Internet Explorer 4.0 supports and an X beside features that it doesn't support. The third column is for Netscape Communicator.

Table B.18   CSS1 Property Support

Property	IE 4.0	NC
Background Properties		
background	✓	✓
background-attachment	X	✓
background-color	✓	✓
background-image	✓	✓
background-position	X	X
background-repeat	X	✓
color	✓	✓
Box Properties		
backgr	✓	✓
border	X	✓
border-color	X	✓
border-width	X	✓
border-bottom	X	X
border-bottom-width	X	✓
border-left	X	X
border-left-width	X	✓
border-right	X	X
border-right-width	X	✓
border-style	X	✓
border-top	X	X
border-top-width	X	✓
clear	X	✓

continues

App

B

Table B.18   Continued

Property	IE 4.0	NC
Box Properties		
float	X	✓
height	✓	✓
margin	✓	✓
margin-bottom	X	✓
margin-left	✓	✓
margin-right	✓	✓
margin-top	X	✓
padding	X	✓
padding-bottom	X	✓
padding-left	X	X
padding-right	X	✓
padding-top	X	✓
width	✓	✓
Classification Properties		
list-style-image	X	✓
list-style-position	X	✓
list-style-type	X	✓
white-space	X	✓
Font Properties		
font	✓	✓
font-family	✓	✓
font-size	✓	✓
font-style	✓	✓
font-variant	✓	X
font-weight	✓	✓

Property	IE 4.0	NC
Text Properties		
letter-spacing	✓	X
line-height	✓	✓
text-align	✓	✓
text-decoration	✓	✓
text-indent	✓	✓
text-transform	✓	✓
vertical-align	✓	X
word-spacing	X	X

App

B

JavaScript Keyword Reference

by Rick Darnell

In this chapter

Key Differences Between VB and VBScript

You didn't run out to the computer store and buy a copy of VBScript. You didn't install a VBScript disk on your computer, either. All you did was install the Internet Explorer browser, which supports VBScript, on your computer—just like millions of other folks. Everyone of them has the VBScript engine on their computer, and everyone of them has the ability to create Web pages with VBScript.

So where's the integrated development environment that you're used to using in Visual Basic? Keep looking, because there isn't one. All you have is your favorite text editor, the ActiveX Control Pad, and a Web browser. That in itself is the single largest difference between Visual Basic and VBScript. It leads to some specific differences, too. Here's what they are:

- Debugging   VBScript doesn't have a debugger like Visual Basic. You'll resort to using lots of message boxes, instead.

- Event-handlers   You don't have an editor in which you select an object and event to edit an event-procedure. You have to name event-procedures in your scripts so that the scripting engine can find the appropriate handler when an object fires an event.

- Forms   VBScript doesn't have a forms editor. It doesn't need one, because you can't display forms anyway. You put forms and controls on the Web page, instead. You can use the ActiveX Control pad to insert all those nasty `<OBJECT>` tags in your Web page, however.

You don't compile a VBScript program into an EXE file like you do with a Visual Basic program. You distribute your scripts as plain, old text embedded in HTML files. Everyone and his uncle can read your scripts. The script engine interprets this text into intermediate code when it loads the Web page. It also creates a symbol table so that it can quickly look up things such as event-procedures and variable names. The scripting engine uses the ActiveX Scripting technology to interact with the browser.

> **N O T E**   You'll find a plethora of nit-picky differences between Visual Basic and VBScript, too. You have to use the `value` property to query an objects value, for example. Thus, instead of reading a text box's value using `form.text`, you have to read it using `form.text.value`. These subtle differences are too numerous to document in this appendix. Go to Microsoft's Web site (**www.microsoft.com**) and their knowledge base for further explanation of these differences. ■

Another significant difference between Visual Basic and VBScript is the keywords that Microsoft omitted from VBScript. You'll learn more about the keywords included in VBScript in the next section. You'll learn about the keywords that Microsoft omitted from VBScript in "Visual Basic Keywords Omitted from VBScript," later in this appendix.

Visual Basic Keywords Included in VBScript

VBScript includes all the keywords and features that you need to activate a Web page. You can't read or write files, as you'll learn later in this appendix, but you can handle any event that an object fires. You can also handle just about any type of data that you'll find on a Web page and manipulate the Web page in anyway you want.

Table C.1 describes each keyword or feature available in VBScript. I've divided this table into broad categories, with each entry under a category describing a single feature. I've used the same categories that Microsoft uses so that you can keep this information straight as you bounce back and forth between Microsoft's Web site and this book. If you don't find a feature that you expect to see, check out Table C.2 to see if that feature is in the list of Visual Basic features omitted from VBScript.

You can find more information about VBScript's features at Microsoft's VBScript Web site: **http://www.microsoft.com/vbscript**.

Table C.1   VBScript Keywords

Keyword/Feature	Description
Array handling	
IsArray	Returns True if a variable is an array
Erase	Reinitilizes a fixed-size array
LBound	Returns the lower bound of an array
UBound	Returns the upper bound of an array
Assignments	
=	Assigns a value to a variable
Let	Assigns a value to a variable
Set	Assigns an object to a variable
Comments	
'	Includes inline comments in your script
Rem	Includes comments in your script
Constants/Literals	
Empty	Indicates an uninitialized variable
Nothing	Disassociates a variable with an object
Null	Indicates a variable with no data
True	Boolean True
False	Boolean False

continues

Table C.1 Continued

Keyword/Feature	Description
Control flow	
Do...Loop	Repeats a block of statements
For...Next	Repeats a block of statements
For Each...Next	Repeats a block of statements
If...Then...Else	Conditionally executes statements
Select Case	Conditionally executes statements
While...Wend	Repeats a block of statements
Conversions	
Abs	Returns absolute value of a number
Asc	Returns the ASCII code of a character
AscB	Returns the ASCII code of a character
AscW	Returns the ASCII code of a character
Chr	Returns a character from an ASCII code
ChrB	Returns a character from an ASCII code
ChrW	Returns a character from an ASCII code
CBool	Converts a variant to a boolean
CByte	Converts a variant to a byte
CDate	Converts a variant to a date
CDbl	Converts a variant to a double
Cint	Converts a variant to an integer
CLng	Converts a variant to a long
CSng	Converts a variant to a single
CStr	Converts a variant to a string
DateSerial	Converts a variant to a date
DateValue	Converts a variant to a date
Hex	Converts a variant to a hex string
Oct	Converts a variant to an octal string
Fix	Converts a variant to a fixed string
Int	Converts a variant to an integer string

Keyword/Feature	Description
Conversions	
Sgn	Converts a variant to a single string
TimeSerial	Converts a variant to a time
TimeValue	Converts a variant to a time
Dates/Times	
Date	Returns the current date
Time	Returns the current time
DateSerial	Returns a date from its parts
DateValue	Returns a date from its value
Day	Returns day from a date
Month	Returns month from a date
Weekday	Returns weekday from a date
Year	Returns year from a date
Hour	Returns hour from a time
Minute	Returns minute from a time
Second	Returns seconds from a time
Now	Returns current date and time
TimeSerial	Returns a time from its parts
TimeValue	Returns a time from its value
Declarations	
Dim	Declares a variable
Private	Declares script-level private variable
Public	Declares public-level public variable
ReDim	Reallocates an array
Function	Declares a function
Sub	Declares a subprocedure
Error Handling	
On Error	Enables error handling
Err	Contains information about last error

App

C

continues

Table C.1   Continued

Keyword/Feature	Description
Input/Output	
InputBox	Prompts the user for input
MsgBox	Displays a message to the user
Math	
Atn	Returns the Arctangent of a number
Cos	Returns the cosine of a number
Sin	Returns the sine of a number
Tan	Returns the tangent of a number
Exp	Returns the exponent of a number
Log	Returns the logarithm of a number
Sqr	Returns the square root of a number
Randomize	Reseeds the randomizer
Rnd	Returns a random number
Operators	
+	Addition
–	Subtraction
^	Exponentiation
Mod	Modulus arithmetic
*	Multiplication
/	Division
\	Integer Division
–	Negation
&	String concatenation
=	Equality
<>	Inequality
<	Less Than
<=	Less Than or Equal To
>	Greater Than
>=	Greater Than or Equal To

Keyword/Feature	Description
Operators	
Is	Compares expressions
And	Compares expressions
Or	Compares expressions
Xor	Compares expressions
Eqv	Compares expressions
Imp	Compares expressions
Objects	
CreateObject	Creates reference to an OLE object
IsObject	Returns True if object is valid
Options	
Option Explicit	Forces explicit variable declaration
Procedures	
Call	Invokes a subprocedure
Function	Declares a function
Sub	Declares a subprocedure
Strings	
Instr	Returns index of a string in another
InStrB	Returns index of a string in another
Len	Returns the length of a string
LenB	Returns the length of a string
Lcase	Converts a string to lowercase
Ucase	Converts a string to uppercase
Left	Returns the left portion of a string
LeftB	Returns the left portion of a string
Mid	Returns the mid portion of a string
MidB	Returns the mid portion of a string
Right	Returns the right portion of a string
RightB	Returns the right portion of a string
Space	Pads a string with spaces

App
C

continues

Table C.1   Continued

Keyword/Feature	Description
Strings	
StrComp	Compares two strings
String	Pads a string with a character
Ltrim	Removes leading spaces from a string
Rtrim	Removes trailing spaces from a string
Trim	Removes leading and trailing spaces
Variants	
IsArray	Returns True if variable is an array
IsDate	Returns True if variable is a date
IsEmpty	Returns True if variable is empty
IsNull	Returns True if variable is null.
IsNumeric	Returns True if variable is a number
IsObject	Returns True if variable is an object
VarType	Indicates a variable's type

Visual Basic Keywords Omitted from VBScript

VBScript leaves out a bunch of Visual Basic keywords such as DoEvents, Print, and Shell. You can't read or write files, either, and you can't do much graphical programming. This won't stop you from creating great Web pages with VBScript, though, because VBScript provides every feature you need to do just about anything you want on the Web page. For example, you can dynamically change the contents of the Web page itself and you can interact with every object on the Web page.

Don't look at the list of omitted keywords and features yet. You need to understand why Microsoft didn't include them so that you'll understand why each feature is on this list. Take a look:

■ Portability   Microsoft intends to make VBScript available on a variety of platforms including Windows, Mac, UNIX, and so on. They've wisely removed keywords and features that make VBScript less portable to these platforms.

■ Performance   You've heard it before: speed or features—pick one. Microsoft removed many nonessential features from VBScript so scripts load and run faster.

■ Safety   You should be concerned with security on the Internet. You don't want to open a Web page and discover that it contains a script which crashes your drive, do you?

Microsoft removed any Visual Basic feature that might cause a security problem with scripts such as file I/O. You can still get access to these features, however, if you create an ActiveX object which you control with VBScript.

Table C.1 describes each keyword or feature available in Visual Basic but omitted from VBScript. I've divided this table into broad categories, with each entry under a category describing a single feature. I've used Microsoft's categories so that you can keep the list on Microsoft's Web site in sync with this list.

N O T E The Internet Explorer Script Error dialog box tells you that it found a statement in your script which couldn't interpret. I'm sure that you've seen error messages such as "Expected while or until" or nested comments that just don't make any sense. When VBScript encounters a keyword it doesn't recognize, it spews out all sorts of garbage like the previous example. It usually points to the offending keyword, however, by placing a caret (^) directly underneath it. The next time you get one of these unexplained errors, look up the keyword in Table C.2 to see if Microsoft omitted it from VBScript. ▓

App

C

Table C.2   Visual Basic Keywords Not in VBScript

Keyword/Feature	Description
Array Handling	
Option Base	Declares default lower bound
Arrays with lower bound <> 0	All arrays must have 0 lower bound
Clipboard	
Clipboard object	Provides access to the clipboard
Clear	Clears the contents of the clipboard
GetFormat	Determines format of clipboard object
GetData	Returns data from the clipboard
SetData	Stores data in the clipboard
GetText	Returns text from the clipboard
SetText	Stores text in the clipboard
Collection	
Add	Adds an item to a collection
Count	Returns number of items in collection
Item	Returns an item from a collection

continues

Table C.2   Continued

Keyword/Feature	Description
Collection	
Remove	Removes an item from a collection
Access collections using ! character	Accesses a collection with !
Conditional Compilation	
#Const	Defines a compiler constant
#If...Then...#Else	Conditional compilation
Constants/Literals	
Const	Defines a constant
All intrinsic	Predefined constants such as vbOK constants
Exponent-based	Real numbers using exponents real number
Trailing data type characters	Defines data types implicitly
Control Flow	
DoEvents	Yields execution to Windows
GoSub...Return	Branches to a label in a procedure
GoTo	Goes to a label in a procedure
On Error GoTo	Goes to a label on an error
On...GoSub	Branches to a label on an index
On...GoTo	Goes to a label on an index
Line numbers	Line numbers
Line labels	Labels define GoTo/GoSub targets
With...End With	Provides easy access to an object
Conversion	
Chr$	Returns a character from an ASCII code
Hex$	Returns string hex from a number
Oct$	Returns string octal from a number
Ccur	Converts expression to currency

Keyword/Feature	Description
Conversion	
Cvar	Converts expression to a variant
CVDate	Converts an expression to a date
Format	Formats a string
Format$	Formats a string
Str	Returns a string form of a number
Str$	Returns a string form of a number
Val	Returns a number from a string
Data Types	
All intrinsic data types except variant	Data types such as Date
Type...End Type	Defines user-defined data type
Date/Time	
Date statement	Returns the current date
Time statement	Returns the current time
Date$	Returns the current date
Time$	Returns the current time
Timer	Returns seconds elapsed since midnight
DDE	
LinkExecute	Sends command during DDE conversation
LinkPoke	Sends data during a DDE conversation
LinkRequest	Receives data during DDE conversation
LinkSend	Sends data during a DDE conversation
Debugging	
Debug.Print	Prints to the debugging window
End	Shuts down the application
Stop	Stops the application
Declaration	
Declare	Declares a DLL
Property Get	Defines a user-defined class

App
C

continues

Table C.2   Continued

Keyword/Feature	Description
Declaration	
Property Let	Defines a user-defined class
Property Set	Defines a user-defined class
Public	Declares a public variable
Private	Declares a private variable
ParamArray	Accepts a variable number of arguments
Optional	Specifies an optional argument
New	Creates a new object
Error Handling	
Erl	Returns the line number of an error
Error	Returns an error message
Error$	Returns an error message
On Error...Resume	Enables error handling
Resume	Resumes after an error
Resume Next	Resumes after an error
File Input/Output	
All	Opens, reads, writes, and closes files
Financial	
All financial	Financial function such as Rate functions.
Graphics	
Cls	Clears the screen
Circle	Draws a circle
Line	Draws a line
Point	Draws a point
Pset	Changes a point's color
Scale	Defines the coordinate system
Print	Prints to a file
Spc	Position output using Print

Keyword/Feature	Description
Graphics	
Tab	Inserts a tab character
TextHeight	Returns height of a text string
TextWidth	Returns width of a text string
LoadPicture	Loads a picture from disk
SavePicture	Saves a picture to disk
QBColor	Returns an RGB color code
RGB	Combines RGB color codes
Manipulating Objects	
Arrange	Arranges windows
Zorder	Changes z-order of windows
SetFocus	Sets focus to a window
InputBox$	Prompts the user for a string
Drag	Begins a drag-and-drop operation
Hide	Hides a form
Show	Shows a form
Load	Loads a form
Unload	Unloads a form
Move	Moves a form
PrintForm	Prints a form
Refresh	Repaints a form
AddItem	Adds item to list box
RemoveItem	Removes item from a list box
Miscellaneous	
Environ	Returns the user's environment
Environ$	Returns the user's environment
SendKeys	Sends keystrokes to a window
Command	Returns the command line parameters
Command$	Returns the command line parameters
AppActivate	Activates an application's window

App

C

continues

Table C.2 Continued

Keyword/Feature	Description
Miscellaneous	
Shell	Launches another program
Beep	Beeps the speaker
Object Manipulation	
GetObject	Returns an OLE object from a file
TypeOf	Returns the type of an object
Operators	
Like	Compares to strings
Options	
def *type*	Sets default data type for variables
Option Base	Sets default lower bound for arrays
Option Compare	Defines default comparison method
Option Private	Defines default scope module
Printing	
TextHeight	Returns height of a text string
TextWidth	Returns width of a text string
EndDoc	Terminates a print operation
NewPage	Ejects the current page
PrintForm	Prints a form
Strings	
All fixed-length	Strings with a fixed length
LCase$	Converts a string to lowercase
UCase$	Converts a string to uppercase
Lset	Left-aligns a string
Rset	Right-aligns a string
Space$	Pads a string with spaces
String$	Pads a string with a character
Format	Formats a string
Format$	Formats a string

Keyword/Feature	Description
Strings	
Left$	Returns left portion of a string
Mid$	Returns middle portion of a string
Right$	Returns right portion of a string
Mid Statement	Replaces a portion of a string
Trim$	Removes leading and trailing spaces
LTrim$	Removes leading spaces from a string
RTrim$	Removes trailing spaces from a string
StrConv	Performs various conversions
Using Classes	
TypeName	Defines a user-defined class
Optional Arguments	
IsMissing	Indicates missing optional argument

VBScript Keyword Reference

by Rick Darnell

In this chapter

Terms

While not necessarily JavaScript objects or keywords, the following items can help in your understanding of JavaScript and how it works. These are the general terms that are used in most discussions about JavaScript and its implementation.

Cookie   A special object containing state/status information about the client that can be accessed by the server. Included in that `state` object is a description of the range of URLs for which that state is valid. Future HTTP requests from the client falling within a range of URLs described within the `state` object will include transmission of the current value of the `state` object from the client back to the server.

This simple form of data storage allows the server to provide personalized service to the client. Online merchants can store information about items currently in an electronic shopping basket, services can post registration information and automate functions such as typing a user ID, and user preferences can be saved on the client and retrieved by the server when the site is contacted. For limited-use information, such as shopping services, it is also possible to set a time limit on the life of the cookie information.

CGI scripts are typically used to set and retrieve cookie values. To generate the cookie requires sending an HTTP header in the following format:

```
Set-Cookie: NAME=Value; [EXPIRES=date;] [PATH=pathname;] [DOMAIN=domainname;]
[SECURE]
```

When a request for cookie information is made, the list of cookie information is searched for all URLs which match the current URL. Any matches are returned in this format:

```
cookie: NAME1=string1; NAME2=string2; ...
```

Cookie was an arbitrarily assigned name. For more information about the cookie and its function, see **http://home.netscape.com/newsref/std/cookie_spec.html**.

Event Handler   Attributes of HTML tags embedded in documents. The attribute assigns a JavaScript command or function to execute when the event happens.

Function   A user-defined or built-in set of statements that perform a task. It can also return a value when used with the `return` statement.

Hierarchy   Navigator objects exist in a set relation to each other that reflects the structure of an HTML page. This is referred to as *instance hierarchy* because it only works with specific instances of objects, rather than general classes.

The `window` object is the parent of all other Navigator objects. Underneath `window`, `location`, `history`, and `document` all share precedence. `Document` includes forms, links, and anchors.

Each object is a descendant of the higher object. A form called `orderForm` is an object, but is also a property of `document`. As such, it is referred to as `document.orderForm`.

Java   An object-oriented, platform-independent programming language developed by Sun Microsystems and used to add additional functionality to Web pages. Programming in Java requires a Java Development Kit with compiler and core classes.

Although Java started out as a language intended for writing Web applets, more and more stand-alone Java applications are being created.

JavaScript   A scripting language developed by Netscape for HTML documents. Scripts are performed after specific user-triggered events. Creating JavaScript Web documents requires a text editor and compatible browser.

Literal   An absolute value not assigned to a variable. Examples include `1`, `3.1415927`, `"Bob"`, `true`.

Method   A function assigned to an object. For example, `bigString.toUpperCase()` returns an uppercase version of the string contained in `bigString`.

Object   A construct with properties that are JavaScript variables or other objects. Functions associated with an object are known as the *object's methods.* You access the properties of an object with a simple notation:

`objectName.propertyName`

Both object and property names are case sensitive.

Operator   Performs a function on one or more operands or variables. Operators are divided into two classes: binary and unary. Binary operators need two operands, and unary operands can operate on a single operand.

For example, addition is a binary operand:

`sum = 1 + 1`

Unary operands are often used to update counters. The following example increases the variable by 1:

`counter++`

Property   Used to describe an object. A property is defined by assigning it a value. There are several properties in JavaScript that contain *constants:* values that never change.

Script   One or more JavaScript commands enclosed with a `<script>` tag.

Objects

JavaScript is an object-oriented language, so at its heart are a predefined set of objects which relate to the various components of an HTML page and their relation to each other. To view or manipulate the state of an object requires the use of properties and methods, which are also covered in this appendix. If an object is also used as a property of another object, that relationship is listed following the definition. Related properties, methods, and event handlers for each object are listed following the definition.

anchors   A piece of text that can be the target of a hypertext link. This is a read-only object which is set in HTML with `<A>` tags. To determine how many anchors are included in a document, use the `length` property.

App
D

```
document.anchors.length
```

Unless the anchor name is an integer, the value of `document.anchor[index]` will return `null`.

Property of `document`. See `link` OBJECT; see `anchor` METHOD.

button   An object that is a form element and must be defined within a `<form>` tag and can be used to perform an action.

Property of `form`. See OBJECTS `reset` and `submit`; see PROPERTIES `name` and `value`; see `click` METHOD; see `onClick` EVENT HANDLER.

checkbox   A form element that the user sets to `on` or `off` by clicking and that must be defined in a `<form>` tag. Using the `checkbox` object, you can see if the box is checked and review the name and value.

Property of `form`. See `radio` OBJECT; see PROPERTIES `checked`, `defaultChecked`, `name`, `value`; see `click` METHOD; see `onClick` EVENT HANDLER.

Date   Replaces a normal date type. Although it does not have any properties, it is equipped with a wide range of methods. In its current release, `Date` does not work with dates prior to 1/1/70.

Methods for getting and setting time and date information are divided into four classes: `set`, `get`, `to`, and `parse`/`UTC`.

Except for the date, all numerical representation of date components begin with zero. This should not present a problem except with months, which are represented by zero (January) through 11 (December).

The standard date syntax is `"Thu, 11 Jan 1996 06:20:00 GMT"`. US time zone abbreviations are also understood; but for universal use, specify the time zone offset. For example, `"Thu, 11 Jan 1996 06:20:00 GMT+0530"` is a place five hours and 30 minutes west of the Greenwich meridian.

See METHODS `getDate`, `getDay`, `getHours`, `getMinutes`, `getMonth`, `getSeconds`, `getTime`, `getTimezoneOffset`, `getYear`, `parse`, `setDate`, `setHours`, `setMinutes`, `setMonth`, `setSeconds`, `setTime`, `setYear`, `toGMTString`, `toLocaleString`, `toString`.

document   An object created by Navigator when a page is loaded, containing information on the current document, such as title, background color, and forms. These properties are defined within `<body>` tags. It also provides methods for displaying HTML text to the user.

You can reference the anchors, forms, and links of a document by using the `anchors`, `forms`, and `links` arrays of the `document` object. These arrays contain an entry for each `anchor`, `form`, or `link` in a document.

Property of `window`. See `frame` OBJECT; see PROPERTIES `alinkColor`, `anchors`, `bgColor`, `cookie`, `fgColor`, `forms`, `lastModified`, `linkColor`, `links`, `location`, `referrer`, `title`, vlinkColor; see METHODS `clear`, `close`, `open`, `write`, `writeln`; see `onLoad` and `onUnload` EVENT HANDLERS.

elements An array of `form` elements in source order, including buttons, check boxes, radio buttons, text and text area objects. The elements can be referred to by their index:

```
formName.elements[index]
```

Elements can also be referenced by the element name. For example, a password element called newPassword is the second form element on an HTML page. It's value is accessed in three ways:

```
formName.elements[1].value
formName.elements["newPassword"].value
formName.newPassword.value
```

Values can not be set or changed using the read-only `elements` array.

Property of `form`. See `length` PROPERTY.

form A property of the `document` object. Each form in a document is a separate and distinct object that can be referenced using the `form` object. The `form` object is an array created as forms are defined through HTML tags. If the first `form` in a document is named `orderForm`, then it could be referenced as `document.orderForm` or `document.forms[0]`.

Property of `document`. See hidden OBJECT; see PROPERTIES `action`, `elements`, `encoding`, `forms`, `method`, `name`, `target`; see `submit` METHOD; see `onSubmit` EVENT HANDLER.

frame A window that contains HTML subdocuments that are independently, although not necessarily, scrollable. `Frames` can point to different URLs and be targeted by other frames—all in the same window. Each `frame` is a `window` object defined using the `<frameset>` tag to define the layout that makes up the page. The page is defined from a parent HTML document. All subdocuments are children of the parent.

If a `frame` contains definitions for `SRC` and `NAME` attributes, then the `frame` can be identified from a sibling by using the `parent` object as `parent.frameName` or `parent.frames[index]`.

Property of `window`. See `document` and `window` OBJECTS; see PROPERTIES `defaultStatus`, `frames`, `parent`, `self`, `status`, `top`, `window`; see METHODS `setTimeout` and `clearTimeout`.

hidden A text object suppressed from appearing on an HTML form. `Hidden` objects can be used in addition to `cookies` to pass name/value pairs for client/server communication.

Property of `form`. See PROPERTIES `cookie`, `defaultValue`, `name`, `value`.

history This object is derived from the Go menu and contains URL link information for previously visited pages.

Property of `document`. See `location` OBJECT; see `length` PROPERTY; see METHODS `back`, `forward`, `go`.

link   A `location` object. In addition to providing information about existing hypertext links, the `link` object can also be used to define new links.

Property of `document`. See `anchor` OBJECT; see PROPERTIES `hash`, `host`, `hostname`, `href`, `length`, `pathname`, `port`, `protocol`, `search`, `target`; see `link` METHOD; see `onClick` and `onMouseOver` EVENT HANDLERS.

location   Contains complete URL information for the current document, while each property of `location` contains a different portion of the URL.

Property of `document`. See `history` OBJECT; see PROPERTIES `hash`, `host`, `hostname`, `href`, `location`, `pathname`, `port`, `protocol`, `search`, `target`.

Math   Includes properties for mathematical constants and methods for functions. For example, to access the value of pi in an equation, use:

`Math.PI`

Standard trigonometric, logarithmic, and exponential functions are also included. All arguments in trigonometric functions use radians.

See PROPERTIES `E`, `LN10`, `LN2`, `PI`, `SQRT1_2`, `SQRT2`; see METHODS `abs`, `acos`, `asin`, `atan`, `ceil`, `cos`, `exp`, `floor`, `log`, `max`, `min`, `pow`, `random`, `round`, `sin`, `sqrt`, `tan`.

navigator   Contains information on the current version of Navigator used by the client.

See OBJECTS `link` and `anchors`; see PROPERTIES `appName`, `appCodeName`, `appVersion`, `userAgent`.

option   Objects created within HTML `<form>` tags and represent option buttons. A set of option buttons enables the user to select one item from a list. When it is created, it takes the form of `document.formName.radioName[index]`, where the index is a number representing each button beginning with zero.

Property of `form`. See OBJECTS `checkbox`, `select`; see PROPERTIES `checked`, `defaultChecked`, `index`, `length`, `name`, `value`; see `click` METHOD; see `onClick` EVENT HANDLER.

password   Created by HTML password text fields, and are masked when entered by the user. It must be defined with an HTML `<form>` tag.

Property of `form`. See `text` OBJECT; see PROPERTIES `defaultValue`, `name`, `value`; see METHODS `focus`, `blur`, `select`.

reset   Correlates with an HTML reset button, which resets all `form` objects to their default values. A reset object must be created within a `<form>` tag.

Property of `form`. See OBJECTS `button` and `submit`; see PROPERTIES `name` and `value`; see `click` METHOD; see `onClick` EVENT HANDLER.

select   A selection list or scrolling list on an HTML form. A selection list enables the user to choose one item from a list, while a scrolling list enables the choice of one or more items from a list.

Property of form. See radio OBJECT; see PROPERTIES length, name, options, selectedIndex; see METHODS blur and focus; see EVENT HANDLERS onBlur, onChange, onFocus.

For the options PROPERTY of select, see defaultSelected, index, selected, text, value.

string   A series of characters defined by double or single quotes. For example:

```
myDog = "Brittany Spaniel"
```

returns a string object called myDog with the value "Brittany Spaniel". Quotation marks are not a part of the string's value—they are only used to delimit the string. The object's value is manipulated using methods that return a variation on the string, for example myDog.toUpperCase() returns "BRITTANY SPANIEL". It also includes methods that return HTML versions of the string, such as bold and italics.

See text and text area OBJECTS; see length PROPERTY; see METHODS anchor, big, blink, bold, charAt, fixed, fontcolor, fontsize, indexOf, italics, lastIndexOf, link, small, strike, sub, substring, sup, toLowerCase, toUpperCase.

submit   Causes the form to be submitted to the program specified by the action property. It is created within an HTML <form> tag. It always loads a new page, which may be the same as the current page if an action isn't specified.

Property of form. See OBJECTS button and reset; see PROPERTIES name and value; see METHOD click; see EVENT HANDLER onClick.

text   A one-line input field on an HTML form that accepts characters or numbers. Text objects can be updated by assigning new contents to its value.

Property of form. See OBJECTS password, string, textarea; see PROPERTIES defaultValue, name, value; see METHODS focus, blur, select; see EVENT HANDLERS onBlur, onChange, onFocus, onSelect.

textarea   Similar to a text object, with the addition of multiple lines. A textarea object can also be updated by assigning new contents to its value.

Property of form. See OBJECTS password, string, text; see PROPERTIES defaultValue, name, value; see METHODS focus, blur, select; see EVENT HANDLERS onBlur, onChange, onFocus, onSelect.

window   Created by Navigator when a page is loaded containing properties that apply to the whole window. It is the top-level object for each document, location, and history object. Because its existence is assumed, you do not have to reference the name of the window when referring to its objects, properties, or methods. For example, the following two lines have the same result (printing a message to the status line):

```
status("Go away from here.")
window.status("Go away from here.")
```

A new window is created using the open method:

```
aNewWindow = window.open("URL","Window_Name",["windowFeatures"])
```

App
D

The variable name is used to refer to the window's properties and methods. The window name is used in the target argument of a form or anchor tag.

See OBJECTS document and frame; see PROPERTIES defaultStatus, frames, parent, self, status, top, window; see METHODS alert, close, confirm, open, prompt, setTimeout, clearTimeout; see EVENT HANDLERS onLoad and onUnload.

Properties

Properties are used to view or set the values of objects. An object is simply a vague generality until a property is used to define the values which make it specific.

action   The action property is a reflection of the action attribute in an HTML <form> tag, consisting of a destination URL for the submitted data. This value can be set or changed before or after the document has been loaded and formatted.

In this example, the action for a form called outlineForm is set to the URL contained in the variable outlineURL.

```
outlineForm.action=outlineURL
```

Property of form. See PROPERTIES encoding, method, target.

alinkColor   The color of a link after the mouse button is depressed—but before it's released—and expressed as a hexadecimal RGB triplet or string literal. It cannot be changed after the HTML source is processed. Both of these examples set the color to alice blue.

```
document.alinkColor="aliceblue"
document.alinkColor="F0F8FF"
```

Property of document. See PROPERTIES bgColor, fgColor, linkColor, vlinkColor.

anchors   An array of all defined anchors in the current document. If the length of an anchor array in a document is 5, then the anchors array is represented as document.anchors[0] through document.anchors[4].

Property of document. See anchor OBJECT; see PROPERTIES length and links.

appCodeName   Returns a read-only string with the code name of the browser.

```
document.write("The code name of your browser is " + navigator.appCodeName)
```

For most Netscape Navigator 2.0, this returns:

```
The code name of your browser is Mozilla
```

Property of navigator. See PROPERTIES appName, appVersion, userAgent.

appName   Returns a read-only string with the name of the browser.

Property of navigator. See PROPERTIES appCodeName, appVersion, userAgent.

appVersion Returns a string with the version information of the browser in the format "releaseNumber (platform; country)." For a release of Netscape 2.0:

```
document.write(navigator.appVersion)
```

returns

```
2.0 (Win95; I)
```

This specifies Navigator 2.0 running on Windows 95 with an international release. The U country code specifies a US release, while an I indicates an international release.

Property of `navigator`. See PROPERTIES `appName`, `appCodeName`, `userAgent`.

bgColor The document background color expressed as a hexadecimal RGB triplet or string literal. It can be reset at any time. Both of these examples set the background to alice blue.

```
document.bgColor = "aliceblue"
document.bgColor = "F0F8FF"
```

Property of `document`. See PROPERTIES `alinkColor`, `fgColor`, `linkColor`, `vlinkColor`.

checked A Boolean value (`true` or `false`), indicating whether a check box or radio button is selected. The value is updated immediately when an item is checked. It's used in the following form:

```
formName.checkboxName.checked
formName.radioButtonName[index].checked
```

Property of `checkbox` and `radio`. See `defaultChecked` PROPERTY.

cookie String value of a small piece of information stored by Navigator in a client-side COOKIES.TXT file. The value stored in the `cookie` is found using substring `charAt`, `IndexOf`, and `lastIndexOf`.

For more information, see the discussion under TERMS.

Property of `document`. See `hidden` OBJECT.

defaultChecked A Boolean value (`true` or `false`) indicating whether a check box or radio button is checked by default. Setting a value to `defaultChecked` can override the checked attribute of a form element. The following section of code will reset a group of radio buttons to its original state by finding and setting the default button:

```
for (var i in menuForm.choices) {
   if (menuForm.choices[i].defaultChecked) {
      menuForm.choice[i].defaultChecked = true
   }
}
```

Property of `checkbox` and `radio`. See `form` OBJECT; see `checked` PROPERTY.

defaultSelected A Boolean value (`true` or `false`) representing the default state of an item in a form select element. Setting a value with this property can override the selected attribute of an `<option>` tag. The syntax is identical to `defaultChecked`.

App

D

Property of `options`. See PROPERTIES `index`, `selected`, `selectedIndex`.

defaultStatus The default message displayed in the status bar at the bottom of a Navigator window when nothing else is displayed. This is preempted by a priority or transient message, such as a `mouseOver` event with an `anchor`. For example:

```
window.defaultStatus = "Welcome to my home page"
```

displays the welcome message while the mouse is not over a link, or Netscape is not performing an action that it needs to notify the user about.

Property of `window`. See `status` PROPERTY.

defaultValue The initial contents of `hidden`, `password`, `text`, `textarea`, and `string` form elements. For password elements, it is initially set to null for security reasons, regardless of any set `value`.

Property of `hidden`, `password`, `text`, `textarea`. See `value` PROPERTY.

E The base of natural logarithms, also known as Euler's constant. The value is approximately 2.7182818285...

Property of `Math`. See PROPERTIES `LN2`, `LN10`, `LOG2E`, `LOG10E`, `PI`, `SQRT1_2`, `SQRT2`.

elements An array of objects containing form elements in HTML source order. The array index begins with zero and ends with the number of `form` elements –1.

Property of `form`. See `elements` OBJECT.

encoding Returns a string reflecting the Mime encoding type, which is set in the `enctype` attribute of an HTML `<form>` tag.

Property of `form`. See PROPERTIES `action`, `method`, `target`.

fgColor The color of foreground text represented as a hexadecimal RGB triplet or a string literal. This value cannot be changed after a document is processed. It can take two forms:

```
document.fgColor="aliceblue"
document.fgColor="F0F8FF"
```

Property of `document`. See PROPERTIES `alinkColor`, `bgColor`, `linkColor`, `vlinkColor`; see `fontcolor` METHODS.

forms An array of objects corresponding to named forms in HTML source order and containing an entry for each `form` object in a document.

Property of `document`. See `form` OBJECT; see `length` PROPERTY.

frames An array of objects corresponding to child frame windows created using the `<frameset>` tag. To obtain the number of child frames in a window, use the `length` property.

Property of `window`. See `frame` OBJECT; see `length` PROPERTY.

hash   Returns a string with the portion of a URL beginning with a hash mark (#), which denotes an anchor name fragment. It can be used to set a hash property, although it is safest to set the entire URL as a href property. An error is returned if the hash isn't found in the current location.

Property of link and location. See anchor OBJECT; see PROPERTIES host, hostname, href, pathname, port, protocol, search properties.

host   Returns a string formed by combining the hostname and port properties of a URL and provides a method for changing it.

```
location.host = "www.montna.com:80"
```

Property of link and location. See PROPERTIES hash, hostname, href, pathname, port, protocol, search.

hostname   Returns or changes a string with the domain name or IP address of a URL.

Property of link and location. See PROPERTIES hash, host, href, pathname, port, protocol, search.

href   Returns a string with the entire URL. All other location and link properties are substrings of href, which can be changed at any time.

Property of link and location. See PROPERTIES hash, host, hostname, pathname, port, protocol, search.

index   Returns the index of an option in a select element with zero being the first item.

Property of options. See PROPERTIES defaultSelected, selected, selectedIndex.

lastModified   A read-only string containing the date that the current document was last changed, based on the file attributes. The string is formatted in the standard form used by JavaScript (see Date object). A common usage is:

```
document.write("This page last modified on " + document.lastModified)
```

Property of document.

length   An integer reflecting a length- or size-related property of an object.

Object	Property Measured
history	Length of the history list
string	Integer length of the string; zero for a null string
radio	Number of radio buttons
anchors, forms, frames, links, options	Number of elements in the array

Property of anchors, elements, forms, frame, frames, history, links, options, radio, string, window.

linkColor   The hyperlink color displayed in the document, expressed as a hexadecimal RGB triplet or as a string literal. It corresponds to the `link` attribute in the HTML `<body>` tag, and cannot be changed after the document is processed.

Property of `document`. See PROPERTIES `alinkColor`, `bgColor`, `fgColor`, `vlinkColor`.

links   An array representing `link` objects defined in HTML using `<a href=URL>` tags with the first `link` identified as `document.links[0]`.

See `link` object. See PROPERTIES `anchors` and `length`.

LN2   A constant representing the natural logarithm of 2 (approximately 0.693).

Property of `Math`. See PROPERTIES `E`, `LN10`, `LOG2E`, `LOG10E`, `PI`, `SQRT1_2`, `SQRT2`.

LN10   A constant representing the natural logarithm of 10 (approximately 2.302).

Property of `Math`. See PROPERTIES `E`, `LN2`, `LOG2E`, `LOG10E`, `PI`, `SQRT1_2`, `SQRT2`.

location   Returns a string with the URL of the current document. This read-only property (`document.location`) is different from the location `objects` properties (`window.location.propertyName`), which can be changed.

Property of `document`. See `location` OBJECT.

LOG2E   A constant representing the base 2 logarithm of e (approximately 1.442).

Property of `Math`. See PROPERTIES `E`, `LN2`, `LN10`, `LOG10E`, `PI`, `SQRT1_2`, `SQRT2`.

LOG10E   A constant representing the base 10 logarithm of e (approximately .434).

Property of `Math`. See PROPERTIES `E`, `LN2`, `LN10`, `LOG2E`, `SQRT1_2`, `SQRT2`.

method   Reflects the `method` attribute of an HTML `<form>` tag: either `<GET>` or `<POST>`. It can be set at any time. The first function returns the current value of the form object, while the second function sets the method to the contents of `newMethod`.

```
function getMethod(formObj) {
   return formObj.method
}
function setMethod(formObj,newMethod) {
   formObj.method = newMethod
}
```

Property of `form`. See PROPERTIES `action`, `encoding`, `target`.

name   Returns a string with the `name` attribute of the object. This is the internal name for `button`, `reset` and `submit` objects, not the on-screen label.

For example, after opening a new window with `indexOutline = window.open("http://www.wossamatta.com/outline.html","MenuPage")` and issuing the command `document.write(indexOutline.name)`, JavaScript returns `MenuPage`, which was specified as the name attribute.

Property of `button`, `checkbox`, `frame`, `password`, `radio`, `reset`, `select`, `submit`, `text`, `textarea`, `window`. See `value` PROPERTY.

options   An array of `option` objects created by a `select` form element. The first option's index is zero, the second is 1, and so on.

See `select` OBJECT.

parent   Refers to the calling document in the current frame created by a `<frameset>` tag. Using `parent` allows access to other frames created by the same `<FRAMESET>` tag. For example, two frames invoked are called index and contents. The index frame can write to the contents frame using the syntax:

```
parent.contents.document.write("Kilroy was here.")
```

Property of `frame` and `window`.

pathname   Returns the path portion from a URL. Although the `pathname` can be changed at any time, it is always safer to change the entire URL at once using the `href` property.

Property of `link` and `location`. See PROPERTIES `hash`, `host`, `hostname`, `href`, `port`, `protocol`, `search`.

PI   Returns the value of pi (approximately 3.1415927). This is the ratio of the circumference of a circle to its diameter.

Property of `Math`. See PROPERTIES `E`, `LN2`, `LN10`, `LOG2E`, `LOG10E`, `SQRT1_2`, `SQRT2`.

port   Returns the port number of a URL address, which is a substring of the `host` property in `href`.

Property of `link` and `location`. See PROPERTIES `hash`, `host`, `hostname`, `href`, `pathname`, `protocol`, `search`.

protocol   Returns a string with the initial portion of the URL, up to and including the colon, which indicates the access method (`http`, `ftp`, `mailto`, and so on).

Property of `link` and `location`.

See PROPERTIES `hash`, `host`, `hostname`, `href`, `pathname`, `port`, `search`.

referrer   Returns a read-only URL of the document that called the current document. In conjunction with a CGI script, it can be used to keep track of how users are linked to a page.

```
document.write("You came here from a page at " + document.referrer)
```

Property of `document`.

search   Returns a string containing any query information appended to a URL.

Property of `link` and `location`. See PROPERTIES `hash`, `host`, `hostname`, `href`, `pathname`, `port`, `protocol`.

selected   Returns a Boolean value (`true` or `false`) indicating the current state of an option in a `select` object. The selected property can be changed at any time, and the display will immediately update to reflect the new value. The selected property is useful for `select` elements that are created by using the `multiple` attribute. Using this property, you can view or change the value of any element in an `options` array without changing the value of any other element in the array.

Property of `options`. See PROPERTIES `defaultSelected`, `index`, `selectedIndex`.

selectedIndex   Returns an integer specifying the index of a selected item. The `selectedIndex` property is useful for `select` elements that are created without using the `multiple` attribute. If `selectedIndex` is evaluated when the `multiple` option is selected, the property returns the index of the first option only. Setting the property clears any other options that are selected in the element.

Property of `select`, `options`. See PROPERTIES `defaultSelected`, `index`, `selected`.

self   Refers to the current window or form, and is useful for removing ambiguity when dealing with `window` and `form` properties with the same name.

Property of `frame` and `window`. See `window` PROPERTY.

SQRT1_2   The square root of 1/2, also expressed as the inverse of the square root of 2 (approximately 0.707).

Property of `Math`. See PROPERTIES `E`, `LN2`, `LN10`, `LOG2E`, `LOG10E`, `PI`, `SQRT2`.

SQRT2   The square root of 2 (approximately 1.414).

Property of `Math`. See properties `E`, `LN2`, `LN10`, `LOG2E`, `LOG10E`, `PI`, `SQRT1_2`.

status   Specifies a priority or transient message to display in the status bar at the bottom of the window, usually triggered by a `mouseOver` event from an `anchor`. To display when the mouse pointer is placed over a link, the usage is:

```
<A anchor definition onMouseOver="window.dstatus='Your message.'; return
true">link</A>
```

Note the use of nested quotes and the required `return true` required for operation.

Property of `window`. See `defaultStatus` PROPERTY.

target   A string specifying the name of a window for responses to be posted to after a form is submitted. For a link, `target` returns a string specifying the name of the window that displays the content of a selected hypertext link.

```
homePage.target = "http://www.wossamatta.com/"
```

A literal must be used to set the `target` property. JavaScript expressions and variables are invalid entries.

Property of `form`, `link`, `location`. See PROPERTIES `action`, `encoding`, `method`.

text Returns the value of text following the `<option>` tag in a `select` object. It can also be used to change the value of the option, with an important limitation: while the value is changed, its appearance on screen is not.

Property of `options`.

title Returns the read-only value set within HTML `<title>` tags. If a document doesn't include a title, the value is `null`.

Property of `document`.

top The topmost window, called an ancestor or Web browser window, that contains `frames` or nested `framesets`.

Property of `window`.

userAgent Header sent as part of HTTP protocol from client to server to identify the type of client. The syntax of the returned value is the same as `appVersion`.

Property of `navigator`. See PROPERTIES `appName`, `appVersion`, `appCodeName`.

value The value of an object depends on the type of object it is applied to.

Object	Value Attribute
button, reset, submit	Value attribute that appears on screen, not the button name
checkbox	On if item is selected, off if not
radio	String reflection of value
hidden, text, textarea	Contents of the field
select	Reflection of option value
password	Return a valid default value, but an encrypted version if modified by the user

Changing the value of a `text` or `textarea` object results in an immediate update to the screen. All other `form` objects are not graphically updated when changed.

Property of `button`, `checkbox`, `hidden`, `options`, `password`, `radio`, `reset`, `submit`, `text`, `textarea`.

For `password`, `text`, and `textarea`, see `defaultValue` PROPERTY.

For `button`, `reset`, and `submit`, see `name` PROPERTY.

For `options`, see PROPERTIES `defaultSelected`, `selected`, `selectedIndex`, `text`.

For `checkbox` and `radio`, see PROPERTIES `checked` and `defaultChecked`.

App
D

vlinkColor   Returns or sets the color of visited links using hexadecimal RGB triplets or a string literal. The property cannot be set after the document has been formatted. To override the browser defaults, color settings are used with the onLoad event handler in the <BODY> tag:

```
<BODY onLoad="document.vlinkColor='aliceblue'">
```

Property of document. See PROPERTIES alinkColor, bgColor, fgColor, linkColor.

window   A synonym for the current window to remove ambiguity between a window and form object of the same name. While it also applies to the current frame, it is less ambiguous to use the self property.

Property of frame and window. See self PROPERTY.

Methods

Methods are functions and procedures used to perform an operation on an object, variable, or constant. With the exception of built-in functions, methods must be used with an object:

```
object.method()
```

Even if the method does not require any arguments, the parentheses are still required.

The object which utilizes the method is listed after the definition as "Method of *object*," followed by any cross-references to other methods. Standalone functions that are not used with objects are indicated with an asterisk (*).

abs   Returns the absolute (unsigned) value of its argument.

```
document.write(Math.abs(-10));
document.write(Math.abs(12))
```

These examples return 10 and 12, respectively.

Method of Math.

acos   Returns the arc cosine (from zero to pi radians) of its argument. The argument should be a number between –1 and 1. If the value is outside the valid range, a zero is returned.

Method of Math. See METHODS asin, atan, cos, sin, tan.

alert   Displays a JavaScript Alert dialog box with an OK button and a user-defined message. Before the user can continue, they must press the OK button.

Method of window. See METHODS confirm and prompt.

anchor   Used with write or writeln methods, anchor creates and displays an HTML hypertext target. The syntax is:

```
textString.anchor(anchorName)
```

where textString is what the user sees, and anchorName is equivalent to the name attribute of an HTML <anchor> tag.

Method of `string`. See `link` METHOD.

asin   Returns the arc sine (between –pi/2 and pi/2 radians) of a number between –1 and 1. If the number is outside the range, a zero is returned.

Method of `Math`. See METHODS `acos`, `atan`, `cos`, `sin`, `tan`.

atan   Returns the arc tangent (between –pi/2 and pi/2 radians) of a number between –1 and 1. If the number is outside the range, a zero is returned.

Method of `Math`. See METHODS `acos`, `asin`, `cos`, `sin`, `tan`.

back   Recalls the previous URL from the history list. This method is the same as `history.go(-1)`.

Method of `history`. See METHODS `forward` and `go`.

big   Formats a string object as a big font by encasing it with HTML `<big>` tags. Both of the following examples result in the same output—displaying the message "Welcome to my home page" in a big font:

```
var welcomeMessage = "Welcome to my home page."
document.write(welcomeMessage.big())
```

```
<BIG> Welcome to my home page.</BIG>
```

Method of `string`. See METHODS `fontsize`, `small`.

blink   Formats a `string` object as a blinking line by encasing it with HTML `<blink>` tags. Both of the following examples produce a flashing line that says `Notice`:

```
var attentionMessage = "Notice"
document.write(attentionMessage.blink())
```

```
<BLINK>Notice</BLINK>
```

Method of `string`. See METHODS `bold`, `italics`, `strike`.

blur   Removes focus from the specified `form` element. For example, the following line removes focus from `feedback`:

```
feedback.blur()
```

assuming that `feedback` is defined as:

```
<input type="text" name="feedback">
```

Method of `password`, `select`, `text`, `textarea`. See METHODS `focus` and `select`.

bold   Formats a `string` object in bold text by encasing it with HTML `<b>` tags.

Method of `string`. See METHODS `blink`, `italics`, `strike`.

ceil   Returns the smallest integer greater than, or equal to, its argument. For example:

```
Math.ceil(1.01)
```

returns a 2.

Method of `Math`. See `floor` METHOD.

charAt   Returns the character from a string at the specified index. The first character is at position zero and the last at length –1.

```
var userName = "Bobba Louie"
document.write(userName.charAt(4)
```

returns an a.

Method of `string`. See METHODS `indexOf` and `lastIndexOf`.

clear   Clears the contents of a window, regardless of how the window was filled.

Method of `document`. See METHODS `close`, `open`, `write`, `writeln`.

clearTimeout   Cancels a `timeout` set with the `setTimeout` method. A timeout is set using a unique timeout ID, which must be used to clear it:

```
clearTimeout(waitTime)
```

Method of `frame` and `window`. See `setTimeout` METHOD.

click   Simulates a mouse click on the calling `form` element with the effect dependent on the type of element.

Form Element	Action
`Button`, `Reset`, and `Submit`	Same as clicking button.
`Radio`	Selects option button.
`Checkbox`	Marks check box and sets value to `on`.

Method of `button`, `checkbox`, `radio`, `reset`, `submit`.

close   For a `document` object, closes the current stream of output and forces its display. It also stops the browser winsock animation and displays `Document: Done` in the status bar.

For a `window` object, closes the current window. As with all window commands, the `window` object is assumed. For example:

```
window.close()
close()
self.close()
```

all close the current window.

Method of `document` and `window`. See METHODS `clear`, `open`, `write`, `writeln`.

confirm   Displays a JavaScript confirmation dialog box with a message and buttons for OK and Cancel. Confirm returns a true if the user selects OK and `false` for Cancel. The following example closes and loads a new window if the user presses OK:

```
if (confirm("Are you sure you want to enter.") {
    tourWindow = window.open("http:\\www.haunted.com\","hauntedhouse")
}
```

Method of window. See METHODS alert and prompt.

cos   Returns the cosine of the argument. The angle's size must be expressed in radians.

Method of Math. See METHODS acos, asin, atan, sin, tan.

escape*   Returns ASCII code of its argument based on the ISO Latin-1 character set in the form %xx, where xx is the ASCII code. It is not associated with any other object, but is actually part of the JavaScript language.

See unescape METHOD.

eval*   This built-in function takes a string or numeric expression as its argument. If a string, it attempts to convert it to a numeric expression. Eval then evaluates the expression and returns the value.

```
var x = 10
var y = 20
document.write(eval("x + y"))
```

This method can also be used to perform JavaScript commands included as part of a string.

```
var doThis = "if (x==10) { alert("Your maximum has been reached") }
function checkMax () {
    x++;
    eval(doThis)
}
```

App

D

This can be useful when converting a date from a form (always a string) into a numerical expression or number.

exp   Returns e (Euler's constant) to the power of the argument to compute a natural logarithm.

Method of Math. See METHODS log and pow.

Formats the calling string into a fixed-pitch font by encasing it in HTML <tt> tags.

Method of string.

floor   Returns the integer less than, or equal to, its argument. For example:

```
Math.floor(2.99)
```

returns a 2.

Method of Math. See ceil METHOD.

focus   Navigates to a specific form element and gives it focus. From that point, a value can be entered by JavaScript commands or the user can complete the entry.

Method of password, select, text, textarea. See METHODS blur and select.

fontcolor   Formats the string object to a specific color expressed as a hexadecimal RGB triplet or a string literal, similar to using `<font color=color>`.

Method of `string`.

fontsize   Formats the string object to a specific font size: one of the seven defined sizes using an integer through the `<fontsize=size>` tag. If a string is passed, the size is changed relative to the value set in the `<basefont>` tag.

Method of `string`. See METHODS `big` and `small`.

forward   Loads the next document on the URL history list. This method is the same as `history.go(1)`.

Method of `history`. See methods `back` and `go`.

getDate   Returns the day of the month as an integer between 1 and 31.

Method of `Date`.

See `setDate` method.

getDay   Returns the day of the week as an integer from zero (Sunday) to six (Saturday). There is not a corresponding `setDay` command because the day is automatically computed when the date value is assigned.

Method of `Date`.

getHours   Returns the hour of the day in 24-hour format, from zero (midnight) to 23 (11 PM).

Method of `Date`. See `setHours` METHOD.

getMinutes   Returns the minutes with an integer from zero to 59.

Method of `Date`. See `setMinutes` METHOD.

getMonth   Returns the month of the year as an integer between zero (January) and 11 (December).

Method of `Date`. See `setMonth` METHOD.

getSeconds   Returns the seconds in an integer from zero to 59.

Method of `Date`. See `setSeconds` METHOD.

getTime   Returns an integer representing the current value of the date object. The value is the number of milliseconds since midnight, January 1, 1970. This value can be used to compare the length of time between two date values.

For functions involving computation of dates, it is useful to define variables defining the minutes, hours, and days in milliseconds:

```
var dayMillisec = 1000 * 60 * 60 * 24 //1,000 milliseconds x 60 sec x 60 min x 24
hrs
```

```
var hourMillisec = 1000 * 60 * 60 //1,000 milliseconds x 60 sec x 60 min
var minuteMillisec = 1000 * 60 //1,000 milliseconds x 60 sec
```

Method of Date. See setTime METHOD.

getTimezoneOffset   Returns the difference in minutes between the client machine and Greenwich mean time. This value is a constant except for daylight savings time.

Method of Date.

getYear   Returns the year of the date object minus 1900. For example, 1996 is returned as 96.

Method of Date. See setYear METHOD.

go   Loads a document specified in the history list by its URL or relative to the current position on the list. If the URL is incomplete, the closest match is used. The search is not case sensitive.

Method of history. See METHODS back and forward.

indexOf   Returns the location of a specific character or string, starting the search from a specific location. The first character of the string is specified as zero and the last is the string's length-1. The syntax is:

```
stringName.indexOf([character¦string], [startingPoint])
```

The startingPoint is zero by default.

Method of string. See METHODS charAt and lastIndexof.

isNaN*   For UNIX platforms only, this standalone function returns true if the argument is not a number. On all platforms except Windows, the parseFloat and parseInt return NaN when the argument is not a number.

See METHODS parseFloat and parseInt.

italics   Formats a string object into italics by encasing it an HTML <I> tag.

Method of string. See METHODS blink, bold, strike.

lastIndexOf   Returns the index of a character or string in a string object by looking backwards from the end of the string or a user-specified index.

Method of string. See METHODS charAt and indexOf.

link   Creates a hypertext link to another URL by defining the <href> attribute and the text representing the link to the user.

Method of string. See anchor METHOD.

log   Returns the natural logarithm (base e) of a positive numeric expression greater than zero. An out-of-range number always returns −1.797693134862316e+308.

Method of Math. See METHODS exp and pow.

App

D

max   Returns the greater of its two arguments. For example:

`Math.max(1,100)`

returns `100`.

Method of `Math`. See `min` METHOD.

min   Returns the lesser of its two arguments.

Method of `Math`. See `max` METHOD.

open   For a document, opens a stream to collect the output of `write` or `writeln` methods. If a document already exists in the target window, then the open method clears it. The stream is ended by using the `document.close()` method.

For a window, it opens a new browser window in a similar fashion to choosing File, New Web Browser from the Netscape menu. Using the URL argument, it loads a document into the new window; otherwise, the new window is blank. When used as part of an event handler, the form must include the window object; otherwise, the document is assumed. Window features are defined by a comma-separated list of options with =1 or =yes to enable and =0 or =no to disable. Window features include toolbar, location, directories, status, menubar, scrollbars, resizable, copyhistory, width and height.

Method of `document` and `window`. See METHODS `clear`, `close`, `write`, `writeln`.

parse   Takes a date string, such as `Jan 11, 1996`, and returns the number of milliseconds since midnight, Jan. 1, 1970. This function can be used to set date values based on string values. When passed a string with a time, it returns the time value.

Because `parse` is a static function of Date, it is always used as `Date.parse()` rather than as a method of a created `date` object.

Method of `Date`. See `UTC` METHOD.

parseFloat*   Parses a string argument and returns a floating-point number if the first character is a plus sign, minus sign, decimal point, exponent, or a numeral. If it encounters a character other than one of the valid choices after that point, it returns the value up to that location and ignores all succeeding characters. If the first character is not a valid character, `parseFloat` returns one of two values based on the platform:

Windows	`0`
NonWindows	`NaN`

See `isNaN` METHOD.

parseInt*   Parses a `string` argument and returns an integer based on a specified radix or base. A radix of 10 converts the value to a decimal, while eight converts to octal, and 16 to hexadecimal. Values greater than 10 for bases above 10 are represented with letters (A through F) in place of numbers.

Floating-point values are converted to integers. The rules for evaluating the string are identical to `parseFloat`.

See `isNaN` and `parseFloat` METHODS.

pow   Returns a base raised to an exponent.

Method of `Math`. See `exp` and `log` METHODS.

prompt   Displays a prompt dialog box that accepts user input. If an initial value is not specified for `inputDefault`, the dialog box displays the value `<undefined>`.

Method of `window`. See `alert` and `confirm` METHODS.

random   On UNIX machines only, returns a pseudo-random number between zero and 1.

Method of `Math`.

round   Returns the value of a floating-point argument rounded to the next highest integer if the decimal portion is greater than, or equal to, .5, or the next lowest integer is less than .5.

Method of `Math`.

select   Selects the input area of a specified form element. Used in conjunction with the `focus` method, JavaScript can highlight a field and position the cursor for user input.

Method of `password`, `text`, `textarea`. See METHODS `blur` and `focus`.

setDate   Sets the day of the month.

Method of `Date`. See `getDate` METHOD.

setHours   Sets the hour for the current time.

Method of `Date`. See `getHours` METHOD.

setMinutes   Sets the minutes for the current time.

Method of `Date`. See `getMinutes` METHOD.

setMonth   Sets the month with an integer from zero (January) to 11 (December).

Method of `Date`. See `getMonth` METHOD.

setSeconds   Sets the seconds for the current time.

Method of `Date`. See `getSeconds` METHOD.

setTime   Sets the value of a date object.

Method of `Date`. See `getTime` METHOD.

setTimeout   Evaluates an expression after a specified amount of time, expressed in milliseconds. This is not repeated indefinitely. For example, setting a timeout to three seconds will evaluate the expression once after three seconds—not every three seconds. To call `setTimeout` recursively, reset the timeout as part of the function invoked by the method. Calling the function `startclock` in the following example sets a loop in motion that clears the timeout, displays the current time, and sets the timeout to redisplay the time in one second.

```
var timerID = null;
var timerRunning = false;
function stopclock () {
  if(timerRunning) cleartimeout(timerID);
  timerRunning=false;
}
function startclock () {
  stopclock();
  showtime();
}
function showtime () {
  var now = new Date();
  ...
  document.clock.face.value =   timeValue;
  timerID = setTimeout("showtime()",1000);
  timerRunning = true;
}
```

Method of `window`. See `clearTimeout` METHOD.

setYear   Sets the year in the current date by using an integer representing the year minus 1900.

Method of `Date`. See `getYear` METHOD.

sin   Returns the sine of an argument. The argument is the size of an angle expressed in radians, and the returned value is from –1 to 1.

Method of `Math`. See METHODS `acos`, `asin`, `atan`, `cos`, `tan`.

small   Formats a `string` object into a small font by using the HTML `<small>` tags.

Method of `string`. See METHODS `big` and `fontsize`.

sqrt   Returns the square root of a positive numeric expression. If the argument's value is outside the range, the returned value is zero.

strike   Formats a string object as strikeout text by using the HTML `<strike>` tags.

Method of `string`. See METHODS `blink`, `bold`, `italics`.

sub   Formats a string object into subscript text by using the HTML `<sub>` tags.

Method of `string`. See `sup` METHOD.

submit   Performs the same action as clicking a submit button.

Method of `form`. See `submit` OBJECT; see `onSubmit` EVENT HANDLER.

substring   Returns a subset of a string object based on two indexes. If the indexes are equal, an empty string is returned. Regardless of order, the substring is built from the smallest index to the largest.

Method of string.

sup   Formats a string object into superscript text by using the HTML <sup> tags.

Method of string. See sub METHOD.

tan   Returns the tangent of an argument. The argument is the size of an angle expressed in radians.

Method of Math. See METHODS acos, asin, atan, cos, sin.

toGMTString   Converts a date object to a string by using Internet Greenwich mean time (GMT) conventions. For example, if today is a date object:

```
today.toGMTString()
```

then the string Mon, 18 Dec 1995 17:28:35 GMT is returned. Actual formatting may vary from platform to platform. The time and date is based on the client machine.

Method of Date. See toLocaleString METHOD.

toLocaleString   Converts a date object to a string by using the local conventions, such as *mm/ dd/yy hh:mm:ss*.

Method of Date. See toGMTString METHOD.

toLowerCase   Converts all characters in a string to lowercase.

Method of string. See toUpperCase METHOD.

toString   Converts a date or location object to a string.

Method of Date, location.

toUpperCase   Converts all characters in a string to uppercase.

Method of string.

See toLowerCase method.

unEscape*   Returns a character based on its ASCII value expressed as a string in the format %xxx where xxx is a decimal number between zero and 255, or 0x0 to 0xFF in hex.

See escape METHOD.

UTC   Returns the number of milliseconds for a date in Universal Coordinated Time (UTC) since midnight, January 1, 1970.

UTC is a constant, and is always used as Date.UTC(), not with a created date object.

Method of Date. See parse METHOD.

write   Writes one or more lines to a document window, and can include HTML tags and JavaScript expressions, including numeric, string, and logical values. The write method does not add a new line (
 or /n) character to the end of the output. If called from an event handler, the current document is cleared if a new window is not created for the output.

Method of `document`. See METHODS `close`, `clear`, `open`, `writeln`.

writeln   Writes one or more lines to a document window followed by a new line character, and can include HTML tags and JavaScript expressions, including numeric, string, and logical values. If called from an event handler, the current document is cleared if a new window is not created for the output.

Method of `document`. See methods `close`, `clear`, `open`, `write`.

Event Handlers

Event handlers are where JavaScript gets its power. By looking for specific user actions, JavaScript can confirm or act on input immediately, without waiting for server introduction, since user activity within an HTML page is limited to mouse movement and input on form elements.

onBlur   Blurs occur when a `select`, `text` or `textarea` field on a form loses focus.

Event handler of `select`, `text`, `textarea`. See EVENT HANDLERS `onChange` and `onFocus`.

onChange   A change event happens when a `select`, `text`, or `textarea` element on a form is modified before losing focus.

Event handler of `select`, `text`, `textarea`. See EVENT HANDLERS `onBlur`, `onFocus`.

onClick   Occurs when an object, such as a button or check box, is clicked.

Event handler of `button`, `checkbox`, `radio`, `link`, `reset`, `submit`.

onFocus   A form element receives focus by tabbing to or clicking the input area with the mouse. Selecting within a field results in a `select` event.

Event handler of `select`, `text`, `textarea`. See EVENT HANDLERS `onBlur` and `onChange`.

onLoad   A load event is created when Navigator finishes loading a window or all frames within a `<frameset>` tag.

Event handler of `window`. See `onUnload` EVENT HANDLER.

onMouseOver   Occurs when the mouse pointer is placed over a `link` object. To function with the `status` or `defaultStatus` properties, the event handler must return `true`.

Event handler of `link`.

onSelect   A select event is triggered by selecting some or all of the text in a `text` or `textarea` field.

Event handler of `text`, `textarea`.

onSubmit   Triggered by the user submitting a form. The event handler must return `true` to allow the form to be submitted to the server. Conversely, it returns `false` to block the form's submission.

Event handler of `form`. See `submit` OBJECT and METHOD.

onUnload   Occurs when exiting a document. For proper operation, place the `onUnload` handler in the `<body>` or `<frameset>` tags.

Event handler of `window`. See `onLoad` EVENT HANDLER.

Last Words

On June 26, 1997, a language standard for Internet scripting was announced by ECMA, "an international, Europe-based industry association founded in 1961 and dedicated to the standardization of information and communication systems" (from the ECMA site, which seemed reluctant to divulge just what ECMA stands for). The standard will be known as ECMA-262, or ECMA Script. ECMA Script was derived from Netscape's JavaScript specification.

JavaScript is on its way to standardization. ●

Index

Complete and Return this Card for a *FREE* Computer Book Catalog

Thank you for purchasing this book! You have purchased a superior computer book written expressly for your needs. To continue to provide the kind of up-to-date, pertinent coverage you've come to expect from us, we need to hear from you. Please take a minute to complete and return this self-addressed, postage-paid form. In return, we'll send you a free catalog of all our computer books on topics ranging from word processing to programming and the internet.

☐ Mrs. ☐ Ms. ☐ Dr. ☐

...ne (first) ☐☐☐☐☐☐☐☐☐☐☐ (M.I.) ☐ (last) ☐☐☐☐☐☐☐☐☐☐☐☐☐☐☐☐☐

...dress ☐☐☐☐☐☐☐☐☐☐☐☐☐☐☐☐☐☐☐☐☐☐☐☐☐☐☐☐☐☐☐

☐☐☐☐☐☐☐☐☐☐☐☐☐☐☐☐☐☐☐☐☐☐☐☐☐☐☐☐☐☐☐

...y ☐☐☐☐☐☐☐☐☐☐☐☐☐☐☐ State ☐☐ Zip ☐☐☐☐☐ ☐☐☐☐

...ne ☐☐☐ ☐☐☐ ☐☐☐☐ Fax ☐☐☐ ☐☐☐ ☐☐☐☐

...mpany Name ☐☐☐☐☐☐☐☐☐☐☐☐☐☐☐☐☐☐☐☐☐☐☐☐☐☐☐☐☐☐

...mail address ☐☐☐☐☐☐☐☐☐☐☐☐☐☐☐☐☐☐☐☐☐☐☐☐☐☐☐☐☐☐

...lease check at least (3) influencing factors for ...urchasing this book.

...nt or back cover information on book .... ☐
...cial approach to the content .... ☐
...npleteness of content .... ☐
...hor's reputation .... ☐
...lisher's reputation .... ☐
...k cover design or layout .... ☐
...ex or table of contents of book .... ☐
...e of book .... ☐
...cial effects, graphics, illustrations .... ☐
...er (Please specify): _____ ☐

...ow did you first learn about this book?

...y in Macmillan Computer Publishing catalog .... ☐
...ommended by store personnel .... ☐
...v the book on bookshelf at store .... ☐
...ommended by a friend .... ☐
...eived advertisement in the mail .... ☐
...v an advertisement in: _____ ☐
...d book review in: _____ ☐
...er (Please specify): _____ ☐

...ow many computer books have you ...urchased in the last six months?

...s book only .... ☐   3 to 5 books .... ☐
...ooks .... ☐   More than 5 .... ☐

4. Where did you purchase this book?

Bookstore .... ☐
Computer Store .... ☐
Consumer Electronics Store .... ☐
Department Store .... ☐
Office Club .... ☐
Warehouse Club .... ☐
Mail Order .... ☐
Direct from Publisher .... ☐
Internet site .... ☐
Other (Please specify): _____ ☐

5. How long have you been using a computer?

☐ Less than 6 months   ☐ 6 months to a year
☐ 1 to 3 years   ☐ More than 3 years

6. What is your level of experience with personal computers and with the subject of this book?

	With PCs	With subject of book
New	☐	☐
Casual	☐	☐
Accomplished	☐	☐
Expert	☐	☐

Source Code ISBN: 0-7897-1449-3

7. Which of the following best describes your job title?

Administrative Assistant ☐
Coordinator ☐
Manager/Supervisor ☐
Director ☐
Vice President ☐
President/CEO/COO ☐
Lawyer/Doctor/Medical Professional ☐
Teacher/Educator/Trainer ☐
Engineer/Technician ☐
Consultant ☐
Not employed/Student/Retired ☐
Other (Please specify): _____ ☐

8. Which of the following best describes the area of the company your job title falls under?

Accounting ☐
Engineering ☐
Manufacturing ☐
Operations ☐
Marketing ☐
Sales ☐
Other (Please specify): _____ ☐

9. What is your age?

Under 20 ....
21-29 ....
30-39 ....
40-49 ....
50-59 ....
60-over ....

10. Are you:

Male ....
Female ....

11. Which computer publications do you read regularly? (Please list)

_____
_____
_____
_____
_____
_____
_____
_____
_____

Comments: _____
_____
_____

Fold here and scotch-tape to m

Fold here and scotch-tape to m

Check out Que® Books on the World Wide Web
http://www.quecorp.com

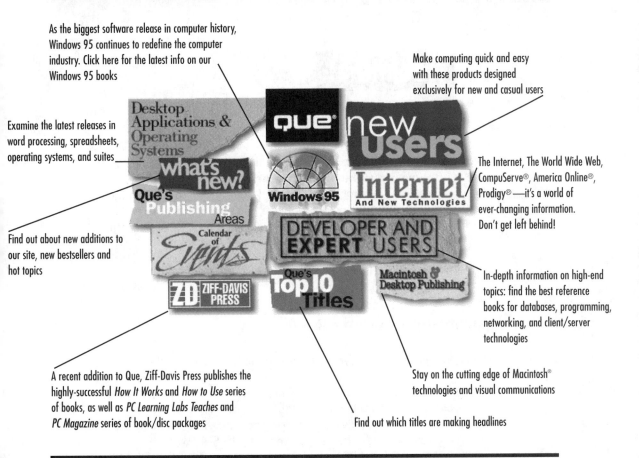

As the biggest software release in computer history, Windows 95 continues to redefine the computer industry. Click here for the latest info on our Windows 95 books

Make computing quick and easy with these products designed exclusively for new and casual users

Examine the latest releases in word processing, spreadsheets, operating systems, and suites

The Internet, The World Wide Web, CompuServe®, America Online®, Prodigy® —it's a world of ever-changing information. Don't get left behind!

Find out about new additions to our site, new bestsellers and hot topics

In-depth information on high-end topics: find the best reference books for databases, programming, networking, and client/server technologies

A recent addition to Que, Ziff-Davis Press publishes the highly-successful *How It Works* and *How to Use* series of books, as well as *PC Learning Labs Teaches* and *PC Magazine* series of book/disc packages

Stay on the cutting edge of Macintosh® technologies and visual communications

Find out which titles are making headlines

With 6 separate publishing groups, Que develops products for many specific market segments and areas of computer technology. Explore our Web Site and you'll find information on best-selling titles, newly published titles, upcoming products, authors, and much more.

- Stay informed on the latest industry trends and products available
- Visit our online bookstore for the latest information and editions
- Download software from Que's library of the best shareware and freeware

MACMILLAN COMPUTER PUBLISHING USA

A VIACOM COMPANY

Technical ---- Support:

If you need assistance with the information in this book or with a CD/Disk accompanying the book, please access the Knowledge Base on our Web site at **http://www.superlibrary.com/general/support**. Our most Frequently Asked Questions are answered there. If you do not find the answer to your questions on our Web site, you may contact Macmillan Technical Support **(317) 581-3833** or e-mail us at **support@mcp.com**.

Licensing Agreement